BLOODLETTERS
AND MEN

APR 1998

BLOODLETTERS AND BADMEN

A NARRATIVE ENCYCLOPEDIA
OF AMERICAN CRIMINALS
FROM THE PILGRIMS
TO THE PRESENT

COMPLETELY REVISED,
UPDATED, AND EXPANDED

JAY ROBERT NASH

M. EVANS AND COMPANY, INC.
NEW YORK

M. Evans and Company, Inc.
216 East 49 Street
New York, New York 10017

Library of Congress Cataloging-in-Publication Data

Nash, Jay Robert.
    Bloodletters and badmen : a narrative encyclopedia of
American criminals from the Pilgrims to the present /
Jay Robert Nash. — Completely revised, updated, and
expanded.
        p. cm.
    Includes bibliographical references and index.
    ISBN 0-87131-777-X (pbk.) : $19.95
    1. Criminals—United States—Biography—Dictionaries. I. Title.
HV6785.N37   1995
364.1'092'273—dc20
    (B)   94-49585
                                                        CIP

Design by Visuality

Manufactured in the United States of America

DEDICATION

THIS BOOK IS FOR ROBERT ABEL, WHO THOUGHT IT NECESSARY; FOR JACK CONROY, NOVELIST AND FRIEND TO YOUNG WRITERS; AND IN MEMORY OF TWO GREAT REPORTERS—WILLIAM L. "TUBBY" TOMS OF THE INDIANAPOLIS NEWS AND RAY BRENNAN OF THE CHICAGO SUN-TIMES.

ACKNOWLEDGMENTS

I wish to thank the following people and organizations for their extensive assistance in helping me research this book and for the wonderful cooperation they extended in providing photos, information, and encouragement: Kevin John Mosley Collection; Roland Restle Collection; Henry Scheafer and Faytonia Fair of UPI's Chicago office; William and Edie Kelly of Wide World's Chicago office; Peter A. Evans, Librarian of the California Historical Society; James H. Davis, Picture Librarian of the Denver Public Library (Western History Department); Mrs. Leona S. Morris, Editorial Secretary of the Missouri Historical Review (State Historical Society of Missouri); G. F. O'Neill, Director of Personnel, Pinkerton's, Inc.; Jack D. Haley, Assistant Curator, Western History Collections, University of Oklahoma; New York Historical Society; Wyoming State Historical Department; Kansas State Historical Society; Arizona Historical Society; Terry Mangan, The State Historical Society of Colorado; Holly B. Ulseth, Curator of Special Exhibits & Collections, Detroit Historical Museum; Malcolm Freiberg, Editor of Publications, Massachusetts Historical Society; William M. Roberts, Reference Librarian, University of California, Berkeley; Ken Burton, *Tucson Daily Citizen*; James, John, and Patrick Agnew; Prof. Andre Moenssens; Raymond Friday Locke, Editor, *Mankind Magazine*; Robert Connelly; Thomas Buckley; Richard Case of the Chicago Historical Society; Jack Paul Schwartz; Mrs. Jerrie L. Klein; Neil H. Nash; Jack J. Klein, Jr.; Ray Puechner; Peter Kotsos; Stan Kaiser; Dr. Richard Talsky; Barry Felcher of the *Chicago Daily News*; Curt Johnson; Leonard Des Jardins; Al Devorin; John Gehlman; Mike Berman; James Small; James Stein; Arthur Von Kluge; Brett Howard; Sidney Harris; Arnold Edwards; Jerry Goldberg of the *Los Angeles Free Press*; Warren Stamer; Arnold L. Kaye; Joseph Pinkston; James McCormick of *Chicago Today*; Jack Lane; Jeff Kamen; Herman Kogan of the *Chicago Sun-Times*; William Kirby, Associate Director of the Louisiana Division of the New Orleans Public Library; the dozens of police force officers of all ranks, criminologists, and penologists across the country who gave their time and information; and to my intrepid typist and friend, Carolyn Zozak, whose fingers ceaselessly danced across her typewriter's keyboard on my behalf.

AUTHOR'S PREFACE

More than thirty years ago, I began to collect a vault of materials dealing with American criminals. This crime memorabilia mounted to tens of thousands of newspaper clippings, books, and magazine articles—as did my own editorial work as a newspaper and magazine editor and writer. My interviews, correspondence, and research into the dark realm of crime broadened from the historical to the contemporary criminal, all of which resulted in this work. This grim, often macabre, background material sparked ideas about the social order and historical development of criminals in the United States. In studying the lives of our most notorious criminals, it became evident that many were treated in their own time as folk heroes. As their lives were embellished into sagas, an offbeat nostalgia was created for those who chose to live outside the law, for those who created a brooding, dark heritage from which one cannot easily turn away.

The notorious lives profiled in this book span four centuries of the New Land and they serve as an introduction to a side of the American character, past and present, that we are still to comprehend. What was once termed "The Frontier Spirit," became umbilically attached to the American criminal. He (or she) was present on the *Mayflower* (John Billington, America's first official murderer), through the Revolution, the settling of the Middle Border, the Civil War, the great westward movement to the Pacific, inside the rising cities, peopling the streets of every new town.

American society easily identified the criminal, outwardly condemning him as being against the common good but marking him for special recognition in a social category reserved for pioneers. He was thought to be as acceptable as the daredevils and wilderness adventurers who came with the bark on. He became an extension of all of these—the loudest, gaudiest, and most dangerous in our patchwork society. He was noise! He was public! And, most importantly, he was ours!

The din has dwindled considerably since the days of Jesse James, John Wesley Hardin, the Daltons, and the Doolins of Oklahoma. Today's criminal prefers shadow and silence, following the code of the underworld and the monolithic national crime syndicate. The link with our violent past, however, remains unbroken, sustained as a kind of tradition in a land where tradition, as well as identity, is hard achieved and preserved.

The criminals portrayed in this book are memorable and do belong to all of us in one way or another. Their passion-evoking crimes instruct, remind, and once again horrify. Many produce in us a logical and collective disgust for our own species. All but a few are unsavory Hydes, but all require our understanding. Those who operated on the periphery of crime have no place in this encyclopedia. The race-track touts, petty gamblers, and minor business cheats more properly belong in the stories of Damon Runyon, but it should be remembered that the shabby glory that Runyon and others brought to such shadowy figures helped to memorialize the more serious criminals. Runyon's Sky Masterson is a heavily cloaked portrait of New York gambler and racketeer Arnold Rothstein, who, indeed, was a serious criminal and not the fanciful Broadway bon vivant of *Guys and Dolls*.

Rothstein was the precursor of the professional gangster. It was the gangster, then the national crime syndicate, that became the most influential force in American crime. In tracing the development of the mob to its present-day status it becomes apparent that personality and character within its ranks have been gutted—all but exterminated by Mafia and syndicate bosses. As the reader will undoubtedly note, this modern-day image is in complete contrast to those first bands of robbers who, following the American Revolution, gathered together in the eastern colonies and along the Natchez Trace, where individuality and personal style were the mark of the successful outlaw.

Unlike Jesse James, America's most famous outlaw, today's syndicate criminal is protected through bribery, blackmail, political connections, and the screen of an economy in which he plays a large part as a legitimate business man, on the one hand, and a secret lawbreaker on the other. James, who was at large for sixteen years, was a public outlaw of his own choosing. He was protected by scores of relatives sympathetic to his "plight."

Jesse James, his brother Frank, the Younger Brothers, and others of his band, fought during the Civil War as Confederate guerrillas. Their myriad relatives in Missouri had also fought with and aided the Southern armies, and when the South finally met defeat, all but the guerrillas were granted amnesty.

Union troops, occupying the border states after

the war, ruthlessly hunted down these Confederate guerrillas, branding them outlaws. Uncles, brothers, cousins, and distant kissing kin threw open their doors to harbor Jesse and the rest to combat this very real persecution. When such oppression ceased, James embarked upon his long criminal career and excused his robberies and murders with claims that he was "driven to it by Yankees." His legions of supporters then contended that he was merely continuing the Civil War on his own, wreaking vengeance on Northern banks and Yankee-owned railroads. He was also of their own blood—family blood—of fierce and loyal pioneers.

Nineteenth-century America was inundated with criminal brotherhoods—the Youngers, the Farringtons, the Sontags, the Renos, the Clantons, the Daltons, and the James boys, to name a few. To the public, Jesse and Frank James typified the truly fraternal outlaw band—hunted brothers pitting their wits and daring against the whole weight of the law, everywhere embodying the heroic American image of the desperado on horseback. The fact that Jesse James was a cold-blooded murderer made little difference in the glowing legend his public demanded.

The hunger for such legends—a greed for sensation peculiarly American—increased in the following century with the rise of gangsters. The more sinister these city-bred criminals appeared, the more popular their exploits became. From horseback to fast cars, the American criminal improvised and adjusted to scientific change and progress. He no longer barged into banks with drawn pistols and scooped money from drawers into grain sacks while his horse waited tethered outside. He became the man behind the submachine gun in the 1920s and 1930s, the killer behind the sophisticated assault weapon of the 1980s and 1990s.

Legendary reputations, however, can often be misleading in the evasive lexicons of crime. For instance, almost every collection of historical crime stories in the last century has included that much harassed spinster Lizzie Borden, whose "forty whacks" have been heard around the world. Lizzie Borden was never convicted of murdering her parents, and suspicion was cast also on the Borden maid who was present in the household at the moment of murder. Lizzie nevertheless is believed to be a savage killer, not from the actual facts of her case and trial but from her axe-wielding legend that dogged her to her dying day.

In assembling the original edition of *Bloodletters and Badmen*, I made a serious attempt to include only those with known and proven criminal records and those whose convictions and crimes were never in doubt. This remains true for this 1995 updated version, too. For this reason, celebrated persons such as Sacco and Vanzetti, Samuel Insull, and a host of others have not been included. I have added Albert DeSalvo in this revised edition where I had excluded him earlier, coming to the belief, after restudying his case, that he was, indeed, the notorious Boston Strangler.

I have not included many whose ongoing trials at this writing have not determined clear guilt or convictions, such as the Menendez Brothers (in their case *which* brother specifically murdered *which* parent), and that of superstar murder suspect O. J. Simpson.

Further, in the last twenty years since this book was originally published, many notorious criminals and crimes have been microscopically reexamined, mostly to prove conspiracy in the case of earth-shaking assassinations. Did James Earl Ray act alone in his murder of Martin Luther King? I believe Ray did the actual shooting, but it is quite possible that his assassination of King was financed by secret and powerful persons, but this is only a suspicion, not a fact.

Was Lee Harvey Oswald the only shooter in Dallas in 1963 when President Kennedy was slain? Oliver Stone's provocative film, *J.F.K.*, insists that several assassins were involved and that Oswald was nothing more than a cleverly positioned scapegoat. Again, this film, along with the dearly held conspiracy theory, is only suspicion, not fact. The proof is lacking, although it is my belief, based on my ongoing research, that Kennedy's murder may have been engineered by a powerful member of Kennedy's own cabinet. Again, however, this remains suspicion until incontrovertible proof is provided.

In many quarters, the American criminal is thought of in separate terms that have little to do with morality, but rather with singular defiance against the habits of conformity. American criminals hold for many a secret, murky fascination. They are part of the collective memory of a nation, part of our lives whether or not they touched those lives directly. Thirty years ago, one out of twenty families in the U.S. were, at one time or another, affected by violent crime. Now, with the rise of myriad street gangs, the proliferation of drugs, and the erosion of the family unit, the figures are more frightening and revealing. Now one out of every four American families is directly touched by violent crime.

A contemporary phenomenon in crime is the serial killer. These singular and devastating murderers have existed in our past, to be sure, but never in such numbers and never before acting with such horrendous regularity. The majority of new entries to this work stem from this breed of cold-blooded murderers: serial killers like Jeffrey Dahmer, Dean Allen Coryl, David Berkowitz, and John Wayne Gacy. These serial killers earned grisly sobriquets through the staggering numbers of their victims, and include Kenneth Bianchi (The Hillside Strangler), Douglas Daniel Clark (The Sunset Slayer), William Bonin (The Freeway Strangler), Vaughan Greenwood (The Skidrow Slasher), Edmund Kemper (The Coed Killer), Randolph Kraft (The Freeway Killer), and Richard Ramirez (The Night Stalker).

Serial killers Walter Kelbach and Henry Lee Lucas bragged of their slayings. In Lucas's case, he vied for the gruesome honor of being America's worst killer, claiming to have slain hundreds in his murderous odyssey across America. Indifference to the taking of human life is a startling hallmark of these modern-day monsters, self-created demons much more frightening than any creature invented by Mary Shelley or Bram Stoker.

In the course of my research, I came to meet and interview many historic and contemporary criminals, including serial killers such as John Wayne Gacy. All were different in character and personality, except the serial killers and mass murderers who were phlegmatic, somber, and dyspeptic. All were the same in that they broke the law with impunity and few had regrets. There was no remorse evident in any of the gangsters of the 1930s I met, such as Alvin Karpis or James "Blackie" Audett, or the syndicate mobsters who murdered "because it is just business." On the other hand, Willie "The Actor" Sutton was reflective and spoke with authority about how "crime does not pay" when we met. He pointed to the many years he had languished in prison in exchange for his useless status as one of America's top bank robbers.

Only the con men reveled in their offbeat fame. These, like the ancient Joseph "Yellow Kid" Weil (who died at the age of 101), excused their criminal careers by blaming the greed of their victims as the root cause of their crimes. "The sucker was greedy, he deserved to be taken," Weil told me many years ago. "He thought he could get something for nothing. Instead, he got nothing for something from me." Weil scammed an estimated eight million dollars from his gullible victims in one fantastic money-making scheme after another. He nevertheless died in poverty and is buried in a pauper's grave.

This was the fate of most of the criminals portrayed in this book. They died broke and miserable. The wealth they sought to accumulate by their wits or by the gun always seemed to elude them. Only a few died peacefully in bed, leaving dubious estates, inheritances seized by successors as ruthless as they had been. There was no glory in their lives; admiration for their legends exists only in those who are ignorant of the truth.

All of these factors should be clear in the profiles within this encyclopedia. The style in which this work is presented is intended to serve the needs of the general reader, the lawman, and students of criminal justice and criminology. By offering a hard-data section preceding the narrative of most notorious criminals, I hoped to give a serviceable and ready reference to each.

I believe that the reader will come away with a new understanding of the depths of inhumanity executed by those sane and mad criminals constantly within our midst. It is hoped that the reader will also come to know better the true character of the American criminal and the workings of his (or her) mind.

Jay Robert Nash

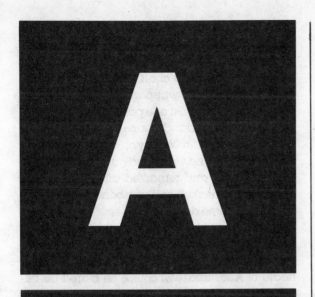

ABBANDANDO, FRANK
Syndicate Gangster ● (1910-1942)

BACKGROUND: HABITUAL CRIMINAL, RAISED IN OCEAN HILL, N.Y., MINOR PUBLIC EDUCATION. ALIASES: THE DASHER. RECORD: SENT TO SEVERAL REFORM SCHOOLS AS A TEEN FOR EXTORTION; SERVED TERM AT ELMIRA, N.Y., REFORMATORY FOR KICKING NEW YORK POLICE OFFICER HAMPTON FERGUSON INTO UNCONSCIOUSNESS IN 1928; WITH HARRY MAIONE AND ABE RELES SHOT AND KILLED RIVAL N.Y. GANGSTERS MEYER AND IRVING SHAPIRO IN 1931; SHOT AND KILLED WILLIE SHAPIRO IN 1934; WITH MAIONE AND RELES STABBED AND AXED TO DEATH GEORGE "WHITEY" RUDNICK IN A BROWNSVILLE, N.Y. GARAGE ON 5/25/37; WITH MAIONE AND VITO GURINO SHOT AND KILLED FELICE ESPOSITO, A WITNESS TO A 1922 GANG MURDER, ON 2/9/39; WITH GURINO AND LEO TOCCI KIDNAPPED AND RAPED A 17-YEAR-OLD GIRL IN BROWNSVILLE ON 8/23/39; CONVICTED OF MURDER AND SENT TO SING SING'S ELECTRIC CHAIR ON 2/19/42.

Few, in any, syndicate killers were more ruthless than Frank "The Dasher" Abbandando. He killed for the sheer love of killing, for the perverse elation it gave him. He showed no remorse for the more than forty lives he took. As he sat down to die in Sing Sing's electric chair, there was a smirk on the lamp-jawed gangster's face that registered only contempt and arrogance.

A native of Ocean Hill, Abbandando quit school at an early age and joined a street gang headed by another vicious hoodlum, Harry "Happy" Maione. He, Maione, and others worked the extortion racket, threatening to burn down shop buildings unless their owners paid them a weekly payoff. Sent to several reform schools, Abbandando could not be reformed. He was mean-spirited and enjoyed beating and bullying others. Apprehended for a minor offense in 1928 by police officer Hampton Ferguson, the hulking Abbandando turned on the officer, knocked him down, and kicked him into unconsciousness before other officers collared him.

This time Abbandando was sent to Elmira (N.Y.) reformatory. The only thing normal practiced by Abbandando at Elmira was to play second base for the reformatory team. He was so fast that he was nicknamed "The Dasher," a moniker he relished. When released from Elmira, Abbandando returned to his stomping grounds in Ocean Hill where he and Maione established lucrative gambling and loan-sharking rackets. Joining this gang was Abe "Kid Twist" Reles, another brutal gangster who aided Abbandando and Maione in battling the powerful Shapiro brothers, who bossed the rackets in neighboring Brownsville.

In 1931, Abbandando, Maione, and Reles shot and killed Meyer and Irving Shapiro, taking over most of the Brownsville rackets controlled by these gangsters. They took full control of this area after murdering Willie Shapiro, the last of the opposing brothers, in 1934. Abbandando, Maione, and Reles put together a large gang of thugs who thought and acted as they did: beat and kill anyone who opposed them, beat and kill anyone who failed to pay their bookies or loan-sharking agents.

So methodical and ruthless were these killers that they quickly came to the attention of the crime czars of Manhattan, particularly those younger gangsters—such as Charles "Lucky" Luciano, Meyer Lansky, Louis "Lepke" Buchalter, and Albert Anastasia—who had put together the newly organized national crime syndicate. Their organization needed a brutal, uncompromising goon squad that would injure or kill without asking questions.

They looked to the gang run by Abbandando, Maione, and Reles that had earned the sobriquet of Brooklyn, Inc. Within a few years, this gang of killers became known as Murder, Inc. Its members received orders from syndicate bosses either to beat up or to kill people they did not know, to go anywhere to enforce syndicate edicts.

The Dasher was one of Murder, Inc.'s most dedicated killers. Inside of a decade, Abbandando killed more than forty people on syndicate orders, slaying them with icepicks, axes, knives, and guns. He never took exception to a "contract" (a syndicate order to kill someone), and made his "hit" (murder) with alacrity and precision, collecting an average payment of $500 per killing.

Suddenly rich, Abbandando lavished himself with a huge wardrobe of blue-striped suits and loud ties. He bought several roadsters and moved into an expensive apartment. The Dasher also serviced a string of expensive call girls, but his sexual appetite was only satiated when forcing sex upon young women. Abbandando would cruise the streets of Brownsville and Ocean Hill in his purring roadster, searching for rape victims.

Typical of Abbandando's sexual offenses was the gang rape he supervised on the night of August 23, 1939. He spotted a tall, well-endowed young woman entering a Brownville bar. He and two of his goons, Vito Gurino and Leo Tocci, followed the girl and, once inside the bar, inveigled her into a back room. They grabbed her and forced her out the back exit and into Abbandando's car. She was driven to a nearby hotel where she was raped again and again by the three men.

When prosecutors confronted the Dasher with his many rape offenses at his murder trial, Abbandando became indignant, snarling: "I never raped nobody!" A prosecutor read an old arrest transcript in which the Dasher all but admitted raping the victim. Shrugging, Abbandando said: "Well, that one doesn't count, really. I married the girl later."

Abbandando murdered in the same fashion as he attacked young women—ruthlessly and without conscience. Such was the case of George "Whitey" Rudnick, who had been earmarked for death because of bad debts and because the mob thought he might be informing on them to police. On May 25, 1937, Abbandando, Reles, and Maione took Rudnick to a Brownville garage and there tortured him by stabbing him sixty-three times with icepicks, strangling him slowly, and then using a meat cleaver to crush his head. The three killers, Reles later related, laughed uproariously as they repeatedly stuck icepicks into Rudnick, counting the blows and delighting in the victim's tortured screams of agony.

The man who meticulously memorized this murder, Abe "Kid Twist" Reles, was the gangster who brought an end to Murder, Inc. Believeing that his bosses intended to kill him, Reles began to inform. He outlined, for the first time, the powerful hierarchy of syndicate members and operations in New York, naming his bosses as Louis Capone (no relation to Chicago's Al Capone), Albert Anastasia, and the overall boss of Murder, Inc., Louis "Lepke" Buchalter.

Reles appeared in court to testify against Ab-

bandando and Maione, who were tried together for the Rudnick and other killings. Both gangsters shouted threats at Reles, who nevertheless damned them from the witness chair. The Dasher was particularly menacing, whispering death threats to anyone he disliked. At one point, when in the witness chair, Abbandando leaned in close to presiding Judge Franklin W. Taylor and told him he would kill him if he was found guilty. Judge Taylor was unmoved and remarked after the Dasher's conviction: "The skull and crossbones of the underworld must come down!"

Unlike Reles, Abbandando had no intention of informing on his bosses. Time and again the Dasher replied to questions about his superior: "I never heard of Anastasia!" Of course he blared his denials so that Anastasia's henchmen, whom he knew were standing in the hallway outside the courtroom, could hear his response and report dutifully back to Anastasia that the Dasher was loyal.

It did Abbandando no good. He was convicted and sent to Sing Sing with Maione to await execution. The Dasher showed his usual bravado to reporters seeing him off at the train for the Castle on the Hudson, saying: "I'm gonna miss the first night ballgame of the season." He then promised that he would be out of prison soon, so confident was Abbandando of the power of the syndicate. He never came out but, instead, on February 19, 1942, was led into the little green room that housed the electric chair. He sat down in it with a smirk of defiance on his face. He said nothing as the black hood was placed over his head. His strapped down body quivered, the only response the Dasher had to the electric current that took his life.

(ALSO SEE Albert Anastasia; Louis Buchalter; Meyer Lansky; Charles Luciano; Harry Maione; Murder, Inc.; Abe Reles.)

ABBOTT, BURTON W.
Murderer ● (1928-1957)

BACKGROUND: BORN AND RAISED IN SAN FRANCISCO, CALIF. MARRIED, WIFE GEORGIA. STUDENT AT THE UNIVERSITY OF CALIFORNIA, MAJORING IN ACCOUNTING. TUBERCULAR SINCE CHILDHOOD (HAD A LUNG AND SEVERAL RIBS REMOVED). DESCRIPTION: 5'8", BROWN EYES, BROWN HAIR, SLIGHT BUILD. ALIASES: NONE. RECORD: STRANGLED AND MURDERED 14-YEAR-OLD STEPHANIE BRYAN IN SAN FRANCISCO 4/28/55; WAS FOUND GUILTY IN A LONG AND SENSATIONAL

Burton W. Abbott went to the gas chamber, convicted of murder, even though he claimed he was the victim of a diabolical frame-up. (UPI)

Burton Abbott was a mild-mannered, almost shy man whose friends called him "Bud" after the comedian. He had led an exemplary life, never had a police record and married an older woman named Georgia. Abbott's recreational habits were more intellectual than common: he was a better-than-average chess player and considered himself a minor master at preparing special cuisine. On weekends, Abbott would drive several hundred miles north of his Alameda home to a small cabin he owned in the Trinity Mountain range for some fishing, small game hunting, and general contemplation.

Though tubercular and frail, Burton Abbott in 1955 was a well-rounded young man, soberly approaching middle age with high values and solid purpose. The great mystery surrounding his brutal killing of fourteen-year-old Stephanie Bryan, therefore, remains doubly arcane.

The girl vanished in front of the Hotel Claremont in Berkeley after walking a classmate home on April 28, 1955. Hours later, dozens of policemen began a desperate search for her throughout Berkeley and Contra Costa County.

Several persons reported seeing a young girl in the area trying to fight off a young man in a car, but identification was skimpy. Thirteen days later a French textbook belonging to Stephanie was found in remote Franklin Canyon. It was the only trace of her.

The mystery would have remained had it not been for the unthinking actions of Burton Abbott's wife Georgia on the evening of July 15, 1955. While Abbott was entertaining a friend, Otto Dezman, (the husband of Leona Dezman for whom Georgia worked in a beauty parlor), Georgia rummaged around in the basement of Abbott's Alameda home. She was searching for costume material for a play she had written. Suddenly, she came across a girl's wallet buried in a box of old clothes.

Standing beneath the glare of a single naked light bulb, Georgia Abbott inspected the wallet finding Stephanie Bryan's identification card, pictures of the girl's schoolmates, and an unfinished letter she had been writing to a friend on the day of her murder. Mrs. Abbott, an avid newspaper reader, realized instantly what she had found and rushed upstairs.

Confronting her husband and Dezman, she held up the wallet and blurted: "Isn't this the girl who disappeared?"

After Dezman inspected the wallet, he called the police. Abbott appeared confused by the discovery, saying nothing. When police came, no one in the Abbott household could offer an explanation. Abbott distractedly played chess while an officer casually asked him a few questions and then went away.

The police returned the next day and carefully began to dig through Abbott's basement, overlooking nothing. While Abbott worked a crossword puzzle upstairs, the police dug up from the earthen floor Stephanie's schoolbooks and her bra.

Confronted with this new evidence, Abbott shrugged. Anyone, he claimed, could have planted that in his basement. In May of that year, he explained, his garage had been used as a polling place and dozens of people would have had access to his house. The police appeared satisfied with this excuse but a newsman, following a hunch, visited Abbott's Trinity Mountain cabin. He brought along a friend with two hunting dogs. The dogs quickly scur-

Abbott's murder victim, fourteen-year-old Stephanie Bryan. (UPI)

ried to a shallow grave and the men began digging.

The badly decomposed but recognizable body of Stephanie Bryan was there. Her head had been crushed and her panties were tied tightly about her neck. The coroner, after being summoned, could not say whether or not she had been sexually molested.

But her presence on Abbott's land sealed his fate. He was arrested and tried for kidnapping and murder.

Burton Abbott's extensive trial was dominated by massive circumstantial evidence against him. He did not considerably improve his chances for acquittal by taking the stand. There, Abbott appeared to take the whole thing lightly, even laughing on the stand when the prosecution insisted that he had intended to rape little Stephanie and killed her when she resisted. The jury didn't care for Abbott's laughter.

It took seven days before the jury found him guilty of Murder One and he was sentenced to death in San Quentin's death chamber. Burton Abbott's real agony began on death row. He was granted several minor stays of execution, some for only hours, while his lawyers prepared weary appeals, all of which were denied.

Even such ardent foes of Capital Punishment as Supreme Court Justice William O. Douglas and Edmund G. "Pat" Brown, then Attorney General, rejected his pleas. Abbott continued to cry out his innocence.

Shortly before his day of execution, the condemned man was visited by San Quentin's psychiatrist, Dr. David Schmidt. When Schmidt asked him about the killing, Abbott tersely replied: "I can't admit it, Doc. Think of what it would do to my mother. She could not take it." This statement, which was kept confidential, was later revealed as Abbott's "confession," creating a political storm in California.

But Abbott never did make a public admission of his guilt and on March 14, 1957, Abbott walked into the small glass death room. At 11:15 a.m. the gas pellets were dropped beneath his chair. As the fumes rose about Burton Abbott the hotline from Governor Goodwin Knight's office began buzzing for San Quentin's warden.

"Hold the execution," one of Knight's aides yelled over the phone.

"Too late," Warden Harry Teets said. "The gas has already been released." Oddly, the Governor's stay was only for an hour anyway. The decision to grant this extra hour was never explained, but it mattered little to Abbott. He was dead by 11:25 a.m.

ABBOTT, JACK HENRY
Murderer ● (1944-   )

BACKGROUND: HABITUAL CRIMINAL. ALIASES: JACK EASTMAN. SENT TO A UTAH REFORM SCHOOL IN 1953 AT AGE NINE. RELEASED IN 1962 AND WAS SHORTLY ARRESTED FOR PASSING BAD CHECKS AND SENT TO THE UTAH STATE PENITENTIARY AS A CONVICTED FORGER. KILLED A FELLOW INMATE IN 1966, WAS CONVICTED AND RECEIVED A FOURTEEN-YEAR SENTENCE FOR MURDER. ESCAPED IN 1961 AND, WHILE AT LARGE FOR SIX WEEKS, ROBBED A BANK. RECAPTURED AND CONVICTED OF BANK ROBBERY. WROTE EXTENSIVE LETTERS TO AUTHOR NORMAN MAILER, OFFERING DETAILS OF PRISON LIFE AND PROMOTING HIMSELF AS AN AUTHOR. THROUGH THE EFFORTS OF MAILER AND OTHERS, WAS GIVEN A CONTRACT FOR A BOOK AND PAROLED ON 6/5/81. KNIFED TO DEATH 22-YEAR-OLD WAITER RICHARD ADAN ON 7/18/81, FLED TO MEXICO, THEN TO LOUISIANA WHERE DETECTIVES LOCATED AND ARRESTED HIM ON 9/23/81. TRIED BEFORE JUDGE IRVING LANG OF THE MANHATTAN SUPREME COURT, PROSECUTED BY JAMES FOGEL AND DEFENDED BY CRIMINAL ATTORNEY IVAN FISHER. GIVEN A MINIMUM SENTENCE, FIFTEEN YEARS TO LIFE. ABBOTT WAS RETURNED TO THE UTAH STATE PENITENTIARY TO SERVE OUT HIS REMAINING EIGHT YEARS BEFORE BEING SENT TO NEW YORK TO SERVE OUT THE MURDER SENTENCE.

One of the shrewdest and deadliest killers of recent times, Jack Henry Abbott spent all but nine months of his adult life behind bars for committing violent crimes. He was a calculating and clever convict who literally wrote himself out of prison with the considerable help of novelist-turned-amateur criminologist, Norman Mailer. His killer's streak ran to the bone marrow, however, and, shortly after winning his freedom through his literary efforts, Abbott inexplicably stabbed a young waiter to death.

Living in foster homes as a child, Abbott proved incorrigible. He was a troublemaker and was given to so many violent outbursts that he was sent to a Utah reform school at age nine. Released at age eighteen, Abbott quickly began passing bad checks and was soon arrested for forgery and convicted. He was sent to the Utah State Penitentiary where, in 1966, he murdered an inmate.

Abbott maintained that he killed in self-defense, that he was the victim of a vicious homosexual attack, but the court failed to believe him. He then feebly tried to prove himself insane by throwing a pitcher of water at the presiding judge. He was examined by psychiatrists who reported him sane. Abbott was found guilty and sentenced to fourteen years for the killing.

Escaping from the Utah State Penitentiary in 1971, Abbott quickly robbed a Denver bank but he did not enjoy the loot for long, being recaptured and becoming a federal prisoner. As a maximum-security prisoner, Abbott's energies turned inward. He began to read endlessly, the subject of philosophy consuming him. He became enamored of Karl Marx and began telling other prisoners, guards, anyone within earshot, that he was a dedicated Marxist. In the course of his reading, Abbott learned that his favorite novelist, Norman Mailer, was writing a book entitled *The Executioner's Song*, a portrait of condemned murderer Gary Gilmore, who was scheduled to die at the Utah State Penitentiary.

It undoubtedly hit upon the conniving Abbott that Mailer was a novice criminologist who would be grateful for inside information dealing with prison life. He began to write to the author, sending him long missives, fifteen pages or more each time. Abbott, in excruciating detail, profiled his own life in prison as a "state-raised" inmate. The prisoner's letters were ingratiating, and, most importantly, written in a clinical style that imitated with astonishing accuracy the writing of Mailer himself, a subtle flattery that the novelist accepted and inter-

preted as talent on Abbott's part. Abbott proved himself a terrier-like researcher, devouring all of Mailer's work and parroting back to the author his own images, even those Abbott found in Mailer's *The Naked and the Dead*.

The nightmare prose Abbott offered Mailer described in horrific detail how he had undergone all manner of prison cruelties, how, standing naked, he had been chained by one arm to his bunk in strip-search cells, eaten cockroaches to survive, beaten by guards who tortured him with antipsychotic drugs. Abbott's seemingly endless correspondence with Mailer fixed upon hate and violence, subjects of the deepest concern to the author.

Mailer became so impressed with Abbott's murky prose that he convinced the editors of the *New York Review of Books* to publish some of the missives in 1980. This led to a book contract with Random House wherein Abbott received a $12,000 advance for a work he entitled, *In the Belly of the Beast*. Mailer wrote prison officials that Abbott was "a powerful and important American writer," lobbying for his release and stating that he had offered the murderer a job as a researcher.

Others joined the chorus to sing Abbott's praises. Errol McDonald, Abbott's editor at Random House, wrote prison officials urging a parole, stating that the killer "could support himself as a professional writer if he were released from prison and that he could very well have a bright future."

The pleas from the powerful brought Abbott's release on June 5, 1981. He was transferred to a Manhattan halfway house and Mailer personally welcomed him when his plane landed. The killer's book was published at this time and it immediately met with torrents of praise from New York's literati. One of those initially applauding Abbott was Jerzy Kosinski, author of *Being There*. Kosinksi, however, was one of the few literary figures to later recant his endorsement of Abbott and express regrets for having praised the killer's written work, likening the kudos showered upon Abbott to the wrongly placed praise the literati had heaped upon the lethal Black Panthers two decades earlier.

In New York Abbott was wined and dined at parties, embraced as a celebrity and peer by *New York Review of Books* editor Robert Silvers, author Jean Malaquais, and powerful literary agent Scott Meredith. He babbled about Camus and Sartre to these and others, cleverly building an image of himself as an intellectual giant. He began to promote among this clique the idea that he should

Jailhouse author and brutal killer Jack Henry Abbott. (AP/Wide World)

be named a writer-in-residence at the esteemed MacDowell Colony in Petersborough, N.H. He was sure that he would acquire this lofty goal through his connections.

When not being feted in posh penthouse apartments, Abbott drifted to the lower depths, moving among his true peers, thieves and prostitutes inhabiting the Lower East Side. After roaming the streets in the early hours of July 18, 1981, Abbott, accompanied by two women, walked into the Bonibon restaurant on Second Avenue and Fifth Street.

The trio sat down and 22-year-old Richard Adan walked up to take their order. The Cuban-born waiter was a struggling actor who had also finished a play about the Lower East Side, which was about to be produced. He was known to be courteous and polite by his customers and friends. Before Adan could take Abbott's order, the killer demanded to use the washroom. Adan explained that the facilities were restricted to employees only because of insurance reasons.

Abbott exploded, screaming abuse, obscenities, and threats. Adan sought to calm him down by asking him to step outside where they could quietly settle the matter. As soon as the pair stepped outside, Abbott drew a knife and, without a word of explanation, plunged it to the hilt into Adan's heart, killing him instantly.

Dashing back into the restaurant, Abbott shouted

to Susan Roxas, one of the women with him: "Let's get out of here! I just killed a man!" He fled and soon vanished from the city.

Police and federal agents searched for Abbott across the country for two months. He was, at that time, holed up in a small Mexican village near the Guatemalan border. Here Abbott languished, unable to speak Spanish or find work. He spent his last dollars to return to the U.S., going to the Louisiana oil fields. Detectives picked up his trail, following his nomadic course through the oil towns of Algiers, Harvey, and Marrero.

Hundreds of itinerant, nameless oil workers were rousted from their beds in rickety dark bunkhouses and examined by flashlight. The officers seemed always to miss their man, often only by a few minutes. Abbott found work by using a social security card that bore the alias of Jack Eastman. He labored sixteen hours a day and was paid four dollars an hour, like the thousands of other drifters who kicked back a third of their wages to the oil firms to sleep in dirty bunkhouses and eat in open-air canteens. The rest of their pay was spent on cheap liquor and the whores who swarmed into the camps at dusk.

Detectives learned that Abbott was working in the oil fields of the Ramos Oil Company in St. Mary's Parish. Pretending to be workers, plainclothes officers approached Abbott as he was unloading pipe from a truck. He stopped to raise his arms and comb his hair. At that moment detectives rushed forward leveling eight shotguns at him.

"Keep your hands in the air!" a detective ordered.

Abbott froze. He was then handcuffed and led away. He wore a filthy T-shirt, pants caked with dried oil, and boots so worn they were falling off his feet.

Flown to New York, Abbott was held at Riker's Island. He was tried before Judge Irving Lang of the Manhattan Supreme Court. His defense lawyer was criminal attorney Ivan Fisher and he was prosecuted by James Fogel. The killer no longer displayed his normal aloof attitude. He appeared nervous, anxious.

Abbott explained his murder of Adan as a "tragic misunderstanding." He then used the same excuse he had used after killing a prison inmate, that he had only acted in self-defense, that he had anticipated an attack from Adan.

"You intended to do it, you scum!" shouted a courtroom spectator who had jumped to his feet. The man was the father-in-law of the dead Adan,

Henry Howard. Judge Lang ordered Howard removed from the courtroom. Throughout the trial, the frustrated Howard languished in the hallway, waiting for justice to be done.

Among the several prosecution witnesses, Wayne Larsen proved to be the most damning of Abbott. He testified that he witnessed Abbott's ruthless knife thrust into the helpless Adan, an impact Larsen claimed "still rings in my ears."

Fisher portrayed his client as the victim of the inhuman prison system that had created him, the same plaintive plea Abbott had so successfully used in engineering his release from prison. "He was mistreated for so long and in so horrible a way," argued Fisher. "If it was, in fact, the poison of prison that brought about these events, how can it be urged that a lot more is the cure?"

Prosecutor Fogel minced no words: "This is a killer, a killer by habit, a killer by inclination, a killer by philosophy, a killer by desire." Fogel asked for a maximum sentence of life.

Abbott was found guilty of first degree manslaughter. Judge Lang had earlier ruled that Abbott's previous convictions had qualified him as a "persistent violent felon." He nevertheless gave the killer the minimum sentence of fifteen years to life. Judge Lang stated that Abbott's conviction was, in part, "an indictment which brutalized instead of rehabilitating. . . . It's perfectly clear that the defendant could not cope with the reality of a non-prison existence."

Norman Mailer had been present throughout the trial. He had pled for a lenient sentence. "Culture is worth a little risk," he implored the court. "A major sentence would destroy him." Even after hearing Lang's minimum sentence, Mailer complained that it was so long as to be "killing." Carped the 59-year-old Mailer: "At the point he gets out, he'll be as old as I am now."

Lang's sentence enraged Henry Howard: "In twenty-four years Jack Abbott will be back on the street and he will kill again. Why are his rights better than Richard Adan's rights?"

The answer to that question might be easily found in the facts that Jack Abbott had been raised to literary stardom, that his book sold 40,000 copies and subsequently earned him $500,000 and that he had powerful friends whose influence was undoutedly effective. Abbott was returned to the Utah State Penitentiary to serve out his remaining eight years. He was then returned to New York to serve out the fifteen-year sentence for ruthlessly killing a hopeful 22-year-old actor-playwright whose

own writing never produced enough money to pay for his burial.

Jack Henry Abbott is scheduled for release in the year 2006.

ABDULLAH, MOHAMMED (JOSEPH HOWK, JR.)
Murderer ● (1939-   )

BACKGROUND: BORN OF A WHITE FATHER AND NEGRO MOTHER, AND RAISED IN LONG BEACH, CALIF. GRADUATED HIGH SCHOOL AT 15 WITH AN IQ OF 140. ATTENDED LONG BEACH CITY COLLEGE IN 1954; ATTENDED THE UNIVERSITY OF CALIFORNIA, BERKELEY, 1958-60, MAJORING IN NEAR EASTERN LANGUAGES AND ISLAMIC CULTURE; CHANGED HIS NAME IN 1956 TO MOHAMMED ABDULLAH AND EMBRACED MOHAMMEDANISM IN 1956. DESCRIPTION: 5'11", BROWN EYES, BLACK HAIR, HEAVYSET. ALIASES: NONE. RECORD: SHOT AND KILLED BERKELEY STUDENT SONJA LILLIAN HOFF OUTSIDE THE UNIVERSITY OF CALIF. LIBRARY, BERKELEY 7/13/60; ATTEMPTED SUICIDE, BUT RECOVERED; TRIED AND SENTENCED TO DEATH; SENTENCE COMMUTED TO LIFE IMPRISONMENT WITHOUT PAROLE BY CALIF. GOVERNOR EDMUND G. BROWN ON REASONS OF INSANITY.

He was a brilliant child who began to read at the age of three and consumed myriad volumes of books before he was eight years old. By fifteen he had graduated from high school at the head of his class.

Howk's bookishness, however, did not tend to calm his emotions. He attempted to hang himself at age nine; the reason was never explained. At sixteen, the boy tried to burn down his parents' home after a violent argument with his mother. He was examined and studied at the Camarillo State Hospital and was diagnosed schizoid. No psychiatric care was provided, though it was recommended.

The racial differences in Howk's home have been suggested as the reason for the boy's discontent. Howk never openly talked about it but his unpredictable changes of religious beliefs tend to endorse this theory. First, he was a Roman Catholic. At fifteen he was an ardent Nazi, dropping out of Long Beach City College because his theories of Nordic supremacy were not supported in courses there.

Inside of two years, Howk swung completely over to Mohammedanism, becoming a fanatic

Islamic follower and changing his name to Mohammed Abdullah.

Abdullah put on weight and began to sport a fez. He arrived in the Berkeley area in 1958 with a scholarship to the University of California. Overnight he became an habitué of the coffee houses by then more Beatnik than Bohemian. In one of these Abdullah met and befriended drifter and local eccentric Martin Horowitz, 34, a high school dropout who had himself been in and out of psychiatric care.

Horowitz began to practice his own weird brand of psychiatry on Abdullah, and the two became inseparable until 1959 when Abdullah met pretty, statuesque Sonja Hoff, 21, a home economics major intent upon entering social work. Her fascination with minority groups may have led her into her association with Abdullah, a group study in himself by some standards.

One reason given for their meeting was that Sonja wanted help with her course in Persian and the brilliant Abdullah volunteered. His tutoring soon blossomed into love and the pair dated heavily. Abdullah was a jealous man, however, and after seeing Sonja with other male students, he wrote in his diary, April 6, 1960: "Tonight I tried to kill myself, but Sonja put herself between my knife and my throat. Next time I suspect her of liking another man, I shall kill her quickly and without warning." Two weeks later, Abdullah again caught Sonja with another student; he threatened to murder her. She reported the incident to the Berkeley police and he was subsequently ordered off campus. He did not, however, leave town.

Abdullah continued to threaten Sonja's life and that of an Iranian student she was dating. She left town at the end of the semester but made the mistake of returning in July to take a job as a waitress near the Berkeley campus.

The lovesick Abdullah spotted her on July 11, 1960, in the restaurant where she was working. He begged her to come to his apartment, where he secretly planned to cut her throat and then stick his head in the oven, turning on the gas. She refused to go with him.

Frustrated, Abdullah turned to his only friend, Martin Horowitz. His friend gave him a loaded .38 caliber pistol. Horowitz later explained that he did this because the mere possession of the weapon by Abdullah and his knowledge that he had the means to murder would distract him from the actual deed and

"soothe his tensions." Later statements claimed that Abdullah stole the gun from Horowitz. Abdullah said at one time that he bought it. No matter. It was the weapon that would end Sonja Hoff's life.

On July 13, 1960, Abdullah went to the University library, rented a typewriter, and tapped out a lengthy confession of the murder and suicide he was about to enact. Following the ornamental style of Near East scripts, Abdullah carefully worded his pain and regret. ". . . In the name of God, beneficent and merciful, I have stolen a pistol to kill my beloved and myself."

He then walked to the main reading room and approached Sonja, who was studying. He asked her to step outside where they could talk and, incredibly, considering the number of threats he had made against her life, she consented. Abdullah whispered the words "I love you" in Sonja's ear as they walked out. Once on the steps of the library, he whipped out the pistol and, holding it only inches from her head, he fired, killing her instantly. He fired another shot at the dead girl as she fell, but missed. Then he turned the weapon on himself and sent a bullet into his right temple.

Though the bullet remained lodged in his brain, Abdullah lived, blinded in one eye. Upon his recovery he and Horowitz were tried for murder, January 3, 1961. Abdullah was found guilty and sentenced to die in the gas chamber, an end he devoutly wished. Horowitz, sobbing, was sentenced to ten years at San Quentin for manslaughter.

Shortly before the date of his execution, Mohammed Abdullah was deprived of his self-envisioned paradise (where he believed God would give him his Sonja). Governor Brown commuted his sentence to life imprisonment without parole on the grounds that he had been insane all his life.

There was no comment from the prisoner.

ACCARDO, ANTHONY JOSEPH
Syndicate Gangster ● (1906-1992)

BACKGROUND: BORN 4/28/06 IN CHICAGO, ILL. AS ANTONIO LEONARDO ACCARDO. PUBLIC EDUCATION TO SIXTH GRADE. DESCRIPTION: 5'9½", BROWN EYES, BLACK HAIR, SWARTHY. ALIASES: JOE BATTERS, JOE BATTY, BIG TUNA.

Tony Accardo, present-day boss of Chicago's syndicate. (UPI)

RECORD: ARRESTED 27 TIMES SINCE 1922 FOR CARRYING CONCEALED WEAPONS, GAMBLING, EXTORTION, KIDNAPPING, AND MURDER; NEVER FINED OR IMPRISONED; LISTED AS A SUSPECT IN THE MURDERS OF JOSEPH AIELLO, "MIKE DE PIKE" HEITLER, AND JACK ZUTA BY THE CHICAGO CRIME COMMISSION IN 1931. ALSO SUSPECTED OF BEING ONE OF THE MACHINEGUNNERS AT THE ST. VALENTINE'S DAY MASSACRE; TOOK THE FIFTH AMENDMENT 144 TIMES WHEN APPEARING BEFORE THE KEFAUVER COMMITTEE AND CITED FOR CONTEMPT OF CONGRESS.

Accardo served as a bodyguard to Al Capone in the late 1920s and early 1930s. Known in the underworld as Joe Batters because of his reputed skill in handling a baseball bat, Accardo rose in the old Capone mob ranks to become boss of the Chicago family of the Mafia in 1943, following the suicide of Frank "The Enforcer" Nitti.

Sam Giancana, also a one-time Capone torpedo, aided Accardo in his assertion of power but wrested it away from him in 1957. Following Giancana's 1966 flight to Mexico to avoid prosecution, Accardo took back control.

The appellative Big Tuna was tacked onto Accardo's name by an inventive Chicago newspaperman—Ray Brennan—after he had learned that the gangster was fond of fishing and had posed beside some prize Florida catches. Accardo had enormous investments in Arizona, California, Florida, Nevada and South America—trucking, coal, lumber, hotels, and restaurants.

Accardo retired to Arizona in the 1980s, and lived out his life in luxury and comfort as the elder statesman of the Chicago branch of the Mafia-Syndicate. He died of natural causes on May 27, 1992, which left the Chicago outfit without a clear leader, but a hierarchy of bosses who essentially rule the rackets at this writing.

ADAMS, CALEB
Murderer ● (1785-1803)

Adams was a "street youth" of Windham, Conn., where a five-year-old neighbor boy, Oliver Woodworth plagued Adams with too many questions and was in the habit of following him.

One day the eighteen-year-old Adams took an axe to little Oliver, striking him on the head. Adams then produced a knife and slit the boy's throat because, as Adams later explained: "He annoyed me."

Adams was promptly convicted and sentenced to hang. On the day of his hanging, November 29, 1803, the youth stood for close to an hour on the gallows before a great throng as the Rev. Elijah Waterman delivered a sermon, pointing out Adams' dissolute life, recounting every crime the boy had confessed to over his brief life span, which included stealing twenty-five cents.

After Adams' spirit had been properly cleansed by Waterman's sermon, he was hanged.

ADAMS, MILLICENT
Murderer ● (1942-   )

A wealthy Philadelphia socialite, Millicent Adams attended Bryn Mawr and moved through uppercrust realms, as did Axel Schmidt, her lover. Schmidt, an engineering student, was a social climber and jilted Adams for another, more socially prominent young woman.

The scorned Adams later claimed that this rejection so depressed her that she intended to commit suicide. She purchased a gun and a St. Bernard. She took the dog to an unused servant's room in her family home and shot it with a .22-caliber Smith & Wesson, just to see if the weapon would work.

Adams then met Schmidt on an October night in 1962 for the last time. As they went to bed, she produced the gun and shot Schmidt dead, although she later claimed that she originally intended to shoot herself while in his embrace.

Pleading guilty to manslaughter, the court leniently sentenced her to ten years probation on the condition that Adams commit herself to a mental health center. All of this was part of a surprising plea-bargaining arrangement. Adams gave birth to a child, fathered by the very man she had slain. She was released in three years and resettled in the comfortable home of West Coast relatives.

ADAMSON, JOHN HARVEY
Murderer ● (1944-   )

Phoenix, Arizona, newsman Don Bolles, who had just recently received a Pulitzer Prize nomination for his investigative reporting, received an urgent phone call on June 2, 1976. The caller asked him to come to a hotel immediately to get information that linked top Republican politicians to the Mafia and enormous land fraud schemes.

Bolles drove to the hotel, met with the caller, then returned to his car. When he started the engine, the car blew up, fatally injuring Bolles. Someone had fixed a crude dynamite bomb to the car's ignition. The reporter lingered for eleven days, undergoing six painful operations. He lost both legs and his right arm. As he lay dying on June 13, 1976, Bolles uttered his last words: "Mafia . . . Emprise . . . They finally got me . . . John Adamson, find him."

The nation's press responded quickly. Star investigative reporters from all the major newspapers flocked to Phoenix and began their own investigation into the murder of one of their own. A $100,000

special prosecution fund was established to pinpoint Bolles's killer or killers.

Adamson was the target, the man Bolles had named in his deathbed statement. Moreover, it was proven, Adamson was the very man who had called Bolles to the hotel meeting. Adamson was charged with murder and pled not guilty at a preliminary hearing on June 21, 1976.

The prosecution brought forth two witnesses. The first was Gail Owens, one-time girlfriend of Adamson, who stated that she was with him when Adamson bought a remote control device, telling her that it was a gift for a friend. The second witness, ex-convict Robert Lettiere, testified that he drove with Adamson to a Phoenix parking lot to identify Bolles's car only five days before the lethal explosion.

Adamson then pled guilty to planting the bomb but only after he had plea bargained for protection against the death penalty. This he accomplished by implicating two others, Max Dunlap, a wealthy contractor, and James Robison, a plumber. Adamson insisted that both men had detonated the bomb with a remote control radio transmitter used for model airplanes.

Though both Dunlap and Robison were convicted and sentenced to death on January 10, 1977, the U.S. Supreme Court overturned these convictions on grounds that Dunlap and Robison were denied their constitutional right to face Adamson, their accuser.

In November 1980, Adamson was then resentenced to die in the Arizona gas chamber. The U.S. Court of Appeals for the Ninth Circuit in San Francisco struck down this sentence, stating that the trial judge had originally imposed a prison sentence as appropriate and could not later add the death penalty. Adamson is currently serving a twenty-year prison sentence.

ADONIS, JOE ("JOEY A")
Syndicate Gangster ● (1902-1972)

Born November 22, 1906, in Montemarano, Italy, Adonis (also known as Adone, real name Joseph Doto), entered this country illegally as a teenager. He joined a

New Jersey rackets boss Joe Adonis (right) sat on the board of the national crime syndicate for twenty years; he was deported to Italy in 1953.

New York street gang at an early age, and was arrested in 1922 for rape.

With a group of notorious young hoodlums—Albert Anastasia, Lucky Luciano, Vito Genovese—Adonis rose rapidly in the newly-formed syndicate during the early 1930s, specializing in hijacking and gambling, his area of operations centered in the Broadway district.

Adonis sat as a regular member on the national syndicate board for two decades, issuing murder contracts, infiltrating clothing and foodstuff businesses. It was once said of him by gangster-turned-police-informant Abe "Kid Twist" Reles: "Cross Joey Adonis and you cross the national combination."

In 1951, while Adonis was in charge of most of New Jersey's rackets, he was convicted of conspiracy to violate gambling laws and was sentenced to a two-to-three-year prison term. After learning that his immigration to the U.S. had been illegal, authorities successfully deported him to Italy August 5, 1953.

AIELLO, JOSEPH
Bootlegger ● (1891-1930)

After the Genna gang had been smashed in Chicago by Al Capone, Milwaukee-bred Joey Aiello and his brothers, Dominick, Antonio and Andrew, attempted to seize control of the *Unione Siciliane*, fraternal organization which controlled Sicilian rackets in Chicago. Aiello reorganized the old Genna mob in October, 1927, and joined forces with North and West Side gangs under the leadership of hoodlums George "Bugs" Moran, William Skidmore, Barney Bertsche and Jack Zuta.

Capone, who coveted the presidency of the *Unione*, went to war with Aiello. It was a short one. The Aiellos tried to bribe the chef at the Little Italy Cafe where Capone regularly dined. They wanted him to put prussic acid in Capone's soup and offered the chef $10,000. The nervous cook weepily told Capone of the treachery and the plot failed.

Next, Aiello offered $50,000 to any Chicago hoodlum who would "show us a Capone notch."

"Nobody puts a price on my head and lives!" Capone reportedly screamed when he heard of the Aiello-offered bounty. Weeks later, when Scarface learned that Joe Aiello had been picked up for questioning in a murder, he sent a troop of gunmen to the Chicago Detective Bureau headquarters.

As detectives on duty watched, eight taxis drew up in front of the Bureau. More than twenty men, all Capone gangsters, climbed out.

"What the hell do they think they're gonna do?" one officer stated, "lay siege to this building?"

Three men headed straight for the door of the headquarters. One was recognized as Louis "Little New York" Campagna, Big Al's personal bodyguard.

"It's the Capone crowd!" a detective yelled; he and some others ran to the street and arrested Campagna, Frank Perry and Sam Marcus for carrying guns. The three thugs were all placed in a cell next to Aiello's which turned out to be their real intent.

A policeman, who understood Italian, was hidden next to the cells heard the following:

Joey Aiello offered $50,000 to any gunman who could kill Al Capone during Chicago's 1920s bootleg wars; Scarface got him first on 10/23/30 with machine guns. (UPI)

Aiello: "Can't we settle this? Give me just fifteen days—just fifteen days—and I will sell my stores and house and leave everything in your hands. Think of my wife and baby and let me go."

Louis Campagna laughed and then spat: "You dirty rat! You started this. We'll end it. You're as good as dead!"

Aiello was terrified and, upon his release from jail, did exactly as he had promised the Capone henchmen. He disappeared from Chicago for eighteen months. In his absence, his brother Dominick was shot to death by Capone men. When Aiello did return, he caused no damage to either Capone's empire or prestige.

For three years, Aiello dodged Scarface's triggermen. They finally caught up with him October 23, 1930, when he emerged from the home of one of his aides, Pasquale Prestigiocomo (alias Presto). Several bursts from machine guns tore Aiello to pieces.

Aiello's futile thrust to take over the Chicago rackets ended all serious underworld opposition to Capone.

AIUPPA, JOSEPH JOHN
Syndicate Gangster ● (1907-   )

Another Phi Beta Capone man, Aiuppa worked his way up in the Chicago mob from muscleman at the Hawthorn Hotel, Capone's old Cicero headquarters, to Mafia boss of Cicero.

Aiuppa (alias Joey O'Brien, J. Buonoma, James Spano, Tom O'Brien) was arrested, since 1935, for assault with intent to kill, bribery, and gambling. He has served in federal prisons for failing to register as a dealer in gambling devices, oddly enough, also for illegally transporting hundreds of mourning doves to Chicago from Kansas.

He is, at this writing, still the boss in Cicero.

Present-day syndicate boss of Cicero, Ill. Joseph Aiuppa, a graduate of the old Capone mob.

ALBANESE, CHARLES, JR.
Murderer ● (1937-   )

In the films *The List of Adrian Messenger* and *Kind Hearts and Coronets*, distant relatives to vast fortunes attempt to murder family members in order to inherit great wealth. This fantastic scheme came to grim reality in the case of Charles Albanese, a Chicago businessman. It was Albanese's sinister scheme to kill off elderly relatives of his wife's and of his own family so that the inheritances would fall into his hands.

On August 6, 1980, 87-year-old Mary Lambert died of an apparent heart attack. Her daughter, 69-year-old Marion K. Mueller, succumbed to the same fate on August 18, 1980. More than $150,000 in inheritance monies went to Virginia Albanese, the granddaughter and daughter of the deceased. Virginia was the wife of Charles Albanese.

In 1981 Michael A. Albanese, Sr., died of an unknown illness. His estate, valued at more than $250,000, went to his two sons, Michael, Jr., and Charles. The senior Albanese also left insurance monies of $200,000 to his wife Clare. Should she die, the money would go to her son Charles.

Then Michael A. Albanese, Jr., fell ill, displaying the same symptons his father had shown before his death. Authorities began to look closer at the family deaths and discovered that heavy traces of arsenic were found in bodies of the deceased. The same poison was found to be in the suffering Michael Albanese, Jr.

Police closed in on Charles Albanese just as he, his wife Virginia, and his mother Clare were about to leave on a vacation to Jamaica. Detectives feared that once Albanese reached that sultry island he would quickly murder his wife and mother and gain another $500,000.

Albanese was charged with poisoning Lambert, Mueller, and his father to death and was found guilty on all counts. He was sentenced to death. At this writing, Albanese still resides on Death Row, having used up all of his appeals to stay alive.

"Milwaukee Phil" Alderisio, another Midwest board member and highest-ranking hit man in the entire American *Cosa Nostra*; died in prison in 1971 while serving a term for extortion.

ALDERISIO, FELIX ANTHONY
Syndicate Gangster ● (1922-1971)

Known in mobdom as Milwaukee Phil, Alderisio (alias Philip Aldi, Phil Gato, Felix Alerise, Aderist, Aldresse, Phil Elderise), was one of the top "hit" men of the Chicago mob for a dozen years.

In 1962, Alderisio and Charles Nicoletti were arrested by Chicago police while they crouched on the floor of a black, specially-equipped "hit" car. Switches that could alternately turn out the car's rear and front lights had been installed to trick police tails. Police also found a secret compartment in a backrest with clamps fixed to hold shotguns, pistols, and rifles. Nicoletti and Alderisio, who explained they were "waiting for a friend," were dressed in black pants and black leather jackets. Fortunately for their "friend," the police showed up before he did.

At that time, Alderisio had been arrested thirty-six times since 1929 for burglary, vagrancy, gambling, assault and battery, and murder. Police credited Milwaukee Phil with no less than fourteen murders, all estimated to be "contract" killings on behalf of the syndicate.

Milwaukee Phil died in prison in 1971 while serving a term for extortion.

ALEX, GUS ("GUSSIE")
Syndicate Gangster ● (1916-   )

Alex (alias Ryan, Sam Taylor, Paul Benson, Gus Johnson) has a criminal career that trails back to 1930 with arrests for bribery, assault with intent to kill, manslaughter, kidnapping, and murder.

Born April 1, 1916, Chicago-bred Alex is reportedly the syndicate boss of the Loop and was named as slayer by two murder victims in deathbed identifications (no convictions). Three others who testified that Alex had sent them threats of death were later killed (no convictions).

Alex testified before the McClellan Committee and took the Fifth Amendment thirty-nine times. He has been mysteriously "underground" in Chicago for several years; one report has it that Alex has suffered a series of nervous breakdowns.

A gangster with problems—Gus Alex of the Chicago syndicate; shown before the McClellan Committee, where he took the Fifth thirty-nine times. (UPI)

ALLAWAY, EDWARD CHARLES
Mass Murderer ● (1939-   )

In July 1976, Edward Allaway, who worked as a janitor at the California State University Library at Fullerton, purchased a .22-caliber semiautomatic rifle. A week later he entered the library, roaming through the basement and ground floor of the building, shooting any and all males he accused of "messing around with my wife." He killed seven people and wounded two others before police were summoned to subdue him.

Allaway's wife Bonnie had recently informed him that she intended to end their marriage and the janitor believed that some co-worker at the library had stolen her away from him. A deadlocked jury failed to convict the mass murderer and the judge declared Allaway not guilty by reason of insanity. Allaway was sent to the Atascadero State Hospital for psychiatric study.

ALLEN, FLOYD
Mass Murderer ● (? -1913)

The Allen clan of Carroll County, Va., was a sprawling family that numbered its members in the hundreds. Its patriarch, Floyd Allen, was the political czar of the county and he did as he pleased, thinking himself not only above the law but the very law itself. A Democrat, Allen boasted that he had knocked down every important Republican in the county. He used his fists on sheriffs and deputies, anyone who displeased him, anyone who stood in his way as he walked down sidewalks.

By the turn of the century, Allen's power in Carroll County was thought to be supreme. This was clearly demonstrated after Allen struck a lawman and was ordered to spend an hour in jail. He refused to enter a jail cell and, instead, sent a messenger to the governor of the state who immediately issued a full pardon for Allen.

In 1912, Allen's enemies pursued two of his nephews into North Carolina, arresting them for attacking students in their Virginia school. When this posse crossed the Virginia border with the boys in tow, it was met by a horde of Allen family members, all bearing guns and led by Floyd Allen who ordered his nephews released, rightly stating that the posse had no authority to arrest his relatives in another state.

A fierce gun battle ensued in which several people were seriously wounded. Allen was indicted for assault and battery and brought to trial in Hillsville,

Va., at the Carroll County Courthouse. After three trials, a jury was to bring in a verdict on March 14, 1912. Jury members in this trial had been brought in from distant counties to avoid being influenced by Allen's goons.

Allen entered the courtroom with a host of family members who lined the walls and packed the pews. Most had guns hidden beneath their coats. Allen himself was not searched, thought to be too important a man for such indignities. He had two pistols under a heavy sweater. His attorney was Judge Bolen, a former magistrate who had argued mightily for Allen's innocence.

Enemies of the Allen family were present and also carryied weapons, most of these being deputies of Sheriff Webb, an avowed Allen foe, as was the state's attorney who prosecuted Allen, Commonwealth Foster. Webb's 'deputies ringed the courtroom and the courthouse grounds, all bearing revolvers, rifles, shotguns. On the bench sat Judge Thornton L. Massie, a magistrate whose animosities toward Allen were deeply rooted and long-known.

C. L. Howard, the jury foreman, handed over the verdict to Judge Massie, who confronted the grim-faced Allen and read: "Guilty as charged in the indictment—one year in the penitentiary."

Allen froze in his chair, gripping the armrests with white knuckles.

"Take it easy, Floyd," cautioned attorney Bolen. "There are better days ahead."

"The sheriff will take charge of the prisoner," ordered Judge Massie.

Allen stood up and began to fumble with his sweater, saying: "Gentlemen, I don't aim to go." He jerked forth two pistols and the rest of the Allen clan produced weapons at the same time.

The courtroom was suddenly filled with black smoke as the Allens opened fire and the deputies returned fire. Firing at the deputies, jury, and the judge were Floyd Allen, Sidna Allen, and Floyd's son Claude.

Spectators stampeded toward the door, knocking down benches, chairs and tables, trampling each other in their frantic effort to reach the exit. Little Bettie Ayers, a member of the Allen clan, screamed: "Let me out of here!" She ran toward the doorway and spun in mid-air as a bullet slammed into her back.

Judge Massie sat frozen in horror as he witnessed his courtroom turn into a slaughterhouse. A bullet thudded into his chest and he collapsed, his head slamming onto the bench, blood spreading forth to stain the jury's written verdict.

Prosecutor Foster, who had expected trouble and had armed himself, traded shots with Floyd Allen and was struck several times. Allen turned his weapons in the direction of Deputy Queensberry, who stood in the doorway of the witness room, firing at the clan leader.

Struck in the thigh with a bullet, Allen suddenly toppled backward to crash through a rail and on top of his attorney, Bolen. The panicked lawyer screamed at his client: "For God's sake, get off me before they kill me shooting at you!"

A clerk named Goad fired his weapon repeatedly at the Allens. Sidna and Claude Allen returned fire, their bullets striking Goad eleven times, one bullet smashing through Goad's mouth, knocking out teeth and exiting through the back of his neck. Incredibly, the dogged clerk remained standing, firing wildly back.

Floyd Allen staggered to his feet and reeled backward down the aisle where his kinsman Sidna Allen stood firing at deputies. "I'm hit bad," Floyd shouted to Sidna, ordering him to give him a gun since his own were now empty. He took another weapon and fired at deputies as he hobbled from the courtroom.

Running down the courtroom stairs to his horse, Allen turned his wounded leg on a rock, breaking it. He begged relatives to help him mount. Once in the saddle, he passed out, revived, and then asked relatives to get him a carriage in which he might escape. He was taken to a nearby stable where he was placed on hay. His relatives gathered around, expecting him to die.

Inside the smoky courtroom, moans and screams were heard everywhere. Judge Massie was dying on the bench, held by juror Daniel Thomas. "Sidna Allen shot me," Massie croaked. "Give me a drink of water . . . tell my wife." Sheriff Webb was also dead, dozens of bullets riddling his body. He was found clenching a toothpick in his mouth.

Prosecutor Foster had been struck by a bullet in the head but still managed to stagger into the jury room where he collapsed on a couch. His wife ran to his side just as he dropped an empty gun he had been clutching. A huge man, it took several men to lift Foster up. As they did so, dozens of bullets spilled from his pockets. Foster had anticipated a battle and he had gotten one.

In addition to Massie, Webb, Foster, and a juror named Fowler, Bettie Ayers was carried away to also die of her wound. Sixteen others were seriously wounded.

Allen was quickly surrounded in the stable by Webb's deputies. Before he was taken away to the jail cell he so bitterly battled to avoid, Allen was confronted by his son Victor who had taken no part in the battle and who had shunned violence all his life.

"This thing hurts me," Victor Allen said to his father as he kneeled next to the wounded man. "I've always tried to do right."

Floyd Allen told his son: "I made my peace with God about seven years gone and methinks I see him now."

"No," replied Victor, shaking his head, "it's the devil that you see."

Floyd Allen recovered from his wounds and then stood trial for murder, as did his two sons, Claude and Victor, as well as Sidna Allen. Floyd and Claude were convicted and sentenced to death, going to Virginia's electric chair in 1913. Sidna Allen went to prison for fifteen years but was pardoned by Governor Harry Byrd in 1926. Victor Allen was acquitted.

Clay Allison, an alcoholic gunslinger who terrorized New Mexico in the 1870s. (Western Historical Collections, U. of Okla. Library)

ALLISON, CLAY
Gunman, Outlaw ● (1840-1877)

BACKGROUND: BORN IN RURAL TENNESSEE. MINOR PUBLIC EDUCATION. ORIGINAL OCCUPATION, COWBOY. HIRED OUT AS A GUNMAN TO VARIOUS CATTLE BARONS IN NEW MEXICO IN THE 1870S. DESCRIPTION: 6', BLUE EYES, BROWN HAIR, SLENDER. ALIASES: NONE, RECORD: SHOT AND KILLED AN ESTIMATED FIFTEEN GUNMEN MOSTLY IN THE NEW MEXICO TERRITORY IN A TEN-YEAR SPAN, BEGINNING ABOUT 1867.

No historian ever doubted Clay Allison's ability as a fast gun. What most historians either refuse or neglect to state is that this handsome daredevil of an outlaw, popularized as a champion of justice, was a roaring alcoholic who seldom if ever gave his opponents a chance in a standup fight.

Allison was a bully who delighted in terrorizing small towns and aging sheriffs. One story has Allison, drunk to the marrow, charging up and down the main street of Canadian, Texas, naked except for his wide-brim hat, boots and six guns, shooting out store windows.

Another is not as capricious. The deputy sheriff of Las Animas, Col. once attempted to disarm Allison and his brother John, and nervously squeezed the trigger of his shotgun. John Allison was shot in the arm and Clay, swearing vengeance, sent a bullet into the deputy's forehead. The killing was ruled self-defense.

Most of Allison's time was spent trying to nurture his small ranch on the Washita River in New Mexico. To make extra money, he would hire out his gun to enforce the boundary rights of large ranches. His reputation as a fast gun stemmed from run-ins such as those he had with Chunk Colbert and Francisco "Pancho" Griego.

In Colbert's case it was a matter of two old friends getting together for dinner to murder each other. The two gunfighters sat down to dinner one night at the Clifton House at Red River Station in Texas. One biographer claims the two stirred their coffee with the muzzles of their six guns as they eye-balled each other.

When Allison saw Chunk drop his hand from sight, he tilted his chair back, firing as he fell and hitting Colbert between the eyes. Getting up, Clay finished his steak without even glancing up to see his enemy's body hauled away.

Griego went faster and without any ceremony. Allison thought it peculiar that the Mexican outlaw fan himself with his large sombrero during one of Cimmaron's coldest days. Obviously Griego was going for his gun hidden behind the hat and, just as obviously, Allison drilled him dead.

The stories of Allison backing down lawmen Wyatt Earp and Bat Masterson in Dodge City are apocryphal; Clay Allison was not a man to face marshals in open combat. He was clever and his fame with a gun was earned through stealth and guile.

It was probably fitting that this border terrorist met with an inglorious and ironic end. While on his way to kill John McCullough, a neighbor, Allison got drunk and fell out of his wagon. He was killed when the heavily-loaded vehicle rolled over his neck.

Supposedly Allison respected his grisly occupation. "I never killed a man who didn't need it," he once said, claiming that in the course of shooting more than a dozen men he was "protecting the property holders of the country from thieves, outlaws and murderers."

ALMAREZ, STELLA DELORES
Murderer ● (1951-   )

When her marriage failed, Stella Delores Almarez of Norfolk, Neb., killed her two youngest girls by slashing their throats on June 18, 1980. Then she shot her two oldest girls, ages seven and ten. She then attempted suicide, according to one report, but failed.

Almarez was charged with murdering her children but, in November 1980, a Madison County jury found her not guilty by reason of insanity. She was sent to the Lincoln Regional Center, a medical institution.

The verdict in the Almarez case caused a sensation, resulting in the burden of proof for a person's insanity being shifted from the prosecution to the defense. Nebraska law was further altered by this case in that it became mandatory for a judge, not

hospital officials, to sign a written order for the defendant's release from a mental facility.

Almarez was released unconditionally on October 2, 1985, on the written order of Judge Merritt Warren, who declared her no longer a danger to herself or society. Almarez had served only five years in a comfortable medical institution where she was permitted to wander the grounds at will and even work outside the hospital. Those rules were also tightened after this killer's release.

ALMY, FRANK C.
Murderer, Burglar ● (? -1892)

For years, Almy operated as a burglar in the New England area under the name of George Abbott. He was apprehended and was sentenced to serve a fifteen-year term in the New Hampshire State Prison, but he escaped.

After having a marriage proposal turned down, Almy murdered Christie Warden July 17, 1891, near Hanover, N.H. Curiously, while armed bands of men sought him, Almy hid out for almost a month in the Warden barn. He was ultimately discovered and brought to trial in 1892, convicted following his confession, and sentenced to death.

ALTERIE, LOUIS ("TWO-GUN")
Bootlegger ● (1892-1935)

Of all Dion O'Bannion's daffy gunners in his Prohibition-fed North Side Chicago gang, Louis Alterie (nee Leland Verain) was the wackiest. He was born in Colorado and owned a small ranch there before moving Eastward to join O'Bannion in the early 1920s.

Alterie was a minor partner in O'Bannion's wide-open gambling casinos and bootlegging operations and was addicted to wearing two pistols Western-style on his hips.

One of Alterie's close pals in the church-going, sentimental O'Bannion organization was Samuel J. "Nails" Morton who fronted for the mob, a well-dressed, cultured gentleman who had won the *Croix de Guerre* during the First World War after leading several heroic charges against German machine-gun emplacements. Morton was a horseman of some note, riding each day along the Lincoln Park bridle path. On one of these rides, a spirited horse threw him and kicked him to death.

Louis "Two Gun" Alterie hijacked beer trucks for Chicago gangster Dion O'Bannion during Prohibition; he offered to shoot it out with his boss's killers in the heart of the Loop at high noon but left for his Colorado ranch when things got too hot in 1924. (UPI)

Hearing his pal was dead, Alterie went berserk; he went to the stables, re ted the same horse and, taking it to the exact spot where Nails had been killed, shot the animal through the head (a scene repeated in the classic gangster film, *Public Enemy*).

Alterie then called the stable owner and said: "We taught that goddamn horse of yours a lesson. If you want the saddle, go and get it."

Even more infuriating for Two-Gun was the assassination of his chief, Dion O'Bannion, in 1924. He wept openly at O'Bannion's funeral and then, in a rage, turned to reporters and said: "I have no idea who killed Deanie, but I would die smiling if only I had a chance to meet the guys who did, any time, any place they mention and I would get at least two or three of them before they got me. If I knew who killed Deanie, I'd shoot it out with the gang of killers before the sun rose in the morning and some of us, maybe all of us, would be lying on slabs in the undertaker's place."

The logical dueling ground, he pointed out, would be the world's busiest corner—Madison and State Streets—at high noon.

Reform Mayor Dever was flabbergasted when he heard of the Alterie challenge. "Are we still abiding by the code of the dark ages?" he stormed.

The brag had created heat for the North Side Mob and its new nominal leader, George "Bugs" Moran, went to Alterie and told him: "You're getting us in bad. You talk too much. Beat it."

Alterie took the hint and caught the next train west to his Colorado ranch, where he lived out his days in obscurity.

[ALSO SEE Dion O'Bannion.]

ANASTASIA, ALBERT
Mafia Chief, Murderer ● (1903-1957)

Known as the "Lord High Executioner" of the Mafia in New York and New Jersey for three decades, Anastasia headed up the reorganized Murder, Inc. after its near-destruction following the revelations of informant Abe "Kid Twist" Reles. (It was Anastasia who ordered Reles killed and also sent out twelve murder contracts for those gangleaders Lepke thought might talk when he went underground to avoid prosecution for murder in 1937.)

Anastasia, who came up through the old "Joe the Boss" Masseria outfit, was an intimate of Luciano's and was one of the four assassins who murdered Masseria in 1931 (the others being Vito Genovese, Bugsy Siegel and Joe Adonis). His role in this killing assured him of a top position in the newly-formed syndicate which, after Meyer Lansky and Bugsy Siegel branched out into gambling interests in California, Florida and Cuba, was the directorship of Murder, Inc. Anastasia was also Luciano's partner in a lucrative narcotics and brothel empire.

In the late 1940s, Anastasia became head of the Vincent Mangano Mafia family, one of the five families ruling New York rackets (upon his death he was succeeded by Carlo Gambino). He closed the books on Mafia membership in the early 1950s and backed up this edict with several murders issued through Murder, Inc., and with his lofty membership on the board of directors of the polyglot national crime syndicate.

Following the decline of Frank Costello's power in the late 1950s, Anastasia, a Costello ally, became the prime target for ruthlessly ambitious Vito Genovese. Genovese proceeded with caution against "The Mad Hatter" of crime, as Anastasia was aptly called. No one knew better than Genovese what kill-crazy wrath Anastasia could muster when angered.

Once, when watching TV, Anastasia happened to see a news report dealing with Arnold Schuster, a Brooklyn resident. Schuster had spotted the notorious bank robber Willie Sutton on the subway one evening, remembering him from wanted posters he had seen. He informed the police, who quickly apprehended the much-wanted Sutton.

Anastasia, watching Schuster being interviewed, suddenly catapulted from his chair and yelled to three of his stooges who were in the room: "I can't stand squealers! Hit that guy!"

Schuster was not a mob man, nor had he ever been connected with any criminal activities; he was merely a citizen doing what he

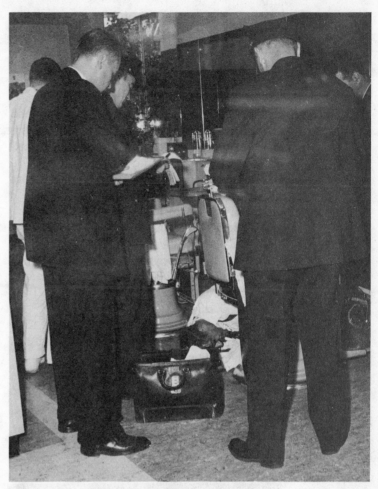

"Lord High Executioner" of Murder, Inc., Albert Anastasia (on floor between barber chairs) minutes after being shot to death by Vito Genovese's gunmen, 10/25/57.

thought to be his duty. He was "hit" and killed March 8, 1952. He had the misfortune to fall beneath the gaze of the lunatic Anastasia.

Carefully, then, Genovese engineered Anastasia's end; it was bloody and in the best gangster tradition of the rub-out. Santo Trafficante, a Genovese henchman, had dinner with Anastasia at the Park Sheraton Hotel (where Trafficante was staying) and reportedly gave him "the kiss of death," following the meal—a slight peck to the cheek upon departure.

The next day, October 25, 1957, Anastasia strolled into the Sheraton basement barbershop and told proprietor Arthur Grasso to give him "a quick haircut." He closed his eyes.

In moments, two men, named later by Joseph Valachi as Carlo Gambino and Joseph Biondo (alias Joe Bandy), entered the shop with scarves covering their faces. One of them whispered to barber Grasso, "Keep your mouth shut if you don't want your head blown off."

Anastasia, his eyes still closed, was wholly unprotected. His chief bodyguard had conveniently called in sick. The two gunmen stepped behind the chair in which he sat and pumped ten bullets into him at close range. Anastasia, a bull of a man, still lived and jerked upward out of the chair, kicking away the footrest. On his feet, he made a wild lunge at the two killers and awkwardly stumbled into a mirror. As it shattered, two more shots hit him in the back of the head.

He fell between the barber chairs without a word as his murderers ran from the shop, throwing their pistols to the gutter, and disappeared into the heavy pedestrian traffic outside. They were never apprehended.

It was the kind of professional killing Anastasia would have devilishly appreciated . . . under different circumstances.

[ALSO SEE Louis "Lepke" Buchalter, Vito Genovese, Charles "Lucky" Luciano.]

William "Bloody Bill" Anderson led Civil War guerrillas in murderous raids into Missouri and Kansas. (State Historical Society of Missouri)

ANDERSON, WILLIAM ("BLOODY BILL")
Guerrilla, Murderer ● (? -1864)

Anderson was one of the ruthless lieutenants who served under William Clarke Quantrill's guerrilla band which raided the Missouri-Kansas border towns during the Civil War, ostensibly for the Confederacy. In reality, Quantrill's band, never exceeding 450 men, were terrorists, robbers and murderers. Anderson was the bloodiest of the lot, a raider who enjoyed shooting down unarmed men and boys he thought loyal to the Union.

When Quantrill led his guerillas into Lawrence, Kansas on a bloodthirsty raid August 23, 1863, Bill Anderson was at his side directing a column of men which included Frank James and Cole Younger. For two hours, Quantrill and Anderson led their marauders through Lawrence's unprotected streets, shooting every

man and boy in sight, almost all of whom were unarmed. Only one young boy was spared. Anderson took great pride in compelling the women and girls of the town to watch the slaughter as a "lesson."

Bloody Bill always insisted on a display of violence. He himself was a walking arsenal advertising death and war. At times he carried eight revolvers stuck around his belt, a hatchet, and a saber. On his horse were four rifles and two saddle bags full of pistols.

In the fall of 1864, Anderson split away from Quantrill to lead his own raid against Centralia, Missouri. With him went thirty of his most ruthless killers, including a seventeen-year-old beardless youth named Jesse Woodson James. They struck Centralia on September 26, 1864, destroying the stores and burning the railroad station. A train pulled into the small town at noon carrying twenty-five Union soldiers. They were quickly disarmed; Anderson ordered them to strip to their underclothes. He then lined them up and asked if any were officers. One Thomas Goodwin said he was (he was only a sergeant) and Anderson ordered him out of the rank. He alone was spared the fate of his comrades.

Turning to his most trusted executioner, Arch Clement, a good friend of Frank and Jesse James, Anderson said: "Muster out the rest of these men, Arch."

Delighted with his task, the diminutive Clement stepped forward smiling. At point blank range he shot dead each man in the line. Some of Anderson's men helped him kill the helpless troopers. Young Jesse James stood and watched.

In October, 1864, Anderson ran into a troop of regular Union soldiers while fleeing through Ray County, Mo. Commander S. P. Cox led a charge against the guerrillas, personally shooting Anderson dead from the saddle.

[ALSO SEE Jesse Woodson James, William Clark Quantrill.]

Anderson's bloody executioner at Centralia, "Little Arch" Clement. (State Historical Society of Missouri)

ANDREWS, LOWELL LEE
Murderer ● (c1940-1959)

An honor student, Lowell Lee Andrews was considered to be the model son. He never drank and went to church regularly. He never dated girls but this may have been attributed to the 18-year-old's tremendous bulk. He weighed more than 300 pounds. The local paper in Wolcott, Kansas, once described Andrews as "the nicest boy" in town.

A loner, Andrews kept to his room at home, nurturing a secret dream, which was to travel to Chicago to become a gangster, wear pin-strip suits, and carry guns. He needed money. To get it, he decided to kill his well-to-do farming parents, along with his sister. After their deaths, he would sell the farm, fulfill his dream, travel to Chicago in style, and set himself up as a gang chief.

With that thought cramming his brain, Andrews entered the living room as his family watched television. He carried a rifle and a revolver. Wordlessly, he shot his sister between the eyes and then pumped bullets into his mother and father. He was a bad shot. Both his parents were still alive and he had to reload his weapons, firing more bullets into his helpless victims.

At first the killings were blamed on unknown invaders but Andrews, a few days later, went to his local pastor and confessed the murders. He was quickly tried, convicted, and condemned, despite overwhelming medical evidence that he was a hopeless schizophrenic. Andrews was executed by hanging at Leavenworth Prison in 1959.

ANNENBERG, MOSES
Tax Evader ● (1878-1942)

The establishment of one of America's greatest family fortunes was built by Moses Annenberg, who began his career as a lowly circulation booster for the *Chicago Tribune*, becoming that newspaper's circulation manager by 1904. He left the *Tribune* and went to work for William Randolph Hearst's *Examiner* and *American* newspapers, becoming the head of a huge gang of thugs who attacked and beat up, sometimes murdered, distribution agents and newsmen selling opposition papers.

Annenberg ran a school for circulation enforcers which focused on assault and battery. Most of his men carried guns and did not stop short of using them. Several murders during the bloody newspaper circulation wars of 1910-1911 in Chicago were performed by Annenberg's goons who later became much-feared Prohibition gangsters, men like Charles Dion O'Bannion, George "Bugs" Moran, and Frankie McErlane, the latter being the first to use a submachine gun during the bootleg wars of the Roaring Twenties.

Through the very men he hired to muscle his newspaper distribution, Annenberg grew powerful. By 1922, he had formed an association with the then crime czar of Chicago, Johnny Torrio, reportedly borrowing a large sum of money from Torrio to purchase a tip sheet, the *Daily Racing Form*. With increasing profits from this publication, Annenberg began to purchase other publications, including the *Philadelphia Inquirer*. His main source of revenues, however, flowed from Nationwide News Service, which provided all the results of racetracks throughout the country.

Nationwide was the perfect conduit through which organized crime could control the results from every racetrack in America. In 1929, Chicago crime czar Al Capone set up a meeting of all the important crime bosses in the country. The meeting, the first summit conference of organized crime, was held in Atlantic City and Capone brought Moses Annenberg with him. Annenberg addressed the top mob leaders of the country, pointing out that millions could be gleaned if all the gangs subscribed to his Nationwide News Service. Nationwide was then reorganized in association with a number of East Coast syndicate members, including Frank Erickson, Meyer Lansky, Frank Costello, and Charles "Lucky" Luciano.

The monopoly on racing results were sent to thousands of syndicate bookie joints, gambling dens, and poolrooms across the country over AT&T wires. Millions poured into Annenberg's coffers. Like his mentor, Capone, Annenberg felt he owed his government nothing and he paid little or no income taxes. In 1939, Annenberg and his son Walter were indicted on income tax evasion charges.

Investigators charged that in 1932, for example,

Annenberg paid only a few hundred dollars in taxes when his vast income dictated a payment of at least $300,000. In 1936, Annenberg paid less than $500,000 when he should have paid $1,500,000, according to federal authorities. Overall, Annenberg owed $9.5 million. As usual, Moses settled the matter by making a deal. In exchange for all charges being dropped against his son Walter, Moses Annenberg would pay the $9.5 million and enter a guilty plea.

When charges against Walter Annenberg were dropped, Moses paid the fine, pled guilty and received a three-year prison term. Annenberg served his time in comfort and when he was released he retired to a life of luxury. His estate passed on to his son, the Annenberg fortune estimated to be one of the fourth or fifth largest in America at this time, a fortune built upon illegal gambling and syndicate power.

APACHE KID, THE
Murderer, Robber ● (1867- ?)

At age twenty, the Indian known as the Apache Kid was the pride of his nation, a fearless sergeant of scouts on the San Carlos, N. M. reservation. He worked under the command of Indian fighter and scout Al Sieber, and his exploits concerning the arrests of rum-runners and gun smugglers were legendary in that part of the West.

When the Kid's father was killed by a renegade, he took tribal revenge by slaying the murderer. The Kid then surrendered to Sieber but later, justly fearing shabby treatment in the white man's courts, fled with some followers. For two years the Kid hid out; he was finally captured, tried, and convicted of murder, but President Cleveland pardoned him.

The running had changed the Kid, and he turned away from the lawful life, angrily killing a whiskey drummer who attempted to sell fire water to his people. He was tried a second time and received a seven-year jail term. On his way to the Yuma jail, the Kid broke away and killed two of his guards, deputies Glen Reynolds and Bill Holmes, on November 1,

The Apache Kid, cavalry scout gone wrong. (Arizona Historical Society Library)

1889. Eugene Middleton, a survivor, staggered back to Globe, Ariz., badly wounded, with the news.

Authorities placed a $5,000 reward for the capture of the Apache Kid dead or alive, but no one ever collected the bounty. For two years the Kid and some members of his tribe roamed the New Mexico territory, robbing gold and horses from prospectors, and raping a number of defenseless settlers' wives. The Kid took a wife and lived high in the hills of the Sierra Madre in Mexico, crossing the border when in need of supplies and money.

In 1894, a prospector named Edward A. Clark, reported shooting two Indians, a man and woman, who had invaded his camp one night, just north of Tucson, Ariz. He had killed the squaw, he reported, and wounded the man. He claimed it was the Apache Kid and was positive the Indian's back wound was fatal.

"He crawled away to die somewhere, I know," Clark stated.

Clark may have been right. The Apache Kid never appeared after that, though some historians claim that it was another Indian Clark wounded and the Kid, a practical soul, merely settled down in Mexico, raised a family and lived unknown into the twentieth century.

APPO, QUIMBY
Murderer ● (1814-1912)

The strangest prisoner to ever be locked inside the old New York Tombs jail was a bizarre little Chinese man named Lee Ah Bow, who was better known to the press and police as Quimby Appo. He was also known in his long heyday of mayhem and murder as the "Chinese Devilman," and "Devil Appo." He was also known to be extremely violent and incurably insane.

Appo, despite claims to the contrary, was not among the first Chinese to arrive in New York. The first Chinese to arrive in the city were entertainers whose showboat, the junk Ki Ying, caught fire while docked in the East River, and stranded the troupe. These Chinese took rooms on Mott Street between Chatham and Pell; this area later became the foundation for New York City's Chinatown. It was a good seven years later when Appo arrived from California as the personal slave of a wealthy businessman. He possessed, even then, a murderous temperament.

In 1840, Appo entered a New York shop and began arguing with the owner over the price of goods, suddenly attacking the man. Arrested and thrown into the New York Tombs, Appo was visited in his cell by missionaries who pled his case as a befuddled foreigner and who won him a quick release. This charitable action somehow led Appo to believe that he could perform any kind of violence and be championed by his friends the missionaries.

Over a period of twenty years, Appo was arrested repeatedly, at least a dozen times, for violent and inexplicable assaults and attempted murder. On March 9, 1859, Appo attacked his mistress, stabbing her when she served him a cold dinner. Another guest in the boardinghouse rushed into the room and Appo drove a knife into this woman's heart. He then rushed down the back stairs shouting incoherently. The heavyset landlady barred his path at the bottom of the stairs and when she turned away briefly Appo stabbed her in the buttock.

Arrested for murder, Appo was then returned to the Tombs. He was convicted and scheduled to hang. Again, Appo's missionary friends appeared and begged authorities for leniency. Incredibly, Appo's sentence was reduced to a seven-year term. He made those seven years a living hell for his jailors. He would bite the hands of jailors nervously shoving his food through the bars of his cell. He would claw at anyone coming close to his cell, including the missionaries who visited him.

Appo was released in 1867 and, a short time later, stabbed Lizzie Williams, a landlady who had the nerve to demand her rent. Missionaries hired a lawyer for the Devilman and he was soon released. In 1872, Appo dug up a cobblestone from the street and brought this crashing down on the head of John Linkowski, crushing his victim's skull.

Thrown into the Tombs for the Linkowski murder, Appo was soon released due to the zealous efforts of the missionaires who swore that the Devilman was about to embrace the cross. In 1875 Appo stabbed a Bowery prostitute, one Cork Maggie, but since she survived the attack, the missionaries pointed out, there was no point in prosecuting Appo. Police did not even bother to arrest the Devilman for this offense.

On October 21, 1876, the Devilman sat down to play poker with John Kelly and others. After losing a few hands, Appo leaped to his feet and accused Kelly of cheating him. He dove across the table and drove a dirk many times into the gambler's chest, killing him on the spot.

Before the missionaries could mount a campaign to protect their pet killer, authorities ruled Appo to be a lunatic and sent him to Mattewan, the state prison for the insane. He lived at this institution for the next 36 years, among such notorious criminals as train robber Oliver Curtis Perry and millionaire killer Harry K. Thaw.

Appo would stand at his cell window every evening, waiting for the Hudson River Nightboat to come into view. When he spotted its searchlight, he would scream: "Here comes my diamond!" Shortly before his death, a Mattewan spokesman reported that the Devilman "believes that he has grand hotels, palaces, servants, and horses outside the asylum. He believes that he is King of the World and Omnipotent, the Second God, that he commands the wind and the sun, that Tom Sharkey and General Coxey are his military staff, and that he must suffer for Ireland."

All of these hallucinations came to an end when, on June 23, 1912, the Devilman died of old age. He was 98. No one claimed the body, which was buried on the grounds of the asylum.

(ALSO SEE Oliver Curtis Perry, Harry K. Thaw)

ARCHER-GILLIGAN, AMELIA
Murderer ● (1869-1928)

A self-styled nurse, Amelia Archer-Gillian, who liked to be called Sister Amy, purchased a run-down boarding house in Windsor, Connecticut some time around 1912. She advertised that she would take tender care of the elderly and at bargain basement prices. Customers flocked to her, their elderly relatives in tow.

Sister Amy insisted that all of her patients sign over their wills to her, explaining that this was the only way in which she could recoup her considerable expenses that were certainly not covered in the meager costs of supporting her elderly charges. She even married five old men, all of whom died shortly after taking their vows with Sister Amy.

Sister Amy's nursing home was really nothing more than a murder house. All of her anicent husbands perished at her hands, authorities later learned. At least a dozen or more women were also killed by Sister Amy, only months after after each had signed over their wills to her. She either poisoned her victims by dosing their scant meals or, to save money on the meals, simply used a pillow to suffocate her patients.

Greed was Archer-Gilligan's undoing. She lost patience with her charges, killing them in her murder factory almost as quickly as they walked through the door. In one instance, a relative learned that the aunt placed in the charge of Sister Amy had died only a few days after taking up residence in the nursing home and only an hour after the aunt signed over her will to Archer-Gilligan. The relative did some research and then went to the police, expressing her suspicions and pointing out that the death rate at the Archer-Gilligan center was ten times higher than other homes for the aged.

Police placed an undercover worker inside the home who witnessed Sister Amy dosing her patients' food with poison. Archer-Gilligan was arrested and was convicted of several murders in 1914. She received a life sentence and was sent to Weathersfield Prison where Sister Amy tried to poison not only the warden but all of the guards. She was removed to a lunatic asylum where, in 1928, she died in her padded cell.

ARMISTEAD, NORMA JEAN
Murderer ● (1930-   )

Nurse Norma Jean Armistead slipped into the medical records section of the Kaiser Hospital in Los Angeles in October 1974. She wrote an entry into the general ledger, recording her own pregnancy, a falsehood that would make no sense until the following year. When the entry was discovered, the medical staff believed that the entry had been made by a resident physician. Some sneering comments were made that Norma Armistead was, at age 44, too old to have a child, and then the matter was forgotten.

Armistead, with hospital knowledge of those women who were expecting to give birth, on May 15, 1975, visited 28-year-old Kathryn Viramontes in her apartment. The pregnant woman was nearing the end of her term of pregnancy and expected to give birth any day. Nurse Armistead suddenly attacked Viramontes with a knife, slashing her to death. She then performed a crude caesarian operation and removed the living child from her victim's womb, fleeing the Van Nuys apartment with the child.

The killer immediately checked into the hospital, telling the medical staff that she had given premature birth to the boy at home. Her story was treated with disbelief and when the Viramontes woman was found slain, authorities quickly determined the truth.

Armistead was charged with homicide and a

battle ensued over her sanity at the time of the slaying. The courts determined the nurse to be sane and she was convicted of murder and sent to prison in one of the most bizarre murder cases in recent times.

ARNOLD, STEPHEN
Murderer ● (Circa 1775- ?)

Slightly touched with lunacy, Stephen Arnold, as a schoolteacher in Cooperstown, N. Y., flew into a rage every time a pupil made a mistake. He found it intolerable, therefore, when his own niece, six-year-old Betsy Van Amburgh, could not spell the word "gig."

Arnold, who was taking care of Betsy for his brother, beat her wildly with a club, killing her. Regaining his senses, the schoolteacher fled to Pittsburgh, Pa. There he was captured and returned to New York for trial in 1805.

Quickly convicted, Arnold was sentenced to hang. His public execution was bloated with pomp. Thousands came to Cooperstown to view the hanging; bands played as Arnold marched to the gallows. He was preceded by a battalion of infantry and a company of artillery, their caissons gayly bedecked with bunting and flowers.

Quavering, with the rope about his neck, Arnold listened to a minister give a lengthy sermon admonishing his evil deed, the speech sprinkled with Arnold's own words of caution to young men warning them to curb their tempers.

Just before the trap was sprung, the sheriff stepped forth and ceremoniously flung the rope from Arnold's neck while the stunned spectators blinked. The sheriff then produced a reprieve from the governor, a document he had kept in his pocket all morning. His explanation for concealing the document was that he wanted Arnold to experience the dread of death for his sin and also that he did not wish to disappoint the crowd of some excitement. (The throng was disappointed.)

Arnold, for reasons of temporary insanity, later received a pardon.

ATTEBERY (OR ATTEBURY), IRA
Murderer ● (1915-1979)

A retired trucker living in a small San Antonio, Tex., trailer park, Attebery faithfully attended the town's annual Battle of the Flowers parade, which snaked past his home. A loner, Attebery stood silently throughout the festivities every year, then returned to his trailer.

He drastically altered his procedure on April 27, 1979, when he gathered six automatic rifles and dozens of bullet clips inside his trailer. As the parade ensued, Attebery inexplicably began firing at random into a crowd of about five thousand persons nearby. He would fire, duck, then fire again, shouting: "Traitors! Traitors!" For more than 30 minutes, the 64-year-old man blasted fleeing people. When police closed in, the retired truck driver turned a gun on himself.

Attebery had killed two people and seriously wounded another 50 parade spectators. An autopsy may have revealed the motive for the murderer's suddenly berserk behavior. Considerable quantities of PCP were found in Attebery's system. Known as "angel dust," this deadly drug is known to bring about homocidal and suicidal behavior in drug addicts.

AULISIO, JOSEPH
Murderer ● (1966-   )

A ccording to his high school principal, Joseph Aulisio was a model student who was known be obedient, well-mannered, and helpful. Like many other boys in the small town of Forge, Pa., he tinkered with cars and was expected to become a mechanic. His father, Robert Aulisio, was a biology teacher in the high school attended by Joseph. All seemed normal and happy in the boy's life.

Then the Aulisios suffered the tragedy of losing their three-month-old child to illness. Strained relations led to a divorce action. Joseph grew withdrawn, sullen, angry. His school grades declined and he began cutting classes.

On July 26, 1981, fifteen-year-old Aulisio abducted two children, eight-year-old Cheryl Ziemba and her four-year-old brother Christopher, from their home outside Scranton, Pa. Their bodies were found in an abandoned strip mine two days later. Both had been shotgunned to death.

Aulisio was identified as the abductor. Convicted of first degree murder, he was sentenced to death. Death penalty opponents roared protest against sending the boy to the electric chair. Countered Judge James Walsh of the Lackawanna County Common Pleas Court: "We're reading more and more about vicious crimes by younger and younger people. Incidents like that are causing a lot of people to say that if they are guilty of adult criminal activity they should be subject to adult punishment."

In 1982, Aulisio was sent to Death Row to await execution, one of the youngest prisoners ever to face electrocution in Pennsylvania. A long series of appeals began and Aulisio was eventually sent to the State Correctional Institution at Huntingdon, Pa.

BAILEY, HARVEY ("OLD HARVE")
Bankrobber ● (1889-1979)

BACKGROUND: BORN AND RAISED IN OKLAHOMA. MINOR PUBLIC EDUCATION. ORIGINAL OCCUPATION, SALESMAN. DESCRIPTION: 5'11", BROWN EYES, GREY-BROWN HAIR, ATHLETIC BUILD. ALIASES: UNKNOWN. RECORD: PRACTICED SEVERAL CONFIDENCE GAMES BEFORE 1920 IN THE SOUTHWEST; ROBBED SEVERAL SMALL TOWN BANKS IN THE SOUTHWEST, PARTICULARLY OKLAHOMA, TEXAS, AND NEW MEXICO IN THE EARLY 1920S; ROBBED THE U.S. DENVER MINT WITH JAMES RIPLEY IN 1922 (GETTING AN ESTIMATED $500,000); ROBBED THE LINCOLN NATIONAL BANK AND TRUST COMPANY IN 1931 WITH EDDIE BENTZ (FOR $1,000,000 IN CASH AND NEGOTIABLE SECURITIES); ROBBED THE BANK IN FORT SCOTT, KAN., MAY, 1932; CAPTURED WEEKS LATER IN KANSAS CITY AND SENT TO THE KANSAS STATE PENITENTIARY, ESCAPING 5/31/33; RECAPTURED IN PARADISE, TEX. 8/12/33 BY FBI AGENTS; ESCAPED FROM THE DALLAS JAIL 9/4/33; RECAPTURED DAYS LATER; TRIED AND CONVICTED AS AN ACCOMPLICE IN THE CHARLES URSCHEL KIDNAPPING; SENTENCED TO LIFE IMPRISONMENT AT LEAVENWORTH; PAROLED IN 1965.

Considered the most professional bankrobber of the 1920s, Harvey Bailey (shown shackled at feet, recaptured after a sensational jail break in Dallas in 1933). (UPI)

During the wild bankrobbing days of the 1920s the king of heist men was Harvey Bailey. An elusive bandit from the Southwest, Bailey preferred to work alone or with the same gang only one time. His thinking was that the weaker the contact with the other criminals the better chance he stood of remaining at large. This maneuver worked well for twenty years.

Bailey's reputation in the underworld was matchless. Where the bankrobber was con-sidered the top man of crime, Bailey was considered the only bankrobber in the nation without peers. He had pulled off some of the biggest robberies in America.

A cool-headed bandit who preferred to avoid gunplay, Bailey robbed the U.S. Denver Mint in 1922, with Jim Ripley and others of more than a half million in untraceable bills. Gigantic hauls like this kept Bailey out of circulation for long spells, which was much to his liking. With his good friend Eddie Bentz (another gentleman bankrobber who retired after each job to a quiet home and a massive library), Bailey knocked over the Lincoln National Bank and Trust Company in Lincoln, Neb. in 1931. Up to that time it was the largest robbery ever committed in the country, the take being more than $1,000,000 in cash and securities.

There were a half dozen other heist men in on that spectacular theft and, beyond their shares, there were huge amounts of money spent on cars, hideouts, and fences to handle the negotiable securities. In the end, there was considerably less to retire on than Bailey had expected. He was compelled to look up Ma Barker and her wild brood of boys for more action. In May, 1932, he got it.

Though Ma's group of raiders was too large for Bailey's liking, he joined in their plan to rob the bank in Fort Scott, Kansas. The gang included Freddie Barker, Alvin Karpis, Larry De-Vol, Phil Courtney, Tommy Holden and Bailey. And Ma Barker would get her "cut" as usual for helping to organize the job.

The plan seemed amateurish from the start but Bailey needed money so he let the hotheaded Barkers do the talking and bungling. Everything seemed to go wrong. A few minutes after Bailey had entered the bank with DeVol, Courtney, Barker and Karpis, a teller hit an alarm button.

Freddie Barker, always the lethal lunatic, began yelling that he was going to "shoot everybody in the place!" Bailey looked out a window to see a still-deserted street. "Take it easy, Fred," he said soothingly to the neurotic gangster. "Just get the money." Barker and DeVol scooped up $47,000 from the tellers' cages into two bags and ran for the door. Tommy Holden roared up before the bank in the long getaway sedan.

"Look at that," Karpis said, and pointed down the street where a dozen lawmen were racing toward them.

"Grab these girls!" Barker screamed, and hustled three girls in the bank out the door. One became so terrified that she fainted on the sidewalk. Bailey did as he was ordered but without enthusiasm. This wasn't his kind of bank robbery. He ushered a girl out to the Hudson where the gang waited and told her, almost apologetically, to stand on the running board. "It's only for a few miles," he whispered.

With that he slid into the back seat and Holden stomped on the accelerator. A motorcycle cop gave chase, but a burst from Barker's machinegun held him back until they escaped. The girls were dropped off a few miles further down the road, after the car had

kicked up so much dust that they were gagging. Bailey had to argue Barker into letting them go. They thanked him as the gang sped away.

Bailey's split was a little less than $4,000 from this raid, a pittance of what he was used to stealing. He decided to forget the whole thing and go golfing with Holden and two other old pro bankrobbers, Francis Keating and Frank "Jelly" Nash. It was his undoing.

The FBI had gotten a tip that the older bankrobbers were golf addicts and agents were haunting the links around their suspected hideout in Kansas City, Kan. Their vigilance was rewarded when they spotted the four gangsters about to tee off at the Old Mission Golf Course.

Never was there a foursome of such embarrassed bankrobbers, captured without a gun between them, sheepishly led from the course in their sporty knickers and bright blazers. The Barkers, out of underworld gratitude for his help, tried to free Bailey through legal maneuvers but failed. Old Harve was convicted of the Fort Scott robbery and sent to the Kansas State penitentiary.

Bailey was mad. He should never have thrown in with the wild Barkers, he concluded. "Their kind of heat burned everybody," he confided years later. The old professional immediately organized an escape group of hard types such as Wilbur Underhill, Bob Brady, Jim Clark and Ed Davis.

This gang crashed out of the penitentiary on Memorial Day 1933. Robbing a series of small-town banks on the way, the gang headed southwest; Underhill and the others were all Oklahoma bandits and wanted to reach the protection of their own Cookson Hills. Bailey had another destination in mind, away from the crowd. The year 1933 was alive with the new breed of killer outlaws—the Barkers, the Barrows, Machine Gun Kelly. Bandits were popping open twenty banks every week. John Dillinger had just begun his crime spree in the Midwest. Pretty Boy Floyd was roaming all over the Southwest. There was only one way out for old Harvey Bailey—Mexico.

As Underhill and the rest neared Oklahoma's Cookson Hills, a posse sent to capture them came out of nowhere. The gang battled fiercely, had a few members killed, and then fought through.

Bailey did not go into the hills. There he would be a virtual captive, he reasoned, surrounded on all sides by lawmen. He split away from the group and, purchasing a second-hand car, leisurely drove to the Shannon Ranch in Paradise, Texas. The Shannon Ranch was a notorious hideout for bandits on the run. It was owned by R. G. "Boss" Shannon, Katherine Kelly's stepfather.

By the time Bailey reached the Shannon Ranch he had already exchanged shots with a small posse and had been wounded in the leg. Worse, he arrived while Machine Gun Kelly and his wife were still holding kidnap victim Charles Urschel and attempting to negotiate his ransom.

It seemed as if Bailey's luck was fast disappearing. Instead of finding a cooling-off place, he had stopped at one of the most sought-after hideouts in America. Everybody was looking for Urschel, including the police of four states and the FBI. But Bailey's wound prevented him from doing anything else but resting in one of Boss Shannon's broken-down cottages.

It was there Albert Bates, Kelly's co-conspirator in the kidnapping, discovered him only hours after Urschel had been released. He was startled to find the bankrobber on his back.

"Listen, Harve," Bates said. "This place is hot. I told the others [the Kellys] to get out. Why didn't you go with them?"

Bailey hooked a thumb in the direction of his shattered leg. Bates yanked a mammoth wad of bills out of his pocket, his cut of the Urschel ransom money, and threw $500 down on the bed. "Take this, go see a doctor, Harve," Bates said as he nervously made his way to the screen door of the cottage. "You better get to running, Harve."

But Bailey's running days were almost over. His leg was not mending and he barely managed to get around his small cottage. He knew that day after day, while he sat about swatting flies, the FBI was closing in on Shannon Ranch. There was nothing he could do but wait.

The heat on August 12, 1933 was intense. Bailey dragged his cot onto the porch of his cottage. Just as he fell asleep with a loaded .45 automatic and a rifle at his side, he felt someone shaking him. "Get up, Harvey!"

Bailey's eyes blinked open and he saw the familiar face of FBI agent Gus T. Jones, one of those who had arrested him in Kansas City. Jones glanced at the weapons. Bailey only crossed his legs.

"If you try for the guns, I'll riddle you," Jones said calmly as he held a gun next to the bank-robber's head.

Maintaining the underworld code, Bailey said, "I'm here alone. You've got me." Then his habitually turned down lips inched upward toward a faint smile. "Well, a fellow has to sleep some time." Agents went through Bailey's pockets. He had a little more than $1200 on him, $500 of which was part of the Urschel ransom money.

After being handcuffed to a post, Bailey watched disgustedly as the truculent Shannons were rounded up at the main house. Mrs. Ora Shannon saw her son Armon in conversation with an FBI man. Her face grew red with anger.

"Armon, keep your goddamned mouth shut!" she called. Armon, however, upon seeing Urschel himself at the scene to identify the place of his captivity to the federal officers, quickly confessed and named his sister and her husband, Mr. and Mrs. George "Machine Gun" Kelly, as the leaders of the gang.

The entire scene brought only clucks from Harvey Bailey. First it was getting mixed up in the Barker lunacy; now he had become an unwitting accomplice to Machine Gun Kelly's botched kidnapping. Unbearable luck.

Bailey was taken into custody and charged with complicity in the Urschel snatch. He was placed on the tenth floor of the Dallas County jail. It was called, as usual, "escape-proof." Old Harve, however, had not given up the thought of reaching Mexico. In two weeks, he had talked his slow-witted guard, Deputy Sheriff Thomas L. Manion, into smuggling him a saw. Bailey promised Manion an equal cut on his next three bank jobs.

Before dawn on September 4, 1933, Bailey was almost through the last bar of his cell. Manion even took turns helping him saw. When the bar proved too strong, Manion obtained a Stillson wrench and with it Bailey was able to break into a hallway.

From there, the aging bankrobber took the elevator to the sixth floor after locking up five guards. He accosted Deputy Sheriff Nicholas Tresp and forced the lawman at gunpoint to escort him from the jail. The two got into a fast car and Bailey headed the opposite direction from Mexico—the Cookson Hills.

Dozens of posses had fanned out looking for the famous outlaw. Over a hundred men encircled his car after a wild chase just outside of Ardmore, Okla. He was captured without a fight ("What does bloodshed get you but more bloodshed?") and taken back to Dallas under heavy guard, manacled hand and foot. Old Harve seemed almost grateful. He was tired of running. The Dallas break was his last and he knew it.

"What did you think you would prove, Harvey?" a guard asked him.

"Well, I got out, didn't I?"

Though he had not participated in the Urschel kidnapping, Bailey refused to testify against the perpetrators. He, along with Albert Bates, the Kellys, and the Shannons were sentenced to life imprisonment.

Harvey Bailey served his sentence in Leavenworth until 1965 when he was paroled. He retired to cabinet making, famous for a crime he did not commit.

[ALSO SEE the Barkers, George "Machine Gun" Kelly.]

BAKER, JOSEPH
Murderer, Pirate ● (? -1800)

Canadian by birth, whose real name was Boulanger, Baker mutinied against his captain, William Wheland, aboard the U.S. schooner, *Eliza* in 1800. Leading two other sailors, LaCroix and Berrouse, Baker killed the ship's first mate and wounded Captain Wheland. The captain was allowed to live after giving his promise that he would navigate the ship into pirate waters.

Biding his time, Wheland finally managed to trap LaCroix and Berrouse below deck, locking them up. Wielding an axe, Captain Wheland drove Baker into the rigging of the ship, where he stayed aloft for sixteen days until the captain brought the *Eliza* to port.

April 25, 1800, Baker was tried in Philadelphia along with Berrouse and LaCroix, for murder and piracy committed on the high seas. All three were sentenced to hang and they mounted the gallows May 9 of that year, confessing their crimes to priests.

BALL, JOSEPH
Serial Killer ● (1894-1938)

Joe Ball killed for love, or at least that is is what police figured when investigating this strange serial killer's past. Ball was the proprietor of a roadhouse called "The Sociable Inn" outside of Elmendorf, Texas. For the twenty or more women who lost their lives in this hellhole, the place was anything but sociable.

Ball received his education at the University of Texas but was not interested in legitimate pursuits. In 1920, when Prohibition began, Ball became a bootlegger and amassed enough money to buy a large house in Elmendorf. Oddly, Ball came from a wealthy family that had vast holdings in real estate and cattle. He had been offered all manner of lucrative jobs by family members but turned these down. He busied himself by making his own rotgut alcohol, selling the liquor for five dollars a gallon.

The house was always filthy and Ball was seen wearing only a bathrobe as he padded about the place. New, attractive blondes came and went. Ball spent most of his time in bed with these women, a plate of fried chicken (his favorite food), always on his bedstand. He was a man of few words. When clients arrived to pick up their orders of bootleg liquor, Ball's only words were: "Got the cash?"

He bought The Sociable Inn in the late 1920s. This roadhouse outside of Elmendorf stood 50 feet back of U.S. Highway 181. Behind the broken-down saloon, Ball built a large cement pool into which he placed five new pet alligators. When drunk, Ball would take favorite customers out back and amuse himself by throwing raw hunks of meat into the pool, which caused the reptiles to lunge about wildly, thrashing the water with their tails as they fought for the food.

Ball took in stray cats and dogs and threw these hapless animals into the pool, also before horrified customers. A large, hulking man, well over six feet, Ball began to put on weight and his rough ways intensified. He shouted instead of talking and he threatened anyone with a beating if they disagreed with him about the most trivial issue.

Customers came to The Sociable Inn not to see Ball but the many young and attractive females serving tables. Ball paid these beautiful girls more money than they could make elsewhere. All became his mistresses, a few his wives, but he tired of them quickly and they soon disappeared. The rapid disappearance of these women, particularly favorites such as Minnie Mae Gotthardt and Hazel Brown, puzzled a local constable and neighbor of Ball's.

When the constable asked about the missing barmaids, Ball exploded, pulling a gun and jamming the weapon into the lawman's face. "You meddle in my affairs again and I'll kill you!" roared Ball. The constable backed off and never reported this incident.

This was not the case with Lee Miller, a Texas Ranger who had received several reports about the missing women. He and several deputies entered The Sociable Inn on the night of September 24, 1938. Ball asked the officers if they wanted some beer.

"No, Joe," replied Miller. "We're here to ask you some questions about Hazel Brown."

Ball, who was standing behind the bar, immediately went to the cash register and withdrew a revolver. The officers, thinking Ball was about to fire at them, all drew their weapons and aimed them at the bar owner. Ball shrugged and grinned. He then put the revolver to his temple and fired, blowing off the top of his head.

Deputies dragged the dead man outside and began searching the grounds. They found human flesh floating in a large water barrel behind the inn and human remains inside the alligator pool. Clifford Wheeler, Ball's handyman, came forward. He shook with terror as he looked down upon the corpse of his former employer, then blurted how Ball had murdered at least twenty women, maybe more, including two of his own wives.

Wheeler explained that Ball had chopped up their bodies and fed the remains to his pet alligators as a way of disposing of the evidence. The handyman admitted that he had helped Ball in his grisly chores. He had remained silent under death threats from his employer. Wheeler, who was later given a four-year prison sentence as an accessory to murder, told the rangers how Ball would fall in love with his victims, impregnate them, and then kill them when they insisted he marry them. "Joe, he weren't no marrying man," concluded Wheeler.

BANISZEWSKI, GERTRUDE WRIGHT
Murderer ● (1929-   )

BACKGROUND: BORN IN INDIANA, 1929. MINOR PUBLIC EDUCATION. DIVORCED. HOUSEWIFE. DESCRIPTION: 5'3", BROWN EYES, BROWN HAIR, SLIGHT. ALIASES: NONE. RECORD: SUPERVISED THE TORTURE-MURDER OF 16-YEAR-OLD SYLVIA LIKENS IN INDIANAPOLIS, IND., 10/26/65; SENTENCED TO LIFE IMPRISONMENT IN 1966; RETRIED IN 1971, CONVICTION UPHELD.

Gertrude Baniszewski never proved herself to be a very bright person but there was nothing in her prosaic makeup to ever suggest the murderous nightmare she would create out of her own mind in the summer of 1965. Until that time, Gertrude was merely a lonely, aging housewife, living with her teenage children Stephanie, Paula, and Johnny in a quiet suburb of Indianapolis, Ind.

Her income was skimpy, and to improve her lot Mrs. Baniszewski agreed to take in two children for the summer while their parents traveled with a circus. Sylvia Likens, 16, and her crippled sister Jenny, 15, were left with Mrs. Baniszewski for the summer months. Their parents were to provide $20 a week for their upkeep.

During the first week of their stay, the girls were barely fed any food—two pieces of toast for breakfast, no lunch, a bowl of soup for dinner. Toward the end of the week, Mrs. Baniszewski dragged both of the girls to an upstairs bedroom of her home. "Well," she ranted, "I took care of you two bitches for a week for nothing!" She hit them in the face until her hand ached.

Money from the parents arrived the following day, the first of a series of payments.

As weeks went by, Gertrude's strange anger mounted, until the mere sight of the Likens girls threw her into a rage. Her sadism became more pronounced each day, particularly as practiced on Sylvia. The temporary foster child was bewildered but she complied with the punishments meted by Mrs. Baniszewski. First came the regular beatings. Then, whenever the whim urged her, Gertrude took a paddle to her, then a board.

Her sordid acts were openly displayed in front of other neighboring teenagers. Gertrude

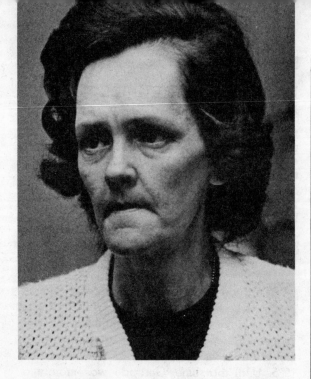

Child-killer Gertrude Baniszewski thought she'd teach her victim, Sylvia Likens, sixteen, a lesson by branding her a prostitute.

burned Sylvia's fingers with matches and encouraged teenagers Coy Hubbard and Richard Hobbs to put their cigarettes out on Sylvia's body, "to teach her a lesson." The boys also practiced judo on Sylvia, slamming her against walls and concrete floors.

The Baniszewski daughters were also encouraged to beat Sylvia whenever they felt in the mood. Paula broke her hand while punching the poor girl. After her hand was put in a plaster cast to heal, Paula used the cast to further beat Sylvia.

Then, inexplicably, Mrs. Baniszewski got it into her head that Sylvia was a whore and began to tell the neighborhood boys she was a confirmed prostitute. Keeping her tied up in the basement of her home, Gertrude would release the suffering teenager only to compel her to dance naked before Hobbs, Hubbard, and her son Johnny, performing, on command, lewd gestures she dictated in a shrill, snapping voice.

The frustrated housewife continued her bizarre attacks against Sylvia Likens until a final madness overcame her and, with the help of Ricky Hobbs, using a white-hot needle, Mrs. Baniszewski branded Sylvia's stomach with the words: "I am a prostitute and proud of it." Following this fiendish torture, Gertrude hit the

girl with such force that upon hitting the concrete floor of the basement, Sylvia died.

Seized by panic, Mrs. Baniszewski called the Indianapolis police, telling officer Melvin Dixon, who came to investigate, that Sylvia had just returned after running off with a gang of boys. The gang, she claimed, had mutilated her body. Her daughters and son parroted her story. Out of fear, so did Sylvia's sister Jenny. When alone, however, with Dixon, Jenny hobbled frantically toward the door whispering to the policeman: "Get me out of here and I'll tell you everything." She did.

Months later, at her trial, the truth about Sylvia's torture murder was unraveled. Mrs. Baniszewski was sentenced to life in prison, the teenagers turned over to juvenile authorities. To this day, Gertrude refuses to give a reason for the killing, vaguely repeating the same line—"to show her a lesson, to show her a lesson."

BANKS, JOHN
Murderer ● (? -1806)

Most murderers find themselves killing out of passion, or for money. John Banks killed for food.

Banks resided in New York City with his wife Margaret, whose cooking and general housekeeping left much to be desired. She also drank heavily and was usually found staggering about by the time Banks came home from his labors.

One spring evening in 1806, Banks returned home to find Margaret blind drunk. When he asked for some coffee, he later related at his trial, May 29, 1806, she gave him "pot-liquor." This was too much. Banks grabbed a coal shovel and beaned his wife, and then, the furies upon him, slit her throat with a butcher knife.

One account stated that Banks "had brought some peanuts and ordered her to brown them . . . and that when he did return with some eggs, he found she had done nothing. These were his provocations [for killing her]."

Banks was speedily tried, and executed July 11, 1806.

BARKER, ARIZONA DONNIE CLARK ("KATE," "MA")
Gangleader ● (1872-1935)

BACKGROUND: BORN NEAR SPRINGFIELD, MO., 1872. MARRIED GEORGE BARKER, A SHARECROPPING FARMER, IN 1892. GAVE BIRTH TO FOUR SONS, THE NOTORIOUS BARKER BROTHERS: HERMAN, LLOYD, ARTHUR, AND FRED. DESCRIPTION: 5'2", BROWN EYES, BROWN HAIR, STOUT. ALIASES: UNKNOWN. RECORD: PLANNED SEVERAL BANK ROBBERIES IN THE MIDDLE 1920S AND RAN A HIDEOUT IN TULSA, OKLA. DURING THIS PERIOD FOR ESCAPED CONVICTS AND BANK-ROBBERS BEING SOUGHT; UPON THE RELEASE OF HER SONS FREDDIE AND DOC FROM PRISON, MA BARKER PLANNED SEVERAL PAYROLL, POST OFFICE AND BANK ROBBERIES IN THE EARLY 1930S; FINALIZED PLANS FOR THE HAMM AND BREMER KIDNAPPINGS OF 1933 AND 1934. MA BARKER AND HER SON FREDDIE WERE KILLED IN A WILD GUN BATTLE WITH FBI MEN IN A REMOTE RESORT ON LAKE WEIR OUTSIDE OF OKLA-WAHA, FLORIDA, 1/16/35. MA BARKER HAD NEVER BEEN ARRESTED FOR ANY CRIME DURING HER LIFE-TIME, REMAINING BEHIND THE SCENE AND SENDING OUT HER SONS AND OTHER CRIMINALS TO PERFORM ROBBERIES.

The grandmotherly woman shown in these snapshots (the only photos ever taken of her during her lifetime) is "Ma" Barker with paramour Arthur V. Dunlop; she organized bankrobberies and kidnappings for her killer sons. (UPI)

The "Bloody Barkers" (left to right)—Herman, Arthur ("Doc"), and Freddie, 1930s kidnappers and bankrobbers. (UPI)

BARKER, ARTHUR ("DOCK" OR "DOC")
Murderer, Bankrobber ● (1899-1939)

BACKGROUND: BORN IN AURORA, MO., 1899. MINOR PUBLIC EDUCATION. DESCRIPTION: 5'3", BROWN EYES, BLACK HAIR, STOCKY BUILD. ALIASES: UNKNOWN. RECORD: ARRESTED SEVERAL TIMES ON ADOLESCENT CHARGES, 1910-15, IN WEBB CITY, MO.; RELEASED TO THE CUSTODY OF HIS MOTHER; STOLE A GOVERNMENT-OWNED CAR, 1918, ESCAPED, WAS RECAPTURED; ESCAPED; KILLED A NIGHT WATCHMAN AT THE ST. JOHN'S HOSPITAL IN TULSA WHILE ATTEMPTING TO STEAL A DRUG SHIPMENT; SENT TO THE OKLAHOMA STATE PENITENTIARY FOR LIFE WHERE HE SERVED THIRTEEN YEARS BEFORE BEING PAROLED 9/27/32 BY WILLIAM H. "ALFALFA BILL" MURRAY, GOVERNOR OF OKLAHOMA; ROBBED WITH HIS BROTHER FRED, ALVIN KARPIS, JESS DOYLE, BILL WEAVER, VERNE MILLER, AND LARRY DEVOL THE THIRD NORTHWESTERN BANK IN MINNEAPOLIS, MINN. ($20,000) 12/16/32, KILLING TWO POLICEMEN WITH MACHINEGUNS AND WOUNDED A CIVILIAN; ROBBED WITH HIS BROTHER FRED, ALVIN KARPIS, JESS DOYLE, FRANK NASH, VOLNEY DAVIS, AND EARL CHRISTMAN THE FAIRBURY, NEBRASKA BANK ($151,350), WOUNDING A BANK PRESIDENT AND GUARD (CHRISTMAN WOUNDED BY THE GUARD, DYING A DAY LATER IN VERNE MILLER'S KANSAS CITY HIDE-OUT) IN APRIL, 1933; KIDNAPPED WILLIAM A. HAMM, JR. IN ST. PAUL, MINN. WITH HIS BROTHER FRED, ALVIN KARPIS, MONTY BOLTON, FRED GOETZ ("SHOTGUN ZIEGLER") AND CHARLES J. FITZGERALD 6/15/33, DE-MANDING $100,000 RANSOM; RANSOM PAID 6/17/33 AND HAMM RELEASED 6/18/33 (ROGER TOUHY, CHI-CAGO BOOTLEGGER, MISTAKENLY TRIED BY THE JUS-TICE DEPARTMENT FOR THE CRIME); ROBBED THE SWIFT

COMPANY PAYROLL AT THE SOUTH ST. PAUL, MINN. POST OFFICE WITH HIS BROTHER FRED, ALVIN KARPIS, LARRY DEVOL AND CHARLES J. FITZGERALD, ($30,000), KILLING ONE POLICEMAN AND WOUNDING ANOTHER, 8/15/33; ROBBED WITH HIS BROTHER FRED, MONTY BOLTON, BILL "LAPLAND WILLIE" WEAVER, AND FRED GOETZ A FEDERAL RESERVE MAIL TRUCK IN CHICAGO (GETTING SEVERAL SACKS OF USELESS CHECKS), BOLTON KILLED PATROLMAN MILES A. CUNNINGHAM AND WOUNDED ANOTHER OFFICER, 8/22/33; KIDNAPPED WITH HIS BROTHER FRED, ALVIN KARPIS, VOLNEY DAVIS, FRED GOETZ, BILL WEAVER, AND HARRY CAMPBELL MILLIONAIRE BANKER EDWARD G. BREMER IN MINNEAPOLIS, MINN. 1/17/34, HOLDING HIM FOR $200,000 RANSOM; RANSOM PAID 2/7/34 AT WHICH TIME BREMER WAS RELEASED; KILLED DR. JOSEPH P. "DOC" MORAN WITH HIS BROTHER FRED, AUGUST, 1934, CAPTURD BY FBI MEN, LED BY SPECIAL AGENT MELVIN PURVIS, IN CHICAGO 1/8/35; CONVICTED OF THE BREMER KIDNAPPING AND SENTENCED TO LIFE IMPRISONMENT AT ALCATRAZ; KILLED IN AN ATTEMPTED ESCAPE FROM "THE ROCK" 6/13/39.

BARKER, FRED
Murderer, Bankrobber ● (1902-1935)

BACKGROUND: BORN IN AURORA, MO., 1902. MINOR PUBLIC EDUCATION. DESCRIPTION: 5'4", BROWN EYES, BROWN HAIR, SLIGHT BUILD. SEVERAL GOLD-FILLED TEETH. PLASTIC SURGERY SCAR ON FACE. ALIASES: UNKNOWN. RECORD: ARRESTED IN HIS YOUTH FOR VAGRANCY AND ROBBERY, RELEASED TO HIS MOTHER'S CUSTODY; ARRESTED FOR ROBBING THE BANK IN WINDFIELD, KANSAS, 1926; RECEIVED FIVE-TO-TEN YEAR SENTENCE IN THE KANSAS STATE PENITENTIARY AT LANSING WHERE HE MET AND FORMED HIS ASSOCIATION WITH BURGLAR AND SNEAK-THIEF ALVIN KARPIS; PAROLED 3/20/31; ROBBED WITH KARPIS SEVERAL JEWELRY AND CLOTHING SHOPS IN MISSOURI AND KANSAS, SUMMER, 1931; ARRESTED FOR BURGLARY IN CLAREMORE, OKLA., SUMMER, 1931. ESCAPED; ROBBED STORE IN WEST PLAINS, MO., WITH ALVIN KARPIS, JULY, 1931, KILLING THE LOCAL SHERIFF, C. R. KELLY; ROBBED THE MOUNTAIN VIEW, MO. BANK WITH ALVIN KARPIS, BILL WEAVER AND JAMES WILSON ($7,000) EARLY FALL, 1931; STOLE CLOTHING, CARS, CIGARETTES (BY THE TRUCK LOAD), HIJACKED WHISKEY (FENCED BY ST. PAUL, MINN. CRIME KINGPIN, JACK PEIFER), AND CRACKED SAFES THROUGHOUT THE FALL OF 1931 WITH ALVIN KARPIS IN MINNESOTA; KILLED CHIEF OF POLICE MANLEY JACKSON OF POCAHOLTAS, ARK., NOV. 1931, SHOOTING HIM FIVE TIMES IN THE BACK; ROBBED A BRANCH OF THE NORTHWESTERN NATIONAL BANK OF MINNEAPOLIS WITH ALVIN KARPIS, ($81,000 CASH, $185,000 BONDS); ROBBED OTHER BANKS IN THE WINTER OF 1932 IN BELOIT, WISC., FLANDREAU, S.D., REDWOOD FALLS, MINN. WITH ALVIN KARPIS, LARRY DEVOL AND ONE OR TWO OTHER MINOR HOODLUMS; ROBBED THE FORT SCOTT, KAN. BANK IN MAY, 1932 WITH ALVIN KARPIS, LARRY DEVOL, PHIL COURTNEY, AND HARVEY BAILEY, ($47,000);

THREE ESCAPEES FROM THE OKLAHOMA STATE PENITENTIARY AT THIS TIME—JAMES CLARK, EDWARD DAVIS, AND FRANK SAWYER—MISTAKENLY ARRESTED FOR THE FORT SCOTT RAID AND RECEIVED TWENTY TO ONE HUNDRED YEARS AT LANSING STATE PRISON IN KANSAS; ROBBED THE WAHPETON, N.D. BANK IN LATE JUNE, 1932 WITH ALVIN KARPIS, JESS DOYLE, HIS BROTHER DOC, AND LARRY DEVOL ($7,000); ROBBED THE CLOUD COUNTY BANK AT CONCORDIA, KAN., ($250,000) 7/25/32 WITH ALVIN KARPIS, JESS DOYLE, FRANK NASH, EARL CHRISTMAN, AND LARRY DEVOL; ROBBED THE CITIZEN'S SECURITY BANK, BIXBY, OKLA., ($1,000) 8/8/32 WITH VOLNEY DAVIS AND LARRY DEVOL; ROBBED SEVERAL BANKS AND PARTICIPATED IN TWO KIDNAPPINGS 1932-34 (SEE ARTHUR "DOC" BARKER FOR DETAILS); KILLED WITH HIS MOTHER, "MA" BARKER, AT LAKE WEIR IN FLORIDA 1/16/35 IN A 45-MINUTE GUN BATTLE WITH FBI AGENTS.

BARKER, HERMAN
Murderer, Bankrobber ● (1894-1927)

BACKGROUND: BORN IN AURORA, MO., 1894. MINOR PUBLIC EDUCATION. DESCRIPTION: 5'5", BROWN EYES, BLACK HAIR, STOCKY BUILD. ALIASES: UNKNOWN. RECORD: ARRESTED FOR PETTY THEFT WHILE A YOUTH; RELEASED TO THE CUSTODY OF HIS MOTHR; ORGANIZED THE CENTRAL PARK GANG IN TULSA, OKLA., 1910, AN ADOLESCENT GROUP DEDICATED TO MINOR BURGLARIES; ARRESTED IN 1915 FOR ROBBERY IN JOPLIN, MO., RELEASED TO THE CUSTODY OF HIS MOTHER; BECAME A MEMBER OF THE KIMES-TERRILL GANG IN EARLY 1920S, ROBBING BANKS IN TEXAS, OKLAHOMA AND MISSOURI. SEVERELY WOUNDED AFTER ROBBING A STORE IN NEWTON, KAN. AND KILLING POLICEMAN J. E. MARSHALL, HERMAN BARKER TURNED HIS LUGER ON HIMSELF, COMMITTING SUICIDE 9/19/27.

BARKER, LLOYD
Robber ● (1896-1949)

BACKGROUND: BORN IN AURORA, MO., 1896; MINOR PUBLIC EDUCATION. DESCRIPTION: 5'4", BROWN EYES, BROWN HAIR, SLENDER. ALIASES: UNKNOWN. RECORD: ARRESTED FOR PETTY THEFT WHILE A YOUTH, RELEASED TO THE CUSTODY OF HIS MOTHER; ORGANIZED THE CENTRAL PARK GANG IN TULSA, OKLA., 1910; CAUGHT WHILE ROBBING A POST OFFICE IN RURAL OKLAHOMA, 1922 AND SENT TO LEAVENWORTH FOR TWENTY-FIVE YEARS; SERVED ALL HIS TIME AND WAS RELEASED IN 1947. LLOYD WAS THE ONLY MEMBER OF THE BARKER BROTHERS WHO DID NOT JOIN A GANG. FOLLOWING THE RELEASE FROM LEAVENWORTH, HE WAS EMPLOYED AS AN ASSISTANT MANAGER OF A SNACK SHOP IN RURAL COLORADO; KILLED BY HIS WIFE IN 1949.

No other outlaw gang of the 1930s so baffled law enforcement officials as the Barkers. Unlike other bankrobbers such as "Pretty Boy" Floyd, Dillinger, and the Barrow gang, the Barkers operated with great stealth allowing others to grab the headlines and the credit. They robbed without pattern. Geographically, the gang—its members rarely the same in number or personnel—roamed from the far northwoods of Minnesota to Texas and Oklahoma, from Illinois to Nebraska (they steered clear of Indiana as that was almost the exclusive province of John Dillinger). The types of robberies committed by the Barkers were far from consistent. One day they might knock over a bank for $250,000, a job expertly cased, well-equipped and selectively-manned. The next day they would appear rashly unprepared in another state, heisting a jewelry store for only several hundred dollars. Then they would switch to a totally new field of crime such as kidnapping.

It was this kind of unpredictability that made it so difficult to identify them and link them to specific crimes. Their crazy-quilt crime wave was more the result of neuroticism rather than planned modus operandi. The Barkers, especially Doc and Fred, were dedicated criminals who would strike happily on all levels.

Fred Barker's willingness to kill, whether or not circumstances demanded it, typified the murderous insanity that ran through the blood of the Barker breed. His brother Doc was just as wildly lethal. "Ma" Barker was slightly more level-headed, but she, too, never flinched when murder seemed the most expeditious method of handling a problem.

Also, unlike the lone bandits of their era, the Barkers found protection in cities like St. Paul, Minn., Kansas City, Kan., Hot Springs, Ark., Joplin, Mo. (towns that were almost wholly owned by local bootleggers and corrupt politicians). Here, for a cut of their enormous profits, politicians, lawyers, and police officials gave them sanctuary, informing them of any impending raid against them far enough in advance to allow them to escape. The Barkers contributed mightily to the campaign chests of politicians running for office.

Contacts were everything with the Barkers. Though they were never part of the embryonic criminal syndicate blossoming during the 1930s, the national crime cartel encouraged and shielded them. The reason, of course, was the money. The Barkers, under Ma's intuitive criminal genius, accumulated at least $3 million in their collective criminal careers and fenced huge amounts of ransom monies through political contacts, who took large percentages (without having to take any serious risk). The gang even gave certain officials their money for safekeeping, drawing funds from them when needed as one would from a bank. In turn, the political hacks would recruit dependable men for the gang, experts in safe-blowing, bank-robbing, burglary—mostly ex-convicts whose records proved them committed to crime. Political hacks would also "finger" jobs.

Even with such influential men to help them, the Barkers would, no doubt, have floundered early and been picked off one by one had it not been for the shrewd thinking and meticulous planning of Ma Barker. Though bankrobber and kidnapper Alvin Karpis, after his release from prison, denied Ma Barker's role as leader of the gang, (perhaps unwilling to think of himself being ordered about by an elderly woman) the fact is evident from all records and accounts.

Ma Barker has been portrayed from every slant imaginable: as a kind and protective mother whose boys grew up poor and got into bad company, as a bloody mama type who planned robberies and kidnappings for her boys at the cold and methodical pace of an IBM machine working overtime; as a thick-witted, slow-moving, silly old woman who knew nothing about the activities of her murderous sons and was used by them as a front.

Which story is true? Probably, a little of each.

Born 18 miles northwest of Springfield, Missouri in 1872, Arizona Donnie Clark grew up in the heartland that nursed Jesse and Frank James. Her childhood hero, Jesse, was killed by Bob Ford when she was ten, but she never forgot the handsome bandit. She had seen him ride through nearby Carthage once with the Younger brothers at his side. The image would never leave her.

Arizona Kate (or "Arrie" as friends called her) was Ozark Mountains tough and grew into a pretty, hard young woman who read her Bible and played the fiddle. She could always be found at the church "sing" on Sunday.

Kate was twenty in 1892 when the Dalton brothers were shot full of holes in Coffeyville, Kansas, after trying to take two banks at one time. That year, Kate married a farm laborer,

George Barker, and moved to Aurora, Missouri.

There the four Barker boys were born: Herman, Lloyd, Arthur (nicknamed Doc) and her favorite, Freddie. Shortly after Herman and Lloyd were school age, the Barkers moved to Webb City, Mo., a mining boomtown.

The family lived in a broken-down tar-paper house and in a few years the boys, growing up wild, got into trouble. Small stuff was first: window-breaking and fights. Next came pilfering and then outright thievery. Ma always defended them against complaints.

Their father, George Barker, brushed aside his paternal responsibilities with, "You'll have to talk with Mother. She handles the boys." Years later, George Barker would recall: "She'd pack up those boys and take them to Sunday school every week. I don't know just why. Because when I tried to straighten them up, she'd fly into me. She never would let me do with them what I wanted to."

But Mother had become Ma and didn't handle the boys at all; she let them run wild and refused to see them as they were, apprentice hoodlums. Even slight criticism of her brood would inflame Ma Barker to rage. She stopped attending church with the words: "If the good people of this town don't like my boys, then the good people know what they can do."

Herman was the first to get into serious trouble. Webb City police arrested him for petty thievery in 1910. Ma raised hell in the police station and the unnerved cops released him.

In 1915, Herman was again arrested for highway robbery. Again, Ma appeared before authorities and got him released. By now, Kate Barker knew she had best get the boys out of Webb City. "They're marked," she told neighbors. "The cops here won't ever stop persecuting my boys."

The Barkers moved to Tulsa, Oklahoma, but the boys grew worse, not better. Her boys were being picked up regularly for all sorts of adolescent crimes, yet Ma always managed to get them off with tantrums, rage, tears, and promises.

After Freddie Barker visited ex-con Herb Farmer, who ran a hideout in Joplin, Mo., he invited several fugitives to stay at Ma's in Tulsa. They started to show up in 1915, people like bank robber Al Spencer. Other big-time heist men like Frank Nash, Ray Terrill, and Earl Thayer appeared. Chicago-bred holdup men Francis Keating and Thomas Holden also used Ma's Tulsa home to lay low.

It became not only a cooling-off place for fugitives but also a hotbed of plans for bank jobs and robberies. Naturally the boys were affected. The first to leave the clan was Herman who drove off with Ray Terrill to knock over banks.

Lloyd tried to hold up a post office in 1922 and was captured. He got 25 years in Leavenworth. Doc's career was not going too good, either; he was nabbed for stealing a government car in 1918, and was in and out of jail through the 1920s. The same year that Lloyd went to Leavenworth, Doc was sent to the Oklahoma State Prison for life. He was charged with killing a night watchman at a hospital in Tulsa.

Ma and Doc always insisted he didn't do it. For once, they were right. Many years later a California thief admitted the killing.

Freddie went to prison next, after dozens of arrests ranging from bank robbery to assault with intent to kill. He got 5-to-10 in the Kansas State Penitentiary in Lansing.

Herman Barker was the only son still free, but his end came abruptly and violently. After being captured with Ray Terrill while trying to rob a Missouri bank, both men escaped custody and with a stolen car raced for the Kansas border. After a holdup in Newton, Kansas, cops flagged down a suspicious-looking car traveling at high speeds. Herman Barker was driving and guns blazed from all the windows.

As police returned fire, officer J. E. Marshall fell dead. But Herman didn't escape; police caught him in another trap. After emptying his gun at them in a blistering shootout, he pulled out his "lucky piece"—a spare bullet—inserted it into his gun and sent it into his brain.

Ma denied it was suicide: "A Barker don't do things like that." She screamed that it was a police execution. But officials still listed Herman as dead by his own hand.

It was Herman's suicide and the imprisonment of her other three sons that, in the words of FBI chief, J. Edgar Hoover, changed Ma Barker "from an animal mother of the she-wolf type to a veritable beast of prey." Perhaps the transformation was not that acute, but Ma's desire to see her boys free never waned.

At 55, gone fat and gray, her face sagging, Ma was alone. But she hadn't lost her perseverance. Kate left George Barker and raised tens of thousands of dollars by running a regular hideout for escaped cons and wanted robbers. She needed the money to pay lawyers who were seeking her sons' release.

For years Ma Barker hounded and haunted the parole boards, wardens, and governors. Finally, on March 20, 1931, her efforts paid off. Freddie was released from Lansing. He brought along his friend and cell-mate, Alvin Karpis, who had also been set free.

They both moved in with Ma and her lover, Arthur V. Dunlop. Alvin Karpis, whom Freddie called "Old Creepy" because of his strange and sinister smile, was well-liked by Ma. He reminded her of her own boys and he was after the same things she taught them to desire.

"What I wanted," Karpis later admitted, "was big automobiles like rich people had and everything like that. I didn't see how I was going to get them by making a fool of myself and working all my life. So I decided to take what I wanted."

And with Ma's help at planning and picking jobs, that's exactly what Old Creepy and Freddie did. Ma would then relax, listening to hillbilly music on the radio and working crossword puzzles.

Alvin and Freddie started small. They robbed a store in West Plains, Missouri. When C. R. Kelly the local sheriff spotted the robbery car with two men sitting in it two days later, he investigated. Freddie and Alvin let him have it.

Kelly was killed instantly.

Now the boys were hot and Ma decided to go to one of the country's cooling-off spots for criminals, St. Paul, Minnesota. They took old man Dunlop along, too, but he didn't like it and complained incessantly.

Ma was tired of Dunlop and his complaining. So were the boys. His bullet-ridden body was discovered floating along the shores of isolated Lake Freasted in upstate Wisconsin in 1932, shot up by gangsters working for the St. Paul political fixer and bootlegger Jack Peifer. Dunlop had talked too much about the gang's operations after getting drunk one night. The gang had done many jobs for Peifer and he "knocked off Dunlop as a kind of return favor to us," Karpis later remembered.

Peifer used his club, the Hollyhocks, as a sort of clearing house for criminal operations in St. Paul. Harry Sawyer (nee Sandlovich), another crime cartel operator in St. Paul, ran the Green Lantern. It was here that every hoodlum on the lam had to check in. After letting Sawyer know he was in town, the criminal was free to operate alone, available, perhaps, for some job Sawyer might dream up.

The Green Lantern became the hangout for almost all Barker mobsters. Young, nervy toughs such as Volney Davis, part Cherokee, born in Tulsa and friend of Doc Barker's who had been sentenced with Doc for killing the night watchman, came into Sawyer's Green Lantern. Davis began his criminal career by stealing a pair of shoes and getting a three-year sentence for it. Ma Barker had arranged for his parole. Davis' eccentric girl friend, Edna "The Kissing Bandit" Murray (who had escaped from the Missouri Penitentiary) enjoyed Ma Barker's wrath. Mother Barker hated all female competition. Davis would get life in prison for his part in the Bremer kidnapping.

William Weaver, a vicious gunsel from Arkansas and one-time cell-mate of Freddie Barker's at Lansing, would also get life at Alcatraz for the Bremer kidnapping (dropping dead of a heart attack in the prison laundry in 1954). Weaver was also known as "Lapland Willie" and "Phoenix Donald."

The other major and younger members of the Barker gang included Lawrence "Larry" De-Vol, a hell-bent killer who was finally killed by lawmen during a holdup; Phil Courtney, an ex-motorcycle cop turned bandit; Earl Christman, who, after being wounded in the Fairbury Bank holdup in 1933, would be buried secretly by the Barkers in Kansas City; Jess Doyle, and James Wilson.

Also in Sawyer's wide-open saloon strutted the older pros of bankrobbing who periodically teamed up with the Barkers—Harvey Bailey, the dean of American bank robbers; Thomas Holden; Francis Keating; Gus Winkler (later killed by syndicate hitmen); Fred Goetz, alias "Shotgun Ziegler," reputed to have been one of the machinegunners at the St. Valentine's Day Massacre (killed by syndicate hoods with a full shotgun blast a foot away from his face while starting his car on a Chicago street); Homer "Big Potatoes" Wilson, who had robbed banks for two decades without ever being apprehended; Tommy Gannon; Tom Philbin; Tommy Banks; Kid Can; and Frank "Jelly" Nash, one of the most notorious and durable bankrobbers in the nation, who was to meet his grimly ironic end at the Kansas City Massacre.

It was from this amazing assortment of stick-up men, bankrobbers, and killers that Ma Barker and her sons selected their helpmates.

After working several successful bank jobs in the northwest, the Barkers filtered down to Kansas City. From there Ma planned the raid against the Fort Scott, Kansas, bank. The boys got $47,000 there in May, 1932 with the help of gunmen Larry DeVol, Phil Courtney, Alvin Karpis, and Harvey Bailey.

Soon, however, police were on the trail and Ma and the boys headed back to St. Paul; once in St. Paul they planned another big job in Kansas. Mobility was everything then, and Ma knew it.

Freddie and Doc Barker (who had been paroled through Ma's persuasiveness in time to help pull the Fort Scott job), Karpis, and expert gunmen Frank Nash, DeVol, and Earl Christman, then knocked over the Cloud County Bank in Concordia, Kansas.

The take was $250,000.

In December, 1932, the boys robbed the Third Northwestern Bank of $20,000. Machine-gunner Volney Davis was in on that one.

In April of 1933, after wintering in luxury in Reno, Nevada, the Barkers robbed the bank at Fairbury, Nebraska. Again the take was impressive: $151,350.

Shortly after that, Ma became inspiration-struck. They would kidnap wealthy St. Paul brewer William A. Hamm, Jr. and ransom him for $100,000. There were less risks in kidnapping, she reasoned.

They took Hamm quickly on June 14 and within three days released him forty miles north of St. Paul after getting the ransom. As in almost all of their robberies up to this point, someone else was blamed; Roger Touhy got the nod from the authorities.

Kidnapping worked so well, Ma got greedy. They would now, she said, snatch Edward G. Bremer, a wealthy Minneapolis banker, and get twice as much for him—$200,000. The following year they pulled it off, but Doc Barker left a fingerprint and the gang was now identified.

In the spring of 1934, the Barkers, feeling local and federal heat for the first time, became desperate. They were out in the open, known. Pictures of Doc and Freddie Barker, Alvin Karpis, and other gang members were prominently displayed in such magazines as *Liberty* and *True Detective*, as well as upon the thousands of FBI wanted posters.

Freddie Barker and Karpis decided to change their appearances. The two gangsters went to Joseph P. "Doc" Moran, a practicing physician who operated on the other side of the law at high fees. Moran, who maintained offices on Irving Park Blvd. in Chicago, specialized in plastic surgery and fingertip alterations. He had also spent some time in Illinois' Joliet prison for illegal abortions performed on syndicate whores.

After injecting Barker and Karpis with heavy doses of morphine, Moran worked on their noses, chins and jowls. He froze their fingertips with cocaine and scraped them with a scalpel, "sharpening the ends of my fingers just like you'd sharpen a pencil," Karpis added later.

The operations were not successful: both Karpis and Barker were in a good deal of pain and did not notice any appreciable change in their make-up. Both developed ghastly scars that would not heal on their faces. Barker's thumbs became infected and swelled. Ma and Dolores Delaney, Karpis's girl, nursed them as best they could.

One night, Fred yelled out in pain: "I'm going to kill that guy [Moran] as soon as I can hold a gun!"

But Moran, a man in his late thirties whose addiction to liquor made him look twenty years older, had not lost his usefulness. He had been paid $1,250 for the two operations but was told he could make a lot more by helping to unload the hot ransom money from the Bremer kidnapping.

Dope addict Russell "Slim Gray" Gibson acted as the go-between for underworld figures such as "Boss" John J. McLaughlin, a Chicago politician, and Moran, doling out thousands of dollars in exchange for small percentages of "safe" money. The strain on Moran became intense, especially when McLaughlin was picked up by the FBI who had traced a hot Barker hundred-dollar bill to him. The gang, taking Moran along, moved to Toledo, Ohio, where their strong contacts with the Licavoli syndicate gang would afford them cover.

Once more, Moran drank himself into a permanent stupor while living in a Toledo whorehouse. Once, he bragged to the madam: "I've got this gang in the hollow of my hand—right there!" He offered a cupped palm. "In the hollow of my hand!" The madam called Barker and Karpis.

In late August, Doc and Freddie Barker took

Moran for a ride; he never came back. Freddie told Karpis: "Doc and I shot the son of a bitch. Anybody who talks to whores is too dangerous to live. We dug a hole in Michigan and dropped him in and covered the hole with lime. I don't think anybody's going to come across Doc Moran again."

Things got hot after Moran's death and everybody scattered. Doc Barker was trailed to Chicago and taken without a fight on the night of January 8, 1935. Doc was surrounded on Surf Street by Melvin Purvis and a dozen other FBI agents after gang member "Slim Gray" Gibson, had informed on him.

Barker was taking his usual evening stroll. As agents searched him, Doc merely smirked. He had no weapon.

Purvis studied him. "Where's your gun?"

Doc half smiled. "Home . . . and ain't that a hell of a place for it?"

Purvis hustled his prize catch to FBI headquarters at the Bankers' Building in downtown Chicago. Agents grilled him hour after hour as to the whereabouts of the rest of the gang. Barker gave them nothing. Purvis wrote later: "He sat in a chair, his jaw clenched, and looked straight ahead. He was not impressive-looking; only his eyes told the story of an innate savagery." Being hand-cuffed for eight days and nights to that chair still couldn't budge Doc's memory.

He spent the rest of his life at Alcatraz until he was killed trying to make a break on June 13, 1939. He had made it over the high walls of Alcatraz and to the rocky beach of San Francisco Bay. Frantically, he assembled what strewn waterlogged timber there was, tieing it together with strips of his shirt, attempting to build a raft.

"Barker!" a voice from the guard's tower above him yelled down through a bullhorn, "throw your hands in the air."

Doc Barker glanced up at the tower only once and then went back to his frenzied work, pushing out a little until the water was at his knees. Police guns from the tower barked and Doc spun in the air, riddled, falling with a splash and dying instantly.

The FBI, through a marked map of Florida found in Doc's apartment, tracked down Ma

Freddie (left) and Ma Barker in the morgue after shooting it out with federal agents in a remote Florida resort, 1935. (UPI)

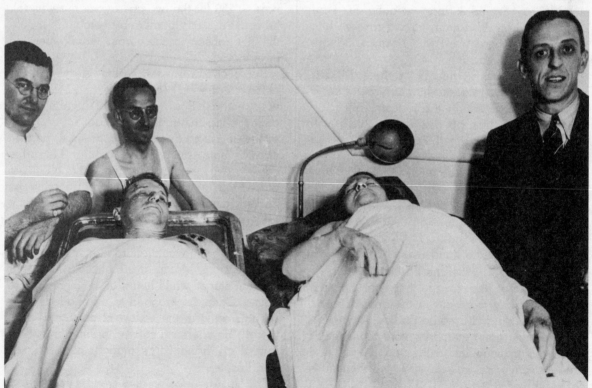

and Freddie to a southern resort in Oklawaha on Lake Weir in Florida. Guns drawn, they asked the Barkers to come out of their cottage. Suddenly, they heard Kate Ma Barker give her youngest son his last command: "All right! Go ahead!"

After a moment, the Barkers opened up on the G-Men. FBI agents returned their fire and inside of 45 minutes the cottage was a sieve. The Barkers had stopped firing. So had the agents, who were out of ammunition, having to send for more from a Jacksonville armory.

Agents then sent a Negro handyman, Willie Woodbury, who worked for the Barkers, into the cabin. The elderly man hesitantly walked inside. Moments later he called out from an upstairs window: "Dey's heah, boss. Dey's dead." (Quote as written by FBI agent Melvin Purvis.) Entering, the agents found Ma and Freddie shot to pieces in an upstairs bedroom. They had died fighting, Fred still holding his Thompson sub-machinegun. A .300 gas-operated rifle with 40 of its 94 rounds gone was next to Ma.

Freddie had been hit eleven times, Ma three, one directly through the heart. This shot, some reported, had been self-inflicted. It's not hard to believe that Ma would end her life the same way her son Herman had chosen.

There was $10,200 in clean currency found in Ma Barker's handbag. Born of a poor family, she died comparatively rich.

George Barker, the man Ma and her four sons had deserted, remained to receive the bodies of his family in the small town of Welch, Oklahoma where they all now rest. Herman was dead. Freddie was dead. Ma was dead. Doc was dead. Lloyd, finally paroled from Leavenworth in 1947, died two years later, killed by his wife.

George Barker buried them all in an open field not far from where he ran a clapboard filling station. New superhighways skirted the dirt road by which it squatted, but sometimes a rare tourist would come by, kicking up dust. George Barker would amble up from his chair in the sun, fill the tank, and study the lonely road.

Once a tourist noticed the clump of graves, their markers poking oddly above the tall reeds about them.

"What's that? A graveyard?"

"That's Ma and the boys," George Barker said.

[ALSO SEE Alvin Karpis]

BARROW, CLYDE
Murderer, Robber ● (1909-1934)

BACKGROUND: BORN IN TELICE, TEXAS 3/24/09 TO HENRY AND CUMIE BARROW, ONE OF EIGHT CHILDREN. MINOR PUBLIC EDUCATION. ORIGINAL OCCUPATION: FARMER. DESCRIPTION: 5'6¾", BROWN EYES, BROWN HAIR, SLIGHT BUILD. ALIASES: NONE. RECORD: COMMITTED TO HARRIS COUNTY SCHOOL FOR BOYS, 1918 AS "AN INCORRIGIBLE TRUANT, THIEF, AND RUNAWAY"; RELEASED IN HIS TEENS; ALONG WITH RAY HAMILTON AND FRANK CLAUSE JOINED THE SNEAKTHIEF SQUARE ROOT GANG IN HOUSTON, SPECIALIZING IN PETTY BURGLARIES; BEGAN ROBBING GROCERY STORES AND GAS STATIONS WITH HIS BROTHER IVAN MARVIN (BUCK) BARROW IN THE DALLAS AREA DURING THE LATE 1920S; ESCAPED POLICE DRAGNET AT DENTON, TEX., BUCK WOUNDED AND CAPTURED, 1928; BUCK SENT TO EASTHAM PRISON FARM FOR A FIVE-YEAR TERM; MET BONNIE PARKER IN JANUARY, 1930 IN DALLAS (BONNIE BORN 1911, ROWENA, TEX.); ARRESTED, 1930 FOR BURGLARY IN WACO, TEXAS, CONVICTED AND SENTENCED TO TWO YEARS IN THE WACO JAIL; DAYS AFTER BUCK BARROW ESCAPED EASTHAM 3/2/30, CLYDE, USING A GUN SMUGGLED TO HIM BY BONNIE PARKER, ESCAPED; RECAPTURED IN MIDDLETON, O., SENT TO EASTHAM PRISON FARM; KILLED FELLOW INMATE, ED CROWDER, 1931; PAROLED 2/2/32; STOLE A CAR IN MARCH, 1932 WITH BONNIE PARKER, PURSUED BY POLICE AND OVERTAKEN IN MABANK, TEX.; BONNIE CAPTURED AND SENTENCED TO THREE MONTHS IN JAIL AT KAUFMAN, TEX.; CLYDE, WITH RAY HAMILTON, ROBBED THE SIMS OIL COMPANY IN DALLAS, 3/25/32 ($300); ROBBED A JEWELRY STORE IN HILLSBORO, TEX., ($40), KILLING JEWELER JOHN N. BUCHER; ROBBED WITH HAMILTON AND FRANK CLAUSE SEVERAL GAS STATIONS IN THE LUFKIN, TEX. AREA IN MAY, 1932; ROBBED A DALLAS LIQUOR STORE 5/12/32 ($76); KILLED SHERIFF, C. G. MAXWELL AND DEPUTY EUGENE MOORE AT A BARN DANCE, ATOKA, OKLA. 8/5/32; ROBBED THE NEUHOFF PACKING COMPANY 8/12/32 ($1,100); BONNIE PARKER REJOINED CLYDE 8/12/32; TOOK SHERIFF JOE JOHNS OF CARLSBAD, NEW MEXICO HOSTAGE 8/13/32, DROPPING HIM OFF THE NEXT DAY IN SAN ANTONIO, TEX.; ESCAPED POLICE DRAGNET ON THE COLORADO RIVER BRIDGE AT WHARTON, 8/14/32; RAIDED WITH HAMILTON THE NATIONAL GUARD ARMORY AT FORT WORTH, STEALING BOXES OF MACHINEGUNS, AUTOMATIC RIFLES, AND SHOTGUNS, SEPTEMBER, 1932; ROBBED THE ABILENE STATE BANK ($1,400) 10/8/32; ROBBED GROCERY STORE IN SHERMAN, TEX. 10/10/32 ($50), KILLING BUTCHER HOWARD HALL; ROBBED WITH BONNIE THE ORONOGO, MISSOURI BANK ($200), 11/9/32; STOLE FORD V-8 IN TEMPLE, TEX., 12/23/32, KILLING ITS OWNER DOYLE JOHNSON; ESCAPED POLICE TRAP IN DALLAS 1/6/33, KILLING DEPUTY MALCOLM DAVIS; HELD STATE MOTORCYCLE POLICEMAN THOMAS PERSELL HOSTAGE 1/9/33; BUCK BARROW, WHO HAD BEEN RECAPTURED IN 1931 PAROLED 3/20/33, JOINED CLYDE, BONNIE AND W. D. JONES; BARROW GANG ROBBED A JEWELRY STORE IN NEOSHO, MO., RAIDED A FEDERAL

ARMORY IN SPRINGFIELD, MO. AND STUCK UP A LOAN OFFICE IN KANSAS CITY, KAN. IN MARCH-APRIL, 1933; ESCAPED POLICE TRAP IN JOPLIN, MO. 4/13/33, KILLING TWO POLICEMEN, WES HARRYMAN AND HARRY L. MCGINNIS; HELD H. D. DARBY AND SOPHIE STONE HOSTAGE 4/27/33, LATER RELEASED THEM UNHARMED; ROBBED THE LUCERNE STATE BANK IN INDIANA 5/8/33 ($300); ROBBED THE FIRST STATE BANK OF OKABENA, MINN. 5/16/33 ($1,500); ROBBED THE ALMA STATE BANK, TEX. 6/22/33; ROBBED A PIGGLY WIGGLY STORE, FAYETTEVILLE, TEX. 6/23/33; KILLED MARSHAL H. D. HUMPHREY NEAR ALMA 6/23/33; KILLED TRAFFIC OF-FICER, OKLAHOMA CITY, OKLA., JULY, 1933; STOLE A CAR, RAIDED THE NATIONAL GUARD ARMORY AT ENID, OKLA., JULY, 1933; ROBBED THREE GAS STATIONS 7/18/33, FORT DODGE, IOWA; ESCAPED POSSE, LED BY ARMORED CAR, NEAR PLATTE CITY, IOWA, BUCK AND BLANCHE BARROW WOUNDED; POSSE SURROUNDED BARROW GANG AT PICNIC GROUNDS OUTSIDE OF DEXTER, IA., 7/24/33, BLANCHE AND BUCK BARROW CAPTURED, BUCK DIED OF SIX BULLET WOUNDS IN THIS FIGHT FIVE DAYS LATER; W. D. JONES, CLYDE BARROW, BONNIE PARKER ALL WOUNDED BUT ES-CAPED; ELUDED POSSE NEAR GRAND PRAIRIE, TEX. 11/22/33, BOTH BONNIE AND CLYDE WOUNDED IN LEGS; BROKE RAY HAMILTON, JOE PALMER AND HENRY METHVIN OUT OF EASTHAM PRISON 1/16/34; ROBBED A BANK IN LANCASTER, TEX. 1/20/34; ESCAPED PO-LICE DRAGNET OF 1,000 POLICE AND NATIONAL GUARDSMEN IN THE COOKSON HILLS, 2/17/34; KILLED TWO STATE MOTORCYCLE POLICEMEN, E. G. WHEELER AND H. D. MURPHY, WHO INTERRUPTED A PICNIC NEAR GRAPEVINE, TEX. 4/1/34; KILLED BY POSSE ON THE ROAD BETWEEN SAILES AND GIBSLAND, LA., 5/23/34.

T he year was 1933 and the place, Okla-homa City, Oklahoma. It was hot and the young, somewhat well-dressed couple in the black Ford had the windows rolled down.

As they came to a corner, the young woman driving braked the car to a stop and glanced at the corner traffic cop with his white helmet worn against the blazing hot sun. An unnatural smile twisted upward on the right side of her face. She poked her companion, a sleepy-eyed youth.

"Watch this," she said to him as she worked the sawed-off shotgun upward from the driver's well until it rested between her legs. She moved the car forward slowly, pausing in the intersection.

"How do I get to Sixth and Main?" she said innocently in a sweet voice.

The traffic cop gave her the directions, smiled and touched the tip of his helmet. Then the girl brought out the shotgun and, firing both barrels, blew his head off. The headless, bloody corpse swooned slowly in the hot Oklahoma sun and then toppled backward toward the ce-ment.

The girl let out a squeal, the youth chuckled, and they drove off. This was the real Bonnie and Clyde.

There never was, in the annals of American crime, a more pathetic, illogical, and murder-ous pair of social truants.

These two penny-ante outlaws—they never robbed anything but gas stations, luncheonettes and a few small-town banks—epitomized the hardscrabble 1930s and the grubbing poor dust bowl Okies from which they came.

Unlike the legend, Bonnie and Clyde were far from Robin Hood types. They preyed on their fellow poor and killed them ruthlessly, thoughtlessly. They were hated by their own kind.

The biggest haul the Barrow gang ever gleaned was $1,500. John Dillinger, who read about their southwestern exploits in 1933 while he was still waiting to be released from the Michigan City, Indiana Penitentiary, called them "a couple of punks. They're giving bank-robbing a bad name!"

They never entered John Dillinger's class or matched his heists—his biggest being $74,000 at Greencastle, Indiana in 1933. But they pos-sessed, for those who did not know them, the devastating and down-home image of the dis-placed person whose cool resignation to obliv-ion was embodied in their slogan: "They wouldn't give up till they died."

Born into a brutally poor farm family in Tel-ice, Texas in 1909, Clyde was the third young-est of eight children. His boyhood was pock-marked with pranks and just plain trouble. His older brother Buck was his bad example and Buck was hellbent for young death, progress-ing early from selling stolen turkeys to stealing cars. Clyde was right behind him.

At an early age, Clyde developed a taste for music, so he stole a saxophone. As a teen-ager, Clyde went to Houston, Texas, where he rolled drunks, stole cars, and enjoyed some "high livin."

But the high living cost money, so Clyde, armed with an old horse pistol that wouldn't fire, held up a gambling den. The take was small but he managed to get his hands on two very real .38s. From then on it was running all the way.

Clyde, joined by his brother Buck, pulled a string of robberies in the Dallas area. Then the boys held up a gas station in Denton, Texas. The law jumped them and a highspeed pursuit at 90 mph developed with Clyde, who was normally an excellent driver, at the wheel. Taking a sharp turn, the car rammed into a ditch, breaking both axles. Buck had been wounded during the chase and Clyde left him for the law. Buck received a five year term at Eastham prison farm.

Clyde went on with his smalltime holdups and in January, 1930, he met five-foot, golden-haired, 90-pound Bonnie Parker. He walked into a little Dallas cafe where she was a waitress. Bonnie was nineteen years old and married to Roy Thornton, a convict at Eastham prison farm doing a 99-year term for murder.

Bonnie had not been faithful to Thornton, even though she had his name and two hearts tatooed on her right thigh. She dated everybody and that included Clyde.

Life in Dallas in 1930 was tedious and, in her own words, Bonnie was "bored crapless." Clyde Barrow was a mover and shaker to her. He was doing something, even if it was outside the law. They began living together. Bonnie liked it that way; Clyde was going somewhere.

He certainly was . . . straight to jail. Dallas lawmen came for him while he and Bonnie were necking on the sofa in a small, threadbare apartment. Clyde was arrested for a burglary committed in Waco, Texas, where he had neglected to wear gloves; the fingerprints he left behind convicted him. He received two years in the Waco jail.

Then Buck escaped from Eastham prison on March 2, 1930. Good old Buck, he knew how to work things out, Clyde thought as he planned his own escape. A few days later, Bonnie Parker walked into the Waco jail with a .38 Colt equipped with a Bisley handle thin enough to squeeze through bars. She had it taped to her thigh and slipped it to Barrow. He forced his way out that night and headed for Abilene, leaving Bonnie behind. Clyde ran as far as Middleton, Ohio, where train police grabbed him as soon as he jumped from a fast freight. This time he was sent to Eastham, known as "The Burning Hell."

If his poverty-stricken home life didn't make Clyde Barrow into a criminal, then Eastham surely did.

At Eastham, Clyde was beaten with whips and tortured on the "barrel cavalry"—made to mount a pickle barrel on top of a sawhorse and sit until he collapsed in the burning sun. There he also killed his first man.

An informer, Ed Crowder, told prison authorities Clyde had been gambling. Later, after being punished, Barrow armed himself with a lead pipe and smashed Crowder's head to pulp.

After Clyde had served twenty months in this sore-festering prison, his mother, Mrs. Cummie Barrow, went to Texas Governor Ross Sterling. She pleaded for his release. A month later, the governor granted it.

It was February 2, 1932 and Clyde Barrow would never see the inside of another prison. "I'll die first," he said. He did.

Clowning it up, Bonnie Parker "gets the drop" on Clyde, 1933. (UPI)

Bonnie teamed up with Clyde in March, 1932, but after they stole a car lawmen sighted them and another spectacular chase developed. Clyde crashed the car into a tree and the two ran across the fields attempting to escape. Deputies caught Bonnie, locked her in jail for three months, and then released her. Meanwhile, Clyde went on robbing tank town cafes and filling stations throughout Texas. His take for the month: $76. In Hillsboro, Texas, Clyde shot 65-year-old John M. Bucher to death while robbing him of ten dollars in his jewelry store.

Governor Sterling put a $250 reward on Clyde's head, but this didn't stop Clyde from shooting Sheriff C. G. Maxwell and Deputy Eugene Moore in Atoka, Oklahoma at a barn dance. The officers had the nerve to ask him what he was doing there lurking in the shad-

A typical picnic for Bonnie Parker and her mass slayer boyfriend, Clyde Barrow (shown cleaning part of his arsenal). This photo was taken by Buck Barrow in a wooded area near Dexter, Iowa, 7/24/33; minutes later a hundred-man posse burst through the trees behind them. Buck, mortally wounded, and his wife Blanche were captured; Bonnie and Clyde got away.

ows. Clyde killed them both.

Bonnie and Clyde, with a gunsel named Ray Hamilton, headed for New Mexico where Bonnie had relatives. It was the fall of 1932 and Bonnie and Clyde had twenty-one months to live.

Their life together on the open road was a strange one. Though Clyde was portrayed as being impotent, his real bent was homosexuality; that was another "lesson" he learned at Eastham. It was Ray Hamilton who slept with Bonnie . . . and Clyde. Later W. D. Jones, the gas-station attendant who joined the Barrow gang for kicks, would serve as lovers to both. Bonnie bordered on nymphomania and she slipped across that border many times.

All through 1932, Bonnie and Clyde went their wild, reckless way. On October 8, 1932, they knocked over the Abilene State Bank for $1,400. It was small pickings but times were tough.

Stopping for groceries a few days later in Red River Valley, Clyde tussled with a butcher whom he tried to rob. The man attacked him with a cleaver but missed. Clyde fired six rounds into him from his .45, scooped up some tin goods and took $50 from the till. The butcher died hours later.

The two young outlaws slept in the open, made coffee over campfires and ate peanut-butter-and-jelly sandwiches. The only real beds they knew were in remote tourist cabins and fishing grounds.

On November 14, 1932, while Bonnie manned the wheel of the car, Clyde robbed the Oronogo, Missouri state bank. The take was awful, a few hundred dollars. Then the two, homesick, sped to Dallas to see Bonnie's relatives.

It was on this trip that Bonnie and Clyde picked up the gas station attendant turned apprentice robber, W. D. Jones. The awe-struck Jones joined them immediately and began to live through "18 months of hell," as he later described it.

He was forced to rob banks, fire a machine-gun and was constantly ravaged by both Bonnie and Clyde. They even tied him up at night with chains so he couldn't escape. That was his tale, at least.

The trio drifted aimlessly in and about the Southwest through the early part of 1933, continuing to hold up small-town banks and stores. Then, Blanche Barrow, Buck's wife, went to the Texas Governor, wept and carried on. She had three children and no support and another baby on the way. Please, please, please release Buck, she begged.

Governor Sterling had been replaced by kind-hearted Mrs. Miriam A. "Ma" Ferguson who was absolutely wild about pardons—she had given out two thousand of them in her first term during the Twenties. Buck Barrow got one, too.

Buck and Blanche immediately joined brother Clyde, Bonnie and W.D. They headed straight for the federal armory in Springfield, Missouri. Days later, brandishing their new machineguns, the Barrow gang held up a loan office in Kansas City.

They were roaring now and the nation's press lavished front-page stories on their most meager exploits. Clyde, who was named the "Texas Rattlesnake," received most of the attention. But Bonnie wasn't far behind. An enterprising newsman dubbed her "Suicide Sal."

The Barrows were snapshot fanatics and would often pose menacingly with automatic rifles, pistols, and other assorted weapons of their vast arsenal. Bonnie posed once with Clyde, both holding pistols on each other, grinning. On one occasion Bonnie dangled a pistol from her hip and clenched a cigar in her mouth, portraying the deadly gun moll.

Later, Bonnie told one of the gang's many hostages, Police Chief Percy Boyd: "Tell the public I don't smoke cigars. It's the bunk."

But Bonnie enjoyed her publicity, and she wrote a long poem about their exploits which was published in many newspapers. By then, she had begun to realize that instead of "going some place" with Clyde Barrow, she was "just going." And she also knew death wasn't far behind.

Bonnie told her mother in the early months of 1934, "When they kill us, Mama, bring me home. Please don't let them lay me out in a funeral parlor."

The Barrow gang roared on through all the small towns, hiding, hitting, running. Bonnie knew death was closing in when they barely escaped a trap in Joplin, Missouri. In a wild shoot-out the Barrows escaped, killing two lawmen, constable Wes Harryman and detective Harry McGinnis.

After the escape, lawmen found Bonnie's poem on the kitchen table, unfinished. She later completed it. Her doggerel was a curious blend of self-exoneration and fatal prophecy:

THE STORY OF SUICIDE SAL
by "Bonnie" Parker

We, each of us, have a good alibi
For being down here in the joint;
But few of them are really justified,
If you get right down to the point.

You have heard of a woman's glory
Being spent on a downright cur.
Still you can't always judge the story
As true being told by her.

As long as I stayed on the island
And heard confidence tales from the gals,
There was only one interesting and truthful,
It was the story of Suicide Sal.

Now Sal was a girl of rare beauty,
Though her features were somewhat tough,
She never once faltered from duty,
To play on the up and up.

Sal told me this tale on the evening
Before she was turned out free,
And I'll do my best to relate it,
Just as she told it to me.

I was born on a ranch in Wyoming,
Not treated like Helen of Troy,
Was taught that rods were rulers,
And ranked with greasy cowboys . . .

The Joplin raid interrupted the poem at this point. Bonnie finished her tale weeks later and mailed it to a newspaper. The last stanzas read:

You have heard the story of Jesse James,
Of how he lived and died.
If you still are in need of something to read,
Here is the story of Bonnie and Clyde.

Now Bonnie and Clyde are the Barrow gang.
I'm sure you all have read
How they rob and steal,
And how those who squeal,
Are usually found dying or dead.

There are lots of untruths to their write-ups,
They are not so merciless as that;
They hate all the laws,
The stool-pigeons, spotters and rats.

If a policeman is killed in Dallas
And they have no clues to guide—
If they can't find a fiend,
They just wipe the slate clean,
And hang it on Bonnie and Clyde.

If they try to act like citizens,
And rent them a nice little flat,
About the third night they are invited to fight,
By a submachinegun rat-tat-tat.

A newsboy once said to his buddy:
"I wish old Clyde would get jumped;
"In these awful hard times,
"We'd make a few dimes
"If five or six cops would get bumped."

They class them as cold-blooded killers,
They say they are heartless and mean,
But I say this with pride,
That once I knew Clyde
When he was honest and upright and clean.

But the law fooled around,
Kept tracking him down,
And locking him up in a cell,
Till he said to me,
"I will never be free,
"So I will meet a few of them in hell."

This road was so dimly lighted
There were no highway signs to guide,
But they made up their minds
If the roads were all blind
They wouldn't give up till they died.

The road gets dimmer and dimmer,
Sometimes you can hardly see,
Still it's fight man to man,
And do all you can,
For they know they can never be free.

They don't think they are too tough or des-
    perate,
They know the law always wins,
They have been shot at before
But they do not ignore
That death is the wages of sin.

"It's the bunk about me smoking cigars," Bonnie Parker
told a police hostage after this photo (found in a Joplin,
Mo. apartment along with Bonnie's poem, "Suicide Sal")
was widely published by newspapers in 1933. (UPI)

From heartbreaks some people have suffered,
From weariness some people have died,
But take it all in all,
Our troubles are small,
Till we get like Bonnie and Clyde.

Some day they will go down together,
And they will bury them side by side.
To a few it means grief,
To the law it's relief,
But it's death to Bonnie and Clyde.

The police closed in fast after Joplin. They captured Blanche Barrow and shot holes into Buck in Dexter, Iowa, July 24, 1933 on a deserted fair grounds where the gang had been hiding. Bonnie and Clyde got away, Bonnie wounded.

Throughout 1934, the two were on the run, but on May 23, set up for a trap by a friend, Henry Methvin, the two were killed at a roadblock ambush near Gibland, Louisiana. A well-armed posse led by Texas Ranger Frank Hamer pumped 187 shells, such was their fierce legend, into Bonnie and Clyde, killing them instantly. Clyde had been driving in his socks and Bonnie had a sandwich in her mouth.

Hamer had tracked the two outlaws for 102 days. His telephone report of the shooting to the Texas Highway Patrol was laconic: "There wasn't much to it. They just drove into the wrong place. Both of them died with their guns in their hands, but they didn't have a chance to use them."

Unlike Bonnie's prediction, the killer-lovers were not buried side by side. Clyde was buried next to his brother Buck in West Dallas cemetery. Bonnie was first buried miles away in Fish Trap Cemetery and later removed to Crown Hill Memorial Park.

At Bonnie's burial, a local quartet sang "Beautiful Isle of Somewhere." On her tombstone ran the mawkish verse (not her own):

As the flowers are all made sweeter
By the sunshine and the dew,
So this old world is made brighter
By the lives of folks like you.

BARTER, RICHARD ("RATTLESNAKE DICK")
Robber ● (1834-1859)

Born in England, Barter immigrated to the U.S. as a youth and traveled to California shortly after the great Gold Rush period. There, tiring of panning gold for syndicates, he became a petty thief. In 1856 he hit upon a scheme to steal $80,000 in one swooping robbery. He and his gang would stop the gold convoy that regularly traveled by mule down from the Trinity Mountains.

For Rattlesnake Dick it was a gigantic undertaking. The robbery succeeded, but never netted Barter a dime, oddly enough. The outlaw did not deign to perform the deed himself but sent an accomplice, George Skinner, and two other members of his band out to stop the convoy. After Skinner made off with the gold, half-way down the mountain trail near Ureka, the mules gave out and Skinner buried most of the treasure.

Carrying what he could, Skinner and two others straggled down the mountain to keep a rendezvous with Barter. The outlaw chief didn't show up; he was already in jail with Skinner's brother Cy, imprisoned for stealing mules.

A posse intercepted George Skinner and killed him following a wild gunfight. When Rattlesnake Dick and Cy Skinner escaped jail, they fruitlessly searched for the gold taken in the robbery Barter had designed; they never found it (nor has anyone else) and the bandit returned to robbing stages. He was shot and killed by lawmen in 1859.

BASS, SAM
Stagerobber, Trainrobber ● (1851-1878)

BACKGROUND: BORN IN WOODVILLE, INDIANA, ONE OF TEN CHILDREN. NO PUBLIC EDUCATION. FOLLOWING THE DEATH OF HIS MOTHER AND FATHER WHEN HE WAS 13, BASS WAS, ALONG WITH HIS BROTHERS AND SISTERS, BOARDED OUT TO AN UNCLE DAVID SHEEKS. ORIGINAL OCCUPATIONS FARMER, MILLHAND, FREIGHT-HANDLER, COWBOY. DESCRIPTION: 5'9", BROWN EYES, BROWN HAIR, HEAVY MUSTACHE, SOLID. ALIASES: NONE. RECORD: ATTEMPTED TO ROB THE DEADWOOD STAGECOACH JUST OUTSIDE OF DEADWOOD, S.D. IN THE SPRING OF 1876 AT WHICH TIME ITS SHOTGUN RIDER JOHN SLAUGHTER WAS KILLED; ROBBED SEVERAL STAGECOACHES IN THE BLACK HILLS AREA IN 1876-77 FOR PIDDLING AMOUNTS; ROBBED WITH JOEL COLLINS, JIM BERRY, TOM NIXON, AND OTHERS THE UNION PACIFIC TRAIN NEAR BIG SPRINGS, NEB., 9/18/77 (TAKING $60,000 IN GOLD PIECES BEING SHIPPED EAST FROM THE SAN FRANCISCO MINT, $458 FROM THE RAILROAD SAFE AND $1,300 FROM THE PASSENGERS); ROBBED THE STAGE NEAR MARY'S CREEK OUTSIDE OF FORT WORTH, TEX. IN OCT., 1877 ($43); ROBBED THE HOUSTON & TEXAS CENTRAL EXPRESS WITH HENRY UNDERWOOD, FRANK JACKSON, SEABORN BARNES, AND TOM SPOTSWOOD, 2/23/78 ($1,280); ROBBED TWO MORE TEXAS TRAINS THAT SPRING WITH THE SAME BAND FOR SMALL AMOUNTS; ATTEMPTED TO ROB THE BANK AT ROUND ROCK, TEX. 7/19/78 BUT WAS BETRAYED BY A MEMBER OF HIS GANG; WOUNDED IN THE RAID AND DIED ON A CABIN PORCH NEAR BUSHY CREEK.

Sam Bass, as outlaws go, was not a man blessed with luck. From the beginning of his young life on a farm in Indiana, events were against him. His mother, Elizabeth Sheeks Bass, died giving birth to her tenth child. Sam was only ten then. His father Dan died three years later of illness. His uncle, David Sheeks, a petty tyrant, took in the Bass children and worked them like day laborers on his farm. Sam's scant legacy from his parents consisted of a bull calf and a worn-out saddle, both amounting to $11.

At eighteen, Sam ran away and took odd jobs in his wanderings. He worked as a millhand in Mississippi, earning enough money to stake him to a trip West where he longed to become a cowboy. By 1874, he made it to Denton, Texas, where he became a freighthandler for Sheriff William "Dad" Egan. He did some cowpunching, too, for the local ranchers.

Acquiring a fast pony, Bass entered her in all the local races for small prize money and won. He and his friend, Henry Underwood, then rode through Southwest Texas, the Indian territories, and Mexico, pitting the animal against local entries and easily winning races. On a trip to San Antonio, Bass befriended Joel Collins, a one-time bartender and cowboy, who convinced him that race-horsing for prizes was penny-ante. It also amounted to hard labor,

Collins argued. He had a six-gun. All Bass had to do was draw it from his holster to earn big money.

While helping to drive a large herd of Texas cattle to Kansas in 1876, Bass and Collins deserted and entered the Black Hills. There they attempted to stop the Deadwood Stage, but failed. Someone fired a shotgun in anger at the stage's guard, Johnny Slaughter, and killed him. (One of their confederates fired the shot and Bass and Collins drove him away; they didn't want trigger-happy outlaws in their band.)

Bass soon realized that stage robbing proved to be a dirt cheap way of starving. His gang never seemed to hit a stage carrying any gold shipments. The passengers were as impoverished as the outlaws. One stage had no passengers at all. Four passengers on the next stage could offer only $30 between them. Another stage brought the bandits only $3 and a gold watch.

Sam could not resist the gallant *beau geste* during these sorties. He had known poverty and he never let his victims ride off without returning $1 each to them for breakfast. It became his trademark. Though the outlaws were masked, as soon as their leader coughed back eating money passengers knew they had been robbed by Sam Bass.

Bass grew tired of the whole scheme. Stage robbing was a bust. He and Collins thought they'd try holding up a train. Collins set forth his plan to rob the Union Pacific express coming from San Francisco. He and Bass collected four other outlaws, the toughest in the Nebraska territory—Jim Berry, Tom Nixon, Jack Davis and Bill Heffridge.

The six men, following the railroad's timetable, rode out to Big Springs on the morning of August 18, 1877, and stopped the train as it was going up a steep grade. Collins and Bass jumped into the Wells Fargo freight car and ordered clerk Charles Miller to open the safe. He said it couldn't be done, that the safe had a time lock on it. Infuriated, Bass grabbed an axe from the car's wall and began to hammer heavy blows on the safe. He couldn't dent the solid iron structure.

Pausing from his labors, Bass wiped the sweat from his brow and, at that moment, happened to see clerk Miller nervously eyeing three boxes on the floor. "What's in them?" Bass asked, resting his hand on his pistol.

Sam Bass at sixteen. (Western History Collections, U. of Okla. Library)

Miller stammered ignorance. "I think some kind of hardware," he finally managed.

Bass swung down his axe on one of the boxes caving in the top. He staggered back, amazed. The box was jam-packed with $20 gold pieces, fresh from the mint in San Francisco, scheduled for delivery to New York banks.

"My God," Bass exclaimed, realizing that with one swing of the axe his fortunes had changed. Quickly, he broke into the other two boxes. They, too, were brimming with $20 gold pieces, $60,000 in all (a great fortune in that era).

Collins ordered Berry and Nixon to stand guard over the treasure. Collins and Heffridge then went to work on the regular Wells Fargo safe (they never did find out what the bigger safe contained) from which they finally extracted $458.

Bass and Jack Davis raced through the coaches, scooping up about $1,300 from the wealthy trans-continental passengers. With their saddle bags full and jingling, the outlaws then rode away whooping with joy.

The Big Springs raid was a sensation in the press and it brought down dozens of posses, railroad detectives, and the greatly feared Pinkertons on Sam Bass's trail. He had not been recognized but someone on the train identified the much-wanted Tom Nixon. He was well-known in the Black Hills as an outlaw friend of Joel Collins and Sam Bass.

The six men rode southward for their lives, each carrying about $10,000. The men split into pairs just after the raid, all heading back to Texas by various routes. Collins and Heffridge were jumped by a troop of soldiers near Fort Hays, Kan. After the two were wounded several times, the soldiers demanded their surrender.

"I'm going down with my six-guns!" Collins bravely yelled out. In minutes he and Heffridge were dead.

Berry and Nixon were next. A posse trapped them outside of Mexico, Mo. Nixon escaped but Berry stood his ground and was killed by Sheriff Walter Glasscock. Nixon apparently took most of Berry's money with him because only $3,000 was found on the dead outlaw. With his saddle bags bursting with gold, Tom Nixon rode out of Western history forever. No one ever found him again, despite a nation-wide manhunt conducted for years by the dogged Pinkerton Detective Agency.

Sam Bass and Jack Davis rode through Texas, dodging lawmen all the way. There, Davis also disappeared forever. It is quite likely that he and Nixon, both frugal cowboys, settled down to inconspicuous living to end their years in comfort and peace.

Sam Bass alone went on with his larger-than-life reputation staked openly and defiantly against the law. At Denton, Tex., he raised another outlaw band which included his old friend Henry Underwood and some other local boys—Frank Jackson, Seaborn Barnes, and Tom Spotswood.

These five hit the Houston and Texas Central express February 23, 1878 near Allen Station, Tex. The take, compared with the Big Springs job, was petty: only $1,280. Two more train robberies that spring involving the same band netted only $600. Train robbing for Sam Bass was proving as meagerly profitable as stopping stages. He decided to turn to banks.

Holed up in his almost impregnable lair, a natural fortress of steep hills and bluffs known as Cove Hollow near Denton, Bass and his bandits planned the robbery of the Round Rock, Texas bank. The outlaw chieftain had taken in a new recruit, Jim Murphy. Seaman Barnes didn't trust Murphy and told Bass so. Sam was a loyal sort and refused to think ill of his new addition to the gang.

Barnes was right. Murphy, a local boy whose family had been pressured by the authorities to turn over Bass (on threat of prosecution for once harboring him), decided to become a traitor. Murphy's deal with Texas Ranger Major John B. Jones also included a considerable reward.

Another ranger, Captain Lee Hall, in the true tradition of the West, wanted no part of the sellout, branding Murphy a "veritable Judas in every sense of the word." But Jones had his way and Murphy waited for his chance.

When Bass and his band rode out of Cove Hollow to raid the Round Rock bank, Murphy went with them. They stopped in a small Texas town to water their horses. Murphy managed to get off a wire to Jones: "We are on our way to Round Rock to rob the bank. For God's sake get there."

By the time Bass arrived in Round Rock, the rangers were waiting. Murphy said he was going "to look around for lawmen" and quickly vanished. Bass, followed by Barnes and Jackson, went into a grocery store for tobacco. They planned to familiarize themselves with the town and rob the bank the next day.

Two local lawmen then walked into Koppel's store. Deputy Sheriff A. W. Grimes approached the outlaws. "Now you know you men ain't supposed to be wearing sidearms in town," he said. Deputy Sheriff M. Moore stood behind Grimes, fingering his six-gun.

With one nervous look between them, Bass, Barnes, and Jackson went for their guns. Grimes went down with six bullets in him. A bullet hit Moore in the chest and he went down firing; one of his shots hit Bass in the stomach. The outlaws ran from the store just as a swarm of rangers ran up the street toward them.

Barnes was shot dead while mounting his horse. Jackson pushed Bass up onto his mount and the two raced down the street. Jim Murphy watched them from hiding. He saw Sam Bass' saddle coated with blood and reported to the rangers that his leader had been severely wounded. His story was supported that night when a local farmer came into town and told authorities that an outlaw was dying on the front porch of his cabin near Bushy Creek.

Ranger Jones and his men rode to the farmer's place and found Sam Bass. His right hand had been smashed by a bullet and he had lost a great amount of blood from the stomach wound. A doctor who rode out with the posse stated that Bass' case was hopeless.

Jones begged the outlaw to tell him who was with him on the raid. Sam Bass responded in a fashion that was to become part of the Code of the West and, generations later, that of the modern American criminal. "It's agin my trade to blow on my pals. If a man knows anything, he ought to die with it in him."

Jones kept asking for names.

"Let me go," Sam Bass said. "The world is bobbing around."

Then he was gone.

BATTAGLIA, SAM ("TEETS")
Syndicate Gangster ● (1908-1973)

A burglar and muscleman for the Chicago outfit since 1924, Battaglia had been one of the ranking members of the Midwest Mafia (one Chicago family controls a tri-state area—Illinois, Wisconsin, Indiana) for several decades. He had been arrested twenty-five times since 1924 on charges from robbery to suspicion of murder (seven homicides).

Battaglia was Chicago's "juice king" until imprisoned for a term of fifteen years following a conviction for extortion. When called before the McClellan Committee, he took the Fifth Amendment sixty times.

Chicago authorities believed that when and if Battaglia, a Giancana henchman, was set free, he would assume the Mafia-syndicate leadership now held by Accardo.

BEADLE, WILLIAM
Murderer ● (? -1783)

For a long period of time, something had been troubling William Beadle of Weathersfield, Conn. He seldom spoke to his wife Lydia or his four children in the last year of his life, and developed the habit of taking an axe and a carving knife to bed with him each night. (Ominous as this sign might be, Mrs. Beadle failed to realize that all was not right with Mr. Beadle.)

On the morning of December 11, 1783, Beadle slaughtered his entire family and then slit his own throat.

BEAUCHAMP, JEREBOAM O.
Murderer ● (1803-1826)

BACKGROUND: BORN IN KENTUCKY, 1803. BECAME AN ATTORNEY AT LAW, 1823. MARRIED ANN COOKE, 1824. DESCRIPTION: TALL, ROBUST. ALIASES: NONE. RECORD: MURDERED COLONEL SOLOMON P. SHARP IN 1826; CONFESSED AT HIS TRIAL, SENTENCED TO THE GALLOWS; HANGED 7/7/26 AT FRANKFORT, KY.

A woman's honor meant everything to Jereboam Beauchamp, born and raised after the genteel tradition in the antebellum South. Beauchamp would do anything to defend that honor, including murder.

Ann Cooke, an aging belle from Virginia, became engaged to Beauchamp when he was only twenty-one years old (she was thirty-eight). Before she would marry the promising young attorney, however, Ann insisted that her honor be avenged. She had been seduced and made pregnant, she claimed, by Colonel Solomon P. Sharp, a member of the Kentucky House of Representatives and a former attorney general of the state.

The heated political campaign of 1826 also involved Ann Cooke. Solomon's political foes used her seduction story against him, openly branding him a scoundrel. The Colonel remained mute on the subject but Jereboam

Beauchamp did not. Two years after marrying Ann (there was no child) Beauchamp, no doubt brooding about Ann Cooke's charges then rekindled in the election, confronted Sharp, demanding that he meet him in a duel. The Colonel declined.

Days later, wearing a red hood over his head, Beauchamp appeared at Sharp's estate. When the Colonel opened the door, Beauchamp plunged a dagger into his chest several times until the politician fell dead.

Beauchamp, however, was recognized and his apprehension followed almost immediately. He was imprisoned in the Frankfort jail, a dungeon-like affair with no windows, pitch-black, which had to be entered by letting down a ladder. Here, Ann visited him to pour out her gratitude for effecting her revenge.

After his confession, Beauchamp was speedily tried and sentenced by the Frankfort Circuit Court in May, 1826. He was sentenced to die on the gallows in July. While waiting for the hangman, Jereboam and Ann decided they would commit suicide together. Ann smuggled poison into Jereboam's cell and both took large doses, but they only succeeded in getting sick.

On July 7, 1826, the day of the hanging, the two ate a final breakfast of chipped beef and tea. Then each took turns with a knife, plunging it into each other's stomachs. As Ann died in Jereboam's arms, thousands of people from all over the county gathered outside the jail to await the hanging.

When jailers entered the cell, Jereboam, still alive, dramatically cried out: "Tell my Father that my wife and myself are going straight to Heaven—we are dying." But, severely wounded that he was, Jereboam was not dying. Angry jailers dragged him from his cell, his dead wife clasped in his arms.

Jereboam's last moments on earth were intended to entertain the thousands of spectators who had come to the execution, many with picnic baskets, kites, and small children. He had been expected to sit on top of his own coffin in an open cart and be led ceremoniously to the gallows in a nearby field while bugles, fifes, and drums heralded his last ride.

But Jereboam Beauchamp was too weak for that; he disappointed the crowd by riding in a closed carriage, wrapped with a blanket soaked with blood from his wound. He clung to the body of his dead wife in the carriage, saying to her: "Farewell, child of sorrow! For you I have lived; for you I die!"

Jailers and hangman had to help the weakened man up the stairs of the gallows where the rope was placed about his head with much ceremony. Following the custom of the day, hangman, jailers, the crowd, and the condemned man paused from their ghastly chore. They stood silently for moments, Beauchamp supported in a half-swoon, while a band played a popular air of the day, "Bonaparte's Retreat from Moscow," Beauchamp's last request.

Then the hangman kicked open the trap door and Jereboam joined his "child of sorrow." His body was quickly taken down and Beauchamp was placed in his coffin. His wife, Ann, was placed next to him, her head resting on his shoulder.

They were both buried that day outside of Frankfort. A giant flat slab of Kentucky River sandstone was placed above their common grave as a marker. On the stone was chiseled a poem Ann Cooke Beauchamp had written in the Frankfort jail:

> He heard her tale of matchless woe,
> And burning for revenge he rose,
> And laid her base seducer low,
> And struck dismay to virtue's foes.

> Daughter of virtue! Moist thy tear.
> This tomb of love and honor claim;
> For thy defense the husband here,
> Laid down in youth his life and fame.

BECK, MARTHA JULIE
Serial Killer ● (1921-1951)

Fat and calculating, Martha Julie Beck had nothing to offer society. She hated all women more attractive than herself and had a pathological devotion to a hollow-eyed, balding man, Raymond Martinez Fernandez (1914-1951). This inconspicuous couple preyed upon single women and became infamous as the Lonely Hearts Killers.

Lonelyhearts killers Martha Beck and Raymond Fernandez, flanking an officer, joking while in custody.

Fernandez had been born in Hawaii of Spanish parents. He had reportely served with British Intelligence during the Second World War, until being discharged after receiving a head wound that drastically changed his personality from happy-go-lucky to morose and brooding. He supported himself by making love to lonely women, conning them out of their savings, and deserting them. He wore a cheap black wig to hide his almost bald head and police later described him as "a seedy Charles Boyer."

He was anything but that to Martha Beck, one of his victims. Beck, a nurse who had been divorced since 1944, operated a run-down home for crippled children in Pensacola, Fla. In 1947, Beck placed an ad in one of the local lovelorn columns and Ferandez replied.

The sleazy con man inexplicably fell in love with the unattractive Martha, and even confessed that he intended to bilk her out of her savings. To his surprise, Martha approved of his crooked ways and offered to join him in his lonely hearts schemes. The couple immediately traveled north looking for victims in the lovelorn columns.

Fernandez wooed and won the hearts of dozens of women; some reports later claimed that his victims numbered more than a hundred. He would promise marriage and then depart before the nuptials with his victims' savings. Often as not during these whirlwind courtships, Fernandez would introduce Beck as his sister. Beck usually moved in with Fernandez when he went to live with his victims. She had no complaints about her lover being with women who were in their fifties or sixties, the age group to which most of the victims belonged.

But when Fernandez roped a younger, more attractive woman, Beck became jealous. This was the case with 28-year-old Mrs. Delphine Dowling of Grand Rapids, Michigan, who had a 2-year-old daughter. Beck moved with Fernandez into the Dowling house but was consumed with hatred for Mrs. Dowling, especially since she slept in a bedroom next to that in which Fernandez slept with his victim.

Mrs. Dowling promised her hand to Fernandez but wanted to wait to see if he was, indeed, sincere. Martha Beck told Fernandez they would not wait, that Mrs. Dowling and her little girl had to be killed. Both disappeared in January 1949. When police investigated they were met by Beck and Fernandez, who told detectives that they had no idea where Mrs. Dowling and her daughter had gone.

Suspicious officers asked for permission to search the house. Beck and Fernandez only shrugged. In the basement detectives found a fresh patch of cement, "the size of a grave," as one of them described it. They dug up the bodies of Mrs. Dowling and her little girl.

Beck and Fernandez did not deny killing the pair. The talkative Martha freely explained that she had dosed Mrs. Dowling with sleeping pills but the young woman revived and Fernandez shot her in the head. They never planned to kill the little girl, Martha pointed out. They even bought her a puppy but she would not be placated and kept crying for her mother. Martha then filled the bathroom tub with water, threw the child into it, and held her under water until she drowned.

Dubbed the Lonely Hearts Killers by the press, Beck and Fernandez reveled in their notoriety. They bragged about killing at least seventeen others. "I'm no average killer," boasted Fernandez. "I only got five hundred off the Dowling woman, but take Mrs. Jane Thompson. I got six thousand off of her." He went to explain how he took Mrs. Thompson to Spain on a vacation and murdered her with doses of digitalis. Fernandez then said that his lover's line was so effective that it worked on Mrs. Thompson's mother, Mrs. Wilson, and that he moved in with this woman, too, and then murdered her.

Fernandez confessed murders one after another, talking so rapidly that he began to sweat and had to remove his wig to wipe the perspiration from his bald head. He told how he married Mrs. Myrtle Young in 1948 and took her to Chicago on a honeymoon where the elderly woman died in bed with him. "Poor woman," laughed Fernandez, "she died of overexertion!"

Beck interrupted to rattle off another string of murders, claiming that she, not Fernandez, was the chief architect of their killings. She explained through giggles that they had killed Mrs. Janet Fay of Manhattan because the 66-year-old woman had cried out for Fernandez when Beck and Fernandez were leaving the victim. It so incensed Beck that another woman displayed affection for her lover that she grabbed a hammer and crushed Mrs. Fay's head with it. "I turned to Raymond," Beck said calmly, "and said 'look what I have done,' and then he strangled her with a scarf."

The couple admitted their killings in the belief that they would be tried and imprisoned in Michigan, where there was no death penalty. To their surprise, Michigan allowed the state of New York to extradite the murderous pair, where they were tried for killing Mrs. Fay. They were even more amazed when their plea of not guilty by reason of

insanity was dismissed after both were examined and judged sane. Both were found guilty and sentenced to death.

Through appeals the Lonely Hearts Killers delayed their rendezvous with Sing Sing's electric chair until March 8, 1951. On the night of his execution Fernandez refused to order a meal, saying he could not keep the food down. He smoked a big Havana cigar down to a stub and then had to be half-carried to the chair to die.

Martha Beck was next, as the tradition was to take the strongest last. She told female warders that she was sick and tired of being portrayed as a flabby, overweight person. She would show the world that she had discipline and would not gorge herself with a last meal. She ordered fried chicken, fried potatoes and a salad, then changed her mind and ordered a double portion of each. When she entered the death chamber she smirked through her three chins and plopped her great weight down so heavily in the electric chair that it creaked and heaved.

Fernandez had the last comment through a note he handed a guard as he sat down in the chair. Later widely published, it read: "People want to know if I still love Martha. But of course I do. I want to shout it out. I love Martha. What do the public know about love?"

BECKER, BARENT
Murderer ● (? -1815)

Becker, a farmer living in Mayfield, New York, grew tired of his wife Ann and disposed of her by following an age-old tradition. Becker prepared his specialty, stewed tomatoes, and served it to her loaded with enough arsenic to annihilate a regiment. She consumed the dish with relish and promptly died.

The farmer confessed and was hanged October 6, 1815, after he delivered a maudlin farewell to his relatives from the gallows. A special hymn, which Becker had composed, was sung.

BECKER, CHARLES
Murderer, Extortionist ● (1869-1915)

BACKGROUND: BORN AND RAISED IN NEW YORK CITY.
MARRIED. ROSE THROUGH THE RANKS OF THE NEW
YORK CITY POLICE DEPARTMENT, REACHING THE RANK
OF LIEUTENANT. MINOR PUBLIC EDUCATION. DESCRIP-
TION: 6'2", BROWN EYES, BROWN HAIR, HEAVYSET,
SWARTHY. ALIASES: NONE. RECORD: EXTORTED MONEY
FROM ILLEGAL GAMBLING CASINOS IN THE BROAD-
WAY, TENDERLOIN, AND HELL'S KITCHEN AREAS OF
NEW YORK FOR YEARS. ORDERED THE KILLING OF
GAMBLER HERMAN "BEANSIE" ROSENTHAL ON 7/21/12.
AFTER TWO LENGTHY TRIALS, BECKER WAS CONVICTED
OF MURDER AND SENTENCED TO DEATH; EXECUTED IN
THE ELECTRIC CHAIR AT SING SING PRISON, 7/7/15.

New York Police lieutenant Charles Becker (shown in 1911) was the king of graft in Manhattan, ruthlessly ordering death for anyone, such as gambler Herman Rosenthal, who displeased him. (UPI)

One of America's greatest novelists, Stephen Crane, watched horrified one evening in the 1890s as a patrolman—tall, massive-shouldered, and with the largest pair of hands he had ever seen—sauntered up to a small, white-faced prostitute. He demanded his share of money from her latest job. She shook her head at the burly extortionist. The patrolman's gigantic hands doubled into fists and began to beat her with hammer-like blows until she crumpled to the ground, her face ripped to a bloody pulp.

Before Crane could move, the huge cop had scooped up the prostitute's miserable change and walked away. This man was not an ordinary cop as Stephen Crane and the rest of the country would later discover. He was Charles Becker "the crookedest cop who ever stood behind a shield."

Although Crane would write Becker into his novel about the little New York prostitute: *Maggie: A Girl of the Streets*, the world was yet to really know this most brutal of men.

When dapper Rhinelander Waldo became New York's police commissioner in 1911, he made Becker a lieutenant and his aide. The big cop had charmed his way into the post. He then charmed the gullible Waldo into naming him as the head of Special Squad Number One.

This squad had but one assignment: crack down on the wide-open graft, gambling and prostitution then rampant in New York. Under Becker's greedy direction this police squad became a strong-arm gang of terrorists promoting its own graft and corruption.

Becker's take came mostly from kickbacks on prostitution and gambling; under his "protection," gambling dens flourished in the Tenderloin and Broadway strips. Becker's "protection" assured him of twenty-five cents on the dollar.

When gamblers refused to kick back, Becker's squad raided their casinos, destroying everything in sight. With particularly stubborn customers, the squad faked evidence and brought in convictions, making Becker appear reliable and upright. It was cheaper, the gamblers learned, to pay off the big cop.

To collect his graft, Becker employed some of the strangest bagmen ever seen in the underworld. One was "Billiard Ball" Jack Rose, who didn't have a single hair on his head. Another was a professional killer from the Lower East Side, "Big Jack" Zelig.

Also making the rounds for Becker were Bridgie Weber, Sam Schepps and a man who had a face like a character out of Bram Stoker's *Dracula*, Harry Vallon. These unsavory criminals were immune to prosecution. "Nothing you do for me will get you in trouble with the law," Becker had promised. The big cop enjoyed his role of enforcer as he swaggered throughout Manhattan, well-tailored, glib, demanding tribute from the corner of his mouth.

Becker had been closely associated with gambler Herman "Beansie" Rosenthal for years. Rosenthal owned a gambling spa called The Hesper and, once each week, kicked back half of his take to Becker. Suddenly, as was Becker's habit over real or imagined slights, the ham-fisted cop took a dislike to "pasty-face" Rosenthal. "He's a goddamn coward and he talks too much," Becker said one day to Vallon.

Even though he owned a large piece of the Hesper, Becker demanded more of the take and Rosenthal balked. Becker went into an hysterical rage and ordered his flying squad to smash Beansie's gambling casino. Every stick of furniture was broken. No one said no to Charles Becker.

He placed a policeman on duty outside the closed gambling den and, incredibly, one in Rosenthal's apartment—twenty-four hours a day. Rosenthal's wife underwent a nervous breakdown and Beansie almost went berserk staring at the cop sitting placidly in his living room.

With his business closed and his house invaded, Rosenthal finally launched a plan to retaliate against his oppressor Becker. The gambler knew that Charles S. Whitman, New York City's young and aggressive District Attorney, wanted to break Becker's criminal stranglehold on Manhattan. Rosenthal also knew that Whitman had no evidence against Becker. His hatred for Becker bubbling over, Rosenthal went to the District Attorney and gave him everything he needed to indict the crooked cop—names, places, dates, the amounts of graft the Becker ring had collected for years.

Whitman moved immediately to have a grand jury convene to indict Becker. Through the well-greased grapevine that fed the crooked cop his information, however, Becker learned of the impending indictment and Rosenthal's betrayal. He gathered his murderous clan, including Billiard Ball Jack Rose and Jack Zelig. Zelig brought in four East Side killers: Gyp the Blood (Harry Horowitz), Dago Frank (Frank Cirofici), Lefty Louis (Louis Rosenberg), and Whitey Lewis (Jacob Siedenshner).

"I want Rosenthal croaked!" Becker screamed at the group. "Kill him anywhere. Do it in front of a policeman and it will be all right. I'll take care of everything."

Herman Rosenthal had the habit of stopping by the Cafe Metropole for a late night coffee and brandy. The Metropole on West 43rd Street was a gambler's hangout and Beansie would trade talk there with his fellow high rollers. But when Rosenthal entered the cafe late on the night of July 21, 1911, no one would talk to him; the gamblers, gangsters, and racetrack touts thought him a turncoat.

None of the angry looks or snarling remarks his friends gave him upset the small gambler. He moved about freely, ignorantly showing everyone a newspaper which told his tale in bold headlines. "That's what the newspapers think of me," he commented.

At 2 a.m., a voice from the doorway called out, "Herman, somebody wants to see you."

Without a sign of apprehension, Rosenthal casually walked out the door and stood blinking under the bright marquee lights of the cafe.

Another voice called out from the darkness: "Over here, Beansie."

As Rosenthal moved in the direction of the voice, four shots quickly rang out and the gambler collapsed to the cement. Then one of Charles Becker's murder group ran forward and leveled his pistol at Rosenthal's head while he lay bleeding on the sidewalk. The killer blew away part of Beansie's skull with the final shot.

The killing occurred in full view of dozens of Metropole customers. It was one of the most blatant and ill-conceived murders in American crime, yet the killers were confident that Becker would protect them.

Becker had boldly instructed police to "lose" the license number of the murder car should some zealous citizen turn it in. Smugly, he thought his order would be sufficient to quash any investigation. But District Attorney Whitman spoiled the killer cop's arrangements. Through a tipster, Whitman learned that police were hiding an eyewitness to the Rosenthal slaying in a back cell of a remote station. He appeared, demanding to talk to the witness.

Ludicrously, there was even a scuffle with the sergeant in command before Whitman spirited his witness away. Through this man, the District Attorney was able to trace the license number of the murder car to its owner, Billiard Ball Jack Rose.

Brought in for questioning, Rose admitted nothing. Ten days passed and when Becker did not intervene on his behalf as promised, Rose panicked. "I'm being thrown to the wolves," he wailed and then asked to see Whitman.

Billiard Ball's mouth didn't close until he had named Rosenthal's killers. Gyp the Blood and the others were quickly arrested. They, too, named Becker as their boss. Rose was given immunity for his testimony but the gunmen were promptly convicted and electrocuted.

The two trials of Lieutenant Becker dragged on for almost three years. Finally, he was sentenced to death after being found guilty of planning Rosenthal's murder.

The powerfully-built Becker was led into the electrocution room at Ossining on July 7, 1915 and several jolts of electricity were sent through his massive body. He was so strong, however, that it required repeated jolts to finally kill him. The execution was one of the clumsiest in Sing Sing's history.

By the time Becker came to be executed, Whitman had become Governor of New York, largely on the strength of convicting the crooked cop. He refused to stay Becker's death sentence.

After the execution, Becker's faithful wife had a plaque (later removed) placed on the crooked cop's tombstone which read:

> CHARLES BECKER
> Murdered July 7, 1915
> By Governor Whitman

BELACHHEB, ABDELKRIM
Mass Murderer ● (1945-   )

In the early morning of June 28, 1984, Abdelkrim Belachheb, a 39-year-old from Morocco, entered Ianni's Restaurant and Club in North Dallas, Tex. He asked a woman to dance but once on the dance floor, the woman pushed Belachheb away from her, complaining that he was being too frisky with his hands. The rebuffed Belachheb blew her a kiss and walked outside to his car where he loaded a Smith & Wesson .459 pistol.

Belachheb then walked back inside the restaurant and coolly shot and killed the woman. He walked back to his car, reloaded his weapon, then returned to the club where he shot six other patrons at random. All died. Belaccheb fled in his station wagon, which he wrecked in an accident. He then went to a fellow Muslim's home, prayed through the last hours of Ramadan, a Muslim holiday, then called police.

Belachheb was charged and convicted of multiple murder and attempted murder. He was sent to prison for life on November 15, 1984. His mass killings were described as "the worst multiple killing in the city's history in modern times."

BEMBENEK, LAWRENCIA
(LAURIE, BAMBI)
Murderer ● (1959-   )

One-time detective and ex-Playboy bunny Lawrencia "Laurie" Bemenek was convicted of murdering her husband's ex-wife in 1981. On May 28 of that year Christine Schultz was shot dead in her Milwaukee, Wis., home. The next month Bembenek, who was married to Elfred Schultz, was charged with the murder. Prosecutors claimed that Bembenek had killed Christine Schultz because she was jealous over the alimony being paid by her husband to the ex-Mrs. Schultz.

The victim's young children testified that the killer invading their house wore a green jogging suit and army jacket, items Bembenek owned. Moreover, hairs from a wig found hidden in Bembenek's closet matched those found next to the victim. In a fifteen-day trial, Bambi Bembenek was found guilty and was given a life sentence. She later claimed she was the victim of a police frame-up because other officers had resented her being on the Milwaukee Police Force and that some other person had killed Mrs. Schultz.

Bambi later escaped and was the object of a sensational manhunt, which resulted in her recapture and return to prison.

BENDERS, THE
Murderers, Robbers

BACKGROUND: THE BENDER FAMILY, CONSISTING OF FATHER AND MOTHER, AGES APPROXIMATELY 60 AND 50, ONE SON IN THE LATE TWENTIES, AND A DAUGHTER NAMED KATE, ABOUT 23, ARRIVED NEAR CHERRYVALE, IN LABETTE COUNTY, KANSAS, IN 1872 ESTABLISHING AN INN AND GENERAL STORE. DESCRIPTION: ALL FOUR MEMBERS OF THE FAMILY WERE TALL, LARGE-BONED PEOPLE, THOUGHT TO BE GERMAN IMMIGRANTS (THEY ALL SPOKE WITH HEAVY, GUTTERAL ACCENTS). ALIASES: UNKNOWN. RECORD: THE BENDERS FROM 1872-73 KILLED AND ROBBED AT LEAST ELEVEN TRAVELERS WHO STOPPED AT THEIR INN, THE MOST NOTABLE VICTIM BEING DR. WILLIAM YORK; THE MURDEROUS FAMILY ESCAPED A POSSE BY ONLY A FEW DAYS, DISAPPEARING COMPLETELY.

The Benders of Kansas have become the classic American family of murder but when they rode quietly into Cherryvale, in south-eastern Kansas in the spring of 1872, no one took any special notice. Like many immigrants of the period, they had come west to make new lives and new fortunes. Their methods were different from those of most homesteaders.

Between the towns of Thayer and Cherryvale, Kansas, the Benders erected a small log cabin, twenty feet long and sixteen feet wide. The one room was divided by a canvas curtain which separated the living room-grocery store-inn from the family bedroom. Old man Bender, his wife, and their dull-witted son spoke little to the strangers who passed their way, selling them canned goods and coffee, with an occasional grunt for a greeting.

Their tall, buxom daughter Kate, however, was outgoing and aggressive. She fancied herself a spiritualist who could contact the dead and cure serious illnesses (for a price). As "Professor Miss Kate Bender," she eventually held public seances.

Kate appeared in several small Kansas towns with her spiritualistic show. She became quite popular with the more rakish members of the audience. Some of these unfortunate men traveled out to the Bender Inn to visit her and never returned.

The alarming aspect of the living arrangements at the Bender inn was a canvas wall.

Some travelers complained that as they sat with their backs to the canvas they heard odd noises behind them. One man insisted on sitting on the other side of the table to eat his meal. Kate suddenly grew angry and began to shout at him—"you sit where you are!" He heard whispers behind the canvas and, frightened, jumped up and ran from the inn.

Others were not as intuitive. If an overnight guest appeared to be wealthy, he was given a hearty meat-and-potatoes meal by Kate and as he ate, Old Man Bender or his son, wielding a sledge hammer, would direct a savage blow against the spot of canvas where the traveler's head rested, instantly crushing his skull.

The body was then dragged beneath the canvas and the corpse was stripped. A trap door leading to a small earthen cellar was thrown open and the body was then dumped into this area until the Benders could find time to bury the victim on the prairie.

This murder system worked well for eighteen months. Then Dr. William York stopped at the inn in the spring of 1873. He had stopped there before and had informed his brother, Colonel York, whom he had been visiting at Fort Scott, that he would again stay with the Benders on his return trip.

Dr. York never reached his home. Shortly after his disappearance, Colonel York arrived at the Bender home, asking about his brother. He knew his brother had stayed with them. Had they seen him?

Father Bender said no, Dr. York never visited their humble inn. "Maybe it's the Indians," he muttered. "And Jesse James is about, you know."

To allay Colonel York's suspicions, Bender and his son offered to help drag a stream not far from the inn.

Colonel York thanked them and rode away. The Benders were now alarmed; one of their victims had been trailed right to their doorstep. They wasted no time. On May 5, 1873, they cleared out, taking their cattle with them.

York, still suspicious, returned to the Bender place five days later with a posse. Finding the inn deserted, York entered the building. He inspected the cellar, noting with alarm that the earthen floor was coated with dried blood. The stench was overpowering.

Then York inspected the open fields about the inn. He found eleven oblong mounds of earth. "Boys," he said slowly, "those look like graves." The posse began to dig and Colonel York was proved correct. The mutilated corpse of his brother was in the first grave opened.

A frantic search by dozens of posses throughout Kansas then began, but the Benders had too much of a head start and were never officially found. They had robbed close to $10,000 from their victims, it was estimated, a small fortune for those days, one which could take them anywhere in comfort. Authorities searched for fifty years for the Benders without success. Once, in 1889, two women identified as Kate and Ma Bender were extradited to Kansas from Detroit but their identification was incomplete and a trial was never held.

It was later claimed that a small posse did catch up with the blood-thirsty family and killed them, shooting them and then burning their bodies, saving Kate for the last and burning her alive—a deed so horrible that the posse members vowed silence. This report was never confirmed.

BERKOWITZ, DAVID (SON OF SAM)
Serial Killer ● (1953-   )

BACKGROUND: BORN 6/1/53, ILLEGITIMATE, GIVEN UP FOR ADOPTION. MINOR PUBLIC EDUCATION IN NEW YORK, N.Y. RECORD: ATTACKED TWO GIRLS IN SEPARATE INCIDENTS ON 12/24/75, SERIOUSLY WOUNDING ONE GIRL. ATTACKED TWO GIRLS ON 7/29/76, SHOOTING TO DEATH DONNA LAURIA AND WOUNDING JODI VALENTI IN THE BRONX; ON 10/23/76 SHOT AND WOUNDED CARL DENARO; SHOT AND WOUNDED TWO MORE GIRLS, DONNA DEMASI AND JOANNE LOMINO ON 11/26/76 IN QUEENS; ON 1/30/77 BERKOWITZ SHOT AND KILLED CHRISTINE FREUND AS SHE SAT IN A CAR WITH HER BOYFRIEND; ON 3/8/77, SHOT AND KILLED STUDENT VIRGINIA VOSKERICHIAN; ON 4/17/77 SHOT AND KILLED VALENTIA SURIANI AND MORTALLY WOUNDED ALEXANDER ESAU IN THE BRONX; ON 6/26/77 SHOT AND WOUNDED JUDY PLACIDO AND SALVATORE LUPO IN QUEENS; ON 7/31/77 SHOT AND KILLED STACY MOSKOWITZ AND BLINDED HER BOYFRIEND, ROBERT VIOLANTE, AS THEY SAT IN A CAR PARKED IN BROOKLYN; APPREHENDED BY POLICE INSPECTOR TIMOTHY DOWD OUTSIDE BERKOWITZ'S YONKERS APARTMENT ON 8/2/77; PLED GUILTY AT ARRAIGNMENT AND SENTENCED TO 365 YEARS IN PRISON.

A serial killer who struck terror in New York in 1976-1977, David Berkowitz was, without a gun, a cringing loner who dwelled in filth

and poverty, frightened of rejection, and hating women of all ages. He had been born a bastard and his mother quickly put him up for adoption. His early years were filled with lonliness and his adoptive parents showed him little affection, according to Berkowitz. His stepfather, Nate Berkowitz, who owned a Bronx hardware store, retired to Florida and left David to live on alone in New York.

Berkowitz dwelled in a squalid little apartment. He supported himself with odd jobs and grew increasingly paranoid. He wrote his stepfather that a neighbor's barking dog and trucks rolling by in the street kept him up all night. He complained that strangers passing him on the street looked at him with hatred in their eyes and spat at him. His special wrath was reserved for women. "The girls call me ugly," he wrote, "and they bother me the most."

His mother's abandonment and several rejections by girls led Berkowitz to lash out at females; any females, it was later conjectured. His first recorded aggressive action occured on Christmas Eve 1975 when he attacked two young girls with a knife. The first frightened him off with her screams but the second, a fifteen-year-old schoolgirl, failed to fight him off. Berkowitz viciously drove a knife into her lung, wounding her.

On July 29, 1976, Berkowitz, prowling Buhre Avenue in the Bronx, found two girls chatting in a car. He slowly withdrew a gun he was carrying in a paper bag and fired five shots into the car at close range. He bullets smacked into Donna Lauria, killing her. One of his shots struck Jody Valenti, wounding her seriously in the leg.

Police became alarmed at this shooting, believing that some lunatic was at large, seeking anonymous victims to kill just for the love of killing. Berkowitz proved this theory correct when he next, on October 23, crawled up to a car parked in front of a Flushing bar. In the auto sat Carl Denaro who was with his girlfriend Rosemary Keenan. Berkowitz quickly jumped up, firing rapidly. After wounding Denaro he fled.

On November 26, 1976, Berkowitz struck again, this time selecting two girls, Joanne Lomino and Donna DeMasi. The girls were chatting, sitting on the stoop of a house in the Floral Park section of Queens. The killer approached them, asking for directions. Suddenly, Berkowitz stopped in midsentence. He reached into a brown paper bag and jerked for a gun, which he blindly fired at the girls. Then he fled.

Lomino was the more seriously wounded of the pair, a bullet lodged next to her spine, paralyzing her. Police dug out bullets from the wooden stoop and matched these to those in the Lauria-Valenti shooting. They knew they were dealing with the same killer but his description was fuzzy and leads were scant.

Berkowitz roamed through Ridgewood on the night of January 30, 1977, seeking more victims. He found a couple necking in a car and pulled his gun from the brown paper bag, firing a bullet into the head of Christine Freund. The girl fell into the arms of her boyfriend, John Diehl. Taken to a hospital, Freund was pronounced dead a few hours later.

The killings went on while police frantically tried to trace the gun and piece together some sort of identity of the murderer. They drew a blank. The kind of killer they were seeking was, they knew, the most difficult to catch. He had no apparent motive and slew strangers who could not be traced to him. He killed alone, which eliminated the possibility of a confederate informing on him.

On March 8, 1977, Virginia Voskerichian, an Armenian student, was walking down a Forest Hills street. Berkowitz was suddenly standing in front of her, a girl he had never met. Wordlessly, he drew the gun from his brown paper bag and fired point blank into the girl's face, killing her instantly. This time witnesses got a good look at the slayer and described him as five feet, ten inches tall, with black hair combed straight back. Police warned females not to travel about New York City alone at night and broadcast a description of the man they were seeking, labeling him "a savage killer."

Berkowitz did nothing for a month. Then, on April 17, prowling the streets only a short distance from where he had shot Lauria and Valenti in the Bronx, he came upon a parked car in which sat Valentina Suriani and Alexander Esau. Whipping out his gun, Berkowitz shot both at close range. Suriani died instantly and Esau, with three bullets in his head, was rushed to a hospital. He died a few hours later.

A short time later Police Captain Joseph Burrelli was given a note from the killer. Burrelli had made many statements about the ruthless killer to the press. To this man Berkowitz wrote: "I am deeply hurt by your calling me a weman-hater (sic). I am not. But I am a monster. I am the Son of Sam. I am a little brat. . . . I love to hunt, prowling the streets, looking for fair game . . . tasty meat. . . . The weman (sic) are prettyist of all." Berkowitz wrote in the same letter that he had been brutalized by his father and that his father had told him to go into the streets to murder.

He sent a similar letter to newsman Jimmy Breslin, who had been extensively covering the killings. In both instances, the letters smacked of imitating the horrific messages Jack the Ripper had sent to officials a century earlier, when that monstrous murderer prowled through the dark streets of London looking for victims.

On June 26, Berkowitz shot Salvatore Lupo and Judy Placido as they sat in a car parked in Queens, but this time his aim was poor and the couple received only minor wounds. Police intensified their patrols throughout Queens and the Bronx, the favorite stomping grounds of the killer. Berkowitz saw them everywhere and he then began prowling through Brooklyn. There, on July 31, 1977, he found Stacy Moskowitz and Robert Violante sitting in a car with the windows rolled up. Berkowitz fired four times through the window. His bullets killed Moskowitz and blinded Violante.

As Berkowitz ran to his car, a woman walking her dog watched him jump in and speed away. She was able to tell police that there was a parking ticket on the windshield of the killer's auto. Police checked and found that only four tickets had been issued in that area. A carbon copy of one of the tickets bore the name of David Berkowitz, a resident of Yonkers.

Captain Dowd and others waited at Berkowitz's address on August 2, 1977. When the killer walked up to his car, Dowd said: "Hello, David."

Berkowitz stood frozen for a moment as he stared at the officer. He then gave him a crooked smile and, recognizing Dowd from his newspaper photos, blurted: "Captain Dowd! You finally got me!" He gave no struggle as he was taken into custody.

At first Berkowitz tried to claim he was insane but psychiatrists who examined him later testified that Berkowitz was faking lunacy. The origin of the name "Son of Sam" then came to light. Berkowitz had used the name of a neighbor Sam Carr. It was Carr's dog who had kept Berkowitz up nights with its barking. The killer had shot the dog but it recovered and when it did, Berkowitz claimed, the dog spoke to him, ordering him into the streets to murder.

Berkowitz pled guilty at his arraignment and was never tried. He was sentenced to 365 years in prison where he presently resides without any hope of parole. Following Berkowitz's arrest, his garbage-littered apartment was mobbed by souvenir hunters who looted anything that could be taken away, including old magazines, empty soup cans, and rolls of toilet paper.

BIANCHI, KENNETH (THE HILLSIDE STRANGLER)
Serial Killer ● (1952-   )

BACKGROUND: BORN ROCHESTER, N.Y., RAISED BY FOSTER PARENTS. MOVED TO LOS ANGELES IN 1977, LIVED WITH ANGELO BUONO, JR. RECORD: EMBARKED ON KILLING SPREE WITH BUONO, MURDERING ELISSA TERESA KASTIN ON 10/6/77. KILLED YOLANDA WASHINGTON, WHOSE BODY WAS FOUND NEAR FOREST LAWN CEMETERY ON 10/18/77. KILLED JUDITH LYNN MILLER WHOSE BODY WAS FOUND 10/31/77 ON A GLENDALE HILLSIDE. ON 11/20/77 MURDERED THREE WOMEN, CHRISTINA WECKLER, DOLORES CEPEDA, AND SONJA JOHNSON. KILLED JANE EVELYN KING 11/23/77; MURDERED LAUREN RAE WAGNER ON 11/29/77. KILLED KIMBERLY DIANE MARTIN ON 11/29/77. SLEW CINDY LEE HUDSPETH, WHOSE BODY WAS FOUND ON 2/17/78. ALONE, IN JANUARY 1979, BIANCHI SLEW TWO COEDS, DIANE WILDER AND KAREN MANDIC, WAS ARRESTED, AND TRIED. BIANCHI WAS GIVEN A LIFE SENTENCE IN WASHINGTON AND BUONO, TRIED SEPARATELY, WAS CONVICTED AND GIVEN A LIFE SENTENCE ON 1/9/84.

Insidious and calculating, Kenneth Bianchi typified the modern-day serial killer who murdered out of the sheer joy of killing. He and his bestial cousin, Angelo Buono, Jr., murdered ten women from 1977 to 1979 without the slightest trace of remorse. These young men were torturers, rapists, sodomites, and murderers who, for the most part, selected streetwalking prostitutes as their victims. Bianchi came to be called "The Hillside Strangler" because of penchant for dumping corpses on hillsides, no doubt because he could better display to the world his heinous crimes, posing the naked, ravished bodies in lacivious positions.

Bianchi was born in Rochester, N.Y., where he was raised by foster parents. In 1977, he moved to Los Angeles to live with his cousin, Angelo Buono, Jr., an upholsterer who worked out of his own home, repairing chairs and sofas in his garage. Buono bragged to his neighbors that being Italian meant proving his manhood. He flew an Italian flag outside his house. Long before Bianchi arrived, Buono was seen arriving regularly with prostitutes on hand.

Drinking beer one night, the cousins began talking about killing people, particularly young women who would not be missed, such as young girls who flocked to Los Angeles every day seeking film careers but quickly opted for prostitution to survive. They planned to pick up girls and bring them to Buono's house where they would indulge any kind of perversion before killing their victims.

The pair began their murderous adventures on October 6, 1977, when they picked up 21-year-old Elissa Teresa Kastin. After raping her, they strangled their victim, then drove to Glendale and dumped the naked body on Chevy Chase Drive. Yolanda Washington, nineteen, was next. Police found her naked body sprawled in a lacivious position, cleaned by the killers so as to eliminate clues and evidence, on the slopes of Forest Lawn Cemetery, the resting place of Hollywood stars.

Police next found the naked body of fifteen-year-old Judith Lynn Miller on October 31, placed on a Glendale hillside close to a road. As was the case with Yolanda Washington, the Miller girl's neck, ankles, and wrists bore rope marks. Detectives easily concluded that Miller had been bound before being raped, sodomized, and finally strangled. Her condition was the hallmark of future victims of Bianchi and Buono. Because Miller's body had been found on a hillside, the press dubbed the murderer "The Hillside Strangler."

Miller's body had been thoroughly scrubbed, which told the police that the killer or killers were being careful not leave any clues. Since the bodies were also left sprawled in the open and close to police stations, detectives rightly concluded that they were dealing with someone who arrogantly defied authorities to apprehend them.

November 20, 1977, was a red-letter day for the killers. On that day they abducted, abused, and killed three females: Dolores Cepeda, twelve; Sonja Johnson, fourteen; and Kristina Weckler, twenty. Weckler's naked body was dumped on a slope in Highland Park. The nude bodies of Cepeda and Johnson were found in Elysian Park. Three days later, their bloodlust at fever pitch, Bianchi and Buono killed Jane Evelyn King, 28. They threw her naked body onto an offramp of the southbound Golden State Freeway.

On November 29, 1977, the killers slew Lauren Rae Wagner, eighteen, dumping her naked body on Cliff Drive in Glassell Park. Kimberly Diane Martin, eighteen, was found next by police. The killings stopped through the holidays but the slayers resumed their gruesome chores the following year. On February 17, 1978, police found the naked body of Cindy Lee Hudspeth in the trunk of a car.

On a map in the police homicide department, detectives had placed pins at the points where all the bodies had been found. The pins formed a circle and detectives theorized that the killer lived inside of that circle. They were right. All the victims were killed in Buono's home and then taken to various points from the house and dumped for public view.

Police routinely reported that they had several suspects and expected to break the case shortly but all of their leads evaporated. When the killings ceased, detectives were baffled and most of those seeking the killers were reassigned to other duties. The reason the murders stopped at this point had to do with the relationship between Bianchi and Buono. The cousins had grown to dislike each other. Bianchi complained about Buono's filthy habits, leaving garbage strewn about his house for days and never bathing.

Bianchi went to Bellingham, Washington. There he had the nerve to apply for a job as an officer with the Bellingham Police Department. He stated on his application that he had been an applicant to the Los Angeles Police Department but had not gotten the job. This was true. Ironically, while he and Buono were killing hapless whores in Los Angeles, Bianchi not only tried to become an L.A.P.D. officer but had driven about with officers in their cars, even some investigating the very murders he had committed.

Bellingham police turned down Bianchi but he managed to obtain a job as a security guard. While working in Bellingham, Bianchi resorted to his killer instincts. He encountered two college girls, Diane Wilder and Karen Mandic. He raped both of them, strangled them, then locked their bodies inside the trunk of Mandic's auto. This time, police had a path to follow. Witnesses came forward to identify Bianchi as having been with his victims shortly before their deaths.

Bianchi was arrested and immediately claimed to be insane. This was his plan. He had, for years, read himself to sleep by pouring over psychiatric studies and was particularly knowledgeable about split personalities. In addition, he had read and reread two books, *Sybil* and *The Three Faces of Eve*. To prison psychiatrists, Bianchi presented all the symptoms of the split-personality mind. He claimed to have blackouts and loss of memory. He stated that he had several personalities and one of them, which he could not control, was a ruthless killer of women.

Psychiatrists saw through the act and Bianchi was pronounced sane and held for trial. Knowing he was facing a death sentence for his Bellingham killings, Bianchi then desperately tried to make a deal. He would testify against his cousin Buono, whom he said was the real Hillside Strangler, if he were returned to California and did not have to face death by hanging in Washington.

Washington authorities agreed but on the condition that Bianchi plead guilty. He did and was given a life sentence. He was then shipped to California where he implicated Buono. He related how he and Buono drove about in Buono's car, stopping naive young girls and flashing fake police badges, claiming that Buono's car was really an unmarked police detective car.

Their victims were ordered into the car and were driven to Buono's house where the two sexually attacked them. They were then tortured and strangled. Both men then scrubbed down the bodies to eliminate any clues. Placing the bodies in the back of Buono's car, the pair drove about, looking for grassy hillsides where they could dump the bodies, almost as if they wished to display them as trophies to a public they took delight in horrifying.

Cursing and struggling, the brutish Buono was arrested in 1979 shortly after Bianchi's Washington arrest. His trial began in 1981 and did not conclude until November 14, 1983. Buno's prolonged trial was a judicial extravaganza that cost millions. More than 400 witnesses testified and 55,000 pages of trial transcript were assembled. Throughout, Buono insisted that he was innocent. He defied authorities to find anything in his home that would implicate him in the murders.

Buono's home, indeed, was spotless. Not in keeping with his hygenic behavior, the killer had thoroughly cleaned his house before his anticipated arrest. Not one fingerprint of the victims was found. Oddly, not even Buono's own fingerprints could be found, so meticulously had he scrubbed the floors and walls. Forensic officials were as meticulous as Buono. Incredibly, they found a single eyelash belonging to one of the victims in Buono's home. Moreover, they found a few fibers from one of Buono's chairs on the bodies of some of the victims.

One of the endless stream of witnesses was a surprise to the defense. It was 27-year-old Catherine Lorre, daughter of Peter Lorre, the famous character actor. She stated that Bianchi and Buono had stopped her on a Hollywood street, showed her their phony detective badges, and demanded she show them some identification. She showed them her driver's license and beside that was a photo of a little girl sitting in her father's lap. Bianchi admitted that when he saw this photo, he decided to let the woman go on her way, stating that he feared that abducting and killing the daughter of a celebrity would bring down intense police heat on him and Buono.

Finally, Buono was convicted and Judge Ronald George gave him a life sentence without the possibility of parole. Bianchi was sent to Walla Walla, Washington, to serve out his life sentence. He will not be eligible for parole until the year 2005. Remarked Judge George at the sentencing: "I'm sure Mr. Buono and Mr. Bianchi, that you will only get your thrills by reliving over and over the tortures and murders of your victims, being incapable, as I believe you to be, of ever feeling any remorse."

BILLINGTON, JOHN
Murderer ● (? -1630)

John Billington's singular though infamous distinction as an American criminal was permanently established when he became this country's first murderer, arriving with the original band of 102 pilgrims on the *Mayflower* at Plymouth Rock in 1620.

Billington and his family came from London—a rowdy, foul-speaking lot who more than once on the voyage over had been reprimanded by Captain Miles Standish. The good Captain, finding Billington's blasphemous harangues more than he could stand, had the offender's feet and neck tied together as an example of a sin-struck man possessed of a Devil's tongue.

This humiliating and painful punishment did not soften Billington's rough ways. He continued to be the black sheep of the Pilgrim colony at Plymouth, starting violent arguments and fights. One of John Billington's bitterest enemies was John Newcomen, a neighboring settler. Their feud raged for a number of years until 1630 when Billington decided to end it with murder.

Hiding behind a rock, Billington waited in the woods until Newcomen, hunting for game, appeared. Leveling his blunderbuss, Billington shot and killed him at close range. He was quickly tried by the little band of pilgrims and hanged.

Ironically, dozens of present-day Americans lay claim to being related to Billington, murderer or not.

BIM BOOM GANG

The Bim Boom gang was a particularly violent group of teenage street thugs who dominated a large area of the near South Side of Chicago in the mid-1920s. Members specialized in petty thievery and violent assaults on other gangs; each foray often resulted in several deaths.

The gang's main opposition in those years was the Garfield Park gang known as the Thistles, another known as the Deadshots, and the savage band of youthful terrorists led by Danny O'Hara.

Bim Boom leaders employed BB guns, .22-caliber rifles, and shotguns in their gang fights. The shotguns were loaded with rock salt, and when fired, produced a paralyzing effect on the person shot. It was an exclusive Bim Boom creation.

BISHOP, ARTHUR GARY
Serial Killer ● (1951-1988)

Born in Hinckley, Utah, Bishop was a popular student who made the honor roll. He was devoutly religious and served as a missionary for the Mormons in the Philippines. In 1974, for unspecified reasons, Bishop was suddenly kicked out of the Mormon Church. He took a job with a Ford dealership in Murray, Utah. In 1981, after being arrested for embezzling $9,000 by forging the owner's signature to a check, Bishop disappeared.

Taking the alias of Lynn E. Jones and later Roger W. Downs, Bishop dropped all contact with his family. Then, small children began to disappear. Alonzo Davis, four, was abducted from the front lawn of his Salt Lake City, Utah, home on October 16, 1979. On November 27, 1980, Kim Peterson vanished. Next to disappear was four-year-old Danny Davis on October 20, 1981. Troy Ward, six, vanished on June 22, 1983, as did Graeme Cunningham, thirteen, on July 14, 1983.

Ten days after the last disappearance, police arrested Arthur Gary Bishop, charging him with

Convicted on five counts of murder and sentenced to death, the child killer was offered by Utah law the option of either a firing squad or lethal injection. He chose the latter. Bishop was injected with a lethal drug on June 10, 1988. Shortly before his death, Bishop read from the *Book of Mormon* and expressed his remorse over killing the children.

BISHOP, WILLIAM BRADFORD, JR.
Mass Murderer ● (1937- ?)

A promising foreign service officer in the State Department in Washington, D.C., William Bradford Bishop, Jr., suddenly went to pieces on March 1, 1976. On that day, Bishop drove his station wagon into a Texaco service station where he chatted with attendants as he filled a five-gallon drum of gasoline, and then, officials later concluded, he returned home where he beat to death his wife, Annette, his three children, and his 68-year-old mother Lobelia Bishop.

Bishop then carried the bodies to the station wagon and drove to a deserted area outside of Columbia, N.C. Bishop dumped the bodies in a ditch, poured gasoline over them, and set them afire. The smoke from the burning bodies attracted motorists but by the time police were summoned, Bishop had vanished.

Two weeks later, Bishop's station wagon was found deserted near Gatlinburg, Tenn., in the Great Smoky Mountain range. FBI agents tracking Bishop discovered that he had used one of his credit cards on March 2, 1976, in a Jacksonville, N.C., sporting goods store, where he outfitted himself with all sorts of camping equipment.

Agents theorized that Bishop, an experienced camper, planned to lose himself deep in the Smoky Mountains. Some later said Bishop intended to commit suicide in the woods he had loved as a boy. In July 1978, however, Bishop was reportedly seen in Sweden, a country he could have easily reached through his foreign service contacts. The FBI has not closed the books on the Bishop case; he is still wanted as a federal fugitive and he is still wanted on murder charges.

Arthur Gary Bishop, child killer, who was executed in 1988.

embezzling $10,000 from one of his many employers. In searching his home, detectives found explicit sexual photographs that showed some of the children who had vanished in Salt Lake City area. Confronted with this evidence, Bishop confessed to abducting all five children, sexually abusing them, and then killing them. He led officers to shallow graves near his residence.

BITTAKER, LAWRENCE SIGMOND
Serial Killer ● (1941-   )

A sadistic and bloodthirsty murderer, Lawrence Sigmond Bittaker kidnapped, raped, and killed five teenage girls between June and October 1979. All of his victims were killed in Los Angeles suburbs. Arrested after his last attack, Bittaker was convicted on February 17, 1981, and sentenced to death. An accomplice, Roy Lewis Norris, was given a 45-year-sentence in return for testifying against Bittaker.

Bittaker's victims were Jacqueline Leah Lamp, thirteen, and Jackie Gilliam, fifteen, both from Redondo Beach; Shirley Ledford, sixteen, of Sun Valley; Lucinda Schaefer, sixteen, of Torrance; and Andrea Hall, eighteen, of Tujunga. The killer filed many appeals but the California Supreme Court upheld the death sentence on June 22, 1989. Bittaker still awaits the gas chamber at this writing.

BJORKLAND, PENNY
Murderer ● (1941-   )

T hough raised in comparatively good surroundings by her family in Daly City, Calif., Penny Bjorkland (born Rosemarie Diane) was bent on murder while still in her teens. There was never an adequate reason given—either by herself or psychiatrists baffled at her deed—for her slaying of gardener August Norry on February 1, 1959. Her only comment on the murder was chillingly laconic— "Just to see if I could, and not worry about it afterwards."

Penny, an attractive eighteen-year-old blonde, worked as a file clerk at a publisher's service bureau. She was conscientious in her work habits and considered an asset to the firm. Her weekends, however, were fitful. She bit her nails horribly and slept for twenty-five hour stretches; she would dream of murdering someone, anyone.

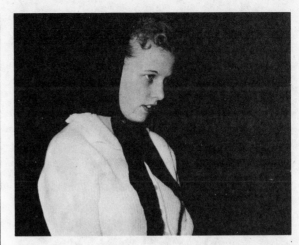

She suddenly decided to murder—Penny Bjorkland stares at a California judge in 1959 while being arraigned. (Wide World Photos)

On the day of the murder, Penny awakened abruptly and said audibly to herself: "This is the day I will kill someone. If I meet anyone that will be it."

After breakfasting with her mother, an unusually beautiful woman (some claim it was Penny's jealousy for her mother which caused her hatred for society and bloodlust), Penny went into her room, got dressed and, after taking out her .38-caliber pistol, which she used for target practice, went hunting for someone to kill in the hills about San Francisco.

She found landscape gardener August Norry, 27, married and the father of two children. The young man was dumping some refuse from his car when Penny walked up to him. He offered her a lift and slid behind the wheel.

"Thank you," Penny Bjorkland replied and pulled out her pistol, pumping six shots into the startled gardener. She then ran around the car and, reloading, fired another six bullets into the dead body.

Penny reached upward, grabbed the corpse by the neck and pulled it from the car. She reloaded her weapon and fired yet another six shots into the dead man. After staring at the body for a while, pleased, Penny jumped into the car—the bloody seat didn't appear to bother her—and drove it wildly down through the hills. It was found hours later in a lover's lane. A boy told police he had seen "a freckle-faced blonde" driving Norry's vehicle "like mad" away from the murder spot.

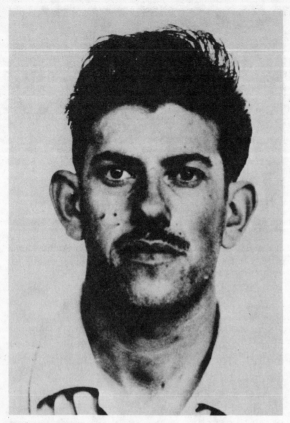

Gardener August Norry was picked at random by Penny and killed. (UPI)

The brutal murder stymied police. Penny tried to help them by sending a letter to a San Francisco newspaper, telling the editor that "her friend" killed Norry—but she did not reveal her identity or any names. A month later, Penny turned to her co-workers at the publisher's service bureau and blandly stated, "I'm the blonde they're looking for in the Daly City murder." Her friends laughed uproariously.

Police did have one clue, however. From Norry's body, they took eighteen unusual slugs, known to ballistic experts as "wadcutters," a kind of bullet used in target shooting. These were somewhat rare and were subsequently traced to a San Francisco gunshop owned by Lawrence Schultze. The proprietor, after attempting not "to get involved" admitted selling fifty rounds of "wadcutters" to a teenage blonde. He had her name on his receipt files. Yes. Here it is. Penny Bjorkland.

In a matter of hours, on April 15, 1959, police arrested the disturbed young girl and took her to the San Mateo County jail where she sobbingly confessed her crime to a matron the following morning.

Penny waived jury trial and admitted the killing, throwing herself on the mercy of the court. A four-month trial followed, weighed down with tedious psychiatric examinations, theories, and cross-examinations. On August 6, 1959, Superior Court Judge Frank Blum of Redwood City determined that the Norry killing was a "willful, wanton murder," and sentenced the girl to life in prison.

"This is not what I expected," Penny told reporters. She was removed to Corona Prison. Years later, a reporter visited with her. She ended the interview brightly with: "I consider myself a normal, average girl."

BLACK HAND, THE

Contrary to popular belief, The Black Hand was anything but a single organization officially associated with such secret brotherhood groups as the Mafia and the Camorra. It was essentially an extortion racket practiced by Sicilian and Italian gangsters (many of whom were members of the evil brotherhoods) for approximately thirty years—1890 to 1920 —against the unschooled, superstitious immigrants of the "Little Italy" settlements sequestered in major Eastern, Southern, and Midwestern cities.

The racket consisted of sending an unsigned note to a prominent and well-to-do member of the Italian or Sicilian community, demanding money under the penalty of death. The sender usually threatened to kill the victim's family and, to create an air of outright terror, would mark the extortion letter with ominous symbols such as daggers, skull and crossbones, hatchets, and sabers dripping blood. In most cases, the outline of a hand dipped in heavy black ink was impressed at the bottom of the note. This was usually sufficient to frighten the recipient into delivering large amounts of extortion monies to the Blackhander at a specified secret place.

New York, Chicago, New Orleans, St. Louis,

and Kansas City were centers of this activity, all of these metropolitan areas containing the largest segments of Italian and Sicilian immigrants in the country.

In New York, the top Blackhander for three decades was Ignazio Saietta, known to inhabitants of Little Italy as Lupo the Wolf. Others who operated in Brooklyn and Manhattan during Saietta's Black Hand supremacy were Frankie Yale (Uale), Johnny Torrio, and Ciro Terranova, who later became the rackets czar known as "The Artichoke King."

Saietta concentrated his Black Hand terror against Sicilians living in the Harlem district; he was more than once arrested for Blackhanding by Lieutenant Joseph Petrosino, the intrepid head of the NYPD's special Italian squad, whose almost impossible job it was to track down the extortionists. Saietta's Black Hand fortune, however, permitted him the best lawyers in the community and he squeaked past one indictment after another. He was finally put out of action by his own greed when he thought counterfeiting would be more lucrative than extortion; he was caught by Secret Service agents and sent to prison for thirty years.

Lieutenant Petrosino got it into his head that most of the Blackhanders probably had criminal records in Sicily. If the New York authorities could prove nothing against these extortionists, he reasoned, they could at least be permanently deported to Sicily if they were wanted there. He began lengthy correspondence with Sicilian authorities, sending them the NYPD records of Sicilians arrested for Blackhanding. His work paid off. Police in Palermo, Sicily sent back wanted sheets on many of these, and more than 500 Sicilian gangsters were subsequently deported to their native country to face prosecution and imprisonment.

In some instances, Petrosino, a hulking six feet, 200 pounds, did not wait for the mail from Sicily. When his good friend, the internationally famous tenor, Enrico Caruso, received a Black Hand note, Joe tracked down the sender by himself. He broke the man's arms and personally threw him onto a boat headed for Sicily with the warning that he would "blow out" the man's brains if he ever came back to the U.S.

The guile which personified the Blackhanders was not for Joe Petrosino. He faced

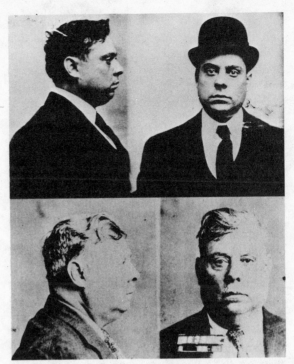

New York's Ignazio Saietta, a vicious Blackhander known to the Italian community he terrorized as Lupo the Wolf. (UPI)

the extortionists squarely in alleys and dark hallways, most often alone, and handled them with his fists and police revolver. On one occasion he tracked down Enrico Alfano, a ranking member of the murderous Camorra brotherhood of criminals, who had killed several helpless persons in New York after they refused to pay Black Hand notes. Alfano was wanted, Italian police notified Petrosino, for killing and mutilating an entire family in Naples.

It was the kind of job Petrosino liked. He located Alfano's room. Drawing his .38 caliber service revolver, Petrosino raised his heavy foot and slammed it against the door. It banged down on two men who were waiting on the other side with drawn guns. Petrosino jumped onto their stomachs with each foot and leveled his gun at Alfano who was making for a window.

"Go ahead, rat!" the policeman yelled. "My bullet will take away your head." Alfano meekly dropped his gun and surrendered. Petrosino roped all three Blackhanders together with their own ties and a bedsheet and dragged them down four flights of stairs and through the gutters of Little Italy on Mulberry Street for two blocks to the station, telling the startled Italian spectators along the way: "Is this what you're afraid of, these gutter rats? How fierce is the Black Hand now? Spit on them!" But none dared to spit.

Petrosino's life was lived against razor-thin odds. He himself received over a thousand Black Hand notes telling him to leave New York or die. He was repeatedly shot at on the street. Knives flashed in bustling crowds, slashing out at him. Poison was put into his food in restaurants. But still he lived, honored by the city of New York and by the Italian and Sicilian governments for his service. Italian authorities presented him with an enscribed gold watch.

Petrosino decided that instead of sending makesheets on those suspected of Blackhanding in New York to Sicily and Italy, he himself would journey to Palermo. There, he concluded, it would be easier if he merely went through the police files checking mugshots to locate wanted criminals he knew were living in the U.S.

Joe convinced Police Commissioner Bingham to send him to Palermo, Sicily in 1909. Arriving in Palermo, Petrosino energetically tackled the police archives there, unearthing hundreds of wanted cards on fugitives known to the NYPD. These he mailed in large batches to Bingham, who promptly had the criminals arrested and arraigned for deportation.

But Petrosino was living inside a hornet's nest. His investigation ran headlong into the core of the Mafia and the Mafia dons wanted him exterminated; he was getting too close to knowledge concerning their own activities and power. *Capo di tutti capi* (boss of bosses) "Don" Paulo Marchese, head of the Mafia's Grand Council in Sicily, actually entertained Petrosino in an exclusive restaurant to learn if the policeman knew of the Mafia hierarchy. When he discovered that Petrosino was hot on the trail, he ordered him murdered.

The next evening, March 12, 1909, Petrosino waited at the base of the Garibaldi statue in the large Piazza Marina in the very center of Palermo. He had been tipped that an informant would meet him there with a complete list of all the important Mafia chiefs in Sicily and the U.S. He was met, however, by more than a hundred shots fired from the darkness and killed.

His death caused an international uproar and produced profuse apologies from the Italian Government. His killers were never apprehended.

Petrosino's effects were shipped to his wife Adelina (who was given a permanent $1,000-a-year pension by the NYPD and $10,000 from friends for the care of her young son). The courageous policeman's belongings were returned to her; they consisted of one "gold watch and chain, pair gold cuff links, cane, two dress suitcases containing personal effects, package of letters and a check for $12.40." After 26 years in desperate pursuit of the Black Hand, this was Joseph Petrosino's legacy.

Marchese, who found Sicily too hot for him after the killing, immigrated to the U.S., living briefly in New York under the name Paul Di Cristina. He then journeyed to New Orleans where he plied the Black Hand trade.

As head of the Mafia in New Orleans, Di Cristina felt powerful enough to operate openly. He delivered his Black Hand notes in person. Fearing instant death, none dared resist —none except stubborn Pietro Pepitone, a grocer. After Pepitone told Di Cristina's strong-arm men that he would not pay any Black Hand money, the boss himself showed up to collect. As Di Cristina casually alighted from his wagon, drawn up in front of the grocer's store, Pepitone stepped out to the sidewalk with a shot gun and emptied it into the boss Blackhander, killing him. This killing touched off one of the fiercest vendettas ever experienced in America by Mafia factions (see MAFIA). Pepitone got twenty years in the Louisiana State Penitentiary but was paroled in six years.

The Italians of Kansas City were plagued by Blackhanders from 1912 to the early 1920s, the most notable offender being Joseph "Scarface" DiGiovanni. Sicilian-born in 1888, DiGiovanni immigrated to K.C. in 1912 and only days after receiving his naturalization papers there went into the Black Hand business, with his brother Peter "Sugarhouse Pete" DiGiovanni. The brothers were arrested by Kansas City detective Louis Olivero in 1915 after the police received complaints from about twenty Black Hand victims. Detective Olivero was shot in the back and killed days later. The victims wilted in court and remembered nothing.

Black Hand thugs made it a practice to at-

Joseph "Scarface" DiGiovanni, notorious Kansas City Blackhander, who was horribly disfigured when a still blew up in his face.

tend any and all court cases involving Blackhanders. Witnesses against them were silenced in seconds after getting the high sign from one of the thugs. The sign was delivered in many ways—drawing a finger across the throat, displaying a red handkerchief, pointing an index finger to the temple—all of them meant death to any witness who dared to testify.

Chicago's history of the Black Hand, like New York's, dated back to about 1890. The violence displayed by Chicago Blackhanders against their victims was devastating; it consisted mostly of bombings that destroyed whole buildings and several families in each attack. Little Italy—the area contained within Oak and Taylor Streets and Grand and Wentworth Avenues—was a Black Hand playground, more appropriately a slaughterhouse.

For years, it seemed that Blackhanders were more interested in annihilating their victims than in extorting money from them. Black Hand killings reached a peak around 1910-11 in Chicago. At one intersection, Oak and Milton Streets, which the Italians named "Death Corner," thirty-eight Black Hand victims were shot to death between January 1, 1910 and March 26, 1911. At least fifteen of those killed were dispatched by a professional Black Hand assassin referred to by the residents as "Shotgun Man." This killer, never apprehended, walked about openly in Little Italy and was well known. He had no loyalty to either victim or Blackhander. He hired out his gun and would murder without flinching, carrying out death sentences decreed by Blackhanders who

could not collect. Blackhanders paid him handsomely for his services.

One criminal historian estimated that close to eighty Black Hand gangs terrorized Chicago's Little Italy during the first two decades of the present century. Some of these gangs, wholly unrelated to each other signed their notes as "The Mysterious Hand," or "The Secret Hand," but it meant the same thing: Pay or Die.

The notes Chicago Blackhanders sent their victims were couched in unbearably polite words, making them all the more sinister. The letter received by a wealthy Italian businessman typified the courteous but deadly Blackhander of this era:

"Most gentle Mr. Silvani: Hoping that the present will not impress you much, you will be so good as to send me $2,000 if your life is dear to you. So I beg you warmly to put them on your door within four days. But if not, I swear this week's time not even the dust of your family will exist. With regards, believe me to be your friends."

This letter was not signed but police still managed to trace it to one Joseph Genite (who was discharged for lack of evidence), in whose house they found a stockpile of dynamite, two dozen revolvers, several sawed-off shotguns, and other assorted weapons.

Other Black Hand notes were less formal:

"You got some cash. I need $1,000. You place the $100 bills in an envelope and place it underneath a board in the northeast corner of Sixtyninth Street and Euclid Avenue at eleven o'clock tonight. If you place the money there, you will live. If you don't, you die. If you report this to the police, I'll kill you when I get out. They may save you the money, but they won't save you your life."

The police in most instances were helpless; the notes were all but impossible to trace. When witnesses did come forward they quickly retracted their statements after being contacted by Black Hand enforcers. In desperation, police raided Chicago's Little Italy in January, 1910, and rounded up close to two hundred known Sicilian gangsters suspected of running Black Hand extortion rackets. All were released within twelve hours for lack of evidence.

For a five-year period—1907 to 1912—upstanding business leaders of the Italian community banded together to form the White Hand Society which actually supplied its own police force and money to prosecute Black Handers. Many extortionists were put in prison, but were shortly paroled through contacts with corrupt local and state officials. Dr. Joseph Dimiani, one of the White Hand leaders, explained why the Society threw in the sponge. "They [the White Handers] were so discouraged by the lax administrations of justice that they were refusing to advance further money to prosecute men arrested on their complaints."

A rash of bombings came next. Experts used by the Black Hand were brutal enforcers such as Sam Cardinelli, his chief lieutenant, eighteen-year-old Nicholas Viana, known as "The Choir Boy," and dim-witted Frank Campione. The three, all later hanged for murder, were responsible for at least twenty bombings in which dozens of Italians were killed. One police estimation reported that more than 800 bombs were directed against Black Hand victims in Chicago between 1900 and 1930, most of them during the period from 1915 to 1918.

A whole generation of professional bombers who had once worked for Black Hand gangs found heavy-duty work in the dawn-of-the-1920s bootleg wars between gangs in Chicago. Many of these were used in Chicago union wars, as well. The Italian and Sicilian Black Handers in earlier days preferred to use non-Italian bombers to prevent identification. When the Black Hand operations fell off in the early 1920s, these non-Italian bombers went to work for union gangsters. One of these, Andrew Kerr, was arrested in 1921 and boasted that he employed the best bombers in the business to enforce his edicts over the Steam and Operating Engineers union.

Kerr named Jim Sweeney as a boss bomber. Sweeney's group of killers included "Soup" Bartlett and "Con" Shea, who had murdered whole families with bombs for decades. Shea, Kerr swore, had been a professional bomber since he was sixteen years old.

Boss of the barber's union in Chicago, Joseph Sangerman took Sweeney's position as king of the bombers after Sweeney was ar-

rested and sent to prison. Sangerman's top bomber was George Matrisciano (alias Martini) who manufactured his own "infernal machines" of black powder. This berserk bomber, who had terrorized Black Hand victims for twenty-five years, always walked about with two sticks of dynamite in his pockets. Before Sangerman had him killed, Matrisciano could be seen approaching total strangers in Little Italy and proudly showing them a newspaper clipping which described him as "a terrorist."

A sharp decline of Black Hand operations followed Matrisciano's death, and finally the racket ceased to flourish. Police had failed to snuff out the Black Hand terror; it was the coming of Prohibition and its big-moneyed rackets which ended the terrible extortions. Like stock market investors, almost everybody happily plunged into bootlegging—even the courteous murderers of Little Italy, much to the gratitude of its hounded residents.

BOISE, THOMAS
Murderer ● (? -1864)

Normally Thomas Boise was only a common drunk whose antics in Wood County, West Va. served to annoy local residents. One night, however, Boise, while in the company of Mortimore Gibbony and Daniel Grogran, drank himself into a rage and, following a chance remark, shot Abram Deem, a local farmer.

The three men were tried; Gibbony escaped. Boise and Grogan were scheduled to hang in Parkersburg, West Va., but a curious problem developed. Each prisoner argued passionately with the sheriff that the other should be hanged first. The sheriff attempted to hang them both at the same time but the rope broke. Grogan, yelling he had a right to watch Boise die, was then hanged first while his partner laughed madly. Gibbony was apprehended later and hanged.

BOLTON, CHARLES E. ("BLACK BART")
Stagerobber ● (Circa 1820- ?)

BACKGROUND: BORN AND RAISED IN RURAL UPSTATE NEW YORK. MOVED WITH HIS PARENTS TO THE WEST AT AGE 10. LEGITIMATE OCCUPATION UNKNOWN. DESCRIPTION: TALL, BLUE EYES, WHITE HAIR, ERECT MILITARY BEARING. ALIASES: BLACK BART. RECORD: ROBBED THE WELLS FARGO STAGE OUTSIDE OF FORT ROSS, CALIF. NEAR THE RUSSIAN RIVER 8/3/1877 ($605.52 IN CASH AND CHECKS); STOPPED AND ROBBED THE QUINCEY TO OROVILLE, CALIF. STAGE 7/26/78 ($379 IN CASH AND COIN, A $200 DIAMOND RING AND $25 WATCH); ROBBED THE WELLS FARGO STAGE MONTHS LATER BETWEEN SONORA AND MILTON NEAR COPPEROPOLIS ($4,800); TRACED THROUGH A LAUNDRY MARK AND ARRESTED WEEKS LATER; CONFESSED AND SENTENCED TO A SHORT PRISON TERM IN THE STATE PENITENTIARY; DISAPPEARED UPON BEING PAROLED; DATE OF DEATH UNKNOWN.

Charles E. Bolton, best known along the California trails of the late 1870s as the hooded stagerobber, Black Bart. (Western History Collection, U. of Okla. Library)

He was a tired old man, almost sixty, when he began stopping stages, but he was a joker at heart. Charles E. Bolton, better known to the West as "Black Bart," always had enough energy to scribble out some insulting doggerel which he left to vex his pursuers.

Little is known of Bolton's beginnings or even middle life. He moved West with his family at age ten around 1830-31. He was believed to have been first a farmer and then a medicine drummer. He finally settled for city life, moving periodically between Los Angeles and San Francisco with occasional trips into the gold fields to seek his fortune.

The gold fields were panned out by the time Bolton got there and his dreams of luxury were fast fading. Yet Bolton still emulated the rich in dress and manner; he read good books, lived in fancy hotels, wore stylish clothes. To finance these pleasures, Bolton had simply become Black Bart, the terror of California's Wells Fargo stages, a strange-looking robber who never fired a shot.

Bart first struck August 3, 1877, when he stopped the stage from Fort Ross. His appearance, rather than the rifle he pointed, frightened the driver. Bart was wearing a long, ghostly-looking white duster. Over his head was a flour sack with holes poked through for his eyes.

At this time, as upon all other occasions, Bart snorted only one order: "Throw down the box!" The Wells Fargo box—a small safe made of wood, reinforced by iron and padlocked—was thrown down and Bart joyfully scurried off to his horse with its contents, $300 in cash and a check for $305.52.

A posse found the box days later while combing the brush near the site of the holdup. Inside it, they discovered a note written by the bandit. It read:

I've labored long and hard for bread,
For honor and for riches
But on my corns too long you've tred,
You fine-haired sons-of-bitches.

Beneath this bit of doggerel was the odd signature, "Black Bart, PO-8," which served to only further mystify the lawmen.

The meager haul was apparently enough to satisfy Bart for almost a year. He did not strike again until July 26, 1878, when he stopped the stage to Oronville, Calif. He wore the same outfit, the duster and flour sack. His voice, as during the previous holdup, was described by the driver as "hollow and deep." He made off with the strong box which contained $379. This time he took a passenger's $200 diamond ring and a $25 gold watch.

Again, lawmen found a note waiting for them in the empty box. Black Bart had written:

Here I lay me down to sleep
To wait the coming morrow,
Perhaps success, perhaps defeat
And everlasting sorrow,
Yet come what will, I'll try it once,
My conditions can't be worse,
And if there's money in that box,
'Tis munney in my purse.

It would be Bart's last jeer at the law and the Wells Fargo express stages. While attempting another holdup, the Sonora stage bound for Milton, Bart ran into trouble. Moments after the strongbox had been thrown down to him he cut his hand while trying to break it open. He covered the wound with a handkerchief. Just then a lone rider came down the road.

Using the rider's gun, the stagedriver fired at Bart and he barely managed to get away with the $4,800 cash shipment. But he had dropped his handkerchief and the Pinkertons, finding a laundry mark on it, traced it to a laundry (they checked through ninety establishments before having any success). It belonged to an elderly gentleman named Charles E. Bolton.

He was quickly taken into custody. Bolton confessed to the robberies but became indignant when detectives called him an outlaw. "I am a gentleman," he said, and twirled his gold-knobbed cane for good measure.

Bolton was sent to the California State penitentiary but, because of his advanced age, was soon released. The last report of him came from Nevada where he was seeking a new fortune.

BONANNO, JOSEPH ("JOE BANANAS") Mafia Family Chief ● (1905-)

BACKGROUND: BORN IN SICILY, MARRIED, TWO CHILDREN. NO FORMAL EDUCATION. DESCRIPTION: 6'1", BROWN EYES, THIN GRAY HAIR, HEAVYSET. ALIASES: NONE. RECORD: ARRESTED FOR GRAND LARCENY, ILLEGAL POSSESSION OF A GUN, AND OBSTRUCTION OF JUSTICE. IDENTIFIED AS HEAD OF A COSA NOSTRA FAMILY IN NEW YORK BY JOSEPH VALACHI.

Joe was tired, he told them. And rich. So it was time he retire, he told them. The Board members of the Brotherhood blinked, said nothing, and sighed in vast relief. Joe Bonanno, better known as Joe Bananas to his fellow chieftans in the Mafia, was safely out of the picture.

That was in the spring of 1953 and Bonanno, who had entered the U.S. illegally by way of Havana and Miami in 1924, went to live on his plush estate just outside Tucson, Arizona. The eyes of his Cosa Nostra brothers were still on him, but they figured Bonanno was a long way from those days in Chicago when he was Capone's top hijacker and rumrunner. Bonanno was through. He said so, didn't he?

Bonanno lounged about his Tucson estate for a week. His angling brain mixed the past with the future. He had everything now, including the perverse delight of having survived a dozen gang wars, attempted hits, and federal deportation. He had been clever about that.

After Lucky Luciano went to prison and Lepke was on the run, Bonanno had skipped the country in 1938, returning to his native Sicily. Then he came back, again illegally via Canada and Detroit, to set up operations. As insurance against what happened to Lucky, he became a naturalized citizen in 1945. That was smart, that was clever.

In the 1920s, Joe took orders from Al Capone. He kept his mouth shut, did his work without fanfare and then moved out of Chicago to join Salvatore Maranzano in his Mafia war against Giuseppe "Joe the Boss" Masseria in the early 1930s. When that human fireplug killer Joe Valachi was initiated into the Cosa Nostra at Maranzano's upstate New York mansion in 1930, it was Joe Bananas who was picked as Valachi's sponsor, his godfather.

After Joe the Boss was killed by his own lieutenants, Luciano and Genovese, Bonanno carved out a great empire in loan-sharking and gambling. He began first with Manhattan and then branched out these activities as far as Montreal and Haiti. He didn't make a great show out of it, but Bonanno wanted to be the boss of bosses, always.

He took his time and did his dogged best to solve Mafia problems. One troublesome thing was how to get rid of all those people the Brotherhood had killed and didn't want discovered. Bonanno solved that. He bought a funeral home—in fact, several—and constructed special coffins.

When a legitimate corpse was being buried, the mourners never knew that the extremely heavy casket containing their loved one had a cleverly-designed false bottom. Inside this area, under each legitimate corpse, was another body, a Cosa Nostra murder victim.

The only conviction Bananas ever had was for violating the Federal Wage and Hour Law. Every other arrest for more than a 30-year period was dismissed.

In Tucson, Bonanno lived the quiet life of a retired millionaire, but he had decided he was far from being retired. He looked East with greed and anger. Then he got on the phone and called New York. His old sidekick and enforcer, Giuseppe Magliocco, heard him order something incredible.

"I want the following hit immediately," Bonanno said cooly. "Frank DiSimone, Thomas Lucchese, Carlo Gambino and Steve Maggadino."

Magliocco huffed and sweated at the other end of the line. His great hulking body grew hot and he could feel his problem blood pressure rising.

Joe Bananas must be insane, he thought. He had ordered the deaths of the Cosa Nostra's entire top board members and elder statesmen: the dons, the consiglieri who ruled America's crime empire. DiSimone headed California's Mafia; Lucchese—known as "Three-Finger Brown"—headed the New York/New Jersey family; Gambino ruled the Brooklyn Cosa Nostra, and Maggadino headed the Mafia clan in Buffalo, New York.

But Magliocco didn't argue with Joe Bananas. He knew too well about those false-bottomed

Joseph "Joe Bananas" Bonanno, though ousted from the New York Mafia, is still a power in the national crime syndicate. (UPI)

caskets and how one got into them. "Okay, Joe, anything you say."

Minutes later, Magliocco contacted syndicate assassin, Joe Columbo and gave him the contracts for the Mafia chieftans. "It's from the top," he told Columbo. "Bananas."

Columbo agreed to fill the contracts immediately, hung up and called members of the Mafia Board. "It's war. Joe Bananas is trying to take over everything."

Lucchese didn't believe it. He and Joe went back twenty years together. "Joe wouldn't do that. Capone would, that's his style, but not Joe."

Columbo finally convinced the members, and a high-level meeting was held at the luxurious home of Thomas "Tommy Ryan" Eboli on September 18, 1964. Everybody who was anybody in the Mafia was there . . . except for Joe Bananas.

They had even sent for him, an invitation to thrash problems out. But he didn't come.

Steve Maggadino exploded at the meeting: "Next he'll be planting flags all over the world!"

His snake-eyes gleaming, Chicago mob boss Momo Giancana could think of only one thing. "For God's sake, why not just kill the guy?"

But it was a question, not a suggestion. Bananas was Mafia don and he had a coast-to-coast army to back him up. The commission dropped the problem for a moment and turned to fat Magliocco who had been brought in for questioning.

He confessed that he had ordered the hits through Columbo but the mobsters were extremely lenient with him. He got off with a $50,000 fine and banishment from the outfit. It wasn't such a strange decision, however, since Magliocco died soon afterward when his blood pressure popped.

The board's decision about Bananas was also curious. They were going to give him one last chance to talk it all out. After all, Bonanno had been one of the pillars upon which the modern Mafia was built. You had to respect a man like that.

After finishing his second steak in a swanky Manhattan restaurant on the night of October 21, 1964, and surrounded by six bodyguards, Joe Bananas walked out into the rain. He had come East on business and felt confident. He was surrounded by loyal mafioso and was as big a boss as they come.

As Bonanno and his mobsters crawled into a waiting cab, one of his bodyguards, Mike Zaffarano, slipped away, walked casually down the street, and got into another car with two men inside.

Zaffarano and his friends raced to the corner of 37th Street and Park Avenue, and waited. This was the street where Joe Bananas kept a year-round luxury suite for his New York "business" trips.

They didn't have long to wait. A cab pulled up near the corner and Bonanno and his lawyer, William P. Maloney, got out and headed for the apartment house entrance. Bonanno, hurrying out of the rain, got there first and by then Zaffarano was waiting with his friends. They grabbed the boss mobster by the arms.

"What the hell's going on, Mike?" Joe said, staring unbelievably at his trusted aide.

Zaffarano shot him a quick glance and hustled him over to his car, grunting, "the boss wants to see you, Joe." He didn't mention who the boss was but it was quite clear to Joe Bananas that Zaffarano wasn't working for him anymore. They shoved him rudely into the car.

As it began to move off, lawyer Maloney ran up, protesting the abduction of his client. Zaffarano leaned from a window, gun in hand. He fired one shot, which missed the lawyer and slammed into the apartment house wall. Then the car roared into the darkness.

Nobody heard from or about Joe Bananas for eighteen months. For six weeks, he was held a prisoner by his Mafia brothers in a secluded Catskill resort in upper New York State. They told him he was going to die. Nobody could order hits on their board members, not even a fellow board member, and live.

But Joe Bonanno was a clever fellow. He knew of one way to live, to survive the edict of death that had been handed down. It was a big price tag, but it was worth it. The boys wanted his crime empire and the estimated two billion dollars a year that went with it.

He threatened them that total warfare would break out if he was killed, but it was no good. They could take care of that—he would just vanish like all the men Joe Bananas had made vanish for thirty years.

But the rackets and the money Joe controlled, that was another thing. Finally, the Mafia board agreed to terms. Bonanno had to give up everything—the loan-shark rackets, the gambling, the narcotics—and get out of the country. If he did this, he could live . . . and so could his son and wife. Joe said, yes, take it, damn it, take it all.

Then for over a year Bonanno lived like a monk in Haiti, hating the men who had exiled him—but he had given his word to stay out of the rackets. Then word came that four men had tried to kill his son Salvatore in a wild Brooklyn shoot-out, chasing the Bonanno boy through a basement apartment while witnesses screamed and dodged over thirty shots.

Joe Bananas erupted like old Vesuvius. It was war, then, full-scale, old-fashioned war like Capone and Dutch Schultz had waged. The battlefield was Joe's old stomping grounds, Brooklyn.

On November 10, 1967, James and Tom D'Angelo and Francisco "Frank the 500" Terelli were eating spaghetti and drinking dark chianti in their favorite Brooklyn restaurant, the Cypress Gardens. They had been Bonanno men but had gone over to Paul Sciacca. Sciacca had been placed, at the Mafia board's orders, at the head of Joe Bananas's family.

A man dressed in black entered the Cypress Gardens restaurant and approached the three henchmen. He stopped ten feet from their table and whipped a submachinegun from beneath his coat. From his short burst of twenty-two .45-caliber slugs, nineteen found their mark. All three Sciacca mobsters were riddled, huge plates of spaghetti and shattered wine glasses their shrouds.

Peter Crociata, another hood who had left the Bananas clan for Sciacca, ducked one bullet meant for his head and was hit by another in the throat on March 4, 1968 as he was parking his car.

Sciacca fought back by killing Sam Perrone four days later. Perrone had been Bonanno's friend and bodyguard for years, and was now his son's chauffeur. Joe Bananas sent out a warning—"Next time they hit one of my men, they lose one of their capos (chiefs) . . . first in one family, then in another."

To prove his sincerity, Bonanno ordered the immediate execution of a capo in Joe Columbo's family, Cologero Lo Cicero. A gunman wielding the Bananas trademark, a machinegun, walked into a soda fountain where the elderly capo was sipping a strawberry malted and fired a burst into Lo Cicero's face. The twelve slugs that ripped into his face made him unrecognizable.

It became evident to the Mafia that Joe Bananas, once back at his Tucson estate, had no intention of stopping the war, which dragged on for several years and claimed dozens of lives. Bonanno finally tired of the costly battles, quit the New York rackets altogether, and settled into permanent retirement, much to the sighing relief of his Mafia adversaries.

BONIN, WILLIAM
(THE FREEWAY STRANGLER)
Serial Killer ● (1947-   )

William Bonin committed his first criminal offenses at age ten. He was in and out of detention homes throughout his formative years. His father was a drunken gambler with a vicious temper and his mother dominated him. It was later conjectured that these homelife factors contributed to Bonin's development, particularly his many acts of perversions and murders.

Jailed for several sex offenses, Bonin later became a truck driver, and with accomplices like Vernon Butts, he molested and killed by his own estimate at least 21 teenage boys in the Los Angeles area between 1978 and 1980. Butts later testified against the brutal Bonin, saying that the killer had a hypnotic hold on him and that "after the first one (murder) I couldn't do anything about it."

Bonin used his truck to cruise the freeways in Los Angeles and Orange counties, picking up young boys, sexually molesting them, torturing them, then strangling them to death before dumping their bodies on the on–off ramps of Los Angeles freeways. He was thus dubbed "The Freeway Strangler."

When Butts dropped out of sight, Bonin enlisted other accomplices and one of these, a seventeen-year-old drifter Bonin had picked up in Hollywood, informed police. Bonin was arrested and tried, being convicted of fourteen counts of murder. Butts testified against him, saying he participated in five of the sadistic killings. Butts hanged himself in his cell. Bonin was sentenced to death on March 12, 1982.

BONNEY, WILLIAM H.
("BILLY THE KID")
Robber, Murderer ● (1859-1881)

BACKGROUND: BORN IN NEW YORK CITY, 11/23/1859. MOVED WITH HIS PARENTS TO COFFEYVILLE, KAN. IN 1862, AND THEN TO COLORADO UPON THE DEATH OF WM. BONNEY, SR. NO PUBLIC EDUCATION. MOVED WEST WHILE STILL A TEENAGER THROUGH TEX., ARIZ., N.M., AND MEXICO. ORIGINAL OCCUPATION, COWBOY. DESCRIPTION: 5'7", BLUE EYES, LIGHT BROWN HAIR, SLENDER. ALIASES: NONE. RECORD: REPORTEDLY SHOT AND KILLED TWENTY-ONE MEN BY THE TIME OF HIS TWENTY-FIRST BIRTHDAY, INCLUDING AN UNKNOWN GUNFIGHTER IN COFFEYVILLE WHEN HE WAS FOURTEEN, THREE APACHE BRAVES ON THE CHIRACAHUA RESERVATION IN ARIZONA A FEW YEARS LATER, A NEGRO BLACKSMITH IN CAMP BOWIE, THREE CARD DEALERS IN MEXICO, TWO MORE INDIANS IN THE GUADALUPE MOUNTAINS, COWBOYS BILLY MORTON, FRANK BAKER, AND ANDREW L. "BUCKSHOT" ROBERTS IN 1876, SHERIFF WILLIAM BRADY AND HIS DEPUTY GEORGE HINDMAN 4/1/78, CATTLEMAN ROBERT W. BECKWITH 7/17/78, GUNMEN JOE GRANT AND JIMMY CARLYLE SOMETIME IN 1879; INDIAN AGENT JOSEPH BERNSTEIN; DEPUTIES AND WARDENS J. W. BELL AND

Of all the legends of the Old West, that of Billy the Kid is the most confusing and impenetrable, so laced is it with dime novel romance, heroic embellishments, and fabulous fiction created by his own friends and enemies. Almost from birth, Billy was a migrant, a drifter who aimlessly rode through the West without roots, family, or purpose. His travels were rarely documented, and attempting to record his life is similar to watching the flashing, powdery cards of an old crank-handled penny peep show machine: the image is there but it is only a fascinating blur, devilishly designed, it seems, by those who insist on perpetuating a sort of noble glory of the Old West, Billy's West. This is the story, shored up with the shaky timbers of the Kid's own legend.

The New York City tenement in which William H. Bonney was born November 23, 1859 was crowded and seamy with poverty and disease; it was no wonder that Bill Bonney moved his wife and son to Coffeyville, Kan. in 1862 to escape. He died there and his widow moved again to Colorado where she married mine-worker William Antrim.

Antrim was a wanderlusting man who yearned to strike it big on his own. He moved the family to Silver City, N.M., where he again worked the mines. Mrs. Antrim ran a small boarding house. Little Billy played in the mud-caked streets, learning the rough ways of streetfighters and gunslingers at an early age. There was no school in Silver City; Billy's education consisted of petty thefts, bloody, knock-down streetfights, and visions of violent, drunken men shooting each other to death.

According to one of Mrs. Antrim's boarders, Ash Upson, a rowdy gunfighter named Ed Moulton took a liking to wild little Billy. He became the self-appointed protector of Billy and his mother while old man Antrim was away working the mines. One day, when Billy was fourteen, a drunk called his mother a name. The boy hit him and then tried to club him with a rock. But the bully was too big to fight and Billy ran. The drunk after him. Ed Moulton stepped in and knocked the man flat.

The boy showed his gratitude to Moulton weeks later when he found two men fighting with his protector. Using a pen knife, Billy repeatedly stabbed one of the men in the back until he died. Even in the free-wheeling Silver City of 1871, Billy's action was branded murder; he needed Moulton's help to escape capture, riding out alone into the Wild West to seek his fortune.

The years between Billy's fourteenth and seventeenth birthdays are sketchy. Information about his whereabouts and activities is documented only by pamphleteers whose facts concerning the Kid were fanciful and unreliable. Ash Upson, who later collaborated with Pat Garrett, Billy's killer, on a highly romanticized version of the Kid's life, portrayed him as a one-man army of righteous wrath slaying hordes of venomous Indians and crooked Mexican card dealers.

Upson and Garrett insisted that the teenager would take offense from no man in these apprentice-gunslinger years. A Negro blacksmith, they stated, was playing cards with Billy in Camp Bowie and the Kid caught him cheating. "You're a Billy Goat," the blacksmith roared when Billy confronted him. The Kid's gun roared and the blacksmith was sent to eternity with a bullet in his forehead.

When the Government opened up public lands in Southeastern New Mexico, the rush was on. Along with armies of bad men from Texas and points north who came to fleece and rob the homesteaders, cattlemen and farmers raced for their parcels of earth. Billy went with them, showing up in Lincoln County around 1875 where he went to work for an immense ranch owned by L. G. Murphy and J. J. Dolan. These men were in open battle with another giant ranch run by Alexander McSween and an Englishman, John Tunstall. McSween and Tunstall had the support of the great cattle baron, John Chisum.

The Kid's work for the Murphy-Dolan forces consisted of rustling Chisum's cattle from his Jinglebob Ranch. These Murphy sold to the Indians.

Billy probably would have continued being nothing more than a rowdy ranch hand, had it not been for his accidental meeting with the sophisticated John Tunstall. The Englishman was refined, educated, and humane: something new to the West. He was a gentleman rancher who told Billy he would have a great future in cattle. Billy idolized him and went to work at his ranch near the Rio Feliz.

There was nothing Billy wouldn't do for Tunstall. The Kid once remarked that "he [Tunstall] was the only man that ever treated me like I was free-born and white." According to George Coe, a cowpuncher in the area, Tunstall gladly repaid the compliment, stating: "That's the finest lad I ever met. He's a revelation to me every day and would do anything on earth to please me. I'm going to make a man of that boy yet."

Tunstall never got the chance. A so-called posse made up of Murphy-Dolan riders stopped him on the morning of February 18, 1878, as he was returning to his ranch from Lincoln. Sheriff William Brady, a Murphy-Dolan man, had deputized a band of gunslingers who rode against the McSween-Tunstall combine, most of them Billy's friends before he switched sides—Billy Morton, Frank Baker, Jesse Evans, and Jim McDaniel.

Evans told Tunstall they had orders to take a part of his herd, that the cattle belonged to Murphy. When the Englishman objected, the posse men pulled out their guns and ordered Tunstall to surrender. The Englishman told them that he did not want any bloodshed. He dismounted and handed over his six-gun but as he did so, Jesse Evans sent a bullet into him. Then, as he pitched forward, Billy Morton fired a shot into Tunstall's head, killing him.

Billy the Kid was roaring mad at Tunstall's murder; the gentle Englishman had been a father-figure to him, the only man for whom he had felt genuine love. Vengeance hissed through his gritted teeth as he watched Tunstall lowered in his grave: "I'll get every son-of-a-bitch who helped kill John if it's the last thing I do."

The Murphy-Dolan clan heard of Billy's oath and did not take it lightly. The slender, bucktoothed boy was fast on the draw, awfully fast; this they knew. He was cagey, too, an expert bushwacker. Some reported that the phony possemen still believed Billy was their friend. He had ridden with them and that should count for something.

In the Kid's mind, it added up to nothing.

Billy the Kid, the great legend of the West. (Western History Collection, U. of Okla. Library)

He caught up with Baker and Morton at a place aptly called Dead Man's Hole, a watering spot between Lincoln and Roswell, N.M. Billy sent each to his Maker, firing only one bullet at each man. Next came Andrew L. "Buckshot" Roberts, a Murphy lieutenant.

The Kid, along with Dick Brewer, Charlie Bowdre and George Coe, trapped Roberts at Blazer's Sawmill. The doomed man, just before the Kid's gang rode up, picked this unfortunate moment to answer nature's call and he found himself surrounded in an outhouse. Roberts, however, hadn't neglected to take his rifle and six-gun with him and he put up a great fight from the unlikely bastion. Brewer was killed outright. Bowdre and Coe were wounded. Such was the intensity of Roberts' gunfire that he actually drove off the band, but Billy fired a parting shot which proved lucky and fatal to "Buckshot" Roberts.

Tunstall's murderers were dying right and left before the Kid's guns, but the man who engineered the Englishman's murder, Sheriff Brady of Lincoln, was still alive. Billy the Kid announced that he would correct this oversight.

On April 1, 1878, waiting in ambush behind an adobe wall in Lincoln, the Kid and some others watched as Sheriff Brady and his three deputies—George Hindman, George W. "Dad" Peppin and Billy Matthews—walked out into the noonday sun, heading for the courthouse.

Billy took aim at Brady's back and then fired several shots into the Sheriff who toppled forward, dead. Hindman was next and the Kid's shots hit him several times. He crawled to the front of the Church of San Juan. Dad Peppin and Matthews took cover and began answering the rapid fire unleashed by the Kid and his gang.

Suddenly, Billy leaped over the wall and darted for Brady's body. As he ran he heard the mortally wounded Hindman cry out for water but kept going: the sheriff's expensive weapons were the Kid's goal, especially Brady's shiny new Winchester rifle. A few moments after he picked up the rifle, a well-aimed shot from Billy Matthews slammed into his hand. The Kid dropped the weapon and raced back to the cover of the adobe wall: After a final glance at his victims, he ordered his gang to retreat.

Brady and Hindman brought the count of Billy's dead to seventeen; he was eighteen years old. There were four more deaths to go, according to the legend, and three more years to live.

Sixteen days after Brady and Hindman were murdered, Peppin became the new sheriff and led a huge posse against the Kid's fourteen-member gang, who were barricaded in Alexander McSween's mansion. Thousands of rounds of ammunition were spent as each side shot it out for three days. (Some say five days.)

A troop of cavalry from Fort Stanton then arrived under the command of Col. Nathan Dudley to make peace. The colonel ordered a small cannon trained on the McSween home before calling for a cease fire. During the lull, Peppin's men sneaked behind the mansion and put it to the torch. The Kid, seeing the mounting flames, told his men to run for it.

McSween dashed from the rear of the building carrying only a Bible. Bob Beckwith, a cattleowner deputized by Dad Peppin, shot McSween down in cold blood. The Kid came upon the scene and cursed wildly as he emptied his six-shooter into Beckwith, killing him. Somehow the Kid escaped both posse and cavalry.

Billy was running fast now, indicted for the murder of Sheriff Brady and wanted all over New Mexico. He stopped long enough to steal horses from the Mescalero Indian Reservation; when government agent Morris J. Bernstein tried to stop him, he was shot dead in his tracks.

The Lincoln County war had spread throughout New Mexico, and an anxious President Hayes replaced Governor Axtell with Lew Wallace. Just after Wallace took office, the Kid was watching when Huston Chapman, a lawyer for the McSween faction, was shot down on the streets of Lincoln; William Matthews, William Campbell and James Dolan did the killing. But instead of going for his six-gun, Billy unexplainably rode to see Governor Wallace, offering himself as a witness against the three murderers.

Perhaps the Kid's move was not so puzzling after all, but a shrewdly thought-out plan. When Wallace took over the state, he declared a general amnesty for all those who had participated in the Lincoln County war. This applied to everyone except those who had been indicted for murder, which meant Billy the Kid. By turning state's evidence, however, the Kid hoped to obtain a full pardon.

Wallace and Billy met on March 17, 1879, in the home of one John B. Wilson. The Kid walked through the front door promptly at 9 a.m., the designated time. In his left hand was a menacing Winchester rifle, in the other a six-gun.

"I was sent for to meet the Governor at nine o'clock. Is he here?"

Wallace looked the boy over, finding it hard to believe that he was the most devastating killer in the far West. "I'm Governor Wallace."

"Your note gave me a promise of absolute protection," Billy said glancing about.

"Yes," Wallace nodded. "And I've been true to my promise." Wallace pointed to John Wilson. "This man, whom, of course, you know, and I are the only persons in the house."

The two men then made a deal. If Billy would surrender and testify against Huston Chapman's killers the Governor promised to set him free with a full pardon.

Billy didn't like the idea of surrendering. It was against his personal code, he said. It would look terrible to the folks in Lincoln.

He would be arrested then, the Governor said. The arrest would be phony but appear genuine to the residents of Lincoln. Billy agreed on that condition.

In a matter of weeks, Billy was arrested in Lincoln. As a star witness he was wined and dined in a local store where he was kept prisoner. The Kid testified against Matthews, Dolan and Campbell, but he didn't stop there. He provided lawmen with complete details on the operations and identities of dozens of outlaws then in New Mexico. His non-stop tongue defied the code of silence, but with all the publicity he was receiving, William Bonney must have realized he was above such breaches of criminal conduct; he was Billy the Kid and he did as he pleased.

He also ignored part of his bargain with Wallace. He had agreed to stand trial for the shooting of Sheriff Brady. The Governor had promised that he would be set free, but Billy distrusted Wallace. One day he merely walked out of the store where he was kept "prisoner," and rode off on somebody else's horse, heading for Fort Sumner where he had friends.

At Fort Sumner, Billy ran smack into a Texas gunman named Joe Grant. Billy's reputation as a gunfighter had spread throughout the West by then and Grant decided to face him down. First, the two got roaring drunk, or, at least, Grant did. Billy, pretending to be drunk, praised Grant's courage and told him how much he admired Grant's expensive six-gun. Grant, at Billy's request, showed the Kid his weapon. While fondling it, the Kid turned the barrel around to an empty chamber, so the story goes, and when the two did draw on each other, Grant's gun only clicked and Billy's went off with a roar. Scratch Joe Grant.

After making some raids for horses and a few dollars around White Oaks, N. M., Billy and his band were holed up in a ranchhouse. A posse rode up and a terrific gun battle ensued. Hours later, the Kid shouted from a window: "I want to talk about surrendering."

Gunslinger Jimmy Carlyle, who knew Billy, said he would negotiate for the posse and

stepped from cover. The Kid shot him dead. This was enough to scare off the posse and Billy's gang leisurely rode out of the area.

Until Pat Garrett was elected sheriff of Lincoln County in 1880, the residents despaired of ever ridding the area of Billy the Kid. Garrett had known Billy well when they had run steers for old Pete Maxwell near Fort Sumner. They had been pals (Garrett later stated), drinking and gambling in town together on their days off.

Garrett went after the Kid almost from the moment he pinned on his badge. Governor Wallace wanted him brought in, offering a $500 reward for his capture. Garrett came close one night after setting a trap near Fort Sumner.

The Kid's right-hand man, Tom O'Folliard, was riding point that night and he ran straight into Garrett's posse. A dozen guns barked and O'Folliard toppled from his horse dead. Billy and the others reined up when they heard the shots and rode off in a different direction.

But the six-foot-four-inch Garrett was a determined man and days later, on December 21, 1880, his men surrounded a deserted farmhouse at Stinking Spring. Trapped inside were Billy the Kid, Tom Pickett, Charlie Bowdre, Dave Rudabaugh and Billy Wilson. Garrett called for their surrender. The Kid and his gang answered with a roar of guns. The posse let them have it, peppering the house with intense fire from rifles and six-guns. There was a scream. Charlie Bowdre was hit several times as he tried to cross in front of an open window.

Brutally, Billy propped Bowdre up and threw open the farmhouse door, shoving his wounded friend outside. The Kid shouted after Bowdre: "They have murdered you, Charlie, but you can get revenge! Kill some of the sons-of-bitches before you go!" Charlie Bowdre wasn't killing anyone. He barely had the strength to take a few steps forward before he fell on his face, murmuring, "I wish . . . I wish . . . I wish . . ." Both sides resumed firing over Bowdre's corpse.

Garrett finally called off the siege and withdrew a hundred yards or so where he and his men made camp. The big sheriff decided to starve out Billy and his band. Days later, panting for water and food, the gang surrendered. Garrett brought the Kid and his gang into Santa Fe where he was thrown in jail and placed under heavy guard.

Billy fired off a letter to Governor Wallace reminding him of his promise to set him free. Wallace ignored the Kid's plea and told newsmen that Billy had run away before standing trial for the Brady killing. All deals were off. The Kid was soon taken to Mesilla, N. M., where he was tried for killing Buckshot Roberts.

Mesilla looked to be the end of the line. Billy was convicted of the Roberts murder and Judge Warren Bristol dramatically sentenced him to hang until "you are dead, dead, dead."

One story reports that Billy, upon hearing the sentence, turned defiantly in court while being led away and shouted: "And you can go to hell, hell, hell."

The famous bandit consented to give the *Mesilla News* an interview at which time he said that "mob law" had convicted him, that he hadn't anticipated a fair trial nor a proper execution. "I expect to be lynched," he said sarcastically. "It's wrong that I should be the only one to suffer the extreme penalties of the law." He was referring to all those who had fought in the Lincoln County war, and he was proved right. Billy the Kid was the only warrior surviving that battle who was tried and convicted.

Two of Garrett's top guns, J. W. Bell and Bob Ollinger, were sent to bring Billy back to Lincoln. The two guards brought him back in an open buckboard. Ollinger, who had fought with the Murphy-Dolan faction during the Lincoln County war, hated Billy and kept poking him with a shotgun.

Somewhat of a sadist, Ollinger encouraged his prisoner to escape. "I can save you from the hangman," he reportedly urged the Kid. "Just make a run for it . . . I'd love putting a load of buckshot in your back!"

Bell had to keep telling Ollinger to "leave the Kid alone" on the trip back to Lincoln. Billy sat quietly in the buckboard taking Ollinger's insults without comment. In Lincoln, he was placed in the old Murphy Store which was used as a courthouse and jail. He was shackled hand and foot and placed in a second-story cell.

Ollinger sat outside the cell taunting him every day, telling him how it would be with the hangman. Billy said nothing.

Early in the afternoon of April 28, 1881, the Kid somehow got hold of a pistol and shot Bell dead. How he managed this is speculative. One story reported that he asked Bell to help him to the outside latrine and, when returning to the courthouse, pushed Bell down with his shoulder. While wearing leg irons, the Kid hobbled into Garrett's gun room, snatched up a pistol, and shot Bell dead as he came running inside. Another story reports that a Mexican girl who was in love with Billy had hidden the gun in the latrine.

Ollinger, who was drinking beer in a local bar down the street, heard the shot and went on the run to the courthouse. As he approached the building, he heard a friendly voice call out "hello, Bob." He turned to see Billy the Kid holding his shotgun straight at his head. The manacles on Billy's hands clanked as he pulled back the triggers. Ollinger, petrified, could only wait for the blast. When it came he was hurtled far into the street. A handyman walked in on Billy and the Kid ordered him to find an axe; when the man returned with the tool, Billy grabbed it and smashed the irons from his legs and arms. He took a Winchester and several pistols from the gun room.

Mounting a horse tethered outside, the Kid rode up to Ollinger's body and dropped the shotgun next to it. The few townspeople who had dared to come onto the street did nothing but stare at the boy bandit. He smiled at them, swept off his hat and shouted: "*Adios, compadres!*" Then he rode off.

The daring escape received thunderous press, most of the newspapers off-handedly praising the Kid for getting away and doing in his tormentor, Ollinger. Billy escaped two weeks ahead of the hangman, but he could not put enough distance between himself and Pat Garrett.

The sheriff was a strong-jawed lawman who prided himself on fair play and his ability to enforce the laws of New Mexico. He organized a posse and once again rode after Billy the Kid. For three months he tracked and re-tracked the Kid's movements. Finally, on the bright moonlit night of July 14, 1881, following a tip, Garrett had his man. He found Billy on the old Maxwell ranch where they had spent so many good days together in the past.

According to Garrett, he went into a bedroom which opened on the front of the main ranch house and sat waiting on the bed. Some of his possemen waited outside in the front, lurking in the shadows.

Billy came out of another room facing the long front porch and moved down the porchway trying to distinguish the figures in the shadows. He carried, according to Garrett, a pistol and a long hunting knife. Posseman John Poe heard him call out "Quien es?" (Who is it?). No one answered.

Billy kept moving down the porch. "Quien es? . . . Quien es?" he repeated in a loud whisper. A figure moved in the shadows and the Kid suddenly backed into the front bedroom where Garrett waited. Two shots rang out. Garrett stated that Billy had turned when inside the room and saw him: ". . . he came there armed with a pistol and knife expressly to kill me if he could . . . I had no alternative but to kill him, or suffer death at his hands."

Garrett's first shot ploughed into Billy slightly above the heart, killing him instantly. The second shot missed. In a few moments, the possemen were startled to see Sheriff Pat Garrett run from the bedroom, screaming, "I killed the Kid! I killed the Kid!"

Garrett stood in front of the house and trembled. Then he returned to the bedroom. Pretty Deluvina Maxwell was cradling the lifeless body in her arms. She looked up at Garrett and spat: "You didn't have the nerve to kill him face to face."

Some called it murder but a coroner's jury acquitted Garrett's act as "justifiable homicide." The $500 reward for Billy's capture did not come easy. Garrett had to have his friends in the state legislature pass a special act before he received it. The lawman lived an up and down life after that and was himself shot to death on February 29, 1908, by an angry tenant who had been working on his land.

Billy was buried first at the Maxwell ranch. Deluvina dressed him in a borrowed white shirt five sizes too big for him. The girl had a cross made for his grave. The marker bore her words *Duerme bien, Querido* (Sleep well, beloved). His body was later removed, to avoid the thousands of curious souvenir hunters, to a common grave near Fort Sumner where his remains were placed with two of his old gang, Tom O'Folliard and Charlie Bowdre. The word "Pals" was etched into the stone years later.

Whether or not Billy the Kid killed twenty-one men in his twenty-one years is no longer important; neither is debate over his slayings and his fast draw. What is important is that history, in his case, insists upon a legend gigantic and solid, romantic and dashing. So be it.

BOOTH, JOHN WILKES
Assassin ● (1839-1865)

BACKGROUND: BORN AND RAISED IN MARYLAND. TRAINED AS AN ACTOR FROM CHILDHOOD BY FATHER JUNIUS BRUTUS BOOTH AND OLDER BROTHER EDWIN BOOTH, THE MOST RENOWNED ACTORS OF THE ERA. DESCRIPTION: 5'7", DARK BROWN EYES, BLACK HAIR, SOLIDLY BUILT. ALIASES: UNKNOWN. RECORD: SHOT AND KILLED PRESIDENT ABRAHAM LINCOLN AT FORD'S THEATRE IN WASHINGTON, D.C., 4/14/1865 AS PART OF A CONSPIRACY TO ELIMINATE UNION LEADERS PURPORTEDLY ON BEHALF OF THE CONFEDERACY; FELLOW CONSPIRATORS INCLUDED GEORGE ATZERODT, LEWIS PAINE, MARY E. SURRATT, DAVID E. HEROLD (ALL HANGED AFTER BEING TRIED AND CONVICTED BY A MILITARY COMMISSION; LINCOLN'S ASSASSINATION WAS CONSIDERED A MILITARY CRIME AT THE TIME SINCE HE WAS COMMANDER-IN-CHIEF OF THE ARMY ESSENTIALLY STILL AT WAR); PAINE (BORN LEWIS THORNTON POWELL) ALSO ATTEMPTED TO MURDER SECRETARY OF STATE WILLIAM SEWARD ON THE NIGHT OF LINCOLN'S ASSASSINATION BUT ONLY SUCCEEDED IN WOUNDING HIM WITH A KNIFE; BOOTH TRACKED DOWN BY UNION TROOPS IN A BARN OWNED BY RICHARD GARRETT LOCATED BETWEEN PORT ROYAL AND BOWLING GREEN, VA., 4/26/65, WHERE HE WAS SHOT AND KILLED. BOOTH'S CO-LEADER IN THE CONSPIRACY, JOHN H. SURRATT, A CONFEDERATE SPY, ESCAPED THE COUNTRY UNDER MYSTERIOUS CIRCUMSTANCES AND WHEN ULTIMATELY CAPTURED AND RETURNED TO THE U.S. WAS SET FREE AFTER AN EQUALLY MYSTERIOUS (AND DUBIOUS) TRIAL.

He was mad with his own ego, possessed of a theatrical vanity that gnawed incessantly for fame. As an actor, John Wilkes Booth already owned national recognition, but he lusted after a kind of immortality completely unrelated to his profession. He desperately wanted to be remembered as a political and military hero, a savior of his romanticized version of the Old South.

His assassination of President Lincoln earned him the contempt and wrath of the country and a perpetual infamy husbanded by all

John Wilkes Booth, the actor turned assassin who thought of himself as the South's avenging angel. (National Archives)

succeeding American generations. His was a fatal miscalculation of history's judgment.

As a young man—he was twenty-six years old at the time of the assassination—Booth's acting career soared whenever he played the theaters of the South before the war. He enjoyed a popularity few actors could claim with discerning Southern audiences. He was the darling of the plantation owners whose linen-suited, cultured, leisurely lives he wished to emulate. Swimming through the cream of Southern society, Booth became convinced that slavery was necessary and good.

When the Civil War broke out, Booth, however, did not rush to enlist in Confederate ranks, but stayed in the North. There, though he continued to act, his success was not equal to the flowery, pompous praise once showered upon him by his Confederate friends. He grew bitter. Then angry. As the Union forces steadily crushed the Southern armies, his words of sympathy for the South became louder; he flaunted his support for Jefferson Davis and Robert E. Lee. His public dismissed his remarks as those typical of an eccentric but talented actor.

Some did not shrug off Booth's Southern sympathies so lightly. Samuel B. Arnold, 28,

and Michael O'Laughlin, 27, two of Booth's boyhood friends, listened intently to Booth's ravings against Lincoln after he sought them out in Baltimore, Md. in September, 1864. Booth hatched an insane plot to kidnap President Lincoln and turn him over to Confederate authorities, so that the President could be ransomed for Southern prisoners and possibly a negotiated peace.

Arnold and O'Laughlin had once served in the Confederate army—Arnold had left because of illness, O'Laughlin had deserted—and both agreed that John Wilkes Booth had a plan that might bring their side victory. Booth's plot had been developed slowly, until he became convinced that it could bring success. He had written a relative months before: "My love (as things stand today) is for the South alone. Nor do I deem it a dishonor in attempting to make for her a prisoner of this man [Lincoln], to whom she owes so much misery."

Booth's successful theatrical career had made him a rich man. He threw money about wildly while discussing his kidnapping plan with Arnold and O'Laughlin, promising them small fortunes if they would participate. They agreed and waited for the actor to enlarge his group of conspirators.

The next recruit was the mysterious John H. Surratt, 20, a wily, highly intelligent Confederate spy whose mother owned and operated a boarding house in Washington, D. C. Booth had met Surratt through a Maryland landowner, Dr. Samuel A. Mudd. The spy agreed to work with Booth and enlisted two more men, George Atzerodt, 33, and David Herold, 23.

Atzerodt was a coachmaker who knew the waters of the Potomac River well; he had ferried contraband to the South at Port Tobacco which was along the route Booth intended to take the kidnapped President. Herold had no special ability but he idolized Booth and his role seemed to be that of soothing the actor's megalomania. Herold had been a drugstore clerk in Washington but was incapable of holding that or any other job. Doctors examining him later reported that he was feeble-minded, possessing the mental age of an 11-year-old.

The last, and perhaps the most important addition to Booth's kidnapping ring was Lewis Paine, 20, a giant of a man who had broken away from the domination of his father, a Baptist minister. Paine, born Lewis Thornton

Powell, was mentally disturbed and has been described as a "half-wit" by doctors and historians. The only subject that seemed to jar him from his melancholy moods was the kidnapping of President Lincoln. He hated the Union and Negroes.

Paine had fought on the Confederate side at Gettysburg, had been severely wounded and captured. After a daring escape, he went to Baltimore. There police answered the screams of a Negro maid who was beaten half to death by Paine on a dark street. He was ordered by authorities to leave the city.

Booth met with these six men on the night of March 17, 1865, in a Washington saloon. The actor was careful to pay for all the food and liquor consumed by the group, which enthusiastically debated the plot. At this time, John Surratt began to argue that abducting Lincoln was too risky; there were guards all around him. Booth insisted that his kidnapping plan was sound. He had learned that the President would visit the Soldier's Home in three days. They could waylay and take him there, he told the group.

Surratt finally agreed to this plan and the plotters assembled to kidnap Lincoln three days later. The President, who had been having "premonitions," however, changed his plans and the kidnapping attempt fizzled.

The next month Lee surrendered to Grant in Virginia. Booth was incensed. He now concluded that the only way to deliver the South from the Union was to kill Lincoln. Hastily, he summoned the conspirators together. His plan called for the assassination of Lincoln by himself, the killing of Vice President Johnson by Atzerodt and the murdering of Secretary of State William Seward by Paine.

The conspirators struck on the evening of April 14, 1865. Ten days before, the President had had a dream where he saw his own assassination. He joked about it later, telling his wife, Mary : "What does anybody want to assassinate me for? If anyone wants to do so, he can do it any day or night, if he is ready to give his life for mine. It is nonsense."

As the light comedy *Our American Cousins* was being played out on the stage of Ford's Theater, John Wilkes Booth walked quietly down a Washington Street and into Taltavul's bar. Hours before, in the darkened theater, he had bored a small hole in the door leading to the Presidential box, knowing Lincoln

Mary E. Surratt, in whose boarding house the Lincoln conspirators met; many argued for her innocence but she was hanged nevertheless. (U.S. Signal Corps, Brady Collection)

would attend that night. He had also arranged to have a horse waiting for him outside the theater. An illiterate chore boy, "Peanuts" John Burrough, was, at the moment, holding onto the horse's reins at the theater's side entrance.

There was, incredibly, no guard outside of the President's box. Lincoln's protector that night, John F. Parker, had left his position. He later explained that the play bored him and he went to a nearby saloon for a drink! (He was never reprimanded, dismissed, or prosecuted for this gross misconduct.)

Booth drank heavily until a little after 10 p.m. Then he casually walked to Ford's Theater, where he was well known, and entered. An actress, Jennie Gourlay, spotted him. Though she called out, Booth walked past her without comment with what she later described as "a wild look in his eyes."

The assassin was greatly disturbed as he made his way upstairs. The thought of killing Lincoln did not alarm him. The fact that Atzerodt had backed out of his promise to kill Vice President Johnson did. Only hours earlier, the conspirators had met, holding a frenzied conversation. Atzerodt was visibly shaken by their plan.

Lewis Paine botched his assignment to kill Secretary of State Seward; David Herold escaped with Booth, but was captured; George Atzerodt backed down from the job of killing Vice President Johnson. They were all hanged together. (U.S. Signal Corps, Brady Collection)

He hung his head and murmured, "I cannot kill Johnson, I cannot perform such a deed, I cannot become a murderer."

"You're a fool," Booth lashed out at him. "You'll be hanged anyway." He and Paine then set out to complete their gruesome tasks.

When Booth came up to the unguarded door of the President's box it was 10:15 p.m. He peered through the peep hole he had made. Inside, he could see Lincoln sitting in a rocking chair, his wife Mary close by, and to their right Clara Harris and her fiance, Major Rathbone. He opened the door noiselessly and entered, clutching a small pistol and a knife.

In a moment he had fired a single shot into the back of Lincoln's head. Rathbone leaped up and struggled with Booth but the assassin's knife slashed out at him and severely wounded him in the arm. Booth stood for a second on the box's railing as the audience screamed in terror. "Sic semper tyrannis!" (Ever thus to tyrants) boomed Booth, ever the actor, and with that he leaped to the stage. His spur caught a flag draped next to the box and he landed with a crash, badly injuring his leg. He staggered up and hobbled off the stage, yelling above the pandemonium: "The South is avenged!"

As Booth stumbled from the theater's side entrance he realized that his left shinbone was fractured. "Peanuts" John Burrough was saucer-eyed at seeing the actor in his condition but obediently helped him to mount his horse. Booth dashed away down the street.

Lincoln's horrible headwound was untreatable. He died the following morning at 7:22

a.m. in a small room near the theater.

While Booth was enacting his self-designed drama, Lewis Paine clumsily attempted to kill Secretary of State Seward. Paine, who had learned that Seward had been injured in a fall from his carriage days earlier, arrived at the Secretary's home, stating that he had brought medicine and "must deliver it personally to him."

He was halted at the foot of the stairs by Frederick Seward, the Secretary's oldest son. Frederick told him that under no circumstances could Paine see his father. The would-be assassin meekly turned to leave and then suddenly whirled about and brought the butt of his pistol crashing down on young Seward's head, knocking him senseless. Paine then dashed up the stairs three at a time and rushed into the Secretary's bedroom.

The helpless Seward could only let out a weak cry as Paine drove a knife into him several times. Seward's young son and male nurse ran in and pushed Paine from the bedroom. The wild-eyed conspirator then ran down the stairs past servants and Frederick Seward, then just staggering to his feet. Paine was screaming hysterically, "I'm mad! I'm mad!"

Paine had no horse awaiting him; he merely ran up the street and into Mary Surratt's boarding house, where he hid beneath a bed. He was taken prisoner a short time later, as were Edman Spangler, the stage hand who had arranged to have Booth's horse waiting for him at Ford's theater, Atzerodt, Arnold, O'Laughlin and Mrs. Mary E. Surratt, 48, John's mother. Mrs. Surratt's case was odd in that authorities never proved that she was in any way part of the conspirators' plot to kill Lincoln, yet she was executed on the claim that the plot had been hatched in her boarding house.

Three of the plotters were missing. Booth had ridden furiously southward with David Herold into Virginia, first stopping at Dr. Mudd's Maryland home where his injury was treated (Mudd placed splints about his leg and sent him on his way). He and Herold finally hid out in a barn on a large farm owned by a Confederate sympathizer Richard Garrett.

John Surratt could not be found anywhere. Thousands of Union troops spread through Maryland and Virginia following each report of Booth's escape route, questioning hundreds of persons who claimed to have seen the frantic rider pass. A Lieutenant Baker, leading a company of troops hot on Booth's trail, tracked him to the Garrett farm on April 26, 1865.

Baker told Booth and Herold to surrender or be burned out of the barn.

Booth yelled: "Let us have a little time to consider it."

Baker gave them five minutes.

Then Booth shouted: "Captain, I know you to be a brave man, and I believe you to be honorable; I am a cripple. I have got but one leg; if you will withdraw your men in one line one hundred yards from the door, I will come out and fight you!"

"We will do no such thing," Baker shouted back.

"Well, my brave boys," Booth yelled, "prepare a stretcher for me . . . one more stain on the old banner!"

Inside the barn, David Herold was cracking, pleading with Booth to surrender. Baker and his troopers heard the actor shout at his hapless follower: "You damned coward! Will you leave me now? Go, go, I would not have you stay with me!" Then, to the troops: "There's a man in here who wants to come out!"

The barn door creaked slowly open and Herold, shaking with fear, walked out and surrendered.

Baker ordered the barn set fire and troopers brought dry brush and piled it against the building. The flame soared upward with great speed. The men outside watched Booth's shadowy figure hobble toward the open door. Just as he reached it a shot rang out and Booth

toppled forward. Who fired this shot was never learned. Some claim it was self-inflicted, others point to a Union zealot, soldier Boston Corbett.

Booth's body was dragged from the flames. The actor, barely alive, managed before he died to whisper the words: "Tell my mother I died for my country."

Lieutenant Baker searched the assassin and withdrew Booth's diary. It revealed a tormented mind haunted by the image of his pursuers, a self-pitying chant seeking to justify the assassination. Excerpts: "After being hunted like a dog through swamps, woods, and last night being chased by gunboats till I was forced to return wet, cold, and starving, with every man's hand against me, I am here in despair and why? For doing what Brutus was honored for—what made Tell a hero. And yet I, for striking down a greater tyrant than they ever knew, am looked upon as a common cutthroat. My action was purer than either of theirs. One hoped to be great. The other had not only his country's, but his own, wrongs to avenge. I hope for no gain. I knew no private wrong. I struck for my country and that alone. A country that groaned beneath this tyranny, and prayed for this end, and yet now behold the cold hand they extend me. God cannot pardon me if I have done wrong. Yet I cannot see my wrong, except in serving a degenerate people. The little, the very little I left behind to clear my name, the government will not allow to be printed. So ends all. For my coun-

With troops and civilians witnessing, four of the major conspirators (left to right)—Mrs. Surratt (the first woman in U.S. history to die on the gallows), Paine, Herold, Atzerodt—were hanged on July 7, 1865. (Alexander Gardner, National Archives)

try I have given up all that makes life sweet and holy, brought misery upon my family, and am sure there is no pardon in the Heaven for me, since man condemns me so. I have only heard of what has been done (except what I did myself), and it fills me with horror. God, try and forgive me, and bless my mother. To-night I will once more try the river with the intent to cross. Though I have a greater desire and almost a mind to return to Washington, and in a measure clear my name—which I feel I can do. I do not repent the blow I struck. I may before my God, but not to man. I think I have done well. Though I am abandoned, with the curse of Cain upon me, when, if the world knew my heart, that one blow would have made me great, though I did desire no greatness. Tonight I try to escape these bloodhounds once more. Who, who can read his fate? God's will be done. I have too great a soul to die like a criminal. Oh, may He, may He spare me that, and let me die bravely. I bless the entire world. Have never hated or

wronged anyone. This last was not a wrong, unless God deems it so, and it's with Him to damn or bless me. As for this boy with me [Herold], who often prays (yes, before and since) with a true and sincere heart—was it crime in him? If so, why can he pray the same? I do not wish to shed a drop of blood, but 'I must fight the course. 'Tis all that's left to me.' "

On July 17, 1865, George Atzerodt, Lewis Paine, David Herold and Mary Surratt were taken up the steep gallow steps in the grimly bare yard of Washington's Old Penitentiary, ironically being shaded from the sun by umbrellas. There they were hanged. Mrs. Surratt's execution was never fully justified. She was convicted on the testimony of an infamous drunk and a known liar. On the scaffold, big-boned Lewis Paine pleaded with the executioner for the woman's life. "If I had two lives to give, I'd give one gladly to save Mrs. Surratt," he begged. "I know that she is innocent, and would never die in this way if I hadn't been found in her house. She knew nothing about the conspiracy at all . . ." Paine's death prattle was ignored. Mrs. Surratt was hanged anyway, the first female executed by the rope in the U.S. (Arnold was sentenced to life imprisonment and was paroled in 1869. O'Laughlin went to jail for life and died there; Dr. Mudd began serving a life sentence and was pardoned by President Johnson in 1868; Spangler got six years of hard labor.)

Her son John Surratt fled the country to Canada. His escape has baffled and confused historians to this day. He was seen several times on his way through New England to freedom but government agents sent to follow him were given contradictory orders emanating from that curiously truculent Secretary of War, Edwin Stanton.

The Secretary's actions immediately following the assassination appeared to be as hysterical as that of Washington's mobs. He ramrodded the conspirators' trials and hastened their execution. Stanton, who at times had acted more as an adversary to Lincoln than as one of his cabinet members during the President's administration, did strange things following Lincoln's death. For one, he confiscated the only photograph showing the President in his coffin, a photo taken while Lincoln lay in state in New York's City Hall. He had the master plate destroyed and burned all but one print of this picture, keeping it among his personal effects. The photo was accidentally found eighty-seven years later.

What was more peculiar was the way Stanton handled the case of John H. Surratt. Several times government agents located the fugitive and informed Stanton of his whereabouts. The Secretary refused to order his arrest or delayed decision. Tracking down Surratt developed into a world chase. He was located in Italy where he was serving in the Swiss Guards. He escaped. He was finally found in Egypt and was returned to the U.S.

Surratt's eventual trial was a farce. His lawyers, who were oddly enough, friends of Stanton's, cleverly picked apart the law and through various loopholes (the absence of certain key witnesses also helped), got him off. Surratt lived out an inconspicuous life in Baltimore where he died, just after the turn of the century, unidentified to his neighbors as the co-chief of the great plot to murder Abraham Lincoln.

BOSTON, PATIENCE
Murderer ● (1713-1735)

Patience Boston, in her short twenty-three years of life had, according to her final confession, committed every kind of sin conceivable in early Puritan Maine—lying, stealing, swearing, drunkenness and finally, murder.

She senselessly killed eight-year-old Benjamin Trot in Falmouth, Maine. As if by whim, Patience picked up the child and threw him down a well in which he drowned.

Patience, who was part Indian, was executed for this murder in York, Me., July 24, 1735.

BOTKIN, CORDELIA
Murderer ● (1854-1910)

BACKGROUND: BORN AND RAISED IN CALIFORNIA. MINOR PUBLIC EDUCATION. MARRIED WELCOME A. BOTKIN OF STOCKTON, CALIF., A BUSINESSMAN. GAVE BIRTH TO ONE SON, BEVERLY. DESERTED HER HUSBAND IN THE EARLY 1890S, LIVING A BOHEMIAN LIFE IN SAN FRANCISCO. DESCRIPTION: 5'2", BROWN EYES, BROWN HAIR, HEAVYSET. ALIASES: NONE. RECORD: MURDERED MRS. ELIZABETH DUNNING AND (BY ACCIDENT) MRS. JOSHUA DEANE BY MAILING THEM A GIFT OF HOME-MADE BONBONS LOADED WITH ARSENIC; APPREHENDED THROUGH HANDWRITING AND TRIED IN THE STATE OF CALIFORNIA IN 1898; FOUND GUILTY AND SENTENCED TO LIFE IMPRISONMENT, FIRST IN THE BRANCH COUNTY JAIL IN SAN FRANCISCO AND THEN IN SAN QUENTIN WHERE SHE DIED IN 1910.

John Presley Dunning led an enviable life in 1895. To some he had the best of two worlds—a lovely wife and child and a responsible, well-paying job as Bureau Chief of the Associated Press in San Francisco. He also had a mistress with whom he enjoyed the seamy side of life.

The wife was patient, Victorian-bred Elizabeth Pennington Dunning, the pretty daughter of a U.S. Congressman from Dover, Del. Elizabeth married John Dunning in Dover in

1891 and gave birth to a daughter later that year. For four years the couple lived quietly but when Dunning was offered the post as head of the AP office in San Francisco, he jumped at the offer. Then life changed radically for the Dunnings.

Enter the mistress, one Cordelia Botkin, a dumpy pigeon-breasted woman a full ten years older than Dunning. Cordelia was a promiscuous soul who had left her husband, businessman Welcome A. Botkin, in Stockton, Calif. several years past and moved with her obese son, Beverly, to San Francisco. There Cordelia hurtled herself into the wild revelries of the Bohemian quarters, drinking and partying all night, sleeping during the day, living off the money her simple-minded husband sent to her.

Dunning and Cordelia met in one of San Francisco's small parks. He was riding a bicycle, then fashionable, to his office when it broke down near the park bench upon which Cordelia sat. The frowsy little woman rolled her dark eyes just once and Dunning was lost. What drew him to this woman is unknown. Cordelia was rather a dull person as well as being homely.

But there was a hidden wild streak in Dunning which apparently pronounced itself every few years. He admitted later that he was prone to gambling, drinking, and whoring binges that went on for months. Dunning met Cordelia secretly for a year and then, ignoring all propriety, the journalist moved into an apartment with Cordelia, Beverly, and Beverly's mistress, 40-year-old Louise Seeley, his mother's best friend. They were a merry group, drinking and dancing into the early hours of the morning, every morning. Cordelia would dance wildly about the small apartment, leaping awkwardly and, to the consternation of the tenants below, landing with heavy crashes on the floor. Her specialty was telling the other three "racy stories," as she later termed them, while all four stretched out across two beds.

Mrs. Dunning, meanwhile, was left to sit and wait at home with her daughter. Her husband's ridiculous affair went on for more than a year. He lost his job and lived off the money Cordelia kept receiving from cuckolded Welcome Botkin. Elizabeth finally called it quits in 1896. She sold her furniture and jewels to obtain passage money for her journey back East to her parents' home in Delaware. John Dunning did nothing to prevent her from leaving; he was elated by her decision. Now he would have no guilty feelings at all, he told himself. To earn money he concentrated on gambling, but his racetrack losses mounted and his life with Cordelia became a hit-and-miss proposition.

Elizabeth settled down with her daughter and parents to live a quiet life in Dover, waiting for John Dunning to come to his senses. In the summer of 1897, the journalist's long-suffering wife received the first of many letters from San Francisco, but not from Dunning. The missive described how her husband was cavorting with an "interesting and pretty woman . . . an Englishwoman . . . a lady by birth and education" who was introducing Dunning to "the extreme delight of a quiet Bohemian life." The writer warned Elizabeth not to "renew living" with her husband and signed the letter, "A friend."

Mrs. Dunning received letters written in the same handwriting all summer long but turned them over unread to her father for safekeeping. Her husband was sent a copy of the first letter and he identified the handwriting as Cordelia's but, upon confrontation, the slatternly Bohemian shrieked an emphatic denial.

The affair ended when the Associated Press contacted its former employee in 1898. The Spanish-American war had broken out and the news service was in desperate need of experienced reporters. Would he go? Would he! Dunning left Cordelia and her friends flat, departing for what was then called Porto Rico.

Cordelia's loneliness for her missing lover was acute. She insisted on being by his side and to that end applied for a position as a front-line nurse but was rejected. For weeks Cordelia sank into depression. She listlessly walked the streets of San Francisco, brooding. She thought much of sweet Elizabeth Dunning. Jack Dunning had talked lovingly about her before leaving for the war zone. She would be the one he returned to, Cordelia concluded. He had had his fling. Now work and war would sober him. He would return to his wife and child, that was certain.

Then the mistress developed a plan. She had deviled Elizabeth by mail. Why not let the Post Office eliminate her competition? Cordelia went to a drugstore and purchased two ounces of arsenic. The clerk asked her why she was buying the poison (signing a register for the purchase of poison did not become mandatory until 1907 when The Poison Act went into effect).

"I want to clean a straw hat," Cordelia replied.

Though the clerk had never heard of using arsenic for such purposes, he shrugged and sold the woman the poison. He did keep an informal sales record and entered a "Mrs. Bothin," of the Hotel Victoria, in his book.

Next, the lovesick woman went to George Haas's candy store, where she bought a box of candy. Cordelia returned to the Hotel Victoria and, to the puzzlement of the servants, did not emerge from her room for several days. When she did, she carried a large box wrapped securely for mailing. She walked to the Ferry Post Office in San Francisco and sent her "gift" east to Elizabeth Dunning.

The Pennington family were cooling themselves on their front porch on the blisteringly hot day of September 9, 1898, when the package arrived.

Elizabeth opened the parcel. Inside a glazed and colorful box marked "bonbons," she found a cheap lace handkerchief with a twenty-five cents price tag still affixed to it, and beneath that some odd-looking candy. This she passed around to those on the porch. Her parents declined, but her sister, Mrs. Joshua Deane, Mrs. Deane's child, and Elizabeth's daughter tasted some. Mrs. Dunning and Mrs. Deane ate several pieces. They made a few unkindly remarks about the gritty lumps inside the chocolates. At the bottom of the box, Elizabeth found a scribbled note which read: "With love to yourself and baby, Mrs. C."

"Oh, it must be from that lovely Mrs. Corbally," she remarked, thinking of a close friend in San Francisco.

The following day, the two women and children were taken ill. The children, who had only nibbled at the chocolate, recovered. The sisters grew worse and finally, after suffering violent spasms of pain Mrs. Dunning and Mrs. Deane died, September 12, 1898.

A physician had first diagnosed the illness as "cholera morbus," (a medical catchall) as a result of eating corn fritters. When a specialist was called in, he told Mr. Pennington that he believed the women had been poisoned. By then it was too late to save them. Pennington, fortunately, had saved the box of candy, the

San Francisco's Cordelia Botkin chose poison to eliminate her rival, John Dunning's wife, in 1898.

wrapping, and the note. The handwriting on the wrapping was the same as that in the letters Elizabeth had received from San Francisco the previous year.

Dunning, who had been contacted, rushed to Dover from the front lines and, upon seeing the letters and the note in the candy box, insisted that they were all penned by the same person—Cordelia Botkin.

Isaiah W. Less, San Francisco's Chief of Police, personally tracked down Cordelia and arrested her. A thorough search of her room at the Hotel Victoria unearthed a wrapping from the George Haas candy store.

On the strength of Dunning's statements, the wrapping, a sales clerk who worked at the City of Paris department store where the lace handkerchief was purchased, and the drugstore clerk, Cordelia was identified as the murderer of Mrs. Dunning and her sister. (Handwriting was not then admissible as evidence in California.)

The pathetic woman was sentenced to life imprisonment in December, 1898. Oddly enough, the judge who sentenced her, Carroll Cook, was amazed to see Mrs. Botkin alight from a cable car in San Francisco in which he was riding in the summer of 1901. He followed her to the Branch County Jail where she was supposed to be a prisoner.

Cook became enraged when he learned that Cordelia had employed her considerable feminine charm with her jailers to obtain special favors. Her cell was made up like an apartment where she received gentleman callers at night: her wardens. In return for her favors, Cordelia was permitted to take "two days off" during each week, at which time she could freely travel through San Francisco.

Judge Cook put an end to this and Cordelia was moved into an ordinary cell. Following the mass devastation wreaked upon San Francisco by its now famous earthquake, the old Branch County Jail was destroyed. Cordelia survived the holocaust, however, and was sent to San Quentin. She died there in 1910 without ever confessing her terrible deed.

BOYD, JABEZ
Murderer ● (? -1845)

Boyd, who was thought to be a deeply religious man in his community, practiced highway robbery at night. One evening, in Westchester, Pa., he robbed Wesley Patton. When the victim put up a fight, Boyd beat him to death with a club.

Boyd was recognized and found the next day in church. According to one report, Boyd was sitting in a pew "with a hymn book in his hand, and from which he was singing with apparent composure."

He was hanged in 1845.

BRAND, SAMUEL
Murderer ● (? -1773)

Following an argument, Samuel Brand set fire to his farmhouse while his elderly parents slept. He entered the flaming building with a loaded gun and confronted his brother, who sat in the kitchen staring at him.

"I'll shoot thee," one narrative reported Brand as saying.

"Shoot if thou wilt," replied Brand's stoic brother. The narrative continues, "This simple and inconsiderate answer did but the more provoke his fury, so that he fired off, and the poor victim fell dead on the spot."

Brand was quickly apprehended, convicted, and hanged December 18, 1773, in Lancaster, Pa.

BRAUN, THOMAS EUGENE
Murderer ● (1945-   )

BACKGROUND: BORN IN RURAL WASHINGTON STATE, 1945, ORPHANED AT AN EARLY AGE. MINOR PUBLIC EDUCATION. ORIGINAL OCCUPATION, GAS STATION ATTENDANT. DESCRIPTION; 6', BROWN EYES, BROWN HAIR, SOLID BUILD. ALIASES: MIKE FORD. RECORD; MURDERED MRS. DEANNA BUSE OUTSIDE REDMOND, WASH., 8/19/67; MURDERED SAMUEL LEDGERWOOD IN OREGON DAYS LATER; MURDERED TIMOTHY LUCE AND PERMANENTLY CRIPPLED SUSAN BARTOLOMEI IN NORTHERN CALIFORNIA, 8/24/67; APPREHENDED WITH HIS ACCOMPLICE, LEONARD MAINE, IN JAMESTOWN, CALIF., 8/27/67; CONFESSED TO KILLINGS, RECEIVED DEATH SENTENCE, WHICH WAS LATER COMMUTED TO LIFE IMPRISONMENT. MAINE ALSO RECEIVED A LIFE SENTENCE.

Maybe it began when Tom Braun's father, half-drunk, made him shoot his own dog. "He's a chicken-killer and he's got to die," the old man explained. Or maybe it began with old Braun locking young Tom and his sister in a battered truck while he hit the taverns for hours. Perhaps it was Tom's mother dying hard and painful under the knife of a butchering abortionist.

But it did begin somewhere—and it ended with the slaughter of three people and the permanent crippling of a young girl, a swath of blood that cut through three states and 1,000 miles in five hot summer days.

On August 17, 1967, long-haired Tom Braun left his job as a gas pump jockey in Ritzville, Washington. He paused to scoop up his sometime friend, runty Leonard Maine.

With his German-made Borgward sedan wide open, Braun and Lennie blasted out of Ritzville with two weapons—an automatic .22-

caliber Luger and a Frontier Colt single-action .22 caliber pistol, plus enough ammunition for a small war.

The two 18-year-old boys made for Seattle at full speed. There, on the evening of Aug. 18, they went to the first rooming house they spotted.

Maine approached the housekeeper and asked for a room.

She described later what happened: "I saw a shadow in front of me." It was Thomas Braun.

"I looked up and he was pointing a gun at me. Then I screamed and stepped into an adjoining room and shut the door."

The boys fled back to their car and zoomed off.

Next day, the boys were headed down Route 202 outside Redmond, Wash. Suddenly, they spotted an attractive, 22-year-old woman driving a maroon Skylark ahead of them. They looked at each other and smiled.

Braun stepped on the gas and came alongside Deanna Buse, married less than a year and returning from her job on her way to her mother's house.

His wild hair swirling in the rush of air from the open window, Maine signalled frantically to Deanna that something was wrong with her tires. Frightened, Mrs. Buse slowed down and Braun's ancient Borgward eased her car over to a stop on the embankment.

The young woman got out of her car while the boys looked over her shapely figure. She walked around the Skylark, bending and examining each tire as they watched her.

She didn't understand. There was nothing wrong.

She stood up—and let out a gasp. Thomas Braun was pointing a gun at her head. Braun ordered her into her own car and told Maine to follow them in the Borgward.

The two cars went slowly down the highway and turned off, winding through narrow roads until they reached a dirt trail that deadended in the woods near Echo Lake. Braun got out and shoved Mrs. Buse in front of him.

Lennie Maine stood there while Braun ordered Mrs. Buse into the woods. Maine watched them disappear into the thick overgrowth. Later, he was to confess that he heard five sharp cracks—pistol shots. Seconds later Braun came back to the cars alone.

Braun and Maine then drove both cars into Seattle and parked on a busy street. They emptied articles from the Borgward to the Skylark and then drove off in Mrs. Buse's car.

Four days later, Police Sgt. Hart inspected the abandoned Borgward and found five .22-caliber shell casings. He impounded the old black car and began to wonder.

Just 22 miles south of Seattle, in Fife, Wash., Braun and Maine stopped again, visiting Maine's uncle and asking him the quickest way to Portland, Ore.

Next morning the pair crossed the Oregon border. Tired, they tried to register at a motel along the scenic coast.

But the motel manager was suspicious of the wild-haired, wide-eyed youths. He quizzed them about their car registration, and asked for other information they were reluctant to give. Finally the two backed away, hurried to their car, and roared off again down the road.

Samuel Ledgerwood had just finished an enjoyable day fishing in his favorite lake and was headed home in his late-model green Buick.

He noticed two young men alongside the country road trying to change a tire. Being a charitable man, Ledgerwood pulled over to help them. It was to be the last act he would ever perform.

Braun put two bullets into Ledgerwood's head, killing him. As he lay dead on the isolated logging road, the two youths set fire to Mrs. Buse's Skylark by firing several bullets into the gas tank. They then got casually into Ledgerwood's gleaming Buick and drove off.

As if on a summer vacation, the two meandered southward along the beautiful Pacific coastline, finally arriving in northern California.

There, along deserted and mountainous Route 120, they met two young hitch-hikers, Susan Bartolomei and Timothy Luce. Amiably, the boys picked up the youngsters—both only seventeen—and drove off with them.

On the same highway at six the next morning, a Mr. and Mrs. Mease, their daughter and nephew, all headed for Santa Barbara, saw a body lying in the road.

They stopped. It was Susan Bartolomei. Mrs. Mease bent over the girl and felt her pulse. She was still alive.

Susan gasped that "they" had shot her and killed her boyfriend.

"They" were "two youths about 18," named "Mike" and "John" from Oklahoma, she said.

Soon an ambulance arrived and Susan retold her story to police at a nearby hospital, where she wavered day after day between life and death.

Back in Washington, searchers found the body of Deanna Buse in the woods where Braun had left her. She was naked and her clothes were piled neatly next to her. She had been shot five times, bullets entering her eye and behind her ear. An autopsy showed she had not been raped.

But Susan Bartolomei had been raped—several times—before being shot. She came out of her coma now and then to tell police about it while others still searched for her boyfriend Tim.

His body, face up in a pool of blood, was found along the highway by an archaeologist looking for Indian arrowheads. He had been shot several times as he tried to stop Braun from raping his girl.

In his anger, Braun had not only killed the boy but proved his lust for blood beyond any doubt. There were tire track marks over Timothy Luce's chest where Braun had repeatedly run over him with the Buick, crushing him.

Then Oregon police found Samuel Ledgerwood's body and the manhunt was on for the car Susan had described.

Piece by piece, police of three states put it all together in a matter of hours.

A few days later, in the hamlet of Jamestown, Calif., Constable Ed Chafin, making his early morning rounds, spotted a green Buick with Oregon plates in front of the town's small hotel.

Mass murderer Thomas Eugene Braun (left front) followed by Leonard Maine moments after their arrest in 1967. (Wide World Photos)

Chafin had heard the alarm and description Susan gave of the killers (in her confusion, she had said the killers drove a Mercury).

Chafin looked over the Buick.

"Even though this car was a Buick and the girl had said that the suspects drove a Mercury, I had a feeling—sometimes when you've been in law enforcement long enough, this happens—and I knew that I was looking at the getaway car," he said later.

Chafin immediately radioed for help. Three officers answered and were in front of the hotel in minutes. Checking the hotel's register, Chafin discovered that "Mike and John Ford" were in rooms 19 and 26.

The cops went up cautiously, guns drawn.

They went quietly to room 19, slipped a passkey into the lock and swung the door open a few inches where it was.stopped by a chain-lock.

They could see a young man—Maine—asleep in the bed.

One of the officers, Lt. Andre, shoved his pistol through the crack and barked, "Put your hands up! Come over here and unlock this chain."

Meekly, Lennie Maine walked to the door in his underwear, unlocked the door and was grabbed by the officers.

They then went to room 26 and kicked the door open, the chain lock breaking loose.

There was Thomas Eugene Braun, his hands beneath a pillow. He had a clear shot at the officers.

One of the officers suspected a trick. "His hands, watch his hands!" he yelled and Andre jumped Braun just as the killer was about to grab for his gun.

The bloodbath was all over.

Three months later, Braun and Maine sat immobile in court, their faces expressionless, now with short haircuts.

They watched as the prosecution paraded one damning witness after another. They watched as movies and still photos were shown of those Braun had mercilessly killed. Then they confessed.

Thomas Braun got the death sentence, which was later commuted to life imprisonment; Maine received the same sentence. They admitted everything: how they killed each one of their victims, where and when. But they never answered the one question everyone wanted to hear—why?

BRISBON, HENRY, JR. (THE I-57 KILLER)
Mass Murderer ● (1956-   )

On June 3, 1973, Brisbon was traveling in a car with three other men along Interstate Highway 57, just south of Chicago. They forced a car driven by a woman off the road. The woman was stripped naked and ordered to run for her life. She was shot between the legs, then the head, the final shot killing her. Less than an hour later, Dorothy Cerny and James Schmidt, both 25 and engaged to be married, were forced off the road by the same four men.

Forced to lie on the side of the road, the couple pleaded for mercy but they were blasted to death by a shotgun. Henry Brisbon, Jr., seventeen, was convicted and given a life term for these killings. Capital punishment had been overturned by the U.S. Supreme Court at the time, which prevented a death sentence being ordered. Brisbon later killed a fellow inmate, Richard Morgan, at Stateville Penitentiary at Joliet, Ill, and was sentenced to death for the murder in 1982.

As he was being led out of the courtroom, Brisbon screamed: "You'll never get me! I'll kill again! And then you'll have another long trial. And I'll do it again." Brisbon tried to kill fellow inmate and serial killer John Wayne Gacy in 1983, but he failed. In 1985 the Illinois Supreme Court overtuned Brisbon's death sentence, saying that the prosecution had prejudiced the jury in the Morgan case by introducing inflammatory evidence from the I-57 killings.

Brisbon was resentenced on October 7, 1986, again to death. He is presently appealing this sentence. Brisbon, who was once described as "a very, very terrible human being, a walking testimonial for the death sentence," has caused a prison riot and has attacked guards and inmates dozens of times during his prison term.

BROCIUS, WILLIAM ("CURLY BILL")
Cattle Rustler, Gunfighter ● (1857-1882)

Born William B. Graham, this Arizona outlaw belonged to the McLowery-Clanton faction that faced Wyatt Earp, his brothers, and Doc Holliday in the legendary gunfight at Tombstone's O.K. Corral in 1881. Brocius was not present for this fight but he had participated in several cattle raids and shoot-outs in and about Tombstone earlier.

Brocius is best remembered for his shooting and killing of Tombstone's Sheriff Fred White in October, 1881, when he used a new and deadly trick that later gunfighters (notably John Wesley Hardin of Texas) employed—the gun spin.

One abysmally hot evening, Sheriff White and his deputy, Virgil Earp (Wyatt's brother), stepped out onto Tombstone's streets to quell a minor riot. Dozens of cowboys from nearby ranches were whooping up a gun party, racing up and down the streets on their ponies and shooting wildly into the air.

White and Earp drove the boisterous cowboys from town. But one, Curly Bill, remained standing defiantly in the middle of the street. White walked up to Curly Bill and asked him to turn over his six-gun. Brocius smiled and, according to the story, held out his weapon butt first. As the Sheriff reached for it, Curly Bill spun the gun around his index finger holding the guard, the butt winding up in his hand.

At this moment, Curly Bill later stated in court, Earp jumped him from behind, attempting to lock his arms, and his gun's hair trigger went off, sending a bullet into Sheriff White and killing him. Another version, Earp's, reported that after spinning the gun back into position, Brocius merely squeezed off a round, murdering White in cold blood.

Some witnesses to the shooting claimed that the sheriff caused his own death when, after being angered by Brocius' fancy gun-spin, he grabbed the cocked six-gun by the barrel and set it off himself.

Brocius was tried days later. The prosecution had to admit that Curly Bill's pistol had five shells in it after White had been shot, and that he was therefore not "hurrahing" the town with the other cowboys and so not guilty of prompting White's action. The gunfighter was released and White's death was ruled an accidental homicide.

When the Clanton-Earp war erupted months later, Curly Bill Brocius was mixed up in several forays, always lined up against the Earps. In another bushwacking following the dramatic gun battle at the O.K. Corral, Earp's brother Morgan was ambushed and Virgil crippled for life. Wyatt tracked down, according to his own version, all of the outlaws responsible for the attacks. Curly Bill, one of his prime suspects, was no exception.

The end was a strange affair. Earp and his men met another posse led by Brocius at Iron Springs outside of Tombstone, in the shadow of the Whetstone Mountains. Both groups had stopped at the spring to water their horses. Brocius claimed he had been deputized by Tombstone Sheriff Johnny Behan, an Earp rival, to bring in the Earp posse for violating certain local laws. When Wyatt refused to turn over his six-guns, Brocius went for his irons. Earp was faster and drilled the young outlaw dead. He was the last serious foe Wyatt Earp faced in Tombstone.

[ALSO SEE O.K. Corral]

BROTHERS, LEO VINCENT
Gangster, Murderer ● (1899-1951)

On June 9, 1930, a rare event in the underworld occurred. Jake Lingle, a $65-a-week legman-reporter for the *Chicago Tribune*, was shot and killed gangland style at the Illinois Central train station underpass at Randolph and Michigan Avenue—at the height of rush hour and before dozens of stunned witnesses. It was the first time a newsman, considered sacrosanct by the mobs, had been killed for what was initially thought to be investigations into Chicago gang operations.

The *Tribune's* legman, it turned out, was anything but a hard-working reporter laboring along the beat of crime. He lived in a luxurious suite at the Stevens Hotel where he usually slept till noon each day. He was driven about in a chauffeur-wheeled limousine and it was nothing for Lingle to spend $1,000 a day at the track betting the ponies.

His long association with Al Capone came to light (Lingle wore a diamond-studded belt buckle, a gift from Scarface), and his paper sorrowfully had to admit that the newsman had been living a double life: reporter by day and front man for Capone at night, working as a liaison between the Capone gang and Lingle's boyhood friend, Police Commissioner William P. Russell (who resigned when the facts were made public).

Jake, who was reportedly in debt to Capone for $100,000 over gambling debts, had tried to extort money from members of his and Bugs Moran's gang, using his considerable influence to barter gambling and liquor licenses via police contacts. "I fixed the price of beer in this town," he once boasted. Capone might tolerate a braggart but never an extortionist. He ordered Lingle killed.

Leo Vincent Brothers, (alias Leo Bader) known across the country to mob leaders as "Buster," was called in from St. Louis to do the job. The tall blond killer was a master of disguises and, after weeks of tailing Lingle to and from the racetrack, got his man as he was about to board a train.

Dozens of witnesses saw a blond-haired priest run up behind Lingle, who was reading a racing form, and fire point-blank into the back of his head, killing him. The imposing clerical costume gave pedestrians enough pause—and Brothers enough time—for his escape through the massive crowds.

One of the most intensive manhunts in Chicago's history culminated four months later when, through an informant, Brothers was picked up and charged with the murder. His record, authorities learned, was a long and deadly one. He had been a labor terrorist in St. Louis and had been arrested for bombing, arson, robbery, and murder. Apparently Capone's murder contracts went cheap in those days since Brothers was found in a third-rate room, almost penniless, when arrested.

Four witnesses positively identified him as the killer, yet Brothers denied any role in the Lingle shooting throughout his long trial March 16, 1931 to April 2, 1931. Finally, after a 27-hour deliberation, the jury found him guilty and he was sentenced to serve fourteen years in prison. The sentence, the most lenient possible, gave rise to the belief that Brothers was "taking a fall" for the real killers and that the court was acting accordingly.

The convicted killer smiled confidently as he was led from the court. When asked about the sentence Brothers's only comment was: "I can do that standing on my head."

He was paroled within eight years and soon faded into obscurity, a gunman who not only got away with murder, but also proved that the mob's savage sword was mightier than the press in Capone's Chicago.

BUCCIERI, FIORE ("FIFI")
Syndicate Gangster ● (1904-1973)

A ranking enforcer in the Chicago syndicate, Buccieri has a record dating back to 1925, when he first began working for the Capone gang as a minor thug. Arrests include carrying a concealed weapon, bribery, larceny, and murder—with only two convictions for minor offenses.

Buccieri was named by federal lawmen in 1966 as "lord high executioner" of the Chicago mob. At that time, over one hundred top mobsters from around the country met at Chicago's old Edgewater Beach Hotel to pay him honor on his sixty-second birthday. The event was also considered an important summit meeting for the syndicate.

BUCHALTER, LOUIS ("LEPKE")
Racketeer, Murderer ● (1897-1944)

BACKGROUND: BORN LOUIS BOOKHOUSE IN MANHATTAN. MINOR PUBLIC EDUCATION. NO OCCUPATION OTHER THAN CRIME. DESCRIPTION: 5'7½", BROWN EYES, BROWN HAIR, SLENDER. ALIASES: LEPKE. RECORD: ARRESTED SEVERAL TIMES IN 1913 AT AGE 16 FOR ROBBING PUSHCART PEDDLERS IN NEW YORK; SEVERAL MORE ARRESTS FOLLOWED BUT NO CONVICTIONS. IN 1917, WORKING WITH HIS PARTNER JACOB "GURRAH" SHAPIRO, LEPKE MOVED INTO THE GARMENT INDUSTRY, SETTING UP A CORRUPT TRADE UNION AND

COMPELLING, THROUGH BLACKMAIL, WORKERS AND EMPLOYERS TO JOIN; BECAME A MEMBER OF THE NATIONAL CRIME SYNDICATE'S BOARD OF DIRECTORS IN THE EARLY 1930S AND CHIEF OF THE SYNDICATE'S ENFORCEMENT ARM, MURDER, INC.; WITH SHAPIRO, KILLED NEW YORK RACKETEER JACOB "LITTLE AUGIE" ORGEN, WOUNDING HIS PARTNER JACK "LEGS" DIAMOND 10/15/26; ARRESTED WITH GURRAH, TRIED AND CONVICTED OF VIOLATING ANTI-TRUST LAWS IN 1933; FINED $1,000 AND SENTENCED TO TWO YEARS IN JAIL; LEPKE'S CONVICTION REVERSED IN A HIGHER COURT BY JUDGE MARTIN T. MANTON; ARRESTED 8/24/39 BY THE FBI ON A FEDERAL NARCOTICS CHARGE, SENTENCED TO 14 YEARS IN LEAVENWORTH; RETRIED IN 1940 FOR ORDERING THE MURDER OF JOSEPH ROSEN AND CONVICTED ON THE TESTIMONY OF FORMER ASSOCIATES IN MURDER SUCH AS ABE "KID TWIST" RELES AND MAX RUBIN. FOLLOWING EXTENSIVE LEGAL MANEUVERS, LEPKE WAS ELECTROCUTED, ALONG WITH TWO OF HIS LIEUTENANTS, MENDY WEISS AND LOUIS CAPONE, IN SING SING PRISON 3/4/44 AT AGE 47.

From sneak thief to criminal empire builder, Louis Lepke Buchalter, more than any other single man, was responsible for the establishment of the national crime syndicate. In 1913, when he was first arrested for robbing pushcarts on Manhattan's Lower East Side, Lepke was so miserably poor that policemen who caught him found that he was wearing stolen shoes—both for the left foot. In twenty years, the same man was netting close to $50 million a year as total czar of New York's industrial and business rackets, kingpin of narcotics smuggling, and head of the most deadliest organization ever known in America—Murder, Inc.

His rise was attributable to two characteristics basic to Lepke's nature: patience and intelligent planning. The rest was all muscle and money.

The bantam-weight Lepke met another sneak thief, hulking marbled-mouth Jacob Shapiro, when they both attempted to rob the same pushcart one day in 1914. Shapiro was known in the neighborhood as "Gurrah." His favorite expression was "get out of here," but once the words escaped his tongue the line sounded more like "gurrah."

It was a perfect union. Lepke needed Gurrah's ape-like strength to enforce his petty rackets; Gurrah needed Lepke's brain. The two began to organize their own protection racket, forcing pushcart peddlers and small store owners to pay weekly tribute to them or suffer arson, slashings, and even death.

Lepke and Gurrah came to the attention of a hoodlum on the rise, Jacob "Little Augie" Orgen. He recruited them for his Lower East Side gang, allowing them to independently continue their own pushcart racket. The gang was an ethnic hodge-podge of young Irish, Italian, and Jewish mobsters. Each of them had their own criminal practices but worked under Little Augie's banner to establish a city-wide extortion ring in the garment industry. Charles "Lucky" Luciano was a member of this group. So were Waxey Gorden and the terrible Diamond brothers, Eddie and Jack, better known as "Legs."

Their plan was simple enough. Terrorize local unions—through beatings and a few exemplary murders—into turning over stewardship to the gang, and then raking in kickbacks from dues-paying members. Next, employers would be extorted of huge sums to prevent the gang-controlled union members from striking.

Orgen labored long in the vineyards of the garment industry, disposing of one gang after another that attempted to encroach on his territory. When he finally eliminated his arch rival, Nathan "Kid Dropper" Kaplan in 1923, the lucrative racket was all his . . . for three years. While getting into a cab with his partner and bodyguard, Legs Diamond, on October 15, 1926, Little Augie met with unexpected fate. The cabdriver was Gurrah Shapiro; the man crouched low in the back seat holding a machinegun was Lepke. As soon as Little Augie opened the hack's door a heavy spray of .45 caliber shells cut him down, wounding Diamond.

After that, Lepke's rise in the industrial rackets was unopposed. He took over the cutter's union in 1927. This union was at the very core of the garment industry, numbering only 1,900 men. Without the cutters, men's suits could not be made in the entire city of New York. Work for more than 50,000 men would halt. Profits amounting to millions of dollars a month would cease. The garment people paid off and joined Lepke's unions.

Shrewd Lepke began to build up his own strike force of gunmen, divorcing from other mobs mostly Jewish gangsters who remained loyal to him. Killers like Mendy Weiss, Curly Holtz, Danny Fields, and Paul Berger were his emissaries sent to muscle other unions.

Their influence and extortion reached to the very heart of the powerful Amalgamated Clothing Workers Union numbering close to 400,000 members then, representing dozens of smaller unions, and captained by much-honored Sidney Hillman.

Next Lepke moved into the truckers' unions (not then affiliated with the Teamsters) hauling machinery, furs, and baked goods. He took over the Motion Pictures Operators union. With his good friend, Lucky Luciano, Lepke financed wholesale liquor smuggling during Prohibition and, following Repeal, he funded the largest dope-smuggling ring in the world (he received a third of all profits; Luciano controlled all drug traffic once shipments were delivered inside the U.S.).

To enforce his giant criminal industries, Lepke built the largest force of sluggers and killers in the underworld. His Manhattan complement alone numbered 250 top gunsels. Some of these were not content with their average $30-40,000-a-year income. Danny Fields, making $250,000 a year as one of Lepke's contact men with unions, talked too much. He was shot to death. Curly Holtz, who was Lepke's narcotics buyer in foreign markets, traveled regularly to Europe to purchase heroin. The mobster carried tens of thousands of dollars with him each trip. It was Holtz and Yasha Katzenburg, known as "King of the Smugglers," who, in four days, brought in six quick shipments of morphine and heroin from China worth more than $10 million.

Curly became greed-struck once and sent back only a partial shipment of heroin to New York, pocketing the bulk of the purchase money. He attempted to cover up his theft by having the heroin appropriated after tipping customs officials to the shipment, but Curly was caught. Mr. Holtz was stabbed to death and dumped in the East River, where he still resides.

Lepke, by 1932, had joined forces with Luciano in the establishment of a national crime syndicate. As a member of the board of directors, Lepke was called "Judge Louis." He sat in on every major decision that came before the board. Other members included Abner "Longy" Zwillman who controlled New Jersey's rackets, Meyer Lansky of the Bug & Meyer mob (his partner being the infamous Benjamin "Bugsy" Siegel) who controlled Philadelphia rackets and certain strong-arm duties in New York, elder criminal statesman Johnny Torrio, who had given up his mob leadership in Chicago but who still had powerful interests there, Frank Costello, Joe Adonis, Albert Anastasia, and Gurrah.

During the board's summit meetings—the Mafia was then only a faction of the crime cartel—Lepke was the most verbal member, as well as its most wealthy sponsor. Luciano listened while Lepke talked. They saw eye to eye on almost everything, particularly on keeping away from each other's interests.

It was Lepke's decision (of which the board approved) to murder Dutch Schultz in 1935 when the Dutchman (also an early member) insisted that New York's District Attorney Thomas Dewey, then zeroing in on Schultz's numbers rackets in Harlem, be killed.

Coolly, Lepke tried to talk the Dutchman out of his wild plan to kill Dewey, explaining that if Dewey unearthed too much evidence against him, he could still "go anywhere. You kill him and it will be too hot for you to be anywhere. And then it will be our turn."

"The son-of-a-bitch has got to be hit!" the Dutchman screamed. "If you won't go with me on this, I'll do it myself!" He stalked out of the meeting. Dutch Schultz was never a man to court tolerance. Moments after Schultz left the summit meeting, Lepke rose and calmly stated: "I move we take steps to protect Dewey's life."

Schultz and three henchman were killed in a New Jersey chop house days later by one of Lepke's top killers, Charlie "The Bug" Workman. Lepke's move to save Dewey's life proved to be ironic in that the District Attorney, working with Brooklyn authorities, became the man who guaranteed Lepke's appointment with the electric chair.

Lepke's army of killers became top heavy in his overall organization by 1933. It was then that he proposed to the syndicate board that the cream of his enforcers, those professional "hit" men under the commands of Albert Anastasia in Brooklyn and Louis Capone (no relation to Chicago's Scarface Al) and Abe "Kid Twist" Reles in Brownsville, become the organization's national enforcement arm. Bluntly, Judge Louis stated that these men could be sent anywhere in the U.S. to kill any and all who opposed the syndicate's edicts. As a sideline, to keep the killer troops in shape and money, he outlined a new business, an enterprise so gruesome that even the Borgias would have flinched at the thought of it. Murder for profit. Anyone who had been cleared by the syndicate officers as being "safe" could order anyone else (except syndicate members) to be killed for a price.

Luciano, the most influential member on the board of directors next to Lepke, liked the plan and approved. Murder, Inc. was born.

Lepke's millions kept him out of trouble until 1933. He and Gurrah were then indicted and convicted, along with 158 others, of violating anti-trust laws. The unholy twosome were fined $1,000 each and sentenced to a year in jail. Presiding Federal Judge John Knox complained that the sentence was merely a "slap on the wrist. But that's the maximum for these violations."

Though denied bail, Lepke and Gurrah were on the streets in two weeks. U.S. Circuit Court of Appeals Judge Martin T. Manton reviewed the case and allowed bail. He then reversed Lepke's conviction. Manton's decision was not a surprise to insiders. For years he had been handing down decisions that favored gangsters, including bootlegger Big Bill Dwyer and Frank Costello, soon to become the syndicate's "prime minister."

By 1937, Lepke's criminal empire became so vast that controlling it was a serious problem. Basically, he was overstaffed with killers and hoodlums and some, to save their own hides after doing Lepke's dirty work, began talking. His narcotics smuggling rings cracked. His union organizations began to crumble.

New York police made it unbearable for Lepke. His phones were tapped. He was followed everywhere. For a while the arch killer played cat-and-mouse with his pursuers. He met his henchmen in hotel and building lobbies, giving his orders in terse, hurried sentences. They met on subway platforms and in the washrooms of cheap restaurants. It was not befitting a crime czar's conduct.

Lepke complained to Paul Berger, one of his labor organizers, that he was getting tired of "sneaking away from the cops . . . I lose them . . . mostly in the subway." Midsummer came to Manhattan and there was no relief in sight for Lepke; the police hounded him mercilessly. They were ruining his business.

"Things are getting too hot here," Lepke whispered to Berger in the lobby of the Flat-iron Building one day. "I'll have to lam. Be careful."

Then he disappeared. Anastasia, Louis Capone, and Kid Twist Reles put him up in a secret apartment specially built above the Oriental Palace, a cheap dance hall in Brooklyn. From there, Lepke issued dozens of murder "contracts" for those he suspected might talk about his activities.

He moved about regularly, under the very eyes of New York Police. In a year, Lepke's dope-smuggling ring was exposed and federal warrants were issued for his arrest. There was a $50,000 price tag placed on his head. Lepke moved into an apartment (also specially equipped with secret panels and hidden rooms) in Flatbush, living with the widow of slain gangster Fatty Walker, a man whom he had personally ordered killed. Mrs. Dorothy Walker became his cover.

Thomas "Three-Fingered Brown" Lucchese, an important Mafia member and close ally of Luciano's, wanted in on Lepke's garment rackets, now that the kingpin was on the run. When Judge Louis discovered this, he exploded. "Nobody moved in on me when I was on the outside and nobody is gonna do it just because I'm on the lam," he shouted at Anastasia and Reles. "You tell Lucky and Brown that the clothing thing is mine. There is no argument."

There wasn't. Luciano and Brown backed away. Lepke, through Anastasia and Meyer Lansky, still controlled Murder, Inc., a force so formidable that it prevented opposition to Lepke's rackets by any syndicate director.

But even that group of dedicated killers who had murdered so ardently for their chief deserted Lepke one by one. Reles, finally apprehended for an old murder, cracked first and involved Lepke in several killings. Then Max Rubin, an old labor slammer, implicated Lepke, Mendy Weiss, and Louis Capone in the murder of one Joseph Rosen.

By that time Lepke had surrendered to the FBI and was comfortably doing a fourteen-year sentence in Leavenworth on a narcotics conviction. He was brought out for trial and sentenced to death in Sing Sing for the Rosen murder.

But Lepke's influence and resources were still powerful and he successfully fought off the sentence for four years. It wasn't until

1944 when federal authorities turned Judge Louis over to the State of New York for execution.

While awaiting the death sentence in Sing Sing's dance hall, Lepke continued to issue death sentences to all those who had betrayed him. Reles conveniently went out of a window in a Coney Island hotel where he was being guarded. Moey Wolinsky, alias "Dimples," had advised Lepke to surrender to Hoover in 1939, passing down the decree of the syndicate's board members (Gurrah and Anastasia were the only dissenting members). Wolinsky, Lepke realized, had double-crossed him. Dimples had stated that the fix was in. The federal government would imprison him for narcotics offenses and he would never be turned over to New York authorities to stand trial for the Rosen murder, Dimples told him. Wolinsky was shot to pieces in a mid-Manhattan restaurant in 1943. As expected, Lucchese took over Lepke's garment rackets and Charlie Lucky got a piece, even though he himself was then in prison.

Last appeals for commutation of Lepke's death sentence were used up in March, 1944. Lepke and his two loyal killers, Louis Capone and Mendy Weiss were all scheduled to die on March 2, 1944. The three were placed in separate cells only 25 feet from the electric chair. Mendy and Capone were nervous, anxiously asking the boss what he was going to do.

Lepke whispered that he still had the fix in. Only hours before the trio was to be executed, Lepke confidently stated: "Something can happen yet. I can feel it."

His killers nodded. They were obedient down to the last meal. Lepke ordered roast chicken, shoestring potatoes and a salad. "I'll have the same," both Mendy and Capone echoed.

An hour before Lepke was to walk to the chair, his "something" happened. He was granted a 48-hour stay of execution while his lawyers made a final appeal for the condemned trio.

But it was for only forty-eight hours. Warden William E. Snyder of Sing Sing came to the three men on March 4, a Saturday night. This time there would be no stay. At 11:02 p.m. Louis Capone was led into the death chamber and, without comment, meekly sat

Louis "Lepke" Buchalter, head of Murder, Inc., on trial in 1941; he went to the electric chair three years later. (UPI)

down in the electric chair. He was pronounced dead three minutes later. Mendy Weiss was next. The giant gangster walked heavily to the chair chewing a thick wad of gum.

"Can I say something?" he asked Warden Snyder as the electrodes were being clamped onto his legs. Snyder nodded. Mendy stared at the newspapermen present. "All I want to say is I'm innocent. I'm here on a framed-up case. Give my love to my family and everything." He was dead inside of two minutes.

Lepke, still the boss, came last. As the small figure of the crime czar appeared in the death chamber the newsmen began to scribble furiously. He said nothing. He walked quickly to the electric chair and, in one last act of defiance, wheeled about sharply and fairly threw himself into it.

The muscles of his jaw worked slightly and his eyes rolled up to see the head electrode descend upon him. There would be no more miracles to save Louis Lepke Buchalter.

Snyder dropped his hand and the unseen executioner pulled the switch that sent 2,200 volts of electricity into the most ruthless criminal of the Twentieth Century, the only ranking member of the national crime syndicate ever to be executed.

The newsmen stared, astonished, as the prison doctor approached the lifeless 165-pound body, pronouncing it dead. It seemed incredible. Nobody expected Lepke to die; he was too big, too powerful, too wealthy, too omnipotent to kill. But he was there, dead in the chair.

Reporter Frank Coniff accorded the crime king a terse, horrible obituary: "You look at the face and cannot tear your eyes away. Sweat beads his forehead. Saliva drools from the corner of his lips. The face is discolored. It is not a pretty sight."

[ALSO SEE Charles Lucky Luciano, Murder, Inc., Dutch Schultz, The Syndicate.]

BUCK GANG

Rufus Buck and the four young men who followed him into a thirteen-day nightmare of murder and rape were illiterate part Creek Indians who suddenly and inexplicably rose against the law in the old Indian territory of Arkansas-Oklahoma on July 28, 1895.

The outrages committed by the five youths (the others included Luckey Davis, Lewis Davis, Maomi July, and Sam Sampson) were sporadic and unthinking. First, the five turned their rifles on a deputy who was looking at them suspiciously and shot him to death. Then, between Muskogee and Fort Smith, Ark.,

They were hanged high—The Rufus Buck gang in captivity on 7/1/96 before members went to the gallows at Fort Smith, Ark. for murder, robbery, and rape (left to right): Maomi July, Sam Sampson, Rufus Buck, Lucky Davis, and Louis Davis. (Western History Collection, U. of Okla. Library)

the band held up ranchers and small store owners with lightning speed. Coming upon a widow named Wilson driving to town in her wagon, the gang raped her. Next they invaded the Hassan Farm and put the farmer under guard while they took his wife, Rosetta into the bedroom.

The woman begged the boys not to part her from her children. Luckey Davis only snorted: "You'll have to go with me," and pointed to the bedroom, threatening her that if she did not comply, they would "throw the goddamn brats into the creek."

The next day they held up a drummer named Callahan and shot in the back a Negro boy who worked for him. The boy died instantly. A giant posse aided by a company of Creek Indian police surrounded the gang in a cave and, following a gun battle, took them into custody, August 10, 1895.

Their fate was already sealed by the time they appeared before Judge Isaac Parker in Fort Smith. Parker, known as the "hanging judge," appointed five attorneys to defend them. In a whirlwind trial, all of the members of the Buck Gang were found guilty and sentenced to hang.

The words uttered by defense attorney William Cravens were lame-dog terse: "You have heard the evidence and I have nothing to say."

Neither did Rufus Buck or any member of his gang and they were led, one by one, to the gallows and hanged. A warden found a picture of Buck's mother on the wall of his cell after the execution. The bandit had written a poem (entitled "My Dream") on the back of the picture which read:

I dreamt I was in Heaven
Among the Angels fair;
I'd ne'er seen none so handsome,
That twine in golden hair.
They look so neat and sang so sweet
And played the Golden Harp.
I was about to pick an angel out
And take her to my heart:
But the moment I began to plea,
I thought of you, my love.
There was none I'd ever seen so beautiful
On earth or Heaven above,
Goodbye my dear wife and Mother.
Also my sister.

BULLOCK, DAVID
Murderer ● (1960-   )

Manhattan street hustler and male prostitute David Bullock killed six people in late 1981, all during robberies. He killed without compunction or remorse. He shot and killed 42-year-old actor James Weber, stole his wallet, and left the body in Central Park. Two weeks later, on December 22, 1981, Bullock slew Herberto Morales. When Bullock was tried for this killing and five others, he told Justice Burton Roberts that the murders made him happy.

Following his plea of guilty, Bullock was given six consecutive sentences of 25 years to life by Justice Roberts, who added from the bench: "You are going to die in prison and then go before the Supreme Judge of us all and let Him impose whatever additional sentence He feels you so rightfully deserve."

BUNCH, EUGENE
Trainrobber ● (? -1889)

An obscure country school teacher, Eugene Bunch decided to better his lot in 1888; he began to rob trains in Louisiana, Mississippi, and Texas. Always the Southern gentleman, Bunch introduced himself to his victims as "Captain Gerald," and spoke in a soft, melodious voice when demanding express car guards to open their safes or have their "brains blown out."

He is credited with robbing at least six trains for a total of $18,000. His biggest haul came in November, 1888, when he took $10,000 from the New Orleans Flyer.

After a brief spell of the "straight" life (he edited a newspaper in Dallas, Texas for six months) and a quick love affair with the daughter of a former governor of the Lone Star State, Bunch was off to Mississippi, where he recruited a gang of toughs and resumed robbing trains.

Pinkerton and train detectives trailed the Bunch gang to Jefferson County, Mississippi in 1889, and trapped them on a small island in the swamps. Bunch and two others were killed in a gunfight with the posse.

BUNDY, THEODORE
Serial Killer ● (1947-1989)

BACKGROUND: EDUCATED AT STANFORD UNIVERSITY, GRADUATED 1972 WITH A BACHELOR OF SCIENCE DEGREE, WORKED AS ASST. DIRECTOR OF THE SEATTLE, WASH., CRIME COMMISSION. ALIASES: CHRIS HAGEN. RECORD: KNOWN MURDERS INCLUDE LYNDA ANN HEALY, 21, 2/1/74; DONNA GAIL MANSON, 19, 3/12/74; SUSAN RANCOURT, 18, 4/17/74; ROBERTA KATHLEEN PARKS, 22, 5/6/74; BRENDA BALL, 22, 6/1/74; GEORGEANN HAWKINS, 18, 6/11/74; JANICE OTT, 23, 7/14/74; DENISE NASLUND, 19, 7/14/74; CAROL VALENZUELA, 20, 8/2/74; NANCY WILCOX, 16, 10/2/74; MELISSA SMITH, 17, 10/18/74; LAURIE AIMEE, 17, 10/31/74; DEBBIE KENT, 17, 11/8/74; CARYN CAMPBELL, 23, 1/12/75; JULIE CUNNINGHAM, 26, 3/15/75; DENISE OLIVERSON, 25, 4/6/75; LISA LEVY, 20, 1/15/78; MARGARET BOWMAN, 21, 1/15/78; KIMBERLY LEACH, 12, 2/9/78. ARRESTED IN 1979, CONVICTED OF THE LEVY AND BOWMAN KILLINGS AND, AFTER TEN YEARS OF APPEALS, EXECUTED IN FLORIDA'S ELECTRIC CHAIR ON 1/24/89.

A charming, handsome, well-educated man, Theodore Bundy was the most unlikely serial killer in America, or so he seemed to be. A brilliant student, Bundy attended Stanford University where he received a scholarship in Chinese studies. He received his B.S. in 1972 and—in a grimly ironic twist, in light of the heinous crimes he was to commit—got a job as assistant director of the Crime Commission in Seattle, Washington.

Crime and its commissions preoccupied Bundy from an early age. He considered himself more than an amateur psychologist and criminologist. He claimed to understand the dark side of man's nature but, perhaps, he was only probing his own innermost cravings to commit capital offenses and, given his arrogant posture and supreme self-confidence, get away with such crimes.

Bundy lived alone and was seldom, if ever, seen to regularly date women. His preference in females could later easily be determined, as most of his victims bear a striking similarity in appearance. Almost all of them had long, straight, black hair, parted in the middle. Their eyebrows were slightly arched, their lips full, their faces oblong. Most were in their late teens to their early twenties.

A glib talker, Bundy easily established a friendly rapport with strangers. He had a quick wit and his sense of humor was infectious. Women found him attractive, too much so, and many of those females became the victims of Bundy's hidden violence. The year 1974 marked the beginning of Bundy's murderous rampage. The first to feel Bundy's rage was Sharon Clarke of Seattle. She was attacked as she slept in her bed. Someone entered her bedroom and struck her repeatedly with a heavy metal rod. Her skull was crushed and she could tell police nothing about the attacker. The rod, bearing no fingerprints, was left in the room, a useless clue.

On January 31, 1974, Lynda Ann Healy, who lived only a few blocks from Clarke, and attended the University of Washington, vanished from her rented room. Similar disappearances began. On March 4, 1974, Donna Gail Manson, a student at Evergreen College in Olympia, Wash., vanished en route to a concert. On April 17, Susan Rancourt, who attended Washington State, went to see a foreign film in Ellensburg and utterly disappeared.

In Corvallis, on the night of May 6, Oregon State University student, Roberta Kathleen Parks, went out for a walk and never came back. On June 1, Brenda Ball left the Flame Tavern near the Seattle Airport on the arm of an unknown man and she, too, vanished. On the evening of June 11, Georgeann Hawkins left her boyfriend and began walking back to her sorority house at the University of Washington. She never arrived.

In Lake Sammanish, Wash., a number of attractive young women were approached by a handsome stranger with his arm in a sling on July 14. He asked them to help him load a small sailboat on top of his Volkswagen. He gave his name as Ted. One woman agreed to help him but when he told her they had to drive to the top of a hill to get the boat, she refused. So did several others. Janice Ott agreed to help and vanished. So did a few other females, including Denise Naslund. She, too, disappeared.

Not until September 7, 1974, were Ott and Naslund found. Two hunters stumbled over their bodies, as well as another female corpse that remains unidentified. The women had been raped and killed and their badly decomposed bodies were in pieces, as if wild animals had been at them.

Police fanned out through the state of Washington, realizing that they were looking for a devastat-

ing serial killer. Women all over the state gave reports of being stopped by a handsome young man wearing an arm sling. One woman said that when she told the young man she would not get into his car, he nonchalantly removed an uninjured arm from the arm sling, then drove off using both hands on the steering wheel. Another woman said she had to walk on a neighbor's lawn to avoid the Volkswagen the same young man had driven onto the sidewalk to block her path.

The badly decomposed corpse of Carol Valenzuela, who had vanished some months earlier, was then found in northern Washington, as was the remains of an unidentifiable female. Thousands of leads were followed and several suspects arrested, then released. Officials were baffled. The disappearances and murders in Washington ceased.

Then young college women in Utah began to disappear, their bodies later discovered. On October 2, Nancy Wilcox vanished. On October 18, Melissa Smith, daughter of the chief of police in Midvale, Utah, vanished. On October 27, Smith's raped and strangled body was discovered in the Wassatch Mountains, east of Salt Lake City. Laura Aimee of Orem, Utah, went to a Halloween party on the night of October 31, and disappeared.

Carol DeRonch was leaving a Salt Lake City shopping mall on November 8, 1974, when a young man approached her, explaining that he was a police detective and that he was verifying a license plate of a car someone had tried to break into. DeRonch accompanied the man to her car, which was undisturbed. The man insisted that she accompany him to police headquarters to finish his report and she got into his Volkswagen.

The man suddenly stopped the car and placed a handcuff on DeRonch's wrist. She screamed and the man jerked a gun from his pocket and jammed it to her head, ordering her to be quiet. DeRonch was not, however, the kind of submissive female Ted Bundy had accosted and murdered in recent months. She was a fighter.

DeRonch opened the car door and jumped out, running down a street, Bundy running after her with a crowbar in his hand. He caught up with her and swung the weapon downward at her skull, but DeRonch caught the crowbar in mid-air and struggled with Bundy. She saw a car coming and leaped in front of it. When it stopped, she jumped inside and the car drove off. Bundy ran after it, then gave up.

Young women throughout the Salt Lake City area kept on vanishing, then three young women in Colorado disappeared and their bodies were later discovered. All had been sexually attacked before being killed. Police intensified their search for the killer and, on August 16, 1975, they found Ted Bundy. He was driving his Volkswagen slowly down a street, inspecting homes carefully. A police car followed him, officers aware that a rash of burglaries had been committed in the area. They suspected the driver of the Volkswagen as being the burglar.

When the officers signaled for Bundy to pull over, he sped up and a chase ensued. His car was curbed and Bundy was arrested. He informed police that he was studying law in Salt Lake City, lived in Seattle, and had high political influence in Washington. A search of his room found nothing incriminating except new maps of Colorado, especially of the areas where three young women had been abducted and murdered. A hair was found in Bundy's car that matched that of Midvale, Utah, victim Melissa Smith.

Bundy was taken to Aspen, Colorado, however, where he was charged with killing the Colorado victims. He quickly charmed his guards into allowing him the freedom of the local law library. Once in the library, he merely opened a window, dropped twenty feet to the ground and escaped. It took police eight days to locate him in the wilds of Smuggler's Mountain. He was returned to Aspen where he was closely guarded.

Bundy claimed that he was a victim of circumstance, that he merely happened to be in the areas where the women were killed. He would defend himself and prove his own innocence, he pronounced. Meanwhile, Bundy somehow obtained a hacksaw and, on the night of December 30, 1977, he escaped from his jail cell and fled. He moved to Chicago, then Ann Arbor, Michigan, then Atlanta, finally going to Tallahassee, Florida.

Bundy took a room in a boarding house close to the sorority houses of Florida State University. On January 15, 1978, Bundy broke into a sorority house where he raped Margaret Bowman and Lisa Levy. He strangled Bowman with her own pantyhose. When found, Levy was still alive but her head had been so thoroughly crushed by the killer that she died in the ambulance rushing her to a hospital.

On February 9, 1979, twelve-year-old Kimberly Leach left her classroom in Jacksonville and vanished. A few days later Bundy left his Tallahassee room where he owed back rent, stole an orange Volkswagen, and drove to Pensacola where a policeman stopped him to check the car's license

Doomed serial killer Ted Bundy, formerly on the FBI's ten most wanted list, at the time of his arrest in July 1978. (AP/Wide World)

plates. Bundy bolted but the officer tackled him. At first Bundy told police that his name was Chris Hagen and that he was a student living in Tallahassee. Then he admitted he was really Ted Bundy and was wanted in Colorado on murder charges.

The body of Kimberly Leach was then found. She had been raped and strangled. Bundy refused to admit killing her or anyone else. He strutted about his cell, vain, arrogant, and insisting he was innocent. On April 27, 1979, police experts entered his cell and told Bundy that they were going to take a wax impression of his teeth. The killer went berserk, striking out, kicking, screaming. He knew what would happen next. It did.

After forcefully taking an impression of Bundy's teeth, the experts matched it perfectly to bite marks found on the buttocks of Lisa Levy, one of the strangest but most convincing pieces of evidence ever introduced in a murder trial. Though Bundy defended himself convincingly, he could not overcome the teeth marks and other evidence brought against him. He was convicted of murdering Lisa

Levy and condemned to death. He was also convicted and condemned for killing the Leach girl.

Bundy, who had once said to guards that "I feel like a vampire," then went to work filing appeal after appeal. He was the subject of several books that glamorized his so-called "intellectual thought process," and his "psychological makeup." For eleven years, Bundy successfully fought off electrocution but he finally exhausted all his appeals. On January 24, 1989, with a large crowd assembled outside the Florida State Prison to cheer his end, Theodore "Ted" Bundy sat down in the electric chair. More than 2,000 volts of electricity was sent into his body, ending his life.

When the crowd learned Bundy was dead, they applauded and waved signs that read "Buckle Up Bundy," and "Roast in Peace!" One person in the crowd told a reporter: "I waited eleven years to see that creep fry."

BURKE, ELMER ("TRIGGER")
Professional Killer ● (1917-1958)

The youngest of six children, Burke grew up in New York's Hell's Kitchen, raised by his older crime-prone brother Charlie following the deaths of his parents. Elmer was not a bright lad and obediently followed his older brother's orders, which included committing petty robberies and secreting guns for older mobsters on the run from police.

Burke was sent to Elmira Reformatory in 1941 after being caught breaking into the same grocery store for a third time. At his brother's suggestion, Elmer volunteered for army duty to escape Elmira and was accepted into a ranger battalion.

At the invasion of Anzio, Italy in 1943, Burke, cradling a Thompson submachinegun, his favorite weapon, advanced across an open field firing steadily as he went at a well-entrenched German machinegun nest. He killed eight Nazis. When his commanding officer ran up to him, he found Burke still riddling the dead bodies.

"All right, soldier," the lieutenant said. "Enough. Those bastards are dead."

"You're goddamn right they are," Elmer Burke said and walked off.

After being mustered out of the army, Burke returned to his old Manhattan haunts, pulling a number of small stick-ups in the late 1940s. Proficient with a machinegun, he became a free-lance killer for various mobs and soon earned the nickname "Trigger."

Burke robbed a liquor store in 1946 and strolled out to the street holding the money in one hand and a loaded pistol in the other. A passing patrolman walked up to him and arrested Trigger as he was counting his loot. Burke was sent to Sing Sing for two years.

While Burke did time, rival gunmen shot and killed his brother Charlie. Trigger swore revenge. Though he had no clues to the killers, he finally settled (without proof) on a hoodlum named George Goll. Upon release, Burke hunted Goll through the Manhattan streets and found him on the night of February 24, 1953, at which time he shot two bullets into the back of Goll's head.

Burke's was a savage reputation; he became one of the most sought-after professional killers in gangland, his standard fee for murder fixed at $1,000. Sometimes the job would be free, as in the case of Edward "Poochy" Walsh, a bartender who aggravated Trigger's sensitive pride.

Burke had an argument in Walsh's saloon one evening with an associate, Joseph "Jumbo"' Lancia. Trigger knocked Lancia to the floor and kicked him several times.

"You should punch him, Elmer," Walsh reprimanded the gangster, "but you had no call to go stomping him all over the floor."

Burke glared at Walsh for a moment and then left the bar. Within minutes he returned, shoved an automatic into Walsh's face and said: "Poochy, you shouldn't have interfered." He fired three shots into Walsh at point blank range and the bartender was dead before he fell.

On June 10, 1954, Trigger Burke got orders from the mob which engineered the $1,219,000 Brinks robbery in Boston, and went hunting Joseph "Specs" O'Keefe. Burke's employers were fearful that O'Keefe, a wayward member of their mob, was going to inform police of details and personnel; they ordered him killed.

In a wild shoot-out in and about the streets of Boston's Dorchester housing project area, Burke, unleashing burst after burst at his quarry, succeeded only in wounding O'Keefe in the arm and chest.

O'Keefe escaped down a darkened street, leaving a trail of blood. Burke, thinking he had killed his man, calmly dismantled his machine-gun, carefully placed it in a small traveling case, and walked out of the area past dozens of wailing squad cars. "Those coppers looked pretty stupid," he later commented. Police learned from O'Keefe, found near death in a rooming house, that they were looking for the notorious Trigger Burke.

Patrolman Frank Crawford stopped a suspicious-looking man eight days later and asked him his name.

The tough-looking character stared stonily at him and said, "Elmer Burke."

"Oh, my God," Crawford said and went for his gun. Burke never moved a muscle. Trembling, Crawford held Burke at gunpoint next to a wall and unzipped a handbag the gangster had been carrying. He found a submachine-gun in three sections inside the bag.

In custody at the Back Bay police station, Trigger Burke gladly gave interviews to the press. As he strutted in his cell, Burke chest-thumped his career for reporter Don Hogan.

Hogan reminded the gunman that ninety shots had been fired from his machinegun when he sprayed the street in his attempt to kill Specs O'Keefe, and that one of these bullets missed a child's crib by inches. "You damned near killed a baby, Elmer," Hogan told Burke.

"Christ," he said, "if Trigger Burke had killed a baby, no cops would have to catch him. He would have turned himself in. You're sure the kid's okay, huh?"

Burke, who disliked being called Elmer, insisted Hogan address him as Trigger. Whenever the newsman touched upon Burke's sinister background, the killer would squint and say, always referring to himself in the third person: "Trigger doesn't like that."

"Look," the gunman concluded, "you can talk to Trigger about baseball and things like that and Trigger will talk about baseball. But don't bother him none about professional matters."

The next day Burke was moved to the ancient Charles Street Jail, from which he quickly escaped with the help of two gunmen who sawed away the bars of an old door leading to the street.

Elmer "Trigger" Burke in custody, 1955; he loved machine-guns. (UPI)

A year later Burke was arrested by FBI agents who cornered him on a Charleston, S. C. street as he waited for a bus. He was unarmed and offered no resistance.

He was extradited to New York to stand trial for the Walsh slaying. Burke, who wanted to be returned to Massachusetts (where he was wanted for carrying a machinegun and knew he would receive a much lighter sentence) complained bitterly at his extradition hearing. "It ain't fair," he told the judge. "My reputation is being used against me."

Trigger was convicted of killing Walsh and sentenced to death in the electric chair. On death row, he admitted nothing except that he was the sensation of the underworld.

Appeals took up more than two years time, at the end of which Burke was told he would be executed on January 9, 1958. He went wordlessly to the chair at 11 p.m. that night, after a giant steak dinner and six cigars. Before walking the last mile, Elmer "Trigger" Burke told the warden to preserve the 144 different newspaper clippings dealing with his zany exploits . . . "for history's sake."

BURROW GANG

For many years Alabama-born Reuben Houston Burrow was a tiller of the soil in Arkansas where he lived on a small farm with a wife and two children. In 1887, Rube Burrow decided to change all that and take his chances with the gun. Collecting his brother Jim and the neighboring Brock brothers, W. L. and Leonard (already a wanted felon who traveled under the alias of Waldrip), Rube led the gang in their first holdup outside of Genoa Station, Ark., December 9, 1887. They boarded the St. Louis, Arkansas, and Texas R.R. bound north for St. Louis, and forced the Southern Express Company messenger to open the safe. They took $3,500.

The gang next struck near Bellevue, Tex., where the bandits stopped a train in early January, 1888, forced open the Fort Worth and Denver Express car, and looted the safe. While Jim Burrow held the express guard at bay, Rube and the Brock brothers ambled through the passenger cars scooping up wallets and watches at gunpoint; the total take was $3,000.

Weeks later, the same gang stopped a Texas and Pacific express train and got $2,000. One of the bandits left behind a brand new black raincoat which the Pinkertons traced to a Burrow confederate. For months, the detectives raced after the fast-moving Burrow gang and finally caught up with them in a mountainous retreat near Nashville, Tenn. Jim Burrow and the Brock brothers were captured, but Rube shot his way to freedom.

Pacing in his cell, Jim Burrow growled to reporters: "Give us Burrows a gun apiece and we will not be afraid of any man alive." But Jim never got his hands on another gun and died of consumption within a year inside the jail at Little Rock, Ark.

For a short while his brother became the subject of a desperate manhunt. Hundreds of detectives and possemen searched the Southern wilds for him. Elaborate "Wanted" posters in which every minute habit of Rube Burrow was detailed were printed up and distributed by the thousands.

The Pinkerton Detective Agency outdid itself with their own flyer on Burrow:

"REUBEN HOUSTON BURROW is about 32 years of age, 6 feet in height, weighs about 160 pounds, blue eyes which do not look a person full in the face, round head, wears 7 1/4 hat, full forehead, face broad under the ears but thin near the mouth, short, inclined to pug-shaped nose, swarthy or sandy complexion, light sandy hair, thin light moustache, uses Hair Vigor to darken hair; left arm is a little shorter than the right, caused by having been broken at bend of arm; rather a lounging gait, carrying his hands in his pockets in a leisurely way.

"Usually wears dark clothes and woolen shirts, a No. 8 boot, but no jewelry. Does not use tobacco; drinks, but not to excess; does not gamble, but can play the game of seven-up; is somewhat of a country story teller, relating stories of snake, dog and cat fights, etc. . . . ."

In 1890, Rube Burrow, alone, robbed another train. As he strolled away from the train to his horse, gingerly swinging a sackful of loot and whistling, a wily detective for the Southern Express Company blew off his head with a shotgun.

Trainrobbers Rube and Jim Burrow

CAMORRA, THE

A criminal organization that dated back to the Bourbons, the Camorra was inaugurated about 1417 in Spain and was imported to Naples and some parts of Sicily a few years later by the conquering French. This secret brotherhood flourished in Southern Italy and became over the years a Neapolitan organization. Unlike its Sicilian counter-group, the Mafia, the Camorra did not begin as a high-minded nationalistic movement.

The brotherhood was strictly an organization of thieves and cutthroats who hired out to murder and rob, particularly for their reluctant sponsors, the Bourbons. Political assassination was the brotherhood's specialty for centuries.

The Camorra became so powerful in Naples at one time that it virtually controlled the government and recruited young apprentice Camorristi from the best Neapolitan families. These young men, taught the ways of murder and robbery, considered membership an honor.

By 1907, the brotherhood was so powerful that only King Victor Emmanuel II could stamp out its influence—and then only by massive, wholesale arrests. Thousands of Camorristi were thrown into jail. The brotherhood responded by murdering dozens of prominent politicians and Neapolitan citizens opposed to its existence. Those in prison merely took over the jails.

The Italian Government led troops of armed men against the Camorra strongholds, fighting pitched battles. The pressure to rid Southern Italy of the brotherhood became so intense that by 1910 most of the Camorra's leaders had fled to America, where through Black Hand rackets they preyed upon fellow Italian immigrants.

There existed an historically intense hatred between the Camorra and the Mafia, inspired by nothing more than attempts at supremacy in their field. Both factions periodically indulged in bloody warfare. In the U.S., particularly within New York City, the Camorra and Mafia battled openly on the streets. One of the most prominent Camorristas in New York was Alessandro Vollero, who was convicted of murder in 1918 (he killed a Mafia lieutenant).

At Vollero's trial, a gang member testified that he and other members of Vollero's Camorra mob were obligated to give as their standard toast the words: "Health to all Neapolitans and death and destruction to all Sicilians!"

Vollero, who was sent to Sing Sing for life, had in the mid-1920s as his cell mate future informer Joseph Valachi. The old "don" told Valachi "if there is one thing that we who are from Naples must always remember, it is that if you hang out with a Sicilian for twenty years and you have trouble with another Sicilian, the Sicilian that you hung out with all that time will turn on you. In other words, you can never trust them. Talk to me just before you get out of here, and I will send you to a Neapolitan. His name is Capone. He's from Brooklyn, but he's in Chicago now." (Valachi did not go to Chicago; there was enough trouble waiting for him in New York.)

Vollero's seething hatred for the Mafia was a rank-and-file emotion of the Camorra. This feeling boiled over into vendetta warfare just before Vollero's trial. Dozens of Camorra and Mafia members slaughtered each other, vying for control of food rackets, extortion, and blackmail.

The war was touched off when a leading Camorrista, Nick Del Gaudio, was killed by Mafia hoodlums in Harlem in 1916. His close friends were Pelligrino Morano, owner of a restaurant in Coney Island and a gambling czar, along with the "don" of Brooklyn and boss of bosses, Alessandro Vollero, head of the Camorra in this country.

The Camorra held a summit meeting. All leading members from various cities were summoned and obediently attended, squatting at the tables in Morano's big Santa Lucia Restaurant. Andrea Ricca, Camorra chief of Philadelphia, was there. So were out-of-towners Eugenio Bizzaro, Leopoldo Lauritano, Salvatore Costa, Albert Esposito, Salvatore Coppolo, Alberto Altieri, Luigi Turriese, Tom Corillo, and top gunmen such as Aniello Peretti, Alfonso "The Butch" Sgroi, Tony "The Shoemaker" Paretti, and Tony Notaro. These men held a council of war and decided on trapping top Mafia members in a cafe Vollero owned in Manhattan.

Their plan was aimed at the Morello brothers: Nicholas, the top Mafia leader in Manhattan, and his brothers Vincent and Ciro (later known as Ciro Terranova). It took six months before Nick Morello and his lieutenant Charles Umbriaco were cornered and shot to death. Pelligrino Morano did the killing. Dozens more on both sides followed.

Torpedo Tony Notaro was trapped by the law, indicted for one of the shootings. To save himself, Notaro talked, revealing for the first time the initiation rites of the Camorra (the rites for both the Camorra and Mafia were similar, both blood oaths, but not until Valachi's much-publicized admissions did the Mafia oath come to light).

Notaro's expose of the Camorra's oath of membership came while he was a witness in the murder trial of Pelligrino Morano in 1918. The rite, Notaro stated, took place on 15th Street in Manhattan in the home of one John Mancini, shortly after Easter, 1916.

Notaro recalled that on that occasion, "Tony the Shoemaker said to me, 'Now we're going to make a Camorrista and give you a title.' He said, 'The leader of the society, the boss [for Brooklyn], is Pelligrino Morano, and Vincenzo Paragallo is the second boss.' Then Pelligrino Morano said to me, 'Do you consent to become a Camorrista and receive the title that we give you?' I answered 'Yes.' He then said to me, 'Whatever is done between us, not a word should be breathed on the outside. You have to respect the bosses. When you are ordered to do a job or kill anybody, or whatever it is, even if you are arrested, never say a word and do not talk at all. And do not be afraid and do not speak to the police. If you speak to the police, you are discharged from this society, and you have to pay attention to what the bosses—those that have been here before —will say.' I then answered 'Yes.' He said, 'In whatever town you might find yourself—Boston, Philadelphia, Pittsburgh, Chicago, Buffalo —in any town, simply mention my name and you will be respected, because they all know me everywhere.' I said, 'Yes.' Then Tony the Shoemaker gave me a penknife. He gave me a little penknife, so big [described the dimensions with his fingers]. There was so much of a blade outside [again described the dimensions]. There was a piece of string attached to that penknife. He had one. Tony the Shoemaker extended his arm in this fashion [illustrated]. He said to me, 'Strike here.' I did with the penknife, and just a little blood came out. Pelligrino went near the Shoemaker's arm and sucked the blood, and a little more blood came out. He said to me, 'You have gained.' "

The only difference between the Mafia and Camorra oaths appears to be that the Camorra's initiation was centered about the spilling of another's blood and the Mafia's about the spilling of one's own.

As a result of Notaro's confession, Vollero and Morano left the court under heavy guard. Dozens of Italians charged up to Morano and planted heavy, wet kisses on his hands and face. One of them explained to the thunderstruck police officers that Morano was being congratulated for "not being convicted of murder in the first degree," and avoiding death in the electric chair.

Tony the Shoemaker Paretti was not so lucky. He went to the electric chair in 1926 for murdering a Mafia gunman. His last visitor in Sing Sing was an aggressive ambitious immigrant from Naples, Vito Genovese.

By then Tony Notaro, released from custody for turning state's evidence, completely disappeared, never to be seen again. This was the report whispered to Paretti by Genovese.

The Camorra-Mafia war by then was long over. The two factions, fearing a sweeping purge of all Italian and Sicilian mobsters in the U.S. by local and federal government, made peace and joined hands. The Camorra eventually faded when Luciano, Genovese, and younger Neapolitans who took control of the rackets and the national crime syndicate expressed no interest in promoting the Camorra's existence. The Mafia was left alone to develop and spread.

[ALSO SEE The Mafia, Vito Genovese, Charles "Lucky" Luciano, Joseph Valachi.]

CAPONE, ALPHONSE ("SCARFACE")
Murderer, Crime Czar ● (1899-1947)

BACKGROUND: BORN IN NYC, 1/17/1899 OF GABRIEL AND TERESA CAPONE (PRONOUNCED CAP-OWN, NEE CAPONI) WHO IMMIGRATED TO THE U.S. IN 1893 FROM NAPLES, ITALY. CAPONE WAS THE FOURTH OLDEST OF NINE CHILDREN INCLUDING JAMES, RALPH ("BOTTLES"), FRANK, JOHN ("MIMI"), ALBERT JOHN, MATTHEW NICHOLAS, ROSE, AND MAFALDA. MARRIED MAE COUGHLIN 12/18/18. SON ALBERT FRANCIS ("SONNY") BORN IN 1919. MINOR PUBLIC EDUCATION. DESCRIPTION: 5'10½", GRAY EYES, DARK BROWN HAIR, STOUT BUILD, OBLIQUE SCAR OF 4" ACROSS LEFT CHEEK 2" IN FRONT OF LEFT EAR; VERTICAL SCAR OF 2½" ON LEFT JAW; OBLIQUE SCAR OF 2½", 2" UNDER LEFT EAR. ALIASES: AL BROWN, ALFRED CAPONI, A. COSTA. RECORD: ARRESTED FOR DISORDERLY CONDUCT IN OLEAN, N.Y., 1919, DISCHARGED; ARRESTED FOR SUSPICION OF MURDER IN NYC, 1919, DISMISSED; ARRESTED FOR ASSAULT WITH AN AUTOMOBILE, DRIVING WHILE INTOXICATED, CARRYING A CONCEALED WEAPON, CHICAGO, 1922, CHARGES DROPPED AND EXPUNGED FROM POLICE RECORDS; ARRESTED FOR BLOCKING TRAFFIC, CHICAGO, CHARGE DISMISSED, 1923; ARRESTED FOR SUSPICION OF MURDER, CHICAGO, 5/8/24, RELEASED; ARRESTED FOR SUSPICION OF MURDER, NYC, DECEMBER, 1925, DISMISSED; ARRESTED FOR VIOLATION OF THE NATIONAL PROHIBITION ACT, CHICAGO 6/7/26, DISMISSED; ARRESTED FOR MURDER, CHICAGO 7/28/26, CHARGE WITHDRAWN; ARRESTED FOR VIOLATION OF THE NATIONAL PROHIBITION ACT, CHICAGO 10/1/26, DISMISSED; ARRESTED FOR REFUSING TO TESTIFY IN KILLING, CHICAGO, 11/12/27, DISMISSED; ARRESTED FOR CARRYING A CONCEALED WEAPON, JOLIET, ILL., 12/22/27, FINED $2,600 AND DISMISSED; ARRESTED WITH BODYGUARD, FRANK RIO (ALIAS KLINE) FOR BEING A SUSPICIOUS CHARACTER AND CARRYING A CONCEALED WEAPON, PHILADELPHIA, PA., 5/17/29, SENTENCED TO ONE YEAR IN PHILADELPHIA'S HOLMESBURG COUNTY PRISON BY JUDGE JOHN E. WALSH IN THE CRIMINAL DIVISION OF THE MUNICIPAL COURT, TRANSFERRED TO EASTERN PENITENTIARY, AUGUST, 1929, RELEASED FOR GOOD BEHAVIOR 3/17/30; ARRESTED FOUR TIMES IN MAY, 1930, MIAMI, FLORIDA FOR "VAGRANCY," DISMISSED; ARRESTED FOR INCOME TAX EVASION AND CONVICTED 10/24/31, SENTENCED TO FEDERAL PRISON FOR ELEVEN YEARS WITH FINES OF $50,000 AND COURT COSTS OF $30,000; SERVED EIGHT YEARS IN FEDERAL PRISONS IN ATLANTA, LEAVENWORTH, AND ALCATRAZ; RELEASED BECAUSE OF GOOD BEHAVIOR AND ILLNESS, 11/16/39; DIED 1/25/47 OF BRONCHIAL PNEUMONIA AND BRAIN HEMORRHAGE AT ESTATE IN PALM ISLAND, FLA.; BURIED AT MOUNT OLIVET CEMETERY IN CHICAGO,

BODY LATER SECRETLY REMOVED TO MOUNT CARMEL CEMETERY.

All of the doors of the Hawthorn Hotel in Cicero, Ill., were barred. The windows were sealed and draped expensively. Inside, at a long table in the private dining room, dozens of swarthy men in tight tuxedos gulped blood-red wine and devoured *linguine* coated with shrimp sauce. Al "Scarface" Capone sat smiling at the head of the table.

At the other end of the table sat three equally happy men—John Scalise, Albert Anselmi, and Joseph "Hop Toad" Giunta. These men were Big Al's ace gunners, a trio of cold-eyed killers who had, for the past ten years, mercilessly chopped down rival gangsters and balking politicans by the scores. Scarface was grateful.

"Saluto, Joe," Capone said to Giunta and raised his brimming glass of chianti.

"Saluto, Scalise, saluto, Anselmi!"

The three men raised their glasses in glee at the boss' toast. Al was such a wonderful guy.

"These are my boys," Capone bawled and with a sweep of the arm took in his three guests who beamed. "Such good boys, too. Always loyal to Al. Never a question. Tell 'em to do this, do that, and they do it." Capone pushed back from the table and got up leisurely, still smiling.

"If it wasn't for these three fine boys, where would I be, I ask you?" Capone held onto his smile but his stare was like ice as he took in the now frozen band of gangsters. "Yes, where would I be?"

Capone walked heavily around the table as his three honored guests clung to half smiles, amused. "I'll tell you where I would be," Capone said softly. And then he screamed, "I would be safe from a bullet in the head!"

He was quick for his five feet ten inches and 225 pounds. He reached beneath the banquet table and withdrew a baseball bat and then raced around the table behind his now petrified three guests.

"Bastards! You were gonna get me killed and take over, huh? Bastards!"

Crash, the bat came down on Joe Giunta's head, crushing his skull and killing him instantly. He moved over to Scalise next and slammed the ballbat down to cave in his head also. Eyes begging and lips bitten so hard the blood ran down his chin, Albert Anselmi took the same death blow looking straight ahead.

Capone's eyes bulged and his porcine, florid face glistened with sweat. He breathed heavily, hushed swearwords gushing from his mouth like spittle. He glared down at the three corpses and noted the splashes of blood from their heads staining the starched tablecloth. "Get 'em outa here!" he roared and several men scrambled to remove the bodies.

This was a typical Capone dinner in Chicago, May 7, 1929, a few short months after the very men Scarface murdered had killed seven of Bugs Moran's gang for him in the St. Valentine's Day Massacre.

The three murdered men had been disloyal and Al Capone liked to think of himself as a loyal man. In the space of a dozen bullet-torn years he rose from an obscure bouncer in Big Jim Colosimo's posh restaurant on Wabash Avenue, to the total blood-drenched ruler of Chicago. By then he was only thirty years old and he made $5,000,000 a year.

"Scarface" was born in Brooklyn in 1899. He was raised in the violent hell of Brooklyn's Williamsburg section. Always a large, chunky kid with murderously big hands, Al climbed rapidly through the hierarchy of the street gangs and became a member of the notorious Five Points Gang. He was a labor union "slammer" who muscled union leaders unwilling to kick back dues to the gang.

Early in his Brooklyn days, Capone took a job as bouncer and bartender in a notorious brothel-saloon, the Harvard Inn. One evening he passed an uncomplimentary remark about one of the girls at the bar. Unfortunately for Capone, the girl's brother, Frank Galluccio, a known felon, suddenly leaped over the bar, stiletto in hand, slashing out revenge. The result of Galluccio's fast carving became Capone's involuntary trade-mark for life—three ugly, jagged scars on the left side of his face that stood out white and hairless (Capone used mountains of talcum powder to soften the appearance.)

Capone never sought revenge for the act against Galluccio. Ironically, Capone later hired his attacker as a bodyguard at $100-a-week, proving again, when it was important to his press, that he could be magnanimous. Al claimed (and several criminal historians bought

the story) that he had been wounded by shrapnel while fighting with the famous "Lost Battalion" in France, but this, like so many of his self-constructed legends, was created to gain him sympathy.

Capone's career as an apprentice hoodlum in Brooklyn was mainly directed and inspired by an older boy, Johnny Torrio. Before he went West to help his wife's cousin—Big Jim Colosimo of Chicago—run his immense brothel empire, Torrio was the leader of the Five Points Gang in Brooklyn. Al worshipped the bantam killer, called him "Johnny Papa," and once told newsmen: "I'd go the limit for Johnny." He did, including murder.

Torrio never tired of playing *patron* to his hulking protege. After both men married Irish girls ("They make the best wives, Al; they don't run around."), Torrio became the godfather to Capone's only son, Albert Francis, nicknamed Sonny. Every year on his birthday, Torrio bought his godson a $5,000 bond.

Once situated with Colosimo in Chicago—in charge of Big Jim's hundreds of brothels in the Red Light districts—Torrio sent for his boy Capone. Al was happy to leave Brooklyn. A police officer had been pistol-whipped to death there and Capone was wanted for questioning.

So in through the gilt-edged doors of Colosimo's nightspot came Scarface in the year 1919 wearing a thirty-dollar suit, scuffed shoes, and no tie. His only baggage was a .38 pistol tucked inside his waistband.

Capone was only 19 then, crude, loud, and Torrio's gunman ... . as Colosimo was to find out too late. Big Jim taught Al an appreciation for life's finer things: a taste for opera (his favorite was Verdi), tailored clothes, expensive cars, society contacts.

The Scarface went to work, first as a bouncer at Colosimo's plush cafe, then as a gun toting aide-de-camp for Torrio, policing brothels, keeping all the madams in line, bagging the daily take and, incidentally, sleeping with Chicago's best whores. He began as a $75-a-week tough and by 1922 he was raking in two thousand a week.

Capone's "front" was printed on his business card which read: "Alphonse Capone, Second Hand Furniture Dealer, 2222 S. Wabash." To make the front seem more real, Capone even put up a few cheap displays of broken-down furniture in the bay windows of some of the whorehouses he managed for Big Jim and Torrio.

When Prohibition became law in 1920, Torrio realized the golden opportunity. Everyone wanted to drink and bootlegging would be big business. There would be millions! But Big Jim Colosimo with his fine clothes and swanky restaurants and well-paying whorehouses couldn't see it. He was making money, life was sweet and he had his reserved seat at the opera. Why go looking for trouble?

"It's business, it's business, Jim," Torrio argued.

"I don't understand it. We stay out. That's final."

It was final. A few days later, Alphonse Capone waited behind the glass doors of a telephone booth in Colosimo's nightclub . . . doing a favor for "Johnny Papa." Big Jim never knew what hit him as he crashed to the tile floor of his club's vestibule. Capone fired through the glass of the door, catching his boss with a shot under the left ear, killing him instantly. Al stepped from the phone booth, tore Big Jim's clothes apart as if a robber had been searching for a money belt, and then quietly left the restaurant.

Torrio and Capone were hauled into police headquarters for questioning. They were angry and tears streamed down their faces. "Big Jim was like a father to me. Colosimo was the kindest man I ever met . . . who would want to hurt Big Jim? God, captain, it's terrible, killing that wonderful old man, a cultured gentleman like that." They were released. "No evidence"—a phrase which was to become standard for Chicago's gang murders during the next ten years.

The day following Colosimo's execution—March 21, 1920—Torrio, with Capone as his right-hand man sharing in 25% of all profits, took over Big Jim's empire.

Capone's first arrest was in 1922. Drunk, his car loaded with several ladies of the night, Scarface smashed into a taxicab. He was doing sixty miles an hour down Wabash Avenue. Three bodyguards sat in the back of his car.

The cabdriver staggered from his taxi holding his head and cursing, "You crazy son-of-a-bitch! You almost killed me!"

Capone jumped from his expensive car and rushed the driver. His pistol was out and pointed at the amazed cabbie. "Goddamn you little bastard, don't talk that way to me!"

"Hey, now wait a minute, fella. How come you got a gun on me?"

Capone stopped and thought a moment. Then he produced a special deputy sheriff's badge. "I'm a law officer."

This was too much for Capone's nervous companions, who could hear the approaching clang of police gongs. They left the hot-head on the street and took off.

Police collared Capone and took him in while cabdriver Fred Drause had his head bandaged. The arrest—Scarface was booked as "Alfred Caponi"—came to nothing. The clout was in by then—Torrio and Capone owned too many judges and police chiefs for notice to be made of such "mischief."

The kind of protection from the law enjoyed by Torrio, Capone, and other Chicago gangsters of the era was never more in evidence than on the night of May 8, 1924. That night in Heinie Jacobs' bistro on South Wabash, "Ragtime" Joe Howard was boasting of how easy it was to hijack beer trucks, particularly those owned by Johnny Torrio.

Howard was a criminal product of another age. He did not carry a gun: such a weapon was not necessary in his day at the turn of the century, and it wasn't necessary in 1924, he told his pal Heinie. "Brass knuckles to the jaw is good enough. Them wop beerboys fold up like old newspapers after one chop."

At that moment, Howard spotted Jake "Greasy Thumb" Guzik, Capone's financial wizard, ambling out of the bar. Howard barred his way. "This is one of them wop workers," Ragtime Joe said. He slapped the small, portly Guzik across his wattles and then added a couple of kicks to his shins. Terrified, Guzik merely took the abuse and then sheepishly walked away—straight to Al Capone.

Minutes later, Capone walked through the doors of Heinie Jacobs' place and Howard, apparently expressing a change of heart toward Italian bootleggers, smiled and put out his hand. "Hello, Al," he said affably.

Grabbing Howard by his coat, Capone shook the independent hijacker. "Why did you kick Jake around, Joe?" he yelled.

Howard, still smiling, became indignant at being manhandled in front of his friends. "Aww, go back to your girls, you dago pimp!"

Capone produced a pistol, placed it to Joe Howard's temple, and emptied all six bullets into his head. Scarface then sauntered out of the saloon.

Three amazed witnesses at that late hour—
Heinie Jacobs and two customers, George Bilton and David Runelsbeck, stared at the floor
where Ragtime Joe lay, still grinning. When police arrived they immediately inventoried Joe's
estate: "1 pair cuff buttons; cash $17." The
witnesses swore in anger that Al Capone had
been the killer.

The Chicago Tribune published Capone's
picture the next morning for the first time, a
face that would become synonymous with Chicago and such inglorious terms as "the rub-
out," "the one-way ride," and "the cement overcoat." A month went by before Capone walked
into a police station, stating, "I hear the police
have been looking for me. What for?"

Captain James McMahon of the Cottage
Grove Avenue station instantly hustled Capone
to the Criminal Courts Building, where he
was interrogated by a young assistant state attorney, William H. McSwiggin.

"You killed Joseph Howard, Capone," Mc-
Swiggin charged. "We've got witnesses."

"Who, me?" Capone responded with raised
eyebrows. "Why, I'm a respectable businessman. I'm a second-hand furniture dealer. I'm
no gangster. I don't know this fellow Torrio. I
haven't anything to do with the Four Deuces.
Anyway, I was out of town the day Howard
was bumped off. You had better do your talking to my lawyer."

McSwiggin's witnesses suddenly lost their
memories. Bilton disappeared. Runelsbeck
couldn't identify the killer; Heinie Jacobs was
at the end of the bar when the shooting occurred.

The coroner's jury at Howard's inquest
handed down a familiar verdict: "Joe Howard
came to his death at the hand or hands of one
or more *unknown*, white male persons . . ."

A year and ten months after Howard's death,
State Attorney McSwiggin, along with two
West Side gangsters, James J. Doherty and
Tom Duffy, was slain by a machinegunner out-
side of a Cicero saloon. The heavyset man
wielding the "chopper" was identified as Al
Capone. This charge, too, was dismissed.

After Big Jim Colosimo's $20,000 funeral—the
first of the splashy gangster send-offs—Torrio
and Capone celebrated. Big Jim was dead and
they had his rackets, his nightclub and his
women. They could also run their booze into
the Windy City. Chicago was all theirs. Well,
almost.

A tough, church-going, street-fighting Irishman on Chicago's North Side had different
ideas. His name was Dion O'Bannion and he
knew what Prohibition meant, too. And Deanie,
as his fellow Irish mobsters affectionately
called him, wasn't alone.

Facing Torrio and Capone were whole armies of ambitious gangsters cutting themselves
in on the boozy empire of Prohibition. Allied
with the Torrio-Capone mob were the six terrible Genna brothers, killers all. The Italians
could also count on Ralph Sheldon, Frankie
Lake, Frank McErlane, and Terry Druggan.

But the rest . . . "those Irish bastards," Capone would complain, were Deanie's boys.
There were the South Side O'Donnell brothers,
six of them to match the Gennas. Then there
were the West Side O'Donnells, Klondike and
Miles.

The North Side, naturally, was all O'Bannion's. His hired hijackers and killers and rum-
runners were the most colorful. Earl "Hymie"
Weiss was his right-hand man—a shrewd murderer with an obsession for showgirls. Vincent
"The Schemer" Drucci would yank out his cannon in broad daylight, threaten a cop writing
him a traffic ticket, and get away with it. Two-
gun Louis Alterie actually wore two six-guns
which he would whip out instantly, twirl, and
replace and was called the Cowboy because
he owned a ranch in Colorado. George "Bugs"
Moran, Deanie's enforcer, was known as "The
Shootin' Fool."

It was a frightening array of killers that stood
in Torrio's path. He could count, however, on
Capone's 300 top gunsels.

For four years these underworld armies
worked their own territories by mutual agreement. O'Bannion had Chicago's North Side,
Torrio-Capone, the South Side—Madison Street
was the dividing line—with smaller gangs to
the west and southwest, snatching what they
could from the other side of the fence. But it
was not open warfare. Torrio and Capone had
seen to that by holding a gangster summit
meeting where the city was cut up like a pie
and everybody agreed not to get out of line or
kill each other.

Capone always had eyes for the North Side.
"O'Bannion's nuts," he said once to "Machine-
Gun" Jack McGurn. "Not one cat house up
there. The phony church-going turkeyneck.
Says it's immoral. Whores immoral? What the
hell kind a guy is that, I ask you, Jack? Cat

Five of Capone's top gunmen who made Scarface's power in Chicago for a decade (left to right): William "Klondike" O'Donnell, William "Three-Fingered Jack" White, Murray "The Camel" Humphreys, Marcus Looney, and Charles Fischetti. (UPI)

houses mean money! The buck! Business."

So Capone tried to cut into Deanie's territory in the 42nd and 43rd wards, installing his high-priced prostitutes. O'Bannion, who had been a choir boy at Holy Name Cathedral (and across from which he had his "front"—a flower shop) learned about it and exploded.

He was also upset that Capone had done in his friends the O'Donnells and taken over their South Side territory. The O'Donnells had re-ferred to Capone as a "dago punk" and a "stinking greaseball." Scarface didn't care for that so he sent Danny McFall and Frank Mc-Erlane out and they sprayed the whole O'Don-nell gang with machinegun fire. Within weeks, only Spike O'Donnell was alive.

"Those killings weren't Torrio's orders," O'Bannion said later in his flower shop. Hymie Weiss nodded. "They were all done by that dirty atheistic dago! Did you see poor Jerry O'Connor's face at the funeral home. It was blown off. Nothing left to it. And Walter O'Don-nell, too. And all those other lads. That Capone

kills like a beast in the jungle!" The ever-faith-ful Weiss nodded to that, too.

O'Bannion was addressing a Capone associ-ate who was friendly with the Irishman. Then Weiss turned to the Capone man and said, "You can tell Capone this for me. If he ever pulls anything like that on us, I'm going to get him if I have to kill everybody in front of him to do it. You can tell him that, and if I see him I'll tell him." The message was delivered and Al Capone started to sweat.

O'Bannion and his boys weren't like the O'Donnells. Deanie had congressmen and judges and half the police force on his payroll. His army of torpedoes was almost as large as the Italian contingent. Capone also remem-bered the words of Chicago Police Chief Mor-gan Collins: "Dion O'Bannion is Chicago's arch criminal who has killed or seen to the killing of at least twenty-five men."

Before Capone moved North, O'Bannion came up with a scheme to "take them spaghet-ti-benders," as he called Torrio and company.

He called "Johnny Papa" and told him that he wanted to sell one of his breweries—Siebens by name—and would Torrio be interested. Hell, yes.

Torrio gave O'Bannion $500,000 cash for the brewery. Only days later, police, led by a chief reportedly on O'Bannion's payroll,. raided the place and locked up Torrio who was taking inventory of his new property. Coincidence? Capone didn't think so.

Deanie had also been hijacking Genna beer. Weiss told him that the terrible Gennas might begin a full-scale war. "Aw," O'Bannion said, "to hell with them Sicilians."

Scarface heard about the remark and didn't think that was a nice way to talk. O'Bannion had to go.

On November 8, 1924, three men—New York gangster Frankie Yale, imported especially for this occasion, John Scalise, and Albert Anselmi —walked into O'Bannion's flower shop on North State Street. Deanie, who had three guns on him at all times (in specially-sewn pockets of his pants) was holding a pair of shears. He had been trimming chrysanthemums.

O'Bannion had no apprehensions. Mike Merlo, president of the Unione Siciliane had just died (a natural demise) and all of gangdom was ordering flowers from his shop for the funeral. "Hello, boys," the Irish killer said and held out his hand to Yale. "You come for Mike Merlo's wreath?"

Yale smiled and took O'Bannion's hand and held onto it. Scalise and Anselmi came up fast on either side firing rapidly into Deanie. The gangster hit the floor, his head in a bucket of flowers. Yale leaned forward and made sure. He fired a bullet into O'Bannion's head. The three calmly walked out of the shop and drove away.

"Hymie Weiss became a raving lunatic," one report says, "when he heard the news of Dion's murder. He took a solemn oath to kill Capone, and Torrio and everyone else in the Syndicate he could find."

And little Hymie tried his best. Weiss, Moran, and Drucci caught up with Johnny Torrio as he was coming home one night, January 24, 1925, after shopping with his wife.

"Shotguns, Johnny!" Torrio's wife screamed, but Torrio was leaning into his car for packages and didn't move fast enough. Moran and Drucci let him have four barrels from ten feet away.

Moran ran up and put a pistol to "Johnny Papa's" head. He squeezed the trigger. "Goddammit!" Bugs yelled. The gun was jammed. A truck was grinding down the South Side Street and the O'Bannion mobsters thought it was the police. They took off on a run.

When the police did arrive, Torrio looked up weakly. He had been hit in the abdomen, chest, jaw and arm. "Bullets . . . tipped with . . . garlic," he managed to say before passing out.

Though given up for dead by doctors, Torrio managed to survive, but he knew what was coming. He had had Chicago. "It's all yours, Al," he told Capone, and packed. After serving a short term in jail for his Sieben brewery operations, he and his wife left for Italy.

Now Capone, at twenty-five years of age, was the Number One Man in Chicago. He was chairman of the board with an income of $5,000,000 a year, but he had a full-scale war on his hands.

Weiss was a fanatic. He almost got Torrio. At least he drove him out of town. He got on the phone to Capone and demanded that he turn over Scalise and Anselmi to him.

"What? I wouldn't do that to a yellow dog!" Capone yelled back. He slammed the phone down and turned to a bodyguard. "You hear that?"

"Yeah," the bodyguard said.

"Hymie's gotta go," Al said.

Scarface was too slow. Weiss, Moran, and the boys planned their next move.

Capone was sitting with his tough bodyguard Frank Rio in the restaurant of the Hawthorn Hotel. It was September 20, 1926. His hot coffee steamed before him and just as he hooked his thumb around the cup and leaned forward, he heard it. "Typewriters," he gasped and his hand slid into his coat to the left armpit where his gun rested.

This was Cicero, Scarface's fortress to the west of Chicago. He ruled supreme here yet the sound of machineguns came drilling down the street. Rio stood up and looked out the window. People were yelling and running down the sidewalk. The restaurant waiters scampered for the kitchen. A lone car cruised past the hotel, stitching it with machinegun bullets.

Capone started to rise but Rio was quick. He pushed Al down to the floor and shielded him with his body. "It's a stall, boss," he said, "to get you out. The real stuff hasn't started.

You stay here."

The real stuff was another eight touring cars brimming with machinegunners. It was crazy; the bootleg war had reached its peak of fury. Here in broad daylight was an open attack on Big Al's stronghold. At high noon! The eight cars came abreast of the hotel spraying everything in sight. Not only that; they stopped and little Hymie Weiss got out and stood boldly in front of the hotel holding his Thompson; Moran was right behind him.

Capone controlled the hotel and all the shops around it. He had 100 men there, all armed. But they dove for cover rather than face the withering fire. Weiss took careful aim and fired from the hip into the hotel's entranceway.

"He used a ukelele with one hundred shells, and his typewriter was set for rapid fire," a newsman wrote. "That means six hundred shots a minute, including reloading, as an expert can slide in a new drum in four seconds . . ."

Weiss' aim was perfect. "As he pressed the trigger he moved the gun slowly back and forth the width of the passageway. The results are still visible—neat horizontal lines of .45-caliber bullet holes against the wall, some the height of a man's waist, some breast-high."

After Hymie finished his serenade to Scarface, he calmly walked back to his car. Three honks on the horn and the cavalcade drove off leisurely. Every glass pane in the hotel was shattered. But surprisingly, no one was killed.

Capone got up slowly from the restaurant floor, bug-eyed, trembling. "Those goddamn bastards! Comin' in here, in here!" He grabbed Rio. "Frank, did you see 'em. Huh?"

"Yeah," Rio said. "It was Weiss. It was Drucci. It was Moran."

"Those bastards are dead," Scarface screamed as he ran through the hotel lobby to inspect the awful damage. His torpedoes gathered about him. They were all shaken. "They're all dead, do you hear me? Dead! Dead! Dead!"

Weiss had his moment of glory and revenge for Deanie's murder. He went down before two Capone gunmen—Scalise and Anselmi—in front of O'Bannion's flower shop. "Hymie," Capone explained to newsmen openly, "is dead because he was a bullhead.

"Forty times I've tried to arrange things so we'd have peace and life would be worth living but he couldn't be told anything!" Drucci went next, killed by a young cop.

Two-gun Louis Alterie was through. His partners on the North Side had no staying power. He retired to his Colorado ranch.

That left only George "Bugs" Moran. Outnumbered and outgunned, Moran knew he was the only real threat left to Scarface but he wouldn't give an inch. He earned the name Bugs the hard way.

Capone took care of Moran by long distance. While living it up in his half million dollar Palm Island retreat outside Miami, he called Chicago. He had some fresh work for Scalise and Anselmi . . . sort of a Valentine.

Early in the morning of February 14, 1929, five men parked a squad car outside a garage at 2122 N. Clark Street. Two were in plainclothes and three were dressed as police officers.

The five marched into the garage—Moran's bootleg headquarters—and lined up seven of the Irish mobsters, who were waiting for a shipment of booze, against the wall. Moran's boys didn't think it unusual, a routine pinch. Bugs would bail them out by noon.

Arriving late, Bugs himself had seen the cops go into the garage and ducked into a nearby coffee shop to wait out the pinch. Inside, however, the "cops" leveled their machineguns at the Moran gang and systematically raked them. They fell away from the wall like lifeless dolls, six of them killed instantly.

Frank Gusenberg lived for a few hours. When questioned, all he had to say was, "Coppers done it."

Moran had more to say, for the first time breaking the underworld code of silence. When he learned of the massacre, he spat out: "Only Capone kills like that!"

Capone's empire was crumbling. Even the hangers-on were getting big ideas. A kinky newspaperman, Jake Lingle of the *Chicago Tribune*, bragged, "I fixed the price of beer in this town!" And he was on Capone's payroll.

Lingle was found in a subway underpass on Michigan Avenue, his brains blown out. Capone, who had given Jake a diamond-studded belt-buckle, lamented in public (as he always did). "Jake was a dear friend of mine," he said. Jake had also taken $50,000 from Capone, promising to use his influence to clear a dog track operation with the city. He never delivered.

Still it seemed nothing could touch Big Al, the Butcher. He had a fortune of $50,000,000, an island estate off Miami, two armored-plated

Capone hired St. Louis killer Leo Vincent Brothers (shown looking at camera while on trial) to murder *Chicago Tribune* newsman Jake Lingle in 1930; Brothers got fourteen years and said: "I can do that standing on my head." (UPI)

Chicago's king of crime, Al Capone plays cards with a federal guard on a train taking him to Leavenworth in 1932. (UPI)

McFarland cars especially made at $12,500 a-piece. He was supreme.

But for all his wealth and street savvy, Al had forgotten one thing. He had neglected to pay his income taxes for ten years. Urged by the press and an enraged public at the mass killing on North Clark Street, federal agents moved in.

After offering the government $4,000,000 to forget his income tax oversight (which was promptly turned down), Al Capone went to trial.

Scarface sweated while the government built a strong case against him. He talked freely to the press, trying to explain his position. "All I ever did was to sell beer and whiskey to our best people . . . Why some of the leading judges use the stuff . . . If people did not want beer and wouldn't drink it, a fellow would be crazy for going around trying to sell it.

"I've seen gambling houses, too, in my travels, you understand, and I never saw anyone point a gun at a man and make him go in . . ."

But the government ignored Al's little-boy-innocent act and found him guilty of tax evasion. He was sentenced to eleven years and $80,000 in fines and court costs. They sent Scarface to Leavenworth and then the Rock, Alcatraz, where he served out eight years.

Paroled in 1939, Capone was a physical wreck. His high living in the 1920s had made a shambles of his body. He had contracted syphilis years ago from one of "Johnny Papa's" whores. It developed into paresis of the brain and the bug ate him alive. He lived, a power-

less recluse, at Palm Island until 1947. He was 48 when he died.

Al Capone had ordered the deaths of over 500 men in Chicago, and more than 1,000 were killed in his bootleg wars. The wholesale slaughterhouse Scarface had made of Chicago was a strange and ironic monument to his own words: "I want peace and I will live and let live!"

[ALSO SEE James "Big Jim" Colosimo, Vincent "The Schemer" Drucci, "Machine Gun" Jack McGurn, George "Bugs" Moran, Dion O'Bannion, O'Donnell Brothers (Chicago, South Side), O'Donnell Brothers (Chicago, West Side), Johnny Torrio, Earl "Hymie" Weiss.]

CAPONE GANG

By the mid-Twenties, Al Capone's army of killers—never numbering less than 300—was the most formidable in the Chicago underworld. Those few who survived Capone's beer wars, such as Tony Accardo and Paul "The Waiter" Ricca, rose to unchallengeable positions as overlords of the modern-day Mafia.

Here are but a few of the torpedoes whose allegiance to Scarface was unto death:

—Louis Barko (alias Valerie), Capone's bag man, who collected hefty sums from the many Capone-Torrio brothels, gambling casinos, racetracks, and saloons. Barko, in the company of two others, tried twice to kill the Northsiders, Hymie Weiss and Vincent Drucci, but was unsuccessful. He was the only Caponite injured (wounded in the arm) when the O'Bannion gang led a daylight raid September 20, 1926 against Capone's citadel in Cicero, the Hawthorn Hotel, at which men in eight touring cars fired over 1000 machinegun bullets hoping one would find Scarface.

—The Barton brothers, Robert and Sylvester, were chauffeur bodyguards for Torrio and Capone. Sylvester was wounded in the back on January 12, 1925, while driving Capone to a restaurant at State and 55th streets; Weiss, Drucci, and Bugs Moran drove up to Capone's car just after Scarface had entered the restaurant and raked the bossman's car. As one policeman remarked: "They let it have everything but the kitchen stove." On January 23, the same North Siders waylayed Johnny Torrio as he was alighting from his limousine in front of his South Side residence, 7011 Clyde Avenue, with his wife. Torrio was seriously wounded and Robert Barton was hit in the leg below the knee.

—James Belcastro was Capone's top "pineapple man." He was known as "King of the Bombers." This veteran Blackhander would insure Capone's beer territory against the encroachment of other gangs by merely dynamiting any new rival breweries that appeared or by blowing up the saloons (with customers) of those truculent bartender-owners who refused to take Capone's beer. (O'Bannion's beer, produced by Sieben's Brewery on Chicago's North Side was considered the best in town during the Prohibition era.)

Largely to Belcastro's dubious credit goes the sobriquet "The Pineapple Primary" of 1927, when Capone's men intimidated and killed dozens of voters who worked against the election of Scarface's ally, William Hale "Big Bill" Thompson, twice mayor of Chicago.

On primary day, April 10, Belcastro caught up with a Negro lawyer, Octavius Granady, who had openly challenged the candidacy of Morris Eller, Thompson's pick for Republican committeeman of the Twentieth Ward. Belcastro and three others drove up to where Granady was talking with friends on the sidewalk and opened fire. Their aim was poor; Granady leaped into his car and sped down the street. Belcastro turned his own car about and gave

chase. Granady's car smashed into a tree as Belcastro's auto came up, shotguns blazing from the windows. As the lawyer staggered from the wreck, he was caught in the headlights of the mobster's car and was ripped to ribbons by dozens of shells. Belcastro was arrested for the murder and tried. He was acquitted.

—Fred R. "Killer" Burke, one of the most deadly of Capone's gunmen, was definitely one of the machinegunners of the St. Valentine's Day Massacre. Burke was an alumnus of the old Egan's Rats gang, a known murderer and bankrobber. He and his side-kick, James Ray, had robbed several Ohio banks dressed as policemen (the modus operandi employed to kill the seven Moran men on St. Valentine's Day, 1929).

After the North Clark Street slaughter, Burke was spotted December 14, 1929, by policeman Charles Skelly in St. Joseph, Michigan, while fleeing from a hit-and-run accident. Skelly curbed Burke's car and jumped on the running board. Burke shot him three times in the stomach and drove away. Skelly died an hour later.

The gunman was badly unnerved, however, and crashed his car into a telephone pole where police found it and traced the car to Burke's address. There they found one of the machineguns— traced by Calvin H. Goddard, the top authority on forensic ballistics—used to wipe out the Moran mob. Burke, captured in April, 1930, never stood trial for the mass slaughter. He was convicted of Patrolman Skelly's murder and was sent to the Michigan State Penitentiary for life.

—Louis "Little New York" Campagna, a graduate of Capone's old Five Points gang imported from Brooklyn to guard Scarface, intimidated Capone's enemies and applied muscle when necessary. For years, Campagna slept on a cot outside of Capone's bedroom with a brace of pistols in hand lest some assassin attack in the night. Campagna prospered in the ranks of the syndicate and with Charles "Cherry Nose" Gioe became an underworld boss on the West Coast, specializing in mulcting the movie industry. In 1953, Campagna died of a heart attack in bed.

—Louis Consentino, Capone muscleman and early organizer of the national syndicate. Rose through the Mafia ranks after joining Capone in 1924 in his Cicero stronghold, a retreat established by Torrio and Capone to thwart the clean-up drives by reform Mayor Dever.

—Tommy Cuiringione (alias Rossi). Replacing Capone's bodyguard chauffeur, Sylvester Barton, Cuiringione was kidnapped in 1925 by Earl "Hymie" Weiss and other North Siders. He was grilled as to the best location where Capone could be ambushed but revealed nothing to his inquisitors. His body was found in a Southwest Side cistern, coated with cigarette burns. Cuiringione was doubled over a concrete slab with his wrists and ankles bound so deep with wire that the flesh was cut to the bone. Five bullets in the head finished Tommy's loyal but short career.

—Phil D'Andrea, Capone's favorite bodyguard. A marksman, it was said of D'Andrea that he "could split a quarter in midair" with a rifle. D'Andrea carried a Municipal Court bailiff's badge and was paid $200 a month by the City of Chicago.

A member of the much-coveted *Unione Siciliane* (or Italo-American National Union) which controlled the vast alky-cooking concerns in Italian communities of Chicago, D'Andrea became one of the few of its presidents who was not killed in office. He was arrested during Capone's income-tax evasion trial for carrying a concealed weapon into court (he would stare menacingly at the jury for hours). Though he flashed a deputy sheriff's badge when arrested, he was nevertheless convicted and sentenced to six months in jail. In the Forties, D'Andrea, Willie Bioff, and Jake Guzik took control of the International Alliance of Theatrical Stage Employees, blackmailing Hollywood studios into paying huge sums to avoid labor strife. D'Andrea died in bed in the Fifties.

—Frank Diamond (nee Maritote) held the rank of captain of Capone's bodyguard contingent and was married to Scarface's sister Rose. Diamond, who was named with Capone as one of the killers who ambushed State's Attorney William McSwiggin (by McSwiggin's father, Chicago police sergeant Anthony McSwiggin), was number eleven on the 1925 Chicago Crime commission's "public enemy" list. His boss, Capone, was, of course, first. By 1930 Diamond was in Scarface's hierarchy and was openly demanding a larger percentage of the syndicate's complete monthly take. He got it and went on to remain a syndicate kingpin until his death in the Fifties, another Capone henchman who died in bed.

—The Fischetti brothers, Charles and Rocco, were Capone's cousins, also imported from Brooklyn, who became top leaders of his gang. They were convenient bodyguards since they lived with Capone for a while in his South Wabash Street apartment. In March of 1924, Charlie Fischetti and Al and Frank Capone led goon squads into Cicero to control the election. Squads of special police from Chicago were sent to aid the beleaguered suburban police. Open battle culminated on March 31. Police and gangsters shot it out all day. That evening, a squad of detectives saw Fischetti and the Capones with drawn automatics pistol-whipping voters who had not marked their ballots for the Democrats, the party Capone controlled in Cicero. Advancing on Frank Capone, officers McGlynn and Grogan saw the gangster raise his automatic and aim at them; it misfired. They leveled their shotguns at him, emptying the barrels. Frank Capone dropped dead before he hit the cement. Al Capone fled down an alley where he ran into another squad of police. They dove for cover at the sight of his two guns and he escaped. Charlie Fischetti was captured but was released by the Capone-owned courts. The Fischettis were elevated to the position of liquor distributors for the Capone outfit and, with Guzik, Frank Nitti, and others, headed the Chicago syndicate until the late 1950s.

—Peter von Frantzius was Al Capone's armorer and owned a sporting goods store, Sports, Inc. on Diversey Parkway. Von Frantzius, a graduate of the Northwestern University Law School, supplied Capone with machineguns, grenades, and automatic weapons of all kinds for use in the beer wars.

—Giuseppe "Hop Toad" Giunta, one-time president of the *Unione Siciliane*, plotted with machinegunners Scalise and Anselmi to kill his boss, Capone, but was killed instead by Capone in 1929. (Capone's rage at their treachery apparently extended to his own men, who worked over the corpses of all three until not one square inch of their bodies escaped a bruise; their bones were reduced to pulp.)

—The Guzik brothers, Harry and Jake, were both longtime whoremasters and white slavers who from the early 1900s in Chicago's red light districts busied themselves at kidnapping young girls and transforming them into captive prostitutes. Both served jail sentences for such crimes. Harry Guzik continued as a whoremaster for Capone, but Jake, called "Greasy Thumb" (he had once been a waiter and his thumb continually dipped into soup bowls), became one of the moguls of Capone's criminal cartel, its chief accountant and financier. When Capone was released from prison in 1939, reporters asked Guzik if Scarface would return to Chicago to take back command of his syndicate, and he imperiously replied: "Al is nutty as a fruitcake." Yet Guzik remained loyal to Capone, sending money when Scarface could no longer function after the ravages of syphilis had taken its toll. Guzik ultimately buried his old boss. He, too, died in bed.

—Michael "Mike de Pike" Heitler was also a Capone whoremaster but did not enjoy Al's friendship and trust as did the penguin-like Guziks. Heitler, vengeful over the fact that he had been demoted and ignored by Capone in 1931, wrote a letter to State's Attorney John A. Swanson in which he disclosed all he knew about Capone's city-wide brothel operations. Days later, Capone had Heitler brought to his headquarters at the Lexington Hotel and threw the unsigned letter in the old pander's face. "Only you could have done this," Scarface yelled. "You're through." Capone never explained how he had obtained the letter. On April 29, 1931, Heitler's corpse was found in a burned-out house in nearby Barrington. Mike de Pike had been roasted alive.

—Murray "The Camel" Humphreys began as a lowly Capone torpedo addicted to camel's hair coats and expensive cars. He later became one of the directors of the board of the Chicago syndicate, and died of a heart attack while opening his Marina City apartment door to a process server.

—Samuel McPherson "Golf Bag" Hunt got his name after police discovered he was carrying a shotgun in a golfing bag. Hunt's explanation was that he "was going to shoot some pheasants." Hunt, had, however, shot Leo Mongoven, a Bugs Moran man, who survived. Police also found in Hunt's cornucopia-like golf bag a .38-caliber revolver, mounted on a .45-caliber frame. Both shotgun and pistol had the symbol # stamped over and obliterating the serial numbers, a known Capone technique. Hunt outlived the gang wars to be a pallbearer at Capone's funeral. He died in bed with at least fifteen murders credited to him.

—The LaCava brothers, Joseph and Louis, were both top gunmen for Capone's early out-

fit. Later, Louis LaCava attempted to appropriate Cicero territory for himself and was exiled to New York. For services rendered, Capone chose this banishment in lieu of execution.

—Lawrence "Dago Lawrence" Mangano started as a member of a Capone muscle squad terrorizing saloonkeepers to take Capone beer and rose to become, with Charlie Fischetti, Capone's director of liquor distribution.

—Frank "The Enforcer" Nitti headed up Capone's special machinegun squad and figured in dozens of murders as Scarface's frontline general in the bootleg war. He slowly worked his way from gunsel to the outfit's treasurer. It was Nitti who assumed command of the Chicago syndicate after serving a tax-evasion sentence in Leavenworth and while awaiting Capone's release. Nitti continued to run things when Capone was paroled, since the boss was now reduced, by his sickness, to uncontrollable humming and singing jags. In 1944, faced with another stiff sentence for tax evasion, Nitti committed suicide: a rare end for one of his breed.

—Frank Rio (alias Frank Kline, Cline, Gline) proved to be Capone's most loyal bodyguard, not only saving his boss' life during the Cicero raid led by Weiss, Drucci, and Moran, but also voluntarily following his leader to jail in Philadelphia. It was Rio who learned of the plot by Giunta, Scalise, and Anselmi to kill Capone.

After Giunta had been installed as the president of *Unione Siciliane* with Scalise and Anselmi as his two vice presidents, Rio overheard Scalise boast that he was "the big shot now." Rio convinced Capone of the plot after a fake argument in which Capone slapped Rio in front of Scalise and Anselmi. Scalise later approached Rio and told him that the Aiello brothers had a $50,000 reward for anyone who would gun down General Al the Scarface. Would Rio join with them to collect the reward? Three days later Capone killed his would-be assassins.

Rio's loyalty apparently waned during Capone's tax trial. One report has it that Rio quietly eyed Capone being fitted for new suits by a tailor at the Lexington Hotel between court sessions.

"You don't need to be ordering fancy duds," Rio allegedly said." You're going to prison. Why don't you have a suit made with stripes on it?"

"The hell I am!" Capone exploded. "I'm going to Florida for a nice, long rest, and I need some new clothes before I go." Capone did go to jail, not to Florida. Frank Rio vanished shortly after.

—Tony "Mops" Volpe was reputed to be one of the most vicious hit men in Capone's early syndicate. He, like Scalise and Anselmi, rubbed garlic on his bullets, hoping that if his aim was poor, the victim would die of gangrene (a popular misconception). Volpe was named as Public Enemy Number Two after Capone in the 1923 Chicago Crime Commission's report. He faded at the end of the bootleg era.

—William Jack "Three-Fingered" White, a Capone gunner, could only shoot with his left hand, but even one-handed was an expert with a pistol. As a youth, White lost two fingers on his right hand when a brick from a building under construction fell on it. He wore gloves at all times, stuffing the empty fingers of the right hand with cotton. White was convicted of murdering a Chicago policeman in 1924, and after two lengthy trials went to prison for life.

—Jack Zuta was one of Capone's heavy connections with City Hall. A whoremaster and political backer, Zuta contributed $50,000 (mostly Capone's money) to William Hale Thompson's reelection campaign chest in 1927. Zuta boasted: "I'm for Big Bill hook, line, and sinker and Bill's for me hook, line, and sinker." Zuta later teamed up with Joey Aiello to kill Capone. He added further insult by assuming the role of Bugs Moran's business manager and financier (still using Capone's money).

Reportedly, it was Zuta who helped to recruit one James "Red" Forsythe, an out-of-town killer, to murder Chicago Tribune reporter Jake Lingle after Lingle threatened to close down a Moran gambling spa unless he received 50 per cent of the profits. This, at least, was a story Capone himself leaked after he had Lingle killed for betraying him to Moran. Forsythe, if he ever had been in Chicago, disappeared after Lingle's murder.

Chicago police captain John Stege, however, swallowed Capone's fake story and brought Zuta in for questioning June 30, 1928. He terrified Zuta by saying: "You're doomed. I've told that to fourteen other hoodlums who have sat on that same chair you're sitting on and all of them are dead."

Though Zuta told curious detectives nothing, a story leaked out that he was talking. Both Moran and Capone had reason to worry. The next evening Zuta was released but begged for a police escort. Police lieutenant George Barker took pity on the quaking gangster and agreed to drive him home.

On the way, Zuta spotted a blue sedan coming up fast on Barker's car. A trim young man wearing a tan suit with a boutonniere in his lapel and a panama hat yanked low over his forehead stood on the sedan's running board. It was 10:30 p.m. and both cars were passing through still busy parts of the Loop.

"They're after us!" Zuta yelled to Barker and dove between the seats of the car. Barker didn't believe the whoremonger until the blue sedan roared abreast of his Pontiac and the young man on the running board calmly jerked forth an automatic, emptying it into the Pontiac's tonneau. Both cars came to a halt and Barker jumped out, his gun blazing. Several shots were traded. A bank guard was wounded. A motorman was also shot and died of his wound in the hospital.

After the gangsters had emptied their guns at Barker they drove off up State Street. Barker saw that Zuta had disappeared; he then pursued the assailants. But, by 1928, Chicago gangsters had become extremely innovative. The gangster car escaped Barker by laying out a massive black cloud—a smoke screen that covered the entire street—which was achieved by a unique injection pump that forced huge amounts of oil through the intake manifold.

Living in fear under the nom de guerre of J. H. Goodman, Zuta hid out at an obscure resort, the Lake View Hotel, next to the waters of Wisconsin's Upper Nemahbin Lake close to Milwaukee. As several local couples did the Lindy Hop about the resort's dancehall on the night of August 1, 1928, Zuta methodically fed the coin-operated player piano.

He never saw the five men who filed into the bar holding tommy guns, shotguns, and pistols. Their barrage hit him full force (sixteen bullets found the mark) just as he inserted another nickel into the piano. Zuta crashed onto the keys as the dancers froze. The five killers put up their weapons and quietly filed out. The player piano continued to bump out a popular hit song of the day: "Good for You, Bad for Me."

A year later, when Capone learned of the $50,000 pricetag Joey Aiello had placed on his head, he roared, "Nobody's gonna Zuta me!" And Al Capone knew whereof he spoke.

CARBO, FRANKIE
Syndicate Gangster • (1904-1976)

Born Paul John Carbo on the Lower East Side of New York in 1904, he received little education except for the streets where he joined various street gangs at an early age. He was sent to several reform schools for assault and grand larceny and, by the time he was twenty in 1924, Carbo had murdered his first man, a cab driver who refused to pay him protection money.

Carbo pled guilty to manslaughter and served only twenty months. By the 1930s, he had gotten a reputation as a ruthless killer who hired his gun to various mobsters. In 1931 Carbo killed Philadelphia mobster Mickey Duffy in Atlantic City. Though Carbo was indicted for this killing, witnesses suddenly disappeared and Carbo was released.

Throughout the 1930s Carbo worked as a hit man for Louis "Lepke" Buchalter, who headed Murder, Inc. He was responsible for a number of mob killings, including those of Max Haskell and Max Greenberg, two former members of the bootlegging gang once headed by Waxey Gordon. Again, Carbo was charged in 1936 for these killings but witnesses refused to testify and he went free.

In 1939, "Big Harry" (or "Greenie") Greenberg was murdered by Carbo and others because he had been talking to police on the West Coast. Again, Carbo escaped punishment through lack of evidence and frightened witnesses. Named by Abe "Kid Twist" Reles as one of Murder, Inc.'s most productive killers, Carbo was arrested five times for murder but he was never convicted. His line of work, he figured, was becoming too dangerous, so Carbo entered a new field of opportunity, boxing.

In the 1940s, thanks to his connections in the underworld which, by then, controlled the most important matches in boxing, Carbo became a fight manager. Within a few years, he was "the underworld czar of boxing." He controlled the sport through a huge bookie network and his personal ownership of many top prizefighters.

The law caught up with Carbo in 1958 when he served a short sentence on Riker's Island for managing three boxers without a license. That year Don Jordan won the welterweight championship and Carbo muscled in on the fighter's earnings. In 1960, Carbo was brought before a Senate investigating committee and asked about his connections to Jordan and other fighters. "I cannot be compelled to be a witness against myself," Carbo told the committee. He repeated this line 25 times until committee members dismissed him in disgust.

The next year, however, Carbo was convicted of conspiracy and extortion in the Jordan case and he was sentenced to 25 years at McNeil Island Penitentiary. Growing ill, Carbo was released early. He retired to life of luxury in Miami Beach where he died peacefully on November 9, 1976.

CARITATIVO, BART
Murderer • (1906-1958)

BACKGROUND: BORN AND RAISED IN THE PHILIPPINES. IMMIGRATED TO THE U.S. IN 1926 AND STUDIED AT OAKLAND TECH HIGH IN CALIFORNIA; RETURNED TO THE PHILIPPINES BRIEFLY IN 1930 WHERE HE MARRIED (A SON WAS BORN LATER) BEFORE COMING BACK TO THE U.S. ORIGINAL OCCUPATION, HOUSEBOY AND COOK. DESCRIPTION: 5'5", BROWN EYES, BROWN HAIR, SLENDER BUILD. ALIASES: NONE. RECORD: MURDERED CAMILLE AND JOSEPH BANKS AT STINSON BEACH, CALIF., 9/10/54 IN AN ATTEMPT TO GAIN THEIR ESTATE THROUGH FORGED DOCUMENTS; TRIED AND CONVICTED, SENTENCED TO DEATH; EXECUTED 10/24/58 IN THE GAS CHAMBER OF SAN QUENTIN PRISON.

Bart Caritativo was forty years old when he came to the exclusive sun-baked resort area known as Stinson Beach, California, a suburb of the rich and idle just north of San Francisco. An itinerant worker, his life had been studded with odd jobs and hand-me-down luck. Bart's luck irrevocably changed at Stinson Beach. There he was to make his fortune and meet his doom.

At first, Bart went to work as a cook and houseboy for S. Laz Lansburgh, a wealthy lawyer. He ingratiated himself to the point where the Lansburghs became protective if not possessive of their most obedient Filipino charge. When his clothes wore out, the Lansburghs bought him a new wardrobe. When he told them that his son and wife in the Philippines were hard-pressed, Mr. Lansburgh loaned him several thousand dollars (which Bart, to his credit, repaid bit by bit from his salary).

The Lansburgh house was next to a sprawling ten-acre estate known as Sea Downs. Mistress of Sea Downs was Camille Banks. Camille had arrived in the area three years before Bart, then equally unemployed. After working briefly as housekeeper for well-to-do Theodore Malmgren, she married her employer. He promptly died, leaving his lands and fortune to her.

Though Camille remarried—to an Englishman, Joseph Banks—she remained good friends with Bart Caritativo. Both had literary ambitions and read each other's rejected stories. Mrs. Banks entertained Bart as a guest several times at her cottage parties, where Filipino dishes prepared by Bart were served.

The trouble in this paradise was Joseph Banks. He was seldom seen in public; he drank. Mr. Banks' alcoholism became so acute (Camille also drank heavily) that his fun-loving wife divorced him in 1954. Oddly, the couple continued to live together at Sea Downs. Bart Caritativo also continued to enjoy Mrs. Banks' company.

Days before she was scheduled to depart on a pleasure tour of the South Seas, Mrs. Banks received a visit from a neighbor, Mrs. Grunert, on September 17, 1954. Mrs. Banks was not receiving—ever again. Mrs. Grunert found Camille in the bedroom with her skull split open, quite dead. In the living room, the hysterical

woman discovered Joseph Banks sprawled on a couch, empty whiskey bottles all around him. From his stomach jutted a large knife. His limp, bloody hand encircled the handle.

After the police arrived to survey the grisly scene, Don Midyett, an inspector for the San Rafael sheriff's department, uncovered three suspicious-looking documents. One was a note written in pencil, allegedly scribbled by Mr. Banks. "I had been pushed long enough," it read. "This is the end. I am responsible to what you see and find. Joseph Banks."

The note's grammatical structure puzzled Inspector Midyett. Also alarming were two more documents, a letter and a typed will, in which Camille Banks left her entire estate to none other than her Filipino friend Bart Caritativo. They, too, were loaded with misspellings and grammatical mistakes.

Upon investigation, Midyett learned that both Camille and Joseph Banks were well-educated. The gross errors found in the documents could not have been made by them, Midyett reasoned. He grilled Caritativo.

"I don't know why she left me the money," he said. "I was surprised. Maybe it was because I chauffeured her a little."

Midyett was still suspicious and obtained several samples of Bart's handwriting. He took these along with the Banks' documents to handwriting experts. All concluded that Caritativo had written the suicide note, the letter, and the will. Bart was immediately arrested.

Caritativo acted in a bewildered fashion throughout his trial. He pleaded not guilty, and his defense tried to pin the murder on Joseph Banks, pointing out that Camille had twice committed him to an insane asylum. The prosecution eliminated Banks as a suspect by reading reports from the asylum stating that Banks was merely an alcoholic drying out there; he was not insane.

Caritativo changed lawyers in mid-stream. He told the court that "I have lost the confidence, the faith and the trust to my attorneys." It was noted that he had used the wrong preposition just as had the author of Joseph Banks' suicide note.

Noted criminal lawyer George T. Davis took on Caritativo's case but with reservations. He was overheard to say that he thought Bart insane.

The prosecution then brought in their heavy witnesses. First a pathologist testified that an

Houseboy Bart Caritativo murdered for money and land and wound up in the gas chamber. (UPI)

autopsy of Joseph Banks' body revealed that he was totally drunk at the time of the murder, so drunk that he could not have committed suicide, let alone have killed his wife.

Next, a stream of handwriting experts testified that the death documents found in the Banks home at the time of the murder were authored by Bart Caritativo. The small Filipino became jittery. "In my heart," he nervously explained between sessions, "I know that I am innocent. I feel that something is going on, something is going wrong with my case."

Bart was right. He was losing.

Davis attempted to destroy the prosecution's testimony, but it appeared too staggering to overcome. The jury deliberated only a little over four hours before returning a verdict: guilty of murder in the first degree. Bart was sentenced to die in San Quentin's gas chamber.

Days before his execution, Caritativo received a visit from the prison psychiatrist, Dr. David Schmidt, who was in the habit of exacting confessions of sorts from condemned prisoners (see BURTON ABBOTT) and then releasing these "confessions" to the press following the execution of the prisoners. He had a brief conversation with Caritativo in the condemned man's cell.

After a few preliminary questions as to Bart's mental well-being, Caritativo dove for the floor of his cell and there, on his knees, began to pray loudly, tearfully, ending his hossanahs to the Almighty with the words: "Oh Lord, if I had known it would be this hard, I would never have carried out my mission."

This remark then, made public days after Bart's death, served as his confession. What the ex-houseboy meant by his "mission" was never explained.

On October 24, 1958, Bart Caritativo was strapped into the gas chamber chair at San Quentin. As the fumes rose about him, he cried out sobbing over and over again until he died, "God bless you all . . . God bless you all."

CARLISI, SAM ANTHONY
Syndicate Boss ● (1921-   )

Since the death of Anthony "Big Tuna" Accardo in 1992, Sam Carlisi, once a syndicate runner, has emerged as one of the top Mafia-Syndicate bosses in the Chicago area. He began as a strong-arm man for Chicago crime boss Joseph "Doves" Aiuppa. When Aiuppa went to jail, Carlisi began his climb up the mob ladder. Carlisi earned the sobriquet of "Wings" from his ability to swiftly make contact with top echelon mobsters and carry their orders to the rank-and-file street mobsters.

Convicted of tax fraud in 1984, Carlisi nevertheless emerged as one of the top syndicate bosses controlling gambling. So notorious did he become that he was barred from all the racetracks in and about the city. Wings Carlisi affected the image of the old-style gangster, flamboyantly wearing a fedora even when sitting down to dinner in some of Chicago's finer restaurants.

Though he is considered to be Chicago's top mobster at this writing, he continues to practice his lifelong habit of penny-pinching. He is known to travel coach class and fly across the country at three in the morning to save money on his fare. His chauffeurs must buy the gas in the limousines that drive him about Chicago. Dinner is always on someone else. He does not leave a tip.

(ALSO SEE Joseph Accardo; Joseph Aiuppa)

CARPENTER, RICHARD
Murderer, Robber ● (1929-1956)

BACKGROUND: BORN IN WISCONSIN AND RAISED IN A MILWAUKEE ORPHANAGE, CARPENTER SERVED BRIEFLY IN THE ARMY AFTER DROPPING OUT OF HIGH SCHOOL. HE WAS DISCHARGED AS AN UNDESIRABLE. DESCRIPTION: 5'11', BROWN EYES, BROWN HAIR, MUSCULAR. ALIASES: NONE. RECORD: ARRESTED FOR ROBBING A TAXI DRIVER IN CHICAGO, ($8), CONVICTED AND SENTENCED TO A YEAR IN JAIL, 1951; STOLE A CAR AND ROBBED A GROCERY STORE IN CHICAGO ($100), AND ESCAPED, 12/4/53; SHOT AND KILLED POLICE DETECTIVE MURPHY, CHICAGO, AFTER THE POLICEMAN ATTEMPTED TO ARREST HIM FOR A STRING

OF BAR-STORE-LAUNDROMAT ROBBERIES, IN AUGUST, 1955; SHOT AND WOUNDED CHICAGO POLICEMAN CLARENCE KERR, WHO ATTEMPTED TO ARREST HIM IN A LOOP THEATER, AUGUST, 1955; HELD LEONARD POWELL, HIS WIFE, AND TWO CHILDREN CAPTIVE HOURS LATER WHICH WAS FOLLOWED BY A WILD SHOOT-OUT WITH CHICAGO POLICEMEN WHO SURROUNDED THE POWELL RESIDENCE; CONVICTED AND SENTENCED TO DIE IN THE ELECTRIC CHAIR FOR THE MURDER OF OFFICER MURPHY; EXECUTED 3/16/56 AT THE JOLIET STATE PRISON.

His routine was always the same. Richard Carpenter would wait until closing time when the customers had cleared out of their favorite neighborhood saloon and then walk in quietly.

It was no different when he sauntered into the small bar on Wrightwood Avenue on Chicago's North Side and approached bartender-owner Martin Chowanski. Carpenter looked about and saw one other person in the bar.

"You're lucky," Chowanski said. "I was just closing up. You got time for one drink. What'll it be?"

Carpenter smiled crookedly. He pulled two guns from his pockets and pushed them to only a few inches of Chowanski's face. "What about the money?" he said.

The fact that the other customer in the bar was patrolman Medard Bosacki dressed in his civilian clothes on his night off didn't bother Carpenter. He saw Bosacki go for his gun.

Coolly, the robber said, "You'd better put that gat on the bar or someone will die here tonight."

Chowanski had a pained look on his face as he looked at his friend and customer Bosacki. "Listen," he told the officer. "Put that gun away. I don't want any killing here. I'd rather give this guy the money I got in the cash register."

Carpenter liked that. He clicked the hammers of his two revolvers just to ensure enough fear in both men. Then, still acting out his movie tough-guy role, the youth snarled, "Slide the gun down the bar to me."

Bosacki slid the gun down the bar and Richard Carpenter pocketed the weapon. Then he turned to the bartender. "Listen," he said, "you'd better be smart, too—give me all the money; all the green stuff, and don't bother with the silver."

Chowanski nervously did as he was told and when Carpenter had stuffed the money—about $60—into his pocket, he ran.

Bosacki waited a minute and then ran after him but the streets outside were empty. The gunman could have disappeared up any one of a dozen alleys.

Bosacki reported later to his superior, Lieutenant John Flannagan, "That guy ran faster than anyone I've ever seen before."

It was April 1, 1955 and Richard Carpenter, the product of a broken home and a shabby life, had been running from the police for close to a year and a half. The description of the gunman Bosacki offered matched perfectly with that of Richard Carpenter, who had been robbing small grocery stores, bars and laundromats.

The Wrightwood Inn robbery was his seventieth successful heist. Police officials estimated that Carpenter had averaged $25 a day in his crime career to date—about $14,000. It wasn't big by bank-robbing standards, but it was consistent and a lot safer.

Even though the police knew who they were looking for, they got nowhere. Carpenter, then 26, had disappeared from his home one night in December, 1953 to go on his robbing rampage; he had simply melted into the city's millions.

He had never been back to see the mother he so doted upon or the three sisters he so cherished or the grandfather to whom he brought "three good cigars every day."

Carpenter practiced no bad habits, so police knew they would never trap him in a whorehouse or gambling den. They knew that, as a cabdriver, he had even refused fares to gambling casinos and bordellos, such was his puritanical streak. He was a loner which ruled out friendly informers.

Carpenter was not one to lose his head either, and police rated him with a high intelligence. He would calmly reason with those he robbed.

He told one victim: "Use your brains and don't get upset or nervous. See how calm I am, and you'd better stay calm, too. I don't want to kill you, but you'll get it in the guts if you make a wrong move."

Carpenter was so clever in one bar, sipping a single beer for hours until closing time when the night's proceeds would be in the till, that he didn't have to wait for all the customers to clear out. "He took $300 off me," the bartender reported, "and my customers didn't even know it. Cool."

That best described Carpenter—cool. Once, when almost trapped after robbing a bar, Carpenter escaped by jumping into a taxi. The alarmed driver refused to take him as he noticed a heavyset man approaching the cab on the run and yelling.

"You gotta help me, pal," Carpenter pleaded with the taxi driver. "I've been romancing a girl and I just found out that she's married. That's her husband coming and he's planning on killing me. Please."

The cabdriver grinned and stepped on the accelerator. The cab roared off. The cabbie thought he was doing Carpenter a good turn —saving his life from an irate husband. His good deed got him one thin dime as a tip!

For eighteen months, Carpenter eluded the law. Police officials knew that he was determined to continue his criminal activities; his robberies occurred too regularly for them to think otherwise.

Lieutenant Flannagan knew something else: no man could brandish two guns Western style like Carpenter did, without having to shoot and possibly kill someone some time.

That time came in August, 1955. Detective Murphy, who had attended all the police meetings concerned with capturing Carpenter, recognized the poorly-dressed robber on the subway. The mild-mannered bespectacled detective calmly walked over to his seat and arrested him.

The two got off at the Roosevelt and State Streets stop. Murphy wanted to be sure of his prisoner. As he pulled out an identification poster on Carpenter, his eyes were averted for a moment.

It was enough time for Carpenter to pull a gun and fire off a single round which slammed into Murphy's chest, killing him instantly. The cop-killer raced for the exit and jumped into a limousine parked there.

Driver Charles A. Koerper blinked in terror. Carpenter's voice was solemn, "I've just killed a man, and I'll kill you, too, unless you drive on and keep quiet."

Koerper drove away and kept his mouth shut. Carpenter jumped from the limousine at Chicago's busiest corner—Madison and State —and disappeared into the moving sea of humanity.

Lone bandit and murderer Richard Carpenter being led into court in 1955 where he was found guilty of killing a Chicago policeman. (UPI)

Now police stepped up their efforts to capture Richard Carpenter. He had not only murdered, but he had killed a cop, and the entire force was fanatically determined to get him.

Three days after Murphy was gunned down, policeman Clarence Kerr went to a downtown theater with his wife to see a movie called *Call Me Lucky*. The name, as events proved, was ironic.

Kerr spotted and recognized Carpenter asleep in the back row. He sent his wife out of the theater and approached the killer. Kerr drew his gun.

"How come you're sleeping here?" he said, nudging the youth.

Carpenter answered slowly, "It's none of your business."

"I'm a police officer. Follow me to the lobby."

The killer got up slowly, pretending drowsiness and stumbled out to the lobby, muttering, "I just wanted to cool off. That's not against the law."

As the two came into the lobby, Carpenter pretended to stumble. He came up with his gun blazing and a shot hit Kerr in the chest. As the courageous policeman fell he got off one shot at the fleeing Carpenter. It hit the killer in the leg but he managed to once again disappear into the Chicago crowds outside.

Kerr's wife rushed to her husband who, before passing out, yelled: "It was Carpenter—Carpenter—I know it was Carpenter."

He was rushed to the hospital and survived by a heartbeat. His heart had contracted at the time Carpenter's bullet struck. The famous heart surgeon Dr. Edward A. Avery, who saved Kerr's life, stated: "If it [the heart] had been expanded, the bullet would have nicked the heart and killed him. He'll live now."

The question was, as usual, where was Carpenter?

A few hours after the theater shooting, a truckdriver, Leonard Powell, heard a knock at his back door. He went into the kitchen and through the screen door saw a ragged youth pointing a gun at him.

The Powell TV was blaring in the next room, spurting out the news of Carpenter's latest escape.

"I guess you know who I am," Carpenter said.

"Yeah," Powell replied and stared at the gun in the killer's hand.

"I've just shot another policeman. If you do as I say, nothing will happen—nothing, I promise—but if you refuse to open this door, I'll shoot you now. Open up and let me in!"

Powell, who stood six-foot-four-inches and outweighed Carpenter by 60 pounds, was helpless. He let the outlaw inside. Mrs. Powell came into the kitchen and her husband explained: "Darling, don't get excited. This man is Carpenter and he says that if we do as he asks he won't shoot and no harm will come to us. Don't scream."

Mrs. Powell didn't scream. Calmly, she told Carpenter that their son Bobby was watching TV. If the boy saw the guns—there were now two of them in Carpenter's hands—he would yell. It was better if the gunman pretended to be a friend of the family.

That was the way it went in the Powell home for a night and a day. Carpenter never revealed his identity to either Bobby Powell or to three-year-old Diane Powell. He slept in the living room, or rather sat in it with the Powells, holding them at gunpoint, fighting off sleep, watching with a crooked grin as TV announcers talked about his murderous exploits.

The family could hear police sirens wailing down Chicago's streets.

Finally, obviously looking for the same kind of sympathy his mother had once lavished upon him, Carpenter told the Powells: "I guess you don't think much of me . . . I just want you to know that I was not the first to shoot . . . but I don't care anything about it anyway."

The TV broadcasters were still rattling off Carpenter's pathetic life story. The killer watched the television screen, momentarily transfixed. "I'm sorry about one thing," Carpenter said half to himself. "I didn't do a single thing to make my mother and my sisters proud . . . It was a lousy life I led—but it's too late now. Either the cops will kill me or I'll go to the chair, but I hope I can see my mother before I die."

Powell tried the psychological approach. "I think you could be a nice fellow," the truckdriver stated, "and I'm sorry you are in such a terrible mess."

The sympathy worked. Carpenter never harmed the couple. The next day he bandaged his slight flesh wound in the leg. Believing the Powells to be his friends, he allowed them to step outside to get some air.

Then the family made a running escape. Powell shouted to his neighbors who were taking the air on their front stoops: "Get out of here quick and into your homes! There's a gunman about!"

The family escaped without injury and called police. Within three minutes 30 patrol cars were outside the Powell house.

"Carpenter!" Sergeant Micklas shouted through his megaphone. "Carpenter! Carpenter! Come out with your hands in the air! We've got you covered! You haven't a chance!"

Micklas was answered by a blast from Carpenter's gun as the killer flitted past a window.

The police guns roared, shattering the window, but Carpenter was not through. He managed to climb to the roof and leap to another roof nearby. He moved down to another apartment. He fired another shot from a window and the police return fire was thunderous.

Several officers burst into the room from which Carpenter had fired his second shot. A young man was groveling on the floor. "It's not me you want!" he screamed. "I live here!"

"It's you we want, Carpenter."

Richard Carpenter got his wish, before he went to the electric chair in 1956. First, he saw his mother.

CASEY, JAMES P.
Murderer ● (? -1856)

San Francisco was a rough town in the Nineteenth Century, even for civilized people. Though James Casey was the editor of the *Sunday Times*, his position did not prevent him from calling his enemies out into the street for fistfights or shootouts.

One arch-foe Casey found particularly intolerable was James King, who edited the rival *Evening Bulletin*. Spotting King on a San Francisco street May 14, 1856, Casey yanked out a revolver and shouted: "Draw and defend yourself!" But he gave King no time to do so (King was unarmed anyway) and immediately fired at him, killing him on the spot.

While Casey was awaiting trial, San Francisco's Vigilance Committee stormed the jail and dragged him outside, along with three other prisoners—Charles Cora, Philander Brace, and Joseph Heatherington. In a wild torchlight ceremony, all four men were pronounced guilty of various crimes—Casey's killing of King given prominence—and were then promptly hanged while 20,000 good citizens cheered.

CASSIDY, "BUTCH"
(ROBERT PARKER)
Bankrobber, Trainrobber ● (1866- ?)

BACKGROUND: BORN ROBERT LEROY PARKER IN CIRCLEVILLE, UTAH, 4/6/1866, ONE OF TEN CHILDREN. NO PUBLIC EDUCATION. ORIGINAL OCCUPATION, COWBOY. DESCRIPTION: 5'9", BLUE EYES, LIGHT BROWN HAIR, MEDIUM BUILD, MUSTACHE (ON OCCASIONS), TWO SCARS ON BACK OF HEAD, SMALL SCAR UNDER LEFT EYE. ALIASES: "BUTCH" CASSIDY, GEORGE CASSIDY, INGERFIELD, MAXWELL, LOWE. RECORD: BEGAN RUSTLING CATTLE WITH OUTLAW MIKE CASSIDY IN THE UTAH-COLORADO RANGES WHILE STILL A TEENAGER; ROBBED WITH TOM AND BILL MCCARTY THE DENVER AND RIO GRANDE TRAIN NEAR GRAND JUNCTION, COLO., 11/3/1887; ROBBED WITH THE MCCARTY BROTHERS AND MATT WARNER (WILLIARD CHRISTIANSEN), THE FIRST NATIONAL BANK IN DENVER, COLO., 3/30/89, ($20,000); ROBBED WITH THE MCCARTY BROTHERS THE SAN MIGUEL BANK IN TELLURIDE, COLO., 6/24/89, ($10,500); ARRESTED BY SHERIFF JOHN WARD IN AFTON, WYO. IN 1894 AND SENTENCED TO TWO YEARS IN THE STATE PENITENTIARY FOR RUNNING A PROTECTION RACKET IN WYO.; RELEASED 1/19/96; RODE TO DIAMOND MOUNTAIN, COLO. WHERE NOTORIOUS OUTLAWS HID OUT AT THE HOLE-IN-THE-WALL, A VAST MOUNTAIN FORTRESS PROTECTED ON THREE SIDES BY SHEER CLIFFS, WITH OUTLAWS ELZA LAY AND BOB MEEKS; ROBBED WITH ELZA LAY A PAYMASTER IN CASTLE GATE, UTAH IN APRIL, 1897, ($8,000); ROBBED THE UNION PACIFIC'S OVERLAND FLYER WITH GEORGE CURRY, HARVEY LOGAN ("KID CURRY") AND ELZA LAY, BLOWING UP THE EXPRESS CAR WITH DYNAMITE, 4/25/98, ($30,000); ROBBED WITH HARVEY LOGAN, CHARLES HANKS ("DEAF CHARLEY"), AND BILL CARVER UNION PACIFIC'S TRAIN NO. 3 AT TABLE ROCK, NEAR TIPTON, WYO., 9/29/1900, ($5,014); ALLEGED TO HAVE ROBBED THE FIRST NATIONAL BANK OF WINNEMUCCA, NEV., WITH HARRY LONGBAUGH (OR LONGABAUGH, ALIAS "THE SUNDANCE KID") 9/19/1900; ROBBED WITH HARVEY LOGAN, HARRY LONGBAUGH, CHARLES HANKS THE GREAT NORTHERN TRAIN NEAR WAGNER, MONT., 7/3/01, ($40,000); FLED TO SOUTH AMERICA WHERE HE AND LONGBAUGH PURPORTEDLY ROBBED SEVERAL BANKS AND THE PAYROLLS OF AMERICAN BUSINESSES IN ARGENTINA AMOUNTING TO $20,000-$30,000; ALLEGEDLY KILLED BY BOLIVIAN SOLDIERS IN SAN VICENTE, BOLIVIA AFTER ATTEMPTING A MINE HOLDUP IN 1908. SOME OF CASSIDY'S RELATIVES INSIST TO THIS DAY THAT BUTCH RETURNED TO THE U.S. ABOUT 1910 AND LIVED OUT A QUIET LIFE ON A WESTERN RANCH.

Butch Cassidy is unique in the annals of Western outlawry. Not only did he begin late as a train and bank thief, robbing successfully from one century and into another, but he imported his considerable criminal skills to another country where he was just as successful. And there is still the strong possibility that Butch survived the many attempts made on his life by determined posses, and died of old age in a West grown modern.

Cassidy was born Robert LeRoy Parker on a small farm in Circleville, Utah, one of ten children. All but two of the Parker brood, Robert and his younger brother Daniel, became law-abiding citizens. Robert turned to criminal activities in his early teens.

Mike Cassidy, a Western outlaw who had survived many a shoot-out since the 1850s, was a neighbor; young Parker grew so fond of him that he subsequently took the name Cassidy himself. Mike taught his young protege how to shoot better than any apprentice outlaw in the territory. Some stories had it that the teenager became so accurate with a six-gun that he could shoot a playing card dead center from fifty paces away. He was fast on the draw, too.

The elder Cassidy soon introduced his charge to cattle rustling, taking him on long drives in and about the Henry and Colorado Mountain ranges. Soon Butch assumed second-in-command of the Cassidy gang. He took over completely when Mike Cassidy disappeared into Texas after shooting down an angry Wyoming rancher.

Butch was a natural leader—calm, easy-going, soft-spoken, always reluctant to draw his gun in an argument. Violent, much-sought-after outlaws rode into Robber's Roost, his mountain retreat. There Cassidy met the train-robbing McCarty brothers, Tom and Bill, and Matt Warner, whose real name was Williard Christiansen. Warner was the son of a Mormon bishop.

Cassidy didn't hesitate when the McCarty brothers asked him to come along to Grand Junction, Colo., on a train raid they had planned. Butch's first robbery was a bust. The McCartys and Butch stopped the Denver and Rio Grande express on November 3, 1887. However the express guard gave them trouble from the start by not opening the safe as ordered. The McCartys pointed their six-guns at his head and he still refused.

"Should we kill him?" one of the brothers said.

"Let's vote," Butch said.

The vote went in favor of the guard and he was allowed to live. The train roared off leaving the bandits with nothing and cursing the obstinate guard. The trio switched to bank-robbing the following spring, hitting the large First National Bank of Denver, March 30, 1889.

Tom McCarty, who apparently possessed a macabre sense of humor, coolly approached the bank president and said: "Excuse me sir, but I just overheard a plot to rob this bank."

The bank president became apoplectic. "Lord," he finally managed. "How did you learn of this plot?"

"I planned it," the bandit said. "Put up your hands!"

The take was better this time. Butch, Matt Warner, and the McCarty brothers walked out of the bank without a shot being fired— and with $20,000 in notes. Matt Warner used his share of the robbery to open a saloon. Behind the bar he nailed a $10,000 bank note to the wall. Its denomination prevented any gang member from cashing it.

Next came the bank in Telluride, Colo. Butch and the McCartys brought $10,500 in currency out in a sack, again without gunplay, on June 24, 1889. The lawmen in the area, however, were leading massive posses against the raiders and the bandits decided to lay low.

Cassidy spent two years, from 1890 to 1892, working small ranches in Colorado and Utah as a cowboy. In Rock Springs, Wyoming he even put in some time as a butcher in a local store—from which sprang his nickname. But going legitimate was not for Butch. A drunk picked a fight with him one night and Cassidy knocked him out; a local lawman locked him up for disturbing the peace.

After his release, Butch vowed never to work for a living again. Teaming up with a small-time cattle thief, Al Rainer, Cassidy rode about the ranches in Colorado selling, of all things, "protection." If ranchers wanted to avoid having their cattle stolen, they could pay Butch and Rainer a fee. They would drive off any rustlers, Cassidy promised. If the ranchers refused, Butch and Rainer drove off the cattle. It was the kind of extortion that became a specialty with Al Capone, the Black Hand, and modern-day gangsters half a century later.

Sheriff John Ward of Wyoming tracked down the two protection specialists in early 1894, arresting them with stolen cattle near Afton. Ward crept up on Rainer and quickly had him tied to a tree. Butch was in a cabin. Ward went in after him with gun in hand. Cassidy dove for a chair where his pistol was holstered, but two fast shots from the Sheriff's gun creased his scalp and sent him flying unconscious to the floor.

Butch got two years in the Wyoming State Prison. There he heard about a fabulous hide-out and gathering place for the toughest gun-men and bandits in the West called the Hole-in-the-Wall, a mountain fortress in Colorado. When released from prison on January 19, 1896, this is exactly where Butch headed, along with two other ex-convicts: crafty, self-taught Elza Lay and gunman Bob Meeks.

There Butch met every notorious gunman and thief still operating in the West. The Lo-gan brothers, Harvey and his younger brother Lonnie, were already experienced bandits by their early twenties. Harvey Logan, the deadliest killer in the Wild Bunch, was also known as Kid Curry, taking his name from an older outlaw, Big Nose George Curry, who also hid out in Hole-in-the-Wall.

Butch got word, while in the mountains, that his old friends the McCartys had met disaster while attempting to rob the bank in Delta, Colo. Bill and Fred McCarty were shot to pieces by the townspeople, who had been informed of their raid by a gang member. The McCartys were displayed dead for one and all on wooden planks. Matt Warner was lucky. He was captured and sent off to do a long prison term for robbery (he would reform, however, and live to a ripe age, dying in 1937).

With Elza Lay as his lone companion, Butch struck the mining camp at Castle Gate, Utah in April, 1897, robbing the paymaster there of $8,000. The take was not as much as Butch expected, so he decided to go back to train-robbing.

Butch, George Curry, Harvey Logan, and Elza Lay stopped the Union Pacific's Overland Flyer on a small trestle near Wilcox, Wyo., June 2, 1889. There were problems right from the beginning when engineer W. R. Jones refused to uncouple the express car after the train ground to a halt. Though Logan viciously pistol-whipped Jones, Elza Lay finally had to move the train himself, jamming down the throttle.

The gang forgot a charge of dynamite they had placed beneath the trestle, but fortunately Lay got the train moving in time. The trestle exploded into fragments just as the Flyer got across.

Surrounding the express car, Cassidy and his men called to the guard inside, a man named Woodcock, to open up and come out.

"Come in and get me!" came Woodcock's brave reply.

A charge of dynamite was placed next to the car and the gang scattered. When it went off, the whole side of the express car was blown away and Woodcock was thrown out unconscious. Logan wanted to kill him, but Cassidy stepped in front of his guns. "Leave him be, Kid," Butch is quoted as saying. "A man with his nerve deserves not to be shot."

After blowing up the safe, the bandits had to scurry along the tracks, picking up bills that had been scattered by the blast. Their haul was substantial—$30,000 in currency and

Butch Cassidy of the Wild Bunch, a most happy-go-lucky outlaw. (Wyoming State Archives and Historical Department)

bonds.

This last raid brought in the Pinkertons; such relentless pursuers as Charlie Siringo and N. K. Boswell were soon on their trail. A posse cornered Logan, Curry, and Lay at Teapot Creek in Wyoming but the trio shot their way through; Harvey Logan shot and killed the posse's leader, Sheriff Joe Hazen, when the lawman was foolish enough to lead a frontal attack against the outlaws as they hid behind the rocks.

Butch and his gang struck next outside of Tipton, Wyo., by stopping Train No. 3 of the Union Pacific Railroad. By mere chance, the same guard, Woodcock, was in the express car. Cassidy was nonplussed for a minute; then he told the engineer to inform the guard "to open up the door or this time we'll blow him and the car sky-high."

The engineer pleaded and the plucky Woodcock submitted. The outlaws blew the safe with dynamite and made off with more than $50,000. A superposse headed by the feared Joe Lefors was hot on Cassidy's trail, but the gang escaped once again into its impenetrable hideout, the Hole-in-the-Wall.

From there, the gang rode out once more

Harry Longbaugh, known as The Sundance Kid, the fastest gun in the West.

—Cassidy, Logan, Deaf Charley Hanks, and a new man, an outlaw whose draw was the fastest ever seen in the West—Harry Longbaugh, better known as the Sundance Kid.

Longbaugh had served eighteen months in the Sundance jail in Wyoming when a boy, for horse stealing; he took the name The Sundance Kid from this experience. He wore only one gun but his aim was deadly. No member of the Wild Bunch ever tangled with Sundance. While Butch was raiding with the McCarty boys, Sundance had been robbing trains and banks. He held up the Great Northern train at Malta, Mont., in December, 1892 with Bill Madden and Harry Bass. Madden and Bass were captured and got ten years in jail; Sundance escaped, teaming up with Harvey Logan, Tom O'Day and Walt Putney to rob the bank in Belle Bourche, S. D. on June 27, 1897. The entire gang was captured. Longbaugh was booked under the alias of Frank Jones. He and Logan escaped from the Deadwood, S. D. jail October 31, 1897, just before their trial.

Some time in 1900, Sundance and Cassidy met at the Hole-in-the-Wall and became great friends. Both men were somewhat introverted, casual and hard to anger.

The gang hit the Great Northern Flyer almost in the same spot where Sundance had once waylaid the train near Malta, Mont. on July 3, 1901. Logan sneaked into the baggage car. Sundance sat in one of the coaches until it reached the outskirts of Wagner. There Logan jumped from the tender into the locomotive cab and, bristling two six-guns, ordered the engineer to stop the train. The Sundance Kid ran up and down the passenger cars, firing his pistol occasionally into the ceiling and yelling to riders; "Keep your heads inside!"

Butch and Charley Hanks got on the train when it came to a stop over a small bridge. The two had been staying at a nearby ranch. With them was one of the girls, Laura Bullion, who periodically stayed with the gang at Hole-in-the-Wall. Laura tended the horses while Butch and Hanks joined Logan and Sundance. Butch, employing his favorite tool, set a massive charge of dynamite under the Adams express car and blew off its side. The take was more than $40,000 in incomplete bank notes. The fact that the notes lacked the bank president's signature meant little to the gang. They merely forged a signature and cashed the notes.

A hundred-man posse chased after Butch and the gang following the Wagner robbery. Cassidy and company rode fast mounts and knew the territory well. They again escaped, this time heading for Fort Worth, Texas, where they stayed in Fannie Porter's luxurious brothel.

It was while languishing at Fannie's that Butch took up bicycle riding and Sundance took up with Etta Place, an uncommonly beautiful teacher and housewife who craved excitement.

Fort Worth was the end of this last great cowboy-outlaw band. Harvey Logan and others rode North in search of more plump banks to rob; Cassidy and Sundance decided against it. Butch tried to explain to Kid Curry that their free-booting days in the West were numbered. There were too many lawmen and law-abiding communities, and too few places left where outlaws could hide.

When some of the gang spent notes taken from the Wagner job, Fort Worth detectives began asking around town about the strangers from up North. Butch and Sundance decided to leave for South America. Etta Place went with them.

Etta Place, schoolteacher turned robber's accomplice; she traveled to South America with Butch and The Sundance Kid when they made their escape. (Pinkerton, Inc.)

The Pinkerton Detective Agency, which had so relentlessly pursued Cassidy and Sundance over the years, completely lost their trail. Then they picked it up in Argentina when banks there were suddenly robbed by two American cowboys.

Etta Place acted as a scout on these raids, entering the South American banks ostensibly to open an account, casing each bank and its guards, and then making her report to her two outlaw friends. For a while Butch and Sundance worked at the American-owned Concordia tin mine in Bolivia as day laborers. It was as good a dodge as any.

But their employer, Percy Seibert, discovered their identities and they departed after two years of legitimate work. In 1907, tired of the reckless life with her two bandits, Etta asked to go home. Sundance accompanied her to New York, where she had an appendicitis operation, and then on to Denver to recuperate. There Harry Longbaugh got drunk, shot up a saloon, and left his girl forever, making his way back to New York and then to the Grand Hotel in La Paz, Bolivia to once more join up with Butch.

It has been reported that the two friends continued their robbing and were finally trapped by a mounted company of soldiers near San Vincente, Bolivia in 1908, where the two men were passing themselves off as the Lowe brothers. Surrounded, the two bandits made a dash for their rifles and ammunition, which were on the other side of a large, open patio. As they ran, the story goes, the soldiers fired repeatedly, shooting Sundance several times. He fell in the dust and died. Butch, upon seeing his friend dead, simply turned his six-gun to his temple and fired.

Another story has it that Cassidy alone survived the Bolivian ambush and made his way back to the U.S., visiting his family in Utah as late as 1929 and dying about 1937 in Johnie, Nevada, where some claim his grave is located.

[ALSO SEE The Wild Bunch]

CERONE, JOHN PHILIP
Syndicate Gangster • (1914-   )

A former chauffeur for Chicago Mafia chief Tony Accardo, Cerone is considered a "master fixer" and West Side Chicago gambling boss. "Jackie the Lackie" Cerone has a record dating back to 1933, studded with nineteen arrests for gambling, bookmaking, robbery, armed robbery, and suspicion of murder (four homicides).

Cerone became the number-two man in the Chicago mob and ran a gambling operation out of his own home that reached across the country. He was arrested and sent to prison in 1970 and was released in 1973. Using vicious assassins such as Joseph Ferriola to take over new territory in 1979, Cerone vied with Aiuppa for total control of the rackets in Chicago, but he was outmaneuvered when he was assigned to oversee the Chicago mob's interests in Las Vegas.

He and other Chicago mobsters continued their skimming of money, millions, from Las Vegas casinos such as the Stardust, but Cerone and the others were too open in their taking of pretax profits.

Cerone, his nominal boss Aiuppa, Joseph "The Clown" Lombardo, a Chicago West Side crime boss, and Angelo LaPietra, a First Ward syndicate lieutenant, were all found guilty and given long prison terms. On March 25, 1986, following his trial in Kansas City, Mo., Cerone was given a 28-1/2-year term by U.S. District Judge Joseph E. Stevens, Jr. Cerone resides in prison at this writing.

(ALSO SEE Joseph Aiuppa.)

CHADWICK, CASSIE L.
Swindler ● (? -1907)

Her beginnings were indescribably poor, yet she would rise to the dizzy heights of millionaire's row through one of the most subtle swindles in American crime.

Born Elizabeth Bigley on a Canadian farm, Cassie moved alone to Toronto as a teenager.

Swindler Cassie Chadwick in 1894, the year she was caught after bilking millions from banks as the fake daughter of tycoon Andrew Carnegie. (UPI)

She ordered calling cards printed which read, "Miss Bigley—Heiress to $15,000" and handed these out at various department stores. Naive managers showered her with grand wardrobes, graciously accepting her worthless cards as promissory notes to pay.

Naturally, Cassie, bedecked in the latest fineries, skipped town. Crossing into the U.S., this auburn-haired, green-eyed seductress bilked, through fraud and blackmail, dozens of prosperous American businessmen. One historian estimated the young vamp made more than $1,000 a week from gullible Pullman car travelers.

Authorities finally overtook her; she was quickly tried and convicted of fraud, and sent to prison for three years. Upon her release, penniless, Cassie fielded about for more victims but her fleshy charm had dissipated. She turned to prostitution and, while working in a run-down whorehouse, met dimwitted Dr. Leroy Chadwick of Cleveland, Ohio.

The good doctor believed Cassie when she told him that she was merely on hand in the bordello to instruct the girls in courtly manners. He fell in love with the scheming trollop and married her.

Cassie, once established as Mrs. Leroy Chadwick, traveled to New York, taking a plush suite of rooms at the Holland House, a hostelry favored by socialities. In the lobby, she "accidentally" bumped into a prominent Ohio lawyer named Dillon. They knew each other slightly and Cassie asked if he would be good enough to escort her to the home of her father. Dillon agreed and an hour later sat stunned in an open carriage as Cassie Chadwick alighted and walked into the majestic Fifth Avenue mansion of Andrew Carnegie, the wealthiest man in the country.

Mrs. Chadwick stayed close to twenty-five minutes inside the Carnegie palace while Dillon waited and wondered. She had brazenly pushed aside the butler and, once past the front door, demanded to speak to the housekeeper. When the puzzled woman arrived, Cassie grilled her about the background of a domestic maid she was thinking of hiring.

Though the housekeeper denied that such a girl ever worked for Mr. Carnegie, Cassie kept chattering; her object was to consume time and she accomplished that feat quite neatly by slowly explaining how she must have been the victim of a hoax.

As she left the mansion, Dillon saw her wave to someone in the hallway; he assumed, Carnegie (it was the butler). Cassie had difficulty reentering the carriage and a slip of paper fell from her hand. When Dillon picked it up he was close to being struck dumb—it was a $2 million promissory note signed by the great Carnegie.

Apologetically, demurely, hesitantly, Mrs. Chadwick explained that she was really the multi-millionaire's illegitimate daughter and as such, Carnegie's guilt compelled him to foist huge sums of money upon her. Cassie stated that there was another $7 million in promissory notes from her "father" at home in Cleveland tucked away in a desk drawer. This was nothing, of course, said Mrs. Chadwick offhandedly, to the $400,000,000 she would inherit outright upon Carnegie's death.

Dillon, upon returning to Cleveland, and sworn to secrecy, immediately told everyone and anyone of importance about Cassie "Carnegie" Chadwick, as Cassie knew he would. At his insistence, Cassie took a sealed envelope to the biggest bank in town for safekeeping in a deposit box. Her scheme to swindle millions through this hoax was based heavily upon the fact that no one would dare embarrass tycoon Carnegie by asking that he verify the existence of an illegitimate daughter, namely Mrs. Chadwick. In this, Cassie was right.

The cashier at the bank, confident of Mr. Dillon's assurances, gave Mrs. Chadwick a receipt for $7 million without ever opening the envelope. In a short time, unscrupulous bankers all but forced her to take enormous loans against her notes. She pretended to be naive and accepted, correctly reasoning that the loans were attached with such illegally high interest rates that the bankers would never admit to making them. It was a high stakes flim-flam game that paid Cassie Chadwick off in millions.

She became the empress of Ohio as the duped bankers showered her with over $1,000,000 a year, never bothering to call the loans—delightedly watching the interest grow to staggering sums. When Carnegie died, they reasoned, Cassie Chadwick would pay . . . and pay handsomely.

Mrs. Chadwick thoroughly enjoyed her millions, reportedly spending $100,000 on a single dinner party; she bought diamond necklaces for the same amount, carriages, golden organs, thirty wardrobe closets full of the finest gowns in America. But never once did Cassie attempt to capitalize on her crooked fortune by investing. She got what she wanted—the money. To her it was to be spent.

Banks in New York and Cleveland never dared to question her loans, but after she applied for and received a $190,000 loan from a Boston bank, its meticulous New England president looked into Mrs. Chadwick's background.

He was aghast at the gigantic loans other banks had made to her and called his loan in. Cassie couldn't pay. The press blared the news and an Oberlin, Ohio bank which had given her $800,000 suffered a run so drastic that it closed its door forever.

Carnegie, a long-time bachelor (he had promised his mother, the story goes, that he would never marry while she lived), issued a statement through one of his aides when he heard of Mrs. Chadwick's preposterous swindle. "Mr. Carnegie does not know Mrs. Chadwick of Cleveland," the statement read. "Mr. Carnegie has not signed a note for more than thirty years."

It was the end of the golden dream. Cassie was arrested in 1904 and was convicted of swindling millions. She was sentenced to ten years in prison, where she died three years later as she had begun, forgotten and impoverished.

CHAPMAN, GERALD
Murderer, Robber, Jewel Thief ●
(1890-1926)

BACKGROUND: BORN AND RAISED IN BROOKLYN, N.Y. OF IRISH-AMERICAN PARENTS (NEE CHARTRES). MINOR PUBLIC EDUCATION. DESCRIPTION: 5'9". BLUE EYES, LIGHT BROWN HAIR, THIN, WIRY. ALIASES: NONE. RECORD: ARRESTED IN 1907, NYC, FOR PETTY THEFT; IN AND OUT OF PRISON FOR UNSUCCESSFUL ROBBERIES IN THE NYC AREA UP TO 1920; MOST SENTENCES SERVED AT NEW YORK'S AUBURN PRISON; ROBBED, WITH DUTCH ANDERSON (IVAN DAHL VON TELLER), A MAIL TRUCK OF THE PARK ROW POST OFFICE 10/24/21 ($1,454,129) CONTAINING REGISTERED MAIL—THE LARGEST THEFT IN AMERICAN HISTORY TO THAT DATE; APPREHENDED AND ESCAPED DAYS LATER FROM THE NYC JAIL, RECAPTURED; AFTER BEING CONVICTED AND SENTENCED TO ATLANTA PENITENTIARY, CHAPMAN

T here was nothing unusual about the birth of Gerald Chapman in 1890. His family name had originally been Chartres and he was raised in one of New York's more motley Irish districts where apple-stealing and street gang warfare was as ordinary as taking a breath.

Perhaps Chapman, who from 1907 to 1920 amassed a long series of arrests, would have wound up as a common and forgotten thief if he hadn't been locked in the same cell with a European dandy.

While waiting out a stretch in Auburn Prison in upstate New York, a criminally warped man from Denmark named Ivan Dahl von Teller was shown into Chapman's cell as his new mate. Von Teller's name in America was George "Dutch" Anderson.

Anderson was one of the most twisted men ever held in an American prison. He was cunning and intellectual. The son of a wealthy Dutch family, Anderson had attended such European citadels of learning as the Universities of Heidelberg and Upsala.

Dignified, aristocratic, Anderson glibly spoke five languages. His polish and worldly airs deeply impressed Chapman, who idolized the crafty crook. Anderson, in turn, took Chapman under his wing.

A swindler, con man, and embezzler, Anderson taught his young protege Chapman the

Dapper Gerald Chapman, who pulled off a $1 million mail robbery in 1921, is shown in his jail cell five years later, pensive and waiting to be hanged for murder. (UPI)

refinements and high art of crime. When Chapman was finally released, he did not resume his normal routine. He bought some fancy clothes, several homburg hats, and bided his time until Anderson was released. When Dutch was finally paroled, he and Chapman moved to the Midwest, where they fleeced suckers by the dozen. In the space of several months they were $100,000 richer.

They then moved back to New York and took a swanky apartment in Gramercy Park to live the high life of leisured gentlemen. Chapman took to dressing like his mentor Anderson, wearing spats, waist-tight tailored suits, and a monocle. He even carried a stylish and expensive cane.

Gerald Chapman had become every inch the gentleman . . . yet underneath his glossy exterior there lurked the pathological robber and killer.

The good food, fancy nightclubs, and Broadway chorus girls were expensive and soon the pair were short of funds. While casting about for some activity, Anderson and Chapman ran into an old crony of Auburn days, a cheap purse-snatcher, Charles Loeber.

Loeber had a plan. He explained that he had watched several unguarded mail trucks moving from Wall Street to the main New York post office.

"Inside those trucks there's millions, registered mail with money orders, bonds, securities . . . a fortune. But the job's too big for me alone . . . now with the three of us . . ."

Loeber had to say no more. The trio immediately made plans to rob the U.S. mails. They watched several mail trucks taking the Wall Street route to the main post office and then, in a stolen Cleveland car, on the night of October 24, 1921, they made their move.

Mail truck driver Frank Havernack slowly geared his truck up deserted Broadway. He paid no attention to the approaching Cleveland which suddenly swerved from behind and raced alongside his truck. A drunk, Havernack thought, and let the big car zoom in front.

Then the car dropped back again so that it was pacing the truck. Havernack was annoyed but decided to ignore the pesty motorist. Suddenly, the car door on the right swung open and Gerald Chapman, always agile, jumped onto the running board of the mail truck.

"Pull over and don't make any noise," Chapman ordered. There was a big, ugly pistol in his hand pointed at Havernack's stomach. The mail truck driver pulled over, got out, and opened the back of the truck, on Chapman's orders.

The trio pushed Havernack aside, tying him up with a laundry sack about his head. Then, digging under 33 sacks of regular mail, the robbers found five sacks of registered mail. Quickly, they scooped them up and fled.

They didn't know it until the sacks were opened, but the robbers had made the greatest haul in mail theft history to date, $1,424,-129!

In their hideout on Long Island, the thieves unhappily discovered that only $27,000 of their loot was in cash, the rest being in securities. These could be converted to cash but the process was long and complicated.

And it would cost them. Fences would demand as much as 40¢ on the dollar. But the thieves had no other choice, so Anderson and Chapman left for Muncie, Indiana where they had a contact.

Holed up on a farm owned by Ben Hance, Chapman and Anderson converted $100,000 of the stolen bonds. Then they returned to Broadway and lived it up, spending upward of $1,000 a day on expensive cars and women.

Their butler and chauffeur was none other than their partner in crime, Charlie Loeber. His lack of brains, Chapman and Anderson figured, rated him a reduction in status. His lack of brains also got them caught.

Loeber did not have the contacts out of town that his partners had, so he foolishly tried to convert his share of the mail robbery loot in New York. This quickly led to his arrest by detectives. He immediately blabbed about Anderson and Chapman and each were speedily picked up.

While waiting to stand trial in New York, Chapman attempted to escape by climbing along a ledge 75 feet above the ground. Though he was apprehended, newsmen inflated his image to that of another Jesse James. Chapman, never tired of having his picture taken, appeared in the New York papers behind bars. He posed with dignity, a gentleman crook, the image he liked best.

Both Chapman and Anderson were convicted and sent to prison for 25 years. The penitentiary to which they were sent was a tough one—Atlanta, but this didn't worry Chapman.

He vowed to escape. The massive publicity he had received while under detention in New York had gone to his head.

Shortly after Chapman went into his cell in Atlanta he planned his escape. He drank an entire bottle of disinfectant and was sent to the prison hospital with a very sore throat. Once there, he slugged an unsuspecting guard, sawed through the bars, and slid to the yard on a rope made of tied-together bedsheets.

Chapman's sensational escape made headlines throughout the country, but he was captured two days later. Police had to shoot him three times before he would surrender.

Following his recovery, Chapman again escaped from Atlanta, again using his bedsheet trick. This time he was successful and went immediately to the Hance farm in Indiana to hide out.

Dutch Anderson soon joined him after he, too, escaped from Atlanta by tunneling his way under the prison wall. This time the confederates thought to reverse their roles. They would commit crimes in the East and live in Chicago.

The two teamed up with an apprentice hoodlum, Walter Shean, and soon they attempted another big caper. They attempted to rob the largest department store in New Britain, Conn., but police intervened and the escaping robbers shot it out, killing one officer.

Shean was soon captured and bragged to police: "My pal was Gerald Chapman."

Chapman was captured in Muncie and taken to Hartford. Avid news readers waited daily for the latter-day Jimmy Valentine to escape just once more—but he didn't.

At his trial, Shean and others identified Chapman as the man who had killed the New Britain cop and he was convicted, sentenced to hang.

Chapman's reaction was laconic. "Death itself isn't dreadful," he said, "but hanging seems an awkward way of entering the adventure." Chapman went awkwardly into death on April 5, 1926.

Dutch Anderson, still at large, lost his mind at the death of his younger associate and convinced himself that the farmer Ben Hance had betrayed Chapman. He was wrong, but he killed Hance and his wife anyway and set their house on fire.

Dutch tried to kill Shean as well, but the

informer was too well guarded. This one-man vendetta was finally halted when a policeman in Muskegon, Michigan recognized Anderson, even though he was wearing one of his many disguises. Both men fired at the same time and killed each other.

CHAPMAN, MARK DAVID
Murderer ● (1955-   )

Texas-born Mark Chapman was a devoted Beatles fan, so absorbed by the life of John Lennon that he came to believe that he really was Lennon. As a teenager he religiously followed the careers of the four young men that made up the group, but he concentrated on Lennon.

Later, when the rather arrogant Lennon remarked that the Beatles were "more popular than Jesus," Chapman was deeply offended. By then Chapman had become a born-again Christian and he took Lennon's remark as that of an anti-Christ. Chapman's own life, however, was anything but religious. He traveled about the country, holding odd jobs. He was arrested for kidnapping, possession of drugs, and armed robbery. Each time he managed to wriggle free of the law. At one point, Chapman tried to commit suicide.

He married a travel agent and moved to Hawaii where he kept his wife a virtual prisoner of his own habits. She was not allowed to watch television or read newspapers. Chapman often stood outside of certain churches shouting abuse.

Later while working as a security guard, Chapman replaced the name plate on his uniform to read "John Lennon." He signed in and out of his job as "John Lennon." Psychiatrists later theorized that Chapman had totally assumed the singer's identity and resented the real Lennon's existence, so much so that he had to kill him to really replace him.

On December 6, 1980, Chapman flew to New York City on borrowed funds. He went to the Dakota, the apartment building where Lennon lived with his wife, Yoko Ono, and their young son. Chapman kept a two-day vigil and, at 11 P.M. on the night of December 8, 1980, when Lennon was returning home with his wife, Chapman accosted him, shouting: "Mr. Lennon!" As the singer turned Chapman shot him five times in the chest.

A patrolman grabbed the singer and put him into a squad car to rush him to a hospital. Lennon died before the squad got there.

Following the shooting, Chapman sat down in front of the apartment building and continued reading a novel, J. D. Salinger's *The Catcher in the Rye*. He was arrested and meekly went into custody, later saying: "I did not want to kill anybody, and I really don't know why I did."

On July 21, 1981, Chapman, after pleading guilty against his lawyer's suggestion, was sentenced to twenty years to life in prison. Chapman's only response was to read a passage from the Salinger novel. He was sent to Attica State Prison where he went to work as a janitor.

CHASE, RICHARD TRENTON
Serial Killer ● (1950-1980)

Between January 23 and 27, 1978, Richard Trenton Chase murdered six people in Sacramento, Calif. He was found naked and covered with the blood of a cow he had slain. Upon questioning, Chase admitted to killing six people and told investigators that he had drunk the blood of the last person he killed.

In 1979, Chase was put on trial that lasted for five months. Ferris Salamy, a public defender, pleaded Chase not guilty by reason of insanity but the court found him sane and convicted him. Chase was sent to prison for life and died in his cell on December 26, 1980.

CHESSMAN, CARYL
Robber, Sex-Offender ● (1921-1960)

Caryl Chessman, the alleged "Red Light Bandit" of Los Angeles, lived twelve agonizing years in San Quentin's death row before being executed.

Chessman's case was one of the most celebrated during the late 1940s. An habitual criminal, Chessman was a four-time loser (he entered a reformatory at 16) by the time he committed the robbery-rapes in a Los Angeles lover's lane in late 1947, crimes which labeled him the infamous "Red Light Bandit." On at least two occasions, Chessman was identified as the man who approached a parked car, flashing a red light on the occupants, and at gunpoint robbed the driver and compelled the woman to perform sexual acts with him.

He was apprehended on January 23, 1948, while driving a stolen car in Los Angeles, a capture which involved a wild chase through Los Angeles streets and ended with the auto being smashed to pieces. He was convicted of seventeen out of eighteen charges May 18, 1948, and in what was considered by many the harshest judgment ever meted out to a felon not having committed murder or kidnapping, sentenced to death the following July.

For twelve years, Chessman fought the death penalty and went through countless agonizing stays of execution. During this period he wrote his autobiography, *Cell 2455*, a moving and penetrating document. The fight to save his life was waged by thousands of persons from writers to housewives, but Governor Pat Brown, a reported foe of capital punishment, stated he felt the condemned man was guilty and would not stay the execution date in 1960, when Caryl Chessman walked into the gas chamber at San Quentin Prison.

There is no doubt that Chessman's prolonged suffering on death row was unusually cruel punishment which he himself succinctly and poignantly summed up in his own writing: "While I have waited this eternity to die, one woman [Barbara Graham] and sixty-nine men have been executed in that 'Green Room' below. Others have gone mad. A demented few have cheated the executioner by violently taking their own forfeited lives. I myself have been within hours of having my life snuffed out before desperate legal action abruptly halted the execution.

"I am not disturbed by outraged assurances that I am headed straight for the hottest and most horrible part of hell the moment I inhale those lethal cyanide fumes. Whenever and however it comes, my physical death will mean only a total cessation of consciousness. And if this Christian hell, by some one-in-ten-billion chance, turns out to be an afterlife reality, I am convinced that the Prince of Darkness will be taxed to devise a torture I would regard as merely an annoyance after my conditioning by the sovereign State of California . . ."

CHRISTIE, NED
Bandit ● (? -1892)

An Oklahoma bandit, rumrunner, and horsethief, Christie began his criminal career in 1885 and was the terror of the Oklahoma territory. Seven years later, the renowned marshal Heck Thomas laid siege to an ancient but sturdy wooden fort near Tahlequah in which the outlaw and his gang had taken refuge.

Thomas brought in an army cannon and fired dozens of shells into the fort, but its

Ned Christie, Oklahoma bandit, fought it out with lawmen and lost; he is shown here, propped up with a rifle in his hands, after having been killed in a gun battle. (Western History Collctions, U. of Okla. Library)

double-wall construction prevented any damage. Next, Thomas ordered his sharpshooters to open up. After 2,000 bullets had whanged into the wooden edifice, the marshal resorted to dynamite. When a breach was finally made, Christie rode out through a cloud of smoke firing his rifle. Fifty guns wielded by possemen were trained on him; he was blasted dead from the saddle.

CIRCUS GANG

A satellite of the Capone gang during the 1920s, the Circus Gang was headed up by J. E. "Screwy" Moore (alias Claude Maddox) with headquarters on Chi-

cago's Northwest Side. Maddox hailed from Missouri and had had a criminal record since he was seventeen years old.

This gang functioned as a sort of "service" outfit, equipping Capone with criminals who specialized in safe-cracking, such as Red Rudensky, and with arms suppliers like Peter von Frantzius, who first introduced the use of the machinegun to Prohibition mobsters.

Its members were later absorbed into the national crime syndicate.

CIUCCI, VINCENT
Murderer ● (1925-1962)

Ciucci, a grocery store owner in Chicago, fell in love with pretty eighteen-year-old Carol Amora. In an effort to free himself from his family, Ciucci chloroformed his wife Anne and his three children on the night of December 4, 1953, and then shot all four in the head. He then faked a fire, setting ablaze his three-room apartment which was located behind his grocery store.

As firemen arrived, Ciucci stumbled from his apartment claiming that he had been overcome by the fumes. He appeared surprised when friends informed him that his wife and children were dead. It was a stupid murder plan, for autopsies of the bodies soon disclosed that they had been shot.

Vincent Ciucci, shown in his 1953 Chicago trial, denied murdering his wife and children, but overwhelming evidence convicted him; he died in the electric chair in 1962, the last man to be executed in Illinois. (UPI)

Ciucci was charged with the killings. "I admit I'm a gambler," he pleaded, "and I like to fool around with women, but I wouldn't do a thing like that . . . How could a man kill his own children? He would kill himself instead!"

At his trial, Ciucci claimed that he was framed, that parties unknown entered his apartment, killed his family, and set fire to his house. The jury disbelieved his story.

Ciucci was sentenced to death. Appeals for commutation dragged on for years. Finally, in 1962, Vincent Ciucci had run out of time and appeals. He was electrocuted, the last man in the State of Illinois to die in the electric chair.

CLARK, DOUGLAS DANIEL
(THE SUNSET SLAYER)
Serial Killer ● (1959-   )

A sex pervert and wanton killer, Douglas Clark hungered after young blonde girls to kill in Los Angeles. Oddly, he was aided in his gruesome pasttime by an older woman, Carol Bundy (1943-   ), who did her utmost to satisfy Clark's sexual fantasies. Bundy was a former Burbank nurse and the mother of two children. When she met Clark in 1980, the young factory worker explained to the older woman that he felt compelled to murder young women.

This somehow excited Bundy, who quickly disposed of her then-lover, John Robert Murray, by decapitating him. Next, she took up with Clark, abandoning her children to relatives. In the spring of 1980, Bundy cruised L.A. streets, chiefly Sunset Boulevard, picking up young blonde prostitutes and delivering these women to Clark.

Clark shot the women, then had sex with their corpses. By his own estimate, this vicious killer murdered 50 women. Bundy later claimed that Clark's goal was to kill 100 women, then quit. He never got to that number.

Arrested on August 11, 1980, Clark was not tried until January 1983. He was convicted of killing six women and sentenced to death on February 15, 1983. Bundy received a 52-year sentence for murdering Murray.

CLARK, MICHAEL
Mass Murderer ● (1949-1965)

A sixteen-year-old boy suddenly decided to play "King of the Hill" in the Spring of 1965, a game that took the lives of three people and wounded a half-dozen more. Without explanation, Michael Clark took his father's Swedish Mauser deer rifle and several boxes of armor-piercing bullets and jumped into the family Cadillac. He drove 150 miles north from Los Angeles up Highway 101, ramming the car into a guard rail.

Clark took the rifle and ammunition to the top of a hill overlooking the highway and waited. The next morning he began shooting at the first cars that came into view. He missed the first car but struck William Reida, driver of the second car. A bullet smacked into Reida's neck, wounding him. Another bullet struck Reida's five-year-old son Kevin in the head and killed him.

Reida's frantic wife stopped two more passing cars, begging the drivers to help her family. When the drivers got out of their cars, Clark picked them off, killing both persons. Cars began to pile up as Clark let loose a terrible barrage that wounded another three people, including a police officer. Six more were injured by shards of glass flying from car windows shattered by Clark's bullets.

Police arrived at the highway in force and began storming up the hill where Clark stood firing. The boy shouted down the hill to them: "Come and get me!" As officers closed in, Clark put the rifle to his head and pulled the trigger. He fell to the earth dead, What motivated this seemingly normal, happy youth to turn mass murderer was never learned.

COHEN, MICKEY
Syndicate Gangster ● (1913-1976)

He was small and stocky, a hot-headed, loud-mouthed goon who enjoyed flashing his guns and frightening young girls and

Los Angeles gangster Mickey Cohen, right, with body-guard Johnnie Stompanato.

old ladies. Mickey Cohen was also a dandy who had earned a fortune by running a successful bookmaking operation in Los Angeles.

Benjamin "Bugsy" Siegel arrived in Los Angeles in the late 1930s and Cohen became his chauffeur and bodyguard. When Siegel was murdered in a mob hit ordered by Charles "Lucky" Luciano and others for reneging on loans they had made to fund Siegel's Las Vegas casino, Cohen went berserk.

He drove madly about Los Angeles looking for the killers of his boss. He marched into the Roosevelt Hotel where he believed the slayers were hiding, and stood in the lobby shouting for the hit men to meet him in the street. He took out two .45-caliber automatics and loudly emptied them into the ceiling of the foyer but this failed to produce Siegel's killers.

The mantle of syndicate leadership fell to Frankie Carbo, not the posturing, diminuative Cohen. This irked Cohen who went about town proclaiming that he ran things in L.A. His actions caused investigations by state and federal authorities into the affairs of Carbo and the Dragna Family. The enraged Carbo marked Cohen for death.

Cohen's luxury home was bombed and several attempts were made on his life. Cohen announced that he would do battle with Carbo or anyone else who dared to attack him. He equipped his home with floodlights and an elaborate alarm system. He kept attack dogs on the place and his private arsenal was almost as large as the closet that held his more than 200 tailor-made suits.

He also hired John Stompanato as a bodyguard and was incensed that this gangster was killed

in a domestic fight in actress Lana Turner's home, one in which Turner's fourteen-year-old daughter, Cheryl Crane, stabbed Stompanato to death with a butcher knife on April 4, 1958.

What particularly enraged Cohen was that Turner refused to pay for her ex-lover's funeral and Cohen had to foot the bill. He bought a cheap wooden coffin for Stompanato. Then, he vindictively gave the press Turner's love letters to Stompanato.

Cohen's gambling operations continued to pour a fortune into his pockets, and he gained some personal security after he agreed to keep his mouth shut and pay heavy tribute to Carbo. His life tumbled down, however, when he was convicted of income tax evasion and was given a four-year sentence. Upon his release he attempted to reestablish his gambling operations but was again jailed for tax evasion, this time for ten years.

Prison life was unkind to Mickey Cohen. He was surly and picked fights with other prisoners, strutting his five-foot-five-inch body about as if he were the boss. A fellow inmate crashed a lead pipe down on Cohen's head, crushing it and permanently damaging Cohen's mind. When he was released, Cohen, his brains scrambled, was shamelessly used by certain members of the press to condemn prison violence. He stood before cameras and mumble-mouthed incoherent sentences while his eyes rolled in his head. Cohen died of a heart attack two years later in 1976.

(ALSO SEE Carbo, Frankie; Crane, Cheryl; Siegel, Benjamin.)

COLE, CARROLL
Serial Killer • (? -1985)

From 1971 to 1980, Carroll Cole drifted through Texas, California, Nevada, Oklahoma, and Wyoming. He was a drunk, a degenerate, and a necrophiliac. He murdered at least seven women and later bragged that he had slain 35 females. He hated his mother, he told authorities after his arrest in 1979. He murdered what he termed "loose women" who reminded him of his mother: "I think I kill her through them."

First brought to trial in Texas in 1981, Cole was

found guilty and sentenced to three life terms for three separate murders to which he confessed. He also stated that he was drunk each time he killed and that after murdering each woman, he had sex with their corpses. Cole was dissatisfied with the verdict. He did not want to spend the rest of his life in a cell. Death was what he craved.

Cole blurted out a confession of killing two more women in Nevada and that state extradited him for trial in Las Vegas. Cole asked for a bench trial, believing that a judge would be more likely to send him to his death than would a jury. He was correct. Found guilty of strangling 51-year-old Marnie Cushman to death in a Las Vegas hotel room in 1979, Cole was sentenced to death, a verdict he greeted with delight, smiling when he heard it, and saying "Thanks, Judge." He was executed by lethal injection on December 6, 1985, at Carson City, Nevada.

COLEMAN, ALTON
Serial Killer, Kidnapper ● (1955-   )

Alton Coleman began his one-man crime wave on May 29, 1984, when he kidnapped nine-year-old Vernita Wheat of Kenosha, Washington. The Wheat girl was found strangled to death in the bathroom of an unoccupied building in Waukegan, Ill., on June 19. Coleman was identified as the kidnapper-killer, along with nineteen-year-old Debra Brown, his accomplice. Because Coleman had transported the Wheat child across a state line for immoral purposes, he had violated federal law and this allowed FBI agents to join in the manhunt for him.

The hunt led to Gary, Ind., where, on June 18, Coleman strangled to death Tameka Turks, seven, and raped and tried to kill her cousin, nine-year-old Annie Hillard. The Hillard girl escaped the ropes binding her, and was found walking dazed along a road. She gave a full description of Coleman.

A Gary hairdresser, Donna Williams, vanished at this time and it was believed that Coleman kidnapped her when stealing her car, which was found in Detroit on June 26. Coleman and Brown had occupied an apartment close to the salon where Williams had worked.

Two days before the Williams car was found, Coleman stopped a woman and stole her car, driving it to Inkster, a Detroit suburb. In Dearborn Heights, later that week, Coleman and Brown invaded a home, beat its occupants, and stole their car, which was found at the Detroit Airport. The couple flew to Cincinnati where Coleman reportedly suffocated to death fifteen-year-old Tonnie Storey. On July 15, Coleman and Brown invaded another home in Norwood, a Cincinnati suburb, where they beat Harry Waters and murdered his 44-year-old wife, Marlene.

Five days later, Coleman and Brown were trapped in an Evanston, Ill., park and police took them into custody. Both were extradicted to Ohio where, in 1985, they were found guilty of killing Storey and Waters. Each received a death sentence.

In Indiana, on April 6, 1986, Coleman was convicted of murdering Tameka Turks and raping Hillard. He received another death sentence. He was tried again in Illinois where he acted as his own attorney. He was convicted and sentenced to death. "I am a dead man," Coleman moaned after the sentence. "I am dead already. I was a fool to represent myself and I admit it." He did not admit to the gruesome killings he had committed. Coleman was the only man facing four separate death sentences in the U.S. Through appeals, he has put off his exeution.

COLI, ECO JAMES
Syndicate Gangster ● (1922-   )

Considered by authorities to be a high-ranking labor terrorist and Chicago West Side boss, Coli's record of arrests dates back to 1945 and includes attempted hijacking, assault, and several murder investigations in which he was the prime suspect.

Coli was convicted of contributing to the delinquency of minors and placed on probation. His second conviction for armed robbery in 1952 led to an eight-to-ten-year term in the Illinois State Prison in Joliet. After serving three years he was paroled by the Illinois Supreme Court.

COLL, VINCENT ("MAD DOG")
Gangster, Murderer ● (1909-1932)

BACKGROUND: BORN AND RAISED IN NEW YORK CITY, THE SECOND SON OF IMMIGRANT PARENTS FROM COUNTY KILDARE, IRELAND. MINOR PUBLIC EDUCATION. DESCRIPTION: 6'1", BLUE EYES, BROWN HAIR, SLENDER. ALIASES: UNKNOWN. RECORD: ARRESTED WHILE A TEENAGER AS A DISORDERLY CHILD AND PLACED IN IMMACULATE VIRGIN MISSION; ARRESTED BEFORE HIS 21ST BIRTHDAY FOR BREAKING AND ENTERING, THEFT, GRAND LARCENY, AND VIOLATION OF PAROLE; SENT TO ELMIRA, N.Y. REFORMATORY FOR A SHORT PERIOD; FROM 1930-32, BECAME A BOOTLEGGER AND POLICY RACKETS GANGSTER; MURDERED VINCENT BARELLI AND HIS GIRL FRIEND MARY SMITH, 1931; KILLED FIVE-YEAR-OLD MICHAEL VENGALLI, 1932 IN AN ATTEMPT TO SLAY ANOTHER GANGSTER; KILLED IN A TELEPHONE BOOTH IN A MANHATTAN DRUGSTORE IN 1932 BY GUNMEN ON ORDERS FROM THE MOBSTER LEADER DUTCH SCHULTZ.

Vincent "Mad Dog" Coll (center) shakes hands with his lawyer, Samuel Leibowitz, following a 1931 acquittal for murder. (UPI)

The short bitter life of Vincent Coll was marked by incredible violence that caused revulsion even in his fellow gangsters. Coll more than earned the sobriquet "Mad Dog" in his brief and awesome twenty-three years.

In the Irish ghetto poverty of Hell's Kitchen, stealing soon became second nature to Coll and his brother Peter. Their childhood twisted from one petty theft to another, from overturned pushcarts to looting department stores. Coll's rise was similar to that of Jack "Legs" Diamond in that it was meteoric and ruled by the gun. His span of criminal success and notoriety, however, was considerably less than Diamond's.

After a number of petty arrests and a hitch in the reformatory at Elmira, Coll became determined to make the big money; he hired out to Dutch Schultz as a gunman and rumrunner at $150-a-week. He enforced the Dutchman's mandate in every saloon that squatted in Schultz's Bronx and Harlem territories. Friends described Coll as mentally unbalanced, a sadistic brutal young man who enjoyed beating up bartenders.

Although Coll enjoyed his job, he disliked working for Schultz, or anybody else for that matter. He had ideas of his own. He, Vinnie Coll, would form his own gang and steal the Dutchman's empire. Enlisting his brother Peter and two young hoodlums, Arthur Palumbo and Frank Giordano, Coll went foraging for an army. His first selection was a trusted Schultz lieutenant, Vincent Barelli, who had solid connections on the bootleg front.

Barelli turned out to be a loyal sort and twice refused to join Coll's embryonic gang. The second time Barelli and his girl Mary Smith met Coll in 1931 guns exploded. When Barelli again turned Coll down, the youthful mobster yanked out a pistol and shot both Barelli and Miss Smith dead.

To make matters worse with the Dutchman, Coll had the impudence to set up headquarters in a speakeasy only a half block from Schultz's office. From this vantage point, Coll began pirating several top gunmen from the Dutchman's employ.

Schultz thought to teach his ex-aide a lesson. He kidnapped Peter Coll and had him shot to death on a quiet street in Harlem.

"That yellow rat!" Coll screamed when he heard how his brother had died. "I'm gonna burn the Dutchman to hell!" Vinnie went to work with unbridled passion. He stole the Dutchman's beer trucks by the dozens and killed the drivers. He took over a huge section of Schultz's Manhattan policy racket. He didn't stop at Schultz but attacked and made inroads against the rackets controlled by crime czars such as Owney Madden and Legs Diamond, who were the Dutchman's friends and associates. He kidnapped Madden's second-in-command, George "Big Frenchy" DeMange and held him captive until receiving $35,000 in ransom money. But his vengeance was mostly vented on Schultz. He harassed the gangster so much that the Dutchman placed a $50,000 reward for Coll's dead body and moaned to his men: "Get Coll off my back! Get the Mick off my back!"

One of Dutch's men attempted to do exactly that. Joey Rao, Schultz's enforcer in the policy racket, took two of his best gunmen and stalked Vincent Coll through the streets of New York. Coll, on the other hand, had learned of the price on his head and Rao's intent. He and his men went looking for Rao.

In July of 1932, Coll spotted Rao and his two henchmen walking down East 107th Street. It was a hot day and every child in the neighborhood was on the sidewalk playing. Rao wended his way through the playing groups of children. Just as he approached one group, a car suddenly swept past and Coll, holding a machinegun out the car's window, sprayed the street.

Rao and his bodyguards ducked but the children didn't. Residents were horrified to see five small children, ages two to four, writhing on the sidewalk, some of them shot four and five times. All survived except five-year-old Michael Vengalli, whose stomach had been blown away by Coll's .45-caliber slugs.

Coll was identified and the newspapers screamed he was a "Mad Dog Killer" who had to be eradicated. The young murderer knew it would be only a matter of time before he was caught and tried. He wanted the best lawyer in town for that: Samuel Leibowitz, but lawyers like Leibowitz were expensive. To raise a defense fund, Coll kidnapped another top aide of Owney Madden's and held him for ransom. Bootlegger Madden paid $30,000 and got his man back. Coll paid Leibowitz and got an acquittal.

To celebrate his freedom, Coll married heavyset Lottie Kreisberger, his chorus girl sweetheart. The honeymoon was brief.

Four of Dutch Schultz's gunmen, one of them Rao (who reportedly swore vengeance on Coll for killing the Vengalli child), caught up with the Mad Dog as he was talking on the phone to none other than Owney Madden, then one of Coll's shakedown victims.

Coll was jabbering threats to Owney's life from a phone booth in a drugstore located on West Twenty-Third Street. Schultz's torpedo merely stepped up to the booth and yanked a submachinegun from beneath his coat. Coll's eyes grew big behind the small glass doors of the booth as he watched the man raise the weapon and aim. There was no room for Vincent Coll to draw his own gun and when the burst of .45-caliber shells tore into him he could do nothing but die helplessly.

Oddly enough, Vincent Coll had been hired by Salvatore Maranzano to kill Lucky Luciano and Vito Genovese during the Mafia's 1930 Castellammarese War in New York. Maranzano, however, was murdered by Luciano and Genovese first. One wonders how the national crime cartel would have developed if the Mad Dog had fulfilled his "contracts."

The mobster who wanted to be a big shot had been hit by fifteen bullets in the head and chest. Police found a miserable $101 in his pockets. Vincent Mad Dog Coll was down on his luck to the last.

COLLINS, JOHN NORMAN (THE YPSILANTI KILLER)
Serial Killer ● (1947-   )

Seven young women were raped and murdered near the campus of the University of Michigan between July 1967 and July 1969. The citizens of Ypsilanti and Ann Arbor, where the savaged bodies were found, were terrified and demanded police find the berserk killer.

The victims were invariably reported as being picked up by someone driving either a car or motorcycle. All were found sexually assaulted and strangled. Some were mutilated. Without clues, officials reached out to anyone who might help them, including Peter Hurkos, the famous psychic.

Hurkos studied the effects of the slain women and other murder artifacts and reported to police that the killer was about 25 years old and was heavyset but he could provide nothing more, except a chilling prediction. The slayer would strike again. He did, on July 23, 1969, murdering eighteen-year-old Sue Beineman, a freshman at EMU (Eastern Michigan University). Beineman was last seen riding with a man on a motorcycle. Her body was found on July 26.

Following leads, police shortly tracked down John Norman Collins, an EMU student who was well known to be obsessed with women, and that his behavior could be definitely defined as aberrant. His girlfriends described Collins as "oversexed." Collins was officially charged with killing Beineman after recently cut hairs were found in her panties. The hairs came from the children of State Police Sergeant David Leik, whose wife was Collins's aunt. Collins had recently cut the hair of the Leik children.

Collins was tried at Ann Arbor where he was described as a "bondage freak" who constantly fantasized about torturing women. His mother, Loretta Collins, had mortgaged her home to pay for her son's defense, repeatedly stating that "I know my boy didn't do it." Collins was nevertheless convicted on July 31, 1969. Judge John W. Conlin sentenced him to life imprisonment.

COLOMBO, JOSEPH, SR.
Mafia Boss • (1914-1978)

Beginning as a member of the New York Mafia family of Joseph Bonnano, Colombo was an effective enforcer and rose to the rank of lieutenant. In 1964, when Bonnano decided to kill all the bosses of rival Mafia families in New York, Colombo was selected as the man to direct the executions.

When Colombo looked over the hit list, which included Thomas "Three-Finger Brown" Lucchese, Carlo Gambino, and several others, he saw that half the ruling members of the syndicate had been marked for murder. Colombo instantly realized that to attempt such a slaughter would mean his own death.

Colombo immediately informed all those on the list that Bonnano had marked them for death. The bosses had "Joe Bananas" kidnapped and released him only after he promised to retire from the rackets. Bonnano, however, began open war in New York, using Colombo to seek revenge for his humiliation.

Pretending to carry out Bonnano's orders, Colombo really worked for his boss's rivals and was eventually rewarded for this betrayal by being named head of the Joe Profaci family when Profaci died. He proved inept. Colombo short-changed his own mob members, insisting they pay him a share of the profits from their petty rackets, which had previously been theirs to keep.

When the Gallo Brothers asked for a larger share from the rackets they managed for Colombo, the crime boss refused. This led to a bloody gang war that took the lives of many. Colombo next made the crucial mistake of stepping into the public eye.

He suddenly felt it necessary to champion the image of Italians and Sicilians everywhere, creating an organization he called the Italian-American Civil Rights League, much to the chagrin of the other Mafia family bosses. It was Colombo's aim to create a shield for his own Mafia operations with an organization that opposed all those who associated any Italian or Sicilian with underworld operations. He undoubtedly took his idea from the old *Unione Siciliane*, which did much the same thing in the 1920s but was controlled wholly by Mafia dons such as Frankie Yale.

Colombo staged enormous rallies in downtown New York in an attempt to establish his League. He named New York Governor Nelson Rockefeller as an honorary member and began drawing up lists of important personalities who would receive similar honors. Joey Gallo also made up a list with Colombo's name at the top, a murder list. Knowing that he could not appear at the next rally, which was to be held on June 28, 1971, since he would be recognized by Colombo's bodyguards, Gallo enlisted the aid of a professional killer from Harlem.

Jerome A. Johnson was the black assassin Gallo recruited from his underworld contacts in Harlem. Wearing a fake press badge on the day of the rally, Johnson got very close to Colombo and fired three shots into the Mafia leader before he himself was shot to death by Colombo's gunmen. Colombo survived but a bullet had permanently damaged his brain and he was no longer a factor in the syndicate. He died in 1978, and with him the fantastic dream of creating a powerful Italian-American civic league that would front for the sinister doings of the Mafia.

(ALSO SEE Joseph Bonnano; Unione Siciliane; Frankie Yale)

COLOSIMO, JAMES ("BIG JIM")
Gangster, Brothel Keeper ● (1877-1920)

Immigrating with his father Luigi from Consenza, Italy in 1895, Colosimo began humbly as a newspaper boy in Chicago who shined shoes on the side. He also labored long as a section-gang water boy and then graduated to the sanitation department, pushing a broom through the streets of the notorious First Ward, known in the Nineties as the Levee, a vice-ridden red light district crawling with crime and overlorded by two of the most colorfully corrupt politicians of the era—Alderman Michael "Hinky Dink" Kenna and his erstwhile side-kick Bathhouse (he once worked as a rubber) John Coughlin.

Colosimo, who had tried his hand at petty thievery and pickpocketing, attempted to make a living as a pimp but was arrested at eighteen and went to work for Kenna and Coughlin instead, serving as their bagman. It was Colosimo's chore to collect the kickbacks of those brothels operating in the First Ward.

In this capacity, Colosimo met Victoria Moresco, an obese and aging madam who ran an Amour Avenue whorehouse and was attracted to his swarthy animal magnetism. She offered him the managership of her brothel and he immediately accepted, marrying Victoria two weeks later in the bargain.

From 1902 Colosimo's fortunes grew. He added one new brothel after another to his chain with the blessings of his political sponsors Kenna and Coughlin. Big Jim became the king of pimps, owning thirty to forty $1 and $2 cribs and two swanky brothels, the Saratoga and the Victoria (named for his wife), which were frequented by every high roller of the day. Kenna and Coughlin received handsome kickbacks.

The take for Colosimo was colossal. He raked in $1.20 for every $2 trick. Dozens of Colosimo saloons, connected to his brothels via side-doors and tunnels, added to his daily coffers. As a labor racketeer he had also moved strong-armed thugs into a dozen unions, skimming mightily from union membership dues. He became a young millionaire. Jim took to wearing well-tailored suits and ostentatious arrays of diamonds—diamond belt buckles, diamond shirt studs, diamond rings, diamond cufflinks.

To add to his personal glitter, the gangster opened the gaudiest, poshest, most elegant nightclub west of the Alleghenies—Colosimo's Cafe at 2126 South Wabash Avenue. It boasted a mahogany and glass bar unequalled in craftsmanship, and a dining room of green velvet walls trimmed with gilded filigree. The sky-blue ceiling was adorned with baroque paintings of nymphs, pucks, and pans frolicking among Nirvana-like surroundings; solid gold chandeliers hung overhead. Crystal chandeliers graced the dancehall, which featured a dance floor that was lowered or raised by a hydraulic lift.

Colosimo made it a point to hire the best entertainment available; the cream of Chicago's society rushed in to sit at his elbow-jamming tables where out-of-town personalities and close friends of Big Jim's like opera stars Amelita Galli-Curci, Luisa Tetrazzini, Cleofonte Campanini, and Enrico Caruso would regularly be seen.

Here the elite of society mixed with the elite of the underworld. Social butterflies played name-games as they pointed out tuxedoed gangsters such as "Issy the Rat" Buchalsky; Vincenzo "Sunny Jim" Cosmano, a notorious Blackhander who had often extorted money from Big Jim; gamblers Mont Tennes and Julius "Lovin' Putty" Annixter; union overlords like Joey D'Andrea and *Unione Sicil-*

Big Jim Colosimo brought Johnny Torrio and Al Capone to Chicago from New York to run his rackets for him; it cost him his life. (UPI)

iane chief Mike Merlo; and whoremasters such as Charlie Genker, Dennis "Duke" Cooney, and "Mike de Pike" Heitler; political bosses Kenna and Coughlin; newspaper reporters Jack Lait, Ben Hecht, Ring Lardner; gunmen Tommy O'Connor, Samuel J. "Nails" Morton, Dion O'Bannion—a polyglot *Who's Who* that would stagger the mind of any dedicated reformer.

As Colosimo's empire spread out through the Levee and other areas of the city, his enforcement arm blossomed. To keep tight control of his vast interests, Big Jim enlisted the aid of some of the toughest gunmen in the Midwest. His bully boys included Jim "Duffy the Goat" Franche, Mac Fitzpatrick (alias W. E. Frazier), Joseph "Jew Kid" Grabiner, Billy Leathers, Harry Gullet, and his pistol-packing brother-in-law Joseph Moresco. These men swore to die to defend Big Jim in an elaborate ceremony which included taking the oath on Colosimo's family Bible.

Irrespective of this formidable assemblage of muscle and gunpower, Big Jim was easy prey for Blackhanders who threatened to blow up his cafe or whorehouses unless he forked over sizable amounts of money. At first, Colosimo and his troops fought back by dumping the payoffs at specified secret spots and then ambushing the extortionists when they came to collect, but it proved too hazardous.

To correct the problem, Colosimo, in 1910, sent for his gangster nephew, Johnny Torrio, who led the ruthless Five Points gang in New York. Torrio, fleeing a murder charge in Brownsville, eagerly accepted the new post and the Blackhanding stopped months after his arrival.

For a decade, Big Jim enjoyed his wealth and power. He divorced his fat whorehouse wife, Victoria, and married showgirl Dale Winter, a sweet-faced, nineteen-year-old ingenue from Ohio who had starred in the roadshow of *Madame Sherry*, a comic operetta.

Colosimo doted on Miss Winter and became not only her husband but sponsor, arranging music lessons for her, introducing her to Caruso, escorting her to Chicago's most dazzling social functions. Instead of attending to his brothels, Big Jim spent most of his time either with Dale or inside his plush cafe hob-nobbing with celebrities. His taciturn, organization-minded nephew, Torrio, was left to run everything.

Torrio, who was once called "the father of modern American gangsterdom," did run everything, pocketing $1 million a year from Colosimo's booze and brothel kingdom. But he was not the boss and Johnny Torrio was an ambitious man.

In 1919, Torrio all but got on his knees before his opera-loving uncle, begging Big Jim to branch out into hijacking and bootlegging. The National Prohibition Act, Torrio argued, was heaven-sent for the likes of them; there would be millions, super millions, to be made by selling illegal hootch. But Colosimo had grown fat and content with what he had. "We stay with the whores, Johnny," he said and scoffed at Torrio's wild schemes.

Sorrowfully, Torrio sent for a bloodthirsty plug-ugly who had served as his enforcer in the old Five Points gang—a heavyset, cheek-scarred, egostistical gangster named Al Capone. Ostensibly, Capone's new job with Torrio was that of a bouncer and bag man for Big Jim's brothels. His real mission in Chicago was to kill Colosimo, a job for which Torrio had neither the stomach nor the heart.

On May 11, 1920, Torrio called his uncle and told him that a shipment of whiskey would be delivered to his cafe that afternoon, promptly at 4 p.m. Big Jim would have to sign for it personally. Colosimo was there, waiting in the vestibule of his club at precisely that time.

Capone was hiding at that moment in a glass-paneled telephone booth. He fired two shots through the glass when Colosimo passed him, the first bullet entering Big Jim's head behind the right ear, the second slamming into a wall.

Big Jim toppled heavily to the tiled floor of the vestibule, face down, dead. Capone rushed from his hiding spot, turned the crime czar over, ripped open his shirt front, withdrew his money-crammed wallet, and fled. (A porter at the cafe had seen Capone enter but testified to police that the man was a "stranger.")

Old World crime ceased in Chicago after that. Big Jim's idea of enforcement was brass knuckles; Torrio and Capone would employ the machinegun. Big Jim's flashy showmanship gave away to Torrio's secrecy and Capone's stealth.

It was still quite fashionable to be a gangster after Colosimo's murder, but it was no longer "a safe bet."

[ALSO SEE Al Capone, Johnny Torrio, *Unione Siciliane.*]

COLUMBO, PATRICIA
Mass Murderer ● (1957-   )

Patricia Columbo, convicted of murdering her parents and brother.

At eighteen, Patty Columbo was tall and darkly attractive. She was also in love with her boss, 38-year-old Frank DeLuca, an Elk Grove, Ill., pharmicist who was married and had five children. This did not deter the strong-willed Patty who moved into an apartment with DeLuca, even though her parents strongly disapproved of the relationship.

So upset with the affair was Patty's father, Frank Columbo, 43, that he cornered DeLuca in front of his pharmacy one evening and jammed the butt of a rifle into the lover's mouth, chipping DeLuca's teeth. He ordered him to stop seeing his daughter. Patty and DeLuca continued their affair, even though Patty began to worry that her parents would disinherit her from a considerable fortune.

So concerned was she that she would lose the family money, Patty met with Lanyon Mitchell in October 1975. A one-time employee of the Cook County Sheriff's office, Mitchell, along with his friend Roman Sobcynski, were to kill her parents. Patty would repay them with sexual favors. She and the two men participated in sex orgies for several months but the would-be killers stalled Columbo.

They demanded photos of the victims, Patty's parents and her young brother. Then they wanted floor plans of the Columbo house. Next they insisted upon being receiving money they knew Patty could never pay. Finally, Columbo and DeLuca decided to murder the Columbo family themselves.

On May 4, 1976, Columbo and DeLuca entered the Columbo house. They shot Frank Columbo four times and crushed his head. They shot his wife, Patty's mother, Mary Columbo between the eyes, killing her. Then Patty stabbed her younger brother to death, stabbing the child 83 times.

Frank DeLuca went to work the next morning and was seen by some of his employees as he washed his bloodstained clothing. He proudly told them about the murders, then quickly added that if anyone talked they and their children would die. When police grilled Patty she blurted that kids high on drugs must have killed her family.

Then detectives inspecting Frank Columbo's car found the print of a three-fingered hand. DeLuca had only three fingers on one hand as the result of an accident. Then one of Patty's friends told police about Lanyon Mitchell and Mitchell told detectives how Patty had tried to hire him and Sobcynski to kill her parents.

Columbo and DeLuca were arrested and put on trial for murder in 1977. After six weeks, on July 1, 1977, a jury found the couple guilty on three counts of murder. They were each sentenced to 200 to 300 years in prison.

Sultry, sexy Patty Columbo did not take to prison life. In 1979, to gain favors and special considerations at the Dwight, Ill., correctional center, she arranged sex orgies for inmates and prison officials alike, with herself as the main attraction.

It was reported in recent years that Patty Columbo had reformed and adjusted to prison life but she has never apologized for the murder of her parents or for the savage slaying the young boy who had been her brother. She remains in the eyes of most criminologists, the writer included, a scheming, vicious mass murderer who willingly and enthusiastically spilled her family's blood to enrich her own life.

COOK, WILLIAM
Murderer, Robber ● (1929-1952)

BACKGROUND: BORN IN JOPLIN, MO., 1929. RAISED IN FOSTER HOMES, MISSOURI REFORM SCHOOLS. MINOR PUBLIC EDUCATION. DESCRIPTION: 5'5", BROWN EYES, BROWN HAIR, STOCKY. ALIASES: NONE. RECORD: ROBBED A ST. LOUIS CABDRIVER ($11) IN 1947; WAS SENTENCED TO FIVE YEARS IN A REFORM SCHOOL, TRANSFERRED TO THE MISSOURI STATE PENITENTIARY, RELEASED IN 1950; ABDUCTED CARL MOSSER, HIS WIFE AND THREE CHILDREN 12/31/50, KILLED THEM ALL NEAR JOPLIN, MO.; ABDUCTED AND KILLED SALESMAN ROBERT H. DEWEY, JANUARY, 1951; APPREHENDED BY MEXICAN POLICE 600 MILES SOUTH OF TIJUANA, 1/15/51; TRIED AND CONVICTED FOR THE DEWEY SLAYING IN SAN DIEGO, CALIF., SENTENCED TO DEATH; EXECUTED 12/12/51 IN THE GAS CHAMBER OF SAN QUENTIN PRISON.

William Cook, one of the most terrifying killers in modern times, marked the fingers of his left hand with the words, "HARD LUCK." And he meant it.

Born in 1929 near Joplin, Missouri little Billy Cook had a hard time growing up. He was raised with his seven brothers and sisters in horrible conditions. His father was an uneducated mine worker and, after the death of his wife, raised his children in an abandoned mine shaft.

One night, after staggering out of a local tavern, the old man hopped a freight and left his children to survive alone. Authorities found the poor little wretches living like animals in the cave.

Welfare workers managed to find foster homes for all of the Cook children except Billy. He didn't look just right—something was wrong with his right eye. He had been born with a sinister-looking affliction: he was not able to close the right lid.

It gave him an Evil Eye personality and no one wanted him.

The courts finally offered to pay for Billy's board if someone would take him in. One woman did, but purely for financial gain, and this marred the relationship from the beginning. For example, Billy two Christmases in succession received a new bicycle from his guardian—only to have it snatched back by the stores after the woman failed to make payments.

As he grew older, Cook stayed out nights, seeking trouble. He found it in petty thievery, was caught, and when taken before a judge, he yelled that he preferred reform school to the foster home. He got his wish.

After being released from this institution, Cook immediately robbed a cabdriver of $11 and stole a car. His apprehension was swift and he was sentenced to five years, again in reform school.

While serving his time, Cook managed to become one of the institution's roughest customers and was sent to the Missouri Penitentiary, where he was much feared. He did crazy things. Once he beat a fellow inmate with a baseball bat so that he almost died. The inmate had passed a remark about Cook's drooping eyelid.

In 1950, William Cook was released and the 22-year-old made directly for Joplin, Missouri to look up his wayward father. It was a strange reunion: a wild hateful boy who had never known love or family, and an alcoholic father who had abandoned him.

"I'm gonna live by the gun and roam," Cook told his father and then ran wildly screaming down the street. He hitched rides all through the Southwest and finally wound up in Blythe, California. By then he had picked up a companion in El Paso, Texas, a snubnosed .32 caliber pistol which he kept tucked away in his pocket.

The only job Cook ever held was in Blythe . . . washing dishes in a small cafe. It didn't take long before Cook wearied of this one stint of legitimate work and he began to roam again, heading for Texas.

On December 30, 1950, Cook found himself stranded at an all-night service station just outside of Lubbock, Texas. He sat on the pavement watching the road.

Two lights from a moving car blinked in the distance and a weary motorist pulled into the station for gas.

Cook ambled over to the driver as gas gurgled into the car's tank. "Where you headed?" he said casually.

The driver looked him over. "Tulsa."

"I want to get to Joplin," Cook said with the same dull voice. At first the motorist hesitated. There was something wrong with this man's face, that strange, drooping eyelid, but, it was a long, lonely drive to Tulsa and some company would be welcome against sleep and the night.

For miles, the driver chattered on but Cook was sullen and quiet. Then the motorist felt the .32's barrel slide up his ribs. He grimaced and stopped the car.

Cook took his money and followed him from the car. The young man unlocked the car's trunk. "Here," he pointed, "get in here."

The victim swallowed hard, looked at the menacing pistol and crawled into the trunk. Cook then drove off at high speeds. The terrified motorist collected his wits and after finding a jackhandle worked on the trunk's lock until the lid came free.

He held it down until he noticed Cook driving off the main highway and onto an unused dusty secondary road. "My God," the driver whispered to himself, "he means to kill me." There was only one chance for him and when Cook slowed the car, he took it by throwing open the trunk and jumping.

Cook heard a noise and stopped. He spun out of the car to see his captive running across the flatland toward the horizon.

"Ya better stop, Mister." He aimed the pistol. "I'm gonna kill ya for sure!" Cook yelled but the figure kept running even faster. After a long, hateful squint, Cook figured he would be wasting his ammunition. He slammed the trunk closed, got behind the wheel and spun off into the darkness.

Cook drove to a lonely stretch of Highway 66 between Claremore and Tulsa, Oklahoma before the stolen car was out of gas. He left the car at the side of the road and walked on. Minutes later he saw a 1949 Chevrolet traveling slowly toward him. Cook waved frantically, as if he were in highway trouble.

Carl Mosser saw the young man and generously came to a stop; he wanted to help. In the car with him was his wife Thelma and the three Mosser children—Ronald, seven, Gary, five, and Pamela, three.

The short, stocky man moved quickly to the car, grinning crookedly, his eyelid squinting. Carl Mosser felt a pang of fear in his stomach when he saw the gun in Cook's hand.

Cook forced Mrs. Mosser to open the door and he climbed inside. Cook didn't ask for their money; in fact, he said nothing for a long while. Mosser finally said nervously, "What do you want with us?"

Silence.

After about an hour, Cook lamely said,

"Drive me around." Mosser kept driving.

Cook had Mosser drive aimlessly through the Southwest, zigzagging and backtracking in a crazyquilt pattern until the motorist became frantic over the lives of his family. He hoped that his twin brother Chris, who lived in Albuquerque, New Mexico and was expecting Mosser and his family for a visit, would become alarmed and notify authorities.

Cook had forced him to drive past Tulsa to Oklahoma City. From there, Mosser drove to Wichita Falls, Texas. He kept thinking of ways to get rid of the brooding armed maniac in the seat next to his wife.

An opportunity came in Wichita Falls. Mosser pointed to the gas gauge. "We'll run out if we don't get gas," he told the gunman. Cook looked at the gauge.

The children complained that they were hungry.

"Yeah," Cook said. "I'm hungry, too. Drive into that gas station. It's got a grocery."

Mosser pulled into the station and told the elderly attendant to fill up the tank. When he asked, at Cook's orders, that some lunch meat be brought out to the car, the attendant told him he would have to get it himself.

Mosser was followed closely by Cook, who leveled the pistol at his captive from inside his black leather jacket. The two walked into the grocery annex. It was then that Mosser made his move by jumping the gunman and holding him from behind.

"Help me," Mosser yelled at the elderly attendant. Frightened, the attendant yanked out an old-fashioned .44 caliber pistol, nervously waving it at the two struggling men. "He's been in my car all day!" Mosser continued to yell. "He's got a gun and says that he'll kill us!" "Turn him loose," the old man said.

Mosser yelled that he was afraid Cook would draw his gun and held on.

"Then get out of my store." The two men battled out of the store and Cook broke away, throwing Mosser into a plate glass window and smashing it.

The old man, now terrified, locked himself in and Cook ordered Mosser back into his car. As Mosser obeyed and the car moved off, the old man jumped into his pickup truck and gave chase.

Cook saw him coming and fired several shots from his pistol. The old man gave up.

A seething, uncontrollable anger overcame

Cook. He told Mosser to drive immediately to Carlsbad, New Mexico. From there, it was El Paso, Texas; from there it was Houston, Texas and then Winthrop, Arkansas.

Then Cook told Mosser to head toward his old stomping grounds, Joplin, Missouri. After 72 hours of nightmare with this hellion, Mrs. Mosser broke down and became hysterical. The children screamed and Cook gagged everyone except Carl Mosser.

After noticing a police car paying too much attention to the Mosser car, Cook realized the deadly and insane game he had been playing. He ordered Mosser to stop the car and quickly turned the .32 on the family, emptying his pistol into them until they were all quite dead.

He even shot the family dog in the back seat. Some psychologists explained later that this was William Cook's savage reprisal against a society that never gave him a normal family life of his own.

Whatever, it was mass murder and Cook reacted to it by driving into Joplin, a town which he knew, and dropping the bodies down an old mine shaft.

After the Mosser car broke down in Osage County, Oklahoma, Cook stopped Deputy Sheriff Warren Smith, disarmed him, and tied him up. He roared off in the police car only to stop Robert H. Dewey and commandeer his car after wounding him and then struggling with Dewey as the driverless car roared across open desert.

Cook ended the struggle by sending a bullet into Dewey's brain. He threw the body into a ditch.

Mass murderer William Cook in custody of Mexican police, Tijuana, 1951.

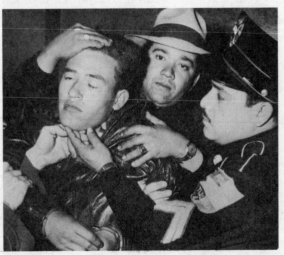

By this time, authorities had identified the mad-dog killer and over a thousand men were hunting him throughout the Southwest. But Cook had driven to Tijuana, Mexico. From there, he headed south.

On January 15, 1951, Police Chief Francisco Morales spotted Cook's car and calmly walked up to the killer and snatched the pistol from his belt.

It was all over. The Mexican police turned Cook over to the FBI. The Mosser family had been found, but the Justice Department turned the murderer over to the State of California where he was prosecuted for killing Robert Dewey.

William Cook displayed as much remorse for his grisly crimes as he had passion for his victims—none. And the Court played it the same way.

He was sentenced to death in the gas chamber. On December 12, 1952, in the glass cage at San Quentin, William Cook went to his dubious rewards . . . without a word.

COPELAND, JAMES
Murderer ● (? -1857)

Known in the 1840s as the "great Southern land pirate," James Copeland was an early outlaw in Mississippi whose gun could be purchased by the highest bidder. Copeland worked for the wealthy and corrupt Wages family who owned vast tracts of land around Augusta, Mississippi.

Copeland generally operated as a common highwayman, but he also murdered for profit. When two of his own band, Gale H. Wages and Charles McGrath, were shot and killed by James A. Harvey, Copeland received $1,000 from Old Man Wages to murder his son's killer. Copeland accepted this assignment with alacrity and dispatched Harvey on July 15, 1848, shooting him in the head.

Though apprehended, found guilty, and sentenced to death, Copeland remained alive for almost ten years, such was the influence of the Wages clan in Mississippi. He was finally hanged October 30, 1857.

COPELAND, RAYMOND
Serial Killer ● (1914-   )

Farmer Raymond Copeland and his wife Faye, in custody in Missouri. He murdered migrant workers; she made a quilt from the clothes of her husband's victims.

Ray Copeland and his 69-year-old wife Faye ran a number of farms near Chillocothe, Mo. A quiet, innocuous couple, they would never have come to the attention of authorities had it not been for a call from one of their workers who said he had found a skull on their property. In October 1989, a curious sheriff began to investigate and found that Copeland never hired local help, always transients.

Digging up the ground in one of the many farms leased by Copeland, police unearthed five bodies, all men who had worked for Copeland at one time or another. All had been murdered, shot in the back. A ledger was found in Copeland's farmhouse that listed the workers. Copeland had drawn an "X" through each one of their names after he had killed them.

Copeland and his wife were charged with murder but defense attorneys argued that Faye Copeland knew nothing of her husband's affairs, that she was a meek, dominated housewife. This was quickly disproved when records in the "Death Ledger" proved to be in her handwriting. Also, a detective examined a curious quilt Mrs. Copeland had on her bed and discovered that she had stitched it together from the old clothes of the men her husband had murdered.

Faye Copeland was convicted of murder in 1990. Her husband was found guilty of murder in 1991 and both were sentenced to death, the oldest couple in Missouri ever to be condemned.

COPPOLA, MICHAEL
("TRIGGER MIKE")
Syndicate Gangster ● (1904-1966)

Coppola was a long-time Vito Genovese henchman who worked his way up in the New York rackets during the 1920s and 1930s. When Dutch Schultz was killed in 1935, Coppola helped Genovese take over the Dutchman's million-dollar numbers racket in Harlem. Evenutally, following Genovese's flight to Italy in 1937, Coppola took over the entire racket, gleaning an estimated income of $1,000,000 a year.

Though lucrative his rackets may have been, Coppola never had any luck with his wives. The first Mrs. Coppola, Doris, had the misfortune to barge into her living room when Trigger Mike was discussing the future murder of a New York politician with an aide. The politician was dead seven days later.

Doris, pregnant, was called to testify against her husband in the case but her hospitalization postponed the trial. She conveniently died the day after she gave birth to a daughter.

In 1955, Coppola met and fell in love with Ann Drahmann (who later insisted that her husband had arranged to have his first wife, Doris, killed in her hospital bed). Mrs. Drahmann, born in 1921 in Cincinnati, was a ravishingly beautiful widow—her husband Charlie, a smalltime hoodlum from Kentucky, had been killed in an airplane crash in 1952.

Trigger Mike had Mrs. Drahmann flown to New York for the Marciano-Moore fight in 1955 so he could study her at ringside and also enjoy his favorite sport. He liked what he saw and, in the next few days, deluged her with jewels, fur coats, flowers, and pounds of candy. They were married December 28,

"Trigger Mike" Coppola, 1947, no lady's man. (UPI)

1955. A $1,000 reception followed in Lawrenceburg, Ind. for "a few friends."

They honeymooned in Miami Beach, where Coppola purchased a small palace. Within weeks, Ann accidentally came across several oddities in her new home—secret hiding places behind movable bookcases and sliding panels where hundreds of thousands of dollars from the New York numbers racket were stored. When she foolishly asked her husband about it, he exploded and lashed out at her, beating her so severely that she bled from a dozen open wounds made by Mike's diamond rings.

From that moment, hatred and revenge bubbled in Coppola's Italian-born mate. Ann began to keep a diary into which she poured her loathing. "I met Mike Coppola—the swine —September 20, 1955," she began. "He pursued me like I don't think too many women have been pursued."

At one Miami fete—the couple's honeymoon party—Coppola rose from the dinner table, drunk, and in front of several guests told his wife that she was "flat-nosed and frog-eyed." He ran from the room and came back with a gun, squeezing off a round in her direction. "Unfortunately," Ann cynically scribbled into her diary, "God made me duck!"

Ann Coppola also recorded her husband's various sadistic fetishes, not the least of which were four horrible abortions. Each time Ann became pregnant, Coppola called in an underworld quack who performed an abortion on his wife while she lay on the kitchen table. Trigger Mike frothily delighted in these miserable operations, helping the "doctor" with his chore and getting, it was later interpreted,

sexual gratification from the deed. The abortionist was always paid with a crisp $1,000 bill.

"Death shall be a blessing to me," Ann later wrote. "Mike and I shall both pay . . . One must have compassion, love and conscience to break . . ." Mrs. Coppola, however, did not take her beatings lying down. She began to hoard the glut of money Trigger Mike gave her, and she wheedled jewels and furs from him that totaled $250,000. Her stashed loot came to $277,100 inside of four years.

Coppola raked in so many millions that he often forgot where he stored the money. Once Trigger Mike returned from his favorite haunt, the Midtown Social Club, and blurted a startled "My God!" moments after he had settled down for the night. Ann watched him rush to the phone and order the manager of the club to send over the package he had forgotten in the kitchen's freezer. The package was delivered within the hour and Coppola spent the rest of the night thawing out $219,-000 in cash.

In 1960 this stormy mobster's marriage came to an end when Ann Coppola discovered her husband had been secretly giving her attractive teenage daughter (by another marriage) drugs. She moved out but it was Coppola who filed for divorce, claiming that in front of his children (by his first wife), Ann had used "vile and abusive language."

The divorce mushroomed into an IRS case against Coppola. Ann was a reluctant witness against him, not out of love but out of fear. "I learned at an early age it was most admirable not to be a stool pigeon," she stated. But she testified that Trigger Mike had given her more than a quarter of a million dollars during the years he claimed he only made a little more than $46,000 (naturally, at the track).

Trigger Mike sent out his goon squads and had his wife kidnapped from her hotel, beaten close to death, and left on a lonely beach. She recovered and continued to testify.

When the case against Coppola bogged down in November, 1961, his wife decided to take matters into her own delicate hands. IRS agents had to take a pistol from her purse on a flight to Miami. She was on her way to kill Trigger Mike. If the law couldn't deal with this reptile, she would dispose of him herself!

Coppola threw in the towel in 1962 and pleaded guilty to tax evasion. He received a year's sentence in Atlanta and a $40,000 fine. Ann Coppola's life was tension-stretched following the conviction. She moved erratically through Europe, avoiding mobmen whose obvious assignment was to kill her. She stopped running in 1962 in Rome. Fatigued and harassed, Ann Coppola scrawled in lipstick above her hotel room bed: "I have always suffered, I am going to kill myself. Forget me."

She wrote a last letter to the Internal Revenue Service, addressing some sections to then Attorney General Robert Kennedy. Her final outpourings were for her imprisoned husband: "Mike Coppola, someday, somehow, a person or God or the law shall catch up with you, you yellow-bellied bastard. You are the lowest and biggest coward I have had the misfortune to meet."

Ann Coppola then gulped down a dozen Nembutal tablets with a heavy scotch chaser, stretched out across her bed while the blinding Italian sun slanted through the magnificent windows of her suite, and slipped longingly into death.

Trigger Mike, released nine months after he walked behind the walls of the Atlanta Penitentiary (where cell-mates Vito Genovese and Joseph Valachi still resided), resumed his nefarious syndicate career, dying of undisclosed causes in October, 1966.

COPPOLINO, CARL
Murderer ● (1933-   )

Brooklyn-born anesthesiologist, Carl Coppolino, retired from his practice while complaining of a heart ailment. Though it suspected the physician was faking, an insurance company reluctantly paid him $22,000 a year in benefits.

Dr. Coppolino lived the easy life, his income supplemented by his wife, Mary Gibson, a 38-year-old divorcee. Mary was his second wife, his first, Carmela Musetto, having died in 1965 of a heart attack. After Coppolino's marriage to Mary Gibson, his former lover, Majorie Farber, told authorities that

Coppolino had murdered Carmela. The jilted lover also insisted that Dr. Coppolino had injected her own husband, an army colonel, with a chemical substance, then used a pillow to suffocate him when the Farbers lived in New Jersey.

Coppolino was indicted in New Jersey and Florida. In Colonel Farber's case, medical evidence was confusing and Coppolino was exonerated. But it was a different case when it came to Carmela Coppolina. Her body was exhumed and carefully examined. It was determined that she had been in perfect health at the time of her death and had no heart problems.

Moreover, it was known that Coppolino had injected Carmela with some kind of chemical before her death. Toxicologists determined this to be succinic acid, the substance that took her life. Despite the considerable efforts of defense attorney F. Lee Bailey, Coppolino was convicted in 1967 of second-degree murder and was sent to the Avon Park Correctional Institution to serve a life term.

Bailey was so incensed at the prosecution and its witnesses that he openly assailed them. He was suspended for a year from practicing in New Jersey. Coppolino, however, was a model prisoner and was paroled on October 16, 1979.

CORYLL, DEAN ALLEN
Serial Killer ● (1939-1973)

The Pasadena, Tex., Police Department received a strange call on August 8, 1973. On the other end of the phone was a weak-voiced Elmer Wayne Henley who informed police that he had just shot and killed Dean Allen Coryll, his best friend. When officers arrived at Coryll's residence they found him lying on his face with six bullets in his shoulder and back.

Henley (1956-   ) immediately confessed that he and David Owen Brooks (1955-   ) had aided Coryll in his sadistic murders of 27 teenage boys, beginning in 1970. In that year Coryll picked up a hitch-hiking University of Texas student, Jeffrey Konen, and took him to his home where he attacked him sexually and then murdered him.

Coryll, the product of a broken home, was an unhappy youth, even more resentful when he was drafted by the Army in 1964. By 1969 he was working for the Lighting and Power Company of Houston. He spent most of his off hours with two high school dropouts, Henley and Brooks, and they consumed their hours by sniffing glue.

Henley and Brooks were used by Coryll to pick up teenage boys and bring them to his small, run-down house. Coryll promised them $200 for every victim they brought to him but he usually reneged on his word. Boys were lured to the Coryll house on the promise that they were going to a drug and alcohol party. After they fell unconscious, Coryll tied them up, sexually abused them, then killed them. The slayer hid the bodies in a boat shed he had rented in Southwest Houston.

On August 8, 1973, Henley arrived at Coryll's home with a girl, fifteen-year-old runaway Rhonda Williams. Coryll exploded, accusing Henley of breaking a cardinal rule: "You weren't supposed to bring any girl!" he yelled. Also present was sixteen-year-old Timothy Kerley. The group sniffed varnish and when Henley awoke he was tied up with Williams and Kerley. Coryll was standing over him.

Henley pleaded for his life, promising Coryll that he would rape and kill Williams while Coryll killed Kerley if Coryll untied him. When he was free, Henley grabbed a .22-caliber pistol and emptied its six bullets into Coryll, killing him. He then called police.

Investigators followed Henley's instructions and went to shed number eleven at the Southwest Boat Storage and there dug up 27 bodies before they called off the search. The numbers of bodies established a gruesome national record up to that time, eclipsing the 25 migrant workers known to have been murdered by Juan Corona.

Though Houston parents whose children were missing begged the police to continue the search, investigators were reluctant to continue. Houston had been stained enough. On August 11, 1973, Henley and Brooks were charged with murder. Their trial opened in San Antonio in July 1974. Both were convicted of murdering six out of the 27 victims and each received a life term.

CORONA, JUAN VALLEJO
Serial Killer ● (1933-   )

Juan Corona thought of himself as a self-made man, a penniless Mexican migrant worker who arrived in Yuba City, Calif., in the 1950s and who, by the 1970s, was making big money as a labor contractor. Corona, however, did not enjoy life, except in pursuing his perversions. He was a pronounced sadist and had been diagnosed as have a severe case of schizophrenia. Oddly, Corona was also married with children.

Corona made his fortune by hiring elderly migrant workers and driving them hard to bring in crops. These men were elderly alcoholics, for the most part, social dropouts, and misfits. Corona housed them on the Sullivan ranch near Yuba City in a seedy barracks-like structure. In early May 1971, these men began to disappear.

On May 19, a Japanese fruit farmer discovered a seven-foot, three-and-a-half feet deep hole had been dug on his land. When he returned the next evening he found the hole had been filled in. He called police who dug up what was obviously a fresh grave. Inside of it they found Kenneth Whitacre, a hobo who had worked briefly for Juan Corona. Homosexual literature was found inside of Whitacre's back pocket. He had been sodomized and stabbed to death. His head was almost severed with what officials determined had been a machete.

More fresh graves were found in the area and police kept digging until June 4, 1971, unearthing a total of twenty-five bodies, all men. They had all been sodomized then stabbed to death. Only one had been shot. All of them had suffered horrible wounds in the head with chops from a machete. Police found in one grave a meat market receipt made out to "Juan V. Corona." Inside of this grave was John Henry Jackson, an old migrant worker who had been seen riding in the back of Corona's pickup.

Corona was arrested and charged with murder. His defense attorney argued that another person had done the killings but no one was ever charged, other than Corona. All the evidence—receipts, eye witnesses, and bodies—led to him.

The 200-pound Corona had simply driven along

the dusty roads of Marysville and Yuba City, picking up elderly men who stumbled along looking for work. He worked them a few days and when it came time to pay them, he sexually assaulted them, then killed them. Prosecutors proved that it had all been premeditated, that Corona had dug the graves of his victims in advance and had even kept a ledger wherein he recorded their names and the dates he murdered them.

Convicted, Corona was sentenced to 25 life sentences in January 1973 by Judge Richard E. Patton. In prison, Corona was attacked repeatedly by inmates and, on one occasion, was stabbed 32 times. He lost the sight of one eye. Corona won an appeal later, claiming he was improperly defended at his trial, that his lawyer should have pleaded insanity. Corona was removed from prison and placed in an asylum for the criminally insane.

COSTELLO, FRANK
Syndicate Racketeer ● (1893-1973)

BACKGROUND: BORN FRANCESCO SERIGLIA 1/26/93 IN CALABRIA, ITALY. MINOR PUBLIC EDUCATION. MIGRATED TO THE U.S. WTH HIS PARENTS SHORTLY AFTER HIS BIRTH. DESCRIPTION: 5'11', BROWN EYES, GREY HAIR, SOLID BUILD. ALIASES: UNKNOWN, RECORD: COSTELLO AT AN EARLY AGE JOINED A STREET GANG IN EAST HARLEM; ARRESTS BEGAN IN 1908 INCLUDING ASSAULT, ROBBERY, AND IN 1919 CARRYING A CONCEALED WEAPON; SENTENCED TO A YEAR IN JAIL; BECAME A RUMRUNNER FOR BIG BILL DWYER'S GANG IN 1920 (AN OPERATION FINANCED BY NEW YORK GAMBLER ARNOLD ROTHSTEIN); TOOK OVER GAMBLING INTERESTS UPON ROTHSTEIN'S DEATH AND, AS A MEMBER OF LUCIANO'S COSA NOSTRA FAMILY, CONSOLIDATED GAMBLING INTERESTS THROUGHOUT THE U.S. IN THE 1930S, CONCENTRATING ON NEW YORK, FLORIDA (WHERE DANDY PHIL KASTEL BECAME HIS PARTNER), AND LAS VEGAS; LATER ARRESTED FOR CONSPIRACY, CONTEMPT, AND INCOME TAX EVASION IN THE LATE 1950S; OUSTED FROM CONTROL BY VITO GENOVESE IN LATE 1950S AND WENT INTO SEMI-RETIREMENT.

Frank Costello proved to be one of the most durable founders of the national crime syndicate. He began, as did most of his confederates, in the slums of New York practicing petty thievery from pushcarts and grocery stores. He then graduated to robbery and in 1919 was picked up carrying a pistol under his coat. This led to a year in jail.

Costello was determined never to go back. He sought the protection of politically-connected William Vincent "Big Bill" Dwyer, working as a rumrunner. Dwyer had begun his career on the docks of New York as a stevedore. At the dawn of Prohibition, Dwyer's waterfront connections were ideal for lucrative bootlegging activities.

Costello became one of Dwyer's most trusted aides. Through Big Bill, he came to meet every important New York hoodlum in that era—Owney Madden, George "Big Frenchy" DeMange, Vannie Higgins, William J. "Big Bill" Duffy, and Waxey Gorden (Irving Wexler).

These men introduced Costello to the political bosses of Tammany Hall such as the powerful Jimmy Hines. Through Hines, Costello met and cemented friendships with other important political bigwigs. Costello also maintained his Mafia alliance with Lucky Luciano through the 1920s. While Charley Lucky moved into control of narcotics and coast-to-coast brothel operations, Costello branched out into gambling interests in New York and Florida, concentrating on slot machines. He became Luciano's right-hand man (Vito Genovese began to operate alone) after the killing of Mafia boss Salvatore Maranzano in 1931.

Lucky particularly liked the way Costello avoided publicity. Unlike Vannie Higgins, Dwyer's wacky lieutenant in charge of Big Bill's speakeasies, Costello stayed in the background . . . and lived. Higgins was the kind of showoff the new crime syndicate could do without, Luciano warned.

He snorted derision when Higgins, crazily courting the press in the manner of the flashy 1920s gangster, flew his private plane to upstate New York where he ceremoniously had dinner with Joseph H. Wilson, warden of the Comstock Prison, and caused then-Governor Franklin D. Roosevelt to explode in indignation. Such antics were not for serious men of crime. Vannie proved he wasn't taken seriously at all in 1932 when he was ambushed on a dark Manhattan Street and shot to pieces.

"Costello," Luciano used to say, "—now there is a man who knows how to keep his mouth shut and tend to business." And he did. Under Lucky's guidance, Costello branched out into the gem-smuggling business,

Charles "Vannie" Higgins, an early Costello associate; he talked too much and was murdered.

making as much as a half million dollars on a single shipment. After Luciano was deported to his native Italy on February 10, 1946, Costello took over his interests, but only as a watchman. Lucky continued to get his share of the profits.

With the rise of Las Vegas in the late 1940s, the Mafia-bred syndicate cut itself in for giant chunks of the gambling receipts. Benjamin "Bugsy" Siegel, who had been sent to California by syndicate board member Lepke in the late 1930s to develop syndicate rackets, began the big Las Vegas gambling boom. Luciano, the Chicago mob, and others took it from there after The Bug was executed gangland style. One of the "others" was Frank Costello, of the Kastel-Costello gambling combine out of Florida.

His activities there brought heat from federal investigators, the most threatening to his enterprises being the 1951 U.S. Senate Crime Investigating Committee headed by Senator Estes Kefauver. The threat caused "The Prime Minister" of national crime, as the Committee labelled Costello, severe internal problems. For decades he had managed to stay out of the limelight. The Senate probe forced him out into the open, even though his answers were empty of information.

Vito Genovese, who had his eyes on Costello's gambling empire, however, used this unwanted publicity to point out that the Prime Minister's days as a power in the syndicate were numbered. Avaricious Genovese wanted Luciano's interests, too, and to obtain this he had to remove Frank Costello, keeper of Lucky's flame.

Willie Moretti, a Costello-Luciano ally since Maranzano's bloody Castellammarese War in 1930, stood in Genovese's way. Though aging and suffering mental disturbances brought on by advanced syphilis, Moretti was a staunch Costello supporter who controlled rackets in New Jersey and some in Manhattan. His army of "soldiers" numbered more than 250 and they were intensely loyal.

Costello, fearful that Moretti's incoherent mental state would reduce him to a quaking, squealing informer if brought before Kefauver's Committee, had his friend moved from one syndicate hide-out to another for over a year until he felt it safe to bring the old man out to testify. Moretti did testify and provided the federal probers with nothing.

Still, his appearance told the story of a mental cripple, a man who, Genovese sadly stated, was not fit to command a *Cosa Nostra* family and should be put out of his misery. Costello argued violently against Moretti's removal.

Cosa Nostra informer Joe Valachi was very close to this situation; his partner in crime, Johnny Roberts (Johnny Robilotto) finally shot and killed Moretti on orders from Genovese.

Valachi was to state: "Vito is like a fox. He takes his time. He wants everything to be legal. He starts talking it up, first among us that are closest to him, which is Tony Bender's [Anthony Strollo] crew, so then we will talk it around and the word will spread, the other members [of the *Cosa Nostra*] will start thinking about it. What Vito says is that Frank Costello is right about a lot of things, but he is wrong about this. He says it is sad about Willie and that it ain't his fault. He is just sick in the head, but if he is allowed to keep talking, he is going to get us all in a jam.

"You see how Vito is agitating to get Willie Moretti killed, and it ain't making Frank Costello look any too good. One time Vito has this meeting with some of us downtown in the Village, and he says, 'What are we, men or mice?' Well, he is scheming like this, saying Willie has got to be hit because he is not well. I remember him telling us, 'He has lost his mind and that is the way life is. If tomorrow I go wrong, I would want to be hit so as not to bring harm to this thing [*Cosa Nostra*] of ours.' Then, after the seed has been planted, it naturally grows, and there is agreement in

Frank Costello in the witness chair, 1951, before the Mc-Clellan Committee. (UPI)

the *Commissions*—meaning all the bosses—that Vito is right."

Willie Moretti was hit and Genovese, along with Abner "Longy" Zwillman, grabbed the dead crime czar's rackets in New Jersey. More importantly, Genovese had weakened Costello's position. The fight for the Las Vegas gambling interests culminated on the night of May 2, 1957. After dining in the swank L'Aiglon Restaurant, Frank Costello walked into his posh New York apartment building on Central Park West.

A giant killer named Vincente "The Chin" Gigante, on Genovese's orders, waited in the lobby with a gun in his hand. "This is for you, Frank," Gigante yelled out dramatically and fired off one round before bolting for the door. The single shot caused Costello to lose a lot of blood, but it was only a grazing wound. Police rushed in to investigate and found a tally sheet of wins and losses to the exact penny of the Tropicana, a Las Vegas casino, which once more put the Prime Minister on the spot.

When Costello refused to answer any questions regarding the casino receipt, or to identify Gigante when the would-be assassin was brought before him, he was held in contempt and sent to jail. Federal authorities then heaped income-tax evasion charges on him and he was sent to prison for that, too.

Costello was through as a Mafia-Syndicate power. Vito Genovese had taken care of him as deftly as he had handled Willie Moretti. Of course, he was an old pro at such business. Costello died in bed February 18, 1973.

[ALSO SEE Vito Genovese, Lucky Luciano, The Mafia, The Syndicate]

COWAN, FREDERICK W.
Mass Murderer ● (1944-1977)

A suspended employee of the Neptune Moving Company in New Rochelle, N.Y., Frederick Cowan marched into his firm's offices on February 28, 1977, armed to the teeth and looking for revenge. He had hand grenades, pistols, a semi-automatic rifle, and bandoliers of ammunition. Cowan shot four employees, singling out black persons, whom he hated.

When police arrived, Cowan shot and killed an officer stepping from a squad car. He moved from window to window in the Neptune building in what became a raging battle. At one time, Cowan shouted that he had "plenty of grenades and other guns to last me all day."

The killer's mother arrived but he would not answer her entreaties as she spoke to him through a loudspeaker. He did pick up a phone at one point and said: "Tell the mayor that I'm sorry to be causing the city so much trouble." A few minutes later Frederick W. Cowan put a gun to his head and killed himself.

Mass murderer Frederick Cowan who killed four in a 1977 rampage.

COY, BERNARD
Murderer ● (1900-1946)

A lifer, Coy and five other inmates of Alcatraz—Cretzer, Hubbard, Carnes, and Thompson—led the most bloody breakout ever attempted on The Rock. On May 2, 1946, Coy and the others overpowered guards in Cell Block D, obtained weapons, and attempted to negotiate their freedom with Warden Johnston.

Stating that he would personally kill the nine guards who were being held as hostages, Coy and the others beat back several attempts to dislodge them as they fought police and troops in a 48-hour battle.

Many attempts had been made to escape Alcatraz—Doc Barker tried in 1939 and was killed, John Bayles tried in 1941—no one succeeded. Bernie Coy failed, too, moments after he told his friends, "It don't matter; I figure I licked The Rock anyway." He, Cretzer, and Hubbard were shot to death during a final assault made by prison guards. Five of the hostages had been murdered.

Hardened Alcatraz cons Clarence Carnes, Bernard Coy, and Joseph Paul Cretzer, along with two other inmates, led the Rock's most bloody breakout attempt in 1946; Coy and Cretzer were killed. (UPI)

CRANE, CHERYL
Murderer ● (1944-   )

The daughter of actress Lana Turner, Cheryl Crane was born to Turner and Stephen Crane, the actress's second husband. She was Turner's only child and lived inside great wealth, a mansion, expensive jewels, servants, limousines. She also reportedly resented her mother's fame or was jealous of it and whispered gossip to her mother about her husbands and the men she dated between marriages.

One of Turner's most ardent lovers was gangster John Stompanato, a bagman and one-time bodyguard and chauffeur for Los Angeles gangster Mickey Cohen. Stompanato was himself jealous of Turner's fame, and even intruded into her moviemaking career, once going onto the set of *Another Time, Another Place* to order Turner's co-star, Sean Connery, to "stay away from Lana!"

Connery turned his back on Stompanato who grabbed the actor, spun him about and waved a gun in his face. Connery brushed aside the gun and punched the gangster. The powerful blow sent Stompanato to the floor. He got up and walked away swearing. That night he raged at Turner, telling her: "When I say jump, you jump!"

He threatened to take a razor the actress's face, to mutilate her, and ruin her career. Cheryl Crane heard these and other threats for many weeks, which continued until April 4, 1958. That night Stompanto demanded that Turner pay his debts, threatening to mutilate her if she did not. "I'll cut you up!" Stompanato yelled. "I'll get your mother and your daughter, too!"

Lana Turner testifying at her daughter's trial.

Stompanato raged in the bedroom and as he was about to strike Turner with a wooden hanger, fourteen-year-old Cheryl Crane came through the bedroom door holding a butcher knife with a nine-inch blade. She drove this into the gangster who fell back onto the plush carpet. He died quickly.

Turner called Hollywood defense lawyer Jerry Giesler who arrived before Beverly Hills police, led by Chief Clinton Anderson. Turner wanted Giesler to tell police that she had killed Stompanato. The lawyer put his arm around Turner and said: "Your daughter has done a courageous thing. Too bad that a man's life is gone, but under the circumstances the child did the only thing she could do to protect her mother from harm."

Giesler had then and there introduced his defense for Cheryl Crane who was locked up in the Juvenile Section of the city jail and charged with murder. Hollywood gossip columnists had a field day. Only Walter Winchell showed sympathy for Turner whom he described as "the girl with a broken heart." Though most of the actress's peers had little or nothing to say, the outspoken Gloria Swanson, glamour queen of the silent era, openly scathed Turner, and attacked Winchell for his defense of her, saying: "You are trying to whitewash Lana. . . . She's not even an actress. . . . She is only a trollop."

When Cheryl Crane appeared before a coroner's jury, charges against her had been reduced to manslaughter. Giesler put Lana Turner on the stand where he softly guided her through the events of the killing. Turner displayed a mother's pain, wiping away perspiration, openly sobbing as she told her story. Some said it was the finest acting job of her career. Cheryl Crane then gave her version of the killing.

The jury was so moved by the testimony of the two females that it rendered a verdict of justifiable homicide. Crane, however, was made a ward of the state and placed in the custody of her grandmother, Mildred Turner. She ran away several times and was placed in a state home for girls.

Both Turner and Crane survived the killing, which was so sensationalized that Turner's next few films were box office hits. Crane later became a successful real estate broker in San Francisco. Only one person at any time had a good word to say about the victim, Stompanato. Mickey Cohen, his one time underworld boss remarked: "Look, this was a great guy!"

(ALSO SEE Mickey Cohen)

CRIMMINS, ALICE
Murderer ● (1941-   )

On the morning of July 14, 1965, Edmund Crimmins went into a room in a Queens, N.Y. apartment to visit his two children, Eddie, five; and Marie, four. The room was empty; the children had disappeared. Alice Crimmins, his wife, had no explanation. She and Edmund had been separated for some time, although Edmund visited the children regularly.

After a desperate search, Marie was found in a vacant lot nearby. She had been strangled to death. Eddie's body was found a mile away a week later, also strangled. Alice Crimmins said she had put the children to bed the night previous to their disappearance after having fed them manicotti and string beans. It was 7:30 p.m. Crimmins said she looked in on the children at midnight and they were sleeping in their beds. She insisted that they had been kidnapped.

Police were suspicious of Mrs. Crimmins from the beginning. She displayed no emotion, never shed a single tear, when learning of her children's fate. Further, the noted pathologist, Dr. Milton Helpern, examined the bodies and discovered that the manicotti and string beans were present but had not been digested. He determined that Marie had died within two hours after eating the food, thus refuting Crimmins's statement.

A neighbor then came forward to state that she had seen Alice Crimmins and an unknown man taking the children to a car on the morning of the killings. Crimmins was charged with murdering her children and placed on trial. A star prosecution witness was Joseph Rorech, who told the court that Alice was his lover and that she went to a motel with him a short time after the murders and there admitted that she had killed her children to prevent her ex-husband from taking custody of them.

A jury convicted Crimmins and she received a life sentence. After appealing, the murder charge was reduced to manslaughter and Crimmins was sent to a release institution in Harlem where she worked as a secretary. Anyone studying the public behavior of Alice Crimmins and Susan Smith, who admitted to drowning her own two small children in 1994, would find striking similarities.
(ALSO SEE Susan Smith)

CROWLEY, FRANCIS ("TWO-GUN")
Murderer, Bankrobber ● (1911-1931)

BACKGROUND: BORN 10/31/11 IN NEW YORK, N.Y.,
PLACED IN A FOSTER HOME AS AN INFANT.
FINISHED THIRD GRADE IN ELEMENTARY SCHOOL; FORCED TO
WORK AS A DAY LABORER AT AGE 12. DESCRIPTION:
5'6", BROWN EYES, BROWN HAIR, SLIGHT BUILD.
ALIASES: NONE. RECORD: PURCHASED A .38-CALIBER
PISTOL ON HIS NINETEENTH BIRTHDAY AND WENT ON
A ROBBERY SPREE IN THE SPRING OF 1931, ROBBING
A BANK AND COMMITTING SEVERAL HOLDUPS, ONE OF
WHICH RESULTED IN HIS MURDERING A STOREKEEPER;
WITH HIS PARTNER RUDOLPH "FATS" DURINGER, MUR-
DERED DANCE HALL HOSTESS VIRGINIA BANNER IN
APRIL, 1931; SHOT AND KILLED PATROLMAN FREDERICK
HIRSCH NEAR NORTH MERRICK, L.I. THE SAME MONTH
WHILE ESCAPING; TRAPPED BY NYPD OFFICERS AT
303 W. 90TH ST. IN AN APARTMENT, SHOOTING IT OUT
WITH THE COPS IN WHAT WAS TERMED "THE SIEGE
OF W. 90TH STREET"; APPREHENDED AFTER BEING
WOUNDED, TRIED FOR MURDER, CONVICTED, AND SEN-
TENCED TO DEATH IN THE ELECTRIC CHAIR AT SING
SING PRISON; EXECUTED A FEW DAYS BEFORE HIS
TWENTIETH BIRTHDAY, 1931.

Francis "Two-Gun" Crowley would probably have remained a smalltime hood
had it not been for his abiding faith in
his own press clippings. From a penny-ante
sneak-thief, Crowley, in his scant lifetime of
nineteen years, managed to rise to the image
of the stand-up and shoot-it-out desperado of
old, fascinating a Depression-torn Manhattan.

Just as he was the product of a broken
home, like many another gangster, Crowley
was also the invention of the press. He
stopped calling himself Francis after the newspapers dubbed him "Two Gun." And he believed himself to be the toughest man in New
York.

Crowley was born just outside of Manhattan, illegitimate. His mother, a German household worker, placed him in a foster home at
an early age. His education was halted at the
third grade and except for what he learned
on New York's streets, and from the pages of
cheap detective magazines and gangster movies, Crowley remained an illiterate.

He hated policemen. His foster mother told
him that his grandfather had been a police
captain, and in his loneliness Crowley looked
upon all policemen as cruel and heartless animals who would abandon their own flesh at
any moment.

Crowley's childhood was uneventful. At age
twelve he was compelled to go to work in a
factory. He was too busy and tired to get into
trouble, conforming to a then-popular theory
that work made men moral and upright: one
strictly subscribed to by Crowley's foster mother. "He would bring his pay envelope home
and give it to me," she later testified. "I did
not suspect anything wrong with him during
all those years, and I'm sure there was nothing
wrong."

Everything seemed right with young Francis
Crowley. He never drank or smoked; he was
never addicted to anything other than hard
rock candy. But he was wildly impressionable.
The gangsters appearing daily in New York
headlines excited him. They had expensive
clothes, fast cars, and the respect and fear of
the city. They were "Big Shots" to Francis.

In his late teens, Crowley fell in with a
dim-witted clod of a man, Rudolph "Fats"
Duringer, whom he referred to as "Big Rudolph." Together, after work, the two planned
and executed several minor holdups in and
about Manhattan. Their take was miserable but
Crowley was delighted. He had found his
milieu in the excitement of robbery and the
risk of death. Like novelist Willard Motley's
Nick Romano in *Knock On Any Door*, he
wanted to "live hard, die young, and have a
good-looking corpse."

Munching on candy, the boy bandit and
Duringer robbed a small bank in early 1931.
Then they knocked over several gas stations
and stores, killing one grocery store owner
when he resisted. Crowley and Duringer took
to hanging around dance halls after Francis
learned that gangster Jack "Legs" Diamond
frequented these nickel-and-dime dives.

Crowley never met Diamond, but he and
his friend Duringer did get friendly with pretty Virginia Banner, a hostess at one of the
halls. When she refused to go out with Duringer, he and Crowley waited for her one night
and after she left the hall, the two shoved
her into their green coupe and drove to an
isolated spot. There Duringer raped her repeatedly. Then Crowley, using the pistol he
had given himself as a present on his nineteenth birthday, shot her to death. Duringer
shot her also for good measure. "I heard she
was going to marry someone else," he later

confessed. "I was jealous of him."

The two raced on with their crime spree. The police were stymied. Ballistic experts matched the bullets from Miss Banner's body with those from the grocery store murder, but clues ended there.

Then on a warm April night just outside North Merrick, N. Y., two officers, Patrolmen Frederick Hirsch and Peter Yodice, drove up to a deserted spot called Black Shirt Lane to shoo away lovers parked in their cars. There was only one car in sight, a dirty green coupe.

"Probably some kids," Hirsch told his partner. "We'd better get them out of here before someone holds them up."

Hirsch got out of the patrol car and advanced on the green coupe with his flashlight bouncing about in the darkness. His thin yellow light settled on a pasty-faced youth sitting next to a pretty teenage girl. Yodice walked to the front of the car and wrote down the license number just in case.

"It's pretty late to be out here," Hirsch said to the youthful driver. "Let me see your license."

"Sure, sure," mumbled the young man and he slowly moved his arm from around the girl. In a moment he opened the car door, slamming Hirsch off balance. As the officer fell backward, Francis Crowley fired three rapid shots into him. Before Hirsch died, he managed to draw his gun and get off one shot which went wild. Crowley jumped from his car and snatched the policeman's pistol, then leaped back into his car and, dodging patrolman Yodice's shots, escaped.

Now police knew who they were looking for and they placed a "shoot-to-kill" order out on Crowley. But he had buried himself in the city. For weeks, it appeared as if the boy murderer had vanished. Then a newspaper reporter for the *New York Journal* tracked down a friend of Crowley's, dance hall girl Billie Dunne. She exploded at the mere mention of the outlaw's name. Crowley, Duringer, and Crowley's girl, sixteen-year-old Helen Walsh, had evicted her from her cheap apartment. They were living there now, she screamed, and she gave the address as 303 W. 90th.

The reporter, along with a photographer, hurried to the apartment after notifying the police. Billie had warned him not to see Crowley. "That guy will shoot his own mother," she said.

News photographer Jerry Frankel didn't wait for the police to arrive. He wanted his pictures for the next edition. After lugging his equipment up the stairs, he stood in front of Billie's apartment and knocked.

A thin voice on the other side yelled out: "Get out of here! We don't want any!"

Before Frankel could reply, police detectives who were hiding in the hall yanked him backward toward the stairs. Suddenly, the door flew open and there stood Francis Crowley, ready for battle. Two guns were strapped to his hips, another was tucked into a shoulder holster. His pants were rolled up to the knees and strapped around each calf were two more guns.

Two-Gun whipped out the pistols on his hips and began shooting down the hallway, his roaring six-guns chunking away plaster that showered down on the policemen as they dove for cover. He emptied his pistols and then jumped back into the apartment, slamming the door and barricading it.

In that moment of eerie silence, policemen raised their heads to peer down the hallway still filled with Crowley's gunsmoke, and heard that oft-delivered classic line snarled from behind the door: "Come and get me, coppers!"

The siege was on. Down in the street, police roped off two blocks and brought an army of officers to train machineguns, shotguns, and high-powered rifles on the apartment. They began to pepper the building as carloads of reinforcements arrived by the minute. (Police were to fire 700 shots throughout the battle.)

Crowley acted out his role in the true Hollywood tradition. Jumping from window to window, he fired a vicious fusillade down to the street, reloading his guns as he ran. Machineguns answered him, shattering the windows overhead; he laughed and brushed away the glass, firing back coolly, plunking his shells dangerously close to where policemen took cover behind parked cars in the street. Then he would dart to the hallway door, spray both ends of the halls with bullets and then return to the windows.

The scene was incredible. Over 300 officers were in the street below, firing back, a tremendously withering fire that chipped away brick, mortar and wood from the building's facade. Two-Gun would wait for a lull and then, from his five-story perch, rapidly squeeze off his rounds, loudly cursing the police below.

Rudolph Duringer and Helen Walsh hid beneath the bed, screaming. Crowley ignored them. He sat on the bed and reloaded. "You're yellow, all yellow," he castigated them.

Fifteen thousand people were in the streets watching the battle. More spectators foolishly watched from neighboring buildings, leaning out of the windows and using pillows for armrests.

While the police regrouped for a final charge preceded by tear-gas, Crowley and Helen prepared to die. Duringer still sobbed beneath the bed as the star-crossed lovers wrote out their farewells to the world.

Two-Gun wrote:

"To Whom It May Concern:
I was born on the thirty-first [of October]. She was born on the thirteenth [Helen was born on the 13th of October]. I guess it was fate that made us mate. When I die put a lily in my hand, let the boys know how they'll look. Under my coat will lay a weary, kind heart that wouldn't hurt anything. I hadn't anything else to do, that's why I went around bumping off cops. *It's the new sensation of the films* [italics added]. Take a tip from me to never let a copper go an inch above your knee. They will tell you they love you and as soon as you turn your back they will club you and say the hell with you. Now that my death is so near there is a couple of bulls at the door saying "come here." I'm behind the door with three thirty-eights—one belongs to my friend in North Merrick [officer Hirsch]—he would have gotten me if his bullets were any good."

Helen wrote:

"To Whom It May Concern:
I was born on the 13 of Oct. and he was born on the 31. If I die and my face you are able to see, wave my hair and make me look pretty and make my face up. Dress me in Black and White in a new dress. Do my nails all over. I don't use this kind of polish. It's too dark. I use a very pale pink. I always wanted everybody to be happy & have a good time—I had some pretty good times myself. Love to all but all my love to Sweets.

[Helen called Crowley Sweets]. Everybody happy & how."

Moments later, the police resumed firing after asking Crowley to come out. Again, he retorted à la James Cagney: "You ain't gonna take me alive, coppers!" and blasted away with his pistols. The police returned his fire with a hail of tear-gas shells which thudded into the apartment. Two-Gun picked up several smoking tear-gas shells and tossed them out the window; some officers below were overcome by their own cannisters. As he threw the tear-gas shells out, Crowley was a perfect target and police bullets hit him again and again, knocking him to the floor.

He staggered up, his eyes swollen from the gas, shooting blindly out the windows. A brave squad of police volunteers finally rushed the apartment door and crashed in. Crowley was staggering blindly about. He leveled his two guns in their direction and squeezed the triggers. Nothing happened. He was out of ammunition. As officers approached him, he swore and collapsed, leaking blood from four bullet wounds. Duringer and Helen Walsh were yanked from beneath the bed.

When Two-Gun Crowley was taken to the hospital the police took no chances. They strapped him to the stretcher and a guard held a gun to his head until he arrived in the emergency room. His trial was anti-climactic.

His faithful sweetheart Helen turned on him, testifying against his defense (she was released). When she stepped from the witness stand she winked at her lover but Two-Gun did not wink back. Duringer, indicted for the killing of Virginia Banner, tried to pin the blame solely on Two-Gun, but he, too, was sentenced to death.

Crowley sat through the entire trial amused and delighted at the attention he received. He smart-cracked for the newsmen. He laughed when the death sentence was pronounced. The only visible sign of annoyance to cross his face occurred when his own lawyer called him "a moral imbecile" before the open court.

The press played up Crowley's bravado. Two-Gun was tough, they said. Two-Gun would go to the chair laughing.

From the moment Crowley entered Death Row at Sing Sing to await his execution, he attempted to prove just how tough he was. Two-Gun was brought through the gates of Sing Sing by a dozen deputies and immedi-

Francis "Two-Gun" Crowley (right) on his way to Sing Sing and the electric chair. (UPI)

ately searched. Inside one of his socks, they found a spoon handle which could have been eventually shaped into a knife.

During his first day on Death Row, Crowley cursed his guards and kicked over his tray of food. The other condemned prisoners applauded him. Thus encouraged, the nineteen-year-old killer proceeded to create pandemonium.

A letter arrived from Helen Walsh. In it she called him yellow. Crowley went berserk. In a matter of days he had destroyed his cell. He stuffed his clothes down the toilet and flooded his cell. Though denied matches, Crowley managed to set fire to everything in sight and a squad of guards had to put out the blaze. He then twisted the wire away from his bunk and wrapped it around a heavy magazine, clubbing one guard unconscious in a futile break.

Warden Lewis Lawes took drastic measures. He had Crowley's cell stripped of everything. Two-Gun was also stripped naked. A mattress was thrown into his cell at night and removed each morning. At first, Crowley only laughed at such punishment. He spent his time trapping flies with sugar from his meals, and then slowly killing them. He was placed in an isolated cell away from the other prisoners and without an audience to goad him on, he became docile. One day a starling flew into his cell, but Two-Gun didn't kill it. Like Robert Stroud, the "Birdman of Alcatraz," he fed it from his food allotment and the bird returned each day.

The bird's appearance seemed to calm the killer. He asked for his clothes and a bunk and Lawes granted these to him. He asked for a sketch pad and began to draw pictures. One of his drawings was of the electric chair.

This Crowley pasted to the wall of his cell. He then drew a figure of a man lying inside of a coffin. He labeled this sketch: "Francis (Two-Gun) Crowley." This drawing too, he stuck up on his wall.

Later, Crowley was taken to New York to testify in a review trial of Rudolph Duringer's case. Before he left, Crowley took one of the death house porters aside and said: "Take all my things. I won't need them again. Once I leave here, I won't come back. You can be sure of that." Two-Gun was planning to make a break but he never got the chance.

Four guards sat around him during the trial. At lunch time, Crowley waited impatiently in the ante-room for his food. "No eats, no testimony," he snarled at a guard. His lunch appeared minutes later. In the afternoon, Crowley played to the gallery, making what he termed "wise cracks." When some of his remarks brought on laughs he began clowning.

"Did you notice how busy those newspapermen got every time I made a hit?" he asked his guards later.

On his return to Sing Sing, Crowley got a good view of the George Washington Bridge. Once back in his cell he asked for some light wood and Lawes gave it to him. Meticulously, with a magazine photo to guide him, he reconstructed the entire bridge. He built a miniature Empire State Building and a rambling structure he labeled "Crowley's Hotel," complete with elevators and miniature workmen. Two-Gun trapped a beetle and, tying it down with a thread, compelled the insect to act as a watchman at Crowley's Hotel.

Two-Gun began to confide in Warden Lawes, one of the best penologists of modern times. He told Lawes that he used to attend church regularly, but that he always wore his two guns, even during the services.

"Why didn't you shoot the minister?" a tough guard sarcastically inquired.

"I never shoot my friends," Crowley said smiling. "Only my enemies—policemen."

Crowley's fame had not subsided. The press kept running a series of articles about his spectacular exploits and just before his execution several requests from newspapers for a final interview with the killer crossed Lawes' desk. One syndicate had written Two-Gun's life story without ever consulting the facts or its subject. It offered $10,000 if Crowley would only sign the phony autobiography. He didn't,

but later Two-Gun told Lawes that "if mother [his foster mother] had that money when I was a kid, maybe things would have been different." He also told Lawes: "I knew when I bought that gun it would land me in the electric chair."

The night he was due to march to the death chair, Lawes came into Crowley's cell to find Two-Gun staring at a water bug shooting about the floor. "See that?" he said. "I was about to kill it. Several times I wanted to crush it. It's a dirty-looking thing. But then I decided to give it a chance and let it live."

Twenty-five newspapermen were on hand in the gallery seated before the electric chair as witnesses when Crowley was led into the chamber. Rudolph Duringer had just been electrocuted minutes before. Noting the journalists, Crowley returned to his swagger and banter.

Two-Gun stopped in his tracks and turned to the warden. "I got a favor to ask you," he said.

"Name it," Lawes said.

"I want a rag," Two-Gun said.

"A rag? What for?"

"I want to wipe off the chair after that rat sat in it."

Lawes had seen this kind of braggadocio displayed many times before by killers on their way to the chair. (He had witnessed all kinds of bizarre behavior, such as the time a Negro murderer was led to the death room humming and whistling, dancing up to the electric chair which he stroked and kissed several times, calling it his "sweet chariot that takes me over Jordan.") Lawes ignored Crowley's remark but the newsmen began to write furiously about the killer they called "the game kid."

Two-Gun was smoking a cigar when he calmly sat down in the chair. He looked at the newsmen who had created the warped legends about him, and, before the straps were applied to his arms, he withdrew the cigar and flipped it at them, hitting one in the middle of the forehead. "You sons-of-bitches," he hissed.

His arms were then strapped down. Just before the black hood was placed over his head, Crowley turned to Warden Lawes and said softly: "Give my love to mother."

Then the executioner jerked a switch downward and the lethal current raced through Francis Two-Gun Crowley, celebrity.

CUNNINGHAM, CHARLES
Murderer ● (1787-1805)

BACKGROUND: BORN IN YORK, PA., PLACED IN A POORHOUSE AS A SMALL CHILD; MADE A "BOUND" SERVANT TO AN INNKEEPER NAMED EICHELBERGER AT AGE 12 IN 1799. NO FORMAL EDUCATION. DESCRIPTION: TALL, DARK, THIN. ALIASES: NONE. RECORD: STRANGLED A YOUTH, JOSEPH ROTHROCK, TO DEATH, 5/16/1805; ARRESTED AND CONFESSED TO THE MURDER; EXECUTED 9/19/05.

Charles Cunningham's life had been anything but pleasant. Born into poverty, he was soon deserted by his mother and placed in a poorhouse—where he was fed one skimpy meal a day and made to slave from dawn till dusk. By the time he was twelve, Cunningham had become an unthinking, insensitive animal. He was sent to an inn in York, Pa. as a "bound" servant, his master being a certain Mr. Eichelberger. The innkeeper did not improve Cunningham's lot.

The youth, at eighteen, had taken to drinking large quantities of the inn's whiskey. Much of the time Cunningham gambled with neighborhood boys in the inn's kitchen. On May 16, 1805, he began a game of hustlecap with two teenage boys—John Heckendorn and Joseph Rothrock. (Hustlecap was a common street game which consisted of shaking and tossing coins into a cap.)

Cunningham and his friends soon left Eichelberger's and walked to another tavern where they continued to gamble, drinking whiskey and cideroyal. Cunningham won Rothrock's money, plus a box, handkerchief, and silver brooch.

Tiring of the game, the boys began to shoot dice. This time Rothrock began to win. Heckendorn said that he wanted to check the dice. The apparent distrust made Cunningham angry. Thinking he was being cheated, the eighteen-year-old shouted at his companions.

Though he had been drinking heavily, Cunningham later swore: "I was in liquor, though as well as in my senses as I am now."

His claimed sobriety, however, did not prevent him from leading his friend Joseph Rothrock into a dark alley and then drawing forth a knife. He intended to slit Joseph's throat. The knife slipped from his hands.

As Rothrock looked at him in horror, Charles jumped forward. In a later confession, the youthful killer admitted: "I sprung upon him, and grasped him by the neck with both my hands, placing both my thumbs in his throat, and squeezing with all my might until he fell down and appeared to be dead."

But Joseph soon revived. Cunningham produced a piece of rough twine and, placing it about Joseph's neck, used it to strangle him to death. "I then committed a most horrid indignity on the dead body, for which I cannot otherwise account than that it was done by the immediate instigation of the Devil," Cunningham later stated.

He grabbed the dead boy's face and slammed it to the cobblestones, face down, until Joseph's features were obliterated.

Swiftly apprehended, Charles Cunningham confessed and was hanged September 19, 1805.

CZOLGOSZ, LEON
Assassin ● (1873-1901)

A 28-year-old laborer, Czolgosz (pronounced *Cholgosh*) was a confirmed anarchist who was impressed with the rash of assassinations sweeping Europe at the turn of the century, particularly the killing of King Humbert of Italy who had been slain by a laborer from New Jersey.

Czolgosz, traveled from the Midwest to the Pan-American Exposition in Buffalo, N. Y. in early September, 1901, with a single thought in mind—to kill the much-loved William McKinley, twenty-fifth President of the United States.

McKinley, an affable hand-shaker, greeted the assembled crowds at the Exposition on September 6, 1901, and stood inside the main temple as lines of citizens pressed forward to clasp his hand. While fifty guards lounged near the President, Czolgosz got in line and slowly inched forward. A white handkerchief was wrapped around his hand but the guards took no notice of it; it was assumed that he had been injured in an accident.

The assassin was not a suspicious-looking person. A guard later stated: "He was the last man in the crowd we would have picked out as dangerous."

Czolgosz reached McKinley at 4:07 p.m. The President, thinking the young man had been injured, reached for the anarchist's left hand. The assassin pushed it aside and dropped the handkerchief wrapped around his right hand to reveal a .32-caliber pistol. Before anyone could react, Czolgosz shoved the barrel to within inches of the President and fired two shots. One ploughed through McKinley's abdomen, a fatal wound.

"I done my duty!" the illiterate killer screamed as guards wrestled him to the floor.

An artist's conception of assassin Leon Czolgosz being led to the electric chair in New York's Auburn Prison on October 29, 1901, (UPI)

Anarchist Leon Czolgosz "thought it would be a good thing" to kill President McKinley and did so in 1901. (UPI)

The President, swooning in the arms of his aides, gave his killer a painful glance and then quietly and magnanimously said: "Be easy with him, boys." He was rushed to a hospital but died eight days later of gangrenous poisoning, a condition brought about through inept medical attention.

Czolgosz was tight-lipped, a prisoner whose only statement on the shooting was, "I thought it would be a good thing for this country to kill the President."

He offered no defense at his trial, sitting mutely in court with a blank expression on his face. In seventeen days he was found guilty and sentenced to death. On October 29, 1901, Leon Czolgosz—wearing a neatly pressed suit, wing-collar, and highly shined shoes sat down in the electric chair in New York's Auburn Prison.

"Anything to say?" the warden asked.

"I am not sorry," Czolgosz muttered as the switch was thrown.

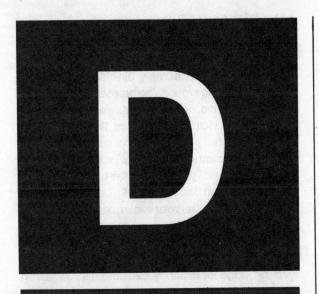

DAHMER, JEFFREY LIONEL
Serial Killer ● (1960-1994)

BACKGROUND: RAISED IN BATH TOWNSHIP, OHIO; GRADU-
ATED HIGH SCHOOL, 1978; SERVED AS MEDIC IN ARMY IN
GERMANY, 1979-1981; WORKED AS NIGHT LABORER IN MIL-
WAUKEE, WIS., FROM 1981; RECORD: AR., BATH TOWNSHIP,
FOR ALCOHOL ABUSE, 1981; CONV. OF LEWD AND LACIVI-
OUS CONDUCT, 3/10/87, RECEIVED ONE-YEAR PROBATION;
AR. 9/26/88 FOR SEXUAL ASSAULT AND ENTICEMENT OF A
CHILD FOR IMMORAL PURPOSES, MILWAUKEE, WIS., GIVEN
ONE-YEAR TERM IN CORRECTIONAL FACILITY ON WORK
RELEASE PROGRAM, 5/204/89; MURDERED NINETEEN-YEAR-
OLD STEVEN HICKS IN BATH TOWNSHIP, OHIO, 1978; ADMIT-
TED KILLING 17 YOUTHS BETWEEN 1978 AND 1991, INCLUD-
ING ANTHONY SEARS, 24; RAYMOND LAMONT SMITH (AKA:
RICKY BEEKS), 33; ERNEST MILLER, 24; CURTIS STRAUGHTER,
18; ERROL LINDSEY, 19; TONY HUGHES, 31; MATT TURNER, 20;
DAVID C. THOMAS, 23; JEREMIAH WEINBERGER, 23; OLIVER
LACY, 23; JOSEPH BRADEHOFT, 25; ANTHONY SEARS, 24;
RICHARD GUERRERO, 22; EDDIE SMITH, 28; KONERAK SIN-
THASOMPHONE; AR. AND CHAR. WITH THESE AND OTHER
MURDERS ON 7/22/91; TRIED IN MILWAUKEE, WIS., 1991;
RECEIVED FIFTEEN LIFE TERMS IN 2/92; MURDERED BY AN
INMATE 11/28/94.

T wo Milwaukee, Wis., police officers making their rounds shortly before midnight on
July 22, 1991, spotted a man running down
the 2500 block of Kilbourn Avenue in the city's
tenement district. His wrists in handcuffs, the young
man frantically flagged down the squad car. Identifying himself as Tracy Edwards, he explained
that he was fleeing from the apartment of Jeffrey L.
Dahmer, a 31-year-old factory worker who had
terrorized him, threatened to kill him "and eat his

heart out." Edwards had been held captive for five
terrifying hours.

Edwards, who insisted that he was not a homosexual, told police that he managed to escape by
gaining Dahmer's trust during a four-hour conversation. "He underestimated me," the 32-year-old
man said. "God sent me there to take care of the
situation."

Edwards led the officers to Dahmer's one-room
apartment at 924 N. 25th St. Inside they found an
apartment littered with human remains. There
were skulls in the freezer, torsos strewn about, and
photographs of dead men, who had been mutilated or completely dismembered. After inspecting
the apartment, Medical Examiner Jeffrey Jentzen
hinted that the remains of the victims "were not
inconsistent with cannibalism."

Jeffrey Dahmer, a shy social outcast who had
been arrested by the Milwaukee authorities on at
least three prior occasions for disorderly conduct,
assault, and child molestation, suddenly became
the focus of international attention as the gruesome crimes of this serial killer unfolded. Police
identified the remains of eleven victims in Dahmer's
apartment, but there was strong evidence that
Dahmer may have committed as many as seventeen killings in Ohio, Wisconsin, and as far away
as West Germany, where he had been assigned
briefly while in the Army. "This guy is really an
aberration even of the abnormal," commented a
Milwaukee mental health professional. "His behavior goes one step beyond. . . . Each element of
the case takes you one step farther into the bizarre."

A chilling psychological profile of a painfully
insecure, alcohol-dependant loner quickly began
to emerge. Dahmer spent much of his early years
growing up in rural Bath Township, Ohio. As a
youth he appeared to be deeply troubled by the
deteriorating marriage of his parents. His mother,
Joyce A. Flint, was considered mentally unstable
by friends and acquaintances. After her divorce,
Mrs. Flint went to live in Fresno, Calif., where she
now works as a case manager for the Central Valley AIDS Team.

In school Dahmer defied conventional behavior
and was described by his high school prom date
as a likely candidate for suicide. "We always saw
him as the type to commit suicide, not harm somebody else," recalled Bridget Geiger. At his parents'
urging, Dahmer entered the military in 1978 and
was stationed as a U.S. Army medic in Baumholder,
West Ger., from July 1979 until his discharge in
March 1981.

Recalling his association with Dahmer in West Germany, former barracks roommate David J. Rodriguez remembered Dahmer's incredible drinking binges. "He'd drink until he passed out. Beginning Friday afternoon, he'd drink all day, pass out, wake up, and start drinking again. He'd have his headphones on, and he'd be in his own little world."

Some weekends Dahmer simply disappeared. Where he went and what he did interested no one until he suddenly burst into the public eye as one of America's most horrendous killers. When news of the Milwaukee murders reached police in Germany, an investigation was launched to determine if Dahmer had been involved in nine unsolved homicides there.

Following his military discharge, Dahmer returned to Bath Township after a brief stopover in Miami, Fla. In October 1981, the Bath police charged him with disorderly conduct and resisting arrest after he was found with an open bottle of alcohol at a local Ramada Inn. It was the first time Dahmer ran afoul of the law.

After visiting his grandmother, Catherine Dahmer, in the Milwaukee suburb of West Allis, Dahmer decided to take up permanent residence in Wisconsin. He found employment with the Ambrosia Chocolate Company as a night laborer, but his work habits were suspect and he was reprimanded for sleeping in the lunchroom and frequent tardiness.

On March 10, 1987, Dahmer was convicted of lewd and lascivious behavior after publicly urinating in front of several children, and was sentenced to one year probation. A year later an Illinois man complained to police that Dahmer had drugged him and stolen his money and jewelry. Lacking hard evidence the case was dropped.

More disturbing allegations were brought against Dahmer in the next two years, but the courts and the state social service agencies seemed unresponsive and indifferent to the potential danger he posed to the community. On Sept. 26, 1988, Dahmer lured a thirteen-year-old boy into his apartment by offering him $50 to pose for a photo. Dahmer drugged his coffee and sexually molested him. The boy, who, ironically, turned out to be the brother of one of his future victims, Konerak Sinthasomphone, managed to escape. Dahmer was arrested and charged with second-degree sexual assault and enticement of a child for immoral purposes. Summarizing the case before Milwaukee County Circuit Judge William D. Gardner, Assistant District Attorney Gail Shelton said that in her judgment, ". . . it is absolutely crystal clear that the prognosis for treatment of Mr. Dahmer within the community is extremely bleak . . . and is just plain not going to work." The prosecutor asked that Dahmer be given a five- or six-year prison sentence, but in Gardner's opinion Dahmer had a better opportunity to benefit from psychiatric treatment if he remained outside of prison, which did not offer a special program for sex offenders.

As a result, on May 24, 1989, Dahmer was ordered to serve a one-year sentence in the Franklin House of Corrections on a work-release program that would allow him to continue to work at the Ambrosia Chocolate Company. Dahmer pleaded with the judge for leniency, blaming his troubles on alcohol. "I can't stress it enough that I desperately want to change my conduct for the rest of my life," he implored.

On March 25, 1989, 24-year-old Anthony Sears of Milwaukee disappeared. He was the first of the eleven victims to be positively identified. Dahmer typically found his victims in local gay bars, shopping malls, or the New Town section of Chicago, which is heavily frequented by homosexuals. Between June 30 and July 19, 1991, Dahmer lured four young men to his apartment, on the pretext of watching videos or paying them to pose for photographs.

On each occasion, after successfully luring his victim to his apartment, Dahmer proceeded to drug, strangle, and dismember him. Police believe that on at least one occasion he engaged in sex with a corpse. When tenants in the building complained of the stench coming from his apartment, Dahmer simply passed it off as rotting meat in the refrigerator, an explanation they accepted. "He even bought a bunch of Pine Sol once like he was really going to get rid of it this time. But it didn't help," recalled Pamela Bass, who lived across the hall from Dahmer.

The most shocking aspect of the case revolved around the Milwaukee Police Department, which was accused of gross negligence for its failure to follow up on a report concerning Dahmer made on May 27, 1991. Two eighteen-year-old women reported that they observed a young Laotian boy running down an alley, naked and bleeding. When three police officers arrived on the scene, Dahmer was chasing the youth. Dahmer told the officers that the teenager was a "house guest" and that he had had too much to drink.

The officers dismissed the incident as a domestic

disturbance between two homosexuals and released the youth to Dahmer. "Police officers do not routinely arrest someone for being intoxicated, especially when they can return him to someplace safe," stated Milwaukee Police Association attorney Laurie Eggert. According to the police officers involved, the youth appeared to them to be eighteen or nineteen years of age and did not attempt to put up a struggle or voice an objection.

The boy, later identified as Konerak Sinthasomphone, was actually too drunk to speak; he was killed minutes after police left him in Dahmer's apartment. Public attention was soon focused on police chief Philip Arreola and the questionable methods employed by his force.

An internal investigation launched by Arreola and Mayor John O. Norquist resulted in departmental charges being filed against Officers John A. Balcerzak, 34, who had been cited for nineteen "noteworthy" arrests during his career; Joseph P. Gabrish, 28; and Richard Porubcan, 25. All three were suspended on July 26. It marked the first time in the history of the Milwaukee Police Department that there were suspensions issued before an investigation commenced. The police tape recordings that were made at the time showed a gross insensitivity on the part of the three officers who spoke with Dahmer and the boy. The men made jokes about the need to be "deloused" after leaving Sinthasomphone with Dahmer.

Chief Arreola delayed his decision on the fate of these three officers until September 6, when he fired Balcerzak and Gabrish, and ordered Porubcan to remain under "close supervision" for one year. "I have concluded the officers failed to properly perform their duties," Arreola said, but the two policemen who lost their jobs maintained that they acted in accordance with departmental procedures. "I wish there had been some other piece of evidence or information available to us," commented Joseph Gabrish. "We handled the call the way we felt it should have been handled."

Once Dahmer was arrested, the focus of the investigation widened. Dahmer, who admitted to as many as seventeen killings, directed police to his boyhood home in Bath Township, outside of Akron, Ohio. There in the backyard, Summit County police found pieces of bone scattered across the property.

Dahmer told the authorities that these were the remains of nineteen-year-old Steven Hicks, a hitchhiker he had picked up and murdered just days after his high school graduation in 1978. After bury-

Milwaukee cannibal and serial killer Jeffrey Dahmer, murdered in prison in 1994. (AP/Wide World)

ing the body, Dahmer apparently had serious concerns about it eventually being unearthed, so he dug up the remains, smashed them with a sledgehammer, then reburied them throughout the 1.7-acre property. Hicks's identity was confirmed by Summit County Coroner William Cox on Sept. 13, 1991.

As Summit County police continued to dig up the yard in Bath Township, Milwaukee police released a list of the eleven victims found in Dahmer's apartment. In addition to Sinthasomphone, they included: Raymond Lamont Smith (AKA: Ricky Beeks), a 33-year-old ex-convict from Milwaukee who was last seen on May 29, 1990; 24-year-old Ernest Miller, who had recently moved from Chicago to Milwaukee to escape "all the violence" there; Curtis Straughter, an 18-year-old Milwaukeean; Errol Lindsey, 19, who disappeared from his Milwaukee home on Apr. 7; Tony Hughes, a 31-year-old deaf mute from Madison, Wis., who was murdered just two days before Konerak Sinthasomphone on May 24, 1991.

The list went on, staggering even the jaded imaginations of police officers: Chicagoan Matt Turner, 20, who was last seen on June 30 at the halfway house where he lived; David C. Thomas, 23, whose photograph was identified among Dahmer's possessions; 23-year-old Jeremiah Weinberger, who was invited to come to Milwaukee from Chicago to pose for pictures and watch videos; Oliver Lacy, 23, of Milwaukee, whose battered remains were found in Dahmer's freezer; Joseph Bradehoft, 25, of Milwaukee who had a wife and three children; 24-year-old restaurant manager Anthony Sears; and Richard Guerrero, 22, who was reported missing on Mar. 29, 1989.

Guerrero and Sears were two of three men Dahmer claimed to have murdered while living at his grandmother's home in West Allis. Dahmer admitted to having murdered 28-year-old Eddie Smith, also of Milwaukee, although the body was not located. Of the first eleven victims, eight were black, one was Asian, and two were white.

Dahmer was taken to the Milwaukee County Jail after initially being charged with four counts of first-degree intentional homicide. Appearing before Milwaukee County Circuit judge Laurence C. Gram, Jr., on September 10, Dahmer and his attorney, Gerald Boyle, entered a not guilty plea by reason of insanity. Boyle admitted that the defense could change the plea before the scheduled startup of the trial on Jan. 27, 1992.

Said Gram at the time: "I think there is a strong likelihood . . . this case may proceed on the Not Guilty by reason of mental defect or disease. But at this junction . . . we're not yet prepared to do that."

According to Wisconsin law, Dahmer would be sent to a mental hospital if he was found not guilty as a result of the insanity plea. If that were to happen, he could petition the courts for his release every six months if he were able to demonstrate that he had regained control of his faculties and was no longer a menace to society. If he were to be found sane and guilty of murder, Dahmer would face a maximum sentence of life imprisonment.

The Jeffrey Dahmer serial murder case had badly shaken the confidence of all Milwaukeeans. "They view it as a national trend in all big cities," said County Supervisor Daniel Cupertino at the time. "But they thought Milwaukee would never get that way. Milwaukee was a clean, safe city."

Dahmer was brought to trial in September 1991 and pleaded not guilty to fifteen murder charges. In each case, he had already confessed to the killing. He promised to plead insanity if convicted of murder. Throughout the early 1992 trial, Gerald Boyle, Dahmer's defense attorney, stressed the gruesomeness of the crimes, as his strategy was to argue that only a madman could commit such heinous murders and thereby prove his client's innocence by reason of insanity.

The prosecution countered the argument, stating that only a sane man with a reasonable fear of being caught and punished would be so clever at avoiding detection for an extended period of time. Dahmer was found guilty. In February 1992, one of

the worst serial killers in our time was sentenced to 15 life terms in prison.

Dahmer was a low-profile prisoner who accepted Christianity behind bars, being baptized in the prison whirlpool. He had considerable enemies, however. In July 1994 an attempt was made on Dahmer's life by another prisoner who stabbed him, but his wounds were only superficial. The next attempt was fatal. On November 28, 1994, while cleaning the washroom at the prison facility in Portage, Wisconsin, Dahmer was murdered by another inmate.

DALITZ, MORRIS BARNEY
Syndicate Boss ● (1899-1989)

One of the few non-Italians to rise to great power in the national crime syndicate, Morris "Moe" Dalitz began at the bottom, as a strong-arm goon in Detroit's infamous Purple Gang. In the 1920s Dalitz moved to Cleveland and there aligned himself with other young, ambitious bootleggers. These included Al and Chuck Polizzi and Frank and Tony Milano.

Dalitz's gang came to be known as the Mayfield Road Gang, named after the highway where its headquarters was located. Dalitz and his fellow gangsters grew powerful and they were known to be ruthless and always lethal to anyone opposing them. They slew the Porello brothers and the entire Leonardo family as they seized control of all of northeast Ohio.

Following Prohibition, Dalitz extended his gambling, protection and prostitution operations into Kentucky, West Virginia, and Indiana. He was named as a member of the board of directors of the national crime syndicate, being one of the only Jewish gangsters to ever rise to such power, the other being Meyer Lansky.

In the 1960s, Dalitz led his Cleveland family to Las Vegas where it bought the Desert Inn and got a foothold on the booming "strip." Within a short time, Dalitz was the most powerful syndicate leader in Nevada and he remained the elder statesman of the syndicate in that state until the IRS began investigating his tax records. Dalitz then retired to a palatial California estate to live out his very long life. He died in Las Vegas of natural causes on September 6, 1989.

DALTON BROTHERS

DALTON, EMMETT
Bankrobber, Trainrobber • (1871-1937)

BACKGROUND: BORN TO LOUIS AND ADELINE (YOUNGER) DALTON IN A FARMHOUSE IN CASS COUNTY, MO., ONE OF FIFTEEN CHILDREN. MINOR EDUCATION. MARRIED JULIA JOHNSON IN 1907. BEGAN A REAL ESTATE BUSINESS IN LOS ANGELES, 1920. WROTE SEVERAL SCENARIOS FOR SILENT MOVIES. AUTHOR: "WHEN THE DALTONS RODE," 1931. DESCRIPTION: 6', BROWN EYES, BROWN HAIR, SOLID BUILD. ALIASES: UNKNOWN. RECORD: STUCK UP A FARO GAME IN NEW MEXICO, 1890 WITH HIS BROTHER BOB; ROBBED THE SANTE FE'S TEXAS EXPRESS WITH BROTHERS BOB AND GRAT, GEORGE "BITTER CREEK" NEWCOMB, CHARLEY "BLACK FACE" BRYANT, NEAR WHARTON, OKLA., 5/9/91 ($14,000); ROBBED A MISSOURI-KANSAS & TEXAS EXPRESS TRAIN NEAR LELIETTA, OKLA. IN THE SUMMER OF 1891 WITH BROTHERS BOB AND GRAT, NEWCOMB, BILL POWERS, CHARLEY PIERCE, WILL MCELHANIE, DICK BROADWELL, AND BILL DOOLIN ($19,000); ROBBED A SANTE FE TRAIN NEAR RED ROCK ON THE CHEROKEE STRIP WEEKS LATER WITH SAME GANG ($11,000); ROBBED AN EXPRESS TRAIN WITH THE SAME BAND NEAR ADAIR, OKLA., 7/14/92, WOUNDING GUARD SID JOHNSON ($17,000); ATTEMPTED TO ROB WITH BROTHERS BOB AND GRAT, DICK BROADWELL, AND BILL POWERS TWO BANKS—THE FIRST NATIONAL AND CONDON BANKS—IN COFFEYVILLE, KAN., 10/5/92. BROTHERS BOB AND GRAT, POWERS AND BROADWELL KILLED BY ARMED CITIZENS, EMMETT SEVERELY WOUNDED AND CAPTURED; TRIED FOR KILLING TWO COFFEYVILLE CITIZENS, GEORGE CUBINE AND LUCIUS BALDWIN (MAINTAINED THEY WERE SHOT BY HIS BROTHER BOB) DURING THE RAID AND FOUND GUILTY; SENTENCED TO LIFE IMPRISONMENT IN THE KANSAS STATE PENITENTIARY IN LANSING, KAN., IN MARCH, 1893; PARDONED BY KANSAS GOVERNOR E. W. HOCH IN 1907; COMPLETELY REFORMED AND BECAME A LEADING BUSINESSMAN IN THE LOS ANGELES COMMUNITY, DYING OF OLD AGE 7/13/37.

DALTON, GRATTON (GRAT)
Trainrobber, Bankrobber • (1862-1892)

BACKGROUND: BORN IN CASS COUNTY, MO. MINOR PUBLIC EDUCATION. SERVED BRIEFLY AS A MARSHAL IN FORT SMITH, ARK., AND LATER WITH THE INDIAN POLICE ON THE OSAGE RESERVATION. DESCRIPTION: 5'9", BROWN EYES, BROWN HAIR, SLENDER BUILD, MUSTACHE. ALIASES: UNKNOWN. RECORD: ATTEMPTED TO ROB TRAIN NO. 17 OF THE SOUTHERN PACIFIC WITH BROTHERS BILL AND BOB, 2/6/91 (DRIVEN OFF BY THE EXPRESS GUARD), CAPTURED WITH BROTHER BILL AND TRIED, SENTENCED TO 25 YEARS IN PRISON, BUT ESCAPED; $6,000 REWARD POSTED FOR GRAT AND BOB (FOR FURTHER INFORMATION, SEE ABOVE); KILLED IN THE COFFEYVILLE RAID 10/5/92.

DALTON, ROBERT (BOB)
Trainrobber, Bankrobber • (1867-1892)

BACKGROUND: BORN IN CASS COUNTY, MO. MINOR PUBLIC EDUCATION. SERVED AS A MARSHAL IN FORT SMITH, ARK. WITH BROTHER GRAT FOR A BRIEF TIME. ALSO SERVED AS A LAWMAN ON THE OSAGE INDIAN RESERVATION. ENGAGED TO EUGENIA MOORE WHO DIED A FEW WEEKS BEFORE HIM, OF CANCER. DESCRIPTION: 5'10", BROWN EYES, BROWN HAIR, SLENDER BUILD. ALIASES: UNKNOWN. RECORD: (SEE INFORMATION UNDER EMMETT AND GRAT DALTON).

DALTON, WILLIAM (BILL)
Trainrobber, Bankrobber • (1873-1893)

BACKGROUND: BORN IN CASS COUNTY, MO. MINOR PUBLIC EDUCATION. TRAVELED TO CALIFORNIA WITH ANOTHER DALTON BROTHER, LITTLETON, MARRIED AND HOMESTEADED. DESCRIPTION: 5'11", BROWN EYES, BROWN HAIR, SOLID BUILD. ALIASES: UNKNOWN. RECORD: ROBBED A CALIFORNIA TRAIN IN 1891 (SEE INFORMATION UNDER GRAT DALTON); ROBBED SEVERAL SMALL TOWN BANKS AND SOME TRAINS WITH THE DOOLIN GANG IN OKLAHOMA; KILLED BY LAWMEN ON HIS FRONT PORCH.

As robbers, the Daltons had a perfect heritage. Their cousins, the Younger brothers, had ridden with Jesse and Frank James. Missouri, the place of their birth, was called "Mother of Bandits." Lower Kansas, around Coffeyville, where they once lived, had been torn apart by Civil War guerrillas and roving bands of thieves and cutthroats. The wild Oklahoma Indian Territory, where their parents finally settled, was overrun with train and bank robbers. The trouble was— the Daltons never realized it until a fateful day in Coffeyville, Kan.—that the border bandit days were gone and they had strapped on their guns too late.

Of the fifteen children Mother Dalton bore, only four turned bad and went against the law. Frank Dalton was a special exception. Frank pinned on a marshal's badge and served on Judge Isaac C. Parker's ("The Hanging Judge") police force in Fort Smith, Ark. He came upon three bandits running illegal whiskey one day and was killed by them.

The older Dalton brothers—Grat, Bob, and Emmett—became so enraged by their brother's murder they also put on stars, but they never caught Frank's killers. Life on the right side of the law was dull. The boys quit their Fort

Smith posts and moved onto the Osage Indian Reservation to serve with the Indian Police. It was lazy duty and they soon turned to rustling a few head of cattle to pick up side money. Grat got tired of the penny-ante stealing, turned in his star, and rode to California to join his brothers Littleton and Bill who had moved there to homestead.

Bob and Emmett Dalton drifted south to New Mexico. The two got into a faro game in a small town there and, suspicious of being cheated, held up the game for a few dollars and raced for Oklahoma. "Wanted" posters were out on them for the first time in 1890.

Emmett returned to the family home in Kingfisher, Okla., but Bob, yearning for adventure, headed for California. There, he teamed up with his brothers Bill and Grat and on February 6, 1891, went after a big score. The boys stopped the Southern Pacific's Train No. 17 which was approaching Los Angeles.

Riding as passengers, they merely got up from their seats, adjusted large red handkerchiefs about their faces, and climbed into the locomotive cab from the tender. Before the train was brought to a halt fireman George Badcliff panicked. One of the bandits shot him in the stomach. He fell to the floor in agony and died hours later.

The brothers ran alongside the halted train to the express car.

Charles C. Haswell, the express guard, was terrified. He rashly pressed his face against the car's window to see the bandits flourishing guns outside.

Bob Dalton, the gang's natural leader, yelled to him: "Open up and be damned quick about it!"

Haswell stalled. One of the outlaws fired a shotgun at the window and buckshot tore across the guard's forehead. In a rage, Haswell grabbed his own shotgun and let the bandits have it. He claimed to have hit one of them before he drove them off.

The first Dalton holdup was a dismal failure. Not only was the gang driven off without getting a dollar but Bill and Grat were soon hunted down and arrested. Bob, racing back to Oklahoma, heard that Bill had been cleared but that Grat had drawn a twenty-year sentence for armed robbery. Then Grat escaped and headed back East to join his brothers.

The Southern Pacific offered $6,000 rewards for the two brothers. Bob later told Emmett that the robbery was a foolish act but that the railroad "put the running iron on our hides" when they posted the rewards. It was the same kind of claim made by the James boys, the Cassidy gang, and hundreds of other outlaws. Whether real or imagined, the old refrain of "they made me a criminal" did nothing to prevent the Daltons from living up to their unsavory publicity.

Bob, Grat, and Emmett rounded up one of the toughest bands of outlaws in Oklahoma's history for a terrifying robbery spree that was destined to last eighteen months and forever be remembered. The handsome and quick-draw gunman George "Bitter Creek" Newcomb joined them. So did "Black-Face" Charley Bryant. His odd monicker resulted after a gunfight when Bryant's face was scarred by powder burns. ("I want to get killed in one hell-firing minute of smoking action," Bryant allegedly stated.) Bill Doolin, who would have a gang of his own one day, Dick Broadwell, Bill Powers, Charley Pierce, and Bill McElhanie, all top gunmen, also joined up.

The first target was, naturally, a railroad. The band held up the Texas Express on the Sante Fe line near Wharton, Okla. in early 1891. They took $14,000 out of the express car without firing a shot. When "Black-Face" Bryant suggested they rob the passengers, the Dalton brothers turned as one and sneered no. In their strange code of honor, the brothers insisted on leaving the passengers alone (a trait not common to their cousins, the Youngers).

With his share of the loot, Bryant rode into the small town of Hennessey, Okla. and happily shot up the town. He was promptly arrested by Marshal Ed Short, who accompanied him on the train to Wichita to stand trial before a federal judge. During the trip, Bryant, held captive in the baggage car, grabbed a gun and both he and Short fired at the same time, killing each other.

Bob Dalton was neither surprised or upset. Bryant asked for it. He was foolish, he told his brothers. But, a little over a year later, Bob would commit one of the most foolish mistakes ever made by a Western badman.

The gang struck again at Lelietta, Okla., smoothly relieving a Missouri-Kansas & Texas express of $19,000 in currency and silver.

Bob Dalton insisted that there be no letup.

He figured every man in the gang would be wealthy enough to retire "inside of twelve months." Bob had a good reason. He was engaged to attractive Eugenia Moore who was no stranger to his robberies. Not until forty years later would it be learned that the reason why the Dalton's struck with such accuracy, just when large shipments of money were being moved, was Eugenia. She worked for Bob (unknown to all except Dalton's brothers) as a sort of advance scout, inquiring at waystations which train would be the best protected. She stated that she wanted to ship some of her own money. Naturally, she was told, the best trains by which to ship her money were those carrying large bank note shipments; they were always heavily protected. Eugenia obtained the proper schedules and passed these to Bob Dalton.

Emmett had a reason to retire, too. Her name was Julia Johnson, a childhood sweetheart. While on the run, Emmett secretly visited her while his brothers stood guard outside the Johnson house in the event a posse should arrive by night. Dalton wanted to marry her but felt it was impossible. "What had I to offer Julia," he wrote later, "a man with a price on his head and no clear way to extricate myself from the compounding results of crime? I rode away. An outlaw has no business having a girl, no business thinking of marriage."

The gang then stuck up a Sante Fe train near Red Rock, taking $11,000 without firing one bullet. The next strike was not so easy. Lawmen learned that the Daltons were going to stop a Texas train July 14, 1892, on its way to Kansas at Pryor Creek, Okla. Bob Dalton, through Eugenia, heard about the fifty-man posse and stopped the train at Adair before it got to the entrapment area. They had to wound Deputy Sid Johnson, an express guard, to get $17,000. Ironically, Johnson had served with the Daltons as a peace officer at Fort Smith.

Bob then planned the biggest raid of his life. Since childhood he had heard romantic stories about how the James and Younger boys tried to rob two banks at the same time in Northfield, Minn. They had failed and were shot to bits, but that didn't mean it couldn't be done, Dalton reasoned. He knew of a small town that had two ripe banks, a town where he and his brothers had briefly lived as small

Bob Dalton, leader of the Dalton brothers, with his sweetheart, Eugenia Moore; she scouted for the gang, setting up robberies. (Western History Collections, U. of Okla. Library)

boys—Coffeyville, Kansas.

Eugenia Moore had no hand in casing this job, unfortunately for the Daltons. She was dead. Suddenly stricken with cancer, Bob's sweetheart died only weeks before the Coffeyville raid. Dalton threw her picture into a campfire. The next day Emmett, Grat, and Bob rode to Kingfisher to see their mother but were afraid to go near the farmhouse. Lawmen, they suspected, might be waiting in the shadows.

The outlaw brothers sat on their horses in the middle of the night and watched their mother move past the windows of their boyhood home. It was bitter nostalgia that moved Emmett to later write: "For a moment we saw her in the distant window, her flitting form, setting the house in order for the night. None of us dared look at each other. With one accord we spurred our horses. And at the sound, I saw her turn her face to the window, listening intently, as if she heard the passing hoofbeats. Such was Bob and Grat's last outspoken salute to the grand old lady who bore them."

Dick Broadwell, Bill Powers, and Bill Doolin made the journey northward the next day with the three Dalton Brothers, heading for Coffeyville, disaster, and eternal Western fame. Only Doolin was to escape that cauldron of death. His horse went lame a few miles from the town. He said he would go to a nearby ranch, steal a horse, and catch up. He didn't.

The other five men rode into Coffeyville on the morning of October 5, 1892, sauntering into the main plaza off Eighth Street at 9:30

Bob and Grat Dalton minutes after their disastrous raid on two Coffeyville, Kan. banks, dead or dying, being held up by lawmen, 10/5/92. (Western History Collections, U. of Okla. Library)

a.m. Each outlaw carried single-action .45s, one on the hip and one in a shoulder holster. After dismounting in an alley behind the jail, the five took out their Winchester rifles and headed up the street.

Stable owner Aleck McKenna recognized the Daltons as they calmly walked past him, spurs jingling. The false beards Bob and Emmett wore didn't fool him; he had known them as boys. He watched, awe-struck, as Grat, Powers, and Broadwell entered the Condon Bank and Bob and Emmett Dalton quickly entered the First National Bank. Through the window of the Condon Bank he saw Grat Dalton raise his weapon and aim it at the cashier.

He let out a terrifying scream: "They're robbing the bank! The Daltons! They're robbing the bank!"

Inside the Condon Bank, Grat was having serious problems. Vice President Charles T. Carpenter, bookkeeper T. C. Babb, and cashier Charles Ball gaped at his leveled guns.

"Open the safe and be quick about it!" Grat ordered.

"It's a time lock. Won't open until 9:45." Ball was lying, playing for time.

Grat put his Winchester only inches from Ball's head. "Open it, or I'll kill you!"

Ball tried to placate the oldest Dalton brother by hauling out a sack containing $4,000 in silver. Grat knew that there was a lot more in the safe—there was, ten times that amount. He looked at his watch. It was 9:42. "That's

only three minutes," Grat said. "I will wait."

Bob and Emmett in the First National held three bank officers and a customer at bay. Tom Ayres, the cashier, attempted to fill the grain sack Bob had tossed to him with coins.

Dalton smiled at Ayres' ploy. "Keep that silver out. It's too heavy to bother with. The vault! The big stuff!"

Quickly, the cashier emptied the vault of $21,000, dumping the cash into the grain sack. Bob and Emmett headed for the door. A slug smashed through a window. The street was crawling with citizens, armed to the teeth, firing on both banks. Dozens of shells crashed in about the two Dalton brothers. Bob slammed the bank's heavy front door closed. "The back way," he ordered and pushed W. H. Sheppard, a customer, in front of him.

In the alley, Bob and Emmett, walking behind Sheppard, saw a man approaching and holding a pistol.

"Look after the money sack," Bob said and tossed it to his younger brother. "I'll do the fighting. I have got to get that man." He raised his rifle and sent a slug into Lucius M. Baldwin, a clerk, who died instantly.

The battle of Coffeyville was on.

As Bob and Emmett raced down side streets to the alley—now known as *Death Alley*—where their horses waited, Grat Dalton, Powers, and Broadwell made a mad dash from the Condon Bank with only $1,500 in small bills. A withering fire from dozens of vigilantes chewed up the dusty street about them as they made for the alley.

Taking their various routes, the boys ran into armed citizens at every corner. Two bootmakers who had made shoes for the boys when they were children—George W. Cubine and Charles Brown—rounded an alley just as Grat came upon them. The bandit shot them both dead.

Bob Dalton, on the run, shot Tom Ayres through the head.

After Bob and Emmett left his bank, Ayres had rushed across the street to a hardware store, grabbed a pistol, and chased after the outlaws. He died trying to recapture the money the bank entrusted to his care.

All five bandits met in the alley. Dozens of men converged on them from either end. The Daltons were doomed and knew it. Grat told them to retreat but there was nowhere to retreat to; every where they turned they met a wall of fire. Powers was shot down first. He got up firing his six-guns. Broadwell went down and got up again. He, too, kept firing his Winchester into the advancing crowds. Bob was hit. Emmett was shot twice. During the battle, Bob turned suddenly and moaned. His brother Grat received a bullet in the chest. He was dead. Before Grat fell he advanced on Marshal Charles T. Connelly, who also stalked the outlaw. Both men's pistols roared as they approached each other and both fell dead.

The next to die was Bill Powers. He managed to mount his horse, but was shot off. His horse galloping madly down the street, Dick Broadwell sagged in his saddle, riddled. He was the only one to escape Death Alley, but fell dead from his horse a few miles outside of the Coffeyville city limits.

Only Bob and Emmett Dalton were left. Sorely wounded in the right arm and hip, Emmett climbed on his horse, still clutching the grain sack full of money. He was about to make his break when he looked back for his brother Bob. His intense loyalty would not allow him to leave the bandit leader.

Bob Dalton was shot to pieces. As Emmett rode back to help him, Bob weakly called up, "Don't mind me, boy. I'm done for. Don't surrender! Die game!"

Emmett reached his shattered arm down from the saddle. Bob shakily reached upward. Just as their hands touched, liveryman John J. Kloehr and the town barber, Carey Seaman, ran up with shotguns and fired a mighty volley at the two brothers. Emmett fell from the saddle. Bob Dalton died instantly.

For moments, as the gunsmoke drifted through the alley, there was an odd silence. Then a hollow-sounding voice called across the street to the main group of vigilantes: "They're all down!"

Emmett Dalton was the only one to survive, wounded more than twenty times. He was sent to prison for life for killing George Cubine and Lucius Baldwin, although Bob had done the shooting. Pardoned in 1907, Emmett led an exemplary life until his death in 1937, a strong testimony to personal reformation.

His younger brother Bill took up the outlaw trail after Coffeyville and rode with the Doolin gang. Emmett sadly related how lawmen crept up on Bill as he was playing with his young daughter on the front porch of his farm and shot him dead from behind.

The remaining Dalton brother, after completing his saga of the bandit brothers, *When the Daltons Rode*, revisited Coffeyville, Kansas in 1931. He stood at the foot of a common grave that held the bodies of Bill Powers and Grat and Bob Dalton. He pointed solemnly to the grave and stated: "I challenge the world to produce the history of an outlaw who ever got anything out of it but that or else be huddled in a prison cell . . . The biggest fool on earth is the one who thinks he can beat the law, that crime can be made to pay. It never paid and it never will and that was the one big lesson of the Coffeyville raid."

[ALSO SEE Bill Doolin, Jesse James]

DANN, LAURIE WASSERMAN
Murderer ● (1957-1988)

Child killer Laurie Danne was mentally disturbed for some time before she stormed into a an elementary school in Chicago's fashionable North Shore and randomly shot six children. The 30-year-old divorcee had gone to pieces after her divorce from Russell Dann in 1986.

Before that time, Dann was described as "unstable," by several young men who dated her when she attended the University of Arizona. She married Dann in 1982 and was divorced four years later. Dann later told police that while the divorce was pending, someone entered his room while he was sleeping and stabbed him with an icepick. He could not be certain but he believed it was Laurie.

The daughter of a prominent Glencoe couple, Dann's behavior worsened. She was arrested for shoplifting. She threatened old boyfriends over the phone. She vandalized apartments and homes where she had once been a babysitter. Though the Danns were well aware of their daughter's unpredictable and dangerous behavioral patterns, they apparently did nothing.

Dann then bought a .357 magnum and, on May 20, 1988, drove frantically about the North Shore delivering free food samples, which she had dosed with arsenic. These she left at the doorsteps of homes where she had once worked as a babysitter. Fortunately, no one ate the samples.

Then she drove to the Ravinia Elementary School where she attempted to set fire to a bag filled with inflammatory liquid but the fire was put out by a janitor. She next went to a daycare center and was seen walking about with a gasoline can but she started no fire. Instead she drove to the home of Padraig and Marian Rushe in Winnetka, Ill.

Dann had worked for the Rushes as a baby-sitter. Once inside the home, Dann locked the two small Rushe children in the basement, setting fire to the stairwell. But Mrs. Rushe was doing laundry and was able to break a window and rescue her children.

Next, Dann drove to the Hubbard Woods Elementary School. Carrying three handguns, she walked into the boy's restroom and shot six-year-old Robert Trossman who managed to crawl into a hallway where he was discovered by a teacher. The police were called, but by then Dann had already entered the second-grade classroom of Amy Moses, 30.

She began firing at students, shooting five of them. One was eight-year-old Nicholas Corwin who later died of his wound. All the rest were to recover. The teacher reportedly struggled to wrestle the gun out of Dann's hand. The killer fled, driving to the home of Ruth Ann Andrew.

Dann did not know Andrew or her twenty-year-old son Philip, a University of Illinois student. She claimed that she had been attacked by a rapist. She then used the Andrew's phone to call her mother. When she refused help from Philip Andrew, he grew suspicious and made a move toward Dann. She shot and wounded him, then ran upstairs. Police arrived and, after hearing a shot, found Dann dead. She had killed herself.

Later, Police Chief Herbert Timm summed up the universal belief that there was no sanctuary in America safe from the Laurie Danns: "If it can happen in an idyllic community like Winnetka, which really does believe it's Camelot, then it can happen anywhere."

D'AUTREMONT BROTHERS
Trainrobbers, Murderers

BACKGROUND: ROY, RAY (TWINS) AND HUGH D'AUTRE-MONT WERE BORN AND RAISED IN RURAL OREGON NEAR THE CITY OF EUGENE. THE THREE BROTHERS RECEIVED MINOR EDUCATION. OCCUPATIONS, LUMBER-JACKS. DESCRIPTION: ALL WERE OF MEDIUM HEIGHT, FAIR COMPLEXIONS. ALIASES: GOODWIN, BRICE, ELLI-OTT. RECORD: STOPPED TRAIN NUMBER 13 OF THE SOUTHERN PACIFIC RAILROAD ON 10/11/1923 BETWEEN PORTLAND AND SAN FRANCISCO NEAR THE TOWN OF SISKIYOU, ORE., IN AN ATTEMPT TO ROB THE MAIL CAR; KILLED FOUR MEMBERS OF THE CREW AND ESCAPED; CAPTURED IN MARCH, 1927; CONFESSED TO THE ROBBERY AND MURDERS AND ALL THREE WERE SENT TO THE OREGON STATE PENITENTIARY FOR LIFE.

Probably no other train robbery in American history was so stupidly mismanaged as that attempted by the D'Autremont brothers in 1923. By then the act was archaic; the dubious art of robbing trains belonged to another age and to a different breed of men long dead. But time had passed by the D'Autremont brothers without impressing upon them the futility and risks of train robbing.

Living out their young lives in the remote wilds of Oregon, however, the D'Autremonts —twins, Roy and Ray, and their older brother Hugh—believed that this was still a good way to get rich quick. Nothing in their combined backgrounds suggested a bent toward crime. They were all hard-working boys who labored in the deep forests of Oregon as lumberjacks. Their decision to rob the Southern Pacific's mail train was, perhaps, a whim.

Since boyhood, the D'Autremonts had watched the mail trains snake in and out of Eugene, Ore., their home. They had even joked about robbing one. After all, Jesse James had been in his grave less than forty years. The memory of his daring train raids were still vivid in the minds of the American young. This idle summer dream became a crazy reality for the D'Autremonts on the morning of October 12, 1923.

An hour before noon on that day the three brothers—Hugh was the nominal leader—got up from their passenger seats on train Number 13 just after it had pulled out of the little station of Siskiyou, Ore. and began to walk to their positions. They wore heavy overcoats and beneath these they carried sawed-off shotguns.

A long tunnel cut through half a mountain outside of Siskiyou. Just as the train, slowing and working its way up a steep grade, entered this tunnel, Roy and Ray D'Autremont wriggled over the engine tender and quietly let themselves down into the locomotive cab where engineer Sidney Bates and fireman Marvin Seng were laboring.

The twins probed the crewmen's backs with their shotguns. Startled, the men turned about. "Stop the train," Roy D'Autremont ordered and waved the engineer toward the brake with his shotgun. Bates obediently grabbed for the brake lever. Half the train was out of the tunnel when it stopped.

Ray D'Autremont then motioned the crewman from the cab. "Get out now. Quick. Come with us." At shotgun point, the two trainmen were forced to walk up a small hill where the twins made them sit down, looking away from them. Bates and Seng then saw another bandit, Hugh D'Autremont, race toward the mail car. He nervously placed a cumbersome package on the window sill of the mail car and ran back into the tunnel. Moments later, the car was rocked by an explosion. The bomb, however, did not perform as expected. Instead of merely blowing away the locked door on the mail car, it caused the entire car to erupt into roaring flames.

The burning mail car was half in and half out of the tunnel. Hugh signaled his brothers to bring their prisoners down the hill. They came on the run.

"We've got to get it out of this tunnel!" Hugh screamed. He held a pistol on Bates and ordered him to climb into the engine's cab. "Get it started. Pull her out a bit." Bates climbed inside the cab and tried to start the engine. It wouldn't move. He explained to the bandits below that he had stopped the train too soon. Certain mechanisms in the old iron horse were jammed.

"Get back down here," Hugh ordered. He was sweating. His brothers were glancing anxiously about. The money and jewels they expected to find in the mail car were being destroyed by the fire. Just then brakeman Charles Johnson, holding a lantern, came running from the tunnel, investigating the sudden stop and subsequent explosion.

"You!" Hugh yelled. "Get over there and uncouple the mail car from the rest of the train." Johnson took one look at Hugh's pistol and complied. He could not uncouple the car. As he was returning to explain his failure,

Hugh D'Autremont, now in a rage at the ridiculous situation, raised his pistol and fired. His shot hit Johnson in the head, killing him. His brothers then turned and, without a murmur, discharged their shotguns into Bates and Seng, killing them, too.

A fourth crewman was already dead. Edwin Daughtery, the mail clerk, had been roasted alive by the fire consuming the mail car.

The brothers stared down at the dead men. Then they panicked. Hugh, who had planned so carefully and long, lost all presence of mind and threw down his pistol, running wildly up the hill next to the tunnel. The twins ran after him.

At the top of the hill, the three men slipped out of the overalls they had donned for the raid. Bundling these, they raced on. Roy D'Autremont's overalls fell from his grasp. He kept running.

The three young men, once back in Eugene, decided to keep on running. The raid had been a fiasco, a bloody crazy mess. Train robbing had brought them nothing but impetuous murder. Hugh decided to join the army; Roy and Ray, always inseparable, would go East and try to find jobs.

When authorities got to train Number 13 they were met with the horrible sight of three men brutally slain, lying next to the still-steaming locomotive. The mail car was a cinder. Clerk Daughtery's remains were charred bones.

Chief of the Southern Pacific's train police, Daniel O'Connell, had never seen anything like it. What was worse, he had no clues to guide him to the identity of the bandits. None of the passengers had gotten so much as a glimpse.

It was days later when a brakeman spotted Hugh's pistol near the roadbed. A farmer brought in Roy's overalls. That was it. O'Connell was stumped. This pistol, the detective was convinced, could not be traced. The first three serial numbers on its face had been filed away. That left him with a pair of overalls, which meant he was left with nothing.

He was about to close out the case as "unsolved" when he remembered an odd little criminologist named Edward Oscar Heinrich, who ran an experimental crime lab in Berkeley, California. O'Connell took the pistol and overalls to Heinrich.

This man, who was to become known as the "Wizard of Berkeley," had a reputation for solving the most baffling criminal cases in modern times. He was an expert in ballistics, chemistry, botany, geology—a master criminologist in the Holmesian tradition. Though his peers jeered at him, O'Connell had confidence in Heinrich's capabilities.

The criminologist asked for two days to work on the clues. At the end of this time, he showed up in O'Connell's office with some astonishing information. "These overalls," he said, holding them out, "were worn by a left-handed lumberjack who has worked around fir trees somewhere in the Pacific Northwest." Heinrich went on to state that the suspect was a white man between the ages of 21 and 25, had medium light brown hair, was not taller than 5'10", weighed about 125 pounds and was "very definitely fastidious in his habits."

When O'Connell recovered his speech, he asked how Heinrich had come to such amazing conclusions. Simple, the criminologist explained. The fir pitch staining the overalls and tiny Douglas fir needles found in the pockets (indigenous to the Northwest territory), which Heinrich examined under a powerful microscope, along with small tree chips found in the righthand pocket of the overalls pointed to the fact that the suspect was a left-handed lumberjack. "A left-handed lumberjack, you know, stands with his right side to the tree he's cutting, and chips fly to the right, not to the left." Heinrich determined the man's size by simply measuring the overalls. The fact that he was "fastidious" was established by Heinrich when he found some neatly cut fingernail slivers in the seam of a pocket. The suspect's age, hair color, and race were determined by examining a hair caught on the button of the overalls.

The Colt pistol was no challenge at all to Heinrich. True, the first three serial numbers had been filed away, but, little known to law officials then, there was another set of serial numbers hidden inside the gun. Heinrich merely dismantled the weapon and found the number. (Manufacturers of firearms had been doing this for a number of years for the explicit purpose of establishing ownership, albeit this process was publicized little.) Heinrich also found a mail receipt tucked into the bib pocket of the overalls.

Armed with this storehouse of information,

O'Connell, the local police, postal inspectors, and the FBI fanned out.

The receipt was for a registered letter, Post Office investigators revealed, sent by a Roy D'Autremont to his brother Hugh. O'Connell's men journeyed to Eugene, Ore. and interviewed Roy's father. His sons were away, he said. He didn't know where. Roy was a lumberjack, yes. He was also left-handed. The detectives scooped up several effects the brothers had left behind, and departed.

The serial number on the Colt pistol led police to a Seattle store. Records showed that a Mr. William Elliott had signed for it. Heinrich, using samples taken from the D'Autremont home, compared this signature with Roy D'Autremont's handwriting and concluded they were one in the same.

Now the authorities knew who they were looking for, but the D'Autremont brothers had vanished.

For four years the search went on. As manhunts go, it was unequalled in modern times. More than two million circulars prominently displaying the photos of the D'Autremont brothers were distributed to almost every city and town in the country. Foreign countries were deluged with wanted posters on the brothers and $15,000 in reward money was offered for their capture.

Sergeant Thomas Reynolds of the U. S. Army finally broke the case in March, 1927. While leafing through some wanted posters, he recognized Hugh D'Autremont as a man who had served with him in the Philippines, known to him at that time as a soldier named Brice. He informed postal authorities and official wires were sent to the army command in Manila. Hugh was arrested and shipped back to the States.

Weeks after Hugh was taken back to Oregon to stand trial, Albert Cullingworth of Steubenville, Ohio, was reading a magazine article about a thrilling train robbery that had occurred in Oregon four years before. He spotted the photos of Roy and Ray D'Autremont and gasped: "The Goodwin twins working at the mill!"

The old man contacted the FBI through a neighbor and the outlaw brothers were arrested and sent to Oregon for trial. There, all three D'Autremonts confessed. Their confession saved them from the rope. The brothers were sent to prison for life.

Trainrobber Hugh D'Autremont upon his release from the Portland Penitentiary in 1958. (UPI)

Hugh was paroled in 1958, dying in March, 1959. Ray was paroled in 1961. Roy D'Autremont, whose discarded overalls betrayed him, still resides in an Oregon mental institution. He is considered just as insane as the criminal adventure which led him there.

DEAD RABBITS GANG

The Dead Rabbits were an early (circa 1850) New York gang of thugs with criminal activities centered in the Lower East Side. Their battle flag when openly warring with other gangs and police was a dead rabbit mounted high on a spear. Members were made up of Irish and Welsh immigrants who specialized in muggings, pickpocketing, and robbery.

In the criminal argot of the day a "dead rabbit" was a fearless and strong hooligan who could not be tamed. The Dead Rabbits gave way to succeeding gangs within two decades.

DE KAPLANY, GEZA
Murderer ● (1926-   )

Few killers approach the cruelty practiced by Dr. Geza de Kaplany. A successful anesthesiologist, de Kaplany was a Hungarian refugee who worked in a San Jose, Calif., hospital. He was vain, arrogant, and aloof. No one called him friend and most of his fellow workers had a hard time talking to him.

De Kaplany spent his off hours pursuing an attractive 25-year-old model and beauty queen in San Jose's Hungarian community. He married her in August 1962 and from that time on, Hajna de Kaplany never had a moment's peace. Her husband, according to his later statements, discovered himself impotent on his wedding night.

The possessive de Kaplany then began to imagine that all of the bachelors in the apartment complex where he lived with Hajna were having affairs with his stunningly beautiful wife. Bloated with jealousy and consumed by paranoia, de Kaplany decided that no other man would ever enjoy his wife's beauty. He would "ruin her, fix her."

To that end, on August 28, 1962, the seething doctor purchased a stereo unit and many speakers, installing these in his apartment. He then manicured his fingernails so they would not puncture the rubber gloves he took home with him. He brought from the hospital several bottles of sulfuric, nitric, and hydrochloric acids and, while his wife slept, arranged them neatly on the bedroom bureau.

Dr. de Kaplany then tied his wife's hands and feet to the bed. He turned up the stereo full blast to drown out the screams he expected. He then began to "operate" on his wife. He made small incisions all over his wife's body as she screamed in agony. Into these horrible wounds he poured various acids. (His savage torture of Hajna later and justifiably earned de Kaplany the sobriquet of "The Acid Doctor.")

The torture went on as de Kaplany cut and slashed his wife's exquisite face, ripped apart her breasts and genitals. His wife, unmercifully, did not pass out but kept on screaming and the doctor kept on turning up the volume of the stereo until neighbors banged on the walls, then called police.

An hour later, police arrived. De Kaplany an-

Dr. De Kaplany in court, staring through dark glasses at the bottles of acid he used to torture his wife, Hajna De Kaplany, inset, to death.

swered the door wearing only his underwear. He stood grinning madly, sweating. He explained that he was busy "working." The officers insisted on entering the apartment and when they entered the bedroom to see the horribly disfigured, naked body of Hajna de Kaplany they staggered backward in shock. Then they arrested the monster.

Mrs. de Kaplany was rushed to a hospital where physicians tried to deal with her third-degree corrosive burns. Attendants tried to apply ointments and burned their hands on the woman's acid-covered body. Hajna de Kaplany survived somehow for twenty-one agonizing days, struggling bravely to cling to life. Her mother stayed at her bedside praying that her horribly mutilated daughter would die and her child's agony would be over. When this finally happened, de Kaplany was charged with murder.

The killer stood trial before Judge Raymond D. Callahan on January 7, 1963, one month after his wife's death. He had been insane when performing his grisly "operation" on his wife, de Kaplany pleaded. He took the witness stand and calmly related how he had no intentions of killing his wife. He only wanted to destroy her beauty, the beauty that had driven him insane.

Prosecutors shattered de Kaplany's quiet composure when they displayed large photos of his wife's mutilated corpse. De Kaplany leaped from his seat, staring at the photos, screaming: "I am a doctor! I loved her! If I did this, and I must have done this, then I am guilty!"

At the end of thirty-five days, a jury found de Kaplany guilty. He was sent to prison for life. Inex-

plicably, the killer was listed as a "special interest" prisoner. He was released prematurely in 1976, six months before being eligible for parole. Startled reporters discovered that de Kaplany had been rushed out of the country, going to work at a hospital in Taiwan as a "cardiac specialist," which he certainly was not.

Ray Procunier, who headed the parole board responsible for reviewing de Kaplany, had no explanation for the monster's release. He resigned his position before he could be interviewed. De Kaplany resides, at this writing, in Taiwan, his patients undoubtedly unaware of the fact that he was America's infamous "Acid Doctor."

DENNISON, STEPHEN
Thief ● (1909-1979)

At the age of sixteen, Dennison impulsively stole a $5 box of candy from a small store in upstate New York. Sent to the reformatory in 1925, Dennison was brutalized by the harsh prison system of the day and was subsequently transferred to the state prison.

Through committing minor infractions of the prison rules, Dennison had years added to his initial sentence. In short, he was buried alive and forgotten in a cell for thirty-four years without ever having committed another crime beyond the candy theft. He was released in 1959. Seven years later, following litigation,

Stephen Dennison, shown after being released from a thirty-four-year prison term; he had stolen a box of candy.

Dennison was awarded $115,000 by the New York State Court of Claims.

The court, in its public apology for this horrible miscarriage of justice, stated: "No amount of money could compensate Dennison for the injuries he suffered and the scars he bears."

DE SALVO, ALBERT HENRY (THE BOSTON STRANGLER)
Serial Killer ● (1931-1973)

BACKGROUND: BORN CHELSEA, MASS., 1931, ONE OF SIX CHILDREN; FATHER SERVED TWO PRISON TERMS FOR THEFT; PARENTS DIV., 1944; AR. FOR THEFT MANY TIMES IN YOUTH; JOINED ARMY AT 17, SERVING IN GERMANY; RETURNED TO U.S., STATIONED AT FORT DIX, N.J.; RECORD: CHARGED WITH MOLESTING NINE-YEAR-OLD GIRL IN 1/55 AT FORT DIX; NO PROSECUTION; AR. IN CAMBRIDGE, MASS., 3/17/60 FOR BREAKING AND ENTERING, SENT. TO TWO YEARS, RELEASED IN TEN MONTHS; RAPED AND STRANGLED TO DEATH THIRTEEN WOMEN FROM 1962 TO 1964, INCLUDING ANNA SLESERS, 55; MARY MULLEN, 85; HELEN BLAKE, 65; NINA NICHOLS; IDA IRGA, 75; JANE SULLIVAN, 67; SOPHIE CLARK, 25; PATRICIA BISSETT, 23; MARY BROWN, 69; BEVERLY SAMANS, 23; EVELYN CORBIN, 58; JOANN GRAFF, 23; MARY SULLIVAN, 19; AR. FOR BREAKING AND ENTERING, 1964, SENT TO THE BRIDGEWATER MENTAL INSTITUTION WHERE HE WAS LATER IDENTIFIED AS "THE BOSTON STRANGLER." NEVER PROSECUTED FOR MURDER BUT TRANSFERRED TO THE WALPOLE STATE PRISON; FOUND DEAD IN HIS CELL ON 11/26/73.

From 1962 to 1964, a sex maniac prowled the streets of Boston and its suburbs, looking for likely victims to rape and then murder. He came to be known as "The Boston Strangler." He was, according to all reliable reports, Albert Henry DeSalvo, who admitted being the fiend.

DeSalvo was born in Chelsea, Mass., one of six children. His father was brutal to all of his family members, beating the children for little or no reason. He was also a thief and served two prison terms. In 1944, DeSalvo's parents divorced and the boy was left on his own.

Taking up his father's habits, DeSalvo was arrested as a juvenile many times for stealing. At age seventeen, however, he joined the Army and was sent to Germany. He fought in the U.S. Army boxing team as a welterweight and married a German girl before being transferred back to the U.S., to be stationed at Fort Dix, N.J.

In January 1955, DeSalvo was arrested and charged with molesting a nine-year-old girl. The girl's mother was frightened of publicity and refused to prosecute. Upon receiving his honorable discharge, DeSalvo returned to Boston with his wife, Irmgard. They had two children, and DeSalvo supported them as a handyman. Every waking hour, when he could spare the time from work, DeSalvo demanded sex from his petite wife. His sex drive overwhelmed her to the point where she asked him to control himself.

To appease his ravenous sexual appetite, DeSalvo invented a scheme whereby he could meet new, attractive females. He would appear at the door of a young woman and introduce himself as representing a modeling agency. He told the woman if she measured up, might be selected to appear in TV commercials, and might even land a movie contract. He would then take the vital statistics of these naive hopefuls with a tape measure, writing down the statistics on a clipboard.

DeSalvo did not make overt gestures toward these women but he later claimed that he seduced a number of them who expected good reports from him to the agency in exchange for their sexual favors. Some of these women, DeSalvo insisted, were so anxious to get the TV modeling job that they seduced him.

Police began to get reports about DeSalvo who had earned the nickname "Measuring Man," from his modus operandi. They believed the man harmless and did not actively pursue him. Their attitude changed on March 17, 1960 when, responding to a call, polic chased DeSalvo down a street in Cambridge, Mass., collaring him. Police saw DeSalvo throw away a screwdriver as he ran and they picked it up. He had been using the screwdriver to force locks in apartment buildings. Found on him was a tailor's measuring tape and a pair of gloves.

At his trial, DeSalvo admitted that he was the notorious "Measuring Man." He was sentenced to two years in prison for breaking and entering but was released in ten months. He returned to his family but instead of subduing his sexual urge he gave it full vent. He broke into hundreds of apartments throughout New England in the next two years, tying up women and raping them. He later estimated his victims of this sexual rampage to be more than one thousand. He was described by his countless victims as "The Green Man," since he invariably wore green workpants and shirt, the uniform of many handymen.

By the summer of 1962, DeSalvo added one

more criminal act to his modus operandi, murder. When he broke into the apartment of Anna Slesers on Gainsborough Street in Boston, he bound and gagged the woman. He then raped her. Then he strangled her to death. He used the belt of her own housecoat to strangle her, tying the ends in a bow beneath her chin. This would be the trademark of the infamous Boston Strangler.

Two weeks later DeSalvo attacked and strangled Mary Mullen, 85. He talked of this killing later but with considerable reluctance since the victim reminded him much of his own grandmother. June Blake, a 65-year-old nurse, was strangled by De-Salvo on June 30, 1962. He then broke into the home of Nina Nichols, a woman in her sixties. De-Salvo attacked this woman from behind but she fought ferociously, digging her nails deeply into the killer's arms.

DeSalvo raped and strangled Ida Irga, 75, on August 19, 1962, He killed Jane Sullivan, 67, the next day. It was during this time, DeSalvo later said, that he underwent sexual urges that almost drove him mad, that the top of his head "was so hot that I thought it would explode."

On December 5, 1962, his wedding anniversary, DeSalvo followed an attractive girl into an apartment building. He tried to get into her apartment but she had deadlocked the door. He went to another door which was answered by Sophie Clark, 25. DeSalvo used his old Measuring Man technique on her and she admitted him. She turned her back on him for a moment and he was shocked by her curvacious body. Leaping forward, De-Salvo raped her, then strangled her. He left her naked corpse propped upward, legs spread. And, again, there was the neat little bow made under her chin by the strangling cord.

Patricia Bissette, a 23-year-old secretary, was next, on December 8, 1962. Oddly, this same woman had met DeSalvo years earlier when he was the Measuring Man. She gave him a cup of coffee and when she turned her back, he attacked her, raping her, then strangling her with her own nylons.

On February 16, 1963, DeSalvo got the shock of his life. He gained entrance to an apartment occupied by a young woman who was home sick from work. When he tried to subdue her, she screamed, kicked, punched, and bit him, fighting like a wildcat. She raised such a clamor that DeSalvo fled in panic. (This woman's name was withheld by authorities to protect her identity but she proved that surrendering meekly to sexual attackers was not the best way to avoid being raped or possibly murdered. She fought and she survived.)

The killing went on. On March 9, 1963, DeSalvo attacked and killed 69-year-old Mary Brown. He gained entrance to her apartment by telling her that the landlord had sent him to fix her stove. He did not rape this woman until after she was dead. He was savage in this instance. He crushed her head with a lead pipe and drove a fork into her left breast several times, leaving it embedded in the flesh. Then he strangled her, although she was long dead by the time he tied the cord into a bow beneath her chin.

While driving to work on May 6, 1963, DeSalvo had what he later termed was "an impulse," and he went hunting women. He spied Beverly Samans, a 23-year-old undergraduate, walking on University Road and followed her to her apartment where, once inside, he tied her to the posts of her bed. He blindfolded her, gagged her, and raped her many times.

Before leaving DeSalvo strangled the girl with her own nylons. Then he got out his jackknife and stabbed the dead girl twenty-two times. He said later: "Once I stabbed her, I couldn't stop. . . . I kept hitting her and hitting her with that knife. . . . She kept bleeding from the throat. . . . I hit her and hit her and hit her . . ." Exhausted, DeSalvo took the knife into the kitchen, wiped the handle clean of blood and left it in the sink. Police found no prints on it.

Evelyn Corbin, 58, was next on September 8, 1963. She was found strangled. This time DeSalvo had used his hands. He had tied the woman's nylons in a bow and affixed this to one of her toes.

Police investigating this last murder were stymied as the lack of clues that might lead them to the killer. A special "Strangler Bureau" was established and every known peeping Tom, mugger, and sex offender in the Boston area was brought in for interrogation. All were released.

Throughout Boston, panic and terror reigned. Police were swamped with calls from terrified women who reported any stranger coming close to their doors. Husbands spent hours on the phone each day checking on their wives, mothers, daughters. Many men stayed home, fearing to leave their loved ones alone.

So desperate were police officials to track down the killer that they asked the noted psychic, Peter Hurkos, to inspect the clothes of the dead women and any other scant clues that had on hand. Hurkos did examine the items and gave a fairly accurate profile of a dark, heavyset killer. Up to the time of the Brown killing, all the victims had been elderly, which caused profile experts to believe that the killer was a young man, in his late teens or early twenties, and that he had a pronounced persecution complex and had a pronounced hatred for his mother. When the young, attractive Brown was strangled that profile was discarded.

Psychologist James Brussel studied the case and provided a remarkably accurate portrait of the strangler, describing him as being strongly built, clean-shaven, about 30 years old. His profile said that the killer was of average height, had thick, dark hair, that he was Italian or Spanish in origin and was a paranoid schizophrenic. Almost all of Brussel's identification points would later fit the profile of Albert DeSalvo.

On November 22, 1963, DeSalvo was riveted to the TV, watching the news stories relating the assassination of President John F. Kennedy. This event so distressed him, he later remarked, that it led him to his next murder the following day, that of dress designer Joann Graff, 23. Once inside her apartment, DeSalvo raped and strangled Graff with her black leotards. He tied the ends in a bow under her chin.

DeSalvo then went home and helped his wife clean up their apartment. He played with the children and then watched a television news report on the Graff killing. He next sat down to dinner. He later reflected on seeing the TV report of his own killing and said: "I knew it was me who did it, but why I did it and everything else, I don't know . . . I wasn't excited. I didn't think about it. I sat down to dinner and I didn't think about it at all."

On January 4, 1964, DeSalvo claimed the life of his last victim, the thirteenth. Mary Sullivan, 19, let DeSalvo into her apartment and seconds later he brandished a knife and tied her up. He raped her, then strangled her with his hands. Propping up her legs, the killer inserted a broom into her and, as a bizarre afterthought, slipped a card he had found in Sullivan's apartment between the victim's toes. It read "Happy New Year."

DeSalvo entered the apartment of a young woman on October 27, 1964. He tied her to a bed and raped her. This time, however, he did not kill. Inexplicably, DeSalvo suddenly backed away from the victim, muttering: "I'm sorry." He fled. When the victim got loose, she called police and gave a detailed description of her assailant. It fit DeSalvo to perfection.

He was identified by police and arrested, held on a $100,000 bond and sent to the mental institution.

Albert DeSalvo, the notorious Boston Strangler. (AP/Wide World)

Police, however, did not connect him to the Boston Strangler, even though the modus operandi of this crime was identical to that of the Strangler. DeSalvo then told hospital officials that he was hearing voices and he was diagnosed as "schizophrenic."

On February 4, 1965, Judge Edward A. Pecce ordered that DeSalvo be detained indeterminately. While at the institution, DeSalvo met George Nassar, who had killed a garage attendant and who had for a time been suspected of having been the Boston Strangler. Nassar listened to DeSalvo rave about sex and violence and then he told his lawyer, F. Lee Bailey, that he thought DeSalvo was the Strangler. Bailey confronted DeSalvo and he admitted being the most sought-after killer in Boston's history. (It is important to note that following DeSalvo's incarceration, the Strangler killings stopped altogether.)

DeSalvo described each of the thirteen killings he had committed, giving details that only the Strangler could provide. He told Bailey of how he had positioned the bodies, how he had tied bows in the cords, belts, and nylons he had used to murder his victims, how he had mutilated some of the bodies, information that only the Strangler and the police knew. DeSalvo even added information on two more murders he had committed, which had not been attributed to the Strangler.

Bailey made his revelations to the Boston officials, who were disinclined to prosecute DeSalvo, giving as their reason that he was a mental patient and that they had no eyewitnesses to the murders. It could easily be assumed that to have dragged DeSalvo through a public trial, the police would have been seen to have bungled matters, that DeSalvo had been in their grasp and they had failed to identify him as the Strangler.

Court officials, however, certainly believed DeSalvo was the Strangler. DeSalvo was brought into court and was convicted of robbery and sex offenses, then given a life term in Walpole State Prison. On November 26, 1973, 42-year-old Albert DeSalvo, the Boston Strangler, was found dead in his cell, stabbed through the heart.

DIAMOND, JOHN THOMAS (JACK "LEGS")
Racketeer ● (1896-1931)

BACKGROUND: BORN AND RAISED IN PHILADELPHIA. (CHRISTENED JOHN T. NOLAND) MINOR PUBLIC EDUCATION. SERVED BRIEFLY IN THE U.S. ARMY (DESERTED) DURING THE FIRST WORLD WAR. ONE BROTHER, EDWARD. MARRIED ALICE KENNY, 1920. ORIGINAL OCCUPATION, LABORER. DESCRIPTION: 5'11", BROWN EYES, BROWN HAIR, THIN. ALIASES: "LEGS," JOHN HIGGINS, JOHN HART, JACK DIAMOND. RECORD: BEFORE 1910, AS A CHILD IN PHILADELPHIA, DIAMOND, WITH HIS BROTHER EDWARD, BELONGED TO THE BOILER GANG WHICH PRACTICED PETTY THIEVERY; UPON MOVING TO NEW YORK CITY WITH HIS BROTHER, JOINED THE HUDSON DUSTERS, A SNEAK-THIEF GROUP SPECIALIZING IN ROBBING PACKAGES FROM DELIVERY TRUCKS; ARRESTED 2/4/14 FOR BURGLARY IN NEW YORK CITY; SENT TO NYC REFORMATORY FOR A BRIEF TERM; ARRESTED FOR ASSAULT AND ROBBERY 5/12/16, DISCHARGED; ARRESTED FOR GRAND LARCENY 5/27/16, DISCHARGED; ARRESTED FOR ASSAULT 7/15/16, DISCHARGED; ARRESTED FOR DESERTION FROM THE U.S. ARMY, 3/24/19; SENTENCED TO ONE YEAR AT GOVERNORS ISLAND DISCIPLINARY BARRACKS, LATER TRANSFERRED TO LEAVENWORTH PENITENTIARY; RELEASED IN EARLY 1920; ARRESTED FOR GRAND LARCENY, 6/1/21, DISCHARGED; ARRESTED FOR ASSAULT AND ROBBERY, 10/27/21, DISCHARGED; ARRESTED FOR BURGLARY, 11/18/21, DISCHARGED; ARRESTED FOR ROBBERY, 11/28/23, DISCHARGED; ARRESTED NEW YORK FOR ROBBERY, 6/14/24, DISCHARGED; WORKED AS A LIEUTENANT TO NEW YORK CITY GANGSTER JACOB "LITTLE AUGIE" ORGEN AS A BOOTLEGGER, NARCOTICS SMUGGLER, AND HIJACKER; ARRESTED FOR SMUGGLING NARCOTICS, 9/9/26 IN MOUNT VERNON, N.Y., DISCHARGED; ARRESTED ON SUSPICION OF MURDER IN OCT., 1928, DISMISSED; SHOT AND KILLED WILLIAM "RED" CASSIDY AND SIMON WALKER, 6/13/29, IN HIS HOTSY TOTSY CLUB WITH CHARLES ENTRATTA, ARRESTED FOR MURDER, DISMISSED; ARRESTED FOR VIOLATING THE NATIONAL PROHIBITION ACT, 5/13/31; RECEIVED AN $11,000 FINE AND SENTENCED TO FOUR YEARS IN PRISON 8/13/31; RELEASED ON $15,000 BAIL BOND PENDING APPEAL; ARRESTED FOR ASSAULTING AND TORTURING BOOT-

LEGGER GROVER PARKS AND KIDNAPPING JAMES DUNCAN, BARTENDER, BOTH OF ALBANY, N.Y., 12/11/31, ACQUITTED; SHOT AND KILLED BY UNKNOWN GANGSTERS (ALLEGED TO BE WORKING FOR DUTCH SCHULTZ) IN AN ALBANY ROOMING HOUSE, 12/18/31.

In the underworld of his day, he was known as the "Clay Pigeon." Jack "Legs" Diamond had been shot at and wounded so many times in his criminal career that even his fellow bootleggers were aghast at his amazing ability to survive. "The bullet hasn't been made that can kill me," Legs once boasted.

Of all the New York gangsters of the 1920s, Legs Diamond was the flashiest, a disarming charmer. He was also the deadliest gunman in the rackets.

Legs got his beginning as a sneak thief and earned his nickname while hanging around the West Side Winona Club owned by racketeer Owney Madden. Diamond, a member of the Hudson Dusters then (about sixteen years old) robbed packages from the backs of delivery trucks parked in front of Madden's swank nightclub. His ability to elude pursuing policeman quickly earned him the name "Legs."

He and his brother Eddie, after moving from Philadelphia, were arrested for a series of petty thefts and burglaries up to the time of the First World War when America called Legs to arms. He was not enthusiastic about serving his country and soon went AWOL. Diamond was apprehended and served a year and a day in Leavenworth as a deserter.

Prison was Diamond's training ground and there he met tough New York mobsters who put him in touch with a showy racketeer, Jacob "Little Augie" Orgen, upon his release. Orgen was a zany killer who had worked his way into the garment industry racket using strong arm goon squads under the command of another rising gangster, Louis Lepke Buchalter. Little Augie was also in need of tough gunmen to help him in his bootlegging enterprises.

Legs Diamond, recently released from prison, with his brother Eddie went to work for Little Augie at the dawn of Prohibition. First, they hijacked beer and liquor trucks carrying Canadian shipments in upstate New York. They worked their way into Little Augie's

Nathan "Kid Dropper" Kaplan; he ruled New York rackets until Legs Diamond figured a way to have him shot to death.

Legs Diamond's first underworld boss: Little Augie Orgen.

smuggling rackets, dealing largely in narcotics and stolen gems.

In the early gang wars Legs more than once proved his nerveless skill with a gun. Little Augie was also surprised at Diamond's ability to organize and plan; he soon made him his chief lieutenant and right-hand man. His first important assignment was getting rid of Nathan "Kid Dropper" Kaplan, Little Augie's chief rival in the labor rackets and bootlegging territories in midtown Manhattan.

Kaplan was no easy prey. He surrounded himself with an army of hoodlums and never hesitated to order a killing either for business or personal reasons. He had even attempted to kill Little Augie once with a knife, when both men were younger and vying for control of a street gang; Kaplan left Orgen with a vicious looking scar that ran from his left ear across his cheek to his nose.

An egotistical gangster, Kaplan insisted that his men and even his wife call him "Kid Dropper," or "Jack the Dropper," after an old-time boxer he had admired. New York's young, tough mobster-gangs were beginning to flourish about the time Diamond and his brother were developing their package thievery. Three men—Owney Madden, Nathan "Kid Dropper" Kaplan, and Johnny Spanish (Joseph Weyler)—were the rising kingpins of New York's underworld.

Madden went to prison for murder in 1915. Spanish and Kaplan followed him there shortly after but were both released in 1917. Then began Manhattan's first bloody gang war. Kid Dropper and Spanish ran the rackets in New York but the competition was tough. The two gangsters sent out platoons of killers and soon open warfare bloodied the streets. For two years, the Dropper-Spanish legions battled. Then, as he emerged from a restaurant on Second Avenue on the night of July 29, 1919, Johnny Spanish was killed. The Dropper and two of his bodyguards merely slipped up behind Spanish and emptied their pistols into his back. Kid Dropper reigned supreme.

The first man to challenge his authority within a year of the Spanish killing was Little Augie Orgen, a product of the Dopey Benny gang on the Lower East Side. Financed by gambler and underworld money man Arnold Rothstein, Orgen moved into the garment racket, amassing a formidable gang of ambitious terrorists culled from the toughest street gangs in the city—Charles "Lucky" Luciano, Lepke and his faithful killer ape, Gurrah, Waxey Gorden, and the Diamond brothers.

This gang clashed openly with Kid Dropper's troops in an industry and bootleg war between 1919 and 1920. In one gun battle between the factions on Essex Street, two bystanders were shot to death. Little Augie still had no luck in getting rid of Kaplan. Legs Diamond came up with a solution.

He proposed that Jacob Gurrah Shapiro file a complaint with the police department, charging Kid Dropper with assault (Dropper had fired at Gurrah in a recent gun battle). When Kid Dropper was brought in to face that charge, the Little Augie gang would simply shoot him. "Get him into court," Diamond insisted. "Once we pinpoint him, we can get to him."

Gurrah filed the complaint and Kid Dropper was brought in for questioning. When police found a gun on the Dropper, Kaplan yelled: "I had to carry it! Self-defense . . . Little Augie and the Diamonds are after me! They want to kill me!"

When the Dropper emerged from the Essex Market Court on August 28, 1923 after listening to Shapiro's charges, Louis Kushner, an Orgen gangster, was waiting for him with a gun in his pocket. Kushner was a hanger-on whom the Little Augies used as a messenger boy. Diamond convinced Kushner that his status in the gang would rise considerably if he killed the Dropper as he came out of court. Kushner didn't need too much urging. Kid Dropper had been blackmailing him for the beating of a garment worker.

As the Dropper walked down the court-house stairs, squads of police swept in about him to escort him to the West Side Court for another hearing. Legs Diamond watched elatedly across the street as Kushner made his way to the back of the police car carrying Kid Dropper. The undersized Kushner awkwardly jumped on the bumper and, in front of hundreds of witnesses, fired rapid shots through the car's back window. The first shot wounded the driver of the car in the ear, the second tore off a straw hat from the head of Police Captain Cornelius Willemse. Seeing Kid Dropper fall to the floor of the car to avoid being hit, Kushner battered out the police car's window to get a better shot.

The Dropper's wife, Veronica, who was standing on the sidewalk, rushed up to the little gangster and tried to hold him, screaming: "Don't shoot him, don't shoot him!" Kushner pushed her down and squeezed off another round into the car, hitting Kid Dropper in the head. "They got me," Jack the Dropper moaned and died.

Dozens of policemen surrounded Kushner, pistols aimed at his head. The killer was ecstatic and proud over his feat. He smiled and handed his gun to an officer. "I got him," he beamed. "May I have a cigarette?"

The bizarre scene, witnessed by a satisfied Legs Diamond from across the street, was not complete until Veronica Kaplan, hysterical, threw herself across the Dropper's body, hanging from a car door, pleading into the dead man's ears: "Nate! Nate! Tell me that you were not what they say you were!" Kushner turned, with a bevy of policemen holding him, and happily posed for the cameras of newsmen who had come to cover Kaplan's hearing. "I got him, I got him," he continued to say as he was led away.

Little Augie was now master of the New York rackets and he had Legs Diamond to thank. He showed his gratitude by giving Diamond lucrative chunks of his bootleg-and-narcotics empire which stretched from Manhattan to Albany, New York.

Suddenly in the big money, Diamond haunted nightclubs, Broadway shows, and dance halls. He had once been a semi-professional dancer, hiring out to wealthy women who wanted to fast-step. Chorus girl Marion "Kiki" Roberts (Marion Strasmick) caught his eye and he quickly made the bosomy, florid-faced jazz baby his mistress.

Diamond's love life never distressed his wife, Alice, who married him in 1920. Alice was the patient sort and proudly sported her wedding ring. Kiki may have had her husband's attentions, she told newsmen, but she possessed the man. Mrs. Diamond hero-worshipped her husband. Pictures of the lean, hollow-eyed gangster adorned every wall of their luxurious apartment. On one above the fireplace, Alice had scrawled in large letters the words: "My Hero."

Kiki Roberts didn't need any photos of her lover, she reasoned. The jewels and money Legs showered on her were enough. Kiki didn't know it, but she was not the only girl-on-the-side Diamond supported. The Hotsy Totsy Club, a second-floor speakeasy on Broadway between 54th and 55th Streets, was owned by Diamond and Hymie Cohen. The place was a veritable Diamond harem. It was also a deathtrap.

Here Legs held court and directed Little Augie's rackets. The speakeasy also served as a killing spot. Several would-be crime czars were lured to the Hotsy Totsy Club only to be carried out hours later, feet first.

By 1927, Legs was a powerful figure in New York's underworld. He ranked with Dutch Schultz, Lepke, Big Bill Dwyer, and Charles "Lucky" Luciano. Top mobsters such as Vannie Higgins, Owney Madden, Waxey Gorden, and Larry Fay, head of the city's mild rackets, paid him homage. Even "Mr. Big"—Arnold Rothstein—took him into his confidence (Diamond had performed bodyguard services for Rothstein while moving up in Little Augie's troop).

But 1927 was also the year in which Legs Diamond's luck turned sour. On October 15, 1927, Diamond was escorting his boss Little Augie from his Lower East Side headquarters near Delancy and Norfolk Streets. The bodyguard chore usually fell to Eddie Diamond but he was in jail, right where Legs wanted him. Diamond, serving as a stand-in bodyguard for Little Augie, explained to his boss that his brother was tubercular and that jail was the best place for his lungs until he could make arrangements for him in a Colorado sanitarium.

Little Augie told Diamond about his present worries, particularly about Lepke Buchalter and Gurrah Shapiro. They were ungrateful punks, kids he himself had trained for the rackets. Now they were muscling in on his garment industry rackets. They would have to be taught a lesson. Diamond nodded.

Moments later, as the gangster pair turned onto Norfolk Street, a fast-moving cab, a Chevrolet, swept past them and stopped. Little Augie was about to get in, when the cab door flew open and a machinegunner, crouched low in the back, opened up on him with a quick, short burst. Twelve bullets went into Orgen and the little hoodlum fell to the sidewalk, dead. Diamond, wounded in the arm and leg, staggered down the street and collapsed inside a doorway. He was ambulanced to Bellevue Hospital where he barely managed to stay alive. He had lost so much blood, doctors at first thought he would certainly die.

The minute Legs was able to talk, police rushed into his hospital room. The gangster weakly propped himself up on an elbow and shouted: "Don't ask me nothin'! You hear me? Don't ask! And don't bring anybody here for me to identify. I won't identify them even if I know they did it!" He fell back on the bed unconscious.

Legs didn't have to point anyone out. He knew the machinegunner in the back of the cab on sight—Lepke Buchalter. And the obese, scowling cabdriver had been none other than Jacob Gurrah Shapiro. Little Augie's troubles with these two gangsters were over.

Upon recovery, Diamond settled for his booze and narcotics rackets, leaving Lepke to take over Little Augie's garment industry interests. But Dutch Schultz, by then the most vicious beer baron of New York, wanted some (perhaps all) of Diamond's territory. War broke out again with a rash of hijackings and killings.

Rothstein backed Diamond in his war against the Dutchman and Legs spent a fortune recruiting gun talent. His goon squads were headed up by a trigger-happy killer named Charles Entratta (alias Charlie Green). Others of Diamond's hit-men troop included A. J. Harry Klein, A. Treager, Salvatore Arcidicio, and a sadistic gangster who enjoyed torturing bartenders reluctant to push Diamond's needle beer, W. Talamo (alias John Scaccio).

For a period of about two years, Legs made great inroads against the Dutchman's empire. He cut a great bootleg swath out of upstate New York, actually controlling several major highways down which Canadian liquor was being bootlegged.

Diamond's fortunes dipped drastically in 1928 following the mysterious murder of his benefactor, Arnold Rothstein. He was then involved in a senseless killing inside his Hotsy Totsy Club.

William "Red" Cassidy, a minor hoodlum, was standing at the bar on the night of June 13, 1929 with a group of friends. Cassidy's demeanor was anything but cordial. He asked for service by banging on the bar with his ham-hock fists and shouting: "C'mon you punks, give me some goddamn service!"

Legs and his favorite henchman, Entratta, were in the bar and jumped up excitedly. "Behave yourself," Diamond warned Cassidy.

"Go to hell, you pimp!" Cassidy roared, throwing a punch in Diamond's direction. Without further word, Diamond and Entratta pulled out their pistols and fired a barrage into Cassidy's group which was advancing upon them, fists raised. When the smoke cleared, gangster Simon Walker, recently paroled from Sing Sing, was dead, his head resting on the bar rail, two loaded .38-caliber revolvers still stuck in his belt. Red Cassidy was badly wounded in several places. His friends frantically dragged him down the Club's stairs to the street where an ambulance was called. He was dead within an hour.

Diamond and Entratta disappeared while police hunted them throughout the state. Dutch Schultz, never a man to miss an opportunity, moved in on Legs' bootleg interests while Diamond was in hiding until the Cassidy murder cooled off. When he did surface and surrender to police he was quickly dismissed of the murder charge for "lack of evidence," (although twenty-five people saw the shootings) but Schultz had grabbed off large portions of his beer territory.

Before the guns roared again, Joey Noe, a Schultz gunman, arranged a truce talk with Diamond in 1929. Both gang leaders were apprehensive of each other.

"I don't trust the Dutchman," Diamond said. "He's a crocodile. He's sneaky. I don't trust him."

"I don't trust Legs," the Dutchman said. "He's nuts. He gets excited and starts pulling a trigger like another guy wipes his nose."

The two arch criminals met in spite of their distrust and agreed to a truce. The meeting took place in the old Harding Hotel. Diamond told Schultz he could keep the midtown beer territory he had stolen if he paid an equitable price for it. Legs wanted out of that area anyway, he said. His other rackets were taking up too much of his time to worry about it. Schultz paid the price, an alleged half million dollars, on the spot and in cash.

Minutes later, as the Dutchman and Noe were walking down the street, two men jumped from an alley and shot Noe down. Schultz whipped out his revolver and drove the two off. The Dutchman then raced off toward the Harding Hotel, leaving Noe to bleed on the sidewalk. Schultz arrived to find the room where he had met Diamond empty. One of his own men was still there.

"The goddamn double-crosser just shot Joey!" Dutch screamed. "I'm gonna kill him for this!" He meant it.

Eddie Diamond, who had traveled to Denver to seek the pure air for his bad lungs, was trapped weeks later in a cabaret his brother Legs had financed. Five gunmen shot him several times and left him for dead. Though Eddie lived, Legs vowed revenge.

Within a year, the five gunmen were dead. Frank "Blubber" Devlin, was shot through the back of the head only once on March 3, 1929, in Somerville, New Jersey. Next Eugene Moran was riddled and his body cremated on a bonfire in August, 1929. James Batto, Monkey Schubert, and Harry Veasey wound up in similar conditions by 1930.

While Diamond was systematically attempting to rub out Schultz's army, the Dutchman made his own plans. Three of his men barged into Kiki Roberts' suite in New York's Hotel Monticello in October, 1929. Kiki and Legs were dining in their pajamas and the gunmen unleashed a wall of shells in their direction. Legs was wounded five times but lived. Kiki was unharmed.

It was getting hot for Legs. Dutch was not going after his men but after him. To avoid such personal attention, Diamond decided to tour Europe. He sailed on the *Baltic* in 1930. Authorities in England, however, aware of the gangster's notorious reputation, refused to let him off the boat. It was the same story in Belgium. Dejected, Legs returned to New York. No sooner was he home with his wife in Acra, N. Y., than Schultz struck again. Legs was shot several times as he emerged

Jack "Legs" Diamond (right), following a court acquittal in 1931; he was shot to death only hours after this photo was taken. (UPI)

from the Aratoga Inn in April, 1931. Again he lived.

The newspapers thought it phenomenal. Diamond had been put on the spot three times and lived. He was a clay pigeon that couldn't be shattered. Schultz started to get nervous. "Can't anybody shoot that guy so he won't bounce back up?"

In early December, 1931, Legs, trying to expand his upstate operations, threatened a bootlegger, Grover Parks, with death unless he turned over his shipments to his men. Parks told Legs to "go to hell." John Scaccio abducted Parks and a partner, James Duncan, one night and took them to an Albany hotel room. There, while Legs and his girlfriend Kiki got drunk, Scaccio and others repeatedly burned the two men with lighted cigarettes, flaming matches jammed beneath their fingernails, and a white hot poker run up their backsides. The two stalwart bootleggers finally gave in and consented to work with Diamond.

Upon their release, however, Parks and Duncan went to the police and reported the whole story. Diamond and Scaccio were arrested and tried in Troy, N. Y. Legs squeaked out of a conviction by sacrificing his henchman Scaccio (who got ten years in Sing Sing and Diamond's promise that he would get him out shortly).

Back in Albany, Legs decided to celebrate. He gave a roaring party at a local speakeasy on the night of December 17, 1931. Dozens of his hoodlum friends, as well as his wife

Alice, were in attendance. About 1 a.m., Legs slipped away from the party to secretly rendezvous with his sweetheart, Kiki Roberts. After spending three and a half hours with her, Diamond, still somewhat drunk, shakily hailed a cab in his employ at Clinton and Tenbroeck and told his man, Jack Storey, to take him home. Home was a small room in a boarding house at 67 Dove Street.

Diamond got out of the cab and staggered upstairs to bed. His driver took off. At 4:45 a.m., the landlady, Mrs. Wood, was suddenly awakened from her bed by five clear shots coming from Diamond's upstairs room. She heard feet running down the stairs and, from her window, saw three men sprint down the street.

Within minutes, Alice Diamond was called; the police came right behind her. They found Legs Diamond still in bed, five bullets in his head and torso, quite dead.

Alice Diamond threw her large body over the corpse, screaming, "Help me, somebody! They've shot Jack! They've killed him!" Great tears swelled up in her green eyes and ran down her face. A police doctor pronounced Diamond dead. Alice shook her head wildly, her long red hair swirling. She dove for the bed, grasping the bedposts. "No! No! You can't have him! He's mine! He belongs to me! Let me stay with Jack . . ."

It took close to ten minutes before two officers could pry Alice's hands loose. They led her sobbing from the room. Before leaving, she turned and said quietly, "I didn't do it."

Detectives found no money on Diamond. His signet ring, brandishing a large D, was in a drawer. Also in the drawer were dozens of letters from women written to Legs at the time of his trial. Most of these ladies wanted to marry and reform him.

When she heard the news of Diamond's death, Kiki Roberts contacted the *New York American*, telling reporters in an exclusive interview: "I was in love with Jack Diamond. I was with him in Albany, New York before he was killed. But I don't know who killed him or anything about the murder."

Apparently, neither did anyone else. Jack Legs Diamond's killers were never apprehended, though most concluded that Dutch Schultz's boys had done the job on orders.

Alice Diamond was the only person to attend her husband's funeral. Marion Kiki Rob-erts had disappeared. Two years later, Alice Diamond was murdered in Brooklyn. Her killer was never found. Kiki Roberts was found at the time of Alice's death. She had resumed her real name, Marion Strasmick, and was living alone in a tenement.

"I don't know anything about those people," Marion insisted. "They were gangsters, weren't they?"

DIAZ, ROBERT
Serial Killer ● (1938-   )

The proclaimed dream of Robert Diaz was to be a doctor. He settled for the role of male nurse. Finishing his schooling at the age of 40, Diaz moved from Gary, Ind., to Apple Valley, Calif. He got a job in Perris at the Community Hospital of the Valley. He seemed professional and conscientious. His manner was confident and he spoke with the authority of a physician.

In late April 1981, the coroner in San Bernadino County received a call from an anonymous female who told him that nineteen people had died at the hospital in Perris and that she suspected that they had been killed. An investigation ensued that determined the premature deaths of twelve patients ranging in age from 52 to 95.

Suspicion fell upon Diaz, as he had been the nurse on duty when those patients died. Moreover, he had predicted to other hospital employees with uncanny accuracy the time those patients would die. All of the patients had died with alarming suddeness and all had an uncommonly high blood acidity.

Many of the medical records for these patients had disappeared and it was known that Diaz had access to these records. Medical experts determined that all of the twelve persons who had died mysteriously had received overdoses of Lidocaine, which would have brought about their instant deaths. All had been attended by Diaz and hospital staff members came forth to state that they had seen Diaz administering injections to these patients.

One of the victims had died at San Gregorio Pass Hospital on the only night when Robert Diaz worked there. Moreover, police inspected Diaz's home and found syringes, morphine, and quantities of the drug Lidocaine. Diaz was arrested and charged with murder. In retaliation, his lawyer filed a multi-million dollar suit against officials, charging defamation of character and violation of Diaz's civil rights.

Diaz, waiving his right to a jury trial, appeared at a bench trial before Judge John H. Barnard. Prosecutors provided 72 witnesses who told how Diaz predicted the deaths of patients who died shortly thereafter and also claimed to have seen him inject these patients before they died. Three syringes used by Diaz were offered as evidence.

The motive for the murders was offered by the prosecuting attorney, Patrick F. Magers, who stated: "He committed these murders for his own entertainment and amusement while playing doctor." Diaz was found guilty on March 29, 1984 and was sentenced to death in the gas chamber on June 15.

DILLINGER, JOHN HERBERT
Bankrobber ● (1903- ?)

BACKGROUND: BORN IN INDIANAPOLIS, INDIANA 6/22/03 TO JOHN AND MOLLIE DILLINGER. ONE SISTER, AUDREY. COMPLETED ELEMENTARY SCHOOL IN INDIANAPOLIS. ORIGINAL OCCUPATION, MACHINIST. SERVED BRIEFLY ON BOARD THE BATTLESHIP "UTAH" IN 1923 AFTER JOINING THE U.S. NAVY. MARRIED BERYL ETHEL HOVIUS IN 1924, DIVORCED IN 1929. DESCRIPTION: 5' 7¼", BLUE EYES, LIGHT BROWN HAIR, MEDIUM BUILD, ½" SCAR ON BACK OF LEFT HAND, SCAR ON MIDDLE OF UPPER LIP. ALIASES: FRANK SULLIVAN, JOSEPH HARRIS, JOHN HALL, "DESPERATE DAN" DILLINGER, JOHN DONOVAN, CARL HELLMAN. RECORD: ARRESTED FOR STEALING A CAR BELONGING TO OLIVER P. MACY OF MOORESVILLE, IND. ON 7/21/23, NO CHARGES MADE; DESERTED U.S. NAVY 12/4/23 IN BOSTON, MASS., $50 REWARD OFFERED FOR HIS CAPTURE; ATTEMPTED TO ROB FRANK MORGAN, A GROCER IN MARTINSVILLE, IND., 9/6/24; SENTENCED 9/15/24 BY JUDGE JOSEPH WILLIAMS OF MARTINSVILLE, AFTER DILLINGER THREW HIMSELF ON THE MERCY OF THE COURT, TO CONCURRENT SENTENCES OF TWO TO FOURTEEN YEARS AND TEN TO TWENTY YEARS FOR CONSPIRACY TO COMMIT A FELONY AND ASSAULT WITH INTENT TO ROB; SENT TO THE INDIANA STATE REFORMATORY AT PENDLETON; ATTEMPTED TO ESCAPE 10/15/24; RECEIVED SIX MORE MONTHS ON TOP OF HIS SENTENCE; ATTEMPTED TO ESCAPE 9/28/24 FROM GUARD AFTER TESTIFYING AGAINST EDGAR SINGLETON, AN ACCOMPLICE IN THE MORGAN ROBBERY AND WHILE BEING RETURNED TO PENDLETON; NAVY OFFICIALS DROPPED CHARGES AGAINST DILLINGER AT THIS TIME FOR DESERTION, ISSUING HIM A DISHONORABLE DISCHARGE; ATTEMPTED TO ESCAPE PENDLETON IN

DECEMBER, 1924; SIX MORE MONTHS ADDED TO HIS SENTENCE; CAUGHT GAMBLING BY REFORMATORY GUARDS 2/25/25, THIRTY DAYS ADDED TO HIS SENTENCE; ACCUSED OF BEING "DISORDERLY" IN AUGUST, 1926, THIRTY MORE DAYS ADDED TO HIS SENTENCE; ACCUSED OF DESTROYING PRISON PROPERTY, 10/17/28, THIRTY DAYS ADDED TO HIS SENTENCE; TRANSFERRED BY INDIANA GOVERNOR HARRY G. LESLIE, AT DILLINGER'S OWN REQUEST, TO MICHIGAN CITY, INDIANA STATE PRISON IN JULY, 1929; PAROLED 5/22/33; ROBBED WITH WILLIAM SHAW SEVERAL SMALL STORES AND FACTORIES IN RURAL INDIANA AND INDIANAPOLIS DURING JUNE, 1933; ROBBED WITH SHAW AND PAUL "LEFTY" PARKER THE NATIONAL BANK OF NEW CARLISLE, IND. 6/10/33 ($10,600); ROBBED WITH HARRY COPELAND THE COMMERCIAL BANK IN DALEVILLE, IND., 7/17/33 ($3,500); ROBBED WITH HARRY COPELAND THE FIRST NATIONAL BANK OF MONTPELIER, IND., 8/4/33 ($10,110); ROBBED WITH HARRY COPELAND AND SAM GOLDSTINE THE CITIZENS NATIONAL BANK IN BLUFFTON, OHIO, 8/14/33 ($2,100); ROBBED WITH HARRY COPELAND AND HILTON CROUCH THE MASSACHUSETTS AVENUE STATE BANK OF INDIANAPOLIS, IND., 9/6/33 ($24,800); ARRESTED BY POLICE OFFICERS IN DAYTON, O., 9/22/33; SENT TO LIMA, O. JAIL TO AWAIT TRIAL FOR THE BLUFFTON ROBBERY; TEN CONVICTS ESCAPED THE MICHIGAN CITY, INDIANA STATE PRISON 9/26/33— A BREAK FINANCED AND ENGINEERED BY DILLINGER— ESCAPEES INCLUDED WALTER DIETRICH, JIM "OKLAHOMA JACK" CLARK, JAMES JENKINS, JOSEPH BURNS, JOSEPH FOX, EDWARD SHOUSE AND DILLINGER'S FORMER CLOSE PRISON ASSOCIATES, BANKROBBERS HARRY PIERPONT, JOHN HAMILTON, RUSSELL CLARK, AND CHARLES "FAT CHARLEY" MAKLEY; TO OBTAIN FUNDS TO FINANCE DILLINGER'S ESCAPE FROM THE LIMA, O. JAIL, PIERPONT, HAMILTON, CLARK, MAKLEY, AND SHOUSE ROBBED THE FIRST NATIONAL BANK IN ST. MARY'S, O. 10/3/33 ($14,000); DILLINGER ESCAPED FROM THE LIMA, O. JAIL 10/12/33, HIS RELEASE EFFECTED BY PIERPONT, MAKLEY, CLARK, HAMILTON AND SHOUSE; PIERPONT AND MAKLEY KILLED SHERIFF JESS SARBER DURING THIS BREAK; ROBBED WITH PIERPONT, MAKLEY, HAMILTON, AND CLARK THE POLICE ARSENAL OF PERU, IND., 10/20/33 (TAKING TWO MACHINEGUNS, TWO SAWED-OFF SHOTGUNS, FOUR .38-CALIBER POLICE SPECIALS, TWO 30.30 WINCHESTER RIFLES, BULLET-PROOF VESTS, THREE POLICE BADGES AND AMMUNITION); ROBBED WITH PIERPONT, MAKLEY, CLARK, AND HAMILTON THE CENTRAL NATIONAL BANK OF GREENCASTLE, IND., 10/23/33 ($75,346 IN CASH AND BONDS); ESCAPED POLICE TRAP IN CHICAGO 11/15/33; ROBBED WITH PIERPONT, MAKLEY, CLARK, AND HAMILTON THE AMERICAN BANK AND TRUST COMPANY OF RACINE, WISCONSIN, 11/20/33 ($27,789); ALLEGEDLY ROBBED WITH HAMILTON THE FIRST NATIONAL BANK IN EAST CHICAGO, IND., 1/15/34 ($20,736) AT WHICH TIME POLICEMAN PATRICK O'MALLEY WAS KILLED BY ONE OF THE BANDITS; ARRESTED WITH MAKLEY, CLARK, PIERPONT IN TUCSON, ARIZ. BY LOCAL POLICE 1/25/34; EXTRADITED TO INDIANA TO STAND TRIAL FOR ROBBERIES THERE AND FOR THE MURDER OF POLICEMAN O'MALLEY; PLACED IN CROWN POINT, IND. JAIL; ESCAPED CROWN POINT JAIL USING A WOODEN GUN 3/3/34; ROBBED WITH BABY FACE

NELSON (LESTER GILLIS), HOMER VAN METER, JOHN HAMILTON, EDDIE GREEN, AND TOMMY CARROLL THE SECURITY NATIONAL BANK IN SIOUX FALLS, S.D., 3/6/34 ($49,000); ROBBED WITH NELSON, VAN METER, HAMILTON, GREEN, AND CARROLL THE FIRST NATIONAL BANK OF MASON CITY, IOWA—DILLINGER AND HAMILTON WOUNDED—ON 3/13/34 ($52,000); ESCAPED FBI TRAP IN ST. PAUL, MINN., 3/31/34; ESCAPED FBI ATTACK AT LITTLE BOHEMIA LODGE NEAR MANITOWISH WATERS, WISCONSIN, 4/22/33; ALLEGEDLY ROBBED THE MERCHANTS NATIONAL BANK OF SOUTH BEND, IND., 6/30/34 ($18,000); FBI CLAIMED TO HAVE KILLED DILLINGER 7/22/34 OUTSIDE THE BIOGRAPH THEATER IN CHICAGO BUT ALL PERTINENT FACTS OF THE SHOOTING CONTRADICT THIS AND POINT TO THE FACT THAT ANOTHER MAN WAS KILLED IN HIS PLACE AND THAT THE INDIANA BANDIT DISAPPEARED COMPLETELY.

John Dillinger, age three, with his sister Audrey.

John Herbert Dillinger is America's classic bankrobber. No other criminal ever approached his exploits and reputation. Within the space of twelve months Dillinger robbed more banks and stole more money than Jesse James did in the sixteen years he was at large. It took the combined forces of five states and the FBI to pressure his operations to a halt and there exists today no real evidence that he was ever finally apprehended and killed.

Unlike the city gangsters of the Thirties, Dillinger sprang from humble rural beginnings. School and work dominated his early life. He was not a "born" criminal in any sense; only a precocious child who could reasonably be considered as average as any man's offspring.

Born in his father's Indianapolis home June 22, 1903, John Dillinger was delivered by a midwife. His mother Mollie was not a well woman and she died prematurely in 1907 following an apoplectic attack and a subsequent operation. Little Johnnie was left to the care of his fifteen-year-old sister Audrey and his father John Wilson Dillinger, who operated a grocery store on Bloyd Street and maintained several houses which he owned and rented.

In 1912, Dillinger's father remarried. His second wife was Elizabeth Fields of Mooresville, Ind. Evidence indicates that Audrey Dillinger spent more time with Johnnie than anyone else during this period. Elizabeth Dillinger gave birth to Hubert Dillinger in 1914, John and Audrey's half-brother. A half-sister, Doris, was born in 1916.

Dillinger's father was a stickler for discipline and sometimes locked the child in the house when he was unruly. One report had it that Johnnie was chained to a bed when he refused to behave. This seems improbable; Dillinger was a quiet child for the most part whose grades in Indianapolis' Washington Elementary School were above average. He was well-liked and at an early age proved to be extraordinarily athletic, excelling at baseball.

As a sixth-grader, Dillinger was hauled into juvenile court one day, charged with stealing coal from the Pennsylvania Railroad yards and selling it to neighbors. He was defiant in court. When the magistrate demanded he stop chewing a wad of gum, Dillinger complied, removing it from his mouth and sticking it to the bill of his cap. "Your mind is crippled!" the judge shouted. Johnnie only grinned.

He was turned back to the custody of his parents. After his graduation from Washington, Dillinger was suddenly uprooted from his Indianapolis home. His father—some later said for reasons of getting John away from corruptive city influences—sold his houses and store and bought a modest farm outside of Mooresville, Indiana, a farming community seventeen miles south of Indianapolis.

Here, everything changed for John Dillinger. He refused to help his father farm and vowed never to return to school. Instead, he took a job in Indianapolis as an apprentice machinist at the Reliance Specialty Company, commuting each day from Mooresville on his prize possession, a motor bike. He did at-

Dillinger as a teenager with his father on the porch of the family farm in Mooresville, Ind.

tempt to return to school, to please his step-mother, but quickly dropped out of his first semester at Mooresville High.

When his father asked him to help work the farm, John merely shrugged and went back to his machinist job. "My people have been farmers for generations," Dillinger's father commented years later. "I liked the land. John never did. Said it was too slow . . . I guess the city kind of got a hold on him. . . ."

When not working in Indianapolis, Dillinger drove south to Martinsville, the county seat, where he had friends. There he played pool in Big John Gebhardt's pool room. He was not good with a cue but took his losses quietly. One man remembered him coming into the pool room, playing for a half hour and regularly losing two dollars to the local sharks. Without a word he would then put on his cap and stroll out.

Dillinger joined the Martinsville baseball team, proving to be a remarkably good second baseman. He dated Frances Thornton, his uncle Everett's stepdaughter. The affair bloomed into love and Dillinger asked his uncle for Frances' hand.

Everett Dillinger refused, the two were too young. The uncle wanted Frances to marry a prosperous boy from Greencastle, Indiana.

Embittered by this rejection, Dillinger re-

turned to Indianapolis where he was seen by neighbors patronizing prostitutes. He contracted gonorrhea. On the night of July 21, 1923, he impulsively stole a car belonging to Oliver P. Macy from the parking lot of the Friends Church in Mooresville. Hours later, Dillinger abandoned the auto in Indianapolis. Fearing arrest, Dillinger enlisted in the U.S. Navy (unknown to John, Macy refused to press charges). He gave his real name and a false St. Louis, Mo., address when enlisting.

After basic training at Great Lakes, fireman third class Dillinger was assigned to the battleship, U.S.S. *Utah* (which would be destroyed at Pearl Harbor in 1941). He went AWOL several times and was thrown in the brig. While the ship was anchored off Boston, Dillinger, on December 4, 1923, permanently jumped ship. The Navy listed him as a deserter and posted a $50 reward for his capture.

Back in Indiana, Dillinger met and courted sixteen-year-old Beryl Ethel Hovius of Martinsville. The young couple married in the spring of 1924 and moved in with Beryl's parents. There wasn't much to it. Dillinger spent more time playing baseball and shooting pool in Gebhardt's than he spent with his wife.

After drinking several beers with Edgar Singleton, 31, a former convict and umpire for the Martinsville baseball team, a robbery plan ensued. Singleton excitedly told John that 65-year-old Frank Morgan, a grocer in Mooresville, carried his week's receipts home late on Saturday nights. It would be terribly easy to waylay him and steal the money.

Dillinger (left) with Navy buddies in 1923 (taken while he was serving on board the battleship *Utah*).

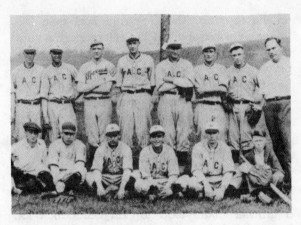

In the spring of 1924, John Dillinger (standing, second from right) played second base for the Martinsville, Ind. baseball team; his first partner in crime, Edgar Singleton, is seated far left.

Dillinger agreed. On the night of September 6, 1924, the two men jumped Morgan in front of the Mooresville Christian Church at 10:30 p.m. as the grocer was making his way home. One of them (it was never determined which) hit Morgan with a large bolt wrapped in a rag, opening his skull. He got up and was hit again. One of the robbers brandished a pistol but the intrepid Morgan knocked it away with his hand and a shot was accidentally fired. The two men, thoroughly frightened, ran.

Morgan's head wound required eleven stitches. He told Deputy Sheriff John Hayworth he couldn't identify his attacker, but the lawman, through information supplied by Mooresville youths, believed John Dillinger was behind the crime and drove out to the family farm. Morgan went with him.

When the grocer confronted John, he recalled how the young man had purchased candy in his store as a child. "Why, John," Morgan said, "You wouldn't hurt me, would you?"

"No, Mr. Morgan," Dillinger replied.

Hayworth took the would-be bandit in for questioning, placing him in the county jail. When Dillinger's father arrived at the jail, John tearfully admitted the hold-up attempt. The prosecutor promised the elder Dillinger that his son would receive a lenient sentence if he threw himself on the mercy of the court. The old man convinced his son to do so and, without counsel, twenty-year-old John Dillinger pleaded guilty.

It was his bad luck to have been brought before Judge Joseph W. Williams, the most severe jurist in the county. Williams gave Dillinger concurrent sentences of two to fourteen years and ten to twenty years on the two charges of conspiracy to commit a felony and assault with intent to rob. He also fined the youth $100 on each charge and disenfranchised him for a period of twelve years. Edgar Singleton, through his lawyer, received a change of venue and a much lighter sentence (he was paroled inside of two years).

Deputy Sheriff Russell Peterson, who delivered Dillinger to the Indiana State Reformatory at Pendleton where he was to serve out his sentence, felt that John "was just a kid. He got a raw deal. You just can't take ten years away from a kid's life."

Dillinger felt the same way. When he faced Warden A. F. Miles at Pendleton for the first time, he calmly stated: "I won't cause you any trouble except to escape."

"I've heard that kind of talk before," Miles reponded.

"Yeah, well, I'll go right over the administration building."

Within weeks, Dillinger tried exactly that but was caught. Next, when Deputy Peterson was returning Dillinger to Pendleton, after he had been escorted to Singleton's trial as a witness, the youth attempted another escape. He kicked over a table in the train station and sent Peterson sprawling. The Deputy chased his charge down a deadend alley and

Inmate 13225 John Dillinger of Michigan City, Indiana State Prison.

Dillinger surrendered after Peterson fired a warning shot into the air.

Dillinger obstinately continued break attempts at Pendleton. On the night of October 10, 1924 he was discovered missing from his cell. Guards located him under a pile of excelsior in the foundry. In November of the same year, working with a makeshift saw, Dillinger broke out of his cell and into a corridor where he was caught. He tried again in 1925 and was captured.

About this time, Dillinger met the man who was to shape his criminal career, handsome Harry Pierpont, a young bankrobber first arrested for trying to kill a man in Terre Haute, Indiana in March, 1922. Pierpont, soft-spoken and considered quite a ladies' man, had knocked over a Kokomo, Ind. bank single-handedly and, upon his capture, was sent to Pendleton.

Inmate 11014 Harry Pierpont, professional bankrobber who taught Dillinger the ropes at Michigan City.

There, Dillinger and Pierpont became close friends and were soon joined by another youthful bankrobber, Homer Van Meter, a crafty habitual criminal who played jester to Pendleton's high court of criminals. Pierpont and Van Meter, who disliked each other, earned Dillinger's admiration by being the toughest, most incorrigible convicts at Pendleton. They spent more time in solitary confinement than in their cells. When officials could no longer control them they were both shipped off to the state prison at Michigan City, Indiana to serve out their long sentences.

After Dillinger's wife divorced him in 1929, he came up before the parole board. His record had been spotty and the board chairman told him that "maybe you'd better go back for a few years."

Dillinger eyed the members of the board. Indiana Governor Harry Leslie was sitting in

on the meeting. The Governor had seen Dillinger play baseball in the reformatory's yard once and remarked: "That kid ought to be playing major league baseball." Dillinger had heard of this and now used Leslie's observation as a ploy to obtain a transfer. He asked that he be sent to Michigan City.

"Why do you want to go to Michigan City?" he was asked.

"Because they have a real team up there," John replied.

Leslie quickly convinced the board that such a transfer might lead to "an occupation for him later." Dillinger was sent to the Big House on July 15, 1929 and happily fell in with Pierpont and Van Meter upon arrival.

His old Pendleton classmates introduced him to John Hamilton, another bankrobber, who was apprehended after stealing a car in 1927. Doing a twenty-five year sentence, Hamilton, 34, began to teach Dillinger, as he had Pierpont, the ins and outs of robbing banks. He was an intelligent tough con who talked quietly and was known to the prison population as "Three-Fingered Jack." Hamilton had lost the index and middle fingers of his right hand years earlier in an accident. (It is interesting to note that though Hamilton was considered a "tough customer" by jailers, he was punished only once at Michigan City and that was for skipping rope in the machine shop in 1932.)

In Pierpont's elite bankrobbing alumni was Charles "Fat Charley" Makley who had been in and out of prison in the last ten years, and who was doing twenty years for robbing a Hammond, Ind. bank. Ohio-born Makley was 44 and the clown of the group when Van Meter wasn't about. There was also Russell Lee Clark, a large, big-boned bankrobber with steely nerves and an introverted disposition. Clark had been sent up in 1927 and had caused prison authorities no end of headaches. He had led attempted prison breaks, riots, and had tried to kill his guards on several occasions.

These men, who would figure in Indiana's largest prison break four years later (an escape engineered by Dillinger), would form a super gang of bankrobbers whose incredible thefts would astound the country.

The group cultivated Dillinger as their future contact man on the outside; he would be up for parole before any of the others. It would be his job to rob a string of small town banks from a list prepared by Pierpont and Hamilton and use funds from these robberies to finance a massive break from Michigan City.

Dillinger's parole came about in the spring of 1933. For four years he had led the life of a model prisoner. In addition, Governor Paul McNutt received a petition from John's Mooresville neighbors, asking that he be released to help out his father on the farm. Even Judge Williams, who had sentenced Dillinger, signed the petition, perhaps regretting the brutal judgment he had handed down in the case.

McNutt relented and signed Dillinger's parole. He was released May 22, 1933 and immediately rushed to his father's Mooresville farm where his stepmother was seriously ill. He arrived an hour after Elizabeth Fields Dillinger died.

The following Sunday Dillinger attended the Friend's Church in Mooresville. Pastor Gertrude M. Reinier saw John sitting with his father in a front pew and immediately launched into a sermon on the Prodigal Son. "Throughout the sermon," Mrs. Reinier later recalled, "young John sat there beside his father crying. Afterward he came to me and said, 'You will never know how much good that sermon has done me.'"

Two weeks later, after recruiting an Indianapolis thug named William Shaw, Dillinger began robbing small stores and companies. Using Pierpont's list, Dillinger, Shaw, and Paul "Lefty" Parker robbed the bank at New Carlisle, Indiana, getting $10,600. (Pierpont's list was somewhat obsolete; many "ripe" banks had already failed during the Depression and Dillinger was met by empty buildings and locked doors.)

Shaw, an egotistical small-time hoodlum, wanted everyone in the gang to don white caps as an identifying symbol sure to strike terror into their victims. Dillinger declined and wore a straw boater. He also insisted that Shaw and Parker call him Dan Dillinger, the only name by which they knew him.

Days later Dillinger and Harry Copeland approached Shaw's home in Indianapolis through an alley. Copeland, a bankrobber from Muncie, Ind., was another ex-convict from Michigan City and had been newly recruited for the gang. Dillinger, driving a stolen Chevrolet, spotted Shaw and Lefty Parker with their hands in the air and a swarm of police about them.

Quickly, Dillinger put the car in reverse and gunned it backward out the alley. Shaw watched him escape. "He drove faster than some people drive forwards," he remembered.

With Copeland as his only aide, Dillinger next struck the small Commercial Bank at Daleville, Ind. on July 17, 1933. It was a one-room red brick affair with a five-foot railing separating the vault and customer areas.

Cashier Margaret Good was the only person in the bank when Dillinger sauntered in wearing his straw boater and a neat blue suit. He pulled out a gun and said to Miss Good: "This is a stick-up, honey." With an agile movement, Dillinger leaped over the railing and entered the vault. Harry Copeland left the getaway car parked in front of the bank and walked inside. He, too, flourished a pistol, lining up customers against a wall as they came into the bank.

Dillinger quickly scooped up $3,500 and then ordered everyone inside the vault. The two bandits casually walked to their car and drove slowly out of town. Miss Good opened the vault door from inside and moments later, trembling, told local police that Dillinger was the most courteous of bankrobbers. "I think he knew I was a kid and was sorry to scare me. He didn't want to scare me any worse than he had to."

Dillinger's identity as the daring, leaping bankrobber was cemented by witnesses, and police throughout Indiana were suddenly searching for him.

John Dillinger with his girl friend Mary Longnaker at Chicago's World Fair, summer, 1933; he had already robbed several banks by then (this photo was taken by an unsuspecting policeman at the Fair, an incident which amused Dillinger no end).

He was by then in another state, Ohio, seeing a new girlfriend, Mary Longnaker, who lived in Dayton. Dillinger took Mary to the World's Fair in Chicago where he humorously photographed a policeman and then impudently asked if he would snap a picture of him and Mary.

On August 4, 1933, Copeland, Dillinger, and another unknown man robbed the National Bank of Montpelier, Indiana. Dillinger was elated to find $10,110 in the bank's small safe and remarked: "This is a good haul." He then spotted the bank president's .45-caliber automatic in a drawer. "And this is a good gun," he added and took that, too.

To supplement the escape fund Dillinger had been assembling for his friends still in Michigan City, he, Copeland, Sam Goldstine, and two other unknown men hit the Citizens National Bank in Bluffton, O. Dillinger and Copeland, wearing straw hats and expensive grey suits, walked into the bank while two other men stood guard outside. "Stand back," Dillinger said to cashier Roscoe Lingler as he drew his gun, "this is a stickup!" He began to go through the tellers' cages gathering up the cash. The take was thin and Dillinger turned to bookkeeper Oliver Locher saying, "You've got more money in here. Where is it?"

Locher pointed a quaking finger at the vault. Just then the bank's alarm went off. One of the lookouts poked his head in the door. "They're after us! Let's go!"

Dillinger ignored the remark and continued filling a sack with small bills. The lookouts started firing aimless shots into the air to frighten away the curious.

After collecting only $2,100, Dillinger and Copeland joined the two men on the street. They hurriedly piled into a large sedan and sped away.

Dillinger was angered over the small take. He required much more to finance the Michigan City break. Again, he and Copeland went searching for a "soft" bank. They settled on the large Massachusetts Avenue State Bank in downtown Indianapolis.

Using Hilton Crouch, a professional race-track driver, as a get-away wheelman, Dillinger and Copeland entered the bank and John immediately vaulted over a high railing and ransacked the tellers' cages. Copeland held a machinegun on at least ten customers.

Dillinger took everything in sight including $500 in half dollars, dumping the coins into a white sack. "Hurry up, will you," Copeland said as he nervously glanced out the bank window. Minutes later the two robbers ran from the bank and Crouch raced the green DeSoto down the street.

With his major share of the $24,800 taken on the Indianapolis raid, Dillinger moved to Chicago where he heavily bribed a foreman of a thread-making company to doctor one of the thread barrels being sent to the shirt shop at Michigan City, Indiana prison. Several guns were placed inside the barrel. It was resealed, and according to a prearranged Pierpont plan, a red "X" was marked on its top in crayon.

This was Dillinger's second attempt to free Pierpont and the others. In early September, 1933, Dillinger had crept up to the Michigan City prison wall under the cover of darkness and tossed three loaded guns wrapped in newspapers over the 30 foot barrier into the athletic field where Pierpont was expected to find them. Other inmates, however, discovered the guns and turned them over to Warden H. D. Claudy.

While the thread barrel was being shipped to Michigan City, Dillinger drove to Dayton once more to see Mary Longnaker. Some one else was looking for the same girl. Dayton police detective Russell K. Pfauhl had been tipped that Dillinger had been seeing a Dayton woman. The tip came from the Pinkerton Detective Agency which had been at work investigating several bank robberies committed by the Indiana bandit. The warden of Michigan City Prison told Pfauhl that Mary Longnaker was James Jenkins' sister. Jenkins was part of the Dillinger-Pierpont clique in Michigan City.

Pfauhl and his partner, Charles E. Gross, staked out Mary's plush rooming house on West First Street in Dayton. At 1:30 a.m., Pfauhl and Gross went in to arrest Dillinger after receiving a call from Lucille Stricker, Mary's landlady, who told them Dillinger was in the house. The two detectives, carrying shotguns, barged into Mary's apartment. A man was standing in the middle of the room holding snapshots. Dillinger had just been showing Mary the photos of them taken at the World's Fair.

"Stick 'em up, Johnnie," Pfauhl ordered and aimed the shotgun square at Dillinger's head.

Police photos of John Dillinger taken in Tucson, Ariz., 1/25/34, following the gang's capture. The diamond stickpin was worth about $4,000.

The photos fluttered to the carpet. Dillinger's hands went upward, then hesitated, and began to inch downward.

"If you do, John," Pfauhl warned, "I'll kill you on the spot."

John Herbert Dillinger was back in custody. Four days later, as Dillinger waited to be indicted for the Bluffton Bank robbery in the Lima, O. jail, his friends came crashing out of Michigan City Prison, wielding the pistols he had smuggled in to them.

The break was massive; ten men in all went out through the gates, stealing two cars parked in front of the administration building. Those escaping were Harry Pierpont, Charles Makley, Russell Clark, John Hamilton, Edward Shouse, Joseph Fox, Joseph Burns, Jim "Oklahoma Jack" Clark (no relation to Russell), Mary Longnaker's brother James Jenkins, and Walter Dietrich.

Pierpont, Makley, Clark, Hamilton, Shouse, and Jenkins took one car and headed for Leipsic, Ohio where Pierpont's family lived. They drove wildly through northern Indiana and near the hamlet of Bean Blossom, a door accidentally flew open and Jenkins fell out. Posses were everywhere hunting the escaped convicts and the gang, thinking vigilantes were in the area, sped on, leaving Jenkins to fend for himself. He walked up the road about a mile and ran into three farmers who were part of the vigilante force.

When Jenkins excitedly pulled out his pistol, the farmers blew him to bits with their shotguns.

Before Dillinger's capture he had left funds with Mary Kinder, a gang contact. Using this money, Pierpont outfitted his men with new clothes, a new car and an arsenal of weapons. To make sure they had enough traveling money, Pierpont led a raid against the First National Bank of St. Mary's, O., on October 3, 1933. St. Mary's was Makley's home town and once inside the bank Makley ran into an old friend, W. O. Smith. Makley passed small talk with bank president Smith like a man casually discussing crops around a cracker barrel. The gang, with $14,000 in a sack, left the bank without firing a shot.

For days, Dillinger had been telling his cell mate, Art Miller, in the Lima jail that his men would deliver him. On October 12, 1933, Pierpont, Makley, Clark, Hamilton, and Shouse did come.

At 6:20 p.m. that night, armed with pistols, Pierpont, Makley, and Clark entered the jail office. Sheriff Jess Sarber, his wife Lucy, and Deputy Wilbur Sharp were reading newspapers after their dinner of pork chops and mashed potatoes. Sarber looked up and spoke pleasantly to the visitors. "What can I do for you?"

"We're officers from Michigan City," Pierpont said. "We want to talk to the prisoner John Dillinger."

Sarber didn't move from his desk. His wife continued working a crossword puzzle. Sharp never put down his paper. "I guess that will be all right," Sarber said. "But first let me see your credentials."

Pierpont's eyes narrowed. Then he drew out a pistol from beneath his expensive suit and aimed it at Sarber. "Here's our credentials."

Sarber's mouth sagged a bit and he put his hand toward the gun as if to ward it away. "Oh, you can't do that," he said.

Pierpont fired two shots. Both hit the Sheriff, one in the stomach, the other in the hip. He sank to the floor. Stunned, Lucy Sarber and Wilbur Sharp stared in wonder.

"Give us the keys to the cells," Pierpont demanded.

Sarber tried to rise on his elbow. Makley dashed forward and brought his gun butt down on the Sheriff's head, opening it to the bone. He hit him a second time.

"I'll get the keys," Lucy Sarber screamed. "Don't hurt him any more."

At the first shots, Dillinger put down the

cards in his hand. Art Miller, the other player, had also heard the firing. "John," he said, "your gang has come for you." Dillinger snatched his coat and went to the cell door. Pierpont, grinning, was there in a minute, opening it and handing him a gun.

"Wanna come?" Dillinger asked Miller.

"No, thanks."

The two men rushed out into the jail office. Other prisoners clamored to be let free. Pierpont stuck his head in the corridor leading to the cells and shouted: "Get back there, you bastards! We came for John. The rest of you can leave when we've gone."

Dillinger knelt down to inspect the damage done to the Sheriff. Sarber, who had been kind to the Indiana bandit, blinked in agony.

"You have to do this?" Dillinger asked without looking at Pierpont.

Handsome Harry made no reply.

Suddenly, Sarber moaned his last: "Oh, men, why did you do this to me?" He then inched his face about slightly to look at his weeping wife and said, "Mother, I believe I'm going to have to leave you."

By then the gang had fled down the jail steps and into a waiting car. Sarber died moments later.

The Terror Gang, as the press first dubbed Dillinger and the others, headed for Indianapolis where Mary Kinder, who had taken up with Harry Pierpont, and Evelyn "Billie" Frechette, a part Menominee Indian girl Dillinger had met in Chicago, were waiting. There the gang made plans to equip themselves for a string of bank raids.

They hit the police arsenal at Peru, Indiana eight days after Dillinger's escape from Lima. Machineguns, bullet-proof vests, shotguns, rifles, super .38-caliber police specials, and bags full of ammunition were taken.

The Peru operation emphasized a new approach in robbery. Dillinger and Pierpont posed as tourists, asking policeman Ambrose Clark what preparations the local lawmen had made in the event the Dillinger gang roared into town.

Proudly Clark and a desk sergeant showed the "tourists" their arsenal and just as proudly Pierpont and Dillinger pulled pistols and relieved them of their guns and equipment, running out to their car with armloads of rifles and machineguns wrapped in blankets. Mary Kinder, who sat in the back seat as a lookout,

gaped at the amount of guns filling up the auto.

"My God," she said to Dillinger. "What are you going to start—a young army?"

There was no real leader of the second and most important Dillinger gang. Pierpont was the most daring and nerveless of the group but his impulsiveness oft-times outweighed his considerable intelligence. Hamilton was the old pro. Whenever any bank job was discussed, he could offer the soundest advice based on experience. Makley and Clark, for the most part, listened.

Pierpont appreciated and more or less encouraged Dillinger's role as leader. He once kidded the Indiana bandit about his name, telling him that it was euphonic and memorable, and it could be employed as a tool to properly unnerve robbery victims. (The name Dillinger, with French-German origins, was actually pronounced with a hard "g," but the press and the public uttered the name with a soft ending which somehow reminded everyone of the pistol, derringer.)

Indiana State Police Captain, Matt Leach, was a dogged pursuer of the Dillinger gang. He thought that by giving statements to the press in which he named Pierpont the leader of the gang, Dillinger and others would be angered and dissension among the members would develop. Nothing of the sort happened.

Many stories surrounding Dillinger and Leach were purely fictitious. Leach stated that Dillinger was a megalomaniac who once called him, stating: "We'll get you. Watch your ass."

Sergeant Frank Reynolds, a member of the specially created "Dillinger Squad" of the Chicago Police Department under the command of Captain John Stege, claimed he had received the same phone call.

Leach went further, saying that Dillinger had mailed him an 1898 publication entitled "How to Be A Detective," but this stunt was performed by two Indiana newsmen who could not abide Leach's pompous statements about how he would snare the Dillinger gang. One of the newspapermen was William L. "Tubby" Toms of the *Indianapolis News*.

Chicago became the base of operations for the gang. They lived in twos and threes in several North Side apartments, changing addresses every two or three weeks. None of the members drank hard liquor, only an occasional beer. Their women did drink liquor but the gangsters frowned on it.

Dillinger never bought liquor for his girl Billie Frechette. "She's an Indian," he told Pierpont. "It's not good for her . . . or for us . . . if she drinks."

While preparing their first major bank robbery together, Dillinger, Pierpont, and Hamilton sat about a dining room table with detailed maps and timetables. While in prison, they had learned from Walter Dietrich (he, Jim Clark, and Joseph Fox were apprehended shortly after the Michigan City break) an amazing formula for robbing banks.

Dietrich had once been a member of a gang headed up by a Prussian ex-officer, who had deserted the Kaiser's service before the First World War, a strange bankrobber named "Baron" Herman K. Lamm (whether or not the term "taking it on the lam" stems from his name is unknown). Lamm immigrated to the U.S. and operated in Utah as a stickup man until his arrest in 1917, spending a year in the state prison. There he perfected what he thought to be a foolproof system of robbing banks.

Upon his release he gathered a gang of experts and initiated his system. First he would case a bank, visiting it several times while posing as a newsman or investor, pinpointing its alarm system, position of guards and the location of safes, vaults and tellers' cages. Then he would draw an actual floor plan of the bank and sometimes the interior of the bank would be created in a vacant warehouse or country barn where his gang members would rehearse their roles. The vital part of the plan was Lamm's stopwatch. He figured the exact time the bandits would have to work safely inside the bank before customers or lawmen could interfere. He insisted that his men leave the bank when the alloted time was up, whether or not they had all the money in the bank.

This kind of precision bank-robbing worked well for thirteen years as Lamm and his gang ran pell mell through the Western states. In 1930, Lamm's incredible exploits came, quite by accident, to a halt.

On December 16, 1930 he entered the Citizens State Bank in Clinton, Ind. with three other men—26-year-old Walter Dietrich, James "Oklahoma Jack" Clark, and G. W. "Dad" Landy, a bankrobber in his late sixties whose criminal career trailed back to stagecoach days. The robbery went off smoothly as the bandits jammed several paper bags with $15,-567 and walked to their getaway car, a large Buick, parked across the street from the bank.

Here, Lamm's third stage of robbing a bank, the carefully planned getaway with all back roads carefully marked and all street lights (if any) timed to the second, fell apart. The driver, upon seeing a vigilante walking toward the bank cradling a shotgun, panicked and made a reckless U-turn, puncturing a tire.

The bandits were forced to commandeer a number of cars and trucks that either broke down or had very little gas. Their trail was quickly picked up and two hundred vigilantes and policemen converged on the group as they stood helplessly around a stalled car next to a cornfield in rural Southern Illinois.

Lamm and his boys decided to fight it out. A wild gun battle raged for several hours. Lamm and his driver were shot dead. Dietrich and Clark surrendered. Old "Dad" Landy hid behind the car while the lawmen called for him to come out. "No prison for me," they heard the old man cry out, "not again." A single shot echoed across the open fields. Landy had sent a bullet into his brain.

Walter Dietrich, who was then sent to Michigan City with Clark for life, was the man who outlined the Lamm strategy for the Dillinger gang. They would use it well.

The super gang drove up to the Central National Bank in Greencastle, Indiana at 2:45 p.m. on October 23, 1933. Clark sat behind the wheel of a Studebaker touring car while Pierpont, Dillinger and Makley went inside. Hamilton stood by the bank's entrance as the "tiger," whose job it was to spot anyone acting suspiciously in the street. Makley stood near the door with a stopwatch. Dillinger and Pierpont knew the bank's interior intimately. They had both acted as "jugmarkers" —casing the bank days before as newsmen— and could have found the vault and important tellers' cages blindfolded.

Dillinger, still the showoff, leaped over a small railing and went rapidly through the cages, scooping money into a sack while Pierpont and Makley held guns on employees. "Keep your hands at your sides and don't move," Pierpont said. "We're not advertising."

Makley kept glancing down at the stopwatch in his hand.

An elderly woman, foreign-born, hurriedly walked out of the bank.

Hamilton, surprised, gently held onto her arm. "Better go back inside, lady," he said.

She pulled away from him and brushed his drawn gun aside. "I go to Penny's and you go to hell," she said and walked off down the street.

Makley called out: "It's five minutes." Dillinger stopped filling his sack—he had just about everything anyway—and abruptly turned about, hopped back over the railing. The bandit spotted a farmer standing at one of the teller's cages. His hands were stiff at his side. In front of him on the counter was a small stack of bills.

Dillinger glanced at the money. "That your money or the bank's?" he asked.

"Mine," the farmer said.

"Keep it. We only want the bank's." (This act was later wrongly attributed to Bonnie and Clyde; even a cursory study of the Barrow gang would reveal that the niggardly Texas thieves would not only have taken the farmer's money but also shot him on the spot for thrills.)

The men quietly left the bank without ever firing a weapon. Taking dirt roads and following pre-coded maps, the gang drove leisurely out of the county, avoiding every major roadblock set up by state and local police.

When they opened the sack in the car, the bandits found they had taken $75,346 in cash and negotiable securities. It was Dillinger's biggest strike.

Newsmen pressing Matt Leach for a lead on the gang were told by the police captain that Dillinger had again called him on the phone, arrogantly shouting: "This is John Dillinger. How are you, you stuttering bastard?" When there were no facts to relay Leach was inclined toward fiction, but it made good copy anyway. The police captain reasoned that if he inflated Dillinger's reputation as a cavalier, wise-gun bandit, his own ego would eventually cause his downfall.

Almost a month later in Chicago, Dillinger came close to doing exactly that. He was suffering from barber's itch, a skin disorder, and went to Dr. Charles Eye for treatment. Ed Shouse, who had been kicked out of the gang because he drank and made advances toward some of the members' women, had been caught and informed Chicago police that Dillinger was being treated by Dr. Eye.

The Dillinger Squad planned to snare the bandit on the night of November 15, 1933. But the wily outlaw, with Billie Frechette at his side, suspected a trap when he saw several unmarked cars next to Dr. Eye's office on Irving Park Boulevard. They were facing the wrong way.

Dillinger was driving his favorite car, a Hudson Terraplane. He quickly changed gears, roaring down the street. In a moment several police cars were on his tail. Flooring the accelerator, Dillinger soon lost all but one police car driven by Sergeant John Artery. With his partner, Art Keller, leaning out the window with a shotgun, Artery brought his car alongside of the Terraplane. Both cars were doing eighty miles an hour down Irving Park, a spin-crazy chase in which they both narrowly avoided several autos, streetcars, and pedestrians.

When the two cars were hood-and-hood, Keller began pumping shells at Dillinger.

"Hey," Billie Frechette said almost lamely, "somebody's shooting at you." Dillinger smiled at her and jammed his foot almost through the floorboard. The Terraplane shot ahead briefly. Spotting a narrow side street, Dillinger whipped the wheel around and took the corner at terrific speed. Artery shot past him down Irving Park. By the time the two officers had turned about, Dillinger's car had disappeared.

"That bird can sure drive," Keller said and disgustedly threw his shotgun in the back seat.

The gang immediately guessed the informant had been Shouse. He had been a troublemaker from the beginning, even attempting to convince John Hamilton to join him in independent bank robberies.

Mary Kinder had overheard Shouse talking and broke in with: "You ain't gonna do a damn thing. There ain't nobody going no place until we all talk it over. This has always been a friendly bunch and you ain't gonna take no two or three and go rob a bank."

Following this incident, Dillinger threw a thousand dollars in a fat wad at Shouse and said, "There's your money. Now get your ass out." Shouse got out. His recklessness led to his capture.

The gang moved to Milwaukee and made plans to rob the bank in Racine, Wisconsin.

It was there they learned that Harry Copeland, who had been with Dillinger on earlier bank robberies, had gotten drunk and arrested.

"We ain't gonna miss neither of them two," Makley commented.

Days later, November 20, 1933, a well-dressed, nonchalant Harry Pierpont walked into the American Bank and Trust Company in Racine just before closing time. Bookkeeper Mrs. Henry Patzke watched, puzzled, as Pierpont unraveled a huge Red Cross poster in the lobby and pasted it in the middle of the bank's large picture window. Mrs. Patzke shrugged and went back to work.

Then Makley, followed by Dillinger and Hamilton, entered.

"Stick 'em up," Makley said to head teller Harold Graham.

"Go to the next window, please," Graham said, thinking the stout man was joking.

"I said stick 'em up," Makley repeated. Graham made a sudden movement and Makley fired, sending a bullet into the teller's elbow and hip. Graham fell and hit the alarm button. The alarm, which did not sound in the bank, went off at Racine Police Headquarters.

Dillinger, Hamilton and Pierpont fairly ran down the aisle behind the cages, gathering up money. "Everybody flat on their stomachs," Pierpont shouted. Everybody in the bank went flat on their stomachs.

Two local policemen, Wilbur Hansen and Cyril Boyard, drove slowly toward the bank after being notified that an alarm had gone off. They were in no hurry. The alarm had gone off accidentally several times before when careless tellers had triggered the button.

When Boyard and Hansen did amble into the bank, Pierpont disarmed them. Hansen took his time surrendering his machinegun and Makley shot him. The women in the bank began screaming. Dillinger came out of the vault. "I've got all of it," he said. An off-duty policeman then walked into the bank. Dillinger poked him with his pistol. "Come on in and join us," he said.

A large crowd had assembled outside when the first shot was fired. Dillinger and the others pushed several women out the front door in front of them as hostages. Policemen were firing at them from across the street, the shots sent high to avoid hitting bystanders.

Dillinger and the others turned around and scurried out a back entrance where Clark was waiting in a large Buick. The gang piled into the car, taking the bank's president and Mrs. Patzke with them as hostages. After several minutes of racing along pre-marked back roads, the two terrified hostages were let out.

Before pulling away, Dillinger looked at Mrs. Patzke and grinned. "Maybe we ought to take you along. Can you cook?"

"After a fashion," Mrs. Patzke said.

"Some other time."

The take from the American Bank and Trust Company was less than what the gang expected—$27,789—but it would have to do. The outlaws decided to winter in Florida and headed for Daytona Beach, where they rented several cottages on the water's edge. They played cards, listened to the radio, fished, and ate steak and potatoes cooked by Mary Kinder and Billie Frechette.

From Daytona Beach, they motored in separate cars to Tucson, Ariz. Between the time the gang left Daytona Beach and the time they arrived in Tucson, the First National Bank of East Chicago, Ind., was robbed of $20,736 on January 15, 1934. A policeman, Patrick O'Malley, attempted to stop two unidentified bandits and was machinegunned to death. The crime was attributed to Dillinger and Hamilton.

Dillinger was named as the killer of O'Malley, but he always denied being there. Mary Kinder to this day denies he ever left the gang to pull this robbery. So did Billie Frechette when interviewed in 1968 before her death by cancer.

Tucson turned out to be a mistake. Clark and Makley were apprehended there first after a fire broke out in their hotel. They paid fireman hundreds of dollars to rescue two of their suitcases. One of the firemen became suspicious when he noticed one of the suitcases was extremely heavy. Opening it, he found a machinegun and several pistols. Pierpont, Dillinger, Billie, and Mary Kinder were soon rounded up and, after being identified, sent back East. Dillinger was extradited to Indiana to stand trial for the East Chicago robbery. Clark, Makley, and Pierpont were sent to Ohio to stand trial for the killing of Sheriff Sarber.

Dillinger was lodged in the Crown Point, Ind. jail, which was termed "escape-proof." Dozens of vigilantes roamed the grounds in front of the jail carrying shotguns and machineguns in case other members of his gang decided to attempt to free him.

But all of the Dillinger gangsters were in prison. He would have to escape alone, he told his lawyer, Louis Piquett. Somehow, the bandit got hold of a razor and using the top of a washboard, carved a crude-looking pistol which he darkened with bootblack.

The pistol looked real enough to attendant Sam Cahoon and Deputy Sheriff Ernest Blunk when Dillinger flashed it on them on the morning of March 3, 1934. "I don't want to kill anyone," the bandit said, letting himself out into a corridor. "Now you do as I tell you."

In minutes, Dillinger had rounded up a dozen guards, made his way down a flight of stairs and, with Herbert Youngblood, a Negro prisoner awaiting trial for murder, escaped in Sheriff Lillian Holley's car, taking Blunk and a mechanic, Ed Saager, along as hostages. He drove on back roads until he crossed into rural Illinois. There he let Blunk and Saager out, giving them $4 for food and carfare. "I'd give you guys more but that's all I can spare."

He drove away. The two men heard him singing, "I'm heading for the last roundup." Before the car turned a bend in the muddy road, Dillinger waved at them.

When Dillinger drove Sheriff Holley's car across state lines, the FBI joined the hunt for him (although agents had been on his trail for months at the request of police in several states).

Chicago seemed to be the most likely place to hunt the bandit, but Dillinger had moved to St. Paul, Minn. Billie Frechette, who had been freed with Mary Kinder after the Tucson arrests, joined him there. Dillinger quickly went to work building a new gang.

Michigan City Prison parolee Homer Van Meter, who had been robbing banks in Michigan and Kentucky, became his right-hand man. Van Meter brought in Eddie Green and Tommy Carroll. John Hamilton, who had gone to Chicago from Daytona Beach, showed up. One more man was needed. A Chicago gangster who had worked with the Capone and Bugs Moran mobs was recruited. He was Lester Gillis, better known as Baby Face Nelson, an insane killer who had been a bootlegger in California and had robbed banks all over the Midwest.

Van Meter and Nelson argued constantly and Dillinger had to step between them more than once before their guns went off. Dillinger didn't like the situation but knew he had to move fast to obtain a large amount of cash and Nelson was important to reach that end. Dillinger had been planning a permanent escape for some time now and he also wanted to help Pierpont, Clark, and Makley, who were standing trial for Sarber's killing.

The new Dillinger gang struck the Security National Bank and Trust Company in Sioux Falls, S. D. on March 6, 1934, only three days after the spectacular escape from Crown Point which had made Dillinger's name a byword in almost every American home.

The robbery went along without incident until Nelson spotted an off-duty policeman getting out of a car. He jumped on a desk and fired several shots through the bank window, wounding Hale Keith. "I got one of them! I got one of them!" he squealed.

Tommy Carroll stood in the middle of the street gripping a machinegun. By the time Dillinger and the others came out of the bank, Carroll had lined up Sioux Falls' entire police force, including the chief. Thousands of spectators milled around the bank, bemused. The good citizens thought the robbery was part of a film being made. A Hollywood producer had been in town a day previous telling everyone that he intended to make a gangster film there. The film producer had been Homer Van Meter!

The gang poured into a large Packard with $49,000 in a white sack and raced out of town. After going several miles, Dillinger ordered the car halted. He got out and, with Hamilton, sprinkled roofing nails all over the road for several yards. "That ought to slow them up," he said. Once again the gang escaped.

Eddie Green was sent out as a jugmarker and soon discovered a plum in Mason City, Iowa, the First National Bank. Green discovered that the bank's vault contained more than $240,000.

On March 13, 1934, the gang entered the bank. Nelson stayed with the getaway car. One complication after another set in from the start. When the bank president, Willis Bagley, saw Van Meter approaching him with a gun he thought "a crazy man was loose." He ran into his office and locked the door. Van Meter, knowing Bagley had the key to the vault, fired several shots through the door but

The Dillinger gang at extradition hearing in Tuscon, 1/25/34: (left to right) Russell Clark, Charles Makley (shielding face), Harry Pierpont (head bent forward), John Dillinger.

Photos of John Dillinger at hearing in Crown Point Jail, Crown Point, Ind., March, 1934; Dillinger escaped from this "escape-proof" jail days later using a wooden gun to bluff his way past guards.

then gave up and began helping Hamilton and Dillinger clear out the cages.

A guard in a specially-equipped seven-foot steel cage above the main lobby then fired a tear-gas shell at Eddie Green. It hit Green in the back, almost knocking him down. He swung his machinegun around and sprayed the cage. Some of the bullets went through a tiny slot and hit guard Tom Walters.

A female customer, minus one shoe, ran from the bank and down an alleyway where she bumped into a short man wearing a cap. "Get to work and notify somebody," she screamed. "The bank is being held up!"

"Lady, you're telling me?" Baby Face Nelson said, and waved her back with his machinegun.

Meanwhile John Hamilton faced a dilemma. Inside the bank, cashier Harry Fisher stood on the other side of a locked, barred door from Hamilton. The vault was to Fisher's back. Since Hamilton could not open the door, he ordered Fisher to pass the money through the bars of the door to him. Fisher wisely began handing him stacks of one dollar bills.

Dillinger was in the street outside, guarding prisoners. An elderly policeman, John Shipley, could see him from his third-floor office. Firing an old pistol, Shipley winged Dillinger in the arm. The outlaw whirled about and let loose a burst from his machinegun. His bullets spattered off the face of the bank building. Shipley was unhurt, having ducked back into his office after firing his one shot.

"Tell them it's time to leave," Dillinger yelled to Van Meter who rushed into the bank.

Hamilton was frantically waving his pistol at Cashier Fisher. The bandit could see stacks and stacks of currency just inside the vault where Fisher stood.

"Open up this door," Hamilton yelled.

"I can't," Fisher lied. "I already told you I don't have the key. All I can do is continue to shove the money out through the bars." He passed several more stacks of one dollar bills to Hamilton.

Van Meter was at the bank door. "Let's go!"

"If you don't hurry up, I'm going to shoot you," Hamilton told Fisher.

"C'mon!" Van Meter yelled.

"Just give me another minute!" Hamilton yelled back. Then to Fisher: "Gimme the big bills!" Fisher kept handing him one dollar bills.

"We're going now!" Van Meter almost screamed.

"It's hell to leave all that money in there!" Hamilton's sack contained only $20,000 in small bills. There was still about $200,000 in full view behind the bars in the vault.

Gritting his teeth John Hamilton turned around and ran from the bank. The crafty Fisher sighed, and closed the vault door, fondly patting it in relief.

The moment Hamilton ran from the bank, Shipley, back at his window, fired another round and wounded the outlaw in the shoulder. He and Dillinger rounded a corner and ran to a large Buick in which the rest of the gang waited. Twenty hostages were on the running boards, fenders, and back bumper, holding on to the back window frame where the glass had been removed.

One hostage was on the ground, bleeding from a leg wound. Dillinger looked at Nelson, who was nearby holding a gun. "Did you have to do that?"

Nelson shrugged.

The car took off at a slow speed, sagging under the weight of the six gang members and twenty hostages. The police did not pursue closely; it was hopeless. Only the hostages would get killed in a running gunfight, thought Police Chief E. J. Patton. Patton's car followed at a safe distance but several times Nelson got out and fired bursts from his machinegun. The police finally gave up, turning into a farmer's driveway.

Taking back roads and moving at twenty-five miles an hour, the Buick let off its last reluctant passenger two hours later. The gang then headed for St. Paul. The raid netted the outlaws a little over $52,000. John Hamilton brooded all the way to the Twin Cities. "I should have killed that man," he finally said.

The city health officer for St. Paul, Dr. N. G. Mortenson, treated the mild shoulder wounds Dillinger and Hamilton had received in the robbery. Mortensen thought of calling the police but was sure Homer Van Meter, who was fondling a machinegun, would return and kill him.

FBI agents, however, had gotten a tip that a Carl Hellman was living in a rooming house somewhere in St. Paul with a woman they thought to be Billie Frechette. Hellman answered Dillinger's description.

While they worked to pinpoint Dillinger's hideout, the outlaw rested, recuperating from his wound and writing letters to his family in Indiana. In one letter to his sister Audrey, Dillinger revealed his sense of self-confidence, boasting easily about his escape from Crown Point. The letter read:

"Dear Sis:

I thought I would write a few lines and let you know I am still perculating. Don't worry about me honey, for that won't help any, and besides I am having a lot of fun. I am sending Emmett [Audrey's husband, Emmett Hancock] my wooden gun and I want him to always keep it. I see that Deputy Blunk says I had a real forty five thats just a lot of hooey to cover up because they don't like to admit that I locked eight deputys and a dozen trustys up with my wooden gun before I got my hands on the two machineguns and you should have seen their faces. Ha! Ha! Ha! Don't part with my wooden gun for any price. For when you feel blue all you have to do is look at the gun and laugh your blues away. Ha! Ha! I will be around to see all of you when the roads are better, it is so hot around Indiana now that I would have trouble getting through so I am sending my wife Billie [Dillinger had not married Billie Frechette]. She will have a hundred dollars for you and a hundred dollars for Norman [another Dillinger relative]. I'll give you enough money for a new car the next time I come around. I told Bud [his half-brother Hubert] I would get him one and I want to get Dad one. Now honey if any of you need any thing I wont forgive you if you dont let me know. I got shot a week ago but I am all right now just a little sore. I bane one tough sweed. Ha! Ha! Well honey I guess I'll close for the time give my love to all and I hope I can see you soon. Lots of love from Johnnie."

Not only was it impossible for Dillinger to go to his family in Indiana but he realized that his friends—Pierpont, Clark, and Makley—were doomed. There was no way to reach them either.

Pierpont's trial in Lima, O. for the murder of Jess Sarber was clear cut. Witnesses testi-

fied seeing him shoot the Sheriff. Pierpont's mother swore her son was with her at home in Leipsic eating dinner at the time the Sheriff was killed. She took great pains to hide Harry behind her scarf when newsmen tried to snap his photo.

On the stand, Pierpont lashed out at the prosecutor: "I'm not the kind of man you are, robbing widows and orphans. You'd probably be like me if you had the nerve."

He was found guilty and sentenced to die in the electric chair.

Makley called to Pierpont from his cell after the trial, "What was it, Harry?"

" Well, what would it be?" Pierpont responded dolefully.

Makley was tried next. He, too, was found guilty of murder and sentenced to death.

When Makley walked past Pierpont's cell, Handsome Harry looked up and asked, "What did you get, Charley?"

Makley proceeded to his cell in a slow shuffle, phlegmatically chewing a large wad of gum. "I got everything." Then he add philosophically, "We all have to die once." Russell Clark was sentenced to life imprisonment.

The guards around the Lima Jail were made up of vigilantes, local and state officers and a company of national guardsmen. Heavy machineguns were mounted on the rooftops about the jail. Gigantic search lights lit up all approaches to the prison. Authorities insisted Dillinger was coming to free his friends with an army of desperadoes.

Dillinger, on the other hand, had his own troubles. Agents R. L. Nalls and R. C. Coulter finally discovered that Dillinger and Billie were living in the Lincoln Court Apartments in St. Paul. They went in after their man on the night of March 31, 1934.

Billie answered their knock and explained that her husband, Carl Hellman was asleep and she was not dressed. They insisted they talk with Carl. Billie told them to wait, relocked the door and ran into the bedroom, telling Dillinger that policemen were outside. He got dressed hurriedly and grabbed a machinegun.

Waiting on the other side of the door, the FBI agents were startled to see a man coming up the stairs.

"Who are you?" Coulter asked the young man.

Homer Van Meter smiled disarmingly. "I'm

a soap salesman."

"Yeah?" Coulter said, eyeing him. "Where are your samples?"

"In my car. Come down stairs and I'll prove my identity to you."

Coulter followed Van Meter down the stairs. At the first floor Van Meter whirled about, displaying an ugly-looking pistol. "You asked for it, so I'll give it to you!"

Coulter ran for the front door and raced down the stairs. The outlaw was so nonplussed that he did not fire. Remembering the other lawman upstairs, Van Meter himself ran out to the street, jumped on a horse-drawn delivery wagon, donned the driver's cap and whipped the horses down the street, a unique getaway for a modern bandit.

Agent Cummings, who had gone downstairs to investigate, left the way clear for Dillinger and Billie to escape via a flight of back stairs. The outlaw sprayed the hallway with his machinegun just to be sure. Cummings followed him out and shot him in the leg from the back door but Dillinger managed to get into his Hudson Terraplane and backed it out of the alleyway at high speed.

Eddie Green found another doctor to treat John's leg wound. The gang then decided to leave St. Paul. It was getting too hot. Pat Reilly, a fringe member of the gang, told Dillinger about a quiet resort he knew of in Wisconsin called Little Bohemia. It wouldn't officially open until May. They could all go there and rest up without being disturbed. Who would look for them at a remote fishing resort?

First Dillinger took a quick trip to Chicago with Billie. He told his lawyer Piquett to keep certain monies available; he would be going on a long trip. From there, Dillinger and Van Meter raided the police station in Warsaw, Indiana, taking several guns and bullet-proof vests.

The gang then drove into the woods of Wisconsin to Little Bohemia Lodge to relax and plan another robbery.

Melvin Purvis, head of the FBI office in Chicago, got a tip from a resort owner in Rhinelander, Wis. that Dillinger was staying at Little Bohemia. Within hours he moved dozens of his agents from Chicago and St. Paul to the Wisconsin woodlands. The group converged upon the lodge on the night of April 22, 1934.

When Purvis led his men against the front of the lodge, three customers emerged and climbed into a parked car. As the car's engine started, Purvis called out for the men to stop, but they failed to hear the warning. A shower of bullets followed and Eugene Boiseneau, a CCC worker, was killed on the spot, his two companions wounded.

Hearing the gunfire, Dillinger, Van Meter, Carroll, and Hamilton raced out the back, running along the shore in the moonlight. Baby Face Nelson, in a cabin nearby with his wife Helen, emerged and fired some random shots at Purvis and then disappeared into the woods.

The FBI pounded the lodge all night thinking the gangsters were still inside. By morning, their only captives were the gang's girls who had been hiding in the basement.

Dillinger, Hamilton, and Van Meter stole a car and drove out of the trap to St. Paul. Nelson, after killing an FBI agent at another resort, stole a car and headed for Chicago. Tommy Carroll stole yet another car and drove to Michigan.

The FBI fiasco put Purvis and J. Edgar Hoover on the spot. The raid did nothing but cause the death of an innocent man, an FBI agent, and the destruction of a fishing lodge.

Hoover placed a shoot-to-kill order out on Dillinger and a $10,000 reward. Another $10,-000 was offered by five states where Dillinger had robbed banks.

In the next two months half a dozen men who looked like Dillinger were arrested or almost shot. The bandit, however, was nowhere to be found. He appeared briefly at his father's farm for a Sunday chicken dinner in May. At that time, the outlaw told the elderly Dillinger that he was going on a long trip and that he wouldn't have "to worry" about him anymore.

When the Merchants National Bank of South Bend, Ind. was robbed on June 30, 1934, the FBI and local police insisted that Dillinger had done the job. Not only that, but his companions in the robbery were identified by police as Baby Face Nelson and Pretty Boy Floyd.

All evidence points to the fact that Dillinger, Nelson, and Floyd did not commit this robbery. Nelson was already on his way to California, thoroughly unnerved by the Little Bohemia raid and seeking isolation. Floyd was in Ohio at the time. And Dillinger was on the road north, heading toward Minnesota to make certain contacts in preparation for a trip West.

In early July, 1934, Chicago Police Captain John Stege was approached by Detective Sergeant Martin Zarkovich of the East Chicago, Ind. Police Dept. Zarkovich told Stege he could, through his long-time friend and whorehouse madam, Anna Sage, deliver Dillinger. There was, however, one condition. Dillinger had to be killed, not taken alive.

Stege refused, kicking Zarkovich out of his office and telling him: "I'd even give John Dillinger a chance to surrender."

Next Zarkovich went to the FBI. Purvis jumped at the plan. Anna Sage would set up Dillinger, Zarkovich stated, but the FBI had to promise to stop deportation proceedings then being enacted against her. Purvis promised.

On the night of July 22, 1934, Anna Sage, the much publicized "Lady in Red," led a young man named "James Lawrence" into the FBI trap outside of the Biograph Theater. He was to shot to death (by Zarkovich) as he left the theater.

The FBI called in the press and announced to the world that John Dillinger was dead.

The author has extensively written about this aspect of the Dillinger case in another book and cannot, for reasons of space, detail the miasmic proportions of this underworld plot. James Lawrence, killed by Martin Zarkovich outside the Biograph Theater could not have been, according to this evidence, John Dillinger.

An autopsy of the dead man (which was missing for three decades) performed by Dr. J. J. Kearns, the Cook County Coroner's chief pathologist, utterly disproved James Lawrence's corpse as being Dillinger's. Lawrence's eyes were brown. Dillinger's eyes were blue. The dead man possessed a rheumatic heart condition chronic since childhood, Dillinger did not. (It would have been impossible for Dillinger to play baseball, join the Navy or perform his athletic bank-robbing feats with such a condition.) Lawrence was shorter and heavier than Dillinger would have been. He also lacked all of Dillinger's scars, wounds and birthmarks. His face was not altered through plastic surgery as explained by the FBI (to compensate for his obvious facial differences

Crooked cop Martin Zarkovich (in car) from East Chicago, Ind., shown with Anna Sage, the so-called "Lady in Red," set up the phony assassination at the Biograph Theater in July, 1934, a killing which effected Dillinger's permanent escape.

with that of Dillinger's).

The fingerprint card offered up by the FBI alleging that Dillinger's and the dead man's fingerprints were one in the same was obviously "planted" in the Cook County Morgue days before the killing.

The FBI was simply duped into believing the dead man was Dillinger and then had to cover up their error after the shooting.

Who then was Jimmy Lawrence? From what this writer has been able to determine he was a small time hoodlum who came from Wisconsin to Chicago about 1930. He was seen in the neighborhood of the Biograph for at least two years, long before John Dillinger, inmate 13225 of the Michigan City Prison, was ever paroled.

That he was involved in an underworld scheme to provide Dillinger with a permanent escape there is no doubt. Whether or not he was a willing dupe to the Sage-Zarkovich plot (both had a fifteen-year record of strong ties to the underworld) is unknown. Perhaps, because of his heart condition, Lawrence may have volunteered for the role. That, too, is unknown.

But it is known that John Herbert Dillinger,

Execution scene, 7/22/34, minutes after "James Lawrence" was shot down four doors south (right in photo) of the Biograph Theater by Martin Zarkovich; swarms of FBI agents led by Melvin Purvis were about the theater that night, claiming they had shot Dillinger.

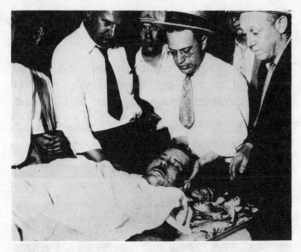

"James Lawrence" in the morgue, his head held up for photos by Dr. Charles D. Parker; dead man had brown eyes, Dillinger's were blue.

a pragmatic but spectacular escape artist, eluded the law in the end.

The last Dillinger gang went to pieces in late 1934. Tommy Carroll was killed by policemen in Waterloo, Iowa, June 5, 1934. Eddie Green was shot in the back by FBI officials April 3, 1934. Homer Van Meter was gunned down in an alleyway, betrayed by friends, in St. Paul, August 23, 1934. Baby Face Nelson, in a wild shoot-out with two FBI men (both killed by him) was shot to death

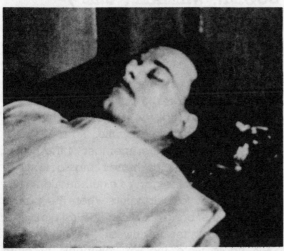

Another morgue photo of "James Lawrence"; to explain the differences in facial appearance between Lawrence and Dillinger, FBI offered preposterous theories about plastic surgery.

Dillinger's favorite girl friend, Evelyn "Billie" Frechette, with a man who bears an amazing resemblance to "James Lawrence"; this photo was taken from Billie's purse when she was arrested in Chicago short months before the Biograph shooting.

near Barrington, Ill., November 27, 1934. John Hamilton's body was never found; reports have it that after receiving a fatal wound in a fight with police, his body was buried in an isolated quarry outside of Aurora, Ill. in April, 1934. Russell Clark was paroled in 1970 and died of cancer months later.

In September, 1934, Pierpont and Makley tried to duplicate Dillinger's Crown Point ruse. They carved pistols from cakes of soap and attempted to escape death row in the Ohio State Penitentiary in Columbus. Makley was shot to death and Pierpont wounded.

The following month Handsome Harry Pierpont sat down almost jubilantly in the electric chair. Through a wide smile he said: "Today I am the only man who knows the 'who's and how's' and as my end comes very shortly, I'll take this little story with me."

[ALSO SEE Baby Face Nelson]

DI VARCO, JOSEPH VINCENT ("LITTLE CAESAR")
Syndicate Gangster ● (1911-1988)

Long connected with Las Vegas gambling, DiVarco was well established in the hierarchy of the Chicago Mafia-syndicate. His record of arrests dates back to 1937 and includes conspiracy to bribe a juror, fraudulent voting, and suspicion of many gang murders. He served one year in the federal prison at Milan, Mich. for counterfeiting.

DiVarco controlled Chicago's lucrative Near North Side, including the Rush Street area.

He is alleged to have fulfilled several murder contracts for mob boss Sam Giancana.

DOANE GANG

Led by rail-thin Moses Doane and his five brothers, the Doanes were the first important outlaw band in the country, rising from the turmoil of the Revolutionary War. The Doanes mounted on fast horses, raided the Bucks County, Pa. area and sometimes roamed as far east as New Jersey, operating at their peak around 1780.

The gang numbered anywhere from sixteen to twenty men, big, raw-boned highwaymen all. The Doanes specialized in robbery, their biggest strike being the raid on Newton, Pa. in October, 1781, when they forced county treasurer John Hart to turn over close to $2,000 to them. (The robbers stopped at the schoolhouse in the center of town and by lantern light counted their loot, giggling like small boys.

Moses, Abe, and Levy Doane (also spelled Doan) were Tories and worked for the British cause when the mood suited them; they struck down colonial tax collectors in the name of England but kept the proceeds for themselves. This gang's reign of terror ended in the late 1780s when several members were appre-

hended and hanged. Abraham and Levy Doane were hanged at Philadelphia Commons in 1788, Moses shortly thereafter.

The most dashing member of the band, James Fitzpatrick, known as "Sandy Flash," eluded several manhunts but was taken in 1787 and hanged.

DONNELLY, EDWARD
Murderer ● (? -1808)

A habitual wife-beater, Donnelly went too far one night in early February, 1808, killing his wife Catherine. Though the poor woman let out piercing screams, the neighbors living in Carlisle, Pa. thought little of it. "There's Ned licking his wife again," one resident was reported to have said.

Donnelly, upon discovering he had murdered his wife, then dissected the body and burned it piece by piece for two days. Teeth and jawbone were discovered in the ashes of his fireplace and this led to his downfall. He confessed at his trial and was hanged February 8, 1808 in Carlisle before a throng of four thousand—who were in a disagreeable temper due to inclement weather.

DOOLIN, WILLIAM ("BILL")
Trainrobber, Bankrobber ● (1863-1896)

Either luck or apprehension caused Bill Doolin's horse to pull up "lame" before he followed the Dalton brothers into the death trap at Coffeyville, Kan. in 1892. He was the only regular member of the Dalton gang to survive that bandit massacre and, upon hearing of the gang's extermination, rode furiously back to Oklahoma where he put together another band of outlaws, the last significant bandit gang in the Southwest.

His riders were the last elements of other

gangs which had been systematically destroyed by an increasingly vigilant citizenry, relentless detective agencies, and modernized law enforcement organizations.

Bill Dalton, last of the outlaw brothers, forsaking his family in California, journeyed East and joined Doolin. Train robber Dan Clifton, known as "Dynamite Dick" came in; so did George "Bitter Creek" Newcomb, George "Red Buck" Weightman, Jack Blake (alias Tulsa Jack), Charley Pierce, "Little Bill" Raidler, Roy Daugherty (alias Arkansas Tom), and Dick West (alias Little Dick).

For more than three years this formidable band swept through the Oklahoma territory robbing stages, banks, and trains. They headquartered in the small town of Ingalls, Okla., where the residents protected them from the prying eyes of Pinkertons, Rangers, and marshals (and where they spent their loot).

On September 1, 1893, a dozen marshals, hidden in a wagon, entered Ingalls for a showdown with the gang. Bitter Creek Newcomb spotted the wagon, called to Doolin and the others, and the battle of Ingalls was on. After several hours of trading lead, the outlaw band moved out, Newcomb and Red Buck wounded and riding double on the horses of their friends. Three marshals had been killed.

Doolin, a good-natured bandit who once prevented the murderous Red Buck from shooting Marshal Bill Tilghman from ambush, hit some big strikes in 1894, his largest haul—$40,000—taken from a bank in East Texas.

A super posse headed by lawmen Chris Madsen, Heck Thomas, and Tilghman went after the gang in a chase that stretched through three states. The Doolins never rested, knowing that the posse, financed by the railroads and banks they had robbed, was always behind them.

Tilghman was so close once that Doolin and his boys barely finished breakfast before an informer rushed into a farm house to announce that the lawmen were thundering toward them, only a few miles distant. Doolin told the farmer, who thought his outlaws part of a posse, that "the other boys" coming up the road would be hungry, too, and that they would pay for the meals.

When Tilghman, Madsen and Thomas appeared on lathered mounts, the farmer greeted them with an affable smile and said: "The others said you'd be along. We got dinner ready." The lawmen ate the dinner and reluctantly paid the price for both meals—their own and what the Doolin gang had eaten before them.

In 1895, the gang separated. Tilghman tracked down Little Bill Raidler in October on a ranch near the Osage Indian territory and brought him in after a wild gun duel in which Raidler was severely wounded. He was given a ten-year prison sentence but was paroled on Tilghman's recommendation when he developed an incurable disease.

Red Buck was next, killed while attempting to rob a bank. Doolin, who had married in 1894, first hid out with his wife and baby, but felt moving about with his family was too risky. He rode alone to Eureka Springs, Ark. Tilghman found him there and, in a slugfest inside of a public bathhouse, subdued the outlaw and brought him back to Guthrie, Okla. to stand trial.

Doolin's reputation was such that when Tilghman arrived with the bandit, 5,000 residents at the train depot cheered wildly—not for the marshal, but the outlaw. The federal jail couldn't hold Bill Doolin; he broke out weeks later and thirty-seven prisoners escaped with him.

His freedom was brief. Doolin joined his wife, bought a small farm and hoped he could live out his life in obscurity. Then Marshal Heck Thomas found him walking down a dirt road one night in 1896 and killed him with a single blast from his shotgun.

Oklahoma trainrobber Bill Doolin, shown dead after being gunned down by Marshal Heck Thomas in 1896. (Western History Collection, U. of Okla. Library)

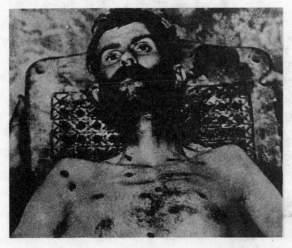

DOSS, NANNIE
Serial Killer ● (1906-1965)

The reason why grandmotherly Nannie Doss murdered eleven people was summed up by the poisoner herself: "I was searching for the perfect mate, the real romance of life." This statement proved puzzling in that only four of Doss's victims had been her husbands. The others included her two infant children, her mother, two sisters, and the nephew of one of her deaceased husbands.

Doss, a native of Tulsa, Oklahoma, was an outgoing, friendly person who married for the first time in 1920 to George Frazer. One day Frazer returned home to find his two small children dead on the floor. They had been "accidentally" poisoned by Nannie. Frazer left town, fearing for his own life.

Nannie's next husband, Frank Harrelson, died of "stomach trouble" a short time after the nuptials. Her third spouse, Arlie Lanning, married Nannie in 1947. He survived until 1952 when he, too, succumbed to "stomach trouble." Richard Morton, Nannie's fourth husband, died of the same persistent ailment shortly after the marriage.

Samuel Doss was next. He died of "stomach trouble" after eating a bowl of Nannie's specially prepared stewed prunes. Unlike the deaths of previous husbands where doctors routinely filled out death certificates mostly dictated by Nannie, Dr. N. Z. Schwelbein became suspicious of the causes that brought death to Sam Doss. He told Nannie that he wanted to conduct an autopsy.

"Whatever he had might kill someone else," Nannie Doss shrugged. "It's best to find out."

Dr. Schwelbein did find out. Doss was loaded with enough arsenic to kill a dozen men. The bodies of Nannie's other husbands and those of other relatives were exhumed and examined. All had been killed with arsenic.

Police interrogated Nannie who had a hard time remembering anything. "I never heard of any Richard Morton," she said when answering questions about her fourth spouse.

"What?" said a detective. "You don't remember your previous husband?"

"Oh, that Richard Morton," replied Nannie. "Yes, I was married to him."

Nannie Doss grew weary of the questioning and finally admitted murdering the husbands and relatives, eleven in number. She remembered feeding Arlie Lanning rat poison for breakfast. She remembered collecting insurance premiums on the lives of her husband but was quick to state that she had not poisoned these men for money alone. "They were dullards," she complained, and not anything like the perfect husbands described in *True Romance*, her favorite magazine.

Nannie Doss went to prison for life where she died of leukemia in 1965. Her cell was strewn with copies of thumb-worn romance magazines.

Tulsa serial killer Nannie Doss with her daughter and grand children at the time of her murder trial.

DRUCCI, VINCENT ("THE SCHEMER")
Bootlegger, Jewel Thief ● (1885-1927)

Close friend of Chicago gangster Dion O'Bannion, Drucci began his criminal career as a teenager by robbing coins from telephone boxes. He graduated to safe-cracking with O'Bannion, George "Bugs" Moran, and Earl "Hymie" Weiss, who formed the leadership of the North Side Irish gang dominating Chicago's Forty-second and Forty-third Wards.

This cold-blooded killer got his sobriquet from his fanciful, wild schemes to rob banks and kidnap wealthy citizens. When O'Bannion went to war with Capone and the Genna brothers over certain Chicago bootleg territories, Drucci, along with Weiss, became a chief enforcer. Drucci was known as the "Shootin' Fool" of the outfit.

He is credited by Chicago Police as being the killer of at least two Capone-Genna gangsters, Giuseppe Nerone, better known as "The Cavalier," a Capone man, on July 8, 1925 and Samuzzo "Samoots" Amatuna, a Genna satellite who had set himself up as president of *Unione Siciliane* and was murdered November 11, 1925.

Drucci and a henchman of the West Side O'Donnell clan, Jim Doherty (the O'Donnells and the O'Bannionites had by then joined forces against the Capone-Genna forces) found Samoots in a Cicero barber shop getting a shave and a haircut. Drucci waded in immediately firing four shots from his pistol. Jim Doherty added another four shots for good measure. Samoots tried to avoid execution by hiding behind the barber chair but was fatally wounded. Hospitalized he begged that he be allowed to marry his childhood sweetheart, Rose Pecorara. Samoots died in his hospital bed, half-way through the wedding ceremony. Drucci sent a large floral piece to his funeral.

In 1926, Capone made a concerted effort to rid himself of the plaguing North Siders. On August 10, 1926, he sent gunman Louis Barko and three others to kill Drucci and Hymie Weiss. At 9 a.m. that morning, Weiss breakfasted with Drucci in the latter's eighth-floor suite at the Congress Hotel. The two gangsters then took a leisurely stroll down Michigan Avenue, heading for the Standard Oil Building on Ninth Street.

At the entrance of the building, four men jumped from a car and ran toward the O'Bannionites with drawn automatics, Barko in the lead. Weiss and Drucci pulled their guns, hiding behind a parked car. The street erupted with gunfire. Windows were smashed. Concrete flew in great chunks from buildings as bullets chipped and whanged into them. Thousands of horrified shoppers saw the shooting. Some ran. Some threw themselves to the pavement. Others merely stood frozen in terror.

Weiss backed away down the line of cars. Drucci did not, advancing toward his sworn enemies, pistol cracking. The four would-be assassins were driven back to their double-parked car by Drucci's fire. They climbed on the running board to get better aim. Drucci, on the sidewalk by then, danced wildly about like a fighter shadow-boxing to avoid their shots. Bullets snapped and clunked at his feet. He laughed hysterically and banged away at the Capone men.

Thirty shots had been fired and none of the participants were hit; James Cardan, a spectator, was slightly wounded in the leg.

A police car roared up with a squad of men and the four Capone gunmen fled in their sedan. Drucci was not content to allow their retreat. He jumped on the running board of a passing auto.

"Follow that goddamn car," he yelled at the driver, wagging his fierce-looking weapon. Police ran after him and dragged him to the pavement.

"What the hell is this, Drucci?" a policeman who recognized the gangster asked.

"It wasn't no gang fight," Schemer blurted. "A stickup, that's all. They wanted my roll." When police searched him they discovered amid "whews" and whistles that Drucci's roll consisted of $13,500. The lawmen surmised that Drucci and Weiss were headed for the offices of Morris Eller, political boss of the Twentieth Ward, to make a protection payoff for their illegal speakeasies.

Eller emphatically denied any such hanky-panky.

Louis Barko (alias Valerie) was picked up by police and brought in front of Drucci. "I never seen him before," The Schemer snarled.

Vincent "The Schemer" Drucci was known as "The Shootin' Fool" of the Dion O'Bannion Gang. (UPI)

All were released.

Five days later, Capone's men tried again, almost at the same time and spot, shooting volley after volley at Drucci and Weiss as they once again tried to enter the Standard Oil Building. This time the pair were attacked as they drove down Michigan Avenue in a large sedan. They elected to run for it, deserting the bullet-smashed car and finding sanctuary in an office building.

Drucci, Weiss, and Moran then gave their violent retort to Scarface Al. On September 20, 1926, the trio led eight cars full of men past Capone's headquarters, the Hawthorn Hotel, and at high noon, stood on the sidewalk with blazing machineguns and riddled the place with more than a thousand bullets.

Louis Barko was the only gang casualty, wounded in the arm as he stood in the hotel lobby—by none other than Vincent "The Schemer" Drucci. When Drucci was brought before him by police, he returned The Schemer's compliment. "Never saw him before," Barko snapped.

During the following election year, Drucci labored hard to get William Hale "Big Bill" Thompson elected. His tactics were a bit unorthodox. The Schemer didn't bother with canvassing voters. He terrorized the political bigwigs backing incumbent Mayor Dever. One such person was Dorsey R. Crowe, Alderman of the Forty-second Ward. Drucci broke into Crowe's offices on April 4, 1927 and wrecked the place, beating up Crowe's secretary. The Schemer had planned to kidnap Alderman Crowe and keep him incommunicado until after the election on April 5.

Police Lieutenant William Liebeck and a squad of men picked Drucci up on the corner of Diversey Parkway and Clark Street that afternoon. With him were two aides, Henry Finkelstein and Albert Single. A .45 automatic was taken from The Schemer's inside pocket; all three men were arrested for creating mayhem and taken to a local station. After twenty minutes of grilling ("I don't know nothin' coppers," was Drucci's favorite response), The Schemer was ordered to go to the Criminal Courts Building where his ever-available lawyer, Maurice Green, was waiting with a writ of *habeas corpus*.

Four officers—Danny Healy, Matthew Cunningham, Dennis Kehoe, and a driver packed up Drucci and his friends for the trip downtown. Healy was a tough cop who abided no back-talk from gangsters. Months before he had shot it out toe-to-toe with three bandits on Armitage Avenue, killing one and driving the others off. A chunky man, Healy had also taken on giant gangster Polack Joe Saltis with his fists and reduced Joe to bleeding pulp. He would tolerate no guff from Drucci and told him so.

The Schemer's violent temper exploded in the police car during the trip. "Nobody talks that way to me, cop," Drucci said, working up his anger. "You son-of-a-bitch. I'll get you. I'll wait on your doorstep for you!"

"Shut your mouth and sit back," Healy ordered.

"Go on, you kid copper. I'll fix you for this!"

Healy held his gun steady on Drucci. "I said shut up."

"You take your gun off me or I'll kick hell out of you!"

Healy only stared. Then Drucci stood up on one leg and swiped his fist down against Healy's right temple, screaming: "I'll take you and your tool [pistol]! I'll fix you!" The Schemer reached down for the revolver in Healy's right hand. The policeman shifted the weapon to his left hand and fired four shots into Drucci at point blank range.

The 31-year-old hoodlum fell to the floor of the police car cursing Healy. He died within minutes, an oddball gangster demise that elated Capone and saved his torpedoes from further gunplay with the Shootin' Fool.

When Maurice Green's client arrived at the Criminal Courts Building, he was a stiffening corpse. Green wanted Healy arrested for murder.

Chief of Detectives William Shoemaker ("Old Shoes") snorted: "I don't know anything about anyone being murdered. I know Drucci was killed trying to take a gun away from an officer. We're having a medal made for Healy."

Drucci's funeral was as lavish as any gangster sendoff of the 1920s. He was placed in a $10,000 silver and aluminum casket and lay in state at Sbarbaro's Funeral Home for a day and a night. (Sbarbaro was also Assistant State Attorney; his funeral home received all the business from the North Side mob. He had buried gangleader Dion O'Bannion and his aide, Hymie Weiss.)

Flowers worth $30,000 surrounded the casket. Drucci's weeping widow, Cecilia, placed a heart of blood-red roses at his feet. Her card read, "To My Darling Husband." A broken wheel of white and purple flowers was placed at his head by gang buddy (and last of the O'Bannion leaders), George "Bugs" Moran, with an inscription reading: "Our Pal."

The Schemer was put to rest at Mount Carmel Cemetery. As Cecilia Drucci, a pretty blonde flapper with beestung lips, walked from the graveyard, she smiled at reporters and quipped: "A policeman murdered him, but we sure gave him a grand funeral."

[ALSO SEE Al Capone, George "Bugs" Moran, Dion O'Bannion, *Union Siciliane*, Earl "Hymie" Weiss.]

DRUGGAN-LAKE GANG (THE VALLEY GANG)

Terry Druggan and his oafish partner Frankie Lake looked at all times like two businessmen down on their luck. These two terrorist-killers controlled a vast West Side area between Chicago's Little Italy and Cicero during Prohibtion and were staunch allies of Al Capone during the bootleg wars, the only Irish gang to side with Scarface.

Their mob was built upon the remnants of the Old Valley Gang, begun in the early 1890s, a group of labor sluggers which included "Big Heinie" Miller, Walter "Runty" Quinlan, and Paddy "The Bear" Ryan—guns for hire to the highest bidder. Druggan, dwarfish in size, and Lake apprenticed with the Valley Gang and by 1919 had taken over, controlling all the rackets in the area, specializing in burglary and booze.

Druggan was the leader, a lisping gangster devoted to wide-brimmed fedoras and horn-rimmed glasses. Lake mimicked his boss' style of dress and obeyed Druggan's every order, whether it was a beating or for murder. Frankie, who had been a fireman and later a railroad switchman, was a bumbling giant who through his awkward antics produced galloping guffaws in the underworld.

Both men were ardent Catholics and took their religion seriously. Once, while hijacking a truckload of beer in front of a church, Druggan identified the drivers as Jewish hoodlums. He and Lake pulled out their guns, jamming them into the driver's faces. Druggan thundered: "Hats off, you Jews when you're passing the house of God or I'll shoot them off!"

Prohibition made Druggan and Lake rich men, especially after wealthy brewer Joseph Stenson gave the pair a fifty per cent interest in his five mammoth breweries. They rode in chauffeur-driven limousines. Druggan's $12,000-a-year apartment boasted such luxuries as solid gold doorknobs and a solid silver toilet seat engraved with the gangster's initials.

In all of the wars with the Genna brothers, with the North Side O'Bannions, and with the South and West Side O'Donnell clans, the

Terry Druggan and Frankie Lake allied themselves with Capone in Chicago's bootleg wars; both went to jail, but

a well-bribed sheriff let them out during the day to conduct business as usual. (UPI)

Druggan-Lake mob fought with Capone. They supplied Capone with the best beer in town (except for the beer in the O'Bannion-controlled Forty-second and Forty-third Wards, which came from the quality-minded Sieben's Brewery). In return Capone surrounded their territory with a protective army of gunsels under the command of Danny Stanton.

Capone got a sizable chunk of the Druggan-Lake beer concessions, an estimated 40 per cent. In turn, Terry Druggan got protection. Capone-Stanton men such as Frank "Dutch" Carpenter, Raymond Cassidy, Thomas Johnson, Hughey "Stubby" McGovern, and the kill-crazy William "Gunner" Padden successfully fought off encroachments of rival gangs seeking to penetrate the Druggan-Lake domain. All of these torpedoes died in this effort before 1925.

With such muscle backing them up, Druggan and Lake operated at whim. Terry Druggan took a liking to a nightspot called Little Bohemia, owned by one Emil Wanatka. He walked into the bar one day and announced: "I'm in, Wanatka; you're out."

The feisty Wanatka told him to go to hell and began to walk up the stairs leading to his second-floor apartment. Druggan followed, scrambling after on stubby legs.

"You don't understand," Druggan yelled. "I'm taking over!" He grabbed at Wanatka's leg. The beefy young proprietor turned angrily about and landed a haymaker which knocked Druggan down the stairs. Druggan never carried a gun, but Frankie Lake and his other

boys did. The elfish gangster scurried off cursing, vowing that his partner would settle this business with Wanatka.

Emil brooded for a half hour and then realized the consequences of his impetuous act. He packed up his family, took the week's receipts out of his safe, hopped into a car, and drove at high speeds for the Wisconsin border. He never came back, establishing another Little Bohemia resort in the North woods of Wisconsin. He wanted no part of Terry Druggan or any other gangster. Ironically, Wanatka was to reluctantly host the John Dillinger gang in April, 1934, a visit that resulted in an abortive FBI raid to capture that gang and which all but destroyed his lodge. There seemed no way for Wanatka to avoid the limelight.

In 1924 a federal injunction against the Druggan-Lake-owned Standard Beverage Corporation was issued, ordering the firm to cease operations. After refusing to comply, both gangsters were sentenced to serve a year in Cook County Jail. They were unperturbed. They had connections. Corrupt Sheriff Peter Hoffman was glad to have the new guests stay at his jail, especially after the pair gave him $20,000 for "conveniences and considerations." To insure good treatment, political boss of the Twentieth Ward Morris Eller, told Hoffman to "treat the boys right."

Hardly a day of their sentence was spent in jail. When a reporter showed up to interview Druggan one morning, a jailer told him that "Mr. Druggan isn't in right now." The reporter asked to see Frankie Lake. "Mr. Lake is also out . . . an appointment downtown. They'll return after dinner."

The press exposed this ridiculous situation and Hoffman was fined $2,500 and sentenced to 30 days in jail. Such unorthodox political conduct in Prohibition-torn Chicago was typical and would remain long after Repeal. A latter-day Chicago alderman, Mathius "Paddy" Bauler, summed it all up with the words: "Chicago ain't ready for reform yet."

The Druggan-Lake machine ground to a halt in 1932 when both men were convicted of income-tax evasion and sent to Leavenworth. Druggan received two and a half years. Lake got eighteen months.

When they were released, the pair found their empire eaten up by other gangsters, particularly by members of the newly-formed syndicate. Big Al, their protector, was gone, doing a long stretch. He also neglected to pay his taxes. The duo became front men for the syndicate and died in obscurity during the 1950s.

DUNBAR, REUBEN A.
Murderer, Robber ● (1829-1850)

The Lester family in Albany, N. Y. was quite well-to-do, their estate including large farmlands and many other holdings. When the widowed Mr. Lester died, his stepson, Reuben A. Dunbar, 21, sought to gain control of the entire estate by killing his two young nephews Stephen V. Lester, 8, and David L. Lester, 10.

Dunbar killed little Stephen with a club and hanged David from a tree. With his relatives out of the way Dunbar filed a claim on the Lester property, but his victims' bodies quickly were discovered. Dunbar was tried and convicted after writing out a confession.

The would-be landowner was hanged September 28, 1850.

DURRANT, WILLIAM HENRY THEODORE ("THEO")
Murderer ● (1874-1898)

BACKGROUND: BORN AND RAISED IN SAN FRANCISCO. A SENIOR MEDICAL STUDENT AT COOPER MEDICAL COLLEGE. WORKED AS AN ASSISTANT SUNDAY SCHOOL SUPERINTENDENT AT THE EMANUEL BAPTIST CHURCH IN SAN FRANCISCO. DESCRIPTION: 5'5", BLUE EYES, BLACK HAIR, HEAVY MUSTACHE, SLENDER BUILD. ALIASES: NONE. RECORD: STRANGLED BLANCHE LAMONT TO DEATH 4/3/1895; KILLED AND MUTILATED MINNIE WILLIAMS 4/13/95; APPREHENDED AND TRIED IN 1895, FOUND GUILTY AND SENTENCED TO HANG; THREE YEARS OF LEGAL APPEALS UNTIL 1/7/98 WHEN THE EXECUTION WAS CARRIED OUT IN SAN FRANCISCO.

Nothing about Theo Durrant suggested impropriety, let alone the compulsion to murder. He was an excellent medical student at San Francisco's reputable Cooper Medical College. He was also a staunch pillar of his local church, Emanuel Baptist.

As an assistant Sunday-school superintendent, Theo was also appointed church librarian, was an usher at masses, and secretary to the church's youth group, Christian Endeavor. Minor duties about the church, located at 22nd and Bartlett Streets, included fixing pews and sealing leaky pipes. To perform these chores, Durrant was given the master key to the church.

Though Theo was the image of virtue to his fellow parishioners, something dark and sinister lurked beneath his religious veneer. The first evidence that all was not right with Theo came to light in early 1895. A young woman of the congregation, at Theo's request, entered the church library after services. He asked her to wait for a moment while he checked on a few things. She waited. Moments later, Theo reappeared before her stark naked, grinning. The woman ran screaming from the church.

The woman's charges of indecency were whispered to her friends but nothing was done. Theo Durrant's reputation with the church congregation was impeccable. Even the gossip that he attempted to kiss young ladies at church socials was pooh-poohed.

On April 3, 1895, at about 4 p.m., several members of the congregation saw Durrant alight from a cable car near the church. One of the prettiest girls in the neighborhood, buxom Blanche Lamont, was with Theo, walking arm-in-arm. Blanche was a senior high school student. As the pair walked into the wooden church, Blanche talked of her dream to become a teacher.

Durrant led Blanche into the library. There, to the young girl's amazement, he stripped. She screamed, but unlike her predecessor, she did not run. Blanche's screams only served to incite Theo's anger—he dove for her neck, his powerful hands squeezing the life from her.

When her limp body fell forward, Theo grabbed Blanche by the waist and, as one would carry a cord of wood, carted her into an ante-room where he dressed. He then carried Blanche's body slowly up the steep stairs leading to the church belfry. He had to make the final ascent with a ladder, hauling Blanche up after him by her waist-length hair.

There, Durrant stripped the body and sexually assaulted it. After indulging himself, Theo put a wooden block under the dead girl's head—a makeshift pillow—folded her arms, and calmly climbed down. Downstairs, an organist, who had arrived early for practice, became alarmed at Durrant's appearance.

"I was fixing a gas jet and inhaled some fumes by mistake," he explained.

When Blanche's disappearance was noted the following day, authorities came to Theo. He had been seen with the girl. Did he know her whereabouts?

Durrant denied any such knowledge and then theorized for police that it was quite possible that poor Blanche had been seized by one of the roving gangs of white slavers then plaguing San Francisco and sold to a brothel in a foreign city.

Implausible as this idea seems today, such events were common in the 1890s, particularly in the still unsettled West Coast. The police were satisfied with Durrant's explanation and the church-going Theo became, for a while, a local celebrity. Young girls excited with the thought of being shanghaied approached Durrant, enamored with his white slaver theories.

One girl was petite Minnie Williams, 21, an attractive blonde. Theo made the same advances toward her as he had toward Blanche but Minnie happily responded. Later evidence revealed that the two met many times in the

church library and had intercourse. The odd thing was that Theo Durrant still killed Minnie.

The reason for his second murder was never given but one report has it that Theo had admitted his murder of Blanche to Minnie and she threatened to tell the police.

Minnie's death was painful. While making love to her, Theo suddenly tore part of her dress away and jammed it violently down the girl's throat, asphyxiating her. Durrant then produced a knife and slashed Minnie's throat, forehead, and wrists. Following this orgy of blood letting, Theo mutilated the body for over an hour with his knife. He was not satiated until he threw himself upon the corpse and had intercourse.

It was not until the next morning that some of the congregation, entering the library, discovered the gory scene. The walls and floor of the library were crusted with blotches of Minnie's blood.

Answering the screams of the church women, police quickly discovered Minnie's body in a closet. One of the detectives followed a hunch and climbed to the belfry where he saw the naked body of Blanche Lamont. "The body was white," he remarked later, "like a piece of marble."

Theo was brought in for questioning. He denied any knowledge of the two hideous murders. Police, however, found Minnie's purse in his closet, stuffed into a suitcoat.

Over one hundred witnesses testified at Durrant's trial. The accused himself testified, still claiming innocence, but the jury quickly condemned him. Appeals dragged on for three years and on January 7, 1898, Durrant's time ran out.

He mounted the scaffold in a dignified manner. As the sheriff approached him, Durrant aloofly stated: "Don't put that rope on, my boy, until I talk." His remark was ignored (and future historians were left to guess what mad Theo might have said). The sheriff ordered the hangman to continue and Durrant was abruptly sent through the trapdoor.

Theo Durrant's strange behavior was matched by that of his parents, who attended the hanging and watched their son die without comment. "They seemed proud of the whole thing," the prison warden commented.

As the Durrants waited for their son's body, the warden asked if they were hungry. They said they were. He had a small dinner brought to them and they calmly sat down, devouring slabs of roast beef and boiled potatoes. The two did not look up as Theo's body was brought into the same room and placed in an open coffin, not more than five feet from the table where they sat eating.

Their son's face was wreathed in a horrible grimace. It was black, the eyes bulged terribly. Durrant's swollen tongue jutted from his mouth, half bitten through.

Mrs. Durrant glanced only once in the direction of the coffin, then turned to her husband and said, "Papa, I'd like some more of that roast."

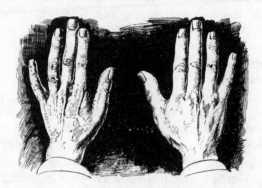

Apprentice newspaper czar William Randolph Hearst touted the gruesome murders of Theo Durrant in his *San Francisco Examiner* by showing the killer's hands on the front page. (N.Y. Historical Society)

DUTARTRE, PETER
Murderer ● (? -1724)

Dutartre was a gullible soul with an equally naive wife. When Christian George, a Swiss religious fanatic, began to preach free love to the residents of Charlestown, S. C., Peter and Judith Dutartre became his followers.

They, along with about a dozen others, joined George in the Orange Quarter of South Carolina, setting up a love commune. Judith Dutartre often slept with George and became pregnant.

When Justice Symmons heard of the coming of "the Devil's child," he rose in anger and, leading a mob of irate and pious citizens, marched on George's barricaded camp. The love group refused to be arrested. Peter Dutartre picked up a musket and fired a shot, killing Justice Symmons. The mob stormed the fort and captured the congregation of lovers.

Following a two-day trial, Dutartre was convicted of murder along with Christian George and Peter Rombert. All three were hanged the following day. The good people of Charlestown returned to their churches, praying for Divine guidance.

EASTMAN GANG

The Eastmans were ruled by a giant of a man, Edward Monk Eastman (nee Osterman) a wild, berserk skull-cracker who delighted in street brawls and murder. The Eastman gang dominated an area in New York City between the Bowery and the East River, Monroe and 14th Streets.

Organized about the turn of the century, the Eastmans practiced wholesale robberies in their area, protected by powerful politicians such as Tammany Hall sachem Big Tim Sullivan. Monk Eastman was a scarred, broken-nosed monster who began as a bouncer in the New Irving dancehall, a dive notorious for its rapes and robberies.

Eastman employed a sawed-off baseball bat in his donnybrooks and sliced a notch into it for every head he had cracked open. One story has it that upon discovering he had forty-nine notches on his club, he jumped up from a barstool and bashed in the head of a fellow drinker, killing him. His explanation: "I wanted to make it an even fifty."

The Eastman gang disolved after Monk was picked out of a line-up and identified as the man who had robbed a grocery store. Tammany didn't shield Eastman this time; he had disregarded Big Tim Sullivan's edict about further street brawls and had recently beaten to death some of Sullivan's cronies. Monk was sent to Sing Sing for ten years.

Monk was release before the First World War, joined the Army, and served with distinction on the Western Front. Upon his discharge, Eastman reformed but was mysteriously shot to death by unknown gangsters on the night of December 26, 1920 as he emerged from the Blue Bird Cafe in Manhattan.

EGAN'S RATS

An old line criminal gang in St. Louis that dated back to the turn of the century, the Rats were first organized by "Jelly-roll" Egan, a strongarm gunsel who was known as a professional "legbreaker" for anti-union business bosses. This mob was revamped in the 1920s by a vicious hoodlum named Dinty Colbeck.

Egan's Rats, under Colbeck's direction, specialized in safecracking, jewel thefts, and bootlegging in the St. Louis-Kansas City area. Colbeck's headquarters was a notorious poolhall called Buckley's frequented by Irish gangsters. Dinty was the cock-of-the-walk in St. Louis for years. He paid off corrupt politicians and policemen with enormous sums of money so that his wide-open rackets could operate unmolested. Colebeck was killed by rival gangsters in the late 1930s.

The most infamous graduate of Egan's Rats was murderer Leo Brothers. Another noted member was safecracker Morris "Red" Rudensky.

ENGLEMAN, GLENNON E.
Serial Killer ● (1927-   )

A dentist from East St. Louis, Ill., Glennon Engleman appeared to be anything but a serial killer. To his blue-collar patients, he was a fine, upstanding citizen who displayed compassion for the poor by often treating them for free. Engleman, however, made up the difference with murder.

Over a period of twenty-two years, the conniving dentist arranged for the murder of seven people, all to share in insurance premiums. Engleman conspired with patients, male and female, to take out insurance policies on their spouses. Engleman would later kill the insured party and benefit from the insurance payment.

The first reported victim of Engleman's sinister scheme was James Bullock who had married Engleman's former wife. Bullock was shot and killed outside an art museum on December 16, 1958. His wife, Ruth Ball Engleman Bullock, collected $64,500 on his life. The widow later invested $15,000 in a dragstrip operated by Engleman. Though police were suspicious and interviewed both the dentist and his ex-wife, no charges were made.

Engleman's next victim was Eric Frey, who was a partner with Engleman in the dragstrip. On September 26, 1963, Fry was killed in a dynamite explosion at the dragstrip. Engleman was the first man to reach Fry and pronounce him dead. The death was ruled an accident and $37,000 was paid to his widow, Saundra Frey, who was Engleman's niece and who, a short time later, invested $16,000 in the dragstrip.

Strange rumors about Engleman reached police ears. He had bragged about killing his partner, it was said. He was involved in insurance schemes that ended in murder and paid off in cash, it was said. Yet, police had no evidence with which to charge the dentist.

The next victim was Peter Halm who was asked by his wife Carmen to go to a wooded area near Pacific, Mo., on September 5, 1976. When he arrived at the deserted spot someone shot Halm in the back and killed him. Carmen Miranda Halm received $60,000 in life insurance benefits. Carmen Halm had known Engleman since she was a child and later became one of his dental assistants.

When investigators later went to Halm she agreed to testify against Engleman, naming him as her husband's murderer, if she were granted immunity. Carmen stated that Engleman actually planned her marriage to Peter Halm so he could later be killed for insurance money. Prosecutor Gorden Ankey was later to remark that the dentist had a strange "hold" over Carmen, adding: "I'll never forget the sadness of Carmen Halm. She wasn't a killer, but he got her involved through manipulation."

Three more murders followed, all of which Engleman engineered, as he would later admit. Arthur and Vernita Guswelle were killed on their farm outside Edwardsville on November 3, 1977. Their son Ron was shot in his garage on March 31, 1977, and his body dumped into a river in East St. Louis. Barbara Guswelle, Ron's wife, stood to inherit more than $500,000 from the combined insurance policies on all three of the dead Guswelles.

As later investigations proved, Barbara Guswelle was another Engleman crony. She had met the dentist in 1960 and she admitted that she had conspired with him to murder the Guswelles for the insurance money. She would later receive a fifty-year prison sentence for her role in the slayings.

Meanwhile, Dr. Engleman went on his murdering ways. On January 14, 1980, Sophie Marie Barrera was killed when her car blew up. Investigators who had been dogging Engleman over the years, soon learned that Barrera ran a dental lab and was suing the dentist over unpaid bills. Then Ruth Bullock, Engleman's ex-wife, went to the police to tell them of her former spouse's history of murder, saying that she had turned informant to protect herself. She feared that Engleman was making ready to kill her.

She agreed to wear a wire and then taped conversations with Engleman wherein he implicated himself in the killings of Barrera and the Guswelles. Charged with murder, Engleman pleaded guilty to three murder counts on June 18, 1985. He was given two fifty-year jail terms.

Richard B. Dempsey, Engleman's attorney, aptly summed up the scheming dentist: "I think probably that his desire to control individuals was his driving force—to make all the little dummies walk in line and sing at the same time."

ENGLISH, CHARLES CARMEN
Syndicate Gangster ● (1914-1985)

Charlie English (nee Englise) was a syndicate leader in Chicago who specialized in jukeboxes and vending machines. His record dates back to 1933 and he was arrested for extortion, robbery, hijacking, loansharking (juice), and murder.

He had vast interests in the Phoenix, Ariz. area

in real estate, public works, and construction. His area of operations in Chicago was the North Side. English appeared before the McClellan Committee and took the Fifth Amendment fifty-six times.

ESPOSITO, JOSEPH ("DIAMOND JOE")
Labor Racketeer, Bootlegger ●
(1872-1928)

BACKGROUND: BORN 4/28/1872 IN ACCERA, ITALY. IMMIGRATED TO THE U.S. AT AGE 23 IN 1895. WORKED AS A DAY LABORER IN BOSTON AND BROOKLYN, SETTLED IN CHICAGO, 1905, OPENING A BAKERY. OCCUPATION, SALOON-RESTAURANT OWNER. DESCRIPTION: 6', BLACK EYES, BLACK HAIR, HEAVY BUILD. ALIASES: NONE. RECORD: ARRESTED IN CHICAGO, 1908 FOR MURDERING MACK GEAQUENTA, CASE DISMISSED THE FOLLOWING YEAR (NO WITNESSES); OPERATED ILLEGAL STILLS IN CHICAGO AND MELROSE PARK DURING PROHIBITION; SOLD SUGAR TO THE ALKY COOKERS CONTROLLED BY THE GENNA BROTHERS; MURDERED 3/21/28 BY RIVAL GANGSTERS.

Diamond Joe Esposito, Chicago labor racketeer, murdered 3/21/28. (UPI)

Diamond Joe Esposito, called "Dimey" by his friends, was not only a local gangster curiosity in Chicago, but, for two decades, a powerful political bigwig whose various enterprises encompassed everything from bootlegging to labor racketeering.

Born dirt poor in a small village near Naples, Esposito immigrated to the U.S. in 1895 where he took any available work, from digging ditches to collecting garbage. He moved to Brooklyn from Boston a few years later, judiciously saving his money. From there he traveled to Chicago in 1905 where he opened a bakery in the Nineteenth Ward (Little Italy).

It was three years before anyone took notice of Joe Esposito. Mack Geaquenta, Joe's barber, got into an argument one day with his client over a woman both men were dating. Esposito became angered and jumped up from the barber's chair, his face coated with lather. He pulled out a gun. Just as Geaquenta was about to protest, Joe shot him in the mouth, killing him instantly.

The murder happened in August, 1908 but Esposito's trial did not take place for a full nine months. During that time witnesses to

the shooting had either disappeared or refused to testify. Little wonder. Esposito's influence had grown considerably in the previous three years. He had organized fellow workers into the International Hod Carriers' Building and Construction Laborers' Union. He was the union's treasurer and agent. Most of Esposito's neighbors belonged to the Circolo Accera Club, members being former natives of Joe's birthplace.

None of these would testify against Dimey, a man they considered their benefactor; he had financed many in new businesses and paid travel expenses for immigrating relatives. Esposito, wearing a massive belt with a buckle studded with $50,000 in diamonds which spelled out his name, gave lavish community parties, fed the poor, and played Santa Claus for the neighborhood children at Christmas.

With the help of his union coffers, Diamond Joe prospered, opening up a swanky cafe at 850 South Halsted, The Bella Napoli. Some said Joe was aping his friend, Big Jim Colosimo, but he ignored such remarks. If Big Jim could open a posh nightclub—Colosimo's Cafe—so could he. If Big Jim wore diamonds on his belt buckle, so could he. Diamond Joe went further and purchased diamond cufflinks, diamond rings, diamond shirt studs. Big Jim knew every important politician and crook in town; Diamond Joe patronized hoodlums, too.

He was no stranger to the underworld. Cuono Coletta, a notorious killer (only one of the many gangsters who frequented Joe's establishment), shot up a pasta party in his saloon once, blowing away Sam Esposito's (Joe's brother) fingertip. One of Diamond Joe's "bodyguards" got up from a table and blew off Coletta's head. New York's Frankie Yale, an infamous gunman, was another of Esposito's friends.

Politically, Esposito was a mighty vote deliverer. He virtually owned Chicago's Nineteenth Ward (now the Twenty-fifth). He could be counted on by his close friend Republican Senator Charles S. Deneen to deliver his ward in one party block. (Oddly enough, Deneen was a reform politician.) Diamond Joe invited the entire ward to his wedding ceremony in 1913 when he married sixteen-year-old Carmela Marchese (he was then 41). The three-day bash cost him $65,000; the wine alone came to $40,000. Diamond Joe knew how to live it big.

In 1920 Esposito, at Deneen's urging, ran for the Republican ward committeeman post in the Nineteenth Ward. He won an overwhelming victory. His celebration party, patrolled by his manager, Tony "Mops" Volpe (one of the most feared killers in the city), exceeded the ceremonies following his opulent wedding. Volpe beat up several uninvited guests, one reporter recalled, but was not arrested. Through his political clout, Esposito arranged Volpe's appointment as a deputy sheriff for the county, which gave Volpe immunity in operating Esposito's vast alky-cooking operations in Melrose Park, Chicago Heights, and Chicago during Prohibition.

Dry agents foiled Esposito briefly in 1923 when they raided the Bella Napoli and closed it up for selling liquor. Diamond Joe's paddy-cake punishment amounted to a $1,000 fine which he happily paid. His place, however, was padlocked for a year.

The action did not separate Diamond Joe from his fortunes. He became the largest supplier of sugar to the Genna brothers' stills; he also set up giant stills throughout the Nineteenth Ward which turned out near-poisonous liquor. His bootleg activities were not without incident. Two Esposito brothers-in-law paid with their lives when the Genna-Capone war broke out. First John Tucillo was riddled and left on Ralph Sheldon's doorstep; Tucillo was Sheldon's key booze runner and Sheldon worked for Capone. Next Phillip Leonatti was machinegunned to death while buying a box of cigars. Leonatti was not a hoodlum. He was only Esposito's brother-in-law. This killing was a personal message from the Gennas to Diamond Joe, who had sided with Capone.

The message became even clearer in 1928 when Esposito was involved in another gang squabble with Scarface Al. On the morning of March 21, 1928, Esposito received a call from a member of the Capone gang. The caller told him, "Get out of town or get killed."

By then the Gennas, Big Jim Colosimo, Johnny Torrio—all of his friends and allies at one time or other—had either been killed or driven out of the city. Diamond Joe's aides urged him to leave.

His bodyguards, the Varchetti brothers, Ralph and Joe, argued with him. "You ought to go down to that farm of yours [located on Cedar Lake] and raise some chickens for a while," Ralph told him.

"I can't go now," Esposito replied. "My boy Joseph was taken down with scarlet fever today. Besides I promised Senator Deneen I would run for ward committeeman."

That night, while Joe was walking toward his home in company with the Varchetti boys, a shot rang out.

"I thought it was a blowout," Ralph Varchetti told police later. Then a hailstorm of bullets burst upon the trio. Esposito, a huge, barrel-chested man, was hit by fifty-eight slugs, all dipped in garlic, police later reported.

The attack came from a large touring car which had crept up on the trio from behind, letting loose its lethal barrage when coming alongside Esposito and the Varchettis. Ralph Varchetti later testified: "Then there were more shots, and Joe says, 'Oh, my God!' and I knew he was hit. I dropped to the sidewalk and lay flat, with my face in the dirt. The shots came in bursts of fire from an automobile . . . When the firing stopped a second, I looked up and they fired again. I dropped flat, and this time waited until they were gone. I got near Dimey and tried to wake him. He was gone."

Carmela Esposito witnessed the assassination. She and three of her children were looking out an open window, watching for Diamond Joe. The 31-year-old widow ran frantically from her home on Oakley Boulevard and threw herself on her husband's lifeless body. "Oh, is it you, Giuseppe?" she screamed. She sobbed hysterically for minutes as the two unharmed and helpless bodyguards stood mute, staring about nervously at the now-empty street.

Then Carmela raised her tear-streaked face and shook her fists at the quiet stars. "He was so good to the Italian people and this is what he got for it! I'll kill! I'll kill them for this!"

Carmela never killed anyone. The coroner wrote out an old Chicago refrain on Diamond Joe's inquest papers—"Slayers not apprehended."

ESSEX, MARK JAMES ROBERT
Mass Murderer ● (1949-1973)

Essex was a black man whose parents raised him with religious zeal in Emporia, Kan. He joined the Navy in 1969 where he encountered racial discrimination. Essex developed an intense hatred for whites. He was discharged early for "character and behaviorial disorders."

Joining black militant political movements, Essex lived in New York, then moved to New Orleans. His hatred for whites consumed him. He had difficulty in holding a job, because, according to one his friends, "he couldn't stand taking orders from whites."

Just before Christmas, 1972, Essex wrote his mother: "The white man is my enemy. I will fight to gain my manhood or die trying."

On January 7, 1973, Essex went to the roof of the seventeen-floor Howard Johnson Motor Lodge, which was located only a few blocks from New Orleans' famous French Quarter. Here, hiding behind a concrete bunker on the roof, he placed a .44-caliber rifle and several thousand rounds of ammunition. He then set fire to several rooms in the hotel to draw occupants outside. He returned to the roof and began to shoot fleeing people.

Of the fleeing guests, Essex shot and killed five. He shot and killed four policemen trying to get to him, including Deputy Police Chief Louis Sirgo. For twelve hours, Essex kept up his barrage of gunfire. He claimed the lives of nine people and wounded another nine until a police helicopter hovered over him and a sharpshooter pumped thirty tracer bullets into him, killing the sniper.

The gun Essex had used was examined. Ballistics experts reported that it was the same weapon used to murder a 19-year-old police cadet in a 1972 New Year's Eve attack on the police.

EVANS, DONALD LEROY
Serial Killer ● (1957-   )

Just as the news of serial killer Jeffrey Dahmer shocked the nation, Donald Leroy Evans burst upon the scene as an even more shocking and prolific serial killer. Evans was arrested in Biloxi, Mississippi in August 1991, charged with the kidnapping, rape, and murder of a homeless 10-year-old child, Beatrice Routh.

Evans confessed to this killing, then confessed to other murders, more than sixty homicides, saying that he had been killing people ever since his discharge from the Marine Corps in 1977. He claimed to have raped and murdered six women in Illinois, California, and Texas. His confessions later encompassed many other states and victims.

The lengthy confessions seemed to be prompted by Evans's remorse over killing the Routh child. Evans offered prosecutors a deal: He would confess to his many killings if he were promised the death penalty. Fred Lusk, his legal advisor, stated: "He said he has lived by the sword and he wants to die by the sword. He does not believe in suicide, so he wants to die by execution."

Authorities began to investigate Evans claims and, at the date of this writing, are still trying to clear up the dozens of murders to which Evans has made chilling claim.

FAIRBANKS, JASON
Murderer ● (1780-1801)

Fairbanks was a 21-year-old rejected suitor, who, after failing to get permission from the parents of Elizabeth Fales to marry her, sought revenge. He led Miss Fales, 19, of Dedham, Mass. to a meadow near her home and slashed her throat, killing her. He then attempted to commit suicide but his efforts were clumsy.

Taken into custody, Fairbanks was quickly tried and convicted. He escaped; he was tracked through New England, and was overtaken in Whitehall, Vermont just as he was preparing to enter Canada. Fairbanks was immediately hanged.

FARRINGTON BROTHERS

Ex-guerillas who fought with Quantrill during the Civil War and had taken part in the bloody raids at Lawrence, Kan. and Centralia, Mo., the Farrington brothers, Levi and Hilary, were brutish bandits with murderous natures and short-lived careers as outlaws.

Following the Civil War, the Farringtons moved back to their native Mississippi, terrorizing the small towns in the swamp country and committing blood-soaked robberies. In 1870, the brothers, accompanied by William Barton and Bill Taylor, stopped the Mobile and Ohio flyer at Union City, Tenn. and stole more than $20,000 from the express car.

The Southern Express Company hired the Pinkerton Detective Agency to recover their money and capture the outlaws. William Pinkerton and train detectives caught up with Hilary Farrington in Verona, Mo. weeks later. The outlaw was holed up in a deserted farmhouse with several rifles. A day-long siege concluded when possemen rushed the place, pistols barking. Farrington was taken alive but, in an effort to escape his captors while being extradited to Tenn. on the steamboat *Illinois*, he struggled with the guards and was knocked overboard. He was crushed to death by the ship's stern paddle.

Levi Farrington was located the following year in the small town of Farmington, Ill. Drunk, Levi shot up the town square, challenging one and all to a duel. A lawman named Brown, affiliated with the Pinkertons, dashed into the square and wrestled the giant outlaw to the ground.

Levi was lynched by the irate citizens of Union City weeks later.

FERGUSON, PAUL ROBERT
Murderer ● (1946-   )

FERGUSON, THOMAS SCOTT
Murderer ● (1951-   )

In the 1920s and 1930s Ramon Novarro earned fame as the "Latin Lover" of screen goddesses such as Greta Garbo. In the 1960s his Hollywood fame lingered but his offscreen lovers were of a decidedly different nature. Novarro had invested his money well in real estate and he lived in luxury. To his Hollywood home he invited all manner of handsome young male hustlers, including the Ferguson brothers, 22-year-old Paul and his 17-

Tom Ferguson, second from left, and Paul Ferguson, far right, conferring with their lawyers at their murder trial.

year-old brother, Tom. They would be his last visitors.

Once the Fergusons were inside Novarro's home they demanded to know where Novarro kept his cash. They had heard a Hollywood rumor that the silent film star kept $5,000 in cash at all times. Paul Ferguson beat and tortured Novarro as Tom Ferguson ransacked the house in search of the money.

Tom Ferguson shredded couches and chairs, tore dozens of valuable paintings from the walls, ripped out drawers. Exhausted, he sat down and called a friend in Chicago, Brenda Lee Metcalf. He talked to her for close to an hour while in the background Metcalf could hear Novarro's screams of torment.

The hustling brothers found no money, only the cash Novarro had in his pockets. They left the actor dead, suffocated by an ornate dildo Novarro had once received as a gift from Rudolph Valentino.

Novarro's secretary, Edward J. Weber, found the body the next day. In their routine investigation, police checked Novarro's long-distance calls and turned up Metcalf. She readily admitted receiving a call from Tom Ferguson and said the brothers were old friends from Chicago. Paul Ferguson had gone to Hollywood to seek his fortune, she said, and Tom had run away from home to join him.

The Fergusons were picked up. Paul Ferguson told police that his younger brother had committed the murder and Tom reluctantly agreed. This had been prearranged by Paul who had told Tom that if they were caught Tom should assume responsibility for the murder because he was underage and would be tried as a juvenile and receive a light sentence.

This was not the case. Juvenile Court authorities decreed that Tom Ferguson would be tried as an adult and both brothers were charged with murder. They were brought to trial in August 1969. The brothers turned on each other, each trying to convice the jury that the other had killed Novarro.

Paul Ferguson had killed Novarro, according to District Attorney James Ideman, who remarked that "it was done cruelly by a man who has no respect for himself or others . . . who has no remorse, no compassion, no regrets . . . and who got his brother to perjure himself."

In the end, both brothers were found guilty. Judge Mark Brandler sentenced them to life in prison, recommending that they never be paroled.

FINCH, BERNARD
Murderer ● (1918-)

"I know he will kill me," the good-looking, 36-year-old blonde said to her lawyer. "I know exactly how it will happen. He will take me to the desert or the mountains in my car and kill me and make it look like an accident."

This was Mrs. Barbara Finch speaking to her lawyer Joseph T. Forno on the morning of May 1, 1959 as she nervously paced his office. Mrs. Finch went on to relate how her husband, Dr. Bernard Finch, a well-to-do Los Angeles physician, had pistol-whipped her and threatened to strangle her to death the night before. "Something," Mrs. Finch said desperately, "will have to be done."

Murder was done to Mrs. Finch two and a half months later.

The Finchs' tangled love affairs had brought homicide to the doorstep of their expensive suburban home in West Covina; on July 18, 1959 Mrs. Finch was killed by her husband, though not in the way she expected.

At age 42, Dr. Bernard Finch was the very epitome of the successful young doctor. He owned and operated his own clinic with his brother-in-law, Dr. Frank Gordon, and possessed an estate of at least $750,000. On the other hand, he had his problems. Several patients had recently sued him for malpractice, one of whom was James A. Pappa who claimed Finch had crippled him for life while operating on a small growth on his knee.

Pappa's young, sexy wife, Carole, met Dr. Finch through her husband but the doctor was concentrating on another woman at that time; Carole would come later.

Finch and his wife Francis were not getting along. Each loved someone else, another couple, Barbara and Forrest Daugherty. Both couples divorced and Finch married Barbara, Forrest married Francis. The Daugherty marriage worked. Barbara and Bernie Finch began to argue, however, from the first, their brawls ending each time when Dr. Finch resorted to beating his wife with his fists.

Into this love mess stepped Carole Tregoff. She was no longer married to Pappa; she, too, had gotten a divorce. Carole became Finch's secretary at his clinic and they began to date heavily. By the spring of 1959, the situation was hopeless. Barbara Finch hired a detective to follow her husband and told her lawyer to prepare divorce papers.

Finch and Carole began to plot. Carole moved to Las Vegas where she got a job as a cocktail waitress. Finch met her there at every opportunity. On July 18, 1959, after the couple recovered from a two-day binge, Carole and Dr. Finch drove to West Covina where, Finch later claimed, they would talk to Barbara about the divorce.

According to Finch, his wife returned home that night at 11 p.m. in her red sports car, while Carole and he sat waiting on the front porch. There was an attaché case nearby on the lawn—police later termed it a "do-it-yourself-murder-kit"—containing two pairs of rubber gloves, two hypodermic needles, two vials of powder, ammunition for a .38-caliber weapon, a flashlight, a long-bladed butcher knife, and some heavy clothesline. (Finch claimed in court he always carried these items on house calls).

Barbara exploded when she saw Finch and Carole, Miss Tregoff later stated. She pulled out a gun and said she would shoot them both if they didn't leave. Carole claimed she ran into the bushes and then heard two shots.

The shots brought the Finch maid to the front door. She saw the doctor standing over his wife with a gun in his hand and began screaming. Finch claimed he had to bang her head against the doorframe to shut her up. When she ran back into the house to call the police, he left.

Five hours later Finch was back in Las Vegas in bed with Carole Tregoff. Carole couldn't sleep and switched on a radio. She heard the news that Mrs. Finch was dead, murdered. Carole woke the snoring Finch from a deep sleep. "What are you going to do?" she asked him. "Your wife is dead. I heard it on the radio. She's dead. What are you going to do?"

"What do you mean," Finch answered drowsily, "what am I going to do?" and turned over and went back to sleep. State police arrested the two the next day and charged them with murder.

Finch and Carole Tregoff faced a jury trial together, their chairs but a few feet apart though they never spoke or even glanced at each other during this time. The prosecution had a field day.

First, ballistics expert Clifford C. Crump stated that Mrs. Finch had been shot in the back, the bullet entering between the shoulder blades and exiting between her breasts. He stated and proved that "the woman was in flight" when shot.

Prosecutor Fred Whichello then held up the so-called "murder kit" and stated that Finch and Carole had gone to the Finch home for the expressed purpose of killing Mrs. Finch, first by injecting an air bubble into her bloodstream and, if that failed, by injecting sodium seconal. They had also planned as an alternative murder plan, Whichello said, to drive the unconscious woman off a cliff at the back of the Finch house.

The most damning witness against Finch and Carole was a petty Los Angeles crook named John Patrick Cody. He stated on the stand that Finch hired him to make love to his wife in order to obtain evidence against her in the up-coming divorce suit.

Cody then stated that Carole Tregoff came to him and offered him $1,400 if he would shoot Mrs. Finch. When he refused, Cody claimed, Miss Tregoff said: "If you don't kill her, Dr. Finch will . . . and if he won't, I'll do it."

Finch himself took the stand toward the end of the trial. He claimed, with tears in his eyes, that he took the gun away from his wife two times, once in her car, and again in the garage. The second time, Finch insisted, he threw the gun over his shoulder and while doing so, it accidentally discharged, fatally

Dr. Bernard Finch in custody, 1960, after murdering his wife. (UPI)

wounding his wife.

Then Finch played to the gallery offering one of the most maudlin crime scenarios ever spoken in open court. He claimed he dropped to his knees next to his dying wife and said: "What happened, Barbara? Are you hurt?"

"Shot in the back," she answered weakly.

"I'll get an ambulance," Finch said.

Great tears rolled down Dr. Finch's ruddy cheeks as he continued. Faint sniffles could be heard in the courtroom. Women took out handkerchiefs and dabbed their moist eyes.

"Wait," Barbara said.

"What is it, Barb?"

"I'm sorry . . . I should have listened to you . . . I love you . . . take care of the kids . . ." and, Dr. Finch said, she died at that moment.

It was a new twist in murder trials. Dr. Bernard Finch had narrated a death scene where his own wife apologized for being killed!

The trial ended with a hung jury. Two more trials dragged through 1961-62. Finally, both Carole and Finch were convicted of second-degree murder March 27, 1961 and both were sentenced to life imprisonment. Carole Tregoff was paroled in 1969 without ever replying once to the letters Finch sent to her while she was in prison (when Finch was leaving the courtroom after the third trial he attempted to kiss her, but she moved her face out of reach).

Finch was released in December, 1971.

Carole Tregoff; Finch murdered for her. (UPI)

FISH, ALBERT
Kidnapper, Cannibal ● (1870-1936)

BACKGROUND: BORN AND RAISED IN AN ORPHANAGE IN WASHINGTON, D.C. MINOR PUBLIC EDUCATION. MARRIED WITH SIX CHILDREN, MORE UNKNOWN. ORIGINAL OCCUPATION: PAINTER AND HANDYMAN. DESCRIPTION: 5'5", BLUE EYES, GREY HAIR, MUSTACHE, FRAIL. ALIASES: FRANK HOWARD, JOHN W. PELL, ROBERT HAYDEN, THOMAS A. SPRAGUE. RECORD: FISH CONFESSED TO MURDERING A MAN IN WILMINGTON, DEL. IN 1910; MUTILATED AND TORTURED TO DEATH A MENTALLY-RETARDED BOY IN 1919 IN NEW YORK; MURDERED A NEGRO BOY ALSO IN 1919 ON A HOUSEBOAT

IN THE GEORGETOWN AREA OF WASHINGTON, D.C.; MOLESTED AND KILLED FOUR-YEAR-OLD WILLIAM GAFFNEY, 2/11/1927; STRANGLED AND BUTCHERED TWELVE-YEAR-OLD GRACE BUDD AFTER ABDUCTING HER FROM HER MANHATTAN HOME IN WHITE PLAINS, N.Y., 6/3/1928; STRANGLED TO DEATH FIVE-YEAR-OLD FRANCIS MCDONELL OUTSIDE OF HIS HOME AT FORT RICHMOND, L.I. IN 1934; TRIED AND CONVICTED OF THE BUDD SLAYING; SENTENCED TO DEATH, EXECUTED IN THE ELECTRIC CHAIR AT SING SING PRISON 1/16/36.

A self-admitted molester of more than 400 children during a span of twenty years, Albert Fish, more than any other American criminal, deserves the title of "inhuman monster." Fish was a sly killer who preyed upon children and, in the words of one of the shocked psychiatrists who examined him, lived a life of "unparalleled perversity. There was no known perversion that he did not practice and practice frequently."

The old man blamed the conditions of his youth for his crimes. Though related to ancestors who fought in the Revolution, Fish was abandoned at an early age and placed in an orphanage where he first saw and experienced brutal acts of sadism. "Misery leads to crime," Fish later wrote. "I saw so many boys whipped it ruined my mind."

Fish's weird, unpredictable behavior surfaced after January of 1917, according to the testimony of one of his children. It was then that Fish's wife ran away with a man named John Straube, who boarded with the family. Fish returned from work and the children from a movie to find the house deserted and stripped of all its furniture.

Mrs. Fish's own behavior was hardly normal. She once returned to her husband with Straube at her side, asking if they could move in with the family. Fish said she could but that Straube could not. The woman agreed and sent Straube away. Days later, Fish discovered that his wife had sneaked Straube into the attic, where she was smuggling him food. Again, he told her that she could stay with the family but that her half-witted lover was to go. They both left and the family never saw Mrs. Fish again.

It was at this time that Albert Fish began to act strangely. He took his children up to the family cottage—hauntingly called Wisteria Cottage—in Westchester County for outings.

They watched him, terrified, as he climbed a hill, struck his fist toward the sky and repeatedly screamed: "I am Christ! I am Christ!"

Pain delighted Fish. Whether inflicting it upon himself or others, he took strange ecstasies from all forms of masochism and sadism. He encouraged his own and neighboring children to paddle his buttocks until they bled. He once told his son, Albert Fish, Jr., when the boy discovered in the old man's room a paddle studded with inch-and-half nails: "I use them on myself. I get certain feelings over me. When I do, I've got to torture myself."

Fish, who had been examined several times in Bellevue by psychiatrists and released as being disturbed but sane, also inserted countless needles into his body. On nights of the full moon, his children later testified, the old man consumed large quantities of raw meat. He even served platters of raw meat to them. "That's the way I like meat," he told them, "and you'll have to eat it that way, too."

Over the years, Fish collected a great amount of published material relating to cannibalism which he avidly read; the choicer, gorier articles he carried about on his person for years until the thumb-worn clippings faded and crumbled.

Fish burned himself constantly with hot needles, irons and pokers. He also answered ads placed by well-endowed widows seeking husbands. His letters—forty-six of them were recovered and entered as evidence at his trial—were black masterpieces of obscenity, some so vile that the prosecution refused to make them public. Basically, Fish told these lovelorn ladies that he wasn't interested in marriage so much as he was their willingness to paddle him. None accepted his offers.

When and where Fish turned to murder is speculative. He confessed to six and referred vaguely to dozens more, the victims, places, and dates lost to his cloudy memory.

The most sensational murder enacted by Fish was the abduction and slaughterhouse killing of twelve-year-old Grace Budd in 1928. Posing as a Mr. Howard, Fish befriended the Budd family, and, after several visits, abducted Grace. Fish told the family he would take the child to a little girls' party a friend was giving for her daughter. Being gullible, the parents agreed. It was the last time they saw their daughter alive.

Fish took the train to White Plains, N. Y.,

Cannibal Albert Fish waylaid scores of little children for ten years, butchered them alive, and then made meals of their remains (shown here, center, looking at his confession in 1934).

June 3, 1928. Grace sat beside him while he told her of the fun she would have at the party. Between them was a box containing what Fish was later to describe as his "instruments of hell"—a cleaver, a butcher knife, and a saw. When the two got off the train, Grace abruptly turned and jumped back on, emerging moments later to hand the old man his box. He had forgotten it.

Fish and Grace trudged the lonely blocks to his isolated Wisteria Cottage. There, while the girl played outside, Fish stripped naked. Grace rushed into the house, saw him and screamed: "I'll tell Momma!" He strangled her on the spot. Using his "tools," he then decapitated the girl, and sawed her in half from the naval down.

Fish graphically described his bestial act later to authorities. The old man happily detailed how he carved up Grace's body and used several sections to prepare a stew which he consumed.

Grace Budd's disappearance baffled police. Mr. Howard could not be found. For six years the family believed that Grace was alive somewhere, and her disappearance might have remained a mystery had it not been for Fish's own inexplicable quirks. He could not resist writing to the Budd family in 1934, telling Mrs. Budd he had killed the girl but oddly emphasizing the fact that he had not sexually violated her.

The letter was Albert Fish's downfall. It was traced and he was arrested. He quickly confessed to killing Grace Budd and five others. He told police that he had "kept track of the case in the papers. If they had accused someone else of the murder, I would have come forward. My best days are over."

Police unearthed what was left of Grace's body in a shallow grave near Wisteria Cottage. The Budd family identified Fish as the Mr. Howard who took their little girl away to a party. The cannibal's fate was sealed . . . almost.

His defense fought desperately to prove him insane. The prosecution provided a host of psychiatrists to prove otherwise. After an exhaustive court battle, Fish was judged sane enough to die in the electric chair for his crimes and was sentenced to death.

He entered Sing Sing prison in 1935 carrying a Bible, handcuffed to another murderer, named Stone, whose forefathers had also

Twelve-year-old Grace Budd of Manhattan (standing extreme right) was abducted by Fish, strangled, and then made into a stew (she is shown with her mother, older sister and little brother circa 1928).

fought in the American Revolution. Dozens of appeals to save Fish were rejected. "The Moon Maniac," as the press dubbed Fish, would die on January 16, 1936.

While awaiting execution on Death Row, the old man told authorities that he was actually looking forward to being electrocuted. With a broad smile on his face he said: "What a thrill that will be if I have to die in the electric chair. It will be the supreme thrill. The only one I haven't tried."

Without aid, Fish entered the death room and walked briskly, perhaps eagerly to the electric chair. He fairly jumped into the seat and readily helped the executioner fix the electrodes to his legs. Dozens of reporters were aghast at his zeal. Here was the oldest man ever to be electrocuted at Sing Sing, barely managing to contain himself in the joy of his own violent death.

It came slowly. When the switch was pulled, the first massive jolt failed to kill Albert Fish, literally producing a small puff of blue smoke about his head. The hundreds of tiny needles in his body apparently created a short circuit. To kill him, another massive charge had to be sent through his quavering body.

While the old man's corpse was being wheeled to the autopsy room, one of the defense attorneys met with reporters. In his hand he held Albert Fish's last statement, several hand-written pages the old man had scribbled only hours before his death. "I shall never show it to anyone," the lawyer said. "It was the most filthy string of obscenities that I have ever read."

FIVE POINTS GANG

From the turn of the century, the bloody Five Points (or Five Pointers) gang ruthlessly controlled a large area of New York's Lower East Side. Its name was derived from a five-pointed intersection between the Bowery and Broadway which later became the intersection of Baxter, Park, and Worth.

This was a terror gang of murderers and cutthroats whose musclemen and gunners were hired by businessmen as strikebreakers or by other mobs who issued them murder contracts.

Some of the most notorious modern-day gangsters served criminal apprenticeships as Five Pointers. Johnny Torrio, Five Point leader from 1903 to 1910, was introduced to the mob by the unshaven, cap-wearing Jack Sirocco, lieutenant of the first leader of the gang, Paul Kelly (nee Paolo Vaccarelli).

Kelly's headquarters was his New Brighton Club, a murky saloon off Third Avenue which attracted socialities eager to shake hands with gangster Paul, whose ferocious street battles with arch rival Monk Eastman were legendary.

Under Kelly's leadership, Torrio developed a sub-gang for the Five Pointers named the James Street gang. Torrio's youthful minions, which included Al Capone, Lucky Luciano, and Frankie Yale (Uale), served initially as runners for the Five Pointers and were gradually absorbed into the older group.

The Five Points gang broke up with the advent of Prohibition in 1920.

FLOYD, CHARLES ARTHUR ("PRETTY BOY")
Bankrobber, Murderer ● (1901-1934)

BACKGROUND: BORN AND RAISED AT AKINS, OKLAHOMA (COOKSON HILLS). MARRIED 16-YEAR-OLD WILMA HARGROVE IN 1921. SON, JACK DEMPSEY FLOYD, BORN 1922. MINOR PUBLIC EDUCATION. ORIGINAL OCCUPATION, FARMER. DESCRIPTION: 6'2", BROWN EYES, BLACK HAIR, HEAVYSET, MUSCULAR. ALIASES: JACK HAMILTON. RECORD: ROBBED PAYROLL SHIPMENT IN ST. LOUIS, MO., 1925; ARRESTED, TRIED, CONVICTED, AND SENTENCED TO MISSOURI STATE PENITENTIARY FOR FIVE YEARS, 1925; PAROLED, 1929; ROBBED SYLVANIA, OHIO BANK 3/11/30; APPREHENDED BY STATE POLICE SAME DAY; SENTENCED TO OHIO STATE PENITENTIARY FOR 15 YEARS ON BANKROBBING CHARGE; ESCAPED FROM GUARDS ON TRAIN 5/25/30 ENROUTE TO PRISON; ESCAPED FROM POLICE TRAP IN KANSAS CITY, MO., 3/23/31; MURDERED WALLACE AND WILLIAM ASH 3/25/31; ROBBED FROM MAY-JUNE, 1931 MOUNT ZION TRUST COMPANY ($4,000), MOUNT ZION, KENTUCKY; ELLISTON BANK ($2,700), ELLISTON, KENTUCKY; WHITEHOUSE BANK ($3,600), WHITEHOUSE, OHIO; KILLED IN EARLY JUNE, 1931, PATROLMAN RALPH CASTNER IN BOWLING GREEN, KENTUCKY DURING GUN BATTLE TO APPREHEND HIM AND FELLOW ROBBER BILL MILLER, ESCAPED; KILLED PROHIBITION AGENT CURTIS C. BURKS 7/21/31 WHEN DISCOVERED IN A KANSAS CITY SPEAKEASY; OCTOBER-NOVEMBER, 1931, FLOYD AND GEORGE BIRDWELL ROBBED THE OKLAHOMA BANKS OF SHAMROCK, MORRIS, KONAWA, MAUD, EARLSBORO, PADEN, CASTLE, TAHLEQUAH FOR SMALL AMOUNTS; ESCAPED POLICE TRAP IN TULSA, OKLAHOMA, 2/11/32; KILLED SPECIAL INVESTIGATOR (FOR THE STATE OF OKLAHOMA) ERV A. KELLEY 4/7/32 WHILE EVADING POLICE TRAP AT BIXBY, OKLAHOMA; ROBBED THE SALLISAW BANK ($2,530), SALLISAW, OKLAHOMA WITH AUSSIE ELLIOTT AND GEORGE BIRDWELL 11/1/32; ROBBED BANK IN HENRYETTA, OKLAHOMA ($11,352.20) 11/7/32 WITH ELLIOTT AND BIRDWELL; ROBBED THE CITIZENS' STATE BANK ($50,000), TUPELO, MISS., 11/30/32; ROBBED DANCE HALL, 3/33 IN WEWOKA, OKLA. WITH ADAM RICHETTI; ABDUCTED SHERIFF JACK KILLINGSWORTH OF BOLIVAR, MO., 6/16/33; CLAIMED TO BE THE

MACHINEGUNNER OF THE KANSAS CITY MASSACRE, 6/17/33, KILLING FBI AGENT RAYMOND CAFFREY AND LOCAL KANSAS CITY DETECTIVES GROOMS, HERMANSON, REED, AND FRANK NASH, A PRISONER UNDER GUARD; CLAIMED TO HAVE ROBBED MERCHANTS NATIONAL BANK ($22,000), SOUTH BEND, INDIANA, 6/30/34 WITH JOHN DILLINGER, BABY FACE NELSON, AND HOMER VAN METER; ESCAPED POLICE TRAP IN RURAL IOWA, 10/11/34; KILLED BY FBI AGENTS NEAR EAST LIVERPOOL, OHIO 10/22/34.

There was very little difference between Charles Arthur "Pretty Boy" Floyd and John Dillinger. Both were poor farm boys, God-fearing and with a Jesse James complex of imagined fair-play about them. And both were professional bankrobbers. The difference was that where Dillinger was romanticized in the newspapers of the day, Pretty Boy got the worst press of any outlaw in the 1930s, and for a crime—the Kansas City Massacre—many believe he never committed.

Like all of the dust-ridden, hard-scrabble people of Oklahoma who were later to be immortalized as "Okies" in John Steinbeck's *Grapes of Wrath*, Floyd began simply enough.

Born and raised near the small town of Akins, Oklahoma, Floyd worked like a dog on his father's dirt-poor farm, clawing at the dust for crops, dust that increased each year through storms and erosion until the area became the "Great Dust Bowl." It was hard work and the unschooled Floyd didn't complain.

In the evenings and on weekends, Floyd would find release in "hellin'" about Akins, nearby Sallisaw, and as far as Siloam Springs and Fort Smith, Arkansas. He loved a local brew called Choctaw Beer so much that he got the nickname Chock. His constant drinking of these downhome suds put more beef onto an already tall and muscular frame.

Wilma Hargrove was only sixteen when Floyd married her in 1921 and she was to be the one true love of his life. But the marriage was hard-pressed from the beginning. Wilma and Chock got along all right. There just wasn't any money to earn in the fast-deteriorating Oklahoma farmlands.

The local banks were small and solid. They practiced a tyranny of foreclosures on farms mortgaged to the treetops. Floyd tried hard at first to stay within the law. Months after his marriage he moved northward, seeking harvest work from farm to farm and usually ending in hobo camps for the night.

He grew bitter and angry at not being able to make a living—he was a strong man and willing one, but there was no work. But Floyd knew where there was money. He obtained a pistol and rode the rails to St. Louis where he committed a quick payroll robbery. Then he raced for Oklahoma and his pregnant wife.

The Floyds had a few weeks of glorious living. They bought new clothes and big meals. Then police arrived, and arrested Floyd for the robbery after recovering some of the St. Louis payroll money on his farm. Floyd was sentenced to five years in the Missouri State Penitentiary in Jefferson City.

While Floyd was being introduced to the hell of the Jeff City pen—an old fashioned Big House that bellowed authority through a leather lash, sweatbox, ball and chain, and cold baths—Wilma gave birth to their son, Jackie. This little boy was to be the dearest thing in Charles Arthur Floyd's short life.

After three agonizing years, Floyd was released, vowing he would never see the inside of a prison again. He kept that promise to himself. Upon returning home, Floyd learned that his father had been shot to death by one Jim Mills, a man who had carried a mountain feud from Kentucky from which the Floyds had fled dozens of years before.

Floyd sat quietly in the Sallisaw Court House and listened as Mills was acquitted of the murder. He went home, loaded his rifle and followed Mills to the nearby Cookson Hills. Mills was never seen again.

"Chock done what he had to," an Akins resident said later. The Okies had their own way of handling things. But the law was looking for Floyd so he fled to Kansas City, "Tom's Town" it was then called, a wide-open, roaring anything-goes city under the protection of boss Tom Pendergast.

It was here in 1929 that Floyd mixed with successful gangsters, heistmen, jugmarkers, hired gunsels, learning the use of the machinegun which was to become his professional tool. A Kansas City madam, Ann Chambers, spotted Floyd immediately when he entered her brothel and said to him, "I want you for myself, pretty boy." The name stuck even though Floyd hated it.

Floyd met Red Lovett, a fellow ex-inmate

from Jeff City, in Kansas City and through him two other bank robbers, Tom Bradley and Jack Atkins. The group had a neat little list of juicy banks in northern Ohio and Floyd joined them to make the Big Money.

Working out of a rented Akron bungalow, the three men knocked over several small-town banks but hit a snag after robbing the bank in Sylvania, Ohio on March 11, 1930. Speeding into Akron, the trio went through a red light and a traffic cop gave chase.

Someone in their car punched out the back window and sprayed patrolman Harlan F. Manes with bullets. The policeman splattered all over the highway but the driver swerved in his haste and the get-away-car smashed into a telephone pole.

Police pried the bankrobbers out and they were tried for murder. Bradley was sent to the electric chair for murdering Manes; Atkins received life imprisonment and Charlie Floyd was acquitted . . . until they connected him with the Sylvania bank job. He was sentenced to fifteen years in the Ohio State Penitentiary.

Floyd apparently remembered his own words after Jeff City and on the way to prison, while deputies dozed in their railcar seats next to him, Floyd kicked out a window and jumped from the speeding train. After rolling down an embankment, Floyd bounced up and ran. By the time the train was halted, he was a half mile away, still running, and heading for Toledo, Ohio.

It was May 25, 1930. While Floyd was bounding through the Ohio cornfield John Dillinger was sleeping in his cell at Michigan City, Indiana State Prison; Clyde Barrow had just chopped off two of his own toes to get out of work detail at Eastham Prison Farm in Texas; George "Machine Gun" Kelly was doing a short term in Leavenworth; and Freddie Barker and Alvin Karpis, bunkmates, had just bedded down in the Kansas State Penitentiary.

Floyd would never stop running after that until the fall of 1934.

Once in Toledo, Floyd teamed up with Bill "The Killer" Miller and the two of them knocked over a string of banks in northern Michigan. They returned to Kansas City, picked up two girls from Mother Ash's whorehouse (after killing the girls' boyfriends, William and Wallace Ash) and headed toward Kentucky.

Floyd and Miller started another bank rob-

bing spree there: Mount Zion Trust Company, $4,000; Elliston, Kentucky bank, $2,700; Whitehouse, Kentucky bank, $3,600. Finally, they rested in Bowling Green, Ohio.

It was here that police chief Galliher grew suspicious of their license plates, checked them out and discovered that they were burning hot. With officer Ralph Castner, he approached Miller and the two girls as they were about to enter a store.

"Hold on there," Galliher shouted and Miller whirled about.

"Duck, Bill," Floyd shouted from across the street where he had planted himself for cover. Miller threw himself down and Floyd, pistols in each hand, blazed away at the two lawmen. Castner crumpled, dead. Galliher darted behind a car. When Miller tried to join Floyd, Galliher ripped half his neck away with a well-placed shot.

Miller spun in mid-air and dropped to the cement, dead. Floyd spread his legs wide apart like an outlaw of the old west and kept blazing away at Galliher. One of the girls, Beulah Baird yelled hysterically and reached for Miller's gun. She aimed it at Galliher but he was quicker and shot her in the head.

Floyd saw the situation was hopeless and dashed down the street to the gang's car, roaring off with gears grinding.

When reporters came with the news to Madam Ash whose two sons Floyd had killed in Kansas City, she asked anxiously, "Did they get Pretty Boy?" The name was electric and it went through the wire services and into almost every headline in the country. Overnight, black fame had come to Charles Arthur Floyd.

After hiding out in Toledo and paying high protection costs to the Licavoli mob, Floyd returned to Kansas City and stayed in a partitioned room above a flower shop—headquarters for a local rum-running operation.

Prohibition agents broke into this secret room on July 21, 1931 and Floyd answered them with two roaring .45s. He blew special agent Curtis C. Burks' head off and ran out in the typical "hail of bullets."

Now Floyd ran for the only place on earth he knew he could find protection—the Cookson Hills of Oklahoma among the hill folk, who had never hurt Floyd because he was one of their own. They remembered how Chock in mad delight had ripped up first mortgages in banks he robbed, hoping they had not been

"The Robin Hood of the Cookson Hills"—bankrobber Charles Arthur "Pretty Boy" Floyd, a folklore hero to his Okie neighbors, a menace to every bank in the Southwest, and a deadly killer to police everywhere. (UPI)

recorded and thereby saving a fellow farmer's homestead.

As John Steinbeck's Pa Joad later said in *The Grapes of Wrath*: "When Floyd was loose and goin' wild, law said we got to give him up—an' nobody give him up. Sometimes a fella got to sift the law."

Floyd stayed with the back county people and became known as "The Robin Hood of the Cookson Hills." He teamed up with George Birdwell, a preacher who "had lost the callin'" and the two of them went on a bank-robbing spree unequalled in the southwest.

The two men robbed the banks in Shamrock, Morris, Konawa, Maud, Earlsboro, Tahlequah, and on December 12, 1931, Floyd did what every bank bandit dreamed of doing. He robbed two banks in one day—the one horsers at Paden and Castle, Oklahoma.

In his home town of Sallisaw, Floyd got casually out of his car and strolled to the bank with a machinegun under his arm. He waved to men he knew lounging outside the local barbershop.

"How de, Chock. What you doin' in town?"

"How you, Newt," Floyd waved. "Going to rob the bank."

"Give 'em hell, Chock," another man yelled admiringly.

He did.

Floyd robbed so many banks that the insurance rates in Oklahoma doubled in one year and the governor of the state went on the airwaves to denounce him and place a $6,000 reward on his head, dead or alive.

Floyd was indignant and wrote to detectives from Altus, Oklahoma: "I have robbed no one but moneyed men."

He was even beginning to believe the image of Robin Hood but that ended on the morning of June 17, 1933.

On that day, five men, one of them FBI agent Raymond Caffrey, were machinegunned to death in the Kansas City train station by three gunmen abortively attempting to deliver desperado Frank Nash. Nash was killed and four lawmen shot to death. Floyd and his new partner Adam Richetti were identified as the killers.

To his dying day, not far off, Floyd insisted he had not been in on the Kansas City Massacre. Blackie Audett, who was there watching the entire massacre wrote later in *Rap Sheet* that the real killers were Maurice Denning, Verne Miller, and William "Solly" Weissman. But the FBI, local police and the press tagged Floyd for the mass slaying.

Time ran out on Pretty Boy on October 22, 1934. Trying to escape a local dragnet, Floyd ran across an Ohio field and FBI bullets cut him down. Melvin Purvis, agent in charge, ran to him as he lay dying.

"Are you Pretty Boy Floyd?" Purvis asked.

"I am Charles Arthur Floyd."

"Were you at the Kansas City Massacre?" another agent asked.

"I didn't do it. I wasn't in on it." He rose defiantly on one elbow. "Who the hell tipped you off? I'm Floyd all right. You've got me this time." And he died there in the open field under a hazy Ohio sun.

Steinbeck's immortal character in *The Grapes of Wrath*, Ma Joad, would have the last word about this Oklahoma bandit who had ten notches on his watch fob for each man he had killed: "I knowed Purty Boy Floyd . . . I knowed his Ma. They was good folks. He was full of hell, sure, like a good boy oughta be . . . He done a little bad thing an' they hurt 'im, caught 'im and hurt 'im so he was mad, an' the next bad thing he done was mad, an' they hurt 'im again. An' purty soon he was mean-mad.

"They shot at him like a varmint, an' he shot back, an' then they run 'im like a coyote, an him a-snappin' an' a-snarlin', mean as a lobo. An' he was mad. He wasn't no boy or no man no more, he was jus' a walkin' chunk a mean-mad.

"But the folks that knowed 'im didn't hurt 'im. He wasn' mad at them. Finally, they run 'im down and killed 'im. No matter how they say it in the paper how he was bad—that's how it was."

FOLKES, ROBERT E. LEE
Murderer ● (1922-1945)

One of America's most sensational and mysterious train murders occured in 1943. During the hectic days of the Second World War, civilians traveling the crowded U.S. rails were sub-ject to being "bumped" from their reservations by servicemen who had priority travel rights. One of these hapless civilians was 21-year-old Martha James, the beautiful blonde wife of Navy Ensign Richard F. James.

Married only four months, Martha James was riding on the Southern Pacific's Oregonian on January 23, 1943, en route to a California naval base to which her husband had been transferred. When the train reached Portland, Oregon, Martha lost her reservation to California-bound servicemen. She caught the next train, the West Coast Limited, 25 minutes later, following her husband's train on the 1,800 mile run between Seattle and Los Angeles.

Assigned to the lower sleeping compartment of berth number 13, Mrs. James fell asleep as the train rattled southward. At 4 a.m. as the Limited neared Tangent, Oregon, halfway between Salem and Eugene, Mrs. James let out a piercing scream that woke 22-year-old Marine Private Harold R. Wilson, who was sleeping in the upper level of berth 13. He heard Mrs. James shriek: "My God, he's killing me!"

Snapping back the curtain on the upper compartment, the half-asleep Wilson spied a dark man moving rapidly down the aisle toward the rear of the train. He later told police that the man was smooth-shaven, had a heavy build, and curly hair combed straight back. He thought it was a black man but he was not sure.

Just as others peeked from the curtains of their berths, the body of Martha James tumbled from her lower berth. Her throat was slashed and gushed blood. Wilson jumped from his berth and followed the path of the dark man, going toward the back of the train. He found no one. Returning to the sleeping car, Wilson stopped in the dining car's galley where he met a black cook dressed in a white uniform.

Wilson told the cook that someone had murdered a woman in his sleeping car. The cook grinned and then asked Wilson: "Have you been drinking, sir?"

"No, and I wasn't dreaming either," replied Wilson.

By the time Wilson returned to the sleeping car a conductor had covered Mrs. James's body with a sheet. When the train pulled into Eugene, police poured into the car and frantically searched the train. Crew members told detectives that someone matching Wilson's description of the dark man had been aboard the train. The man could not be found.

A diligent detective noticed a faint trail of blood spots leading from the murder car all the way to the observation car. The door leading to the small open-air observation platform of the last car was swinging open. It was then theorized that the killer could have leaped from the train as the train slowed in the Tangent railroad yard.

Sheriff Herbert Shelton found what appeared to be bloody footprints in the Tangent railyard and surmised that the murderer had jumped from the slow-moving southbound train and boarded a northbound train. Police, joined by large posses made up of private citizens, combed the freight yard and throughout the town of Tangent but found no one fitting the description that Private Wilson had given.

Mrs. James's body was removed at Eugene. Detectives, however, remained on board the train, grilling the passengers and crew as the Limited made its way toward California. They knew that robbery had not been the motive in the killing, having found Mrs. James's jewelry and more than $100 in cash in her purse still in her berth.

The investigation narrowed down to the only man Wilson had encountered as he followed the dark man through the train, the very cook Wilson had met in the diner. His name was Robert E. Lee Folkes, a self-confident, rather witty individual who denied ever having seen Mrs. James.

At first Folkes was indignant when told he was under suspicion: "That's right, go for the black man. It's always the black man, right?" He insisted that anyone of the passengers in the sleeping car could have done the murder. He even suggested that Private Wilson might be the culprit.

Then detectives received a report from Los Angeles that Folkes had a criminal record which included a sexual assault on a woman, where he had attempted to rip rings off her fingers, and a breaking and entering charge where Folkes had attempted to sexually attack three women. Confronted with this information, Folkes nervously admitted the killing. He then quickly recanted the confession.

Detectives concentrated on crew members in the dining car. Other cooks and waiters related how they had, as was their custom, relaxed after the passengers had gone to sleep, sitting about and drinking. During this party, they talked about the most attractive women on board the train, and the blonde woman in berth 13 was thought to be the most stunning female passenger, especially in the view of Robert Folkes.

Again Folkes was confronted with this report and he admitted that he had seen Mrs. James in the diner. When all were asleep, he said in his second confession, he put an overcoat over his white uniform and went to the Pullman car where Mrs. James was sleeping. He slipped into the lower level of berth thirteen. As he was closing the curtain, Folkes admitted, Mrs. James awakened.

"She wanted to know who I was and told me to get out," Folkes said. He placed a butcher knife to her throat. "I told her to keep still. She hollered and tried to throw me out. So I cut her." Folkes was arrested and charged with murder.

Though he later recanted his second confession, considerable evidence, including a blood-stained knife and Folkes's blood-stained uniform, was used to convict the suave cook. He was sentenced to death in Oregon's gas chamber by Judge L.G. Lewelling on April 26, 1943. Folkes's numerous appeals were denied and he went to the gas chamber at Salem, Oregon on January 5, 1945. As he stepped into the chamber, the ever casual Folkes waved to more than 100 silent witnesses and said with large smile on his face: "So long, everybody!"

FOOY, SAM
Murderer, Robber ● (1844-1875)

A half-breed Indian, Fooy went on a week-long rampage in the Oklahoma territory in 1875, ending with the brutal murder of a school teacher who was reluctant to give up $500 in savings.

Sentenced to death by Judge Isaac Parker in Fort Smith, Ark., Fooy, hours before he died on the gallows, told a reporter he had made peace with God.

"I dreamed I was on the gallows before a great crowd of people," Fooy said, "I was sick and weak and felt like fainting, and thought I could not face death.

"Just then a man stepped up from the crowd, came right up to me and said, 'Look, Sam, don't you be afraid to let them jump you. Jesus is standing under the floor and he will catch you in His arms.'

"That made me feel strong, when the drop came, and I felt no pain. I just fell asleep and woke up in the beautiful garden. It had running waters and stars were dancing on the waves."

Sam Fooy went through the trap on September 3, 1875, sent to his Maker, along with five others that day, by Fort Smith's dreaded executioner, hangman George Maledon. A meticulous man, Maledon made his own hanging ropes from Kentucky hemp and kept them well oiled at all times, using them over and over again on the sixty men he sent to death on the gallows (at $100 per man). He was as cold-blooded as they come. "I never hanged a man," Maledon once said, "who came back to have the job done over."

FORTY THIEVES GANG

A group of professional muggers and pickpockets, this gang operated in the Lower East Side of Manhattan as early as 1820. Its immigrant members were often used as political sluggers who destroyed polling places during elections.

Like many another gang succeeding them, the Forty Thieves encouraged a sub-mob made up of juvenile delinquents dubbed the Forty Little Thieves Gang (from which new talent was recruited). The gang disappeared from view shortly before the Civil War.

FRANKLIN, JOSEPH PAUL
Serial Killer ● (? -   )

Between 1977 and 1980, Joseph Paul Franklin, a rabid supporter of the American Nazi movement, sought out mixed-race couples, whites sympathetic to blacks and black causes, and blacks in general. He killed them at random.

Franklin began hunting his prey in the fall of 1977, seeking to murder a judge who had a reputation for leniencey toward black defendants. Instead, he shot and killed Alphonse Manning and his white girlfriend, Toni Schwenn, in Madison, Wisconsin on August 7, 1977.

On October 21, 1979, Franklin shot and killed Jesse Taylor and Marion Bressette, another mixed-race couple in Oklahoma City, Oklahoma. Franklin was brought in for questioning but released for lack of evidence. It was the same story in January 1980 when Franklin, on two separate occasions, shot and killed two young blacks, Leo Watkins and Lawrence Reese, in Indianapolis, Indiana. He was known to be in Cincinnati on June 8, 1980 when two black teenagers were shot to death.

Moving on to Salt Lake City, Franklin shot and killed two black men, Ted Fields and David Martin, on August 20, 1980, when he saw them jogging with white women. Franklin fled to Florida but this time he had been positively identified as the killer and he was extradicted back to Salt Lake City where he was charged with two counts of murder.

Franklin was convicted and sentenced to four life terms in March 1981. He was brought to trial again in 1986, charged with killing Manning and Schwenn. He received two more life terms.

FRAZIER, JOHN LINLEY
Mass Murderer ● (1946-   )

Only a year after the Manson Family murders in Los Angeles, California was shocked by another massacre, this time in the peaceful town of Santa Cruz, about 40 miles south of San Francisco. On October 19, 1970, the home of wealthy eye surgeon Dr. Victor Ohta burst into flames.

When firemen managed to extinguish the blaze, they discovered five bodies in the smoldering ruins. Found were Dr. Ohta, his wife Virginia, their two children, Taggart, 11, Derrick, 12, and Dorothy Cadwallader, Ohta's secretary.

Investigators found a note attached to Ohta's Rolls Royce which read: "Halloween 1970. Today

WWIII will begin, as brought to you by the people of the Free Universe. From this day forward, anyone and/or company of persons who misuses the natural environment or destroys same will suffer the penalty of death by People of the Free Universe. I and my comrades from this day forth will fight until death or freedom against anyone who does not support natural life on this planet. Materialism must die or mankind must stop." The note was signed: "Knight of Wands—Knight of Pentacles—Knight of Cups—Knight of Swords."

The Ohta family had been slain in a ritualistic fashion, which suggested cult killers similar to the Manson clan. There were many groups of hippies camped in the woods about Santa Cruz and these cultists came under suspicion since they were devout users of Tarot cards. The signature on the note indicated Tarot figures.

Police soon focused upon John Linley Frazier, a 24-year-old garage mechanic and cultist who lived in nearby Felton and who was a fanatical ecologist and Tarot card practicioner. Witnesses came forward to say that they had seen Frazier driving Virginia Ohta's station wagon a day after the murders. Frazier's fingerprints were found on the wheel of the Rolls Royce where the note had been placed.

Charged with the killings, Frazier would not say whether he was guilty or innocent. He was found to be legally sane and was convicted on five murder counts. Frazier was sentenced to death in California's gas chamber but his sentence was commuted to life imprisonment when the state abolished the death penalty in 1971.

FREEMAN, JOHN GILBERT
Mass Murderer ● (1930-　　　)

Thinking a family friend was having an affair with his estranged wife, John Gilbert Freeman, on September 3, 1971, entered the Phoenix, Arizona, home of Novella Bentley. Freeman carried two .38-caliber revolvers. Without explanation, Freeman shot Bentley, her daughter, and her daughter's husband. He found four children sleeping in bedrooms and shot each one of them in the head.

As he was leaving the home, police arrived, summoned by neighbors, and arrested Freeman. He was charged with seven counts of murder, but his defense counsel immediately protested, saying that in 1971 Freeman had been ruled mentally incompetent and it was technically illegal to indict him.

Prosecutors were outraged but soon overcame the argument mounted by the defense, pointing out that the 1971 ruling applied to only a time period of 120 days. Freeman was indicted, convicted, and sentenced to seven consecutive life terms.

FROMME, ALICE (AKA: "SQUEAKY")
Assassin ● (1952-　　　)

A member of the killer cult led by Charles Manson, Alice "Squeaky" Fromm sought to give voice to her political malcontent by attempting to assassinate President Gerald R. Ford on September 5, 1975. On that date, Fromme was present in a large crowd attending a rally for Ford in Sacramento, California. Pulling a .45-caliber automatic from her purse, Fromme aimed the weapon as Ford neared her, and fired. The weapon, however, misfired. Fromme was quickly subdued by presidential bodyguards. She was tried, convicted, and sentenced to prison for life.

GACY, JOHN WAYNE
Serial Killer ● (1942-1992)

BACKGROUND: BORN CHICAGO, ILL, 3/17/42; GRADUATED BUSINESS SCHOOL, BECAME SHOE SALESMAN; MARRIED MARLYNN MYERS, 1964 (DIV.); MARRIED CAROLE HOFF, 1972; WORKED AS BUILDING CONTRACTOR IN DES PLAINES, ILL.; RECORD: SEXUALLY ATTACKED A YOUTH IN WATERLOO, IOWA IN 1968; CONVICTED AND SENTENCED TO TEN YEARS IN PRISON; RELEASED IN 18 MONTHS; SEXUALLY ABUSED AND MURDERED IN LATE 1970S 33 YOUNG MEN, BURYING MOST OF THE BODIES BENEATH THE CRAWL SPACE OF HIS DES PLAINES HOME.

Named after the movie star John Wayne, Gacy was totally unlike his heroic namesake. He was a vicious predator who lured young men into his car, then to his home where, in the late 1970s, he tortured, sexually attacked, and killed them, burying the bodies, or pieces of them, in the shallow earth beneath the crawl space of his home.

Gacy claimed the lives of 33 youths, which made him the third worst killer in Illinois history after Herman Webster Mudgett, who murdered an estimated two hundred women in the early 1890s, and Johann Otto Hoch, who killed an estimated 50 women at the turn of the century. His murders, however, stand as a chilling record in modern times.

Born in Chicago on March 17, 1942, Gacy was severely injured in an accident at age eleven when a swing struck him on the head. For many years afterward he suffered dizzy spells. Some later claimed that this injury altered his mind, which led to his later crimes, not unlike the coast-to-coast killer Earle Leonard Nelson of the late 1920s who suffered a severe head injury in his youth.

After graduating business school, Gacy moved to Iowa. He worked as a shoe salesman and married Marlynn Myers in 1964. By 1968, Gacy was operating a fast food outlet in Waterloo, Iowa. At that time, Gacy lured a young boy into the back room of the store. He offered the boy money to perform oral sex but the youth refused. He then tried to sodomize the boy who managed to escape.

The boy went to the police and Gacy was charged with sexual molestation. Before the trial Gacy gave some thugs money to terrorize the boy into not testifying against him. The stubborn youth was not frightened and did appear as a witness. Gacy was convicted and given a ten-year sentence.

A model prisoner, Gacy was released in eighteen months. By that time his wife had divorced him and his reputation in Iowa was such that he could find no work. He moved back to Chicago in 1971 where he worked in construction. He began his own contracting company and began to make money. He married again to Carole Hoff in 1972 and purchased a home at 8213 West Summerdale Avenue, in Norwood Park, near Des Plaines, Ill.

All seemed well with Gacy. As he prospered he joined the Junior Chamber of Commerce. He also became popular by entertaining children's groups as "Pogo the Clown." Gacy worked diligently for the Democrat Party in Norwood Park's 21st Precinct, and, at one political gathering, posed for a picture with First Lady Rosalyn Carter.

Carole Hoff Gacy, however, realized that her husband possessed a vicious mean streak and a violent temper. She came to fear him, then left him. On his own, Gacy sought company in the form of young men. He drove his big, expensive car into the city and cruised the area near "Bughouse Square," a one-block park across from Newberry Library in the Gold Coast, then a known gathering spot for homosexuals.

Gacy had never attempted to live a normal life. In the year he arrived in Chicago, he had picked up a boy and tried to force him to have sex. Gacy was arrested but released when the boy did not testify against him. By 1977 Gacy stalked young homosexual men with regularity, or lured them to his home on the pretext of hiring them for his construction company.

One young man that year applied for a job at Gacy's home and was confronted by the barrel of a revolver. Gacy tried to force the man to have sex with him, snarling: "I killed a guy before." The young man thought Gacy was fantasizing and departed unmolested. Gacy, however, had not uttered an empty boast. He had killed before, taking the lives of several youths, but the secret life of this vile murderer was yet to be revealed.

In 1978 Gacy let loose his warped passions, attacking and killing most of his victims. On March 21 of that year, Gacy picked up Jeffrey Rignall in Newtown, another area in the city frequented by homosexuals. Rignall looked into the face of a man who had let himself go; Gacy now had a triple chin, puffy, bulging eyes and a bloated stomach.

Gacy suggested that Rignall get into his car, smoke some marijuana, and take a drive. The 27-year-old Chicagoan accepted, one of the worst mistakes of his life. No sooner was Rignall in the car than Gacy wheeled about, locked Rignall's arms in front of him, and covered his face with a chloroform-soaked rag. Rignall passed out, coming to hazily only to realize that he was traveling at high speed on an expressway and groggily noticed an exit sign.

Rignall was not fully conscious until he was in the basement of Gacy's home, immobilized by a pillory-like rack that pinioned his head and arms. He had been stripped. John Wayne Gacy stood naked before him, a grotesque display of a fat, hairy belly. Gacy pranced about, holding up whips and torture instruments, along with sexual devices that Gacy said he was about to use on Rignall.

The monster began torturing Rignall who passed out from the pain. Gacy waited until the young man came to, then tortured him again, sadistically laughing, enjoying his victim's pain. This went on for hours. At one point, Gacy growled to Rignall that he was a policeman and "I'd just as soon shoot you as look at you."

So accute was the pain Gacy inflicted upon him that he wanted to die, Rignall later stated. He begged Gacy to release him, promising that he would leave Chicago and never mention the encounter. His tormentor kept applying chloroform to him and when, hours later, Gacy applied more chloroform, Rignall passed out for the last time in the basement. He awoke in Chicago's Lincoln Park at the base of one of its many statues. Though his wallet and cash were intact, his driver's license was missing.

Rignall was bleeding from the rectum and medical tests later determined that his liver had been permanently damaged from the heavy doses of chloroform administered by Gacy. When Rignall reported the attack to police he was told that noth-

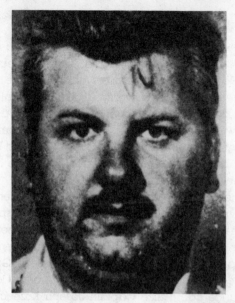

Chicago serial killer John Wayne Gacy, executed in 1994. (AP/Wide World)

ing could be done without the identity of the man, his home address, the license number of his car.

Rignall decided to track the man down himself. He rented a car and drove to the expressway exit ramp he remembered. He parked at this spot and waited for the big, black Oldsmobile to show up. It finally did and Rignall wrote down the license plate. He then used his experience with a law firm and checked real estate records, unearthing the name of John Wayne Gacy.

Taking this information to Chicago police, he managed to get an arrest warrant issued for Gacy but was told that since Gacy lived in Norwood Park, an unincorporated area, Chicago police had no jurisdiction and could not complete the arrest. The frustrated Rignall finally managed to get Gacy arrested on a misdemeanor battery charge on July 15, 1978. Police refused to charge Gacy with a felony. The burly contractor, however, did agree to pay Rignall $3,000 for medical bills which were the result of Gacy's monstrous attack.

Gacy was beginning to lose his composure. He talked about needing more space in his house, of adding more floors. One neighbor said this was foolish, that he should simply sell his house and buy another, larger house. Gacy nodded and said he would sell the house.

It was almost midnight on December 11, 1978 when Mrs. Elizabeth Piest appeared at the Des Plaines police department to report that her fifteen-year-old son Robert was missing. He had told her earlier that day that he was going to see a contractor at a pharmacy to set up a job for the following summer.

Police checked with the pharmacist who told him about a contractor named Gacy. A detective called Gacy the next day and asked him if he had interviewed the Piest boy for a job. "I don't talk to any kids," Gacy replied. "I can't help you. I don't know anything about it." At the very moment Gacy was on the phone, the body of the Piest boy was lying on the floor of his front room. He had killed the boy hours earlier.

The police doggedly went after Gacy after reviewing his record. They were sure he was responsible for abducting Robert Piest. Going to his home, they politely asked Gacy to accompany them to the police station to answer some questions. Gacy stalled, saying he had to make an important long distance call. Police Captain Joseph Kozenczak said they would wait. They did, as Gacy stretched out the call.

Hanging up the phone, he turned to detectives and said angrily: "Hey, I got a lot of important work to do. I can't be going down to the police station. I know the kid is missing but that's not important to me."

"Well, it's important to the parents," replied Kozenczak, who realized that he did not have enough evidence to arrest Gacy. He gave the contractor his card and asked that he drop by the station when he had time.

That night Gacy managed to get the body of the Piest boy into his car. He drove to the Des Plaines river and threw the body into the swirling waters. The killer must have been unnerved by recent events because, when driving home, he went off the road and had to be pulled from a ditch by a tow truck.

A short time later Des Plaines police managed to obtain a search warrant for Gacy's home. They found a receipt from the pharmacy made out to the Piest boy. This proved that Gacy had had contact with the missing youth. Still they did not move to arrest the contractor. They did assign officers to watch Gacy's house night and day.

Gacy peered from his window to see the police car outside at all hours. On December 19, 1978, he boldly walked to the police car and invited the two officers to come inside and have some coffee. They did, and while sitting in the kitchen, detected a peculiar smell. Gacy said it was from his sump pump, which he had opened to free up a clogged drain. The truth was that the water flowing beneath the house had loosened dirt beneath the crawl space and this had exposed parts of the twenty-nine bodies Gacy had buried there over the years.

Another warrant was obtained and the bodies were dug up. Gacy was arrested and held for trial. His victims ranged from a nine-year-old boy to youths in their twenties. The crawl space revealed John Butkovich, a grown man whom Gacy had murdered as early as 1976. Others included John Szyc, Billy Carroll, Greg Godzik, Samuel Stapleton, Randall Reffett, Rich Johnston, Michael Bonnin. Gacy later admitted that he had thrown four other bodies in the Des Plaines river over the years, including the Piest boy.

Tried in 1980 and sentenced to death, John Wayne Gacy clung to life for another fourteen years, filing appeal after exhausing appeal. He took up painting, like another multiple killer, Richard Speck, but when he attempted to sell these less than enviable works of art, authorities stepped in, stopping the sales. Finally, after long years of appeals, delays and stays, Gacy was finally executed by lethal injection on May 10, 1992.

(ALSO SEE: Johann Otto Hoch; Herman Webster Mudgett)

GALANTE, CARMINE
Syndicate Gangster ● (1910-1979)

Considered to have been the most important American Mafioso in the U.S. While doing twenty years for conspiracy to violate narcotics laws, Galante still ranked high as a world Mafia leader, with heavy contacts and allegiance from the Mafia hierarchy in Palermo, Sicily.

Galante's record dates back to 1921. He had been a kingpin in East Coast rackets for dozens of years and was a long-time associate of Vito Genovese and Joseph "Joe Bananas" Bonanno. One report had it that Galante was "a prime candidate for the world Mafia throne." He was shot in New York City in 1979.

GALLEGRO, GERALD ARMAND, JR.
Serial Killer ● (1953-   )

In 1955, the gas chamber in Mississippi claimed the life of Gerald Gallegro, Sr. He had murdered a prison guard. Two decades later, his son Gerald Armand Gallegro, Jr., would slay almost a dozen female hitchhikers between 1978 and 1980.

This serial killer was provided with victims by his own wife, Charlene Williams Gallegro, who would entice young girls on the road into her car with the promise of giving them marijuana. Once inside the car, the girls would be delivered to Gallegro who raped, sexually abused, and then shot them to death.

Gallegro murdered his way through California and Nevada until a witness identified his car to police. He was sentenced to death in both California and Nevada, residing, at this writing, in the latter's Death Row. His wife, the seventh and last woman to marry this monster, testified against him during several trials and received a short prison term.

GALLO, JOSEPH
Syndicate Gangster ● (1929-1972)

Brooklyn born "Crazy Joe" Gallo was first arrested in 1947; his arrests include attempted sodomy, assault, burglary, and kidnapping. As a member of New York's Carlo Gambino family and while working under capo Carmine Lambardozzi, Gallo and his brothers Larry and Albert "Kid Blast," attempted to unseat Joseph Profaci and destroy the power of his Mafia family in the late 1940s and early 1950s.

"Kid Blast" Gallo was shot to death early in the gang war. After a recent prison term, Joey Gallo attempted to resume his war with the Profaci family in 1971-72, but was shot and killed.

GAMBINO, CARLO
Syndicate Gangster ● (1902-1976)

Gambino headed one of the five New York Mafia families and was a director of the national syndicate. He once served close to two years in prison for smuggling narcotics into this country.

A power in Brooklyn, Gambino rose through the revamped Mafia-syndicate ranks with Luciano, Meyer Lansky, and Thomas "Three-Fingered Brown" Lucchese. He was in attendance at the Mafia meeting in Apalachin in 1957.

Reputedly the most powerful Mafia chief in the U.S., New York's Carlo Gambino (wearing hat) is shown in 1970, flanked by FBI agents who arrested him on suspicion of planning a $6 million armored car robbery. (UPI)

GARCIA, MANUEL PHILIP
Murderer, Thief ● (? -1821)

Garcia was a roughneck and thief who, with Jose Demas Garcia Castillano, operated in the Norfolk, Va. area as a burglar and highwayman. When another of his band, Peter Lagoardette, began courting a local girl, Castillano became incensed. The girl, was his he told Garcia, and the two plotted murder.

Enticing Lagoardette to a deserted house in Norfolk March 20, 1820, Garcia and Castillano fell upon him with cutlases, killing him. They dissected the body but authorities, inspecting the premises after neighbors reported smoke coming from the empty house, discovered Lagoardette's head, feet and hands half burned in the fireplace.

Garcia and Castillano, tracked down through laundry marks on clothes left in the deserted house (one of the first instances where such clues were used by police), were tried and hanged in Norfolk June 1, 1821.

GARY, CARLTON
Serial Killer ● (? -   )

Elderly women living in the Columbus, Georgia, were the victims of Carlton Gary. He raped and strangled seven women, between 1977 and 1978. Gary was not apprehended until 1984 when a witness identified him as a jogger running in the area where one of the victims had been slain. He had already served a prison sentence for raping a woman in New York.

Gary strangled his victims with their own stockings, earning the name "The Stocking Strangler." His victims included Ferne Jackson, 60, killed on September 16, 1977; Jean Dimmerstein, 71, murdered on September 24, 1977; Florence Scheible, 89, strangled on October 2, 1977; Martha Thurmond, 69, murdered on October 6, 1977; Kathleen Woodruff, 74, killed on December 29, 1977; Mildred Borom, 78, strangled on February 12, 1978; Janet Cofer, 61, killed on April 29, 1978.

Gary was convicted and sentenced to death by the electric chair in Jackson, Georgia. During the reign of the "Stocking Strangler," another serial killer, William Hance, went to work, provoked by Gary's murders, it was later claimed.

(ALSO SEE: William Hance)

GASKINS, DONALD HENRY
Serial Killer ● (? -   )

Known as "Pee Wee," in the small town of Prospect, S.C., Donald Henry Gaskins stood five-feet-three-inches tall. His disposition had always been mean. Gaskins threatened anyone who displeased him and he drove around town in a hearse, saying without a smile that he was looking for passengers.

At one point, someone had the audacity to ask him why he drove the hearse. Replied Pee Wee: " 'Cause I started my own personal graveyard." He even told the friend where it was, in a wheatfield behind his farmhouse.

After a resident disappeared in 1977, local police began to take Gaskins seriously. They dug up the wheatfield and unearthed nine bodies, all victims of Pee Wee's rage. He had shot Johnny Sellers in the back because the victim owed a small amount of money to one of Pee Wee's friends. He killed Jesse Judy simply because he was with Sellers.

In all, Gaskins admitted to murdering nine people during the 1970s, including Avery Leroy Howard, Doreen Dempsey, and her child, Dennis Bellamy. He was convicted of killing Silas Barnwell Yates, a 45-year-old farmer who had dared to tell Pee Wee to stay off his property.

Gaskins was sentenced to a life term on April 27, 1977. Once at the Central Correctional Institute in Columbia, S.C., Gaskins made friends with convicted murderer Rudolph Tyner, who had killed an elderly couple. The stepson of the victims was dissatisfied with Tyner's sentence and offered Gaskins $400 to kill him.

Pee Wee obtained a plastic explosive called C-4 and then affixed this to the end of a wire he ran through an air vent from his cell to that of Tyner's. He told Tyner that he was installing a cell-to-cell phone system. When the gullible Tyner picked up the "phone," a tin cup attached to the wire, the plastic explosive went off, driving metal slivers into Tyner's brain, killing him.

Gaskins was tried for this murder and condemned to death. During this trial Pee Wee Gaskins was described as "the meanest man in America." The prosecutor of his second trial added that Pee Wee was "a back-stabbing, baby-killing, mangy cur."

GEIN, EDWARD
Murderer, Cannibal ● (1906-1984)

BACKGROUND: BORN AND RAISED IN RURAL WISCONSIN. MINOR PUBLIC EDUCATION. OCCUPATION, FARMER. DESCRIPTION: 5'5", BROWN EYES, BROWN-GREY HAIR, SLENDER BUILD, ALIASES: NONE. RECORD: SHOT AND KILLED MARY HOGAN, 51, NEAR PLAINFIELD, WIS. IN 1954; SHOT AND KILLED MRS. BERNICE WORDEN IN PLAINFIELD IN 1957; ARRESTED SHORTLY THEREAFTER AT HIS FARM OUTSIDE OF PLAINFIELD WHERE OVERWHELMING EVIDENCE (AND HIS OWN ADMISSION) PROVED GEIN TO BE A PRACTICING GHOUL, NECROPHILE, AND CANNIBAL; COMMITTED TO WISCONSIN'S CENTRAL STATE HOSPITAL FOR THE CRIMINALLY INSANE WHERE HE DIED IN 1984.

Ed Gein, for decades, went unnoticed in his home town of Plainfield, Wisconsin: a quiet, unassuming man with a smile for everyone; a hard-working farmer who tended, with his brother Henry, the 160 acres left to him by an ailing mother. Gein's mother, probably, more than any other single factor, contributed to his "problem." From early boyhood, Mrs. Gein had protected her boys from women, convincing them to mind the farm and not to marry.

Two strokes in 1944 and 1945 finally brought Mother Gein to her grave. Later, Henry Gein died screaming, while he fought against a crackling Wisconsin forest fire.

Ed was suddenly alone and in his loneliness began to feed a new and sinister appetite. Without explanation, Gein sealed off his mother's bedroom and the parlor, living only in a small bedroom and the kitchen of the farmhouse where he devoured books on anatomy. Ed didn't have to bother tending the farm anymore; the government gave him a subsidy through the soil-conservation program.

For extra income, Gein worked at odd jobs for many of his 700 neighbors in Plainfield. Another idle farmer named Gus complacently joined Ed in some of his own odd jobs—namely digging up corpses from remote graves. Gein explained that he wanted the bodies (all female) for "experiments." Secretly, Ed wanted the bodies of women to study the anatomical structure of female organs—he wanted to become a woman and was thinking of an operation that would change his sex (inspired, no doubt, by the recent success in this area exhibited by Christine Jorgensen).

Gus never saw what happened to the bodies after he helped Gein carry them to a shed next to the big farmhouse. There Ed skinned each cadaver. He studied his dissected trophies. Then he was inspired to don the skins and wear them for hours as he sat brooding or walked about his kitchen; it gave him a peculiar thrill to perform such bizarre acts.

Burying the bones of each corpse, Gein burned the fleshy parts of the bodies that interested him least. The grisly remainders he kept as trophies—the heads, sex organs, hearts, livers, intestines and various strips of skin that stimulated his senses.

After Gus was taken away to an old people's home, Gein tired of looting graveyards; however, his obsession to obtain his ghoulish prizes increased. He decided to rob the living of their lives and bodies. His first known victim (Gein admitted to only two murders; others he can't remember) was Mary Hogan, 51, who ran a saloon in Pine Grove, Wisconsin. Carrying a .22-caliber pistol, Gein walked into her bar one lonely winter evening and, without a word, shot her in the head. He dragged her corpse back to his farm on a sled.

The next victim Gein remembered killing was Mrs. Bernice Worden, who operated a hardware store in Plainfield. For a week in November of 1957, Gein frequented the store, talking openly with Mrs. Worden's son Frank, who happened to be the town's deputy sheriff. Gein pressed Frank about when he planned to go deer hunting. Worden told him Saturday morning. Gein said he would return in the morning—Saturday—to pick up some antifreeze.

The following morning, while Mrs. Worden was alone in the store, Gein entered. He walked to a gun rack in the store, withdrew a .22 rifle, inserted a single bullet which he had brought along for that purpose and turned the weapon on Mrs. Worden, shooting her dead. After locking the store and taking $41 from the cash register (which he also removed), Gein carted Mrs. Worden's body out the back door and took it to his farm house for further "experiments."

When Frank Worden returned to his mother's store late Saturday, he noticed it was locked; he had to break in. There was no sign of his mother but he saw that the cash register was missing and that there was a small dark pool of blood on the floor. On the counter he saw, in his mother's handwriting, a sales slip written out for a half gallon of antifreeze. Remembering Gein's statement from the previous evening, Worden told his suspicions to his superiors. The sheriff went to Gein's farmhouse. Worden, acting on a hunch, drove to a store in West Plainfield where he knew Gein could usually be found; the proprietor and his wife were friendly with Ed. Worden found the amiable little farmer just finishing supper with the storeowners.

Worden put it to Gein without ceremony: "My mother is missing, Ed. The cash register is missing from the store. There's blood on the floor. I know you were in the store this morning for the antifreeze; I have the sales slip for it . . . Did you do anything to my mother, Ed?"

Gein retained his innocent smile. "I didn't have anything to do with it." The farmer stated that someone had come into his friend's store with the story. "I just heard about it while I was eating supper."

Worden took Gein into custody anyway and waited to hear what the sheriff had found at Ed's farmhouse, seven miles beyond Plainfield's placid streets. He didn't have long to wait. The sheriff was back soon, glassy-eyed and, for a long time, speechless. Then, staring at Gein, the sheriff rattled off the gruesome trophies he had found in Ed's farmhouse: Bracelets made of human skin, four human noses in a cup on the kitchen table, a pair

of human lips on a string dangling from a windowsill, two human shin bones, strips of human skin bracing four chairs, a tom-tom made from a coffee can with human skin stretched over top and bottom, a pair of leggings made from human skin, skin from a woman's torso converted into a vest, nine death masks—the skinned faces of women—mounted on the walls, ten heads belonging to women sawed off above the eyebrows, another head converted into a soup bowl, and a purse with handles made of human skin.

The refrigerator was stocked with human organs, frozen. A human heart was in a pan on the stove. As near as the sheriff could figure, the various pieces of bodies added up to fifteen dead women, maybe more.

Ed Gein stopped smiling. He admitted everything: the grave-robbing, the murders (those he could remember). But he was most concerned about the cash register and the money he took from Mrs. Worden's store.

"I'm no robber," he insisted. "I took the money and the cash register because I wanted to see how it worked."

For years, neighbor boys threw rocks through the windows of Gein's deserted farmouse. They pelted it with snowballs in winter. The large building became a symbol of all that was evil in the world for the townspeople of Plainfield. One night it was torched, its charred, stumpy remains visible to this day. But most of the older residents of Plainfield still refuse to drive past the Gein place. They take another road.

Wisconsin farmer and practicing cannibal, Ed Gein (wearing cap) in custody in 1957. (UPI)

GENNA BROTHERS
Bootleggers, Murderers

BACKGROUND: THE SIX GENNA BROTHERS—ANGELO ("BLOODY ANGELO"), ANTONIO ("TONY THE GENTLEMAN"), MIKE ("THE DEVIL"), PETE, SAM, AND VINCENZO ("JIM")—WERE BORN AND RAISED IN MARSALA, SICILY. IMMIGRATED TO THE U.S. IN 1910, FATHER A RAILROAD SECTION HAND, MOTHER ALREADY DEAD. DIAMOND JOE ESPOSITO, BOSS OF CHICAGO'S NINETEENTH WARD, SPONSORED THE GENNA'S MOVE FROM ITALY. THE ELDERLY GENNA DIED A FEW YEARS AFTER THE FAMILY SETTLED IN CHICAGO. DESCRIPTION: ALL SIX BROTHERS WERE MEDIUM-HEIGHT, SWARTHY, DARK EYED AND BLACK-HAIRED. ALIASES: NONE. RECORD: SAM, ANGELO, AND MIKE GENNA BEGAN THEIR CRIMINAL CAREERS

CIRCA 1912 AS BLACKHANDERS; JIM GENNA OPERATED A BROTHEL ABOUT THIS TIME; ALL SIX BROTHERS ESTABLISHED AN ALKY COOKING EMPIRE IN CHICAGO'S LITTLE ITALY IN 1919, SUPPLYING CHEAP (AND DANGEROUS) LIQUOR TO JOHNNY TORRIO AND AL CAPONE; THE GENNAS WERE INVOLVED IN THE 1921 POLITICAL BATTLE BETWEEN NINETEENTH WARD ALDERMAN JOHN POWERS AND CHALLENGER TONY D'ANDREA. TAKING SIDES WITH THE LATTER AND KILLING SEVERAL POWERS SUPPORTERS: PAUL A. LABRIOLA, 3/8/21, DOMINICK GUTTILLO, 8/27/21, NICOLA ADAMO, 11/26/21; MIKE GENNA WITH ALBERT ANSELMI AND JOHN SCALISE KILLED POLICE OFFICERS HAROLD OLSON AND CHARES WALSH IN A GUNFIGHT ON WESTERN AVENUE 6/13/25; ANGELO GENNA KILLED BY VINCENT "THE SCHEMER" DRUCCI, GEORGE "BUGS" MORAN, AND EARL "HYMIE" WEISS 5/25/25; MIKE GENNA KILLED IN THE ABOVE-MENTIONED POLICE FIGHT; TONY GENNA KILLED BY GIUSEPPE NERONE (TONY SPANO, ALSO CALLED "THE CAVALIER") AND ACCOMPLICES, 7/8/25; SAM AND PETE GENNA WENT INTO HIDING IN 1925, JIM FLED TO MARSALA, ITALY; THE THE THREE BROTHERS EVENTUALLY RETURNED TO CHICAGO, COMPLETELY DIVORCED FROM THE RACKETS, RUNNING AN IMPORT FIRM SPECIALIZING IN CHEESE AND OLIVE OIL. THEY DIED IN OBSCURITY.

Angelo Genna, "Bloody Angelo," stood on the curb with his three bodyguards, watching a man he hated—Paul Labriola—cross the street at Congress and Halsted. Genna had just eaten a mammoth spaghetti lunch and a toothpick hung limply from his scowling mouth. Labriola, a bailiff for the Municipal Court in City Hall, was a strong supporter of incumbent Alderman Johnny Powers (Johnny De Pow) in this election year of 1921. Angelo Genna wanted Tony D'Andrea, the challenger, to win. His methods of achieving such a victory were slightly unorthodox.

As Labriola nervously crossed the intersection, Angelo nodded to Samuzzo "Samoots" Amatuna, Johnny "Two Gun" Guardino, and Frank "Don Chick" Gambino. All four men, without hesitation—before dozens of pedestrians walking past them in the broad, bright afternoon-pulled out pistols and began shooting at Labriola.

The hapless victim fell in the street, his twitching body almost torn in half by the volley.

"He ain't done yet," Bloody Angelo said, and he casually sauntered over to the wounded man, straddling him with his legs. He aimed his pistol at Labriola's head and the revolver jumped three times in his hand. The back of Labriola's head disappeared.

"C'mon," Genna said to his henchmen. "He's done." Angelo threw his toothpick to the ground and the four men got into a large black Lincoln parked at the corner and drove off at a moderate speed.

This was 1921, the streets of Chicago, and whatever Angelo Genna or his five brothers chose to do in Littly Italy was their business. He was a millionaire gangster whose power was so vast and reputation so fearful that he conducted open mayhem and murder with impunity. The dozen witnesses to the Labriola shooting would never testify against him, he was sure. And he was right.

The way of the Gennas, notwithstanding Angelo's public slaughter of Labriola, was normally one of guile, cunning, intrigue. They were masters of hypocrisy and deceit, more likely to ambush their victims than to shoot it out toe-to-toe.

It was an all-Sicilian clan; the Gennas trusted no one—not even their downtown sponsors, Capone and Torrio—except those who hailed from their native land and even these were suspect unless they came from the Genna village of Marsala, such as the treacherous John Scalise and Albert Anselmi.

Scalise and Anselmi were the most dreaded murderers in Chicago in the 1920s. Wanted in Sicily for murder, the unwholesome pair fled to Chicago, going to work for the Gennas as their top enforcers. They were strange-looking together; Anselmi was short, fat and balding, Scalise was tall, railroad thin and had an ugly cast to his right eye—it always appeared to be at the corner of the socket while the other stared straight ahead—creating a sinister appearance guaranteed to unnerve any rival gangster.

They were innovators of crime. Scalise and Anselmi began the practice of coating their bullets with garlic, in the mistaken belief that if their shots were not true, the additive would kill the victim by causing gangrene to set in. Gangland imitated this useless trick for several years.

The pair also inaugurated the hand-shake murder. One would walk up to an unsuspecting victim and warmly clasp him by the hand, smiling and graciously uttering the words: "Meester Joe, my fren'." The other would sneak up behind the victim and shoot him in the back of the head. This technique was ap-

A gathering of the "Terrible Gennas" of Chicago; the brothers (left to right) are Sam, "Bloody Angelo," Peter, Antonio, and Jim. They made bad booze and had their gunmen tip garlic on their bullets. (UPI)

plied on several occasions when the pair was busy eliminating Genna foes, notably when Scalise and Anselmi shot and killed Dion O'Bannion in 1924.

Equally fearsome killers like Orazio "The Scourge" Tropea and Giuseppe Nerone (alias Joe Pavia, Tony Spano, "The Cavalier") toted guns for the Gennas. Tropea led a sub-gang of juvenile killers who preyed on fellow Sicilians and acted as liaison agents between the Gennas and the thousands of Sicilian immigrants who ran the gang's alky-cooking operations in their homes. Tropea, who thought of himself as a sorcerer—the superstitious in Little Italy believed he possessed "The Evil Eye"—made his daily rounds with Tony Finalli, Felipe Gnolfo, Ecola "The Eagle" Baldelli, and Vito Bascone. These men would march peacock-proud down the streets in broad daylight with pistols drawn and shotguns cradled in their arms, unhampered by police (the Gennas reportedly paid $200,000 yearly to the police in their district for "looking the other way").

The Gennas were the chief suppliers of liquor to dives serviced by the Torrio-Capone combine. The quality of Genna liquor was abominable. So inept were the brothers as distillers that their liquor actually possessed a poisonous residue. If an unlucky speakeasy patron purchased a "bad" Genna bottle, he would wind up blind, paralyzed, or dead.

Irrespective of the dangers, Capone and Torrio couldn't buy enough of this awful rotgut, such was the demand in their bootleg domain. The Gennas, to meet the demand, first enlarged their giant Taylor Street distillery. They then turned to fellow Sicilians, installing small copper stills in homes. Day laborers quit their jobs and stayed at home in their kitchens, watching the alky-cookers gurgle at $15 a day. It cost the Gennas 40¢ a gallon to produce their booze. Torrio paid $2 for each gallon and saloons paid $6 a gallon. The money rolled in. There was even a slush fund to handle the funeral arrangements of those hapless alky-cookers killed when defective stills exploded.

The Gennas were as status-seeking as Capone and Big Jim Colosimo. They purchased twelve front-row season tickets to the opera. After performances, they would dine *en masse* in the swanky Pompeian Room of the Congress Hotel where Tony Genna lived with his mistress, Gladys Bagwell. Gladys was the daughter of a Baptist minister in Chester, Ill. who had traveled to Chicago in 1920 seeking a stage career. She became a torch singer instead, in one of the Torrio-owned brothel bars where Gentleman Tony met her. He kept his blonde jazz cutie in a $100-a-week suite in the Congress Hotel and showered her with platinum bracelets, pearl necklaces, diamond rings, and dozens of fur coats. When asked about her relationship with the gangster, Gladys demurely answered, "Why, he's my fiancé."

All went well in the corrupt world of the Gennas until 1925. There had been the gang wars with Dion O'Bannion and other North Siders, but Big Al Capone had backed the Gennas and Big Al was always victorious. Then, a year after the death of Mike Merlo, president of the *Unione Siciliane* (a fraternal order that controlled all the Sicilian-based rackets) the Gennas rose as one man, screaming independence and defying Al Capone.

Capone lusted after the *Unione's* presidency, but the fact that he was a Neapolitan prevented him from taking office. The Gennas moved into the *Unione*, spending heavy chunks of their $300,000-a-month bootleg income to win over high-ranking members. Angelo Genna proclaimed himself President. He also sent his deadliest of killers—Scalise and Anselmi—out to kill Capone.

The murderous pair were often rash in the ways they disposed of their victims, but in 1925 they were reasonable enough to realize that killing Capone would only insure their own deaths. (They did plot to kill Capone in 1929 when Scalise became the *Unione's* president and were, in turn, killed by Capone.) The killers went to Capone and informed him that the Gennas had secretly declared war against him and his powerful organization. They continued to work for the Gennas, but were ever after in Capone's private employ.

Angelo Genna was the first of the scabrous clan to die. In January of 1925, Angelo married Lucille Spingola, daughter of the prestigious lawyer and politician, Henry Spingola. The wedding was another status move. Genna took out ads in newspapers which blared a "come one, come all" invitation to the lavish reception in the Ashland Auditorium. Three thousand people attended, uproariously applauding the twelve-foot, 2,000-pound cake attendants wheeled to the center of the hall. (Designer S. Ferrara gave an on-the-spot press interview stating that it took four days to bake the monstrosity, which contained 400 pounds of sugar, 400 pounds of flour, seven cases of eggs, and buckets and buckets of flavors.)

The couple honeymooned in the Belmont Hotel. Mayor William Hale "Big Bill" Thompson lived across the street. Capone, worried that Genna would form new and solid alliances with the in-power political machine, ordered Angelo killed. Bugs Moran saved his men the trouble.

On May 25, 1925 Angelo kissed his bride goodbye and hopped into his $6,000 roadster with $25,000 in cash bulging in his pocket. He was on his way to buy a house for Henry Spingola's little girl. As he approached Hudson Street on Ogden Avenue, a large sedan roared from a side street, tailing him. At the sedan's wheel was mobster Frank Gusenberg. In the back seat sat "Bugs" Moran, Hymie Weiss, and "Schemer" Drucci, all fondling their shotguns. They still seethed with hatred and vengeance over the killing of their chieftain, Dion O'Bannion, by Genna killers Scalise and Anselmi.

Genna spotted them in his rear-view mirror and stepped on the gas. At Hudson, he swung the auto sharply into a vicious turn; the roadster fish-tailed and then smacked into a lamppost. Pinned behind the wheel, Angelo helplessly watched as the black sedan glided past him, shotguns from the windows emitting a fatal barrage.

At the morgue, there wasn't much left for Mike Genna to identify. He cursed for ten minutes and then called Scalise and Anselmi. They would track down Moran, Drucci, and Weiss if it took years, he told the killers.

It didn't take years for Capone to eliminate Mike. On the pretext that they were aiding Mike in his search for his brother's murderers, Scalise and Anselmi took Genna for a ride on June 13, 1925, intending to kill him. At Forty-seventh and Western, a squad car swung behind Genna's auto. Inside were police detectives Harold Olson, Charles Walsh, Michael Conway, and William Sweeney. They had recognized Genna at the wheel and decided to investigate.

Policeman Olson clanged the police gong as a signal for the gangster car to stop. It sped up. Going close to seventy miles an hour, the cars zigzagged down Western Avenue for a mile and a half. A truck suddenly veered onto the boulevard and Genna jammed down the brakes, the car spinning completely around and jumping the curb where it smashed into a pole. Genna, Scalise, and Anselmi, grabbing shotguns, flung themselves from the car.

They crouched at the ready as the squad car came up, and watched the four plain-clothesmen alight. "How come you didn't stop when you heard our gong?" Conway asked.

Scalise and Anselmi opened up, their loads of buckshot hitting Olson square in the head as he stepped from the car. He was killed instantly. Walsh was half-way out of his seat when Scalise fatally shot him. Anselmi felled Conway with a blast in the chest.

That left young Sweeney.

"He's hiding behind the car," Scalise said. "We'll pick him off when he puts up his head."

Sweeney wasn't waiting to be picked off. With a pistol in each hand, the intrepid cop dove through a door and hurled himself like a javelin at the three killers. He squeezed off his rounds as he came on the run and the startled gangsters panicked and ran down an alley. Sweeney galloped after them.

For heavyset men, Scalise and Anselmi amazed the smaller Genna by sprinting ahead of him and darting down a passageway. Mike, trailing, tried to follow, but Sweeney fired a shot from the alley's mouth and sent a bullet into Genna's leg. Painfully slowed up, Mike the Devil looked about frantically for refuge. He spotted a basement window, bashed out the glass with his shotgun, and dove into the cellar head first.

Joined by two off-duty policemen, George Oakey and Albert Richert, Sweeney broke through the basement door. Genna was lying on a coal pile. Weakly, he raised his revolver and sent a wild shot at the three officers rushing toward him.

They overpowered him and dragged him into the alley. A police ambulance arrived shortly and as attendants were lifting Genna onto a stretcher, Mike raised his good leg in a mighty kick. The attendant received the blow square on the jaw and was knocked unconscious. Genna smiled crookedly. "Take that, you dirty son-of-a-bitch!" he said. These were his last words. The bullet in his leg had severed an artery and he bled to death within two hours.

Scalise and Anselmi, their shirtfronts torn open, their hair, wet with sweat, in their eyes, raced around the block like wild men. They ran north on Western and boarded a trolley car. Just as the trolley moved off, a squad car spotted them and followed. They were picked up at the next stop.

"We don't know nothin' about no shootin'," Scalise insisted.

"We are just a couple boys lookin' for work," Anselmi snorted. "You know where there's jobs?"

"I'd like to give you jobs for life," a sergeant answered and took them into custody. They were released hours later and never brought to trial. Capone got them out and kept them out. They were on his payroll. The assignment that day was to kill Mike Genna. Detective Sweeney had done it for them.

Fear came to Tony Genna. He and his remaining brothers were terrified. The two tough men of the family, Angelo and Mike, had been slaughtered in twenty days. Tony the Gentleman, the real brains behind the Genna family, knew he was next. He locked himself up in his lavish Congress Hotel suite, sending his mistress Gladys out to shop for necessities. He refused to attend meetings with his brothers. Too risky.

Several phone conversations with his chief gunner, Giuseppe Nerone, revealed that Capone was behind his brother Mike's death. Scalise and Anselmi had broken the Sicilian gangster code and had gone over to Big Al; in fact, they were now his personal bodyguards, he was told.

"I got to get out of town," Tony told Nerone.

"No, wait. First we must make plans," Giuseppe argued. "I build up the gang. We take Capone. Then you and the boys can come back. We must meet and talk first."

Tony Genna drove to a rendezvous at Curtis and Grand Avenue. Nerone waved to him from the doorway of Cutillas' grocery store, a Genna front. Genna parked his car, looked up and down the street through large smoky glasses and walked over to Nerone who put out his hand. Tony took it. In a moment, two men—Scalise and Anselmi—ran up behind him and shot him in the back.

Nerone, too, had thought it better to break the code than to buck Al Capone. The three men ran down the street and jumped into a car which roared away. This time, however, Scalise and Anselmi had been sloppy. Tony Genna still lived.

He clung to life for several hours at the County Hospital.

Her mascara running with tears, Gladys Bagwell was at his bedside. "Who shot you, Tony?" she begged.

Genna's eyes fluttered open. "The Cavalier," he hissed and then died.

Police thought Tony had said "Cavallaro" and searched fruitlessly for such a man. By the time they discovered their error, the Cavalier had been machine-gunned to death in his favorite barber chair.

After Tony's slaying, everybody in the Genna cartel went down. Angelo's father-in-law, Lawyer Henry Spingola, was shot to death by Orazio Tropea and others on January 10, 1926. Tropea himself was next. "The Scourge" was hit by two shotgun blasts from a passing car on Halsted Street February 15, 1926. Vito Bascone was trapped by Capone gunners in a remote spot in suburban Stickeney. He begged for his life, hands lifted in prayer. His killers shot his hands off and sent a bullet into his brain. Vito's body was thrown into a ditch. Ecola Baldelli—"The Eagle"—was killed the same day, January 24, 1926. Scalise and Anselmi had a fight on their hands with Baldelli and took special pains, after killing him, to hack his body to pieces. The remains were strewn on a North Chicago garbage heap. Shotguns found Tony Finalli March 7, 1926, ending his career. It took three years for Capone's men to find Felipe Gnolfo; he was dispatched in 1930.

Unlike Angelo Genna, who was buried in a $10,000 bronze casket with $25,000 in flowers strewn about his grave, Tony went into the sod in a cheap wooden box and without a mourner in sight. His brothers had fled the city, their influence forever smashed. (Jim Genna ran all the way back to Marsala, Sicily, where he promptly stole the jewels from a religious statue, was caught, and went to prison for two years.)

A police sergeant at Tony's funeral, which took place at Mount Carmel Cemetery, looked about and was shocked to see Dion O'Bannion's grave only yards away. Sworn enemies in life, these two gangsters now reposed almost side by side. "When Judgement Day comes and them graves are open," the sergeant said ruefully, "there'll be hell to pay in this cemetery."

[ALSO SEE Al Capone, Dion O'Bannion, *Unione Siciliane.*]

GENOVESE, VITO ("DON VITONE")
Mafia Chief, Murderer ● (1897-1969)

BACKGROUND: BORN IN RISIGLIANO, ITALY NEAR NAPLES, 11/21/1897. PUBLIC EDUCATION TO THE EQUIVALENT OF FIFTH GRADE. IMMIGRATED TO THE U.S., 5/23/13 ON BOARD "SS TAORMINA." MARRIED, 1924, WIFE DIED 1929; REMARRIED, 1932 TO ANNA PETILLO, DIVORCED, 1950. ORIGINAL OCCUPATION, LABORER. TWO CHILDREN. DESCRIPTION: 5'6", BROWN EYES, BLACK HAIR, STOCKY BUILD, TWO SMALL SCARS ON RIGHT CHEEK. ALIASES: UNKNOWN. RECORD: ARRESTED, NYC, 1917 FOR CARRYING A CONCEALED WEAPON; SENTENCED TO 60 DAYS IN NYC WORKHOUSE; ARRESTED, 1918, CARRYING CONCEALED WEAPON; FINED $250; WORKED AS LUCKY LUCIANO'S SECOND-IN-COMMAND OF NARCOTICS AND BROTHEL RACKETS IN MANHATTAN IN 1920S; ARRESTED 11 TIMES BETWEEN 1920-1939 ON SUSPICION OF ASSAULT, ROBBERY, MURDER; MURDERED WITH JOE ADONIS (JOSEPH DOTO), ALBERT ANASTASIA AND BENJAMIN "BUGSY" SIEGEL, BROOKLYN MAFIA CHIEFTAIN JOSEPH "JOE THE BOSS" MASSERIA IN SCARPATO'S RESTAURANT, CONEY ISLAND, N.Y., 4/15/31 ON ORDERS FROM LUCKY LUCIANO; REPORTEDLY ORDERED TWO OF HIS GUNMEN—PETER MIONE (ALIAS PETEY MUGGINS) AND MICHAEL BARRESE—TO KILL GERARD VERNOTICO AND ANTONIO LONZO IN MANHATTAN 3/16/32; MEMBER OF THE NATIONAL CRIME SYNDICATE BOARD UNDER LUCIANO; ORDERED THE MURDER OF GANGSTER FERDINAND "THE SHADOW" BOCCIA 10/9/34; AS BOARD MEMBER OF THE NCS VOTED TO KILL DUTCH SCHULTZ 10/23/35 IN NEWARK, N.J. RESTAURANT; ESCAPED TO ITALY TO AVOID PROSECUTION IN THE BOCCIA MURDER CASE IN 1937; ESTABLISHED HIMSELF THERE AS A MAFIA BOSS AND DIRECTED NARCOTICS SMUGGLING INTO U.S.; BECAME A GOOD FRIEND OF DICTATOR BENITO MUSSOLINI, FINANCING FASCIST BUILDINGS; LEADER OF ITALIAN BLACK MARKET OPERATIONS AFTER AMERICAN OCCUPATION; RETURNED TO U.S. TO FACE TRIAL ON BOCCIA MURDER; DISMISSED; ASSUMED OLD POLICY RACKETS IN HARLEM, LUCIANO'S NARCOTICS AND BROTHEL DIRECTORSHIP IN MANHATTAN; ORDERED THE MURDER OF NEW JERSEY MAFIA CHIEF WILLIE MORETTI 10/4/51; ORDERED THE MURDER OF GANGSTER AND POLICE INFORMANT STEVEN FRANSE, 6/19/53; ORDERED THE MURDER OF NCS BOARD MEMBER FRANK COSTELLO 5/2/57 (ATTEMPT BY GUNMAN VINCENTE "THE CHIN" GIGANTE FAILED); ORDERED THE MURDER OF ALBERT ANASTASIA, MAFIA OVERLORD, 10/25/57; INDICTED FOR SMUGGLING, DISTRIBUTING AND SELLING NARCOTICS 7/8/58; CONVICTED IN EARLY 1959 AND SENTENCED TO FIFTEEN YEARS IN THE FEDERAL PENITENTIARY IN ATLANTA, GA., WHERE HE CONTINUED TO RULE HIS CRIME CARTEL, ORDERING THE DEATHS OF ALL WHO OPPOSED HIM, SUCH AS BROOKLYN GANGSTER ERNEST "THE HAWK" RUPOLO, WHOSE HACKED-UP BODY SURFACED IN NEW YORK'S JAMAICA BAY, 8/27/64 (THE HAWK HAD IMPLICATED GENOVESE IN THE 1934 BOCCIA MURDER; HIS BODY WAS PIERCED WITH MORE THAN ONE HUNDRED ICE-

He was forty-nine, had killed countless men, ruled an empire of crime and was about to be released once again, escaping a guilty verdict in a twelve-year-old murder. Judge Leibowitz stared coldly down at the defendant Vito "Don Vitone" Genovese and said: "I cannot speak for the jury, but I believe if there were even a shred of corroborating evidence you would have been condemned to the electric chair. By devious means, among which were the terrorizing of witnesses, kidnapping them, yes, even murdering those who could give evidence against you, you have thwarted justice time and again." Genovese only sneered, pivoted slowly, and walked victoriously from the court, June 11, 1946.

Time and again, the judge had said. How true that statement was, how sadly accurate. Genovese, an arch criminal of organized crime, could once again boast to his underworld minions about his omnipotence and immunity against prosecution. He had aspired to become Capo di tutti Capi—boss of all bosses—and, through murder, terror and torture, he eventually achieved this end.

Genovese began small. Upon arrival from Italy in 1913, he fell in with Lower East Side gangs. There were hundreds of these in New York, all preying upon small shopkeepers and pushcart peddlers, stealing, extorting, selling protection. Genovese met Lucky Luciano in 1917. They began as a burglary and robbery partnership. That year, at age 20, Genovese was first arrested for carrying a revolver and thrown into the workhouse for sixty days. The following year, when he and Luciano were part of Little Augie Orgen's mob, he was arrested again for toting a gun. The second arrest did not disturb Vito. This time he was in the money and simply paid a $250 fine. He was free in two hours.

Genovese and Luciano built up a lucrative business in chain brothels and narcotics, becoming the city's chief suppliers of smuggled heroin by 1925. By then they went to work for Joe "The Boss" Masseria, an old-fashioned gangster who barely spoke English. Masseria was labeled by Genovese, Luciano, and other rising Italian and Sicilian gangsters as a "Mustache Pete."

In 1930, Salvatore Maranzano, a New York Mafia chieftain, declared war on Masseria. For more than a year gunfights in New York chopped down dozens of gangsters on both sides. The war spread to other cities. In Chicago Capone joined the Italian cause headed by Masseria, and Joey Aiello backed Sicilian-bred Maranzano, sending $5,000 a week to New York for the battle chests. Approximately sixty men were killed in twelve months, most of the slaughter taking place in Manhattan.

It was a stand-off for a while. Though Maranzano's forces got the upper hand, Joe the Boss could not be found. He was crafty in that he seldom left his stronghold at 65 Second Avenue and his mere existence continued to spark resistance to Maranzano. Maranzano rejected all efforts to create a settlement even though his two lieutenants, Luciano and Genovese, longed for peace. He would only come to terms if Masseria were killed.

Economically, Genovese and Luciano were suffering. Their neglected rackets were crumbling; they had been too busy murdering their enemies. The two ultimately promised to have their chief killed. Fine, Maranzano said. Good. Then there will be peace.

Luciano connived. Using his considerable persuasiveness, Charley Lucky talked Masseria into having a fat lunch at Joe the Boss' favorite restaurant, Scarpato's in Coney Island. Genovese, Luciano, and Ciro Terranova drove Masseria there on April 15, 1931. Luciano and Joe the Boss dined alone for three hours, settling into a card game after a resplendent meal.

Then Luciano excused himself, pretending to use the toilet. Genovese re-entered the restaurant with three other men, all young hoodlums: Albert Anastasia, Joe Adonis, and Benjamin "Bugsy" Siegel. This was to be a universal murder in the sense that each man represented important and separate gangs who were to unite under Maranzano once Joe the Boss was dead.

Masseria hardly knew what happened. The four gangsters aimed pistols at his head and emptied their guns into him. Shattered, the gangland chief spilled forward onto the table and the assassins walked from the restaurant. When police arrived, Luciano explained that he had been in the men's room washing his hands. No, he didn't see any of the killers. Neither did any of the two dozen customers in the restaurant. The New York Police Dept. closed the book on Joe Masseria, another mobster killed by "persons unknown."

Genovese and Luciano went fast and far after this murder. Within months, they eliminated Maranzano and established a national crime syndicate ruled by a board, no boss of bosses. Unlike Charley Lucky, Genovese made out-of-the-country plans for the future. He took a three-month trip back to his native Italy in the early 1930s, establishing important criminal contacts around Naples, scheming out an escape plan should conditions become too hot in the U.S.

Genovese's first wife had died in 1929 of unknown causes. He fielded about for a good woman, a silent woman. In 1932 he met attractive Anna Petillo Vernotico, a married woman. Her husband Gerard was found weeks later on March 16, 1932, strangled to death on top of a Manhattan building. Antonio Lonzo, who had accidentally stumbled upon this murder, was found a few feet away, dead with a bullet in his brain.

The killers, identified years later by informant Joe Valachi as Michael Barrese and Peter Mione, disappeared, killed on Genovese's orders. Vito was a tidy man. A short time after the murder of her husband, Anna married Vito Genovese, a union which produced two children.

Though Genovese's cut from the brothels and narcotics racket he helped Luciano run was hefty—some reports estimate $200,000 each year—Vito additionally amassed huge on-the-spot fortunes by fleecing wealthy merchants in rigged card games.

In September of 1934, Genovese bilked an Italian businessman for $160,000 in a card game played in the back room of a restaurant owned by one of his mobsters, Ferdinand "The Shadow" Boccia. The rash Boccia demanded a $35,000 cut of the spoils. His boss, Genovese, said he would think it over.

After Vito had meditated, he sent Peter Defeo, Gus Frasca, George Smurra, Mike Mirandi, and Ernest "The Hawk" Rupolo to pay off Boccia with bullets on September 9, 1934.

A small-time Brooklyn mobster and member of Mirandi's troop, Willie Gallo, learned of the killing and Genovese's lieutenants, Mirandi, ordered The Hawk to kill him. Rupolo attempted to comply, pointing his gun at Willie's head one night after the two emerged from a movie. The gun misfired.

"What the hell is this?" Gallo demanded.

Rupolo smiled. "A joke. Look, the gun isn't loaded."

Both men laughed. Returning to Gallo's apartment, The Hawk privately inspected his weapon, oiled the firing pin, reloaded and minutes later, when the pair were once again on the street, fired a bullet into Gallo. Rupolo's aim was poor and his victim lived. The Hawk was sent to prison for twenty years.

Three years later, Genovese heard that Rupolo and another gangster, Peter LaTempa, were about to involve him in the Boccia murder. By then Manhattan's district attorney Thomas E. Dewey had turned on the heat under New York's top racket bosses. Dutch Schultz was the first to go, killed by the national syndicate (Vito voted with Luciano and Lepke for his death) after the Dutchman threatened to kill Dewey in 1935. Lepke and Luciano were next. Dewey relentlessly exposed their operations and both faced long prison terms.

Genovese didn't wait for Dewey's spotlight to find him. Since 1933, when he had visited his home town of Naples, Don Vitone had been secreting enormous funds in European banks, particularly in Switzerland. He skipped with an estimated fortune of $2 million.

For years it was thought that the dreaded Genovese had been killed in the war. But he turned up in Naples in 1944 and, with the usual congenial smile and soft word, talked himself into a job as an interpreter for Army Intelligence. U.S. authorities were gratified at his cooperation. He exposed every important black market operator in and about Southern Italy. It was learned later that Genovese's willingness to inform stemmed from greed. Once the black marketeers were imprisoned, he simply took over their rackets.

Don Vitone's prestige fell sharply with the Army when CID agent Orange Dickey learned that Genovese was a fugitive gangster from America who had fled prosecution in 1937 from a murder case, stylishly coming to Italy with several expensive cars, a retinue of servants and gunmen, and a Monte Cristo fortune which he doled out to Mussolini, his close friend, in an effort to ingratiate himself with the dictator.

The situation was paradoxical. Mussolini had promised the Italian people that he would rid Italy of the Mafia (after the slaying of the dogmatic Maranzano in 1931, the Mafia was no longer a strict Sicilian organization but an amalgamation of Italian and Sicilian gangsters everywhere). Genovese, a leading Mafia figure known to Mussolini, became his close friend and remained so through the war. The gangster simply bought the dictator's favor by contributing more than $250,000 to the fascists, notably for the erection of a lavish party headquarters in Nola, Italy.

Agent Dickey, informed by New York authorities that Genovese was wanted on the Boccia slaying, arrested Genovese and personally escorted him by boat back to the U.S. where he was placed on trial. Don Vitone was undisturbed. The two chief witnesses against him were Rupolo and LaTempa and he knew how to handle them.

Peter LaTempa, placed in a Brooklyn jail under protective custody, suffered from gallstones. He was accustomed to taking painkilling pills. On January 15, 1945, he was given several of these tablets and promptly doubled up and died, his medicine dosed with enough poison "to kill eight horses," police stated.

How and who administered the lethal medicine to LaTempa was never determined, but both the prosecution and underworld knew Don Vitone had engineered the murder. With only Rupolo's testimony against him (under New York law the corroboration of a second witness is necessary for conviction), Genovese relaxed. Judge Leibowitz was forced to set him free June 11, 1946.

The gang chief lost no time in re-establishing his authority over the New York mobs, through his still-viable position in the syndicate. Luciano had been deported and was rendered ineffectual. Loyal lieutenants Tony Bender (Anthony Strollo) and Mike Mirandi still commanded two troops of gunmen-racketeers and these diligently went to work on Genovese's behalf, asserting their leadership once again in narcotics peddling.

A new crop of gangsters had assumed power in Genovese's absence and he systematically had them killed or pacified as he worked his way to the top position of the national crime cartel. First to go was old-line New Jersey Mafia chief Willie Moretti who was aligned with the syndicate's "prime minister," Frank

Vito Genovese, the most ruthless Mafia chief of modern times; shown as he is being led to a federal prison on a narcotics conviction, 1960. (UPI)

Costello, Genovese's real objective. Moretti was shot to death October 4, 1951.

Vito next ordered the death of another Costello ally, Steven Franse, June 19, 1953. Costello's number came up on May 2, 1957, after Genovese sent his 6' 4" killer, Vincent "The Chin" Gigante out to do the job. Gigante was sloppy and only wounded Costello, but the prime minister's power was broken and he was voted out of the syndicate.

Another board member, Albert Anastasia, who had taken control of the old Murder, Inc. organization and was known as the "Mad Hatter" of the Mafia, had been a staunch Costello-Moretti ally. Genovese, fearing Anastasia's berserk wrath, had him killed on October 25, 1957, in a hotel barber shop. Later that year, Genovese called for the notorious Apalachin meeting which was attended by more than 100 top Mafia and syndicate leaders representing every major city in the U.S. Vito's power was supreme. He had achieved his goal: the group recognized him as boss of bosses, the coveted title that had destroyed Masseria, Maranzano, and others.

The publicity surrounding the Apalachin

meeting spurred the Government to heavy action and a solid federal narcotics case was soon established against Genovese. Arrested in 1958, he was sentenced to fifteen years the following year.

Such was the fear Don Vitone generated in the underworld, however, that his power to direct rackets and order murder did not wane behind bars. His henchmen finally found Ernest "The Hawk" Rupolo; he was brutally tortured, killed, and dumped into New York's Jamaica Bay in 1964.

Serving part of his sentence in the federal prison in Atlanta, Genovese was subsequently transferred to Leavenworth. There, in his Spartan cell, he died in 1969 of a heart attack.

In the ten years of Genovese's confinement, the underworld knew no peace. He had ordered dozens of killings. He held court from his cell, issuing directives through the prison grapevine. Hundreds of men lived in terror while Don Vitone served out his sentence. He was a merciless unfeeling killer, utterly dedicated to crime despite the godfatherly appearance he took on in old age. Only one person ever jarred his emotions: his wife Anna.

She had divorced him in 1950, informing authorities of his rackets and secreted bank accounts. Anna was never harmed. "Nobody could understand why Vito didn't do anything about her," Joe Valachi once testified. "The word was all around, why don't he hit her? She had something on him." That "something" undoubtedly had to do with the murder of her former husband.

No matter. Genovese, most vicious of killers, forgave Anna everything. When he spoke of her in the prison yard, great tears welled up in his eyes and uncontrollably streamed down his cheeks. The gangsters who surrounded him during his jailed exile would watch these displays, gaping incredulously. Don Vitone crying! If the boys outside could only have seen it.

[ALSO SEE Frank Costello, Charles Lucky Luciano, The Mafia, Salvatore Maranzano, The Syndicate, Joe Valachi.]

GIANCANA, SAM ("MOMO")
Syndicate Gangster ● (1908-1975)

Giancana was the top Mafia boss of Chicago from 1957 until 1966, when he was released from a one-year prison term he had served for contempt of a federal grand jury. At that point, Giancana found federal surveillance in Chicago too hot and skipped to points unknown in either Mexico or South America. Tony Accardo resumed leadership of the Chicago family at that time.

Momo, or "Sam Mooney," has had seventy arrests since 1925 when he began working for Capone. His record includes assault and battery, burglary, larceny, flight from justice, assault to kill, damage by violence, bookmaking conspiracy, bombing, gambling, and countless arrests under suspicion of murder (three of which occurred before he turned twenty).

Giancana has served thirty days for auto theft, a five-year term at the Illinois State Penitentiary at Joliet for burglary, and four years in the federal penitentiary at Terre Haute, Ind. for operating an illegal still. He was considered the most ruthless Mafia killer in the U.S.

Sam "Momo" Giancana, deposed family head of Midwest.

Outside of Chicago, Momo Giancana had interests in Florida, Nevada and the West Indies. Giancana was expected to take back the mob leadership from Accardo in Chicago. He was shot to death in his Cicero bungalow while frying sausages.

GIBBS, CHARLES
Murderer, Pirate ● (? -1831)

A native of Rhode Island, Charles Gibbs went to sea as a youth and soon fell into evil ways, first pilfering supplies on board ships and then participating in several mutinies and murders (he confessed to killing over 400 men before his execution, although this figure is in doubt and probably exaggerated by the melodramatic reports of the day).

Gibbs' final mutiny took place on board the *Vineyard*, which sailed from New Orleans for Philadelphia November 1, 1830. After spotting $50,000 in precious cargo, Gibbs, joined by a Negro cook, Thomas G. Wansley, killed Captain William Thornby and his mate, William Roberts, throwing them overboard off Hatteras.

Abandoning the ship at Long Island, Gibbs, Wansley and three others made their way ashore in a long boat. Gibbs' shipmates informed authorities of the mutiny and murders and Gibbs and Wansley were arrested, tried and convicted. The two were hanged after a large ceremony on Ellis Island, April 22, 1831.

GILLETTE, CHESTER
Murderer ● (1884-1908)

A t age twenty-two, Chester Gillette saw a new life dawning for himself. He had risen from poverty, orphaned at fourteen by parents who deserted him to spread the word of the Salvation Army throughout the land. Chester never harbored hatred for his religious-zealot parents. Their absence made him free of a home, schooling, and authority; he bummed his way through the country, hopping freights into strange towns and working at odd jobs.

Gillette became so familiar with the rails that he took a job as a railroad brakeman when a yard detective, who had collared him, kindly suggested it. A dull, routine-ridden job, it turned Gillette inward upon his own forgotten loneliness. At twenty, Chester was stirred with ambition and, remembering his uncle, a factory-owner in Courtland, N. Y., he wrote, asking for work. A task-master, the uncle agreed to hire his itinerant nephew if he was willing to begin at the bottom. The boy agreed and soon won promotion to shop foreman of the Gillette skirt factory at a salary of $10 per week.

As a distant member of the well-to-do Gillette family, Chester attended local society functions. At one ball, he met a socially prominent girl and fell in love with her, planning marriage as soon as his fortunes improved.

Petite Grace "Billie" Brown, an eighteen-year-old secretary who worked at the factory, brought Gillette's dreams to doom. Normally a reserved, calculating young man, Chester disregarded his rigid moral code (imbued in him since childhood by his fanatical parents) and seduced Grace.

Gillette forgot about her weeks later. She was a mere farm girl who had traveled to Courtland to earn a miserable $6 a week. He dismissed Grace as an unimportant flirtation, his eyes still focused upon his High Society girl. It was the spring of 1906. He had worked industriously for his uncle for two years. He would better his status by demanding and getting a junior partnership in the Gillette firm, he reasoned, and then be free to marry the girl he loved.

Billie Brown came to him in May and informed him that she was pregnant. She was in tears. He would marry her, wouldn't he? It was the decent, honorable, Christian thing to do. The code of the Edwardian era demanded it or scandal and ruination was assured.

Chester Gillette stalled. Billie was not part of his plans. He was a gentleman now, elegantly attired in a wing collar and expensive suit, a young man on the rise. He couldn't be held back by a milkmaid of a girl, settling for a dowdy, inconspicuous, and socially vacuous marriage.

He convinced Billie to return to her father's farm and be patient. He would work something out very soon and come to her. The girl waited. When he failed to appear, Billie began to write imploring, tear-soaked letters. None were answered. Gillette finally received a letter from Billie in which she threatened to inform his uncle of his careless love-making.

Clutching the letter, Gillette panicked. He informed his uncle in July that he needed a vacation; he was worked out and needed rest, he explained. With $25 of borrowed money in his pocket, Chester journeyed to Utica, N. Y. on July 8, 1906, where he met Billie. They stayed at a hotel overnight as man and wife and then, at Gillette's suggestion, traveled southward into Herkimer County in the Adirondacks. Chester acted aimless. He was unresponsive to Billie's questions about marriage. But he had a plan and it was murder.

First, Gillette took the girl to Tupper Lake where they stayed at a lodge. The lake was crowded; Gillette required isolation. Chester carefully inquired if there was "any old hotel where they have boats to rent." He and Billie moved to the gabled, ramshakled Glenmore Hotel on Big Moose Lake.

The couple did not pretend marriage, oddly enough, when registering at the Glenmore. Gillette wrote down a false name. Billie wrote her real name and address. The management was not shocked since they took separate rooms. On the morning of the next day, July 11, 1906, Chester rented a boat. He placed a suitcase containing a large picnic lunch and a tennis racket in the craft, and he and Billie shoved off into the water at noon.

It was the last time Billie Brown was seen alive.

At about 8 p.m. that night, Gillette, lugging the suitcase, his clothes soaking, was spotted as he walked solemnly through the woods stretching from Big Moose Lake. An hour later he registered at the Arrowhead Inn on Eagle Bay. Still wet, Gillette strolled out to the beach and sat next to a bonfire to dry off. He lifted his melodic voice in song with a group of vacationers.

The desk clerk at the Arrowhead became suspicious of Gillette after the young man approached him and asked: "Has there been a drowning reported on Big Moose Lake?"

"No," came the reply.

Billie Brown's battered body floated to the surface of the lake that day and a coroner ruled her death a homicide. Her face and body had been battered. The suspicious clerk at the Arrowhead Inn called police when he heard of the killing, and Gillette was arrested.

The murder weapon was soon discovered. Searchers found the tennis racket Chester had hastily buried next to the shore of Big Moose Lake. At his sensational trial, Gillette shouted his innocence. Billie committed suicide by leaping into the water, he first claimed. Then he said he had accidentally capsized the boat and Billie, hit on the head by the hull, was drowned. Then he said that, perhaps, she was not unconscious but that she couldn't swim anyway and died in the water.

"But you can swim?" he was asked.

"Yes."

"Well?"

"Yes."

"And yet you made no effort to save her?"

Chester Gillette only shrugged on the stand.

For twenty-two days, the prosecution battled to prove murder. Gillette, to earn money to pay for specially catered dinners, sold autographed pictures of himself from his cell to the curious at $5 each. He cut out pictures of attractive women from newspapers and plastered the walls of his cell with these. Always at ease, he acted like a man still on vacation.

Chester Gillette, who murdered Grace Brown on 7/11/06 on Big Moose Lake in upstate New York, sold this photo of himself to admiring women and used the money for catered meals in his cell. (UPI)

The jury heard more than 100 witnesses testify and finally, on December 4, 1906, found Chester Gillette guilty of murder. He was sentenced to death in the electric chair. He fought off execution through legal appeals for more than a year from his cell in Auburn Prison.

His time ran out on March 30, 1908. Refusing to confess to Billie's murder to the last, Gillette was led silently to the electric chair and executed.

Novelist Theodore Dreiser, basing his classic *An American Tragedy* upon the Gillette case, aptly described the boy's last moments: "And his feet were walking, but automatically, it seemed. And he was conscious of that familiar shuffle—shuffle—as they pushed him on and on toward that door. Now it was here; now it was being opened. There it was—at last—the chair he had so often seen in his dreams—that he so dreaded—to which he was now compelled to go. He was being pushed toward that—into that—on—on—through the door which was now open—to receive him—but which was as quickly closed again on all the earthly life he had ever known."

GILMORE, GARY
Murderer ● (1940-1977)

Eighteen of Gary Gilmore's thirty-seven years on Earth had been spent behind bars. From an early age, he had proven to be a violent criminal who supported himself by armed robbery. He was paroled in 1976 after serving eleven years for armed robbery, a parole that had been cosponsored by Nicole Baker, mother of two. Gilmore and Baker reportedly planned to marry but, upon Gilmore's release, the couple argued and broke up.

Three months later, on July 19, 1976, Gilmore entered an Orem, Utah, gas station and forced attendant Max Jensen, 24, to lie down on the floor while he robbed the till. As he was leaving, Gilmore fired a bullet into Jensen's head, killing him. The next night, Gilmore walked into a motel in the same area and forced night manager Bennie Bushnell, 25, to lie down on the floor while he plundered the cash register.

Again, while walking out, Gilmore killed the night manager by firing a single bullet into the back of Bushnell's head. Both Jensen and Bushnell had been young married men with children. Both were graduates of Brigham Young University.

A short while later Gilmore was caught and put on trial. The chief witness against him was Nicole Baker, whose testimony related her knowledge of the two murders and about Gilmore's conviction. He was sentenced to death, a fate he embraced. So relentless was Gilmore's wish to die that he went on a 25-day hunger strike to protest a stay of execution he had received from the Utah Supreme Court.

He demanded to be shot by a firing squad and waived his rights to an appeal before the U.S. Supreme Court. At 8 A.M., on January 17, 1977, Gilmore was strapped to a wooden chair in front of a wall of sandbags. A hood was placed over his head. From beneath it, Gilmore's voice was clearly heard to say: "Let's do it!"

From a distance of thirty feet, five marksmen fired at a target pinned to Gilmore's clothes in front of where his heart would be. One of the guns contained a blank so that none of the sharpshooters would know who did the actual killing. The four bullets struck Gilmore in the heart and he was pronounced dead four minutes later.

The killer's life and struggle for death was profiled in Norman Mailer's book, *The Executioner's Song*, a work that inspired another Utah prisoner, Jack Henry Abbott, to curry favor with Mailer and subsequently manipulate the author into securing his release and help with the publication of Abbott's own book. Following the publication of this book, Abbott killed again, which led to his eventual capture and imprisonment. Mailer was widely criticized for playing amateur criminologist.

(ALSO SEE: Jack Henry Abbott)

GLATMAN, HARVEY MURRAY
Murderer, Rapist ● (1928-1959)

On a prison I.Q. test conducted in the last hours of his life, Harvey Glatman scored an amazing 130—amazing because Glatman was one of the most sadistic killers ever to step into San Quentin's gas chamber, a man whose intelligence never interferred with his lust for rape and murder.

Harvey loved ropes. Even as a child, he fondled them lovingly. As a Boy Scout, Glatman excelled in knot tying and rope handicraft. He remembered later: "It seems as if I always had a piece of rope in my hands when I was a kid."

He led a docile middle-class life as a child. Everything in Harvey's world was orderly. In school, he was a model student. But there was something secret and strange about him, his mother discovered. Mrs. Glatman later stated that the strangeness became pronounced when her son reached age twelve.

"We noticed one evening, when my husband and I got home, that Harvey's neck was all red with what looked like rope marks. He said he went up in the attic, took a rope, tied it around his neck, and tortured himself . . . In that way he got satisfaction."

A family physician gave the Glatmans some sedatives for their son, advising them to "keep him busy. He'll outgrow it."

At seventeen, Harvey, a shy youth, invented an unusual way to meet girls. He snatched their purses, ran down the street a bit, laughed, and then threw their purses back to them. "It was just his approach," Mrs. Glatman said.

The approach changed in 1945 when Glatman jumped in front of a terrified teenage girl one night in Boulder, Colo., wielding a toy gun. He told her to disrobe. She screamed and he ran. He was picked up by police, but set free on bond. Harvey skipped to the East Coast and was arrested in New York after committing a robbery. He got five years in Sing Sing. He was still receiving psychiatric treatment at the time of his release in 1951.

Glatman had apparently reformed. He moved to Los Angeles and began a modest TV repair shop. He also started a hobby, photography. For six years, Harvey Glatman led a quiet bachelor life. He never dated and seldom spoke to his customers.

The mild-mannered bachelor, however, seethed with thoughts of sex perversion and death. On the afternoon of August 1, 1957, these nightmares became reality. Glatman had met pretty Judy Ann Dull, nineteen and recently married, on one of his calls. When he learned Judy was a professional model, he told her that he was a free-lance photographer on the side and had just recently been given an assignment by a New York detective magazine to photograph women in distress. "The typical bound and gagged stuff, you know," Glatman laughed. There would be $50 in it for Mrs. Dull.

Judy accepted the offer and minutes later got into Glatman's car. He pulled a gun from his pocket. He told Mrs. Dull he would shoot her if she screamed or attempted to escape. Driving with one hand, Glatman took Judy to his apartment, and after raping her several times, tied and gagged her. He placed her in an easy chair and photographed her in her undergarments as the terrified girl strained against her bonds. He then carried the helpless girl to his car and drove to the desert, 125 miles east of Los Angeles near the town of Indio. In a lonely spot he dumped the girl out, took some more photographs of her and then, because he thought "she could identify me later," Glatman strangled her with his favorite rope. He dug a shallow grave, placed the body in it, and left. Wind swept away the sand over the grave, and Mrs. Dull's bleached bones were found in December by hitch-hikers. Authorities were stumped. There were no clues.

Glatman, whose enlarged photos of Mrs. Dull adorned his bedroom walls, tried a different approach to snare another victim. He joined a lonely hearts club in downtown Los Angeles and met Shirley Ann Bridgeford, thirty, a divorcee from Sun Valley, Calif.

Harvey told Mrs. Bridgeford his name was George Williams and that he was a plumber by trade. They made a date. Glatman called for Mrs. Bridgeford at her apartment on March 9, 1958. She wore a semi-formal dress since Harvey told her they would be "dancing at an exclusive club."

Mrs. Bridgeford became somewhat alarmed when Harvey headed the car toward the Anza-Borrego Desert, a state park 55 miles east of San Diego. He explained that the supper club was "out a ways." Once in the desert, Glatman went through a now familiar procedure. He tied her up. "I decided I would kill her the same way I killed Judy," Glatman later explained to stunned officials. "I used the pictures to tie her up without alarming her." Once tied, Mrs. Bridgeford was subjected to several rapes by Glatman. He then took his pictures and strangled her with his rope. He left her body to rot beneath a cactus plant.

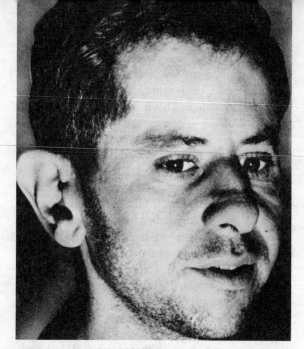

Sex maniac and murderer Harvey Murray Glatman told police that he enjoyed every minute of the sadistic killings he performed. (Wide World Photos)

On July 23, 1958, Glatman, scanning the personal ads in a Los Angeles newspaper, noticed an insert placed by a model and part-time stripper, Ruth Rita Mercado, twenty-four, of Los Angeles. Miss Mercado was seeking model assignments. Harvey went to her apartment. Once inside, he forced Miss Mercado to disrobe and raped her repeatedly. Taking her to the desert, he photographed her slip-covered body. This time, Glatman hesitated. He waited until nightfall. "Late that night, I decided to kill her," he commented later. "She was the one I really liked. I didn't want to kill her. I used the same rope, the same way."

Glatman had killed three pretty Los Angeles women in the space of a year, littering the

Glatman's victims: (left to right) Judy Ann Dull, 19; Mrs. Shirley Bridgeford, 24; and Ruth Mercado, 24. (UPI)

desert sands with their bodies, and yet the police still had no idea who the madman was; he was free to go on murdering.

His next selection was an attractive French model, Joanne Arena, twenty, but she proved to be too cagey for Glatman. She agreed to pose for some pin-up shots but insisted that she drive her own car and bring along a friend. Harvey told her to forget it. Miss Arena's caution saved her life. After Glatman's arrest, Joanne said in deep relief: "I'm not so dumb . . . You know, I think he wanted to kill me . . . I knew it even then."

Harvey's next victim was not as clever but she was a fighter, someone who would not be killed without a struggle. Lorraine Vigil, twenty-eight, a fetching brunette, answered one of Glatman's many ads for models. He told her he would drive her to his studio but when they began to leave the city on the Santa Ana Freeway, Lorraine became alarmed. Glatman swung the car onto the freeway's shoulder and pulled out his .32-caliber pistol. He began to tie the woman's wrists.

"I knew he was going to kill me," Miss Vigil later told police. "I tried to plead but I knew pleading wouldn't do any good." She decided to fight. The plucky woman lunged toward Glatman. "He wasn't very clever. I grabbed his gun."

A shot accidentally went off and wounded Miss Vigil in the thigh, but she continued to hold the gun on Glatman. He dove for her and the two wrestled and bounced out of the car. In a sitting position, the girl jerked up the gun and trained it on Glatman, telling him she would kill him if he came closer. He stood with his rope in his hand, transfixed by the weapon aimed at him.

At that moment, a state policeman, cruising along the freeway, saw the couple and pulled over. He came on the run, firing a shot into the air, just as Glatman was about to spring on his fourth victim. Harvey froze.

In custody hours later, Glatman bragged: "If I wanted to, I could have killed that highway patrolman who arrested me, but I gave up the ghost." The killer proudly recounted each of his rapes and murders, dwelling on the most sordid and perverse details.

He was convicted of murder in three days and went willingly, almost happily, into death row at San Quentin. His lawyers tried to arrange appeals, but Glatman refused to cooperate. He wanted to die, saying: "It's better this way. I knew this is the way it would be." He was put to death in the gas chamber, August 18, 1959.

GOLDSBOROUGH, FITZHUGH COYLE
Murderer ● (1880-1911)

Murderer Fitzhugh Coyle Goldsborough slew novelist David Graham Phillips because he mistakenly thought the writer had maligned his socialite sister in a fanciful tale. (N.Y. Historical Society)

Goldsborough fit the image of the eccentric young man born into wealth during the lazy, fat-cat years at the turn of the century. He was a workless, listless neurotic who squandered time in opulent surroundings. A Philadelphian, he had been trained for leisure. Thin-faced and pale, Fitzhugh kept mostly to himself, spending whole weeks in bed, devouring by the dozen mawkish, maudlin novels of the era.

His socially active sister, a spinster, was Goldsborough's only joy; he doted on her whims and fancies and would tolerate no criticism of her scatterbrain ways, not even from his parents. When the elder Goldsborough mildly chided his daughter, Fitzhugh would explode. He would rage and shout fist-shaking threats at his father. The son's conduct was excused following these rows. He was merely overprotective and sensitive about his sister, the family reasoned. Such affection was touching no matter how volatile its display.

In one reading orgy, Fitzhugh came across a novel written by David Graham Phillips, one of the most popular writers of the day. The novel, *The Fashionable Adventures of Joshua Craig*, dealt with a frivolous, selfish young lady placed well in American High Society. Goldsborough immediately assumed that Phillips' portrait of the spoiled girl was based upon his sister and became incensed.

He made no attempt to learn whether or not Phillips had ever met his sister (he had not). Fitzhugh wrathfully decided the popular novelist had wronged his sister and set out to make amends through murder.

Handsome well-dressed David Graham Phillips was the very essence of the popular man of letters in that Gibson Girl day. Indiana-born, he had gone to Princeton and worked for the *New York World* (once quoted as saying he would "rather be a reporter than president"). His eleven-year career as a novelist produced immensely lucrative best sellers such as *The Great God Success*. At forty-three, Phillips had finished his latest work, a book he considered his best writing to date, *Susan Lenox: Her Fall and Rise* (published in 1917 and thought for years by critics to be a minor masterpiece).

He would never live to see this book published. On January 23, 1911, the writer stepped from his fashionable Gramercy Park apartment for his morning stroll, an important walk this day in that he was on his way to mail a short story to the *Saturday Evening Post*.

As he slowly walked through the park, a well-cut, expensive overcoat shielding him from the brisk, clear day, his path was barred by an ashen-faced, hand-twitching man. For a moment, Phillips thought he was a panhandler, judging from his shabby clothes, unkempt hair and wild, blinking eyes. Just as he was about to reach into his pocket for change, Fitzhugh Coyle Goldsborough pulled forth a pistol.

"Here you go!" Goldsborough screamed and, at close range, shakily shot Phillips, his arm describing a purposely made circle in the air, a self-designed technique to assure several fatal wounds in the victim's head and torso.

Never glancing at Phillips, who had fallen to the sidewalk writhing in pain, Goldsborough shouted for horrified spectators to hear: "Here I go!" He placed the pistol next to his temple and blew away the front of his head. Phillips died days later in the hospital.

Police solved the mystery when Goldsborough's grieving parents came forward, explaining their son's error in thinking Phillips had maligned his sister. It was a thoroughly unromantic end for both men, an end not in keeping with that gentle epoch of hoop skirts and horse-drawn cabs. A sullen and sinister intruder into the world of New York Society, this murder.

GOLDSBY, CRAWFORD ("CHEROKEE BILL")
Murderer, Robber ● (1876-1896)

Goldsby, known in the Oklahoma territory as "Cherokee Bill," was the killer of thirteen men before his death on the gallows at age twenty.

His bloody career began in 1894 when he shot Negro Jake Lewis at a barn dance in Fort Gibson, Okla. He fled, wandering through the Creek and Seminole reservations. There he met and joined the outlaw gang led by Bill and Jim Cook. In June, after several small robberies, the gang rested in Tahlequah, Okla. A posse roared into town seeking the Cook brothers, but they escaped. As they fled from town, Cherokee Bill whipped about in his saddle and threw a shot at the pursuing lawmen. Deputy Sequoyah Houston dropped dead from his horse.

Bill, hiding out, went to stay with his sister Maude. Her husband, George Brown, was not the gentle sort and when Bill came upon him whipping his sister with a leather strap, he shot him. He next killed a railroad agent named Dick Richards who tried to argue him out of robbing a train station. That same day, Bill attempted to rob a train stopped at the station and shot a conductor, Sam Collins, for trying to push him away from the express car.

Cherokee next robbed a general store in Lenepah, Okla. When a local man, Ernest Melton, walked through the door, Bill sent a

Twenty-year-old Crawford Goldsby, called Cherokee Bill, murdered thirteen men before being hanged in 1896. (Western History Collection, U. of Okla. Library)

bullet into his head.

Judge Isaac Parker of Fort Smith offered $1,300 for Bill dead or alive, preferably dead. Two farmers, Clint Scales and Ike Rogers, overpowered the boy bandit in their house on January 29, 1895. He was taken to Fort Smith where he attempted numerous escapes. In one attempt, on June 26, 1896, he shot and killed guard Lawrence Keating, the father of four children.

Cherokee Bill was dragged from his cell weeks later and led to the gallows. He noted the hundreds of spectators gathered about the open yard and commented: "Hell, look at all the people. Something must be going to happen."

On the gallows he looked sharply about and then at the clear blue sky. "This is about as good a day as any to die," he said.

Cherokee's mother, at the bottom of the gallows, began to weep.

"Mother," the killer said, "you ought not to have come."

"I can go anywhere you go," she sobbed back.

"You got anything to say?" a guard said to Bill.

"No. I came here to die, not make a speech." He swung off moments later.

GOPHER GANG

A New York gang operating mostly in the Bowery at the turn of the century, the Gophers came to prominence late in 1905 when their leader, James "Biff" Ellison, an ex-Five Points Gang member, and others, shot up Paul Kelly's saloon, the New Brighton. Kelly was the leader of the Five Pointers.

One of Kelly's henchmen, a man named Harrington, was killed outright by the Gopher barrage; Kelly was wounded in three places. Ellison, who drenched himself each day with perfume, sidled up to the bar, poured himself and his comrades a drink, and walked out whistling.

Ellison was killed shortly thereafter and the Gophers splintered off into other gangs.

GOTTI, JOHN
Syndicate Crime Boss (1940-   )

Reportedly the Boss of Bosses of the five Mafia families in New York, John Gotti was a high profile gangster for two decades. He

New York Mafia boss John Gotti in court, 1990. (AP/Wide World)

favored expensive, tailor-made suits, limousines, and the finer restaurants in Manhattan.

Gotti began as a lowly enforcer in the Carlo Gambino family. He rose in stature by executing a family foe in 1971. In that year, Manny Gambino, the nephew to the then Boss of Bosses, Carlo Gambino, was kidnapped and held for a $350,000 ransom. After part of the ransom was received, the kidnappers killed Manny and threw his corpse in a New Jersey garbage dump.

Carlo Gambino went berserk, ordering every gunman in his employ to hunt down and kill the kidnappers. John Gotti and two others found one of the kidnappers, John McBratney, in a Staten Island bar. They shot and killed him on sight. Gotti was sent to prison for seven years but in the eyes of Carlo Gambino he was a loyal "soldier" who would be rewarded.

When released, Gotti was named as one of the top bosses in the Gambino family. Gotti was ruthless. He told his men that if they failed to obey his orders he would blow up their houses and kill their familes. Though supported by aging Gambino sub-boss Aniello Dellacroce in his climb to power, Gotti's path was blocked by rivals Paul Castellano and Thomas Bilotti.

Gotti reportedly had both men killed on December 2, 1985 as they stepped from a popular Manhattan steak house. From that point onward, John Gotti was the top Mafia don in New York City. His real problems, however, started over a lower Manhattan restaurant, Bankers and Brokers, which was operated by one of his lieutenants, Philip "Philly" Modica.

Modica was renovating the restaurant with non-union workers. This did not sit well with the powerful John O'Connor, vice president and business manager of the Carpenter's Union of New York. He visited the restaurant and was reportedly offered $5,000 by Modica in exchange for his noninterference regarding the reconstruction.

O'Connor was reportedly insulted by being offered so little money and he ordered a gang of union thugs to wreck the restaurant. More than $30,000 in damage was done to the place. Gotti exploded and ordered O'Connor killed. Four gunmen from the Westies, a violent street gang, were sent out to shoot the union leader, on orders of Angelo Ruggiero, one of Gotti's sub-bosses. O'Connor was shot but only wounded in the legs and buttocks. He survived and Gotti went about his business.

Meanwhile, the O'Connor episode prompted Manhattan District Attorney Robert M. Morganthau to go after Gotti. Members of the Westies told officials that they had been hired by Ruggiero, Gotti's man, to kill O'Connor. Further, two of the Westies agreed to wear a wire to record Gotti family members. They did, producing what Morganthau believed was enough evidence to indict Gotti and others for conspiracy.

The indictments were made and Gotti was arrested outside a restaurant on January 24, 1989. Before the sensational trial of John Gotti ensued, a battle royal centered on the admissability of the more than 28,000 taped conversations between informants and Gotti henchmen between March 1985 and May 1986. Many of the tapes were played for the jury at Gotti's trial, which began on January 20, 1990.

Bruce Cutler, Gotti's defense attorney, tried to discredit the tapes that pinpointed Gotti as the supreme ganglord of New York. Cutler had successfully defended Gotti in two previous cases and he was confident that he would win this one. Though the evidence was overwhelming, Cutler proved to be correct. Gotti was acquitted on February 5, 1990.

Prosecutors, however, were not done with the mob boss. He was indicted again on federal charges and he was, after more lengthy trials, convicted and sentenced by Judge Leo Glasser to life in prison. Gotti was immediately sent from a Manhattan jail to the maximum federal security prison at Marion,

Ill. At present, Gotti, the once all-powerful mob boss of New York City, is restricted to near solitary confinement in a seven- by eight-foot cell. He is allowed only one hour out of each day to take exercise outside of his cell. He eats his meals inside that cell and he eats the kind of meals that every prisoner at Marion receives.

(ALSO SEE: Carlo Gambino)

GRAHAM, BARBARA
Murderer ● (1923-1955)

Barbara Graham was a lovely, loveless girl, whose sordid unthinking affairs led her to the depths of human evil and a final nervous walk into San Quentin's gas chamber.

Born in 1923 in a shabby rooming house in Oakland, Calif., Barbara Graham (Barbara Elaine Wood) led a lonely childhood. Her mother, Hortense, was sent to a reformatory as a "wayward girl" when Barbara was two years old. Neighbors raised this beautiful child haphazardly. Her schooling was sporadic. When her mother returned, she gave birth to two more children. Barbara was shut out and she ran away at age nine. It was a pattern she would repeat throughout her adult life.

Barbara's mother took her out of Oakland's public schools when she learned she had been dating boys, and packed her off to a convent. Then Hortense removed her from the convent (where her grades and conduct had improved) and placed her back in the public schools. She was picked up as a vagrant and, with her mother's consent, was sent to the same girl's reformatory in which her mother had spent time. Barbara was released in 1939 with a year of high school to her credit.

She entered a business college, studied for an office job, married, and gave birth to one child. By 1941, she was divorced. Her life fell apart. Between 1941 and 1945, she tramped about California, arrested twice in San Diego for vagrancy and "aggravated lewd and disorderly conduct" and fined $50 with two months in jail, then arrested in San Francisco in 1944 as a prostitute. She married a sailor and was divorced months later. By 1946, almost all of her friends were associated with criminal activities, connections that ran straight to organized crime.

Barbara became a cocktail waitress in Chicago, where she hustled drinks and men. She moved back to San Francisco in 1947 and worked as a call girl for Sally Stanford, the city's most infamous madam. She then perjured herself for two petty crooks—Marck C. Monroe and Thomas M. Sittler, providing them with an alibi when they were charged with theft.

Attempting to reform her life, Barbara became a nurses' aide in the Nye County Hospital at Tonopah, Nev. in 1948. There she married a third time, to a salesman. She opened a hamburger stand but soon moved to Seattle alone. Between 1951 and 1953, Barbara married again to Henry Graham, giving birth to her third son.

Graham introduced her to drugs. "We messed around with some marijuana and some laudanum pills I got from the doctor," he later admitted. He also introduced her to a man named Emmett Perkins, a small-time crook.

Barbara next surfaced with Perkins in Los Angeles. Through Perkins, forty-four and the father of two, she was introduced to three more hoodlums, Baxter Shorter, John L. True, and vicious plug-ugly Jack Santos, who operated a murderous robbery ring in the Los Angeles area.

On about March 9, 1953, True, Perkins, Shorter, and Santos attempted to enter the home of an elderly woman named Monohan in Burbank (they had learned the woman possessed large amounts of expensive jewelry). Barbara Graham led the way. According to True, who later turned state's evidence, Barbara hit Mrs. Monohan several times with the butt of a pistol to gain entry. The gang, True said, stood behind her as Mrs. Monohan screamed, "Oh, no, no, no!" One of the men yelled out, "Give her more!" and Barbara did, cracking Mrs. Monohan's skull and killing her. The gang had been misinformed; there were no jewels.

Barbara, following her arrest, could not provide police with an alibi for the night of the murder. Through a lengthy court battle, she maintained her innocence. True continued to condemn her (he died in an accident in 1958). The prosecution ultimately trapped Barbara

Murderer Barbara Graham fights back tears as she hears sentence condemning her to the gas chamber, 1953. (UPI)

Graham when a police officer posed as an underworld figure in a visit to the jail where she was held, promising that he would provide an alibi for her if she agreed to pay him $25,000. She agreed. The deal was made public in court and Barbara screamed: "Oh, have you ever been desperate? Do you know what it means not to know what to do?"

She was convicted and sentenced to death at San Quentin. Perkins and Santos, who were to follow her the same day, refused to comment on the case; Baxter had already been killed by mobsters to prevent his talking. Exhaustive appeals were made on her behalf; all failed. Days before she was to die, Barbara told a reporter: "In a situation like this, you don't moan, you don't beg, you don't plead—you try to be a woman."

Before walking into the gas chamber on June 3, 1955, Barbara Graham asked for a blindfold. "I don't want to have to look at people," she said through trembling lips. Minutes later she was dead, age thirty-three, her prayers mumbled down into silence.

GRAHAM, GWENDOLYN GAIL
Serial Killer ● (? -   )

A nurse at the Alpine Manor Nursing Home in Walker, Michigan, Gwendolyn Graham, along with her lover, nurse Catherine Wood, began killing elderly women suffering from Alzheimer's disease in 1987. They performed the killings as one would play a game, selecting their victims by their names so that a string of six killings would spell out the word MURDER.

The nurses suffocated all of the six elderly women, ages ranging from 60 to 98. They would then steal one of the victim's trinkets as a souvenir. When they washed down the corpses in preparation for burial, the two women became sexually aroused and made love to each other in the preparation room.

All of this was later related by Wood who told the story to her ex-husband. She said she was afraid that Graham, who hated children, would now start to murder babies in her care. The ex-husband went to police and both Graham and Wood were arrested.

Graham was charged with six murder counts in December 1988 and was convicted on all counts, receiving six life terms. Wood was given a lighter sentence, 20 to 40 years, for informing on her lover.

GRAHAM, HARRISON
Serial Killer ● (1959-   )

Known as "Marty" to his friends, Graham was a handyman living in North Philadelphia. He appeared friendly and outgoing but a little odd. Everywhere he went Graham carried a Cookie Monster puppet. Graham would introduce the puppet as his best friend and he would talk for the puppet in a strange, distorted voice.

The 28-year-old Graham did not lack for girlfriends but they seldom visited his apartment more than once, complaining of the foul odor coming from a back room, the door to which was nailed shut. Graham jokingly explained that the smell was from a bucket kept in the room, one that he had used as a toilet on one occasion. To others he blamed broken sewer pipes.

In August 1987, Graham was evicted from his apartment after neighbors in his building complained about the smell coming from his apartment. The woman downstairs also said that what looked like blood was dripping down her wall from Graham's overhead apartment.

On August 9–10, 1987, investigators searching Graham's apartment found six badly decomposed bodies stacked in the back room. Pieces of a seventh body was found in a closet. All were women. Graham was arrested but he emphatically denied killing anyone. The bodies were in the apartment when he first rented it, he claimed, and he was afraid to tell anyone lest they think he was the murderer.

This ludicrous argument quickly collapsed and Graham admitted to murdering the six young women, saying that he was high on drugs or alcohol when having sex with them and was overcome with an urge to strangle each woman. Graham was tried before Judge Robert A. Latrone and was found guilty. He was given six life terms on May 3, 1988.

GRAHAM, JACK GILBERT
Forger, Murderer ● (1932-1957)

Around dinner time November 1, 1955, United Air Lines Passenger Flight 629, a DC-6B, was blown apart over a beet farm near Longmont, Colo. Eleven minutes before, its forty-four passengers—a crew of five, thirty-eight adults, and an infant—had taken off at Denver's Stapleton Airport en route to Seattle, Wash. Now all forty-four were dead.

The FBI was called to the scene of the crash and fingerprinted each of the dead bodies. These prints were immediately sent on to Washington but failed to reveal any clues. A quick analysis of the plane (or what was left of it) revealed it had been blown apart by a bomb. The FBI agents knew they were looking for a mass murderer.

Checking the insurance policies taken out by the passengers, the agents came across a suspicious name: Jack Gilbert Graham. His mother, Daisie Walker King, fifty-four, had been aboard Flight 629. What made agents single out Graham was the fact that Mrs. King had made out three policies worth $37,500 before taking off, all naming Graham as the beneficiary. The young man also stood to inherit about $150,000 upon his mother's death, from her considerable estate.

Graham's background was also shady. He

had been raised in an orphanage until he was eight. When his mother remarried—to a wealthy Colorado rancher named John Earl King, she recovered her son, providing a good home for him and his half-sister Helen. Though he had the best of care after 1940, Jack proved to be a moody, listless boy who seldom joined in games with his classmates (they called him "Abigail").

He left high school after the first year, running away to Alaska to see his married half-sister. Then he joined the Coast Guard, but the service didn't agree with him; he was AWOL for more than two months out of the total nine months he served. The Coast Guard discharged him when it discovered he was under age.

Back in Denver again in 1951, he took a job as a timekeeper. Here he forged $4,200 in company checks and fled to Texas in a new convertible (purchased with the stolen money). For ten months Graham went on a wild spree of petty crimes which included bootlegging and evading arrest. He was finally apprehended after running a roadblock and returned to Denver authorities. His mother agreed to pay back the stolen money and the charges were dropped.

Graham seemed to settle down after that, marrying a coed, Gloria Elson, whom he met while attending the University of Denver. Then began a series of planned mishaps. First, Graham's service station, financed by his mother, blew up; insurance claims were reluctantly paid. Next, Graham's pick-up truck conveniently stalled in front of an oncoming train and was demolished. That, too, was settled by the insurance people.

Jack Graham's conduct at the airport on the day his mother died had also been suspicious. He had eaten lunch at the airport's snack shop and suddenly became violently ill just after Mrs. King's plane took off. He blamed the food. At home, hours later, when learning of his mother's death, he recalled that Mrs. King had carried a box of shotgun shells on board the plane; she intended to go hunting on her daughter's ranch in Alaska. Jack laughed hysterically for minutes saying: "Can't you just see Mother when all those shells began to go off in the plane?"

Jack Graham was the FBI's primary suspect in the plane bombing.

Webb Burke, agent in charge of the Denver

Mrs. Daisie King, Jack Gilbert Graham's mother; to kill her for insurance money, Graham had to blow up forty-three other persons on a Denver passenger plane. (Wide World Photos)

office, went to work on Graham, grilling him by the hour. Jack told him he had given his mother a going-away present, a box containing tools for making artcraft objects. Then he denied giving his mother any kind of box.

"You've got your facts all mixed up," Graham told Burke. "I had intended buying her a tool set but I couldn't find the right kind, so I didn't buy any."

"But your wife told us you did and that you brought it home with you." Burke said.

"Oh, she's wrong about that," Graham replied. "I'd been talking a lot about the tools and I guess she just supposed I bought them. That's reasonable, isn't it?"

Burke also knew that it was reasonable to assume that Jack Gilbert Graham had given his mother a package covered with Christmas wrapping paper that contained a bomb guaranteed to kill her. Burke told Graham that he was suspected of murdering his mother and that he was not obligated to make a formal statement at that time.

"Of course I'll make a statement!" Graham blurted. "Why shouldn't I? And I'll do a lot more—I'll take a lie detector test if you wish. What's more you have my permission to search my house, my car, or anything else. I haven't done anything wrong."

A search of Graham's house revealed a roll of copper wire used to detonate charges. Confronted with this and the insurance policies taken out by his mother, Graham cracked. He admitted that he had blown up his service station for the insurance. He admitted that he had driven his pick-up truck onto a rail-

Under guard, Jack Gilbert Graham enters death row in the Colorado State Penitentiary in 1956; he would wait a year and a half before going to the gas chamber. (Wide World Photos)

road crossing so it would be hit by a passing train, also for the insurance.

The six-foot, 190-pound Graham broke into a sweat.

Burke asked him: "Now about the plane crash—you did that, too, didn't you?"

Graham's eyes shifted back and forth. He took out a handkerchief, wiped his brow and said nothing.

"You did that, too, didn't you?" Burke repeated.

Graham still said nothing.

"Come now, Graham—the truth. You blew up that plane for your mother's insurance. Let's have the truth."

The killer nodded and said, "Where shall I start?"

"At the beginning."

Graham quickly told Burke how he planted in his mother's suitcase twenty-six sticks of dynamite wired to two electric primer caps, a timer, and a six-volt battery. He had set the timer so the bomb would detonate about ten minutes after the plane took off. It hadn't failed him.

In the months to come, Graham tried to refute this confession, particularly when he was sent to the Colorado Psychopathic Hospital for psychiatric examination. There he told four psychiatrists: "While the FBI men were interviewing me in Denver, I saw a photograph on the wall and it fascinated me. It showed the capture of Nazi saboteurs on the coast of Florida during World War II and FBI men were digging up dynamite. Some-

how that gave me the idea of confessing that I'd used dynamite to blow up the plane but, really, I didn't do it."

It was a fantastic story that no one believed, especially Graham's jury. He was convicted of murder on May 5, 1956, and sentenced to die the following August. His appeals failed at the end of four more months of legal battling. On January 11, 1957, Graham, without a word, entered the gas chamber at the Colorado Penitentiary and was pronounced dead in eight minutes—almost the same amount of time his infernal machine had taken to explode in the clear Colorado skies.

GRAVES, THOMAS THATCHER
Murderer, Thief ● (1843-1893)

The killing of wealthy Josephine Barnaby by Dr. Graves in 1891 became one of America's classic murder mysteries. Mrs. Barnaby was the wife of a wealthy clothing store owner in Providence, R.I. When he died, Mrs. Barnaby, who had been estranged from her husband for a number of years, inherited only $2,500 annually.

Dr. Graves, who had treated Mrs. Barnaby for minor illnesses, learned of her husband's vindictive will. He advised Mrs. Barnaby to contest it, particularly the major parts of the estate left to the two Barnaby daughters. Graves became more than an adviser. Mrs. Barnaby gave him power of attorney over her holdings. When the will was successfully reversed, Graves began to systematically steal Mrs. Barnaby's assets.

To manipulate the estate, Dr. Graves insisted that Mrs. Barnaby travel for her health. He arranged one long trip after another for her. When the old woman grew suspicious, Graves told her that she was not able to handle her own business affairs and that if she attempted to do so, she would be declared incompetent and might be placed in an old people's home.

At one point, Graves boldly wrote to Mrs. Barnaby (while she was away on one of her extended vacations): "I wish to explain what being placed under guardianship means. You could not sign a paper legally, you could not borrow money, you could not have nothing [sic] charged more than a five-year-old, you could never step foot again in the Adirondacks for you could not even leave town, as you could not raise funds; you would have to live in your old home."

Mrs. Barnaby became alarmed by Graves' letter; this was an out-and-out threat. She was determined to return from California and get rid of the bounder. On her return trip, Mrs. Barnaby stopped in Denver to visit a friend, a Mrs. Worrell.

Awaiting her in Denver was a package mailed to the Worrell home from the East. Pasted to the bottle of whiskey in the package was the note: "Wish you a Happy New Year's. Please accept this fine old whiskey from your friend in the woods."

Mrs. Barnaby and Mrs. Worrell mixed drinks from the bottle. Mrs. Worrell sipped her drink. "This is vile stuff," she said but drank down the whiskey as did Mrs. Barnaby.

Following a violent sickness which lasted for six days, both women died April 19, 1891. One of Mrs. Barnaby's daughters, Mrs. Mabel Conrad, when learning of the gift of whiskey, paid $1,000 to have her mother examined. The autopsy proved the old woman had been poisoned. Dr. Graves was immediately suspected and arrested.

While Graves went free on a $30,000 bond, authorities unearthed evidence to convict him of murder. At his trial, the prosecution surprised Graves when they produced a startling witness, one Joseph M. Breslyn. The witness, a young man, stated that Dr. Graves had approached him in November, 1890 (fully five months before the poisonous whiskey was delivered to Mrs. Barnaby in Denver) in the Boston train station and asked him to pen a note, claiming he could not write.

Breslyn agreed and Graves dictated: "Wish you a Happy New Year's. Please accept this fine old whiskey from your friend in the woods." Obviously, Graves did not intend to have his handwriting traced, the prosecution insisted, and the jury agreed. The Doctor was sentenced to die.

While awaiting a new trial in April, 1893, Graves was found dead in his cell. He had committed suicide by taking a heavy dose of poison.

GRAY, HENRY JUDD
Murderer ● (1893-1928)

BACKGROUND: BORN IN NYC, 1893. HIGH SCHOOL EDUCATION. MARRIED WITH ONE DAUGHTER. OCCUPATION, CORSET SALESMAN. DESCRIPTION: 5'8½", BROWN EYES, DARK BROWN HAIR, SLENDER. ALIASES: NONE. RECORD: MURDERED, WITH THE HELP OF RUTH BROWN SNYDER, ALBERT SNYDER, 3/20/27, TRIED, CONVICTED; EXECUTED, ALONG WITH MRS. SNYDER AT SING SING PRISON, 1/12/28.

Albert Snyder was a contented man. In 1927, he owned a sprawling three-story home in Queens, Long Island and made $115 a week as the art editor of *Motor Boating Magazine*. Married, he was relatively sure that his wife Ruth would never go beyond her casual flirtations with salesmen and delivery boys who came to their door.

Ruth was a tall, Nordic-looking woman with voluptuous curves, a hard-set jaw and an icy stare. But she was far from cold. In those flapper days, she could be aptly termed as a "red-hot mama." At thirty-two, her hair a peroxide blonde, Mrs. Ruth Brown Snyder wanted thrills and big-time adventures, not the role of the housewife and mother she compelled herself to play.

Everything in her home life annoyed her. Her husband's obsession for hunting and fishing and boating, the fuddy-duddy house she had to keep up, her nine-year-old daughter Lorraine. Her life was slipping away while the rest of the world went mad and carefree on tinny jazz, bootleg hootch and "Oh, you kid!"

But she had "Lover Boy" and that was something. "Lover Boy" or "Bud" was Henry Judd Gray, a meek-mannered, short and dapper corset salesman who wore shell-rimmed glasses and lived in Orange, New Jersey with a wife and an eleven-year-old daughter.

Ruth Snyder had been seeing Judd for almost two years. She had met salesman Gray in Manhattan in 1925, introduced by a mutual friend. When the sexy housewife learned that Judd Gray sold corsets—or corselettes as they were then called—she told him that, gee, it was odd, but that's exactly what she had come down to Manhattan to buy.

Minutes later, Gray was showing Mrs. Snyder into his offices. "She removed her dress," he stated later, "and I tried on a garment to see if it was the right size and she was very badly sunburned and I offered to get some lotion to fix her shoulders . . ."

It was the beginning of their frowsy love affair. After Gray applied his lotion to Ruth Snyder's bare flesh aquiver with illegal and immoral lust, consummation followed.

They met so regularly in Manhattan hotels that sometimes Ruth would bring her daughter for lack of a baby sitter and the pathetic nine-year-old would have to sit in lobbies while her mother and Lover Boy Gray sexually attacked each other in mad bedroom antics.

Like so many sordid, little, middle-life romances, the Snyder-Gray conversations petered down to comparing notes on their separate married lives between huge gulps of booze. But as the first grey months of 1927 arrived, Ruth Snyder did more than complain to Lover Boy about her husband.

She had plans to do away with her loveless marriage and, between their love-making jousts, and through the babbling baby-talk they gurgled at each other, she told Judd all about it. It was murder, plain and simple. All they had to do was kill Albert Snyder after insuring him for a large amount of money and then they could set up their permanent love nest.

Judd Gray may have fancied himself a debonair ladies' man but the thought of murder gave him the shudders. He began to drink heavily as Ruth continued to insist they do away with her husband.

Gray became such an experienced boozer of rot-gut that he could handle a pint of Mountain Dew (his favorite whiskey) in one swallow. "Momsie," as Gray called his lovemate, kept after Judd to finish off her husband. She nagged, cajoled, begged, threatened.

When Lover Boy repeatedly refused to kill Snyder, Ruth tried several times to poison her husband. All her efforts failed. Again, Ruth went back to Gray. "Do you realize what it would mean in the eyes of God?" he naively asked her.

Eyes or no eyes, Ruth Snyder was a determined woman and she wanted her husband dead. Her insistency finally ground Judd Gray down and he agreed to the murder.

Saturday, March 19, 1927 was a cold, raw day and Judd Gray nerved himself. This was the day he had promised to kill Albert Snyder.

The corset salesman mulled over the murder plan he had cooked up with Ruth.

He was to enter the Snyder home in Queens, Long Island by the back door while the Snyder family attended a late party. He was to hide in a spare room and wait.

Gray was selling corsets in Syracuse on the morning of the 19th. Solemnly, with two bottles of Mountain Dew stuffed into his handsome overcoat, he took the train to New York. There he took a bus to Queens, traveling fifteen miles and taking little nips from his pocketed spirits.

Night had fallen by the time dapper little Judd arrived in Queens. He walked around in the cold, scant blocks from the Snyder house. He acted strangely for a would-be murderer. He stopped several times beneath street lamps, yanking out his bottle and gulping the burning fluid.

Judd Gray acted as if he wanted to be caught breaking the law of the land—Prohibition. No one paid any attention. Finally, Gray entered the Snyder home and went upstairs to the spare room.

There Ruth had already laid out the tools of murder: a heavy sashweight, rubber gloves, chloroform. Gray crouched there in the dark, drinking and waiting.

At 2 a.m., the family returned. Opening the door a crack, Ruth Snyder whispered, "Are you there, Bud, dear?"

"I'm here."

A few minutes more and she returned wearing only a slip. They fell on each other in fierce fornication that consumed an hour.

Then Gray grabbed the sashweight and Ruth led him into the master bedroom. Once there, the love duo decided not to bother with the rubber gloves and chloroform. Judd the Lover Boy raised the sashweight with all his strength and brought it down on the sleeping figure of Albert Snyder.

Gray was indeed puny for the blow merely glanced off Snyder's head, stunning him momentarily. Snyder let out a roar of pain and sat up suddenly, attempting to grab Gray.

Lover Boy became terrified; the whole thing had backfired. His voice came out of his throat like a woman's scream: "Momsie, Momsie, for God's sake, help!"

There was no panic in Ruth Snyder, who stood on the other side of the bed: only determination. With a burst of disgust and anger she wrenched the sashweight out of the quaking hands of her fellow conspirator and crashed it down on her husband's skull, killing him.

With Snyder dead, Ruth and Judd went downstairs. They had some drinks and chatted about the rest of their plan. They faked a robbery attempt by turning over a few chairs and then Gray loosely tied Ruth's hands.

Minutes after Gray left, Ruth Snyder banged on her daughter Lorraine's door. The child ran out and took the gag from her mother's mouth. "Get help!" Ruth yelled to her, and the terrified girl ran to a neighbor's house where the police were called.

For all their planning, the murder-lovers had not presented a convincing robbery. All of the items Ruth said had been taken by the mysterious burglar were found in secret hiding places and detectives began to question her. The stony-hearted Ruth gave way almost at once and confessed. "Poor Judd," she said with her best Nita Naldi theatrics, "I promised not to tell . . ."

Gray was found hours later cringing in his Syracuse hotel room. He shrieked his innocence. "My word, gentlemen," he expressed to police in wounded tones, "when you know me better you'll see how utterly ridiculous it is for a man like me to be in the clutches of the law.

"Why, I've never even been given a ticket for speeding."

Judd's calm attitude broke apart on the train going to New York, and he confessed.

Almost immediately the two lovers blamed each other. Judd said that, at the moment of murder, he had weakened and required Mrs. Snyder's aid. She said she lost all her courage when the deed was done and Gray had performed the killing alone.

Damon Runyon, the celebrated newsman, said they were both inept idiots and called the whole mess The Dumb-bell Murder, "because it was so dumb."

By the time the two were tried, they were at each other's throats, each blaming the other. The trial was an extravaganza. Celebrities by the droves attended: Mary Roberts Rinehart, David Belasco, D. W. Griffith, Will Durant, Peggy Hopkins Joyce, and evangelists Billy Sunday and Aimee Semple McPherson were only a few to appear in court. Sister Ai-

Sedate and somber, sashweight murderer Henry Judd Gray awaits trial in New York in 1927; his mother gave him silent comfort. (Wide World Photos)

mee received a hefty sum of money from the *New York Evening Graphic* to write up the sordid mess. Sister Aimee, involved in a burning scandal of her own a year later, encouraged young men in her column to say, "I want a wife like mother—not a Red-Hot Cutie."

Both defendants had separate counsels arguing for their innocence. Mrs. Snyder's lawyer said that her husband "drove love from out that house" by carrying a torch for a departed sweetheart.

He also said that Gray had tempted her by setting up the $50,000 double indemnity insurance policy on Albert Snyder. "We will prove to you," he droned to a disbelieving court audience and jury, "that Ruth Snyder is not the demimondaine that Gray would like to paint her, but that she is a real, loving wife, a good wife; that it was not her fault that brought about the condition in that home."

Her lawyer, Edgar F. Hazleton, then put the wronged woman on the stand. Over 120 reporters buzzed as she walked forward wearing a simple, black dress. Women reporters related that she looked "chic but decorous."

Ruth played the role of suffering wife and mother as never before. She told how her husband ignored her most of the time, except when taking her to an occasional movie. She was the one, she said proudly, who read the Bible to her daughter Lorraine and took the child to Sunday school, not her unfeeling husband.

Her lawyer glossed over the Gray romance as Ruth's responses were carried via a microphone at her side on the witness stand to hundreds listening in the corridors.

"He was in about the same boat I was," Ruth said of Gray. "He said he was not happy at home." Mrs. Snyder then told how Lover Boy had taken her to such speakeasy hot spots as the Frivolity Club and the Monte Carlo, where she watched him drink himself senseless. She, Ruth insisted, rarely touched even one drink and never, ever, smoked.

Then she swore that Gray insisted she take

Ruth Snyder, who murdered her husband with Judd Gray, was pensive at her 1927 trial. (UPI)

out the heavy insurance policy on her husband. "Once," she said, "he sent me poison and told me to give it to my husband."

At this, the excitable little Judd began jabbering at his lawyers.

Turn about was fair play in this silly melodrama. Gray took the stand after his lawyer blasted Mrs. Snyder good and proper. Attorney Sam Miller described Judd's situation as "the most tragic story that has ever gripped the human heart."

Gray, Miller claimed, was a law-abiding citizen who was fed over twenty shots of whiskey by Mrs. Snyder to steel him for the act of killing.

"He was dominated by a cold, heartless, calculating master mind and master will," Miller chanted. "He was a helpless mendicant of a designing, deadly, conscienceless, abnormal woman, a human serpent, a human fiend in the guise of a woman.

"He became inveigled and drawn into this hopeless chasm when reason was gone, when mind was gone, when manhood was gone, and when his mind was weakened by lust and passion."

Things were looking up for Judd.

He took the witness chair dressed in a snappy double-breasted business suit, playing the victim to the hilt. As he talked, he nervously glanced at his elderly mother sitting in the court next to the famous actress, Nora Bayes, who had come to watch the fun.

Judd Gray said that Mrs. Snyder had tried to kill her husband several times. Once she put knockout drops in his prune whip, but that failed, and then she tried to gas him.

"I told her I thought she was crazy," Gray said innocently and then reported that Ruth had given her husband poison when he had the hiccups. It only made him violently sick.

"I said to her," Gray intoned mildly, "that was a hell of a way to cure hiccups. I criticized her sorely." He then added that Mrs. Snyder tried to kill her husband twice again by administering sleeping powders to him.

He also said that Ruth arranged the insurance policy on her own and had struck the death blow. It was then that Ruth Snyder sobbed loudly and Judd glanced in her direction.

The jury was spared more of this double-crossing banter; they retired. They were out only 98 minutes and came in with a verdict of guilty. Both defendants were stunned. The sentence was death.

The warden came for Judd Gray on the bleak night of January 12, 1928. He sat smiling in his cell. He had received a letter from his wife forgiving him. "I am ready to go," he said to the warden. "I have nothing to fear."

Ruth Snyder followed her faithless lover minutes after she watched the prison lights flicker and signal his death. Reporters remembered, as she was led to the electric chair, that she had said days before that God had forgiven her and she hoped the world would.

An enterprising reporter from the *New York Daily News* smuggled a camera strapped to his ankle into the death chamber and clicked off a photo just as the current raced through Mrs. Snyder's body, hurtling her against the chair straps.

The love affair was still good for one more edition.

GREEN, EDWARD W.
Murderer, Bankrobber ● (1833-1866)

Though many historians insist that the first bank robbers in America were Frank James, the Youngers, and six other Missouri outlaws, this odd distinction belongs to Eddie Green, the postmaster of Malden, Mass. Green, who had been crippled in an accident as a youth, fell heavily into debt and began to drink.

The idea of robbing a bank was a spur-of-the-moment action. When Green walked into the Malden bank on December 15, 1863, he noticed that only Frank E. Converse, seventeen, the bank president's son, was on the premises.

Green returned to his home and got a pistol. Quickly, he went back to the bank and shot Converse twice in the head, killing him. He then helped himself to $5,000 of the bank's cash and fled.

Police received reports that Green was suddenly spending a lot of money and picked him up for questioning. He confessed and was sentenced to die. Execution took place February 27, 1866.

GREEN, HENRY G.
Murderer ● (1823-1845)

A reformed drunk, Green became a temperance advocate. During one high-spirited meeting held to lay "Demon Rum" low, he chanced to meet eighteen-year-old Mary Ann Wyatt, whom he later married in Berlin, N.Y.

Soon after, Green began to have marital problems. His mother hated his wife, telling him that Mary Ann was not a fit life-mate. Apparently Green agreed with his mother, for he shortly gave Mary Ann a fatal dose of arsenic.

He was quickly taken, tried, and convicted. The execution was at Troy, N.Y. September 10, 1845.

GREENWOOD, VAUGHAN ORRIN (THE SKID ROW SLASHER)
Serial Killer ● (1944-   )

Beginning in early 1974, Skid Row derelicts were discovered in alleys and doorways with their throats cut. All were undersized, penniless alcoholics whose throats had been slit with precision. The killer had removed their shoes and placed them so that they pointed to the bodies. He had then, for unknown reasons, spread salt in circle around the corpses.

By January 1975, "The Skid Row Slasher" had claimed nine victims, including two derelicts found in seedy hotels. Police were baffled until February 3, 1975 when a man tried to hatchet to death two other men in a Hollywood home. Arrested for this attack was 31-year-old Vaughan Greenwood.

It took ten months for police to mount evidence and a case against Greenwood who was officially charged with the nine slasher cases and two other murders committed in 1964. On December 29, 1976, Greenwood was convicted of nine counts of murder. Judge Earl C. Broady sentenced Greenwood to life in prison on January 19, 1977.

GRETZLER, DOUGLAS
Serial Killer ● (c1950-   )

Bronx, N.Y., born and bred, Douglas Gretzler met William Steelman in Denver, Colorado. Steelman was a former convict and mental patient. Both men traveled through the Southwest, killing and robbing. In 1973, Gretzler and Steelman killed seven persons in Arizona, two of which were their partners in a drug deal. In Victor, Calif., the two men held nine people hostage until they could loot a store safe of $4,000. They then systematically shot and killed each hostage in the head, including four children.

Gretzler and Steelman were later identified by a Sacramento, Calif., hotel clerk who called police. Gretzler surrendered but Steelman had to be teargased out of his hotel room where he had holed up.

Both serial killers, who may have claimed more than thirty lives, were given life sentences in California, then extradicted to Arizona where they were condemned. They await execution at this writing.

GRINDER, MARTHA
Murderer ● (1815-1866)

Mrs. Grinder, a resident of Pittsburgh, Pa., was a mental case. A raving sadist, she enjoyed any form of punishment and pain endured by others. In her confessions, Mrs. Grinder admitted: "I loved to see death in all its forms and phases, and left no opportunity unimproved to gratify my taste for such sights. Could I have had my own way, probably I should have done more [murder]."

To this end, Mrs. Grinder poisoned her neighbor, a Mrs. Carothers, with arsenic and then "nursed" the poor woman to her death.

She was tried and condemned to death, being executed January 19, 1866.

GUIFOYLE GANG

Martin Guifoyle headed up this Capone satellite gang. His partners were Al Winge, an ex-police lieutenant turned crook, and Matt Kolb, an old wardheeling politician. Guifoyle and his mobsters controlled all the liquor concessions on the near Northwest Side of Chicago from about 1920 to 1929. The gang was later absorbed into the national syndicate.

GUIMARES, ALBERTO SANTOS
Swindler ● (1890-1953)

Guimares figured mysteriously in the much-publicized death of playgirl Dot King (Dorothy Keenan). A petty swindler in New York, Guimares met Miss King sometime in 1922 while she was being kept by a millionaire.

Dot, who had run away from a tenement home in a slum Irish neighborhood in 1915, was a pretty, petite Fifth Avenue model. She was the epitome of the short-skirted, bob-haired flapper of the day.

She balanced her love scales between her millionaire friend, who had given her $30,000 in jewels, and Guimares, who beat her up regularly (acts which Miss King reportedly enjoyed). On March 15, 1923 her maid found Dot King dead in her luxurious suite; she had been chloroformed. Apparently, she had struggled violently with her murderer since her face was considerably bruised and scratched. Her apartment had been ransacked. Police figured burglars were searching for her jewels and furs; these, of course, were gone.

The sugar daddy, a wealthy Boston banker known to Dot only as Mr. Marshall, could not be located. But police did pick up Alberto Guimares. He had an alibi, he told authorities. On the night of the murder he had been wooing socialite Aurelia Drefus. Mrs. Drefus sup-

Swindler and con man Alberto Guimares relaxes on the beach at Atlantic City in 1923; he was considered the prime suspect in the sensational murder of show girl Dot King. (UPI)

ported his story and he was released.

The murder case faded and was all but forgotten until 1924. At that time, Mrs. Drefus dove from the balcony of her Washington hotel. Guimares had been standing next to her on that occasion. She fell, he insisted. It was an accident.

Rummaging through Mrs. Drefus' effects, police uncovered an affidavit signed by Mrs. Drefus in which she swore that she had committed perjury in providing Guimares with an alibi on the night of the Dot King murder.

Again the slippery con man was arrested but authorities had to let him go; more concrete evidence was lacking. Guimares lived on for another three decades, involved in one petty swindle after another. He died penniless, and as far as certain authorities are concerned, unpunished for the murder of his Jazz Age sweetheart.

GUITEAU, CHARLES JULIUS
Assassin ● (1844-1882)

BACKGROUND: BORN AND RAISED IN RURAL ILLINOIS. A SELF-TAUGHT, SELF-APPOINTED LAWYER. MARRIED BRIEFLY TO A SIXTEEN-YEAR-OLD GIRL WHOM HE ABANDONED. DESCRIPTION: APPROXIMATELY 5'9", BROWN EYES, BLACK HAIR, SLIGHT. ALIASES: NONE. RECORD: SHOT AND FATALLY WOUNDED PRESIDENT JAMES A. GARFIELD, 7/1/1881 (GARFIELD DIED 9/18/81); AFTER A LENGTHY TRIAL WHERE HE SERVED AS HIS OWN LAWYER, GUITEAU WAS HANGED 6/30/1882.

Guiteau was the classic political malcontent who would also, by today's standards, certainly be judged insane. A drifter and deadbeat, Guiteau practiced a weird brand of law. He took on small claims cases which gave him the opportunity to vent his hysterical tirades in court. The defendants of these cases rarely saw any compensation. Guiteau kept three-quarters of all settlements. He never paid any of his own bills and was, therefore, being constantly sued.

When hauled into court for his own debts, Guiteau, who fancied himself a powerful evangelist, called upon the Lord to aid him against heathen creditors. Somewhere in the midst of all his hopeless legal battles, dodging landladies, and preaching the true word of God, Guiteau married a sixteen-year-old street waif. He soon abandoned her, moving to Washington, D. C. There the self-styled lawyer patronized street prostitutes, caught syphilis, and decided he had earned an ambassador's appointment to Paris.

Politics interested Guiteau, and in 1880 he ran errands for the Republican group headed by Roscoe Conkling which was working for Grant's nomination at the convention. James A. Garfield finally got the nod and Guiteau switched sides, feverishly writing out a long-winded, erratic speech for Garfield to use in his campaign. After mailing his speech to Garfield, Guiteau had copies printed and these he passed out at meetings.

Garfield never used Guiteau's speech but, after the presidential election, the lawyer concluded that his words alone had swayed the voting public. He went to the White House and demanded his appointment to Paris in return for his unwanted literary efforts.

Though Lincoln had been murdered a scant sixteen years before, no security men, other than a few unarmed male secretaries, were in evidence at the White House. Guiteau entered and left the building at will. The President did see Guiteau once but, when the lawyer pressed for his appointment to Paris, Garfield put him off.

Guiteau then began to harass Secretary of State Blaine. The little man with the high-pitched voice accosted Blaine in White House corridors almost every day. Blaine lost patience and finally shouted: "Never speak to me about the Paris embassy as long as you live!"

According to his irrational thinking, there was nothing left for the political petitioner to do but to seek vengeance by killing the President. Guiteau purchased a .44-caliber pistol and began target practice on the trees lining the Potomac River. When he felt that he had become an accomplished marksman, he began to dog the President's movements.

Assassin Charles Guiteau was placed under arrest moments after fatally shooting President Garfield. (N.Y. Historical Society)

Through the local newspapers which printed the President's daily schedule, Guiteau learned that Garfield would be taking the train to his alma mater, Williams College, to deliver an address on July 1, 1881. He hid in the Baltimore & Potomac train station and when Garfield, accompanied by Blaine, entered the terminal at 9:20 a.m., Guiteau rushed up and fired a bullet into the President.

Aides grabbed Guiteau and in a matter of seconds he was on his way to jail. Garfield's wound (he had been hit in the back, the bullet lodging behind the pancreas) proved fatal and the President died a little more than two months later.

Guiteau's trial in November of 1881 was a sensation. The prosecution quickly proved his premeditation. Wardens testified that Guiteau had inspected the District of Columbia jail before the assassination, stating that it was "an excellent jail." Guiteau endorsed these statements by remarking that he wanted to see what his future home would be like.

The madman also stated that he had kept Garfield in his gun sights for weeks before he killed him. From a bench in a nearby park, he had watched the President leave the White House every day. He had stood behind Garfield in church once ready to kill him there, but had decided against it because the President's wife was with him. (Guiteau called her "that dear soul.")

With bursts of venomous outrage, Guiteau conducted his own defense for more than ten weeks, yelling, screaming, dancing ludicrously about the courtroom floor. His conduct went unchecked. He interrupted prosecution witnesses by calling them "dirty liars." Other times he would run in front of the prosecutor's table yelling that he was "a low-livered whelp," and "an old hog."

At other times, Guiteau appeared to be rational. "I had a very happy holiday," he told the judge after Christmas and New Year's, comments unsolicited by the bench.

Guiteau seemed to enjoy his imprisonment. So did the thrill-seeking people of Washington. He walked peacock-proud back and forth behind the bars while crowds (encouraged by the authorities) gaped at him.

The summation Guiteau delivered at the end of his trial was nothing short of spectacular. He told his jury that God had divined the assassination of President Garfield. When ques-

Charles Julius Guiteau acted as his own attorney at his trial; he mocked the judge and called the prosecutor names. (N.Y. Historical Society)

GUNNESS, BELLE
Murderer, Robber ● (1860-1908?)

BACKGROUND: BORN IN INDIANA IN 1860. MINOR PUBLIC EDUCATION. MARRIED PETER GUNNESS, SETTLED IN LAPORTE, INDIANA. BORE THREE CHILDREN, DISAPPEARED IN A FIRE IN HER FARMHOUSE 4/28/08. DESCRIPTION: 5'5", BLUE EYES, BROWN HAIR, CORPULENT. ALIASES: NONE. RECORD: POISONED ANDREW HELGELIEN AND THIRTEEN OTHER SUITORS IN THEIR SLEEP, STOLE THE MONEY THESE MEN POSSESSED AND DISAPPEARED IN 1908; HER CONFEDERATE, RAY LAMPHERE, WAS SENTENCED TO TWO TO TWENTY-ONE YEARS IN THE INDIANA STATE PENITENTIARY WHERE HE DIED.

tioned about how God let him know this, Guiteau responded with: "God told me to kill." In a shrieking voice the assassin rose from his chair and said: "Let your verdict be, it was the Deity's act, not mine!"

When he heard the jury's death verdict, Guiteau wagged his bony finger at each jurist, growling, "You are all low, consummate jackasses!"

At dawn, June 30, 1882, the day of his execution, Guiteau rolled back the blankets from his face (he suffered fitful nightmares and slept fully covered). Hurriedly, he dressed and then carefully trimmed his scraggly beard. He asked for bootblack and shined his shoes to a high gloss, humming and whistling his satisfaction at their appearance.

All through a mammoth meal, Guiteau carried on a one-sided conversation with God. When jailers came for him, he coolly adjusted his clothes and calmly walked from his cell to the gallows without comment. Once on the scaffold, he began to whimper and sob.

Seeing the rope awaiting him, he suddenly brushed away his tears, smiled, and produced a poem he had written for the occasion. As the executioner moved forward, Charles Julius Guiteau began to recite in a clear, high voice: "I am going to the Lordy. . . ."

The advertising departments of Chicago newspapers loved her. She regularly placed personal ads with them for a husband. She paid on time and her appeals made for interesting reading. But no one seemed to answer Mrs. Belle Gunness' ads.

No one the newspapers ever knew. Belle and her lover handyman Ray Lamphere knew a lot. Almost all of Belle's lovelorn ads hit paydirt and her marriage-seeking correspondents hit only dirt.

All of Belle's matrimonial ads ended with the same essence-of-propriety warning, "triflers need not apply."

To the unsuspecting, Belle Gunness was a good, hard-working widow woman who supported her three fatherless children. Their father, Peter Gunness, had died in an accident.

Well, his death was finally ruled an accident after Belle faced an angry coroner and a curious jury. It seems that Peter Gunness, who ran a small hog farm and butchering shop, had been killed by a blow from the meat grinder which had toppled from a shelf. That was Belle's story.

The coroner of LaPorte, Indiana, didn't believe it. "This is murder!" he said and drew up a special jury to sift the evidence.

One of the Gunness children told a schoolmate: "My momma killed my poppa. She hit him with a cleaver."

Even this hearsay didn't cause a ruffle in Belle's composure. She stuck to her story, and the coroner's jury freed her.

Just after her husband's untimely death, Belle took up with a handyman, Ray Lamphere, who helped out with the family business. He also shared the grieving widow's bed.

About this time, Belle hit upon her highly-successful scheme to bilk lovelorn suitors.

Several men from distant states answered Belle's carefully-worded ads. Some were seen escorting her briefly in the Laporte area; then they disappeared.

The last suitor to appear was Andrew Helgelien who answered Belle's ad in a Norwegian-language newspaper. The thrifty, love-seeking bachelor received a honey-kissed letter from Belle who promised true love and a long life of wedded bliss. She also casually mentioned that she needed $1,000 to pay off a pressing mortgage.

She ended her letter with: "My heart beats in wild rapture for you, come prepared to stay forever." Her words were prophetic to say the least.

Helgelien traveled from South Dakota with his wallet full of money and his heart aching for Belle. Before his arrival, Belle changed from her usual attire of overalls in which she butchered hogs to a flouncy dress. This in itself was a hardship since Belle enjoyed wearing men's clothing. Helgelien showed up and was immediately introduced to Lamphere as the hard-working widow's next husband.

Suddenly Helgelien disappeared.

Nothing more would have been said about the amazing vanishing acts performed by Belle's suitors except that a roaring fire occurred on the night of April 28, 1908 and Belle's farmhouse went up in smoke.

The Gunness place was entirely gutted and the good citizens of LaPorte rocked with tragedy. Belle had been found with her three children, ages eleven, nine, and five.

Upon further investigation, Sheriff Smutzer became puzzled. The body of the woman, burned to a crisp, was oddly shriveled. Belle, who stood 5'5", tipped the scales at 280 pounds. Yet the dead woman found in the Gunness ruins was only 150 pounds.

Smutzer found it impossible to believe that the fire, irrespective of its heat, could have reduced Belle by 130 pounds. What made the job of identification even more difficult was that the dead woman's head was missing!

At first, the coroner had speculated that a falling beam had decapitated the helpless victim. A closer look favored the fact that a murderer had severed the head and set fire to the entire building.

But who?

Ray Lamphere was drinking heavily after the burning of Belle's house. Sheriff Smutzer picked him up. Lamphere bragged to him how he had slept with Belle. Then Smutzer charged him with killing Mrs. Gunness and setting fire to her house.

Lamphere screamed his innocence.

Smutzer knew that Belle had fired Lamphere after Helgelien arrived and that the handyman had repeatedly tried to force himself on her after that. The sheriff also knew that Belle had Lamphere arrested for trespassing on her property.

At that time, Belle had told the arresting officer that "I'm afraid he'll set fire to the place." It was a meaningful statement coming from her.

Just as Sheriff Smutzer was trying to puzzle out the Gunness mystery fire, Helgelien's brother Asle arrived from South Dakota. He insisted Belle had killed his brother Andrew for his life savings. His suspicions increased when diggers, looking for Belle's head in the ruins of her home, began to unearth shocking artifacts.

Found were eight men's watches; also in the rubble were bones and human teeth. Asle Helgelien helped the diggers search and intuitively pointed to Belle's hog pen. "Try here," he told the workmen, pointing to a pen surrounded by a six-foot fence.

The diggers turned up four bodies expertly sliced up and wrapped in oil cloth. One of them was Andrew Helgelien . . . or what was left of him.

The following day three more dissected bodies were unearthed. Fourteen bodies in all were unearthed on Belle's property.

Smutzer pieced the story together this way: Belle had lured her lovesick suitors to LaPorte with promises of marriage and a happy home. Then she drugged them in their sleep, crushed their heads, and cut them up, just as she butchered her hogs.

The sheriff estimated that Belle had stolen over $30,000 from her hapless victims. This was an astronomical sum for the year 1908.

Yet the body of the headless, 150-pound woman remained a mystery to Smutzer. The sheriff figured that Belle must have been a heartless creature to kill her attractive children in the fire if she was responsible for it. There was a good chance that she was.

The woman found in the ashes, the sheriff reasoned, was not Belle. But he needed proof. Smutzer went to a man in LaPorte who had been a prospector in the great California gold rush of 1849.

Smutzer was interested in locating the false teeth Belle was known to have had. The prospector went to work building a sluice. The entire Gunness building, or what remained of it, would be sifted through the sluice in search of Belle's teeth.

Hundreds of LaPorte's citizens turned out for the sluicing operations. Very soon after the water began to flow, charred pages from books dealing with hypnotism and anatomy were identified.

More male teeth and watch parts and clothing were also discovered. Then the prospector hit pay dirt. Belle's porcelain plate, attached to one of her real anchor teeth, turned up. This convinced the sheriff that the 150 pound body was Belle's. The mystery was solved.

Or was it?

Lamphere stood trial for the murder of his murderous lover. The jury exonerated him of the murder of Belle but convicted him of setting fire to the Gunness place. He was sentenced to two to twenty-one years in the state penitentiary.

He never saw freedom again. During his trial, Ray Lamphere developed tuberculosis, and he died in prison.

Before he died, Lamphere confessed the whole sordid story to his cellmate. He knew all about Belle's murders and had, in fact, helped her by burning the bodies of her victims, he said.

But as far as the headless woman found in the burned out ruins of the Gunness home, she definitely was not Belle. Lamphere stated that Belle had lured a drunken derelict from Chicago and killed her by slipping strychnine into her glass of whiskey. She then decapitated the hapless harlot and put her in bed with her pathetic children and burned the house down around them.

As a final touch, Belle had ripped out her own anchor tooth and false plate and tossed

An early dime novel portrayed Mrs. Belle Gunnes approaching her suitor-victims in the dead of night with love and poison. (N.Y. Historical Society)

them into the burning house. Lamphere said she made off with a fortune stolen from the men she had killed. She was supposed to contact the moronic Lamphere later but never did.

"For all I know," Lamphere moaned, "she's living the high life in Chicago or New York or even San Francisco . . . what China blue eyes she had."

Incredible as it may seem, Ray Lamphere died in his cell still in love with this human monster.

And Belle? No one ever heard from or saw her again.

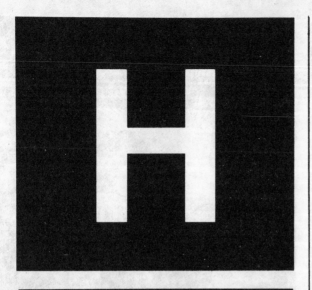

HALBERT, HENRY
Murderer ● (1735-1765)

According to his own confession, Henry Halbert had led a life of sin which included "drinking, whoring, cursing, swearing, breaking the Sabbath, and keeping all manner of debauched company." To this he added the senseless murder of a Philadelphia youth, Jacob Woolman, by cutting his throat one night while drunk.

Halbert was hanged October 19, 1765, in Philadelphia.

HANCE, WILLIAM HENRY
Serial Killer ● (? -   )

Hance was a soldier stationed at Fort Benning, Georgia. In 1978, he became incensed at the Stocking Strangler plaguing Columbus, Georgia. He wrote a letter to a Georgia newspaper threatening to kill black women unless the killer of white elderly women was caught. He signed the letter "The Forces of Evil."

When the Stocking killer was not caught, Hance killed three black women but he was quickly identified as having been drinking with one of the victims. Hance confessed and received the death penalty.

HARDIN, JOHN WESLEY
Murderer ● (1853-1895)

BACKGROUND: BORN IN BONHAM COUNTY, TEX., 5/26/1853, THE SECOND OF TWO SONS (JOSEPH WAS OLDER BY TWO YEARS) TO ELIZABETH AND REV. J. G. HARDIN. MINOR PUBLIC EDUCATION. MARRIED JANE BOWEN IN 1872, WHO BORE HIM TWO GIRLS AND A BOY; JANE HARDIN DIED 11/6/92; REMARRIED TO CALLIE LEWIS 1/8/95. ORIGINAL OCCUPATION, RANCHER. DESCRIPTION: 5'11", BLACK EYES, BLACK HAIR, THIN. ALIASES: J. H. SWAIN. RECORD: KILLED A NEGRO NEAR BONHAM IN 1868 AT AGE 15; REPORTEDLY KILLED THREE SOLDIERS TRACKING HIM FOR THE MURDER WEEKS LATER; WITH SIMP DIXON KILLED TWO MORE SOLDIERS IN 1869; SHOT AND KILLED A CIRCUS HAND MONTHS LATER; KILLED GUNFIGHTER JIM BRADLEY IN 1870; KILLED AN UNKNOWN ROBBER IN KOSSE, TEX., 1871; ARRESTED IN LONGVIEW, TEX. AND CHARGED WITH MURDER (DISCLAIMED BY THE DEFENDANT); ESCAPED, KILLING A HALF-BREED GUARD IN EARLY SPRING, 1871 AND THREE SOLDIERS WHO TRACKED HIM DOWN; KILLED WITH HUGH ANDERSON GUNFIGHTER JUAN BIDENO, IN AUGUST, 1871 (BIDENO WAS WANTED FOR THE MURDER OF TEXAS CATTLEMAN WILLIAM C. COHRON); KILLED AN UNKNOWN GUNFIGHTER IN ABILENE, KAN. LATE 1871; KILLED GONZALES COUNTY POLICEMAN NEGRO GREEN PARAMOOR, AND WOUNDED HIS AIDE, JOHN LACKEY, LATE 1871; ALLEGEDLY KILLED THREE MORE NEGRO POLICEMEN WHO CAME TO ARREST HIM WEEKS LATER; KILLED DEPUTY SHERIFF J. B. MORGAN IN CUERO, TEX., 1873 WHILE INVOLVED IN THE SUTTON-TAYLOR RANGE WAR; KILLED WITH JIM TAYLOR SHERIFF JACK HELM IN DEWITT COUNTY, TEX. IN APRIL, 1873; KILLED BROWN COUNTY, TEX. SHERIFF CHARLES WEBB 5/26/74 IN A GUNFIGHT; CAPTURED BY TEXAS RANGER JOHN B. ARMSTRONG AND POSSE 8/23/77 IN THE PENSACOLA, FLA. TRAIN DEPOT; TRIED IN AUSTIN, TEX. FOR THE WEBB MURDER IN SEPTEMBER, 1877; FOUND GUILTY AND SENTENCED TO TWENTY-FIVE YEARS AT HARD LABOR AT RUSK PRISON IN HUNTSVILLE, TEX.; PARDONED IN 1894; SHOT IN THE BACK AND KILLED BY JOHN SELMAN, SENIOR 8/19/95 IN AN EL PASO, TEX. SALOON.

"**I**f you wish to be successful in life, be temperate and control your passions; if you don't, ruin and death is the inevitable result." This upstanding exhortation was penned by none other than the most notorious gunslinger of the Old West, a man straight out of fiction whose quick-draw duels in dusty Texas streets were real, the twenty-one men (or more) who fell before his guns authentic—the most notorious, whooping, leather-slapping gunfighter of them all—John Wesley Hardin.

Hardin's career parallels that of Jesse James

and Billy the Kid in many respects. Like Jesse, his father had been a preacher, like Billy, he killed his first man as a young teenager. Hardin's bloody Texas trail is almost as hard to follow as Billy's, except that his infamous gun duels were reported (with all the literary embellishments indigenous to the era) in the press and in Hardin's own book, written in dime-novel style, a self-aggrandizing autobiography known more for its colorful flare then for its honesty.

Reportedly, John Wesley Hardin killed more than forty men, almost all in gunfights, but the actual count is somewhere in the twenties, an intimidating record which brands Hardin the most diligent killer of his day.

A product of the South, Hardin and his family felt the Confederate defeat deeply after the Civil War. John Wesley, named after the famous Methodist leader in England, hated all Negroes. At fifteen, while living with his family in Bonham, Tex., Hardin reported that a Negro bully "came at me with a big stick," and so he shot the fellow dead with an old Colt pistol.

Like Billy Bonney, this teenage murder caused him to flee, a fugitive "not from justice," Hardin rationalized, "but from the injustice and misrule of the people who had subjugated the South."

The young firebrand made his way to Navarro Country, after (again by his own report) shooting down three Union soldiers pursuing him for the Bonham killing. In Navarro, Hardin went to work for a ranch as a cowboy. About this time, Hardin, with his cousin Simp Dixon, shot down two more Union soldiers in a quarrel and followed up these killings with a gun duel with gunslinger Jim Bradley. Hardin had taken offense and stood up shooting after Bradley accused him of cheating at cards.

As a teenager, Hardin had developed a fast draw, one of the quickest in the West. He was a rare gunslinger in that he employed a cross-draw. His two holsters were sewn into a vest, the pistol butts pointing inward across his chest. When Hardin drew, he crossed his arms and pulled his guns forth in a wide arch, a one-motion movement rather than reaching down to a hip holster and jerking the pistol upward and outward. He figured it saved him vital seconds and, many times, his life.

After settling an argument with a circus roustabout by shooting him through the head,

John Wesley Hardin of Texas, the top killer of the West. (Western History Collections, U. of Okla. Library)

Hardin headed for Kosse, Tex. where he knew a dance hall girl. When Hardin was in her room, the door burst open and an enraged man identified himself as the girl's lover. The unknown gunman held a pistol on Hardin and demanded $100 or he would kill him. Hardin explained that he possessed only $60 but the robber was welcome to that. The bandit agreed. Hardin clumsily handed the money over, most of the bills falling to the floor.

"When he stooped down to pick it up and as he was straightening up," Hardin later related, "I pulled my pistol and fired. The ball struck him between the eyes and he fell over, a dead robber."

While being taken to Waco, Tex. to stand trial for a murder he emphatically denied committing, Hardin escaped from his guard, killing him. He explained that he had purchased a Colt pistol from a fellow prisoner in Longview where he was first arrested and had secreted the gun on his person before the journey.

Three Yankee soldiers sent to recapture the boy gunman, were slain by Hardin on the open prairie; he was on foot and the three were mounted when they rushed him. The youth made his way to a ranch where he took a job herding cows. The owner, William C. Cohron was shot to death by Juan Bideno, a cattle rustler.

With another ranch hand, Hugh Anderson,

Wild Bill Hickok, "The Prince of Pistoleers"; some said Hardin backed Hickok down in Abilene in 1871 with a quick gun-spin. (The Kansas State Historical Society, Topeka)

Hardin tracked Bideno for weeks, finally catching up with him in early August, 1871. The two charged each other on ponies; Hardin won. Bideno received a bullet in the heart.

Though most of John Wesley Hardin's wild exploits had taken place in small Texas tank towns, his reputation as a fast triggerman preceded him to Abilene, Kansas, where he showed up in 1871. Abilene was a wide-open cattle town with violent gun battles taking place every day on its wagon-rutted dirt streets. The only law came in the personage of 6'2", long-haired James Butler "Wild Bill" Hickok, town marshal and savage gunman.

Hours after Hardin hit town he began to drink, emerging from a saloon in festive spirits. He fired several shots into the air as a way of announcing his arrival, and then turned to face the tall Hickok who stood in his path.

"You can't hurrah me," Hickok said coldly. "I won't have it."

"I haven't come to hurrah you," Hardin replied just as coldly, "but I'm going to stay in Abilene."

Hickok studied the frail-looking poorly-dressed cowboy. "I'll have your guns first," the marshal said.

With that, John Wesley Hardin later claimed, Hickok became a victim of the celebrated "border roll" or gun-spin. Hardin wrote: "I said all right and pulled them out of the scabbard, but while he was reaching for them, I reversed them and whirled them over on him with the muzzles in his face, springing back at the same time. I told him to put his pistols up, which he did."

Facing down Hickok was a heady claim to make, and many Wild Bill enthusiasts refuse to believe Hardin ever performed this trick, but he did stay in Abilene. The fact that Hardin felt no animosity toward Hickok was evidenced one night in the Bull's Head Saloon and Gambling House, owned by Ben Thompson, the scourge of the plains. Thompson, who had had several run-ins with Hickok, reportedly asked Hardin to shoot the marshal down.

Hardin became indignant. He was no hired killer, he insisted. "If Bill needs killin', why don't you do it yourself?" he said. Thompson declined.

The boy gunslinger left Abilene abruptly weeks later. A ruffian who proclaimed his hatred for Texans to one and all in a saloon where Hardin was drinking was drilled on the spot. John Wesley, knowing Hickok would be on the prod for him after the shooting, jumped on his horse and dashed out of town.

He journeyed back to Texas, ranching a bit in Gonzales County. There, two Negro policemen, Green Paramoor and John Lackey, went hunting for him. Hardin shot Paramoor and ran Lackey off after wounding him several times.

In 1872, Hardin's luck came "with the bark on." First, he was wounded in a gunfight with Phil Sublet in a gambling disagreement. Sublet let Hardin have a load of buckshot. A posse came riding into Trinity City after him with a warrant for the Paramoor killing. Hardin, after a furious gun-blasting chase, escaped, but not before one of the pursuing lawmen had shot him in the leg.

Too much, John Wesley decided. The best way to continue living was to surrender, and that he did, turning over his guns to Sheriff Richard Reagan who escorted Hardin to the Gonzales jail. As he was being placed in his cell, a jittery deputy squeezed off a round, wounding the gunfighter again in the knee.

Hardin tired of jail and cut his way through the bars of his cell with a saw smuggled to him by a friend. He returned to his wife Jane, whom he had married only months before.

Connubial life couldn't hold John Wesley for long (although he did manage to sire three children during the lulls of his battles). He soon limped off to neighboring DeWitt County where his relations—the abundant Taylor family—were having trouble with the Suttons. It was a blood feud that dated back to 1868 when clan chieftain William Sutton had shot Buck Taylor from ambush.

Some claimed that the feud dated back two decades before the Civil War, moving with the two families as they settled first in South Carolina, then in Georgia, and finally in Texas, curiously always on neighboring lands. Leaders of the Taylor faction were Pitkin, Creed, Josiah, William, and Rufus Taylor. Against them were the volatile and vehement Suttons whose 200-man army all but dominated the territory and controlled the range. Backing them up were lawman Jack Helm, cattle baron Abel Head "Shanghai" Pierce, and Joe Tumilson.

Hardin first worked for the Clements family, also his cousins and stalwart Taylor supporters. In the small town of Cuero, wedged in the heart of the contested territory, Hardin ran into Sheriff J. B. Morgan, a Sutton man. Morgan, according to Hardin, passed several unkind remarks about his personality, parentage, and physical appearance, all of which caused Hardin to take stern umbrage. In no time, the two reached for their guns. Hardin wrote: "I pulled my pistol and fired, the ball striking him just above the left eye. He fell dead. I went to the stable, got my horse, and left town unmolested."

The war raged on through 1873. Two of Pitkin Taylor's cousins, Bill and Henry Kelly, were arrested by Jack Helm who looked the other way while his two deputies, Doc White and John Meador, shot the prisoners. Helm was booted out of the state police force but that didn't prevent Sutton men from shooting Pitkin Taylor weeks later on his front porch. His son, Hardin's best friend at the time (friendships with gunfighters were as transitory as their addresses), Jim Taylor, swore vengeance: "I will wash my hands in old Bill Sutton's blood!"

Taylor and Hardin set an ambush in Bank's Saloon but Bill Sutton and some of his boys got off with light flesh wounds. Hardin's aim was better a few weeks later when two Sutton partisans, Jake Chrisman and Jim Cox, were shot and killed.

Then, Jack Helm, a man "whose name was a horror to all law-abiding citizens," according to Hardin, came up against Hardin in a blacksmith shop. When Helm jerked forth a knife and tried to plunge it into Jim Taylor's chest, Hardin let him have both barrels from a shotgun he was holding.

The war culminated in a full-scale weeklong battle which raged through the town of Clinton, Tex. Both factions fought from the area of Tumilson House down into the town, some two miles distance. Waves of charge and countercharge finally ebbed at the Clinton Courthouse where a queasy truce was finally accepted by both sides, mediated by Judge Clay Pleasants.

Pot-shooting went on into 1874 but the war came to a blood-soaked end when Jim and Bill Taylor, on a tip from Hardin, located Bill Sutton, his chief aide, Gabe Slaughter, and Sutton's wife and baby, as they were about to board the New Orleans-bound steamer at Indianola. Jim Taylor completed his vow by sending a bullet into Bill Sutton's heart. Gabe Slaughter fell with a ball sent to the same spot by Jim's brother Bill.

The decades-old Sutton-Taylor feud was ended. John Wesley Hardin went home to his wife and children at Commanche, Tex.

But there would be no peace for the gunfighter now; he had killed too many men, one too many for Brown County Sheriff Charlie Webb, a brave lawman who learned Hardin and Jim Taylor were residing in Commanche. Both men, he knew, were wanted, especially Hardin. Almost every sheriff in Texas held warrants for his arrest except Commanche's John Karnes, a friendly marshal who enjoyed playing cards with Hardin in one of the town's six saloons.

It was Hardin's twenty-first birthday when Charlie Webb came to town. The one-street Commanche held races in Hardin's honor and his big bay swept the meets. He had pocketed more than $3,000 and enough cattle, horses, and equipment to outfit a large ranch.

In the midst of the celebration, Sheriff Webb rode up slowly to the saloon. Hardin was on the steps with a drink in his hand, his last of the day. His little brother Jeff sat in a buckboard, waiting to take the outlaw to his ranch and family.

Webb tethered his horse to a hitching post fifteen feet away as Hardin eyed him. The sheriff walked to within five feet of the gunfighter, staring at him, his hands folded behind his back. Hardin spread his coat, revealing his gun butts jutting outward, vest-high. He kept his hands poised outward, limp, bent, as if he were about to drop them lightly upon piano keys and play.

"Have you any papers for my arrest?" Hardin asked Webb.

"I don't know you," the sheriff replied.

"My name is John Wesley Hardin," the outlaw said.

"Now I know you, but I have no papers for your arrest."

Hardin then ceremoniously invited Webb into the saloon for a drink and the lawman accepted with alacrity. Hardin led the way. After taking a step toward the saloon's swinging doors, a friend, Bud Dixon, called to Hardin: "Look out!"

The gunfighter jumped to one side, yanking out his deadly pistols with his turn-about and firing in the same motion. Webb, who had half-drawn his pistol behind Hardin's back (proving him to be one of the slowest guns in the West), was caught flat-footed, and Hardin's first bullet wickedly tore into his left cheek, killing him. Though dead on his feet, the sheriff, before he collapsed, got off a spasmodic shot which wounded Hardin in the side. According to Hardin's count, Webb was his fortieth victim.

It was nothing but running after that. Hardin bade a quick farewell to his small family and, leading a string of mounts, headed East with a posse behind him. A lynch mob caught up with his brother Joe and hanged him. The Dixon brothers, Tom and Bud, were hanged days later. Hardin's friends Ham Anderson and Alex Barrickman were hunted down and shot to death. The name of John Wesley Hardin had become an anathema in Texas. A $4,000 reward was placed on his head.

The Pinkertons took up his trail. So did the Texas Rangers. Dozens of apprentice fast-draw artists were also searching for him. One could make a reputation for one's self by putting a bullet into John Wesley Hardin. But he was no-

where to be found. He had vanished. Lawmen staking out his ranch gave up in disgust after several months. Vague reports drifted in from Georgia, Florida, Louisiana, and Alabama. He had been seen there, robbing trains.

After three years of search and surveillance, the Rangers were rewarded. They determined Hardin would be in Pensacola, Fla. after intercepting a letter he had sent to his wife.

The Pensacola station was jammed to every platform board with Rangers on August 23, 1877, when the train came in. Texas Ranger Lieutenant John B. Armstrong first spotted Hardin sitting at a window, his elbow bent on the sill, his cupped hand cradling a placid, unsuspecting face. The Rangers boarded the car from both ends and converged on Hardin; he struggled fiercely in the narrow train aisle with a dozen lawmen before he was subdued and knocked to the floor.

When he looked up, Armstrong's pistol was aimed at his forehead. Hardin's heroic account has him uttering: "Blow away! You will never blow a more innocent man's brains out, or one that will care less!"

The outlaw then wrote that Armstrong stopped one of his deputies from clubbing him, majestically saying: "Men, we have him now; don't hurt him; he is too brave to kill and the first man that shoots him I'll kill him."

Uninspired reality flagged down such roaring rhetoric. When Armstrong walked down the train's aisle toward Hardin, the outlaw spotted the lawman's raised 7½" barrel Peacemaker, the type of weapon commonly used by the Rangers.

"Texas, by God!" Hardin yelled and yanked for his high-riding pistols while attempting to stand up. He was a ridiculous sight. His guns snagged in his suspenders. "He almost pulled his breeches over his head," Armstrong reported.

While Hardin was trying to untangle himself, one of his companions jumped into the aisle and fired a wild shot at Armstrong which coursed through his wide-brimmed hat. Armstrong aimed carefully and plugged the man square in the chest. He grunted and then dove through a window, got up from the platform and staggered a few feet, dropping dead at the feet of James Duncan, another lawman.

Frustrated, Hardin still hadn't freed his guns. As he stood struggling and cursing, Armstrong reached over and hit him alongside the head, knocking him unconscious. The other three outlaws meekly surrendered their six-guns to the fearless Ranger and were escorted from the train. Hardin had to be carried; he was unconscious for two hours.

John Wesley insisted that he was J. H. Swain all the way back to Texas. He had come to Pensacola to buy timber, he claimed. Who was John Wesley Hardin? By the time he crossed the border into the Lone Star State, Hardin admitted his identity. Taken to the jail in Austin, Hardin passed his idle moments with some infamous fellow prisoners—Johnny Ringo, Manning Clements (who with Joe and John Gipson "Gyp" Clements had fought on the Taylor side in the DeWitt County War), and Bill Taylor.

The courthouse in Gonzales was packed when Hardin was moved there for the murder trial of Sheriff Webb. The eloquent outlaw rose in his own defense on the stand, pleading his case with the sweep and flower of a Shakespearian actor.

"Gentlemen," he began, "I swear before God that I never shot a man except in self-defense. Sheriff Webb came to Commanche for the purpose of arresting me, and I knew it. I met him and defied him to arrest me, but I did not threaten him . . . I knew it was in his mind to kill me, not arrest me. Everybody knows he was a dangerous man with a pistol." He looked about the courtroom with pleading eyes. "I know I don't have any friends here but I don't blame them for being afraid to come out for me. My father is a good man, and my brother who was lynched never harmed a man in his life."

He became solemn, his resonant voice carrying throughout the stilled courtroom, a tall, thin young man dressed all in black like his preacher-father. "People will call me a killer, but I swear to you gentlemen [fixing his wide-set eyes upon the jury], that I have shot only in defense of myself. And when Sheriff Webb drew his pistol I had to draw mine. Anybody else would have done the same thing. Sheriff Webb had shot a lot of men. That's all, gentlemen." He eased himself into his chair and waited.

The jury shuffled from the box and returned in an hour and a half. He was found guilty of second-degree murder. Hardin's flamboyant ability with words had saved his life. He was sentenced to serve twenty-five years of hard labor at Rusk Prison in Huntsville, Tex.

John Wesley Hardin went into the Huntsville prison a boy gunman and was released sixteen years later, reformed, he claimed, in February, 1894. The reformation was painful. Hardin rebelled against the prison authorities for close to ten years. He tried to escape several times, was caught, and whipped. He led revolts and was thrown into solitary confinement, given no food or water for days. Then he conformed, quieted, and began to study law in his cell for hours on end.

He was forty-one when he was set free and he immediately threw himself into law studies. His wife Jane had died while he was in prison; his children had grown up and moved off. Alone, he traveled to El Paso where he worked as a lawyer. Citizens of the modern frontier hailed his rehabilitation with cheers. The *El Paso Times* praised his good citizenship and community leadership.

But there was an unrelenting wild streak in John Wesley Hardin and he was soon back in the saloons gambling and oftimes wearing his irons. He took a pretty new wife, Callie Lewis, a girl who became infatuated with his legendary exploits. The marriage was a bad one. Callie, only eighteen, soon tired of her carousing husband and left him. Hardin began to drink all the more. He lost his ability to hold liquor and was often found, dead drunk, in the gutters that fronted on the sleazier El Paso dives.

His nerve seemed to flee, too. He became enamored with a fun-loving married woman, heavyset Mrs. Martin McRose. Her husband, a wanted cattle rustler, was hiding out across the border in Mexico. When McRose, Vic Queen, Tom Finnessy, and other members of this outlaw band crossed into the U.S., they were shot down by Ranger Jeff Milton and U.S. Marshals George Scarborough and Frank McMahon. Hardin, upon hearing of the incident, boasted in the bars that he had hired the lawmen to shoot McRose so he could have Mrs. McRose to himself.

Milton flew into a wild rage when he heard of this and tracked Hardin down in a bar where he demanded an apology. Hardin said he was not wearing his guns or the Ranger wouldn't speak so to him.

"You're lying again," Milton stormed. "You're always armed. And you can go for your gun right now or tell all these men here and out loud that you lied."

Without hesitation, Hardin turned to the soggy faces in the saloon and swept an encompassing hand before them. "Gentlemen," he intoned, "when I said that about Captain Milton, I lied."

Worse came to Hardin days later. Beyond public humiliation, he endured one of the most inglorious ends to ever befall a feared Texas outlaw.

Following an argument with lawman John Selman, who had the effrontery to throw Mrs. McRose in jail for rowdy conduct, Hardin passed several unpleasant comments about Selman's heritage, calling the policeman's father an assortment of vile names.

Old John Selman's hatred for Hardin went back for years. When he heard that Hardin had stated, "Old John better go fixed at all times," Old John, town constable, picked up his pistol and headed for the Acme Saloon on July 19, 1895. He found Hardin there as he knew he would, and quickly walked up behind him.

Hardin was at the bar, shooting dice with the bartender. "Four sixes to beat," John Wesley said after a roll and at that moment he looked up into a mirror and saw Selman's pistol pointed at him. He never had a chance to move.

The first bullet killed him, splitting open the back of his head. Wordless, the great gunfighter toppled to the floor, dead. Selman was acquitted of murder; his lawyer, Albert Fall (of the future Teapot Dome scandal), successfully pleaded his client innocent, stating he had acted in self-defense. Hardin was going for a gun in a shoulder-holster, Fall maintained.

The death of John Wesley Hardin was ignominious, a weird slur upon his personal credo of honor that demanded gunfighters face each other in fair draw, life awarded to the man with the fastest hands and the sharpest eyes.

He did, however, die with his boots on.

[ALSO SEE Clay Allison, Ben Thompson.]

HARE, JOSEPH THOMPSON
Highwayman ● (? -1818)

A freebooter born in Chester, Pa., Hare, at an early age, gathered a band of cut-throats and preyed upon the stages running between Nashville, Tenn. and Natchez, Miss. He was a legend for a dozen years, totally unknown to lawmen of the day. He was caught in 1813 and sent to prison for five years. Upon his release, Hare immediately resumed his old ways, stopping the Baltimore night coach near Havre de Grace.

The coach was carrying a special bank shipment and Hare made off with more than $15,000, his biggest haul and an enormous prize for those days.

Unfortunately for the bandit, he never lived to spend it. Apprehended only days after the robbery, he was promptly hanged on the yard gallows of the old Baltimore Jail on September 10, 1818.

HARPE BROTHERS

William Micajah "Big" Harpe (born 1768) and his brother, Wiley "Little" Harpe (born 1770), alias Roberts, were the scourge of the Wilderness Trail leading from Knoxville, Tennessee to the unchartered West.

The brothers were tories in North Carolina, their birthplace, and, following the surrender of the British, fled to Tennessee, robbing and killing the Westward-moving settlers working their way along the Wilderness Trail. The two giant, bearded, wild-eyed men were captured time and again but always managed to free themselves from the flimsy frontier jails.

Five particularly vicious murders were attributed to the Harpes in the early 1790s; the brothers attempted to hide the bodies of their victims by disemboweling them, filling them with rocks, and throwing them into the Barren River.

A kingly sum of $300 was offered for their capture in Tennessee but the Harpes, restless robbers, moved on to the Ohio country and made their headquarters at a place called Cave-in-the-Rock, a natural fortress honeycombed with subterranean passages so large that the Harpes hid herds of cattle and horses in them.

Sixty-odd miles south of this hideout, pirates openly freebooted on the Ohio River. The buckskinned brothers, heavily armed and carrying the scalps of Whites and Indians in their belts were described by the Ohio pirates at this time as "men turned into wild wolves."

Dozens of settlers were murdered in their beds by the "Terrible Harpes," one man merely because he snored too loudly. In 1799, a large group of frontiersmen trapped the Harpes in the wilds of Ohio. Wiley escaped but Micajah was blown from his horse by a well-directed volley. Such was the fear of the blood-lusting Harpes that the possemen set upon Micajah with long knives and attempted to cut off his head. As they were sawing, the mammoth killer bellowed at one of the executioners: "You are a Goddamned rough butcher but cut on and be damned!"

Harpe's head bounced along in a saddle bag on horseback as the pioneers made their way back to camp. Lack of provisions caused them to boil "Big" Harpe's head for supper one night; the skull was nailed to a tree and remained there, looming white in the wilderness clearing for years, an ominous warning to those who would take up the highwayman's life.

Wiley Harpe disappeared into the woods, reappearing along the trails to kill and loot. He disappeared some time after 1800, some said as the victim of a wild wolf pack. Ironic justice, settlers grimly joked. The wolves had claimed one of their own.

HARRIS, JEAN STRUVEN
Murderer ● (1923-   )

Her students called her "Integrity Jean," because she stressed self-control, propriety, and commitment to excellence in her lec-

Socialite Jean Struven Harris who killed her lover Dr. Herman Tarnower in 1980.

tures. Yet, Jean Struven Harris, headmistress at the exclusive Madeira school for girls in McLean, Va., broke all her own rules when it came to her chief interest in life, Dr. Herman Tarnower.

Tarnower wrote the best-selling *Scarsdale Diet* which, in 1979, would bring him more than $11 million. But when Tarnower met Harris at a Manhattan cocktail party in 1966, he was only a successful cardiologist and she was a divorced woman with two children. Harris was a brilliant educator who had graduated magna cum laude from Smith College in 1945.

The following year the couple became loosely engaged and there was talk of marriage but nothing "official" developed. The wealthy Tarnower, however, was a womanizer, who dangled marriage to Harris while entertaining several other women at his luxury estate in Purchase, N.Y. By 1977, Tarnower, at age 68, was involved with his medical assistant, 38-year-old Lynne Tryforos.

When Harris learned of Tryforos's liaison with Tarnower, a struggle between the two women for the doctor's attention ensued. Though Tarnower appeared to favor the younger Tryforos, he relied on Harris to edit his diet book, which was just about to go to publication. After the book's success, Tarnower brushed off his 56-year-old mistress.

A patient overheard Tarnower talking to Harris on the phone, saying "Goddamnit, Jean! I want you to stop bothering me!" He accused her of lying and cheating. After some muffled conversation about his money, the patient heard the doctor say, "Well, you're going to inherit $240,000." When Tarnower slammed down the phone he was visibly agitated.

Rather than begin anew, Harris placed a .32-caliber handgun in her purse, got into her car on March 10, 1980, and drove from McLean to the doctor's estate. She arrived close to midnight, just after Tarnower's dinner guests had left. She let herself in with the key she had to the front door, climbed the stairs to Tarnower's bedroom, and pulled out her gun. She fired four shots. Herman Tarnower slumped dead to the floor and Harris fled the estate.

Harris did not get far. Scarsdale police intercepted her and put her under arrest. "He wanted to live," she said. "I wanted to die." She added that she had gone to Tarnower and asked him to shoot her, but in the struggle for the gun, he had been killed. Her sensational trial began in November 1980.

Defense attorneys attempted to portray Harris as the scorned woman who had been driven to kill by the lover who had cruelly jilted her. This argument was lost on a jury that convicted Harris of murder on February 24, 1981. She was given a life sentence on March 20 and became an inmate at the Bedford Hills Correctional Facility.

As a prisoner, Harris worked hard at prison reform and also authored a book, *They Always Call Us Ladies*, which was published in 1988. A few years later, Harris underwent heart surgery. It was thought that she had only a few years to live and, considering her model conduct in prison, she was paroled on January 22, 1993. She presently lectures on the need for prison reform.

HARRIS, ROBERT ALTON
Murderer ● (1953-1992)

One of the most vicious killers on record, Harris ruthlessly murdered two boys in 1978 and spent fourteen years waiting for execution. He is typical of the convicted murderers sentenced to death and who manage to cling to life for years and years, filing endless appeals and receiving stay after stay while begging for the mercy he never showed his victims.

On the morning of July 5, 1978, two 16-year-old boys from Mira Mesa High School in San Diego, California, sat in their car eating hamburgers in the parking lot of a fast food restaurant. Robert Harris and his younger brother, Danny, approached the boys, John Mayeski and Michael Baker, showing them a 9-mm Luger, saying he needed their car to commit a bank robbery. He promised that he would later release them.

Harris forced the boys at gunpoint to drive the car to the Miramar Resevoir. Once at this deserted spot, he ordered the boys from the car, telling them he was going to kill them. One of the boys cried and begged for his life. "Stop crying and die like a man," snorted Harris. With that he shot both boys to death, jumped into their car and fled with his brother. As he drove Harris ate the unfinished hamburgers left by his victims.

Ironically, Harris was arrested for a traffic violation later that day by San Diego policeman Steve Baker who was unaware that Harris had shot and killed his own son. Harris was brought to to trial in 1979. Typical of his self-serving character, Harris blamed his brother Danny for the killings. Danny testified that Robert had committed the cold-blooded murders.

Robert Alton Harris was convicted and sentenced to death in 1979. He avoided San Quentin's gas chamber for fourteen years while the state spent an estimated $400,000 to keep him alive. Through his lawyers he filed endless appeals, dodging four different execution dates.

Only days before his last scheduled execution date, Harris made a final, desperate appeal through his lawyers who claimed that the killer should receive special consideration because he was an abused child, that his brutal father had kicked his pregnant mother, causing her to give premature birth to Harris. Further, they said, Harris's mother was an alcoholic who drank during pregnancy and this left Harris a victim of "fetal alcohol syndrome," which might have affected his mind and, subsequently, caused the killings of the two boys.

This fierce, last argument was typical of Harris. He would squander the last vestiges of his own respect, staining the memory of his father and mother to save his own life. He even persuaded his brother Danny to recant his testimony against him. None of it worked.

Time ran out for Harris on April 21, 1992. He was the first person to be executed by the State of California in 25 years. Prior to Harris, Aaron Mitchell was sent to the gas chamber on April 12, 1967 for killing a Sacramento, California police officer. The American Civil Liberties Union was reportedly given permission to video tape Harris's execution, to use the tape later as an argument against the pain and agony of capital punishment.

A year later, on April 21, 1993, the anniversary of Harris's execution, Steve Baker, who was then retiring from the San Diego Police Department and whose son Michael had been killed by Harris, spoke at a Crime Stoppers luncheon. He said: "Harris was visited by Mother Teresa" while on death row. "Mother Teresa did not visit or offer condolences to the familes of Harris's victims.

"I ask only that in the future, the experience of victims not be forgotten in the heated debate about capital punishment, and that the rights of victims are not ignored."

HART, PEARL
Stagerobber ● (? -1925)

Pearl was a young hellion living in the Globe, Ariz. area in the late 1890s. She had become enamored of the Wild West after reading thrilling tales of Jesse James and Butch Cassidy and moved to Arizona from the East where she had been a student.

Miss Hart, in her twenties, adorned her curvacious body with two giant six-guns at the hips and several more stuck into ammunition belts. Carrying a rifle almost as long as she was tall, she convinced a town drunk, Joe Boot, to help her rob the local stage.

The two unlikely outlaws, days later, stopped the Globe stage and took about $450 from the passengers—Wells Fargo had discontinued the shipping of money in strong boxes at that late date.

The pair subsequently got lost in their getaway and were quickly arrested and tried. Pearl got five years in the Yuma Territorial Prison for her prank robbery. Upon her release, she disappeared for two decades, returning to the scene of her crime decades later on a nostalgic visit.

Pearl Hart would be forgotten today if it were not for the fact that she pulled off the last stagecoach robbery in the history of the

Pearl Hart, the last bandit to rob a stage in America. (Arizona Historical Society Library)

West, an impulsive and foolish crime that nevertheless earned for her an odd if not enviable distinction.

HARVEY, DONALD
Serial Killer ● (? -   )

Working as a hospital orderly, Donald Harvey was responsible for more than fifty murders by his own admission. When John Powell, a patient at the Drake Memorial Hospital in Cincinnati, Ohio, died suddenly in March 1987, suspicion immediately fell on Donald Harvey. The orderly had been present when many other patients had suddenly and inexplicably died.

Confronted by police, Harvey confessed that he not only administered cyanide to Powell, but had done so with twenty-four others. Before confessing, Harvey had plea bargained for life in prison instead of execution for his crimes. He went on to admit to killing eight patients in Kentucky where he had worked at one time. In the end, it was learned that more than fifty people had been poisoned to death by Harvey.

The hospital orderly at first insisted that he had committed mercy killings only, but this was contradicted when it was discovered that he had also poisoned neighbors who annoyed him. Harvey received twenty life prison terms.

HATCHER, CHARLES
Serial Killer ● (? -1984)

Between 1961 and 1982, Charles Hatcher, a decidedly deranged killer, murdered fourteen people, mostly small boys. Hatcher kidnapped, sexually attacked, and strangled these children in Missouri, California, Nebraska, and Illinois. He was given a life term in Missouri, despite asking that the court sentence him to death. He brought about his own execution by hanging himself in his cell on December 7, 1984.

HAUPTMANN, BRUNO RICHARD
Murderer, Kidnapper ● (1899-1936)

BACKGROUND: BORN 11/26/1899 IN SAXONY, GERMANY. GRADUATED ELEMENTARY SCHOOL AND ENTERED A TRADE SCHOOL. SERVED AS AN APPRENTICE CARPENTER AT AGE 14 IN KAMENZ, GERMANY. AT AGE 17 SERVED IN A MACHINE-GUN BATTALION IN THE GERMAN ARMY DURING THE FIRST WORLD WAR; WAS WOUNDED SLIGHTLY AND GASSED; DISCHARGED CHRISTMAS, 1918. IMMIGRATED TO THE U.S. IN 1923. MARRIED ANNA SCHOEFFLER IN 1924. SON, MANFRED, BORN IN 1931. DESCRIPTION: 6'2", GREY EYES, BROWN HAIR, THIN. ALIASES: CEMETERY JOHN. RECORD: ARRESTED AND CONVICTED OF BREAKING AND ENTERING THE HOME OF THE MAYOR OF KAMENZ, GERMANY, 3/15/19; ARRESTED FOR DEALING IN STOLEN GOODS IN KAMENZ, 1922; ESCAPED DAYS AFTER HIS APPREHENSION; ARRESTED TWICE IN 1923 FOR ILLEGAL ENTRY INTO THE U.S. AS A STOWAWAY ON GERMAN FREIGHTERS; KIDNAPPED AND MURDERED CHARLES A. LINDBERGH, JR., 3/1/32; ARRESTED 9/15/34 FOR THE LINDBERGH MURDER; TRIED AND CONVICTED OF THIS CRIME 1/2/35—2/13/35; SENTENCED TO DEATH AND ELECTROCUTED AT THE STATE PRISON IN TRENTON, NEW JERSEY, 4/3/36.

When Charles Lindbergh flew the Atlantic in 1927, the world went mad with worship. The Lone Eagle, as Lindbergh was called by the press, became the single most important hero in America, the clean-cut, good-looking, well-mannered boy down the block who courageously took his *Spirit of St. Louis* to Paris alone, all alone.

This same man, heaped with glory, financial success, and national reverence, suffered the ultimate of tragedies on March 1, 1932 when his only son, Charles Augustus Lindbergh, Jr. was kidnapped.

On that night, six persons occupied the Lindbergh country estate home at Sourlands, New Jersey, a few miles from the town of Hopewell. At nine o'clock Mrs. Lindbergh looked in on her twenty-month-old son as he slept in the upstairs nursery.

She had been worried over the cold he had developed, but the child was sleeping soundly in his crib. Several minutes later, Colonel Lindbergh heard some sounds outside the downstairs library.

The noise didn't alarm Lindbergh as he worked on his notes. He knew that the shutter outside the baby's nursery was broken and banging in the wind.

Betty Gow, an attractive, dark-haired English nurse of twenty-eight who had been employed to look after the child, went up to check on the baby at ten minutes to ten. He was missing from his crib.

The nurse didn't let out any scream of panic. This had happened before. The Colonel, she knew, was a practical joker. Months before, he had taken the baby out of his crib and hidden him in a closet, badly frightening the family for twenty minutes until he revealed his hoax.

But this time it wasn't a hoax. Lindbergh, after frantically searching the house with Miss Gow, his wife, and the cook and butler, Ollie and Elsie Whately, discovered a crudely-written, ungrammatical ransom note on the inside of the nursery window on the sill.

"Don't let anyone touch it," Lindbergh said to everyone as he pointed to the envelope. He turned to Whately the butler and yelled, "Call the police and tell them the baby has been taken." Then he snatched up a rifle and ran from the house in search of the kidnapper.

Hopewell's chief of police, Harry Wolf, was the first to arrive at the Lindbergh house, but before he could investigate a thing, hordes of state police on motorcycles arrived. They obliterated any trace of vehicles that may have carried the baby away on the mud-rutted backroads about the house.

The state officers clomped through the house, touching everything in sight like visiting souvenir hunters. Even the makeshift ladder which was still outside the nursery window was so stupidly manhandled that over 500 sets of fingerprints on it confused clue-searching detectives.

As the investigation proceeded, Lindbergh himself became a hindrance rather than a help in finding the kidnappers and his own son.

Two ransom letters were sent from mailboxes in a specific area of Brooklyn. Ed Mulrooney, police commissioner, wanted to station a man at each mailbox in the vicinity, suspecting that a third letter would also be sent from the same area.

Lindbergh vetoed the action, saying that he felt that any shadowing of the letter-writer might cause the death of his son. He also added that if Mulrooney went through with his plan he would use his considerable influence to see that he was broken to the ranks.

It was an unfortunate, if understandable decision. The day after Mulrooney proposed his stake-out plan, another ransom letter was sent from the Brooklyn area.

Lindbergh tried everything, and, perhaps too much to attempt to retrieve his tragic curly-haired child. He enlisted the aid of gangsters and speakeasy proprietors to find the kidnappers and act as intermediaries in paying the ransom.

He also used Dr. John F. Condon as a go-between. This seventy-two-year-old teacher and lecturer enjoyed basking in the limelight and playing at cloak-and-dagger. He inserted several ads in newspapers requesting the kidnappers to get in touch with him for delivery of the $70,000 ransom which was demanded.

Cleverly, he thought, he used the name Jafsie which represented his initials J. F. C. when pronounced quickly. Others were busy getting in on the Lindbergh act, now the single most important news item in the nation.

Al Capone said from his jail cell that through his connections he could find the Lindbergh baby. Treasury agents grilled him and his knowledge came to nothing. Scarface only wanted an excuse to get out.

Another would-be hero, "Commodore" John Hughes Curtis, formed a group of socialite searchers from Norfolk, Va. Curtis, enamored by the publicity he was receiving for his efforts, fabricated a story about meeting with four men and a woman—all Nordic sailors who claimed they had the baby on a boat and were awaiting ransom.

When confronted by Police Captain John Lamb in the Lindbergh home, Curtis admitted that no such group existed. Lamb took him to the basement and, in the words of a reporter of the day, "beat the hell out of him."

Another schemer, former FBI agent Gaston Bullock Means, took advantage of socialite Evalyn Walsh McLean, who offered to pay $100,000 for the Lindbergh baby's return.

Means, whose preposterous career included bilking the U.S. government of federal funds, acting as a bagman for the Cabinet crooks of Harding's Tea-pot Dome regime, and authoring a book that Mrs. Harding had poisoned her husband to death, was happy to bilk Mrs. McLean.

He told her that he could obtain the child's release through his contacts in the underworld. After setting up several rendezvous with the mysterious kidnap gang, Means brought a man, known as "The Fox" around to meet Mrs. McLean. The Fox allegedly represented the gang.

The Fox was, of course, a Means associate and part of the ruse. He was finally identified as a one-time lawyer, Norman Whittaker, and he and Means were convicted of fraud and sent to prison.

Meanwhile Jafsie made contact with a man claiming to be the Lindbergh kidnapper. They met in the Woodlawn Cemetery in the Bronx. Jafsie sat with the man—called Cemetery John—for about an hour, noticing that he talked with a heavy German accent.

This tied in to the ransom notes which experts had agreed had been written by someone of German origin.

Cemetery John convinced Jafsie that he was, indeed, the Lindbergh kidnapper when he identified two safety pins as being in the baby's crib and telling the go-between that the child was wearing a nightsuit without a flap in the back.

The newspapers had mistakenly reported that the nightsuit did have a back flap—a purposely misleading clue supplied by authorities to see who could describe the correct garment.

Arrangements were made for the payoff. Authorities wrapped up $50,000 in marked bills, $20,000 of which were in old gold certificates.

On April 2, 1932, Jafsie met again with Cemetery John in the St. Raymond's Cemetery in the Bronx. Jafsie, who could barely make out the kidnapper's face as before, explained that there was a depression on and Lindbergh could only raise $50,000 of the ransom money.

"Yes," replied John, "I know. Fifty thousand will be all right."

Jafsie went to a car where Lindbergh himself sat and retrieved the payoff. He was delighted that he had gypped the kidnapper out of $20,000. After handing over the money, Jafsie was given a note from Cemetery John, who melted away into the shadows. The note said that the Lindbergh child was on a boat named Nelly docked at Martha's Vineyard, Mass.

Lindbergh flew there immediately but there was no such boat anchored in those waters. He realized he was the victim of another hoax.

On May 12, a truckdriver stopped alongside a backroad four miles away from the New Jersey home of Lindbergh, and discovered the pathetic corpse of a child, turned black with decomposition, missing its right foot and its left leg from the knee down.

Lindbergh and the nurse Betty Gow made the identification as that of the Lindbergh baby. The nation wept at the brutality of the crime and the Lindbergh Kidnapping Law was quickly passed, bringing the FBI into the case.

But the G-Men, like so many hundreds of others, were unsuccessful in finding the kidnapper.

Suspect after suspect was picked up and released. Jafsie couldn't identify them or they had alibis.

One suspect, an English maid named Violet Sharpe, was so bothered by police that she committed suicide. So did a much-harrassed German-born gardener, also under suspicion.

When the gold certificates were called in in 1933, Cemetery John—whoever he was—was under new pressure. His ransom money could now be more easily spotted. That is exactly what happened in September of 1934, almost two and a half years after the killing of the Lindbergh child.

A man drove into a Bronx filling station and bought some gas with a gold certificate. The station attendant, who had a list of the Lindbergh notes, compared it to the bill before giving the customer his change. It was on the list. He quickly jotted down the car's license number and it was subsequently turned over to police.

Authorities traced the license number to a car owned by a 36-year-old carpenter named Bruno Richard Hauptmann. He was promptly arrested by New York police.

Several factors had already contributed to Hauptmann's conviction. The ladder found outside the Lindbergh home was unique, experts agreed, in that it was handmade and soundly constructed by a man who had to have knowledge of carpentry.

The top rung of the ladder had been broken, it was estimated, under the killer's weight when he fled back down the ladder with the baby in his arms. Experts built an exact duplicate of the ladder and tested various weights on the top rung until it broke under a total weight of 210 pounds. Since the Lindbergh baby weighed exactly 30 lbs. when abducted, the killer had to weigh 180 lbs. Bruno Richard Hauptmann weighed exactly 180 lbs.

Hauptmann's face also perfectly matched the police composition made up from descriptions given by Jafsie, two cabdrivers who had taken Cemetery John to the ransom meetings, and Mrs. Cecilia Barr, a ticket agent at Loew's Sheridan Square Theater who had sold a ticket to a theater-goer in November of 1933. He had paid for it with one of the Lindbergh notes.

Mrs. Barr identified Hauptmann. One of the taxi-drivers, John Perone, picked him out of a line-up. Two more witnesses who were around the Lindbergh home at the time of the kidnapping, Millard Whited and Amandus Hochmuth, identified Hauptmann as a man who had hung around the grounds then.

Hochmuth went even further and said he had seen a man drive past him close to Sourlands with a three-sectioned ladder strapped to the side of his auto on the day of the kidnapping.

"Do you mind stepping down [from the witness chair] and showing us this man," the prosecution asked Hochmuth. The elderly man, visibly fighting his angry rheumatism, feebly walked forward into the court area, wending his way at an agonizingly slow pace through the maze of desks until he came to the defendant's table. He walked up to Bruno Richard Hauptmann and, in a scene electric with drama, placed his hand on the defendant's shoulder.

"Right here," Hochmuth said solemnly. "This is the man."

Hauptmann's ordinarily cool composure shattered. He whipped his head around to look at his wife who was sitting in the visitor's section. "Der Alter ist verrucht!" he yelled. "The old man is crazy."

It was the only time Hauptmann was to use his native tongue during the course of the trial.

More evidence was mounted against Hauptmann when the prosecution matched the wood of the kidnapping ladder to a missing board in Hauptmann's attic. The clincher came when close to $30,000 of the ransom money was uncovered in the German's home. Also, they found Jafsie the go-between's phone number written on a closet wall in the Hauptmann home.

To counter this mountain of evidence, Hauptmann yelled he was innocent and that he was merely keeping the money for a fellow German, Isidore Fisch, who had returned to Germany in 1933 and died there.

Prosecutor David T. Wilentz took special note of Hauptmann's sardonic smile as he talked of Isidore Fisch, an obvious dead scapegoat.

"This is funny to you, isn't it?" Wilentz asked Hauptmann.

The carpenter held onto his grin as he sat comfortably in the witness chair. "No, no."

"You are having a lot of fun with me, aren't you?" Wilentz said.

"No, that is not true."

"You think you are a big shot, don't you?"

"No. Should I cry?"

"You think you are bigger than everybody, don't you?"

"No, but I know I am innocent."

"You wouldn't tell if they murdered you—"

"No."

Wilentz struck at the German's fierce pride.

Kidnapper and killer of the Lindbergh baby, Bruno Richard Hauptmann, on trial in 1934.

"Will-power is everything with you—"

"No, it is—I feel innocent—that keep me the power to stand up."

"Lying when you swear to God that you will tell the truth. Telling lies doesn't mean anything."

Hauptmann shook his finger at Wilentz. "Stop that!"

"Didn't you swear to untruths in the Bronx Court House?"

"Stop that!"

"Lies, lies, lies about the Lindbergh ransom money—"

"Well, you lied to me, too."

"Where and when?"

"Right in this courtroom here."

"The jury will decide that . . . I see you have stopped smiling. Things have become a little more serious."

"I guess it isn't any place to smile here."

The wily prosecutor then exploded Hauptmann's story about Fisch. The man whom Hauptmann alleged had left the Lindbergh money in his home, now conveniently dead, was, in reality, a pauper, Wilentz stated. The prosecutor said that instead of discovering Fisch's money, he, Hauptmann, had loaned Fisch $5,500. Hauptmann screamed a denial.

"Didn't you write to Mr. Fisch's family in Germany after his death, claiming that you had given Fisch $5,500 from your own private bank account?" Before the defendant could answer, Wilentz produced a letter Hauptmann had written to the Fisch family in Germany demanding the return of just such a sum.

Hauptmann squirmed in his chair. "Well, I—"

"My God," Wilentz sighed. "Don't you ever tell anybody the truth?"

The jury didn't think so. Eight men and four women found Hauptmann guilty and recommended the death penalty. On April 2, 1936, Bruno Richard Hauptmann was led into the New Jersey State Prison's little green room and was promptly electrocuted. He denied his guilt to the end.

HAYWARD, HARRY T.
Murderer, Swindler ● (1864-1894)

Hayward was content to be a common swindler in the Minneapolis, Minn. area during the Gay Nineties; the prospect of $10,000 in one lump sum led him to murder. After his engagement to Catherine M. Ging, Hayward convinced the gullible girl to take out $10,000 in insurance policies, and to make him the benificiary.

Next, Hayward went to Claus Blixt, a janitor who had collaborated with him on previous swindles, and asked him to shoot Catherine for the insurance while pretending to rob her. Murder was too much for Blixt, who begged off.

Determined to realize his scheme, Hayward then went to his brother Adry and asked him to kill Catherine. He, too, refused. Adry Hayward reported the conversation with his brother to an attorney but Harry's reputation as a notorious liar prevented the lawyer from acting.

Hayward carried out his murder plan him-

self and was soon apprehended. Blixt and Adry Hayward testified against him.

Harry Hayward's dying request was probably the most unusual in criminal records. He asked that the rope and the gallows upon which he would be hanged be painted red, his favorite color. The Minneapolis sheriff complied, at least partially. When Hayward ascended the gallows stairs, he was fairly beaming with delight. The scaffold had been painted a bright fire engine red. The rope, however, had not.

HEARST, PATRICIA CAMPBELL (PATTY; AKA: TANIA)
Robber ● (1955-   )

The media had a field day with the Patty Hearst case, one that involved kidnapping, murder, and revolution. At the center of this crime drama was the heiress to one of America's great fortunes. Patty Hearst was kidnapped from her Berkeley, California, apartment on February 4, 1974. At that time, two men broke down the apartment door and beat Stephen Weed, who was Hearst's fiance, and shared the apartment with her.

Patty Hearst was then dragged outside to a waiting car, stuffed into the trunk, and, while the kidnappers fired automatic weapons in the air to frighten off any would-be pursuers, the car sped off with its hostage. Neighbors later reported that they thought the kidnapping had been staged and that Patty's cries for help seemed feeble and feigned.

The media exploded with the news, particularly the Hearst papers and an anxious country awaited the kidnappers' next move, speculation high on how much they would demand from the super-rich Hearst family. The ransom, or extortion money, was staggering. It was soon learned that Hearst was in the hands of a revolutionary group calling itself the Symbionese Liberation Army (SLA), a radical leftist organization that never numbered more than ten people.

Its leader was a 30-year-old malcontent named Donald DeFreeze who was a convicted thief, terrorist, and fugitive. DeFreeze called himself "Cinque" after a nineteenth-century rebellious slave, and he had put together his crazy-quilt leftist philosophy while serving time in prison. The SLA's headquarters were in Oakland, California.

DeFreeze demanded that if Patty's father, newspaper czar William Randolph Hearst, Jr., wanted his daughter safely returned, he was to dole out $70 worth of food to each of the 5.9 million poor people in California, an estimated $400 million. Accompanying DeFreeze's demand was a tape recording of Patty who stated in a weak voice: "These people aren't just a bunch of nuts. They're perfectly willing to die for what they are doing."

Hearst began to deliver the food to the homeless, poverty-stricken, and the elderly. In Oakland more than 5,000 persons rioted, which caused terrified clerks to toss the food parcels wildly into the crowd and escape. With more than $2 million in food handed out, Hearst was accused by the SLA of dragging his feet, not doing enough. Even his own daughter criticized him.

Then a tape was sent to a radio station. On it was the voice of Patty Hearst, saying: "I have never been forced to say anything on tape. Nor have I been brainwashed, tortured, hypnotized or in any way confused." She then denounced her father and criticized her mother for taking a position at the University of California. She stated that she had grown tired of her relationship with Stephen Weed and that she had "an unselfish love for my comrades" in the SLA.

Patty Hearst had gone over to the terrorists, if, indeed, she had not been in collusion with them from the beginning. She stated that she was to be known as "Tania," the name of a woman who had been the consort of revolutionary Che Guevara. On April 15, 1974, Patty Hearst proved to one and all that she was a devout member of a lunatic terrorist group.

On that day, she, three other women, and DeFreeze, all carrying automatic weapons, entered San Francisco's Hibernia Bank in the Sunset District. They robbed it of $10,900. Hearst was captured on the bank's video camera pointing a weapon at terrified customers and shouting orders to them. There was no doubt about the missing heiress. Attorney General William Saxbe labelled her "a common criminal."

Two SLA members, William and Emily Harris, surfaced on May 17, 1974, robbing a sporting goods store, and running outside to their van. When a clerk followed, he was stopped by the withering fire of an automatic weapon wielded by Patty Hearst who was inside the van providing "covering fire," for the fleeing Harris couple. Fortunately, her aim was poor and her more than 30 bullets struck no one.

A short time later, acting on a tip, hundreds of officers surrounded a small stucco house at 1466 East 54th Street, Los Angeles. Inside were DeFreeze and four diehard followers. After a wild gun battle the house caught fire. Rather than surrender, the fanatics died in the flames.

On September 19, 1975, the Harrises were captured and Patty Hearst was taken a few days later. Convicted of robbery, the Harris couple went to prison for twenty-five years. They were paroled in 1984. Patty Hearst was convicted of robbing the Hibernia Bank and went to prison for seven years. She served only a year before being released on bail while an appeal was heard. The appeal was denied and Hearst went back to prison. President Jimmy Carter, however, exercised executive clemency and ordered Patty's release in January 1979. She later married Bernard Shaw.

HEDGEPETH, MARION
Trainrobber, Bankrobber ● (? -1910)

His name was slightly effeminate and he looked like nothing of the Wild West, but Marion Hedgepeth was one of the most raw-boned, gutful gunfighters and bandits of his era, a quick-draw expert so fast, some reports said, that he could outpull and drill a man whose pistol had already cleared the holster. This horse-faced six-footer dressed all in black with a large wing collar, cravat spliced by a diamond stickpin, and a derby hat precariously balanced on his head.

Hedgepeth ran away from his birthplace in Cooper County, Mo. at age fifteen and moved West, becoming a cowboy for brief spells in Wyoming and Colorado.

In 1890 he turned to crime, robbing trains with a ruthless band of outlaws dubbed by lawmen as the "Hedgepeth Four"—Marion, Albert "Bertie" Sly, James "Illinois Jimmy" Francis, and Charles F. "Dink" Burke. The gang first held up a passenger train of the Missouri Pacific near Omaha, Neb. on November 4, 1890, taking a mere $1,000 from the express car. On November 12, 1890 the fast-moving gang hit the Chicago, Milwaukee & St. Paul line. They didn't wait for the express guard to surrender. They placed dynamite beneath the express car. Its walls and roof were blown away in a single blast (the guard somehow survived). Hedgepeth got $5,000 this time.

Weeks later, the four men boarded a St. Louis train, stopped it near Glendale, Mo. and took $50,000 from the express car safe without firing a pistol. Traveling to St. Louis, the gang settled into rented rooms, buried their weapons in a shed and waited for the hard-riding posses to burn out following their purposely misleading trails. A child, however, was their undoing.

Playing in the shed, a small girl dug up the gang's weapons and found the envelopes used to hold the money taken from the Glendale strike.

The discovery led authorities to Marion Hedgepeth's room, where he was staying with a mistress. He was placed under heavy guard and his sensational trial was held in 1892. The dapper bandit was the toast of St. Louis. Droves of women sent him so many flowers that he was almost crowded from his cell by the posies.

It was while awaiting judgment in St. Louis that Hedgepeth met a man named H. H. Holmes from Chicago. Holmes, whose real name was Herman Webster Mudgett, was the then-unknown slayer of more than two hundred gullible females, all butchered for their insurance and doweries in his claptrap Chicago dwelling, later called "Murder Palace."

Holmes, arrested for fraud, asked Hedgepeth if he could suggest a shrewd attorney to get him out of jail. The bankrobber, for an agreed-upon price, did, and Holmes was set free. Hedgepeth, who was later to reveal Holmes' murderous activities to astounded authorities, never collected his payoff and was sent to the state prison at Jefferson City for twelve years.

"That's what a life of graft got me," he lamented at the prison gates, a false signal of reform in Hedgepeth who, when released at the end of his sentence, quickly went to Omaha, Neb. where he was caught redhanded while breaking into a company safe. He went back to jail for two more years.

In 1908, Hedgepeth reappeared in small Western towns with a new gang of thieves. After several small robberies, he traveled to Chicago. There, while drinking in a saloon on January 1, 1910, Marion decided to rob again. He slipped behind the bar, warded off the bartender with an ugly-looking six-gun, and filled his pockets with money from the cash register.

At that moment, a policeman, seeing the robbery from a street window, rushed into the bar with his pistol drawn. "Surrender," the lawman ordered.

Hedgepeth, thin and weak now from TB contacted in prison, coughed just once and then roared a defiant "Never!"

Both men shot at the same time. Hedgepeth's usually deadly aim had been spoiled by years of prison, sickness, and dissipation. He missed. The policeman's aim was true, his shot hitting Hedgepeth squarely in the chest. The outlaw, firing all the rounds of his gun wildly into the sawdust floor, died on his knees.

[ALSO SEE Herman Webster Mudgett.]

HEIRENS, WILLIAM
Murderer, Burglar ● (1929-   )

BACKGROUND: BORN IN 1929 AND RAISED BY ABOVE MIDDLE-INCOME PARENTS IN LINCOLNWOOD, A CHICAGO, ILL. SUBURB. STUDENT AT THE UNIVERSITY OF CHICAGO. DESCRIPTION: 5'10", BROWN EYES, DARK BROWN HAIR, SLIGHT BUILD. ALIASES: GEORGE MURMAN. RECORD: ARRESTED IN 1942 AT AGE 13 FOR POSSESSING AUTOMATIC WEAPONS, RELEASED TO THE CUSTODY OF AN ILLINOIS CORRECTIONAL INSTITUTION; COMMITTED SEVERAL BURGLARIES IN EARLY 1945; MURDERED MRS. JOSEPHINE ALICE ROSS IN CHICAGO 6/3/45 WHEN CAUGHT BURGLARIZING HER APARTMENT; ATTACKED AND BEAT ARMY LIEUTENANT EVELYN PETERSON AFTER LOOTING HER APARTMENT 10/5/45; ROBBED AND KILLED FRANCES BROWN 12/10/45; ABDUCTED FOR RANSOM AND MURDERED 6-YEAR-OLD SUZANNE DEGNAN 1/7/46; CONFESSED TO THESE MURDERS AND SENTENCED TO THREE CONSECUTIVE LIFE IMPRISONMENT TERMS AT JOLIET STATE PENITENTIARY IN ILLINOIS 9/7/46.

When William Heirens was eleven years old he accidentally stumbled across a couple fornicating. Relating his traumatic experience to his puritanical mother, the boy was told: "All sex is dirty. If you touch anyone, you get a disease."

Six years later, Heirens attempted to overcome his hatred for women by petting a girl. He broke into tears in her presence and vomited. Then he took to dressing in women's garments for sexual release while staring at pictures of Nazi leaders Hitler, Goering, and Himmler which he had meticulously pasted into his scrapbook. Heirens' sexual desires still went unfulfilled.

He returned to the only thing that gave him sexual gratification and release: burglary.

When Heirens was thirteen years old, on the eve of his graduation from the eighth grade of St. Mary's-of-the-Lake parochial school in Chicago, police picked him up for carrying a loaded pistol.

Detectives learned from the small boy that he had committed eleven burglaries and set fire to six houses in recent months. Chicago police searched the Heirens home and found William's small-sized arsenal behind the kitchen refrigerator—an army rifle, a .25-caliber pistol, two .38-caliber revolvers. On the roof of the Heirens house four more pistols and another rifle were found.

Heirens' parents were amazed. His mother had given the boy anything he craved. The father was an upstanding businessman, an executive with a steel company (he has since changed his name). When the boy appeared in juvenile court, he was remorseful. After the parents agreed to send the boy to a private correctional institute in Indiana, the judge placed him on probation.

After a year at the correction home, Heirens was permitted to transfer to St. Bede's Academy in Peru, Ill. where he remained for three years. He was a brilliant student and entered the University of Chicago, skipping the entire freshman year to enroll as a sophomore.

All through these years, Heirens perfected his burglary techniques, robbing North Side apartments regularly. Once in custody, Heirens was to explain: "I get sexual satisfaction out of breaking into a place. If I got a real thrill, I didn't take anything."

Heirens went over the edge of burglary and into his first murder in June, 1945. Entering the North Side apartment of Mrs. Josephine Alice Ross, 43 years old and two times divorced. Heirens discovered the woman sleeping in the bedroom.

He began to ransack the place. Mrs. Ross was awakened by the noise and Heirens, performing what was later termed a "reaction" murder, ran to her and slashed her throat from ear to ear. He then stabbed her several times.

Mrs. Ross' blood bothered Heirens. He went to the bathroom and came back with bandages which he used to close the dead woman's severed throat. The wound was still visible. This, too, offended Heirens. He spied a red dress in the bedroom and wrapped it tightly about Mrs. Ross' neck. He then went through her purse, taking $12. Heirens stayed two hours in the apartment, walking slowly from room to room. His role as violent intruder caused him to climax several times, such was the weird nature of his sexual degeneration.

Heirens then hurriedly left the apartment, passing Mrs. Ross' daughter, Jacqueline Miller, who was returning from work.

In October, 1945, Heirens was discovered looting the apartment of an army nurse, Lieutenant Evelyn Peterson. He slugged her and ran, but left fingerprints.

An attractive ex-Wave, Miss Frances Brown, thirty-three, came out of her bathroom after bathing one December evening and caught Heirens, who had entered her apartment via a fire escape, going through her purse. She began screaming.

Heirens fired two shots point blank from his pistol and Miss Brown fell dead. Heirens then ran to the kitchen, got a butcher knife, and returned to the dead girl, stabbing her twice. He left the knife jutting from the second wound.

Miss Brown's bloody body troubled the youth. He dragged the corpse into the bathroom and washed its wounds and placed several soaking-wet towels about the bloody head. Then he threw a housejacket hanging on the bathroom door over Miss Brown's body, now draped over the bathtub. He left her that way.

Police arrived at the Brown apartment and found that the killer had taken pains to wipe away all his fingerprints in the bedroom, but they found a clear set on the bathroom door. They also discovered a terrifying note written on the mirror in lipstick: "For Heaven's sake catch me before I kill more. I cannot control myself."

Detective Chief Storms warned his men: "He's killed twice and will keep on killing until we catch him. We're working against time."

Storms was correct in his assumption. Heirens entered an apartment in north Chicago on January 7, 1946. Six-year-old Suzanne Degnan was awakened in her bed as the stocky youth entered. Heirens, who never harmed anyone who didn't interfere with his burglaries, reacted the same way he had with Mrs. Ross and Miss Brown, only with a new twist. He didn't kill the child immediately.

It was 12:50 a.m., and an upstairs neighbor, Ethel Hargrove, heard the disturbance. She heard Suzanne say, "I don't want to get up. I'm sleepy."

Heirens gagged the child and dragged her down his makeshift ladder. He left a note reading: "Get $20,000 Ready & Waite for Word. Do Not Notify FBI or Police. Bills in 5's and 10's." The other side of the ransom note Heirens left had a postscript reading, "BURN THIS FOR HER SAFETY."

Heirens immediately dragged the child to a nearby basement, killed her, and then dissected her body. He wrapped the pieces of Suzanne's body in her bedclothes and walked, early in the morning from sewer to sewer, dropping the grisly remains through the gratings.

An ex-soldier saw Heirens walking about a block from the Degnan house about 1 a.m. carrying a shopping bag. A janitor in the vicinity doing his early morning chores also noticed the aimlessly wandering youth.

Heirens had left his fingerprints all over Suzanne's bedroom. The ransom was never paid. Police found parts of Suzanne's body and the murder knife Heirens had used. But they still hadn't found the killer.

It wasn't until June 26, 1946, that their search would end. On that night, a North Side apartment house janitor reported a prowler about his building. Detective Tiffin P. Constant answered the call.

Constant found the janitor and Mrs. Leonard Pera, a tenant, grappling with a youth who broke away from them and held them at bay with a pistol. Tiffin moved in and the youth fired twice at the detective. Both were misfires. The policeman lunged toward Heirens and the two struggled until an off-duty policeman, Abner Cunningham, returning from the lake and wearing only a bathing suit, ran up and crashed three flowerpots containing dead geraniums over Heirens' head, finally subduing the killer.

The young killer was brought into custody and immediately questioned after being injected with truth serum. Unknown to the police, Heirens had been injecting himself with truth serum for nine months and had achieved almost total immunity to the drug. His answers to questions incriminated a man named George Murman.

The interrogation began with:
"Did you kill Suzanne Degnan?"
"No, George did it."
"How did George do it?"
"Well, George was robbing a man's home the night before and saw a ladder across the way leaning against the building."
"When did he kill Suzanne? The next night?"
"George went into the yard."
"What yard?"
"The yard where the little girl was killed."
"Did George do anything else?"
"He placed a ladder against the window and climbed in."
"He climbed in the window?"
"Yes. And then he carried her out . . . George is a bad boy."
George, of course, psychiatrists later discov-

Murderer William Heirens behind bars for life after police complied with his request to "catch me before I kill more."

ered was William Heirens, a product of his own mind, the one side of his personality that robbed and killed, (George **Mur**-der-**man**). William Heirens was the good boy. George was the bad boy.

The fingerprints on the doors of the death apartments, the handwriting of the message written on Miss Brown's mirror and the Degnan ransom note all matched those of William Heirens. He finally admitted that he, indeed, was the killer.

Insanity had obviously captured the youth at an early age and his judge and jury knew it. Heirens was sentenced to three consecutive life prison terms, never to be paroled.

He is serving time now in the Illinois State Prison at Stateville. In the same cell with him is his alter ego, George Murman.

"To me he is very real," he said recently, "he exists. You can accept George as being me but—well, it's hard to explain. A couple of times I had talks with him. I suppose I was really talking to myself. I wrote lots of notes to him which I kept."

George never wrote back.

HELLIER, THOMAS
Murderer, Thief ● (? -1678)

Life for Thomas Hellier became unbearable after he was sentenced to bondage on a Virginia plantation following a number of thefts. The master to which he was bound sold him to another gentleman farmer, one Cutbeard Williamson, who owned the ominously-named estate called Hard Labour.

Resenting his intolerable slavery, Hellier waited until the Williamson family was asleep one night and then entered the mansion where, with an axe, he slew Williamson, his wife, and the maid.

Following his hanging, August 5, 1678 at Westover, Va., Hellier was lashed with chains to a tall tree overlooking the James River, a gruesome exhibit for other rebellious bound servants to view as they were carried up the river in barges. The body remained on the tree for several years until it rotted away.

HENDRICKSON, JOHN JR.
Murderer ● (1833-1853)

Shortly after marrying his nineteen-year-old fiancee Maria, Hendrickson decided on murder. Living with seven members of his family in Bethlehem, N. Y., the newlyweds were subjected to constant bickering and arguments.

Hendrickson's relatives stated that it was all caused by Maria, who was possessive and strong-willed. A dim-witted youth, Hendrickson gave his wife a heavy dose of aconite poison (the first known case of such poisoning in the U.S.) to eliminate the family problem.

The family attempted to cover up the murder but local police examined the body and determined Hendrickson's guilt. He was hanged March 6, 1853.

HICKMAN, EDWARD
Kidnapper, Murderer ● (1907-1928)

It had been the most trying ordeal of Perry Parker's life. The Los Angeles businessman's deep love was rooted in his twin twelve-year-old daughters Marian and Marjorie. When Marian was abducted, he first went to the police and then, when the girl was not returned, agreed to pay the $7,500 ransom to the kidnapper, a young man who signed himself "The Fox."

In late December, 1927, Parker, alone in his car, met the young man in an isolated spot at the outskirts of Los Angeles. As both men glared at each other from their autos, Parker asked: "Is my daughter alive?" The curly-headed young man smiled, reached to his side and held up a blanket-wrapped child who appeared to be sleeping.

"Give me the money and I'll leave her down the road away," the kidnapper said softly. Parker threw the money from the window of his car into the young man's auto. The kidnapper's car sped away. Minutes later, following the road, Parker saw the bundle by the side of the road, stopped and ran to his daughter. Throwing back the blanket, he groaned. Marian was dead, strangled, her neck almost severed. Her monstrous killer had insanely and inexplicably cut off both her legs.

The vicious killing shocked the country and ignited one of the greatest manhunts in California history. The killer, twenty-year-old Edward Hickman, had gone to Seattle to vacation on the kidnapping money.

Hickman, a psychopath, mimicked the movie stars of the day and spent a great deal of time pitying himself and weeping over the privations he had endured as a youth. A college student, Hickman desperately fielded about for a way to amass $1,500 for tuition (at least, that was his explanation later). In early December, 1927, he hit upon the idea of kidnapping a wealthy child and holding her for ransom.

He drove about Los Angeles' wealthy suburbs for days and finally selected prosperous Perry Parker. Hickman then went to Marian Parker's school, telling the child that "there's trouble at home," and that her father had sent him to pick her up. He drove her to a lonely shack. There he stood over Marian with a long knife pressed to her back and dictated a letter to her father. Marian, terrified, wrote down everything uttered by the maniacal kidnapper.

"Dear Daddy and Mother:
I wish I could come home. I think I'll die if I have to be like this much longer. Wont someone tell me why all this had to happen to me? Daddy please do what the man tells you or he'll kill me if you don't. Your loving daughter, Marian Parker. P.S. Please Daddy, I want to come home tonight."

After Marian finished scribbling the note, the demoniac Hickman strangled the little girl and, for reasons never explained, cut off her legs. He then mailed the note to Parker and waited. When Parker failed to correctly respond to his phone calls, Hickman began sending him his own carefully-lettered notes. They were headed by the word "DEATH," elaborately scrolled at the top of the page.

One letter read:

Kidnapper and murderer Edward Hickman in January, 1928, combing his hair and admiring himself in his jail cell; he was hanged at San Quentin Prison a month later. (UPI)

"Mr. Parker:
Fox is my name, Very sly you know. Set no traps. I'll watch for them. All the inside guys . . . know that when you play with fire there is cause for burns. Not W. J. Burns [head of the Burns Detective Agency] and his shadowers either—remember that. Get this straight. Your daughter's life hangs by a thread and I have a Gillette [razor] ready and able to handle the situation. This is business. Do you want the girl or the 75 $100 gold certificates U.S. currency? You can't have both and there's no other way out. Believe this and act accordingly. Before the day's over I'll find out how you stand. I am doing a solo so figure on meeting the terms of Mr. Fox, or else FATE."

Hickman's florid ego demanded he send

Parker several of these notes, telling the frantic businessman that "if you want aid against me, ask God, not man."

But several very ordinary men, local police, picked up Hickman at Echo, Oregon, and arrested him for murder after discovering he corresponded to the description offered by Mr. Parker. He was sent southward on the first fast train from Seattle. Hickman was docile in captivity but tried twice to commit suicide in the train's washroom. They were feeble efforts designed to convince his guards and later his jury that he was insane.

Thousands of curious spectators gathered at stations along the route of the train carrying Hickman. The youthful murderer idiotically waved and smiled to them. Some nervously waved back.

His trial was less farcical. The prosecution provided a witness, one of Hickman's fellow cellmates, who testified that the killer had planned to fake insanity to escape the death sentence. After a long trial, extensive psychiatric examinations and last-ditch appeals, Hickman's insanity plea collapsed. He was hanged in San Quentin Prison, February 4, 1928.

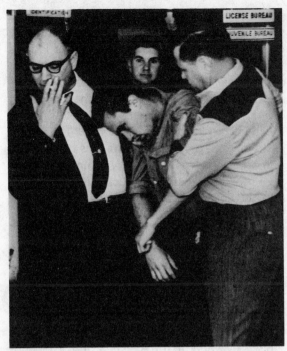

Richard Hickock collapsing into the arms of police after confessing his wholesale slaughter of the Clutter family in 1959.

sentenced to death. They were hanged April 14, 1965.

Novelist Truman Capote chose this senseless, stupid murder as the subject of his best-selling *In Cold Blood*.

HICKOCK, RICHARD E.
Murderer ● (1932-1965)

Learning that well-to-do rancher Herbert W. Clutter, 48, of Holcomb, Kansas, kept large sums of cash in his home, vagrants Richard E. Hickock, 28, and Perry E. Smith, 31, invaded the residence November 15, 1959. After terrorizing the Clutter family—wife Bonnie, 45, daughter Nancy, 16, son Kenyon, 15—the two neurotic thieves killed them with a shotgun and a hunting knife.

The two were trailed to Las Vegas, much through the efforts of detective Al Dewey of Kansas, and picked up there by Nevada police. Hickock, a parolee from the Kansas State Prison, admitted the quadruple slayings moments after his arrest. Both he and Perry, following a long trial, were found guilty and

HINCKLEY, JOHN WARNOCK, JR.
Assassin ● (1956-   )

A drifter with no clear political mindset, John Hinckley was the son of a Denver, Colorado, executive. His brother and sister seemed to have goals in their lives but Hinckley apparently had none. His only obsessions involved actress Jodie Foster and the character played by Robert DeNiro in the violent movie *Taxi Driver*.

For inexplicable reasons, Hinckley found himself in a small crowd in Washington, D.C., on March 30, 1981. He and the others were waiting to see President Ronald Reagan emerge from the Washington Hilton. When the President finished his speech to a group of trade unionists, he stepped outside and was about to enter his limousine when Hinckely quickly produced a .22-caliber revolver loaded with a deadly type of bullet called the Devastator. (These bullets explode after penetration.)

Hinckley fired six shots wildly as the screaming crowd dove for cover and Secret Service Agents raced toward the assassin. Reagan, 70, who had been in office only two months, was hit and was immediately driven to George Washington University Hospital. A bullet had struck a rib on his right side and collapsed a lung. The unexploded bullet was removed, along with a gallon of blood from his chest cavity. He would recover fully.

Also struck by Hinckley's bullets were White House Press Secretary James S. Brady, a presidential bodyguard and a Washington policeman. Brady survived after six hours of surgery, but he would remain partially paralyzed. The law enforcement officers received less serious wounds.

Hinckley went to trial in April 1982 and his defense attorneys made much of his unstable mential condition, a point that undoubtedly caused the jury to return a verdict of not guilty by reason of insanity. The press and public universally condemned the verdict. The court ordered Hinckley confined at St. Elizabeth's Hospital in Washington, D.C.

HOCH, JOHANN OTTO
Serial Killer ● (1862-1906)

Hoch was a "bluebeard" who hunted female victims throughout the Midwest from the 1890s to the turn of the century. His modus operandi was to marry wealthy women, spinsters, or widows—it made no difference—then poison them, hide their bodies, and loot their savings.

It was estimated that Hoch had slain at least fifty females before he was identified and tracked down by a dogged Chicago Police detective, George Shippy. Hoch was convicted of only one killing, that of Marie Walcker. As he was led up the gallows stairs to be hanged on February 3, 1906, Hoch was still shouting his innocence.

HORN, THOMAS
Murderer ● (1861-1903)

Horn was a man completely turned around in life—from lawman to murderer. His is the story of simple corruption. In his twenties, Horn was one of the most fearless men in the Arizona Territory, working scrupulously and doggedly for the Army and later as an agent for the Pinkertons.

Born and raised in Memphis, Mo., Horn thrilled to tales of the border bandit, Jesse James. At age fourteen he ran off to Arizona, working for the pony express, and then traveled to California to try his hand at gold mining. There he met Indian scout Al Sieber in the fields and the two, realizing that myriad prospectors before them had panned out the streams, gave up and rode back to Arizona where they became scouts for Army General Nelson A. Miles, who was then conducting a campaign against the Apaches under Geronimo.

In August, 1886, the Geronimo campaign ended; more than any other man, Tom Horn was responsible for its conclusion. He had tracked the wily Geronimo to his lair high in the Sierra Gordo in Sonora, Mexico. As Chief of Scouts, Horn went in alone to Geronimo's camp and negotiated a surrender to U.S. troops across the border.

Following Geronimo's momentous surrender and subsequent acceptance of peace terms (at which Horn acted as interpreter, the only man the Apache chief would trust), Al Sieber and Horn drifted back to gold digging. Young Tom soon tired of this and went to work as a ranch hand. His prowess as a cowboy was displayed in the Globe, Ariz. rodeo where, in 1888, he captured the world's championship for steer roping.

He was in Wyoming shortly after that, working as a Pinkerton operative. In one spectacular encounter with outlaws in the notorious Hole-in-the-Wall bastion, Horn single-handedly captured a notorious bandit known as Peg Leg Watson (alias McCoy).

Watson had robbed a mail train with his gang and Horn discovered him living in a lonely cabin high in the hills. After exchanging random shots with the outlaw, Horn called out, telling Peg Leg he was coming for him. He gingerly stepped out from behind a rock and crossed a large, open field, his Winchester pointed toward the ground. Peg Leg only stared in awe at the lone lawman.

"He didn't give me much trouble," Horn prosaically stated later, but it was considered one of the most heroic feats in Western law enforcement.

In the early 1890s, Horn quit the detective agency by informing his employers that he "had no more stomach for it." At this time, he moved to Cheyenne, Wyo., and went to work for cattle barons who wanted to settle old scores with their range-war enemies. Horn changed completely from the respected lawman and scout to a hired killer. He grew avaricious. There wasn't anyone he wouldn't kill for the right price.

Dozens of men fell before his guns, victims of his clever bushwackings. Horn preferred stealth in these later years to brazen face-to-face encounters. His reputation as a bloody-handed murderer grew. Ranchers, farmers, and townspeople about Cheyenne knew that Tom Horn would wait weeks or months to get his man. He left an odd trademark in his grisly

Lawman turned killer, Tom Horn, with a rope he made in jail and by which he was hanged. (Denver Public Library)

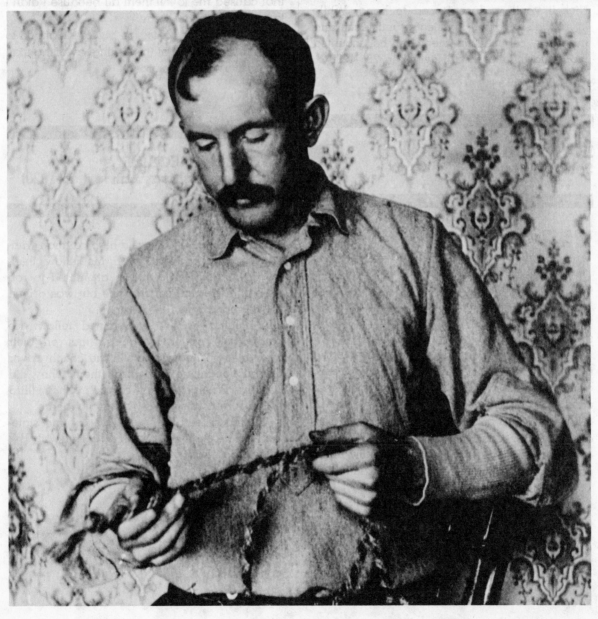

business—a rock placed beneath each dead man's head.

Not until 1902 did the law catch up with Tom Horn. Late that year, Horn shot and killed fourteen-year-old Willie Nickell while lying in wait for the boy's father, a sheep raiser whose death was desired by several local cattlemen.

Though the murder was commonly attributed to Horn in Cheyenne, proof was lacking. Then Joe Lefors, a U.S. Marshal, (the man who had led the super posse in dogged pursuit of Butch Cassidy and the Sundance Kid) got Horn drunk one night and coaxed a confession from him while witnesses jotted down every word.

Horn was quickly convicted of killing the Nickell youth and sentenced to hang. While in jail he shaved off his elegant mustache and hurriedly penned his memoirs; he mounted the gallows and died November 20, 1903.

HOYT, WANETA E.
Serial Killer ● (1947-   )

William Fitzpatrick, a prosecutor in upstate New York, was researching back issues of medical journals in prepartion for a case involving a man charged with murdering his 15-month-old daughter. He read one account of a woman who had lost five children to infant death syndrome between 1965 and 1971.

Said Fitzpatrick: "I was dumbfounded after reading the article. I said: 'These children have been clearly murdered.' I just never forgot about the case."

Fitzpatrick later became District Attorney for Onondaga County and began to investigate the case, even though the article he had originally read only identified the mother as "H." He noted in the article that all the children, except one, had lived less than six months. The exception reached two years of age. The prosecutor concluded that one, perhaps two, infants in the same family might succumb to crib death but not five.

A search of all the death records of neighboring Tioga County revealed the deaths of five children named Hoyt. Fitzpatrick went to his counterpart in Tioga, Robert Simpson, and asked him to investigate Waneta E. Hoyt.

In March 1994, Hoyt was brought in for questioning. At first she denied having anything to do with the deaths of her children—Erik, James, Julie, Molly, and Noah. Then she broke down and confessed that she had smothered all five children because she felt helpless to stop their crying. "It was the thing that caused me to kill them all because I didn't know what to do for them."

Hoyt signed this confession but later claimed to be innocent. She is, at this writing, awaiting trial, facing five counts of murder.

HUTTON, PEREGRINE
Murderer, Highwayman ● (? -1820)

Peregrine Hutton was a highwayman without luck. Along with his fellow thief, Morris N. B. Hull, he attempted to rob the Baltimore mail coach twice but was driven off by shots from the driver.

But Hutton was a determined fellow. He exacted his partner's promise that on their third attempt they would kill the coach driver if they thought he recognized them. They did stop the Baltimore mail coach in their third try and Hutton shot the driver to death.

"He recognized me," was his laconic statement before he was hanged with Hull, July 14, 1820 in Baltimore.

INGENITO, ERNEST
Murderer, Burglar ● (1924-   )

BACKGROUND: BORN IN 1924 IN RURAL PENNSYL-
VANIA. RAISED IN POVERTY, MINOR EDUCATION. MAR-
RIED AT 17, SEPARATED FROM WIFE. SERVED BRIEFLY
IN U.S. ARMY, DISHONORABLY DISCHARGED FOR AT-
TACKING SUPERIOR OFFICERS IN 1943. MARRIED
THERESA MAZZOLI IN 1947, TWO SONS. DESCRIPTION:
5'11", BROWN EYES, BROWN HAIR, STOCKY. ALIASES:
NONE. RECORD: ARRESTED, CONVICTED OF BURGLARY
IN PHILADELPHIA, 1939, SENTENCED TO TWO YEARS IN
THE PENNSYLVANIA STATE REFORMATORY, RELEASED
IN 1941; SHOT EIGHT PERSONS (OF WHICH SEVEN DIED)
11/17/50; JUDGED INSANE AND SENT TO THE NEW
JERSEY STATE HOSPITAL FOR LIFE.

"What's going on here, Ingenito?" The sergeant stood over the good-looking young man who refused to leave his bunk.

"Nothin'. Get lost," Ernie said.

"Get outa there," the sergeant ordered.

Ingenito gave him the raspberries.

"You refusin' to obey orders?"

"Go to hell!"

The sergeant left the barracks and returned with two officers. Ingenito was ordered to get out of his bunk. He did—feet first and fists flailing. The sergeant went down with a hard left to his head. Then one of the officers felt the wind go out of him with a punch from Ernie's big left hand to his solar plexus.

Ingenito jumped on the other officer, knocking him down and battering his face to a bloody pulp before the other two soldiers pinned back his arms.

It was no way to treat U.S. Army officers, let alone a sergeant. Ernest Ingenito learned this the hard way; he received a sentence of two years in a federal prison and, in 1946, received a dishonorable discharge.

This incident was only another sliver added to the cross Ernie Ingenito had been building for himself throughout his sad life.

Born in 1924, Ingenito's parents provided a poor home and even poorer family background punctured daily with round-house fights. By the time he was thirteen, the Ingenitos separated and Ernie went to live with his mother. She couldn't control the boy. In two years, Ernie, who had received a criminal apprenticeship from street gangs, failed miserably in his first attempted burglary. He received a long term in the Pennsylvania State Reformatory.

After his release, Ingenito lived with his mother and settled down a bit until her death in 1941. It was a tragedy Ernie found hard to bear. She had been the only controlling and effective influence on him.

Refusing to live with his father, Ernie married the first girl who winked in his direction.

He eloped at seventeen. His young bride withstood his tirades and physical abuse for a year and then, even though she was pregnant, she packed up and left him.

Ingenito knew he needed authority to survive and the Army provided this—until his habit of sleeping late provoked his fight with superiors.

In 1947 Ingenito met and married an attractive, dark-featured Italian girl, Theresa Mazzoli. Theresa's parents operated and owned a successful truck farm in Gloucester County. Ernie got a job.

Shortly after their marriage, the Ingenitos began to argue constantly. Theresa was a strong-willed young girl used to having her own way. She insisted on living with her parents. Ernie wanted a life apart. Theresa won . . . perhaps the most tragic victory of her young life.

The two moved into the Mazzoli house. Though Ernie got along with his father-in-law, Mike Mazzoli, Theresa's mother Pearl nagged him ceaselessly. Nothing was good enough for her daughter and when, two years later, the young couple were fortunate to have two healthy sons, Ernie's nerves were a shambles.

His mother-in-law kept up a barrage against

Mass killer Ernie Ingenito (center), being led into court, 1951. (UPI)

him to better himself. Ernie sulked.

First, to unleash his pent-up resentment, Ernie tried drinking. With the drinking came fights and then bloody brawls in local bars around Vineland, N. J.

Mike Mazzoli took Ernie's part for a while— he had had problems as a young man, too. But the end came when Ingenito's understanding father-in-law discovered that Ernie had been sleeping with someone else. That was too much. Nobody could treat his daughter like that. He kicked Ernie out.

For most normal men troubled with nagging in-laws, and possessing a steady job, such freedom might be a welcome relief. But Ernie Ingenito was no longer normal.

The strain had twisted his mind. He rented a room in a home located close to the Mazzoli house. He explained that he wanted to be near his two young sons.

But Theresa was having none of that. She refused to let Ernie see his boys and wanted no part of him.

Ernie was confused; resentment was replaced by hatred. He called his lawyer, Fred Gravino of Woodbury, N. J. Gravino told him that he had to get a court order to see his children. Ernie shook his head. That would take too long.

He called another lawyer, William Gallner. The counsel told him the same thing. Runaround, Ernie figured. His anger mounted.

On November 17, Ernie Ingenito found himself wildly rummaging through his room, sorting his collection of weapons. He chose two pistols, one of which was a Luger with a special apparatus that allowed it to fire as a machine gun, and a .32-caliber carbine. After shouldering the carbine and pocketing the pistols, Ernie jammed his pockets with ammunition. He was ready.

With his arsenal bulging in his pockets, Ernie marched over to the Mazzoli home down the block. He still wasn't sure what he was going to do, but he was plenty angry.

Theresa opened the front door to her husband's loud bangings.

"I want to see the kids," Ernie said.

His wife's eyes blazed and her mouth turned into a hostile sneer. "Go away, Ernie. You're not welcome—"

When Theresa saw the Luger in Ernie's hand, her eyes went wide and she instinctively backed away from the door. Mike Mazzoli rushed from the living room. It was bad timing.

Ernie leveled the deadly German automatic at him and fired twice. Mazzoli went down. Ingenito gave the dying man a quick glance and in that moment decided crazily that this was the way to end all of his problems.

He turned the weapon back on his wife. Theresa was petrified. Ernie hated her and without pity he let the Luger spit out his hate. She fell next to her father with two bullets in her.

Ingenito enjoyed the authoritive snap of the weapon, the instant action that made him total master of a fate that had hounded and dogged him. Ernie had killed and liked it and planned to finish the job. Where was Mrs. Mazzoli? She was really the object of his hate. Ernie began to run frantically through the house searching for her.

But Pearl Mazzoli knew what was happening when the first shots rang out. She knew Ernie would seek her out immediately so she fled through a side door to the home of her parents, Armando and Theresa Pioppi, who lived down the block.

After several empty moments of searching, Ingenito realized what had happened. But he knew where Pearl Mazzoli would go; he had lived in her house long enough to remember. He trotted down to the Pioppi home.

Pearl Mazzoli beat him there by only a few minutes. As she ran through the Pioppi home she screamed, "It's Ernie! He's shooting everybody!" She ran upstairs and hid in a bedroom closet.

Gino Pioppi, Pearl's brother, raced for the phone to call the police. Pearl's mother, Theresa, ran to lock the door. Too late. The athletic Ernie bounded through the screen door, guns blazing. Mrs. Pioppi dropped to the floor, dead. Panic struck Gino Pioppi. He dropped the phone and ran for his life out a back door.

His wife, Marion, an attractive woman of twenty-eight, flitted across one of the rooms. Ernie saw her out of the corner of his eye and blasted her twice with fatal accuracy. She was dead before she hit the floor.

Ernie didn't give Marion a second glance. He knew his quarry was upstairs. He found Pearl Mazzoli cowering in a closet. He smiled thinly and then emptied both his guns into her. She crumpled to the floor.

It should have been all over then but Ernie, like a dog gone mad with the first taste of warm chicken blood in his mouth, was now obsessed with killing . . . and there were more Mazzoli relatives alive.

Gino Pioppi had recovered his nerve and began to steal back toward his home. As he approached, he heard two more reports crack out. Ernie had just fired two bullets into his nine-year-old daughter.

Gino's brother John, forty-six, sat in the kitchen with his six-year-old nephew, shielding him in fright against the carnage that had encompassed the house. When Ernie left, John snatched up a knife and followed the berserk killer. Ernie, fleeing on the lawn, saw his pursuer and squeezed off his last rounds into Pioppi, killing him.

Ingenito raced on to his car and drove madly to Minotola, N. J. to kill the Frank Mazzoli family. He caught them at home and rushed inside. Strangely, he brushed past ten-year-old Barbara Mazzoli without harming her, screaming his odd revenge through garbled words, firing his pistols as he ran down the hall.

When Ingenito staggered from the house, both Hilda and Frank Mazzoli lay in pools of their own blood. He began to run to his car, realizing that every cop in New Jersey was probably now on his trail.

Ingenito's reign of terror began at 9 p.m. on November 17, 1950. It was all over at midnight when a patrol car spotted Ernie's battered Ford a few blocks from Mike Mazzoli's home where it all began.

As the officers approached him, Ernie vainly tried to cut into his wrists with a tin can but the police had no intention of letting Ingenito escape into suicide. His wrists were bound up and he was taken into custody.

His wife, Theresa, after being shot twice, had crawled to a phone and called police. Now she was in a hospital and hating the murderer of her family. "I wish they would hang Ernie," she gritted.

But Ernie was not hanged. Psychiatrists pronounced him insane and he was placed in the New Jersey State Hospital for the Insane at Trenton.

IRVING, JOHN
Pickpocket, Gangleader ● (? -1883)

The once-feared Dutch Mob operating east of the Bowery during the 1870s was the invention of a professional sneak thief and pickpocket, Johnny Irving. The Dutch Mob, which at one time counted three hundred professional pickpockets in its ranks, was ultimately broken up by police in 1877. That year a newly appointed police captain, Anthony Allaire, developed a new approach to breaking up gangs. He sent flying squads into the gang-infested area from Houston to Fifth streets, the police members of which clubbed anything in their path resembling a crook.

Irving took the hint and became a freelance crook once more. In 1883, accompanied by friend and fellow thief, Billy Porter, Irving entered the infamous Sixth Avenue saloon owned by bankrobber Shang Draper (he had been implicated in the robbery of the Manhattan Savings Institution). A rival gangleader, Johnny Walsh ("Johnny the Mick") was at the bar.

The two men exchanged glances and then went for their pistols. Walsh was faster and killed Irving on the spot. Billy Porter then drew his gun and killed Walsh. Draper pulled his gun out from behind the bar and shot Porter, who, though severely wounded, escaped.

Irving's sister, Babe, later became a mistress of the notorious bankrobber, George Leslie.

[ALSO SEE George Leslie.]

J

JACKSON, CALVIN
Serial Killer ● (1948-   )

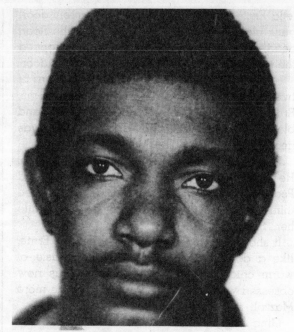

Serial killer Calvin Jackson.

Elderly women rooming at New York's Park Plaza Hotel began to be murdered in April 1973. Nine of these helpless victims would be killed before their lone murderer was apprehended in 1974. Police investigating the deaths at this seedy hotel were less than accurate in their estimation of the murders, believing them all separate crimes and not the work of one man. So shoddy was their investigation that the murders later caused a complete reorganization of the homicide department.

Detectives failed to inspect anyone living at the Park Plaza. If they had, they would have easily unearthed Calvin Jackson, who worked there as a porter and who had a prison record for robbery and drug abuse. Not until Jackson had killed his ninth victim, Mrs. Pauline Spanierman, a 59-year-old widow living in the adjacent building, did police arrest Jackson. Even then he was arrested for possession of stolen property.

Not until Jackson's rooms were searched did police discover the stolen possessions of the Park Plaza victims and charge him with murder. Jackson, a year before the murders began, stole a TV and a stereo from one of his neighbors at the hotel and was arrested. He plea bargained and received a 30-day sentence, instead of the fifteen-year term this offense would normally bring. When he was released, Jackson returned to the hotel and soon embarked on his serial murders.

During his trial it was pointed out how relaxed Jackson felt when committing his robberies and murders. After killing the occupant of an apartment he invariably went to the refrigerator and made himself a meal from the victim's food. He dined for about an hour while watching the body, then left with his loot.

A jury listened to Jackson's five-hour taped confession, and, on May 25, 1976, found him guilty on five counts of murder. He was given two life terms for each victim by Justice Aloysius J. Melia of the State Supreme Court. He will be eligible for parole in the year 2030.

JACKSON, HUMPTY
Murderer, Gangleader ● (? -1914)

A bibliophile, Jackson was partial to the works of Darwin, Voltaire, and Spencer, as well as being one of the most feared New York gang leaders in the 1890s. His extensive library and good education notwithstanding, Jackson led a gang of toughs that controlled the area bounded by First and Second avenues and Twelfth and Thirteenth streets. His headquarters was an old grave-yard.

There, almost each night, Humpty Jackson, whose name was derived from his hunchback, would meet with some of the most notorious hoodlums of the era—the Lobster Kid, Spanish Louie, Nigger Ruhl, and a giant killer ominously known as The Grabber. Humpty would sit on a tombstone and outline plans for a robbery or a paid killing.

Three guns could be found on Humpty at all times. A small revolver was carried in his pocket. Another gun was tucked into a strange-looking holster slung by a strap about his hump. A third was secreted in a special compartment inside his derby. Humpty's usual price for blackjacking a person was $100. Murder cost more.

From 1890 to 1909, Jackson was arrested twenty times and sent to prison following a dozen convictions, but he always managed to obtain parole. Jackson was finally sent to prison in 1909 for twenty years after being convicted of ordering the murder of a man he never met. He died in a cell.

JAMES, JESSE WOODSON
Murderer, Bankrobber, Trainrobber ●
(1847-1882)

BACKGROUND: BORN 9/5/47 IN KEARNEY, CLAY COUNTY, MO. TO ROBERT AND ZERELDA COLE JAMES (BOTH FROM KENTUCKY). MINOR PUBLIC EDUCATION. ONE BROTHER, ALEXANDER FRANKLIN JAMES, BORN 1/10/43. SERVED IN QUANTRILL'S GUERILLAS WITH "BLOODY BILL" ANDERSON DURING THE CIVIL WAR (1864-1865). MARRIED FIRST COUSIN ZERELDA MIMMS 4/23/74; TWO CHILDREN, JESSE JR., MARY. ORIGINAL OCCUPATION, FARMER. DESCRIPTION: 5'11", BLUE EYES, LIGHT BROWN HAIR, MUSCULAR, MISSING TIP OF MIDDLE FINGER ON LEFT HAND (SHOT OFF WHILE CLEANING PISTOL). ALIASES: HOWARD, WOODSON, DINGUS. RECORD: REPORTEDLY ROBBED WITH BROTHER FRANK AND OTHERS THE CLAY COUNTY SAVINGS AND LOAN ASSOCIATION BANK IN LIBERTY, MO., AT WHICH TIME A BYSTANDER, GEORGE WYMORE, WAS KILLED, 2/13/66 ($15,000 IN GOLD, $45,000 IN NON-NEGOTIABLE SECURITIES), INCORRECTLY SAID TO BE THE FIRST DAYLIGHT BANK ROBBERY IN AMERICAN HISTORY; ROBBED WITH HIS BROTHER FRANK AND THE YOUNGER BROTHERS THE ALEXANDER MITCHELL BANK IN LEXINGTON, MO., ON 10/30/66 ($2011.50); ATTEMPTED TO ROB WITH FIVE OTHER RIDERS MCCLAIN'S BANK IN SAVANNAH, MO., 3/2/67, JUDGE WILLIAM MCCLAIN WOUNDED BY THE BANDITS; ROBBED WITH HIS BROTHER FRANK,

COLE, BOB AND JAMES YOUNGER, JAMES WHITE, JOHN WHITE, PAYNE JONES, RICHARD BURNS, ISAAC FLANNERY, ANDREW MAGUIRE, THOMAS LITTLE, THE HUGHES & MASON BANK IN RICHMOND, MO., MAYOR SHAW, B.G. & FRANK GRIFFIN KILLED BY THE BANDITS, 5/22/67 ($4,000 IN GOLD); ROBBED WITH HIS BROTHER FRANK, THE YOUNGER BROTHERS, AND TWO OTHERS THE BANK IN RUSSELVILLE, KEN., 3/20/68 ($14,000); ROBBED WITH BROTHER FRANK AND COLE YOUNGER THE DAVIES COUNTY SAVINGS BANK IN GALLATIN, MO., 12/7/69, BANK CASHIER JOHN W. SHEETS KILLED BY JESSE ($500); ROBBED WITH BROTHER FRANK, COLE, JIM AND JOHN YOUNGER, JIM CUMMINS, CHARLIE PITTS (NEE SAMUEL WELLS), AND ED MILLER THE OCOBOCK BANK IN CORYDON, IOWA, 6/3/71 ($45,000); ROBBED WITH FRANK, COLE YOUNGER, AND CLELL MILLER THE DEPOSIT BANK, COLUMBIA, KY., KILLING R.A.C. MARTIN, BANK CASHIER, 4/29/72 ($600); ROBBED WITH COLE AND BOB YOUNGER, WILLIAM CHADWELL ALIAS BILL STILES THE SAVINGS ASSOCIATION BANK IN STE. GENEVIEVE, MO., 5/23/72 ($4,000); ROBBED WITH BROTHER FRANK AND COLE YOUNGER THE KANSAS CITY FAIR GATE RECEIPTS IN KANSAS CITY, MO., 9/23/72 ($978); ROBBED WITH BROTHER FRANK, COLE & JIM YOUNGER, CLELL MILLER, BOB MOORE, AND COMANCHE TONY AN EXPRESS TRAIN NEAR ADAIR, IOWA, WITH ENGINEER JOHN RAFFERTY KILLED WHEN THE TRAIN WAS DERAILED, 7/21/73 ($2,000); ROBBED WITH BROTHER FRANK, COLE, JIM YOUNGER, CLELL MILLER THE CONCORD STAGE NEAR MALVERN, ARK., 1/15/74 ($4,000 IN CASH AND JEWELRY); ROBBED WITH BROTHER FRANK, COLE, BOB AND JIM YOUNGER, JIM CUMMINS, CLELL AND ED MILLER, SAM HILDEBRAND, ARTHUR MCCOY, AND JIM REED THE LITTLE ROCK EXPRESS TRAIN AT GADSHILL, MO., 1/31/74 ($22,000) (TWO MONTHS LATER, ON 3/16/74, JOHN AND JIM YOUNGER SHOT AND KILLED TWO PINKERTON OPERATIVES, LOUIS J. LULL AND E. B. DANIELS, NEAR OSCEOLA, MO.; JOHN YOUNGER KILLED ON THE SPOT); MURDERED PINKERTON AGENT JOHN W. WHICHER NEAR KEARNEY, MO., IN EARLY 1874 WITH JAMES LATCHE AND CLELL MILLER; ROBBED WITH BROTHER FRANK, COLE, BOB, JIM YOUNGER, CLELL MILLER, AND BUD MCDANIELS THE EXPRESS TRAIN AT MUNCIE, KAN., 12/12/74 ($25,000 IN CASH, GOLD AND JEWELRY); PINKERTON AND RAILROAD OPERATIVES ATTACKED THE FARMHOUSE OWNED BY JESSE'S PARENTS ON THE NIGHT OF 1/26/75, THROWING A BOMB THROUGH A WINDOW WHICH KILLED ARCHIE SAMUEL, JESSE'S EIGHT-YEAR-OLD HALF-BROTHER AND TORE THE ARM FROM HIS MOTHER; ROBBED WITH BROTHER FRANK, COLE, JIM AND BOB YOUNGER THE SAN ANTONIO STAGE NEAR AUSTIN, TEX., 5/12/75 ($3,000); ROBBED WITH BROTHER FRANK, COLE, BOB AND JIM YOUNGER, CLELL MILLER, CHARLIE PITTS, BILL CHADWELL, AND HOBBS KERRY THE MISSOURI-PACIFIC EXPRESS TRAIN NEAR OTTERVILLE, MO., 7/7/75 ($75,000); ATTEMPTED TO ROB WITH HIS BROTHER FRANK, COLE, JIM, AND BOB YOUNGER, CLELL MILLER, CHARLIE PITTS, AND BILL CHADWELL THE FIRST NATIONAL BANK OF NORTHFIELD, MINN., 9/7/76, WHEREUPON THE CITIZENS OF NORTHFIELD TRAPPED THE GANG AND SHOT SEVERAL MEMBERS (FRANK AND JESSE ESCAPED, CHADWELL AND MILLER KILLED DURING THE GUN BATTLE, CHARLIE PITTS

Jesse James at seventeen, wearing three guns; this photo was taken in 1864 when Jesse was riding with Bloody Bill Anderson. (Western History Collection, U. of Okla. Library)

KILLED DAYS LATER IN A FIGHT WITH A POSSE, THE YOUNGER BROTHERS ALL CAPTURED AFTER BEING WOUNDED, AND GIVEN LIFE SENTENCES IN THE MINNESOTA STATE PENITENTIARY); J. L. HEYWOOD AND NICHOLAS GUSTAVSON, NORTHFIELD RESIDENTS, KILLED IN THE ROBBERY ATTEMPT BY OUTLAWS; ROBBED WITH BROTHER FRANK, BILL RYAN ALIAS TOM HILL, DICK LIDDELL ALIAS CHARLES UNDERWOOD, TUCKER BASHAM, ED MILLER, AND WOOD HITE THE CHICAGO & ALTON EXPRESS NEAR GLENDALE, MO., 10/7/79 ($35,000); ROBBED WITH BROTHER FRANK, DICK LIDDELL, BILL RYAN, AND ED MILLER THE STAGE NEAR MUSCLE SHOALS, ALA., IN MARCH, 1881 ($1,400); ROBBED WITH THE SAME GANG THE DAVIS & SEXTON BANK IN RIVERTON, IOWA, 7/10/81 ($5,000); ROBBED WITH THE SAME GANG THE CHICAGO & ROCK ISLAND & PACIFIC RAILROAD EXPRESS OUTSIDE OF WINSTON, MO., 7/15/81, KILLING FRANK MCMILLAN, A PASSENGER, AND ENGINEER WILLIAM WESTPHAL ($600); MISSOURI GOVERNOR THOMAS T. CRITTENDEN PLACED A $10,000 REWARD FOR THE CAPTURE AND CONVICTION OF FRANK AND JESSE JAMES 7/28/81; ROBBED WITH BROTHER FRANK, WOOD AND CLARENCE HITE, DICK LIDDELL, CHARLES FORD THE CHICAGO-ALTON EXPRESS TRAIN NEAR GLENDALE, MO., 8/7/81 ($1,500 IN CURRENCY AND JEWELS); KILLED BY CHARLES AND BOB FORD, 4/3/82 IN HIS HOME IN ST. JOSEPH, MO. (FRANK JAMES PERSONALLY SURRENDERED TO GOVERNOR CRITTENDEN 10/5/82, WAS TRIED FOR A NUMBER OF CRIMES BUT ACQUITTED; HE LIVED OUT AN INCONSPICUOUS LIFE UNTIL HIS DEATH ON 2/18/1915 AT THE SAMUEL FARM. COLE YOUNGER, WHO WAS PAROLED ON 7/11/01 FROM THE MINNESOTA STATE PRISON AT STILLWATER ALONG WITH HIS BROTHER JIM, DIED 3/21/16. JAMES YOUNGER COMMITTED SUICIDE IN 1902; BOB YOUNGER DIED IN PRISON, 8/16/89 OF TUBERCULOSIS).

No other American criminal has so deeply etched his imprint upon our culture as has Jesse Woodson James. Today he is folklore, a sweeping, rustic image of Americana, a Robin Hood about whom sagas have been spun so thickly that the man within is all but obscured. If there can exist such a person as a "great" criminal, then Jesse James was the greatest criminal in America.

Yet, behind the legend, an unimpassioned study reveals Jesse James to be a glinty-eyed murderer, flaunting a boastful, callous, and totally unsympathetic nature: a man whose bark grew to the very center of his being.

Landowners on the Missouri-Kansas border harbored Jesse and his roving outlaws, worshipping them as heroes for close to two decades following the Civil War. The farmers in this area were fiercely loyal to anyone who had served the Southern Cause and, in their down-home way, thought the James boys victimized by Yankee authorities who had taken over control of the railroads, the banks, the very land itself upon which they grew their meager crops. Jesse himself often repeated the tired line, "We were driven to it."

The claim was partly true but wore thin and then disappeared into the haze of sixteen years of robbing and murder, a systematic, dedicated career of crime no rationalization could excuse. Bob Younger, the baby of the clan known as the Younger Brothers who so faithfully followed Jesse in one raid after another, explained the genesis and rationale of this most famous of outlaw gangs when he told a reporter (following his capture after the Northfield raid): "We are rough men and used to rough ways."

Prosaic, yes. But the statement reveals the phlegmatic attitude of Jesse and his boys. They were born and lived and robbed inside a tunnel of time that had not yet broken through to their intimately known and loved wilderness; the sites of their homes, the places of their daring robberies, the areas through which they made their unbelievable escapes represented America's first frontier in the middle of the Nineteenth Century.

While this Middle Frontier stubbornly and shakily resisted the progress of the East, Jesse James and those like him could flourish.

Dime novelists penned the tarnished exploits of the James gang, making them lurid and colorful. New York detective magazines churned out dozens of pamphlet-sized novellas in which Jesse and his men appeared as simple farmers driven to the gun by unscrupulous, vindictive and often sadistic lawmen. Words such as gallant, noble, honorable, so embedded in the nation's mores of this period, quickly came to typify Jesse James in these dime novels. The railroads and banks became the culprits, not poor plagued Jesse, the humble man born in a log cabin. A spellbound country accepted and embraced the image of Jesse as a man fighting all odds.

This national reaction grew to an emotional heritage which exists in many quarters today, a feeling of deep reluctance to damn Jesse, let alone indict him, for his many crimes. Following Jesse's early death at age thirty-four, in 1882, R. T. Bradley aptly summed up the country's overall empathy for the James boys:

"In men whom men condemn as ill
I find so much of goodness still;
In men whom men deem half divine
I find so much of sin and blot;
I hesitate to draw the line
Between the two—where God has not."

The myth of Jesse James grew while the outlaw rode and robbed, years before he met his ignoble end at the hands of a treacherous "friend," Robert Ford and the James legend was nurtured by the outlaw himself in his last years. The claim that he "robbed from the rich and gave to the poor" was embellished by the James gang whenever they visited neighbors and relatives in the western wilds of Missouri while on the run from lawmen. They paid handsomely for their keep and meals. One

story, more than any other, epitomizes the heroic legend of Jesse James.

Returning from one of his hold-ups (the locale changes from the Ozarks to the plains in different versions of this story), Jesse and his gang rest at a lonely widow-woman's cabin. Though impoverished, the widow feeds the outlaw band. Jesse notices tears welling up in the woman's eyes. He asks about her sorrow, and she tells him of her dead husband and the threadbare life she has led. She then explains that even the rickety cabin in which she lives is about to be taken from her. There is a final note on her mortgage due in the amount of $3,000 and an indifferent banker is to arrive that day to collect either the money or foreclose on the small farm.

Jesse smiles and withdraws the amount from his pocket, foisting it upon the stunned widow. She gratefully accepts and the band departs. A few hours later the banker arrives and is astounded when he receives the amount due him. The widow woman demands her note and mortgage (remembering Jesse's warning to do exactly that) and these are handed over to her by the startled banker. Fondling his money, the greedy banker leaves in his buckboard. Three miles from the cabin, Jesse James emerges from the brush, pistol in hand and

Jesse James at the height of his criminal career. (State Historical Society of Missouri)

leveled at the banker. He recoups his $3,000, plus the banker's watch for his trouble, and rides away chuckling.

This story has been told not only of Jesse James but of almost every important outlaw of the Old West. Yet most historians attribute the act to Jesse (Butch Cassidy told it of himself once), even the noteworthy James biographer, Robertus Love, who was once moved to say: "I for one shall continue to applaud his achievement. There was pathos in it, there was chivalric sentiment, there was simple human tenderness . . . and there was humor."

There were other stories, countless tales of Jesse the Brave, Jesse the Kind. This most desperate of men is said to have taken his best riding coat from his own back, to give it to an old man freezing alongside a deserted, windswept Missouri road. This killer of a dozen men is said to have alighted from his favorite race horse, Red Fox, to reduce to a bloody pulp a bully who had beaten a young Easterner half to death. He is said to have delivered his share of the proceeds of a train robbery to an orphanage so that the "little ones will have vittles through the winter." The youth of America, cluttered with ageless sagas of such feats, has always insisted on the truth of these tales. Well, he was Jesse James of the alliterative name, the bravest, boldest bandit ever seen in America. Was he not?

The parents of Frank and Jesse James went West into the frontier to homestead in the early 1840s, settling in untamed Clay County, Mo. near the small and struggling community of Kearney. Robert James, a Baptist missionary, and his sturdy wife Zerelda, (she married at seventeen), built a small log cabin and began to carve from the wilderness a modest farm.

The couple's first child, Alexander Franklin James, was born January 10, 1843. They were blessed by a second son four years later, September 5, 1847, whom they named Jesse Woodson James. The boys' father dreamed of wealth and soon set aside his religious work, leaving the hard-pressed family to fend alone as he made his way to California to labor in the teeming gold fields where he died of pneumonia. Mrs. James remarried. Her second husband, a man named Simms, could not get along with his rambunctious stepsons and this soon brought about a divorce.

Zerelda James Simms was determined that her sons would have some kind of father. She found another man, Dr. Reuben Samuel, a general practitioner and farmer. The marriage worked, basically because Dr. Samuel, a closed-lip type, kept to his work and allowed his wife to raise the James boys.

A few miles from the James homestead, at Lee's Summit, lived their cousins, the Younger brothers, Coleman, James, John, and Robert (the only four of fourteen children to turn to crime), wild hellions who raided many an apple orchard with Frank and Jesse.

The coming of the Civil War disrupted the peaceful farming life in Missouri. Frank James and Cole Younger rode off to join William Clarke Quantrill, the Southern guerrilla leader, and they subsequently participated in the bloody raid on Lawrence, Kan. Jesse joined one of Quantrill's lieutenants, "Bloody Bill" Anderson, when he was old enough, and in 1864, helped to massacre seventy-five unarmed Union soldiers at Centralia. It was his first taste of blood.

The seventeen-year-old Jesse became a wonder to his campmates. He rode a horse better than most men and his marksmanship was uncanny. His hatred for federal troops was unbounding; one story quietly repeated by his comrades was that Union troopers, searching for his brother Frank, had tied him to a tree on the Samuel farm and horsewhipped him in hopes of getting information. Jesse did not talk about this incident, but seethed with anger only abated by the deaths of Yankee soldiers shot down by his own hand.

Hours after the Centralia raid, a Major Johnson led a troop of Union soldiers against the retreating rebel guerrillas. Anderson's irregulars turned on the federals and charged into their midst, slaughtering them. Jesse James, his horse's reins in his teeth, rode furiously into the fleeing Yankee command, firing two pistols. He was credited with shooting down six men, killing three.

The youth made no comment about the battle that night. He sat silently at a campfire cleaning his pistol. Its hair trigger was accidentally bumped by Jesse and a shot was fired that blew away the tip of his left middle finger. The young guerrilla let out a painful cry and said as he stared at his wound: "If that ain't the dingus-dangast thing!" The name "Dingus" stuck but only his closest friends and Civil War comrades called him that. (Frank James

Frank James, an artist's rendering. (State Historical Society of Missouri)

was referred to as "Buck" by his fellow guerrillas.)

The war along the Middle Border between Kansas and Missouri was bloody and embittered. Regular troops fought pitched battles with farmers and irregulars. Homesteaders loyal to both sides were burned out, their families shot and bayoneted to death. The James boys' reputation under Quantrill and Anderson grew to such proportions that Dr. Samuel and his wife were forced by Union soldiers to abandon their farm and were banished to Nebraska. At the close of the war, Frank and Jesse returned to their home to find it vacant. They lived in terror as federal troops searched for them. Regular Southern troops had been pardoned, but guerrillas were considered outlaws and were hunted down and shot.

A general amnesty for guerrillas was issued in early 1865 and Jesse James, leading a band of irregulars, including his brother Frank and Cole Younger, rode toward the small town of Lexington, Mo. under a white flag to surrender. A company of federal troops intercepted them and opened fire on the ex-guerrillas. Jesse was wounded in the chest but managed to take cover in the thick brush. Two Union soldiers pursued him but quickly backed off when he fired a single shot that killed one of their horses.

A farmer found the boy soldier lying in a creek bed soothing his wounds the next day and helped him travel to his family in Nebraska, where he recuperated slowly. At first, Jesse seemed as if he would die of the wound and begged his mother to take him back to Missouri. "I don't want to die in a Northern state," he reportedly said. Mrs. Samuel complied and moved her son to Harlem, Mo., where he was sheltered in a boardinghouse owned by his uncle, John Mimms. His cousin Zerelda (named after his mother), called Zee, nursed Jesse back to health. Before he left for the family farm in Kearney, the two became betrothed, but would not marry for a full nine years.

While the echoes of the war died, Frank and Jesse James peacefully farmed their land, living with guns on their hips. What changed them into the most feared outlaws of their day is uncertain. The war had already begun to change them—the battles, blood, and death made simple farm life boring and uneventful. Whatever the reason, they followed the path many irregulars chose—robbery and murder.

On February 13, 1866, ten men rode into the town of Liberty, Mo. and headed for the Clay County Savings Bank. One bandit approached cashiers Greenup and William Bird, holding pistols. "If you make any noise, you will be shot," the bandit told them (many reported this man later to be Frank James).

The bandit then ordered Greenup Bird into the vault and told him to hand over the money. "I hesitated and began to parley," Bird nervously stated later. "He told me that if I did not go in instantly, he would shoot me down. I went in."

Within minutes the two bandits inside the bank walked casually to the street with a wheat sack crammed with $60,000 of currency and non-negotiable bonds. The pair motioned to the other men standing in strategic positions along the street and the band mounted their horses and began to ride from town.

George "Jolly" Wymore, a student, was just then walking across the town square en route to classes at nearby William Jewell College. The ten men rode solemnly past him. One stared curiously at Wymore and, perhaps suspecting the youth of raising an alarm, drew his pistol and fired several shots into him. Wymore died instantly. With this, the band began whooping and firing their pistols into the air as they rode madly from town.

The horsemen crossed the Missouri River

on the ferry and by the time a posse arrived in pursuit, the outlaws had disappeared in a blinding snowstorm. The Liberty daylight raid was the first bank robbery in America performed by an organized gang (the first daylight robbery of a bank occurred in Massachusetts in 1863—See Edward W. Green).

All evidence points to the fact that Jesse was not in this band but that it probably included his brother Frank and Cole Younger.

The next bank to fall was in Lexington, Mo., on October 30, 1866. A pattern emerged at the robbing of this bank which was to become all too familiar to law enforcement officers seeking Jesse James. A young man entered the Alexander Mitchell and Company banking house early in the morning. Another young man stationed himself at the entrance.

"Can you change this for me," the tall young man asked cashier J. L. Thomas. He held out a $50 bill.

Thomas was suspicious. The Liberty bank raid was still current and terrible news. "No," the cashier said. As he looked about, two more men entered the bank, drew their pistols and aimed them at his heart.

"You've got one hundred thousand dollars in this bank," the tall young robber said quietly. "Unless you turn it over, you'll be killed."

"That's not true," Thomas said.

"Let's have the key to the vault."

"I don't have it."

The robbers searched his pockets and found nothing. Disgusted they scooped up what cash there was in the drawers and left. One of the bandits was definitely identified as young Jesse James "from up Kearney way."

It was almost five months later before the James gang struck again, this time in Savanna Mo. Bank president Judge John McClain offered stiff resistance. He refused to give up the keys to his vault. One of the bandits swore and shot him in the chest before the gang rushed back to their horses. McClain survived his painful wound and the bandits tallied nothing from the raid.

The setback only made the James gang all the more determined. The small, solid Hughes and Mason Bank squatting in the center of Richmond, Mo. became the object of the band's next attack. There was no elaborate ceremony to the raid. Jesse and his men rode into Richmond on May 22, 1867, guerrilla style, racing down the main street, hollering and firing their pistols wildly in the air which soon had pedestrians scurrying for cover.

Six men—Jesse and Frank James, the Younger brothers, and James White—dismounted in front of the locked bank while their confederates continued to terrorize the town. The six battered down the bank's doors, entered, and lined up the quaking tellers. Opening their wheat sack, the outlaws scooped up more than $4,000 from the largest county bank in Missouri.

Mayor Shaw led a small group of armed citizens to the town square and began to battle the outlaws. A group of the bandits rushed Shaw on horseback and killed him in the street with seven bullets. The riders then turned about and headed for the jail where several ex-guerrillas were being detained. They tried to break into the jail, but the solid oak door held. Jailer B. G. Griffin and his fifteen-year-old son, Frank, had taken up positions behind a tree nearby and began exchanging shots with the outlaws. The robbers swept past the pair riddling them. Both were killed by one volley.

Only one of this raiding party was ever tracked down: Payne Jones. His farmhouse was surrounded by lawmen, but Jones dashed directly into the group with two six-guns roaring. A posseman fell from his saddle, dead before he hit the ground. A young girl who had guided the posse to the Jones farm was also hit and died several hours later. The Richmond raid and its aftermath claimed the lives of five innocent persons.

Jones was later shot dead in a gun duel. Richard Burns, another member of the raiding party, who resided near Richmond, was taken in his farmhouse and led to a wooded area, where he was tried by torchlight and then hanged. The same fate befell Andy Maguire and Tom Little, who were apprehended and lynched a few miles outside of Warrensburg, Mo.

Incensed citizens thought of doing the same to Frank and Jesse but were dissuaded by "alibi cards" distributed by their friends—cards upon which Frank and Jesse had scribbled claims that they in no way had been part of the bank raids. These, incredibly, were accepted by local lawmen, who saw no reason to doubt the word of the James brothers.

Though Frank and Jesse James and the Younger brothers were suspected of being in these raids, investigation proved nothing. Their excuse was always the same. They were at home, tending to chores. Townspeople who identified them during the bank raids suddenly lost their memory when questioned later by the authorities. Nowhere in Western Missouri was it possible for a person to threaten the ex-guerrillas, such was the local sympathy for them. If a merchant or farmer did speak the truth he stood to be boycotted by his own neighbors or worse, shot some evening while traveling a lonely road. This silent conspiracy became a way of life in Clay and Ray Counties and lasted until Jesse's assassination.

The James gang, in these early years, really included almost any farmer who wanted to ride along with its hardcore elements—the James boys and the Younger brothers—to pick up a few dollars in a yearly bank raid to obtain seed money for next season's planting. Jesse and his kinsmen were becoming professional robbers but prudently paced themselves, usually performing one or two robberies each year. The desperate robberies in later years came about only when the pressure from lawmen became unbearable and the gang's thrust was aimed at a "big strike" to provide them with enough cash to allow them to escape permanently.

What made the gang's immunity from prosecution steadfast was the facelessness of its members. No pictures existed of the outlaws. The only photo of Jesse James was secreted in a gold locket his mother kept on her person. Identification became almost impossible. The gang would employ its anonymity well.

A year after the Richmond raid, on March 20, 1868, a man who had been using the name Colburn (Frank James) and for several days had pretended to be a cattle dealer from Louisville, entered the bank operated by Nimrod Long and George Norton in Russelville, Ky. He offered Long a $100 note and asked the banker to cash it. Long became suspicious.

"Colburn" jerked a thumb in the direction of the door where a tall, blue-eyed man stood. "I've got to pay off one of my hired hands."

Long examined the note carefully and stated: "This bill is counterfeit, Mr. Colburn."

"I reckon it is," the would-be cattle buyer chuckled after looking at the note. He tucked the bill into a vest pocket and then pulled out a Colt pistol. "But this isn't, Mr. Long. Open the vault!"

Long glanced to the young man in the doorway. He, too, was holding a pistol. The banker suddenly bolted for a rear door. The man in the doorway, Jesse, cursed loudly and sent a bullet in his direction that creased his scalp and dropped him to the floor. The bandit ran to him and began to strike Long on the head with his gun butt. Long, a well-built fellow, spun about and grabbed the bandit's hands. As they rolled about the floor, Frank James moved wildly around them, trying to squeeze off a shot at the banker, yelling to his brother to finish him.

With a burst of strength, the intrepid Long tossed the bandit aside, jumped to his feet, and raced to the door of the bank. Two bullets sent after him lodged in the door but the banker escaped, running down the alley next to the bank and shouting: "They're robbing my bank!"

Outside, three men waiting on horseback—the Younger brothers—calmly watched the terrified banker flee. Frank and Jesse James, within minutes, came from the bank dragging two large wheatsacks full of gold and cash, about $14,000. This they laboriously lifted onto their horses while Russelville citizens dashed about madly looking for water buckets, thinking the bank was on fire.

A wizened old man, confused rather than drunk, staggered blindly down the street between the dashing horses of the bankrobbers. Cole Younger rode up to him and shouted: "Old man, we're having a little serenade here and there's danger of you getting hurt. Just get behind my horse here and you'll be out of the way." With that, Younger edged the old man out of the road using his horse's flanks to push him along.

When Jesse and Frank joined their hooting companions, the outlaw band formed a single line and dashed down the main street as if carrying out a cavalry charge. An hour after they had disappeared, a fifty-man posse was on their trail into Allan County, a James-Younger stronghold.

Pinkerton detectives searched frantically for the James gang without success. They did interview George Hite, whose family was close to the outlaw clans and whose sons often rode with Jesse. Hite operated a store in Adairville and was reported to be one of Jesse's best friends. Hite knew nothing of the Russelville strike, he said, but his memory suddenly erupted fourteen years later following Jesse's death when he wrote how the outlaws worked out their raids: "They'd decide on going somewhere, and then they'd send word to all the others—they always knew where they were, and then went and done it [the robbery]. That's all there was of it."

Hite's statement was only one of many that supported the idea that Jesse was not the actual leader; neither was Frank James. The James boys and the Youngers, with several hand-picked henchmen would gather secretly at a deserted farmhouse or barn and, under the yellow, flickering glow of lantern lights, discuss each proposed robbery, arguing safety and escape factors. It was quite democratic. Jesse was always the most daring of the original gang, and therefore identified as the leader, though it was a nominal role. His willingness to murder, no doubt, inched him above the others as the most ferocious in their ranks. Later, after the Northfield disaster, Jesse would, indeed, come to be the absolute leader of his band, threatening his own brother Frank with death when he dared to criticize him.

Frank James was never the staunch savant-as-older-brother to Jesse that has been often pictured. He was a tight-lipped, sanctimonious sermonizer who spouted Shakespeare and the Bible whenever the whim urged him, much to the annoyance of his fellow outlaws. But none dared tell him to be still. Frank "Buck" James, though cautious and tedious in his manner, was almost as deadly with a gun as his younger brother.

Jesse's calculating ability to kill was never more pronounced than on December 7, 1869, when he, Frank, and Cole Younger rode into the small town of Gallatin, Mo., heading straight for the Davies County Savings Bank. Frank went inside first. He stopped at the teller's cage and offered cashier John W. Sheets a $100 bill to change. Sheets took the bill and turned to his desk.

Jesse then entered the bank as Cole Younger watched the horses outside. Jesse walked up to Sheets and said lightly, "If you will write out a receipt, I will pay you that bill." The banker began to reach for his receipt book and Jesse pulled out his pistol and shot Sheets twice, once through the head and once square in the heart; he was dead before he hit the floor.

Frank James ran behind the counter and threw all the bank's available cash into a sack. A bank clerk, William A. McDowell, bolted for the door and Jesse fired a shot at him that tore through his arm. McDowell managed to stagger into the street and alarm the town.

Jesse and Frank ran from the bank and jumped to their horses. Jesse missed, his foot caught in the stirrup while his horse raced down the street. The struggling outlaw was dragged almost forty feet before he managed to free himself. Frank James, seeing his brother's plight, wheeled his horse about and pulled Jesse up behind him. Hundreds of bullets smacked at their horse's hooves from weapons wielded by the enraged Gallatin townsmen, but the robbers again made a successful escape.

The take from the bloody Gallatin robbery was small, about $500, but Jesse's near-fatal experience unnerved the bandit so much that he and his brother stayed close to the Samuel farm for almost two years without plans for any future raids. There was something else which disturbed Jesse. His horse, an expensive, well-groomed animal, had been found by the good citizens of Gallatin and Jesse had been tentatively identified as one of the robbers. He countered that his animal had been stolen and lived on quietly at his farm, unmolested, planning his next move, his loot buried in a nearby meadow.

Jesse had further covered himself in obscurity following the Gallatin raid. Minutes after the outlaws rode from town, they encountered a Methodist minister named Helm whom they forced at gun point to guide them around an unfamiliar community nearby. Jesse told Helm: "I'm Bill Anderson's brother. I killed S. P. Cox who works in the bank back there in Gallatin. He killed my brother in the war and I got him at last." Thus, Jesse James wrongly identified himself and his victim, John Sheets, whom he knew had been a major in the Union army, to excuse murder.

The James gang remained in hiding for almost two years before riding out again to rob. Jesse and Frank James, Cole, Jim, and John Younger, Jim Cummins, Charlie Pitts, and Ed Miller rode slowly from Missouri into the peaceful town of Corydon, Ia. arriving on June 3, 1871. It was one of the easiest holdups of their careers.

The Ocobock Brothers' Bank off the main square was fairly bursting with money, a little more than $45,000 in gold and cash nestled in its safe. Jesse and Frank James, along with Cole Younger, entered the bank and found only one clerk on duty. The others waited outside, curiously noting the empty streets.

"Where's everybody at?" Frank James asked the clerk.

"Over to the Church," he answered, "listenin to Mr. Dean." The clerk went on to explain that the famous orator Henry Clay Dean was lecturing at the Methodist Church and the entire town had turned out to hear him.

"All the better," Jesse said and pulled his pistol. In a matter of minutes the bank had been cleaned out and the outlaws sauntered their horses lazily up the street. As they came abreast of the church, Jesse flashed his now famous icy, thin smile. He told the outlaws to stop, dismounted and casually walked into the church. Standing in the middle of the aisle, Jesse raised his hand and the golden-throated Dean paused in the middle of his speech.

"What is it, young man?"

"Well, sir," Jesse said slowly, drawing out his words for effect, "some riders were just down to the bank and tied up the cashier. All the drawers are cleaned out. You folks best get down there in a hurry."

The crowd stared at the bandit who blinked back at them with chilling blue eyes. Jesse's mouth crinkled and his head lifted. A short laugh lengthened into a roar like a train getting up steam. He spun on the heels of his shiny boots and walked outside to his horse, mounted, and rode away with his men, all ripping with laughter.

For several seconds, the stunned townspeople merely looked out of the church's door. The silence was finally splintered by a man in their midst who shouted: "For God's sake! It's the James gang! They've just robbed the bank!"

The Corydon residents rushed to the bank, and then quickly organized a posse. The lawmen chased the James band back into Missouri but lost all traces of the outlaws near Clay County.

Though Jesse was again identified as the outlaw leader who led the Corydon robbery, witnesses either disappeared or refused to confront the bandit.

Another year eased into history before the gang struck again, this time at the bank in Columbia, Ky. on April 29, 1872. Jesse and Frank entered while Cole Younger and Clell Miller waited outside with the horses. When cashier R. A. C. Martin became reluctant to turn over the keys to the safe, Jesse shot him three times, killing him where he stood.

Frank cleaned out the cash drawers which only yielded $600 and the gang raced from town. More than one hundred men followed them but the outlaws outfoxed their pursuers by doubling back on their own trail, circling the town twice, and then riding off toward Missouri.

The gang next hit the Savings Association of Ste. Genevieve, Mo. on May 23, 1872. Riding at Jesse's stirrups were Cole and Bob Younger (Bob's first robbery), Clell Miller, and Bill Chadwell (also a new recruit). It was a bloodless raid. Cashier O. D. Harris wisely gave the bandits no arguments when they ordered him to fill their wheat sack with money. The take was $4,000 and the outlaws rode quietly out of town.

Near a small farm, Jesse dismounted to adjust the heavy sack filled with gold hanging from his saddle. Suddenly, his horse dashed away, leaving the bandit standing in the middle of the road and looking quite foolish. A passing farmer was ordered to retrieve the horse by the gang. When he refused, several pistols were aimed in his direction.

The farmer chased the frightened animal through a field, caught it, and returned it to its owner. He smiled toothlessly up at Jesse and then said in a heavy accent: "I catch der horse. Vot do I get for dot, yah?"

Jesse gave him back his own thin smile. "Your life, Dutchy. Vot do you tink, yah?"

This oft-repeated story may be apocryphal, yet it becomes consistent with Jesse's sense of humor and his increasing consciousness of his own exploited myth. As his career spun forward he grew careless in protecting his own identity until he became indifferent, then strangely proud of his role as America's Robin Hood.

On September 26, 1872, Jesse, Frank, and Cole Younger rode leisurely into the giant fairgrounds of Kansas City, Mo. while more than ten thousand people milled about. They approached the main gate. Jesse dismounted and walked up to the cashier.

"What if I was to say I was Jesse James," he said to the cashier, "and told you to hand out that tin box of money—what would you say?"

The cashier, Ben Wallace, spat back: "I'd say I'd see you in hell first."

"Well, that's just who I am, Jesse James, and you had better hand it out pretty damned quick or—" Jesse brought his pistol to aim at Wallace's head.

The tin box, containing $978, was emptied into the traditional wheat sack. Jesse cursed at having gotten so little. Frank, who had scouted the fair for days before the raid, had reported that at least $10,000 would be on hand. He had been right, but only minutes before the outlaws struck thousands of dollars had been taken to a local bank for safe-keeping.

As the bandits threaded their horses through the throng, Wallace jumped from his booth and raced after them, clutching Jesse's leg in the stirrup and shouting: "It's the James gang!" The outlaw drew his pistol and sent a bullet toward Wallace which missed him and hit a small girl in the leg. The shot caused the fairgoers to run pell-mell in all directions and open a large space through which the thieves galloped to freedom.

The miserable proceeds from the fair made Jesse all the more determined to snare a large amount of money. Banks were hit-and-miss propositions. Trains, on the other hand, carried enormous amounts of cash, gold, and silver. The act of robbing trains was not new and certainly, contrary to popular belief, not invented by Jesse James. The first train robbery had been committed by the Reno brothers of Indiana in 1868. Seven years later Jesse and Frank James decided to go into the train-robbing business.

The brothers—Frank found time to put aside a copy of Pilgrim's Progress which he was reading—gathered up Cole and Jim Younger, Clell Miller, Bob Moore, and a half-breed outlaw from Texas named Commanche Tony and headed for Adair, Iowa in late July, 1873.

Frank and Cole had scouted as far as Omaha, Nebraska weeks before and had learned that the Chicago, Rock Island, and Pacific Express racing through Adair on July 21, 1873 would be carrying more than $100,000 in gold for Eastern banks. At dusk on that day, the gang loosened a rail in the tracks just outside of Adair. When the train came around a curve, engineer John Rafferty spotted the disjointed piece of track and threw his engine into reverse. It was too late; the engine soared

through the break and crunched over on its side, killing Rafferty.

The seven bandits plunged from a wooded area and two of them—Frank and Jesse James —jumped into the baggage car and ordered the clerks to open the safe under gunpoint. There was no $100,000 inside, only a few thousand dollars in federal notes. The bandits rode away swearing. Jesse learned that the gold shipment train had been rescheduled for just such an emergency and had gone through Adair four hours before the robbery.

Though Jesse was reported to be the leader of the gang, no action was taken against him. Again, the James-Younger clan waited till the turn of the year before pulling another job. On January 15, 1874 the band traveled to Arkansas and held up the Concord Stage a few miles outside of Malvern, taking $4,000 in cash and jewels from the wealthy passengers.

During this robbery, Cole Younger proved that he, too, could practice that special flamboyance peculiar to this outlaw band. One passenger turned over his gold watch while protesting with a strong Southern accent.

Younger looked him over as he dangled the gold watch from his hamhock hand. "Are you a Southerner?"

"Yes, suh."

"Were you in the Confederate Army?"

"I had that distinction, suh."

"State your rank, regiment, and commanding officer."

The startled passenger did and was then shocked to see the giant bandit hand him back his watch.

"We are all Confederate soldiers," Younger said, garnishing his beau geste, "We don't rob Southerners, especially Confederate soldiers." He wagged a finger of warning at the rest of the passengers cringing in their seats. "But Yankees and detectives are not exempt."

Fifteen days later, on January 31, 1874, the James gang showed up in tiny Gadshill, Mo., a flag station for the Iron Mountain Railroad. Jesse, Frank, the Youngers, and five others took over the depot and flagged down the Little Rock Express train. The train's safe yielded a great haul—$22,000 in cash and gold.

As Jesse rode alongside the train after he and others had pilfered the passenger cars, he shouted to Cole Younger who had the engineer under guard: "Give her a toot, Cole!" Younger yanked the whistle chord several times.

Before the gang departed, one story has it that Jesse threw a piece of paper wrapped about a stick to the engineer. "Give this to the newspapers," he shouted. "We like to do things in style."

The paper contained the bandit's own press release of the robbery, written carefully by Jesse only hours before the outlaws had struck. Jesse had penned:

"THE MOST DARING TRAIN ROBBERY ON RECORD!"

"The southbound train of the Iron Mountain Railroad was stopped here this evening by five [there were ten] heavily armed men and robbed of——dollars. The robbers arrived at the station a few minutes before the arrival of the train and arrested the agent and put him under guard and then threw the train on the switch. The robbers were all large men, all being slightly under six feet. After robbing the train they started in a southerly direction. They were all mounted on handsome horses.

PS: There [sic] a h—— of an excitement in this part of the country."

The robberies ceased. Jesse had decided to marry his cousin Zee after nine years of clandestine meetings in woods and lonely cabins. A reporter for the *St. Louis Dispatch* interviewed the bandit in Galveston, Texas where he and his bride allegedly awaited a steamer to take them to Vera Cruz where they planned to settle. The first-hand report stated:

"On the 23rd of April, 1874, I was married to Miss Zee Mimms, of Kansas City, and at the house of a friend there. About fifty of our mutual friends were present on the occasion and quite a noted Methodist minister [Reverend William James, an uncle] performed the ceremonies. We had been engaged for nine years, and through good and evil report, and not withstanding the lies that had been told upon me and the crimes laid at my door, her devotion to me has never wavered for a moment. You can say that both of us married for love, and that there cannot be any sort of doubt about our marriage being a happy one."

The *Dispatch* ran this improbable account under the subhead of, "All the World Loves a Lover."

But Jesse and Zee did not depart for Vera Cruz. Instead, they made their way back to Missouri, settling in a small cabin near Kearney, Mo. Jesse was tied to the roots of his birthplace and bound by habit to a life of crime. Married or not, the outlaw was by then dedicated to his ill-chosen career. No record today indicates his wife's attitude concerning his thieving, but several intimates later stated that she "looked the other way . . . out of love."

Wood Hite, when asked by a reporter in later years if Jesse loved his wife, thought a moment and then said, "Yes, I believe he did . . ." The couple produced two children, Jesse Jr. and Mary, and Jesse doted upon them.

Frank James also married, eloping with a Jackson County farmer's daughter, seventeen-year-old Annie Ralston. The farmer first disowned his child but later accepted the couple whose marriage produced one son, Robert James, named after the outlaw brothers' father.

The Pinkertons and local law enforcement officers in Western Missouri were by then hot on Jesse's trail. They stalked him everywhere, lying in wait about his favorite haunts, surrounding his mother's farm.

On January 26, 1875, acting on a tip that the James boys were visiting the Samuel place, several Pinkerton detectives and local lawmen tossed a bomb through the window of the cabin. The explosion tore away most of Mrs. Samuel's right arm and a fragment embedded itself in the side of eight-year-old Archie Peyton Samuel, Jesse's half brother. The boy died in writhing agony inside of an hour.

The vicious bombing instigated a national hatred for the Pinkertons and the detective agency was vilified by the press as perpetrating an "inexcusable and cowardly deed." Jesse went further. He planned his revenge carefully, traveling to Chicago where he shadowed the head of the detective agency, Allan Pinkerton (who repeatedly denied that his men had thrown a bomb into the Samuel's place). Jesse's friend George Hite told reporters after the outlaw's death that James "went to Chicago to kill Allan Pinkerton and stayed there for four months but he never had a chance to do it like he wanted to. That was after the Pinkertons made a raid on his mother's house, blew off her arm and killed his step brother. He said he could have killed the younger one [one of Pinkerton's sons, William or Robert] but didn't care to. 'I want him to know who did

John Younger, killed in an 1874 gun duel with Pinkerton detectives. (State Historical Society of Missouri)

it,' he said. 'It wouldn't do me no good if I couldn't tell him about it before he died. I had a dozen chances to kill him when he didn't know it. I wanted to give him a fair chance but the opportunity never came.' Jesse left Chicago without doing it but I heard him often say: 'I know that God will some day deliver Allan Pinkerton into my hands.' "

Later that year, Frank James, who had been brooding over events and a violent argument he had had with his brother—some reported Frank had tried to convince Jesse of settling down and quitting crime—wrote a long letter to the editor of the *Pleasant Hill Missouri Review* disavowing his participation in the robberies attributed to him. He wrote that he and "Dingus" (his pet name for Jesse) "were not good friends at the time [of the K. C. fair grounds robbery] and have not been for several years."

Frank went on to complain about the Pinkertons hounding his family and shooting down John Younger the year before. (John and Jim Younger had shot it out with two Pinkerton operatives, Louis J. Lull and E. B. Daniels, in the woods near Osceola, Mo., on March 16, 1874; John had been killed. Frank did not mention the fact that his brother, along with Clell Miller and a local farmer, James Latche,

had murdered Pinkerton detective John W. Whicher about a month later.)

Frank James concluded his self-alibis with ". . . the day is coming when the secrets of all hearts will be laid open before the All-Seeing Eye and every act of our lives will be scrutinized, then will his soul be white as the driven snow, while those of the accusers will be doubly dark."

Whatever the feud between the James brothers, it was apparently forgotten; the two were soon leading the Youngers and others in one robbery after another. While in Texas, the gang held up the San Antonio Stage, May 12, 1875, taking $3,000 in cash and jewelry from the passengers. Cole Younger had to be coaxed into this robbery, lured away from his amorous adventures with Belle Starr, a notorious bandit herself who lived in Collins County on a ranch owned by her father, John Shirley.

Cole, outgoing and friendly, even thought of settling down near Dallas and briefly became a census taker. But Jesse soon talked him out of such peaceful activities and he was off with his brothers riding behind Jesse and Frank back to Missouri. Word went out to Clell Miller, Charlie Pitts, and Bill Chadwell to meet at the Samuel place. There Jesse outlined his plans for stealing $100,000 from the Missouri Pacific Railroad.

He had gotten word from a bribed railroad employee that on July 7, 1875 the United Express Company was shipping a gigantic amount of gold East. When the train slowed down to cross a rickety bridge east of Otterville, Mo., Jesse explained, they would be waiting for it.

Everything went according to plan until Jesse, Cole, and Bob Younger approached the Adams Express safe inside the baggage car. Jesse ordered John Bushnell, the safe guard, to open it.

"It can't be done," he apologized. "I don't have the keys to it. It's locked all the way through and the keys are at the other end of the run."

Jesse turned to Bob Younger and told him to "get an axe." Within minutes Younger was wielding a fire axe which only succeeded in making tiny dents in the sturdy safe.

Burly Cole Younger stepped forward. "Let me have it," he said. Younger, a towering 200-lb. man, slammed the axe hard against the safe for a full ten minutes until a small hole was made in its top. Jesse, whose hands were smaller, reached inside and drew up a leather pouch which was slit. Bob Younger then worked stacks of money from the pouch until their wheat sack was bulging with $75,000. The outlaws dragged the sack to the open door of the baggage car and lifted it onto a waiting horse, brought up by Frank and the others.

Before the band hurried off into the darkness, Jesse called up to the frightened baggage car guard: "If you see any of the Pinkertons, tell 'em to come and get us."

The success of the Otterville raid convinced Jesse that big money could be gotten if the gang planned its moves carefully and employed scouts to obtain intelligence about their strikes far in advance. Bill Chadwell acted as a scout in casing the Northfield, Minnesota First National Bank. Chadwell, a one-time Minnesota resident, insisted that it was the wealthiest bank in the Midwest. What further enticed the outlaws was the fact that its principal stockholders were General William Butler and W. A. Ames, the most hated men in the South during the Civil War, Butler as a Union General who persecuted the hapless Confederates under his occupation of New Orleans and Ames who was thought to be the worst carpetbagger south of the Mason-Dixon Line.

The long trip from Missouri to Northfield began in August, 1876. Flush with money and confidence, the James-Younger gang set out on well-groomed, expensive horses with scabbards holding new carbines banging their flanks. Each man in the eight-man gang wore a pressed riding suit and new, shiny, black boots. They wore linen dusters to hide the deadly Colt pistols at their sides. Jesse wore extra pistols in shoulder holsters.

The eight outlaws—Jesse and Frank James, Cole, Jim, and Bob Younger, Charlie Pitts, Clell Miller, and the scout, Bill Chadwell— formed the hard core of the band that had existed for close to ten years, the most experienced bandits of their time. But the town they entered on September 7, 1876 was unlike any other they had ever raided.

Northfield was the center of a rich farming community and its citizens were of hardy pioneer stock. It was a trouble-free town where law and order prevailed, robberies were unknown, and the churchgoing populace zealously guarded their hard-earned savings. Unlike the residents of Missouri, that state aptly called "The Mother of Bandits," Minnesota's citizens were unused to daring bank raids and lawlessness in their streets, so unused to it that once such bedlam began the citizens turned out to defend what they owned with guns in hand rather than cower behind locked doors.

Just after two o'clock, Jesse James, followed by Bob Younger and Charlie Pitts, walked into the First National Bank. Clell Miller and Cole Younger waited outside the bank to watch for trouble and mind the horses. Frank James, Jim Younger and Bill Chadwell sat on their horses at the end of the street to guard the gang's escape route.

Trouble for the outlaws came instantly. Owner of a hardware store, J. A. Allen, noticed the activity around the bank and walked over to investigate. Clell Miller grabbed him by the arm as he was about to enter the bank and told him: "Keep your goddamned mouth shut!"

Allen broke away and began to scream: "Get your guns, boys! They're robbing the bank!"

Henry Wheeler, a university student home on vacation, lounging in a chair nearby, saw Allen and he, too, ran into the street yelling, "Robbery! Robbery! Robbery! They're at the bank!"

Cole Younger and Miller mounted their horses and were soon joined by Frank James, Jim Younger, and Chadwell. The five horsemen rode furiously up and down the street shouting to every one to "Get in! Get in!" But the citizens did not "get in." They came out of their homes, offices, and stores with pistols and shotguns.

Inside the bank Joseph Lee Heywood, acting bank cashier, was about to greet Jesse James when he noticed the pistol in the outlaw's hand. "Don't holler," Jesse told him. "There's forty men outside this bank."

Heywood nodded, stunned.

"Open the safe goddamned quick or I'll blow your head off," Jesse said.

"I can't do that," Heywood said. "There's a time lock on it."

Pitts raced up and sliced the cashier's throat with a hunting knife, inflicting a slight wound. Then he and Bob Younger took turns jamming their pistols into his stomach and ordering him to open the safe. Still Heywood refused, claiming he had no way of opening the safe. Oddly, the bankrobbers didn't bother checking the safe; it was already open.

The bandits were distracted when another clerk, A. E. Bunker, dashed through the director's room and out a back door. Pitts fired at him but missed. Bob Younger, cursing loudly, was able to find only a small amount of money in a cash drawer.

Charlie Pitts panicked. He ran to the front door and saw that citizens all along the street were shooting at their five companions outside. "The game's up," he shouted to Jesse. "Pull out or they'll be killing our men!" He ran outside.

Jesse and Bob Younger followed. One of them—it was never learned which—turned around at the door and, in an act of reckless vengeance, took deliberate aim at Heywood then attempting to stand up while holding his wounded throat, and sent a bullet into his head, killing him.

The street reeked of carnage. Elias Stacy, a resident, had shot Clell Miller full in the face with a load of buckshot. The outlaw was unrecognizable, his shirtfront sopped with blood. He rode crazily up and down the street moaning and shooting his six-gun blindly. One of his shots hit and killed a terrified immigrant, Nicholas Gustavson, who was trying to run for cover across the street.

Cole Younger took a bullet in the shoulder. Another citizen, named Manning, shot Bill Chadwell square in the heart and the outlaw toppled dead into the dust of the street. Miller, still blinded by his face wound, was next, shot to death by Henry Wheeler, the university student. Wheeler then saw Bob Younger stalking Manning and shot him in the right hand. Younger changed his gun to his left hand and kept firing.

Frank and Jesse James, Cole and Jim Younger, and Charlie Pitts were now charging up and down the main street with reins in their teeth and each firing two pistols at the townspeople. The cross-fire through which they rode was murderous. Pitts was wounded and then Jim Younger and then, again, Cole Younger.

Jesse surveyed the slaughter. "It's no use, men!" he shouted. "Let's go." Bob Younger, whose mount had been shot in front of the bank, climbed up behind his brother Cole and the gang thundered down the street as dozens of unarmed citizens ran forward stoning them with rocks.

A few miles from Northfield, Jesse examined

Clell Miller, dead at Northfield. (State Historical Society of Missouri)

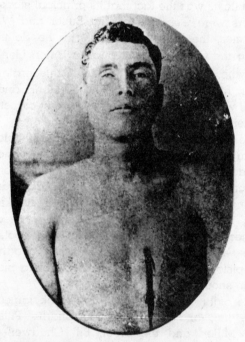

Bill Chadwell, dead at Northfield. (State Historical Society of Missouri)

Bob Younger's wound. The baby of the Younger clan was losing a lot of blood. Jesse turned to big brother Cole and told him that he thought it was best either to leave Bob behind or "put him out of his misery," much the way he would have killed a horse with a broken leg. For the first time in his life, Cole Younger blazed with anger at his cousin Jesse James. The two, hands

Bob Younger, following his capture in 1876. (State Historical Society of Missouri)

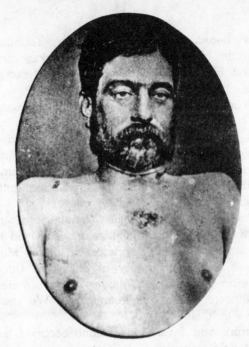

Charlie Pitts, dead, killed by possemen. (State Historical Society of Missouri)

Cole Younger just after surrendering to a posse following the Northfield raid in 1876. (State Historical Society of Missouri)

Jim Younger, bleeding from wound, after his capture. (State Historical Society of Missouri)

fingering pistols, glared at each other. Younger then told Jesse that he would never desert his brother and suggested they split up.

Frank and Jesse went one way, the Youngers and Charlie Pitts another. The Youngers were slowed down by the conditions of their wounds and, fourteen days later outside the small town of Madelia, Minn., were surrounded by posse-

men. A full-scale battle ensued. After several hours of intense fighting, Sheriff Glispin, leader of the vigilantes, called out to the outlaws who were lying behind a log in a small swamp: "Do you men surrender?"

In the lull, nervous possemen reloaded and listened to the noises of the swamp birds and animals. Then a voice from behind the log was heard. "I surrender." Bob Younger, wounded five times, stood up shakily and raised his hands. "They're all down except me."

When the lawmen rushed up, they found Cole Younger with eleven bullets in him but still alive. Jim Younger had been wounded five times but he, too, still lived. Charlie Pitts, who had used up every bullet in his belt and in the pistol in his hand, lay still and quite dead with five bullets in his chest.

Taken into custody, the Younger brothers were given medical attention and survived to be sentenced to life imprisonment at the Minnesota State Penitentiary at Stillwater. Upon entering prison, Cole Younger told a reporter, "We were victims of circumstance. We were drove to it, sir."

Frank and Jesse James alone escaped the Northfield debacle. They rode southward for three weeks, stealing horses, living in barns, moving only at night, eating raw vegetables from the fields. Missouri was too hot for the James boys now. The entire nation had been alarmed at the Northfield raid and murders. The brothers decided to move to Tennessee and were driven by relatives in covered wagons to Nashville where they settled on small farms. For three years, the brothers tilled the land and lived quietly. Jesse, living under the name Howard, even entered his favorite horse, Red Fox, in local Nashville races, winning several events.

Then, in the fall of 1879, Jesse organized a new gang which included Frank, Bill Ryan, Dick Liddell, Tucker Basham, Ed Miller (Clell's brother), and Wood Hite. The gang roamed back through Missouri where they held up the Glendale train on October 7, 1879 for $35,000 and then as far south as Muscle Shoals, Ala., where they held up a stage for a paltry $1,400.

On July 10, 1881, Jesse led his men into Riverton, Iowa and held up the Davis and Sexton Bank, taking $5,000. Only five days later, Jesse struck the Chicago, Rock Island, and Pacific Railroad Express near Winston, Mo. Here, he killed a passenger, Frank McMillan, who attempted to interfere with the robbery, and Engineer William Westphal.

The brutality of the raid and the cold-blooded killing of McMillan and Westphal stirred Governor Thomas T. Crittenden to offer a $10,000 reward for the capture and conviction of Frank and Jesse James. It was an unheard-of sum in those days and one to tempt even members of Jesse's own gang. The outlaw band Jesse and Frank had originally ridden with would never have dreamed of turning in either man. First, they had been protected by their cousins, the Youngers. Secondly, all the members of the gang were tied to Jesse and Frank through long years in the guerrilla service and were life-long residents of the farming community in which they lived, and living would no longer be possible should one betray the boys; Jesse's loyal kinsmen would see to that.

But after Northfield, Jesse was forced to go far afield to recruit new members for his gang. These new followers, especially the shifty brothers Ford, owed no particular allegiance to the outlaw. In fact, they openly criticized him and often came close to drawing their pistols against him. Crittenden's offer merely gave Robert and Charles Ford an additional reason to eliminate a man they personally disliked.

Robert Ford was never a full-fledged member of the second James gang. He moved within the periphery of associates who aided the outlaws in hiding out or escaping after a robbery. Charles Ford, however, did manage to be taken into the gang as a working member in time to participate in one of the strangest train robberies in American history.

On August 7, 1881 Jesse led his brother Frank, Wood and Clarence Hite, Dick Liddell, and Charles Ford to Blue Cut near Glendale, Mo., a few miles from his train robbery of 1879; the gang busied themselves with piling timber upon the tracks. At the sight of the obstruction, an engineer named Foote halted the Chicago, Alton Express.

A tall, bearded man with blinking blue eyes jumped into the locomotive's cab and formally introduced himself. "I'm Jesse James," he said. Then, motioning Foote down from the cab with his pistols, he ordered the engineer toward the express car.

Inside of the car, Jesse, enjoying the popularity the dime novels had established for him, smiled widely and said, introducing the members of his gang, "This is Frank James, Wood Hite, Clarence Hite, Dick Liddell, and Charlie Ford." Each man smiled and gave a brief nod. The mood of the outlaws changed when they realized that their total take was slightly more than $1,500. They rode off grumbling. It was to be Jesse's last raid.

The Ford brothers had been secretly planning to kill him for months. They rode with him back to his mother's home while Frank stayed on at his Tennessee farm three miles from Nashville. Jesse, suspicious that Pinkertons might be watching the house, slept in the barn with his horse. The Fords stayed with him. The next morning, while Jesse ate breakfast in his mother's house for the last time, the Fords, according to Robert, "discussed the matter again and how we would kill him," for the reward.

That day Jesse left for St. Joseph, Mo. with the Ford brothers flanking him. Once in his small home, a quaint cottage on a hilltop overlooking St. Joseph, Jesse settled down for a while with his wife and children. The Fords stayed for several days and then went off on Jesse's orders to scout prospective robbery sites.

The second James gang, pressured by hundreds of lawmen and Pinkertons searching for them, became unnerved and finally began to dissolve. First Ed Miller's body was found on a lonely Missouri road. Jim Cummins, one-time James gang member, swore Jesse had killed him when Miller told him he wanted to surrender to the law. Next Wood Hite was killed by Dick Liddell and Bob Ford in an argument over $100 missing from the loot of the second Glendale train robbery. Dick Liddell then surrendered to lawmen on January 24, 1882. Liddell's confession implicated Clarence Hite, who was arrested, tried, and sentenced to prison for twenty-five years.

Only Jesse and Frank James and the Ford brothers were still at large. Jesse met the Fords in his home on the morning of April 3, 1882. He quietly outlined his plan for robbing the Platte County Bank. The three bandits ate breakfast prepared by Mrs. James as Jesse's children romped in the yard. Following breakfast, Jesse pulled out a newspaper and read about Dick Liddell's confession in which he implicated Jesse and Frank in several robberies. Though he spoke not a word, Bob Ford later stated that the look on Jesse's face was bone-chilling. Ford suddenly became terrified as he thought about what might happen to him if James learned how he and his brother Charlie had contacted Governor Crittenden and told him they would deliver Jesse James for amnesty and the reward money.

"I knew then I had placed my head in the lion's mouth," Bob Ford recalled at the inquest of Jesse James. "How could I safely remove it?"

His chance came minutes after Jesse tossed the paper aside. The bandit walked to the window, looked at his children playing and then turned around. He spotted a picture high on the wall which was tilted. He moved toward it. For a reason never explained, Jesse unbuckled his gun belts—he wore two, one about the hips and a shoulder holster, four guns in all—and placed them on a chair.

As he began to adjust the picture, Jesse's unprotected back offered a perfect target to the Fords. Robert Ford raised his pistol with a quaking hand and fired several times. The outlaw spun about with a wild look in his eyes and toppled forward. Mrs. James rushed into the room, fell to her knees and, weeping, cradled the head of her murdered husband in her arms.

Bob Ford stood in the middle of the room, holding his pistol up for examination. "The gun went off accidentally," he told Mrs. James.

Through tear-streaming eyes, Zerelda Mimms James looked up at her husband's murderer and said: "Yes, I guess it did go off on purpose."

The Ford brothers dashed from the house, Robert screaming at the top of his lungs, "I have killed Jesse James! I killed him! I killed him! I have killed Jesse James!"

The Fords got their reward, the newspapers their headlines, and Jesse Woodson James his immortality.

Newspapers from New York to Texas, from Missouri to California bannered the news. "Jesse by Jehovah," yelled the *St. Joseph Gazette*. "Good-Bye, Jesse!" lamented the *Kansas City Journal*.

Robert Ford and his brother Charles attended the coroner's inquest and gave unimpassioned testimony. Ford mounted the witness stand and calmly responded to the coroner's question "concerning the particulars of the killing."

"After breakfast, between eight and nine o'clock," Bob Ford stated, "he, my brother and myself were in the room. He pulled off his pistols and got up on a chair to dust off some picture frames and I drew my pistol and shot him."

"How close were you to him?"

"About six feet away."

Charlie Ford rode with Jesse, then betrayed him. (State Historical Society of Missouri)

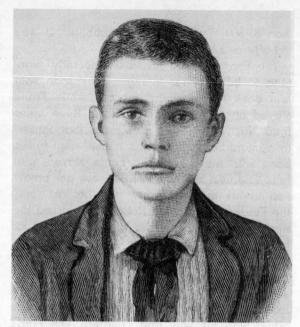

Bob Ford shot Jesse James in the back and collected the reward. (State Historical Society of Missouri)

"How close was the hand to him which held the pistol?"

"About four feet I should think."

"Did he say anything?"

Bob Ford paused and then said almost inaudibly, "He started to turn his head but didn't say a word."

"Was Jesse James unarmed when you killed him?'

"Yes, sir."

Hours later, aging Mrs. Zerelda Samuel entered the courtroom. She took the stand and said: "I live in Clay County, and am the mother of Jesse James." Then the mother who had protected her outlaw sons to the end, broke into deep moaning and sobs. "My poor boy . . . I have seen the body since my arrival and have recognized it as that of my son, Jesse . . . the lady by my side is my daughter-in-law and the children hers . . . he was a kind husband and son."

As the old woman was led from the courtroom in her grief, she saw Dick Liddell and the Fords sitting together. She stopped and in the hushed courtroom, her eyes fierce, steady, and fixed upon the three men, she raised the stump of her right arm and shouted in a half scream: "Traitors!"

The blood drained from the trio's faces and they hurried out of the courtroom via a side entrance. Jesse's mother and wife purchased a $500 coffin and took the outlaw home to

Kearney where he was buried in a quiet field on the Samuel farm beneath a coffeebean tree.

A gleaming, white marble tombstone was placed above the grave which read:

Jesse W. James
Died April 3, 1882
Aged 34 years, 6 months, 28 days
Murdered by a traitor and a coward
whose name is not worthy to
appear here.

Five months later, the last of the infamous James gang, Alexander Franklin James, surrendered personally to Governor Crittenden in his Jefferson City office, October 5, 1882. He was then thirty-nine, a thin, tall man with a wispy mustache. He marched into the Governor's office and took off his gunbelt which held a single .44-caliber Colt pistol.

"Governor Crittenden," James said solemnly, "I want to hand over to you that which no other living man except myself has been permitted to touch since 1861." The outlaw pointed to the buckle on the belt which carried a U.S. stamp. "The cartridge belt has been mine for eighteen years. I got it in Centralia in 1861."

Crittenden promised James protection and a fair trial. As he was being led to jail, an enterprising reporter from the *Sedalia Dispatch* interviewed Frank James.

"Why did you surrender?" the reporter buzzed. "No one knew where you were in hiding, nor could anyone find out."

Frank shot back: "What of that? I was tired of an outlaw's life. I have been hunted for twenty-one years. I have literally lived in the saddle. I have never known a day of perfect peace. It was one long, anxious, inexorable, eternal vigil. When I slept it was literally in the midst of an arsenal. If I heard dogs bark more fiercely than usual, or the feet of horses in a greater volume of sound than usual, I stood to my arms. Have you any idea of what a man must endure who leads such a life? No, you cannot. No one can unless he lives it for himself."

The unscrupulous shooting of Jesse James so aroused the nation and, especially, the residents of Missouri that it improved Frank's chances of acquittal by a jury. After a series of trials, he was freed and returned to his farm. He lived without incident until February 18, 1915, when he died on the Samuel farm in the room where he had been born.

The Younger brothers were not freed until 1901. Bob Younger, who developed tuberculosis while in prison, died September 16, 1889 at age thirty-two. His sister, Retta, visited him at his deathbed in the Stillwater prison. His last whispered words were: "Don't weep for me." Cole and James Younger were paroled from the Minnesota State Penitentiary, July 10, 1901. Jim stayed in St. Paul, courting a young newswoman. When she rejected him, the ex-bandit committed suicide.

Cole Younger returned to Lee's Summit, Missouri to live out a quiet life. He and Frank James sometimes appeared at local fairs, running horse races and recalling the days of their youth. Younger lived the longest, dying from a heart attack March 21, 1916.

There was never any peace for the Ford brothers after the death of Jesse James. Charlie, plagued with the thought that he would be killed by one of Jesse's relatives, got drunk one night and blew away the top of his skull with his six-gun. Bob Ford drifted about the country, appearing in vaudeville shows and retelling the story of how he killed America's most famous bad man.

During the silver rush, Ford opened a saloon in Creede, Colo. One night, June 24, 1892, Ed O. Kelly, a distant relative of the Younger brothers, walked into Ford's saloon and emptied his shotgun into the killer of Jesse James.

Almost from the moment Jesse was placed in his grave, claimants would come forward to state that another man had been killed and that they were, in reality, the bandit. All were exposed as frauds, the latest pretender appearing in 1948 under the name of J. Frank Dalton, who insisted that he was 101 years old and the real Jesse James. He failed, however, to explain to skeptics how he had managed to grow a new tip to his left middle finger, the same finger which Jesse had blown off accidentally while cleaning his pistol when he rode with "Bloody Bill" Anderson.

These claims, however, were not unexpected, particularly when one realizes that almost every boy in America at one time or another wanted to be Jesse James, the strong, fearless bandit who came to symbolize the individuality of the American West (the murders he committed ignored as being unspeakable for a man of his courageous reputation). After generations, the man, Jesse James, has vanished and has been replaced by a dream image, rising from the blood-soaked earth of Missouri and towering with a long, nostalgic shadow that reaches into our considerably imperfect history as a nation.

And the history of that one man has become interminable and arcane, so hellishly involved with our collective emotions that his ghostly memory becomes something warm, delightfully indistinguishable and irretrievably rooted to a good past. In the end he becomes mistakenly worthy and honorable, this American killer.

A day after Jesse's death, a melodramatic ballad appeared as if by magic, attesting to the strange immortality gained by this strangest of outlaws:

Jesse James was a lad who killed many
    a man.
He robbed the Glendale train.
He stole from the rich and he gave to the
    poor,
He'd a hand and a heart and a brain.

(Chorus)
Jesse had a wife to mourn for his life,
Two children, they were brave,
But that dirty little coward that shot Mister
    Howard,
Has laid poor Jesse in his grave.

It was Robert Ford, that dirty little coward,
I wonder how does he feel,
For he ate of Jesse's bread and he slept
in Jesse's bed,
Then he laid Jesse James in his grave.

Jesse was a man, a friend to the poor.
He'd never see a man suffer pain,
And with his brother Frank he robbed the
Gallatin bank
And stopped the Glendale train.

It was on a Wednesday night, the moon
was shining bright.
He stopped the Glendale train.
And the people all did say for many miles
away,
It was robbed by Frank and Jesse James.

It was on a Saturday night, Jesse was at
home,
Talking to his family brave,
Robert Ford came along like a thief in the
night,
And laid Jesse James in his grave.

The people held their breath when they
heard of Jesse's death,
And wondered how he ever came to die,
It was one of the gang called little Robert
Ford,
That shot Jesse James on the sly.

Jesse went to his rest with his hand on his
breast,
The devil will be upon his knee,
He was born one day in the county of Shea
And he came from a solitary race.

This song was made by Billy Garshade,
As soon as the news did arrive,
He said there was no man with the law in
his hand
Could take Jesse James when alive.

The author was never found.

[ALSO SEE William "Bloody Bill" Anderson, Al
Jennings, William Clarke Quantrill.]

JAMES, ROBERT
Murderer ● (1895-1942)

Robert James was an ambitious barber who pocketed considerable side money from insurance schemes that involved killing his relatives. Born Raymond Lisemba in rural Alabama, James grew up a sharecropper's son, baling cotton until his back ached. Then a miracle occured. He inherited $4,000 from two uncles who died and left him the sole beneficiary of their insurance policies.

He traveled to Birmingham where he changed his name to James and went to barber college. There, in 1921, James married Maud Duncan, but the union dissolved a short time later after his wife filed for divorce, claiming extreme cruelty. She stated that James was a sadomasachist and had, among other tortures, stuck hot curling irons under her fingernails to stimulate his sex drive.

James moved to Emporia, Kansas, opening a barber shop and marrying again. He fled the shop and his wife when the father of a young girl he had made pregnant came hunting for him with a shotgun. Arriving in Fargo, N.D., James bought another barbershop and committed bigamy by marrying a third time to Winona Wallace. James had not bothered to divorce his second wife.

Running low on funds, James was ever mindful of how he came by the original windfalls that sent him to Birmingham, life insurance policies. He heavily insured Winona, then took her to Pike's Peak on a honeymoon. She almost fell to her doom while the couple scaled the mountain. They retired to a remote Canadian cabin but a short time later James arrived at a police station to report that his poor wife had drowned in a bathtub. He explained that she must have still been dizzy from the mountain mishap and slipped unconscious beneath the bath water.

James collected $14,000 on Winona's life from an insurance policy he had taken out only a day before he married her. He moved back to Alabama and married a fourth time, but his wife, who knew his background, became wary when James told her he was going to insure her life for a large amount of money. "People you insure," she told him, "always die of something strange." She divorced James who next looked about for another victim.

He found that person in the form of his dim-witted nephew, Cornelius Wright, a sailor stationed in San Diego, Calif. Wright had a long history of being accident prone. He had been hit by several cars, scaffolding had collapsed on him, and he had even been knocked unconscious by a line drive while attending a baseball game. He was the perfect subject for James's insurance murder scheme.

James invited his nephew to visit him when on leave. At the time, he insured the youth, then played the generous uncle by loaning Wright his car, telling him to have a good time driving it around. Wright promptly drove off a cliff, killing himself. The mechanic who towed the wreck back to James told him that something was wrong with the steering wheel but James failed to mention this when collecting the premium on his nephew's life.

Moving to Los Angeles, James opened a very large barber shop, employing tall, blonde 25-year-old Mary Bush as his manicurist. He was soon carrying on a torrid affair with Bush whom he later married then quickly insured.

A few weeks later, in July 1935, James took aside Charlie Hope, a thick-headed friend and asked him to find some poisonous snakes. He told Hope that he had a friend with a troublesome wife. "The snakes will take care of her," he said. Hope went to "Snake Joe" Houtebrink, a reptile collector and purchased two Crotalus Atrox rattlers.

James then admitted that the poisonous reptiles were for his own wife and that if Hope helped him eliminate Mary he would share the insurance money with him. Hope nodded and the pair went to James home that night. James introduced Hope as an "eminent physician," who was there to advise her on her pregnancy. Hope looked over Mrs. James and suggested she have an immediate abortion. In fact, he, Hope said, could perform the operation that night on the kitchen table.

The naive woman agreed. Then Hope apologized that he had no anesthetic with which to knock her out. James suggested that she drink herself into unconsciousness. The trio drank whiskey for some hours until Mary passed out. Then James and Hope brought out the snakes, opened the box and stuck Mary's foot into it.

James and Hope then left the woman for several hours. When James returned alone, he discovered his wife still alive. He removed her leg from the snake box and hid the snakes. Mrs. James regained consciousness and complained of terrible pains in her leg which had swollen to twice its former size. She also wondered why the abortion had not been performed.

Robert James, seated, testifying at his 1936 murder trial.

"Conditions weren't right," James mumbled. He then put his wife to bed and called Hope, telling him: "The damned snakes didn't work. Find something stronger." Hope showed up later with a deadly, black widow spider.

James placed this in the bed with his wife and it stung the still intoxicated Mrs. James several times but she miraculously survived. Her murderous husband later figured that she had drunk so much alcohol that it made her immune to the snake and spider poison.

Mrs. James's leg was so swollen that she could not walk for days. Meanwhile, James was running out of ideas. He finally helped his wife to the bathtub, which he had filled. He helped her into it, then yanked her legs high into the air which forced her head down. She drowned in the tub, the same fate that had befallen James's third wife, Winona Wallace.

This time Mary Bush James was finally dead. James dressed the body and Hope arrived to help him carry it to the back yard of the James home. There they placed the body face down in a small lily pond to make it appear that the drunken woman had gotten dizzy, fallen down, and accidentally drowned in the pond.

James went to work at the barber shop where he remained all day. He invited two guests to dine with him and his wife that night, pretending to arrange things with his wife on the phone while

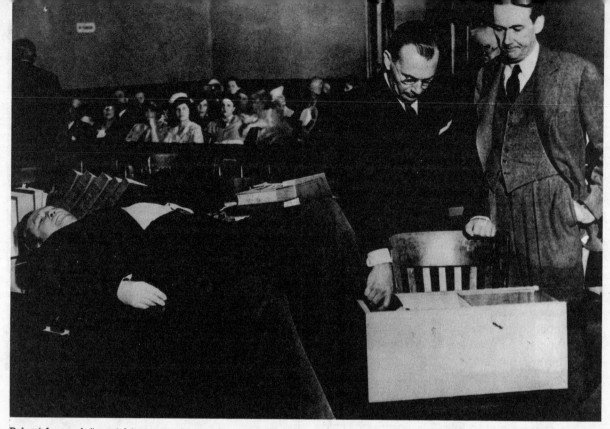

Robert James, left, watching a court room demonstration of his deadly snake box which he used in trying to kill his wife.

the friends stood nearby. When James and his friends arrived for dinner they discovered Mrs. James face down in the lily pond. The death was reported as an accident and James put in for the insurance.

Jack Southard, Captain of Detectives for the Los Angeles Police Department, thought something strange about the case when, three months later, he received a report that James had been arrested for propositioning a woman. He thought it curious that a grieving man so recently widowed would be picked up for mashing. He began to investigate. He learned that Hope might be involved and searched Hope's apartment, finding a receipt for two rattlesnakes. He checked the coroner's report on Mrs. Mary James and saw that it listed snake bites on the one leg of the body.

He arrested Hope on suspicion of murder and Hope immediately informed on James. In May 1936, James was placed on trial. The snakes, spider, and other murder implements were displayed as evidence. James murderous past was exposed and he was convicted and condemned. Hope received a life sentence.

For the next four years James remained in the Los Angeles County Jail as he filed a host of appeals. He was finally sent to San Quentin but James again

filed appeals that he be executed in the recently completed gas chamber, not by hanging, as had been the practice. This appeal failed. James was to be hanged since he was sentenced to death at the time that this form of exeuction was in force. On May 1, 1942, the inventive Robert James mounted the gallows stairs in San Quentin and became the last man to be hanged in California.

JAMESON, JAMES
Murderer, Burglar ● (? -1807)

With his partner, James M'Gowan, Jameson earned his dubious living as a burglar in the Harrisburg, Pa. area. The pair's undoing occurred August 28, 1806, when they attempted to rob Jacob Eshelman of Hummelstown, Pa. He resisted and the burglars clubbed him to death with tree limbs.

They were quickly taken into custody; Eshelman's savings—$500—was found on their persons. They were sentenced to death. M'Gowan was hanged December 29, 1806, but Jameson escaped from the Dauphin County Jail. He was recaptured days later, discovered hiding under his mother's bed in Reading, Pa.

He was hanged January 10, 1807, in Harrisburg.

JEFFERSON, LEROY
Narcotics Peddler ● (1919-   )

Leroy Jefferson is one of the top syndicate narcotics peddlers operating on the West Coast. He is considered the chief supplier for other high ranking Negro narcotics traffickers in Washington, Oregon, and California. Jefferson's contacts in Mexico have enabled him to obtain vast amounts of narcotics.

Originally an overlord in vice, Jefferson, according to U.S. Senate crime probes, was actually fought over by elements of the Mafia who were eager to have him handle the syndicate's funneling of heroin to pushers.

JENNINGS, AL
Trainrobber ● (1863-1961)

Jennings began late as a robber and his exploits were anything but awe-inspiring: comic would be more like it. The four Jennings brothers—Al, Frank, Ed, and John—were roustabout cowboys who lived at Kiowa Creek, Oklahoma, near Woodward. Al first met a shoddy-looking outlaw named "Little Dick" about 1885 and was goaded into several awkward attempts at robbery, more on a dare than through a desire to steal and kill.

Al and his brothers first pretended to be U.S. marshals and levied a toll against gullible ranchers driving cattle through the still-wild Oklahoma Territory. They soon tired of this

and tried to rob two trains near Woodward.

Jennings attempted to flag the engineer to a stop but was ignored; he was almost crushed by the locomotive. The second attempt was even more ridiculous. Jennings and his brothers rode alongside a roaring train for several minutes firing their pistols in the air as a way of signaling the engineer to halt. The engineer merely waved a friendly hello and kept going.

The boys finally stumbled on a small passenger train taking on wood at a water stop, and robbed the express car of $60. Of the four men in this band, Frank and Al Jennings were captured a day later by lawman Bud Ledbetter who never fired a shot. He ordered the brothers to throw down their guns and tie themselves up. They did.

Ed and John Jennings rode to a nearby town and entered a saloon where famed lawman Temple Houston was sipping whiskey. The Jennings boys began an argument with Houston, who promptly shot them both. Ed was killed outright; John was wounded and lived to return to his small ranch.

Both Al and Frank Jennings were given life sentences for their absurd robbery. Al was freed in five years, Frank in seven. In the mid-1890s, Al Jennings rode out of the Oklahoma Territory and traveled to California, where he permanently settled. In his muddled mind, he somehow transformed himself from a bungling bandit to a much-feared outlaw.

Sheriff Jim Herron of Oklahoma later stated: "Old Al Jennings was around California for years, stuffing dudes with nonsense and telling them wild yarns about himself in the early days." One of the stories Jennings told of himself was that he could, in his prime, hit a can tossed in the air from one hundred paces without ever missing.

Ex - Rough Rider and World War I commander, General Roy Hoffman clucked his tongue at this Jennings tale. "I knew Al Jennings personally," he once said, "and his marksmanship was notoriously poor. He was one of the kind of fellows who could have qualified as the traditional bad shot who couldn't hit the side of a barn."

Jennings' lurid tales of the Old West were strengthened when, in 1948, 101-years-old J. Frank Dalton appeared, claiming to be the real Jesse James. Jennings, then 85, hurried to his side, took one look at the ancient pretender, and shouted to AP reporters: "It's him!

Al Jennings of Oklahoma, the West's most awkward bandit. (Oklahoma Historical Society)

It's Jesse!"

Both men posed holding pistols. Jennings stated that "there isn't a bit of doubt on earth," that Dalton was the true Jesse James. He neglected to inform the press that he had never met Jesse James and that Dalton had miraculously grown a new left middle fingertip, one which the real Jesse James had accidentally blown off while cleaning a pistol when he rode with "Bloody Bill" Anderson.

Jennings died in 1961, raving about deadly shootouts that had occurred only in his fruitful imagination. As a tribute to his ability as a teller of tall tales, Hollywood believed every word and made a motion picture based on his life . . . or the life he thought he had led.

JIMMY CURLY GANG

The gangs along Fifty-ninth Street in New York just before the First World War were some of the toughest in the city. The most dreaded in this area was the Jimmy Curly Gang, led by an ambitious youth named "Gold Mine" Jimmy Carrigio.

Another, much older gang, The Gas Housers, met the Jimmy Curly Gang in 1914 in an all-out street battle for supremacy of the area. Gas House leader Tommy Lynch was murdered (some said by Carrigio himself) and the Jimmy Curly mob controlled the street. They meted out extortion, blackmail, and murder until the close of the War when members were absorbed into other gangs.

JOE THE GREASER GANG

A heavily armed band of East Side sluggers, this gang operated exclusively as strike-breakers, or union organizers with lead pipes, whichever befitted the job they were paid to perform. They were led by a thug named Joe the Greaser and were active in New York prior to the First World War.

During the great union battles of 1913, Joe the Greaser allied himself with the powerful Dopey Benny gang to exclude independent mobsters such as Pinchey Paul and William Lustig from sharing in the spoils of paid union slugging.

The gangsters of this era were brass knuckle types, using firearms on rare occasions, which accounted for their poor marksmanship. A good example of this was a street battle between the Joe the Greaser gang and the Pinchey Paul mob at Grand and Forsyth streets in late 1913. More than one hundred gang members participated in a wild hour-long shoot-out there, but no one was even wounded.

Joe the Greaser learned that a man named Jewbach had agitated Pinchey Paul into the fight and sent one of his most ruthless killers, Nigger Benny Snyder, to kill him. Jewbach survived a knife slashing and openly vowed to testify against Snyder in court. Joe the Greaser and a dozen men visited Jewbach days later and the gang leader chopped a piece of Jewbach's tongue away, yelling: "Let that learn you not to talk so much!"

Jewbach didn't talk, but Joe the Greaser's friend Snyder did. He was picked up later for killing Pinchey Paul and, to save himself, blamed Joe the Greaser for the murder, telling police that he committed the slaying at Joe's orders.

When Joe the Greaser was brought in for questioning, he shook his head disgustedly at his lieutenant. He pleaded guilty to manslaughter when in court. Snyder was sent to prison for twenty years. Joe the Greaser received a ten-year sentence in Sing Sing in December, 1915. Upon his release, he faded into obscurity, his gang long since dismembered.

JOHNSON, JOHN
Murderer, Robber ● (? -1824)

Publicity surrounding the trial of murderer John Johnson in New York City was tremendous. His victim, James Murray, had been his roommate. Johnson, seeking

The strange murder tale of Richard Johnson was recounted in this 1828 booklet. (N.Y. Historical Society)

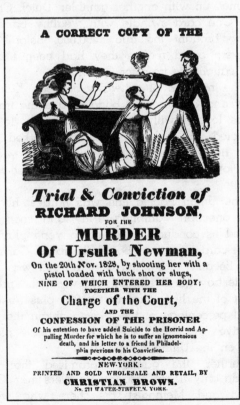

A CORRECT COPY OF THE

Trial & Conviction of
RICHARD JOHNSON,
FOR THE
MURDER
Of Ursula Newman,
On the 20th Nov. 1828, by shooting her with a
pistol loaded with buck shot or slugs,
NINE OF WHICH ENTERED HER BODY;
TOGETHER WITH THE
Charge of the Court,
AND THE
CONFESSION OF THE PRISONER
Of his intention to have added Suicide to the Horrid and Appalling Murder for which he is to suffer an ignomenious
death, and his letter to a friend in Philadelphia previous to his Conviction.
NEW-YORK:
PRINTED AND SOLD WHOLESALE AND RETAIL, BY
CHRISTIAN BROWN,
No. 211 WATER-STREET, N. YORK.

Murray's purse, murdered him in his sleep by splitting his skull with a hatchet.

He wrapped the body in a blanket and carried it toward the harbor, intending to dispose of the corpse there. A curious policeman called to Johnson and the killer dropped his grim load and ran.

Murray was unknown and authorities seeking his identification displayed his corpse at City Hall Park for days, hoping that someone would recognize the body. Someone did and this led to Johnson's arrest and speedy trial on March 16, 1824. He confessed and was sentenced to death.

Johnson's execution was a circus-like affair in the heart of New York City. Fifty thousand spectators came to watch him hang at Thirteenth Street and Second Avenue, April 2, 1824.

JOHNSON, RICHARD
Murderer ● (? -1829)

Frustration was the root of Johnson's murderous discontent. Though his strange mistress, Mrs. Ursula Newman, had given birth to his child, she refused to marry him. The peculiar woman even refused to admit that the child was his. When he demanded she give the child his name, Mrs. Newman laughed at him.

In a rage, Johnson grabbed a pistol loaded with buckshot and fired it into his beloved on the evening of November 20, 1828, killing her instantly (nine slugs were removed from Mrs. Newman's body). Moments later, Johnson thought of committing suicide but discarded this idea.

Another report had it that Johnson suffered from a strange malady—that he imagined Mrs. Newman's child was his own (as he did many others'). According to this version of the story, her jibes at his fantasy were what caused Johnson to kill her.

He was tried in New York City and confessed to the crime. Johnson was hanged May 7, 1829 on Blackwell's Island. Dying on the gallows with Johnson the same day was Catharine Cashiere, a Negro servant who had gotten drunk and stabbed another woman, Susan Anthony, to death. (The judge who sentenced Catharine to the gallows made several testy remarks about the increasing number of saloons in New York City.)

JONES, GENENE
Serial Killer ● (1951-   )

A fifteen-month-old baby died of cardiac arrest in Kerrville, Texas in September 1982. This aroused the suspicions of officials since the child had had an examination by a competent pediatrician and was in perfect health. A powerful drug, Anectine, had been administered to the infant girl and this had not been perscribed.

Investigators pinpointed Genene Jones, the nurse on duty when the child died. Examining Jones's past, it was learned that more than two dozen babies in her care had died under similar circumstances. A hospital employee came forth, saying that she believed Jones had been killing babies so that she could create "life and death situations," which increased the drama of her work.

At a San Antonio hospital where Jones had once worked, more horrors were discovered. More than a dozen children had died of cardiac arrest, all of whom having been injected with Anectine by "The Death Nurse," as Jones came to be called.

On February 15, 1984, Jones was convicted of murder and sent to prison for 99 years.

JONES, WILLIAM ("CANADA BILL")
Gambler ● (? -1877)

A longtime card sharping partner of the notorious gambler George H. Devol, Jones was a habitué of the Mississippi river boats. His expertise with cards earned him the reputation as the greatest three-card monte player in the country. He was known as Canada Bill and Devol later described him in his memoirs as "medium-sized, chicken-headed, tow-haired, with mild blue eyes, and a mouth nearly from ear to ear, who walked with a shuffling, half-apologetic sort of gait; and, who, when his countenance was in repose, resembled an idiot . . . he had a squawking, boyish voice, and awkward manners, and a way of asking fool questions and putting on a good-natured sort of grin that led everybody to believe that he was the rankest kind of sucker—the greenest sort of country jake."

Canada Bill was anything but that. Born in England to gypsy parents, Bill migrated to Canada where he learned his card playing from a leading crook, Dick Cady. He fleeced the gullible there for years in three-card monte, the proverbial bent card utilized to tip him off as to which card to play. He ran his luck dry in Canada by 1850 and moved south.

First Bill moved to the Mississippi area. After meeting Devol in New Orleans, the pair worked the elegant paddle wheelers for years through the 1850s. By the Civil War, the bet-a-million gamblers had disappeared. At this time, Bill learned that Devol was attempting to con him out of their jointly pooled funds and departed for Kansas City, where he teamed up with another gambler, Dutch Charlie. One card swindle with wealthy bankers there brought the duo $200,000. Before the players could realize they had been taken, Bill caught the train for Omaha.

The network of railways between Kansas City and Omaha was budding and the trains were loaded with greenhorns begging to be cheated. Bill obliged them and worked the iron horse trade for more than fifteen years, employing his nefarious skills with three-card monte.

The Union Pacific line was hardest hit by this one-man gambling army and soon ordered its conductors to eject anyone playing three-card monte on board its trains. Canada Bill became indignant. The railroad was out to destroy his livelihood. He wrote the president of the line, offering $10,000 plus an annual percentage of his take to obtain the exclusive "franchise" to three-card monte playing on the Union Pacific rails.

Further, the gambler promised that he would only fleece wealthy travelers from Chicago and Methodist preachers who were known to carry large sums and whom he personally disliked. The president of the line declined to sell Bill the franchise.

In 1874, Bill traveled to Chicago and with gamblers Jimmy Porter and "Colonel" Charles Starr, established four infamously crooked gambling dens in the Red Light district. There, Canada Bill amassed $150,000 within six months but, being an inveterate gambler himself, lost almost every penny to crooked casino dealers.

Bill ambled on to Cleveland where he met with little success; his reputation preceded him and he could find little action. His last stop was the Charity Hospital in Reading, Pa., where he died in 1877. Gamblers by the dozens attended the quick-hand artist's funeral. One even offered to bet $1,000 to $500 that "Bill was not in the box."

His gambler's eulogy was delivered dramatically by a friend:

"O, when I die, just bury me
In a box-back coat and hat,
Put a twenty dollar gold piece on my watch
   chain
To let the Lord know I'm standing pat."

JUDD, WINNIE RUTH
Murderer ● (1909-   )

BACKGROUND: BORN AND RAISED IN ILLINOIS. DEVELOPED TB AT AN EARLY AGE AND MOVED TO A SANITARIUM FOR CURE IN PHOENIX, ARIZONA. MARRIED TO DR. WILLIAM J. JUDD. DESCRIPTION: APPROXIMATELY 5'2", BLUE EYES, SANDY HAIR. ALIASES: NONE. RECORD: SURRENDERED TO LOS ANGELES POLICE 10/23/32 AFTER KILLING AND DISSECTING MISS HELWIG (SAMMY) SAMUELSON, AND MRS. AGNES LEROI IN PHOENIX, ARIZONA AND SHIPPING THEIR DISMEMBERED BODIES IN A TRUNK TO LOS ANGELES; TRIED FOR MURDER IN PHOENIX, ARIZ., 11/12/32; SENTENCED TO DEATH BY HANGING; DECISION REVERSED AT SPECIAL SANITY HEARING ORDERED BY THE GOVERNOR OF ARIZONA; RE-SENTENCED TO LIFE IMPRISONMENT IN THE ARIZONA STATE MENTAL HOSPITAL; RELEASED FROM ARIZONA STATE PRISON, 12/22/71; LIFE SENTENCE COMMUTED BY THE ARIZONA BOARD OF PARDONS AND PAROLES; MOVED TO SOUTHERN CALIFORNIA.

In the fall of 1932, an attractive brunette entered the baggage room of the Southern Pacific Railroad in Los Angeles. Sweetly she asked the attendant to help her load a small case, a metal locker and a huge trunk into her car.

While handling the trunk, the agent stopped, puzzled. He saw something red dripping through a crack in the trunk.

"Say, lady," he said, suspicious that it contained contraband deer meat, "what's in this?"

The pretty girl replied that the trunk keys were in her car and she would have to get them. She went to her car. Then she drove off, but the alert agent jotted down the car's license number.

He waited several hours before he pried open the trunk. Inside, in horror, he found the hacked-up bodies of two women, one completely dismembered, their faces smashed beyond recognition.

The hunt was on. The license number was traced to a student, who stated that the trunk belonged to his sister, Winnie Ruth Judd, a resident of Phoenix, Ariz., who had traveled from Illinois for a TB cure.

When winsome Winnie turned herself in, she told a neurotic tale of killing the two women, Agnes LeRoi and Helwig "Sammy" Samuelson, in self-defense. But police discovered a letter proving murder. Winnie's own words sealed her verdict:

". . . she ["Sammy"] came in with my gun and said she would shoot me if I went hunting with this friend. I threw my hand over the mouth of the gun and grabbed the breadknife. She shot [there was a bullet hole in Winnie's hand to prove it]. I jumped on her

The trunk Winnie Judd used to store her dismembered victims.

Axe murderer Winnie Ruth Judd at her 1932 trial posed dramatically for cameramen while exhibiting a wounded hand; she was shot while disarming one of her victims. (UPI)

with all my weight and knocked her down in the dining room—Ann [Agnes] yelled at us. I fired twice. . . ."

Winnie's trial was brief. She was sentenced to death by the rope. Then the wild show began. The governor of Arizona granted a stay from the gallows and a sanity hearing began.

Winnie laughed uproariously, clapped her hands and, at one time, rose up and said of the jury, "They're all gangsters!" Another time, she said loudly to her husband, Dr. William J. Judd: "Let me throw myself out that window!"

In desperation, Winnie's mother clawed away at the prosecution by taking the stand to state that insanity ran like a wild river through her family. The elderly woman said she herself had a feeble mind and her daughter had "been more or less insane all her life."

Then Winnie's father testified that his paternal grandmother, 125 years ago in Scotland, had lost her mind and rattled off numerous other loonies in his family tree. All the while, Winnie pulled at her clothes, tore her hair and raged.

Though she was finally removed forcibly from the hearing, Winnie won. Her sentence was altered to life imprisonment in the state mental hospital.

There, she became a smiling, charming, and model prisoner. And she also plotted. Using boxes, bottles, and soapcakes, she made a "sleeping dummy" of herself and escaped.

Found later wandering about shoeless and run-down, she told a story of being taken in by kind strangers who believed her weird tales. A witness then stated, "When she looked at you with those great big eyes brimming with tears, you would believe anything she told you."

Winnie obtained a passkey and tried again. She wandered about the state. Again, more people helped her before she was apprehended. After another spectacular escape in 1952—she made seven successful escapes in all—Winnie was taken before a grand jury to testify about hospital conditions.

Amazed doctors found another key hidden in her hair and a razor blade under her tongue!

In 1962, Winnie escaped again and lived with a California couple for eight years before she was discovered. She had been working for the couple and made extra money as a baby sitter.

Internationally-known lawyer Melvin Belli fought Winnie's extradition from California to Arizona in 1969 but Governor Reagan sent her back.

Doctors then decided that she was sane and sent her to prison.

The Arizona Parole Board released her on December 22, 1971, commuting her life sentence.

Winnie Ruth Judd moved to California where she now resides.

When thinking of the crime that made her the infamous "trunk murderess," she told the parole board, "I'm terribly sorry."

Oklahoma bandit Frank "Jelly" Nash, the gangster the Kansas City killers were allegedly attempting to liberate from federal custody, was shot to death in the massacre. (UPI)

KANSAS CITY MASSACRE

When Frank "Jelly" Nash, one of the most successful bankrobbers of the 1920s, escaped from Leavenworth in 1930, he became the subject of a nation-wide manhunt led by the FBI and local police officers in five states. He participated in several bank robberies engineered by the Barker-Karpis gang, but when police began to close in on the Barkers, the ever-elusive Nash broke away from the gang and went into hiding in Hot Springs, Ark.

FBI agents trapped him there in early 1933. From Hot Springs the bandit would be returned to Leavenworth to finish his twenty-five year sentence. At the moment of his capture, Nash spotted gambler and pool-hall owner Dick Galatas and gave him the high sign, indicating that he was being arrested by federal agents. Galatas called Nash's wife, Frances, and then placed several long-distance calls, attempting to learn where FBI men were taking Nash.

Galatas contacted lawman-turned-bankrobber Verne Miller in Kansas City. Miller, who had robbed with the Barkers, was an old friend of Jelly's. He told Galatas: "You have Frances call me as soon as she finds out what route they'll be taking to Leavenworth."

Through connections on the Hot Springs police department, Galatas learned the agents would be driving with their prisoner along the Joplin (Missouri) Road. Galatas and Frances Nash hired a plane and flew to Joplin where they met another underworld fence, gunsmith, and hideout operator, Herbert Farmer. They learned at that moment that the FBI had gone by another route, U.S. 64, and, at Fort Smith, Ark., had boarded the Missouri Pacific Flyer en route to Kansas City.

The agents joked in their stateroom with Nash about his new disguise, a red wig to cover his bald head. "I paid a hundred bucks for it in Chicago. You do what you can," Nash explained. He went on to state that he had had his nose straightened and then asked the lawmen not to pull his mustache because that was real.

In Kansas City, Verne Miller had learned that the prisoner was heading his way on board a train. He made preparations to greet it in the morning. On June 17, 1933, there were a number of people waiting to see Frank "Jelly" Nash. FBI agents Raymond Caffrey and R. E. Vetterli and city detectives W. J. "Red" Grooms and Frank Hermanson were waiting to escort Nash to Leavenworth in their car.

Also waiting in the busy train station were five or more gangsters, the would-be deliverers of Frank Nash. One of them was definitely Verne Miller. The identities of the others are in serious doubt to this day. Just as the Flyer pulled into the station, the gangsters went out to the parking lot and took positions next to parked autos. They were not noticed by the lawmen waiting at the curb next to their own car.

Nash was led from the train by FBI agents F. J. Lackey, Frank Smith, and Otto Reed, police chief of McAlester, Okla. The bandit was

Spectators view the carnage of the Kansas City Massacre, 6/17/33; the bodies of Kansas City detectives William Grooms and Frank Hermanson lie between the two bullet-smashed cars in the Union Station Plaza parking lot. (UPI)

still wearing his red wig; it kept slipping off. Lackey and Smith carried shotguns. The trio, joined by the four lawmen, began to get into a Chevrolet parked in the plaza. Nash got in the front seat. Lackey, Smith, and Reed got in the back. Agent Caffrey walked around the car to the driver's side and had his hand on the door handle when a booming voice yelled to the lawmen from across the plaza: "Up! Up! Get 'em up!"

Shocked and motionless, the agents and detectives looked up to see three men standing on the running boards of cars, pointing machineguns in their direction. A heavyset man aiming his machinegun at them, the man who had yelled out the order, waved his weapon slightly. For moments, dozens of people in the parking lot stood transfixed by the incredible scene. Police detective Red Grooms then broke the spell by jerking his pistol out and squeezing off two shots at the heavyset man, hitting him in the arm.

The heavyset gangster never faltered. "Let 'em have it!" he shouted to the others and opened up on the lawmen. The deadly spray of machinegun bullets splattered the Chevrolet, a torrent of lead that raked the car from back to front. Agent Caffrey fell to the cement, dead. Police Chief Reed took a chest full of slugs and toppled to the floor of the car, dead. Also inside the car agents Smith and Lackey fell forward, each shot several times.

Lackey struggled up courageously with his service revolver in his hand and tried to get off a shot from the window. The weapon was shot out of his grip. Agent Vetterli and detectives Grooms and Hermanson were all wounded, pressed to the pavement for cover.

Inside the car, Nash waved frantically at the machinegunners with handcuffed wrists. "For God's sake!" he shouted. "Don't shoot me!" The overlapping bursts of machinegun fire quieted him forever as his head was blown away.

Mrs. Lottie West, a caseworker for the Traveler's Aid Society, witnessed the entire shooting from the station. She spotted a patrolman she knew, Mike Fanning, who had entered the lot to investigate the awful racket. "They're killing everybody!" Mrs. West screamed to him.

Slugs were now bouncing into the pavement in front of the car. They tore into the already wounded, prone lawmen, killing detectives Grooms and Hermanson.

Mrs. West screamed to Officer Fanning: "Shoot the fat man, Mike! Shoot the fat man!"

"I knew she meant the big man whose machinegun was doing such bloody work," Fanning later recalled. "I aimed at him and fired. He whirled around and dropped to the ground. I don't know whether I hit him or whether he fell to escape. In any event he got up, fired another volley into the car, and ran toward a light Oldsmobile car, which roared west toward Broadway. As the car raced out of the parking lot I saw three men in it and there may have been more."

Just as Fanning was about to walk to the lawmen's car, another auto, a 1933 Chevrolet, with more gunners swooped past the parked car and riddled it from the rear.

Fanning ran to the lawmen's auto and peered inside. "It was a shambles. In the front seat a man was dead under the steering wheel [Nash]. On the left of the rear seat was another dead man [Chief Reed]. On the right was an unconscious man but he was groaning. A third man lay face down on the floor. I could see that he was alive."

Agent Vetterli, holding a wounded arm, staggered up, staring at the blood from the bodies of Hermanson and Grooms gathering in pools at his feet. Five men were dead—FBI agent Caffrey, Chief Reed, detectives Hermanson and Grooms, and Frank "Jelly" Nash, the man the shooting supposedly had been designed to set free.

One woman, unable to take her eyes from the carnage, groaned, "It's like Chicago."

In hours, newspapers across the country were screaming headlines that read "Kansas City Massacre." The public outcry against the slaughter was deafening. Contingents of FBI men and armies of police scoured the Kansas City area searching for the killers.

Frances Nash, Dick Galatas, and Herb Farmer were traced to Joplin, Mo. through long-distance calls they had made and were soon arrested. Witnesses tentatively identified one of the machinegunners as Verne Miller. Mrs. West was sure that the "fat man" had been Charles Arthur "Pretty Boy" Floyd. FBI officials and police immediately deduced that the third gunner had been Floyd's sidekick, Adam Richetti.

When Floyd and Richetti were finally brought to ground in October, 1934, the FBI announced that they had captured the perpetrators of the Kansas City Massacre. From all subsequent reports, however, it appears that the FBI was mistaken.

According to the 1954 statements of underworld figure Blackie Audett, Floyd and Richetti had nothing to do with the K.C. killings. "I knowed better," Audett wrote, "because I seen with my own eyes who was in that car. Both of them that was in it got clean away." Audett named Verne Miller, Maurice Denning, and William "Solly" Weissman.

Events immediately following the mass killing proved Audett's claim to a great degree. Police trailed Miller to his home only hours after the shooting but found that he had fled. They also found bloody rags in his living room.

Miller's naked and mangled body was discovered in a ditch near Detroit on November 29, 1933. His death had all the earmarks of a syndicate killing. It appeared that hot flatirons had scorched his skin. He was tied up head to toe and icepicks had punctured his tongue and cheeks.

Two weeks later Weissman's body was found in the same condition on the outskirts of Chicago. Denning's corpse never surfaced. It was apparent that all three men had been killed not because they failed to effect Nash's release but because they knew who had ordered Nash killed. They also knew that Jelly was marked for death because he knew too much. It was impossible for them to mistake Nash as he sat in the front seat of the auto waving his handcuffed hands. The killing was simply a syndicate hit. The killers had been paid a considerable sum to perform the job so their attack was not made out of loyalty to Nash. Once the hit was accomplished, the killers were murdered to silence them.

The syndicate had taken root throughout the country by then; a formal board of directors would be established early the following year. Local syndicate gang bosses controlled many local politicians. In Kansas City, the local gangleaders were thickly associated with the political machine run by Tom Pendergast. From later reports it appears that everyone in power in Kansas City knew about the impending killing.

Pendergast's "front man" in K. C. was City Manager Henry McElroy. Audett stated that McElroy's daughter, Mary, had been informed of the shooting hours before it happened, and it was Mary who invited Blackie to the station to view the grisly affair. "Me and Mary Mc-

Elroy watched the whole thing from less than fifty yards away," Blackie later commented.

Everything and anything went in Kansas City in those days, except a formal invitation to watch a mass murder. You had to know a special friend for something like that.

[ALSO SEE Charles Arthur "Pretty Boy" Floyd.]

KARPIS, ALVIN ("OLD CREEPY")
Bankrobber, Burglar, Kidnapper ● (1908-1979)

BACKGROUND: BORN ALVIN KARPOWICZ IN MONTREAL, 1908, TO JOHN AND ANNA KARPOWICZ, WHO IMMIGRATED FROM LITHUANIA FIRST TO LONDON, ENGLAND, THEN TO MONTREAL, CAN., THEN TO GRAND RAPIDS, MICH., THEN TO TOPEKA, KAN. SECOND OF FOUR CHILDREN, INCLUDING MIHALIN, EMILY, CLARA. MINOR PUBLIC EDUCATION. MARRIED DOROTHY SLAYMAN, 1931; ONE SON, RAYMOND ALVIN, BORN TO KARPIS AND HIS COMMON-LAW WIFE DELORES DELANEY IN 1935. ORIGINAL OCCUPATION, SHIPPING CLERK. DESCRIPTION: 5'6", BLUE EYES, LIGHT BROWN HAIR, SLENDER, PLASTIC SURGERY SCARS ON FACE, FINGERTIPS ALTERED BY ACID. ALIASES: UNKNOWN. RECORD: BURGLARIZED A TOPEKA, KAN., GROCERY STORE IN 1918 AT AGE TEN, TUTORED IN CRIME BY A LOCAL TOUGH, ARTHUR WITCHEY; WENT ON A PENNY-ANTE CRIME SPREE IN TOPEKA AND CHICAGO FOR FIVE YEARS UNTIL TAKING A LEGITIMATE JOB AS A SHIPPING CLERK; ARRESTED IN FLORIDA, 1925, FOR VAGRANCY AND ILLEGALLY RIDING THE PAN AMERICAN EXPRESS, SENTENCED TO THIRTY DAYS ON A FLORIDA CHAIN GANG; ARRESTED FOR BURGLARIZING A WAREHOUSE IN RURAL KANSAS, 1926, SENTENCED TO FIVE-TO-TEN YEARS IN THE HUTCHINSON, KAN. REFORMATORY; ESCAPED WITH ANOTHER INMATE, LARRY DEVOL, ALIAS O'KEEFE, FROM HUTCHINSON IN THE SPRING OF 1929; STOLE A CAR IN PUEBLO, COLO. SHORTLY AFTER THIS BREAK; ROBBED SEVERAL STORES IN OKLAHOMA; DEVOL ARRESTED LATER THAT YEAR IN CHICAGO AND RETURNED TO HUTCHINSON; STOLE SEVERAL CARS IN AND ABOUT CHICAGO AND HELD UP SEVERAL FILLING STATIONS THROUGH 1929; TEAMED UP WITH DEVOL IN 1930 AFTER THE LATTER WAS RELEASED FROM HUTCHINSON AND ROBBED SEVERAL OKLAHOMA AND KANSAS STORES IN SMALL TOWNS (DEVOL KILLED A NIGHT WATCHMAN IN PERRY, OKLA, AND A POLICE OFFICER IN EARLY 1930 WHILE ROBBING A RESTAURANT IN LEXINGTON, MO.); ARRESTED IN MARCH, 1930 BY POLICE IN KANSAS CITY, KAN. AND RETURNED TO HUTCHINSON TO FINISH SENTENCE; TRANSFERRED TO THE KANSAS STATE PENITENTIARY AT LANSING, KAN. WHERE HE MET FREDDIE BARKER, WHO WAS CONVICTED FOR BURGLARY IN 1926 AND SERVING A FIVE-TO-TEN-YEAR SENTENCE; DIS-CHARGED 5/2/31; ROBBED MANY BANKS AND PARTICIPATED IN THE HAMM AND BREMER KIDNAPPINGS FROM 1931-35 (SEE FRED BARKER); WENT INTO HIDING, FIRST IN MIAMI, FLA., THEN ATLANTIC CITY, N.J. FOLLOWING THE FBI'S KILLING OF FREDDIE AND MA BARKER, 1/16/35; ESCAPED WITH HARRY CAMPBELL POLICE TRAP IN ATLANTIC CITY WEEKS LATER; ABDUCTED DR. HORACE HUNSICKER IN HIS CAR AND USED HIM AS A HOSTAGE TO ESCAPE INTO OHIO; ROBBED WITH HARRY CAMPBELL AND JOSEPH RICH, THE YOUNGSTOWN SHEET & TUBE PLANT PAYROLL 4/25/35 ($70,000); ROBBED THE ERIE MAIL TRAIN, NO. 622 AT GARRETTSVILLE, O. WITH BEN GRAYSON, HARRY CAMPBELL, FRED HUNTER AND A MAN NAMED BROCK IN WARREN, O., NOVEMBER, 1935 ($34,000); ESCAPED DRAGNET IN A PRIVATE PLANE TO HOT SPRINGS, ARK.; ARRESTED WITH FRED HUNTER BY FBI AGENTS IN NEW ORLEANS, 5/1/36; SENTENCED TO LIFE IMPRISONMENT FOR KIDNAPPING AND BANK ROBBERY; BEGAN SERVING SENTENCE IN ALCATRAZ, 8/7/36; TRANSFERRED TO FEDERAL PENITENTIARY ON MCNEIL ISLAND IN 1962; PAROLED, JANUARY, 1969 AND DEPORTED TO CANADA. HE DIED IN EUROPE.

Alvin Karpis was perhaps the most shifty, evasive Public Enemy of the 1930s. He was considered (at least by himself) the last important free-lance bandit of the gangster era following the wholesale destruction of the bankrobbing gangs by 1935. Karpis once boldly stated: "My profession was robbing banks, knocking off payrolls, and kidnapping rich men. I was good at it."

Karpis, born Alvin Karpowicz in Montreal in 1908 of Lithuanian immigrants, began his criminal career early. (His name was arbitrarily changed to Karpis by a grade school teacher because it was easier to pronounce.) At age ten, he was busy burglarizing small stores in Topeka, Kan., where his family had settled following brief stays in Canada and Michigan. The boy's tutor in crime was an eighteen-year-old thief named Arthur Witchey who had done time in the state reformatory and who taught him, among other things, to take what he wanted from store windows by merely tossing a brick through the glass, scooping up the loot, and running down the nearest alley.

For five years, Karpis worked hard at his penny-ante thievery. When his parents moved to Chicago, he did a short stint as a shipping clerk. He later worked briefly in a bakery. These were the only two legitimate jobs Alvin Karpis would ever hold.

At seventeen, Karpis returned to Topeka and there operated with an associate a shabby roadhouse where hot goods were fenced and rotgut booze served under the table. He soon tired of his minor bootlegging activities and began to hop freight trains, traveling throughout the South and Midwest. In these travels, the youth familiarized himself with small towns in a dozen states, noting stores and warehouses which he would later burglarize. Karpis' love affair with trains ended abruptly in Florida where he was arrested as a vagrant and given thirty days on a chain gang.

Upon his release, Karpis traveled to Kansas and attempted to burglarize a warehouse in the first small town he visited; he was caught. He was given a five-to-ten-year sentence in the Hutchinson, Kansas State Reformatory in 1926. No sooner was he inside than he struck up a friendship with Larry DeVol, an instinctive murderer and an habitual criminal.

Karpis looked upon his prison life as a preparatory school where he could learn invaluable secrets of crime. DeVol, a specialist in burglarizing banks, taught Karpis how to crack open safes. In 1929, the two men, whose cells adjoined each other, broke out of Hutchinson by sawing their way through a barred door (the saws were easily obtained in the prison workshop!). The duo went on a crime spree through Kansas, Oklahoma, and Missouri for close to a year, burglarizing dozens of stores, shops, and warehouses.

DeVol was picked up later that year in Chicago and returned to Hutchinson. He asked for a transfer to the state prison in Lansing and worked in the coal mine there. Authorities had established the unusual policy of knocking off time from a prisoner's term if he volunteered for mine work. Because of this, DeVol was paroled in a matter of months and rejoined Karpis in their robbing spree.

DeVol, who often used the alias O'Keefe, made separate sorties into Oklahoma and Missouri. In Perry, Oklahoma, he shot and killed a night watchman who interrupted his burglary of a drugstore. He shot and killed another policeman in Lexington, Mo., when he and another burglar named "Dago" Howard were leaving a restaurant with their loot.

Karpis and DeVol were apprehended in Kansas City by suspicious police who investigated their car and found several weapons and a complete set of burglary tools. Karpis was returned to Hutchinson to complete his sentence. Once there, he schemed his way into getting

transferred to the state penitentiary at Lansing where, employing DeVol's trick, he volunteered for the coal mine. He actually bought some time from lifers in the mine, accruing six month's time within the space of sixty days.

He was given a discharge on May 2, 1931. Karpis had befriended the notorious Freddie Barker at Lansing and when Barker was paroled in fall, 1931, the two teamed up to rob several jewelry stores in Kansas and Missouri. Next came bankrobbing. Karpis became a full-fledged member of the Barker gang. Ma Barker thought of him as one of her own sons and Karpis returned the feeling. Freddie Barker nicknamed Karpis "Old Creepy" because of the gangster's constant dour expression; it was a sobriquet that would become famous in the underworld and synonymous with bankrobbing and kidnapping.

With Freddie, and later Doc Barker, Karpis helped to form the nucleus of one of the most deadly gangs of the 1930s, its erratic robberies and kidnappings planned by Ma Barker for the most part. From 1931 to 1935, Karpis participated in almost every major crime perpetrated by this mob, including the infamous Hamm and Bremer kidnappings (See Barker Gang for details).

When Freddie and Ma Barker were killed by FBI agents in a wild shootout in Lake Weir, Florida, January 16, 1935, Karpis struck out on his own, listed as Public Enemy Number One by J. Edgar Hoover. He went into hiding with Harry Campbell, another remaining member of the Barker crowd, first in Miami, Florida and then in Atlantic City.

Atlantic City police almost captured Karpis and Campbell and their molls, Delores Delaney and Wynona Burdette (whose ambition it was to become a singer of radio commercials) at the Danmore Hotel in early 1935.

Karpis had undergone extensive plastic surgery and had had his fingertips altered through painful acid operations in 1934. The doctor who had performed these operations, Dr. Joseph P. "Doc" Moran, had been killed by Freddie and Doc Barker and his weighted body tossed into Lake Michigan. (Karpis denies having anything to do with this or any other killing committed by the savage Barkers.)

In addition to such surgery, Karpis had his hair cropped short and wore glasses with owl-like lenses. His disguise was apparently ineffective. Led by the housekeeper of the Danmore Hotel, a Mrs. Moreley, police surprised Karpis and Delores Delaney (youngest sister to outlaw Pat Riley, a fringe member of the Dillinger gang), in their room.

Karpis feigned ignorance. He asked if they had come because of a loud party he had thrown the previous evening. With guns aimed at the bankrobber, detectives asked about "the other man," Harry Campbell.

Old Creepy practically shouted out his conversation with the police so that Campbell, in the next room, would be alerted.

"Come out of there with your hands up!" a detective yelled to Campbell through the door.

Karpis thought quickly and then said, "He's probably a little hung-over. We had a party last night and he drank too much. Is that why you're here? Did we make too much noise?" The detectives were taken aback and appeared slightly confused. Karpis offered to go in and get his friend. "He's probably still drunk," he explained. "He doesn't realize that you guys are policemen. I'll get him."

"All right," one of the detectives said, "go in and bring him out but remember we're leveling these guns on you every minute."

Karpis threw open Campbell's door and, as he expected, the gangster was waiting on the other side with a machinegun in hand which he proceeded to fire into the hallway the moment after Old Creepy jumped inside. The burst of gunfire sent the detectives fleeing down the hallway. Huge fragments of plaster flew from the wall and one piece wounded a detective who was taken downstairs for treatment.

Karpis ran to his room, threw on a pair of pants, shoes, and an overcoat, grabbed an automatic and then he, Campbell and the two women made their way down the hotel's back stairs. Delores Delaney had been wounded in the leg by Campbell's wild gunplay. The two women hid beneath a back stairwell but were caught within an hour. The two men ran to a garage across the street from their hotel where their car was parked. Dozens of detectives and FBI men milling about in the street saw them and opened fire. Karpis jumped into the car behind the wheel, Campbell sat in the rear seat, firing his machinegun at the police as the souped-up Ford lurched into the street and swung back and forth until it disappeared down an alley.

Karpis, unfamiliar with Atlantic City streets, led the police in a wild hour-long chase, a running gun battle that inflicted no damage to either side. Zooming in and out of back streets, Karpis finally found a highway leading from town. Police patrols were already on the road, however, and Karpis noticed an unmarked detective car in front of his own.

"I stepped on the gas," he later wrote, "and Harry leaned out the window aiming that big, mean machinegun of his. We caught the cops flatfooted. We'd seen them first, and they didn't make a move. They looked at Harry's gun. Then they looked the other way, as if to pretend they weren't cops. We really embarrassed them, and I thought to myself that those cops wouldn't have the nerve even to report that they'd seen us pass by."

Heading for Toledo, one of his favorite hiding out spots, Karpis abducted Dr. Horace Hunsicker near Allentown, Pa. The doctor's car was emblazoned with medical stickers and Karpis and Campbell thought the vehicle a perfect cover. The gunmen let the doctor out in Wadsworth, Ohio and went on to the bordello madam Edith Barry ran in Toledo.

Karpis' special hide-outs were usually whorehouses, particularly in Toledo, and in Hot Springs, Ark., where Grace Goldstein ran a posh brothel. Once inside Edith Barry's establishment, Karpis and Campbell planned a payroll robbery set up by Oklahoma bandit Fred Hunter. The Youngstown Sheet and Tube Plant would be shipping close to $100,000 through Warren, Ohio in early April, 1935, Hunter told Karpis. Old Creepy made plans to rob it.

Hunter was compelled to exclude himself since he had been a one-time resident of Warren and feared identification as a wanted felon. It was a simple operation. Karpis, Campbell, and a small time heist man named Joseph Rich stopped a mail truck on April 25, 1935 in Warren and plucked a payroll shipment of $70,000. The robbery went according to Karpis' plans and without incident. J. Edgar Hoover exploded and vowed he would capture Karpis himself.

The next and last raid, made by Alvin Karpis in middle November, 1935 was more elaborate. He decided to rob a train, a criminal act unlike the pattern of his fellow bankrobbers but typically imaginative for Karpis once he was out from under the plodding direction of the Barkers.

For months the gangster recruited a hand-picked band of robbers, traveling between Cleveland and Toledo. A peripheral associate of Cleveland's Licavoli mob, and a notorious dipsomaniac, Burrhead Keady, supplied a professional robber named Brock. Karpis himself found aging bankrobber Ben Grayson, recently released from prison. Harry Campbell and Fred Hunter would make up the rest of the holdup unit.

The prodigious plan Karpis worked out even called for his own escape from Ohio to Hot Springs, Ark. in a private plane (a Stinson aircraft which he purchased for the occasion) to be piloted by a maverick airman named Al Zetzer.

After briefing members of his gang on the robbery, Karpis waited for questions. Only Ben Grayson spoke. "Just one thing," the elderly bandit intoned. "Who the hell robs a train in this day and age?"

Old Creepy smiled. This job was going to be done for posterity. "I was going to take a mail train," he would write later. "I thought of the great bandits of the old West, the James brothers, the Dalton boys, and all the rest of them. They knocked over trains, and I was going to pull the same stunt."

The gangster was not unique in his odd nostalgia for Jesse James. He was competing with the dead Missouri bandit, a boyish practice common with 1930s outlaws. Pretty Boy Floyd once wrote a letter to newspaperman R. J. Scott, thanking him for comparing him with Jesse James in an editorial. "Jesse James was no punk himself," Floyd opined.

In mid-November, 1935, Karpis and his gang waited for the Erie Train No. 622 in the small town of Garrettsville, Ohio. When the train stopped in the small station, Karpis and the others waited for all the passengers to alight. The bandits eyed the mail car, the object of the robbery. Its massive door slid back and two clerks poked their heads out, taking the fresh air.

Grayson, wearing a phony mustache and rouged cheeks to disguise himself, climbed into the engineer's cab and placed the two trainmen there under guard. Fred Hunter stayed in the parking lot, guarding the gang's escape route. Brock marched like a sentinel with a shotgun in his hands, overseeing the station's platform. Harry Campbell and Karpis approached the mail car and from beneath long overcoats swung out two machineguns and trained them on the astonished clerks. Unexpectedly, the two clerks ran to the back of the car and cowered among the mail sacks.

Old Creepy ordered them to come out. When they didn't he took out a piece of dynamite and threw it into the mail car. The dynamite stick landed with a loud thump. "I'm gonna heave another stick in," Karpis called to the clerks, "and it will be burning. You've got five and I'm counting now . . . One, two, three . . ."

His bluff worked. The two clerks, plus another mail guard, rushed to the door and plunged out. Karpis jumped into the car, bringing the head clerk along with him. He stood surrounded by mountains of mailbags, not knowing which contained the payroll money he sought. The clerk refused to identify the sacks.

Karpis pointed out that there was another train due on the same tracks and if he didn't get what he had come for, he was perfectly willing to do nothing to prevent the collision. ". . . there'll be a lot of dead people," he told the clerk. "I don't care about that, but you might." The clerk pointed out the sacks.

A Warren, Ohio payroll was discovered in one of the sacks, but the Youngstown payroll, the one from which Karpis expected to glean as much as $200,000, enough with which to retire, was not in the mail car. Old Creepy clutched the machinegun angrily. He was close to killing the mail clerk. The clerk hastily retrieved his ledger to show the gangster that he had signed for only one payroll, the Youngstown money having been shipped on an earlier express. Disgustedly, Karpis and Campbell hauled off the Warren payroll and five regular mail sacks which they loaded into a large Plymouth touring car parked in the station's lot. The gang sped away from Garrettsville along premarked roads, wending their car into Port Clinton where they dragged the mail sacks into a rented cottage.

Inside the sacks, Karpis found only "a lousy $34,000. I'd been expecting six times that amount." He settled for what he had and was soon taking off in Zetzer's Stinson, flying south to Hot Springs. The plane landed on a deserted airstrip and Karpis went immediately into hiding, living at Grace Goldstein's whorehouse. The gangster consoled himself with the thought that he had "held up a train in fine style just like the famous old Western bandits."

The FBI was frantically searching for Karpis throughout Ohio. The thin gangster, meanwhile, moved from Hot Springs to a sharecropper's farm in Paris, Texas owned by Grace Goldstein's brother. Through his excellent underworld contacts, Karpis learned that FBI agents had swarmed through his old hide-outs in Ohio and Arkansas. They were looking for him in New York City, in Chicago; Alvin Karpis was now the subject of the greatest FBI manhunt in history with the possible exception of the search agents had conducted for Dillinger.

J. Edgar Hoover considered Karpis the last of the big shot gangsters and vowed to bring him in dead or alive. The FBI director stated that he had received a letter from Karpis, following the shooting of Ma and Freddie Barker, in which Old Creepy threatened to kill him. (Karpis has always denied this charge.)

As the year turned, Old Creepy, moving with Fred Hunter through Texas and then doubling back to Hot Springs, didn't dare live longer than a week in any apartment or cottage. Sometimes he moved every day. He became jittery, his nerves frayed. A squeal of a car's tires in the night had him reaching for his weapons. His anxiety mounted.

Hoover's anxiety mounted, too. In early 1936, Senator Kenneth McKellar of Tennessee grilled him unmercifully when the FBI director appeared before an appropriations committee. The Senator humbled Hoover in that he compelled the Director to admit that he had never personally made an arrest. Hoover angrily made plans to do exactly that. The gangster in his sights was his imagined nemesis, Alvin "Old Creepy" Karpis.

FBI men tracked him through Arkansas, Florida, Mississippi, Tennessee, and finally, through an underworld informant, located him in New Orleans. Once the outlaw was pinpointed, FBI agents called Hoover who took a fast plane to Louisiana. On May 1, 1936, Karpis and Fred Hunter were surrounded by dozens of agents as they sat in their car in front of their apartment.

According to Karpis, Hoover was called from the cover of a building once the bandits were in custody so that he could personally make his own arrest as a way of vindicating himself of McKellar's charges. When the FBI chief ordered Karpis handcuffed his agents blanched.

Alvin "Old Creepy" Karpis (in shirt) is led to jail here in 1936 an hour after his capture in New Orleans; FBI's J. Edgar Hoover is in foreground. (UPI)

None had remembered to bring handcuffs. An agent's tie was used to bind Karpis' wrists.

Hoover and several agents flew with Karpis to St. Paul where he would stand trial for the kidnapping of wealthy brewer William Hamm. During the trip, according to one report, Karpis took umbrage at Hoover calling him a hood.

"I'm no hood!" Karpis insisted. "And I don't like to be called a hood. I'm a thief."

Hoover refused to see the difference, declining to note that Karpis was a free-lance bandit rather than a member of organized crime, as well as declining to note that organized crime existed in the U.S. He continued to call Karpis a "hoodlum" throughout the air trip.

Karpis attempted to enlighten the FBI chief. "You don't understand," he stated. "I was offered a job as a hoodlum and I turned it down cold. A thief is anybody who gets out and works for his living, like robbing a bank or breaking into a place and stealing stuff, or kidnapping somebody. He really gives some effort to it. A hoodlum is a pretty lousy sort of scum. He works for gangsters and bumps guys off after they have been put on the spot. Why, after I'd made my rep, some of the Chicago Syndicate wanted me to go to work for them as a hood—you know, handling a machinegun. They offered me two hundred and fifty dollars a week and all the protection I needed. I was on the lam at the time and not able to work at my regular line. But I wouldn't consider it. 'I'm a thief,' I said, 'I'm no lousy hoodlum.' "

After five days and nights of interrogation in St. Paul, agents gave up trying to break Karpis; he wouldn't talk about Harry Campbell or any other criminal associate at large or in prison. He was charged with the Bremer and Hamm kidnappings on May 6, 1936, and his bail was fixed at $500,000.

"Do you care to make this bond today?" a court clerk asked Karpis.

"Well, hardly," he said. It was the largest amount of bail ever set for a criminal to that date.

There was no trial for Karpis. He pleaded guilty in hopes of drawing a sentence light enough to permit him to apply for parole years later. He was sentenced to a life term which he began serving in Alcatraz August 7, 1936. Karpis stayed on The Rock until 1962 when he was transferred to McNeil Island, the federal penitentiary in Puget Sound. He was finally paroled and deported to Canada in 1969 where he penned his bloody memoirs and presently resides.

Only months after Karpis went to prison, the remnants of the once powerful, well-protected maverick gangsters were rounded up, primarily through informants. Once the hideout masters and brothel owners were pressured, cracks in underworld secrecy developed into gigantic breaches.

Fred Hunter received a long jail term. Harry Campbell was caught and sent to prison. Larry DeVol was convicted of killing a policeman in Minneapolis and died in prison after receiving a life term. Ma and Freddie Barker,

Earl Christman, and others of the Barker clan were felled by police bullets. Those who sold protection and rented hideout spots to the bankrobbers soon felt the pinch of the law.

Owners of the notorious Harvard Club in Cleveland, Art Hererandt and Anthony Amerback, were closed down. So were Ted and Burt Angus in Toledo, Edith Barry, Joseph Roscoe, and James McGraw.

Boss men who fingered jobs for the robbers such as John J. McLaughlin, Harry Sawyer, and Jack Peifer received long prison sentences. Peifer committed suicide in his cell.

The era's limelight on independent gangsters fizzled and died, leaving the members of the national crime syndicate to flourish in the darkness.

[ALSO SEE The Barkers.]

KATZ, ARTHUR
Murderer ● (1934-1987)

The world of high finance intrigued Arthur Katz all his life. He became involved in a stock manipulation scheme in the 1970s but received immunity for his testimony against others in the scheme. As part of the witness protection program, Katz relocated to Miami, Florida, where he worked as a Social Security claims adjuster. He also used his savings to dabble in the stock market.

When the stock market plummeted in 1987, Katz lost most of the money that he had invested through a Miami office of the Merrill Lynch brokerage firm. On October 26, Katz entered the Merrill Lynch offices and withdrew a gun from his briefcase. He shot and killed his broker, Lloyd Kolokoff, 38, and Jose Argilagos, 51. Then, just as calmly, he put the gun to his head and killed himself.

KEARNEY, PATRICK WAYNE
Serial Killer • (1940-   )

Police in Redondo Beach, Calif., were startled when, on July 1, 1977, Patrick Wayne Kearney and David D. Hill sauntered into a precinct station, pointed to a wanted poster bearing their pictures and said: "We're them." Both men were wanted on charges of killing dozens of homosexual men.

Charges against Hill were subsequently dropped for lack of evidence, but Kearney was another matter. Kearney worked as an electronics engineer for the Hughes Aircraft Company in Los Angeles. The bespectacled, balding little man appeared to be anything but the savage killer he was.

Kearney preyed on transient young homosexuals, finding them in gay hangouts in Los Angeles and Hollywood. His first victim was Albert Rivera, 21. Kearney murdered Rivera in 1975, then stripped his body and placed the naked corpse in a plastic bag, dumping this along the highway.

This was the way in which Kearney killed Arturo Marquez, 24, and John LeMay, 17, in 1976. He continued killing homosexuals and dumping their bodies along the highway from Los Angeles to the border of Mexico. On December 21, 1977, Kearney pleaded guilty to the murders of Rivera, Marquez, and LeMay and was sentenced to life in prison by Judge John Hughes.

Prosecutors were not satisfied, however, realizing that Kearney had killed many more young men and they began preparing additional cases against him that would certainly bring a death sentence. To avoid California's gas chamber, Kearney struck a deal with them. He would provide information on many additional killings he had committed and plead guilty, but only on the proviso that he not be given the death sentence. To solve the old homicides, prosecutors agreed.

On February 21, 1978 Kearney appeared before Judge Dickran Tevrizzian, Jr. He pleaded guilty to slaying eighteen more young men and boys, providing details on the deaths and pinpointing where the bodies could be found. Moreover, Kearney provided information to prosecutors that resolved the murders of another eleven homosexual men, which brought his murder record to a total of thirty-two, one less than that committed by John Wayne Gacy of Illinois.

(ALSO SEE: John Wayne Gacy)

KEATING, CHARLES H., JR.
Swindler • (1924-   )

After Irvine, California-based Lincoln Savings & Loan collapsed, its chairman, Charles H. Keating, Jr., was the target of a federal civil suit involving violations of the Racketeer Influenced and Corrupt Organizations Act (RICO). Keating and his fellow executives of American Continental Corp. were accused of buying the hapless savings and loan in order to divert its funds to themselves through "illegal, fraudulent, and imprudent acts." According to the federal regulators who filed the suit, these acts included concealment of illegal cash payments, forgery, and false and misleading statements made to the regulators.

Following the suit, it was learned that Keating had made substantial campaign contributions to five United States senators, who, in turn, had lobbied the federal regulators not to pursue their investigation of Lincoln's finances too closely. The senators, Alan Cranston of California, Dennis DeConcini and John McCain of Arizona, John Glenn of Ohio, and Donald Riegle of Michigan, were cleared of any wrongdoing, but having their names dragged into the S&L scandal as the "Keating Five" cast a pall over their political reputations.

Keating's troubles continued in November of 1989, when more than sixty federal agents and plainclothes Phoenix, Arizona, police officers seized two luxury hotels that had been centerpieces of Keating's financial empire. As if to signal the end of his economic power, the agents sealed off Keating's office and proclaimed that he would no longer function as president of the hotel management company.

When a congressional committee investigating Lincoln's economic collapse subpoenaed Keating to testify less than a week later, Keating pleaded the Fifth Amendment, stating, "On the advice of counsel, I respectfully exercise my constitutional prerogative and privilege and decline to answer questions here today." His silence during a ten-hour House Banking Committee session served to punctuate the trouble in which regulators found themselves.

Danny Wall, director of the federal Office of Thrift Supervision, testifying before the committee the same day, acknowledged that he and other regulators made mistakes in not having caught illegal activities at Lincoln earlier, but that fraudulent statments by Lincoln's officers had misled them. Political pressure had not influenced the regulators' procedures, Wall testified, but the circumstances of the hearing cast Wall and his colleagues more as investigative subjects themselves than as the lawmen who brought a fraud to light.

Said Congressman Jim Leach of Iowa, a member of the Banking Committee, "Keating is at fault because he is a bank robber, but we in Washington made it, in part, a legal bank robbery."

But there is no such thing as a legal robbery. On September 18, 1990, Keating was indicted on criminal fraud charges in a Los Angeles court. In keeping with his status as a monetary mogul, bail was set at $5 million. Indicted with him were 42-year-old Judy Wischer, who had been president of American Continental; 32-year-old Ray Charles Fidel, the former president of Lincoln; and 37-year-old Robin Scott Symes, Lincoln's one-time chief executive officer. There were those who thought it symbolic of an age of greed that Keating's co-defendants were all a generation younger than he was.

Keating and his henchmen got a break in November 1990, when twenty-two of the forty-two charges were dropped due to their being "too vague." Despite this legalistic leniency, however, the trial went ahead in the summer of 1991. Keating was accused of selling "junk bonds," high-risk but potentially high-yield securities that promised the possibility of profit for investors, but then keeping the proceeds himself.

A highlight of the courtroom proceedings occurred on August 2, 1991, the first day of trial, when a diminutive 90-year-old former Lincoln investor lost her composure and began screaming at the six-foot, five-inch Keating, then grabbed the lapels of his tailored suit and demanded her money back. Before bailiffs were able to escort her from the courtroom, she also punched Wischer's defense attorney, Abbe Lowell, in the stomach.

Superior Court Judge Lance A. Ito, who was later to preside at the sensational 1994 O.J. Simpson murder trial, said he might order searches of anyone entering the court from then until the end of the trial. Outside Ito's courtroom, demonstrators heckled Keating with taunts of "Pay it back, Charlie," and "Mr. Cheating, where's our money?"

Throughout the proceedings, Keating maintained his innocence. After a trial, in which the defense called no witnesses, Keating was convicted on seventeen counts of securities fraud. Keating, his son, Charles H. Keating III, 36; Wischer; Robert M. Wurzelbacher, 37; and Andrew F. Liggett, 34; all former American Continental officers, were indicted anew in December 1991 on charges that they conspired to operate an illegal financial scheme.

When that case went to trial in Tucson in March 1992, Keating again took the Fifth Amendment. Nevertheless, Keating was again convicted. Before his sentencing, more than 120 people wrote letters to the judge to plead for clemency, including Mother Teresa, who vouched for Keating's generosity in support of her charitable works in Calcutta.

On April 10, 1992, Judge Ito sentenced Keating, by now 68 years old, to ten years in state prison and a quarter-million-dollar fine. As Ito explained, Keating deserved the maximum sentence he received because of the large number of victims of Keating's fraud—more than 17,000—and the vast amount of money, an estimated $250,000,000, they collectively lost.

Keating and his son were on trial yet again the following winter. A federal jury in Los Angeles convicted the elder Keating of seventy-three more counts of racketeering, fraud, conspiracy, and transporting stolen property. His son was convicted on sixty-four counts.

Regarding the veracity of Keating's testimony at this trial, which denied wrongdoing and accused regulators of pursuing a personal vendetta, one juror remarked afterward, "I don't want to hurt his feelings, but we all felt we would have liked to have one of those fake expanding noses that grows longer and longer. We just didn't think any of it was valid."

KEATING'S SALOON, BATTLE OF

As Western gunfights go, the battle of Keating's Saloon in El Paso, April 15, 1881, was an awkward melee spawned by drink and racism. The events leading to this reckless shootout began weeks earlier when the notorious Manning brothers were suspected of rustling Mexican cattle and driving them across the border near El Paso to sell them at high prices.

Ed Fitch, a Texas Ranger, and two Mexican vaqueros named Juarique and Sanchez from the raided Mexican ranch, investigated the Manning spread. The Mexicans, who had gone off on their own, were shot to death by hidden gunmen. Seventy-five heavily armed Mexican riders then crossed the border and entered El Paso, their leader demanding an inquest and investigation.

On April 15, 1881, Gus Krempkau, a Spanish-speaking El Paso constable, acted as interpreter during the inquest. At noon, Krempkau left the judge's chambers and walked to Keating's saloon where he retrieved his rifle (no firearms were allowed at the inquest). Pushing out through the swinging doors of the saloon, Krempkau spotted George Campbell, a small-time outlaw and a friend of the Manning brothers who was prone to excessive drinking and nurtured a surly disposition.

Campbell was standing in the middle of the street, shouting at the top of his lungs that El Paso's marshal should have arrested the armed Mexicans who rode into town earlier that day. The marshal was none other than the redoubtable Dallas Stoudenmire, one of the most feared lawmen in the Southwest. Stoudenmire, at the time Campbell began his play, was eating beef stew in the Globe Restaurant, two hundred yards away.

Krempkau was a peace-loving man who tried to avoid trouble when possible. He ignored Campbell's taunts and walked to his horse, tethered in front of the saloon, where he slipped his rifle into its scabbard.

Campbell weaved in the middle of the road, obviously drunk, eyeing Krempkau's back. He shouted: "Any American who would befriend the Mexicans should be hanged!"

Krempkau craned his head about and gave the roughneck a long look. "George," he said slowly, "I hope you don't mean me."

"If the shoe fits you wear it, Gus."

Krempkau ignored the remark, readying his saddle.

Another town drunk and troublemaker, John Hale, staggering from Keating's moments before had heard the heated words and suddenly decided to throw in with his friend Campbell. He dashed up to Krempkau with a drawn gun which he jammed under the lawman's arm. "Turn loose, Campbell," Hale called to his friend. "I've got him covered." Inexplicably, Hale then fired one bullet into Krempkau who sagged to the ground, shot through the lungs.

Hale blinked in amazement at the stricken Krempkau and then, obviously realizing the rashness of his act, ran behind a post in front of Keating's Saloon to hide. Marshal Stoudenmire came on the run when he heard the pistol shot. Two guns were in his hands.

Stoudenmire evaluated the situation immediately when he saw Krempkau dying on the steps of the saloon and Hale hiding behind the post. He fired two shots at Hale as he ran. One wounded a bystander. The second shot was perfect, hitting Hale in the head as he peered around the post, killing him.

Campbell sobered quickly when he saw Stoudenmire. To a crowd collected in front of him which he attempted to flag away with a drawn pistol, Campbell nervously yelled, "Gentlemen, this is not my fight!"

The mortally wounded Krempkau thought differently. He managed to pull forth his pistol and with his last drams of strength squeezed off all six rounds, wounding Campbell in the toe and wrist. Campbell dropped his gun into his other hand and aimed at Krempkau who slumped against the steps leading to the saloon and who was already dead.

Stoudenmire turned and fired three shots into Campbell who dropped to the dust. The marshal walked over to Campbell and rolled him over on his back. With his last breath, the outlaw moaned: "You big son-of-a-bitch, you murdered me."

Another barfly, Patrick Shea, who was completely drunk, ambled from Keating's, crossed the street on wobbly legs, and knelt down next to his friend Campbell. He picked up the outlaw's weapon, an attractive pistol he had much coveted, and said with slurred words, "George, d'ya want your gun?"

Marshal Stoudenmire spat into the street in disgust, wiggled his pistols in Shea's direction and said: "Move on, you little rat." Shea moved on.

Though three men were killed in this zany dispute, it was never learned who murdered the two Mexican riders.

KELBACH, WALTER
Robber-Murderer ● (1938-   )

Hardened criminals and homosexual lovers, Walter Kelbach and Myron Lance (1941-   ) went on a robbery–killing spree in Salt Lake City, Utah, on the night of December 17, 1966. After consuming large quantities of drugs, they robbed a gas station of $147 and forced the young attendant into their car where they forced him to have sex, then Kelbach killed him, repeatedly stabbing the victim. Kelbach and Lance dumped the body along the roadside.

Their next victim was Michael Holtz, another gas station attendant. After robbing Holtz, they forced him to have sex, then brutally killed him. Police by this time had issued an all-points warning on the killers and ordered all gas stations in Salt Lake City closed.

Four days before Christmas 1966, Kelbach and Lance got into a Salt Lake City taxi driven by Grant Creed Strong. Before picking up the pair, Strong thought they looked suspicious. He told his radio dispatcher that if he had trouble he would click the microphone twice.

Kelbach told Strong to drive to for a few blocks, then ordered him to pull to the curb. When Strong did so, Lance put a gun to the taxi driver's head, demanding all his money. Strong handed over only nine dollars. "This all you got, you crumb!" shouted Lance. He then fired a bullet into Strong's head, killing him. The taxi driver never got the chance to click his microphone.

The killers then went to Lolly's Tavern, which was near the airport. The two men stepped inside and Lance said in a loud voice: "This is a stickup!"

"Yeah, sure," remarked one of the patrons at the bar.

Lance casually walked up to the man, 47-year-old James Sizemore, and shot him through the head.

The men went behind the bar and took $300 from the till. As they began to leave the tavern, Kelbach and Lance aimed their weapons at the customers frozen in terror and opened fire, spraying the place with bullets, which killed Beverly Mace, 24, and Fred William Lillie, 20.

Police were called and they quickly set up a roadblock. One of the first cars to be stopped was

Serial killers Walter Kelbach, left, and Myron Lance, center, under arrest in 1966.

occupied by Kelbach and Lance who surrendered meekly. Charged with first degree murder, both men were convicted and condemned to death. Their sentences were commuted to life when the U.S. Supreme Court abolished capital punishment.

Both men still reside at the Utah State Penitentiary. Neither of them have a bit of remorse over the six known lives they took. "I haven't any feelings toward the victims," Lance remarked at one time. Added Kelbach: "I don't mind people getting hurt because I just like to watch it."

KELLY, GEORGE R. ("MACHINE-GUN")
Bootlegger, Kidnapper ● (1897-1954)

BACKGROUND: BORN IN TENNESSEE, 1897, RAISED IN LOWER-INCOME ENVIRONMENT. MINOR PUBLIC EDUCATION. MARRIED KATHRYN COLEMAN THORNE IN 1927. ORIGINAL OCCUPATION, SALESMAN. DESCRIPTION: 6'1", BLUE EYES, BLACK HAIR, HEAVYSET. ALIASES: J. C. TICHENOR, E. W. MOORE. RECORD: KNOWN AS A "SOCIETY BOOTLEGGER" IN MEMPHIS DURING THE MIDDLE 1920S, KELLY WAS RUN OUT OF THAT TOWN AND TOOK UP BOOTLEGGING IN NEW MEXICO, ARRESTED IN 1925, CONVICTED AND SERVED THREE MONTHS IN THE NEW MEXICO STATE PRISON; MOVED TO THE OKLAHOMA CITY AREA AND ARRESTED THERE FOR SELLING LIQUOR TO INDIANS; CONVICTED FOR VIOLATING THE NATIONAL PROHIBITION ACT AND SENTENCED TO ONE YEAR IN LEAVENWORTH, 1930; RELEASED IN 1931; ROBBED SEVERAL SMALL TOWN BANKS 1931-33, INCLUDING THE BANKS IN TUPELO, MISS. AND WILMER, TEX., TAKING SMALL AMOUNTS; KIDNAPPED WITH ALBERT BATES, A SMALLTIME SWINDLER AND CON MAN, MILLIONAIRE OILMAN CHARLES F.

URSCHEL IN OKLAHOMA CITY, 7/22/33 AND HELD HIM FOR $200,000 RANSOM; CAPTURED 9/26/33 IN MEMPHIS BY MEMPHIS POLICE; TRIED WITH HIS WIFE KATHRYN, ALBERT BATES, MR. AND MRS. R. G. SHANNON (KATHRYN'S PARENTS WHO HAD HELPED TO GUARD URSCHEL); ALL RECEIVED LIFE SENTENCES; KELLY IMPRISONED FIRST AT LEAVENWORTH, THEN AT ALCATRAZ WHERE HE DIED IN 1954; KATHRYN KELLY RELEASED IN 1958.

There was nothing spectacular about George Kelly. He was a big, almost lovable braggart who nearly drank up more of his own bootleg hooch than he peddled in the 1920s. He was stupid, too. But Cleo Coleman Shannon changed all that . . . with a machinegun.

Cleo was born in Saltilo, Mississippi in 1904, a pretty, fetching, dark-haired girl who fantasized from childhood a life of glamor, money, and power. Her parents were dirt-poor and little Cleo would imagine her ragged homespuns to be the delicate gowns of princesses. Like many of the underfed, emotionally deprived children of the South and Southwest of those days, Cleo lived in a dream world she snatched desperately from the penny movies. There was nothing else.

When her avaricious mother deserted her father, Cleo packed her skimpy wardrobe and tagged along. Mother knew best.

By the time she was fifteen, Cleo had changed her name to the more romantic "Kathryn" and had married, giving birth to a daughter. She was divorced in 1917 and went to live with her mother.

By 1921, the seventeen-year-old girl was running booze from Fort Worth, Texas to her mother's hotel, where women as well as rooms were for rent. In 1924, Kathryn met bootlegger Charlie Thorne and it was love at first lunge.

That marriage lasted three years. One sultry night in 1927, Kathryn, her sixteen-cylinder roadster purring, stopped at a gas station in Fort Worth, Texas. She was fuming.

"Hey, Kate, what's the matter?" the attendant said.

She gave him a burning stare. "I'm bound for Coleman [Texas] to kill that goddamned Charlie Thorne." It wasn't an unusual threat since the couple carried on animal warfare with each other all the time.

But the filling station attendant was a little alarmed to hear the next day that Charlie Thorne had committed suicide. He left behind a conspicuous and not-too-believable note which read: "I can't live with her or without her, hence I am departing this life." Charlie went out with a bullet in the left temple.

That same year, 1927, George Kelly entered Kathryn's less-than-dull life.

Kelly was a big man, over six feet, with broad shoulders, a pudgy, smiling face, and a growling tough guy's voice copied from gangsters he had met. But George wasn't tough at all and Kathryn knew it.

Introduced to her in Forth Worth as a "society bootlegger," George had the criminal habits of a small-time punk and was as soft as a three-day-old cream puff in a blast furnace. "No copper will ever take me alive," Kelly was fond of sneering out of the corner of his mouth.

Kathryn became enamored of George's phony underworld image and set out to promote him as a hardnosed, high-living bank robber. There was a problem though: George had never robbed a bank.

Throughout the late 1920s and early 1930s, George Kelly had been running rotgut booze into New Mexico, Oklahoma, and Texas. He was happy with his work; as an amiable drunk who impersonated a big time mobster he was content to peddle illegal liquor to smalltown druggists. George didn't even like guns. He never hurt anyone.

"But, you've got to be able to hurt people," Kathryn would plead. "You've got to be tough or nobody will respect you. You gotta have the respect, George. And I know something that will get you the respect." Kathryn went out and bought George a brand new, shiny machine gun.

Next came target practice. In the baking sun that beat down on her mother's new ranch—the E. G. Shannon Ranch of Paradise, Texas—Kathryn set up walnuts on a fence. Months went by before he knocked the walnuts off, but finally George actually became a marksman with the deadly weapon.

Kathryn was proud of him and introduced him to several of the gangsters who paid $50 a night to hide out at the Shannon ranch while they were dodging the law. Sometimes she would drive into Forth Worth and hit the big time speakeasies there.

Kathryn would go along and carry a fistful

Kathryn Kelly built up her husband's desperado image and nagged him into kidnapping Oklahoma millionaire Charles Urschel. (UPI)

of .45-caliber cartridges. She would hand these out to special underworld friends with a whisper: "Here's a souvenir I brought you. It's a cartridge fired by George's machine gun—Machine Gun Kelly, you know."

And the name became the legend. But when asked where George was, Kathryn would imply he was away—up north pulling some high class heist jobs. Meanwhile, the legend was in a small, dirty room on the Shannon ranch, fighting off a bad case of the DT's.

In 1931, George Kelly drove a truckload of whiskey onto an Indian reservation and was promptly picked up without a fight by Prohibition agents. He got a short stretch in Leavenworth Federal Penitentiary. Again Kathryn humped the PR trail, pumping up George's reputation, telling her underworld friends that " 'Machine Gun' is in Kentucky robbing banks."

Kelly's attitude changed in Leavenworth; he began to believe the image Kathryn had been systematically building for him. When he met safecracker Morris "Red" Rudensky outside of his cell one day, he couldn't resist the urge to lie about his exploits and financial assets.

"This place is getting on my nerves, Red," Kelly snarled at Rudensky. "I've got fifty grand sitting on the outside and I could throw a party that'd last for a year. But I can't get at it."

"Why don't you go over the wall," Rudensky suggested.

The thought of escape frightened Kelly. He laughed off the idea. "Hell, Red. I'm too old for that. I'll be out in a year. But if you get any ideas, I'll help you for laughs. You young guys are the ones who should be licking your chops over busting out. And if you do, you might help old George make the wheels spin a little faster."

After Kelly was released, Kathryn married her would-be desperado, took him home to the ramshackle Shannon ranch, and showed him a pile of newspaper clippings. The Barrows and the Barkers and Pretty Boy Floyd were making headlines. They robbed banks with ease. They had made the Big Time.

She got out his machine gun and after a bit more training, Kathryn landed George a job with a two-bit bankrobbing gang. Reluctantly, George hit the jug-knocker's trail.

The first Kathryn heard of him was when he and the boys hit the bank in Tupelo, Mississippi for a few thousand dollars. The take was even less when they knocked over the hayseed bank in Wilmer, Texas. And here a security guard had been machine-gunned to death.

Kathryn was proud of her roving bank robber, her own creation, and she beamed when someone whispered that the guard on the Wilmer job had been sprayed to death by none other than the hard-as-nails killer, Machine Gun Kelly.

But bankrobbing was slim pickings in the early 1930s and as the years ground on, Kathryn got tired of the small takes, George's drinking, and watching the big name outlaws grab the newspaper glory. Her clever mind whirled.

One day, George woke out of his usual drunken stupor to discover a table laden with more newspaper clippings. This time they all dealt with kidnapping. Kathryn was studying them.

Carefully, she pored over the recent Mary McElroy kidnapping, the Charles Boettcher kidnapping in Denver, the William Hamm, Jr., kidnapping in St. Paul with its $200,000 payoff.

"We've got to put the snatch on one of these birds, George," Kathryn told him. "It's the only way to make any money these days."

"Too risky," Machine Gun said.

"We're going to do it, George."

George nodded obediently.

The first person Machine Gun and Kathryn thought of kidnapping was a wealthy South Bend, Indiana businessman. But their plan failed from the start. Kathryn got drunk in Fort Worth and told of the plot to two local detectives—Ed Weatherford and J. W. Swinney—whom she thought were crooked. They weren't and a ring of security guards was thrown around the businessman's house.

The irony of the situation was that the Indiana businessman was broke and the Kellys couldn't have gotten $50 in ransom money.

The next victim of Kathryn's scheming was better off; he was millionaire oilman Charles F. Urschel of Oklahoma City. On the night of July 22, 1933, Machine Gun Kelly and a sidekick, Albert Bates, brushed past the screen door on the porch of the Urschel home. The Urschels were playing cards on the porch with neighbors and looked up startled.

"Stick 'em up," Kelly snarled in his best gangster voice as he aimed his machinegun at the card players. "Which one's Urschel?"

Walter Jarrett, who was sitting with Urschel, remained silent. "All right," Kelly said. "We'll take both of you."

A few miles out of town Kelly had the two men empty their wallets and identified Urschel. Jarrett was thrown out on the empty road and the kidnappers drove off with their captive.

Hoover and the FBI were on the trail hours after getting a call from Mrs. Urschel and the Oklahoma City area was blanketed with agents. But they drew a blank.

The Kellys and Bates then played a cops-and-robbers game of collecting the $200,000 ransom (all in marked bills). They made a date with Urschel's friend, E. E. Kirkpatrick, to deliver the goods. He was to deliver the money by boarding the fast train, The Sooner, speeding from Oklahoma City to Kansas City. After spotting two field fires on the way, Kirkpatrick was to toss the briefcase containing the money from the observation car at the end of the train. But, like most everything else he tried to do in life, Machine Gun botched the deal. He flooded the gang's car and the delay caused the kidnappers to arrive late at the rendezvous without lighting their field fires. They watched helplessly as the train and $200,000 shot past them.

The kidnappers finally made contact with Kirkpatrick in Kansas City. The pickup was awkward. Kelly was so nervous he almost fumbled his relatively easy chore. As Kirkpatrick walked down Linwood Avenue, he noticed a tall, solidly-built man step from a car parked next to the curb. The large man walked abreast of him several feet, nervously glancing at the large, black bag Kirkpatrick carried which contained the $200,000 in ransom money.

"I'll take that bag, Mr. Kincaid [Kirkpatrick's cover name]," the heavyset man whispered.

"How do I know you're the right man?" Kirkpatrick said coolly.

"Hell, you know damned well I am."

The man's appearance was natty. Kirkpatrick studied the rich summer suit he wore, the rakish Panama hat creased sharply down in front, the two-tone shoes. "Two hundred thousand dollars is a lot of money," Kirkpatrick said. "I want some kind of assurance Mr. Urschel will not be harmed."

Kelly growled: "Don't argue with me! The boys are waiting!" Well, one boy was waiting anyway; meek, middle-aged Albert Bates sat blinking anxiously in a nearby car.

But Kirkpatrick held his ground. "I want a definite answer I can give to Mrs. Urschel. When will her husband be home?"

Machine Gun Kelly's huge body seemed to jangle nervously as he shifted from one foot to another. He eyed the black bag. "He'll be home in twelve hours," the kidnapper blurted.

Kirkpatrick dropped the bag to the sidewalk and strode away without turning around. Kelly scooped up the ransom and ran to the car where Bates waited.

Urschel was then released from captivity at the Shannon ranch—Machine Gun had to argue Kathryn out of killing the old man. He was driven to the outskirts of Oklahoma City, handed a hat and $10, and told to grab a cab.

Immediately, Kathryn and Kelly ran north to Chicago and St. Paul, spending their loot like drunken sailors instead of lying low. It didn't take long before the two local detectives Kathryn had blabbed to in Fort Worth led the FBI to the Shannon ranch. Picked up at the Shannon hideout was bankrobber Harvey Bailey, who was recovering from a leg wound. Bates was soon picked up in Denver.

The FBI took Mr. and Mrs. R. G. ("Boss") Shannon into custody and when Kelly learned of the apprehension of his in-laws, he exploded, foolishly writing threats to Urschel and blaming him for their arrest. One letter read:

"Ignorant Charles—
If the Shannons are convicted look out, and God help you for He is the only one that will be able to do you any good. In the event of my arrest I've already formed an outfit to take care of and destroy you and yours the same as if I was there. I am spending your money to have you and your family killed—nice, eh? You are bucking people who have cash—planes, bombs and unlimited connections both here and abroad . . . Now, sap—it is up to you, if the Shannons are convicted you can get you another rich wife in Hell because that will be the only place you can use one. Adios, smart one.
                    Your worst enemy,
                    Geo. R. Kelly
I will put my prints below so you can't say some crank wrote this."

He did. But such bravado was only superficial. Kelly did not enjoy either freedom or the ransom money. When he learned that Bates had been arrested by feds in Denver he shouted to Kathryn, "Oh, my God, it's all over!"

Before the Kellys had a chance to spend all their ransom money, it was over for them, too. The FBI tells the story that when surrounded in a Memphis flophouse, George "Machine Gun" Kelly cowered like a rat caught in floodlights, screaming "Don't shoot, G-Man!"

In reality, it was local police sergeant W. J. Raney who broke into Machine Gun's room and shoved a shotgun into the outlaw's paunch. "I've been waiting for you," Kelly said softly and smiled.

The rest was anti-climactic. The Kellys tore at each other during their resulting trial, each blaming the other. Kelly and Bates got life in prison. Kathryn got the same.

In 1954, after Kelly had been removed from Alcatraz to Leavenworth, he wrote his old victim, Charles Urschel. "These five words seem written in fire on the walls of my cell," Machine Gun lamented. "Nothing can be worth this!" And nothing was. Kelly died in prison.

Kathryn Kelly survived, however, and she was released from the Cincinnati Workhouse in 1958. Like all the other gun molls of the 1930s, this once desperate woman, who saw

Kidnapper George "Machine Gun" Kelly (with dyed hair), happy to be in custody and away from his shrewish wife. (UPI)

herself as a modern Belle Starr, faded unheralded into the kind of social oblivion from which she sprang.

From all reports, she is alive today with the wilting vision of the outlaw she created, a man who came to be known, sadly and tragically, as "Pop Gun Kelly."

KEMPER, EDMUND EMIL III (THE COED KILLER)
Serial Killer ● (1948-   )

Always big and bungling, Edmund Emil Kemper III was a social misfit from early age. He was prone to violence and was absorbed with the images of mutilated corpses. Inside Kemper was a wide streak of sadism that manifested itself at an early age when he mutilated his sister's doll. He then tortured and killed the family cat.

His divorced mother, Clarnell Kemper, was a secretary at the University of California at Santa Cruz. She found it impossible to handle her overgrown boy so she bundled him off to live with his grandparents.

A year later, on August 27, 1964, Kemper crept up quietly behind his grandmother as she was reading a magazine and fired a bullet from a .22-caliber rifle into the back of her head. She fell to the floor and the tall, heavyset boy stood over her, firing two more bullets into her prone body. When his grandfather returned from work, Kemper shot and killed him, then locked the body in the garage.

Kemper then went to the phone and called his mother, telling her what he had done. "I just wondered how it would feel to shoot grandma," he said calmly. His mother told him to call the police. He did, waiting on the porch of his grandparents' house for officers to arrive. Police found him cradling the gun, which he turned over to them without comment.

Sent to the Atascadero State Hospital, Kemper was kept under observation. A file kept on Kemper by the California Youth Authority contained a psychiatric recommendation that Kemper never be released to the custody of his mother. Yet, in 1969, the Authority did exactly that, sending this brutal, towering killer to live with a woman psychiatrists knew he hated.

At that time, Kemper was a giant, standing six feet nine inches tall and weighing 280 pounds. He was not yet twenty years old. When Kemper moved back in with is mother, the indulgent woman did all she could to make her son comfortable. She got him a car and got him a university parking sticker so he could park on campus where he did some odd jobs.

Kemper had no idea of reforming. He studied and learned routes of every back road in the area between Santa Cruz and San Francisco to the north. He then rigged the door on the passenger side of his car so that it could not be opened from the inside. In 1972, Kemper left his mother's home and moved to San Francisco where he began "practicing" a routine whereby he would lure victims into his car.

Cruising along a highway on May 7, 1972, Kemper picked up Anita Luchese and Mary Anne Pesce, two youg coeds from Fresno State College who were hitchhiking. He flourished a knife and assaulted them but surprisingly found himself outside his own car and unable to get back inside.

Amazingly, Mary Anne Pesce actually opened the door and let the killer back into the car. He quickly killed them, then cut off their heads. After dumping the torsos in the mountains near Santa Cruz, Kemper drove back to his room where he kept the heads. To him, the heads of these two girls were souvenirs. Excited at what he had done, Kemper went looking for new victims and found Aiko Koo, who was hitchhiking to her San Francisco dance class. She befell the same fate as Luchesse and Pesce.

Kemper kept hunting for and finding victims, cutting off their heads and hiding the torsos. He added the head of each new victim to his collection. He would later boast that he had sex with these heads since decapitation sexually aroused him. One head bothered him, he later claimed, so he buried it in his yard facing his bedroom so he could talk to it at night.

The killer also practiced cannibalism with the bodies of some of his victims, eating part of the flesh. He refined his modus operandi and studied ways in which to avoid detection, avidly watching the TV show *Police Story* to pick up tips.

Meanwhile, the headless bodies were found and police began a manhunt for the maniac killer. Kemper amused himself by dropping by lunch stands where cops on the case stopped by. He chatted with them and even joined them on a few occasions in their hunt for the "Coed Killer." (This kind of "try-and-catch me" arrogance was displayed five decades earlier by Richard Loeb, killer of Bobbie Franks, who accompanied Chicago police as they searched for him and his fellow murderer, Nathan Leopold.)

A thought began to nag Kemper. He had found killing and escape so easy that he thought he would let down his guard and commit a murder so blatant he would be caught. He did just that on Easter Sunday 1973 when he murdered his mother.

Kemper crept into his mother's bedroom and crushed her head with a hammer. He then cut off her head and removed her larynx, which he tossed into the garbage disposal in the kitchen sink. He then called Sara Hallet, his mother's best friend, and told her his mother wanted her to come to dinner. When Hallet arrived, Kemper strangled her. He decapitated her also. Putting the heads into a sack, he carried these gruesome souvenirs to his car and drove to Pueblo, Colorado. He took a room and waited for the manhunt to begin.

Nothing happened. Kemper read the newspapers. He watched endless TV news programs. There was no mention of his hellish crimes. He could no longer wait. Kemper called Santa Cruz police and told them the whole story. It sounded so preposterous that the police operator hung up several times but Kemper was persistent that he be caught this time. He kept calling back until his confession was believed.

Arrested in Pueblo, he was returned to California, where, in April 1973, "Big Ed" Kemper was arraigned on eight counts of first-degree murder. Kemper asked for the death penalty but he did not get his way. He was sent to prison for life behind the walls of Folsom Prison, one of the worst institutions in California where every inmate has to do "hard time," every day and every night.

KENNEDY, JAMES ("SPIKE")
Murderer ● (1855- ?)

In the days Wyatt Earp clamped law down upon the wild Kansas town of Dodge City, the reigning queen of the saloons was Dora Hand alias Fannie Keenan, a stunning showgirl who sang and danced her way to local fame. Dora, once described as "the most graciously beautiful woman to reach the camp in the heyday of its iniquity," was much sought after by Dodge's mayor, James H. "Dog" Kelley.

Vying for the singer's attentions was the son of one of the wealthiest cattlemen in the West, James W. Kennedy, called "Spike" by his friends. Kelley had his bouncers toss Kennedy into the street one night in 1878 after the young gunslinger paid too much attention to his star attraction.

Just before dawn on an October morning, Kennedy returned and fired a single shot into Kelley's bedroom window. The bullet hit Dora Hand, asleep on a couch, killing her. Kennedy, without stopping to see whom he had shot, whooped it out of town on his pinto.

Four of the most renowned lawmen in Dodge City (or anywhere else) set out after Kennedy—Earp, Charlie Bassett, Bat Masterson, and Bill Tilghman. The frantic chase led across more than a hundred miles of open range. The lawmen rode extra horses in relays in a day and night pursuit. Kennedy rode a single

mount and he rode him to death.

Near Meade City, Kennedy's horse collapsed. The report of his pistol cracking a mercy bullet into his mount brought the lawmen to him. A wild fight ensued with Kennedy holding off the four man posse, potshooting from behind his dead horse. Masterson, a crack shot, finally pumped a bullet from his rifle into Kennedy's arm. The young man was taken without further struggle. As the four lawmen walked toward him, he shouted across the dark plain: "You sons-of-bitches! I'll get even with you for this!"

Minutes later, Wyatt Earp told Kennedy: "Your shot killed Dora, not Kelley."

Kennedy fell to weeping and sobbed, "I wish you had killed me."

He was returned to Dodge City where he was quickly tried and acquitted "for lack of evidence." Spike Kennedy left Dodge forever after the trial, returning first to his father's ranch and then becoming a drifter along the many cow trails, disappearing in the 1880s.

KERRIGAN, MICHAEL
Bankrobber ● (? -1895)

Known in New York underworld as Johnny Dobbs, Kerrigan was one of the most remarkable bankrobbers of his day, a burglar who entered privately-owned banks, cracked the safes in seconds, and was gone. The number of banks he did rob was never determined but it is known that he

Safecracker and fence Michael Kerrigan was one of the most infamous bankrobbers of his day; he died an alcoholic.

fenced more than $2 million in securities (of which he realized a third) over the bar of his saloon on Mott Street.

Kerrigan was a loquacious sort who was once asked by police why so many crooks centered their activities near police headquarters. "The nearer the church the closer to God," Kerrigan quipped.

High living, a series of expensive mistresses, and a gigantic thirst finally brought Kerrigan down. He died in 1895 in the alcoholic ward in Bellevue Hospital. One of the mistresses sold an expensive broach he had given to her, to pay for his funeral.

KERRYONIANS GANG

Exclusive to natives of County Kerry, Ireland, the Kerryonians existed in New York about 1825, one of the earliest organized criminal gangs. The members headquartered on Center Street (now Worth) at Rosanna Peer grocery store. The Kerryonians spent most of their time mugging and beating up Englishmen.

KETCHUM, THOMAS ("BLACK JACK")
Murderer, Trainrobber ● (1866-1901)

BACKGROUND: BORN AND RAISED IN NEW MEXICO. NO PUBLIC EDUCATION. ONE BROTHER, SAMUEL. ORIGINAL OCCUPATION, COWBOY. DESCRIPTION: 6', BROWN EYES, BLACK HAIR, SLENDER. ALIASES: BLACK JACK. RECORD: FORMED AN OUTLAW BAND AT WYOMING'S HOLE-IN-THE-WALL, CIRCA 1898, AND ROBBED SEVERAL STAGES AND SMALL BANKS IN NEW MEXICO THAT YEAR; REPORTEDLY KILLED TWO MINERS 7/2/99 NEAR CAMP VERDE, ARIZ.; ROBBED WITH ELZA LAY (ALIAS BILL MCGINNIS) AND G. W. FRANKS FOUR TRAINS IN ALMOST THE SAME LOCATION NEAR TWIN MOUN-TAINS, N.M. 1898-99 FOR SMALL AMOUNTS; CAPTURED OUTSIDE OF CIMARRON, N.M. 7/13/99 AT WHICH TIME HE KILLED SHERIFF EDWARD FARR OF COLORADO AND ANOTHER DEPUTY, W. H. LOVE; CONVICTED OF TRAIN-ROBBING; EXECUTED ON THE GALLOWS 4/25/01.

Black Jack Ketchum was probably the most unimaginative robber who ever held up a train. Late in 1898, Ketchum, G. W. Franks, and Elza Lay, a member of the Butch Cassidy gang, held up an express train near Twin Mountain, N. M. The take was small, only a few hundred dollars, but Ketchum never looked down his nose or beyond his bushy, black mustache at a good thing. With the same two accomplices, Black Jack held up the same train three more times almost in the same spot, the last raid occurring July 11, 1899.

Ketchum's robbery methods never varied, which surprised no one, including Butch Cassidy and his more professional Wild Bunch riders. Black Jack and his brother Sam (who was also called "Black Jack" at times) had always been aimless cowpunchers who merely drifted into crime when times got tough.

Tom Ketchum was simply unlucky. He drank heavily and could not hold a job. Neither could he hold a woman. He was also a bit crazy. When a girl named Cora two-timed him, Ketchum went berserk. He received a letter from her in which she told him that her lover watched him kiss her goodbye before going off to a cattle drive. "No more than you were out of sight then we went to Stanton and got married." The cruelty of the letter produced an odd reaction in Tom Ketchum. He took out his pistol and, to the amazement of cowboys around him, began to beat himself on the head with the gun butt. Between blows, he yelled at himself, saying, "You will, will you? Take that! And that!"

Then Black Jack Ketchum marched down to the nearby Perico River, loudly damning all women, and gave himself another severe beating with a saddle rope while teetering at the water's edge.

Weeks later, Black Jack and his brother Sam rode to Wyoming's Hole-in-the-Wall with robbery on their minds. Butch Cassidy's men would have nothing to do with the demented bandit, but Elza Lay finally joined him. G. W. Franks, another small-time outlaw, also followed Black Jack to New Mexico where the foursome pulled several minor robberies. Then came the four train robberies of the Sante Fe Railroad near Twin Mountains.

Before the last train strike, Ketchum rode to Camp Verde, Ariz. where he killed two miners in an argument over cards. A large posse

Black Jack Ketchum, being executed for train robbery at Clayton, New Mexico, 4/25/1901. (Western History Collection, U. of Okla. Library)

tracked down the Ketchum gang in Turkey Canyon near Cimarron, N. M. on July 13, 1899. There was a wild gun battle in which two lawmen, Edward Farr and W. H. Love, were killed. Ketchum, wounded in the shoulder, was captured with Lay; Franks escaped.

While Black Jack was in custody and awaiting trial for the trainrobbing his brother Sam displayed his own inventiveness by attempting to hold up the same Sante Fe train his brother had robbed four times. Sam was shot by an alert train conductor named Frank Harrington, but escaped to a nearby ranch. Blood poisoning set in and his arm was amputated. The surgery was badly performed by a cowboy and Sam died of shock hours later.

Though convicted of trainrobbery, Black Jack screamed his innocence while waiting to be executed on the gallows. He watched the erection of the scaffold from his prison cell with interest and when it was done called out to workmen: "You did a fine job, boys, but why not tear down the stockade so the fellows can see a man hang who never killed anyone?"

He had no words for the priest who came to visit him on the day of his execution, insisting that he was "going to die as I've lived." When the warden asked Black Jack if he had any last requests, the darkly handsome outlaw smiled and said: "Have someone play a fiddle when I swing off."

Ketchum's bravado held up all through the ceremonies. He fairly ran up the steps leading to the hangman's noose and once there smiled broadly for the few witnesses standing beneath him. "I'll be in hell before you start breakfast, boys!" A black hood was put over Black Jack's head and from beneath that sinister-looking shroud came the outlaw's last words: "Let her rip!"

The rope did exactly that. When the trap was sprung, the tall bandit shot down through space and the poorly placed weights caused a terrific jolt, tearing Black Jack Ketchum's head from his torso. The outlaw's desire for self-inflicted punishment could not have been more devastating or final.

KING, ALVIN LEE III
Mass Murderer ● (1934-1982)

One-time high school math teacher Alvin King went to pieces in October 1979 when his own nineteen-year-old daughter Cynthia accused him of incest. His trial was to begin on June 23, 1980. The day before his court date, King decided to take vengeance on those who had condemned him before he had been legally judged, those living in his own community of Dangerfield, Texas.

Early in the morning of June 22, King tied up his wife. Loading up his pickup truck with an automatic carbine, automatic rifle, several revolvers, and wearing a flak jacket and helmet from the Second World War, King drove to the First Baptist Church in Dangerfield.

He burst through the church doors and screamed: "This is war!" With that, King opened fire on the congregation. He shot and killed 7-year-old Gina Linam, Gene Gandy, 48, and Thelma Robinson, 78. Three men tried to tackle him as he fled down the stairs of the church. King shot and killed James Y. "Red" McDaniel, 53, and Kenneth Truitt, 49, who was a city councilman.

Running from the church, King shot himself in the head but he survived the wound. While awaiting his trial for murdering five people and wounding nine others, King tore a towel in half and used the strips to make a noose in his cell where he hanged himself on January 19, 1982.

KNAPP, JOSEPH
Murderer ● (? -1830)

Seafaring captain Joseph Knapp lived with his wife in a sprawling New England home at Salem, Mass. along with several other relatives, and a Captain Joseph White, another retired sea captain in his late eighties. White had accumulated great wealth and Knapp conspired to steal it, arranging for the aged captain's murder.

Enlisting the aid of his brother John Francis Knapp and Richard and George Crowinshield, Joseph opened a window in the White home on the night of April 6, 1830. Richard Crowinshield crept inside and made his way to White's bedroom. The old man still had enough strength to resist and Crowinshield was compelled to knock him out with a club. He then drove a stiletto thirteen times into White's chest, killing him.

The Crowinshield brothers, who had been suspected of other murders in the Salem area, were immediately questioned by authorities. Then a letter, written by a convict attempting to extort the Knapp brothers for their part in the murder (the convict had learned of the deed through the Crowinshields) fell into police hands.

The Knapp and Crowinshield brothers were all arrested and tried. Joseph Knapp was promised immunity if he testified against the others. He agreed and named Richard Crowinshield as the murderer. Crowinshield hanged himself in his cell. Then John Francis Knapp was tried, prosecuted by no less a personage than Daniel Webster, who considered the murder

"a most extraordinary case."

It took two trials to convict Knapp; then he was hanged. Since Joseph refused to testify against his brother, he lost his immunity and was also tried and hanged. George Crowinshield was acquitted after his mistress and her friend testified that he was in bed with them at the time of the murder. Crowinshield was set free and died a natural death in Salem decades later.

KNOWLES, PAUL JOHN
Serial Killer ● (1946-1974)

A small-time thief, Paul Knowles spent most of his life behind bars. He was serving time in Florida's Raiford Penitentiary, when he struck up a correspondence with Angela Covic of San Francisco. She found his letters so appealing that she agreed to marry him. Covic got Knowles a lawyer who secured his parole. She then sent him airplane tickets so he could fly to San Francisco.

Once Covic met Knowles, however, her attitude changed drastically. She became so uneasy around him that she broke off their relationship and sent him back to Jacksonville, Florida. Knowles immediately got into a bar fight and was locked up. On July 26, 1974, he picked the lock on his cell and escaped.

Only hours after his escape, Knowles broke into the home of Alice Curtis. He tied her up, stuffed a gag in her mouth, then stole her money and car. Knowles had forced the gag too far down the woman's throat. She suffocated to death. A few days later the fugitive abducted two girls, Mylette Anderson, 7, and her sister Lillian, 11. He killed them because, as he later said, they had recognized him.

Knowles drove to Atlanta Beach where he strangled Marjorie Howe in her home. He stole her TV. Two days later he picked up a hitchhiker whom he raped and killed. On August 23, 1974, Knowles drove into Musella, Florida where he broke into the home of Katherine Pierce and strangled her to death in front of her 3-year-old son.

Driving to Ohio, Knowles met William Bates whom he killed. Bates's naked body would be found a month later. He was strangled. Knowles then drove to Nevada, stopping at a trailer camp in Ely, where he shot and killed an elderly couple. As he drove eastward again, Knowles accosted a woman walking along a road. He raped and strangled her.

Reaching Birmingham, Alabama, Knowles met Ann Dawson. They enjoyed each other's company and Knowles spent six days with the woman, spending all the money she had before he killed her. Knowles then drove to Connecticut, randomly picking out a house in Marlborough. He knocked on the door. When teenager Dawn Wine answered, Knowles forced his way inside. He raped the girl for more than an hour and when her mother Karen came home, he attacked the mother, raping her before her daughter. He then strangled both females to death with a nylon stocking.

Knowles drove to Virginia, breaking into the home of Doris Hovey. He ordered her to get a gun from her husband's gun cabinet. She brought him a .22-rifle and ammunition. Knowles slowly loaded the weapon, then shot Mrs. Hovey dead. Knowles wiped the gun clean and left it beside his victim. Oddly, he took nothing from this house.

Driving to Miami, Knowles contacted his lawyer, Sheldon Yavitz, telling him that he was growing tired of killing people, and that he had murdered fourteen persons. Yavitz tried to persuade Knowles to surrender himself but the killer refused. He did agree to tape his confession before he left to resume his crime spree. Yavitz immediately called the police but by that time, Knowles had already driven out of Miami.

Carswell Carr then met Knowles in a gay bar and took him home to spend the night. It was Carr's last night on earth. Knowles not only strangled Carr to death but he also killed Carr's 15-year-daughter. A short time later, in Key West, Knowles took Barbara Tucker hostage. He left her bound and gagged in a motel room as he drove off in her Volkswagen.

Tucker broke free and called police who sent out an all-points bulletin. An officer named Campbell spotted the Volkswagen and pulled it over to the curb. Knowles jumped out, pointing a gun at Campbell, then jumped into the squad car and sped off with Campbell as a hostage.

Overtaking a new car driven by businessman James Meyer, Knowles handcuffed Meyer and then, with Campbell and Meyer as hostages, drove off in Meyer's car. He drove to a wooded area, forced the two men out of the car and handcuffed them to a tree. He then shot each man in the back of the head, killing them.

Paul John Knowles was now known to almost every law enforcement officer in America. His four-month crime wave through dozens of states had claimed the lives of eighteen people. Hundreds of officers sought him throughout Florida and other southern states where he was reported to have been.

On November 17, 1974, Knowles attempted to break through a police roadblock. His car went off the road and crashed into a tree. Knowles leaped from the car and began running through open country. More than 200 policemen and possemen ran after him. Terry Clark, one of the possemen, dashed in pursuit, knocking down the serial killer with the butt end of his shotgun. Knowles tried to get up and attack Clark who smashed the stock of the gun into the cheek and nose of the murderer.

Once in custody, the sneering, arrogant Knowles bragged how he would escape any jail or prison. On November 18, as he was being transported to a jail, Knowles picked the lock on his handcuff and dove for a sheriff's gun. FBI Agent Ron Angel was faster, shooting and killing Paul Knowles on the spot.

KRAFT, RANDOLPH
(THE FREEWAY KILLER)
Serial Killer (1945-)

From 1982 to 1983, Randy Kraft, a computer programmer, preyed on homosexual Marines in southern California, torturing, mutilating, and murdering his victims. Kraft killed sixteen men in California and perhaps as many more in New York, Michigan, Ohio, Washington, Oregon, and California before he was apprehended.

On May 14, 1983, two highway patrol officers stopped Kraft's car, which was swerving along the road. Kraft got out of the car and walked to the officers and tried to tell them that nothing was wrong. It was apparent that he was trying to keep the officers from his car. When they looked inside of it, they found the dead body of Terry Lee Gambrel, a Marine. Gambrel had died of an overdose from a powerful drug.

Taken into custody, Kraft remained mute. He would admit to nothing. He did not even attempt to explain what a body was doing in his own car. All of Kraft's victims had been tortured and castrated. It was theorized that Kraft hated being a homosexual and loathed his sex partners, that he castrated them to make them into women, but this notion was dismissed as far-fetched by some psychiatrists.

Refusing to admit his guilt, Kraft stood trial in Orange County, California and was convicted on sixteen counts of murder. On November 29, 1989, Kraft was sentenced to die in San Quentin's gas chamber. He has already begun the usual appeal process.

The appeal process, at this writing, now provides condemned prisoners about fourteen years of life behind bars before all legal action is exhausted. It is interesting to note that before 1920 in Chicago condemned prisoners had an appeal period of about a month before they were hanged.

Today, society spends between $400,000 to $500,000 keeping each such killer alive, as was the case with John Wayne Gacy and Robert Alton Harris, both executed in 1992. These ruthless killers managed to squeeze more than a decade of life out of a judicial system hopelessly malfucntioning and enriching only the lives of the convicted and their lawyers.

KRIST, GARY STEVEN
Kidnapper ● (1945-   )

On the evening of December 17, 1968, Gary Krist and Ruth Eisemann-Schier kidnapped Barbara Mackle, daughter of wealthy real estate firm owner, Robert F. Mackle of Miami, Fla.

Krist had a long record of thefts and burglaries before he was twenty-one. Ruth Eisemann-Schier, who acted as his accomplice in the kidnapping, explained to authorities later that they were looking for "kicks."

Barbara Mackle was buried alive by Krist in a box lowered into a nine-foot pit on a hillside near Atlanta, breathing through a tube for 83 hours until Krist collected $500,000 in ransom from Robert Mackle. The ransom, in twenty dollar bills, was delivered to a deserted spot near a causeway leading to Fair Island, Fla.

Kidnapper Gary Steven Krist, convicted of abducting Barbara Jane Mackle, is led smiling to prison for life in Decatur, Georgia in 1969. (UPI)

The girl was released upon receipt of the money and Krist made an escape attempt by sailing across the Gulf of Mexico; he was captured by FBI agents near Hog Island, Fla. after his ship sank. Ruth Eisemann-Schier was also apprehended and found guilty. Krist, who was sentenced to life on a Georgia chain gang, was silent at his trial. Upon hearing his sentence he caustically stated: "Kidnapping? The only kidnapping I know anything about is Robert Louis Stevenson's."

LANSKY, MEYER
Crime Syndicate Chief ● (1902-1983)

BACKGROUND: BORN IN GRODNO, RUSSIA AS MAIER SUCHOWLJANSKY ON 7/4/02 TO MAX AND YETTA SUCHOWLJANSKY. IMMIGRATED WITH HIS FAMILY, INCLUDING A SISTER AND BROTHER, TO NEW YORK. IN 1911. GRADUATED FROM EIGHTH GRADE, 1917, PS 34. BECAME A NATURALIZED AMERICAN CITIZEN, 9/27/28. MARRIED ANNA CITRON, 5/9/29. THREE CHILDREN, BERNARD, BORN 1/15/30; PAUL, BORN 9/22/32; SANDRA, BORN 12/6/37. DIVORCED, 2/14/47. MARRIED AGAIN, 12/16/48, TO DIVORCEE THELMA SCHEER SCHWARTZ, A MANICURIST. ORIGINAL OCCUPATION, TOOL AND DYE MAKER. DESCRIPTION: 5'4¼", BROWN EYES, BROWN HAIR, SLIGHT BUILD. ALIASES: MEYER LANSKY, MEYER THE BUG. RECORD: ARRESTED 10/24/18 FOR BRAWLING WITH SALVATORE LUCANIA (CHARLES LUCKY LUCIANO), SPENT FOUR DAYS IN JAIL, FINED $2; WITH BENJAMIN "BUGSY" SIEGEL ESTABLISHED STOLEN CAR RING WHICH SUPPLIED CARS AND TRUCKS TO NYC MOBSTERS, ALSO PROVIDED GOON SQUADS WHO ADMINISTERED BEATINGS AND LATER COMMITTED MURDER ON ORDER OF INDEPENDENT GANGSTERS (THIS ORGANIZATION WAS TO BECOME THE ORIGINAL MURDER, INC. UNDER THE DIRECTION OF LANSKY AND SIEGEL, LATER LED BY ALBERT ANASTASIA); ATTEMPTED TO KILL FUR THIEF JOHN BARRETT, CIRCA 1923; ATTEMPTED TO KILL HIS OWN GUNMAN, DANIEL FRANCIS AHERN 3/3/28, CHARGED WITH FELONIOUS ASSAULT IN NYC; CHARGED WITH THE MURDER OF PETE BENDER, ANOTHER GUNMAN; BOTH CHARGES DISMISSED; ORGANIZED FIRST BINDING GANG AFFILIATION KNOWN AS "THE COMBINATION," WHICH INCLUDED BOSSES OF NEW ENGLAND STATES CHARLES "KING" SOLOMON (BOSTON), JOSEPH LINSEY, HYMAN ABRAMS, MICKEY ROCCO, AND GANG LEADERS IN THE CLEVELAND AREA—MORRIS KLEINMAN, LOUIS ROTHKOPF, MOE DALITZ, SAM TUCKER, AL AND CHARLES POLIZZI, AND ANTHONY AND FRANK MILANO IN THE LATE 1920S, CONSOLIDATING EFFORTS TO SMUGGLE CANADIAN LIQUOR INTO THE U.S.; SUS-

PECTED OF MURDERING CHICAGO RUMRUNNER SAMUEL BLOOM (A CAPONITE) TO ACQUIRE HIS ILLEGAL INTERESTS IN THE BAHAMAS IN 1929; INSTITUTED GIANT DISTILLERY CONCERNS DURING PROHIBITION, CIRCA 1929, IN AND ABOUT HOBOKEN, N.J. UNDER THE COVER OF MOLASKA, INC., A FIRM ALLEGEDLY MAKING POWDERED MOLASSES; ORGANIZED THE FIRST NATIONAL GANGSTER ENCLAVE AT ATLANTIC CITY, N.J. IN 1929 UNDER THE PROTECTION OF LOCAL GANGSTER BOSS ENOCH "NUCKY" (FOR BRASS KNUCKLES) JOHNSON; THOSE IN ATTENDANCE INCLUDED AL CAPONE, JACK GUZIK (CHICAGO), LUCKY LUCIANO, FRANK COSTELLO, JOE ADONIS, LANSKY, LEPKE BUCHALTER, FRANK ERICKSON, LARRY FAY (NEW YORK), ABE BERNSTEIN OF THE PURPLE GANG (DETROIT), MOE DALITZ, LOUIS ROTHKOPF AND CHARLES POLIZZI (CLEVELAND), CHARLES SOLOMON (BOSTON), JOHNNY LAZIA (KANSAS CITY), ABNER "LONGY" ZWILLMAN (NEW JERSEY), MAX "BOO BOO" HOFF AND NIG ROSEN (PHILADELPHIA), WHO AGREED TO COOPERATE IN CONTROLLING NATIONAL BOOTLEGGING AND GAMBLING UNDER MUTUALLY EQUITABLE REGULATIONS AT THE HOTEL PRESIDENT; ARRESTED WITH LUCIANO AT THE CONGRESS HOTEL IN CHICAGO, 4/19/32 WHILE IN THE MIDST OF A JUNIOR SUMMIT CONFERENCE WITH MAFIA MOBSTERS ROCCO FISCHETTI AND PAUL "THE WAITER" RICCA; RELEASED TWO DAYS LATER; ORGANIZED WITH LUCIANO AND LEPKE A NATIONAL CRIME SYNDICATE IN SPRING, 1934 AT THE WALDORF-ASTORIA; THOSE ATTENDING INCLUDED LANSKY, LUCIANO, LEPKE, JOHNNY TORRIO (NEW YORK), PHILIP "DANDY PHIL" KASTEL (NEW ORLEANS), ABNER "LONGY" ZWILLMAN (NEW JERSEY), ANTHONY "LITTLE AUGIE" CARFANO (ALSO PISANO, MIAMI), HARRY STROMBERG, ALIAS NIG ROSEN (PHILADELPHIA), MOE DALITZ, ALIAS DAVIS (CLEVELAND), ISADORE BLUMENFIELD, ALIAS KID CAN (MINNEAPOLIS), HYMAN ABRAMS (BOSTON), PAUL "THE WAITER" RICCA (CHICAGO); A PERMANENT, MUTUALLY-COOPERATIVE SYNDICATE WITH BOARD MEMBERS REPRESENTING EACH IMPORTANT CITY CONVENING ON ALL IMPORTANT CRIMINAL ACTIVITIES AND DECISIONS; ORGANIZED BOOKMAKING, SLOT MACHINES, FLOATING CRAP GAMES IN NEW ORLEANS, CIRCA 1936 UNDER THE DIRECTION OF LOCAL MAFIA BOSS CARLOS MARCELLO, SEYMOUR WEISS (WHO REPRESENTED THE THEN-POWERFUL HUEY LONG) AND PHIL KASTEL; ORGANIZED GAMBLING IN FLORIDA IN THE EARLY 1930S; ORGANIZED, WITH THE AID OF RULING STRONGMAN BATISTA, THE GAMBLING CONCESSIONS IN HAVANA, CUBA IN MID-1930S; ORDERED THE KILLING OF HARRY "BIG GREENIE" GREENBERG IN LOS ANGELES, CALIF. BY BENJAMIN "BUGSY" SIEGEL, ALBERT "ALLIE" TANNENBAUM, AND FRANKIE CARBO, 11/22/39; ORDERED THE KILLING OF BENJAMIN "BUGSY" SIEGEL IN LOS ANGELES, 6/20/47; TESTIFIED BEFORE THE KEFAUVER COMMITTEE, 1951; ORDERED THE KILLING OF LITTLE AUGIE CARFANO 9/25/59 IN NYC; ALLEGEDLY BECAME "CHAIRMAN OF THE BOARD" OF THE NATIONAL CRIME SYNDICATE FOLLOWING CARFANO'S DEATH; MOVED TO THE BAHAMAS IN THE EARLY 1960S AND ORGANIZED WIDE-SPREAD GAMBLING THERE; MOVED TO MIAMI IN LATE 1960S; TRIED FOR ILLEGAL POSSESSION OF BARBITURATES 6/17/70 IN FLORIDA, ACQUITTED; FLED TO TEL AVIV, ISRAEL IN 1970 TO AVOID

Meyer Lansky, the most durable member of the original 1934 national crime syndicate. (UPI)

INDICTMENT FOR INCOME-TAX EVASION TO LIVE IN THE DAN HOTEL, BUILT BY HIS OWN FLORIDA HOTEL CONSTRUCTION ORGANIZATION; LANSKY RETURNED TO U.S. IN LATE 1972 AND WAS ARRESTED BY FEDERAL AGENTS ON INCOME-TAX EVASION CHARGES.

For his turbulent era, Lansky proved to be an uncommon gangster. That he survived the mass slaughter between mobsters in the 1920s, the purges of the 1930s, and that he endured and grew all-powerful in the modern epoch of crime is attributable to his organizational genius. Lansky, at present, is the only bathtub gin gangster to emerge unscathed and prominent still in a computer-run, impersonal world. Yet, the dehumanized role of today's ambiguous personality burrowing mole-like through life is the exact role Meyer Lansky created for himself. More than fifty years ago Lansky slipped through the back door of crime, a subtle, cunning, murderous elf, a promoter of rainbows that arched to violent death instead of his promised pot of gold.

The beginning was anything but preordained. When Max and Yetta Suchowljansky left the squalid streets of Grodno, Russia in 1911 to immigrate to the U.S., they were determined to raise their three children as upright and substantial American citizens. They settled in New York.

Lansky, who shortened his name from Suchowljanksy early in life, completed PS 34 with honors. His eighth-grade education enabled him to become an apprentice tool and dye maker. Up to this time, little Meyer had no black marks against him. He had stolen nothing. He had side-stepped truancy. He was a "good boy."

Then, on October 24, 1918, while returning home from work with his tools in hand, Lansky's honest life came to an abrupt end. Passing a deserted brownstone, he heard screams. Lansky rushed into the building and found a woman and boy half naked. Before them stood another man who swore loudly and kicked the woman repeatedly. The boy was fourteen-year-old Benjamin "Bugsy" Siegel and he had been sexually enjoying the older prostitute, a whore in the employ of the young man who stood cursing and kicking. His name was Salvatore Lucania who would become Charles Lucky Luciano.

Luciano was about to kick the prostitute again when Siegel, an ineffectual pen knife in his hand, rushed the apprentice hoodlum. Luciano tossed him aside. Lansky, using one of his tools, advanced on Luciano and hit him in the head, sending Luciano reeling. At that moment, police rushed through the door and arrested all three for disorderly conduct.

Luciano and, because of his age, Siegel, were released within hours. Lansky was held for two days and then discharged after he paid a $2 fine. The episode was to lead to Lansky's permanent departure from a legitimate way of life and his willing entry into lucrative and sinister crime. Siegel, who became his devoted follower, helped Lansky to organize a floating crap game which became so successful that the two youngsters were soon taken under the wing of gangster "Little Augie" Orgen and, later, Joe the Boss Masseria.

They received protection against police interference from the gangsters in return for a forty per cent kickback from the crap game's profits. The two hoodlums supplemented their income by stealing from stores and pushcarts and then fencing the goods.

Lansky finally reasoned that the uptown gangsters weren't needed. He could supply his own muscle to protect his gambling interests. His most faithful "slammer" in those days was Phil "Little Farvel" (also "The Stick") Kovolick, a hulking brute.

In one free-for-all led by Kovolick, several Mafia collectors attempting to muscle in on Lansky's operations were sent to the hospital. Little Meyer was arrested and once more fined the nominal sum of $2 for disorderly conduct. As he walked from the courtroom, he was stopped by none other than Lucky Luciano, the man he had once beaned in the head.

Instead of battling, the two men, at Luciano's insistence, held a night-long conference at which Lucky outlined his plans to some day consolidate all the young mobsters in New York in a loose but cooperative "combination." This program concurred with Lansky's ideas but it was realized that the reigning gangsters, the Kid Droppers, the Owney Maddens, the "Mustache Petes" of the old world Mafia, would have to be deposed. That would take time, both knew. They would wait, plan, and organize gangs of devoted followers. Their time would come, Luciano said.

Lansky's first recruit and unquestioning liegeman was Benjamin "Bugsy" Siegel. The two began small as suppliers of fast cars to various gangs. Lansky then branched into handling stolen cars. He became an expert at changing the appearance and serial numbers of any car.

These cars were then sold outright to unsuspecting persons or used by gangsters. Siegel did the stealing, Lansky the remodeling. By 1921, the pair reaped tens of thousands of dollars from their hot car racket. In addition to renting out their stolen cars, the Bug and Meyer franchised fleets of trucks to haul illegal whiskey.

When the gang became larger, Lansky rented out his men as professional murderers, killers who, for the right price, would dispose of anyone fingered by a mobster. The killing was done on a contractual basis and the new service came to be known as Murder, Inc., the most feared organization in the underworld.

In 1923, Lansky and Siegel masterminded elaborate burglaries, their men specializing in stealing furs from warehouses. One of their gunmen, an ex-con named John Barrett, held out on Lansky after a successful fur haul. He was brought before a sort of tribunal headed up by Louis Buchalter, labor racketeer and one

of Lansky's closest friends. The tribunal was Lansky's idea and by placing Buchalter, the leader of a different gang, at its head, little Meyer had conveniently established an air of impartiality in any judgment handed down.

Barrett admitted he had held back several expensive furs from the robbery. He explained his reasons to the fish-eyed Lepke: "It ain't fair, for us to take all the risks while he [Lansky] gets most of the gravy."

"Bull," Bugsy Siegel shouted.

The situation was serious. Barrett had committed a serious offense, far more serious than holding out a few furs for himself; he had mutinied against his boss. After Barrett was sent from the room, Lepke and Lansky decided to kill him.

With Bugsy Siegel behind the wheel of a car, Barrett was ordered into the back seat. Meyer, and his brother Jake, got in with him. So did their chief torpedo, Sam "Red" Levine.

Levine was about to shoot Barrett but Lansky whispered that killing him in the car would get the seat bloody. He told Siegel to stop the car. "Get out!" Lansky ordered Barrett. The terrified gunman jumped from the auto and began to run. Levine, as the car pulled away from the curb, leaned out the window and shot the running Barrett several times.

Barrett was picked up minutes later, rushed to a hospital and then agreed to sign a complaint charging Siegel, Levine, and Lansky with attempted murder. Days before he was about to be released from the hospital, however, Barrett received a visitor, Daniel Francis Ahearn, a Lansky associate. Ahearn brought Barrett a tasty-looking plate of *chiboni*. The wounded gunman told Ahearn that he was too weak to eat the food but to leave it. When the gangster left, Barrett had the food examined and it was discovered to be loaded with strychnine.

The would-be informer changed his mind and refused to identify anyone. He returned the stolen furs to Lansky, meekly apologized, and was taken back into the gang. As far as Lansky was concerned, Barrett had learned his lesson.

Daniel Ahearn, on the other hand, received a similar lesson concerned with the pecking order of Lansky's gang. Ahearn, much concerned with elevating his position with Lansky, was once present in 1928 when Bugsy Siegel and

Lansky fell to arguing. He seriously misjudged the common feeling the two gangsters shared for each other, intervened, and slapped Siegel in the face. To his amazement, both Siegel and Lansky left the room without saying a word.

The following night Ahearn saw a car screech to a halt next to him as he walked along a deserted street. Jake Lansky was at the wheel. The man he had once tried to poison on Meyer Lansky's orders, Barrett, was in the back seat. In front, aiming a pistol straight at his head was Bugsy Siegel. Ahearn took a few steps away from the car and Siegel fired twice, hitting Ahearn in the face and arm. The hoodlums roared off in their car, leaving the wounded man for dead. When found by police, Ahearn named Lansky as his assailant.

Several phone calls were made to Ahearn to his hospital bed from unknown persons and he suddenly lost his memory, recanting his accusation. He broke from the gang on his release. A close Ahearn associate, Peter Bender, however, was determined to avenge his wounded friend. He grabbed two pistols following the Ahearn shooting and stated he would kill Meyer Lansky. It was the last anyone ever heard of Pete Bender.

Lansky's ruthless control over his own gang was tempered with establishing a hierarchy of authority. There was never a boss of bosses in what has been termed the Jewish mobs, particularly those of Lansky's and Lepke's. Their men were allowed, for services rendered, to rise through the ranks to positions of self-satisfying power as did Bugsy Siegel with Lansky and Jacob "Gurrah" Shapiro with Lepke.

As the 1920s closed, Lansky extended this attitude in his relationships with Mafia-controlled gangs, such as that headed by Joe the Boss Masseria in which his friend and fellow dreamer, Lucky Luciano had clawed his way to second-in-command. When Masseria was marked for murder by Luciano to appease rival Mafia gangster Salvatore Maranzano as well as to place Luciano in a position of absolute authority, it was Lansky who proposed the killing of Joe the Boss by a "universal" execution squad made up of members from different New York gangs. It was Lansky's first attempt, in 1931, at the unification of the underworld. He loaned Bugsy Siegel to Luciano for this express purpose.

Lansky had already brought together various gang chiefs from other cities in the late 1920s to establish state-to-state cooperation in bootlegging and gambling. He and Luciano had organized the 1929 Atlantic City convention which was attended by such underworld powers as Al Capone, Frank Costello, Joe Adonis, Charles Solomon, Johnny Lazia, and Abner Zwillman, all representing the most important cities in America.

In 1934, Lansky took time from his lucrative gambling interests to organize with Luciano the original national crime syndicate. He became a board member, representing certain underworld interests and participated in all major decisions, such as ordering the death of Dutch Schultz in 1935.

By 1936, Lansky had branched out his gambling empire to include Florida and Cuba. He worked out a careful deal with Cuban dictator Fulgencio Batista by which he was given a complete monopoly of gambling in Havana in return for kicking back fifty per cent of profits to the ruling military junta, namely Batista.

New Orleans became another city where Lansky's gaming operations flourished, much to the cooperation of Huey Long, according to one report. The inconspicuous-looking Meyer Lansky then became the syndicate's banker, secreting millions of dollars in foreign banks. He was content to allow Luciano and others to bully the leadership of the crime cartel. In dealing with the Italians, Lansky always took the self-deprecating role, praising the Lucianos and the Genoveses and demeaning non-Latin gangsters. He once remarked to syndicate gangsters Marshall Caifano and California powerhouse Jack I. Dragna, when "Russian Louis" Strauss vanished after trying to pocket board funds: "That's the last time a Jew will cheat a Sicilian in this town [Las Vegas]."

When Luciano went to prison after being convicted of directing wholesale vice in New York City, Lansky and Frank Costello looked after Lucky's interests. It was Lansky who acted as one of the go-betweens who formed the queer alliance of Luciano and U.S. Navy Intelligence chiefs that strengthened waterfront security and provided information vital to military authorities for the invasion of Sicily in 1943.

Lansky, ever the server, saw Luciano off at the dock in 1946 when Lucky was deported to Italy, and was one of those who went to

Havana the following year when Lucky sneaked into Cuba to call together a gangster enclave there.

His old friendship with Bugsy Siegel was strained to the breaking point in 1947 when the Bug defied the national syndicate and refused both to repay a huge loan the organization had made to him to build the Flamingo Hotel and Casino in Las Vegas, and to turn over his interests in certain wire services handling betting results to Chicago mobsters.

Siegel had been given a huge bankroll and the blessings of the syndicate when departing for California under orders to establish rackets there in 1937. He had moved into the movie colony and through blackmail, extortion, and pure threat had reaped a fortune. He was the first big time hoodlum to begin the development of Las Vegas as a high roller gambling spa. His success went to his head and his defiance of syndicate orders to "cooperate" embarrassed his sponsor, Lansky.

Little Meyer tried to talk the egotistical Siegel into obeying orders. When the Bug refused, he was killed. "I had no choice," Lansky is reported as saying following Siegel's execution in his mistress' home on June 20, 1947.

Lansky's willingness to cooperate with Italian elements of the syndicate, even to disposing of his friend Siegel, resulted in his present-day status, one of immunity and immense power. When Mafia-bred Little Augie Carfano (nee Pisano) attempted to grab off Lansky's Florida gambling interests in 1959, the Italian members of the board looked the other way, letting Lansky and his associate Vincent "Jimmy Blue Eyes" Alo, handle things. Carfano and Mrs. Janice Drake were shot to death by unknown assassins, February 25, 1959, as they were being driven to the New York apartment of Vincent Alo.

While the Mafia dealt with its unruly elements in the 1960s—concentrating on the pacification of certain Eastern Young Turk factions such as the Gallo brothers—Lansky broadened his gambling cartel to the Bahamas where he purchased interests in several casinos.

Though he traveled widely for the syndicate during the early 1960s, Lansky had become the invisible gangster. Not once in five years from 1960 to 1965 was his name ever mentioned in the American press. He and his gambling cohorts—literally hundreds of ca-

Little Augie Carfano tried to muscle in on Lansky's gambling interests in Florida and wound up murdered on 2/25/59.

sino operators, professional card sharps, dealers, skimmers—moved into various South American countries such as Colombia and Venezuela. He cemented connections with syndicate-inspired casinos in Hong Kong (an important source of narcotics). He moved into Haiti when his gambling empire was swallowed up in Cuba by Fidel Castro. He was a busy man, and he made millions.

Just how far Lansky's connections reach into the American government has yet to be determined, but it is a fact that he has success-

Meyer Lansky, head of the board for the American South and also for the national syndicate's banking operations. He returned to the United States in 1972 and was arrested by federal agents on income-tax evasion charges.

fully dodged every effort to jail him on deportation and income-tax charges. When he feared indictment of income tax evasion in 1970, Lansky fled to Tel Aviv, Israel to take up residence in the swanky Dan Hotel. He returned to the U.S. in late 1972 and was arrested on the charge of income-tax evasion.

Lansky's gambling interests spanned the world and so did his bank accounts (his holdings were estimated to be close to $300,000,000). Little Meyer had outfoxed the government, gang rivals, ambitious police authorities, and the most calculating minds of the underworld. His faith in the monster syndicate he, Luciano, Lepke, and others spawned was unabiding. "We're bigger than U.S. Steel," he once boasted. He had three ulcers to prove it.

[ALSO SEE Louis "Lepke" Buchalter, John "Legs" Diamond, Charles "Lucky" Luciano, Dutch Schultz, Benjamin "Bugsy" Siegel, Joseph "Doc" Stacher, The Syndicate, Abner "Longy" Zwillman.]

LAPAGE, JOSEPH
Murderer ● (? -1875)

A French-Canadian lumberjack, Lapage worked at odd jobs in New England. In 1874, Lapage killed and mutilated Miss Marietta Ball, a school teacher, near St. Albans, Vt.

A year later, Lapage hit seventeen-year-old Josie Langmaid over the head with a club as she was on her way to school in Pembroke, N. H. After dragging her body into the woods, Lapage decapitated the girl with an axe and then proceeded to mutilate her. He then ravished the corpse.

Lapage was apprehended, tried, and convicted. He was hanged in 1875.

LATHAM, JAMES DOUGLAS
Serial Killer ● (1942-65)

Just as Mark Essex went on a killing rampage in New Orleans because he hated whites, James Douglas Latham and George Ronald York (1943–1965) decided to "wage war against the world," killing mostly blacks in their 1961 crime spree. Both men were under 20, Latham 19 and York 18, when they broke out of the guard house at Fort Hood, Texas, on May 24, 1961.

Both buck privates hated serving under black officers and decided to escape the Army. They murdered seven people in five states—Florida, Tennessee, Illinois, Kansas, and Utah, mostly in robberies. They were finally apprehended at a Kansas roadblock. One of the revolvers found in their car had eight notches on it.

Kansas tried and convicted the pair for killing Otto Ziegler, a 62-year-old farmer who had stopped to help them when he thought they were having car trouble.

Latham and York were glib and defiant at their trial. They asked for no favors, except one. They wanted to be executed together. Convicted and condemned, both men went to the gallows at Lansing, Kansas on June 23, 1965.

LATIMER, IRVING
Murderer ● (1866-1946)

BACKGROUND: BORN AND RAISED IN JACKSON, MICH.
OF WELL-TO-DO PARENTS. COLLEGE EDUCATED. OCCU-
PATION, PHARMACIST. DESCRIPTION: 5'10", BROWN
EYES, BLACK HAIR, SLENDER BUILD. ALIASES: NONE.
RECORD: MURDERED HIS MOTHER 1/24/1889 FOR HER
ESTATE (SOME REPORTS HAVE IT THAT HE ALSO MUR-
DERED HIS FATHER PREVIOUSLY TO COME INTO CER-
TAIN INHERITANCE MONIES); TRIED AND CONVICTED
OF MURDER IN THE FIRST DEGREE; SENTENCED TO LIFE
IMPRISONMENT IN MICHIGAN STATE PRISON IN JACK-
SON; PARDONED 5/11/35; DIED IN ELOISE STATE HOS-
PITAL, 1946.

The web of invented facts which Irving Latimer spun round himself at the time of his mother's murder was intended to protect him with a foolproof alibi. Instead, it entrapped him.

That Latimer was a clever, handsome, dashing young man in 1889 there can be no doubt. Women at Jackson's high society balls vied for his attention. He was also known to the fair belles of that city as a bit of a rake. Yet, at 23, he was a pillar of the community. He owned his own drugstore and taught Sunday School.

It seems that Latimer's tastes were rich, for he had been sinking heavily into debt. His mother had advanced him $3,000 to pay some of his creditors.

But this loan had nothing to do with maternal indulgence. Mrs. Latimer, ever the straight-laced Victorian, held her son's note, a handwritten I.O.U. which she fully intended to collect on January 31, 1889. She never lived that long.

On the night of January 24, 1889, someone broke into the Latimer home through a cellar door. From the basement, the intruder carefully walked upstairs to the second floor, entered Mrs. Latimer's bedroom and, as the woman woke hazily from her sleep, reduced her head to a bloody pulp with a heavy instrument and then shot her. The invader, without disturbing her considerable jewelry and other valuables, then retraced his steps and left the premises again by the cellar door. The family watchdog, Gyp, made no attempt to stop the killer or sound a warning.

The next morning, curious neighbors who noted that Mrs. Latimer did not let Gyp outside for his morning ritual as was her habit, inspected the house. They found the broken cellar door. They pounded and rang for Mrs. Latimer but got no answer. Police were summoned and the body of Mrs. Latimer was quickly discovered. Where, authorities wanted to know, was Irving?

They were told that Mrs. Latimer's fun-loving son was in Detroit. One thing puzzled Jackson Police Chief John Boyle. He was unable to find Latimer at Detroit's exclusive Cadillac Hotel, where he was known to stay. Instead, he found the young man registered at the second-rate Griswold Hotel. Latimer rushed home as soon as he was notified of his mother's death.

Latimer's untimely trip aroused Boyle's suspicions from the beginning. Irving had told the boy who helped him in the drugstore that he was going to the big city to attend a funeral. Upon his return, Latimer denied that there had been any funeral. He said he only used that excuse because he didn't want his employee to know his business. His business? Irving admitted it was a girl, a peccadillo named Trixy. He said he was embarrassed to talk about getting emotionally involved with a professional tart.

The Police Chief nodded understandingly. Then he went to check on Latimer's story, systematically running down witnesses who might have seen him. There were many between Jackson and Detroit, Michigan, all unwittingly hostile to Latimer's claim.

In Detroit, Boyle found a porter at the Griswold who recognized Latimer from photos as the man he saw sneaking out a side entrance of the hotel at 10 p.m. on the night of the murder. Two conductors of the Michigan Central railroad then verified that it was Latimer who frantically hopped aboard the 10:10 p.m. train for Jackson that night, getting off at Ypsilanti and then catching another train to take him on to Jackson where he arrived shortly before midnight, a half hour before Mrs. Latimer's murder.

Solid witnesses then cropped up faster than those summoned by Scratch to face Daniel Webster in his dynamic duel with the Devil. Their statements damned the young Latimer phrase by phrase.

Another conductor for the railroad stated

that at 6:20 a.m. on the morning of January 25, 1889, only hours after Mrs. Latimer had been slaughtered, before her neighbors became suspicious of her silent house, he had picked up a young man who demanded a sleeper on the Detroit-bound train, paid for it on the train, and dove into it, immediately drawing the curtains. A porter supported the conductor's remarks. The man was identified from photos as Irving Latimer. The young man's strange conduct was further emphasized when he leaped from the slow-moving train in West Detroit fifteen minutes before the train came to a halt in the main station.

Boyle went back to the Griswold Hotel. A chamber maid stated that she had gone into Latimer's room on the morning of the 25th to make up the bed. It had not been slept in. As she left Room 34 and walked down the passage, she turned to see Latimer, nervously scanning the hallway as he let himself into his room. A barber whose shop was next to the Griswold Hotel testified that at 10 a.m. the same morning, Latimer had entered his premises and demanded a shave. He wore no cuffs on his shirt (in those days cuffs were detachable as were the collars of shirts; Latimer prided himself on his shirtcuffs because of the diamond cufflinks he habitually sported). There was blood on his coat. Latimer told the barber that he had had a nosebleed earlier that morning.

Boyle's excellent investigative prowess turned up one more damning piece of evidence. Aside from the terrible beating Mrs. Latimer had taken about her head, an autopsy revealed that she had been shot twice. Two .32-caliber bullets were recovered from her brain. Boyle found a .32-caliber revolver in a desk drawer in Latimer's drugstore.

The young man was arrested. His marvelous cufflinks were in his pocket, but he possessed no cuffs. His shoes and clothing were splattered with blood. It was the nosebleed, Latimer explained.

At his trial Irving Latimer continued to defend his elaborately-constructed alibi. He explained his night flight to Ypsilanti as an effort to find his love-mate Trixy, who had run away from him in Detroit. He had then gone on to Jackson to get some sleep on a cot in the rear of the drugstore which was sometimes his habit. Early on the morning of the 25th, he had remembered that his clothes and

bags were still in Detroit and he took the early train back there to retrieve them. He had not gone near his mother's house, he insisted, during the night of her murder.

No one believed Irving Latimer, least of all the jury. In a record twenty minutes they returned a verdict of first degree parricide and he was sentenced to life imprisonment, Michigan having no death penalty.

Latimer became a model prisoner. He was made a trusty, and pharmacist's aide. As such he had access to deadly drugs. On the night of March 26, 1893 Latimer served his guards a midnight lunch of sardines and lemonade. The lemonade was lethal; he had dosed it with prussic acid and opium. It killed one guard and rendered the other unconscious.

Irving escaped but was picked up days later. He hadn't meant to kill the guard, he explained. It was an "accident." Too much prussic acid got into the lemonade, he said. It wasn't his fault.

There would be no parole for Latimer now. He would rot in prison. The calm, finely-mannered inmate did his time well. By 1907 he had become a trusty again and was placed in charge of landscaping the prison grounds. By the mid-1920s he had become the prison's most celebrated old con, giving out interviews to the press on the decline of class prisoners: "We used to have train bandits, bankrobbers, safe blowers—all fairly intelligent men. Now what do we have? A mob of ignorant, half-educated boys who think they know it all."

Years dragged on and changes came. The state prison was moved to new quarters but Irving Latimer declined to go. His cell was virtually a modest apartment with books, plants, desk. He liked it there. It was his home. The state considered him a harmless old man and allowed him to stay on as a watchman for the deserted prison. In 1935, he was set free after spending 46 years in prison. He loitered about Jackson's Depression-torn streets, and was picked up several times for vagrancy. There was no place for him on either side of prison walls anymore. He was finally taken in by a state-run old people's home where he died in 1946 still claiming his innocence as a victim of circumstances, a man chasing an imaginary tart named Trixy down through five decades.

LAWSON, BENNIE L.
Mass Murderer ● (1969-1994)

The proliferation of guns and their availability to anyone in the U.S., including felons, has contributed greatly to the increase in street slaughter in the past decade. Lethal proof of this problem was Bennie L. Lawson, a former college student from the District of Columbia.

On November 22, 1994, Lawson walked into the D.C. Police Department with semi-automatic weapons and, once in the homicide division, opened fire. He killed a police sergeant and two FBI agents who were working on unsolved murders in the D.C. area, before he himself was killed. Two other persons, including an FBI agent were wounded as Lawson sprayed the area with bullets.

Lawson had a long criminal record, including convictions on thirteen weapons and ammunition charges. Earlier in the day of the shooting Lawson had been brought in for questioning about a triple homicide occuring the week before. He was released after investigators failed to get a confession from him, but his car was kept as evidence in that case.

This was what incensed the killer, according to police, and prompted him to return to police headquarters seeking vengeance. Oddly, the police department building in Washington, D.C. was, at the time of the shooting, the only law enforcement building in the city that did not have metal detectors, which would have quickly identified the concealed weapons Lawson was carrying.

LE BLANC, ANTOINE
Murderer ● (? -1833)

Arriving from France April 26, 1833, LeBlanc took a job with the Sayre family in rural New Jersey as a common laborer. He resented his lowly position, especially the fact that he was compelled to sleep in a woodshed.

On May 2, 1833, LeBlanc decided to better his way of life and invaded the Sayre home with intent to rob them. He beat both Mr. and Mrs. Sayre to death with a shovel and placed their bodies under a heap of manure.

Hearing noises in the Sayre house he rushed to the attic where he found the Negro maid and killed her. Visitors to the Sayre place apprehended him and he was quickly tried; he was executed on the gallows September 6, 1833 at Morristown, N. J.

LeBlanc was a roguishly handsome fellow who, apparently, had a way with the ladies. As one historian's account has it, his execution took place on the Morristown green and "twelve thousand persons were present, of which the majority were females."

LECHLER, JOHN
Murderer ● (? -1822)

Mary Lechler was about as unfaithful a wife as one could be, particularly when her neighbor, a Mr. Haag, arrived at her front doorstep. Unfortunately, her husband John, who caught Haag and his wife in bed, was not an understanding fellow. He threatened to kill them both.

In desperation, Haag offered Lechler a large sum of money, writing out a promissory note. When he later refused to pay, Lechler went berserk, rushing home where he strangled his wife and then hanged her from an attic beam. He then charged to Haag's home, pistols in hand.

When Haag refused to come out, Lechler fired through his front door, shooting and killing Mrs. Haag.

Lechler was hanged in Lancaster, Pa. October 25, 1822.

LEE, JOHN D.
Murderer ● (? -1877)

When Mormon Bishop John D. Lee became an Indian agent in Utah in the early 1850s, he had more on his mind then keeping the peace. Arming his wards and enlisting the aid of white renegades dressed as Indians, Lee began leading attacks on wagon trains heading for California.

With a large body of such men, Lee, in September of 1857, jumped a wagon train of 140 immigrants. The foreigners valiantly fought off the attack for almost three days. Then Lee sent word that if they surrendered to him, giving up their gold and some livestock, they could continue their trip.

The immigrants threw down their arms and came out of their wagon circle, only to be slaughtered at Lee's command. Only seventeen children were spared.

It wasn't until 1875 that Lee was accused of the Mountain Meadows massacre and was tried. His second trial proved him guilty and he was condemned to death. Lee was shot by a firing squad near Salt Lake City, Utah, March 23, 1877.

LENOX AVENUE GANG

Harry "Gyp the Blood" Horowitz headed up the Lenox Avenue gang just after the turn of the century. The gang was composed of professional pickpockets and burglars who centered activities on 125th Street in Manhattan.

This was a short-lived gang which police broke up after making several arrests and getting lengthy convictions. Gyp the Blood, however, did recruit special killer bodyguards Frank "Dago Frank" Cirofici and Whitey Lewis from the Lenox Avenue mob (who helped Horowitz murder gambler Herman Rosenthal on Police Lieutenant Charles Becker's orders).

[ALSO SEE Charles Becker.]

LEOPOLD, NATHAN F. JR. ("BABE")
Murderer, Kidnapper ● (1906-1971)

BACKGROUND: SON OF MULTI-MILLIONAIRE NATHAN F. LEOPOLD, A SHIPPING MAGNATE. BORN AND RAISED IN THE EXCLUSIVE KENWOOD DISTRICT OF CHICAGO, ILL. GRADUATE OF UNIVERSITY OF CHICAGO, 1924, AT AGE 18. EXPERT IN ORNITHOLOGY, BOTANY, AND LANGUAGES. AUTHOR OF "LIFE PLUS 99 YEARS," 1958. DESCRIPTION: 5'8", BROWN EYES, BLACK HAIR, STOOPED, ROUND-SHOULDERED. ALIASES: MORTON D. BALLARD, GEORGE JOHNSON. RECORD: ARRESTED FOR KIDNAPPING AND MURDER OF FOURTEEN-YEAR-OLD BOBBIE FRANKS, 5/24 IN CHICAGO, ILL.; PLEADED GUILTY BEFORE JUDGE JOHN R. CAVERLY, CHIEF JUSTICE OF THE CRIMINAL COURT OF COOK COUNTY 7/21/24; DEFENDED BY COUNSEL CLARENCE DARROW IN BENCH TRIAL; SENTENCED TO LIFE IMPRISONMENT FOR MURDER PLUS 99 YEARS FOR KIDNAPPING AT NORTHERN ILLINOIS PENITENTIARY AT STATEVILLE, ILL.; PAROLED 3/13/58, DIED OF HEART FAILURE 8/30/71 IN PUERTO RICO.

LOEB, RICHARD A.
Murderer, Kidnapper ● (1907-1936)

BACKGROUND: SON OF ALBERT H. LOEB, WEALTHY VICE-PRESIDENT OF SEARS, ROEBUCK AND COMPANY. BORN AND RAISED IN EXCLUSIVE KENWOOD DISTRICT OF CHICAGO, ILL. GRADUATE OF UNIVERSITY OF MICHIGAN, 1924, AT AGE 17. DESCRIPTION: 5'11", BROWN EYES, BLACK HAIR, LEAN, ATHLETIC BUILD. ALIASES: LOUIS MASON, GEORGE JOHNSON. RECORD: ARRESTED FOR KIDNAPPING AND MURDER OF FOURTEEN-YEAR-OLD BOBBIE FRANKS, 5/24 IN CHICAGO, ILL.; PLEADED GUILTY BEFORE JUDGE JOHN R. CAVERLY, CHIEF JUSTICE OF THE CRIMINAL COURT OF COOK COUNTY 7/21/24; DEFENDED BY COUNSEL CLARENCE DARROW IN BENCH TRIAL; SENTENCED TO LIFE IMPRISONMENT FOR MURDER PLUS 99 YEARS FOR KIDNAPPING AT NORTHERN ILLINOIS PENITENTIARY AT STATEVILLE, ILL.; MURDERED BY FELLOW INMATE, JAMES DAY, 1/36.

In the spring of 1924, a Morton D. Ballard checked into the Morrison Hotel in Chicago as a salesman from Peoria. He was a short, stooped young man with bulging eyes and an even more bulging wallet. He was soft-spoken and a big tipper but he was no salesman and he had never been in Peoria. The wealthy youth was Nathan F. Leopold Jr. acting out the first stage of America's strangest, almost perfect murder.

Almost immediately after checking into his hotel, Leopold went to the Rent-A-Car Agency in Chicago and rented a sedan from its president, Mr. Jacobs, who asked for a reference.

Leopold was glad to supply him the name and phone number of one Louis Mason who was, in actuality, his friend, Richard Loeb. Jacobs made the call and Loeb gave "Ballard" a glowing reference.

Leopold then deposited $50 security payment for the car and drove it around for a two hour test. He would pick it up when he needed it, he told Jacobs. Once back at the Morrison, Leopold had a lot to ponder about —he was about to become a murderer for no other reason than "intellectual" fun.

Born in 1906 to millionaire transport magnate Nathan Leopold, Babe, as the boy was called by his friends, had never been quite right. He was internally malformed with diseased adrenal, pineal, and thymus glands.

He had an overactive thyroid gland, was undersized, round-shouldered and a sexual deviate at fourteen, when he became the eager butt of thirteen-year-old Dickie Loeb's pederastic leanings.

This sexual abnormality was not developed solely by the two boys; Leopold had plenty of help from a sexually perverted governess. This sub-normal woman encouraged Leopold at an early age to practice sexual perversions on her which she, in kind, returned.

Leopold's parents showered him with gifts, money, and freedom, but they noticed his unwillingness to associate with girls. In their rank ignorance, they placed their son (along with the sex-crazed governess) into an all-girls school. To completely collapse Leopold's struggling normal sexual growth, his mother died while he was an adolescent. With his "Madonna" gone, the boy concentrated on studies, for where his physical and emotional deformities were pronounced, his mental capacities were enormous.

There is no doubt that Nathan Leopold was a brilliant student, perhaps a genius with an I.Q. of 200. By the time he was eighteen, he had graduated from the University of Chicago with a B. Ph.—the youngest ever to do so— was an expert ornithologist and botanist, and spoke nine languages fluently.

His family life was never as rewarding. Leopold lived in a loveless home and his father compensated for his lack of fatherly direction with a shower of wealth. Leopold was given $3,000 to tour Europe before entering Harvard Law School. His father also gave him a car of his own and $125-a-week allowance.

He still wasn't happy. He had devoured Friedrich Nietzsche, and the German philosopher's theory of the superman became Leopold's flaming ideal. According to historian Irving Stone, Leopold did not feel he could ever be such a superman so, instead, he longed to be "a superwoman, a female slave to some big, handsome, powerful king."

Leopold found his king in Richard Loeb, whose father was as wealthy as Babe's. As the son of the Vice President of Sears, Roebuck and Company, Dickie Loeb was given everything he wanted and even more. His weekly allowance was $250, far surpassing the monthly wage that most American men made at that time.

Where Leopold was brilliant, Loeb was clever. But where Leopold was undersized and withdrawn, seventeen-year-old Loeb was athletic, tall, handsome, a charming conversationalist. He, too, had his physical defects—stuttering, a nervous tic, fainting spells (which sometimes were interpreted as the petit mal of epilepsy) and a suicidal trend. Loeb, as his last grim days testify, was also a pronounced homosexual.

Intellectual prowess and egotism abounded in Loeb as it did in Leopold. Dickie, at seventeen, was the youngest graduate of the University of Michigan. He fancied himself a criminal detective and his dream had always been to commit the perfect crime.

Perfection for the boys was a joint obsession. To them it meant being above all others —which their station in life endorsed; they felt total immunity from laws and criticism— they were perfect.

Well, almost perfect. Both had insatiable appetites. Loeb's was crime; Leopold's, abnormal sex. These "moral imbeciles," as they were later to be called, played one desire against the next to reach their personal fulfillment.

When Leopold got down on his knees and begged his god-hero, Loeb, to satisfy his pederastic lust, he was, at first, rebuked. Then the ever-cunning Loeb had an idea.

He knew that Leopold's love for him would goad him into any kind of agreement. So Loeb said that he would be willing to submit to Leopold's sexual eccentricities if he, in turn, would agree to begin a career of crime with him. The two actually signed a formal pact to that exchange.

During the next four years, the two boys, always under Loeb's leadership, committed petty thefts, set fires, turned in false alarms, vandalized property, and even devised a system to cheat at bridge. All through this adolescent period, violent arguments took place. Both threatened to kill each other. Loeb threatened to commit suicide.

Richard Loeb's most fanatic dream was to commit an important crime perfectly. A criminal at heart, which Leopold apparently was not, Loeb insisted his sex-mate join with him in a last titanic act before Leopold went on an extended vacation to Europe.

To plan a perfect crime appealed to Leopold's Nietzchean bent. He wrote Loeb once: "The superman is not liable for anything he may do, except for the one crime that it is possible for him to commit—to make a mistake."

In this way, these two pampered, spoiled children of vast wealth and twisted intelligence, groped toward murder.

For weeks Leopold and Loeb made intricate murder plans. They decided that whoever their victim was—his identity was of no concern to the youths—he would be kidnapped, killed, and then a ransom would be collected.

The ransom notes were to be written on a typewriter Loeb had stolen from his fraternity house at Ann Arbor, in November, 1923 when the boys attended a football game there.

Obviously they did not want to use Leopold's car for the abduction, so the Ballard-Mason identities were set up to rent a car. Further, under these aliases they opened bank accounts into which they intended to deposit the ransom money.

For several weeks Leopold and Loeb boarded the three o'clock train for Michigan City, Indiana and Loeb practiced throwing off boxes of the correct dimension and weight at places Leopold had selected (areas he had known through his bird-watching expeditions). This is how the ransom would be delivered to them.

On May 20, 1924, the boys drove the rented car to a hardware store at 43rd and Cottage Avenue where they purchased some rope, a chisel, and hydrochloric acid.

They planned to garrote their unknown victim, stab him with the chisel, if necessary, and then destroy his identity with the acid. So detailed was their plan that Loeb and Leopold argued whether or not to use sulphuric acid before deciding on hydrochloric.

The following day, the plotters met at Nathan Leopold's home where Babe took some adhesive tape and wrapped it tightly about the chisel for a better grip. They also gathered up a lap robe and rag strips with which to bundle and gag their victim.

Nothing was overlooked. Leopold also placed a pair of wading boots in the rented car. These hip boots would be worn while the victim was disposed of in a swamp the boys had already selected.

Each boy carried a loaded pistol. They read over the already-typed ransom note demanding $10,000 in cash. Although the last thing they needed on earth was cash, this would convince authorities that the kidnappers were from a lowly, money-grubbing station.

The only thing missing was the victim.

Quietly—what must have been the most macabre scene in the annals of American crime—the boys ran down a list of possible victims. First, it was suggested that they kill Loeb's younger brother Tommy, but they dismissed that idea—only on the grounds that it would be difficult for the older brother to collect the ransom from his own family without arousing suspicion.

Then they came up with little William Deutsch, grandson of millionaire-philanthropist Julius Rosenwald. But that was also still too close to home: Rosenwald was president of Sears, Roebuck and Company.

They almost agreed to kill their friend Richard Rubel who had lunch with them regularly, but they dropped him since they thought his father, a known penny-pincher, would not pay the ransom.

They shrugged. Across from Leopold's home was the Harvard Preparatory School, an exclusive institution for the sons of Chicago's wealthy. The boys decided to cruise around the school and search for a likely subject.

Loeb and Leopold agreed that their victim be small since neither felt they possessed enough strength to subdue a strong child and one determined to fight for his life. Little John Levison was the boy they selected. They spotted him playing in the school yard.

Levison's life was spared through an oversight. The dedicated killers didn't know his address and where the ransom note could be sent. They drove away to a drugstore and looked up his address. When they returned, the Levison boy had disappeared.

Leopold spotted him across a field with his spyglasses (brought along for that purpose). As they followed him home, Levison vanished up an alley.

After more driving, Leopold pointed out some boys near Ellis Avenue. Loeb identified one of them, fourteen-year-old Bobbie Franks, as one of his distant relatives. The Franks boy was ideal for their grotesque plans. His father, Jacob Franks, was a retired millionaire who had made his mammoth fortune in the manufacturing of boxes.

Richard Loeb called to the Franks boy, who walked over to the car. He invited the youth for a ride but Bobbie said no. He must have felt some apprehension since he caught Leopold's cold stare and said he did not know the other man anyway and had to get home.

Loeb was smooth. He had played tennis with Bobbie several times and finally persuaded the boy to get into the car to discuss a new tennis racket.

Bobbie Franks got into the car.

Although at their trial both denied being the actual killer, Leopold was at the wheel of the car and Dickie Loeb was in the back, wielding the murder weapon (which he later admitted).

As Leopold drove northward in heavy traffic, Loeb dropped the idea of using the rope on the boy as being too cumbersome. Quickly, ruthlessly, Loeb lashed out at the startled boy, stabbing him four times from behind with the chisel. All of the blows were to Bobbie's head and he dropped instantly to the floor, gushing blood.

When Leopold saw the Franks boy go down, he gasped, "Oh, God, I didn't know it would be like this!"

Richard Loeb ignored him. He was all business. Even though Bobbie was unconscious, Loeb stuffed his mouth with rags. Then he wrapped the boy's body in the lap robe. As Leopold drove through twenty miles of heavy traffic, the boy slowly bled to death on the floor of the car.

While waiting for darkness to cover their body-hiding routine, the youths parked the car and had sandwiches. Leopold called his home and told his father he would return late that evening.

The boys then went to another restaurant and ate a heavy meal. After that they leisurely drove to the Panhandle tracks at 118th Street. Here a swamp drained into an open culvert, their prearranged burial site.

Leopold slipped into his hip boots and carried the Franks boy to the culvert through the mud. Both killers had stripped him. Loeb had poured the hydrochloric acid over Bobbie. Leopold struggled to shove the naked corpse into the pipe. He took off his coat to make the job easier which was to prove his "one crime . . . to make a mistake."

After stuffing Bobbie into the pipe with his foot, Leopold squished slowly back to the car. The killers felt secure that the body would not be found until long after they had received the ransom money. But in the deep darkness, Leopold failed to see one small foot edging from the culvert.

Parking the rented car next to a large apartment building, the killers went to Leopold's house. Bobbie's blood, which had seeped through the lap robe, now stained the car's upholstery. After hiding the lap robe in a yard, the youths burned Bobbie's clothes and typed out the Franks' address on the prepared ransom note.

Again in the car, the boys drove to Indiana where they buried the shoes Bobbie had worn along with everything of his made of metal, including his belt-buckle and class pin.

Then the confident pair returned to Chicago where Leopold immediately called the Franks home. "Your boy has been kidnapped," he told Bobbie's terrified mother. "He is safe and unharmed. Tell the police and he will be killed at once. You will receive a ransom note with instructions tomorrow." He hung up.

The following day, a ransom note signed "George Johnson" was delivered to Franks demanding $10,000 in old, unmarked 20 and 50 dollar bills which should be wrapped in a small cigar box, in turn wrapped in white paper and sealed with sealing wax. More instructions would follow after 1 p.m.

Meanwhile, police had been notified through Franks' lawyer. They promised no publicity.

Leopold and Loeb went on with the elaborate preparations they had worked out the night previous while sipping drinks and playing cards till midnight in Babe's room.

The next day they parked the rented car in the Leopold garage and tried to clean away the bloodstains on the car seat. The Leopold chauffeur, Englund, saw them and the boys explained that they were trying to remove a stain caused by wine they had accidentally spilled.

Englund, who had no love for the boys, would later testify that Leopold's car never left the family garage on the murder night when Babe claimed he and Loeb used it to pick up two girls.

The boys took the lap robe to an empty lot outside of Chicago and there burned it. Driving to Jackson Park, Loeb yanked the keys from his typewriter. These he threw into the lagoon; the typewriter was thrown into another.

That afternoon, Richard Loeb took another train ride to Michigan City, leaving a note addressed to Franks in the telegram slot of a stationery desk in the observation car. On the envelope he had written in long-hand: "Should anyone else find this note, please leave it alone. The letter is very important."

He then got off the train at 63rd Street and rejoined the waiting Leopold. Andy Russo, a yardman, found the letter and it was speedily sent to Franks.

Jacob Franks, however, would follow no more instructions. Bobbie's body had been found by a railroad maintenance man who spotted his foot sticking from the culvert. Police notified Franks who sent his brother-in-law to identify the pathetic little body. It was Bobbie all right and newspapers screamed extras of the murder hours later. The ransom was never delivered.

Then began one of the wildest manhunts Chicago had ever seen, witnesses and suspects picked up by the scores. Leopold said nothing, keeping to his room. Loeb, on the other hand, immediately got involved in the search, accompanying police everywhere and spouting his amateur theories about crime. Officers grew suspicious when he suddenly blurted: "If I were going to pick out a boy to kidnap or murder, that's just the kind of cocky little son-of-a-bitch I would pick," meaning Bobbie, of course.

There followed, much to the killers' apprehension, several discoveries. The typewriter was found, the keys to same, the bloody chisel wrapped with tape, and a pair of horn-rimmed glasses were picked up near the culvert where Bobbie had been hidden. Police traced the glasses to Albert Coe and Company who stated that only three pair of glasses with such unusual rims were sold.

One pair was owned by a lawyer who was in Europe. Another belonged to a woman. She was wearing them when questioned by the police. The third pair had been sold to Nathan Leopold.

Police brought both boys in for questioning. Each was gently interviewed in separate rooms.

Leopold was confronted with the glasses but he reacted shrewdly by saying that he must have lost them near the culvert days ago while on one of his bird-hunting trips.

Police Captain Wolff reported that it had rained hard the past few days. How was it that the glasses were spotless?

Leopold shook his head. He tried to ward off the next terrible question: "He was a nice little boy. What motive did I have for killing him? I didn't need the money; my father is rich. Whenever I want money all I have to do is ask for it. And I earn money myself teaching ornithology."

The boy-killer then explained that he and Loeb had been riding around with two girls they had picked up—"May and Edna."

Pushing harder, Wolff insisted that the boys produce their girl friends. They could not. Then two novice reporters, Al Goldstein and Jim Mulroy, earned themselves a Pulitzer Prize. They obtained letters Richard Loeb had written on the stolen typewriter. The letters matched the typing of the ransom note. At that point, the youthful killers confessed.

Loeb broke down first, saying the murder was a lark, an experiment in crime to see if the "perfect murder" could be accomplished in Chicago. He then condemned, in a long tirade, Leopold's perverted sex habits. He denied being the killer; he said he had driven the car and Nathan Leopold had slashed Bobbie Franks to death.

Hearing this, Leopold said that he was the driver of the car and even posed, with police close by, in the driver's seat later as if to offer proof.

Bobbie Franks being carried from his home by boyhood friends who served as pall bearers, all sons of wealthy neighbors, 5/25/24, four days after his murder. Richard Loeb, still free, was driving home and parked across the street to view this very scene. He commented later that these "small white faced boys" made him feel "a little bit uncomfortable."

ment and understanding and faith that all life is worth living and that mercy is the highest attribute of man . . . If I can succeed . . . I have done something for the tens of thousands of other boys, for the countless unfortunates who must tread the same road in blind childhood . . ."

Nathan Leopold (second row, fifth from right) and Richard Loeb (third row, third from right) listen to a Chicago coroner's jury indict them for the murder of Bobbie Franks, 6/2/24. Their lawyer, Clarence Darrow, sits at right, head of table, leaning forward.

The boys were brought together. Loeb took one look at his partner-in-crime and stuttered, "We're both in for the same ride, Babe, so we might as well ride together."

Leopold insisted that Loeb was the killer. Loeb sneered: "He's only a weakling after all."

Then both confessed the killing.

Loeb's family immediately disowned him, his father dying two months after Richard was sentenced. Leopold's father went to the only man he felt could save his son. He literally got down on his knees and begged the greatest lawyer in the land—Clarence Darrow—to take the case.

Darrow, accepted stating, "While the State is trying Loeb and Leopold I will try capital punishment."

For 33 days, Darrow, who knew there was no chance for mercy from a jury, pleaded before Judge John R. Caverly in a bench trial. He pleaded his clients guilty and delivered one of the most eloquent appeals ever heard in an American courtroom.

He fought with all the vigor and brilliance in him, ending with: "I am pleading for the future . . . I am pleading for a time when hatred and cruelty will not control the hearts of men, when we can learn by reason and judg-

Caverly was much moved by Darrow's pleading but he stated that his decision was based on the defendants' youth and the fact that the state of Illinois had never executed boys of their age. He sentenced them each to life imprisonment on the charge of murder and 99 years each for the crime of kidnapping.

The judge stated that neither was to be paroled and that they were to be kept separated for the rest of their lives.

Though Darrow had won, he had to wait seven months for his fee (rumored to be $1,000,000). He was finally paid $30,000 by Leopold's father—the same man who had begged him to take the case—with the thankless remark: "The world is full of eminent lawyers who would have paid a fortune for a chance to distinguish themselves in this case."

Loeb and Leopold were sent to the Northern Illinois Penitentiary at Stateville just outside

Nathan Leopold, Jr. sitting on the floor of the Chicago County Jail's "bull pen," listening to a jazz concert, 6/9/24.

Leopold (second from left) stands next to Loeb before the bench of Chief Justice Caverly while being arraigned for murder. They pleaded "not guilty," 6/11/24.

Joliet. Here, Judge Caverly's orders were instantly ignored.

The "fun killers" lived in luxury. Loeb's expansive cell contained rows of books on geometry and poetry, an expensive filing case and a large glass-top desk, plus toilet articles unknown to any other convict . . . except Nathan Leopold, who also enjoyed the same, if not more, special treatment.

Both men ate separately from the rest of the prisoners in the officer's lounge and their meals were cooked to their specifications. Their so-called cells were usually open and they had passes to visit each other at any time, which they did.

Leopold and Loeb washed in the officers' shower room and roamed outside the walls of the prison to visit Leopold's garden where they gathered flowers. They were brought bootleg hootch and jolts of narcotics at $1 a shot.

Special visitors could see the wealthy prisoners at almost any time. Both young prisoners were allowed to make personal phone calls from the prison storeroom at almost any time. Of course, it was the money.

Everybody, from guards up, was bribed. Loeb was the worst offender, strutting about the prison as if it were his country estate. He flaunted his homosexuality, attacking whom he liked when he liked while guards turned their backs.

Loeb spotted a young prisoner doing a seven-year term. The young man, James Day, appealed to Loeb's sexual lust and he began offering Day cigarettes and food.

Day finally got the drift when Loeb grabbed him one day in the prison library, telling him of his love and to be "broad-minded and be nice to me." Disgusted, the young prisoner pushed Loeb away and walked out.

From that moment, Loeb hounded the man. "I never had a peaceful day," the prisoner said later. "He was always after me. I became desperate. I had to get him off my back. I was looking for the right day."

It came in January of 1936. Day, after the bloodletting, described it in all its terror and gore:

"This morning after breakfast I asked Loeb if I could talk to him. Loeb was eating breakfast in his cell with Leopold. He said, 'Surely.' After dinner he came to my cell and said he was on his way to take a bath and I could see him in the bathroom.

"I went to the bathroom and waited. Loeb came in in five minutes and locked the door. He said, 'What is on your mind. Get it off quickly. I'm warning you it won't do any good as far as my attitude toward you is concerned.'

"He started taking off all his clothes. I was leaning against the wash basin. His back was to me and he bundled the clothes . . . in a towel.

"He got between me and the door and I noticed he had a razor in his hand. He had taken it out of the bundle. He said, 'Keep your mouth shut. Get your clothes off.'

"I knew the door was locked. Loeb said, 'Get your clothes off before I start in on you.' I started undressing. I got off all my clothes and left them in the shower. I decided to pretend that I had given in so I could watch my chance to do something. He followed me in the shower. He took two steps and stepped over the sill of the shower. I kicked him in the groin. He grabbed for his groin with his free hand and slashed at my face with the razor as he fell. He missed me by inches.

"I hit him on the neck with my fist. The hand in which he had the razor hit the sill and the razor fell. He grabbed for it as I jumped over his body, and as he turned around at me I caught him by the wrist and throat and we fell to the floor together. He dropped the razor again.

"I grabbed the razor and jumped over him. He got up and swung his fist at me. It caught me on the left side of the face. I slashed at him. Blood flew in my face as he locked his arms around me. I remembered slashing at him as I fell back across the sill and felt the sharp sting across my left kidney.

"I dropped the razor. Loeb fell on top of me and he got the razor and caught me with one hand by the throat. Something told me that I would die there unless by super-human efforts I could get out from under him.

"Somehow, I threw him off. He swung at me, laughing and saying I could fight when I had to. I got up with the razor in my hand. I slashed at him and he backed under the shower and turned on the hot water. I stepped in after him. Steam was in my eyes. I kept slashing.

"After what seemed like several minutes of fighting under the shower, he sank into a sit-ting position and in a funny way used two fingers of his right hand to push in some of the flesh of the abdomen, which was cut open.

"I turned to leave the shower. He started to get up. His eyes were big and staring. He lunged at me with everything he had. His hands were clenched like claws. I slashed at him some more and kept on slashing until he fell mumbling.

"I turned off the hot water. Turning on some cold, I stepped under the shower to wash off the blood. My whole body was red. I left the shower and wiped the water out of my hair and eyes. I heard laughter or a groan. Loeb stood straight up. He lunged at me and knocked me down. His body slipped over me and fell by the door.

"He got up and fumbled with the key. He ran out to the dining room tunnel. I did not see him after that."

It was one of the most shocking confessions ever heard and proved the Rasputin-like insanity that lurked in Richard Loeb.

Loeb didn't have the strength to run far. He had been slashed 56 times and guards found him sprawled in the corridor, his blood running as freely as did that of Bobbie Franks twelve years before.

Loeb's mother rushed to the prison with the family physician. Leopold stood by his lover's bedside. Loeb's eyes fluttered only once when he said, "I think I'm going to make it," and then he died.

When Clarence Darrow was told of Loeb's death, he commented, "He is better off dead . . . for him death is an easier sentence."

A bizarre photo diagram created by a Chicago phrenologist, which alleges Nathan Leopold, Jr. to be an intellectual "slave," 7/28/24.

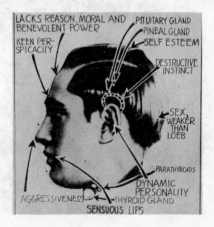

LACKS REASON, MORAL AND BENEVOLENT POWER
KEEN PERSPICACITY
PITUITARY GLAND
PINEAL GLAND
SELF ESTEEM
DESTRUCTIVE INSTINCT
SEX WEAKER THAN LOEB
PARATHYROIDS
DYNAMIC PERSONALITY
AGGRESSIVENESS
THYROID GLAND
SENSUOUS LIPS

Poet Carl Sandburg appearing before Illinois State Pardon and Parole Board in Stateville Penitentiary as a witness for Nathan Leopold, Jr. Sandburg supported Leopold's fourth appeal for freedom, saying that Leopold had been "struggling for the light for 33 years." The poet also stated that he would be willing to have Leopold in his home, 2/5/58.

Leopold survived to live out the long years in prison and finally be paroled on March 13, 1958. He was allowed to travel to Puerto Rico where he became a laboratory technician at a local church. In 1961, Leopold married a widow, Trudi Feldman Garcia de Quevedo, who owned a flower shop.

When Leopold was released he stated: "I am a broken old man. I want a chance to find redemption for myself and to help others."

Nathan Leopold, Jr., (right) waits for the plane that will take him to a $10-a-month hospital technician job in Puerto Rico after being paroled, 3/15/58.

When Leopold was living in Puerto Rico and writing a sequel to his 1958 book *Life Plus 99 Years*, he gave an interview which pointed to the fact that he was still constantly hounded by the almost "perfect murder" he and Dickie Loeb committed those long decades ago.

"The crime," he said, "is definitely still the central part of my consciousness. Very often it occupies the forefront of my attention and I can think of nothing else. More often, it is not in the center of my attention, but it always is present in the background."

Nathan "Babe" Leopold died of heart failure August 30, 1971, in Puerto Rico.

LESLIE, GEORGE LEONIDAS
Bankrobber ● (1842-1884)

BACKGROUND: BORN IN CINCINNATI, OHIO, THE SON OF A BREWER. GRADUATED UNIVERSITY OF CINCINNATI WITH A DEGREE IN ARCHITECTURE, HONORS. MOVED TO NEW YORK AT THE CLOSE OF THE CIVIL WAR. DESCRIPTION: TALL, FAIR-COMPLEXIONED, SLENDER. ALIASES: GEORGE HOWARD, WESTERN GEORGE. RECORD: CONSIDERED BY NEW YORK CITY POLICE TO BE THE MOST SUCCESSFUL BANK ROBBER IN THE EAST FOR TWENTY YEARS, ROBBING AN ESTIMATED $12,000,000 FROM VARIOUS BANKING INSTITUTIONS WHICH INCLUDED THE SOUTH KENSINGTON NATIONAL BANK OF PHILADELPHIA, THE THIRD NATIONAL BANK OF BALTIMORE, THE SARATOGA COUNTY BANK OF WATERFORD, N.Y., AND THE WELLSBORO BANK OF PHILADELPHIA; ROBBED WITH GILBERT YOST A JEWELRY STORE IN NORRISTOWN, PA., IN 1870, CAPTURED, RELEASED ON BAIL, JUMPED BOND; LESLIE'S SCORES WERE THE OCEAN NATIONAL BANK OF NYC ON 6/27/69 ($787,879) AND THE MANHATTAN SAVINGS INSTITUTION ON 10/27/78 ($2,747,000); MURDERED BY MEMBERS OF HIS OWN GANG IN 1884.

At his mother's death, college-trained Leslie moved to New York in 1865. He was easily accepted into exclusive clubs because of his family's social distinction, and soon acquired the reputation of a bon vivant. But George Leslie, while top-hatting it with New York's four hundred, lived a double life, one which put him squarely in the social register and another that heralded him as a criminal genius in the underworld, a man destined to be called "King of the Bankrobbers."

Leslie's technique in robbing banks was fairly simple. He merely acquired the architectural plans of a bank from some of his social contacts to "study" and then determined where a break-in could be best achieved. If plans were unavailable, Leslie would visit a bank he intended to rob, pretending to be a new depositor. From his observations he would then proceed to draw intricate plans of the bank's interior.

New York Police Superintendent George Walling was suspicious of the youthful dandy from the beginning but proof of his involvement in some of the most shocking bank robberies of the century was lacking. Leslie was apprehended once, in Norristown, Pa., in 1870, while burglarizing a jewelry store with a common thief named Gilbert Yost, but his political contacts in Philadelphia had the case against him quashed. (Yost was convicted and went to prison for two years.)

To further ensure success in his robberies, the ingenious Leslie established social contacts with bank presidents and then convinced them to hire some "down and out chap of my slight acquaintance" as a guard or porter. These "chaps," of course, were members of Leslie's mob who included such infamous thieves as James "Jimmy" Hope, Abe Coakley, Shang Draper, Johnny Dobbs (nee Michael Kerrigan), Jimmy Brady, Banjo Pete Emerson, Red Leary, and Worcester Sam Perris.

Leslie would assemble these men in a Manhattan room which had been fitted to duplicate the interior of the bank to be robbed. He rehearsed his men in their various assigned tasks, criticizing them on their timing and movements. In addition to such training, Leslie went to master tool makers and, according to his own specifications, ordered the finest

New York bankrobber Worcester Sam Perris belonged to Leslie's gang and helped to kill his leader over a love dispute.

burglar equipment ever seen in America. The tools used to burglarize the Manhattan Savings Institution alone cost Leslie $3,000.

After completing several successful robberies, Leslie engineered the robbery of the Ocean National Bank at Greenwich and Fulton Streets on June 27, 1869. The take was overwhelming, even beyond the robbers' expectations—$786,879. Fortified with a staggering amount of money, Leslie settled down to plan the biggest robbery of his life.

He took three years in planning his attack on the mammoth Manhattan Savings Institution, one of the largest banks in the world. The bank's vault possessed one of the most intricate combination locks ever made. Leslie learned from a friend in one of the clubs he had joined, the style of the combination and then purchased a copy from its manufacturers, Valentine & Butler.

Leslie then spent hours practicing with the combination lock until he discovered it could be thrown out of gear and the notches of the tumblers aligned by boring a hole under the indicator and then working the tumblers with a hair-like piece of steel.

An unimportant member of his gang, Pat Shevlin, was placed in the bank as a guard through Leslie's connections and the master thief was allowed inside one night by Shevlin six months later. He and Shevlin placed a black screen in front of the vault and then Leslie went to work. He fiddled with the combination for hours before boring his hole under the indicator. It was dawn and he had not completed his task. He puttied up the hole and left, hoping to return the next night.

The tumblers, however, had not been replaced and bank officials found it impossible to open the vault the next morning. A new lock plate was installed that day and when Leslie returned he discovered he could not move the tumblers. Leslie left the bank in disgust, determined to rob it within a week with only the means left to him—force.

On October 27, 1878, Leslie returned to the Manhattan Savings Institution with four men —Pete Emerson, Jimmy Hope, Abe Coakley, and a strong man named Bill Kelly who was supposed to handle any situation involving a beating. The policeman on duty, John Nugent, had been bribed to be away from the bank area during the time of the robbery, and, if necessary, to cover the gang's retreat.

The gang gained access to the bank through the apartment of night watchman Louis Werckle, tied up the Werckle family, and then entered the bank's main offices. There, Leslie and the others worked for three hours behind their black screen to break into the vault.

Patrolman Van Orden, on his way home from work, peered into the bank to see the black screen in front of the vault. Then he saw a cleaning man dusting desks. The cleaning man looked up at him with a smile and waved. Van Orden waved back and continued homeward, unconcerned. The cleaning man was master thief Abe Coakley.

Working their way into various compartments within the vault, the gang extricated a whopping $2,747,000 in cash and securities which they stuffed into satchels. As they escaped out a back entrance, one of these satchels was given to patrolman Nugent to carry.

Ironically, the gang failed to notice more than $2 million in cash encased in sacks on the vault floor behind. The cash realized from the robbery amounted only to $11,000. More than $2 million in bonds were non-negotiable, but it was still an enormous haul and Leslie's fame in the underworld as a super bankrobber was firmly entrenched.

Following the Manhattan robbery, Leslie acted as an adviser to bankrobbers for close to six years. His fee for approving plans and suggesting methods was $20,000 a robbery. Police figured that Leslie was the consultant on fifty or more of the nation's most sensational bank burglaries between 1879 and 1883 coast to coast.

Despite his criminal windfalls, Leslie was soon near broke, having spent small fortunes on his mistresses, Babe Irving, younger sister to gangleader Johnny Irving and, subsequently, Shang Draper's girl. Draper, a vicious thug, sought revenge when his girl left him for Leslie and he plotted the bankrobber's death. Draper, Johnny Dobbs, Worcester Sam, and Ed Goodie barged into Leslie's Brooklyn rooming house one night in 1884 and shot him through the head.

The badly decomposed corpse of the King of the Bankrobbers was found on June 4, 1884 by a patrolman on horseback at the base of Tramp's Rock near the Bronx River. New York society reeled in shock. Police Superintendent Walling only shrugged and said: "I told you so."

[ALSO SEE Fredericka "Marm" Mandelbaum.]

LICATA, NICHOLAS ("NICK")
Syndicate Gangster ● (1897-1974)

Reputed boss of the syndicate in southern California (assuming control upon the death of Frank DiSimone), Licata immigrated to the U.S. in 1913 from Camporeale, Tampani, Italy. Strong contacts in the underworld over the years have included Louis Dragna, James Fratianno, and Frank Bompensiero.

Licata's criminal record is scant. He received a small fine in 1945 for a minor offense. He was cited for contempt for refusal to answer questions put to him by a California State Assembly subcommittee investigating rackets in California.

LIEBSCHER, WILLIAM JR.
Bankrobber ● (1918-   )

There was nothing distinguished about Liebscher, a resident of Fairfax, California, except that he was a good actor in the amateur theater group he attended once a week. He and his wife lived in an expensive house in Fairfax's best suburb and he earned his living as an auto salesman.

The car business was bad in 1956 and, with debts creeping miserably upon him, Liebscher attempted to put to good use the acting experience he had gotten in Fairfax. From February 3, 1956 to September 11, 1957, Liebscher became a part-time bankrobber.

He made his face up to look ten years older than he was and began robbing banks of small amounts. They were not wholesale robberies, but piecemeal thefts nibbled from a single teller's window, amounts ranging from $700 to $2,500. His modus operandi never varied.

His face made up with a drawn-on pencil mustache and lines suggesting deep furrows and crow's feet, he would walk to a teller's window with the muzzle of a toy pistol barely jutting from a piece of cloth and hidden from everyone's view save that of the teller.

Next would come a printed note which said: "Be calm and I won't shoot. Give me your 20s, 10s, and 5s." The tellers never failed to hand over the money in their drawer. The teller at the Westlake Branch of the Bank of America at Daly City, near San Francisco, handed over $1,750 on July 18, 1956. The teller at the Bank of America branch in Napa City handed over $2,555 on May 10, 1957. The teller at the First Western Bank in Fairfield, Calif., handed over $2,555 on June 14, 1957. The teller at a branch of American Trust Company in San Francisco handed over $700 on July 10, 1957. Thirteen banks in all had been robbed in the same routine for a total of $27,765.

Following each robbery Liebscher returned to his auto franchise and resumed selling cars. He complimented himself several times on his foolproof robbery system but Liebscher neglected one small item at the very beginning of his criminal jaunt.

In the July 18, 1956 robbery in Daly City,

the thief had forgotten to take back a hand-written money order he had filled out and shoved beneath the bent head of a busy clerk to get her attention. This small scrap of paper was sent to the FBI. This, coupled to a partial license number on a car suspected as that being driven by the robber, led agents to Liebscher's auto agency in Fairfax.

A much younger man than that described by the bank tellers affably greeted the agents. They confronted him with the crimes and, without hesitation, William Liebscher Jr. confessed. "I'm sorry, gentlemen," he said, "for all the trouble I've caused you." The theatrical bankrobber received fifteen years in prison.

Just after his arrest, Liebscher asked if he could call his wife. When she picked up the phone, he said: "I won't be home for a long time. I'm in trouble. I'm with the FBI. I hate to tell you this, but I've been robbing banks for a year and a half."

LINGLEY, WILLIAM ("BIG BILL") Murderer, Gang Chief ● (? -1915)

Big Bill Lingley and his murderous side-kick, Freddie "The Kid" Muehfeldt were the chief organizers of New York's Car Barn Gang which controlled a huge territory that ran from 90th to 100th Streets and from Third Avenue to the East River. Lingley and Muehfeldt recruited thirty to forty of the most awesome dock fighters and killers in the city and formally announced the gang's existence by posting the following notice on a pole near the old car barns at Second Avenue and 97th Street:

Notice
COPS KEEP OUT!
No policemen will hereafter
be allowed on this block.
By Order of
THE CAR BARN GANG.

As a way of proving their intention, Lingley and Muehfeldt led a dozen men during the fall of 1911 through the area at night, clubbing

California used car salesman William Liebscher, Jr. robbed banks on the side for eighteen months until FBI agents trapped him in 1957. (UPI)

and kicking policemen unconscious. Police finally had to move their men through the district in squads of six men, almost back to back, fighting off showers of bricks as they patrolled their beats.

The Car Barners terrorized storekeepers in their domain to pay protection (from themselves, naturally) and set up relays of muggers beginning each day at noon and operating in shifts till dawn. The lawless Car Barners were dissolved four years later when Lingley and Muehfeldt killed a Bronx liquor dealer in a shakedown argument, were caught, and went to the electric chair in Sing Sing.

LONGLEY, WILLIAM P.
Murderer, Gunfighter ● (1850-1877)

BACKGROUND: BORN AND RAISED NEAR EVERGREEN, TEX. NO FORMAL EDUCATION. ORIGINAL OCCUPATION, COWBOY. DESCRIPTION: 5'11', BROWN EYES, BLACK HAIR, SLENDER. ALIASES: UNKNOWN. RECORD: MORE THAN THIRTY MEN, INCLUDING SEVERAL NEGRO POLICEMEN, POSSE MEMBERS AND GUNSLINGERS, WERE KILLED BY LONGLEY IN THE EARLY 1870S; LAST MURDER ATTRIBUTED TO HIM WAS THAT OF RANCHER WILSON ANDERSON IN APRIL, 1875; CAPTURED TWO YEARS LATER AND HANGED AT GIDDINGS, TEX.

No gunfighter believed more intensely in the myth of the Old South (with the possible exception of John Wesley Hardin) than did William P. Longley, a devout hater of Negroes, Yankees, and carpetbagging lawmen. Almost all of Longley's brutal slayings were explained away by the gunman as merely arguments in which he was protecting the honor and dignity of the defunct Confederate "Cause."

Longley, who occasionally worked as a cowboy to earn money for bullets and gambling, rode through New Mexico, Arizona, and Texas, like a grim reaper on horseback. An accurate count of the bodies he left littering small Western towns is unavailable, but most sources credit this fast gunman with killing more than thirty men (a record only John Wesley Hardin topped—by ten).

A rancher named Wilson Anderson had

Texas gunfighter William P. Longley.
(Denver Public Library)

feuded with Longley and his family for several years. When one of the gunfighter's cousins was shot from ambush in April, 1875, Longley returned to his birthplace, Evergreen, Tex., and killed Anderson, whom he suspected of his kinsman's murder.

He was caught about two years later and was sentenced to die on the gallows. Awaiting death in the small jail at Giddings, Tex., Longley wrote an embittered letter to the Governor of the state. One of his complaints was that gunfighter John Wesley Hardin received only twenty-five years in prison for his many killings and he, Longley, had been condemned to hang. Why? The Governor declined to respond and Longley was hanged on schedule.

Standing on the gallows in his Sunday suit, the goateed killer brought himself erect and said clearly: "I deserve this fate. It is a debt I owe for a wild and reckless life. So long, everybody!"

LOOMIS, GEORGE WASHINGTON, JR.
Murderer, Robber ● (1813-1865)

BACKGROUND: BORN NEAR SANGERFIELD CENTER, N.Y., TO GEORGE WASHINGTON LOOMIS, SR. AND RHODA MARIE MALLETT. FIVE BROTHERS AND THREE SISTERS (ALL OF THE BROTHERS, GROVER, WILLIAM, WHELLER, PLUMB, DENIO, AND ONE SISTER, CORNELIA, TURNED OUTLAW WITH "WASH"). DESCRIPTION: TALL, DARK, HEAVYSET. ALIASES: UNKNOWN. RECORD: ROBBED AND MURDERED THROUGHOUT THE MOHAWK AND CHENANGO VALLEYS FROM THE 1840S TO 1865, LEADING HIS BROTHERS IN RAIDS AGAINST LOCAL FARMERS FOR LIVESTOCK WHICH WAS RESOLD TO CITIZENS AND THE U.S. ARMY; KILLED IN A RAID AGAINST THE LOOMIS STRONGHOLD IN NINE-MILE SWAMP IN 1865 BY VIGILANTES LED BY CONSTABLE JAMES FILKINS OF NEARBY BROOKFIELD.

For a half century, the Loomis gang dominated the upper New York State area, concentrating their outlaw exploits in the Mohawk and Chenango Valleys. Their leader, George Washington Loomis, Jr., called "Wash" by his friends and family, was the off-spring of a notorious horse thief who had plundered farms in Vermont and Connecticut in the 1790s.

Loomis' mother, a French Canadian, schooled her six sons in criminal pursuits early in life, encouraging them to pilfer anything they wanted. Wash later stated that his mother sanctioned "stealing little things. As long as we were not caught, it was all right. If we got caught, we got licked."

By the early 1840s, the Loomis farmhouse, a rambling two-story structure, became the home of bandits, escaped convicts, and wanted murderers, all in the employ of Wash and his brothers who raided neighboring farms at will, driving off livestock to be resold. Often they killed the inhabitants.

The Loomis brothers used their mother's home to store stolen furs, equipment, and food. Their unwed sister, wild Cornelia, rode with the boys in many of their murderous raids and attacked several farmers who dared to call her brothers outlaws.

The Loomis farmhouse was raided in 1857 by a band of vigilantes and huge quantities of stolen goods were found secreted in hidden panels and closed-off rooms. The brothers were taken to Waterville, N. Y. but indictments against them disappeared. During their trial,
court records were burned nightly by their armed bands who broke into the courthouse. Witnesses against the Loomis brothers vanished, only to be found days later hanging from trees. The Loomis boys were released.

Grover Loomis was arrested for counterfeiting bills drawn on the Onondaga Bank in Oneida County but was soon released when his brothers beat up the local district attorney.

At the time of the Civil War, the Loomis gang concentrated on horse stealing. It was big business. The U.S. Army was paying top prices for horses. The Loomis bunch stole every horse in sight along the Mohawk Valley and moved them to New York City through their own shipping system—on "thief boats" along the Erie Canal. Once in NYC, their stolen goods were handled by aging prostitute and super fence, Fredericka "Marm" Mandelbaum, who became a millionaire by reselling hot goods.

No legal methods worked against the Loomis brothers, though Plumb and Grover had been arrested numerous times. The frustrated constable of Brookfield, N. Y., James Filkins, finally took matters into his own hands and led a posse to the Loomis farmhouse in 1865. The lawmen crashed through the barricaded door and fell upon Wash Loomis, beating him about the head with guns and pipes. He was literally stomped to death.

Plumb Loomis was also beaten and then thrown onto a large fire in front of the farmhouse. When the posse departed to search for the other Loomis brothers, Mrs. Loomis raced from her home and dragged her son from the fire. He lived.

Another raid against the farmhouse took place in Summer, 1867. This time, Grover and Plumb Loomis were strung up by their hands over fires until they confessed to the crimes vigilantes insisted they had committed. When Grover died in 1870, Denio Loomis took control of the outlaw band. Denio and Plumb Loomis died in the early 1880s but their sister Cornelia continued to plan and order raids. The last of the Loomis gang members disappeared after Cornelia's death in 1897.

Constable Filkins, who almost single-handedly fought this terror gang for forty years, outlived them all, dying peacefully in 1911.

[ALSO SEE Fredericka "Marm" Mandelbaum.]

Rowdy Joe Lowe, saloon keeper by trade, killer by instinct.
(Kansas State Historical Society, Topeka)

LOWE, JOSEPH ("ROWDY JOE")
Gambler, Gunfighter, Procurer
(? -1880)

"Rowdy Joe" Lowe showed up in the wide-open cattle town of Wichita, Kan. about 1870 where he opened a saloon. Joe's wife Kathryn, known as "Rowdy Kate," operated a whorehouse on the second floor of the saloon and carried, like her husband, two guns at her sides at all times.

Lowe's gaming tables were rigged; whenever customers mumbled complaints of being cheated, Rowdy Joe leaped over his bar and pistol-whipped the offender into unconsciousness. Lowe's reputation became so bad that he packed up Kate, her girls, his fixtures, and moved his bar to Newton, Kan. in 1871. No sooner was he established there than he was involved in a battle with a gunslinger named A. M. Sweet.

The gunman was attracted to Rowdy Kate and, on several occasions, had pawed her.

Kate Lowe reminded Sweet that such hanky-panky was reserved for the girls in her husband's establishment, but the amorous gunfighter insisted on having Kate. Lowe, watching from behind his bar with his ever-present top hat askew on his head, reached for his pistol and drilled Sweet dead on the spot. The Lowes departed Newton shortly thereafter, returning to Wichita.

In 1873, it was the same story all over again. Another saloonkeeper, E. T. "Red" Beard, battled Rowdy Joe over Kate in an hour-long gun duel inside the latter's bar. Beard was finally killed in the smoke-filled dive after an estimated fifty shots had been fired. Lowe was released from custody after it was determined that no one had seen him shoot Beard although the two combatants were the only ones present in the bar during the shootout, the customers having fled to a more serene atmosphere.

Lowe was finally killed in Denver in a gunfight, again over his wife's ample charms. Rowdy Kate disappeared days later. Rumors had it that she traveled to San Francisco and, under a different name, married a wealthy railroader who was a distinguished member of Nob Hill society.

LUCAS, HENRY LEE
Serial Killer ● (1937-   )

The life story of Henry Lucas is written in obscenity, matricide, and the blood of three hundred victims, if the killer's claims were to be believed. Lucas never knew a father. He was born to Viola Lucas, a Virginia prostitute (a double amputee) and, as a child, he had to remain in the same room where his mother entertained her male clients.

When in his early twenties, Lucas moved to Michigan with his mother. There Lucas met a sixteen-year-old girl he wanted to marry but his mother so ridiculed the idea that Lucas went berserk and killed his mother by driving a knife into her heart. He was sent to prison to serve a life term.

In 1975 Michigan officials paroled Lucas, even though he pleaded with them, or so he later claimed, not to release him, saying he would only kill more people. He made good his promise when he killed a man a short time after he left prison. He would add three hundred more victims to the list, murdering them throughout the country.

According to the serial killer's later statements, he traveled west from Michigan, killing people at random and dumping their bodies on prairies, in deserts and inside mountain canyons. His manner of murder varied. He suffocated, strangled, shot, stabbed, and bludgeoned his victims to death. He sometimes, if the mood struck him, tortured his victims, then savagely mutilated the bodies.

On the bum in Florida, Lucas went to a soup kitchen and there met Ottis Toole, an ugly degenerate who was also a serial killer of homosexuals, and who had a proclivity for pyromania. At first they schemed to murder each other. Then they became lovers and embarked on a killing rampage, selecting both male and female victims at random.

Lucas and Toole traveled together cross country for many months and eventually separated in Florida. Toole abducted six-year-old Adam Walsh from a shopping mall and killed him. Lucas, on the other hand, went to Texas, where he lived with his nine-year-old niece Frieda "Becky" Powell.

After having sex with the child, Lucas stabbed her to death in a field outside Stoneburg, Texas. Police found him sitting next to the body on June 11, 1983 when they came to arrest him on an illegal weapons charge. He was charged with killing a neighbor, 80-year-old Katherine Rich, along with Powell.

Convicted of the Rich killing, Lucas began his recitation of murders and had chronicled twelve of his murders before being brought to trial for killing his niece. Lucas implicated Toole in many of the slayings he recalled and then, over the next few years, directed officers to more than two hundred murder sites in thirty states. By 1984 Lucas had admitted to killing 360 people. In June of that year he was convicted of five murders and had been sentenced to death for slaying a female hitchhiker in San Angelo, Texas.

LUCCHESE, THOMAS ("THREE-FINGER BROWN")
Syndicate Chief ● (1903-1967)

When three fingers were accidentally cut from his hand as a youth in 1915, Lucchese acquired the moniker of "Three-Finger Brown," after a popular baseball pitcher of the same name. The name was not to Lucchese's liking and anyone who uttered it was in serious trouble with this feared New York gunman and murderer. "I never heard anyone call him 'Three-Finger Brown' to his face," Joe Valachi, a one-time Lucchese aide-de-camp, testified later.

Lucchese first began as a bodyguard to Lucky Luciano in the early 1920s when both of them worked for Joe the Boss Masseria. Three-Finger was adept at avoiding arrest though he was reportedly involved in no less than thirty murders, mostly involving the Cosa Nostra or Mafia. In 1923, Lucchese was convicted of grand larceny but served only a light sentence.

In 1925, Lucchese was named as a killer by both the wife and the mother of the victim. Before police could obtain signed statements from the two women, Lucchese's men paid them a visit. No complaints were ever signed.

During the 1930-31 war between Salvatore Maranzano and Joe the Boss Masseria over the control of the New York Mafia, Lucchese

New York Mafia chieftain Thomas Lucchese, also known as "Three Finger Brown," in 1952. (UPI)

became Luciano's favorite killer, disposing of several Maranzano men. He was responsible for the death of Maranzano aide, Joe Pinzolo, on September 9, 1930. Almost a year later to the date, September 10, 1931, Lucchese and three others, acting under Luciano's orders, entered Salvatore Maranzano's Manhattan office and shot and stabbed him to death.

Lucchese moved into the garment industry rackets, taken over from Lepke Buchalter after Lepke was electrocuted in Sing Sing. He reaped millions from union kickbacks, narcotics smuggling (taking over part of Luciano's network when Lucky was deported to Italy in 1946), and gambling interests in the East.

From a lowly Sicilian gunman of the 1920s, Lucchese rose through the Cosa Nostra-Mafia ranks. Of the five Mafia "families" established in the mid-1930s, Lucchese became a high-ranking Mafioso in that of Tom Gagliano (the other original four families were headed by Luciano, Joseph Profaci, Joseph Bonanno, and Vince Mangano). By 1960, Lucchese had completely taken over the Gagliano family.

Lucchese, unlike most of his counterparts, stayed out of the limelight, one of the most secretive men the Mafia ever bred. His last arrest was in 1923. From that year to 1967, when he died of cancer in the deep comfort of a $100,000 home, Thomas "Three-Finger Brown" Lucchese never saw the inside of a courtroom.

[ALSO SEE Salvatore Maranzano.]

LUCIANO, CHARLES ("LUCKY")
Crime Syndicate Chief ● (1897-1962)

BACKGROUND: BORN 11/24/97 IN THE SMALL SICILIAN HAMLET OF LERCARA FRIDDI TO ANTONIO AND ROSALIA LUCANIA (CHRISTENED NAME, SALVATORE LUCANIA). TWO BROTHERS, ONE SISTER. IMMIGRATED WITH FAMILY IN 1907. ATTENDED PS 19 IN NYC; COMPLETED SIXTH GRADE. ORIGINAL OCCUPATION, SHIPPING CLERK. DESCRIPTION: 5'7", BROWN EYES, BLACK HAIR, SLENDER, DROOPING RIGHT EYELID, KNIFE SCARS ON FACE ABOUT NECK, EARS, CHIN. ALIASES: CHARLES LANE, CHARLES ROSS, LUCKY, CHARLIE LUCKY, "THREE-TWELVE." RECORD: ARRESTED AT AGE TEN IN NYC FOR SHOPLIFTING IN 1907, RELEASED; ARRESTED SEVERAL TIMES UP TO 1915 FOR MINOR THEFTS; ARRESTED IN 1915 FOR PEDDLING NARCOTICS IN NYC, SENTENCED TO ONE YEAR IN JAIL, RELEASED IN SIX MONTHS; JOINED THE FIVE POINTS GANG IN 1916; PARTICIPATED IN SEVERAL GANG WARS BETWEEN FIVE POINTERS AND THE MONK EASTMAN GANG, SEVERAL BEATINGS AND MURDERS ATTRIBUTED TO HIM BY POLICE; FREELANCED WITH THE KID DROPPER AND LITTLE AUGIE ORGEN GANGS TO 1920; WENT TO WORK AS A RUMRUNNER, BROTHEL-KEEPER AND NARCOTICS PEDDLER FOR NEW MAFIA CHIEFTAIN GIUSEPPE "JOE THE BOSS" MASSERIA IN LATE 1920; PARTICIPATED IN SEVERAL GANG WARS BETWEEN MAFIA FACTIONS, 1922-30, SUSPECTED OF KILLING SALVATORE MAURO AND SILVA TAGLIAGAMBA OVER CONTROL OF MANHATTAN BOOTLEG TERRITORIES IN 1922; ARRESTED BY FEDERAL AGENTS IN NYC IN 1923 FOR PEDDLING NARCOTICS, RELEASED AFTER TURNING INFORMANT; ARRESTED IN 1924 IN JERSEY CITY, N.J. FOR CARRYING CONCEALED WEAPON, RELEASED; BECAME MASSERIA'S CHIEF LIEUTENANT IN 1925; ALSO WORKED AS A LIEUTENANT TO JACK "LEGS" DIAMOND, CIRCA 1924-29; ARRESTED IN NOVEMBER, 1928 ON SUSPICION OF MURDERING GAMBLER ARNOLD ROTHSTEIN, DISMISSED; ARRESTED ON SUSPICION OF MURDERING WILLIAM "RED" CASSIDY AND SIMON WALKER IN LEGS DIAMOND'S HOTSY TOTSY CLUB, 6/13/29, RELEASED; BECAME MAFIA CHIEF OF DOWNTOWN MANHATTAN THAT SAME YEAR; ATTACKED BY RIVAL GANGSTERS VYING FOR BOOTLEG CONCESSIONS IN OCTOBER, 1929, ALMOST KILLED (BLAMED "THE COPS" FOR THIS ATTACK ON HIS LIFE IN 1953 INTERVIEW); ORDERED THE KILLING OF GIUSEPPE "JOE THE BOSS" MASSERIA IN A CONEY ISLAND RESTAURANT 4/15/31; JOINED SALVATORE MARANZANO'S ONE-FAMILY MAFIA ORGANIZATION IN 1931; ORDERED THE KILLING OF SALVATORE MARANZANO IN HIS OFFICE 9/10/31; ESTABLISHED TOTAL CONTROL OVER NARCOTICS, BROTHELS AND RESTAURANT RACKETS IN NYC, 1932-36; ESTABLISHED WITH MEYER LANSKY,

LOUIS "LEPKE" BUCHALTER, JOE ADONIS, ABNER "LONGY" ZWILLMAN, DUTCH SCHULTZ, ALBERT ANASTASIA, JACOB "GURRAH" SHAPIRO THE NATIONAL CRIME SYNDICATE, BECOMING A DIRECTOR; ORDERED WITH OTHER BOARD MEMBERS OF THE SYNDICATE, THE MURDER OF DUTCH SCHULTZ 10/23/35 IN A NEWARK, N.J. CHOPHOUSE (THREE OF SCHULTZ'S MEN ALSO KILLED AT THIS TIME BY CHARLES WORKMAN AND MENDY WEISS, SYNDICATE GUNMEN); ARRESTED IN HOT SPRINGS, ARK. IN 1936 AND RETURNED TO NYC WHERE A GRAND JURY INDICTED HIM ON NINETY COUNTS OF EXTORTION AND DIRECTION OF HARLOTRY, BAIL SET AT $350,000; CONVICTED AND SENTENCED TO THE CLINTON STATE PRISON AT DANNEMORA, N.Y. TO FROM THIRTY TO FIFTY YEARS; APPEALED FOR PAROLE IN APRIL, 1938, DENIED; APPEALED FOR PAROLE 2/8/43, DENIED; PAROLE APPROVED IN LATE 1945; DEPORTED TO ITALY 2/10/46; APPEARED IN HAVANA, CUBA IN FEBRUARY, 1947 TO DIRECT AN ENCLAVE OF UNDERWORLD CHIEFS INCLUDING FRANK COSTELLO, WILLIE MORETTI, MEYER LANSKY, CHARLES FISCHETTI; ORDERED TO RETURN TO ITALY WEEKS LATER; DIRECTED NARCOTIC, ALIEN, AUTO SMUGGLING TO U.S. FROM EUROPE 1947-61; DIED OF A HEART ATTACK AT CAPODICHINO AIRPORT IN NAPLES, 1/26/62.

F Scott Fitzgerald's hero Jay Gatsby and Charles "Lucky" Luciano had the same fascination with jewels, money, expensive clothes, and women of unreal beauty. Like Gatsby, Luciano, in his palmy days, spent hours powdering himself and selecting the day's apparel from three wall-length closets where hundreds of $500 suits were draped. But there the similarity rudely ended. Unlike the mysterious and sentimental Gatsby, Luciano was thoroughly corrupt, an openly diabolical killer who traded in humans as the most notorious vice lord in the annals of American crime.

Living in a posh suite of rooms—39-C—at the Waldorf-Astoria Hotel under the alias Charles Ross (following his move from the equally swank Barbizon-Plaza where he was known as Charles Lane), Luciano exercised unlimited power throughout the underworld of the East as the unchallenged boss of bosses from 1932 to 1936. He owned every prostitute in New York City; all gambling and narcotics peddling were under his control; he led the New York Mafia and was one of the "big three" (including Lepke and Lansky) who organized and directed the Machiavellian national crime syndicate.

From the beginning, women were the tools with which Charlie Lucky constructed his criminal cartel. And women—lowly whores who at gunpoint surrendered half their pathetic income to Luciano goons—would one day pull this crime czar from his vulture's perch.

The first woman in Luciano's life, his mother Rosalia, lost her son to the slum streets of New York when he was ten. Months after the Lucania family traveled in steerage in 1907 from poverty-torn Sicily to the U.S., little Salvatore Lucania was stealing food, clothes and trinkets on a wholesale basis from stores and pushcarts. He could barely speak English when first arrested. He was returned to the custody of his parents and the next day he was running with Lower East Side gangs, rolling drunks and holding up terrified Sicilian grocers at knife point.

Luciano quit grade school at fourteen and became a narcotics peddler for a member of the Five Points gang known only as Cherry Nose. While delivering a package of heroin to a Bowery bar, he was arrested by an off-duty policeman and was tried and convicted. He spent six months in jail. Upon his release, Luciano was rewarded for not identifying other members of the dope ring by being taken into the infamous Five Points gang as a full-fledged member.

His mentor was Johnny Torrio, soon to move to Chicago where he would first work for his uncle Big Jim Colosimo and then take over the Windy City rackets. Luciano rubbed elbows with Frankie Uale (later Yale) and a hulking killer named Al Capone. He became expert with icepick, bat, and gun, relishing the bloody battles the Five Pointers waged with a rival mob, the Eastman gang.

Though accused of murdering several henchmen who bashed for Monk Eastman, Luciano was always set free. His uncanny fortunes with the law coupled to his phenomenal ability to win at craps earned him the name "Lucky." After several police bookings, Charlie dropped the Salvatore and then, up to 1931, altered his last name until Lucania became Luciano.

Gambling not only became Luciano's first pleasure but when asked by police to specify his occupation he invariably replied "gambler." On rare occasions he referred to himself as a fruit dealer, chauffeur, or salesman. His real occupation and the source of his large income: extortion of prostitutes.

After leaving the Five Points gang in 1920 and joining Giuseppe "Joe the Boss" Masseria's

Mafia clan, Lucky muscled his way into the prostitution racket. His techniques were uncomplicated. Employing several goon squads, Luciano sent his toughs around to brothels to sell them protection. Protection against what, the madams wanted to know? They were already paying off the police. Protection against thieves, Lucky's boys replied.

Some bordello matrons didn't get the point. Days later, strong-arm men Davey Betillo and Jimmy Frederico [alias Fredericks] would invade the brothels of obstinate owners, rob the till, burn up some beds, and break the legs of some of the in-house prostitutes. The madams paid up handsomely after that, fifty per cent of their take, plus fifty per cent of each girl's share. Lucky grew rich.

Those whoremasters like Pete Harris who didn't get into line were simply killed. By the mid-1920s, Lucky virtually owned prostitution in Manhattan. He offered, through his madams and Broadway connections, three types of women to anxious, well-fixed males. Showgirls, culled from the nightclub reviews and theater extravaganzas, were available strictly as escorts from $20 (for dinner only) to $75 for a full evening on the town. Call girls, a step down in status, but no less attractive than the dancers and singers of the first bracket, were on tap for a flat $100 a night, all night. Luciano's stable of whores, an average of 5,000 women hustling each and every night with fifty per cent of their take going to Lucky, operated on different levels, right down to the $2-for-a-half-hour variety.

Cornering the brothel market made Luciano a millionaire by 1927; his annual income was then estimated to be a cool non-taxable (not declared) $1 million. To appease the IRS in later years, Luciano unswervingly filed a $22,-500 return, based on income from "wagers." Lucky's hoodlums were scant compared to the troops in the employ of such arch criminals as Lepke, who owned the garment industry and controlled most of the city's unions, and Lansky's loan-sharking and gambling legions. But no one ever leaned on Lucky. Whenever he needed more strong-arm slammers, he called on his friends Lepke and Lansky or Albert Anastasia whose Murder, Inc. troop in Brooklyn handled any untoward situation.

There was one problematical event in October, 1929, that none in this hoodlum empire could prevent from happening to Charlie

Lucky. Inspecting a load of heroin being smuggled into Manhattan from the docks of the Hudson River, Luciano was suddenly jumped by four men. He was thrown into a car which sped off.

In the car, the four men in the back seat viciously worked over the gang chieftain. He was hit in the face and on the head repeatedly with fists, blackjacks, and gun butts. He passed out and then came to when slapped in the face. Again, while the long, black touring car zig-zagged through the streets of Brooklyn, he was beaten senseless. While he was lying on the floor of the car, one of his attackers leaned forward and taped his mouth. The unconscious Luciano was then hit square in the eyes. Another man flashed a long-bladed knife and sliced Luciano about the chin, and the ears. He cut the gangster's throat but missed the jugular vein. Another gangster leaned forth wielding an icepick and drove it a dozen times into Lucky's back until Luciano's expensive tweed suit was pockmarked with holes seeping blood.

The death car was driven about for hours and then roared away after its grisly cargo was dumped on Huguenot Beach on Staten Island. At dawn, the mobster rose shakily to his feet and staggered off the beach and down a deserted street. A beat cop named Blanke spotted him and caught the little gangleader just as he collapsed unconscious. He was rushed to a hospital.

Hours later, several detectives sat at Luciano's bedside, ramming questions. Luciano shook his head wearily. "I dunno who, where, what, nuthin'."

"What's your name?" asked Detective Charles Schley.

"I'm Charlie Luciana," Luciano said, already beginning to alter his name.

"What happened?"

"Accident."

"What happened?"

"I'm standin' on the corner of Fiftieth and Sixth when this car pulls up. The curtains are yanked down. I can see nuthin' in the windows. Don't pay much attention. I'm waitin' for a girl. Then three guys get out and put guns on me. They shove me in the car, and take off."

Luciano described the beating he took until he lost consciousness. The police grilled him for hours. No, Luciano knew nothing about anything. No, he didn't know who had beat him up. No, he couldn't identify anyone. It was dark. The curtains in the car were drawn.

Luciano smiled, showing even, straight teeth. "Look," he said, "I'm pals with everybody. Nobody's after me. Everybody likes me."

Following his release from the hospital, Luciano got in touch with some of his old "pals" in the Legs Diamond gang. Diamond had once hired Lucky to smuggle narcotics to his pushers. Legs also lusted after a piece of Luciano's brothel racket. Though Lucky was to claim in an interview in 1953 that the 1929 beating was received at the hands of "the cops," it is probable that members of the Diamond gang had taken Luciano for a ride. (Lucky was the only known underworld character ever to survive such a trip.)

Through 1928 and 1929, members of Diamond's mob began to disappear. Their bodies turned up in alleyways, in gutters, in rivers, and, half-burned, in basements of tenement houses, stuffed into furnaces. Diamond himself went on the spot December 18, 1931, shot to death while drunk in bed in a cheap Albany rooming house, by persons unknown. Those persons were very likely Luciano's gunmen (if not those of Dutch Schultz who also had a good reason to hate Diamond; Legs had been hijacking the Dutchman's beer trucks in record numbers).

It was the last attempt on Luciano's life by the underworld or anyone else. Lucky's sponsor, Joe the Boss Masseria, became more and more dependent on the sycophantic Luciano, appointing him his chief lieutenant and Mafia boss of downtown Manhattan in 1929. For two years, Luciano and his own lieutenant, Vito Genovese, served Masseria faithfully, enforcing his edicts, doling out portions of their own rackets to him, and supplying him with gunmen to protect his restaurant and bootleg empire.

In early 1930, a Mustache Pete (as younger Mafiosi referred to the older "dons" who still dominated the ritualistic Mafia families) named Salvatore Maranzano, decided to unify all Mafia members under his command. He began an open, bloody war with Joe the Boss.

The young Turks such as Luciano, Genovese, Willie Moretti (alias Willie Moore), Joe Adonis, and Frank Costello worked for Masseria. Joe the Boss was also allied with Al Capone in Chicago. Opposing Masseria were such Maranzano stalwarts as Joseph Profaci, Joseph "Joe Bananas" Bonanno, Stefano Magaddino in Buffalo, and Joe Aiello in Chicago, all staunch supporters of the traditional "family" system inaugurated by the Sicilian Mafia centuries before.

Masseria got wind of the impending war and opened up. His first victim was Gaetano (Tom) Reina, one of his own men whom he suspected was going over to Maranzano. Reina was blown apart by shotguns on the evening of February 26, 1930, in the Bronx. Maranzano countered by killing a Masseria henchman, Pietro Morello, in Palisades, N. J., August 15, 1930. The New Yorkers were reaching into other states by then to eliminate their factional enemies. The Morello killing was performed by a man identified later by Joseph Valachi only as "Buster from Chicago." (There is every indication that "Buster from Chicago" was none other than freebooter Leo Vincent Brothers, a ruthless St. Louis gunman who was later to kill *Chicago Tribune* reporter Jake Lingle and who was known throughout the underworld as "Buster.")

Joseph Pinzolo, a Maranzano Mustache Pete, was next, murdered in the Brokaw Building in Manhattan, September 9, 1930. Masseria's ally in Chicago, Al Capone, then took care of Joseph Aiello who was shotgunned to death in front of his home on October 23, 1930. Aiello had been sending $5,000 a week to Maranzano to finance the war.

The forces of Maranzano struck back in a flurry of killings. Two of Luciano's best gunmen, Steven Ferrigno (alias Sam Ferraro) and Al Mineo were blasted off a Manhattan street in the middle of the afternoon on November 5, 1930. The shooting was performed by "Buster from Chicago," Girolamo Santucci (alias Bobby Doyle), and Nick Capuzzi.

At this point, the Masseria-Luciano faction began to lose not only their best gunmen but also their money and prestige. Lucky began to waver. Masseria, he concluded, was a marked man, whose death could profit him by peace with Maranzano. When Joe the Boss' best friend, Joseph Catania (alias Joe Baker) was found on February 3, 1931 with six bullets in his head, Luciano decided to dispose of his boss, Masseria.

Luciano felt no loyalties binding him to Joe the Boss; the only code he adhered to was the code of self-survival. Once, when picked up on a narcotics charge in 1923, he had turned in several Italian heroin pushers to gain his freedom.

On April 15, 1931, Luciano lured Joe the Boss to one of Masseria's favorite restaurants, the remotely situated Scarpato's in Coney Island, Brooklyn. Lucky dawdled through the heavy old-fashioned Italian meal with its endless courses. He watched coldly as Joe the Boss downed glass after glass of red wine, slurping and sloshing it onto his chin.

Masseria became sentimental and talked of old times, how he began as a professional killer in New York in 1907, the year Lucky immigrated to the U.S. He praised Luciano for his loyalty throughout the present "troubles." When the belching Masseria attempted to heave his heavy frame from his chair, Lucky stopped him.

"How about a little *brisco*, Joe?" Luciano asked. "It's early. We got a little time, yet."

Masseria beamed. *Brisco* was his favorite card game. He gladly consented and the cards were brought to Joe the Boss' table. He and Lucky played for forty-five minutes. Outside the restaurant, four gangsters representing different gangs in New York—a sort of universal "hit" squad—got out of a touring car. Vito Genovese, Albert Anastasia, Joe Adonis, and Bugsy Siegel fingered their pistols, checking before entering Scarpato's.

Luciano was checking, too. He glanced at his watch and then excused himself, telling Masseria that he had to go to the men's room and they would leave when he returned. Once in the washroom, Luciano locked the door and turned on the taps. Past the locked door marched the four killers. They walked straight up to Masseria who was fiddling with an ace of diamonds in one hand and lifting a glass of wine to his lips with the other.

Each man fired one bullet into Joe the Boss' head. The heavy little man crashed forward onto the table. Anastasia gave Masseria the *coup de grace*, one more shot in the back of the head. The four assassins walked out of the restaurant. Luciano turned off the water in the men's room, and emerged to see Scarpato's filling up with policemen.

He quickly explained that he had been in the men's room when the shooting occurred, washing his hands. Yes, he had heard the noise but thought nothing of it. It was too bad about Masseria. They had been close pals.

Nicola Gentile and another ranking Mafia member, Toto Lo Verde, arrived at the restaurant minutes after the shooting. The two gunmen, unaware of the assassination, were surprised to see a crowd outside the restaurant. Upon questioning someone, the two were told that "they have killed Joe Masseria."

Gentile, a Luciano flunky, later wrote with typical old-world flair: "Quickly we went to the house of Lucky Luciano. In the meantime, Troia [Vincenzo Troia] arrived and Lucky turned to him and said: 'Don Vincenzo, tell your *compare*, Maranzano, we have killed Masseria not to serve him but for our own personal reasons. Tell him besides, that if he should touch even a hair of even a personal enemy of ours we will wage war to the end, and tell him also that within twenty-four hours he must give us an affirmative answer for the locality [the site of a truce settlement between the two Mafia factions] which we, this time, will pick out.' "

Luciano's valiant stand aside, a truce was signed and Maranzano named himself boss of bosses. Luciano had other ideas. He nodded agreement to all Maranzano's orders, waiting until the elderly "don" was comfortably settled into his imperial role. On September 10, 1931, four men, acting on Lucky's orders, entered the Manhattan offices of Salvatore Maranzano and shot and stabbed him to death.

Charles Lucky Luciano now reigned supreme in New York. He consolidated the Mafia members into one family, his own, and then moved on to strengthen his already deep ties to independent gangsters such as Lepke Buchalter, Meyer Lansky, and even the temperamental beer baron, Dutch Schultz.

His absolute control of narcotics and the brothels brought Luciano millions each year—and he spent lavishly. He, like Arnold Rothstein before him, purchased a stable of horses. According to his own statement, he also bought a piece of former bantamweight champ Lou Salica on the sly. Everything with Luciano was on the sly, even his love affairs.

He was in the habit of calling his favorite women on the phone early in the morning, demanding they visit him in his Waldorf-Astoria suite. These included Nancy Presser, a onetime showgirl Lucky had reduced to a $2 prostitute; Russian dancer and singer Gay Orlova; and a worn-out tart named Cokey Flo whose real name was Florence Brown. Sometimes he would avail himself of their charms but mostly Luciano consistently broke the Mafia code of *omerta* by talking to them, particularly about his business. Lucky was clever. He couched his problems obscurely, careful not to reveal the kind of information the Mafia feared most to reveal—names, dates and places of various robberies, killings, narcotics shipments.

It was a strange life for these women. One moment they would be working with brothel customers at a furious pace. The next would find them in the quiet, luxurious surroundings of Charlie Lucky's impressive suite. No matter to them. They always went away from Luciano with a crisp $100 bill for services rendered.

When going on the town, Luciano was always seen with a stunning Broadway showgirl (many of whom migrated to Hollywood, a few becoming top stars in films). He could be spotted regularly in such nightclubs as the Vilanova on Sixth Avenue, where seafood was a specialty, or Dave's Blue Room on Seventh. Sometimes he visited his old neighborhood on Mulberry Street to dine *en famille* with his cronies, laboring through a heavy Italian meal at Celano's. Mostly he strolled along Broadway, frequenting the Paradise and the Hollywood.

On almost every occasion, police dogged Luciano's footsteps, shadowing those he met. They found nothing. Luciano's business transactions with his men took place in his Waldorf suite early in the morning (he was a chronic insomniac) and, for only minutes, at a drugstore at Forty-ninth and Seventh owned by Moe Ducore. Lucky, in his daily stroll, invariably turned in at this pharmacy to give Ducore verbal orders to pass along.

Other times, Luciano handled his business on the phone, especially anything having to do with vice. When using the phone for this purpose, Luciano always identified himself as "Three-Twelve," numbers corresponding to those letters of the alphabet that were his initials. Lucky employed this audible razzle-dazzle to prevent identification by any possible phone tap. He liked to play it safe.

On the other hand, safety last was the motto of Arthur Flegenheimer, better known as Dutch Schultz. When Luciano formed the national crime syndicate in 1934 with Lepke, Lansky, Adonis, and others, he reluctantly agreed to take Dutch Schultz in as a full member. The beer baron's power in Manhattan was staggering, what with his army of 500 gunsels protecting the largest and most lucrative police and restaurant rackets in town.

Schultz was constantly needling Luciano. On one occasion in Lucky's suite, the site of a mob conference, Luciano graciously provided some statuesque girls. None of the mobsters accepted any of the women except Schultz, who proceeded into a bedroom and took part in the meeting by shouting out his opinions from there. Following this gathering, Schultz ambled from the bedroom, the blonde on his arm, and threw $100 at Luciano, saying, "This is for the broad."

It was not the kind of gesture Luciano thought endearing. The cool ganglord only smiled at Schultz's obvious crassness. He could wait. He had waited for Legs Diamond, he had waited for Masseria, and he would wait for Schultz.

In 1935, police heat, fanned by a new district attorney, Thomas E. Dewey, intensified in Manhattan. Raids on numbers games, brothels, narcotics storage areas, became common. Dutch Schultz raged at one of the syndicate's board meetings that "Dewey has got to be hit." The directors voted on this proposition but turned the idea down as being too risky. Schultz, ever the hothead, stormed from the room, swearing that he would "hit him myself."

The unruffled board members took only a few minutes after the Dutchman's departure to decide to kill him. Dewey's assassination would mean destruction for them all, they concluded; besides, it meant death to go against any top level syndicate decision. Schultz was doomed.

On October 23, 1935, Charlie "The Bug" Workman, Mendy Weiss, and a get-away driver identified only as "Piggy," drove up to the Palace Chophouse in Newark, N. J. All three men were professional killers in troops controlled by the Bug-and-Meyer mob (Bugsy Siegel and Meyer Lansky). Workman got out of the car dressed in a conservative business suit (much like that Charlie Lucky habitually wore) and marched into the chophouse, two guns in his hands. He first opened the door to the men's room (a favorite niche for gangsters in those days) and found Schultz washing his hands. He shot him several times. Workman then proceeded to a back room where

Charles "Lucky" Luciano, king of the New York rackets (center, wearing hat), being led to jail in 1936 following his conviction as a vice lord. (UPI)

he sprayed a table around which sat three Schultz henchmen, Abe Landau, Lulu Rosencranz, and Otto "Abbadabba" Berman, a mathematical genius whose computer-like brain tallied Schultz's dizzy earnings from his rackets. All three men were dead or dying in a matter of seconds. Schultz died raving the next day in a hospital.

The publicity resulting from the Schultz rubout was blistering. Dewey then turned his attention to the rackets controlled by Luciano. Lucky fled by a private plane to Hot Springs, Ark. Dewey denounced the gangleader as being "Public Enemy Number One in New York, and the man who succeeded Al Capone in the West!"

The police pressured the madams and girls who had been kicking back their income for half a decade to Luciano. They began to talk. A grand jury indicted Lucky on ninety counts of extortion and direction of harlotry. After a bitter fight, Luciano was extradited from Arkansas. The "King of the Pimps" spent hundreds of thousands of dollars to wiggle out of the charges but was finally convicted and sent

to Clinton Prison at Dannemora for a thirty-to-fifty year term.

Luciano never stopped trying to get out. His application for parole was turned down twice, once in 1938, again in 1942. Then an oddball event took place which would bring about this mobster's release.

When the luxury liner *Normandie* blew up at a Hudson River pier in 1942 just as it was being refitted as a troopship, the U.S. Navy's intelligence unit made a desperate move to stabilize waterfront security. The waterfront was still controlled by the crime syndicate, and, in particular, Luciano, even from his small prison cell. No one along the docks would cooperate with the Navy. Authorities went to see Lucky and asked for his help. It was understood that if he "sent out the word" for the mobsters to prevent sabotage and turn in any Mafia types working for the fascists, Luciano would benefit mightily following the war. Lucky sent out the word. The mobsters cooperated fully with the Navy and sabotage along the docks became non-existent.

The following year, through his powerful grapevine, Luciano, at the request of military authorities, contacted Mafia Don Calogero Vizzini in Palermo, Sicily, asking him to cooperate with U.S. forces once they landed there. The request was both acknowledged and carried out. Calogero's men led U.S. troops through passes and across rivers, providing vital intelligence information on enemy troop locations.

In 1945, the New York State Prison Parole Board showed its gratitude to Luciano. He was freed but on the condition that he be permanently deported to his native Italy. Luciano boarded the groaning Liberty Ship, *Laura Keane* on February 10, 1946. Frank Costello and Meyer Lansky came to see him off, carrying two suitcases. In one was a new wardrobe. In the other, a reported half million in cash. Costello would remain Luciano's chief lieutenant in the U.S. until his ouster from the syndicate by avaricious Vito Genovese in the late 1950s.

Luciano landed in Naples weeks later and took up residency in the once regal Quirinale Hotel once he arrived in Rome. Lucky, however, had no intention of remaining in Italy. Obtaining a traveling visa, he flew to Havana, Cuba in February, 1947. Havana was Meyer Lansky's town—the runty gangster controlled all the wide-open gambling and vice there, splitting all earnings with the corrupt Batista regime.

From a swanky hotel where he was registered under his given name, Salvatore Lucania, Lucky sent out the word to the states that he wanted to meet with all syndicate heads. They came on the run—Costello, Willie Moretti, Meyer Lansky, the Fischetti brothers from Chicago, even Bugsy Siegel from Las Vegas. All paid the gangleader homage, and cash.

Siegel, who was in debt to several top syndicate leaders for millions over the financing of his posh Flamingo Hotel and Casino in Las Vegas, fell into an oath-calling argument with Luciano when Lucky asked him to pay his boys back. Siegel stormed out swearing. He was murdered months later.

An enterprising reporter from Havana's *Tiempo de Cuba* newspaper discovered Luciano's presence in Havana. The story made headlines across the U.S. Under pressure from Washington, Batista's officials ordered Luciano out of Cuba. He left on a tramp Turkish steamer, the *Bakir*, traveled to Brazil and Venezuela where he was refused entry, and finally sailed back to Italy. The Italian government, embarrassed over the incident, as well as alarmed by Luciano's newly-established rackets in Rome, barred him forever from the Eternal City. Lucky moved to Naples where he lived out the remainder of his life, granting interviews to visiting American newsmen and smugly playing out the role of an exiled king of the underworld.

His complaints and whining never varied. "The American press is disgraceful," he told newsman Sid Feder in one interview. "There is too much freedom of the press in America . . . Someday, I'm gonna write my own memories . . . Then the real story is gonna come out . . . I'm gonna write about my side of it . . . But the time ain't right yet."

The time would never be right for Charles Lucky Luciano, a man who scorned all legitimate job holders as "chumps." The ganglord continued to control all drug traffic flowing into the U.S., as well as the wholesale smuggling of thousands of aliens into America. But it was apparent that Charlie Lucky ceased to enjoy his criminal status. He grew listless. He even entertained ideas of marrying his mistress, Igea Lissoni.

All that remained for him was a gnawing vanity that insisted his life was worth an epic movie. He agreed to meet with movie and TV producer Martin Gosch. On January 26, 1962, Luciano stepped from his limousine at Naple's Capodichino Airport and walked across a runway to greet Gosch. Lucky's wide smile suddenly turned into a grimace. He grabbed frantically at his shirt front and then fell to the pavement, dead of a heart attack. It was *omerta* to the end.

[ALSO SEE Louis Lepke Buchalter, Frank Costello, Vito Genovese, Meyer Lansky, The Mafia, Salvatore Maranzano, Benjamin "Bugsy" Siegel, Dutch Schultz, The Syndicate, Joseph Valachi.]

LUETGERT, ADOLPH LOUIS
Murderer ● (1848-1911)

BACKGROUND: BORN IN GERMANY, IMMIGRATED TO U.S. IN EARLY 1870S. SETTLED IN CHICAGO WHERE HE PURSUED SEVERAL TRADES INCLUDING FARMING, TANNING, AND EVENTUALLY SAUSAGEMAKING. MARRIED LOUISA BICKNESE IN 1880S. MINOR PUBLIC EDUCATION. DESCRIPTION: 6'3", BROWN EYES, BROWN HAIR, EXTREMELY HEAVYSET. ALIASES: NONE. RECORD: MURDERED HIS WIFE ON MAY 1, 1897, TRIED FOR THIS MURDER IN TWO TRIALS IN CHICAGO; CONVICTED BY JURY 2/9/1898 AND SENTENCED TO LIFE IMPRISONMENT AT JOLIET STATE PENITENTIARY WHERE HE SUBSEQUENTLY DIED.

Adolph Louis Luetgert was an unhappy man, a hard-working, powerfully built German immigrant bent on sweaty success. For years he had been building up his sausage factory in Chicago. His first wife died leaving him with one child. He married again to Louisa Bicknese. Why Luetgert married Louisa is uncertain; that he planned her grisly murder in a most unique way was very certain indeed.

Luetgert's sexual appetite was enormous. He made no bones about it. Any woman he could manage to engineer under his massive 240 pound frame in a love bed in his factory was merely another prize.

There was his wife's maid, Mary Simering. Luetgert slept regularly with her. There was also his mistress Mrs. Christine Feldt, a wealthy German women. Luetgert slept regularly with her. Then there was Mrs. Agathia Tosch, who owned a saloon with her husband on Chicago's North Side close to the sausagemaker's factory. Luetgert slept regularly with her also.

As Luetgert pursued his lustful objectives, his business began to slip away from him. Though his huge factory on Hermitage and Diversey turned out great quantities of sausages, Luetgert discovered that he could not meet his supplier's costs. Instead of shoring up his losses, Luetgert and his business advisor William Charles planned to expand.

They attempted to secure more capital to enlarge the factory and suddenly, Luetgert had visions of becoming the sausage king of America. But by May, 1897, the plans came to failure. As usual Luetgert sought solace in sex orgies with his many mistresses.

As Matthew W. Pinkerton of the renowned detective agency judged: "He was an immoral man and was often visited by women of extremely doubtful character." An understatement at the least.

Louisa Luetgert, a normally placid, nondescript person, suddenly became outraged at her husband's extravagant sex life. The cold-eyed, egotistical German sausagemaker responded to her indignation by immediately taking her by the throat and choking her. Before the poor woman collapsed, the butcher thought better of his rage and released her. He noticed alarmed neighbors watching him through the parlor windows of his home. A few days later Luetgert was seen chasing his wife down the street, shouting threats, a revolver quaking in his hand. Again, his angry burst came to nothing.

Then the butcher began to plan. On March 11, 1897, the sausagemaker went to Lor Owen & Company, a wholesale drug firm, and ordered 325 pounds of crude potash plus 50 pounds of arsenic. This was delivered to his factory the next day.

On April 24, Luetgert asked one of his employees, Frank Odorowsky, known as "Smokehouse Frank," to come into his office. There he told the worker to remove the barrel of potash in the shipping room to the factory basement where there were three huge vats used to boil down sausage material.

"This is strong stuff, this potash," Luetgert

warned his employee. "Be careful not to burn yourself."

"Smokehouse Frank" and another employee, following Luetgert's orders, crushed the potash into small pieces with a hatchet and a hammer. Both burned their hands and faces badly.

Luetgert and "Smokehouse Frank" then placed the "strong stuff" in the middle vat in the basement. The sausagemaker then turned on the steam under the middle vat until the material dissolved into liquid.

On May 1, 1897, Luetgert called his night watchman, Frank Bialk, gave him a dollar and told him to go to a nearby drugstore and buy a bottle of celery compound. When the watchman returned with the medicine, he was amazed to find the door leading to the main factory barricaded. Luetgert appeared and took the medicine.

"All right, Frank, go back to the engine room," he said.

At ten that evening Luetgert again summoned the watchman and sent him back to the drugstore to buy a bottle of Hunyadi water.

While the watchman was running errands, Luetgert worked alone in the factory basement. He turned on the steam under the middle vat about a quarter before nine.

As she was later to testify, a young German girl named Emma Schiemicke, who was passing the factory on the night of May 1, at about 10:30 p.m. with her sister, saw Luetgert leading his wife up the alleyway behind the factory.

Luetgert stayed in the basement of his factory until two the following morning. Watchman Bialk found him fully dressed in his office the next day.

"Should I let the fires go out under the vat?" he asked his employer.

"Bank the fires at fifty pounds of steam pressure," the huge man told him. The watchman went down to the basement. There he saw a hose running water into the middle vat. On the floor in front of the vat was a sticky, glue-like substance. Bending down, Bialk noticed that the substance appeared to contain flakes of bone.

He thought nothing of it. Luetgert used all sorts of waste meats to make his sausage. Following the weekend, May 3, "Smokehouse Frank" also noticed the unusual slime on the floor of the basement. He ran to his employer, surprised.

"I don't know what that is, Mr. Luetgert. Somebody maybe came into the factory and—"

Luetgert spoke rapidly: "Don't say a word, Frank, don't say anything about it, and I'll see that you have a good job as long as you live."

The sausagemaker's employees went to work cleaning the brown slime from the floor. They scraped the gooey substance into a nearby drain that led to a sewer. The larger chunks of waste they placed in a barrel.

"What do I do with the stuff that won't go down the drain," Odorowsky said to Luetgert.

"Take the barrel out to the railroad tracks and scatter it around out there."

Odorowsky obeyed.

The following day, Diedrich Bicknese, Louisa's brother, came to Chicago and called on her at home. The maid, Mary Simering, told him that Mrs. Luetgert was not home. He came back later and his sister still had not appeared. That evening, he found Luetgert at home and demanded to know where his sister was.

Luetgert calmly told the brother that his wife had disappeared, that she left the house on May 1 and had never returned.

"Why didn't you go to the police?"

"I don't want a scandal," Luetgert replied. "I paid five dollars to two detectives to find her."

Bicknese then seriously began to search for his sister. He went to Kankakee, Illinois, thinking she might be visiting friends there. He found nothing. He returned to Chicago and discovered that Louisa still hadn't returned home. Then he went to the police.

Police Captain Schuettler had to summon the sausagemaker twice to the station. He knew the butcher well and also knew about his violent arguments with his wife. When Luetgert arrived, the captain began to question him.

"You made a vigorous appeal to me to find a lost dog for you not long ago. Why did you not report the absence of your wife?"

Luetgert was calm. "I expected her to come back. I wished to avoid any disgrace. I'm a prominent businessman and can't afford to have this sort of scandal about my household."

The police allowed Luetgert to return to his factory. Then they began dragging the river and searching the alleyways of Chicago. On May 7, police visited the factory and inter-

Adolph Louis Luetgert boiled his wife's body down to sludge in his Chicago sausage factory; discovery of her teeth led to his arrest and conviction. (N.Y. Historical Society)

rogated watchman Bialk and "Smokehouse Frank."

Their story of the running water and the slime found in front of the middle vat in the factory's basement sparked Captain Schuettler's imagination. By May 15 he was back at the factory and began a thorough search of the basement, particularly the middle vat.

Schuettler's discovery was one of the most gruesome in the annals of murder. The middle vat was two-thirds full of brownish fluid. They drained the vat after using gunny sacks to act as filters. The catch was awful.

They found several pieces of bone and two gold rings. One was a small, badly tarnished friendship ring; the other was a heavy clean ring with the initials "L.L." engraved on it.

Both rings had been worn by Mrs. Luetgert.

Under analysis, the bones discovered in the vat were definitely human—a human third rib, part of a humerus or great bone of the arm, a bone from the palm of a human hand, a bone from the fourth toe of a human right foot, fragments of a human temporal bone, a bone from a human ear, and a sesamoid bone from a human foot.

After Luetgert was arrested and brought to trial, he maintained these bones were those of animals, that he purchased these scraps to boil down to make soft soap by which he could clean up his factory.

The defense's argument, of course, was ridiculous, argued the prosecution. Why would Luetgert buy $40 worth of potash and waste materials to scrub down his factory when $1 (at that time) worth of soft soap would have done the job?

All this circumstantial evidence was crowned by witnesses who damned the heavy German sausagemaker.

Luetgert's mistresses turned on him in womanly rage. First came Mrs. Agatha Tosch who stated that she asked Luetgert where his wife was shortly after she had disappeared while he was gulping huge amounts of beer in her saloon.

He became pale and excited, she said, and blurted: "I don't know. I am as innocent as the southern skies!"

The jury smiled grimly. It was obvious to everyone that if Luetgert didn't know where his wife was there was nothing over which to claim his innocence.

Mrs. Tosch further told the jury that Luetgert once stated that he hated his wife and that "I could take her and crush her." Another time, the witness said, Luetgert sent for a doctor to attend his sick wife. At that time, sitting in Mrs. Tosch's bar, he told her, "If I had waited a little longer, the dead, rotten beast would have croaked!"

Another witness, a woman, reported that the sausagemaker told her that "If it were not for Mary Simering I would not stay at home."

Then Luetgert's favorite mistress, Mrs. Christine Feldt took the stand. This was the woman for whom he felt, or once stated he felt, true love: "If you forsake me, Chrisine, I will take my own life; I do not care to live."

Christine Feldt, unfortunately for the sausagemaker, did not feel the same way about him.

She produced all the mawkish, love-gushing letters the heavyset man had written to her. He blushed in court, the only change in his calm demeanor throughout his two lengthy trials.

Mrs. Feldt also stated that Luetgert had given her $4,000 for "safe-keeping" shortly before Mrs. Luetgert's disappearance. The crushing evidence came when the sausagemaker's mistress also stated that Luetgert had given her a blood-stained knife without explanation the day after his wife vanished. Mrs. Feldt produced the knife.

Though the butcher never admitted his guilt, the evidence overwhelmingly supported the fact that Luetgert had murdered his wife and then boiled her body down to a gluey residue in his sausage machine.

He was sentenced to life in prison, where he died still claiming his innocence.

LUTHERLAND, THOMAS
Murderer ● (? -1691)

A convicted felon, Lutherland was sent as a bound servant from England to work in New Jersey. Not long after his arrival, he was convicted of stealing. Months later, John Clark, a boat trader, was found dead and his supplies stolen. It was an obvious murder.

The goods from Clark's trading boat were found in Lutherland's home. The superstition rampant in the New World at that time was evidenced at Lutherland's trial. The corpse of John Clark was brought forth and the accused man was ordered to touch it. If Lutherland was guilty, the court reasoned, the body would bleed. It did not, but Lutherland was sentenced to die anyway, being executed February 23, 1691.

LYLES, ANJETTE DONOVAN
Serial Killer ● (1917-   )

Insurance money was the motive behind the many murders committed by Anjette Lyles. Housewife, mother and restaurant proprietor, Lyles appeared to her friends and customers in

Macon, Georgia, an outgoing, well-adjusted person. She was, however, plagued by family deaths that occured without explanation.

Two of Anjette's husbands and a mother-in-law had died from mysterious illnesses. Then her young daughter Marcia grew strangely ill and no amount of medication seemed to make her better. A short time after Marcia became sick, the Macon police received an anonymous letter that stated that Anjette Lyles was a poisoner and that she had murdered two previous husbands, the mother-in-law, and was now slowly killing her daughter Marcia by slowing administering arsenic to her. (The letter had been written by Lyles's cook, Carrie Jackson.)

Authorities acted immediately but they were too late to save little Marcia who died from arsenic poisoning. Mrs. Lyles had only one explanation for her daughter's death—that the little girl must have beeing playing "doctor and nurse" and had somehow ingested arsenic.

The bodies of Lyles's husbands were exhumed and arsenic was again found. Lyles was put on trial and charged with four counts of murder. She was found guilty and sentenced to death. State psychiatrists later certified her as insane and she was removed to the State Hospital at Milledgeville, Georgia.

Killer of four, Anjette Lyles with her children Marcia, left, whom she poisoned, and Carla.

MC CONAGHY, ROBERT
Murderer ● (? -1840)

Plagued with family problems, McConaghy lost his mind May 30, 1840, and slaughtered his wife's family after an

Mass murderer Robert McConaghy was described in this 1840 pamphlet as being hanged twice for the slaying of his six relatives. (N.Y. Historical Society)

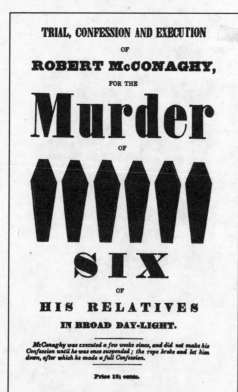

TRIAL, CONFESSION AND EXECUTION
OF
ROBERT McCONAGHY,
FOR THE
Murder
OF
SIX
OF
HIS RELATIVES
IN BROAD DAY-LIGHT.

McConaghy was executed a few weeks since, and did not make his Confession until he was once suspended; the rope broke and let him down, after which he made a full Confession.

Price 12½ cents.

argument. He strangled his mother-in-law, Mrs. William Brown, and beat and shot her four children whose ages ranged from 10 to 21 years old.

Quickly taken into custody, McConaghy stubbornly refused to confess his guilt during his trial. He was sentenced to death on the gallows. On the day of his execution, November 6, 1840 at Huntington, Pa., the rope broke as McConaghy dropped through the trap door. He was carried up to the scaffold again and, as another rope was placed about his neck, he loudly confessed his murders.

He again shot down into space, this time a self-admitted killer. The second rope held; McConaghy joined his hapless relatives.

MC GURN, "MACHINE GUN" JACK
Murderer, Gangster ● (1904-1936)

BACKGROUND: BORN IN CHICAGO'S LITTLE ITALY IN 1904. GIVEN NAME, JAMES VINCENZO DE MORA. MINOR PUBLIC EDUCATION. MARRIED SHOWGIRL LOUISE ROLFE, 1929. DESCRIPTION: 5'10", BROWN EYES, BLACK HAIR, STURDY BUILD. ALIASES: VINCENT GEBARDI. RECORD: ARRESTED IN CHICAGO, 1923, CARRYING CONCEALED WEAPON, DISMISSED; ARRESTED, CHICAGO, 1924, ALONG WITH HIS BROTHER ANTONIO IN A WEST SIDE HOTEL ROOM (APPARENTLY WAITING TO AMBUSH ONE OF THE WEST SIDE O'DONNELLS) WITH A SMALL ARSENAL CONSISTING OF A THOMPSON SUBMACHINEGUN WITH LOADED MAGAZINE, A .45-CALIBER AUTOMATIC PISTOL, A RIFLE AND LARGE QUANTITIES OF DUMDUM SHELLS, DISMISSED; ARRESTED TWICE ON SUSPICION OF MURDER, 1927, RELEASED; ARRESTED ON SUSPICION OF MURDER, 1929 (FOR THE ST. VALENTINE'S DAY MASSACRE), NEVER BROUGHT TO TRIAL; KILLED IN A CHICAGO BOWLING ALLEY, 1936.

The story of "Machine Gun" Jack McGurn is the age-old tale of the good boy turned gangster, so dear to the hearts of Warner Bros. script writers. McGurn was truly a product of the 1920s, beginning his career as a clean cut kid from the slums battling for a slice of dignity in the ring as a promising welterweight.

McGurn's elementary education showed he possessed deep qualities of leadership and a retentive memory. Boxing fascinated McGurn and as a teenager he won a series of impressive victories at a local amateur athletic club. Fight promoter Emil Thiery discovered him and soon promoted him to the ranks of professional fighters. It was at Thiery's suggestion, James Vincenzo De Mora adopted the ring name of Jack McGurn. The "Machine Gun" would come later.

While McGurn was proving that he "had the true fighting heart," as one sports writer claimed, his father, Angelo De Mora, a grocer whose store squatted in Little Italy on Halsted Street, was running into trouble with the terrible Genna brothers. At the advent of Prohibition, the Gennas had transformed all of Little Italy into a vast commercial area of alky cookers. Stills bubbled and gurgled in almost every home, franchised by the Gennas, making the raw, rotgut gin and bourbon so popular and sometimes lethal in the neighborhood speakeasies.

Angelo De Mora sold sugar to the Gennas for their alky operations, a comparatively safe enterprise until some ugly, unknown competitors appeared on January 8, 1923. On the morning of that day Angelo was found shot dead in front of his store. McGurn rushed home as soon as he heard of his father's death. He was then nineteen but he immediately assumed the role as head of the household, standing before policemen, shielding his mother and five younger brothers.

"Do you know who killed your father?" one officer asked.

"No," McGurn said solemnly.

"Are you afraid for your own life now that you're head of the house?"

Young Jack McGurn's dark eyes smoldered as he said ominously, "I'm big enough to take care of this case myself."

McGurn never went back to the ring. He took up the gun and began working for Al Capone who regarded him as his most trustworthy gunner, a torpedo of invincible nerve who could be counted on to carry out the most grisly and hazardous assignments without mistake. Five years later, "Machine Gun" (his preferred weapon), Jack McGurn was the most feared of Capone's killers.

Following the slaughter of Moran's gang on North Clark Street in 1929, Cook County Coroner Dr. Herman N. Bundesen wrote: "It is known he [McGurn] is suspected of having a hand in the killing of some fifteen other gangsters [the seven killed on St. Valentine's Day would have made twenty-two]. He is generally regarded as an expert machine gunner. It

is believed he got his start as a killer after his father was shot to death."

Six of those notches on McGurn's gun were carved in 1928. The Gennas had risen against Capone, and Scarface had assigned McGurn the job of obliterating the Sicilian clan's army. McGurn relished the job since several on Capone's list had been involved in his father's death. Within a month and a half, McGurn wiped out six of the Gennas' top men: Lawrence La Presta, June 1; Diego Attlomionte, June 29; Numio Jamericco and Lorenzo Alagno, June 30; Giovanni Blaudins, July 11; Dominic Cinderella, July 17.

The dedicated young killer had learned that one of these men had referred to his father as "a nickel and dimer." After each man had been machinegunned to death, McGurn had pressed a nickel into each victim's palm, his sign of utter contempt and a trademark forever linked with his brand of killing.

The previous August had also seen McGurn's handiwork in full view. Joey Aiello's feud with Capone over certain West Side beer territories reached its peak when Aiello offered $50,000 reward for Al Capone's lifeless body. He imported four out-of-town killers to do the job when no one in Chicago took up his offer. Days after their arrival, the imported gunsels ran smack into the smiling "Machine Gun" Jack McGurn. The lights went out for Antonio Torchio of New York, Anthony K. Russo and Vincent Spicuzza of St. Louis, and Sam Valente of Cleveland. All of them were found riddled with machine gun slugs. There were five-cent pieces in all their hands.

Capone was delighted with his youthful killer. Next to Phil D'Andrea, McGurn became Scarface's constant companion. The gunner, the sides of his suitcoat bulging from the weight of two automatics, sat one seat behind his chief at the ball park and at ringside. At other times McGurn could usually be found skipping rope and working out in the special gym Capone had equipped at his headquarters in the Hotel Metropole, 2300 South Michigan Avenue. He, like most of Scarface's troop, kept trim and fit for the unsavory jobs handed down by the chief.

When not on assignment from Capone, McGurn frequented most of the hotter jazz spots in Chicago. He collected blonde chorus girls and part ownerships of the better nightspots, through intimidation and broken legs. McGurn

Comedian Joe E. Lewis shows knife scars he received from hoodlums when he refused to work in McGurn's nightclub.

fancied himself a jazz-age sheik, pomading his curly black hair down flat and parting it in the middle. He strummed a ukulele and did snake dances in cabarets. Sporting wide-checked suits heavily padded in the shoulders, flower-bedecked neckties, and pointed patent-leather shoes, McGurn imitated his idol, Rudolph Valentino.

By the time he was twenty-three, McGurn owned pieces of at least five nightclubs as well as other lucrative properties that had come his way without ceremony or worry while he was working for Capone.

When McGurn bought 25 per cent of the Green Mill cabaret in 1927, he became incensed that the club's star attraction, singer-comedian Joe E. Lewis, refused to renew his contract, stating he was going to work for a rival club. Lewis opened to packed houses at the New Rendezvous. Days later, McGurn drew Lewis aside as he was about to enter his hotel, The New Commonwealth. McGurn had two friends with him. All three men kept their hands in their pockets, fingering guns.

"We miss you, Joe," McGurn purred. "The old Mill's a morgue without you."

"You'll get another act," Lewis replied.

"You made your point, Joe. You said you'd

open and you did." He paused. "It's time to come back now." McGurn had previously told Lewis that he "would never live to open" his new act.

"Not a chance, Jack," Lewis said bravely and walked away.

On November 10, 1927, three of McGurn's troop burst into Lewis' hotel suite, pistol-whipped him, and cut his throat almost ear to ear. The comedian lived, however, and through a titanic effort regained his voice and renewed his glittering career. Capone, incensed at McGurn's action (so the story goes) advanced Lewis $10,000 until he could get back on his feet.

Capone, nevertheless, could not bring himself to rebuke his most devoted killer.

McGurn had gone on the spot twice for Capone, both attempts on his life being made by the "Bugs" Moran gang. The Gusenberg brothers, Pete and Frank, ace Moran machine-gunners, once caught McGurn in a phone booth inside the McCormick Hotel. Several bursts from the Gusenbergs' tommy guns almost ended McGurn's spectacular career, but major surgery and a long period of guarded recuperation saved the killer.

It was McGurn who visited Capone at his Palm Island, Florida resort early in February, 1929 for very important conferences concerning the rising threat of the North Side gang led by Bugs Moran who boldly challenged Scarface's beer strongholds. Ten days later, the St. Valentine's Day Massacre occurred.

Of the five men who walked into Moran's headquarters on North Clark Street that bloody day to slaughter seven men, only two men were ever identified—Fred R. "Killer" Burke and Jack McGurn.

George Brichet, a teenager, was walking past the Moran warehouse when the five men entered that day and overheard one man say to another: "Come on, Mac." He picked out McGurn's picture from police mug shots. Armed with an arrest warrant, police broke into McGurn's suite of rooms at the Stevens Hotel on February 27, 1929. Before hauling the gangster away, officers were treated to an invective-filled tirade from McGurn's sweetheart, showgirl Louise Rolfe.

Miss Rolfe, a statuesque blonde—"the blonde alibi" as the press dubbed her—swore that McGurn had been with her all during the time of the Massacre. McGurn was neverthe-

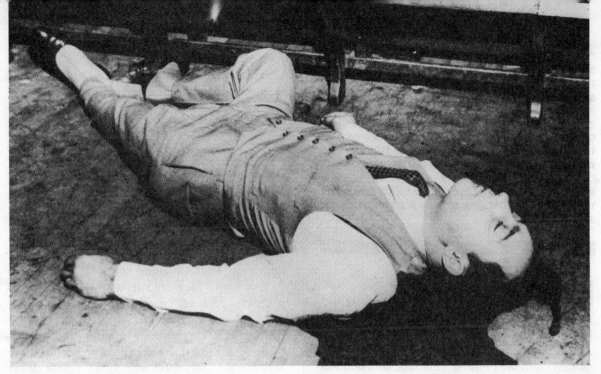

"Machine Gun" Jack McGurn, Al Capone's top triggerman, killed in a Chicago bowling alley on the eve of St. Valentine's Day, 1936. (UPI)

less indicted for perjury but the gangster got around that by marrying his blonde love baby. As McGurn's wife, Miss Rolfe could not testify against him.

Defense attorneys for McGurn four times insisted that their client be tried. Each time, the prosecution stated that it was not ready to proceed. Under Illinois law the prosecution has only four legal delays of this kind. Following these, the state must drop the case. On December 2, 1929, it did, and McGurn was set free.

McGurn's role in the St. Valentine's Day Massacre caused Capone to put him "on ice." He was too hot to use again as an enforcer. He was seen less and less with Capone and not at all during Scarface's tax trial, the role of bodyguard given over exclusively to Phil D'Andrea.

Following Capone's jail sentence, McGurn's prestige dipped. He busied himself with his various nightclubs, which all collapsed during the Depression years. Louise Rolfe left her gunman-lover when the money ran out. Alone and near penniless, McGurn met his ironic fate on February 13, 1936—the eve of the anniversary of the St. Valentine's Day Massacre.

Two unidentified men, remnants of the old Moran gang, finally caught up with McGurn in a Chicago bowling alley, shooting him to death with machineguns. In his left hand, the killers placed a comic valentine, its verse reading:

> You've lost your job,
> You've lost your dough,
> Your jewels and handsome houses.
> But things could be worse, you know.
> You haven't lost your trousers.

Into the palm of "Machine Gun" Jack McGurn's right hand they pressed a nickel.

[ALSO SEE Al Capone, St. Valentine's Day Massacre.]

MADDEN, OWEN ("OWNEY")
Murderer, Bootlegger ● (1892-1964)

BACKGROUND: BORN IN LIVERPOOL, ENGLAND. IMMIGRATED WITH PARENTS TO U.S. IN 1903. MINOR PUBLIC EDUCATION. DESCRIPTION: 5'6", BROWN EYES, BROWN HAIR, SLENDER. ALIASES: OWNEY MADDEN, OWNEY THE KILLER. RECORD: BECAME A MEMBER OF THE NOTORIOUS GOPHER GANG WHICH DOMINATED A LARGE WEST SIDE AREA OF NEW YORK KNOWN AS HELL'S KITCHEN; RAN UP FORTY-FOUR ARRESTS BY THE TIME HE WAS TWENTY-TWO, NONE OF WHICH CAUSED HIM TO SPEND A DAY IN JAIL; HEADED THE GOPHER GANG IN 1909 AND WAS SUSPECTED OF KILLING FIVE RIVAL GANGSTERS IN THE HUDSON DUSTERS GANG FROM 1910 TO 1915; CONVICTED OF KILLING PATRICK

"LITTLE PATSY" DOYLE, A LEADER FOR THE HUDSON DUSTERS GANG, ON 11/28/14; SENTENCED TO SERVE TEN TO TWENTY YEARS IN SING SING; PAROLED IN JANUARY, 1923; UPON RELEASE BECAME A COMPANY-PAID BLACKJACKER OF UNION ORGANIZERS OF CAB DRIVERS; ORGANIZED A HIJACKING GANG IN 1923, OPENED SEVERAL SPEAKEASIES AND BECAME ONE OF THE TOP BOOTLEGGERS IN MANHATTAN THROUGHOUT THE 1920S; JAILED BRIEFLY IN 1932 FOR PAROLE VIOLATION; QUIT THE RACKETS TO RETIRE TO HOT SPRINGS, ARK., A LONG-TIME COOLING OFF PLACE FOR THE UNDERWORLD, WHERE HE DIED A NATURAL DEATH IN 1964.

Outwardly, Owney Madden in his youth appeared to be a friendly, smiling lad who could safely be described as a "clean-cut kid." He was anything but that. As a member of the Gopher Gang in NYC at age eleven, Madden was a cunning, evil-minded thief who murdered for the pure pleasure of killing. He was once called "that little banty rooster out of hell," and he lived up to every word of it.

Madden was a wiry youth who taught himself early how to wield a lead pipe wrapped in newspapers, brass knuckles, a blackjack, a slingshot and, with great delight, a pistol. Of all the gangsters of his era, Madden was considered the best shot in New York. He proved his marksmanship time and again in gang wars with the rival Hudson Dusters mob. At seventeen he had murdered his first man and acquired the unsavory title of "Owney the Killer." At eighteen he captained a faction of the Gophers. At twenty-three he had killed five men.

Madden prided himself on the fact that he had never worked a day in his life. As a leader of the Gophers, he accepted daily tribute from his stooges, raking in at least $200 a day for the robberies, union beatings, killings, and inter-gang raids he planned. He received extortion money from dozens of storekeepers who paid rather than have their shopfronts destroyed by a bomb.

A newsman once asked Madden how he managed to live in luxury without working. "I don't work," Owney replied.

"What do you do all day long?" the reporter asked.

Madden grinned and then sat down at a desk in police headquarters, where he was being momentarily detained, and wrote a brief journal for the newsman. His entries included:

"Thursday—Went to a dance in the afternoon. Went to a dance at night and then to a cabaret. Took some girls home. Went to a restaurant and stayed there until seven o'clock Friday morning.

"Friday—Spent the day with Freda Horner. Looked at some fancy pigeons. Met some friends in a saloon early in the evening and stayed with them until five o'clock in the morning.

"Saturday—Slept all day. Went to a dance in the Bronx late in the afternoon, and to a dance on Park Avenue at night.

"Sunday—Slept until three o'clock. Went to a dance in the afternoon and to another in the same place at night. After that I went to a cabaret and stayed there almost all night."

Madden was girl happy. Any girl he knew was *his* girl. Any man who made a pass at his girl was beaten senseless; some, like innocuous William Henshaw, a clerk, were killed. Madden learned that Henshaw had asked one of his girls on a date. He followed the clerk on board a trolley car and shot him in full view of a dozen passengers. Before fleeing, Madden paused to ring the trolley's bell.

Henshaw lived long enough to identify his killer as Owney Madden. Two weeks later police spotted Madden in Hell's Kitchen and finally captured him after Owney led them in a desperate chase across several rooftops. The murder charge against Owney collapsed when no witnesses came forward.

With Tanner Smith, Madden opened his wild Winona Club, a second-story bistro which served as a meeting place for the Gophers and became the scene of countless sluggings, robberies, and murders. When Dennis Keating, the building owner, complained of the noise emanating each night from Madden's club, he was thrown face first down the stairs.

The Winona Club became a Gopher stronghold, so fiercely protected by Madden and his goons that police were fearful to enter. One squad of eight men did attempt to gain entry and were driven back under a hail of bullets. Madden screamed from his second-floor barricade: "We'll shoot the gizzard out of any cop who tries to get in here!"

Another squad of police broke through the back entrance and, after an hour fight with fifteen hoodlums, brought the Gophers into headquarters. Madden was released the next day under a $500 bond. The charge of disorderly conduct was dropped six months later.

Tanner Smith was also released and, after convincing New York Mayor William J. Gaynor to order police not to use their clubs against "suspected criminals" (as a result of the bruises he displayed to the Mayor), became the idol of the underworld. Smith subsequently served a year in prison for carrying a concealed weapon and ostensibly reformed upon his release in 1914. He became a contractor and his fortunes grew, but he was killed in 1919 by a berserk worker in his employ. Smith left $100,000 in his estate. Owney Madden would leave thirty times that amount.

Madden built up the Gopher gang from 1911 to 1914, enlisting the aid of such killers as Chick Hyland, Eddie Egan, and Bill Tammany. Each of these was eventually sent to Sing Sing for carrying out Owney the Killer's orders. Madden was unconcerned. His ambition was to be king of all the gangs in New York, a dream Joe the Boss Masseria would realize almost fifteen years later—along with five bullets in the head.

There was a streak of hard-core hate in Owney which he substituted for courage. He had been in hundreds of gang fights where he had been injured, but he always managed to walk away. His closest shave was on the night of November 6, 1912 when he attended a dance at the Arbor Dance Hall on Fifty-Second street. Lured to the hall's balcony by an attractive woman, Owney failed to see eleven men—members of the rival Hudson Dusters gang—take seats all around him. When the woman left, Madden caught sight of them.

He stood up and shouted: "Come on, youse guys! Youse wouldn't shoot nobody! Who did you ever bump off?" Madden went for his gun and the eleven men drew theirs. Owney the Killer went down in the shootout, eight bullets in his body.

The eleven mobsters fled with the rest of the terrified dancers and police found Owney bleeding to death, alone in the hall. On the way to the hospital, police quizzed him about his assassins.

"Nothin' doing," the banty gangster choked out. "The boys'll get 'em. It's nobody's business but mine who put these slugs into me!" Before Madden recuperated, six of his attackers had been killed.

In late 1914, Owney had more girl problems.

He had stolen Freda Horner away from Little Patsy Doyle, a ranking member of the Hudson Dusters. Doyle, in retaliation, began informing police about Madden's operations. He also beat and stabbed Madden's close friend, Tony Romanello. Upon learning this, Owney the Killer marked Doyle for death.

On the night of November 28, 1914, a friend of Freda Horner's, Margaret Everdeane, called Doyle and told him that Freda was "all busted up over the way she treated you." When Margaret told Doyle that Freda was pining to see him, the little gangster came on the run to a pre-appointed rendezvous, a backroom of a saloon on Eighth Avenue.

He spotted Margaret Everdeane sitting alone. "Where's Freda?" Doyle said.

"Gone for a minute," Margaret explained. "She'll be right back. Sit down for a minute, Patsy. Sit down."

The bartender came into the room. "There's a guy outside wantsa see youse," he said to Doyle and left.

Patsy shouted after him: "Who wants to see me?"

Owney Madden stepped through the door. "I do, rat!" Madden fired one shot that hit Doyle in the lung. Doyle stood up, clutching for his pistol. Two more shots hit him. Bug-eyed, Doyle staggered past Madden, through the saloon, and out into the street. There he dropped dead of his wounds.

In the days that followed, police had broken down the stories of Margaret Everdeane and Freda Horner and, to save themselves, they gave evidence against Madden who was quickly arrested, convicted and sentenced to Sing Sing for ten to twenty years. Owney was paroled in January, 1923 only to find his gang completely decimated. His two top men, Johnny McArdle and Arthur Biedler, were both in prison. The rest were dead of gang battles, in prison, or had joined the Prohibition mobs.

Madden went recruiting and was soon in the bootlegging business. He teamed up with Dutch Schultz to become the most important bootlegger and speakeasy owner in New York until the end of the 1920s. He and Schultz battled Legs Diamond, Waxey Gordon (Irving Wexler), and Vincent "Mad Dog" Coll throughout the wild era. Coll once kidnapped Madden's partner Big French DeMange, and held him for a large ransom.

By 1931, with Repeal on its way, Madden

went into the fight rackets with Bill Duffy and the two promoted the powderpuff giant Primo Carnera to his dubiously-earned heavyweight championship.

The following year, Owney was arrested again on a parole violation charge. "Piddling," he said. It was part of a new program to harass Prohibition gangsters out of town. Disgusted with countless minor arrests—fifty-seven in NYC alone—Owney Madden gave up the rackets and retired at forty years of age, moving to Hot Springs, Ark., where he died in 1964.

Some said he retired with more than $3,000,-000, which wasn't bad, figuring that Primo Carnera won an estimated $2,000,000 from purses and retired penniless.

[ALSO SEE Vincent "Mad Dog" Coll, John Thomas "Legs" Diamond, Dutch Schultz.]

Manhattan gangster Owney Madden (left) once again in custody, 1940. (UPI)

MAFIA, THE

Of all the sinister and evil secret societies and brotherhoods——from the Thugee cult of India to Aleister Crowley's clique of devil worshippers—the Mafia has emerged as the most feared, the most powerful, and the most malignant. It was not always so.

The present-day Mafia is a vile perversion of a once patriotic and partisan secret brotherhood dedicated to freeing its native Sicily from the oppressive rule of the French Angevins in 1282. The Society's battle slogan, was, according to legend, *"Morte alla Francia Italia anela!"* ("Death to the French is Italy's cry!") The initial letters of this slogan formed the word Mafia and came to symbolize the violently anti-French movement.

For centuries the Mafia became a champion of its people, waging guerrilla warfare against the French and other invaders of Sicily. The island country's chief city, Palermo, became the hub of Mafia activities and from here the "dons" of the secret organization sent out recruiters to the country, culling from the land the young and ardent patriots who were taught the deadly uses of the dagger, the rope, and the sword.

Early members of the Mafia were experts at mutilating their enemies with the knife in order to extract information from them, a practice learned from Moslem invaders years before. Stealth, guile, and murder became the Mafia's stock in trade.

The early organization, strictly confined to those born in Sicily, absorbed all sub-secret societies in the country, including the centuries-old Camorra (although this criminal fraternity continued to operate independently in mainland Italy, its leaders vowing eternal blood feuds with the Mafia).

By the turn of the Nineteenth Century, the Mafia had evolved from a benevolent society which fed the starving and sheltered the homeless to a monolithic beast of prey that extorted money and power on a grand scale from both wealthy landowners and peasants. Its leaders, known as *capos*, directed its political destiny with businesslike methods, infiltrating politics, the police system, and even the small Sicilian army.

The brotherhood was and is organized along militaristic lines. Centuries ago, Sicily was divided into areas of responsibility by the Mafia, each faction accountable for a certain province and all factions answerable to the chief Mafia overlord in Palermo. The *Stoppaglieri* faction controlled Palermo and the province of Morreale, its rules enforced by a gang of young thugs known as the *Fratuzzi* (Little

Brothers). The large agrarian province of Messina was controlled by the *Beati Paoli*; the province of Caltanisetta was dominated by the *Fratellanza* (Brotherhood).

Usually ten Mafia members constituted a unit. From these a *capo*, or leader, was elected through democratic voting. The *capos*, in turn, elected a chief of the province or "family" known as *capo famiglia*. The family or province chiefs then elected their Mafia king, or, as he would be known in the U.S., boss of bosses—*capo dei capi* or *capo de tutti capi*.

Naturally, the position of Mafia king became the most enviable and powerful position in all of Sicily. The holding of such power in Sicily mostly required the ability to make nerveless decisions and a steady diet; it was life-long. In the U.S., such a position was risky. Once elevated to this underworld throne, a *capo de tutti capi* had to guard against ruthless, ambitious Mafiosi who disregarded Old World tradition and pursued the position through the undemocratic process of murder.

For the first four decades of the Mafia's encroachment into the United States' underworld, Sicilian Mafia leaders considered the American chapter of the brotherhood irresponsible and perverted, since it paid little or no allegiance to its parent group. Ties today are much stronger, particularly through the use of the Mafia-controlled European drug traffic channeled into the U.S.

However, the *Mafiosi* who immigrated to the U.S. in the last quarter of the Nineteenth Century upheld the basic rules that governed the paternal Sicilian organization:

1. Reciprocal assistance to any Mafia faction in need without question.
2. Total obedience to the boss.
3. An attack on any Mafia member to be considered an attack on all members, to be avenged irrespective of circumstance.
4. No dealings with authorities in any circumstances.
5. The code of *omerta* (silence) to be maintained under penalty of death; the identity of Mafia members and the brotherhood's rites to be kept secret at all costs.

This fanatical credo was kept amazingly intact for five decades in America until Nicola Gentile, a Mafia member, disclosed the brotherhood's working apparatus in the late 1930s.

Joseph Valachi was to do the same twenty years later when he outlined the Society's rites and pecking order. Up to the time of these revelations, the only hard core information provided to U.S. authorities about the Mafia came from the tidbits and scraps pieced together by outsiders, albeit the knowledge of an existing Mafia in America had been established as early as 1889.

Early in that year, on January 24, 1889, authorities of New Orleans came into contact with the evil operations of the Mafia quite inadvertently when investigating the murder of Vincenzo Ottumvo, a Mafia member. Vincenzo's throat was cut from ear to ear while he was playing cards.

Police Chief David Peter Hennessey suspected the existence of a powerful brotherhood in New Orleans after questioning several Sicilian immigrants who hinted darkly that a "secret society" had ordered Ottumvo's death. The puzzled Hennessey (who had an avowed dislike for all Italians and Sicilians) was further troubled a month later when investigating the brutal slaying of another immigrant, Giuseppe Mataino, whose throat had also been cut and his head shoved into the fireplace of his home and set afire.

Four months later Camillo Victoria was shot through the head by a bullet from a rifle poked through a window of his home one warm June night. Hennessey was plagued by citizens' groups demanding he solve the murders. The only leads his department developed ran to the existence of a secret society. Witnesses whispered in his ear and then vanished. For a year, Hennessey's detectives attempted to penetrate this organization but met small success.

Then, on May 1, 1890, Tony Matranga was shot and wounded as he coaxed his horse-drawn wagon down Esplanade Avenue. Through this shooting, Hennessey learned that Charles and Anthony Matranga were the *capos* of the New Orleans Mafia faction. Tony had been shot by opposing Camorra leaders, members of the Provenzo family, who were hotly contesting the lucrative New Orleans dock rackets.

To learn more of the Mafia, Hennessey openly sided with the Provenzos and, when the case was scheduled for court in October, 1890, the chief of police announced that he would take the stand and relate what he had learned about the Matranga-controlled Mafia

New Orleans Police Chief David Peter Hennessey accidentally stumbled upon the existence of America's first powerful Mafia faction but was murdered by Mafia killers on October 15, 1890 before he could fully expose their operations.

organization. Hennessey, like his New York counterpart, Police Lt. Joseph Petrosino, wrote to authorities in Palermo, Sicily, sending them names and descriptions of suspected Sicilian criminals residing in New Orleans. He learned, by return mail, "that more than one hundred escaped convicts are in New Orleans." Hennessey went on to state: "I am now prepared to break the Mafia in New Orleans . . . The Mafia doesn't scare me. I will tear it out by the roots before I'm finished." The burly policeman never got to the witness stand.

Peter Hennessey was a tall, fearless cop who brazenly walked New Orleans' most perilous streets alone. He defied the underworld to molest him. Usually armed with two pistols, Hennessey marched down the middle of the street late at night, solemn, proud, a Wyatt Earp dangerously out of his own time.

Following this habit, Hennessey, on October 15, 1890, walked to his home around midnight. The giant policeman took no notice of the small boy skipping and whistling a few yards in front of him. As he was about to enter his home, a series of shotgun blasts tore into him. He turned and staggered down the steps, drawing his service pistol and firing at moving shadows on the dark street.

Wounded six times, Hennessey toppled to the ground. One of his assailants rushed up to him, knelt down, and carefully fired a shotgun charge into his back. With a roar, Hennessey got to his feet, blasting away with his pistol, lurching down the middle of the street. Several men ran along the opposite side of the street, following him like wolves and discharging blast after blast from shotguns, many of which found the target.

The raging battle was heard by another off-duty policeman, Captain William J. O'Connor, who came on the run. He found his police chief sitting on a curb, dying; his attackers had disappeared.

"Who did this?" O'Connor said, holding Hennessey in his arms.

Hennessey was close to passing out but managed to blurt: "The Dagoes . . . Billy, oh, Billy, they have given it to me and I gave them back the best I could!" Hours later Hennessey was dead.

The killing of Police Chief Hennessey served to be the undoing of the early New Orleans Mafia faction. It was a rule that local authorities were never to be attacked and the Mafiosi, out of fear that Hennessey would reveal what he had learned of them, had broken their own rule.

Nineteen Mafia members, including the boy who had run in front of Hennessey on the night of the shooting, Aspero Marchese, were indicted for murder. Their number was subsequently reduced to nine by the state—J. P. Macheca, Charles "Millionaire Charlie" Matranga, Aspero Marchese, Antonio Bagnetto, Antonio Marchese, Bastiano Incardona, Pietro Monastero, Antonio Scaffidi, and Manuel Polizzi (who confessed to the crime but whose confession was not accepted by the district attorney, who insisted on a mass conviction).

The grand juries that indicted these men studied Hennessey's elaborate records and came forth with a statement that shocked the country and made the ensuing trial the hub of national attention: "The extended range of our researches has developed the existence of the secret organization styled 'Mafia.' The evidence comes from several sources fully competent in themselves to attest its truth, while the fact is supported by the long record of bloodcurdling crimes . . .

"As if to guard against exposure, the dagger or the stiletto is selected as the deadly weapon

Mafioso Antonio Banetto, lynched.

Mafioso Bastiano Incardona,
lynched and shot.

When several thousand New Orleans
citizens stormed the Parish Prison on
March 14, 1891, Antonio Marchese attempted to hide with other prisoners
but was rooted out by the mob and
lynched.

Mafioso Antonio Scaffidi was shot in
the throat in the visitor's room of New
Orleans' Parish Prison by an irate
friend of Chief Hennessey's.

Mafioso Pietro Monastero, lynched.

Manuel Polizzi, Mafia member, admitted
to killing Hennessey but his confession
was ignored, the prosecution insisted
on the conviction of all nine murder
suspects being held.

to plunge into the breast or back of the victim
and silently do its work . . . The officers of
the Mafia and many of its members are known
. . . The larger number of the Society is composed of Italians or Sicilians [it was not then
known that the Mafia was an exclusive Sicilian
society] who have left their native land, in
most instances under assumed names to avoid
conviction for crimes there committed . . ."

The astounding aspect of this indictment is

that the organization was exposed in 1890, decades before U.S. Senate crime committees began their probes.

To determine the existence of the Mafia and learn its secrets, police and Pinkerton Detective operatives were placed in jail cells next to the Sicilians in custody. One, Frank Dimaio, a Pinkerton operative, was put in with the Mafia prisoners in the Old Parish Prison at Conti and Orleans Streets. He befriended Polizzi, posing as a convicted Sicilian counterfeiter under the alias of Anthony Ruggiero.

Polizzi was the most frightened of the Mafia group, telling Dimaio that the leader, "Millionaire Charlie" Matrango, wanted to kill him because of his nervousness. Dimaio convinced Polizzi that the Mafiosi intended to poison his prison food and the terrified Mafioso began to talk.

"Why me, Tony?" Polizzi asked Dimaio. "Why are they picking on me? I did a lot for them. They know that."

"What did you do for them?"

"Murder, Tony, murder." Later, Polizzi became more explicit, telling Dimaio that "we murdered Hennessey . . . They think I will betray the Society."

The widespread publicity on the case circulated by the local and national press had whipped public indignation over Hennessey's murder into frenzy. Thomas Duffy, the eighteen-year-old son of a prominent New Orleans businessman and friend of the slain police chief, took matters into his own hands, went to the prison, and asked to see Antonio Scaffidi. When the prisoner arrived, Duffy drew a gun and promptly shot Scaffidi in the neck, wounding him severely.

Arrested, Duffy was given a mild six-month sentence. "I'm willing to hang," Duffy shouted at the warden, "if one of those Dagoes die and I wish there were seventy-five men more like me." There were.

When 1800 more Sicilian immigrants landed on the docks of New Orleans days later, the town panicked. Coupled to the arrival of the immigrants (many of whom Mayor Shakespeare stated were known criminals) was the surprising fact that a jury exonerated nine men standing trial for Hennessey's killing. The nine, however, were still held in jail pending technical arrangements for their release.

Dozens of angry citizens formed groups and talked openly of lynching the nine Sicilians. Suddenly, posters appeared all over New Orleans asking "all good citizens to appear at Clay Statue to remedy the failure of Justice in the Hennessey case." Thousands of citizens did appear on March 14, 1891, at which time W. S. Parkerson, a New Orleans attorney and firebrand, mounted a tree stump and yelled: "When courts fail, the people must act!" Parkerson studied the quiet throng and then began to harangue the crowd with a loud and throaty speech.

"What protection or assurances of protection is there left us when the very head of our police department, our chief of police, is assassinated in our very midst by the Mafia Society, and his assassins again turned loose on the community? The time has come for the people of New Orleans to say whether they are going to stand these outrages by organized bands of assassins, for the people to say whether they permit it to continue." The attorney stopped talking and then exploded with: "Will every man here follow me and see the murder of Hennessey vindicated? Men and citizens of New Orleans, follow me! I will be your leader!" The mob roared its approval and set off down the street behind the fast-walking Parkerson.

First, the crowd broke into the city arsenal and withdrew weapons. Next, the mob stormed the Old Parish Prison, tossing aside what few guards were on duty. The cries of

The Old Parish Prison in New Orleans to which civic zealot W. S. Parkerson led thousands of citizens on March 14, 1891; the mob, incensed over the murder of Chief Hennessey, broke inside and dragged out eleven men whom they promptly hanged.

"We want the Dagoes!" echoed through the gloom-filled corridors of the prison. Captain of the guards, Lem Davis, ordered all prisoners out into the back courtyard. The Sicilians, housed on the second floor, were to be kept separate. Davis opened their cells and told them to "hide the best you can" inside the prison.

Of course, there was no place to hide. Marchese, Scaffidi, and Macheca ran to the third floor, hoping to hide with prisoners there, but they had been removed. Alone in the cell block, the three men were easily visible to the mob in the street who began shooting at them. Macheca was hit several times and killed.

Outside, a large black man came at one of the locked doors with a massive paving stone; the door was broken to bits on impact. Thirty of the vigilantes ran into the building and raced up the stairs for the prisoners.

Polizzi was found by a man named Ross, hiding in a doghouse the warden kept beneath a stairwell. He was dragged to the corner of Treme and St. Anne streets where he was quickly hanged. Dozens of armed men in the mob shot at him with rifles until he dangled lifeless in the March breeze. Bagnetto was next, hanged next to Polizzi. Eleven men (two of whom were not under the final murder indictment) were shot and hanged.

With the dead bodies of the Mafiosi hanging from trees and littering the ground about the prison, Parkerson once more addressed the crowd: "Mob violence is the most terrible thing on the face of the earth. I called you together for a duty. You have performed that duty. . . . I have performed the most painful duty of my life today. . . . Now go to your homes and if I need you, I will call you. If you have confidence in me and in the gentlemen associated with me, I ask you to disperse and go quietly to your homes. God bless you."

"God bless you, Mr. Parkerson," echoed the massive crowd. The good citizens of New Orleans dispersed and trundled home.

The New Orleans incident ignited international explosions felt in Italy, Sicily, and Washington, D.C. Though the White House chastised the residents of New Orleans for the lynchings, Italy was not offered a formal apology despite the demands of Baron Fava, the Italian Ambassador. Neither Parkerson nor any of his followers was ever arrested for the lynchings.

The purge of the Mafia in New Orleans far from stamped out the Society's growth in the U.S. By 1905 there were huge Mafia families in almost every major American city, with networks of communications connecting each faction. Outside of the usual vendettas practiced between the Mafia and its rival Camorra, there were no internecine battles inside the brotherhood until 1909 when a New Orleans grocer, Pietro Pepitone, shot and killed Mafia boss of the city, Paul di Cristina (nee Marchese) who was attempting to extort funds from him through Black Hand threats.

After serving six years in the Louisiana State Penitentiary for the shooting, Pepitone was released. The Mafia had not forgotten. A paid killer, known only as "Doc" Mumfre (whether or not his background was Italian was never learned) was sent to kill Pepitone. This was done in 1915. The Pepitone family struck back and several small-time Mafiosi were slain. Between 1916 and 1920 Mumfre, on orders from the Mafia faction, then systematically murdered, according to reports, twelve members of the Pepitone family, using an axe to bash in each victim's head. More than two dozen Mafia members met their violent deaths in this tribal vendetta which subsided when Prohibition was established.

Kansas City, not Chicago, became the Mafia's Mid-western hub during the 1920s. Capone ruled Chicago in those days and Capone was a Neapolitan and therefore a non-Mafia criminal who was never admitted into the Society even though some reported that he attempted to gain membership on numerous occasions.

Under Boss Tom Pendergast's protection, Mafia chieftains such as Frank "Chee Chee" DeMayo and Johnny Lazia (murdered in 1934) ostensibly ran the rackets in K.C. during the roaring Twenties. Vincenzo Carrollo headed the family until 1940 when he was sent to prison. Charles Binaggio's gambling and narcotics rackets alone brought him in an estimated $34,000,000 a year.

The real power in K.C. was Joseph "Scarface" DiGiovanni, who, along with his brother Pete "Sugarhouse Pete" DiGiovanni and James Balestrere, headed up the Black Hand rings, dominated bootlegging during Probhibition, and then controlled the narcotics traffic and gambling.

In nearby St. Louis, the Mafia throughout

the Prohibition era was led by John and Vito Giannola and Alphonse Palizzola, whose family members were referred to as "The Green Ones" because its leaders immigrated from Sicily's farming communities. The Green Ones infiltrated labor unions and the food industry, levying tribute on every item sold in Italian and Sicilian groceries.

Once established, the Mafia battled openly with such independent groups as Egan's Rats, led by Dinty Colbeck, for control of the lucrative bootleg business in St. Louis. Dozens of bootleggers were slaughtered. The Mafia's favorite methods then consisted of stabbing their victims to death and working over the dead bodies with baseball bats. Many times the victims were dragged by the neck behind cars. Colbeck's crew was finally eliminated when The Green Ones arranged a police trap for the gang at the moment its members were enacting a mail robbery. The entire mob was sent to prison.

A gang called "The Cuckoos," a group of ambitious young St. Louis toughs, then took on The Green Ones in bloody gang warfare that lasted until 1930, at which time the Cuckoos were all but eliminated. St. Louis became a Mafia fiefdom.

The larger cities, New York and Chicago, did not come under the criminal control of the Mafia until after the Second World War. There were too many non-Italian, non-Sicilian gangsters, absorbed by the National Crime Syndicate at its inception in 1933, who opposed its domination. Neapolitans such as Vito Genovese and Charles "Lucky" Luciano also resisted a complete Mafia takeover during the period of their reign.

Not until Luciano was deported, Lepke Buchalter executed, and other non-Mafia gang leaders such as Meyer Lansky, Bugsy Siegel, and Abner "Longy" Zwillman were conveniently killed or shuttled to the sidelines, did the Mafia dominate organized crime in the U.S.

The last war of any consequence within Mafia ranks occurred in the early 1960s when New York gangster-brothers Larry ("The Blond"), Joseph ("Crazy Joe"), and Albert ("Kid Blast") Gallo, all members of the Joseph Profaci family, rose up against their leaders and forced many slayings. All three brothers were defeated while attempting to take over this family, which subsequently came under the leadership of Joe Columbo following the

death by cancer of Profaci in 1962.

The date of the Mafia's complete takeover of the national crime syndicate was November 14, 1957, when more than 100 top Mafia members from across the country met, following Vito Genovese's order, at the Apalachin, N. Y. estate of Joseph Barbara. By then the American Mafia had relaxed its nationalistic exclusivity and Genovese, a Neapolitan, was elected *capo de tutti capi*. His image of power was punctured moments after the voting when state police raided the Barbara home on a tip that the gangster conclave was meeting there. The most feared criminals in America went dashing through doors and slipping out of windows, racing madly through the woods, shredding their $500 suits, and scuffling their imported shoes. Dozens were arrested.

Since then, Genovese has died in prison and the old leaders of the Mafia families in New York have followed him. Ailing Carlo Gambino is now the Mafia's elder statesman in America, if not its boss of bosses.

The statements of long-time Mafia member Joseph Valachi, who turned informer in 1962 and disclosed the rites and existence of the American Mafia under the nom de guerre of *La Cosa Nostra*, presented few new facts about the Society other than the details of the Maranzano-Masseria war in New York during the early 1930s.

[ALSO SEE The Black Hand, The Camorra, Al Capone, Vito Genovese, Charles "Lucky" Luciano, Salvatore Maranzano, The Syndicate, Unione Siciliane, Joseph Valachi.]

MAGADDINO, STEFANO (STEVE)
Syndicate Gangster ● (1891-1974)

Born in Castellammare, Sicily, October 10, 1891, Magaddino was one of the elder "dons" of the American Cosa Nostra-Mafia. He was one of those who sided with Salvatore Maranzano in the 1930-31 Castelammarese War with Joe the Boss Masseria in New York.

Long a ruler of organized crime in Buffalo, N.Y., Magaddino was first arrested in 1921 for evading a charge of murder in Avon, N.J. His "family" has long been involved in narcotics trafficking, gambling, and vice. Considered by many authorities to have sat on the board of the national syndicate, Magaddino was reportedly in attendance at the notorious criminal summit meeting at Apalachin in 1957.

MAIONE, HARRY (HAPPY)
Syndicate Gangster ● (? -1942)

Maione was a petty thief who teamed up with Frank Abbandando in the late 1930s to form a killer-for-hire gang, which later became known as Murder, Inc. Maione was a ruthless thug who cared nothing for life. He murdered without remorse. In fact, he so much enjoyed killing rival mobsters that he would giggle and laugh while shooting, stabbing, or mutilating them, thus earning the sobriquet of "Happy."

At least a dozen persons were murdered by Maione before he was arrested and charged with several killings. He was convicted, as was Abbandando, on the testimony of Abe "Kid Twist" Reles, and was sent to the electric chair in 1942.

(ALSO SEE Frank Abbandando; Abe Reles)

MANDELBAUM, FREDERICKA ("MARM") Fence ● (1818-1889)

BACKGROUND: BORN IN NEW YORK, 1818. MARRIED WOLFE MANDELBAUM. GAVE BIRTH TO TWO DAUGHTERS AND ONE SON. MINOR PUBLIC EDUCATION. DESCRIPTION: 5'1", BLACK EYES, BLACK HAIR, FAT (APPROX. 250 LBS.). ALIASES: MARM MANDELBAUM, MOTHER MANDELBAUM. RECORD: OPERATED THE MOST SUCCESSFUL FENCING OPERATIONS IN THE EAST COAST, CENTERED IN NYC, FROM 1862 TO 1884, HANDLING AN ESTIMATED $12,000,000 IN STOLEN GOODS; FENCED THE NEGOTIABLE BONDS TAKEN IN THE MANHATTAN SAVINGS INSTITUTION THEFT ON 10/27/78; HANDLED ALL THE STOLEN GOODS—AN ESTIMATED $500,000 WORTH—SENT TO HER BY THE NOTORIOUS LOOMIS GANG OF UPSTATE NEW YORK THROUGH THE 1870S; INDICTED FOR GRAND LARCENY AND RECEIVING STOLEN GOODS IN 1884; FLED TO CANADA WHERE SHE DIED SOMETIME IN 1889.

Marm Mandelbaum was as colorful a crook as they came, an authentic forerunner to Damon Runyon's "Apple Annie," except that she operated on a scale so vast police were never able to determine the exact amount of stolen goods she handled in her twenty-two years as America's super fence. They estimated around $12,000,000 but the sum was likely higher.

Marrying early in life to Wolfe Mandelbaum, a drifter, Marm produced three healthy children and then decided in her halcyon years to enter a life of crime. At forty-four, Marm purchased a three-story brownstone house at 79 Clinton Street and spread the word through underworld contacts she had established that she would handle any kind of stolen goods available, from diamonds to horses. The boodle flowed into her home from dawn to dusk.

Within the space of two years, Marm had become a millionaire and had safely fenced $4 million in stolen loot. Grateful thieves who wished to remain in her favor then began to steal the most exquisite furniture and furnishings from the landed gentry of the East to give as gifts to Marm. She accepted these and furnished her house with them; it became the showplace of the underworld.

The most important criminals of the era flocked to Marm Mandelbaum's place, attending her famous balls and fetes. George Leonidas Leslie, who became America's first superbankrobber and who fenced millions of dollars in securities through Marm, was usually in attendance; so were Banjo Peter Emerson, Mark Shinburn, Shang Draper, and the infamous burglars, Bill Mosher and Joseph Douglas. Mosher and Douglas, at the behest of king of the kidnappers, William Westervelt, had abducted little Charley Ross from his home in Germantown, Pa., July 1, 1874 and held him for ransom. They subsequently turned him over to Westervelt, from whose custody he disappeared.

Shinburn was one of Marm's favorite burglars; he brought her so much stolen goods that she put him under exclusive contract to her.

He was a deft safecracker and burglar who detested the company of other crooks. They were beneath him, he told Marm, ordinary scum with haphazard talents. For years he fenced his stolen wares through Marm, sent money to relatives in Germany, and eventually retired in Monaco under the auspicious title of Baron Shindell.

With her fencing racket so lucrative, Marm invested time in promoting the cause of female criminals, teaching lady pickpockets, burglars, and confidence workers how to improve their trades. Her graduates included Black Lena Kleinschmidt, Ellen Clegg, Kid Glove Rosey, Old Mother Hubbard, Sophie Lyons, and Queen Liz.

Two of her graduates, Sophie Lyons and Black Lena, went on to the big time. Sophie, married to a bank burglar named Ned Lyons, ultimately became the most famous confidence woman in America, plying her trade exclusively in Pullman cars. Black Lena blackmailed her way to wealth, moved to Hackensack, N. J., and entered high society under an alias.

Marm went on to establish a female Fagin school on the third floor of her home. Here, a staff of experienced criminals taught youngsters how to pick pockets and become expert sneak thieves. She later introduced them to the professional methods of safecracking, blackmailing, and burglary.

The reign of Marm Mandelbaum came to an abrupt end when a reform party came to power in New York in 1884 and indictments against her for grand larceny and handling stolen goods were drawn up. Marm's famous legal firm of Howe & Hummell were powerless to prevent the indictments and she fled with her furnishings, family, and an estimated $10 million to an unknown spot in Canada.

There, she lived out her days in quiet luxury, traveling to New York in disguise, reports have it, to visit some of her fond underworld associates. Marm died a nostalgic woman.

[ALSO SEE George Leonidas Leslie, George Washington Loomis, Jr.]

MANSON, CHARLES
Murderer ● (1934-   )

BACKGROUND: BORN 11/11/34 IN CINCINNATI, O. TO UNWED KATHLEEN MODDOX OF ASHLAND, KEN., DESERTED BY MOTHER, RAISED BY GRANDMOTHER IN MCMECHEN, W.VA., SUBSEQUENTLY SENT TO BOYS TOWN IN NEBRASKA FOR A BRIEF STAY. MINOR PUBLIC EDUCATION. ORIGINAL OCCUPATION, GAS STATION ATTENDANT. DESCRIPTION: 5'6", BROWN EYES, BROWN HAIR, SLIGHT. ALIASES: UNKNOWN. RECORD: FIRST ARRESTED IN PEORIA, ILL. FOR STEALING FOOD; SENT TO INDIANA BOYS SCHOOL REFORMATORY AT PLAINFIELD, ESCAPED EIGHTEEN TIMES; ARRESTED IN BEAVER CITY, U., IN 1951, SENT TO SEVERAL FEDERAL REFORMATORIES OVER A THREE-YEAR PERIOD INCLUDING THE NATIONAL TRAINING SCHOOL FOR BOYS IN WASHINGTON, D.C.; PAROLED FROM THE CHILLICOTHE, O. FEDERAL REFORMATORY IN NOV., 1954; MARRIED ROSALIE JEAN WILLIS IN 1955; ARRESTED IN 1955 FOR TRANSPORTING STOLEN AUTOS ACROSS STATE LINES, SENT TO SAN PEDRO'S TERMINAL ISLAND PRISON OUTSIDE OF LOS ANGELES FOR A PERIOD OF THREE YEARS; RELEASED IN 1958; BECAME A PROCURER AND RECEIVED SEVERAL SHORT JAIL SENTENCES FOR TRANSPORTING WOMEN ACROSS STATE LINES FOR IMMORAL PURPOSES; ARRESTED, TRIED AND CONVICTED OF FORGING GOVERNMENT CHECKS IN 1960, SENTENCED TO TEN YEARS IN THE FEDERAL PENITENTIARY ON MCNEIL ISLAND, WASHINGTON; RELEASED, MARCH, 1967; ORGANIZED COMMUNE-LIKE HOSTELRY AT SPAHN RANCH, NEAR LOS ANGELES, CALIF., DIRECTED CULTISTS IN HIS GROUP IN THE KILLING OF ACTRESS SHARON TATE, MILLIONAIRE COFFEE HEIRESS ABIGAIL FOLGER, VOITYCK FROKOWSKY, JAY SEBRING, AND STEVEN PARENT ON 8/8-9/69 AND TWO DAYS LATER THAT OF LENO AND ROSEMARY LA BIANCA; CONVICTED OF THE KILLINGS ALONG WITH SUSAN ATKINS, PATRICIA KRENWINKEL, AND LESLIE VAN HOUTEN 1/25/71; SENTENCED TO DEATH IN GAS CHAMBER. WHEN THE U.S. SUPREME COURT ABOLISHED THE DEATH PENALTY, ALL DEATH SENTENCES WERE COMMUTED TO LIFE TERMS WHICH WERE NOT ALTERED WHEN THE STATE OF CALIFORNIA LATER REINSTITUTED THE DEATH PENALTY UNDER A NEW EDICT FROM THE U.S. SUPREME COURT.

The much-celebrated Charles Manson case probably received more publicity from 1969 to early 1971 than any other in California criminal history. Sadly enough, the notoriety appeared to be enjoyed by Manson, a wandering vagrant who had been in and out of reform schools and prisons for a decade.

Establishing a self-aggrandizing cult (much like the killer sect of India, *Thugee*), Manson had collected a shiftless, unemployed group of

Hippie cultist Charles Manson mugs wildly for cameras while being tried for mass murder in 1970. (UPI)

hippies at a place called Spahn Ranch near Los Angeles, used at one time as a filming location by Hollywood studios. There Manson practiced assorted brands of free love, polygamy, and pseudo-religious ceremonies centering about his self-appointed role as Christ-like leader (often referred to by his fanatical followers as Death or the Devil).

Manson's "family" was supported in several instances by contributions from several Hollywood personalities who supplied money with which to purchase food and other necessities. Some reports have it that Manson fathered several illegitimate children with a number of the women in his drug-consuming sect.

Spouting Manson's indoctrinational gibberish about "peace . . . love . . . death," several members of his group, reportedly led by Charles "Tex" Watson, broke into the plush Hollywood residence of film director Roman Polansky on August 8-9, 1969 and slaughtered five persons there—Polansky's pregnant wife, Sharon Tate, Abigail Folger, Voityck Frokowsky, Jay Sebring, and Steven Parent.

The leader of the killer band, reportedly Watson, used a pistol to shoot most of the victims, screaming: "I am the devil and I have come to do the devil's work!" The five victims were shot and stabbed to death; demented slogans were then written on the walls of the house with the blood of those slain.

This senseless killing spree was repeated 48 hours later when the same group invaded the home of Leno and Rosemary La Bianca, killing both and scrawling out the same kind of idiotic messages ("pig," etc.) with their blood.

Manson, who had a long criminal record, was shortly identified as the leader of this crackpot ring and was brought to trial, along with three of his mistresses—Susan Atkins, Patricia Krenwinkel, and Leslie Van Houten. (Watson was tried separately.) All were found guilty and sentenced to death but when the U.S. Supreme Court later abolished the death penalty, all received life terms. California was one of the states that reinstituted the death penalty under a new Supreme Court ruling but this was not retroactive and the Manson clan survived to serve out life terms.

MARANZANO, SALVATORE
Founder of La Cosa Nostra ●
(1868-1931)

BACKGROUND: BORN IN CASTELLAMMARE DEL GOLFO, SICILY. COLLEGE-TRAINED. STUDIED FOR PRIESTHOOD EARLY IN LIFE. IMMIGRATED TO U.S. FOLLOWING FIRST WORLD WAR. ORIGINAL OCCUPATION, REAL ESTATE BROKER. DESCRIPTION: TALL, DARK, SLENDER. ALIASES: UNKNOWN. RECORD: A BOSS OF THE CASTELLAMMARESE FACTION OF THE MAFIA BEFORE IMMIGRATION; CONTINUED IN THIS ROLE WHEN RESETTLED IN U.S.; OPERATED VARIOUS ILLEGAL ENTERPRISES INCLUDING GAMBLING, ILLEGAL DISTRIBUTION OF LIQUOR

DURING PROHIBITION, PORTIONS OF THE ITALIAN LOT-
TERY IN NYC, BURGLARIZING WAREHOUSES; ORGAN-
IZED RESISTANCE TO JOE THE BOSS MASSERIA IN
1930-31 IN WHAT WAS TO BE LATER KNOWN AS THE
CASTELLAMMARESE WAR WHICH BEGAN IN NYC AND
SPREAD TO VARIOUS OTHER STATES SUCH AS NEW
JERSEY AND ILLINOIS; ORDERED THE DEATHS OF SEV-
ERAL MASSERIA HENCHMEN 1930-31, AND MASSERIA
HIMSELF ON 4/15/31; KILLED BY LUCIANO-GENOVESE
MURDER SQUAD 9/10/31.

Maranzano held a deep grudge against members of the Sicilian Mafia when he immigrated to the U.S. following the First World War. The society had paid little or no attention to his Mafia faction in remote Castellammare; members from his district, including clan chief Maranzano, were looked upon as country bumpkins, hinterland primitives, incapable of ever assuming responsible roles in the organization's hierarchy.

Once established in New York, Maranzano gathered about him those Sicilian-born American criminals who, like himself, came from Castellammare, seeking vindication and honor for their Mafia chapter. A rank egomaniac, Maranzano was enamored and steeped in the life and times of Julius Caesar, a man who set for him an inspired example of benevolent dictatorship and whose death enacted unparalleled political fratricide.

Maranzano's aim in the American underworld was to bring the Mafia to dominance under a new code of ruthless ethics, strict organization, and the establishment of regimented allegiance to a super boss, a *capo de tutti capi*, a dictator, himself. He carried with him into the New World warped concepts of old-line Napoleonic honor which he childishly but eloquently foisted upon those who thought him sage. He demanded the practice of his high theories of crime, theories totally incongruous with the new breed of American criminals. Clearly, Salvatore Maranzano was behind and ahead of his time.

Though a Mustache Pete himself, a Mafia man filled with the Old World traditions, he advocated the destruction of all Mustache Petes in America so that his New Order of crime could flourish unhampered by plodding customs. Naturally, the elimination of all Mustache Petes allowed for the existence of only one remaining Mafia patriarch. That man would be Salvatore Maranzano.

Maranzano busied himself during the 1920s with interests in gambling, bootlegging, and burglaries, which he directed from his real estate office in Manhattan. His gang of freebooters roamed the city, invading the territory of jealous gangsters, but he was tolerated as an ineffectual and aging Sicilian mob man merely trying to turn a dollar. Non-Italian hoodlums such as Owney Madden, Dutch Schultz, Waxey Gordon, Legs Diamond were unaware of his presence. Sicilian and Italian gangsters like Joe the Boss Masseria, Luciano, and others merely shrugged at his name—"Yeah, old man Maranzano. . . ."

With the rise of Giuseppe "Joe the Boss" Masseria as crime overlord of New York, Maranzano grew apprehensive. Masseria, on many occasions, had talked of his dislike for Mafiosi from Castellammare. Masseria also coveted the rich spoils certain Castellammarese men such as Brooklyn's Joseph "Joe Bananas" Bonanno and Joseph Profaci reaped from their Italian-based rackets. At the zenith of his criminal stature, Masseria declared war on them. The year was 1930 and the Castellammarese War, as the internecine battle would later be termed by informant Joseph Valachi, would cause dozens of gang deaths throughout the country, sweep Masseria's gun-wagging regime away, and establish a newly-constructed Mafia, much like the one that presently exists in the U.S.

Gathering such Mafia sub-dons as Profaci, Bonanno, Stefano Magaddino from Buffalo, and Joe Aiello in Chicago to his ranks, Maranzano organized and fought back. Death squads on both sides established machinegun nests throughout Manhattan and waited for their prey to arrive. Opposing gangsters patroled the streets daily, searching for each other and, upon confrontation, opening up with shotguns, machineguns, and pistols. The toll was excruciating.

Both sides suffered the loss of top men: Gaetano (Tom) Reina, a Masseria man, killed August 15, 1930; Joseph Pinzolo, a Maranzano man, murdered September 9, 1930; Maranzano ally Joe Aiello, killed in Chicago, October 23, 1930; Steven Ferrigno (alias Sam Ferraro), and Al Mineo, Masseria gunmen, killed November 5, 1930; Masseria lieutenant Joseph Catania (alias Joe Baker), murdered February 3, 1931; Joe the Boss Masseria himself executed by his own men at Lucky Luciano's orders on

April 15, 1931.

Only upon Masseria's death would Maranzano make peace with Joe the Boss' lieutenants Charles Lucky Luciano and Vito Genovese. This done, Maranzano pompously called the members of both factions together in late 1931. He rented a large hall on Washington Avenue in the Bronx to which flocked more than five hundred gunmen involved in the war.

Maranzano, conservatively dressed in vested suit with silver watch chain dangling and wing collar jutting, looked more like a professor than an overlord of crime. He sat in a throne chair on the stage with a huge cross mounted on the wall behind him. "He had done this," Valachi stated, "so that if outsiders wondered what the meeting was about, they would think we belonged to some kind of holy society."

Once the phalanxes of gunmen were seated, Maranzano stood up and delivered an attack on the recently murdered Masseria, stating that Joe the Boss was destined to die because he had been "shaking down" Italians everywhere and because he had dared to declare war on the all-powerful Castellammarese, unjustly sentencing them to death.

"Now it will be different," Maranzano roared. "I will be your *capo de tutti capi* [boss of bosses]. New families will be set up and each family will have a boss and an underboss. Under them will be *caporegimes* [lieutenants]. The rest of you will be soldiers. You will each be assigned to a lieutenant. When you learn who he is you will meet all the other men in your crew."

The boss of bosses then outlined the order of command and explicitly pointed out that soldiers of this new crime federation must never go to the boss of a family without first seeking the permission of his immediate superior, his lieutenant. For minor infractions of the new fraternity's rules, each man would be judged by a tribunal and given punishment, such as being cut off from the Society's payroll for long periods of time.

There were cardinal rules in the new organization that could never be broken, unless a member wished to face death. For violating any member's wife, death! For talking about the Society and its secret rites, death! For talking to wives about the Society, death! For failing to obey an order from a superior, death! Such crafty murderers as Luciano, Genovese, Thomas Lucchese, squirmed in their seats at such *ex cathedra* directives, but nodded approval just the same.

Maranzano concluded with: "Whatever happened in the past is over. There is to be no more ill feeling among us. If you lost someone in this past war of ours, you must forgive and forget. If your own brother was killed, don't try to find out who did it or get even. If you do, you pay with your life!"

Throughout the speech, Maranzano employed a term colloquially used in Castellammare to describe the Mafia—"La Cosa Nostra." Literally translated, it meant, "this thing of ours." The term would be one of the most closely guarded secrets in the Italian underworld for more than thirty years, revealed later by Joseph Valachi. The Cosa Nostra was, however, a term strictly used by New York Mafia members and was not adopted universally throughout the country.

It was really Maranzano's personal term, many concluded, and Salvatore Maranzano was to die in the same fashion he had ordained for others. Luciano and his scheming Iago, Genovese, had no intention of serving a boss of bosses (although they did later adopt Maranzano's five family plan for the New York Mafia as well as his system of authority).

Guarded only by a small troop of men, which included Valachi, Steve Runnelli, and the infamous Girolamo Santucci (alias Bobby Doyle), Maranzano became extremely vulnerable, although he felt confident of his authority after triumphing over Masseria. Luciano paid him lip service and planned his death.

The boss of bosses was not unaware of Luciano and Vito Genovese. "I can't get along with those two guys," he once told Valachi.

Giuseppe "Joe the Boss" Masseria, Maranzano's arch rival in the Castellemmarese War of 1930-31.

"We got to get rid of them before we can control anything." His "hit" list also included Al Capone, Frank Costello, Willie Moretti, Joe Adonis, and Dutch Schultz.

Thomas "Three-Finger Brown" Lucchese learned that Maranzano, not trusting the inner circle of his self-invented Cosa Nostra, had gone outside Mafia ranks to employ Vincent "Mad Dog" Coll to kill Luciano, Genovese, and others. Luciano was in no mood to wait for Coll to come calling.

At 2:50 p.m. on September 10, 1931, four men entered the Manhattan offices of real estate broker Salvatore Maranzano in the Eagle Building at 230 Park Avenue. The four men flashed police badges, asking for the boss. Bobby Doyle, who was sitting in the outer office, shook his head, as if nonplussed. Maranzano opened the door of his office.

"Who can we talk to?" one would-be policeman asked him, flashing the badge.

"You can talk to me," Maranzano answered and waved them into his office. Once inside, the fake policemen pulled pistols, but Red Levine of Meyer Lansky's troop—loaned out especially for the occasion—told the others that a knife would be silent and yanked out a blade. He advanced on Maranzano who surprisingly turned on him, hitting Levine several times. Levine kept plunging the blade into the boss of bosses, six times in all. Still alive, Maranzano cursed the quartet and dove for the three men holding pistols. They fired at the same time and Maranzano fell to the floor dead, his dream of being another Julius Caesar blubbering incoherently from frothy lips.

Levine, who watched, fascinated for a moment by Maranzano's death throes, then ordered the other three men from the room. Various reports identified the other killers as Bugsy Siegel, Albert Anastasia, and Thomas Lucchese.

When police arrived they found Maranzano dead of four bullet wounds and six knife thrusts. There were no witnesses. Bodyguard Bobby Doyle had fled after hearing the first gun fired. Doyle, Valachi, and other Maranzano guards went into hiding. Some did not.

Two hours after Maranzano's bloody execution, one of his lieutenants, James Marino (alias James LaPore) was shot six times and killed as he emerged from a Bronx barbershop. Three days later, the bodies of two more Maranzano supporters, brutally mangled, washed ashore

The knife-gashed, bullet-riddled body of Salvatore Maranzano, founder of New York's *Cosa Nostra*, lies sprawled in his private office, 9/10/31. (UPI)

in Newark Bay. They were identified as Samuel Monaco and Louis Russo. Both men showed signs of horrible torture. Their heads were crushed, their throats slashed, and parts of their bodies were missing, hacked away as if by a cleaver. Valachi, terrified for his own life, heard, in gory details, of the twin slaying. He later reported that "Sam [Monaco] had an iron pipe hammered up his ass."

Luciano had carefully worked out the mass extermination of Salvatore Maranzano's allies throughout the country. The same day Maranzano was killed more than forty Cosa Nostra leaders were slain nationwide. They were killed in their beds, at lunch tables, in washrooms, on the streets, and sitting on their front porches.

It was the beginning of the modern era of organized crime and the end of the Mustache Petes.

[ALSO SEE Vito Genovese, Thomas "Three Finger Brown" Lucchese, Charles "Lucky" Luciano, Joseph Valachi.]

MARKET STREET GANG

This gang of sluggers, pickpockets and thieves existed in Chicago's 42nd and 43rd Wards before the First World War. Members, also known as the Little Hellions, were juveniles who specialized in rolling drunks and attacking single women for their purses. The most infamous member of this gang was Dion "Deanie" O'Bannion, who would rise to the precarious position of Al Capone's only significant rival for control of the city's bootlegging and gambling rackets during the 1920s.

The Market Streeters disappeared by 1919 with the advent of Prohibition, its members joining adult gangs.

MARKLE, JOHN
Swindler, Mass Murderer ● (1942-1987)

The son of actress Mercedes McCambridge, John Markle was vice president of Stephen's Inc., of Little Rock, Arkansas. Stephen's was the fifteenth largest investment banking firm in America and the largest off Wall Street. Markle handled his own mother's accounts at the firm, along with many others.

Markle handled his mother's investments as an out-of-state account. He was also responsible for the firm's in-house accounts. He reportedly made no distinction between the two. He would make investments for both accounts at the same time. If the investments made money, Markle credited his mother's account. If they lost money, he would place the losses on the Stephen's accounts.

The firm discovered Markle's account juggling and fired him on November 13, 1987. He returned to his luxury home and brooded about the ruinous publicity sure to follow his dismissal. Markle had had an unhappy childhood as the son of a distinguished actress. His parents had divorced when he was five and he spent most of his early years in a boarding school.

On November 15, 1987, Markle shot and killed his wife Chris, 45, and his two daughters, Suzanne, nine and Amy, thirteen. He then called his lawyer and told him that he was going to kill himself. When police arrived at the Markle home fifteen minutes later, they found the investment broker dead.

The mass killings had an eerie undertone. A scary Halloween mask lay next to Markle's body. On a video recorder nearby, the horror film, *Nightmare on Elm Street*, was ready to play. It was remembered that McCambridge, who had won an Oscar for her supporting role in *All the King's Men*, was best remembered as the voice of the devil in *The Exorcist*.

Markle's sad fate and that of his family seemed to sum up the clutch-and-run attitude of the 1980s where money overpowered any concept of family unity and human survival. To live without wealth was a death certificate. The coronor in the case was kind. Steve Nawojczyk labelled the murderer's suicide "an act of macabre benevolence. He wanted to spare the girls the publicity."

MARTIN, MICHAEL ("CAPTAIN LIGHTFOOT")
Highwayman ● (1775-1822)

BACKGROUND: BORN IN CONNEHY, IRELAND, 4/9/75, TO A WEALTHY LANDOWNER. MINOR EDUCATION. IMMIGRATED TO THE U.S., 6/17/18. ORIGINAL OCCUPATION, BREWERY OWNER. DESCRIPTION: TALL, MUSCULAR. ALIASES: CAPTAIN LIGHTFOOT. RECORD: BECAME A HIGHWAYMAN IN IRELAND, CIRCA 1792 IN COMPANY WITH ANOTHER, MORE EXPERIENCED BANDIT KNOWN ONLY AS "CAPTAIN THUNDERBOLT"; THE TWO MEN ROBBED COACHES, TRAVELERS AND PUBS THROUGHOUT IRELAND AND SCOTLAND FOR CLOSE TO TWENTY-SIX YEARS; MARTIN LEFT IRELAND ON 4/12/18 TO AVOID CAPTURE AND IMMIGRATED TO THE U.S.; ROBBED COACHES AND LONE TRAVELERS THROUGHOUT NEW ENGLAND STATES 1819-22; HANGED AS A HORSE THIEF IN CAMBRIDGE, MASS., 12/22/22.

The life of a highwayman in the late Eighteenth Century was a full time occupation that called for nerve, daring, and an unquenchable thirst for adventure. Boys of that era thought of becoming highwaymen just as youths in America would later imagine themselves fireman, baseball players, or cowboys. In this sense, Irish-born Michael Martin could be considered normal.

At age seventeen he ran away from his Connehy farm to Dublin where, in his own words he met and befriended "profligate men and women." Though he was soon compelled to return to his father's farm, Martin was wooed into a life of crime when a traveler stopped to water his horse, a man known throughout Ireland as the boldest bandit on the roads, "Captain Thunderbolt."

Martin rode off with the older man and for twenty-six years, became Thunderbolt's right-hand man, riding stirrup to stirrup with him on countless raids and hold ups in Ireland and Scotland. Martin, who had taken on the sobriquet "Captain Lightfoot," fled to America in 1818 aboard the brig *Maria* when government troops were put on his trail.

Landing in Salem, Mass. on June 17, 1818, Martin decided to live an honest life, first buying a farm which went broke, and then a brewery which no one patronized. An ill-starred love affair finally caused him to return to crime.

Dressed as a Quaker and armed with two pistols and a swordcane, Martin began to ride the roads of Connecticut, where in early 1819 he robbed a traveling merchant of $70, hitting the man on the head for good measure.

For three years, Martin roamed at will, robbing coaches and travelers for small sums. His territory was vast, all of New England. No one was safe from his hold ups. Martin even robbed Indians as far north as Canada. Rewards for his capture offered $50 to any brave man who could bring in "the most notorious scoundrel."

Martin, or "Captain Lightfoot," as he still liked to be called, stopped one of the governor's coaches in 1821 and held up the passengers. When a woman handed him her watch he quickly returned it, stating, "I do not rob women, ma'am." It was the kind of beau geste in which Martin delighted, thinking himself, as would Jesse James and Pretty Boy Floyd centuries later, to be an American Robin Hood.

The governor of Massachusetts exploded upon hearing that his personal coach had been pilfered by the highwayman. He ordered an all-out manhunt which culminated in Martin's bloodless capture in a barn outside Springfield. Injured, he had fallen asleep after eluding several posses. A fall from his horse caused him to break his shoulder. He had then stolen a horse to continue his flight.

A posse of farmers delivered Martin to the Letchmere Point jail near Cambridge, Mass. in October, 1821. Here, he was condemned to die as a horse thief, a capital offense in those days. Days later, he broke out of his chains and smashed through three jail doors, but was soon recaptured in a cornfield.

Days before his execution on December 22, 1822, hundreds of curious spectators gathered near Letchmere jail to see him die. Writers of the period were on hand to describe the handsome highwayman as "romantic and unreal."

His death was real enough. He was placed upon a horse-drawn cart beneath a tree limb with a noose around his neck (which he unconcernedly helped to adjust). Taking a piece of cloth from his pocket, Martin looked at the executioner. "When shall I drop the handkerchief?" he asked politely.

"Whenever you're ready," came the reply.

Martin studied his audience, a crowd of hundreds who gasped as he held the handkerchief aloft in the crisp, cold air. With a shrug of indifference, Michael Martin let the wispy cloth slip from his fingers. The cart driver snapped a whip, the horse jerked forward, and Captain Lightfoot was gone.

MASON, EBENEZER
Murderer ● (? -1802)

Insanity was deep in Mason and the neighbors of William Pitt Allen, for whom he worked, knew it. Mason always responded in a surly fashion at every order Allen gave him. The fact that Allen was his brother-in-law only increased Mason's resentment, which bubbled over into murder on May 18, 1802, when Allen told his in-law to hurry as he was scraping muck from a farm wagon.

Mason turned on Allen with an iron shovel in his hand and struck him dead. Ebenezer Mason was executed October 7, 1802, at Dedham, Mass.

MASON, SAM
Robber, Murderer ● (? -1803)

A rough river man, Mason robbed and killed for several years along the Natchez Trace. After being captured in Natchez and sent from that city in tar and feathers, Mason organized a vicious band of cutthroats and plagued the residents with rapes, robberies, and murders from 1800 to 1802.

He was finally tracked down by a professional bounty hunter, Bill Setten, who brought the outlaw's head back from the wilderness in a jar as a way of proving his kill. Setten, however, received no rewards from the governors of Mississippi and Louisiana who had offered huge amounts for Mason's capture. The bounty hunter was accused of being none other than Wiley Harpe, one of the murderous Harpe brothers who had pillaged the countryside for years.

Though he mightily protested his innocence, Setten was hanged on February 8, 1804. The bounty hunter's true identity was never established, but many thereafter believed they had hanged the wrong man, especially when reports of Wiley Harpe's presence in the area continued long years after the execution.

MASSIE, THOMAS
Murderer ● (1900-1944)

Lt. Thomas H. Massie of the U.S. Navy was considered a patient man, a soft-spoken officer who conscientiously performed his duties while stationed in Hawaii. During the fall of 1931, however, an event occurred that shattered his life and that of several others.

One night in September, 1931, Massie's attractive wife, Thalia, stepped from their beach bungalow to stroll alone upon the star-lit sands sprawling into the ocean before her. Five beach boys of Japanese-Hawaiian ancestry found her with her skirts up and splashing naked legs in the water. They raped her.

The mass assault on Thalia Massie produced the arrest of the five boys who were imprisoned in Honolulu and then released on bond pending a trial. Feeling ran so high in the American colony against the five Hawaiians that one, Horace Ida, was reportedly kidnapped by sailors, beaten until his back was raw, and then released, the attack on Ida occuring in December, 1931.

Lt. Massie, normally an easy-going man, became extremely agitated while awaiting the trial. Several officers slyly suggested that his wife had encouraged the boys. For the most part, Massie became an outcast in a class-conscious society apprehensive of a scandal involving one of their own. "Everyone shunned me and avoided me like hell," Massie later stated.

He then got the idea of confronting one of the beach boys before the trial opened, thinking to extract a confession from him. He sent

Lt. Thomas Massie (extreme left) and his wife Thalia were the leading figures in one of the most sensational murder trials of the 1930s, also shown here in 1932 (left to right): Mrs. Granville Fortesque, Sheriff Gordon Ross, Seaman A. O. Jones and E. J. Lord and their lawyer, Clarence Darrow, who defended them in Hawaii.

two of his men, sailors Albert O. Jones and Edward J. Lord, to find one of the boys. They returned to his beach house with Joseph Kahawawai. The boy stood impassively before Massie as Jones, Lord, and Mrs. Granville Fortescue, Thalia's mother, looked on.

Massie was blunt. From a sitting position behind his desk he asked Kahawawai: "Did you assault my wife?"

The boy did not hesitate. "It is true. We done it."

At that moment, according to his later statements, Massie lost complete control of his faculties and, in a blind rage, drew his service revolver and fired a shot directly into the Hawaiian's heart, killing him instantly.

"My God, Lieutenant," Seaman Jones yelled as he inspected the dead beach boy, "you're a damned fool!"

"Everyone was in a daze," Massie later reported, but none opposed the idea of dumping Kahawawai's body from a bluff near Koko Head. Massie, the two enlisted men, and Mrs. Fortescue attempted to drive to the lonely spot, concealing the corpse in the back seat. Authorities stopped the car before Massie could reach his destination.

One of the most controversial trials of the decade commenced with Mrs. Fortescue, a well-known socialite from New York and Washington, D.C., calling in the famous Clarence

Darrow for the defense. Massie's testimony, concerned with the unwritten law, was moving but unconvincing. A polyglot jury of Americans, Chinese, Hawaiians and others found the defendants, Massie, Jones, Lord, and Mrs. Fortescue, guilty of murder in the second degree.

The prisoners were kept in custody at Pearl Harbor while race riots throughout the U.S. and Hawaii ensued. Darrow talked of taking the case to the Supreme Court. Judge Davis had sentenced all the defendants to ten years in jail. Governor Judd of Hawaii, thinking to quell public anger, commuted the sentences to one hour each which the defendants served in the courtroom dock. Then they were freed.

Massie, his wife, and his mother-in-law slipped out of Hawaii that day on a steamship heading for San Francisco. Neither Mrs. Fortescue nor Massie ever received full pardons for the killing. Massie, however, stayed in the Navy, first serving on the *U.S.S. New Mexico* and then assigned to duty in California where he faded into obscurity.

Thalia Massie grew estranged from her husband several years later and went to Reno for a divorce. Reporters swamped her outside a courtroom. One asked: "Do you think you'll marry again?"

The ex-Mrs. Massie fixed a large stare at him and snapped: "Of course. I'm going to marry Clark Gable, didn't you hear?"

MATHER (OR MATHERS), DAVID ("MYSTERIOUS DAVE")
Murderer, Robber ● (1844- ?)

Mather was considered a "killer of killers" during the 1880s, a rough, uncompromising gunslinger who, upon telling a man he would kill him, "was sure to do it."

An unknown background and a tight lip earned Mather the name "Mysterious Dave." Some of his exploits were not as cryptic. It was known that he had been a horse thief and had been suspected of robbing trains in Texas and New Mexico. Mather possessed a violent temper and would not tolerate the slightest of threats. While serving as a constable in Las Vegas, N. M. on January 25, 1880, Mysterious Dave came upon a drunken railroad worker named Joseph Costello. Mather ordered him to move off the street and the drunk fumbled for his gun. Mysterious Dave shot him through the heart, an abrupt act which no doubt made the Las Vegas residents apprehensive of his law enforcement policies and led to his dismissal as a constable.

Mather was next seen in Dodge City, Kan. in the company of such hell-raisers as Charlie Basset, riding into the roaring cattle town about April, 1880. Stories told of him by street gossips had it that Mysterious Dave had broken three friends out of a New Mexico jail; had stuck up a whorehouse in Forth Worth, Tex., barely saving his life from an avenging madam who attacked him with a butcher knife and shotgun; and had been involved in a number of killings throughout the Southwest.

His reputation notwithstanding, Mather was appointed Assistant Marshal in Dodge in June, 1883. He was soon replaced through an open election which favored a new marshal, William "Bill" Tilghman, who would prove to be one of the finest lawmen in the Old West. Tilghman replaced Mather with Thomas Nixon, a famous buffalo hunter who had reputedly brought down 120 of the great beasts in one day, a record far in excess of that claimed by Buffalo Bill Cody.

Nixon and Mather both owned saloons in Dodge City. They went into a price war. Nixon gave his customers two beers for a quarter. Mather then offered the same at twenty cents. Nixon then reportedly bribed a distributor to cut off Mather's supply of beer. Mather strapped on his guns and went looking for Nixon.

The Assistant City Marshal was warned that Mysterious Dave was looking for him and on July 18, 1884, waited in hiding near Mather's saloon until he came outside. Nixon sent a bullet whizzing past Mysterious Dave and then fled down an alley.

Nixon, who at first thought he had killed Mather, was brought in for questioning but released when Mysterious Dave refused to make a formal charge against him. David Mather had other plans through which to enact his revenge. On the night of July 21, 1884, Mather found Nixon lounging outside a saloon on Front Street, came silently up behind him and said in a near whisper, "Hello, Tom." He then pumped four bullets into Nixon's back, killing him instantly.

Gambler and gunfighter Bat Masterson rushed from a nearby saloon and cradled the dead man's head in his arms. They had been friends. Before Masterson could bring about his own revenge, Mather was arrested by Tilghman and subsequently tried for the murder of Nixon. The trial took place at Kinsley, Kan. Mather's lawyers claimed he could not receive a fair trial in Dodge. The jury played out the rules of the West. Though Mather had murdered Nixon in cold blood, the jury felt

Mysterious Dave Mather, a killer of killers, was the terror of Dodge City in the early 1880s. (Western History Collection, U. of Okla. Library)

that the dead man had initiated the argument by firing the first shot.

Mather was acquitted and shortly thereafter vanished as mysteriously as he had appeared in the wild frontier towns.

MEACHAM, JEREMIAH
Murderer ● (? -1715)

On the morning of March 22, 1715, Jeremiah Meacham climbed to the roof of his house outside of Newport, R. I. for no apparent reason. He sat there for several hours brooding while his family—his wife and her sister—begged him to come down.

Suddenly, Meacham, who had no history of violence, jumped from the roof and killed both women with an axe. He tossed their bodies into the house and set it on fire.

Meacham was hanged at Newport, April 12, 1715.

MERRICK, SUDS
Robber ● (? -1884)

Merrick, along with Tommy Shay, James Coffee, and Terry Le Strange, was the organizer of the notorious Hooker Gang which robbed virtually at will in the Fourth Ward of New York City during the late 1860s and early 1870s. At one time Merrick had at least one hundred experienced thieves working for him, dominating an area from Fourteenth Street to the Battery.

The gang specialized in looting cargo boats docked in the East River. In 1874 Merrick led three of his top crooks—Tom Bonner, Sam McCracken, and Johnny Gallagher—on board a canal boat operated by Thomas H. Brick. The robbers tied up Brick and took hours carrying off everything on the boat that wasn't nailed down.

Police interrupted the quartet as they were about to depart, and all were captured, except Merrick, who fled. His three best men were sent to Auburn prison for long terms, and as a result, Merrick lost face with the other Hooker gang leaders and quit. He struck out alone, burglarizing and mugging for almost ten years until he was mysteriously killed in the Bowery in 1884.

METESKY, GEORGE PETER
Bomber ● (1903-1990)

For a short, anxious period, George Peter Metesky was "the most dangerous man in New York City," according to police seeking his whereabouts. That Metesky was mentally deranged was certain, particularly when he sought to settle an old feud with Consolidated Edison by secreting bombs all over the city.

Metesky began planting bombs, harmless duds for the most part, in 1940-41. He then sent notes to Consolidated Edison, blasting the firm with invective. He signed these erratically written missives "Fair Play." None of his early bombs went off, but the mad bomber, like the one who terrorized the city in the early 1930s and called himself "3-X," created enough stir to give the bomb and arson squads the jitters for a year. Without reason, his bombs and notes ceased as quickly as they had appeared.

It was ten years before Metesky resumed his bomb-planting. Why he waited so long to replay his lunatic hand remains a mystery, but he did begin again in 1951, planting live bombs in Radio City Music Hall, Grand Central Station, and several theaters. The bombs, some of which exploded, were followed by notes which raved against Consolidated Edison. Perhaps, it was reasoned, Metesky took a decade to learn how to construct a bomb that would actually explode.

Explode they did. A porter in Penn Station was crippled for life when Metesky's infernal machine went off there. Seven more people were seriously injured as they filed from a theater where a Metesky-planted bomb ignited.

The hundreds of special detectives assigned to catching the mad bomber had no clues to follow until Metesky wrote a letter to a newspaper in which he claimed that Consolidated Edison was responsible for his getting tuberculosis. An exhaustive check through the utility firm's files unearthed the record of George Peter Metesky, who had had an accident with the firm in 1931 and had previously claimed that through this he had contracted the disease. Thus, his hatred for Consolidated Edison.

Metesky was soon apprehended at his home in Waterbury, Connecticut, and charged with attempted murder. Psychiatric examinations established that he was a homicidal maniac. He is presently under guard in a New York State hospital for the criminally insane.

MILKEN, MICHAEL R.
Swindler ● (1947-   )

The economic excesses and greed of the 1980s was probably best personified by the career of Michael Milken, a high-powered financial wizard credited with the invention of the junk bond. As a bond trader for Drexel Burnham Lambert, a New York-based securities house, Milken engineered leveraged buyouts, made huge fortunes, and gutted formerly productive corporations with reckless abandon.

Prior to Milken's rise to prominence, a "junk bond" was a securities issue made by a troubled industry giant that might, with a new influx of capital, become competitive again. Milken's financial instinct told him that because small and midsized companies had much greater difficulty borrowing money than a giant had, such issues would make a dynamic difference in making smaller companies more profitable.

In helping smaller companies resolve debts by selling the debts off to speculators, Milken ushered in the era of coporate raiders—super-rich traders

Manhattan's "mad bomber," George Peter Metesky (getting out of car) happily smiled for cameras in 1957. (Wide World Photos)

who could buy up a company's debts, then use the economic leverage they gained to take over proprietorship of the company. In some cases, this led to a newly invigorated business. All too often, however, the corporate raiders swooped down like vultures to suck the life's blood of profits from dying businesses, while thousands of loyal workers were laid off or fired.

Milken's financial empire became so extensive that at one point he was able to add $500,000,000 to his personal fortune. Then, in 1989, the roller coaster ride came crashing down. Milken was indicted on 98 counts of securities violations in federal court. He was implicated in the national Savings and Loan scandal when the Congressional House Banking Committee subpoenaed his records of land deals with Irvine, California's Lincoln Savings and Loan Association, which was chaired by Charles H. Keating, Jr., another financier whose ethics were being questioned.

In 1990, Milken pleaded guilty to six counts of "technical" violations (while denying any deliberate fraud), and was sentenced by Judge Kimba M. Wood to ten years in prison. Judge Wood later acknowledged that she intended Milken's actual jail time to be less than half that, with the sentence meted out on the assumption that Milken would qualify for parole much earlier than the full sentence prescribed. Later, Judge Wood recommended Milken for just such a parole.

Milken reported to the minimum-security Federal Correctional Institution at Pleasanton, California, where his federal prisoner number was 16126-054, in early March 1991. While there, he was appointed camp tutor for inmates seeking high school equivalency diplomas, reorganized the prison law library, created educational puzzles for other inmates' children, and worked toward settling hundreds of millions of dollars worth of civil suits brought against him by angry investors burned in leveraged buyouts.

Altogether, Milken was estimated to pay around $900 million dollars in settlements and penalties, with Drexel Burnham Lambert adding another $300 million, and insurers $100 million to make good the losses to others in the scandal.

In June 1992, Milken testified against a former colleague, Alan E. Rosenthal, in the latter's federal conspiracy trial in Manhattan. Although officials of the Securities and Exchange Commission questioned whether Milken's testimony really helped the prosecution's case against Rosenthal, it was taken into consideration when Judge Wood ruled two months later that his sentence could be commuted.

Milken was released after less than two years in prison. He left the Correctional Institution, where he was regarded a model prisoner, for a halfway house in Los Angeles in early January 1993.

The last portion of Milken's sentence was yet to come. He was expected to perform eighteen hundred hours of unspecified community service. He announced that, over the next three years, part of his service would be to teach mathmatical skills to children in poor Los Angeles neighborhoods.

Friends of Milken believe that he was made a scapegoat for the economic troubles of the 1980s.

They also point out to the hustler's credit that his plea agreement included a clause that all charges against his brother, who also worked at Drexel, be dropped. Drexel itself went out of business during Milken's stay in prison.

According to Milken's lawyers, he had given over $360,000,000 to charity in the 1980s. But charity for Michael Milken always began at home. He left prison with an estimated half-billion-dollar fortune intact. Milken has been barred from securities trading for life.

MINA, LINO AMALIA ESPOS Y
Murderer, Thief ● (1809-1832)

BACKGROUND: CLAIMED SPANISH HERITAGE AND TO BE THE SON OF THE SPANISH GOVERNOR OF CALIFORNIA, CONSIDERING HIMSELF A "DON." DESCRIPTION: 5'2", BROWN EYES, BLACK HAIR, SLIGHT BUILD. ALIASES: CAROLINO ESPOS. RECORD: KILLED WEALTHY PHILADELPHIAN DR. WILLIAM CHAPMAN BY ADMINISTERING MASSIVE DOSAGES OF ARSENIC TO HIM IN HIS FOOD IN 1831; TRIED AND CONVICTED 2/25/32 IN DOYLESTOWN, PA.; EXECUTED 6/21/32.

In the early fall of 1831 a slender, dark-eyed Spaniard who called himself Carolino Espos visited the home of Dr. William Chapman, headmaster of a prominent Philadelphia school. The young man explained that he was the son of the Spanish governor of California and that he was trying to rejoin his family in the West but lacked the funds to do so. He bluntly asked if he could board with the family until funds arrived to make his journey possible.

The socially conscious Chapmans agreed, or rather, Mrs. Lucretia Chapman, an attractive woman in her forties who was quite charmed by Mina, insisted that he stay in their home. Dr. Chapman, a weak-willed man, accepted this strange arrangement without argument. In the following weeks Mina was seen by the Chapman children and servants embracing and kissing Mrs. Chapman, who appeared quite receptive to the Spaniard's advances.

Dr. Chapman remained the complete gentleman and looked the other way, silencing the stories whispered to him by his household help.

Within five weeks of his arrival at the Chapman residence, Mina went to a druggist in Philadelphia and ordered a quarter pound of arsenic. The druggist wanted to know how Mina intended to use the poison.

"It is for the stuffing of birds," the Spaniard replied.

The next day, Dr. Chapman ate a heavy meal and retired early, feeling sick. His illness continued for four days before he died. Oddly enough, Mina insisted on personally shaving the corpse before it was buried.

Two weeks after Dr. Chapman died, Mina married Mrs. Chapman in New York. Then small treasures in the Chapman household began to disappear, and even the family's silver vanished. Mina, of course, had stolen the goods (along with Mrs. Chapman's jewelry and certain bank assets). Swindles in which Mina posed as Chapman to complete financial deals alerted the Philadlphia police.

Authorities suspicious of Mina ordered Dr. Chapman's body dug up and an autopsy performed. Massive amounts of arsenic were discovered in the corpse, and both Mina and Mrs. Chapman were arrested and tried.

A weeping Lucretia sobbed that she had been victimized and hoodwinked into loving a thief and murderer. Mrs. Chapman was acquitted of murder by a chivalrous jury.

Mina was promptly convicted and labeled a notorious foreign cad who had violated an American home and marriage. He was hanged.

MINER, WILLIAM ("OLD BILL")
Stagerobber, Trainrobber ●
(1847-1913)

BACKGROUND: BORN IN JACKSON, KY. MOTHER A SCHOOLTEACHER, FATHER A MINER. MINOR PUBLIC EDUCATION. RAN AWAY IN 1860 TO BECOME A COWBOY. BECAME A MESSENGER FOR THE U.S. ARMY IN 1863. LATER ORGANIZED A ONE-MAN PONY EXPRESS FROM SAN DIEGO TO POINTS EAST. DESCRIPTION: TALL, SLENDER, THICK MUSTACHE. ALIASES WILLIAM MORGAN, GEORGE ANDERSON, SAM ANDERSON, G. W. EDWARDS, CALIFORNIA BILLY, BUDD, OLD BILL. RECORD: ROBBED THE SONORA STAGE IN 1869 ($200); CAPTURED AND SENTENCED TO FIFTEEN YEARS IN SAN QUENTIN; RELEASED IN 1879; ROBBED WITH WILLIAM LEROY A HALF DOZEN TRAINS AND COACHES IN THE COLORADO AREA; VIGILANTES CAPTURED LEROY AND HANGED HIM; TRAVELED TO TURKEY AND SPENT A BRIEF TIME AS A SLAVE TRADER; TRAVELED TO SOUTH AMERICA WHERE HE RAN GUNS TO INSURRECTIONISTS FOR A SHORT TIME; RETURNED TO U.S. AND ROBBED THE SONORA STAGE 11/8/80 ($3,000); ROBBED THE DEL NORTE STAGE IN COLORADO IN LATE NOVEMBER, 1880 ($2,000 IN GOLD DUST); ROBBED WITH STANTON T. JONES THE DEL NORTE STAGE THE FOLLOWING YEAR; ROBBED THE SONORA STAGE 11/7/81; CAPTURED AND SENT TO SAN QUENTIN PRISON FOR TWENTY-FIVE YEARS; PAROLED 6/17/01; ROBBED A TRAIN ALONE AT CORBETT, ORE., 9/23/03; ROBBED A CANADIAN PACIFIC TRAIN AT MISSION JUNCTION, BRITISH COLUMBIA, IN SEPTEMBER, 1904 ($10,000); ROBBED THE TRANSCONTINENTAL EXPRESS OF THE CANADIAN PACIFIC 5/8/06, NEAR FURRER, B.C.; CAPTURED BY NORTHWEST MOUNTED POLICE; RECEIVED A LIFE SENTENCE; ESCAPED FROM THE NEW WESTMINISTER PENITENTIARY 8/9/07; ROBBED A PORTLAND, ORE., BANK IN JULY, 1909 ($12,000); ROBBED THE SOUTHERN RAILWAY EXPRESS WITH FIVE OTHER BANDITS NEAR WHITE SULPHUR, GA., 2/18/11 ($3,500); SENTENCED TO LIFE IMPRISONMENT; ESCAPED THREE TIMES FROM THE GEORGIA STATE PENITENTIARY AT MILLEDGEVILLE; RECAPTURED EACH TIME; DIED IN HIS CELL IN 1913.

The criminal profession of William "Old Bill" Miner spanned almost a half century and three continents. At the height of his career as a robber he was a wizened geezer who doggedly refused to follow any other path than that of an armed bandit. More than thirty years of his adult life were lived behind bars, but imprisonment failed to reform him. He was still robbing banks and trains when well into his sixties.

After running away from his home in Jackson, Kentucky, Miner rode west in the early 1860s. He reached San Diego in 1863 just as a savage war between the U.S. Army and the Apaches broke out, and he soon became a messenger for General Wright. The hazards Miner faced while riding through hostile Indian territory convinced him that he should be paid handsomely. He agreed to deliver letters from San Diego citizens to points east for hefty charges that ranged up to $25 per letter. Miner accumulated a small fortune, which he promptly spent on liquor and women. He soon realized that to maintain his newly developed standard of living, he had to earn more money. There was big money to be had, he concluded, in robbing stages.

Alone, in 1869, he stopped the Sonora stage, getting $200. Miner had selected a poor mount, however, and the horse dropped dead from overexertion a few miles beyond the site of the robbery. A posse took him without a fight. Sentenced to fifteen years in San Quentin, Miner got out in ten for good behavior.

California was unlucky for Miner, so he rode to Colorado, where he teamed up with Bill Leroy, an experienced bandit. The two robbed several stages and trains, obtaining small amounts of money. Vigilantes closed in on the outlaws' camp one night and a fight took place. Miner shot three possemen who rushed him and fled into the night. Leroy was captured and hanged on the spot.

Packing his bags and loot, Miner took a leave of absence from crime and went to Europe, where he treated himself to a grand tour. He wound up in Turkey in early 1880 and, according to his memoirs, did a brief stint as a slave trader. Later that year he sailed to Rio de Janeiro and employed himself as a gunrunner. He then sailed back to the United States in time to rob the Sonora stage of $3,000 in late November. Days later, in Colorado, he stopped the Del Norte stage, taking about $3,000 from the strongbox.

Again Miner went sightseeing, this time to Chicago, where he met a young bankrobber named Stanton T. Jones. The pair rode back to Colorado and stopped the Del Norte stage, but the take was poor. They went away with only a few hundred dollars and a giant posse on their trail. At one point, the lawmen drew close enough for Jones and Miner to twist in their saddles and shoot three of them from their horses.

Miner returned to California, where his luck ran out again when he once more robbed the Sonora stage and was captured days later by a posse. This time Miner got twenty-five years in San Quentin.

On June 17, 1901, at age fifty-four, Old Bill was released. He tried his hand at various legitimate pursuits for two years and then gave up, returning to outlawry. His first strike was near Corbett, Oregon, on September 23, 1903, where, alone, he stopped a small passenger train and carried off only a few hundred dollars. Miner then decided to test his luck in Canada and rode into British Columbia in 1904. He stopped the Canadian Pacific express at Mission Junction and took $10,000 from the safe, a gigantic haul for those days.

Dressed in the finest clothes, Miner lived in the best hotels and passed himself off as a rich, retired cattleman. His money ran out in 1906, and on May 8, 1906, he again hit the Canadian Pacific, holding up the Transcontinental Express near Furrer, B. C. It took the Mounties one month to capture him, and he was sentenced on June 1, 1906, to life imprisonment in the New Westminster Penitentiary at Victoria. In less than a year Miner had dug a thirty-foot tunnel from his cell to the other side of the prison wall. He successfully made his escape on August 9, 1907.

Two years later, in July, 1909, Miner robbed a Portland, Oregon, bank of $12,000. He next appeared in White Sulphur, Georgia, on February 18, 1911, and with several other men stole $3,500 from the Southern Railroad Express.

The railroad hired the redoubtable Pinkerton Detective Agency to track down Old Bill, and he was captured in a swamp by several operatives led by agent W. H. Minster. Miner received a life sentence at the Georgia State Penitentiary. This time, there would be no escape—not that Old Bill didn't try. Following his capture after a third break attempt, Miner was led through the swamps back to prison. On the way, he remarked caustically to one of his guards: "You know, I'm really getting too old for this sort of thing."

Old Bill Miner died in his cell in 1913, a recalcitrant bandit to the end.

MIRANDA, MICHELE
Syndicate Gangster ● (1896-1973)

With a record that dates back to 1915 (shortly after his immigration to the United States from Naples, Italy), Miranda was a high-ranking Mafia member whose status in the New York area permitted him to attend the notorious criminal summit meeting in Apalachin in 1957.

He had long been identified with industrial racketeering, and was active in the garment industry which was once the province of Thomas Lucchese and Lepke Buchalter.

MITCHELL, WILLIAM
Murderer, Gunfighter ● (1853-1928)

Bill Mitchell, better known to the criminal world under his alias, Baldy Russell, was an inconspicuous gunman in Texas until 1874, when a neighboring family named Truitt invaded his father's farm. Mitchell and a handyman, Mit Graves, returned the Truitt raid by staging one of their own and killing two members of the Truitt family.

Fleeing the law, Mitchell went into hiding. His father was blamed for the killings and was hanged by a vigilante committee. A year later, Mitchell came out of hiding and rode three hundred miles to shoot down James Truitt, the last member of the clan. He then irregularly rode with small outlaw bands in the Southwest, robbing stages and stores under the name Baldy Russell.

Still wanted for the Truitt killings, Mitchell managed to evade a murder charge. Arrested many times, he gave aliases and then went free on bond, which allowed him to escape. Mitchell was finally captured in 1912 and sentenced to life imprisonment for the Truitt slayings. He escaped within months and lived out his life a hunted man, dying in 1928, and thus establishing an endurance record for a wanted criminal remaining at large and on the run.

MOLASSES GANG

Jimmy Dunnigan, Blind Mahoney, and Bill Morgan were the founders of the zany Molasses Gang whose members operated throughout New York City in the early 1870s. The gangsters were basically store thieves and pickpockets, and their gang name came about through their simple, comic method of robbery.

Dunnigan, Morgan, and Mahoney would enter a store and hold out a soft hat, asking the proprietor to fill it with sorghum molasses. Yes, they knew it was crazy, they said, but it was a bet, you see, to determine if they were right in guessing how much molasses the hat would hold. The proprietor usually shrugged and filled the hat.

When full, one of the gang members would grab it and force it over the proprietor's head, the molasses blinding him until the others could rob the till and depart. Members were rounded up about 1877, and the gang ceased to exist.

MOLINEUX, ROLAND B.
Murderer ● (1868-1917)

BACKGROUND: BORN AND RAISED IN NEW YORK, N.Y., THE SON OF A BRIGADIER GENERAL WHO HAD A DISTINGUISHED SERVICE RECORD, NOTABLY IN THE CIVIL WAR. COLLEGE-TRAINED. MARRIED BLANCHE CHEESEBOROUGH, 1898. ORIGINAL OCCUPATION, MANAGER OF A COLOR FACTORY; LATER A NEWSMAN AND WRITER. DESCRIPTION: ABOUT 5'10", BROWN EYES, BROWN HAIR, ATHLETIC BUILD. ALIASES: NONE. RECORD: POISONED HENRY C. BARNET IN 1898, N.Y.C.; ATTEMPTED TO POISON HARRY CORNISH, 1898, N.Y.C. (KILLING MRS. KATHARINE ADAMS, CORNISH'S LANDLADY, BY ACCIDENT); CONVICTED AND SENTENCED TO DEATH AT SING SING PRISON AT OSSINING, N.Y., WHERE HE WAS IMPRISONED FOR EIGHTEEN MONTHS AWAITING EXECUTION IN THE ELECTRIC CHAIR; GRANTED A NEW TRIAL IN 1902 AND RELEASED ON A TECHNICALITY; DIED IN KING'S PARK HOSPITAL FOR THE INSANE, 1917.

Molineux was the product of New York society in the Gay Nineties. He flaunted his wealth, prestige, and power. He was an aloof aristocrat used to having his own way. When his way was barred, he chose the ungentlemanly art of murder to dispose of his foes.

The seven-story Victorian building squatting at the corner of Madison Avenue and 45th Street in 1898 represented everything opulent and powerful in New York. It was the exclusive Knickerbocker Athletic Club, which catered solely to members of high society.

One of these was Roland B. Molineux, age thirty, whose father, General Molineux, was a club member and had wangled his son's admission. Roland spent a great deal of time at the club, occasionally traveling to Newark, New Jersey, where he managed a factory that made

Wealthy, aristocratic Roland B. Molineux, a prominent member of New York's high society in the 1890s, chose to poison those he didn't like; he died in an insane asylum. . (N.Y. Historical Society)

color dyes, a family business interest.

A handsome, well-built man, Molineux was later described as having a "feline appearance." This, no doubt, stemmed from the fact that his movements were graceful and catlike.

There was something catty about his personality, too. Molineux was constantly plaguing the club's board of directors to get rid of certain members who displeased him. His charges were dismissed as the whims of an eccentric young man yet to discover his purpose in life, or, as the super rich of those days put it, his destiny.

But Roland would not be put off when it came to matters of the heart. A fellow member, Henry C. Barnet, who resided at the club, was courting a beautiful, young debutante, one Blanche Cheeseborough, a girl Molineux secretly planned to marry.

In October, 1898, Barnet died. The club's doctor diagnosed Barnet's death as being caused by diphtheria, but there was a great deal of rumor and mystery surrounding the passing of Henry Barnet. While delirious, he had mumbled to the doctor something about receiving a strange bottle sent by mail. The doctor ignored the remark. A few weeks later, Roland Molineux married Blanche Cheeseborough.

Weeks later, Molineux had a run-in with the club's athletic director, Harry Cornish. It seems that Cornish had bested Molineux in a dumbbell-lifting contest. Such public humiliations were unbearable to handsome Roland, who rushed to the club's board members, demanding that they put Cornish on the street. "Fire him or I resign," he shouted.

The athletic director stayed and Molineux quit the club. On December 23, 1898, Cornish received a bottle of Bromo Seltzer along with a silver holder generally used for toothpicks. Cornish thought it a joke, one of the members undoubtedly pointing out his need for relief at the height of a champagne holiday.

Cornish took the bottle home with him to his boarding house and forgot about it. When his landlady, Mrs. Katharine Adams, awoke on December 28, 1898, with a thumping headache, Cornish remembered the Bromo Seltzer and poured out a glass, giving it to Mrs. Adams.

"It tastes bitter," she said.

"Let me try," Cornish replied and took a sip. "Seems all right."

Mrs. Adams then gulped down the potion. To Cornish's amazement, his landlady suddenly fell from her chair in wild convulsions. He himself became so queasy that he barely managed to stagger outside for help. A doctor arrived, but could do nothing. Mrs. Adams was already dead. Cornish, who was taken to his club, was deathly ill for days but survived.

The club's doctor now remembered Barnet's ravings about receiving a bottle and went to Cornish's boarding house. There, he analyzed the Bromo Seltzer and discovered it was loaded with cyanide of mercury, a deadly poison. He called in detectives who virtually ransacked the Knickerbocker Club, much to the annoyance of its crusty members.

In Cornish's office they found the original wrapper used to mail the poison. Comparing the writing on the wrapper with the writing of club members, they quickly determined that Roland B. Molineux was their man.

A sensation trial ensued. The prosecution spent over $200,000 to convict Molineux. His father spent even more to save him. The young man steadfastly cried out his innocence, but his case was hopeless.

Fourteen experts testified that it was Molineux's handwriting on the package Cornish had received. Moreover, the prosecution proved that Roland had, before the poisonings, rented two mailboxes. One was in the name of H. C. Barnet. The other was in the name of Harry Cornish.

Using Barnet's name, Molineux, it was proved, ordered a shipment of Kutnow's Stomach Powder from a Cincinnati firm (the handwriting on this order was also identified as Molineux's). Roland, the prosecution insisted, had replaced the powder with poison and sent it to Barnet.

The prosecution also proved that Molineux had ordered a shipment of cyanide of mercury, ostensibly for his factory.

Roland the handsome was doomed. Though more than 500 persons, all males, were interrogated about their open-mindedness before the jury was formed, the twelve jurists carefully selected and screened by the defense found Molineux guilty, and he was sentenced to die in the electric chair at Sing Sing.

He sat on death row for eighteen months until he was granted a new trial on a technicality. The court ruled that testimony concerning Barnet in the Cornish-Adams case was inadmissible. While watching one condemned man after another walk to the electric chair, Molineux coolly penned a small book entitled *The Room With the Little Door*. It was published and was heralded as a minor masterpiece.

Shrewdly, Molineux's lawyers dragged their feet, stalling off the second trial, which did not occur until 1902. By then public rage had subsided. Witnesses were missing. When Roland Molineux entered the courtroom, he was the picture of a victimized man, suffering from the oppression of the masses jealous of his wealth and prestige (as would be the case with Harry Thaw), a sensitive writer of great talent whose attractive wife had been visited by unjust misery.

Molineux was relaxed and smiling in court. A jury, reportedly unconcerned with the real facts of the case, responded emotionally and set him free in four minutes, a record deliberation.

Life was good to Roland Molineux after that, kinder than he had been to it; he prospered and his stature as an author grew. Ironically, he became a writer for several newspapers, exclusively covering murder stories. Theatrical impresario David Belasco even produced one of his plays.

After Blanche divorced him, Molineux remarried. For a while his life appeared stable, but following a relapse, Molineux was committed to an insane asylum in 1913, where he died four years later.

A curious footnote to the Molineux case was his biography in *Who's Who*. For the years 1898 to 1902—the time of the poisonings and his imprisonment—the biographical sketch merely stated: "Out of employment."

MORAN, GEORGE ("BUGS")
Bootlegger, Burglar ● (1893-1957)

BACKGROUND: BORN OF POLISH-IRISH PARENTS IN MINNESOTA IN 1893. MINOR PUBLIC EDUCATION. MARRIED, NO CHILDREN. DESCRIPTION: 6', BROWN EYES, BROWN HAIR, HEAVYSET. ALIASES: GEORGE MILLER, BUGS. RECORD: COMMITTED TWENTY-SIX ROBBERIES IN THE CHICAGO AREA BEFORE HIS TWENTY-FIRST BIRTHDAY; FIRST ARRESTED IN 1910, SENT TO JOLIET PRISON FOR ROBBERY 9/17/10, PAROLED 6/18/12; ARRESTED IN 1913 FOR BURGLARY AND LARCENY, RECEIVED

MINOR SENTENCE; ARRESTED IN 1917 FOR ROBBERY, FORFEITED BAIL BOND, CHARGE STRICKEN FROM RECORD; ARRESTED FOR ROBBERY, EARLY 1918, SENT TO STATE PRISON 5/24/18, PAROLED 2/1/23; JOINED WITH DION O'BANNION, EARL "HYMIE" WEISS, AND VINCENT "THE SCHEMER" DRUCCI IN ORGANIZING THE NOTORIOUS NORTH SIDE GANG IN CHICAGO, CIRCA 1914, BECAME CLOSE FRIENDS WITH O'BANNION AND ROBBED SEVERAL WAREHOUSES AND SAFES WITH "DEANIE" (THE O'BANNION-MORAN-WEISS-DRUCCI DOMAIN RESTED IN THE 42ND AND 43RD WARDS); INVOLVED IN DOZENS OF KILLINGS·DURING THE PROHIBITION ERA, ALL CAPONE HENCHMEN; SUSPECTED OF THE ATTEMPTED MURDER OF JOHNNY TORRIO 1/24/25; KILLED, WITH VINCENT DRUCCI AND FRANK GUSENBERG, ANGELO GENNA, A CAPONE ALLY, 5/25/25 ON CHICAGO'S HUDSON AVENUE AFTER A HIGH-SPEED PURSUIT; WOUNDED WITH DRUCCI ON 6/13/25 IN A SHOOT-OUT WITH MIKE GENNA, SAMOOTS AMATUNA, JOHN SCALISE, AND ALBERT ANSELMI; MEMBER OF THE TEN-CAR CAVALCADE WHICH SHOT UP AL CAPONE'S HEADQUARTERS, THE HAWTHORN HOTEL IN CICERO, AT HIGH NOON, 9/20/26, WOUNDING CAPONE HENCHMAN LOUIS BARKO AND A PASSER-BY, MRS. CLYDE FREEMAN; REPORTEDLY KILLED EIGHT CAPONE MEN FROM 1926 TO 1932; FOLLOWING THE WHOLESALE DESTRUCTION OF HIS GANG ON 2/14/29 (ST. VALENTINE'S DAY MASSACRE), PRESTIGE AND PROWESS DECLINED DURING 1930S; REDUCED TO PETTY BURGLARIES; ROBBED WITH VIRGIL SUMMERS AND ALBERT FOUTS A BANK MESSENGER IN DAYTON, O., 6/26/46 ($10,000); ARRESTED IN HENDERSON, KY., 7/6/46 WITH SUMMERS AND FOUTS; SENTENCED TO OHIO STATE PRISON, RELEASED 1956; ARRESTED BY FBI DAYS LATER ON AN OLD BANK-ROBBERY CHARGE; SENTENCED TO TEN YEARS IN LEAVENWORTH FEDERAL PENITENTIARY; DIED IN LEAVENWORTH IN FEBRUARY, 1957, OF LUNG CANCER.

He was a cool, somber-looking kid with large, brown eyes and a deep cleft in his chin. Big-boned and tall, George Moran moved to Chicago before the turn of the century with his parents and was soon a member of one of the many Irish gangs that roamed and robbed the North Side of Chicago.

At age sixteen Moran took a leaf from the annals of the Old West. He unhitched horses from delivery wagons, led them to a secret stable, and held them for ransom. Zany as his racket might have been, Moran claimed it was a living until something better showed up. Something better arrived the following year in the personage of an Irish strong boy, Dion "Deanie" O'Bannion, the criminal "Cock-of-the-Walk" on the North Side.

O'Bannion was an expert safecracker and burglar, with natural instincts and abilities as a leader. Dion led; Moran followed. After robbing several warehouses together, O'Bannion and Moran attempted to crack a delicate safe. A night watchman interrupted their labors and Moran was caught. O'Bannion escaped, his crippled leg—a result of a childhood accident —not hindering his speedy departure.

Moran proved his loyalty to the older boy, O'Bannion. He maintained the gangster's code of silence and took the rap alone. After serving almost two years in the state prison at Joliet, Moran was released. He was nineteen and not a bit enlightened by his experience. He returned to robbing warehouses with O'Bannion, was caught in the act in 1913, and received a light sentence.

Taking the fall for charming Deanie became a habit with Moran. He was apprehended by police in a robbery in 1917 (again O'Bannion escaped). Proving his loyalty to Moran, Deanie put up bail bond. Moran jumped bail and did not appear in court. O'Bannion, who by then could afford expensive lawyers and payoffs to crooked judges, had his friend's arrest stricken from the record. There was little the Irish gangleader could do the following year, however, when Moran was again, foolishly, caught robbing a department store. It cost the awkward burglar almost five more years in state prison.

When Moran, known as "Bugs" because of his uncontrollable temper, was finally released in early 1923, he joined O'Bannion's then formidable North Side gang, which had gone into the bootlegging business in a big way. O'Bannion, Hymie Weiss, and Vincent Drucci had built up a powerful organization that controlled all gambling and dispersing of illegal booze in the wealthy 42nd and 43rd wards, known as the Gold Coast. Moran became an O'Bannion stalwart, hijacking Capone's beer trucks at will.

Mimicking the leader he idolized, Moran began to sport a well-tailored wardrobe. His daily attire usually consisted of a white snap-brimmed hat, immaculate blue serge suit (with vest), finely striped shirt, conservative tie held by a diamond stickpin, and his habitual pearl-gray spats. Where O'Bannion wore three guns, Moran played the role of vassal correctly; he wore only two, secreted in pockets specially fitted into his suit coats. He used them often in Deanie's employ. When attending social events in the evenings, Moran wore, like his boss, a tuxedo at all times. The two guns never varied.

Usually Moran gave the appearance of a quiet, retiring type, uttering few words and remaining unobtrusive in the long and sinister shadow of O'Bannion. When Deanie was murdered in 1924 amid the posies of his flower shop, Moran, along with Weiss and Drucci, vowed vengeance on the slayers—Al Capone's hit men.

The first target was Capone's ally and mentor, Johnny Torrio. "Papa Johnny" was brought down by the North Side trio in a wild shotgun affair outside his home at 7011 South Clyde Avenue, Chicago, on January 24, 1925. Moran, seeing that Drucci and Weiss had hit the Italian gangleader, ran to Torrio, leaned over him with a pistol, and pulled the trigger. Torrio, blinking up in horror, heard only a click. Moran's pistol had misfired. The sound of running feet, the inevitable interested spectators, sobered Moran, and he fled before administering the coup de grace. He didn't miss a few months later, however, when he and Drucci chased Angelo Genna in an 80 mph pursuit, with guns blazing, down Hudson Avenue in broad daylight on May 25, 1925. Genna was shot to pieces. By then, Torrio had quit the city, and Capone was in charge of the South Side. Capone had ordered O'Bannion's death, and the Genna brothers had loaned him Albert Anselmi and John Scalise to perform the murder. The Gennas began to die.

Mike Genna, before his own death at the hands of Capone murderers, fought back, ambushing Drucci and Moran on June 13, 1925, in another daylight shooting. The North Siders were wounded and managed to drive their car to Congress Street, where they ran it onto a curb. Drucci and Moran ran for a block with blood from their wounds splattering the sidewalk until they reached a doctor's office. After a short recuperative period, both were back in action.

The action was something out of a First World War bayonet charge. On September 20, 1926, Weiss, Moran, and Drucci filled ten touring cars with machine gunners and drove into Cicero, Capone's stronghold. As they passed his headquarters, the gunners raked the Hawthorn Hotel with thousands of bullets, shattering every window in the block. Weiss, Moran, and Drucci stepped from the last car and stood on the sidewalk spraying the entire place, while Capone was sprawled on the floor of the hotel's coffee shop; Frank Rio, his bodyguard, squatting on Scarface to protect him.

The bizarre noonday attack produced only two casualties. Louis Barko, a Capone flunky, was wounded in the arm, and a passer-by, Mrs. Clyde Freeman, was injured when a splinter of glass flew into her eye. The raid, however, terrified Capone and the city at large. Only the North Siders were crazy enough to pull a stunt like that, Capone reasoned (several of his henchmen had spotted Weiss, Moran, and Drucci wielding machineguns). He would take care of them, he bellowed. Scarface's execution squad was headed by Louis Barko. Twice Barko attempted to shoot down Drucci and Weiss on Michigan Avenue, again in broad daylight. He missed both times.

Scalise, Anselmi, and others, who had been lying in wait for Weiss for weeks, did not miss on October 11, 1926. He was machine-gunned to death with several aides while crossing State Street to enter Dion O'Bannion's flower shop, headquarters of the North Side gang.

Next came the turn of Vincent Drucci. The Schemer, irate at being arrested on April 4, 1927, attempted to club policeman Danny Healy while being taken to headquarters. Healy shot and killed him in the squad car.

George "Bugs" Moran was now all alone against the might of General Al the Scarface. Moran was a gutsy gangster with more moxie than sense. He swore an eternal vendetta against Capone, whom he called "The Pimp," "The Beast," and "The Behemoth." Bugs gave public interviews in which he spewed forth his venom for Big Al. He was proud of the fact that he and his cohorts restricted themselves to bootlegging and gambling. Moran, like O'Bannion and Weiss before him, was a churchgoer who abhorred prostitution. It was a fact that during the reign of the North Siders not one brothel was in operation in their territory. That kind of low life was for Capone, Moran said.

In one interview with the Reverend Elmer Williams, a Methodist minister who published a reform broadsheet entitled Lightning, Moran delighted in explaining the difference between himself, an upright gangster trying to turn a dollar, and Al Capone, the scum of the earth.

" 'The Beast,' " Moran explained, "uses his musclemen to peddle rot-gut alcohol and green beer. I'm a legitimate salesman of good beer and pure whisky. He [Capone] trusts nobody

Chicago gangster George "Bugs" Moran (center) at one of his many court appearances. (UPI)

and suspects everybody. He always has guards. I travel around with a couple of pals. The 'Behemoth' can't sleep nights. If you ask me, he's on dope. Me, I don't even need an aspirin."

Heady talk. Yet Capone only snickered and continued his plans to take over the opulent North Side. It would take him close to two years to achieve his goal, the wholesale slaughter of the Moran gang. During the interim, Moran built up his gang with ace gunners, crack gamblers, and speakeasy managers who operated his many casinos and saloons. He cut into Capone's dog-racing monopoly by building a racetrack in downstate Illinois. When Capone mobsters burned down the stands, Moran and two of his men, Willie Marks and Ted Newbury, burned down part of Capone's dog track.

At the height of his underworld fame, Moran married. He fearlessly drove about in an expensive touring car with his wife, daring Capone to blow him up. Unlike most gangsters, Moran informed anyone who cared to know where he would be during the day.

Leaving police headquarters one day, the dapper Moran swept an expansive hand past a stunning brunette sitting in his car. "Gentlemen," he said to several newspaper reporters, "my wife. If anybody comes looking for me you can tell them that this is our wedding anniversary and we're going roller skating."

A sight to behold! George "Bugs" Moran, two guns bulging beneath his expensive jacket, racing about a rink on roller skates.

Though not endowed with criminal genius, Moran possessed a certain boyish charm, an impish sense of humor that once even caught the fancy of reformer Judge H. Lyle, one of the few honest jurists in Prohibition-torn Chicago.

On one occasion when Moran was brought before Lyle, the judge peered down from his bench and recognized an apprehensive look in Bugs' eyes. "What's the matter?" Lyle asked. "Don't you like me, Moran?"

Bugs cracked a wide grin. "I like you, Your Honor . . . but I am suspicious of you."

Another time, Moran came up to Lyle at the Cubs' baseball park. "Judge," the gangster said, "that's a beautiful diamond ring you're wearing. If it's snatched some night promise you won't go hunting me. I'm telling you now I'm innocent."

The Irish pixie in Moran could turn monster at any moment. Judge Lyle's court was interrupted one morning by a terrific racket in a nearby bullpen. Investigating, Lyle found Moran battling three bailiffs. They had mistakenly arrested Bugs when he appeared in court to sign some routine papers. Moran hadn't bothered to explain his presence to the bailiffs. After one bailiff had locked handcuffs on him, Moran used them as brass knuckles to knock out his three attackers.

Staring at Lyle, Moran said: "Sorry, Judge, but these clowns were trying to throw me back in the can."

By early 1929 Moran had sided with Joe Aiello in an all-out war against Capone. Aiello offered $50,000 to any gunman who would kill Scarface. Then, on January 8, 1929, Aiello and, reportedly, Bugs Moran shot down Pasquilino Lolordo, a Capone stooge who headed up the powerful *Unione Siciliane*.

For Capone, it was the final act of defiance by Moran. He ordered Bugs and his entire gang to be destroyed on February 14, 1929.

Moran, who had survived a dozen shootings, was again lucky. He would miss the St. Valentine's Day slaughter by five minutes. He, Ted Newbury, and Willie Marks arrived just in time to see a police wagon draw up to his gang headquarters, the S-M-C Cartage Company at 2122 North Clark Street. Thinking it a raid, the trio darted into a coffee shop and waited. When crowds began to mill around outside the garage an hour later, Moran and his two men fled to their hideouts.

Inside the garage, Capone had wrought the most awful carnage of the Chicago gang wars. Seven men were dead, machine-gunned in one burst after another against the garage wall, including the much-feared Moran gunmen, Pete and Frank Gusenberg (SEE St. Valentine's Day Massacre).

Moran had inadvertently set up the slaughter the previous night after receiving a phone call from a man he trusted, a man never named by either Capone or Moran, who told him that a special shipment of Canadian liquor would be delivered to the North Siders the next morning. Moran had okayed the shipment. Now most of his best gunmen were dead.

Reporters tracked down Moran days later and badgered him about the shooting. For once, Bugs was nervous and upset. He kept shaking his head at every question. "I don't know, I don't know anything about it," he repeated rapidly. Finally, he looked up at the newsmen and shouted: "Only Capone kills like that!"

Capone was languishing at the side of his swimming pool in Palm Island, Florida, at the time of the shooting. He had distance and an estate full of guests as alibis. The sports editor of the New York Post, Jack Kofoed, interviewed Capone the following day at poolside. Scarface had several newspapers spread about him. He had circled the remark made by Bugs Moran in red pencil.

While his wife, Marie, cavorted in Capone's pool, Kofoed chatted for a time and then got around to the reason he was there. "Al," he said anxiously, "did you have anything to do with it?"

Scarface bunched up his ample cheeks in a fat-lipped smile. Through halting laughter he said, "The only man who kills like that is Bugs Moran."

The North Clark Street shooting spelled the decline and fall of George Moran. With the remnants of his gang he attempted to assert his authority in the 42nd and 43rd wards, but Capone's army of gunmen beat him back on every corner. His lot did not improve when Capone was sent to jail in 1931 for income-tax evasion. He drifted into gangster oblivion.

Moran did have one effectual stroke of vengeance in 1936. According to most reports, it was Bugs and two others who caught up with Machine Gun Jack McGurn, one of those who had done the shooting at the garage, on the seventh anniversary of the St. Valentine's Day Massacre. Bugs found McGurn with his coat off, his sleeves rolled up, and a bowling ball in his hand. Those in the Chicago bowling alley ran for cover when Moran's men opened up with machine guns. McGurn was killed in the first burst. Moran was not brought to trial for this murder.

The once mighty Bugs, who boasted a personal bootleg fortune of $500,000, was reduced to petty burglaries by the end of the Second World War. He moved first to downstate Illinois and then to Ohio, where, with bank robbers Virgil Summers and Albert Fouts, he stuck up a bank messenger, stealing a little more than $10,000, a sum considerably beneath him in his palmy days. He was arrested by FBI agents in early July, 1946, and drew a ten-year sentence. Released briefly in 1956, Moran was rearrested for an earlier bank robbery and was sentenced to Leavenworth, where he died in February of the following year.

Moran's old friendly enemy, Judge Lyle, read about the Prohibition gangster's death by lung cancer and figured that Bugs, more than any of his ilk, would have repented before death. He wrote the prison chaplain, Father O'Connor replied:

"George Moran died a very peaceful death and was strengthened with the full Last Rites (Penance—Extreme Unction—Holy Viaticum —Apostolic Blessing) of the Catholic Church while he was fully conscious. This happened some days before he died and was not a 'last ditch' stand. Your theory certainly proved out very satisfactory in his case. I am sure that God in His mercy was very kind to him in his judgment."

Missing from Moran's funeral were all the trappings of the typical gangster burial of the Roaring Twenties. Bugs and the boys had sent Dion O'Bannion off in style with a $75,000 funeral. Moran, Weiss, Drucci, Louis "Two-Gun" Alterie, Maxie Eisen, and Frank Gusenberg had borne their leader to the grave wearing tuxedos. Six convicts in gray lugged Moran to the prison cemetery in a $35 casket.

For George "Bugs" Moran there wasn't even the traditional wreath he himself had often given, inscribed with that universal farewell: "So long, pal."

[ALSO SEE Joseph Aiello, Louis "Two-Gun"

Alterie, Al Capone, Vincent "The Schemer" Drucci, Genna Brothers, Dion O'Bannion, St. Valentine's Day Massacre, John Torrio, *Unione Siciliane*, Earl "Hymie" Weiss.]

MORAN, THOMAS B. ("BUTTERFINGERS")
Pickpocket ● (1892-1971)

BACKGROUND: BORN IN BOSTON, MASS., 1892. MINOR PUBLIC EDUCATION. DESCRIPTION: 5'5", BROWN EYES, BROWN HAIR, STOCKY. ALIASES: NONE. RECORD: ARRESTED SIXTY-FOUR TIMES FOR PICK-POCKETING SINCE 1906, SERVING SMALL JAIL SENTENCES WHICH AMOUNTED TO A TOTAL OF EIGHT YEARS THROUGH HIS LIFETIME, HIS LAST ARREST BEING IN 1970.

Long considered America's dean of pickpockets, "Butterfingers" Moran began his criminal career in San Francisco only hours after the earthquake subsided. Never a member of any gang, Moran taught himself to pick pockets until he became an expert, always denying he ever snatched a woman's purse in the pursuit of his trade. "That's strictly for amateurs," he sneered.

Asked once to divulge his method of picking pockets, Moran only smiled. "You just do it," he said from his prison cell. "You don't need anybody to show you."

Moran usually wintered in Florida and moved, like the birds, north during spring. In 1967, the aging pickpocket remarked that his trade gave him "a chance to travel." "I've been in every big city in the country and I must have at least 10,000 friends scattered around."

A twinkle-eyed, grandfatherly type, Moran plied his trade at racetracks, in subways, and on busy downtown streets. A rough estimate of his lifelong success was 50,000 wallets picked, or $500,000 at $10 per wallet, a career record for pickpockets.

Moran died in a charity bed at the Miami Rescue Mission, Miami, Florida, on September 14, 1971. "He had been arrested in every state on the continent and Canada, too," said Miami police sergeant Edward MacDermott, an old acquaintance (Moran had spent many a night in the Dade County stockade).

Moran had no regrets concerning his life or chosen profession. At the end he had only one complaint: "I've never forgiven that smart alecky reporter who named me Butterfingers. To me, it's not funny."

MORS, FREDERICK
Serial Killer ● (1885- ?)

Arriving in New York from Vienna on June 26, 1914, Frederick Mors announced, to those curious about his strange attire, that he was the most famous hunter in Austria. He wore leather leggings, a long leather coat, and carried a large knife in a leather sheaf. He intended to travel to the Rockies, he said, where he would become America's most celebrated hunter.

Instead Mors took a job as a porter in a home for the elderly in the Bronx. While he was on duty, from August 9, 1914 to January 4, 1915, the death rate increased at the home in alarming proportions. Seventeen aging people had died, apparently of being chloroformed.

Police were called and Mors was brought before one of the toughest cops in New York, Captain Cornelius W. Willemse, who had learned that Mors had been passing himself off as a doctor and had virtually ruled the nursing home, striking fear in anyone who opposed his will by casting upon them "the evil eye," as one terrified patient put it.

Willemse asked Mors for his real name and Mors replied: "I do not care to give it."

Mors claimed he was a professional in the medical field. Willemse asked him what university he had attended when studying medicine.

"I do not care to give it," Mors responded.

"How about all these deaths up here," Willemse inquired.

Frederick Mors replied in a calm voice. "Oh, I killed them." He went on to explain that he felt he had to "put them out of their misery. Take the first one I killed, for instance, Christian Hitgers. I mean I had to change his bedclothes several times a day and I got tired of it . . . I gave him a glass of beer, which contained arsenic. I should have known better. He got convulsions and became paralyzed. It was several days before he died. I made up my mind that the next one would not cause that much trouble."

Mors then stated that it was easier to kill off the patients with chloroform. He was proud to inform the captain that he had helped the patients into the next world to ease their suffering. His mercy killing was coupled to self-serving ends, of course. "All of them were suffering and all of them were great nuisances. So I got rid of them."

Incarcerated at Bellevue Hospital, Mors was examined by Dr. Menas Gregory. The killer stood at a window in the doctor's office, staring down coldly at the derelicts and cripples moving about the hospital yard.

Mors then turned to Gregory and said solemnly. "I'd like to get a job here, Doctor. I'd clean up that yard for you quick."

Declared a criminal lunatic, Mors was sent to Mattewan State Prison for the Insane, the same institution that would house such celebrated criminals as millionaire murderer Harry K. Thaw, the berserk killer Quimby Appo, and trainrobber Oliver Curtis Perry.

Mors remained at Mattewan for a decade, telling other inmates that he would some day escape and continue performing his mercy killings, his kind of charity. In the late 1920s Mors disappeared from the institution and was never found again, leaving many to apprehensively believe that the maniac might be in any nursing home in America, carrying out what he had termed his "good deeds."

(ALSO SEE Quimby Appo; Oliver Curtis Perry; Harry K. Thaw)

MUDGETT, HERMAN WEBSTER
Murderer, Robber, Arsonist ● (? -1896)

BACKGROUND: BORN AND RAISED IN GILMANTOWN, N.H., OF YANKEE LINEAGE. STUDIED MEDICINE AT ANN ARBOR MEDICAL SCHOOL IN MICHIGAN. WORKED AS A DRUGGIST IN SOUTH CHICAGO IN THE EARLY 1890S. PROPRIETOR OF THE INFAMOUS "MURDER CASTLE" DURING THE CHICAGO FAIR OF 1893. DESCRIPTION: APPROXIMATELY 6', BROWN EYES, SANDY HAIR, HEAVY BUILD, MUSTACHE, IN HIS THIRTIES. ALIASES: H. H. HOLMES, H. M. HOWARD. RECORD: ARRESTED ON SUSPICION OF MURDER 11/17/94 IN BOSTON, MASS. (SUSPECTED, AND LATER PROVEN GUILTY, OF MURDERING MORE THAN TWO HUNDRED WOMEN IN CHICAGO) TRIED FOR THE MURDER OF BENJAMIN F. PITEZEL IN

THE COURT OF OYER AND TERMINER AND GENERAL DELIVERY JAIL AND QUARTER SESSIONS OF THE PEACE, PHILADELPHIA, PA., 10/28-11/2/95; SENTENCED TO DEATH BY HANGING; EXECUTED ON THE GALLOWS OF MOYAMENSING PRISON 5/7/96.

He was the criminal of the nineteenth century, the archfiend of America and the all-time mass killer who slaughtered by the dozen. And he was the nicest man you'd ever want to meet.

Born Herman W. Mudgett, this subtle, charming murderer dropped his given name early and adopted the more rakish Harry Howard Holmes (one of many aliases). A sharp-minded but lazy student in New Hampshire, Holmes was always scheming ways to profit by the stupidity of others.

As a student of medicine at the University of Michigan, he finally struck pay dirt . . . or cemetery ground. Holmes hit upon the idea of taking out large insurance policies under different names.

Next, he would filch cadavers from the university's dissecting room and plant the bodies in various spots. Then he would collect the insurance on the unrecognizable bodies (he was by then a master of acid methods). His fortunes grew.

But this nineteenth century ghoul was caught one night dragging the body of a young woman from the medical lab. A campus policeman was astounded. "My God, what are you doing there?" he demanded.

Holmes cracked a crooked smile and answered, "Taking my girl for a walk, you idiot."

The body was returned to the university morgue, and Holmes, dragged before a sputtering dean, aghast in his nightgown, was expelled immediately.

He shrugged, packed his bags, and headed for Chicago. Once there, he became, among many other names and disguises, Dr. Harry Howard Holmes. His time was spent ingeniously as a swindler—later he would graduate to being a professional polygamist, rapist, and sadist, and a mass murderer unequaled anywhere in the world.

At first, Holmes made his money by purchasing furniture on credit, then selling it overnight. It was easy, fast work, but it required constant changing of addresses. Dr. Harry was the movingest man in Chicago.

Herman Webster Mudgett, alias H. H. Holmes, America's most prolific murderer, he claimed the lives of at least two hundred victims. (UPI)

He soon tired of the furniture "race," and, not letting his medical background go to waste, landed a job in a drugstore on Chicago's South Side. By then he was a tall, handsome, and utterly charming gentleman with a long, well-waxed mustache and piercing snake eyes.

His looks, manners, and knowledge of medicine made business boom. It got so good that Holmes bought the drugstore. But operating a legitimate business was not enough for Holmes. He found honest success boring.

Holmes instituted a program of alcoholism cures, special self-bottled elixirs of colored cinnamon water. He also dashed off fictional get-rich-quick stories and published them in pamphlet form. The money rolled in.

There were moments when Harry would stare coldly at the empty lot across the roadway from the drugstore on 63rd Street. Once, caught eyeing the vacant property, he murmured, "I want that vacant lot . . . I've got plans."

He purchased the land the next day and then went to work designing one of the strangest buildings ever erected on the American continent. It had turrets, bay windows, and several entrances.

The three-story building was a monstrosity, crazily conceived, but it was all according to Holmes's plan. During the construction there was some talk about his strange behavior. No sooner would one work crew finish a section of the building than they would be fired and another crew of workmen hired.

Systematically, Holmes was creating a madhatter's castle that would go undetected. When completed, this crazy-quilt structure had hidden rooms, concealed stairways, trap doors, false walls and ceilings. There were closets and rooms without doors, and doors that opened up to solid brick walls. There was an elevator that had no shaft, and an elevator shaft without an elevator. And there was a chute that led to the basement.

In the basement Holmes installed a mammoth dissecting table made of huge planks, a giant stove-crematory, and yawning pits that could be (and were) filled with quicklime and acid. Now Dr. Harry was ready.

Murder may have been on his mind, but money was the plan. Holmes went to several employment agencies and asked for secretary-typists. "He liked nice, green girls fresh from business college," one account states.

The parade of pretty young girls began through Dr. Harry's horror house. He explained away all this activity with a simple excuse: "The World's Fair [of 1893] is coming and that means tourists. That's why such a big building. Rents will go high with tourists coming into Chicago. By me, it's smart business."

But it was the devil's business. . . . in a devil's house. As each pretty young thing was hired, Holmes began instant suggestive advances, which always ended with him leading the young girl up the stairs to his bedroom on the third floor.

There, after properly wooing her, and with the promise of marriage drooling from his lips, Holmes would convince each girl to sign over her insurance and savings and to make out a will in his favor.

As a reward, he allowed each would-be wife to spend an entire night in his bed. He would awaken early, go to his "laboratory" on the same floor, and return to the bedside with a container of chloroform. As the girl dreamed in ecstatic reverie, Dr. Harry gently deepened her sleep with a heavy dose of the anesthetic.

Holmes would then lift his victim carefully, almost lovingly and carry her to the elevator shaft, into which he rudely dumped her. Slipping a glass lid over the shaft, he sat down and waited until the girl became conscious. He watched silently with snake eyes gleaming as she awoke and realized the trap, clawing helplessly, frenzied and hysterical, at the doorless walls.

"It's time," he would say and retrieve a hose which he inserted into a small hole in the glass lid. He then pumped lethal gas into the horror shaft and settled back to watch the girl gasp out her final breath.

The next move required some strength, but Holmes was always up to it. He would loop a rope around the girl's neck and drag her up, then unceremoniously threw her down his special chute and listen to the body slide its way to the basement.

Down the wooden steps he would stomp through a concealed trap door in his personal bathroom. Once in the basement, its walls lined with containers of deadly gases and poisonous powders, Holmes would go to work on the dead girl, using many of the surgical tools that hung on the walls. He dissected the body methodically on his large bench. Those parts of the anatomy that attracted him most were pushed into one heap (he would later take them to his third-floor "lab" for grisly experiments), and the rest of the body was hacked and sawed to pieces. These unwanted remains would then be dropped into the huge stove for cremation.

As he stirred the fires slowly, he would notice hunks of body that refused to burn. These he placed into the vats on the concrete floor and poured quicklime and acid over them.

His daily chore complete, Dr. H. H. Holmes fiendishly gathered up the pieces of body saved and, humming a peculiar melody (overheard often by his janitor), began his climb upward to his quarters, hands outstretched and clutching his quivering "specimens."

Meanwhile, the World's Fair roared open and Chicago was jammed with tourists. Nobody noticed the girls—reported to approach the incredible number of 150—who went into Holmes' odd castle, never to be seen again.

Sometimes Holmes did away with all formality and merely butchered the girls alive and screaming. Who could hear? One of his rooms was completely soundproof, lined with asbestos.

In 1893 an alarmingly beautiful young woman, Minnie Williams, left her hometown in Texas to come to the World's Fair, seeking a career as an actress. She was to spoil everything for Dr. Holmes.

Minnie had been left a hefty piece of land by her rancher father, valued at $60,000, no mean sum in 1893. The first building she went to after reading an ad was the "crazy-looking house" on 63rd Street.

Dr. Harry welcomed her with open arms as a new boarder. When he learned of her assets, he advanced like the proverbial bull, taking her again and again in his elegantly appointed bedroom. He loved her, he adored her, he revered her, he cherished her. And Minnie believed him.

But when it came to turning over her land to Holmes, Minnie balked. First, she had to write her sister Nannie back in Texas and tell her about her wonderful husband-to-be.

Fine. Write sister Nannie.

Nannie showed up in Chicago weeks later, and Holmes, wearing the best finery of the day, was a perfect gentleman. He squired the two Texas beauties to the World's Fair. They also went shopping in the fashionable stores in the Loop.

Days later, when the girls were shopping alone, they ran into one of Nannie's friends. She introduced her lovely sister, saying, "Minnie is soon to be Mrs. Holmes."

"Holmes?" the friend said. "That's curious. I know a woman who lives in Wilmette, the wife of a Dr. Harry Holmes. Are they related?"

The sisters blinked in amazement at each other. Could they be?

That night Minnie, remembering that her betrothed owned property in Wilmette and often went there on business (sometimes staying overnight), confronted Dr. Harry.

The janitor who worked in the building (he was never allowed into the basement or any of the special rooms) heard Minnie and Holmes arguing.

"You're married, aren't you, Harry?" he heard the young girl say. "That woman in Wilmette . . . she's your wife . . . isn't that so, Harry?"

"Ridiculous, absurd. Who told you such nonsense?"

"It's true, it's true, it's true, isn't it, Harry?"

The janitor heard no more.

Of course it was true. Dr. H. H. Holmes did have a wife in Wilmette, comfortably tucked away in a luxurious $50,000 house. What of it? He also had a wife in Indiana. There was a Mrs. Holmes in Philadelphia, too. Well, the woman in Philadelphia wasn't really a wife anymore. She was dead, hacked to bits years ago.

One thing was certain: Minnie would not be Mrs. Holmes Number Four. The night after the janitor overheard the argument, the two Texas sisters disappeared. The groom lamented. Handsome Harry had been jilted, he said to all.

One of those consoling Harry was a petty thief named Ben Pitezel. The smalltimer was not unaware of the good doctor's line of work. In fact, after this gruesome story was finally pieced together by a remarkable detective, it was learned that Pitezel had often helped his benefactor in his bizarre Murder Castle work.

Holmes complained to Pitezel that his horror house was not taking in enough loot. "Lord knows, I've worked hard, Ben. But the damnable place has cost me $50,000 to operate. I'm going broke in this business!"

Yes, life was rough for Holmes, but he pulled himself together and cooked up another wild scheme. Pitezel would travel to Philadelphia, Holmes explained, and set himself up as a wealthy patent agent, taking out a $10,000 insurance policy. Once established, Holmes would show up, steal a corpse from the local morgue, disfigure it beyond recognition, and leave it to be discovered in Pitezel's home. They would then claim the insurance and be back on their feet.

"A sound plan, Harry." Pitezel even went further and offered the loan of his wife and three children, eight-year-old Howard, Alice, fourteen, and Nellie, thirteen, for a cover. The bereaved widow, Pitezel's own wife, would claim the phony body.

Pitezel packed and rushed off to Philadelphia to begin his career as a patent agent. Holmes, however, decided to pick up some quick money first. He torched Murder Castle so badly that it had to be boarded up. Then he attempted to collect the insurance on the building.

Overcurious police inspectors messed up this plan. They insisted on examining his structure before the insurance company paid off.

Holmes, standing in a police station, never lost his composure. He was indignant. "Now, see here. I'm a tax-paying, law-abiding citizen and I'm entitled to my claim."

"Of course, Dr. Holmes, but we must inspect the premises. It's a formality. You'll have to unlock your building."

"That's an insult. Are you accusing me of something?"

"Of course not. It's only a formality, doctor."

What must have been in the mind of Herman Mudgett at that moment? What visions of those awful rooms, that hideous basement, and the ghastly fragments hidden there must have flashed through his mind? Dr. Harry thought better of it and told the police he would have to reconsider; he was busy and would return later.

He never did. Instead Holmes headed for Texas and tried, unsuccessfully, to obtain Minnie Williams' $60,000 property, but the Texas lawyers representing the estate were too shrewd for him. They demanded proof that Minnie was his wife and had died by natural causes.

Holmes hung around Fort Worth for weeks trying to figure an angle, until his money ran out. Then, this highly intelligent criminal made his first mistake. Acting like an ordinary thief, he stole a horse, his only means of getting out of Texas, and fled.

St. Louis was as far as he got. Once there, a common swindle backfired and Holmes was arrested for the first time in his life. He gave the name of H. M. Howard. He shared a St. Louis cell with the notorious train robber (they were still running wild in those days), Marion Hedgepeth.

Mr. "Howard" asked the bandit if he knew of a reliable, crooked lawyer, explaining his impending insurance scheme with Pitezel, who was waiting in Philadelphia. He offered $500 to Hedgepeth for the right lawyer and told him he would pay after he received the insurance money. The bandit gave him the name of Jeptha D. Howe. Soon, Holmes was out on bail and skipped off to Chicago to prepare for his next murderous adventure.

On Tuesday, September 4, 1894, a Mr. Perry, who had set up a patent office and whose only known client was a Mr. Holmes in Chicago, was found very dead, his face charred beyond recognition. A pipe, a box of matches, and a benzine bottle were found nearby. Poor Mr. Perry. How unfortunate. He blew most of his face away on his back porch while lighting his pipe too close to the benzine bottle. Poor soul.

A medical examiner grew suspicious. He inspected the body and reported that Mr. Perry had died of poisoning. A coroner's jury, however, ruled death by accident.

Almost immediately, attorney Jeptha D. Howe stepped forward representing Mrs. Benjamin D. Pitezel. The woman said that the dead man was really her husband—Ben Pitezel. They were claiming the insurance. But the company had second thoughts. So the insurance people wrote Perry's only client, now back in Chicago, the ubiquitous Mr. Holmes.

Would he come and identify the body? Certainly, if he were to be paid a fee. It was agreed, and, incredibly, Holmes went to Philadelphia to identify the body of his ex-partner in crime. He brought Ben's fourteen-year-old daughter, who made the identification through rivers of tears, and the insurance was paid. The couple disappeared.

It was then that convict Hedgepeth blew the whistle on Mr. "Howard," telling the warden of the St. Louis jail how he gave Holmes the name of the crooked lawyer to set up the phony insurance deal.

"So I give him the name of my lawyer. And that's the last I seen of him. He got out on bail the next day and skipped out. I heard by the grapevine that he collected the insurance money but he ain't been near me to pay the five hundred dollars!"

That's when Philadelphia policeman Frank P. Geyer, a super-detective by anyone's standards, was hired by the insurance people to track down the nefarious Mr. "Howard."

Geyer inspected boarded-up Murder Castle, but did not enter. He checked the Illinois license records and they led back to the University of Michigan. There he was given Holmes' birthplace—Gilmantown, New Hamshire.

Nobody in Gilmantown had ever heard of Holmes. Geyer described the handsome, tall man with the glib tongue. "That fits Herman Mudgett to a T," one officer said, and Geyer was directed to the Mudgett home.

Mrs. Mudgett explained that her son was away, busy. "He's an inventor, you know."

"Yes, I know," the wily detective said. "He's invented some marvelous things. Do you know where I can find him?" She told Geyer that Herman was in Boston on business, and the

H. H. Holmes' "Murder Castle" in which he slaughtered a reported two hundred or more gullible females during the time of Chicago's World's Fair. (N.Y. Historical Society)

detective caught up with him there on November 17, 1894. He was with Mrs. Pitezel and both were arrested.

Mudgett refused to be returned to Philadelphia, and under questioning, Mrs. Pitezel admitted that she didn't have the insurance money. She had signed it over to Herman.

Then a warrant for Mudgett's arrest arrived from Fort Worth for horse stealing. "Take your choice," Geyer told Mudgett. "It's back to Philadelphia or to Texas for horse stealing."

Mudgett sweated. Horse stealing was a hanging offense in Texas. "I'll go back to Philadelphia." Once in Philadelphia, Mudgett told incessant lies. He said that Pitezel was alive in South America and that he had stolen the corpse known as Mr. Perry from a medical school. The records were checked, and the medical-school-cadaver story was thrown out.

Next, Mudgett said, "All right. The man was Pitezel. He was supposed to steal a cadaver, lost his nerve and got despondent. So he drank chloroform. When I discovered that, I decided to make it appear an accident so his poor widow could collect the insurance."

"What about the Pitezel children? We can't find them."

"I've told you everything, so help me God."

God, on the other hand, was far from helping Mudgett. Again, Geyer went to work, tracking through all the cities Mudgett had dragged the helpless, hopeless Pitezel children —Chicago, Detroit, Cincinnati.

In a rented house in Indianapolis, leased by Mudgett (as Holmes), Geyer sifted through the ashes in a large stove. He found bones and the skull of a small boy—Howard Pitezel. In Toronto he discovered another Mudgett-rented house and in its basement a trunk containing the two Pitezel girls. They had been locked inside, and gas, piped into the trunk, had killed them.

"It was a foul murder!" raged Herman Mudgett when Geyer confronted him. "Who was the fiend?"

Geyer only stared at the good-looking face behind the bars, a face that hid the real sight of a monster. He still had no proof linking Mudgett to murder. Then he remembered the big house in Chicago.

With the help of Chicago police, Geyer broke into Murder Castle, and in the stench-reeking basement, grown men dug, fainted, then dug again until they had unearthed the remains of over *two hundred corpses*.

"Untrue! A lie! Villainous slander!" Mudgett yelled, but they had him on the Ben Pitezel murder, for he did, it was proved, kill his partner in crime. It was all over . . . or was it?

Herman Mudgett invited the press in and confessed in detail to murder after murder in Murder Castle. He described his gory slaughterhouse, and as the papers sopped up his words and spread his name across a shocked nation, he reveled in his terrible fame. "My sole object," he said in a gross misstatement, "is to vindicate my name from the horrible aspersions cast upon it."

The date of his hanging cut short his "memoirs"—he had only gotten to victim number twenty-seven—and on May 7, 1896, Herman Mudgett, alias Dr. Harry Holmes, staggered up the thirteen steps to the gallows.

As the noose was slipped around his neck, there came a high, almost inhuman voice wailing, "As God is my witness, I was responsible for the death of only two women. I didn't kill Minnie Williams! Minnie killed her—"

At that moment, the trap sprang open and the large, heavy rope sliced into Mudgett's last words, silencing him forever. But what did he mean with that last, unfinished statement? Did Minnie kill her sister? Was she in league with her killer-lover?

We shall never know . . . which is exactly what this archfiend of the century may have wanted after all. Was it the truth or a lie on his lips at the last. The final baffling mystery

left unsolved—that would fit Herman Mudgett to a T.

[ALSO SEE Marion Hedgepeth.]

MULLIN, HERBERT WILLIAM
Serial Killer ● (1947-   )

The son of a Marine colonel, Mullin spent most of his time smoking marijuana and taking LSD in his native town of Santa Cruz, California. When he was 25, he later insisted, he began to hear voices telling him that he could prevent the massive earthquakes predicted for southern California if he sacrificed human lives.

To that maniac end, between October 1972 and February 1973, Mullin mudered a tramp he encountered in the mountains around Santa Cruz, a girl whose body he mutilated, four campers, a priest in a confessional, the couple who introduced him to drugs, a woman and her two children, and an old man working in his back yard.

The last killing was done in broad daylight, which quickly led to Mullin's arrest. At his trial, Mullin was shown to have voluntarily entered five different mental hospitals. He had been diagnosed as a violent paranoid schezophrenic. Those examining him on each occasion recommended that Mullin never be released, that he was a danger to society. Instead, in every instance, he was given some drugs and sent home. Mullin was given a life term. The jury recommended that he never be released.

MURDER, INC.

With the growth of organized crime in the early 1930's, the czars of the newly formed syndicate—Charles "Lucky" Luciano, Vito Genovese, Louis "Lepke" Buchalter, Abner "Longy" Zwillman, Meyer

Lansky, and Frank Costello—established an enforcement arm to protect their growing interests against lone rival mobsters. At first this strong-arm goon squad was headed by Benjamin "Bugsy" Siegel and his partner, wily little Meyer Lansky. This flying squad was available to every syndicate organization throughout the United States.

The troop of killers was used regularly, flying into a city and disposing of a victim fingered by the local gang (as strangers these killers could not be identified, and police could not trace motives). By the time Louis "Lepke" Buchalter, labor rackets kingpin, took over the enforcement squad, it had become known as Murder, Inc., and its bloodthirsty members, recruited from the tough, gangster-ridden sections of Ocean City, Brownsville, and East New York, were for hire to almost anyone.

Murder became big business under Buchalter's guidance. The mob employed business terms to describe their bloody work and to confound police. A "contract" was an assignment to murder. A "hit" was the actual killing. The "bum" was always the victim. Each assassin usually got from $1,000 to $5,000 for a hit, depending upon the risk involved and the importance of the person to be killed. Huge sums of money were regularly (and still are) funneled into the national syndicate's war chest by all local gangs to pay these killers.

One of the most energetic of these killers was Pittsburgh Phil (Harry Strauss), a hulking murderer addicted to expensive, flashy clothes.

Phil enjoyed his work, and delighted in telling his fellow goons about the clever ways in which he disposed of many of his victims. (Pittsburgh Phil, it was reported, murdered at least 500 people as a professional killer for hire from the late 1920s to 1940, when the group was finally exposed.)

Once, in Jacksonville, Florida, Phil followed his victim doggedly. "Even if it takes all day, I'll tail him and find the right spot," Phil bragged to his associates. He finally trailed his man into a movie house. Like most of Murder, Inc.'s assassins, Pittsburgh Phil never carried a weapon in case the local police picked him up on suspicion. He would cast about, once he had selected his murder spot, for any tool handy that would do the job. In the case of the man in the movie theater, Phil noticed a fire axe in a glass case.

"It was an easy 'pop' [killing]," Phil stated. "I take the axe and sink it in the guy's head. It's the kind of thing that will make a lot of holler. Dames and guys will make a run out of there. I just run with them—and the getaway is a cinch. This is a natural."

On other occasions, such as in 1937 when Phil and Happy Maione received a contract to murder Detroit gangster Harry Millman, conventional means were employed. Maione and Phil found Millman dining in a crowded restaurant and merely waded in, each with two pistols, and pumped twelve slugs into him (also wounding five others) then sauntered outside, disappearing on a dark street.

Murder, Inc. took care of its employees. There was a contingency fund, an insurance fund, a family fund. When two of Siegel's top killers—Joseph Schaefer and George Young—fired seven bullets into Abe Wagner in St. Paul in 1932 (Wagner had run from the mob in New York, but they traced him to St. Paul, where he was living under the name of Loeb and pushing a fruit cart), and were apprehended, "Bugsy" immediately made plans to have them set free.

Since there was no legal method open to him, Siegel gave another killer, known only as "Dandy Jack," $35,000 to "set those two guys out on the street." Apparently, Dandy Jack meant to blast a hole in the prison so that the killers could escape, but the expensive jailbreak never materialized (Dandy Jack disappeared shortly thereafter).

The organization could be equally enthusiastic in punishing a wayward member. In the summer of 1937 Walter Sage, manager of Murder, Inc.'s slot-machine enterprises in upstate New York, was discovered skimming money from the take. Mob "purification" was swift. Pittsburgh Phil, Gangy Cohen, "Pretty" Levine, and Jack Drucker took Sage for a ride. Drucker, sitting in the back seat, leaned forward and placed one arm around Sage's neck. With his free hand he drove an ice pick thirty-two times into Sage's chest.

The body was then tied to a pinball machine and dumped into a lake. But the killers learned a valuable lesson. They had neglected to open the victim's intestinal tract, and the body gases caused Sage's corpse to surface some days later. They never made that mistake again.

"Think of that," Pittsburgh Phil commented.

"With this bum you gotta be a doctor or he floats!"

The hit troop never lacked for murder specialists. There were the giant Vito "Socko" Gurino, Angelo "Julie" Catalano, Dasher Abbadando, Happy Maione, Abe "Kid Twist" Reles, Blue Jaw Magoon, Pittsburgh Phil, Buggsy Goldstein, Dukey Maffetore, and dozens of others. There was even a women's auxiliary corps for the more delicate assignments, led by Evelyn Mittelman.

Their lieutenants were ruthless killers, too: Mendy Weiss, Louis Capone, Dandy Phil Kastel, Luciano, Lepke, Jacob "Gurrah" Shapiro, Bugsy Siegel.

The group even had their own undertakers to handle the hundreds of slain corpses and hidden gang cemeteries—specially selected swamps, deserted farms, and warehouses.

It was an army of professional killers that operated for a decade in total secrecy, until, trapped by the confessions of confederates, one of Murder, Inc.'s high-ranking murderers began to talk, unraveling one of the most ghastly tales of human carnage for profit ever witnessed in America.

In the spring of 1940 a smalltime hood named Abe "Kid Twist" Reles was brought into custody for interrogation on a murder charge.

Killer Abe "Kid Twist" Reles told all he knew about Murder, Inc. and then went out a window to his death. (UPI)

This arrest came about after Burton B. Turkus, assistant district attorney for New York City, received a letter from an inmate of the City Workhouse on Riker's Island. "Dear Sir," the letter began, "I am doing a bit here. I would like to talk to the district attorney. I know somehing about a murder in East New York." It was signed "Harry Rudolph."

Turkus went to Riker's Island and saw Rudolph. The man exploded in his face. "Those bastards from Brownsville! Those rats killed my friend Red Albert [alias Alex Alpert, called "Red," a nineteen-year-old hoodlum killed in New York on November 25, 1933]. I saw them do it. I'll tell you who did it, too. Those Brownsville guys—Reles and Buggsy and Dukey Maffetore!"

Turkus demanded some sort of proof. Harry Rudolph stood up in his cell and raised his shirt. There, he said, was proof—an old and ugly scar on his abdomen. "That's what they did. They stood two feet away from me and shot me. And I picked the bullet right out with my fingers!"

Abe "Kid Twist" Reles, Buggsy Goldstein, and Dukey Maffetore were picked up for what they thought would be routine questioning. While being held on the Alpert murder indictment, Kid Twist discovered that somebody outside wanted him dead. Dukey had also begun to sing, implicating him in several murders. So for the first time in gangland history, a major syndicate hoodlum told all, to save himself on a promise of immunity from prosecution made by the district attorney.

The song Reles sang for almost two years was long, loud, and gruesome. It was the song of Murder, Inc.

Reles told of murder on a national scale—murder for profit run by Louis "Lepke" Buchalter and Jacob "Gurrah" Shapiro. He admitted to Turkus that he belonged to a troop of men in Brownsville, only one of many that existed solely to carry out murders.

The Kid introduced the chilling new words from the underworld—the "contract," the "hit," the "mark," and the "bum."

The killing, Reles said, was done coast to coast. The Brownsville troop alone accounted for over 1,000 murders in ten years. And it was easy, Reles said, terribly easy. "Since the bum never knew us—say one of us went to Cleveland—he never suspected nothin'. We laughed at the coppers. How could they trace a hit to one of our troop? How? We didn't even have a motive they could follow, see? We never even knew these bums. We get a contract and we make the hit and we get paid. It was a lot easier than working our loan-sharking [juice] and number rackets."

Reles stood fairly high in the hierarchy of the syndicate, and his memory was perfect. He remembered the details of dozens of killings, some a decade old. And he remembered who did the killings, too.

Reles named Happy Maione, Dasher Abbadando, Blue Jaw Magoon, and the worst of the lot, Pittsburgh Phil, the killer who delighted in murder, who begged for contracts, whose bloodlust was never satiated.

"Phil never could get enough hits. He talked about them all the time." Pittsburgh Phil preferred to use an ice pick on his victims. It came to be the most popular murder weapon for his troop, next to the strangling rope.

Sometimes, Reles said, they would happily do the unnecessary in their killings. He admitted strangling a smalltime syndicate mobster named Puggy Feinstein in his own home. "That wasn't enough for Phil, though. He picks up the bum's body and hauls it into a car.

"Then we drive out to the fields back of Brooklyn. Phil dumps the bum out and then brings out some gas and dumps it all over the guy. Then he lights the guy up and watches him burn. 'Puggy makes a nice fire, don't he?' Phil says. 'Yeah,' I says. Whattaya gonna say to somethin' like that? Huh? Phil is nuts."

There were some big-timers who took a bad trip down Kid Twist's memory lane. He named Joe Adonis and Albert Anastasia and Lucky Luciano for the first time as leaders of the crime syndicate. He also named one of America's most vicious gangsters who was also part of the mob rulers—Louis "Lepke" Buchalter.

When Buchalter was in hiding in 1939 with a stack of witnesses lined up against him for his involvement in the rackets, he gave Reles a big order. "Lepke was satisfied real good," Reles cooed.

"Lep give us eleven contracts for witnesses when he was on the lam. We knocked off seven of them before Dewey put him on trial last year."

Reles remembered Lucky Luciano telling him in 1934 of a hit he wanted: "This bum is cutting in on my play with the stuff [narcotics]. You guys take him."

Dutifully, Reles and his troop grabbed Muddy Kasoff, held him for ransom, which was paid, then drove him into the country. The blindfolded Kasoff was told to walk a hundred steps. He started to stumble on his way. Then Reles blew the top of the dopester's head off with a shotgun.

"It handed Phil a laugh," Reles grinned. "We left the bum under a billboard that says, 'Drive Safely.' Lucky was satisfied plenty."

The murders rolled off Reles' tongue like spittle. He told how George "Whitey" Rudnick was hit in Brooklyn in a garage with such savagery that the judge and courtroom gaped open-mouthed. Reles was on the stand staring right into the eyes of his former mobster pals— Happy Maione, Abbadando, and Pittsburgh Phil (whom Reles sometimes called Pep or Big Harry).

"I walk in (into a garage). Over there on the floor Rudnick is laying. Abby is holding him around the shoulders, and Big Harry is putting a rope around his neck.

"Then they strangle him. Rudnick is laying there. Pep has an ice pick. Happy has a meat cleaver . . . It is the kind you chop with . . . you know, a butcher cleaver. Then Abby grabs Rudnick by the feet and drags him over to the car. Pep and Happy grab it by the head. They put it in the car. Somebody says, 'The bum don't fit.' So Abby pushes . . . he buckles it up to make it fit . . . he bent up the legs.

"Just as they push the body in, it gives a little cough or something. With that Pep starts with the ice pick and begins punching away at Whitey. Maione, over there [pointing Happy out in the courtroom], he says, 'Let me hit this bastard one for luck,' and he hits him with the cleaver, someplace on the head."

Whitey's brutalized body was identified by his mother the next day in the morgue. He had sixty-three stab wounds in his head and torso, and Happy Maione's "one for luck" was described by the coroner's physician as "a laceration in the frontal region of the head. The wound gaped and disclosed the bone underneath."

Kid Twist himself blandly admitted killing people by the dozen. Here is only a part of his immense testimony:

Q—Did you kill Jake the Painter?
A—Yes, sir, in 1933 or '34 I think.
Q—Did you kill a labor delegate named Greenblatt?

A—Yes, with somebody else.

Q—Did you know a man named Rocco who was killed?

A—I don't recall the name. [Reles later remembered this man, Rocco Morganti, as the one who was lured to a card game where Kid Twist dealt him a hand and then shot him in the face as he made his first bid.]

Q—Did you kill a man on Columbia Street?

A—I was a party in it. There were two of us pulled triggers.

Q—When Puggy Feinstein was killed, you killed him, didn't you?

A—I helped, I was part of it.

Q—Did you shoot any of the Shapiro Brothers? [Rival gangsters in Brownsville during the early 1930s, who were eliminated by Murder, Inc.)

A—Not alone. I was one of the party.

Q—Did you pull the trigger?

A—I was one of them pulled the trigger and if you want to know the other man, I'll tell you.

He did. As Reles walked smugly from the courtroom that day, his ex-pal and fellow killer Happy Maione lunged wildly at him, screaming, "You stool pigeon son of a bitch!" He shrieked wildly, "I'm gonna kill you . . . I'm gonna tear your throat out!"

The jailers, however, held Maione in check, and Kid Twist was led back to his heavily guarded room at the Half-Moon Hotel in Coney Island.

Everybody in mobdom wanted to do what Happy Maione threatened to do: get at the Kid's throat to stop him from singing. Lepke had a $50,000 contract out for him. So did Lucky Luciano.

But the hotel in which the Kid ate his thick steaks, drank beer, and listened to ball games was a veritable fortress. There were six men in the room with him at all times, three shifts of officers, eighteen policemen in all.

On the morning of November 12, 1941, prosecutor Turkus got a call from an aide.

"Hey, Burt," he said quickly, "Reles just went out the window."

"Out the window? What?"

"No, no, you don't get it. Reles really went out the window . . . out of his sixth-floor window at the hotel. He's deader than a mackerel!"

They found Kid Twist's body splattered all over the roof of the hotel's kitchen extension. Found next to him were two bedsheets tied together, re-enforced with wire. Turkus was told that Reles was trying to escape his police protectors by attempting to get into the vacant room below his (how Reles knew this room was vacant was never explained).

The prosecuting attorney couldn't believe his ears. Six policemen in the room with him and he went out a window? All of the officers had excuses, however, and none was prosecuted.

Did Reles really try to escape? Hardly. Where could he go to escape the syndicate? Besides, his body was found twenty feet from the side of the hotel building. This indicated that Kid Twist left this world with some help, obviously via a big push. No one has ever discovered who did the Reles job, but Lucky Luciano, Vito Genovese, and others breathed a lot easier when the Kid died.

But not Lepke, his chief executioner, Mendy Weiss, and Louis Capone (no relation to Scarface). Based on Reles' testimony, they went to the electric chair. Happy Maione, Abbadando, and Pittsburgh Phil joined them months later.

[ALSO SEE Albert Anastasia, Louis "Lepke" Buchalter, Benjamin "Bugsy" Siegel.]

MURIETA, JOAQUIN
Bandit ● (? -1853)

Practically nothing is known about this most glamorous of California bandits except that fiction writers have heralded his exploits for a hundred years with only threadbare facts to sustain their lurid and ample imaginations.

At the time of Murieta's raids, California was a wild place where upstanding citizens lost their identities in the pandemonium of the gold rushes. It was all but impossible to keep factual records of elusive bandits like Murieta.

There is little doubt, however, that he did exist, robbing gold miners of their hoarded treasure and stopping stages to pilfer passen-

An artist's rendering of the legendary Joaquin Murieta, California's most notorious bandit. (Denver Public Library)

gers. The bandit's one-man crime wave in the early 1850s caused the governor of the state to offer a $1,000 reward for his capture, dead or alive.

One Harry Love, a captain of the Texas Rangers, promised California authorities that he would bring in the bandit. After several expeditions, Love did bring in something—the head of a Mexican preserved in a jar, which the ranger insisted was that of Murieta. The head was displayed in Stockton, California, on June 24, 1853, for the gawking curious.

Rumors persisted for a dozen years following Love's trophy hunt that Murieta was still riding and looting in the California hills. The rumors then faded into gentle folklore.

MURREL, JOHN A.
Bandit ● (1794- ?)

He was known to readers of the *Police Gazette* as "the great Western Land Pirate," but John Murrel was, in reality, a murderous bandit with a head full of fanciful

schemes and a massive ego. Murrel was one of the first horse bandits to organize a gang of cutthroats who robbed and terrorized those living along the Natchez Trace.

In 1834 Murrel met a youth named Virgil Stewart in his travels, and the two men journeyed several miles through the wilderness together. During the trip, Murrel, who passed himself off as a harmless merchant, told Stewart of an "elder brother" who had become a bloodthirsty bandit.

At their camp stops, Murrel painted grisly pictures of killings and robberies committed by his "elder brother," who also stole slaves and resold them. Those slaves who gave him trouble, Murrel said, were killed. One slave, Murrel pointed out, gave his brother so much trouble about being resold that "he took the nigger out on the bank of the river which ran by the farm and shot him through the head and then got rid of him . . . He cuts open the belly and scrapes out the guts, and then he fills him full of sand and throws him into the river to feed the eels . . ."

Hours later, while Stewart was still shivering from such cold-blooded stories, Murrel leaned a shadowy face into the light of a campfire, smiled, and said: "I might as well be out with it. I'm the elder brother I've been telling you about."

Murrel then admitted to Stewart that he had committed countless robberies along the Trace and had killed a number of men who resisted him. He terrified the young man when he outlined his plans for taking over the city of New Orleans by leading a slave revolt. Many of the slaves he had stolen, Murrel said, he had kept and armed for this purpose. When he had accumulated enough slaves to form an army, he would take over the states of Mississippi and Louisiana. He vowed he would kill every aristocrat he found, a class of people he bitterly blamed for beginning his criminal career, and at whose hands he had been beaten and whipped and branded a horse thief. "My blacks will cut all their throats . . . we will swim in rivers of blood!"

Murrel, who thought to recruit Stewart for his insane cause, took the young traveler to his camp, where dozens of armed blacks were drilling as soldiers and preparing for Murrel's coming attacks on nearby settlements. Stewart slipped away during the night and informed authorities of the madman's plot. Murrel was taken without a fight, tried, and sent to the Nashville prison for ten years. His abortive slave revolt began without a leader and soon collapsed following a number of murders along the Natchez Trace.

Murrel was released from prison about 1842 and disappeared.

MUSICA, PHILIP
Swindler ● (1877-1938)

BACKGROUND: BORN IN NAPLES, ITALY, IN 1877, IMMIGRATED WITH PARENTS MARIA AND ANTONIO MUSICA TO N.Y.C. IN 1883. SISTERS—LOUISE, GRACE; BROTHERS—ARTHUR, GEORGE, ROBERT. MINOR PUBLIC EDUCATION. MARRIED CAROLE JENKINS HUBBARD. ORIGINAL OCCUPATION, IMPORTER. DESCRIPTION: 5'5", BROWN EYES, BROWN HAIR, STOCKY, GLASSES. ALIASES: F. (FRANK) DONALD COSTER, FRANK COSTA. RECORD: ARRESTED IN 1909 FOR FAILING TO PAY CUSTOMS DUTIES ON FOODSTUFFS IMPORTED FROM ITALY AND BRIBING OFFICIALS TO SUBSTITUTE FALSE BILLS OF LADING; FINED $5,000 AND SENTENCED TO ONE YEAR IN ELMIRA REFORMATORY; PARDONED IN FIVE MONTHS BY PRESIDENT TAFT IN 1910; ARRESTED AND JAILED FOR THREE YEARS IN 1912 FOR STEALING $500,000 FROM SEVERAL BANKS THROUGH A FALSE COMPANY SWINDLE; ARRESTED FOR PROHIBITION VIOLATION IN 1920, RELEASED AFTER TURNING STATE'S EVIDENCE AGAINST HIS PARTNER, JOSEPH BRANDINO; ESTABLISHED AN AMORPHOUS FIRM UNDER THE NAME GIRARD & CO. IN MOUNT VERNON, N.Y., IN 1923, OSTENSIBLY A HAIR-TONIC COMPANY; PURCHASED LARGE QUANTITIES OF ALCOHOL, SELLING SAME THROUGH DUMMY FIRMS IN HIS CONTROL AND THEN ACTUALLY SELLING THE ALCOHOL TO BOOTLEGGERS; WITH PROFITS FROM THIS ILLEGAL ACTIVITY, BOUGHT IN 1927 THE ESTABLISHED FIRM OF MCKESSON & ROBBINS AND SUBSEQUENTLY USED THIS FIRM'S NAME TO HOAX DOZENS OF DRUG FIRMS INTO FORMING A MERGER; EMBEZZLED FROM HIS OWN FIRM $640,000 IN 1929 TO COVER WALL STREET LOSSES; FRAUDULENT CRUDE-DRUGS DIVISION OF MCKESSON & ROBBINS, EXCLUSIVELY UNDER HIS CONTROL, EXPOSED IN 1938 AS A HOAX; COMMITTED SUICIDE 12/16/38.

Of all the swindlers of America in the twentieth century, not one has yet surpassed the magnitude and complexity involved in the nightmarish schemes of Philip Musica. His own identity would disappear early in life and be replaced by the dignified "F. Donald Coster," drug tycoon, whose frantic manipulations of company funds would bene-fit his personal bank account by millions and whose desperate frauds would unintentionally create one of the most profitable corporations in the United States.

From his slum-tenement beginnings, Philip Musica was determined to "be somebody." Early in manhood Musica convinced his father, Antonio, to invest his small savings in a firm which would import Italian delicacies such as wines and cheese to the United States. The demand for such foodstuffs was heavy in New York's Little Italy, Philip argued, and Antonio Musica agreed.

In 1900 they hung out the shingle of A. Musica & Son and began importing. Philip devised a scheme by which he could defraud the government of customs duties on the sausages and other goods being shipped from Italy to his company. He simply bribed a dock official to substitute the real bills of lading for his goods, made out by the captain of a ship, with false invoices, listing the weight of the shipment as substantially less than what it really was.

When it came time to pick up the goods at a warehouse, Musica paid only a small portion of what was actually due. To many this scheme might appear petty, but when the firm of Musica & Son increased their orders, the unpaid duties reached staggering proportions. With their goods practically duty-free, the Musicas could and did outsell any competitor in Manhattan.

Within three years the firm was grossing almost a half million dollars annually, and the Musicas moved into a mansion in Brooklyn. They rode in ornate carriages, owned their own stable of horses, and socialized with the most prominent families in the area. Philip became a dandy and was often seen with celebrities like Enrico Caruso at Rector's or Delmonico's.

The bubble burst in 1909 when, in a rare check, customs officials investigated the Musicas' phony bills of lading and took to weighing the contents of each shipment. Philip graciously assumed all the blame for the fraud, although his father had also signed dozens of the false invoices. He was fined $5,000 and sent to Elmira Reformatory for a year. His father went free.

Musica's noble stance of assuming the full guilt for the swindle in court touched the heart of President William Howard Taft, who gave him a full pardon after he had served less than six months of his sentence.

The prison sentence had taught Musica only to be more careful in future frauds. His next swindle involved an elaborate scheme of selling human hair, popular with wealthy society matrons who used hairpieces to heighten their appearance. Through phony shipments backed up by equally false shipping invoices, Musica swindled more than $500,000 from several banks. He was caught and convicted and given a three-year prison sentence.

Musica next emerged in New York at the beginning of Prohibition, which proved to be a windfall for his fertile mind. Under the guise of making a hair tonic, Dandrofuge, Musica applied for a permit to buy raw alcohol. This was granted by the Alcohol Tax Unit of the Treasury Department.

Federal agents, who periodically checked on companies with such permits, were shown piles of order forms from bogus firms ordering Dandrofuge hair tonic. Of course, Musica kept a few bottles of the vile-smelling stuff in his offices, but beyond these samples, Dandrofuge existed only in the mind of its inventor. The great quantities of raw alcohol Musica and his partner, Joseph Brandino, ordered were quickly converted into bootleg liquor and sold to gangsters.

Though business was brisk, Musica grew to loathe Brandino and decided to dissolve the partnership by informing the Treasury Department that his partner had been misusing the permit.

The success of Dandrofuge convinced Musica that he had found a sure-fire swindle that, under different circumstances and with different partners, could make him millions. Musica next appeared in Mount Vernon, New York, in 1923. There he instituted another Dandrofuge factory under the name Girard & Co.

Musica, who had changed his name to F. Donald Coster, had created another anomalous firm in Girard & Co. Since his father, Antonio, had died, he stated to one and all that he, as president, operated the firm for the widowed Mrs. Girard, her husband, Horace, having died. Mrs. Girard was impersonated by Coster's mother, Maria. His sister Grace became Mr. Girard's daughter. Naturally, there never was a Horace Girard.

The Musica brothers were brought into the grand scheme, too. Arthur Musica assumed the name George Vernard, chief agent for another nonexistent firm, W. W. Smith & Co. George and Robert Musica changed their last name to Dietrich and became managers under Coster.

Their swindling system was simple and yet devilishly clever. Coster, as president of the Girard firm, required a federal permit to buy large amounts of raw alcohol to make Dandrofuge as well as crude drugs. When federal agents checked, they were handed dozens of orders for the drugs from W. W. Smith & Co., Coster's other bogus firm. The need seemed real, and the alcohol permit was granted.

What followed was a gigantic swindle in which Coster bought raw alcohol to manufacture crude drugs and then distilled it into cheap Scotch. The Scotch was shipped to W. W. Smith & Co., where Vernard (Arthur Musica) sold the booze to bootleggers for staggering amounts of cash—$8 million by the end of Prohibition, according to one estimate.

The shipments of crude drugs from Girard were accounted for by Vernard when he showed his distribution orders from other companies (also nonexistent) to the highly respected auditing firm of Price, Waterhouse & Co., which had been employed by Coster to audit his firm's books. Verification of W. W. Smith's solvency was provided by a forged report allegedly made by Dun & Company, the forerunner of Dun & Bradstreet, which stated W. W. Smith & Co. was worth $7 million.

Incredibly, no one bothered to call the Dun company in Chicago. The much-respected auditing firm did not take any inventory of Girard & Co., a practice not then common. In 1925 it blandly listed Coster's crooked firm as having sales of $1,100,000 and yearly profits of $250,000.

Coster, who had been buying 15,000 gallons of alcohol a month for his phony crude-drug manufacturing, got rich in the swindle. To avert suspicion of his apparent financial wizardry, he purchased the long-established firm of McKesson & Robbins for more than $1,000,000.

Using McKesson & Robbins as a legitimate front for his illegal bootlegging activities, Coster grew even richer, buying a twenty-eight-room mansion for his bride, Carole Jenkins Hubbard, a luxurious yacht, some racing

Dignified looking Philip Musica swindled millions under the alias F. Donald Coster, then took his own life. (UPI)

drugs division, his own domain, out of $640,-000. He covered himself by issuing thousands of bogus inventory invoices which listed millions of drug items through W. W. Smith & Co. As a weird result, when other firms collapsed or were thrown into receivership during the crash, McKesson & Robbins appeared well-stocked with sound assets and weathered the financial destruction on Wall Street.

Coster felt comfortable and safe until 1937, when the board of directors for McKesson & Robbins ordered him to convert $2 million of his crude drugs into cash as part of financial preparations to bolster the firm during another expected depression. In lieu of converting non-existent crude drugs into very real cash, Coster demanded the firm obtain a $3,000,000 loan "for improvements."

The company controller, Julien Thompson, grew suspicious. Why should a firm that appeared immensely successful be compelled to go outside of its own coffers for such monies? He began to investigate and discovered that W. W. Smith & Co. was a false front and that it's fifteen-year-old Dun report was a forgery. When Thompson confronted Coster with this information, as well as knowledge he possessed about Coster's nonexistent crude-drugs inventory, the shrewd swindler accused him of "trying to wreck this company."

Thompson informed officials of the New York Stock Exchange of his findings, and Coster's mammoth scheme was exposed in a matter of days. Though McKesson & Robbins, after a short suspension from the Exchange, eventually recovered to become one of the giants in the drug field, Coster was through.

He locked himself up in his mansion for a week and then, on December 16, 1938, went to his bathroom with a pistol in his hand. Musica-Coster always was a neat, meticulous man. His suicide was as thoroughly planned as his criminal career had been. Before he shot himself, he was careful to stand in such a way that when he fell backward into a large, marble bathtub, none of his blood stained the imported carpet on the floor.

horses, and the finest autos in America. As McKesson & Robbins grew, Coster and his brothers grew with it, selling preferred and common stock and merging with a group of enterprising wholesalers. As president of the firm—the third-largest drug firm in the world—Coster was still responsible to a board of directors.

In 1929 he was faced with a serious dilemma. He had speculated wildly on the bull market, and to cover his losses, he swindled the crude-

N

NEAL, TOM
Murderer ● (1913-1972)

Hollywood actor Tom Neal shown when he was "King of the B Films" in 1952, and, right, when released from prison in 1971.

Actor Tom Neal was called the "King of the B pictures," in his heyday, appearing in numerous low-budget films in the 1940s. Although a handsome, personable young man, Neal possessed a deep streak of jealousy when it came to his wives and sweethearts. His first wife, Vickly Lane, divorced him because of his obsessive jealousy.

Neal took up with blonde, buxom Barbara Payton who appeared in a few films then slipped into crime, later being arrested for intoxication, passing bad checks, and prostitution. Payton tried to manipulate Neal into marrying her by dating actor Franchot Tone. Neal cornered Tone and hammered him senseless with his fists, causing Tone to have a brain concussion from which he never fully recovered, resulting in a speech impediment and an inability to concentrate on his lines, which is apparent in Tone's later films.

Remarrying, Neal's second wife died of cancer in 1958. Three years later Neal met an attractive brunette, the receptionist at the Palm Springs Tennis Club, and married her a short time later. Neal established a successful gardening business and doted on his wife, Gail.

The old nagging doubts then began to gnaw on Neal. He began accusing his wife of flirting with other men, then accusing her of seeing other men and having secret affairs. His jealousy consumed him to the point where, on April 2, 1965, Neal fired a bullet into his wife's head as she lay on a couch.

Neal told Palm Springs police that his wife had pulled a gun on him and when he attempted to take the weapon away from her, it went off, killing her. He was nevertheless charged with Gail's murder and went to trial. After eight witnesses testified, Neal was found guilty of involuntary manslaughter and sent to prison at Chino, California, to serve one to fifteen years.

Paroled in December 1971, Neal attempted to make a comeback in show business, producing a morning TV show called *Apartment Hunters* but the show failed. Neal died in obscurity on August 7, 1972.

NELSON, EARLE LEONARD
Murderer ● (1897-1928)

BACKGROUND: BORN IN PHILADELPHIA, ORPHANED AT AN EARLY AGE, RAISED BY AN AUNT. HIGH-SCHOOL EDUCATION. MARRIED A SCHOOLTEACHER 8/12/19, SEPARATED SHORTLY THEREAFTER. DESCRIPTION: 5'6", BLUE EYES, BLOND HAIR, STOCKY BUILD. ALIASES:

ROGER WILSON. RECORD: ARRESTED AND CONVICTED OF RAPE, PHILADELPHIA, 1918, SENT TO THE STATE PRISON FARM FOR TWO YEARS; ESCAPED, 1918, RECAPTURED THE SAME YEAR; ESCAPED AGAIN IN LATE 1918 FROM THE STATE PENITENTIARY; MURDERED AND RAPED MRS. CLARA NEWMAN 2/20/26 IN SAN FRANCISCO; STRANGLED TO DEATH AND RAPED MRS. LAURA BEALE 3/2/26; KILLED AND RAPED MRS. LILLIAN ST. MARY 6/10/26; MURDERED AND RAPED MRS. GEORGE RUSSELL 6/26/26 IN SANTA BARBARA; STRANGLED AND RAPED MRS. MARY NESBIT 8/16/26 IN OAKLAND, CAL.; MURDERED AND RAPED MRS. BETA WITHERS 10/19/26 IN PORTLAND, ORE.; KILLED AND RAPED MRS. MABEL FLUKE 10/20/26 IN PORTLAND; STRANGLED AND RAPED MRS. VIRGINIA GRANT 10/26/26 IN PORTLAND; KILLED AND RAPED MRS. WILLIAM EDMONDS 11/10/26 IN SAN FRANCISCO; STRANGLED AND RAPED MRS. BLANCHE MYERS 11/15/26 IN PORTLAND; MURDERED AND RAPED MRS. JOHN BERARD 12/23/26 IN COUNCIL BLUFFS, IOWA; KILLED AND RAPED MRS. GERMANIA HARPIN AND HER EIGHT-MONTH-OLD CHILD 12/28/26 IN KANSAS CITY, MO.; MURDERED AND RAPED MARY MCCONNELL 4/27/27 IN PHILADELPHIA; MURDERED AND RAPED JENNIE RANDOLPH 5/1/27 IN BUFFALO, N.Y.; MURDERED AND RAPED TWO SISTERS, MINNIE MAY AND MRS. M. C. ATORTHY, 6/1/27 IN DETROIT, MICH.; KILLED AND RAPED MARY SIETSOME 6/3/27 IN CHICAGO, ILL.; MURDERED AND RAPED LOLA COWAN 6/8/27 IN WINNIPEG, MANITOBA; STRANGLED AND RAPED MRS. EMILY PATTERSON 6/9/27 IN WINNIPEG; ARRESTED IN KILLARNEY, MAN., IN JUNE, 1927; ESCAPED, RECAPTURED HOURS LATER; CONVICTED OF MURDERING MRS. EMILY PATTERSON 11/14/27 IN WINNIPEG; EXECUTED BY HANGING 1/12/28.

America has never seen anything like him before or since. There have been killers who were just as methodical and who carried out their brutal murders with just as much religious fervor—but none had the transcontinental intensity that overflowed from the poisonous wells inside Earle Leonard Nelson.

He was a killer apart, a killer's killer, a mass murderer who worked from coast to coast with a Bible in his hand.

Earle Nelson loved God. He said he did. His words oozed with sanctimonious tones, and his Bible was thumb-worn and ink-stained at his favorite passages.

Nelson carried his Bible everywhere, especially when trying to rent a room from a landlady. It was a disarming device which worked effectively—so effectively that it cost eighteen landladies their lives.

Earle Nelson was a common-looking little boy when his mother died. The orphan was taken in by a kindly aunt, Mrs. Lillian Fabian, whose religious beliefs bordered on fanaticism and who constantly chanted that "Earle will be a minister someday."

Mrs. Fabian encouraged her young charge to read his Bible and say grace at every meal. His whole appearance exuded purity, from his sensitive, slightly quivering mouth to his unblinking blue eyes.

If it hadn't been for a trolley car, Earle Leonard Nelson might have lived up to his aunt's pious expectations.

While playing catch with a playmate one day, Earle raced after a runaway ball and was snared by the cowcatcher of a passing trolley car. The trolley dragged him fifty feet, his head bouncing on the cobblestones, before the car could be braked.

Aunt Lillian and Earle's cousin Rachel stayed at his bedside for five days as little Earle fought death. He recovered slowly, battered and broken as he was. His bones mended, but the doctors continued to worry about the terrible blow to his skull.

Six weeks later, Mrs. Fabian reported that Earle was "all mended and all well. The accident hasn't changed him a bit."

But had Aunt Lillian had the psychic gift to see into Earle's mind, her blood would have run cold. For the little boy's brain had been grotesquely altered, distorted into some unrecognizable blob of horror.

At first, Earle lapsed into sullen moods of brooding silence. He would take his Bible to his room and read it, underscoring passages.

Then he began pulling his cousin's pigtails so viciously that the little girl screamed in pain. At such times, a twisted smile would dart across Earle's mouth.

His aunt scolded him for this, and Earle, playing upon the naive ignorance of his guardian, would drop to his knees and plead for forgiveness, groveling and sniveling. He would then run off to his room and babble over his Bible for hours.

Nothing Mrs. Fabian attempted altered the dark course Earle followed. She began to find him peeping at his cousin Rachel through a keyhole while the blossoming girl was undressing for bed.

Even as a child Earle's hands had been big, almost outsized, and extremely powerful. In celebration of his twenty-first birthday in 1918, Earle Nelson used those massive hands to drag a neighbor girl to her basement, where he tore away her dress and tried to rape her.

Her screams were heard by her father, who raced to the basement. It took two policemen to hold Nelson after he was arrested.

Authorities no longer agreed with Mrs. Fabian that Earle was merely an odd young man whose peculiar manners and attitudes were the result of a tragic accident. He was dangerous, a powerful bully and a threat to the safety of those around him.

The rape charge was upheld, and Nelson was convicted and sent to the state penal farm for two years. Within a week Nelson escaped, only to be recaptured immediately.

Six months later, he broke out again, and police tracked him to Mrs. Fabian's home. They found him standing in the rain, leering at his cousin Rachel as he watched her undress for bed through a bedroom window.

The penal farm couldn't hold Nelson, so he was transferred to the state penitentiary. But the penitentiary couldn't hold him either. He escaped on December 4, 1918.

After that, Earle Leonard Nelson disappeared and didn't resurface for nine years. Police files later revealed that Nelson married a young schoolteacher on August 12, 1919, using the alias Roger Wilson.

The young couple's marital life was anything but blissful. Nelson constantly raged at his wife over the smallest if imagined slights. He accused her of flirting with every male on the street, from salesmen to streetcar conductors.

Like a preaching prophet of old, he screamed in full public view that his wife was a woman of sinful ways, a whore.

The girl finally had a nervous breakdown. But she found no peace in the hospital. Nelson visited her there and, with vulgar expressions pouring from his mouth, tore the sheets from her bed and threw himself on her.

Doctors and nurses ran to Mrs. Nelson's room after hearing her screams. Nelson raved at the doctor for interrupting his carnal pleasures. Then he accused the doctor of having intercourse with his wife. Indignant, Earle left the hospital. His wife, luckily for her, did not see him again for seven years.

The next six years in the life of Earle Nelson remain a blank, a curtain of obscurity that has never been lifted.

Nelson stepped from this maw on February 20, 1926, appearing on the doorstep of a boarding house in San Francisco.

The landlady, Mrs. Clara Newman, watched the young man in rather drab clothes approach her front door.

"Are you Mrs. Clara Newman?" the young man asked. Mrs. Newman looked him over, noticing that he was neat, clean, and of medium build and had piercing blue eyes.

"Are you the lady who has advertised a room for rent?"

"I have three rooms vacant at the moment," Mrs. Newman said.

Something red-hot entered Earle Nelson's mind and caused a glow in his eyes as he watched the attractive Mrs. Newman lead him up the stairs to the room. He ravaged her body with his eyes—the neatly turned ankle, the swaying buttocks beneath her dress.

On the third floor, Mrs. Newman suddenly felt the young man's arm around her throat. He yanked the struggling woman to him and grabbed the pearl necklace around her neck, twisting it into her soft flesh until she hung limp and dead from his arm.

As the pain in his head reached a white-hot pitch, Nelson gave himself up to necrophilia and ravaged the dead woman again and again.

The murdered woman's nephew, Richard Newman, found her and rattled off his story to the police later that evening.

Richard had passed both Nelson and his Aunt Clara on the stairs as the landlady took her prospective boarder to his room. His description was limited because he had only glanced at Nelson: a man standing five-foot-six with dark complexion and blue eyes. That was all.

But the San Francisco officers knew something more about Nelson. He was a maniacal sex pervert with a taste for murder. From the looks of Mrs. Newman's ravished body, he had enjoyed himself and would want more of the same.

Nelson moved South and on March 2, 1926, struck again. Mrs. Laura Beale, strangled and raped, was found dead and naked in one of the rooms of her boarding house. Again, witnesses described a short, dark-complexioned man with strange blue eyes.

On June 10 Mrs. Lillian St. Mary was found ravished and stuffed beneath a bed in her rooming house. Sixteen days later, Nelson's insatiable appetite for sexual fulfillment through death was appeased with the murder of a

Mrs. Beta Withers (shown with her son) of Portland, strangled by Nelson.

Mrs. Mabel Fluke of Portland, strangled by Nelson.

Mrs. Blanche Meyers of Portland, strangled by Nelson.

Santa Barbara landlady, Mrs. George Russell.

On August 16 Nelson raped and strangled an Oakland landlady, Mrs. Mary Nesbit. Then, for several months, he held back. Police thought that his sexual perversion had subsided.

But it had taken Nelson time to work his way up to Portland, Oregon, where he attacked Mrs. Beta Withers on October 19. The following day Nelson killed Mrs. Mabel Fluke. Both victims were boarding-house landladies and both were strangled and ravished after being murdered.

Police intensified their search, but that didn't stop Nelson from killing and then raping Mrs. Virginia Grant, also a Portland landlady.

Nelson's ninth victim was in San Francisco, Mrs. William Edmonds. He then raced back to Portland and murdered and raped Mrs. Blanche Myers.

Ten victims and still no clues. The state of California was panicking, and the heat was so intense that Nelson decided to leave the West Coast. He ambled across the Plains States, and before the year was out, he murdered and violated two more landladies, Mrs. John Berard of Council Bluffs, Iowa, on December 23, and Mrs. Germania Harpin of Kansas City, Missouri, on December 28.

With this last stop, Nelson added one more gruesome and perverted act to his ghoulish list: he strangled and ravished Mrs. Harpin's eight-month-old daughter.

Nelson's bloody trail can be charted by the bodies he left from coast to coast. He struck in the East on April 27, 1927, in Philadelphia, where he strangled Mary McConnell.

The berserk killer moved to Buffalo, New York, where he killed and raped Jennie Randolph. Then he swung back to Detroit and murdered Minnie May and Mrs. M. C. Atorthy on June 1.

While the entire nation was throwing dragnets out for the blue-eyed killer, Nelson moved to Chicago, where he murdered Mrs. Mary Sietsome on June 3. She was his last victim in the United States, and like all his other victims except the Harpin baby, she was a landlady.

Earle Nelson realized he could not forever elude the armies of police looking for him. He headed for Canada, and on June 8 he rented a third-story room from a Winnipeg landlady, Mrs. August Hill.

Mrs. Hill was impressed with her new and devout lodger. He even appeared at her doorstep carrying a Bible.

That night, sixteen-year-old Lola Cowan disappeared. Lola was widely known and loved in Winnipeg. The lovely girl sold artificial flowers made by her crippled sister to support their family.

On June 9, 1927, police began combing the city for the girl. The following evening, a Winnipeg man returned home to find his children at play.

"Where is your mother, children?" William Patterson asked.

The children broke into sobs when they informed him that she had been gone all day. In a quick check of the neighborhood, Patterson could find out nothing.

A devoutly religious man, Patterson went to his bedroom and knelt at his bed in prayer for his wife's safe return. After finishing, he glanced down and saw his wife's hand protruding from beneath the bed. He peered under and gasped in shock.

Emily Patterson lay naked beneath the bed, dead. She had been strangled and then raped after death.

George Smith, Winnipeg's chief of detectives, told his men: "I think that we must operate on the assumption that the madman who has been killing all those landladies in the States has crossed over into Canada. Mrs. Patterson had been strangled by a man with extremely powerful hands and then, after death, she had been sexually molested. It is the same pattern."

Someone pointed out that Mrs. Patterson was not a landlady, and Smith countered that the killer had changed his *modus operandi*. He not only had killed and ravished the Patterson woman but this time had done something he had not done before—he had stolen things: a complete set of Mr. Patterson's clothes, $70 in currency, Mrs. Patterson's wedding ring, and a Bible.

He had also done another strange thing— he had left behind his old clothes.

"Then we do have some clues," a lieutenant put in.

"The clothes he left behind were probably stolen from a clothesline somewhere," Smith said.

Smith kept his men working around the clock for the next few days, and issued bulletins all over Canada that the sex fiend had struck in Manitoba and was probably trying to escape from Winnipeg.

On a routine check of boarding houses detectives interviewed a Mrs. Hill, who denied taking in any suspicious borders recently.

"You're certain that no new lodgers have come to your house lately?" one asked her.

"None since Mr. Wilson last Wednesday."

Mrs. Hill described Mr. Wilson as "rather on the short side, dark, with blue eyes."

The detectives immediately realized that this matched the killer's description and raced to Wilson's room.

There, a thick and sickening smell greeted them. Mrs. Hill apologized for the odor and opened a window.

"Good God, man" an officer cried out to his partner. "Look here!"

Under the bed, they discovered the body of a naked girl. Her body was mutilated almost to the point of obliteration. It was the flower girl, Lola Cowan.

Mrs. Hill's husband, August, comforted his hysterical wife and then turned to the officers, saying, "To think that that fiend lay sleeping in that room for three nights with that poor dead girl under his bed!"

The dragnet that went out for "Roger Wilson" was the most desperate and intense in Canadian history.

But Earle Leonard Nelson was now an expert at escape. He showed up in Regina, 200 miles west, the next day and rented a room. This time, he went after a fellow boarder, an attractive girl who worked at the telephone company.

Her screams, as he tore at her, brought an alert landlady, and Nelson fled, police on his trail within minutes.

In Winnipeg Smith got the report and told his men, "my hunch is that he's trying to get back to the States. Things are becoming much hotter in Canada than he had anticipated. If he's heading for the border, he'll have to cross prairie country. That should make him easy to spot."

Smith was right, and for the first time police began closing in on the most murderous strangler on the American continent.

Two constables, Grey and Sewell, on the alert for the strangler, were patrolling twelve miles north of the international border, outside the small farming community of Killarney.

There they saw a man walking leisurely down the roadway. He wore a plaid shirt and corduroy pants.

Pulling up alongside of him, the officers asked him who he was.

"My name is Wilson. I'm a stock hand and I work on a ranch near here."

"We're looking for a man who is responsible for the deaths of twenty women," Constable Grey blurted. He watched for some telltale sign from the stranger in the road.

A loud laugh greeted him as Nelson coolly said, "I only do my lady-killing on Saturday nights."

"I think you'd better ride back to Killarney

with us," Grey said, "so we can check on your story."

Nelson was nonchalant. "That's fair enough. I guess you fellows have to play it safe when there's a killer on the loose."

Constables Grey and Sewell locked Nelson in the small local jail. They handcuffed him to the bars of his cell and took away his shoes. Then they called Chief Smith in Winnipeg.

Sewell thought they had the wrong man and told Smith so as he and Grey stood in the telephone office. "He sure looks like he might be the killer but he says that his name is Roger Wilson and he works on a ranch near here. Besides that, he is just too calm to be guilty of anything."

Smith exploded. "That must be the strangler!" he shouted wildly at Sewell. "He used the name Roger Wilson here in Winnipeg and once before in San Francisco. It may be a coincidence but I am coming down there to question the man. Is Constable Grey with him now?"

"No, sir. He's here with me in the telephone office."

"What! Don't let that man out of your sight! I want one of you with him at all times! And don't be taken in by his calmness and innocent appearance. Remember, twenty women are

Earle Leonard Nelson (center), who made a habit of strangling landladies in the late 1920s.

now dead because they made the same mistake."

It was only fifteen minutes since the constables had locked up Nelson, but when they rushed back to the jail, he was gone. He had picked the locks from the handcuffs and the jail doors.

A 500-man posse was quickly formed, and all the women of Killarney were locked safely behind doors. Chief Smith sent detectives to the area by plane, and he led fifty men to the isolated village on the next train.

While the frantic search for Nelson went on, he was sleeping like a baby in William Allen's barn, only one block from the jail.

Nelson rose in the morning and calmly walked to the train station. He lounged in the waiting room until the morning express came into view.

With the air of a man confident of escape, Nelson walked slowly to the train. Just as he was about to board it, dozens of men rushed down the steps of the car, Chief Smith pointing out their target.

With his hands bent behind his back, the powerful little man was led away.

Nelson faced trial in Winnipeg for the murder of Mrs. Patterson. All through the damning testimony, the brutal killer displayed not the slightest bit of emotion. His blue eyes gazed in a stare at some inner vision and a smile played subtly about his lips.

His aunt and wife came to visit him in Winnipeg, but he only stared blankly at them, saying nothing.

A verdict of guilty was brought in on November 14, 1927, and he was condemned to death.

Earle Leonard Nelson mounted thirteen steps to the gallows on January 12, 1928. He stood on the gallows, and just before the hangman lowered the black hood over his sensitive face, he broke his strange silence.

His voice was high-pitched, the words tumbling and joining rapidly: "I am innocent. I stand innocent before God and man. I forgive those who have wronged me and ask forgiveness of those I have injured. God have mercy!"

The hood went down, the trap snapped open, and Earle Nelson swung into space.

NELSON, GEORGE ("BABY FACE")
Murderer, Bankrobber ● (1908-1934)

BACKGROUND: BORN IN CHICAGO AS LESTER GILLIS. MINOR PUBLIC EDUCATION. MARRIED HELEN WAWZY-NAK, 1928. DESCRIPTION: 5'4¾", BLUE EYES, LIGHT-BROWN HAIR, STOCKY BUILD. ALIASES: GEORGE NELSON, BABY FACE NELSON, ALEX GILLIS, LESTER GILES, "BIG GEORGE," "NELSON," "JIMMIE." RECORD: ROBBED A CHICAGO, ILL., JEWELRY STORE 1/15/31; ARRESTED DAYS LATER BY CHICAGO POLICE; TRIED, CONVICTED, AND SENTENCED TO ONE YEAR TO LIFE AT THE STATE PENITENTIARY IN JOLIET (INMATE 5437); ESCAPED 2/17/32; ROBBED WITH TOMMY CARROLL AND EDDIE GREEN SMALL-TOWN BANKS IN IOWA, NEBRASKA, AND WISCONSIN DURING 1933; SHOT AND KILLED ST. PAUL, MINN., RESIDENT, THEODORE KIDDER, MARCH, 1934; ROBBED TWO BANKS EARLY IN 1934 WITH JOHN DILLINGER; SHOT AND KILLED FBI AGENT W. CARTER BAUM NEAR LITTLE BOHEMIA LODGE, RHINELANDER, WIS., 4/23/34; SHOT AND KILLED FBI AGENTS HERMAN HOLLIS AND SAM COWLEY 11/27/34 NEAR FOX RIVER GROVE, ILL., AT WHICH TIME NELSON WAS ALSO KILLED.

Lester Gillis looked innocent from the day he was born in 1908 next to the reeking Chicago stockyards.

He grew up tough in the Chicago street gangs, but his height (5'4") was always a source of agitation to him. Snubbed, bullied, and beaten as a boy, Lester wanted recognition more than anything in the world. He got it—as the most bloodthirsty, death-seeking bandit of the Public Enemy Era.

His fame came to him under another name —Baby Face Nelson. As one criminal historian put it, he "was something out of a bad dream." Nightmare would be more apt. Where outlaws such as Pretty Boy Floyd and the Barkers would kill to protect themselves when cornered, Nelson went out of his way to murder —he loved it.

Lester strutted a lot, and his angelic, pear-smooth face never betrayed his instant ability to kill. He wanted to be known as "Big George Nelson," but the underworld called him "Baby Face"—though never, never to his face.

Baby Face learned how to make a fast buck the easy way. He graduated from petty thieving to sticking up brothels and bookie joints and then selling the same establishments protection against his own trespassing.

While working his heist and protection rack-ets in 1928, he met a petite girl named Helen Wawzynak. She was selling hardware in a Chicago Woolworth's store. He said she was his "Million Dollar Baby from the Five and Ten Cen Store."

By 1929 Nelson was working for the racket czar Al Capone. His specialty was labor relations. He could always be counted on to line up labor unions to kick back part of their union dues to gangsters.

Sometimes he got too ambitious and his usually severe beating of a balking labor leader turned into murder. It was all the same to Baby Face.

His strong-arm tactics were finally too much for syndicate operators, and he was dropped from the muster rolls of reliable gunmen in 1931. He went back to his old heist trade, but was apprehended that year for a jewelry store robbery.

Joliet prison couldn't hold Nelson, and he made his escape, running out of Illinois all the way to the West Coast. Once there, Baby Face went to work as a gunman for bootleg boss Joe Parente.

Nelson's right-hand man was John Paul Chase, who chauffered, ran errands, and cleaned up after him. Chase wasn't too bright, but Nelson thought he could count on him. He was loyal.

Nelson left California in 1932 and headed for an underworld gathering place, Long Beach, Indiana, to recruit a bankbusting mob. After Chase, his first member was top-notch machine gunner Tommy Carroll, a light-hearted character who had once been a promising boxer.

Eddie Green, known in the trade as a "jug-marker"—the man who picked and scouted a bank marked for robbery—also joined Nelson. These men were professionals. They had robbed banks all over the Midwest.

With these men, Nelson hit banks in Iowa, Nebraska, and Wisconsin during the fall and winter of 1933.

The take was good, but Nelson was outraged because the publicity mistakenly went to others. All of his jobs were attributed to the Dillinger gang or to Pretty Boy Floyd.

Baby Face felt credit should be given where credit was due. Although he admired the work of the levelheaded Dillinger, he also hated him because of Dillinger's publicity and the impressive rewards offered for his capture.

George "Baby Face" Nelson, berserk bankrobber who killed three FBI agents in 1934. (UPI)

Dillinger was too big to overshadow, Nelson figured, so he went to John's right-hand man, Homer Van Meter, and asked if Dillinger needed another gun.

"We don't know you, Nelson," Van Meter told him. "And we don't trust you."

The story was different the following February, when Van Meter and John Hamilton were the only Dillinger gangsters still at large. The "Super Gang" that Dillinger had led through several bank robberies had broken up.

Bank-busters Harry Pierpont, Charles Makley, and Russell Clark were all in custody in Ohio. Dillinger himself was languishing in the so-called escape-proof Crown Point Jail in Indiana.

This time, Van Meter and Hamilton went to Nelson. They were now interested in a merger. "Johnny's breaking out of that tin can soon," Van meter explained. "Do you have any big action for us?"

"Yeah," the bantam rooster replied. "Eddie Green has marked two jugs in Sioux Falls, South Dakota, and Mason City, Iowa. Big dough there." Nelson gave Van Meter and Hamilton the once over, squinted his eyes, and then said, "Can Dillinger take orders?"

"Why you little . . ."

"They're my men and my jobs," Nelson said, stopping Hamilton.

"Johnny will go along with it," Van Meter said diplomatically.

Little did John Dillinger realize what he was in for when he broke out of Crown Point in early March, 1934, and joined Nelson in St. Paul.

When the five men met in Nelson's hotel room, the runty gangster was obviously starstruck by Dillinger. He covered this up by delivering an insane diatribe on robbing banks.

His theory was basically to roar into a bank, shoot everybody in sight, and then roar out of town, guns blazing.

Van Meter laughed at him, and Nelson went for his machinegun. Only Dillinger's cool presence prevented the two of them from killing each other.

The following day Dillinger was in a car with Nelson as they traveled to Van Meter's room. Nelson, always a poor driver, hit another car in an intersection.

The other driver, Theodore Kidder, jumped from his auto and ran back to Nelson. "Are you blind?" he raged. "You had a stop sign . . ."

Baby Face's gun was already drawn. He sent a .45 slug into Kidder's head right between the eyes, killing him instantly. Then he backed up wildly and roared off.

"Did you have to do that?" Dillinger said.

"Hell, yes!" Baby Face yelled hysterically. "He recognized you."

"Well, a citizen got your number back there," Dillinger said. This threw Nelson into a frenzy of curses.

Baby Face's temperament didn't improve. On March 6, 1934, just three days after his Crown Point break, Dillinger, with Nelson, Hamilton, Van Meter, Green, and Carroll, hit the bank in Sioux Falls, South Dakota.

Though the take was slightly under $50,000, it was a disaster. Dillinger was astounded at the insanity Nelson displayed. No sooner were they in the bank than a teller nudged a security button which touched off a loud, clanging burglar alarm.

Nelson went berserk. While Dillinger, Van Meter, and Green emptied the cages, they could hear the banty outlaw scream over and over again, "I'm gonna kill the bastard who hit that alarm!"

Nelson's attention was distracted by an off-duty policeman who sauntered by a window. Baby Face hurled himself over a railing, jumped on a desk, and blasted four quick shots through a window. The cop fell dead.

"I got one of them! I got one of them!" Nelson yelled in glee.

It was a typical Dillinger getaway, with hostages crowded onto the running boards of his car and roofing nails strewn behind on the road.

The next bank, in Mason City, Iowa, was another setting for Nelson's lunatic tantrums. Here, after the outlaws had scooped up $52,-000, Baby Face wounded the bank's vice president and was only stopped from killing him by Dillinger.

After weeks of running in separate directions, Dillinger collected his gang at the Little Bohemia Resort in northern Wisconsin. On a tip, federal agents raided the place on April 22, 1934. Everybody ran for it but Nelson.

He traded shots with several FBI men and then, ignoring the escape plan, ran the wrong way to Koerner's Resort. Just as he was about to steal Koerner's car, a coupe containing two G-men and a constable roared into the lot.

Nelson leaped from Koerner's car and ran over to the coupe. He held two .45s in his hands. As the agents started to get out, he yelled: "I know you bastards wear bullet-proof vests so I'll give it to you high and low!" He emptied his guns into them, killing Special Agent H. Carter Baum.

He then hopped into the agents' car and drove off at high speed, first to hide out on an Indian reservation, then to find his way back to expensive hideouts in Chicago.

After the Biograph shooting in Chicago in which Dillinger was claimed to have been killed, Nelson went to California to cool off.

He was now Public Enemy Number One, but it made him crazy to think that the reward on his head was a lot less than that offered for Dillinger. He'd fix that, he told John Paul Chase. He would go back to the Midwest and really give the yokels something to remember.

Nelson planned to rob a bank a day for a month! But Tommy Carroll was dead, killed in a gunfight in Waterloo, Iowa. Eddie Green was also dead in St. Paul, Minnesota, at the hands of G-men. John Hamilton was dead, too, in an Illinois quarry, his body almost destroyed by acid to avoid identification. In August, 1934, Homer Van Meter was caught in a St. Paul blind alley and riddled with fifty bullets. Nelson was on his own.

With only John Paul Chase and his wife,

Baby Face returned to the Midwest in September, 1934. He skidded about, hotter than burning griddlecakes. The underworld wanted nothing to do with him. "Die," they told him.

Two FBI agents—Sam Cowley and Herman Hollis—spotted Nelson's car on November 27, 1934, along a lonely country road near Fox River Grove, Illinois. Then began a wild chase with bullets flying from both cars.

Just outside Barrington, Baby Face braked his car. Helen ran into a nearby field to hide. Nelson jumped out with his trusty machine gun. Chase had a BAR.

The FBI car halted, too, and one of the wildest gun battles in modern crime history ensued.

Hollis crouched behind the FBI car with a shotgun, and Cowley threw himself into a ditch, his machine gun ready. Then everyone opened up. Highway-construction workers nearby belly-flopped to the ground as the air was suddenly thick with bullets.

After several minutes, Nelson got disgusted. He swung his machine gun to his hip, stood up, and told Chase, "I'm going over there and get those bastards!"

When the construction workers looked up, their eyes almost popped as they watched Nelson walking casually toward the two G-men, his Thompson spitting death.

"It was just like Jimmy Cagney," one of the workers breathlessly recalled later. "I never seen nothin' like it. That fellow just came right a-comin' at them two lawmen and they must a hit 'im plenty, but nothin' was gonna stop that fellow."

As Nelson plodded forward, Cowley sprayed him several times with his own machinegun. But he did keep coming, like a man in a dream, walking and firing. He reached the ditch where Cowley was and fired directly down at him, almost cutting him in half.

Then he turned and went after Agent Hollis, who pumped several rounds from his shotgun into Nelson's legs. The little gangster walked on, firing short bursts. "Come on, you yellow-belly sonofabitch!" he screamed, delirious. "Come and get it."

Hollis threw down his empty shotgun and ran for the cover of a telephone pole, drawing his pistol.

He emptied his gun at Baby Face, who seemed to grin as he walked forward. One

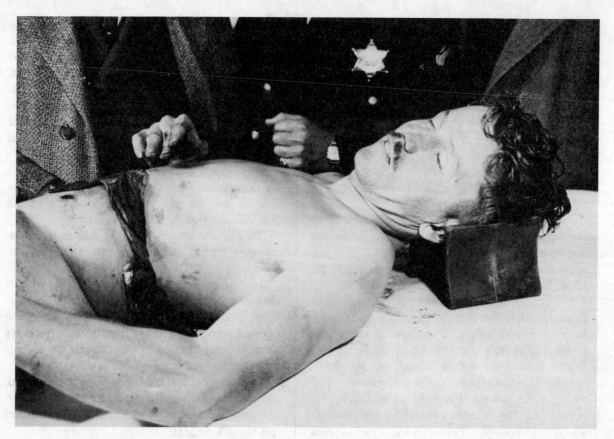

Nelson's naked and bullet-torn body was found on a deserted country road in Illinois, 11/27/34, where his wife and best friend had left him. (UPI)

long burst from his machine gun cut Hollis down like a cracked sapling.

Almost as calmly, Nelson went back to the G-men's car, staggering the last few steps. Chase and Helen joined him, and as they piled in, Nelson said, "You'll have to drive. I'm hit." There were seventeen slugs in him.

Baby Face's shredded body was found the next day in a ditch near Niles, Illinois. Chase had stripped him naked to avoid immediate identification. It didn't matter. John Paul Chase was taken a month later and so was Helen Gillis.

Chase died in a federal penitentiary. Helen Gillis, alias Mrs. George "Baby Face" Nelson, did a year in the Madison, Wisconsin, women's prison and then faded into oblivion.

But little Lester Gillis got his wish after all. Baby Face Nelson would be remembered for a long, long time.

[ALSO SEE John Dillinger.]

NEU, KENNETH
Murderer ● (1910-1935)

An unemployed young nightclub singer and dancer, Kenneth Neu was panhandling in New York's Times Square on September 2, 1933 when he was picked up by a middle-aged man, Lawrence Shead, who owned a number of theaters in Patterson, New Jersey.

Shead promised to hire Neu but, instead, inveigled him into a tryst. Once inside Shead's hotel room, Neu became enraged, or so he later claimed, hitting Shead over the head with an iron. He then strangled the man. He took a shower and put on Shead's finest suit before fleeing.

Using money he stole from Shead, Neu went to New Orleans where he looked for nightclub work. He met waitress Eunice Hotte, promising to take her to New York. "We'll have a big time in the big town." They needed money for the trip, however.

Neu hocked the watch he had also stolen from Shead and bought a blackjack. He used this to sap the head of businessman Sheffield Clark, Sr. Neu had earlier tried to blackmail Clark while the Tennessee businessman stayed at the Yung Hotel. Neu hit Clark too hard and killed him. He stole $300 and Clark's car.

With Eunice Hotte at his side, Neu began driving to New York but he was stopped by suspicious highway patrolmen in New Jersey who identified Clark's stolen car. Neu was taken to a police station where he smilingly admitted to killing Clark. He was asked if he had also killed Shead.

"Sure I killed him," replied Neu affably. "This is his suit I'm wearing now."

Extradicted to Louisiana, Neu stood trial for murdering Clark and was convicted. He was sentenced to die on the gallows but this seemed not to worry the would-be entertainer. As he was led from the courtroom, Neu burst into song, warbling "Sweet Rosie O'Grady."

Before his execution on February 1, 1935, the condemned man gave lengthy interviews with the press. On that day, Kenneth Neu was bright and happy. He had sought fame and now it had come to him. As he stepped from his cell, Neu broke into a tap dance, which he continued all the way up the gallows stairs.

On the scaffold platform, as his last request, Neu was allowed to sing a song of his own creation, one entitled, "I'm Fit As A Fiddle and Ready to Hang." After rendering three choruses of this ditty, song-and-dance-man Kenneth New was sent through the trap door.

Song-and-dance man Kenneth Neu performing for newsmen; he is wearing the suit of the man he murdered.

NEWTON'S GENERAL MASSACRE

This fight began in early August, 1871, on the eve of a referendum concerned with issuing $20,000 in county bonds to help build a long stretch of track for the Wichita and Southwestern Railroad, particularly that section which reached through Newton, Kansas.

Two lawmen were assigned to keep the peace on election day, August 11, 1871. One was a brawler known as Mike McCluskie (alias Art Delaney). The other was gunfighter and gambler William Wilson (alias Billy Bailey). Each man hated the other. McCluskie, some said, was jealous of Wilson's reputation as a gunslinger, belittling the fact that Wilson had gunned down three men in previous duels.

That night in the Red Front Saloon, the two men began to argue over who would buy the drinks and were shortly in the street shooting at each other. Wilson died of his wounds within hours, and McCluskie was warned to flee since the slain man had many friends in Newton. McCluskie departed, but returned on August 19, 1871, and immediately retired to Tuttle's Saloon to drink himself abusive.

Hugh Anderson, son of a wealthy cattleman and long-time friend of William Wilson, led a band of Texans into the bar at 2 a.m. the following morning, shouting vengeance. McCluskie went for his guns and killed John Martin. McCluskie was then hit by a blizzard of bullets and fell dead. His young friend, T. Riley, picked up McCluskie's guns and blazed away at the Texans, killing three of them.

Riley, it was said, was spared death because he was consumptive.

The twenty-minute slaughter took the lives of five men and was referred to as "Newton's General Massacre" by a local paper whose editor sadly concluded "It was worse than Tim Finnegan's wake."

NINETEENTH-STREET GANG

A juvenile mob led by an unholy terror named Little Mike, the Nineteenth-Street Gang operated as pickpockets and sneak thieves in the area about East Thirty-fourth Street and Second Avenue in New York City. At the time of the gang's existence in 1875, this teeming tenement section was known as Misery Row and Poverty Lane.

Little Mike preyed on storekeepers, cripples, and other children, stealing what he could from them. He was particularly fond of leading other Catholics in his gang in raids against Protestant missions and schools. The apprentice thug would throw rocks through the windows of these institutions and, while classes were going on, thrust his gnomelike head through the jagged opening and shout: "Go to hell, you old Protestants!"

Mike and his minions disappeared by the early 1880s, much to the relief of everybody in the neighborhood.

NIXON, ROBERT (THE BRICK MORON) Serial Killer ● (c.1920-1939)

For two years police in Chicago and Los Angeles were baffled by a killer who murdered in the same fashion in both cities. He killed his victims with a brick after looting their apartments, a modus operandi that earned the slayer the sobriquet of "The Brick Moron."

His first known murder victim was Florence Thompson Castle, 24, a cocktail waitress who was found dead in Chicago's Devonshire Hotel on June 29, 1936. The killer had entered Castle's room via a fire escape and had accosted her with a brick. He used his victim's lipstick to write on a bureau mirror: "Black Legion Game." He was seen by the victim's 7-year-old son who was hiding in a closet but the boy gave a hazy description of the killer.

The boy described the killer as a "white man painted black," but, in truth, the killer was a black man named Robert Nixon who had committed a number of juvenile offenses. Following his attack on Castle, Nixon rode the rails to Los Angeles, changing his name to Thomas Crosby. He survived by purse-snatching and shoplifting.

On March 2, 1937, Nixon invaded the Los Angeles home of Rose G. Valdez, 20. He ransacked the place and, when Valdez confronted him, he crushed her head, killing her with a brick. Only a few days later Mrs. Zoe Damrell, who lived in the same area, was attacked in her home but she survived. The assailant left a brick outside a window.

Police were called to an Olive Street home in Los Angeles on April 4, 1937. There they found 48-year-old Edna Worden and her 12-year-old daughter Marguerite. Both had been bludgeoned to death with a brick. Following this killing, Nixon bummed his way back to Chicago. There, on May 27, 1938, he attacked and killed Florence Johnson. Again, he used a brick to crush the woman's head.

Chicago police then received a fingerprint report from Los Angeles officials. Nixon had been arrested in Los Angeles for several minor offenses and had been fingerprinted. His prints matched those found in the Worden home. When news that The Brick Moron had struck again in Chicago, Los Angeles authorities sent the prints to that city.

Nixon was picked up and questioned. At first he

tried to pin the murders on a friend but he finally broke down and confessed to all the murders. He was convicted and condemned for the Johnson murder. After severn stays of execution, Nixon was sent to the electric chair on June 15, 1939.

NORTH, JOHN
Gambler ● (? -1835)

One of the most corrupt gamblers of the ante-bellum South, North ran a notorious saloon-brothel-gambling-house in Vicksburg, Mississippi. North's place was in the center of the criminal-infested Landing area, from which he proposed the taking and looting of Vicksburg. Hundreds of gamblers and thieves rallied to his plan, but the army of criminals was foiled by an alert vigilante group who invaded the Landing on July 6, 1835.

Dozens of gamblers were hanged, but North escaped. He was found the following day and hanged on the highest hill overlooking Vicksburg with practically the entire town looking on. He was not cut down for twenty-four hours. North's crooked roulette wheel was "tied up to his dangling body" as a warning against dishonest gamblers.

NORTHCOTT, GORDON STEWART
Serial Killer ● (? -1930)

Northcott owned a run-down ranch in Riverside County, California. His mother Sarah Northcott and his teenage nephew Stanford Clark lived with Northcott and helped him in his real business of abducting, torturing, and killing children. Some later claimed that Northcott provided these waifs to wealthy Los Angeles perverts to sexually abuse.

In February 1928, the headless body of a Mexican boy was found in Puente. Then two other Mexican boys were reported missing. Detectives learned that they were last seen at a boy's club with Northcott. When police arrived to interview Northcott at his ranch, they discovered that the owner had fled to Canada.

Stanford Clark admitted to police that he had helped the monster abduct boys, and that Northcott beat them to death, cut off their heads and buried them on the ranch. Sarah Northcott was confronted with this story and confessed that she not only aided her lethal son but had participated in one of the murders.

Northcott was found in Canada, extradicted to the U.S. and placed on trial. He was found guilty of three murders and was sentenced to death. His mother was sent to prison for life and Clark was released in exchange for his testimony against Northcott.

Housed at San Quentin, Northcott grew so ill that he thought he would die. He summoned Assistant Warden Clinton Duffy and confessed to seventeen more murders of young boys. Northcott, however, recovered and was fit enough to climb the gallows stairs to be hanged on October 2, 1930.

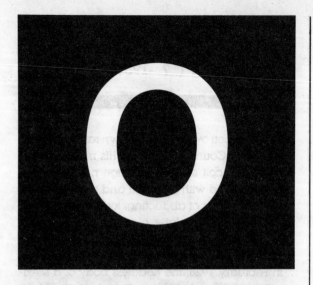

O'BANNION, CHARLES DION ("DEANIE")
Bootlegger ● (1892-1924)

BACKGROUND: BORN IN AURORA, ILL. MOVED WITH PARENTS TO CHICAGO, CIRCA 1899. MINOR PUBLIC EDUCATION. MARRIED VIOLA KANIFF, NO CHILDREN. ORIGINAL OCCUPATION, SINGING WAITER. DESCRIPTION: 5'8", BLUE EYES, LIGHT-BROWN HAIR, SLENDER, LEFT LEG SHORTER THAN RIGHT AS A RESULT OF A BOYHOOD ACCIDENT, WALKED WITH LIMP. ALIASES: UNKNOWN. RECORD: JOINED THE LITTLE HELLIONS, A JUVENILE DIVISION OF THE MARKET STREET GANG WHICH OPERATED ON CHICAGO'S NORTH SIDE IN 1902; BECAME A PICKPOCKET AND DRUNK-ROLLER IN EARLY TEENS; BECAME AN ENFORCER FOR WILLIAM RANDOLPH HEARST'S "HERALD-EXAMINER" IN 1909, BEATING UP NEWSSTAND OWNERS WHO REFUSED TO SELL THE PAPER; ARRESTED FOR ASSAULT, 1909, SERVED THREE MONTHS IN HOUSE OF CORRECTION; ARRESTED FOR ASSAULT, 1911, SERVED SIX MONTHS IN HOUSE OF CORRECTION; ARRESTED IN MARCH, 1921, FOR BURGLARY, STRICKEN OFF WITH LEAVE TO REINSTATE; ARRESTED, MAY, 1921, FOR BURGLARY, STRICKEN OFF WITH LEAVE TO REINSTATE; ARRESTED AGAIN IN MAY, 1921, FOR POSSESSING BURGLAR TOOLS, STRICKEN OFF WITH LEAVE TO REINSTATE; ARRESTED, JULY, 1922, FOR ROBBERY, POSTED BOND OF $10,000, CASE NOLLE PROSSED; ORGANIZED A GANG OF THE MOST FEARED MOBSTERS, NEXT TO CAPONE'S, IN CHICAGO, ABSOLUTELY CONTROLLING THE 42ND AND 43RD WARDS; GANG INCLUDED SUCH NOTORIOUS THIEVES, HIJACKERS, ROBBERS, SAFECRACKERS, AND KILLERS AS GEORGE "BUGS" MORAN, EARL "HYMIE" WEISS, VINCENT "THE SCHEMER" DRUCCI, SAMUEL J. "NAILS" MORTON, LOUIS "TWO-GUN" ALTERIE, MAXIE EISEN, PETE AND FRANK GUSENBERG; AT THE ADVENT OF PROHIBITION BEGAN BREWING BEER, DISTILLING WHISKEY, AND DISTRIBUTING SAME THROUGHOUT CHICAGO'S NORTH SIDE, OPERATING FROM A HEADQUARTERS AT 738 NORTH STATE STREET, A FLOWER SHOP; KILLED 11/10/24 IN HIS FLOWER SHOP BY AL CAPONE'S

GANGSTERS—REPORTEDLY ALBERT ANSELMI, JOHN SCALISE, AND NEW YORK MOBSTER FRANKIE YALE (UALE).

He was a disarming fellow, lovable almost. Chicago's newspaper reporters fawned over him, chronicling his zany antics and quoting his wisecracks and butchered *bons mots*. He was delightfully macabre copy, a walking fiction, the storybook gangster of the 1920s—Charles Dion "Deanie" O'Bannion. He was also, according to Chief of Police Morgan Collins, "Chicago's arch criminal who has killed or seen to the killing of at least twenty-five men."

From the beginning, O'Bannion strove heartily to be unique, despite his dirt-common background. Deanie's father was a hard-drinking Irish immigrant who became a plasterer in Aurora, Illinois. Thankfully, his mother never saw her son rise to the top of his profession, dying when O'Bannion was five. Upon moving to Chicago, Deanie's playground was the street, and his youthful games consisted of pick-pocketing and rolling drunks as a member of the Little Hellions Gang, a division of the Market Streeters.

At the same time, O'Bannion sang in the choir of Holy Name Cathedral—he possessed a fine, lilting Irish tenor voice. Each Sunday he served as an altar boy for Father O'Brien, who thought Deanie's religious zealousness might lead to the priesthood. Although a practicing Catholic, O'Bannion kept his religion in its place, reserving a few hours for God on Sunday mornings throughout his brief life and devoting his remaining hours to robbery and murder.

Graduating to the Market Street adult gang, O'Bannion shunned jackrolling for burglary—"a man's profession." His legitimate front was that of an enforcer for William Randolph Hearst's *Herald Examiner*. His job was to convince various newsstand proprietors to carry the Hearst paper instead of McCormick's *Tribune*. Those who resisted his commercial cooing were beaten senseless by Deanie's hamhock fists.

It was during this period of his life that O'Bannion befriended the knight-errant newspaperman Charles MacArthur, who would pole-vault to fame as the coauthor of such plays as *The Front Page* and *Twentieth Cen-*

tury and a host of film scenarios written with the prolific Ben Hecht. Later, when Deanie became a sort of underworld cause célèbre, he would pick up MacArthur at whatever saloon or poolroom the writer happened to be in, and the two of them would race O'Bannion's flivver down the sidewalks of posh Michigan Avenue as the dawn broke. It was all great fun, but not to MacArthur's editor, the indomitable Walter Howey. On one occasion, when O'Bannion stood like a ghostly Charon framed in the steamy light of a saloon door beckoning to his friend MacArthur, Howey shouted at his protégé: "You're not going with that murderous son-of-a-bitch! You're going home and go to bed."

Almost obediently, MacArthur put down his pool cue, yawned, and said to his editor: "Deanie's my sandman. He'll take me home." He then strolled away with O'Bannion for some early morning high jinks.

In Deanie's newspaper-slugging days, he was arrested only twice for assaulting news dealers. He was thrown into jail for short terms, each time being released in the shadow of the powerful Hearst lawyers. One story has it that O'Bannion stole a mail truck thinking it was a Tribune lorry and, upon discovering that it contained sacks full of negotiable bonds, went into the crime business in a big way.

During his early twenties Deanie became a singing waiter at the McGovern brothers' café and saloon on North Clark Street, hobbling between the tables on his bad left leg (his left leg was noticeably several inches shorter than his right one as a result of falling from a trolley car as a boy) and singing "Where the River Shannon Flows" while balancing a hefty tray of foaming beer steins. McGoverns' was the worst sort of dive. Every other customer was a crook working on a future score.

It was here that Deanie met and befriended such notorious safecrackers and hijackers as George "Bugs" Moran, Earl "Hymie" Weiss, Vincent "The Schemer" Drucci, and Samuel J. "Nails" Morton.

With this crew of fearless Fagins, O'Bannion put together one of the most devastating gangs in Chicago, centering his activities on the northeast side of the 42nd and 43rd wards. O'Bannion's power in these wards, commonly referred to as the Gold Coast—its eastern fringe was lined with the most exclusive homes and apartment dwellings in the city—was

overwhelming by the late 1910s.

His political control of this area was best summed up in an old refrain: "Who'll carry the Forty-Second and Forty-Third?" The answer was always: "O'Bannion in his pistol pockets."

During election time Deanie's boys swarmed through polling places, stuffing ballot boxes, herding floaters and repeaters through the lines, and bribing officials to dump votes for the opposition. If none of these methods achieved O'Bannion's ends, he resorted to employing strong-arm squads who bashed in the heads of stubborn election judges and counters.

Seldom did the O'Bannion gang flash any of their heavy equipment, although Deanie alone carried three pistols on his person at all times. He was ambidextrous and could reach to the left armpit of his suit jacket, the left-outside coat pocket, or his right-front pants pocket for a pistol.

When Prohibition came into being, O'Bannion purchased several of the best distilleries and breweries on the North Side. Where Capone and Torrio on the South Side were compelled to either import beer or whiskey into Chicago at high prices or rely on the rotgut produced by the Genna stills to supply their outlets, O'Bannion had the finest booze and beer available. "The real McCoy," he called it.

Throughout the city, society people and owners of the better restaurants bought from O'Bannion. The quality of his bootlegging wares was superior to anyone else's, and it was thought that he was more trustworthy than Capone, who avidly insisted that his customers also patronize his brothels and floating gambling operations. O'Bannion once signed an agreement to keep his interests north of "The Dividing Line"—Madison Street—but continued to service his special customers south of the line.

At first this encroachment upon Torrio-Capone territory was tolerated. Next, Capone argued that if O'Bannion was to continue running booze into his area, he should, at least, agree to the establishment of Torrio-Capone whorehouses in the Gold Coast. "I ain't no pimp!" O'Bannion snorted to Capone one night in the latter's headquarters, the Four Deuces, at 2222 South State Street. "Besides," he added sincerely, "running prostitutes is against the Holy Mother, the Church!"

Interestingly enough, not one professional brothel was operated in the opulent Northeast section of Chicago during the tenure of the O'Bannion-Weiss-Moran gang. O'Bannion's religious compunctions, however, did not apply to hijacking Capone's trucks, wholesale robberies, gambling casinos, and the killing of anyone who got in his way.

Wide-open bootlegging practiced by O'Bannion did not alter his attitude about liquor. He hated alcohol and beer. He did love flowers, so much so that he purchased a half-interest in the Schofield Flower Shop operated by William Schofield at 738 North State Street, directly across from Holy Name Cathedral, which Deanie continued to visit each morning, stuffing the poor box with fistfuls of dollars culled from his criminal sorties.

"My money goes to those who need it," he once remarked. To prove his point and to ease his sin-struck conscience, O'Bannion filled his large touring car each week with foodstuffs and clothing and drove into the shabby parts of his district to distribute these to the needy. "Deanie's always good for a touch," his devoted bodyguard "Two-Gun" Louis Alterie once said. "The old guys, people who don't have no jobs, the crippled kids, these are the ones Deanie doles his dough to. He's a swell guy, ain't he?"

There was even a story describing how O'Bannion once sent a crippled child to the Mayo Clinic for extensive operations and, learning that the boy was beyond help, provided a trust fund for him for life. O'Bannion once shot a citizen by mistake and paid for the hospital bills.

The shooting became part of Chicago folklore. O'Bannion stopped Edward Dean Sullivan of the *Examiner* one day and asked: "Where can a guy buy a boxful of the best cigars around here?"

"Who's sick?" Sullivan inquired.

Deanie gave Sullivan his saddest face. "This morning I'm going across the Madison Street bridge and I got plenty on my mind. Somebody's been tailing me lately. An automobile crossed the bridge and backfired. I didn't know what it was. I popped at the only guy I saw. I got to send some smokes over to him." O'Bannion had shot Arthur Vadis in the leg when Vadis was on his way to work.

Such indiscriminate shooting on O'Bannion's part was commonplace. A nightclubber who sipped soda, Deanie donned his tuxedo almost every evening, and with his top hat tilted on his head, led his boys into bistros and theaters to enjoy themselves. Moran, Weiss, and Alterie all aped their boss, their tuxedos snug at their hips and bulging from the weight of pistols near their hearts.

One evening, while watching a play at the LaSalle Theater, O'Bannion happened to spot Davy "Yiddles" Miller, a prizefight referee and ex-boxer who had publicly insulted an O'Bannionite, one Yankee Schwartz, weeks before.

O'Bannion excused himself from his party just before the play ended and walked to the lobby. There, as Miller emerged, Deanie calmly withdrew one of his pistols and shot the referee in the stomach. Miller's younger brother Max rushed forward and O'Bannion shot him, too. The second shot, however, did no damage other than paralyzing Max Miller with fright after it bounced harmlessly off his belt buckle.

Then the "Cock-of-the-Walk," as the newspapers called O'Bannion, turned with a grin on his face and strolled from the theater unmolested. He was never arrested, but he did send a nice floral piece to Davy Miller, who was recovering in a nearby hospital.

Next to tending his flowers, O'Bannion's love for safecracking never ceased. He had been a box man most of his adult life and derived great pleasure in splitting cribs, particularly with George "Bugs" Moran (who had been captured several times and convicted of safecracking, taking the fall for O'Bannion, who always managed to escape) and Earl "Hymie" Weiss.

In early 1922 O'Bannion and Weiss were interrupted by police detective John Ryan just at the moment they were about to blow open a Postal Telegraph safe. On the way to the station O'Bannion smilingly explained that "You got it all wrong, Paddy. Me and Hymie were waiting for the manager. You see, Paddy me boy, we heard about what good pay these telegraphers get and wanted to hire on."

"You mean to tell me that you were in that office in the middle of the night to apply for jobs?"

"Ah, that's it, Paddy boy. That's the very thing, you see."

Ryan turned to another detective in the squad car and clucked his tongue. "I've never heard of anything so disgusting in all my days."

The attempted-robbery charge came to nothing, which was usual in O'Bannion's case. Alderman Titus A. Haffa of the 43rd Ward rushed to O'Bannion's side and put up $10,000 bond so that he and Weiss could swagger free out the police-station doors. With an additional $30,000 in well-placed bribes, O'Bannion had indictment No. 28982 on the Chicago Police Department's blotter nol-prossed in court.

Haffa's gesture was not surprising. Politicians throughout Chicago catered to O'Bannion. His power in delivering his borough into Republican hands at each election was so omnipotent that no political favor was too large to grant him. "I deliver my wards as per requirements," O'Bannion once boasted, and the service brought him and his criminal activities unlimited immunity.

A prime example of the way Chicago politicians coddled the Irish gangster was a party given in his honor at the swanky Webster Hotel during the embattled election year of 1924. The guests filing into the dining hall would have caused the eyes of any law-abiding citizen in Chicago to pop.

On one side of a long, long table sat O'Bannion, Weiss, Moran, and Alterie; Cornelius P. Con Shea, murderer and labor racketeer; burglar and gunman Frank Gusenberg; Maxie Eisen, union thug and manager of O'Bannion's Cragin distillery; gambler Jerry O'Connor (not to be confused with the Chicago gunman of the O'Donnell clan of the same name); and William Scott Stewart, Alterie's lawyer and former assistant state's attorney.

The other side of the table was occupied by County Clerk Robert Schweitzer, Chief of Detectives Michael Hughes, Police Lieutenant Charles Egan, and Colonel Albert A. Sprague, the Democratic nominee for U.S. Senator and Commissioner of Public Works. Lesser party hacks trailed to the end of the exquisitely set table.

Sprague spoke briefly and then sat down to enjoy himself. The best Scotch, wines, and beers began to flow. Everyone commented favorably on the decorous red-white-and-blue bunting adorning the walls and chandeliers.

O'Connor, who was vice president of the Theater and Building Janitors' Union, received a $2,500 stickpin from his federation. O'Bannion was given a $1,500 platinum watch "for services rendered." The end of the festivities

was highlighted by Louis Alterie's gun act.

The gangster took note of a waiter passing the hat among the guests for tips, which was the usual custom at the Webster. Alterie jumped up with both pistols in his hands. "Hey you!" he shouted at the startled waiter. "None of that racket stuff goes here!"

Jaws dropped and mouths opened in disbelief. Alterie glanced about him at the distinguished company and asked: "Shall I kill him?"

O'Bannion sat back in his chair in peals of laughter and finally blurted: "Naw, let 'em suffer, Louis lad."

When the "Belshazzar feast," as the clergy dubbed the meeting, was made known, reform mayor Dever exploded and called Hughes before him to explain. The chief of detectives mumbled that he thought the dinner was to be for Jerry O'Connor. He didn't know O'Bannion and his mob would be there, he claimed. "When I recognized a number of notorious characters I had thrown into the detective bureau basement a half dozen times I knew I had been framed, and withdrew almost at once."

Such hand-in-hand fraternization between gangsters and politicians blithely continued in Chicago all the same. O'Bannion flagrantly used the police to cover up one of the most sensational thefts in Chicago history. In 1924 he engineered the robbery of the Sibley warehouse, carting off 1,750 cases of bonded whiskey worth $1 million. The startling aspect of this theft was that a grand jury indicted police lieutenant Michael Grady and four of his sergeants from the detective bureau for providing a protective convoy of police cars which accompanied O'Bannion's truck drivers to their various distribution points. (The charges were subsequently dismissed, and Grady was made a captain.)

Chief Collins was not on O'Bannion's payroll and attempted to foil the bootlegger at every turn, even placing a wiretap on the Irish mobster's flower-shop phone. One evening the tap recorded a call to O'Bannion by one of his truckers who had been stopped on the West Side by two enterprising policemen. "That load of beer we're bringing in, Deanie," he said. "Well, there's two bulls here who want three hundred bucks to release it."

"Three hundred dollars!" O'Bannion screamed. "To them bums? Why, I can have them

Bootlegger Dion "Deanie" O'Bannion was considered "Chicago's arch killer" of the 1920s; he attended church regularly.

knocked off for half that much!"

While squads of police sent out by Collins to arrest the rogue cops and, perhaps, save their lives, were searching frantically through West Side streets, the trucker again called O'Bannion, stating: "Hey, Dion, I just been talkin' to Johnny and he says to let the cops have the three hundred. He says he don't want no trouble."

O'Bannion grunted a reluctant approval and hung up. The "Johnny" referred to in the phone conversation was none other than Johnny Torrio. Only months before, O'Bannion had joined forces with Torrio and Capone in a triumvirate that controlled the entire bootlegging operation in Cicero. His association with the "spaghetti-benders," as he called them, agitated his independent nature. He was also partners with Capone and Torrio in a gambling casino called The Ship, and bitterly complained each week when the three owners met to divide the earnings that certain Sicilian gangsters were allowed to lose heavily without redeeming their markers.

O'Bannion was referring, of course, to Angelo Genna of the murderous Genna brothers, a Capone-Torrio ally and a notoriously poor gambler. When O'Bannion learned that Genna had lost $30,000 at The Ship's roulette table, he called "Bloody Angelo" and told him: "You got one week to pay up, spaghetti-bender!"

Hatred for Italian and Sicilian gangsters ran deep in O'Bannion. At every opportunity, he attempted to ridicule and undermine Capone and Torrio. In May, 1924, Deanie went to the gangster captains of the South Side and offered to sell the lucrative Sieben's brewery to them for $500,000, explaining that he was going to quit the rackets and settle down in his flower shop.

Torrio paid O'Bannion in cash and on May 19, 1924, drove to the brewery to take charge. He was not inside the place for more than twenty minutes before dozens of policemen swarmed through the brewery, arresting Torrio for violating the Prohibition Act.

O'Bannion roared with laughter. He had learned that the police planned to close down his operation and dumped the property on Torrio and Capone for a handsome profit. Between guffaws, O'Bannion told Weiss: "I guess I rubbed that pimp's nose in the mud all right."

Weiss, a cunning gangster with above-average intelligence, pleaded with his boss to "take it easy with them guys."

"Aw, Hymie," O'Bannion snickered. "When you gonna learn, lad? Those people are gutter rats, dumb bastards all of 'em, Torrio, Capone, them Gennas . . . To hell with them Sicilians!"

Capone and the Gennas raged against such insults from O'Bannion, and they told Torrio Deanie would have to be killed. Torrio tried to soothe Scarface and then warned, "It means war, Al." He reminded Capone that Mike Merlo, the founder and president of the all-powerful *Unione Siciliane*—an ethnic federation that controlled Sicilian gangster operations which Capone sought for years to dominate—was a close friend of O'Bannion's. Capone thought better of his intent and waited. When Merlo died in November, 1924, Capone felt his way was clear to kill the Irish gang leader.

On November 10, 1924, James Genna and Carmen Vacco, a city sealer, entered O'Bannion's flower shop and ordered a large wreath for Merlo's funeral. They gave Deanie $750 for the floral arrangement. "We'll send some boys to pick it up later," Genna told him.

Five minutes later the phone rang, and an unknown caller wanted to know if O'Bannion had the flowers ready. "At noon," O'Bannion told them. A few minutes after twelve a blue Jewett touring car pulled up in front of the shop.

Negro porter William Crutchfield, who was at that moment sweeping petals into the back room, glanced up to see three men get out of the car and walk into the shop while another stayed at the wheel.

O'Bannion, dressed in a long white smock and holding a pair of florist's shears in his left hand, lurched forward in his curious rolling limp, his left hand outstretched in greeting.

"Hello, boys," Deanie said. "You from Mike Merlo's?" The three men, walking abreast, approached O'Bannion with smiles. The man in the center was tall, clean-shaven, and wearing an expensive overcoat and fedora; the other two were dark-complexioned, short, and stocky.

"Yes . . . for Merlo's flowers," Crutchfield heard the tall man say before he stepped into the back room. The tall man grabbed O'Bannion's hand in greeting. The two men at his sides moved around Deanie and drew pistols. Then, at close range while the tall man held O'Bannion in a viselike grip, bullets ripped into the Irish gangster—two in the right breast, one through the larynx, another next to that one, another in the right cheek, and a final *coup de grace* shot through the left cheek. So close were the shots fired that powder burns were later found at the opening of each wound.

The three men fled to the car, which drove away slowly once they were inside. O'Bannion crashed, dead on his feet, into a row of geraniums, his three pistols still tucked away unfired in his specially made pockets. The first victim of the handshake-murder method sprawled among his flowers, an incongruous sight for a man known as Chicago's "arch criminal."

Years later O'Bannion's executioners were determined to be Frankie Yale (the man in the center) and John Scalise and Albert Anselmi, the sinister Genna killers loaned to Capone for the occasion. James Genna had placed the order for Merlo's floral piece; it was only logical that when O'Bannion saw the two Genna men enter his shop, he would think they were there to pick up the order.

At least that's what Detective Captain William Shoemaker ("Old Shoes") thought. Although he didn't name Scalise and Anselmi as the murderers, he did state: "O'Bannion, above all things, knew he was marked for death. He knew it might come at any moment. Ordinarily, when talking to strangers, he stood

with feet apart, the right hand on the hip, thumb to rear and fingers down in front. The left was usually in his coat pocket. In this position he was ready for instant action with the automatics in the specially tailored pockets.

"But we have him advancing to meet these fellows without hesitation—his right hand extended. He felt safe. He knew them—at least by sight—and did not suspect them."

The Genna brothers, Capone, and Torrio were all arrested on suspicion of homicide, but were soon released after supplying concrete alibis. Frankie Yale, a good Capone friend from New York, was arrested at La Salle Station as he was about to depart for points east only hours after the shooting. He, too, was ultimately released.

At an elaborate funeral ceremony O'Bannion's minions filed past his body, tough gangsters weeping as they went past his bier in Sbarbaro's Funeral Home. He was placed inside a $10,000 bronze casket fitted with bronze-and-silver double walls. A heavy plate-glass window allowed visitors to peer down at Deanie's patched-up face. "They did a good job on Deanie," Louis Alterie said. "He looked great."

O'Bannion reposed on white satin cushions with a purple cushion beneath his mounted left hand, his shooting hand. One reporter wrote: "Silver angels stood at the head and feet with their heads bowed in the light of ten candles that burned in solid golden candlesticks they held in their hands. Beneath the casket, on the marble slab that supports its glory, is the inscription: 'Suffer little children to come unto me.'"

Deanie's funeral was the most lavish in gangland history, a gaudy show topped with twenty-six truckloads of flowers, his favorite blossoms, worth $50,000, leading the hearse's way to Mount Carmel cemetery. One small wreath among the deluge was labeled "From Al."

The scene at the cemetery was more bizarre than the everyday confrontations occurring between the North and South side gangster factions. On one side of the grave, lowering the body to its rest, were Earl "Hymie" Weiss, George "Bugs" Moran, and Vincent "The Schemer" Drucci; on the other, Al Capone, Johnny Torrio, and Angelo Genna. The O'Bannionites glared at the Italian gangsters, but made no move toward their guns. That would come within days.

Torrio had been right. By killing O'Bannion, Capone had started a war that would claim the lives of at least five hundred gangsters (which the police would appreciate). Following the ceremony, Torrio, Capone, and Genna raced off in their cars. Within six months Torrio would nearly be killed in an ambush by Weiss, Moran, and Drucci; Angelo Genna would be shot to pieces; and Al Capone would slip behind a barricade of gunsels, where he would remain in terror for four years before ordering the slaughter of the entire North Side gang on St. Valentine's Day in 1929.

"If I had known what I was stepping into in Chicago," Capone was later to lament, "I would never have left the Five Points outfit [in New York]."

Fifteen thousand people attended O'Bannion's funeral. "It was one of the most nauseating things I've ever seen happen in Chicago," remarked reform judge John H. Lyle. Though Cardinal George Mundelein refused to allow O'Bannion to be buried in consecrated ground or any last rites administered to his corpse, Father Malloy of Holy Name Cathedral knelt next to O'Bannion's casket as it was being lowered into the unblessed earth by his gangster friends and enemies and said three Hail Marys and the Lord's Prayer. The priest remembered O'Bannion only as the smiling, blue-eyed choirboy in his church, not as the gangster.

Above it all, Viola O'Bannion, the gangster's pretty widow, wailed, "Why, why, oh tell me why?" Why would anyone want to kill her peace-loving husband, a gentle man who enriched people's lives with his beautiful flowers?

To her, he was a quiet businessman whose North Pine Grove Avenue apartment possessed a $15,000 player piano, a symbol of his love for music. "Dean loved his home and spent most of his evenings in it," Viola O'Bannion told the world. "He loved to sit in his slippers, fooling with the radio, singing a song, listening to the player-piano. He never drank. He was not a man to run around nights with women. I was his only sweetheart. We went out often to dinner or the theater, usually with friends. He never left home without telling me where he was going and kissing me goodbye."

[ALSO SEE Louis "Two-Gun" Alterie, Al Capone, Vincent "The Schemer" Drucci, Genna Brothers, George "Bugs" Moran, John Torrio, Earl "Hymie" Weiss, Frank Yale.]

OBERST, OWEN
Mass Murderer ● (1911-   )

A farm boy who lived near Florence, Kansas, Oberst was seventeen when he slew his entire family of seven, all because he was denied the use of the family car. On April 21, 1928, authorities were called to the Oberst farm, which had been gutted by a roaring fire.

Sifting through the embers, police found the charred remains of seven people: Oberst's mother and father, and five younger children. Oberst told detectives that he had been at a Florence movie house when the fire took place and returned home to find his family dead.

Police were suspicious, however, after they found a .22-caliber automatic pistol in the kitchen stove. The weapon had been recently fired. The coroner quickly reported that the Oberst family members had all been shot. Then came a report that the elder Oberst had recently won considerable money in a poker game.

For a while police thought the farmer and his family had been killed by gamblers wanting their money back. When Owen Oberst showed up at the funeral for his family, however, the local sheriff noticed he was wearing an expensive new suit.

Oberst was again questioned. This time he broke down and admitted that he had killed his parents, brothers, and sisters. His father had refused to let him use the family car, he said, and that made him angry. He was sent to prison for life.

O'CONNOR, THOMAS
("TERRIBLE TOMMY")
Murderer, Robber ● (1886- ?)

BACKGROUND: BORN AND RAISED IN IRELAND, IMMIGRATED TO THE U.S., CIRCA 1900. MINOR PUBLIC EDUCATION. ONE SISTER, MARY; BROTHER, DAVID. ORIGINAL OCCUPATION, TAXI DRIVER. DESCRIPTION: 5'9", BROWN EYES, BROWN HAIR, SLENDER. ALIASES: UNKNOWN. RECORD: ARRESTED IN CHICAGO A NUMBER OF TIMES ON MINOR CHARGES FROM 1907-20, INCLUDING BURGLARY, ROBBERY, AND SUSPICION OF MURDER; ARRESTED FOR ROBBING THE ILLINOIS CENTRAL DOWNTOWN STATION, JUNE, 1921, IN WHICH

NIGHT WATCHMAN DENNIS TIERNEY WAS KILLED;
SHOT AND KILLED MEMBER OF POLICE SQUAD, SER-
GEANT PATRICK J. O'NEILL, WHO ATTEMPTED TO AR-
REST HIM AT HIS SISTER MARY'S HOME, 6515 SOUTH
WASHTENAW, DAYS AFTER THE I.C. RAID; TRIED AND
FOUND GUILTY OF MURDER IN THE FIRST DEGREE
10/15/21; SENTENCED TO DIE ON THE GALLOWS
12/15/21; ESCAPED ONLY DAYS BEFORE HE WAS DUE
TO HANG AND COMPLETELY DISAPPEARED; A COURT
ORDER IS STILL IN EFFECT IN CHICAGO CHARGING
AUTHORITIES TO KEEP THE ORIGINAL WOODEN GAL-
LOWS (THEY ARE PRESENTLY STORED IN COOK COUNTY
JAIL) UNTIL O'CONNOR IS APPREHENDED AND HANGED
FROM THEM; O'CONNOR WAS THE LAST MAN TO BE
SENTENCED TO DEATH BY HANGING IN ILLINOIS.

Chicago's "Terrible Tommy" O'Connor in 1921, only days
before he successfully escaped from the Cook County Jail
under a sentence to hang for murder; the gallows have
been preserved to this day should O'Connor ever be found.
(UPI)

Tommy O'Connor broke out of jail almost on the very eve of his execution, while Cook County Sheriff Peters tested the rope that would hang him, grappling it with gnarled hands and dangling his full weight from the noose as the trap sprung open.

"Okay, close it. That will hold the weight of a bull." Sheriff Peters was confident. This was one sentence Terrible Tommy would not escape.

Upstairs, on the fourth floor of the jail, separated from the old Criminal Courts Building on Hubbard and Dearborn by a scant yard encompassed by a twenty-foot wall, O'Connor mingled with prisoners in a bullpen. It was Sunday morning, 11 a.m. December 11, 1921.

"They'll never hang me," O'Connor had said. But, according to twelve good men and true on October 15, 1921, O'Connor was convicted of shooting and killing detective sergeant Patrick J. O'Neill in a gun battle outside his sister's home at 6515 South Washtenaw. Officers had come for Tommy to answer for the Illinois Central holdup earlier that year in which watchman Dennis Tierney was killed.

The charges of the I. C. murder were dropped, but O'Connor was going to answer for the death of O'Neill. The jury recommended death.

Judge Kickham Scanlan thundered down from the bench that Terrible Tommy would meet his legal fate on December 15: ". . . On that day, between the hours of sunrise and sunset, you, the said Thomas O'Connor, be, by the Sheriff of Cook County, according to law within the walls of said jail, or on the grounds

or enclosure adjoining the same, hanged by the neck until you are dead!"

O'Connor paced the bullpen, getting a squint of the outside through the windows, a bleary sky and silent streets this Sunday. It was 11:10 a.m. Seventy-five prisoners moved aimlessly in the bullpen. A guard entered the room. They were getting ready to feed the prisoners.

O'Connor was in the guard's path. His large eyes loomed wide. It was only a few days before he would stand on the waiting gallows downstairs.

He leaped forward. The guard crumbled to the floor, and in the desperate scramble Terrible Tommy rose with his gun. Two more guards rushed into the bullpen. "Move aside, I'm comin' out," O'Connor said. The guards stepped aside and all three were bound by the prisoners.

Terrible Tommy dashed forward down the hall to the freight elevator. Frank Kordecki, an assistant guard, blinked as he stood by the elevator. He thought of stopping O'Connor and two of the prisoners, Edward Darrow and James LaPorte, but there was the big pistol in Tommy's hand. "Stand there or I'll blow you to hell!" O'Connor said. Kordecki stood there and was bound up and thrown onto the elevator floor.

The elevator squealed and chugged downward.

O'Connor was impatient. "C'mon, c'mon, hurry." He kept smashing the basement button.

As the elevator door opened on the basement floor, guard Thomas Wette was about to enter. He stared into the muzzle of O'Connor's gun. He too, was tied and placed in the elevator. Capriciously, a grinning O'Connor sent both bound guards back up to the fourth floor, pushing the button and leaping out between the closing elevator doors.

Using the keys he had taken from Wette, O'Connor unlocked the basement door leading to the jail yard. Beyond the courtyard was a twenty-foot wall. On the other side was sleepy Illinois Street.

How he got over that wall is still not known, and probably never will be, but O'Connor did get over, dropping to the pavement with three other prisoners. The fourth prisoner weighed 233 pounds, and his ankles broke when he hit the sidewalk. That's where frantic police found him twenty minutes later.

Darrow and LaPorte ran down Illinois and turned up Clark Street, running into oblivion.

John Jensen, forty-two, a city electrician, was just starting his car, parked on Illinois next to the ominous wall. Terrible Tommy jumped on the running board, waving the big pistol. "Drive like hell!" he roared. Jensen fumbled with his keys. The car wouldn't start.

Disgusted, O'Connor ran across the street and hopped on the running board of Harry R. Busch's car. Busch, who lived at 509 North Clark, had just come around the corner to make sure his car would start in the cold weather. It did.

O'Connor poked his lean face into Busch's. And there was the gun. "I'm Tommy O'Connor and I've just escaped from the county jail! Drive like hell!" Busch stepped on the gas and drove like hell. Busch said later that Terrible Tommy O'Connor cried huge tears. The car spun around onto Dearborn, sped up to Chicago Avenue, turning there with squealing tires onto North Sedgwick, where O'Connor jumped off as the car raced on.

It was approaching noon, and Paul Sorci of 942 Sedgwick decided to take the family flivver out of the garage and fill up the gas tank. As the car backed out of his driveway, a lean, mustachioed man, hands hard around a gun butt so that his knuckles showed white, jumped

into his car. "Drive it like hell!" he yelled. O'Connor's intent, as well as his vocabulary, was constant.

Sorci jammed the accelerator almost through the floorboard, and the machine screamed up Sedgwick.

"Faster!"

"It's going as fast as it can!"

"Then make it go faster! There's hell behind me."

Sorci's car, whining at top speed, ate up the space of Sedgwick, arched onto West Oak Street, and again turned like a whirlwind onto Townsend. At Larrabee, speed took control of the machine and hurled it into a house.

Steam gushed from the smashed auto, its crumpled front end buried into wood. Both men had been knocked from their seats. As the hapless Sorci rose from the sidewalk, he watched O'Connor race across Larrabee, still holding the gun, his thin legs pumping hard, the long jaw set, a maniacal grin on the narrow lips.

Another car with two women and a man inside slowed down at the corner, and O'Connor jumped onto the running board. Sorci stared unbelievingly as the car sped up. He watched it go all the way up Larrabee, until the man on the running board was a gesturing blur.

No one, it has been said, ever saw Terrible Tommy O'Connor again.

One Chicagoan envisioned the escape thusly: "No plans, no place in particular to head for. That was the best way. Like he'd figured it out and it turned out perfect. Grab the first auto and ride like hell and keep on changing autos and riding around and around in the streets and crawling deeper into the city until the trail was all twisted and buried. . . ."

Though all these trails spun off into nowhere, the hunt for O'Connor went on, spurred by the rampant curiosity of the press, the hot rage of the police, and, for the lowest form of life in the underworld, the informer, a $1,000 reward, dead or alive.

The news of O'Connor's escape brought joy to some.

His sister, Mrs. Mary Foley, clasped her hands and gave high gratitude: "We know nothing about it but we are certainly delighted. We knew that the power of Almighty God would save Tommy, and show the police and all the people who were against him that he was innocent."

Tommy's father piped to a news-bringing reporter, "We're going to have a merry Christmas."

Back at the jail, languishing in his cell and awaiting trial for a minor offense, sat Tommy's brother, "Darling Dave" O'Connor. The day after Tommy had crept into the unknown, "Darling Dave," as the press called him, sneered at his inquisitors.

"I don't have to say anything about Tommy. I stand on my constitutional rights." The guards and the reporters started to leave. The O'Connor brother aimed a glinty eye on one of the guards. "Well," he said, "one O'Connor got away from you. I suppose you think you ought to have some O'Connor around here. Well, you've got me." And he laughed.

Chicago's Chief Fitzmorris didn't get the joke. He was table-thumping angry. "It's all bunk about O'Connor escaping," he said to reporters. "He was turned loose as definitely as though he had been escorted out the front door."

"Can you capture him this time?" a reporter asked the frothy captain.

Fitzmorris, devoted to his office and duty, was first silent and then, out of character, gave an answer still wondered at today. "No. I think that we have seen the last of him."

Through the years, O'Connor's presence has been reported in New York, Los Angeles, and Ireland. One story had it that he returned to the Old Sod and fought and was killed in the Black and Tan wars there in 1922, possibly being killed in the Beal-na-Blath ambush that claimed the life of the Irish patriot Michael Collins.

OCUISH, HANNAH
Murderer ● (1774-1786)

A Pequot Indian girl, Hannah was abandoned at an early age and turned to delinquency in nearby New London, Connecticut. In late 1786 she was arrested for murdering Eunice Bolles, a six-year-old child who, according to reports, angered Hannah by accusing her of stealing her strawberries.

The stern New England court quickly condemned her to death following her murder confession (which she made only after she was confronted with the body of the dead Bolles girl). The half-witted girl hardly responded to the court's sentence. On the scaffold the day she was hanged, December 20, 1786, a contemporary account indifferently stated that "she said very little and appeared greatly afraid, and seemed to want somebody to help her."

O'DONNELL BROTHERS
(CHICAGO, SOUTH SIDE)

W hen arguments fail, use a blackjack!" This was the motto of Edward "Spike" O'Donnell, and the advice he gave to his gun-toting brothers—Steve, Walter, and Tommy—when selling their bootleg beer. The brothers, and a small but devoted group of strong-arm men, centered their bootleg operations in southwest Chicago, in a traditional Irish neighborhood known as Kerry Patch.

They were squeezed between the Torrio-Capone area and the back-of-the-yards southwest section claimed by the dreaded Saltis-McErlane gang. While the oldest brother Spike was in Joliet penitentiary doing a long stretch for complicity in the $12,000 robbery of the Stockyards Trust and Savings Bank, peace reigned between Capone and the O'Donnells. Then, in the summer of 1923, Spike was released from Joliet.

The O'Donnell clout was heavy. Spike's release had been petitioned by no less than six state senators, five state representatives, and a judge of the Cook County Criminal Court. Governor Len Small was only too happy to sign the parole papers for his old friend O'Donnell.

O'Donnell's return to Kerry Patch marked a brief but bloody gang war between Capone and the South Side Irish gang under Spike's leadership. O'Donnell bolstered his bootleg crew with such gunmen as George "Spot" Bucher, George Meeghan, and Jerry O'Connor, who had been doing a life term in Joliet until he, too, was paroled. A New York marksman

"I can lick this bird Capone," Edward "Spike" O'Donnell said in 1923, but he and his brothers were run out of the Chicago rackets within two years. (UPI)

named Henry C. Hasmiller was imported to provide additional gunfire.

At the time of the O'Donnell uprising and encroachment into foreign bootlegging territories in Chicago, the Capone-Torrio organization was closely allied with Polack Joe Saltis and his gun-happy sidekick, Frankie McErlane. After a brief meeting, Scarface convinced Saltis to handle the O'Donnells. "If they get to be too much for you," he said, "we'll come in, too."

The O'Donnells weren't too much for Frankie McErlane. He eagerly waited for an opportunity to put the O'Donnells in their place. His chance came on September 7, 1923.

On that day, Steve, Walter, and Tommy O'Donnell, accompanied by Meeghan, Bucher, and O'Connor, strolled into a saloon operated by ex-pug Jacob Geis at 2154 West 51st Street. Meeghan and Bucher, acting as drummers for O'Donnell beer, had tried to convince Geis to take the Irishmen's brew instead of Capone's. Geis was adamant. He was staying with Capone. Next, Spike sent in his six-man contingent.

Steve O'Donnell approached Geis and his apelike bartender, Nick Gorysko. "We're giving you one more chance," the O'Donnell brother stated. "What say?"

Geis snarled, "Nothin' doin'!"

Six pairs of hands reached across the bar for the two men, and in the presence of a half-

dozen witnesses, Geis and Gorysko were beaten senseless and left unconscious on the floor. Geis' skull was fractured, and he barely survived the beating after lying in Deaconess Hospital for two weeks.

The Irish gang moved off to four more bars that night, slugging owners and bartenders as they went. After knocking Frank Kveton through a plate-glass window when he, too, proved reluctant to switch from Capone beer to O'Donnell brew, the clan withdrew to one of their strongholds, a bar operated by Joseph Klepka at 5358 South Lincoln Street.

Spike was waiting for his bravos in Klepka's with sandwiches and beer, O'Donnell beer naturally. No sooner had the gang entered than Cook County Deputy Sheriff Danny McFall followed them into Klepka's and shouted to them: "Stick up your hands or I'll blow you to hell!" As a way of emphasizing his point, McFall, with two pistols in his hands, sent a bullet whining past Spike O'Donnell's derby.

"Scram!" Spike yelled to his minions, and they dove out the back and side doors. Waiting at the side entrance for whomever might attempt that escape route was a short, stocky man holding a sawed-off shotgun. He was Frankie McErlane. Within seconds, Jerry O'Connor ran right into him and McErlane shot him in the heart.

The O'Donnells dwindled fast after that. On September 17, 1923, beer drummers Bucher and Meeghan stopped their touring car for traffic at Garfield Boulevard. A green auto drew alongside and a stocky man holding a shotgun —Frankie McErlane—blew off their heads. Another killer wielding a pistol, Polack Joe Saltis according to one report, fired several more bullets into Meeghan and Bucher. Police found the dead men minutes later, cigarettes still burning in their hands.

Mayor William E. Dever was incensed over the killings and issued a statement reading: "Until the murderers of Jerry O'Connor and the murderers of these two men have been apprehended and punished and the illegal traffic for control of which they battle has been suppressed, the dignity of the law and the average man's respect for it is imperiled, and every officer of the law and every enforcing agency should lay aside other duties and join in the common cause. . . . The police will follow this case to a finish as they do all others. This guerrilla war between hijackers, rum runners and illicit beer peddlers can and will be crushed. . . ."

Dever's noble intent was but a grunt in a hurricane. Though Daniel McFall was indicted for O'Connor's death, he was speedily acquitted in January, 1924. McErlane wasn't even picked up for questioning.

Spike's hearties continued to fall. In the next few months, Spike O'Donnell was shot at by the McErlane troop at least ten times. Once, his brother Tommy was wounded as he and Spike were driving to church on Sunday. Spike, who readily gave out colorful interviews to the press, commented: "I've been shot and missed so often I've a notion to hire out as a professional target. Life with me is just one bullet after another."

In December, McErlane caught up with Morris Keane, stopping his beer truck and shotgunning him to death. Another O'Donnell driver, William "Shorty" Egan, was also stopped by McErlane and wounded several times. Frankie also got Philip Corrigan, shooting him on the wing as his beer truck sailed past. Dead at the wheel, Corrigan and the truck crashed into an all-night diner, luckily injuring no one.

McErlane was busy throughout 1924 tracking down the O'Donnells. He found Walter O'Donnell and hotshot gunner Henry Hasmiller in a roadhouse in Evergreen Park. Barging through the crowded tables, he walked up to the two men as they were eating and emptied his shotgun into them.

When Spike heard of the double murder, he roared to a sob sister on one of the newspapers: "I can whip this bird Capone with my bare fists any time he wants to step out in the open and fight like a man!" But the days of bare-knuckle battles were long ended, and Spike's enthusiastic but thinning platoon of bootleggers was soon destroyed.

Spike O'Donnell lingered inside Chicago's gang wars for another year, until McErlane took to using a machinegun, the first ever employed by the underworld, on September 25, 1925, when he sprayed a storefront where O'Donnell was standing. Spike, wounded and shaken, decided to quit the rackets and soon settled for more mundane enterprises.

[ALSO SEE Al Capone, Saltis-McErlane Gang.]

O'DONNELL BROTHERS (CHICAGO, WEST SIDE)

The West Side O'Donnells were no less fierce, but perhaps a bit more tactful, than the O'Donnells of the South Side (no relation) in controlling their bootleg barony during the 1920s—a vast area between Madison Street and Grand Avenue that stretched as far west as Cicero. The three brothers—William "Klondike," Bernard, and Myles—were anything but standup gunfighters; rather, they would needlessly and recklessly potshoot at members of the Torrio-Capone forces to make their point.

Their all-Irish gang was small, and they preferred to negotiate their future with Scarface rather than slug it out. When Capone and Torrio took over the suburb of Cicero in the early 1920s to evade pressure from Chicago's new reform mayor Dever, the O'Donnells were placated with promises of sharing the spoils. They would be allowed to retain their own "milk runs"—speakeasies serviced with O'Donnell beer and booze—but all other saloons and casinos would come under Scarface's domination.

Klondike O'Donnell even agreed to provide some muscle for Capone if any of the old-line saloonkeepers refused to take his needle beer. One such was Eddie Tancl, a broken-nosed ex-prizefighter. Myles O'Donnell, Thomas Duffy, and James J. Doherty paid Tancl a call on Klondike O'Donnell's orders and tried to convince him to go along with Capone.

"I buy my beer from the guys I want to buy my beer from," Tancl truculently told them. "That Capone guy makes bad stuff, I don't serve no needle beer in my joint."

"You don't get it, Eddie," Myles O'Donnell reasoned. "If you don't take Al's beer, you don't take no beer at all."

"And you leave Cicero besides," Doherty said.

"Yeah, you leave Cicero in maybe not a healthy state," Myles added.

Tancl gripped the bar and shouted: "Try and put me out! I was in Cicero long before youse guys came!"

Days later, Myles and Doherty were back, entering Tancl's saloon at about 8 a.m. after

Chicago's gang wars took its toll of nerves as well as lives, here, the once fearless Myles O'Donnell goes into a screaming faint after hearing the popping of news cameras; he thought they were pistols. (UPI)

an all-night drinking bout. Both were half-drunk and knocked over several chairs before sitting down and ordering breakfast from waiter Martin Simet.

Tancl and his burly bartender Leo Klimas stood at the bar, alerted for an O'Donnell outburst. It came a half hour later when Myles O'Donnell tore up the check Simet brought him. "You overcharged us, you bastard!" He hit Simet in the face. Tancl rushed forward. "Wait a minute, Myles—"

O'Donnell and Doherty drew their guns. So did Tancl. Four shots went into Eddie Tancl, but before he crashed to the floor of his saloon, he had sent three bullets into Myles O'Donnell and two into Doherty.

O'Donnell, who sagged against the bar, lurched out of the saloon and, to the surprise of the Sunday-morning churchgoers walking by, staggered down the street, his blood splotching the sidewalk. Tancl, with four chest wounds, raised himself from the floor of his bar with superhuman strength and ran wobbly-legged after O'Donnell. He tackled the gangster halfway down the block. Both men lay gasping when bartender Klimas dashed up. "Leo," Tancl choked, "kill the rat! He got me!" Klimas jumped on O'Donnell's back and began to club him with the gangster's own gun. At that moment, the wounded Doherty struggled past the two and, almost as an afterthought, fired a bullet into Klimas' head, killing him. O'Donnell and Doherty then half-crawled to their car and drove away. Both

survived, but Eddie Tancl and his loyal bartender Klimas were quite dead. Neither O'Donnell nor Doherty was arrested for the murders, although there were several eyewitnesses to the shootings.

By the spring of 1926 the O'Donnells were no longer in the good graces of Capone. They had sided with George "Bugs" Moran in his war with Scarface, and Jim Doherty had helped Moran's pal Vincent "The Schemer" Drucci shoot down a Genna-Capone ally, Samuzzo "Samoots" Amatuna, in a Chicago barbershop on November 13, 1925. In addition to several other killings of Capone gunsels by the O'Donnells, Klondike O'Donnell, tired of taking orders from Capone, began to distribute his own beer and booze to Cicero saloons then under Scarface's control.

There was hatred for Capone's strong-arm tactics and bad booze in Cicero. One saloonkeeper, Harry Madigan, stated to the police: "When I wanted to start a saloon in Cicero more than a year ago, Capone wouldn't let me. I finally obtained strong political pressure and was able to open. Then Capone came to me and said I would have to buy his beer, so I did.

"A few months ago Doherty and Myles O'Donnell came to me and told me they could sell me better beer than Capone beer, which was then needled. They did and it only cost $50 a barrel, where Capone charged me $60.

Cicero saloon owner Eddie Tancl stood up to gangster Myles O'Donnell in a toe-to-toe gun battle and lost. (UPI)

I changed and, upon my recommendation, so did several other Cicero saloonkeepers."

Madigan's political connections might have been explained by the presence of assistant state's attorney William H. McSwiggin, who was sitting in a car parked outside his bar on the night of April 27, 1926. Also inside the car, which had just parked, were Myles O'Donnell, Thomas Duffy, James J. Doherty, and Doherty's chauffeur, Edward Hanley. Ironically, McSwiggin had prosecuted Doherty earlier on a murder charge which was dropped.

As Doherty, Duffy, and McSwiggin stepped from the car, another auto, first traveling at top speed and then slowing to a crawl when it came abreast of Madigan's saloon, began to spit lead. A fat, balding machine gunner, shouting obscenities as he fired, leaned from a window.

McSwiggin, Doherty, and Duffy hit the cement, riddled with bullets. Hanley and Myles O'Donnell ducked and were uninjured. Duffy though bleeding from several wounds, crawled down the block and propped himself against a tree, mumbling and fidgeting with a piece of paper which listed sixty bars that carried O'Donnell beer. He died halfway through his odd inventory.

Myles O'Donnell and Hanley dragged McSwiggin and Doherty back into their car and drove off at high speed, thinking the two men could be saved. They died of their wounds in the car, and their bodies were thrown into a ditch in the suburb of Berwyn. The car was abandoned in Oak Park.

Capone, who was identified as the machine gunner, had apparently decided to handle the O'Donnell uprising personally, which he was wont to do in matters he deemed important. Witnesses who spotted him during the shooting, however, predictably vanished, though several newspapers claimed "a secret warrant was issued for Al Capone charging him with murder." Scarface was never indicted.

When reached for comment, affable Al smilingly complained that "they made me the goat. McSwiggin was a friend of mine. Doherty and Duffy were my friends. Why, I used to lend Doherty money. Just a few days before the shooting, my brother Ralph, Doherty, and Myles and Klondike O'Donnell were at a party together."

The O'Donnells ceased to exist as an organized gang following the triple killing, and

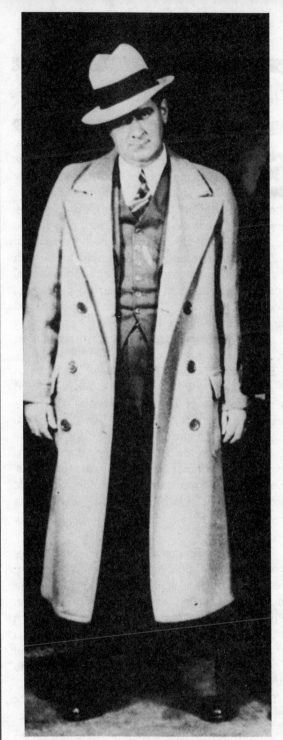

William "Klondike" O'Donnell. (UPI)

Capone dominated Cicero and points south and west completely. For years, however, the cry of "Who killed McSwiggin?" became part of the police idiom in Chicago. Of course, everybody knew.

[ALSO SEE Al Capone, Vincent "The Schemer" Drucci.]

O.K. CORRAL, GUNFIGHT AT THE

By the time Wyatt Earp and his brothers assumed the duty of upholding the law in Tombstone, Arizona, in 1881—the site of the wild shoot-out at the O. K. Corral—the lawman was the most legendary peacemaker in the West. He had appeared in a dozen wild cow towns since 1873, taming them with his fists, his guns, and his considerable verbal persuasion. For most, Earp had no peers; not even the feared Wild Bill Hickok approached the magnitude of his exploits. To some, he was a mean, bushwhacking murderer who gloried in his gunslinger reputation.

Earp was first heard of in Ellsworth, Kansas, in the summer of 1873, when he backed down a motley crew of Texas gunmen (so the story goes) led by quick-tempered Ben Thompson. Earp assumed the duties of sheriff for one day to clean up the town. The following year Earp was made marshal in Wichita and soon dismantled such gun-worthies as the Clements brothers, Abel Head, "Shanghai" Pierce, the rowdy cattle baron, and brutish George Peshaur.

Then came Dodge City, which could justly claim the first Boot Hill in the West. Earp became Dodge's chief deputy at $2.50 per month and earned every penny of it, along with his three aides, Bat and Jim Masterson and Joe Mason. Earp moved to the goldfields around Deadwood, South Dakota, in 1876, but the area was panned out. He returned to Dodge and pinned his star on once again.

Outlaw barons placed a $1,000 reward for anyone who would put Earp in Boot Hill in 1876. Gunman George R. Hoyt tried to collect one night by furiously riding up to the Comique Theater where Earp was lounging after watching comedian Eddie Foy. Hoyt banged six bullets into the railing where Earp sat. The lawman coolly withdrew his pistol and, taking careful aim, shot Hoyt from his skittish horse. The would-be assassin died a month later of lead poisoning.

Earp left Dodge in 1879 and, at the request of Sheriff John E. Behan, rode to distant and chaotic Tombstone, Arizona, founded a dozen years before by prospector Edward Schiefflin,

Wyatt Earp, the legendary lawman, brought the fight to the outlaw McLowery and Clanton brothers at the O.K. Corral in Tombstone, Ariz., 10/26/81. (Kansas State Historical Society, Topeka)

who struck a vein that ultimately yielded more than $30,000,000 of silver. With Wyatt rode his brothers James and Virgil and the dentist-turned-gunfighter John H. "Doc" Holliday. Morgan Earp followed a month later.

Why Behan had bothered to ask Earp to be his deputy at all was never learned. Though Earp had ostensibly been brought in to keep the peace and quell the almost daily riots incurred by the deadliest outlaws of the era, Behan spent his efforts in pooh-poohing the mayhem. Much to Earp's disgust, Behan coddled and patronized the worst gunmen in the territory, attempting to befriend such killers as Curly Bill Brocius, Johnny Ringo (Ringgold), Frank and Tom McLowery, and the three Clanton brothers led by their murderous father, N. H. Clanton.

Behan refused to patrol the streets at night; that chore was left to the Earps and town marshal Fred White. One evening in October, 1881, White and Virgil Earp attempted to arrest Curly Bill Brocius, Pony Deal, Ike and Billie Clanton, the McLowerys, and Frank Patterson when the gunmen began to shoot up the town.

Brocius pretended to surrender his pistol to White, but used a gun-spin to bring the butt of his gun back to his own hand and shot White dead. Virgil Earp knocked Brocius senseless and dragged him to jail.

Later that year, Earp was made deputy U.S. marshal and his chief concern became the protection of the Oriental Saloon, a wide-open gambling spa. The casino's owners paid Earp $1,000 a month to make sure nobody wrecked the place, a daily goal of other saloon owners.

Within months, Earp's friends Bat Masterson and Luke Short came from Kansas to obtain jobs as dealers in the Oriental and, if necessary, back Earp's play against the outlaw faction.

Outside of a few drunken fights, Earp had little to do in Tombstone until the spring of 1881. The Wells Fargo Stage was then held up and its driver, Bud Philpot, shot to death. Shotgun rider Bob Paul told Earp that the raiders had been Luther King, James Crane, Harry Head, and Bill Leonard, all friends of the Clantons.

Alone, Earp rode after Luther King and captured him. When he brought the bandit back to Tombstone, Sheriff Behan ordered Earp to turn King over to him. "He's my prisoner, Wyatt," Behan insisted. Earp reluctantly turned King over to Behan's cutody, and the prisoner escaped two days later.

Then the Clantons stated that Doc Holliday had really led the raid against the stagecoach. Dance-hall trollop Big Nose Kate Fisher (later Doc's lover), who had stayed up all night drinking with the Clantons, made a deposition to the effect that Holliday bragged to her about committing the holdup. Holliday, who was not much given to defending himself with anything other than a six-gun, pointed out that the $80,000 the stage had been carrying at the time of the holdup had not been taken by the outlaws.

"If I had pulled that job," Holliday said wryly to a board of inquiry, "I'd have gotten the eighty thousand." He sauntered out of the jailhouse and into the Oriental. No one dared challenge Holliday, considered one of the meanest, fastest guns in the West.

Holliday, who had a record of grim gunfights in Denver and Dodge City, was consumptive and excessively nervous. It took very little prompting to draw him into a gun duel. According to his sometime friend Bat Master-

Wyatt Earp's intrepidly loyal back-up man was John H. "Doc" Holliday, consumptive, a fast draw, a deadly killer. (Western History Collection, U. of Okla. Library)

son, Holliday "had a mean disposition and an ungovernable temper, and under the influence of liquor was a most dangerous man. . . . Physically [Holliday] was a weakling who could not have whipped a healthy fifteen-year-old boy in a go-as-you-please fist fight, and no one knew this better than himself, and the knowledge of this fact was perhaps why he was so ready to resort to a weapon of some kind whenever he got himself into difficulty. He was hotheaded and impetuous and very much given to both drinking and quarrelling, and, among men who did not fear him, was very much disliked."

Trouble with the McLowery-Clanton gang plagued the Earps throughout the summer and early fall of 1881. Ike Clanton began to tell the tale that Wyatt Earp had attempted to bribe him to turn in Head, Leonard, Crane, and King, and he refused. When Earp confronted Clanton, a notorious loudmouth, the outlaw denied his words. Hours later, Clanton stated: "He offered me the reward for them fellows, all he wanted was credit for capturin' 'em." In June, 1881, Head and Leonard were killed by the Haslett brothers in Eureka, New Mexico. Crane died fighting Mexican regulars in August of that year while attempting to rustle cattle near Huachita.

The feud between the Earps and Clantons boiled over on the night of October 25, 1881, when Doc Holliday (by this time deputized as a deputy U.S. marshal) had a run-in with Ike Clanton. The two were eating steaks in a lunchroom. Morgan Earp sat at the end of the counter with his hand inside his coat, as if resting it on a gun butt. Holliday looked up from his platter. "Still say I robbed that coach, Ike?"

Clanton gave Holliday a sideways glance and snorted an unintelligible reply.

"You're a son-of-a-bitch of a cowboy," Holliday said.

Clanton pushed his plate back, stood up slowly, and walked outside. There he saw Virgil and Wyatt Earp. Morgan Earp and Holliday followed him outside and, according to some reports, taunted him. Clanton turned to Morgan Earp and said, "Don't shoot me in the back, will you, Morg?" He then walked away into the darkness.

Later that evening Clanton joined Tom McLowery and Sheriff Behan in a saloon and played cards until dawn. About 9 a.m. the following morning Clanton approached Virgil Earp in the middle of the street and said: "If you were one of them threatening me last night, you can have your fight." He then walked away.

About noon Virgil and Morgan Earp spotted Clanton and stopped him. Their argument ended when Virgil Earp withdrew his six-gun and slammed it against Clanton's head. The two lawmen then dragged Clanton to the courthouse, where he was fined $25 by Judge Wallace for carrying concealed weapons. Tom McLowery barged into the courtroom shouting oaths. Wyatt Earp stepped up, took out his pistol, and cracked McLowery on the side of the head. He then dragged the outlaw into the street and threw him into the gutter.

An hour later, a town drunk came up to the Earps, all assembled at the courthouse. Doc Holliday stood nearby holding a shotgun. The barfly said: "There are some men want to see you fellas down at the O. K. Corral."

"Who are these men?" Wyatt asked.

"The McLowery brothers, the Clantons, and Billy Claiborne."

Wyatt turned to Morgan Earp and said, "Let's go."

Then began the most famous gun battle in the history of the West. The three tall, mustachioed Earp brothers, dressed all in black, and Doc Holliday, cradling a shotgun in his arms, moved solemnly down the street abreast of one another, heading for Fremont Street and the O. K. Corral. It was the final showdown, and the lawmen had prepared for it for days.

Sheriff Behan, who was getting a shave, raced from a barbershop, the lather still on his cheeks, when he heard of the impending fight. He tried to argue the Earps out of the showdown, but he was brushed aside.

When the lawmen turned the corner to Fremont Street and entered the O. K. Corral, they saw five men waiting for them—Billie and Ike Clanton, Tom and Frank McLowery, and Billy Claiborne.

"You sons-of-bitches, you have been looking for a fight and now you can have it!" roared Wyatt Earp (according to Sheriff Behan's later testimony).

Virgil Earp, who was the town marshal, said: "You men are under arrest. Throw up your hands."

Billie Clanton and Frank McLowery dropped their hands to the pistols at their sides.

"Hold it, I don't mean that," Virgil Earp said. "I've come to disarm you."

Behan, who witnessed the entire confrontation, claimed that Billie Clanton shouted: "Don't shoot me, I don't want to fight." He also later stated that Tom McLowery brushed back his frock coat and said: "I am not armed."

For a moment the two groups glared at each other. Then Wyatt Earp and Billie Clanton went for their pistols. Earp's gun came out of a specially made coat pocket with a leather lining heavily waxed for a fast draw. Clanton and Frank McLowery drew their pistols from holsters. Clanton fired at Wyatt and missed. Wyatt fired at Frank McLowery and hit him in the stomach.

Ike Clanton, the braggart and instigator of the fight, panicked and ran up to Wyatt, grabbing him by the sleeve. "Don't shoot me!" he screamed. "Don't kill me! I'm not fighting!"

"The fighting has now commenced," Earp stoically told him. "Go to fighting or get away." Clanton ran across the street and down an alley.

Though mortally wounded, Frank McLowery managed to stagger across the open lot behind the O. K. Corral, into the street, and onto a sidewalk where he fired off a shot that barely missed Wyatt Earp.

"Throw up your hands!" Virgil Earp continued to shout, but the outlaws kept firing. Billy Claiborne threw up one hand when bullets came dangerously close to him. He sent a shot toward Virgil Earp and then raced down the street and hid inside C. S. Fly's photographic studio. Tom McLowery, who allegedly said he was unarmed, advanced against Morgan Earp and Doc Holliday, firing a very real pistol as he went. Two shots threaded Doc's coat sleeve just as Holliday raised his ugly shotgun and fired both barrels into McLowery, who died in his boots.

Before the second McLowery died, he squeezed off a round that tore into Morgan Earp's shoulder. Billie Clanton, nineteen years old and alone in the Corral, shifted his pistol from his shattered right hand, which had been hit by either Virgil or Morgan Earp, to his left and fired off several shots at the Earps, hitting Virgil in the leg. As he fired he ran in the same direction that Claiborne had fled, collapsing in front of Fly's gallery. By then he had been hit by at least four more bullets from the Earps' roaring pistols. One of Clanton's last shots creased Holliday's back.

Wyatt Earp, the only lawman uninjured, jogged after Clanton and stood over him as the boy tried to lift his pistol to shoot. Clanton kept repeating, "God, God, won't somebody give me some more cartridges for a last shot . . ." Then he died.

From thirty to fifty shots had been fired in the two-to-three-minute gun battle. Three of the outlaws—Frank and Tom McLowery and Billie Clanton—were dead.

Lawmen Wyatt Earp and Doc Holliday were arrested after warrants were sworn out by Sheriff Behan and Ike Clanton. Virgil (discharged as deputy U.S. marshal) and Morgan were not arrested and were bedridden with serious wounds. After a short hearing before Justice of the Peace Wells Spicer, Earp and Holliday were exonerated.

The outlaw clan struck back from ambush within months, when an unknown gunman shot Virgil Earp in the side on the night of November 28, 1881, as he was entering the Oriental Saloon. He was crippled for life. Ike Clan-

Morgan Earp, killed after the O.K. Corral battle by Ike Clanton's friends. (Arizona Society of Pioneers)

Virgil Earp was crippled for life after the gun battle. (Arizona Society of Pioneers)

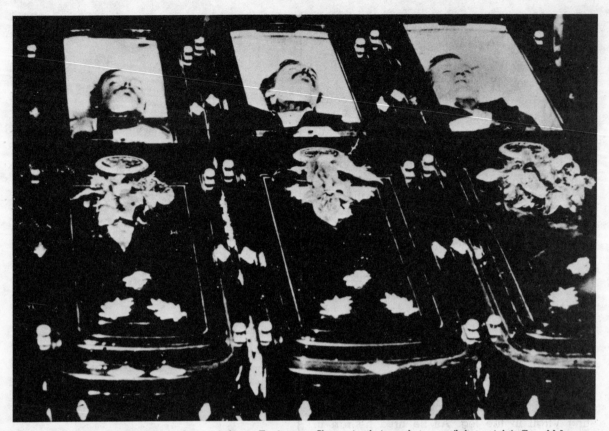

Three dead outlaws resulted from the gunfight in Tombstone. Shown in their caskets are (left to right), Tom McLowery, Frank McLowery, Billie Clanton. (Arizona Historical Society Library)

ton added new guns to his cause, and on the night of March 17, 1882, Hank Swilling, Pete Spence, Frank Stilwell, and Florentino "Indian Charlie" Cruz hid behind a stack of kegs and shot Morgan Earp in the back, killing him, as he played pool in Hatch's Saloon.

Wyatt and Doc Holliay accompanied the wounded Virgil Earp and the body of Morgan Earp on board a train bound for California. James Earp, who had been severely crippled in the Civil War and did not serve as a lawman, went with them. The Earps were going to their family home in Colston, California. Doc Holliday and Wyatt Earp got off the train at Tucson, where they were joined by another Earp brother, Warren, and three noteworthy lawmen—Texas Jack Vermillion, Turkey Creek Jack Johnson, and Sherman McMasters.

Wyatt had been warned that Stilwell and the others planned to ambush the Earp family on the train after it pulled out of Tucson. As the train took on passengers Wyatt and his friends scoured the area around the tracks. Earp, according to his own version, spotted four figures crouching on a flatcar and began shooting at them. One, Pete Spence, ran across the roadbed, and Earp killed him with a single shot.

Earp came face to face with Stilwell, his brother's murderer, in the dark. The famous marshal later stated: "Stilwell caught the barrel of my Wells Fargo gun with both hands . . . I forced the gun down until the muzzle of the right barrel was just underneath Stilwell's heart. He found his voice. 'Morg!' he said and then a second time, 'Morg!' I've often wondered what made him say that . . . I let him have it. The muzzle of one barrel was just underneath the heart. He got the second before he hit the ground."

One by one, Earp tracked down his brother's killers. He found Indian Charlie Cruz outside of Tombstone and killed him after forcing the outlaw to draw on a count of three. He caught up with Curly Bill Brocius at Iron Springs and shot him to pieces. On the western side of the Whetstone Mountains, Wyatt ran down Johnny Ringo and killed him in a close duel, according to one historian.

Then Earp hung up his guns and retired to the peaceful town of Colston, California, to live out a storybook life and mull through awful memories. His close friend and back-up man in a dozen gunfights, John H. "Doc" Holliday, died four years after the gunfight at the O. K. Corral. He was thirty-five, and the cause of death was tuberculosis. Next to his bed was his shotgun, his nickel-plated six-gun, and a bowie knife he had worn about his neck for ten years.

After a final shot of whiskey, Holliday worked himself up on one elbow and looked at his bare feet. "Dammit," he yelled. "Put 'em back on." The nurses of the Glenwood Springs, Colorado, sanitorium searched frantically but were too late. Holliday died with his boots off.

[ALSO SEE Curly Bill Brocius, Ben Thompson.]

OLD BREWERY

Erected in 1792 and originally known as Coulter's Brewery, the Old Brewery was situated in the center of what is now White, Leonard, Lafayette, and Mulberry streets in New York—the old Five Points section. The brewery was a five-story brick building originally painted yellow. Through the years, its dilapidated appearance, according to one writer, "came to resemble nothing so much as a giant toad, with dirty, leprous warts, squatting happily in the filth and squalor of the Points."

In 1837 the cavernous building was transformed into a tenement house with more than 100 rooms. The long hallway between rooms was called Murderer's Row. Irish immigrants inhabited the top floors, Negroes were in the twenty basement rooms. Dozens of children born in the Old Brewery did not see sunlight or inhale fresh air until their teens.

Murder was a pastime at the Old Brewery, a nightmare world in itself, dangerous to enter and lethal to leave. Anyone foolish enough to enter the building was marked for death. Any-

The notorious Old Brewery squatted at the hub of the Five Points; literally thousands were murdered in its murky chambers before it was destroyed in 1852.

one leaving would be stoned or strangled by citizens fearing the building's barbarous inhabitants.

It was truly a nether world of nauseating poverty and compassionless people who were more animal than human. In a fifteen-foot room, ten years prior to the Civil War, twenty-six persons dwelled. When a small girl rashly displayed a penny she had been given, she was murdered for it and her body tossed into a corner, where it stayed unburied for five days. Her mother, weak from starvation, finally managed to scrape out a miserably shallow grave with a spoon and fork and place her child in it.

Negroes, many of whom had reached New York via the slave escape route, came to dwell in the Old Brewery, where they took white wives. Sexually, the place was a free-for-all, flourishing with incest, miscegenation, rape, homosexuality. Almost every denizen of the Old Brewery pursued a criminal trade—pickpocketing, burglary, professional murder.

Drunken revels never ceased; loud voices, the banging of doors, the smashing of bricks, continued on a twenty-four-hour-basis. The building fairly shuddered with the most frightening and ghastly sounds imaginable—wails, whines, shrieks, insane laughter, screams, catcalls, hoots. The mad cacophony could be heard from blocks away.

One historian estimated that there was a murder per night in the Old Brewery for an unbroken period of fifteen years—5,475 lives snuffed out without one police investigation. Police did venture into the building occasionally, but never in numbers less than fifty and then only at great peril to their lives.

It was said that many scions of once great American families who had fallen into disrepute went to live and die in the Old Brewery. Harman Blennerhasset, the man who had so archly sided with Aaron Burr to create an American dictatorship, lost his son to the Old Brewery.

In 1852 the powerful Ladies Home Missionary Society, with the backing of financier and philanthropist Daniel Drew, bought the Old Brewery for $16,000, erecting a mission on the site a year later. Pandemonium erupted when the city police came to eject the Old Brewery's inhabitants on December 2, 1852. Like rats, the murderers—some wanted by the authorities for twenty years—fled into police nets. Women and children cried with joy to be released from the foul social and economic prison. When the grisly work of destroying the building began, workmen removed a hundred sacks of human bones from between the walls and under the floors.

OLIVE, ISON PRENTICE ("PRINT")
Murderer, Gunfighter ● (1840-1886)

BACKGROUND: BORN IN MISSISSIPPI IN 1840. MINOR PUBLIC EDUCATION. SERVED IN HOOD'S TEXAS DIVISION DURING THE CIVIL WAR. ORIGINAL OCCUPATION, CATTLE OWNER AND RANCHER. DESCRIPTION: TALL, SWARTHY, HEAVYSET. ALIASES: NONE. RECORD: INVOLVED IN SEVERAL KILLINGS IN TEXAS FOLLOWING THE CIVIL WAR; MURDERED LUTHER MITCHELL AND AMI KETCHUM, HOMESTEADERS, AT CLEAR CREEK, NEB., IN NOVEMBER, 1878, CLAIMED THE TWO WERE ENCROACHING ON HIS VAST CATTLE RANCH; PLACED ON TRIAL WITH FREDERICK FISHER, FOUND GUILTY OF MURDER AND SENTENCED TO LIFE IMPRISONMENT IN THE NEBRASKA STATE PENITENTIARY; FREED, 1880, ON A TECHNICALITY AND SCHEDULED TO BE RETRIED (A NEW TRIAL NEVER OCCURRED); KILLED IN 1886 IN TRAIL CITY, COLO., BY JOSEPH SPARROW.

Following in the tradition of Abel Head "Shanghai" Pierce, Olive became one of the super cattle barons of the West before homesteaders and farming communities sprang up in the middle of his vast herds and ranges. He ruled his enormous lands by the gun and the lynch rope. His cowboys were hired not only as expert cowpunchers but for their prowess with a pistol.

Violence had been a way of life with Olive, called "Print" by his friends, since his childhood in Mississippi. While still a youth, Print moved with his parents to Texas. When the Civil War broke out, he was one of the first to enlist in the Confederate Army, serving with distinction in Hood's Texas Division and participating in such bloody actions as Gettysburg.

Following the war, Olive moved back to Texas and raised a gigantic herd of cattle which he drove northward. Some of his beef was sold and the rest kept as stock with which to raise even greater herds in the then untamed ranges of Nebraska. Olive cut out a huge territory along the Platte River there, lands that stretched for hundreds of miles. He hired an army of killer cowboys to run his cattle and protect his barony.

Two intrepid homesteaders, Ami Ketchum and Luther Mitchell, moved into Nebraska's Custer County, controlled by Olive, and with their large families established neighboring farms. Olive, along with his brother Robert, who had fled Texas to avoid arrest by the Texas Rangers on a murder charge, rode into Mitchell's farm at the head of a sizable body of men in November, 1878.

The farmers had been prepared for just such a raid after receiving repeated warnings from Print to "get out or get killed." A gun battle erupted in which Robert Olive was killed and the cattlemen driven off.

Through his bribed officials (Olive owned everything in sight along the Platte), Print had Mitchell and Ketchum arrested and then turned over to him. Olive proceeded to mete out his own brand of frontier justice. In a deserted spot near Clear Creek, Olive ordered the two farmers bound with ropes. He then shot Mitchell in the back, saying "That's the way you gave it to my brother."

Both farmers were strung up by their necks from a nearby tree. The lynching did not satisfy the cattle baron, so he ordered a large fire built beneath the swaying, dead bodies. When members of a vigilante committee arrived, they found the corpses charred almost beyond recognition.

Public anger at such raw power and brutality rose against Olive, and, under pressure, the governor ordered his arrest and trial for murder. Olive and one of his top lieutenants, Fred Fisher, were found guilty and sentenced to life imprisonment at the Nebraska State Penitentiary. The outcome of the trial so enraged the hundreds of cowboys who worked for Olive that it was feared they would storm the courthouse where the cattle baron was being held.

No less a personage than President Rutherford B. Hayes was called upon by Nebraska's governor to order troops into the territory to prevent Olive's release by his private army. Several mounted companies of soldiers were sent into deliver Olive and Fisher to jail.

Print Olive boasted he would never stay in prison, and he was right. He spent a large fortune on legal maneuvers, and two years after being put behind bars, he was released. The state supreme court ruled that his trial, and that of Fisher, were improperly conducted since they were not held in Custer County, scene of the Mitchell-Ketchum slayings.

While Olive was in prison, his empire waned. His herds had diminished following incessant raids by rustlers (many of whom were his former employees). An influx of settlers challenged his supremacy, and hatred for him in the Platte River communities was rampant. He took what was left of his herds and crossed into Kansas in 1882.

Kansas, too, was overrun with farmers, members of a farming federation known as The Grange, which all but destroyed Olive's influence in Dodge City, where he attempted to establish himself. Selling his beef, Print moved on to Colorado and purchased a saloon in Trail City.

The once mighty cattle baron came to an unexpected end in 1886 when a cowboy, one Joe Sparrow, who was disgruntled over the fact that Olive owed him $10, entered his saloon and shot him, without warning, in the head. Olive died while standing up, a startled look on his face.

OSWALD, LEE HARVEY
Assassin ● (1939-1963)

A malcontent for most of his life, Lee Harvey Oswald became fascinated with Communism while in the Marine Corps. After his discharge in 1962, Oswald gave up his American citizenship and journeyed to Russia to live. He soon tired of proletarian life and returned to the United States, where he became involved in such quasi-political organizations as The Fair Play for Cuba Committee.

What motivated Oswald to shoot and kill President John F. Kennedy on November 22, 1963, in Dallas, Texas, has never been fully determined, and although the Warren Commission exhaustively sifted through the testimony of hundreds of witnesses, the only conclusion reached was that Oswald acted alone and for vague political reasons.

Days before President Kennedy's arrival in Dallas, Oswald, living on Beckley Avenue under the assumed name O. H. Lee, had learned from an edition of the *Dallas Morning News* that the President's motorcade would pass directly beneath the windows of the seven-story Texas School Book Depository where he was an employee.

Late in the morning of November 22, Oswald positioned himself in a sixth-floor window of this building with a cheap Italian-made rifle he had purchased from a mail-order sporting goods store in Chicago.

President Kennedy, riding in an open car with his wife, Governor John B. Connally, and Connally's wife, passed directly beneath Oswald's gunsights at approximately 12:30 p.m., and the assassin fired three rapid shots.

Just before the first shot, President Kennedy was happily acknowledging the waving, cheering crowds. Mrs. Connally turned and said to him: "Mr. President . . . you can't say Dallas doesn't love you."

He was about to speak to her when the first bullet struck; he clutched at his throat, and an aide thought he heard Kennedy say, "My God, I am hit." The second and third shots followed almost immediately, and the President fell forward. Mrs. Kennedy said: "Oh, my God, they have shot my husband. . . . I have his brains in my hand."

One of the bullets which hit Kennedy passed through his body and hit Governor Connally. The bullet tore through Connally's chest and became embedded in his thigh. Connally yelled, "My God, they're going to kill us all!"

The motorcade speeded up and raced to Parkland Hospital where, realistically, President Kennedy was dead on arrival, although frantic efforts were made to revive him. Following the shooting, Oswald hid his rifle between some packing crates and walked down to the second floor. Police rushed into the building.

Motorcycle policeman Marion L. Baker met superintendent Roy Truly at the second floor. He then saw Oswald entering the lunchroom. "Come here," he told Oswald. Oswald walked calmly up to Baker. "Do you know this man?" Baker asked Truly. The superintendent stated that he did, that Oswald worked in the building. Baker and other policemen then dashed

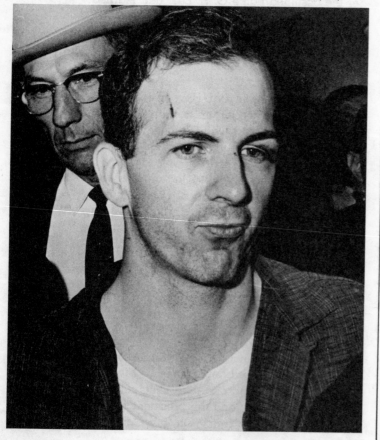

Assassin Lee Harvey Oswald, minutes before he was shot and killed by Jack Ruby in Dallas, 11/24/63. (UPI)

up the stairs. Oswald walked back into the lunchroom, where he bought a soda, sipped it for awhile, and then walked unnoticed from the depository.

He went to his room, changed his jacket, and pocketed a pistol. When he emerged, Officer J. D. Tippit, patrolling in his squad car, called Oswald over to the curb. The assassin leaned over, according to several witnesses, and spoke to Tippit for several minutes through the police car's window. He then straightened and began to walk away. Tippit leaped from his car and shouted after him.

Almost nonchalantly, Oswald withdrew his pistol, turned, and fired four times at Tippit, who died instantly. "Poor dumb cop," Oswald was heard to mutter.

An hour later, police were notified that a strange man had entered the Texas Theater without paying for a ticket. When Oswald spotted officers in the lobby, he took out his gun, aimed it at them, and said: "Well, it's all over now."

The pistol misfired and Oswald was arrested. He apparently had made no attempt to escape, having only $13.87 in his pockets and leaving $170 in his apartment. Though he consistently denied having murdered President Kennedy and patrolman Tippit, Oswald's palm print was found on the murder weapon, and the bullets that had killed President Kennedy and wounded Connally matched those of his rifle.

Two days after he was taken into custody, Dallas police prepared to move Oswald to the county jail in order to provide him with more protection; the FBI office in Dallas had received an anonymous phone call early that morning stating that Oswald would be killed.

In the presence of seventy policemen and before millions of television viewers, Jack Ruby, the owner of a striptease nightclub, stepped in front of Oswald as he was being escorted to a waiting car inside the city-jail garage and shot him in the abdomen. Ruby was convicted of murder and sentenced to death, but died three years later of cancer before he could be executed.

Dozens of claims were later made that Oswald was part of a vast conspiracy to kill President Kennedy, the most notable of which was that put forth by New Orleans district attorney James Garrison, but none of these claims have been proved.

PACKER, ALFRED (OR ALFERD) G.
Murderer, Cannibal, Robber ●
(1847-1907)

BACKGROUND: BORN IN RURAL COLORADO. MINOR PUBLIC EDUCATION. ORIGINAL OCCUPATION, PROSPECTOR. DESCRIPTION: SHORT, HEAVYSET. ALIASES: JOHN SCHWARTZE. RECORD: IN LATE 1873 MURDERED FIVE PROSPECTORS WHOM HE WAS GUIDING TO ALLEGED GOLDFIELDS IN THE MOUNTAINOUS REGION ALONG THE GUNNISON RIVER IN COLORADO; THE FIVE VICTIMS—BELL, HUMPHREYS, NOON, MILLER, AND SWAN—WERE KILLED, ACCORDING TO HIS CONFESSION, TO PROVIDE FOOD; STOLE SEVERAL THOUSAND DOLLARS FROM HIS VICTIMS; ESCAPED FROM THE LOS PINOS INDIAN AGENCY WHERE HE WAS BEING HELD IN FEBRUARY, 1874, AND FLED TO SALT LAKE CITY, UTAH, WHERE HE LIVED UNDER THE ALIAS OF JOHN SCHWARTZE; REARRESTED 3/12/83 IN SALT LAKE CITY; TRIED IN LAKE CITY, COLO., 4/3/83; CONVICTED OF MURDER 4/13/83, CHARGE CHANGED TO MANSLAUGHTER SINCE COLORADO CONSTITUTION HAD NOT PROVIDED FOR PUNISHMENT OF MURDER; SENTENCED TO FORTY YEARS IN THE COLORADO STATE PRISON; BECAME MODEL PRISONER AND WAS RELEASED AFTER SIXTEEN YEARS; PAROLED IN 1901; DIED NEAR DENVER OF NATURAL CAUSES 4/24/07.

Murderer and cannibal Alfred Packer, (Denver Public Library)

The crisp, wind-howling fall of 1873 promised a bitter winter in the West, but the prospects of such mean weather were incidental to twenty gold-seekers who set forth from Salt Lake City to seek their yellow fortune in the San Juan Mountains. All the men were novices, greenhorn prospectors, who had no knowledge of the wild regions they trod—all except one, a self-proclaimed mountain man named Alfred G. Packer, who acted as their guide.

In Colorado the party's original enthusiasm waned and turned to bitter complaints as its members stumbled from one campsite to another, the winter winds and snow following like a stealthy, carnivorous mountain lion. They lost their equipment, their food ran out. Fortunately, since Packer's ability to guide was all brag, the band straggled into the camp of a friendly Indian, Chief Ouray. The humanitarian chief fed them and warned them to go no farther. The mountains were virtually closed for the winter, he said, with endless wastes of snow blocking the trails; they would never find gold, only death, Ouray prophesied.

The group held a council meeting and debated the unlikely future of their expedition. Ten of the prospectors elected to return to Salt Lake City, the other ten were swayed by Packer's belief that there was gold to be had along the Gunnison River. He insisted that they continue to look for a strike. Packer did not reveal the fact that he was broke and did not want to return to Salt Lake City to build up another grubstake.

To bolster his position, Packer convinced

Chief Ouray to give the ten gold-hunters provisions. This Ouray did, but he also warned the men to stay close to the river since venturing into the mountains at that time of year meant certain death. Packer shrugged and pointed out that, if need be, the party could always find shelter at the Los Pinos Indian Agency, a camp not far from their intended diggings.

The following day the ten men led by Packer began to work their way up the Gunnison, but within weeks they were again out of supplies. After some vicious arguments, the party split up. Four men decided to try to make the confines of the Los Pinos Agency (only two arrived there, in haggard condition); five others —named Bell, Humphreys, Miller, Noon, and Swan—were again awed by Packer's earthy rhetoric and promises of finding gold over the mountains near the Rio Grande.

With Packer leading the way, the five men blindly followed. Exhausted and starving, the men groped through blizzards to a lonely trapper's hut high in the mountains. There they ate their last meal and, without saying it, prepared to die. The storms, however, had not conquered the fertile mind of Alfred G. Packer.

When the prospectors fell asleep, Packer reached for his rifle and, moving quietly up behind each man, shot him quickly in the back of the head. From evidence found later, Miller apparently jumped up to defend himself, and Packer dispatched him with a skull-cracking blow so hard that it broke the stock on his rifle. The five dead, Packer then ransacked their packs and emptied their pockets, taking several thousand dollars. Though financially enriched, he still faced the dilemma of starvation. After staring at the bodies for some time, the solution to his problem became grimly obvious. They were his food.

Using a hunting knife, Packer ravenously fell upon the corpses, slicing away the skin, particularly the flesh about the breast, which he cut to the ribs. The ghoulish Packer froze the strips of flesh in a snowbank overnight. The following morning he took the frozen "fresh meat" and packed it into his bundles. Then he set out for the Los Pinos Agency, eating as he went from his ample stores.

Wandering in aimless patterns, Packer reached a bluff overlooking the agency in February, 1874. The remaining contents of his food pack (subsequently described as "human beef jerky") worried him with the sight of civilization before his eyes. "When I espied the agency from the top of the hill," he later said, "I threw away the strips of flesh I had left, and I confess I did so reluctantly as I had grown fond of human flesh, especially that portion around the breast."

The man who walked into the agency that dawn was a human wreck. Inhabitants shuddered to look at him; his face was bloated, his skin mottled, his eyes popped, his clothes were in rags. At first, sympathetic residents diligently cared for him, but thought it strange that he could keep no food in his stomach and that he craved only liquor.

When the commanding officer of the agency, General Adams, returned from a patrol, he questioned Packer at great length about the whereabouts of the men who had been with him. Packer's answers were vague and evasive. The prospector's free-spending habits and pockets jammed with cash made Adams suspicious and he arrested him.

Two Indians from Chief Ouray's camp found, on April 4, 1874, the human strips of flesh Packer had discarded outside the agency the previous February, preserved by the snow. Confronted with this, Packer told Adams a fantastic story, relating how he and his fellow travelers had run out of food weeks after leaving Chief Ouray's compound and had fallen to living off roots. He then made his crime that of the others.

"Strange looks came into the eyes of the men of the party," he said, his features becoming animated. ". . . they all became suspicious of each other, figuring the others were holding out grub. One day I went out for wood for the fire, and when I got back, I found that Mr. Swan, the oldest man in the party, had been struck on the head and killed, the rest of them were in the act of cutting up the body preparatory to cooking and eating it. We divided his money, amounting to two thousand dollars, between us."

Packer related how he had taken Bell aside and the two had agreed to a self-preservation pact wherein whatever happened to the rest, they would not attack each other. ". . . I suggested that Miller be the next one we ate, because of the large amount of flesh he packed around. His skull was split open with a hatchet. . . . Humphreys and Noon were the next to go."

Eventual starvation had driven Bell mad, Packer sadly recounted. His lament sputtered at the thought of Bell's tragic death. "One night," Packer said, while we sat at a small campfire, glaring at each other, Bell suddenly stood up and yelled, 'I can't stand it any longer!' and rushed me like a famished tiger, trying to brain me with his gun. I parried the blow and killed him with a hatchet. . . . I then cut his flesh into strips which I carried with me as I pursued my journey."

Packer agreed to lead authorities to the bodies and set out in an expedition commanded by lawman H. Lauter. It became evident to Lauter that Packer had no intention of finding the bodies as he guided the party in hopeless circles. Packer then attempted to escape, but was caught and sent back to Los Pinos. Lauter and others went on alone and, weeks later, found the mountain shack and the bodies of the five men. Obviously they had been murdered, and Lauter raced back to the agency with the news. Packer, however, had already escaped.

Almost a decade passed while authorities searched for the cannibal. The murderer's luck ran out on March 12, 1883, when a member of the original prospecting group ran into Packer in Salt Lake City.

"You're Alfred Packer," the man said.

"I am not," Packer insisted. "I am John Schwartze. Who is Alfred Packer?"

Police arrested him that day and sent him to Lake City, Colorado, where he was tried for his crimes on April 3, 1883. Packer took the stand and claimed he had acted out of self-defense. He was nevertheless convicted of murder and sentenced to die. Packer appealed the verdict from jail. His lawyers found the perfect loophole. The Colorado constitution, it appeared, had made no provisions for the fate of murderers.

Packer was granted a new trial, on a charge of manslaughter, and was sentenced to forty years in 1885. He was a model prisoner in the state prison and served only sixteen years, being released in 1901. He went to work as a wrangler on a ranch near Denver, Colorado, and died there on April 24, 1907, wheezing restfully in a warm room with a full stomach.

PANCOAST, MARVIN
Murderer ● (1950-   )

Hollywood hustler Marvin Pancoast moved in with an attractive model, Vicki Morgan, when the young woman had trouble paying the rent on her Studio City, California, condominium. Morgan, at that time, had filed a whopping "palimony" suit against the vast estate of Alfred Bloomingdale, the department store tycoon. She had been Bloomingdale's mistress for a number of years and had reportedly been the magnate's companion in innumerable sadomasochistic orgies.

When, in 1982, Morgan's suit against Bloomingdale's estate collapsed, Morgan and Pancoast decided to go their separate ways, having no hope of paying the rent on their luxury apartment. On July 6, 1982, the night before the scheduled move, Pancoast took a baseball bat and crept into the model's bedroom. He beat her to death with it.

Pancoast turned himself into the police a short time later, saying that "I was tired of being her slave boy." Though placed on trial for murder, Pancoast became forgotten as the Morgan–Bloomingdale saga was vented by the nation's press, particularly the weekly tabloids.

Robert Steinberg, a Los Angeles attorney, took stage center by claiming to have seen video tapes of Bloomingdale, Morgan, and many national celebrities performing bizarre sex acts. Then it was claimed that the sensational tapes had been stolen, if they ever existed. Meanwhile, buried on the back pages, was the story that Pancoast had been convicted of killing Morgan. He was sentenced to 26 years in prison.

PANZRAM, CARL
Murderer, Burglar, Robber ●
(1891-1930)

BACKGROUND: BORN 6/28/91 ON A FARM NEAR WARREN, MINN., TO MATHILDE ELIZABETH (BOLDEN) AND JOHN PANZRAM, PRUSSIAN IMMIGRANTS WHO MOVED TO THE U.S. IN 1888. MINOR PUBLIC EDUCATION. THREE BROTHERS—PAUL, ALBERT, LOUIS; ONE SISTER—LOUISE. ORIGINAL OCCUPATION, FARMER. DESCRIPTION: 6', BROWN EYES, BROWN HAIR (RECEDING), HEAVYSET.

MUSTACHE. ALIASES: JEFF DAVIS, JACK ALLEN, JEFFERSON RHOADES, JEFF BALDWIN, JOHN O'LEARY, COPPER JOHN II. RECORD: ARRESTED AT AGE EIGHT FOR BEING DRUNK AND DISORDERLY, DISMISSED; AFTER GOING ON A ROBBING RAMPAGE AT AGE ELEVEN, SENT TO MINNESOTA STATE TRAINING SCHOOL IN RED WING IN 1903; SET FIRE TO A WAREHOUSE IN THE SCHOOL 7/7/05, RESULTING IN $100,000 DAMAGE; RELEASED JANUARY, 1906, TO THE CUSTODY OF HIS MOTHER; AFTER THREATENING A PREACHER WITH A PISTOL IN GRAND FORKS, N.D., RAN AWAY FROM HOME 3/29/06; ARRESTED IN BUTTE, MONT., FOR BURGLARY AND JAILED FOR TWO MONTHS; TRIED, CONVICTED, AND SENT TO MONTANA STATE REFORMATORY AT MILES CITY, MONT.; ESCAPED IN LATE 1906 WITH ANOTHER INMATE, JAMES BENSON; ROBBED AND BURNED, WITH BENSON, SEVERAL CHURCHES IN MONTANA; JOINED THE U.S. ARMY IN 1907; COURT-MARTIALED 4/20/07 FOR ATTEMPTING TO STEAL GOVERNMENT PROPERTY, SENTENCED TO THREE YEARS IN LEAVENWORTH; SERVED THIRTY-SEVEN MONTHS, DISCHARGED IN 1910; TRAVELED THROUGH COLORADO, STEALING AND COMMITTING ARSON; ARRESTED IN JACKSONVILLE, TEX., FOR VAGRANCY, RECEIVED THIRTY DAYS' ROAD-GANG WORK AT RUSK, TEX., ESCAPED; ROBBED A MAN OF $35 NEAR EL PASO, TEX., EARLY 1911, COMMITTING SODOMY UPON HIM; FLED TO MEXICO AND SERVED BRIEFLY UNDER THE COMMAND OF REBEL GENERAL OROZCO; RETURNED TO U.S., STOLE A BICYCLE IN FRESNO, CALIF., APPREHENDED AND SENTENCED TO THIRTY DAYS IN JAIL; SERVED THIRTY DAYS FOR VAGRANCY, 1911, IN SEATTLE, WASH.; ARRESTED FOR HIGHWAY ROBBERY, ASSAULT, AND SODOMY, DALLES, ORE., 1912, SERVED THREE MONTHS IN JAIL, ESCAPED; ATTEMPTED TO BREAK CAL JORDAN, A SAFECRACKER, OUT OF A MOSCOW, IDAHO, JAIL IN 1912, ARRESTED AND GIVEN THIRTY DAYS IN JAIL; ARRESTED FOR VAGRANCY IN HARRISON, IDAHO, RECEIVED LIGHT SENTENCE; ARRESTED UNDER THE ALIAS JEFF DAVIS FOR ARSON, RELEASED; ARRESTED FOR BURGLARY AT CHINOOK, MONT., SENTENCED TO ONE YEAR IN THE STATE PRISON AT DEER LODGE, MONT., ESCAPED IN EIGHT MONTHS; ARRESTED, 1912, IN THREE FORKS, MONT., FOR BURGLARY, UNDER THE ALIAS OF JEFF RHOADES, SENTENCED TO ONE YEAR IN STATE PRISON AT DEER LODGE; RECEIVED AN ADDITIONAL YEAR FOR PREVIOUS ESCAPE; SERVED TWENTY-THREE MONTHS OF SENTENCE; RELEASED IN 1914, MOVED TO ASTORIA, ORE., ARRESTED THERE FOR BURGLARY, SENTENCED TO SEVEN YEARS IN THE STATE PRISON AT SALEM; LED RIOTS AND BECAME INCORRIGIBLE, PROVOKING SEVERAL INCIDENTS, HAD AN ADDITIONAL SEVEN YEARS ADDED TO HIS SENTENCE; ESCAPED MAY, 1918; ROBBED A HOTEL IN FREDERICK, MD., OF $1,200; JOINED THE MERCHANT MARINE UNDER THE ALIAS JOHN O'LEARY, SAILED TO PANAMA ON "JAMES S. WHITNEY," JUMPED SHIP IN PERU, WORKED BRIEFLY IN COPPER MINES THERE; MOVED TO BOCAS DEL TORO, PANAMA, AND WORKED FOR THE SINCLAIR OIL COMPANY; BURNED DOWN AN OIL RIG IN 1919; RETURNED TO U.S., SHIPPED OUT ON ANOTHER FREIGHTER AND SAILED TO SCOTLAND; TRAVELED THROUGH EUROPE AFTER JUMPING SHIP; RETURNED TO U.S. IN EARLY 1920; ROBBED A JEWELRY STORE IN BRIDGEPORT, CONN., 1920 ($7,000); ROBBED THE NEW HAVEN, CONN., HOME OF WILLIAM HOWARD TAFT IN JULY, 1920 ($40,000 IN JEWELRY AND LIBERTY BONDS); PURCHASED SMALL YACHT "AKISTA," 1920; LURED SAILORS TO YACHT DURING 1920 ON THE PROMISE OF WORK, AND, BY HIS OWN ADMISSION, ROBBED AND MURDERED TEN MEN; ARRESTED FOR BURGLARY IN BRIDGEPORT, CONN., SENTENCED TO SIX MONTHS IN JAIL, RELEASED; ARRESTED IN PHILADELPHIA FOR AGGRAVATED ASSAULT, RELEASED ON BAIL, JUMPED BOND AND SAILED TO EUROPE ON FREIGHTER; JOURNEYED TO AFRICA, WORKING FOR THE SINCLAIR OIL COMPANY, CLAIMED TO HAVE KILLED A NEGRO BOY OF TWELVE IN QUIMBAZIE AFTER PERFORMING ACTS OF SODOMY UPON HIM; ALSO CLAIMED TO HAVE KILLED SIX NEGRO MEN NEAR LOBITO BAY (CLAIMED TO HAVE KILLED A TOTAL OF TWENTY-ONE PERSONS IN HIS LIFETIME); RETURNED TO U.S., CIRCA 1922, KILLED TWELVE-YEAR-OLD HENRY MCMAHON IN JULY, 1922, AT SALEM, MASS.; ROBBED SEVERAL YACHTS AT THE NEW HAVEN YACHT CLUB (WHERE HE WORKED AS A WATCHMAN) IN APRIL, 1923; STOLE A YACHT IN PROVIDENCE, R.I., MAY, 1923; KILLED A MAN IN KINGSTON, N.Y., BY HIS OWN ADMISSION, IN JUNE, 1923; ARRESTED WEEKS LATER IN NYACK, N.Y., ON CHARGES OF BURGLARY, ROBBERY, AND SODOMY, RELEASED ON BOND, JUMPED BAIL; KILLED, BY HIS OWN ADMISSION, A BOY IN NEW HAVEN, CONN.; ARRESTED WEEKS LATER IN LARCHMONT, N.Y., BEING CAUGHT IN THE ACT OF ROBBING AN EXPRESS OFFICE; SENTENCED TO FIVE YEARS IN SING SING PRISON; TRANSFERRED TO CLINTON PRISON AT DANNEMORA, N.Y., AS A HARD-CASE INMATE; RELEASED IN 1928; WITHIN A MONTH'S TIME, BY HIS OWN ADMISSION, COMMITTED ELEVEN BURGLARIES AND ONE MURDER IN THE BALTIMORE, MD./WASHINGTON, D.C., AREA; ARRESTED FOR HOUSEBREAKING 8/16/28 IN WASHINGTON, D.C.; WROTE OUT CONFESSION IN JAIL AND AS A RESULT OF THIS RECEIVED A TWENTY-FIVE-YEAR SENTENCE AT LEAVENWORTH; MURDERED CIVILIAN FOREMAN OF LEAVENWORTH'S LAUNDRY, ROBERT G. WARNKE, 6/20/29; HANGED AT LEAVENWORTH 9/5/30.

Carl Panzram was the complete misanthrope. Nowhere in the annals of American crime has there been anyone so dedicated to the wholesale destruction of mankind than Panzram. He enjoyed crime. There was no penance in him for the countless hideous deeds he performed. "I have no desire whatever to reform myself," he stated in his self-written confession-autobiography. "My only desire is to reform people who try to reform me. And I believe that the only way to reform people is to kill 'em."

In a rather blasé fashion, an approach obviously designed to evoke terror and dread in the reader, Panzram callously admitted: "In my lifetime I have murdered 21 human beings.

I have committed thousands of burglaries, robberies, larcenies, arsons and last but not least I have committed sodomy on more than 1,000 male human beings. For all of these things I am not the least bit sorry. I have no conscience so that does not worry me, I don't believe in man, God nor Devil. I hate the whole damned human race including myself."

There was a subtle pride in Panzram's didactic diatribe, similar in many respects to the maniacal passion for killing expressed by Los Angeles' mass murderer of the late 1950s, Stephen Nash, who, at age thirty-three, had killed a half-dozen skid-row bums, children, and unemployed workers. After killing ten-year-old Larry Rice (with twenty-eight knife wounds), Nash told police: "He was a kid. It was all there in front of him . . . His whole life . . . sex, fun, all of it! Why should he have it when I never did? I took it all away from him . . . Besides, I never killed a kid before. I wanted to see how it felt."

Panzram took great delight in murdering, too, but his self-admitted goal in life was the slaughter of whole cities. He stayed awake nights in his cell plotting the demise of thousands. "I used to spend all my time figuring how I could murder the most people with the least harm and expense to myself, and I finally thought of a way to kill off a whole town. . . ." He devised macabre murder systems, such as poisoning a town's reservoir or blowing up passenger trains like the National Limited.

His counterpart, Stephen Nash, thirty-odd years later would say: "Killings are cheap. They cost about $1.35 or $1.40. . . . It's like being on a quiz show . . . When you get to ten, you go for twenty . . . You always want more. . . . When I was in Quentin [San Quentin prison], I borrowed books from the prison library. I was studying the operation of railroads. I planned to run a whole train off a bridge and watch them monkeys go swimming. I'd lie on the river bank and enjoy myself laughing at them."

Panzram was a Minnesota runaway, Nash a New York foundling. Panzram went to the gallows, describing himself as "the most criminal man in the world." Nash entered San Quentin, sentenced to the gas chamber, describing himself thusly: "I'm the king of killers! I'll go to my death like any king should. I have nothing to die for because I had nothing to live for."

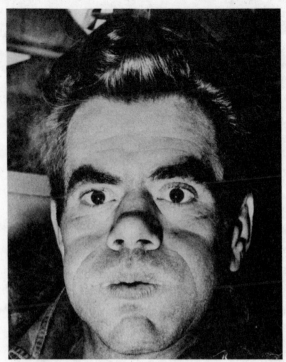

California slayer Stephen Nash was to brag of his countless killings much the same way Panzram had confessed. (UPI)

Where Nash's life had been but a series of vagrancy arrests, drifting, and unemployment, a lifetime of looking through windows as the total outsider, Panzram was brutalized early in life by what he called "Bible-back" disciplinarians and a medieval prison system where heinous tortures and spiritual degradation were the backbone of penal reform.

In one prison where he spent four years, the archaic state prison at Salem, Oregon, Panzram was placed in a strait jacket until his blood ceased to circulate; a torture known as "The Humming Bird" was applied to him—the victim was placed in a steel bathtub filled with water, chained hand and foot, and rubbed down with a sponge connected to an electric battery ("The agony is intense . . . Two or three minutes and the victim is ready for the grave or the mad house")—whipped on the bare back and buttocks and then salt applied to the wounds (done to Panzram while he was working on a road gang in Rusk, Texas); beaten on the bare back, buttocks, and legs by a baseball bat while strapped face down on a cot (in the Montana State Training School); strapped across the chest and by the hands to a steel wall and forced to dangle barefooted for hours (in the U.S. Military Prison at Leavenworth);

chained naked to a wall and hosed down with a water hose that caused his eyes to blacken, his body to welt, and his genitals to swell to enormous proportions (in the Oregon State Prison).

There is no doubt, when viewing Carl Panzram's subsequent crimes, that such unthinking prison bestiality created an unreasoning monster of wrath who killed and pillaged without mercy, a malevolent demon who serenely slumbered untroubled by Coleridge's "avenging angel—dark misgiving, an ominous sinking at the inmost heart."

Born to lower-class parents, Panzram's stark youth was lived in rural Minnesota. His father deserted the family, and one by one, his brothers slipped away from the farm to let his mother till the soil alone (his brother Albert did work in the fields for a while before becoming a policeman). Given little or no attention at all by his slaving mother, little Carl first grew envious of common emotions such as love and compassion; then he developed an early hatred for any kind of affection.

He was brought into juvenile court in 1899 at the age of eight on a charge of being drunk. Dismissed, he quickly began to steal from neighbors and was finally sent as an incorrigible to the Minnesota State Training School in Red Wing, Minnesota. The school was rigid and demanding. Panzram was ordered about in military fashion, made to toil in workshops in his bare feet, and wound up endlessly scrubbing dishes. He reacted by urinating and masturbating into beverages he served officers of the school. He was caught trying to insert rat poison into the coffee of a commander named John Moore.

Seeking to punish those he thought were punishing him, Panzram set fire to the school's warehouse which stored winter clothes and blankets on July 7, 1905. "That night," he stated, "the whole place burned down at a cost of over $100,000. Nice, eh?"

Whipped, beaten, and often starved, Panzram's hatred went down to bone marrow, and by the time he was released in January, 1906, he was well on his way to homicide. He later commented: "I have met thousands of graduates of those kinds of institutions and they were either in, going into or just leaving jails, prisons, mad houses, or the rope and the electric chair was yawning for them as for me."

Panzram went home briefly after being dis-charged, stole a pistol and threatened to kill a preacher with it, and then, on March 29, 1906, hopped a freight train in the yards of East Grand Forks, North Dakota. The rest of his short life was a Gorgonian odyssey into crime.

Stealing and burglarizing his way west (after being gang-raped by four men in a boxcar), Panzram was arrested several times and put into jail, but he always escaped. He and another inmate of the Montana State Reformatory, one James Benson, broke out and robbed and burned several churches throughout the state.

For some inexplicable reason—the future killer attributed it to a fascination for uniforms—Panzram joined the Army in 1907 while drinking beer in a Helena, Montana, bar and listening to an impassioned recruiting sergeant. He was soon punished for insubordination, and on April 20, 1907, he was court-martialed and sentenced to three years in the military prison at old Fort Leavenworth for attempting to steal government property. Panzram served thirty-seven months breaking up rocks under a blistering Kansas sun and was discharged in 1910 ("I was the spirit of meanness personified").

Bumming and robbing across Texas, Panzram reached Mexico, which in 1911 was torn with several revolutions, and served briefly with the insurrectionists led by Pascual Orozco, a satellite of Venustiano Carranza. He then moved on to California, Washington, and Idaho, served several minor sentences for sodomy, assault, highway robbery, safecracking, burglary, and vagrancy.

Under the name Jeff Davis, Panzram was arrested in Chinook, Montana, for burglary and received a year in the Montana State Prison, where he was tortured and beaten; he escaped in eight months. The following year he was arrested under the alias of Jeff Rhoades and sentenced to one year for a burglary in Three Forks, Montana. Authorities learned of his previous escape and added another year to his sentence in the Montana State Prison. Upon his release in 1914, Panzram went to Astoria Oregon, and was there arrested for burglary. He was sentenced to seven years in the state prison at Salem.

Leading a constant revolt against the horrible prison conditions in Salem earned Panzram another seven years. Serving his time under the alias of Jeff Baldwin, Panzram attempted several escapes. In retaliation he was placed in a cage and fed bread and water, which he more than once threw into the face of his guard. He was then beaten and sprayed with a fire hose. In May, 1918, Panzram sawed his way to freedom with crudely made instruments and traveled east.

He next appeared in Frederick, Maryland, using the name John O'Leary. He held up a hotel, taking about $1,200, and then went to New York, where he joined the Marine Firemen's, Oilers', and Water Tenders' Union. He signed on board the *James S. Whitney*, a tanker en route to South America. Jumping ship in Peru, Panzram worked briefly in the copper mines. He traveled to Chile and then to Panama, where he got a job as a foreman for the Sinclair Oil Company.

In Bocas Del Toro, Panzram, out of pique, spite, or whim, burned down an oil rig. The firm offered a $500 reward to anyone who could identify the arsonist, but Panzram went unnoticed as he shipped out in another freighter headed for the United States. His travels then widened. He sailed to Europe and, after robbing his fellow seamen, returned to the United States.

Early in 1920 Panzram robbed a jewelry store in Bridgeport, Connecticut, getting $7,000. That summer he went to New Haven and burglarized the home of William Howard Taft, taking $40,000 worth of jewels and Liberty Bonds. Using the loot from this robbery, Panzram purchased a yacht under the name John O'Leary.

He then lured several sailors (ten in all, he later admitted) to his boat and robbed and killed them. After they had worked hard refitting his ship, the sailors were invited to spend the night on board the docked yacht. ". . . we would wine and dine and when they were drunk enough they would go to bed. When they were asleep I would get my .45 Colt Army Automatic . . . and blow their brains out." He would then take their bodies to the middle of the harbor in his rowboat and drop the weighted corpses into the water.

When Bridgeport police began to grow suspicious of Panzram, he sailed his boat to New Jersey, where it was destroyed in a gale. Days later, like a homing pigeon, Panzram was back in Bridgeport, where he was arrested for burglary and sentenced to spend six months in the local jail, which he did without incident. He next hopped a freight to Philadelphia where he was tossed in jail for inciting a riot in a union dispute. He posted bond and then jumped bail, sailing to Europe on a freighter. From there he went to Africa.

By his own account Panzram worked briefly for the Sinclair Oil Company in Portuguese West Africa, where he murdered a twelve-year-old Negro boy (". . . first I committed sodomy on him and then I killed him . . . His brains were coming out of his ears when I left him and he will never be any deader . . .")

In Lobito Bay, Panzram thought it would be exciting to hunt crocodiles and hired six Negro porters to pole him through the backwaters. (". . . I shot all six of these niggers and dumped 'em in . . . The crocks done the rest . . . It was very much easier for me to kill those six niggers than it was for me to kill only one of the young boys I killed later and some of them were only eleven or twelve years old.")

Murder became an avidly pursued pastime for Panzram. He worked his way back to the United States, and in Salem, Massachusetts, in July, 1922, he attacked twelve-year-old Henry McMahon, killing him with a rock. (". . . I tried a little sodomy on him first . . . I left him laying there with his brains coming out of his ears . . .")

Obtaining a night watchman's job at the New Haven Yacht Club, Panzram looted several ships and then stole a yacht in Providence, Rhode Island, and sailed it to New York. In June, 1923 a man attempted to rob Panzram while on board his boat. He shot the robber twice and dumped the body into the bay at Kingston, New York.

He returned to New Haven after jumping bail for an arrest in Nyack, New York, where he was charged with burglary, sodomy, and robbery. Once again in New Haven, Panzram claimed to have killed another boy. A few weeks later, he decided to rob an express office, but was caught in the act and sentenced to five years in Sing Sing. He proved to be such a thorough malcontent that he was quickly transferred to Clinton Prison at Dannemora in remote upstate New York, a jail especially reserved for hardened criminals.

Carl Panzram was released in 1928 and went on a crime spree in the Baltimore/Washington D.C., area, committing, by his own

Mass murderer Carl Panzram. (UPI)

count, eleven burglaries and one murder. Washington police arrested him for housebreaking on August 16, 1928, and he was thrown into the local jail.

It was there that Panzram wrote out his gruesome memoirs and handed them to a friendly jailer, Henry Lesser. At his subsequent trial, the mass murderer taunted and threatened the jury with: ". . . If I live I'll execute some more of you!" After Judge Walter I. McCoy sentenced him to twenty-five years in Leavenworth, Panzram smiled and shouted to the justice: "Visit me!"

Panzram told Leavenworth's deputy warden Fred Zerbst upon arrival: "I'll kill the first man who bothers me." He was put to work in the laundry.

The prison's laundry at that time was run by a civilian named Robert G. Warnke, a squat, taciturn man who efficaciously went about his business. He never shouted at the prisoners working under his direction, but did scribble out daily infractions on a penalty sheet which was turned into authorities and brought minor punishments to inmates. It may have been for this reason, or because the laundry foreman merely got in Panzram's way, as he had warned, that the killer of twenty men and boys added Warnke to his list. On June 20, 1929, Panzram bashed in Robert Warnke's head with an iron bar, killing him instantly.

He then walked calmly across a prison yard with blood-smeared hands still gripping the iron bar. He stared through the bars of a door leading to the isolation cells. "I just killed Warnke," Panzram told guard Dale Ballard. "Let me in."

Ballard could not take his eyes from the bloody iron bar. "I'll never let you in with that in your hand," he finally managed.

Panzram looked at the bar, as if for the first time, and then said, "Oh. This must be my lucky day." He threw the bar aside and was admitted to the cell block, where he was promptly locked in a cell.

Following a quick trial, Panzram was sentenced to die on the gallows. When the Society for the Abolishment of Capital Punishment attempted to obtain a commutation for Panzram, the convicted murderer wrote to them telling them that he wanted to hang and that in no way should they attempt to save him. He insisted that he was sane and said: "I do not believe that being hanged by the neck until dead is a barbaric or inhuman punishment. I look forward to that as real pleasure and a big relief to me . . . when my last hour comes I will dance out of my dungeon and on to the scaffold with a smile on my face and happiness in my heart . . . the only thanks you or your kind will ever get from me for your efforts on my behalf is that I wish you all had one neck and that I had my hands on it . . . I believe the only way to reform people is to kill 'em . . . My motto is: 'Rob 'em, rape 'em all and kill 'em all!'" He signed his letter COPPER JOHN II, in memory of a copper statue that once stood in front of Auburn Prison in New York.

To ensure his execution, Panzram wrote to President Herbert Hoover, demanding that his "constitutional rights" be observed and that he be hanged on schedule. "I absolutely refuse to accept either a pardon or a commutation should either one or the other be offered me," Panzram wrote Hoover.

Neither was forthcoming. Panzram was true to his word. He fairly bullied his way to death, shoving guards to hurry up as they led him to the gallows in Leavenworth on September 5, 1930. "Let's get going. What are we stalling around for?" he asked Warden T. B. White.

The hangman ran the rope through his hands, eyeing Panzram, and then asked, "Anything you want to say?"

"Yes," the arch-killer replied. "Hurry it up, you Hoosier bastard! I could hang a dozen men while you're fooling around!" He then pulled the hangman up the scaffold steps, spat twice, and was quickly hanged, dying at 6:20 a.m. in the prison yard.

PARSONS, REUBEN
Gambler ● (? -1875)

Parsons, who moved from New England to New York in the 1850s, was known as the "Great American Faro Banker." He was responsible, more than any other, for the rise of infamous sharpers such as John Frink and Henry Coulton, who he backed in dozens of gambling houses. He and Frink inaugurated the policy game in America.

One historian described Parsons thusly: "Plain in his dress, and unassuming in his manners, he associates but little with his class, and is seldom publicly seen in any of his gaming houses, of which, although the actual proprietor, he stands in no fear or danger of legal prosecutions, as it cannot be shown that he is the winner of a dollar."

Parsons retired to a life of wealthy leisure in 1861, but caught the gambling fever a dozen years later when he speculated hundreds of thousands of dollars on Wall Street. He was wiped out in 1875, the year of his death.

PATRIARCA, RAYMOND L. S.
Syndicate Gangster ● (1908-1984)

BACKGROUND, BORN 3/17/08 IN WORCESTER, MASS. MINOR PUBLIC EDUCATION. DESCRIPTION: 59", BLACK EYES, BLACK HAIR, SLENDER. ALIASES: UNKNOWN. RECORD: ARRESTED FOR BURGLARY AND THEFT FOUR TIMES BEFORE 1928; REPORTEDLY ACTIVE IN WHITE SLAVERY IN LATE 1920S; BOOTLEGGING AND SEVERAL ARMED ROBBERIES ATTRIBUTED TO HIM; BECAME A "SOLDIER" FOR FRANK IACONE AND LATER PHILLIP BRUCCOLA IN THE MAFIA-CONTROLLED NEW ENGLAND STATES; ARRESTED FOR ARMED ROBBERY IN 1938, SENTENCED TO FIVE YEARS IN OLD CHARLESTON STATE PRISON, PARDONED BY THE GOVERNOR OF MASSACHUSETTS EIGHTY-FOUR DAYS LATER; PUBLIC OUTCRY OF BRIBERY IN HIGH OFFICE COMPELLED AUTHORITIES TO RETURN HIM TO PRISON FOR A SHORT TERM; ACTIVE IN GAMBLING THROUGHOUT THE NEW ENGLAND STATES DURING THE 1940S AND 1950S, PROTECTED IN THE SYDICATE HIERARCHY BY CLOSE FRIEND FRANK COSTELLO; NAMED BY JOE VALACHI AS THE BOSS OF THE NEW ENGLAND COSA NOSTRA FAMILY IN OCTOBER, 1963; ARRESTED FOR CONSPIRACY TO KILL ROCCO DESIGLIO IN 1966, CONVICTED AND SENTENCED TO FIVE YEARS IN PRISON 3/8/68, FREED ON $25,000 BOND PENDING APPEAL; BEGAN SERVING SENTENCE IN 1970. DIED IN 1984.

Throughout the years he was in prison, Raymond Patriarca still controlled the Mafia-syndicate of New England. Patriarca, or the Padrone as he was called in New England, began his criminal career in the late 1920s with several arrests for burglary.

The first stint Patriarca performed with organized crime was as a bodyguard for motor launches carrying illegal beer and liquor shipments. He promptly accepted a hefty bribe from a rival gang to look the other way while these launches were hijacked. Next, the apprentice gangster moved into the Mafia gang of Frank Iacone, who retired from the rackets about 1933 to allow Patriarca to assume leadership of his "troop." Within fifteen years the wiry hoodlum had taken control of the entire New England area, wresting power from Phillip Bruccola, who also retired to Italy.

Gambling, vice, and loan-sharking became Patriarca's major interests during the 1940s and

New England's Mafia boss, Raymond Patriarca. (UPI)

1950s. He was linked with the Dunes Hotel in Las Vegas at one time shortly after cementing relations with syndicate boss Frank Costello, the "prime minister of organized crime," according to the McClellan Committee.

The Padrone was always careful in avoiding arrests. He slipped up only once after his youthful crimes and that was in 1938, when he was convicted of armed robbery and sent to the Old Charleston jail for five years. He was released by a full pardon from the governor of Massachusetts in eighty-four days, but the hue and cry raised by the press caused an investigation of those who had signed a petition requesting Patriarca's release.

The governor, it appeared, had be persuaded to approve the pardon after receiving an imploring letter from one Father Fagin. Upon checking, it was learned that no such priest existed. Patriarca was sent back to prison and served close to two years of his sentence.

In the early 1940s the Padrone quietly went about building up his rackets. He was spotted one day by a Cosa Nostra hit man from New York, Joe Valachi, who was standing at the rails in Rockingham Park Racetrack in Salem, New Hampshire. Valachi had met Patriarca previously and was later to state that he knew the Padrone was definitely the head of the Mafia family that ruled New England from his offices at the National Cigarette Service Company in Providence.

At their meeting, Valachi intimated to Patriarca that a horse named Hi Bobby was "made" (had been given a speedball and was expected to win). The rising crime kingpin bet $5,000 on the horse, which came in fifth. Patriarca grabbed Valachi by the coat lapels and shouted for all to hear: "So that horse was made! If you come near me again, I'll kill you!"

Ruthlessness is the key attribute of any syndicate leader, and Patriarca exemplified his capacity in this regard when, according to most reports, he annihilated a group of young Irish gangsters headed by Bernard McLaughlin in October, 1961. The tough youngsters had attempted to take over the Mafia's juice racket in Boston, and Patriarca's extermination of the mob earned him a place on the board of directors of the national crime syndicate.

Despite the noonday shooting of McLaughlin, the Padrone was never mentioned by the press for close to twenty-five years. He shunned pub-

licity and sidestepped any direct contact with his crime cartel by giving his orders verbally over the phone from his Providence offices.

This was the case in 1966, according to Mafia informer Joseph "Baron" Barboza, who told a grand jury that Patriarca ordered by phone his Boston front man, Gennaro Anguilo, to kill Rocco DiSiglio, a young Mafiosi who had been fingering syndicate-run crap games for a band of stickup men. DiSiglio was shot several times on the beach near South Boston after being told to "drink the ocean." His dead body was found on June 16, 1966, propped up in his new sports car.

Patriarca was convicted of conspiracy to commit murder and was allowed to post a $25,000 bond pending appeal. After several appeals, Patriarca was finally sent to prison to serve out his term.

(ALSO SEE the Syndicate.)

PAYNE, A.D.
Murderer ● (? -1930)

A successful lawyer in Amarillo, Texas, Payne fell in love with his statuesque secretary, Verona Thompson. The problem was that Payne had a wife and two small children. To rid himself of a tiring wife, Payne, who had studied the use of explosives, fixed a bomb to the family car just before his wife drove to a shopping area.

The car blew up, killing Mrs. Payne and seriously injuring her young son. Police investigating the case soon learned from the children that their father had talked about taking out expensive insurance policies on their mother and themselves. Further, Payne's affair with his secretary was discovered.

Verona Thompson told police that Payne planned to marry her after "he got rid of his wife." When Payne heard Thompson's statement, he confessed, saying he had rigged the bomb. Payne was convicted and sentenced to die in the electric chair, but the shrewd attorney outwitted the executioner. He built a small bomb, strapped this to his chest and, only hours before he was to be executed, detonated the explosive in his cell, which blew out his heart.

PERRY, OLIVER CURTIS
Trainrobber ● (1864-1930)

BACKGROUND: BORN IN NEW YORK. NO PUBLIC EDUCATION. RAN AWAY TO THE WEST, CIRCA 1881, SETTLING BRIEFLY IN WYOMING. ORIGINAL OCCUPATION, COWBOY. DESCRIPTION: TALL, SLENDER, SOMETIMES WORE MUSTACHE. ALIASES: JAMES CURTIS PERRY, CURT PERRY, OLIVER MOORE, RECORD: ALONE, STOPPED THE NEW YORK CENTRAL NO. 31 ON 9/29/91, STEALING SEVERAL THOUSAND DOLLARS' WORTH OF JEWELS AND CASH FROM THE EXPRESS CAR NEAR ALBANY, N.Y.; ROBBED THE NEW YORK CENTRAL TRAIN NEAR SYRACUSE, N.Y., 2/21/92 FOR SMALL AMOUNT OF CASH; ROBBED NEW YORK CENTRAL TRAIN NEAR LYONS, N.Y., FOR SMALL AMOUNT OF CASH; CAPTURED BY A POSSE HOURS LATER NEAR LYONS; SENTENCED TO FORTY-NINE YEARS IN AUBURN PRISON, N.Y.; TRANSFERRED IN 1893 TO THE STATE HOSPITAL FOR THE CRIMINALLY INSANE AT MATTEAWAN, N.Y.; ESCAPED 4/10/95 AND RECAPTURED DAYS LATER IN WEEHAWKEN, N.J.; SENT TO CLINTON PRISON AT DANNEMORA; AFTER SEVERAL ESCAPE ATTEMPTS, PLACED IN SOLITARY CONFINEMENT FOR TWENTY-FIVE YEARS: DIED IN HIS CELL 9/10/30.

"I was only a lad without schooling so I had to take bold strokes with big chances." Thus spoke Oliver Curtis Perry, who claimed to be related to Oliver Hazard Perry of the Battle of Lake Erie fame, and who was also considered "the nerviest outlaw in New York."

Early in his youth, Perry fled the tenement life he was born to in New York and bummed his way west. When he reached the broad, green plains of Wyoming, he became a cowboy, his lifelong dream. The incessant rounds of chores and gulping dust kicked up by cattle soon bored Perry. He quit and then committed several small robberies in the area before traveling back east.

The thought of robbing trains had often occurred to Perry. The success of Wyoming's Wild Bunch convinced him to enter the same profession. Perry wandered through Texas, up to Nebraska, and into Minnesota, robbing, he later claimed, several coaches and trains (this was never verified). When he reached New York State in late 1891, he was determined to rob a train single-handedly.

He bought a ticket on the New York Central's fast flyer, No. 31.

On September 29, 1891, Perry cut a hole in the wall of the baggage car while the train was en route to Albany, New York, squeezed through, and held up the express guards, taking about $2,000 in jewelry and cash. Just outside of Albany, Perry, hanging on by one hand, sawed the train's air hose between two cars, bringing it to a halt. He quickly ran to a nearby woods and escaped.

Small amounts were turned over to the lone bandit when he robbed two more New York Central trains the following year—one on February 21, 1892, near Syracuse, another on September 20, 1892, near Lyons. Perry's last train robbery, reckless though it may have been, possessed all the grit and gumption of latter-day Western film heroes.

press Company's car would be carrying more than $100,000 in gold and jewelry in its safe. He purchased a ticket to Lyons on the day of that shipment and, during an eye-scratching hailstorm, climbed to the top of the express car while the train was hurtling through mountain gorges. He drilled a hole in the top of the car and then screwed a hook into the hole. Through the hook, the bandit threaded a rope. He then slowly let himself down the rope to the side of the express car and, with a spring of his legs, pushed himself outward away from the train and then, returning with full force to its side, crashed through one of the express-car windows.

Guard Daniel T. McInerney blinked in amazement, said, "My God," and then tenaciously threw himself upon the outlaw. The two fought wildly through the length of the car for several minutes until Perry managed to withdraw his pistol, which he bashed against McInerney's head, knocking him senseless. During the fight, however, the valiant guard had pulled the signal rope, and this brought conductor Emil Leass on the run. He found Perry fumbling with the combination of the safe.

Perry, who had robbed the guard and the petty-cash box, looked up, startled, at the conductor, and then dashed to the door of the express car, flung it open, and dove out near Jordan, New York. By the time the train reached Lyons, authorities had been warned of the robbery, and a posse was waiting to board a train to take them back down the line to Jordan. Just as the lawmen were about to embark, the sedulous conductor, Leass, saw Perry calmly waiting for a train outside the station.

With Leass' shriek, the lawmen poured out of the train and began to chase the bandit across the yards. Perry, dashing frantically over the rails, reached a freight engine that already had a full head of steam, its cab deserted. He jumped on board and yanked the throttle. The locomotive ground out of the yards.

The amazed possemen boarded another train and gave pursuit. The chase was risky, especially for Perry, since his locomotive was running on the opposite track and an oncoming train would mean certain collision. When the pursuing locomotive loaded with lawmen came abreast of Perry's engine, the bandit and possemen began trading shots. Perry drove his locomotive with one hand and fired a pistol with the other. Though a dozen rifles were trained on him, the lawmen proved poor shots, their bullets missing Perry repeatedly.

The outlaw threw his locomotive into reverse in an effort to shake off his pursuers, but the experienced engineer in the other engine stayed with him. Back and forth, forward and reverse, the engines huffed and hissed. Stalemated, Perry finally gave up and brought his engine to a halt after spying a large stand of timber. He raced for cover. The lawmen were right behind him.

Perry stole a buggy from a nearby farmhouse and drove it wildly down a country road. The lawmen commandeered carriages and chased him, shots from their rifles echoing strangely through the valley at dusk.

After changing horses several times, Perry quit the twenty-five mile buggy chase and waded into a swamp. The lawmen went in after him. Sheriff J. Collins knew a showdown was at hand, and when he spotted Perry attempting to hide behind a log, he shouted: "Do you want to fight it out, Perry?"

The hard-breathing possemen staunchly clutched their rifles, preparing for a fight to the death. For a full minute nothing stirred in the shadowy swamp, and then Perry's high, almost girlish voice broke the lull: "No. I'm out of bullets . . . I guess it's all up with me."

Once in custody, the lone train robber was rushed to trial and quickly convicted. Perry received forty-nine years in Auburn Prison.

The newspapers played up the bandit's clawing fearlessness. Pinkerton's superintendent George Bangs was quoted as saying Perry's ingenious method of breaking into the New York Central's express car was "the most daring train robbery attempt in criminal history. I would call Perry the nerviest outlaw I ever heard of. There are few western badmen who possessed his courage."

The press fawned over Perry, and his reputation became such that several women proposed marriage to him in long, maudlin letters. One young lady, swept into the mawkish emotion whipped up by the newspapers' inflating of Perry's career, was moved to send him a saw secreted inside a Bible. The prisoner had been removed from Auburn Prison after creating several disturbances and sent to the State Hospital for the Criminally Insane at Matteawan, New York. Here, poorly paid guards were less inclined to check gifts sent to inmates, and the lovesick lady's saw went undetected. Before making his escape on April 10, 1895, the bandit penned a bit of doggerel and placed it on his bunk:

> I don't intend to serve this out,
> Or even let despair,
> Deprive me of my liberty
> Or give me one gray hair.

Within an hour, Perry sawed his way through the bars of his cell, stole a set of keys from a sleeping guard, and released a number of other prisoners. He then forced a window and spotted a drainpipe running down the side of the building. Once again, Perry relied on his athletic prowess. He stood on the windowsill, jumped sideways to grapple the pipe, and then rode it downward for eighty feet to the ground and freedom.

Penniless and hunted by hundreds of lawmen, Perry tramped his way to New York City and then moved to Weehawken, New Jersey. He was arrested by a town constable while roasting over a small fire a rabbit he had killed with a rock.

Authorities took no further chances with Perry. He was sent to the maximum-security prison at Dannemora. The train robber never gave up hope of escaping, but after several futile attempts he was permanently isolated in a narrow solitary-confinement cell where he stayed for twenty-five years.

Driven half-mad by the solitude, Perry built an

odd contraption consisting of a block of wood and two nails which he evenly spaced so that when he dropped the gruesome machine with weights onto his face, both his eyes were pierced, causing permanent blindness.

Weeks later, he dictated a letter to a friend which read: "I was born in the light of day, against my will, of course. I now assert my right to shut out the light."

Perry, totally blind and without speaking a word for six years to his guards, died quietly in his Clinton Prison cell on September 10, 1930.

PHILLIPS, JAMES JETER
Murderer ● (1844-1868)

A well-educated and moderately wealthy young man, Phillips grew tired of his wife, a woman ten years his senior. On the pretense of inspecting his estate in Henrico County, Virginia, Phillips convinced his wife to accompany him in a buckboard. He stopped on a deserted road and shot her with a derringer, throwing her body into a ditch.

Approximately three months later, Mrs. Phillips' body was discovered and her landowner husband charged with murder. He confessed and was quickly executed.

PINELLI, ANTHONY R., SR.
Syndicate Gangster ● (1899-1977)

Pinelli immigrated to the United States in 1913 from Calascibetta, Sicily, settling first in New York City. Named by Robert Kennedy as a Mafia chieftain in Lake County, Indiana, Pinelli had ruled the roost there since 1954. Kennedy's investigations pointed out that this member of the syndicate's board of directors in Chicago had used great sums of money gleaned from gambling and narcotics rackets to buy valuable real estate in California.

Reportedly linked strongly with John S. La-Rocca and Gabriel Mannarino—two of those who attended the 1957 Apalachin meeting—Pinelli has a record that dates back to 1926 and includes six convictions for bootlegging—1926 ($100 fine), 1927 (six-month jail term), 1930 ($500 fine), 1932 (six-month jail term), 1932 ($500 fine), 1933 (six-month jail term).

Pinelli pleaded guilty to income-tax evasion in May, 1966, received a two-year probation, and was fined $2,000.

PIPER, THOMAS W.
Murderer ● (? -1876)

As sexton of the old Warren Avenue Baptist Church in Boston, Thomas Piper had complete access to church buildings and grounds. For years it was rumored that Piper was "not quite right" and had attacked several young girls in the neighborhood, but nothing could be proved against him.

Late in 1875 Piper enticed a young girl, Mabel H. Young, into the tower of the church. There, he turned on the five-year-old child and beat her to death with a cricket bat.

Police discovered the body and soon picked up Piper as a suspect. He was convicted by overwhelming evidence and sentenced to death on the gallows. He was hanged in 1876 after authorities learned that he had murdered at least one other young girl and had, indeed, attacked and raped several children.

PLUG UGLIES GANG

Organized about 1825 in New York City in the Five Points section, the Plug Uglies took their name from the giant plug hats they filled with rags and straw to protect them in gang battles. It was an all-Irish gang at the beginning, and its members were required to be at least six-feet tall.

Each member walked the streets in the symbolic plug hat and carried a brick in one hand and a mammoth club in the other. He usually wore a pistol in his belt and considered his giant hobnailed boots an additional weapon with which to stomp robbery victims and enemies to death.

The Plug Uglies were afoot during the period in which The Chichesters, Roach Guards, Shirt Tails, and Dead Rabbits gangs operated, their leaders being some of the most notorious gangsters in New York. This gang participated in the death-dealing New York City draft riots in 1863 which claimed the lives of hundreds.

The Plug Uglies disappeared about 1900, its members amalgamated into the Five Points gang, the last important street gang in New York before the Prohibition gangsters took over.

PLUMMER, HENRY
Murderer, Robber ● (? -1864)

Plummer headed one of the most vicious gangs of outlaws and murderers in the early Washington Territory. The area in which he and his men operated, the town of Bannock being their headquarters, later became the Idaho Territory and then part of Montana.

Nevada City, California, was the scene of Plummer's first criminal escapades in the late 1850s. The killing of a man married to the woman he was wooing was laid at Plummer's door, and he was found guilty of the murder. Plummer, a man of imposing appearance and considerable charm, had, however, important political contacts, and through these he wangled a pardon from the governor of California.

No sooner was he freed than Plummer joined a gang of bandits and robbed a stage. One man was killed in the robbery, and Plummer was again arrested for murder. There would be no pardon this time, which the outlaw knew, and he soon arranged an escape.

After breaking out of the Nevada City jail with the help of friends, Plummer rode into the goldfields of Washington Territory.

He established headquarters in Lewiston, now in Idaho, and gathered about him the deadliest cutthroats and outlaws in the territory. Plummer acted out the role of a concerned citizen whenever a robbery was committed and donated sums of money to hire lawmen to patrol the community. Under this leader-of-the-community cover, Plummer directed his bandits in one theft after another. In 1861 one member of his gang was captured and a lynch mob formed in the middle of Lewiston's main street. The outlaw Charlie Forbes, was a quick-draw artist who wore his pistol scabbard in the middle of his gun belt and served as Plummer's right-hand man.

Upon seeing Forbes being led down the street to be hanged, Plummer raced to the front of the mob and held up his hands. He delivered an impassioned speech about fair play and "justice" for Forbes. "This man deserves an impartial trial," Plummer insisted.

A shopkeeper in the crowd shook his fist. "Not to hang this man is cowardice!" he yelled at Plummer.

Henry Plummer only stared at the man and then went on with his plea, which convinced the vigilantes to return Forbes to Lewiston's gimcrack jail, from which he easily escaped days later. The pesky shopkeeper was shot to death the following week by members of Plummer's gang at the outlaw leader's orders.

When the Lewiston area was sufficiently plundered, Henry Plummer and his most-trusted aides rode to Bannock, a boom town squatting among the thriving goldfields. Again Plummer played the role of upstanding citizen while organizing the outlaws in the territory into a small army, numbering at times close to two hundred men. Between directing his carefully planned robberies and murders, Plummer found enough time to work for his own election as sheriff of Bannock, which he won on May 24, 1863. He was now not only the town's leading lawbreaker but the law itself.

Wholesale robberies, looting, and stickups followed Plummer's election. His men, absurdly dubbed "The Innocents," attacked stagecoaches almost daily, particularly those marked with an X in chalk, the symbol placed by Plummer's paid informants and spies who worked for the stage lines and knew in advance of the gold shipments each stage would be transporting. Plummer grew rich, and the residents of Bannock grew enraged. Their new sheriff, leaders of Bannock's vigilante committee concluded, was not only ineffective but had to be involved directly with the robberies.

Vigilantes then captured some of the outlaws in Plummer's employ, and they identified him as their leader. Plummer, Forbes, and two others were promptly arrested and lynched on January 10, 1864. Before the hanging, outlaw leader Plummer protested loudly, claiming innocence—"You wouldn't hang your own sheriff, would you?"

Plummer's question was answered with alacrity when one young man in the crowd dashed to the rope dangling from Bannock's odd-looking gallows (three heavy timbers resembling an inverted U) and trailing to a noose around the outlaw's neck, and gave it a violent yank. Others quickly joined the young man, and the vigilantes hauled Henry Plummer up into the air and death.

The irony of the execution was that Plummer had ordered the construction of the gallows before his election as sheriff to prove to the populace that he meant to deal severely with lawbreakers. Two dozen members of Plummer's gang were subsequently hanged from this makeshift gallows, a grim accolade to Plummer's false intent.

POILLON SISTERS

Bunco games and bizarre swindles occupied the lives of the colorful Poillon sisters, Charlotte and Katherine. Both women, born between 1870 and 1872, were huge. Katherine weighed in at about 200 pounds; Charlotte, who fancied herself a semi-professional ring-fighter, tipped the scales at around 210 pounds.

After some stormy marriages, the New York-born sisters developed minor criminal records around the turn of the century. Both well into their thirties, the sisters were fond of bilking elderly men out of their life savings on the promises of marriage.

The first known offense of this type involved Katherine Poillon, who, in 1903, sued William G. Brokaw for $250,000, charging breach of promise. The well-to-do Brokaw settled out of court for $17,500 to avoid publicity. Trapping lonely, wealthy men into promising marriage and then threatening to expose their cadlike actions after they had backed away from their earthy pleasures was a Poillon specialty, demure blackmail of a sort which profited the sisters handsomely for decades.

Katherine and Charlotte were anything but ladylike during their best years. They were arrested and fined $10 on a disorderly-conduct charge in 1907; they had thrown a hotel manager down a flight of stairs when he demanded they pay their bill, months overdue—the sisters would endure no such flagrant insults. The Poillons were sent to jail for three months the following year, convicted of defrauding the Hotel Bristol in New York of $135. When receiving their sentence, the Poillons angrily stated that they had been victimized by a judge named Barlow who had promised to pay their hotel bill following a particularly edifying sexual frolic with the two leviathans.

Hotel bills continued to hound the sisters. They were ousted from one hostelry after another. In 1909 it took six men to eject them from the Hotel Willard. Charlotte, who had once gone four rounds in an exhibition match with Gentleman Jim Corbett, beat up three bellhops so badly that they required medical attention.

The proprietor of the swank Rector's Cafe had Charlotte Poillon carried bodily from his establishment in 1912. She sued the restaurant for $25,000. Rector's won the case after the maitre d' described Charlotte's attire as that of a man's and said she had knocked down two waiters while barging toward a reserved table.

In 1915 the two sisters were again in trouble, arrested for bilking an elderly man out of $75 which he paid for "favors." The case was dismissed. Eight years later, the Poillons again made headlines when seventy-three-year-old Charles Dusenbury, a laundry-chain owner, sued the sisters for defrauding him of $3,000.

Once in court, the sisters refused to plead to anything, rejected a court-appointed lawyer, and cut paper dolls out of newspapers. Judge McIntyre rebuked them for their attitude.

"You can't railroad us, Judge McIntyre," Charlotte said, banging a heavy fist on the table.

"Please remember that you are women or I may forget that you are!" the judge shouted back.

"We want an Irish counselor," screamed Katherine. "We don't think the man you appointed to us, Sam Feldman, is Irish!"

Following several hectic hours in court, Dusenbury broke down in sobs, admitting he had given Katherine Poillon $3,000 out of love. The case was dismissed.

The sisters were back in court months later when W. N. Edelstein charged the sisters of bilking him out of $23,338. The Poillons assumed their usual self-righteous stance, wisecracking at every turn.

"What is your occupation?" inquired the judge of Katherine Poillon.

"What would you characterize a woman who stays home and attends to her business?" she replied.

"I would say that she was a wise woman."

"Then I'm a wise woman. That's my occupation."

This time, the Poillons hired the flamboyant lawyer Bill Fallon to defend them, and he soon had them set free. Fallon, an eccentric in his own right, encouraged the antics of the Poillon sisters. They followed him in and out of courtrooms and often loitered in his offices, working their shady deals over his telephone. Once when he was down on his luck, Fallon called Charlotte Poillon and asked for a loan.

"You loafer!" she screamed at him. "Where do you think we'd get any money? I have half a mind to clean you up! You're making my sister cry. Don't do it again, ever!"

The sisters faded into oblivion in the late 1920s. Charlotte Poillon reappeared briefly in 1929, popping out of a crowd gathered in front of an athletic display in a New York City department store.

A boxer employed for the occasion was pounding away at a punching bag. After several flurries, the fighter heard a booming voice call out, "You stink!"

He turned to see Charlotte Poillon glowering at him, a towering woman of great girth with her hands on her hips.

"You're so rotten, you ought to brain yourself with a toy balloon," Charlotte said.

"I suppose you could do better, lady?" the boxer retorted.

"If I couldn't I'd give myself up to the nearest T. B. hospital!"

The embarrassed fighter quit, and the floor manager hired Charlotte to put on the boxing exhibition. After three weeks of punching the bag, along with a few male customers who passed some unkind remarks, Charlotte quit and vanished forever.

POMEROY, JESSE H.
Murderer ● (1860-1932)

Mentally deranged, Pomeroy was a sadistic bully who lived in the back streets of Boston, an unwashed waif without home or education. He took particular delight in administering vicious beatings to small children, and in 1872 he was arrested by police for nearly killing one small boy. He was sentenced to the Westboro Reformatory, where he remained for eighteen months.

On the streets again at age fourteen, Jesse, on April 22, 1874, waylaid four-year-old Horace Millen and took him to Dorchester Bay, outside of Boston. There, on the beach, Pomeroy beat the little child so badly that he knocked out an eye; he then stabbed the boy fifteen times and slit his throat. He made no attempt to conceal the body.

Police quickly arrested Pomeroy, and he not only confessed to murdering the Millen boy but admitted that he had killed Katie Curran, age nine, several weeks previously. At his direction, police found the child's body buried in the basement of a small shop.

Pomeroy's age mattered little; he was placed on trial and the public clamored for his death. He was convicted and sentenced to die on the gallows. His defense of insanity was ignored.

Then took place one of the strangest series of events involving an American murderer. Governor Gaston refused, for obscure political reasons, to either sign the boy's death warrant or commute his sentence. As a result, Pomeroy stayed in jail for two years until a new governor commuted his sentence to life in prison, with the special order, to appease the many who still demanded the death penalty, that Jesse be kept in solitary confinement for the rest of his life.

He was removed to the Old Charleston Prison (from which Elmer "Trigger" Burke would escape seven decades later) and placed in solitary confinement. He stayed there for forty years. In 1916, at age fifty-four, Pomeroy was released from his lonely cell and allowed to mingle with other prisoners. He became studious and wrote several accounts of his life. Reformed though he may have seemed, he was consistently denied parole.

Pomeroy lived out his life in prison, dying on September 29, 1932. His time of confinement, fifty-eight years, remains the longest record of imprisonment for an American criminal to date.

PONZI, CHARLES
Swindler ● (1878-1949)

BACKGROUND: BORN IN ITALY, IMMIGRATED TO THE U.S., CIRCA 1893. MINOR PUBLIC EDUCATION. MARRIED ROSE PONZI. ORIGINAL OCCUPATION, TRANSLATING CLERK FOR AN IMPORT-EXPORT FIRM. DESCRIPTION: 5'2", BLACK EYES, BLACK HAIR, SLENDER. ALIASES: NONE. RECORD: ARRESTED FOR FORGERY IN MONTREAL, QUE., 1905, RECEIVED MINOR SENTENCE; ARRESTED FOR SMUGGLING ALIENS IN ATLANTA, GA., 1908, RECEIVED MINOR SENTENCE; PERPETRATED A GIANT FINANCIAL INVESTMENT SWINDLE BETWEEN 12/20/19 AND 8/13/20 IN BOSTON; ARRESTED BY FEDERAL AGENTS AND CONVICTED OF USING THE MAILS TO DEFRAUD; SENTENCED TO FOUR YEARS IN PLYMOUTH PRISON; ARRESTED UPON RELEASE FROM FEDERAL PRISON BY MASSACHUSETTS AUTHORITIES AND CONVICTED OF FRAUD; SENTENCED TO A SEVEN-TO-NINE YEAR TERM; POSTED BOND PENDING APPEAL AND FLED TO FLORIDA WHERE HE WAS ARRESTED IN 1925 ATTEMPTING TO DEFRAUD REAL-ESTATE INVESTORS; RECEIVED A YEAR IN JAIL; REARRESTED BY THE STATE OF MASSACHUSETTS UPON RELEASE AND SENT TO PRISON TO SERVE OUT PREVIOUS SENTENCE OF NINE YEARS; RELEASED IN 1934 AND DEPORTED TO ITALY; DIED IN RIO DE JANEIRO IN 1949.

Charles Ponzi was never anything more than a common swindler. His checkered career, however, failed to be lost to the oblivion of petty thievery and awkward frauds because he perpetrated with nerveless emo-

tions and a permanent grin the simplest yet most gigantic financial hoax of the twentieth century. P. T. Barnum's axiom that there was a sucker "born every minute" was not lost on Ponzi.

To put across his fantastic scheme, Ponzi banked on the avariciousness of investors, the gullibility of the press, and the naiveté of Americans who believed all things possible in the free-enterprise system. It was terribly simple: he borrowed from Peter and paid Paul. And it worked . . . until Peter got wise.

After emigrating from Italy to the United States in the early 1890s, Ponzi became a waiter but was soon fired for being garrulous with customers. A Chaplinesque figure, Ponzi longed to dress like the elegantly tailored diners he had served. Jobless, he saw the promised riches of the New World fade. With two dollars in his pocket, he boarded a train bound for Canada. He was there only a short while before he was picked up for forging a check and sentenced to jail for a short term.

Undaunted, Ponzi rode the rails to Atlanta, where he convinced leaders of the Italian community that he could arrange to have members of their families still in Italy transported to America without the bother of immigration regulations. He apparently did manage to slip a few immigrants into the country, because he was shortly arrested and jailed briefly on a charge of smuggling aliens.

In 1914 Ponzi traveled to Boston, disgusted with his faulty get-rich-quick schemes. He met and married the daughter of a wholesale grocer and soon took over the business. The firm, under Ponzi's wacky procedures, floundered almost immediately. "The market just fell out," he explained to his despondent wife, Rose.

A year later, Ponzi became a $16-a-week translator for an import-export firm, J. P. Poole. His knowledge of Italian landed him the job. For two years the little schemer sat at his desk and worked out elaborate plans to bilk people out of millions, but he gave them up as impractical moments after they had hatched in his plotting brain. Then, in June, 1919, the "Ponzi Plan" materialized.

Little Charlie noticed a packet of International Postal Union reply coupons in the office. Upon inquiring, he learned that the coupons were purchased abroad and then sent to the United States or other countries not suffering economic depression and redeemed for a considerably higher rate than when purchased. In Italy or Germany, for instance, where depressed rates for these coupons were in effect, one could purchase a coupon for a penny. These could be redeemed for five cents in the United States, for more than that in other countries.

Ponzi's brain exploded. Here it was, the scheme of a lifetime. He quit his job and went home to work out the details. He first borrowed money and sent this to relatives in Europe, instructing them to buy postal coupons and return them to him. This was done, but when Ponzi attempted to redeem the coupons here, he met with horrendous red tape and his scheme was foiled.

Still, he would not give up the idea. Ponzi went to several Boston friends and told them as he waved his postal coupons on high that he could double their money in ninety days. His elaborate plan made little sense to his first investors, who had never even heard of postal-reply coupons, but they gambled small amounts with him. In ninety days Ponzi had paid back $750 interest on the first due date from initial investments totaling $1,250.

"Incredible . . . I can't believe it," one friend told him.

Ponzi smiled knowingly. "Re-invest and tell your friends."

In days, hundreds rushed to Ponzi with fistfuls of dollars with which to purchase postal-reply coupons. In weeks, thousands were flocking into the offices of Ponzi's new Financial Exchange Company on School Street in the heart of Boston's financial district. The affable wizard couldn't hire people fast enough to count the money, so he stuffed it into desk drawers, suitcases, filing cabinets, wastebaskets.

Forty thousand frenzied investors, mostly little people, dumped their life savings into Ponzi's coffers. The amazing thing was that from December 20, 1919, until he was exposed the following year, Ponzi paid off, first at 50 per cent interest every ninety days and then at 50 per cent interest every forty-five days. His harried clerks—mostly members of his wife's family who barely spoke English let alone knew how to handle delicate investment data—scooped up an estimated $200,000 a day from investors during the firm's peak period.

A financial writer on one of Boston's newspapers dared to suggest that Little Charlie's financial dealings were questionable and that no financier, even the "Great Ponzi," as Charlie liked to be called, could legitimately provide such earnings in so short a time.

Ponzi read the article and sued the writer and the paper for $500,000 damages. His brazenness stunned and quieted the press, nullifying any probes into his business matters for some time. Meanwhile, the Great Ponzi realized his dream of riches and luxury. He bought a twenty-room mansion in Lexington for $100,000; he bought a $12,000, chauffeur-driven Locomobile; he bought the Poole firm where he had spent two years at a job he hated (and upon taking over, fired his old employer); he bought two hundred suits, one hundred pairs of shoes, four dozen Malacca canes with solid-gold handles, two dozen diamond stickpins, one hundred five-dollar ties—Charlies Ponzi bought everything in sight and still he couldn't spend money fast enough to clear it out of every nook and cranny in his spacious offices.

He continued to pay his incredible interest rates on old investments with the money from new investments. By the summer of 1920 Ponzi, who spent most of his time posing for pictures while smoking through a diamond-studded cigarette holder and hustling bags of money to his car, thought it wise to invest elsewhere. He walked into the esteemed Hanover Trust Company with two suitcases full of large bills, totaling $3 million, and bought a controlling interest.

When the Boston Post asked for an interview with the financial genius, Ponzi grew leery and hired a public-relations man, William McMasters, to deal with the press. McMasters became suspicious of his employer from the first moment he walked into Ponzi's offices.

"The man was a financial idiot," the PR man later stated. "He could hardly add. There was money stuffed into every conceivable place in his offices. He sat around with his feet on the desk, talking complete gibberish about postal coupons."

McMasters went to the state authorities, who were already interested in the blossoming financial Ponzi empire that had spread with electrifying rapidity through New England, New York, and New Jersey, where branch offices of the Financial Exchange Company were doing brisk business. At the PR man's urging, state investigators called in Ponzi and his books.

He arrived at the State House in Boston in late July, 1920, carrying a stack of moth-eaten ledgers. Hundreds of his fanatically loyal investors were at the entrance to greet and encourage him. He posed on the steps waving confidently.

"You're the greatest Italian of them all!" one man yelled.

"Oh, no," Ponzi modestly offered. "Columbus and Marconi. Columbus discovered America. Marconi discovered the wireless."

"Sure, but you discovered money!" came the reply.

State auditors labored over Ponzi's labyrinthine books and distractedly reported that they could make nothing out of them. Enormous sums had been entered in the ledgers without dates and the names of investors. Investors' names had been entered without the amounts of their investments.

When some of Ponzi's workers were interviewed, they responded to the simplest questions with stares of wonder. They had no idea how Mr. Ponzi worked his business. They merely paid people who showed up with notes at collection time and took money from those who wanted to give it to Mr. Ponzi.

At this point the *Boston Globe*, whose reporters had been quietly investigating Ponzi's background for months, exposed the financial wizard, citing his former arrests and convictions for smuggling and forgery. The balloon burst, and the Ponzi exchange was inundated with thousands of investors demanding the return of their money on August 13, 1920. Ponzi ordered his clerks to "pay everybody off." Inside of eight months, the diminutive tycoon had taken in $20,000,000. After paying off $15,000,000, his clerks ran out of money.

Thousands of investors trailed from his offices into the street and around several corners, all on the verge of rioting. Desperately, Charlie Ponzi ran about his office, muttering and peeping into boxes, drawers, and cabinets. "There's more here," he was heard to say, "there's gotta be more here." He knew there wasn't; only two days previously, according to one report, he had packed close to $2,000,000 in a suitcase and driven to Saratoga Springs in a last-ditch effort to win enough at the gambling tables to shore up his company. He had lost it all.

Federal agents arrested Ponzi in his mansion days later on charges of using the mails

Charles Ponzi at the zenith of his multi-million dollar swindle in 1920. (UPI)

to defraud. He had sent some of his investors letters reminding them to reinvest in his swindle. He got four years in Plymouth prison. On his release in 1925, Ponzi was arrested by Massachusetts authorities for his swindle and convicted in a speedy trial. He was sentenced to nine years in jail, but posted bond pending appeal and then skipped to Florida, where he attempted to defraud investors in the feverish land boom there. He was again arrested and jailed for a year. Upon his release, the State of Massachusetts claimed him, and he served out his original nine-year term, being paroled in 1934. With his parole went an automatic deportation order to Italy.

Reporters who interviewed him before he sailed saw a different Charles Ponzi. His mouth drooped, his hands twitched, he was dressed in an old suit and unpolished shoes with the heels worn down. His wife Rose had left him, and he was returning to the land of his childhood with empty pockets.

"I bear no grudges," he told reporters. "I hope the world forgives me."

If the world didn't, dictator Benito Mussolini certainly did. He gave Ponzi a high-ranking job in the financial section of his government, but soon learned that little Charlie was unreliable as well as inept. Before charges were brought, Ponzi skipped to South America with a large unstated sum from Mussolini's treasury.

His name all but disappeared until 1949, when his death in a Rio de Janeiro charity ward was reported. There was still a matter of $3,000,000 Ponzi never accounted for, money he took from investors but failed to return. These "Ponzi millions" vanished as completely as did little Charlie's dream of wealth and his amorphous money machine.

POOLE, WILLIAM ("BILL THE BUTCHER")
Murderer, Gangster ● (?-1855)

As one of the leaders of the Bowery Boys —a gang of notorious thugs who operated illegal rackets and administered political drubbings in the Lower East Side of New York for seven decades, from 1830 to 1900—Poole was a brawler and strong-arm slugger who took particular delight in bashing in the heads of any member of the Tammany political group.

Poole, along with such feared bruisers as Tom Hyer, once American heavyweight boxing champion, worked for and was paid handsomely by the Know-Nothing Party. By 1855 Poole headed a gang on New York's West Side, having close to two hundred professional criminals along Christopher Street under his command.

A former butcher, Poole was a six-foot-tall, 200-pound killer who had dispatched many foes with carving knives. On the night of February 24, 1855, Poole entered Stanwix Hall, a new and splendidly gilded bar in the hub of Manhattan's night life at Prince Street and Broadway, across from the old Metropolitan Hotel.

Moments after entering, Poole, in the company of Charley Shay and Charley Lozier, two of his minions, began to argue with three Tammany toughs—Lew Baker, Jim Turner, and Paudeen McLaughlin (whose nose had been

"Bill the Butcher" Poole (on floor of Stanwix Hall saloon) receives a bullet in the heart from his murderer Lew Baker.

bitten off in a to-the-death fight with Five Points gangsters).

McLaughlin threw a drink into Bill the Butcher's face and called him a "black-muzzled bastard." Turner threw off his coat and pulled a pistol, but his draw was so poor he shot himslf in the elbow, whereupon he screamed horribly and fainted. Someone threw a drink into Turner's face. He revived and fired off a shot at Poole, who was advancing toward him, hitting the giant in the leg.

Lew Baker then drew a pistol and said: "I guess I'll take you anyhow," and fired twice. One shot hit Poole in the abdomen, the other went through his heart. The powerfully built man, though mortally wounded, got up from the floor, grabbed Baker, and hurled him against the bar, breaking his arm. Poole, in a daze, grabbed a carving knife from the free-lunch service area and shouted at the terrified Baker: "I'll cut out your heart!" He then collapsed as his assassins fled.

Fourteen days later, with his gang members at his bedside, Poole died. His endurance with a bullet in his heart was a source of wonder to the medical profession. At the last moment he jackknifed from his bed and shouted: "Goodbye, boys. I die a true American!"

Poole's death marked the first of the lavish gangster funerals in the United States. Because of his strong affiliation with the Know-Nothings, five thousand of his cronies and political associates marched behind his flower-bedecked hearse, and ten brass bands heralded his approach to Greenwood Cemetery in Brooklyn.

His killer, Baker, attempted to flee by boat to the Canary Islands, but a sloop was sent after him and he was arrested and returned for trial. After several involved legal and political battles, he was acquitted.

Poole, however, emerged triumphant in death. His last words inspired several melodramas in which he was pictured in the last act as a heroic martyr draped in The Stars and Stripes and shouting patriotically, "Goodbye, boys. I die a true American!"

POWERS, HARRY F.
Serial Killer ● (? -1932)

Powers ran the lovelorn racket for all it was worth. A native of Quiet Dell, a surburb of Clarksburg, W. Virginia, Powers read out-of-town newspapers, hunting for victims in the lovern columns. He would write glowing letters to wealthy widows, promising undying love. They responded like moths to the flames, rushing to his side to wed him, only to have their savings stolen and to be brutally murdered.

Powers ran a delicatessen in Quiet Dell. He was married but operated his lovelorn schemes in secret, using aliases like Herman Drenth and Cornelius O. Pearson, to sign off his love letters to victims. In June 1931, Powers finished building a garage on some remote property owned by his wife.

It was to this place that Powers brought his victims, the first known to be Dorothy Pressler Lemke, a divorcee from Northboro, Massachusetts. Mrs. Lemke traveled to Clarksburg to marry Powers, bringing her savings. Powers put her money in his bank account and promptly drove to his garage where he killed her and then buried the corpse nearby.

The garage had an underground chamber, a "Death Room," the press later dubbed it, where Powers brought his victims whom he had drugged unconscious. In this airless, windowless place he murdered Lemke and also Mrs. Asta Buick Eicher of Park Ridge, Illinois, along with Mrs. Eicher's two children, Annabel, nine, and Harry, twelve.

Sheriff C.O. Duckworth of Clarksburg began to investigate the strange doings of Harry Powers after receiving a phone call from an anonymous woman who reported Powers going to his garage late at night. There was also the smell of "rotting meat," said the woman.

Duckworth investigated, found the "Death Room," and then discovered what appeared to be fresh graves near the garage. His men began to unearth bodies. Powers was arrested and put on trial for murdering Mrs. Lemke. The press ballyhooed Powers as "The Lothario of the West Virginia Hills," but the local residents did not find his gruesome murders entertaining.

A mob of four thousand people collected in front of the Harrison County Jail on the night of September 20, 1931. They demanded that Powers, who was cringing inside of a cell, be turned over to them to be lynched. A group of deputy sheriffs had a hard time holding off the would-be lynch mob, making several arrests after a small bomb went off.

Powers's trial was a sensation, held at the Moore Opera House to accommodate the huge crowds wanting to attend. Evidence proved that he was, indeed, an horrific "bluebeard," one who had wooed and married dozens of females and had slain at least five women and several children in the underground, soundproof room beneath his garage.

Outside the opera house, vendors hawked songs, books and records about "The Bluebeard Slayings at Quiet Dell." On December 11, 1931, Powers was found guilty of murdering Mrs. Lemke. On December 12, he was sentenced to death by Judge John G. Southern. He went to the gallows on March 18, 1932.

PRESCOTT, ABRAHAM
Murderer ● (1816-1836)

On June 23, 1833, when Mrs. Sally Cochran refused to make love to Prescott, the enraged youth, then eighteen, picked up a stake and beat the woman to death with it. His long trial was a sensation. His defense argued that Abraham was a somnambulist (the first attempt at utilizing such a defense) and had killed Mrs. Cochran in his sleep! The suspicious jury and court refused to countenance such a plea (insanity was still widely considered to be a variance of devil possession) and ordered Prescott hanged.

A large throng gathered at Pembroke, New Hampshire, not far from the scene of the killing, to witness Prescott's hanging. When the mob learned that the youth had received a temporary stay of execution, riots occurred, causing several injuries.

Prescott was moved to Hopkinton and was there hanged, on January 6, 1836, without pomp and ceremony.

PRIO, ROSS
Syndicate Gangster ● (1900-1972)

Famed as one of the seven top "power" mobsters in Chicago in a 1963 Senate probe, Prio had a record that dated back to 1929—previous police records on Prio were destroyed by a court order. He had been arrested for bootlegging, murder, arson, and assault, and he took the Fifth Amendment

Ross Prio, on the Midwest board of the *Cosa Nostra*.

ninety times during the McClellan Senate probe into organized crime.

Prio's domain in Chicago covered the entire North Side. He had heavy interests in nightclubs, vending machines, motels, hotels, and currency exchanges, as well as out-of-state gambling interests in Las Vegas.

This much-feared syndicate mobster died on December 22, 1972 of a heart attack.

PROBST, ANTOINE
Murderer ● (? -1866)

Probst worked as a hired hand for Christopher Deering, a wealthy farmer whose estate was outside Philadelphia. Following several bouts of drunkenness, Probst was fired. He brooded over losing his job and then begged it back from the kindhearted Deering.

One spring night in 1866 Probst grabbed an axe and slaughtered the entire Deering family in their beds, including a female house guest and a hired boy, eight persons in all.

He was quickly apprehended and confessed the murders immediately. He was hanged, and as was the custom of the day, parts of his body were turned over to medical colleges for examination and study. Oddly enough, Probst's eyes were removed and carefully examined to prove that the retina of his eye retained the last image seen before death. The "experiment" was a failure.

PUENTE, DOROTHEA MONTALVO
Serial Killer ● (1929-   )

Police arrested Dorothea Puente at the boardinghouse she ran at 1426 F Street in Sacramento, California on November 16, 1988. They had just exhumed seven bodies from the backyard of the Victorian house, including that of

Alvaro "Bert" Montoya, a lodger of Mrs. Puente's, whose social caseworker had reported him missing.

Not until July 1990, however, were California prosecutors ready to lodge a formal charge against her of nine counts of murder. They theorized that the gray-haired, grandmotherly Puente poisoned elderly lodgers in order to receive their social security checks.

In the meantime, extensive press coverage in Sacramento, where preliminary hearings in the case were being heard, inspired Puente's defense team to request a change of venue for her trial, arguing that the depiction of her as a serial killer "dehumanized" her to an extent that a fair trial could not be held there. Superior Court Judge Michael J. Virga selected the compromise of hearing preliminary defense motions in the capital, then moving the case to Monterey for jury selection and the hearing of arguments.

One of the defense motions was to ban from the trial all talk of Dalmane, a prescription sedative found in the systems of all the victims disinterred from Puente's yard. None of the bodies contained enough toxicological information for the coroner to fix a cause of death. However, Ruth F. Munroe, 61, who died at Puente's boardinghouse on April 28, 1982, was determined to have died of Tylenol and codeine intoxication. This was the first death at the F Street location, and the only one reported.

A macabre sequel to Munroe's death occurred on New Year's Day 1986, when the body of Everson T. Gillmouth, another lodger of Puente's, was discovered in a wooden box near the Sacramento River in Yuba County. Puente was charged with their deaths as well as the seven found in the yard. The prosecutors, meanwhile, moved that evidence be included that Puente had also drugged three surviving lodgers in the year before the grisly backyard discovery.

Defense attorney Kevin D. Clymo surprised the prosecution on February 11, 1993 by offering an alternative theory as to why Puente failed to report eight alleged natural deaths (the ninth allegedly being a suicide) at the boardinghouse. "She has a touch of larceny in her heart," he admitted, acknowledging that Puente had served time in a California prison for administering drugs to an older man she'd met at a bar.

A condition of Puente's parole was that she have no contact with elderly or mentally disabled people. Therefore, Clymo argued, when her friend Everson Gillmouth moved in with her, then died suddenly in 1985, Puente was afraid she would go back to prison for a parole violation if she reported it.

Another shocking development occurred six days later, when truck driver David Van Alstine, testifying for the prosecution, identified Alvaro Montoya and fellow victim Benjamin Fink as the two men who helpd him unload a delivery of pre-mixed concrete in the summer of 1988. The concrete was later used to cover some of the grave sites.

Later in the trial the prosecution also introduced a videotape of Montoya talking to his social worker to give the jury a sense of the life that had been lost. Another tenant testified that he complained to Puente about a smell "like death" in the boarding-house four days after Fink's disappearance, only to be told that it was the smell of a sewer backing up. Puente herself testified that she saw Montoya alive after his disappearance, but a check of the sequence of events showed this to be a lie, as Montoya was already buried at the time Puente claimed to have seen him.

The trial continued into March 1993 when former boarder Joyce Peterson testified that after her eviction, Puente pushed her down a flight of stairs when she returned for her belongings and her welfare check. Another ex-boarder, Robert S. French, said that during the winter of 1988 he witnessed Puente lifting 95-pound sacks of concrete in the front yard to move them to shelter. Puente had claimed to detectives that she had a bad heart and could not lift heavy objects, and thefore "couldn't drag a body anyplace."

One of the most gruesome pieces of testimony came from Dr. Gary A. Stuart, a pathologist who examined the remains of victim Dorothy Miller shortly after her exhumation from Puente's yard. Dr. Stuart stated that Miller's body was bound with duct tape and twine, swathed all over with plastic, then wrapped in three layers of fabric. He offered no speculation as to why the body was treated this way, but could not, under cross-examination, rule out the defense contention of death by natural causes.

By April Fools' Day, Social Security records were subpoenaed for use at the trial. These showed that Puente, under her maiden name of Dorothea H. Montalvo, had been diagnosed as schizophrenic in 1978 and approved for disability benefits. She received benefits until the time of her arrest for murder—even during the years 1982–1985, when she was imprisoned after pleading Guilty to forgery, grand theft, and administering stupefying drugs.

By the time the case went to the jury in July

1993, 3100 exhibits were amassed, including photographs of the victims' remains, scale models of the boardinghouse and its surrounding neighborhoods, maps, drawings, and graphs. Tesimony and arguments lasted five months. Jury deliberation lasted a state record 24 days over a five-week period, after which Dorothea Puente was convicted of first degree murder in the cases of Dorothy Miller and Benjamin Fink and second-degree murder in the case of 78-year-old Leona Carpenter. The jury was deadlocked on the other six counts. At no time in her marathon trial did Dorothea Puente take the stand in her own defense. She was sent to prison for life.

PURPLE GANG

Detroit was plagued by this vicious gang of murderous thugs during the Prohibition years. Hundreds of killings in Detroit's bootleg wars were attributed to the Purples, who were led by Abe Bernstein. Other notorious members of the gang included Ed Fletcher, George F. Lewis, and the brothers

Purple Gang members Abe Axler and Ed Fletcher were taken for a one-way ride in 1933 when the national syndicate took over Detroit. (UPI)

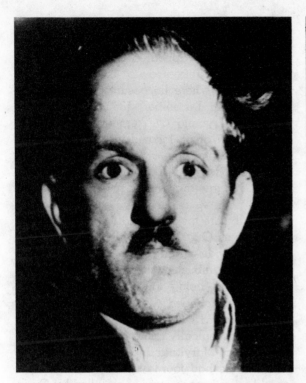

Detroit mobster George F. Lewis, a Purple Gang member, was held for questioning by police in the 1929 St. Valentine's Day Massacre. (UPI)

Harry and Phil Keywell, the latter two suspected of being loaned out to Al Capone as spotters for the hit men who shot down seven of George "Bugs" Moran's gangsters in the St. Valentine's Day Massacre.

The Purples concentrated on bootlegging, hijacking, jewelry thefts, and widespread extortion. The proximity of Detroit to Canada placed the Purple Gang in a strategic position to supply Chicago gangs with Canadian liquor. Capone became the chief importer of Purple Gang whiskey, which was shipped to him under the label "Log Cabin."

Though the gang exported booze and killers to other towns, Bernstein and his lieutenants found it necessary to bring safecracking specialists like Morris "Red" Rudensky to Detroit for important jewelry thefts. Rudensky was paid a straight fee for the jobs he pulled, all marked in advance by the Purples. His fees ran from $5,000 to $15,000. The gang also marked and cased several out-of-town "jugs" and "cribs" (safes) to be broken into by Rudensky and his safecracking partners, Smitty Krueger and "Dago" Vanelli, such as the $1,500,000 jewelry theft in St. Louis in the 1920s.

Later, Bernstein and other Purple Gang members became partners in several Miami gambling casinos with Meyer Lansky and Joe Adonis. When the national crime syndicate was formed by Luciano, Lansky, Lepke, and others in 1934, the Purple Gang was systematically incorporated into the new crime cartel.

[ALSO SEE St. Valentine's Day Massacre.]

PURRINTON, JAMES
Murderer ● (? -1806)

Purrinton was a retired army captain who suddenly went berserk on the night of July 8, 1806, and slaughtered his entire family—his wife and seven children. He had been meditating and reading his Bible, which was allegedly found open to a passage by Ezekiel: "Slay utterly old and young, both maids and children."

The mass murderer then slit his own throat, thus saving Maine authorities the expense of a trial.

QUANTRILL, WILLIAM CLARKE
Murderer, Outlaw ● (1837-1865)

BACKGROUND: BORN IN CANAL DOVER, OHIO, 1837. MOVED TO THE UTAH TERRITORY IN 1857 AND THEN TO KANSAS IN 1859. ORIGINAL OCCUPATION, TEACHER. DESCRIPTION: 5'9", BROWN EYES, BLACK HAIR, SLENDER. ALIASES: CHARLES (OR CHARLEY) QUANTRILL, CHARLES HART. RECORD: WANTED BY AUTHORITIES IN KANSAS IN 1859 FOR HORSE STEALING AND MURDERING SEVERAL PROSLAVERY FARMERS, ALSO NAMED AS A SLAVE STEALER; JOINED CHEROKEE INDIANS AS A RENEGADE AND HELPED TO ATTACK AND KILL REGULAR U.S. ARMY TROOPS AT WILSON'S CREEK IN 1861; ORGANIZED GUERRILLA BAND TO FIGHT UNION FORCES OSTENSIBLY UNDER CONFEDERATE BANNER IN DECEMBER, 1861; BURNED AND LOOTED THE TOWN OF OLATHE, KAN., 9/6/62; RAIDED LAWRENCE, KAN., 8/21/63 WITH 450 MEN WHEREIN HE ORDERED THE MURDER OF MORE THAN 150 DEFENSELESS MEN AND BOYS, BURNED AND LOOTED THE TOWN; LOOTED A WAGON TRAIN NEAR BAXTER SPRINGS, TEX., IN OCTOBER, 1863; KILLED IN EARLY MAY, 1865, IN KENTUCKY IN A FIGHT WITH UNION TROOPS.

Quantrill left his quiet home in Ohio when he was about twenty and journeyed west. His education was better than most youths his age, and he sometimes taught Bible school. Life in rural Ohio, however, was not for him. He longed for adventure and traveled as far as Utah in 1857, where he stole horses to earn a living. He moved back to Kansas two years later and, posing as an antislavery Jayhawker, raided several farms, claiming he wanted to free slaves. The slaves taken into his custody from such raids (along with considerable livestock) were resold to other slaveholders.

When the law appeared to be closing in on Quantrill, he retreated to the refuge of a schoolhouse, where he assumed the duties of a teacher. In December, 1860, Quantrill persuaded five young Quakers to raid the farm of Morgan Walker, located in Jackson County, Missouri, telling the ardent abolitionists that their goal was to free the slaves Morgan owned. His true aim was to resell the slaves at a good price elsewhere.

Hours before the raid, and for reasons never made clear, Quantrill informed slave owners of the impending raid. He then led the Quakers into an ambush which resulted in three of their number being killed. When the slaveholders surrounded Quantrill, he calmly leaned forward on his saddle and, as torches flickered, prosaically told his wary captors that he was from Maryland and was proslavery. He said that he had journeyed to California with an older brother who had been killed by Quakers; he himself had been left for dead. "I have spent my days trailing my brother's murderers," he lied, "and the three dead men you see before you were part of that band."

He was not only believed but became an immediate folk hero to the slave traders. His reputation was such that at the time the Civil War broke out, Quantrill had no trouble in enlisting several men to his pro-Confederate guerrilla banner. These included such arch-murderers as William "Bloody Bill" Anderson, George Todd, and Fletcher Taylor. Coleman Younger and Frank James also joined him. Jesse James, who was too young to enlist at the war's beginning, joined Quantrill's group in 1864.

Quantrill's aim was anything but serving the Confederacy. He busied himself during the war with murder, arson, and robbery, all performed under the guise of fighting for the South. With Todd, William Haller, and William H. Gregg as his lieutenants, Quantrill led his first bloody raid against Olathe, Kansas, which he burned to the ground after carting away gold, cash, and jewelry. A dozen unarmed men were shot to death at his command.

Elected captain by his men, Quantrill never officially existed as an officer in the Confederate Army, though he did journey to Richmond once to seek an appointment with President

Jefferson Davis. Later, in 1864, when regular Confederate officers in Texas challenged his authority, he produced a commission signed by President Davis.

With a band of 450 men, Quantrill set out for Lawrence, Kansas, in August, 1863. Lawrence was a peaceful farming community and the home of James Lane, the notorious Jayhawker and senator. Quantrill had encouraged his men to kill without mercy in this raid to teach Lane a lesson (ever the teacher) and promised his followers that the old Jayhawker would be returned to Missouri and publicly executed by being burned at the stake.

As Quantrill's men moved through Kansas, they ordered residents at gunpoint to lead them through unknown territory and around Union Army camps. These guides were summarily killed once they had performed such duties. The raiders reached Lawrence on August 21, 1863.

Swooping into town, Quantrill and his men found no garrison to oppose them. They searched frantically for Lane, but he had heard their rebel yell and had escaped by running in his nightshirt into a cornfield, where he hid during the massacre.

Men such as Bill Anderson and John McCorkle were particularly bloodthirsty, seeking revenge for the deaths of their sisters. The sisters of both men, along with dozens of other wives, mothers, and daughters of Confederate sympathizers, had been rounded up by Union General Thomas C. Ewing and confined in a three-story building in Kansas City weeks earlier. The top floor, where the women were imprisoned, collapsed, and many of the women were crushed to death, among them Matilda Anderson and Christie McCorkle Kerr.

These and other grievances, real or imagined, spurred Quantrill and his men to mass slaughter. More than 150 men and boys were rounded up in Lawrence. Their hands were tied behind their backs, and then their wives and daughters were made to watch as they were shot to death. The killing went on for two hours and became the worst massacre of the Civil War. William Clarke Quantrill rode among the bodies of the slain, ordering men to shoot those who appeared to be still alive. He then ordered the burning and looting of the town. Several hours later, his band of men, half-drunk in Lawrence's saloons (these were not put to the torch), received word that

Civil War raider William Clarke Quantrill slaughtered 150 helpless men and boys at Lawrence, Kan., 8/21/63. (State Historical Society of Missouri)

Union troops were approaching. Quantrill and his guerrillas rode hurriedly from the smoldering ruins, leaving only one man behind. He was hopelessly drunk and was promptly lynched by the enraged citizenry once the raiders were out of sight.

Lawrence proved to be Quantrill's high point. From Kansas he rode to Texas, where he attacked several defenseless wagon trains and murdered dozens of travelers, robbing them of their goods. He became an anathema to the Confederacy and was shunned by regular Southern officers. With a slowly diminishing band of men, he first made his way back to Missouri for a few skirmishes with Union troops and then moved to Kentucky with a band of about twenty men. Quantrill's plan was to surrender to Union troops there. Knowing the war was coming to an end, he intended to pass himself and his men off as regular Confederate troops, receive a legal pardon, and avoid the certainty of hanging if he capitulated in Missouri or Kansas.

The plan failed. Union troops under the command of Captain Edward Terrill intercepted Quantrill and his men and destroyed them in early May, 1865. William Clarke Quantrill was found dead on the field with a bullet in his back, shot while running away.

[ALSO SEE "Bloody Bill" Anderson, Jesse James.]

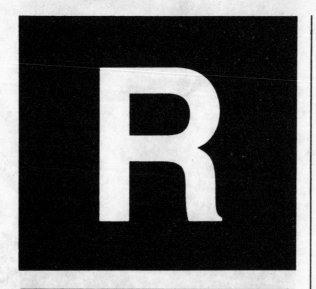

RAGEN'S COLTS

Led by Frank Ragen and originally called Ragen's Athletic and Benevolent Association, a fraternal organization on Chicago's South Side existing in the 1890s, the Colts turned to criminal pursuits at the beginning of the nineteenth century. The gang, which grew to a small army before the First World War (the Colts' motto was "Hit me and you hit 2,000"), specialized in political sluggings, kidnapping, assault, and murder for profit.

Noted Chicago criminals who began with the Colts included Ralph Sheldon, who would later form his own Prohibition era gang and work under Capone's direction; Joseph "Dynamite" Brooks, a dive-keeper who reportedly killed a dozen men; arch-murderer William "Gunner" McPadden; political fixer and poll-booth destroyer Harry Madigan; and gunmen Hugh "Stubby" McGovern, Danny McFall, and Davy "Yiddles" Miller.

The Colts, a violently redneck organization, was largely responsible for the deadly Chicago race riots of 1919 in which more than five hundred were injured and thirty-five killed.

Ragen's Colts faded and then disappeared during the 1920s and the rise of Al Capone.

RAMIREZ, RICHARD (THE NIGHT STALKER)
Serial Killer ● (1960-   )

From June 1984 to August 1985, Richard Ramirez, a vagrant from El Paso, Texas, terrorized middle-class Los Angeles. He entered homes in the middle of the night (thus earning the name "Night Stalker") to shoot or strangle the males present so he could rape and murder females and children.

One of Ramirez's favorite acts of sadism was to kidnap a child from a home he had just robbed, and in which he had killed all the occupants, and let the dazed child loose some distance away to wander back with tales of terror. Bloated with arrogance and self-confidence, Ramirez finally slipped and left his fingerprints on the wheel of a getaway car. The FBI matched the prints to his record and soon every newspaper in the country was running his photo.

In August 1985, Ramirez was seen in several shopping plazas but most of these sightings turned out to be false reports. He did, however go to one shopping plaza and attempt to yank a woman from her car. Her husband arrived, however, and began bashing Ramirez. A large crowd collected, identifying the wanted killer. The crowd pressed forward and Ramirez was punched and kicked into a bloody heap. Police took him away in a half-conscious state.

At his trial, the killer (he may have murdered as many as 25 persons) played to the press. He flashed the palm of his hand where he had drawn a livid sign of the pentagram. On other occasions, as he sat listening to the prosecutors condemn him for his crimes, he placed two upturned fingers on either side of his temples to indicate horns and intoned: "Evil . . . Evil . . . Evil . . ."

Ramirez was convicted of twelve separate counts of first-degree murder, one second-degree murder count and 30 other offenses ranging from burglary to rape. When hearing his conviction, the killer sneered his disdain to the jury, shouting. "You maggots make me sick. I will be avenged! Lucifer dwells within all of us!"

When he was later brought back into court to hear his death sentence, Ramirez was flippant, saying. "Big deal . . . , Death comes with the territory . . . , See you in Disneyland."

RAY, JAMES EARL
Assassin ● (1928-   )

Assassin James Earl Ray shown in various police photos

Martin Luther King had learned to live with fear. The great civil-rights leader had been threatened dozens of times. His home had been bombed. Months before his assassination, Dr. King stated: "Maybe I've got the advantage over most people. I have conquered the fear of death."

His methodical killer, James Earl Ray, had also conquered. From an inept and desultory crook, he suddenly became a highly professional assassin who knew exactly where Dr. King could be found in Memphis, Tennessee, on the night of April 4, 1968, when he sent a single and fatal bullet into him from a little more than two hundred feet away.

Ray's background possessed no suggestion of such a political-racist assassination. He had been a cheap crook since his twenty-first birthday, holding up gas stations and stores. In a 1952 robbery attempt he dropped his wallet, which led to his identification. In another robbery in 1959 he plummeted clownishly into the arms of the law after falling out of his escape car. He served time in the Illinois State Prison at Joliet and the Miami prison, and was sentenced to two terms to the Missouri State prison, from which he escaped on April 23, 1967.

That Ray would even consider killing a man like Dr. King is a grim riddle to most, a criminal acrostic that might be explained by the fact that every crime Ray ever committed was for money, not for political convictions. His convictions concerning civil rights, if any, were never made public. Many suspect that Ray was paid to execute Dr. King, but supportive evidence for this speculation was never provided.

Employing the aliases of Eric Starvo Galt and John Willard, Ray rented several rooms in the Memphis area, one of which was directly across from the motel where Dr. King was staying. Standing at a bathroom window on the evening of April 4, 1968, Ray had a clear shot at the civil-rights leader as he emerged from his second-floor room and stood talking to friends on a balcony. Ray raised his 30.06

Ray during his unsuccessful career as a robber. (UPI)

Remington pump rifle, sighting through a pair of binoculars, and squeezed the trigger only once. The shot hit Dr. King in the neck, passed through his lower jaw, and severed his spinal column, the explosion hurling him against a wall. He died without speaking an hour later in St. Joseph's Hospital.

The moment after firing his weapon, Ray coolly left his possessions in the room and drove out of Memphis, crossing into Canada three days later. He stayed in Toronto for a month, and then, using a Canadian passport for which he had paid $8, Ray, under the alias Sneyd, departed for London, England, on May 6, 1968. He was obviously well-fixed, and the existence of a cabal was not impossible; he received phone calls at his room from unknown persons before leaving Canada.

After spending six days in London, Ray flew to Lisbon. He spent five days in the Hotel Portugal and then returned to London. The Lisbon trip was never explained (like so many bewildering aspects of this assassination). Some reports have advanced the theory that Ray went to Lisbon to receive money for killing Dr. King.

In London, Ray moved erratically from one

hotel to another, first to New Earl's Court, then to the Pax. The FBI had quickly established his identity and had, on April 20, placed his name on their "ten most-wanted fugitives" list. In early June, 1968, Ray called several London newspapers, inquiring how one might go about enlisting in mercenary forces in Africa. Days later, on June 8, London police closed in on him and put him under arrest. On that day, Ray was about to fly to Brussels and was picked up at Heathrow Airport just as he was boarding a plane.

The following events were anticlimactic and confusing. Ray, scheduled to stand trial in Memphis on March 11, 1969, abruptly pleaded guilty after being extradited from England. He was sentenced to ninety-nine years in prison. A two-hour hearing decided his fate.

Months later, Ray recanted his confession and insisted on dropping Percy Forman, his lawyer. His new legal counsel, according to one report, was connected with the Ku Klux Klan. There the matter stands. Ray is serving his sentence, Dr. King has been in his grave for twenty-three years, and no one has yet adequately explained how the murderer was able to finance his expensive assassination and escape, let alone provide a reason for the killing.

Shrouded in mystery, the King case deserves a full-scale investigation, one that might find acute similarities between James Earl Ray and that arcane brigand John Surratt (see John Wilkes Booth), who helped to mastermind the assassination of President Lincoln and escaped the country and eventual punishment through the aid of what could best be described as men in high places.

The assasination of Martin Luther King was never fully solved with the conviction and imprisonment of James Earl Ray. There is little doubt that Ray was King's killer but serious doubts still exist as to who financed the impoverished Ray in his costly flight to escape justice.

RAYNOR, WILLIAM P.
Gunfighter ● (? -1885)

El Paso, in its wildest days, was the scene of more than one mass shoot-out. In the spring of 1885 two gunfighters met their death there over imagined insults and through unprofessional carelessness. Famed lawman Wyatt Earp was a witness to the whole affair without ever drawing a pistol.

Bill Raynor, called "the best-dressed bad man in Texas," was spoiling for a fight on the night of April 14, 1885, as he sat playing faro in the notorious Gem Saloon, site of dozens of gunfights and killings.

Faro dealer Bob Cahill made an odd movement with his hands to which Raynor called attention, stating that Cahill was "a bit too fancy." Cahill said nothing, obviously frightened of the older man, who had been involved in several shootings and was known as a fast-draw artist. Raynor pushed away from the table and joined his friend Charlie "Buck" Linn. Both men had been law-enforcement officers at one time or another—Raynor had been an El Paso constable and Linn was presently a city jailer who was thought to be "crazy" when drunk. The two proceeded to get drunk.

Wyatt Earp, who was visiting a friend in the town, was standing at the bar, quietly drinking. Raynor moved toward him and mildly insulted the lawman. Earp looked at Raynor and said: "I'm not armed." The marshal brushed back his long coat to reveal no pistol at his side. Earp pointed out that he wanted no part of a man who was obviously "glory-hunting."

Raynor then turned his attention to "Cowboy" Bob Rennick, who was playing faro with Cahill. Raynor made several caustic remarks about Rennick's white cowboy hat. Rennick said nothing except to point out that he, too, was unarmed. With a snort of disgust, Raynor moved into the billiard room of the Gem Saloon. Rennick took several drinks and then growled, "I've been imposed upon enough and won't stand for it." He took a pistol from Cahill. Raynor, sitting in a position in the billiard room where he had a full view of Rennick's actions, came running into the saloon with his guns drawn. He fired five or six shots at Rennick, who calmly knelt down and shot twice. Both bullets hit Raynor, one in the shoulder and another in the stomach.

The gunfighter, moaning as he moved, staggered outside past the stoic Earp and managed to stumble aboard a passing horse-drawn streetcar. Collapsing on a seat, he shouted to the driver to tell his mother that he "died game." He was taken to a doctor.

Raynor's friend Linn, who had been drinking in another saloon, then raced into the Gem thinking Cahill had shot his drinking companion. The youthful faro dealer had been warned that Linn was on the prod for him. Before Linn burst through the Gem's swinging doors, Earp gave Cahill a quick lesson in gunfighting.

"He'll come shooting," Earp told him. "Have your gun cocked but don't pull until you're certain what you're shooting at. Aim for his belly, low. The gun'll throw up a bit, but if you hold it tight and wait until he's close enough, you can't miss. Keep cool and take your time."

Cahill had the drop on Linn when the latter burst into the saloon. The faro dealer asked Linn to drop his weapon, which he refused to do. Then both men began firing, until Linn fell to the floor with a bullet in his heart.

Gunfighter Bill Raynor, though mortally wounded, lingered near death for hours. Talk in the Gem Saloon had it that when he recovered, Raynor would kill Cahill and Rennick. Both men rode into Mexico to hide. A courageous drunk at the bar suddenly shouted, "Bill ought to have been killed years ago. I'm damned glad he got it." No one at the bar said a word. The drunk quickly sobered at the sound of his own words, placed his drink on the bar, and moved toward the door. He turned and thoughtfully remarked: "If Bill gets well, what I said don't go."

Raynor died an hour later, much to the relief of El Paso's citizens.

REAVIS, JAMES ADDISON
Swindler, Forger ● (? -1908)

BACKGROUND: BORN IN RURAL GEORGIA. DATE UNKNOWN. MINOR PUBLIC EDUCATION. MARRIED "SOFIA LORETA MICAELA," CIRCA 1882; DIVORCED IN THE LATE 1900S. ORIGINAL OCCUPATION, STREETCAR CONDUCTOR. DESCRIPTION: TALL, SLENDER, BEARDED. ALIASES: BARON DE ARIZONAC, CABALLERO DE LOS COLORADOS. RECORD: FORGED PROPERTY TITLES IN ST. LOUIS IN THE LATE 1860S TO EARN COMMISSIONS; FROM 1868 TO 1870 FORGED DOCUMENTS, CHARTERS, AND LAND GRANTS ALLEGING THAT HUNDREDS OF MILES OF TERRITORY IN THE STATE OF ARIZONA WERE DEEDED TO ONE MIGUEL DE PERALTA, A HISTORICAL PERSONAGE OF HIS OWN INVENTION; POISONED DR. GEORGE WILLING IN PRESCOTT AND SUBSEQUENTLY LAID CLAIM TO THE "PERALTA LANDS"—10,800,000 ACRES IN ARIZONA WHICH HE STATED HE HAD PURCHASED FOR $30,000 FROM WILLING, WHO HAD PURCHASED THE RIGHTS OF THESE LANDS FROM A PERALTA DESCENDANT FOR $1,000; BEGAN TO COLLECT HUGE SUMS FROM RAILROADS AND MINING FIRMS INSIDE THE AREA OF HIS "BARONY"—SOME REPORTS FIXED AMOUNTS AS HIGH AS $300,000 ANNUALLY FOR A DECADE; EXPOSED AND TRIED IN 1895; CONVICTED AND SENTENCED TO SIX YEARS IN THE STATE PENITENTIARY FOR FORGERY AND FRAUD; DIED IN 1908 OF NATURAL CAUSES.

Of all the swindles ever perpetrated in the United States, none was so painstakingly pieced together over such a long period of time as the one concocted by master forger James Addison Reavis. Where most swindlers are content to bilk money from their victims, Reavis laid claim, through delicately forged documents, to a tract of land half the size of the state of Wisconsin and for a decade exacted staggering tribute while frenzied experts and exasperated courts attempted to prove him a fraud. His swindle was in the grand design, and its success was achieved by sheer gall, superb acting, and obdurate patience.

Little is known about Reavis' background. He first appeared on the muster rolls of the Confederate Army during the Civil War, a lowly private with good manners and a penchant for escaping duty. It was at this time that Reavis discovered his ability to forge signatures. He carefully copied the signature of his commanding officer on a pass, and it was accepted by sentries guarding the post. Employing this peculiar talent regularly enabled Reavis to miss most of the war.

About a year after the war ended, Reavis was in St. Louis working as a streetcar conductor. Times were hard, but through his considerable skill as a salesman, Reavis managed to quit the horse-drawn trolley and open a small real-estate business. The few customers who did patronize broker Reavis were not particular how he settled their affairs.

One man stated that there was some question about his ownership of a considerable piece of property. He offered Reavis a hefty commission if he could manage to obtain a quitclaim on the land. The clever forger produced a document of ownership so authentic-looking that it was accepted in court and filed. Reavis got his commission and a new vocation in life. He went on to doctor records and create deeds so quickly that he aroused the suspicion of authorities. To avoid arrest, Reavis closed his handsome bank account and moved West.

A high liver, he was broke by the time he reached Santa Fe. There he applied for a clerical job in the records division of a special commission to handle Spanish and Mexican claims on lands annexed by the United States following the Mexican War. This country had agreed by treaty to honor all legitimate claims and turn back the proper lands to true owners. It was in Santa Fe that Reavis developed the most intricate swindle in American crime.

Essentially, Reavis began to forge ancient Mexican and Spanish documents, creating out of nothing a Spanish nobleman named Miguel de Peralta. In his unique clerical position he was privy to the types of documents and scrolls produced by monks and Spanish padres who had laboriously penned out land grants, marriage certificates, and family histories of Spanish royalty hundreds of years in the past.

Reavis studied the delicate paper and parchment employed in such documentation. He experimented with inks and even whittled quills modeled after those used by royal Spanish historians.

Reavis' fictional Spanish don was related to King Ferdinand. The master forger's vivid imagination portrayed Peralta as a grandee of Spain, a knight heaped with regal honors and possessing an ancestry resplendent with princely titles, enormous wealth, and a very distant strain of the blood royal.

Obsessed with his intricate swindle, Reavis spent years manufacturing documents to prove the existence of the Peraltas; he also created whole families who had descended from the Peraltas. He then prepared the most significant documents involved in his stupendous swindle, those giving the descendants of Peralta a vast tract of land in Arizona, more than ten million acres, which had once been within the province of Spain.

About 1870 the myriad travels of James Addison Reavis become virtually impossible to trace, though it is known that he journeyed to Guadalajara, Mexico City, Lisbon, Madrid, and Seville. How he financed such expensive travel for a period of seven or eight years is unknown, but he did arrive in the ancient capitals of Europe, and there, quietly and stealthily, he lodged his forged documents concerning the Peralta family in archives, libraries, and monasteries where such state papers were zealously preserved and guarded.

Sometime in the late 1870s, Reavis appeared in Prescott, Arizona. There he met and most likely murdered a Dr. George Willing by giving him poison. Willing was another unwitting accomplice to Reavis' grand scheme. Reavis would later claim that Willing, for a mere $1,000, had purchased rights to a vast section of land from Miguel Peralta (whose history was also linked to the original Peraltas by fake documents), a direct descendant of the Spanish nobleman. Reavis then bought the rights to the grant from Willing and his heirs for approximately $30,000. He had the forged documents, of course, to prove it.

In 1881 Reavis filed his claim with the Surveyor General of the United States. His petition was backed up with certified copies of his falsified documents. He then appeared in Phoenix, which was within his claimed realm— as were the cities of Tempe, Silver King, Pinal, Florence, Globe, and Casa Grande—posting notices and demanding taxes and tribute of those living on his land. He also sent word to the powerful Southern Pacific Railroad and the equally commanding Silver King Mine that his rights had been trespassed and that his gold and silver had been mined illegally.

The best legal minds in the country went to work on Reavis' carefully manufactured documents and, after minute inspection, woefully conceded that the "Red Baron of Arizona," as Reavis came to be called, was the real owner of the finest lands in the state.

Reavis' ten years of acicular forgery and secret travels finally paid off. The Southern Pacific gave him $50,000 as a down payment for the right of way along its rail lines; the Silver King Mine paid him $25,000 to continue mining Reavis-owned ore. Thousands of Arizona settlers, ranchers, and businessmen were thrown into a frenzy. Reavis levied claims against their lands and properties, and they were forced to pay.

James Addison Reavis became wealthy overnight, his barony in Arizona yielding hundreds of thousands of dollars each month. Worried that the government would send experts throughout the world to analyze the specious documents he had planted, Reavis found a Mexican waif, sent her to a finishing school, dressed her in jewels and finery, and passed her off as a direct Peralta descendant. He then married his ward and moved into a luxurious hotel in New York, collecting his fabulous rentals all the while.

The marriage produced two sons, twins, who were always attired in princely fashion and escorted by a host of servants wherever they went. And the Reavis family went far and wide, traveling, as would royalty, to Europe where the king of Spain greeted them like long-lost relatives.

For ten volatile years, the Reavis claim withstood all manner of challenges by experts. In 1891, however, Spanish historian and linguist Mallet Prevost followed the trail Reavis had made ten years before and meticulously examined the documents he had planted in monasteries and state libraries. Using special chemicals and a microscope, Prevost found that the first few pages of each document granting lands to the Peraltas were genuine but that succeeding pages were made of parchment much more modern than the documents claimed to be. There was a noticeable difference in ink, too. The genuine script employed by the monks of Spain was written in iron ink, and the doctoring of certain phrases, wherever the name Peralta was mentioned, was penned in dogwood ink.

Reavis was hauled into the Land Grant Court in Santa Fe and exposed as a fraud. He was indicted and tried in 1895 and sentenced to six years in the state penitentiary. Released in 1901, he was a pauper. He had spent his fortune lavishly for a decade, boldly thinking his swindle would never be revealed. His wife had divorced him and gone to live in Denver with her sons, where she disappeared.

Penniless and addle-brained, Reavis spent his remaining years haunting the streets of Santa Fe. A stoop-shouldered man in a threadbare suit, he spent most of his hours reading about his own exploits during his heyday. He was found dead in his shack in 1908.

RED SASH GANG

During the range war between cattlemen and homesteaders, from 1887 to 1892, the Red Sash Gang (so named because of the red sashes they wore) became the most notorious band of rustlers and killers in Wyoming's Powder River territory. The gang was headed at times by gunslinger Frank W. Canton and Major Frank Wolcott. Members preyed on settlers and accounted for a number of murders, the most infamous being the shooting of Nathan Champion and his foreman Nick Rae at the Champion Ranch on April 8, 1892.

Champion and Rae, after barricading themselves in their ranch house, were shot to death by a large party under the command of Wolcott. The house was put to the torch and the two men fled. A gunslinger known as The Texas Kid killed Rae, and Champion was shot down in cold blood by other killers in the raiding party.

The war became so bloody that it reduced the hardened Frank Canton to a nervous

Gunfighter Frank M. Canton, Red Sash Gang member, was driven half mad with the terrors of the Johnson County, Wyo. range war of 1887-92. (Western History Collection, U. of Okla. Library)

wreck. He had nightmares of killings and gun-fights and found it impossible to sleep, often leaping from his hotel bed and screaming so loud that he awakened boarders with: "Can't you hear them, boys? . . . Get to your horses! . . . Get to your guns!"

The U.S. Army arbitrated the dispute under martial law in 1892, until the Johnson County war ended and the Red Sash gang disappeared.

REES, MELVIN DAVID
Murderer ● (1933-1961)

It was a lovely night for a drive. The Army sergeant and his girl, Margaret Harold, had stopped to admire some flowers alongside the road. They were just across the Maryland State line, near Annapolis. It was June 26, 1957, Margaret Harold's last day on earth.

As the two started on their way again, a speeding green Chrysler overtook them and swerved in front. The sergeant pulled over and stopped. The driver of the Chrysler got out and ran over to the sergeant's car.

He was a tall, thin-faced man with long hair. He leered into the window where Margaret Harold sat, and she pulled away nervously.

"What the hell do you want?" the sergeant said, but his words were cut off when he saw the nickel-plated .38 pistol in the man's hand. The man pulled open the back door and climbed in.

The pistol was aimed at the sergeant's head as the man leaned forward and put his long, bony fingers on Margaret's neck. He ran them up into her hair.

It made her shudder, and she groaned in disgust as she pulled away. The thin-faced man twitched in anger and yanked the gun over and fired into the woman's face. She collapsed sideways.

Knowing what was coming next, the sergeant threw open his car door and bolted down the highway, zigzagging and expecting a well-aimed bullet to find his back. It didn't come.

He ran for a mile, until, breathless, he found a farmhouse near Route 450. There he called officials in Annapolis and rattled off his terror-filled story.

When the police arrived, they found Margaret's body just as the killer had left it, with a large bloody hole in the side of her head, her dark hair matted.

A fingerprint-identification squad went over the car from top to bottom and found nothing more than the fingerprints of the sergeant and Miss Harold.

Then police began a thorough search of the area. Nearby, police chief William Wade and Lieutenant Hagner noticed a broken basement window at the side of an unoccupied cinder-block building. They wriggled inside.

The two never expected to witness the scene that awaited them. Covering the basement walls from floor to ceiling was an assembly of pornographic pictures.

As the officers stared bug-eyed at the seemingly endless display, one picture stood out, glaringly different. The picture was that of a very pretty girl fully dressed. It was printed on strange paper.

Wade took the photo from the wall and sent it to Washington for analysis by the FBI labs. The bureau reported that the paper on which the picture was printed was the kind generally used by college yearbooks. FBI agents checked all the colleges in the area around Annapolis and hit pay dirt: the University of Maryland.

The photo was that of Wanda Tipson, a 1955 graduate. When questioned, however, Wanda could provide no clue to the thin-faced man's identity. She had gone on dates with several tall men who had long hair. It was a dead end.

The murder case of Margaret Harold lay dormant for a year and a half. Then the murderer struck again, this time in Virginia.

Carroll Jackson was a big, burly truck driver who stood over six feet tall.

The twenty-nine-year-old Jackson was driving his wife, Mildred, and their two young daughters home after visiting with relatives. Mildred was holding eighteen-month-old Janet while four-year-old Susan sat in the back seat.

In an instant, the bright lights of a car approached from the rear, almost blinding Jackson as he drove along the dirt road. The driver behind Jackson kept his high beam on the car and tailgated.

When Jackson slowed down, so did the other car. After several miles, Jackson pushed the rear-view mirror aside so he could see. Then the car following him shot forward and came alongside, keeping pace with him.

Jackson thought he was dealing with some sort of lunatic, and in order to protect his family, he slowed down to a crawl. The driver of the car roared forward, only to swerve in front of Jackson, forcing him to halt.

Now Carroll Jackson was burning mad. He was going to give the driver a piece of his mind and maybe more if he asked for it. When the tall, thin-faced man came running, long hair waving in the wind, Jackson froze as he got out of his car.

There was a nickel-plated revolver in the man's hand. He waved Jackson back, and the big man took a few steps away from his car.

Then the gunman looked in the car at Mildred Jackson and the two girls, a long, hard look.

"Everybody outside," the gunman ordered. "And turn out those headlights."

Mildred, carrying the baby, helped her little daughter from the back seat. They walked over to Jackson.

"If you want my money . . ."

The man waved the gun menacingly. "Shut up. All of you come on over and get in my car."

Jackson kept looking at the gun, waiting for a chance. There was none, so the family obeyed. The gunman took Jackson's necktie off and tied his hands with it. Then he forced the entire family into the trunk of his car and sped off down the lonely Virginia road.

Carroll Jackson's abandoned car was spotted the next day by Mrs. H. M. Ballard, a worried relative who lived near the Jackson home. She called Sheriff Willis E. Proffitt, who immediately investigated and found the keys still in Jackson's car. Mrs. Jackson's purse and the children's dolls were also in the car.

That, coupled with the skid marks directly in front of the car, meant only one thing to the sheriff—the Jacksons had been forced from their car in a hurry by somebody who was armed.

The local police, county officers, and the FBI came up with nothing. Then, almost two months later, on March 4, James Beach and John Scott got their car stuck in a muddy stretch of road outside of Fredericksburg, Virginia.

When Beach went along the roadway looking for brush to use as traction, he found a man's legs sticking out from the underbrush. It was Carroll Jackson.

When police arrived, they looked over the corpse and discovered a bullet hole in the skull. Even more sinister, the murderer had suffocated eighteen-month-old Janet by placing her under her father's dead body.

Not long after this discovery, two boys playing near the cinder-block house close to where Margaret Harold had been shot to death uncovered a sight of horror.

Digging at what they thought was a gopher hole, the boys swept dirt away from a small mound of earth to see the golden hair of a little girl. Frightened, they ran to get police.

Once again, Chief Wade and Lieutenant Hagner investigated and found Mildred Jackson and her four-year-old daughter Susan under shallow heaps of earth. Susan had died from a fractured skull caused by a blow to the head.

Mildred Jackson had met death either by a beating or by strangulation. The coroner reported that she had been repeatedly raped before she was killed, the sexual assault being one of the most brutal he had ever investigated.

The rape was supported by the fact that Wade found a red button in the cinder-block shack which matched those of Mildred Jackson's dress, proving that the depraved murderer had dragged her into his smut-lined chamber.

Lieutenant Hagner was quoted as saying, "That stocking around Mrs. Jackson's neck, loose as it was, indicates to me that the murderer used it to force her to do something she didn't want to, rather than as a means of slaying her."

Police now knew that the killer of the Jackson family and Margaret Harold were one and the same. The close proximity and description of the killer in both instances fit. The manhunt was on.

Publicity was intense, and this brought several letters from people describing a weird-acting man driving a "blue or green" Ford. One letter coming from a man in Norfolk, Virginia, was the bombshell.

This letter writer accused a young musician

Mass murderer Melvin David Rees posed for this photo with dancer Mrs. Patricia Routt, only days before his capture by the FBI. (Wide World Photos)

named Melvin David Rees of the murders of Margaret Harold and the Jackson family. The writer, a salesman, said that he was a friend of Rees' and that they were together during the Harold slaying. He said that Rees was "hopped-up" on Benzedrine at the time and was acting wild.

The letter writer went on to state that he had asked Rees to his face if he had killed the Jackson family. Rees, instead of denying it, merely evaded the question.

In his letter, Rees' friend described the musician as being tall and thin-faced and having long dark hair and bushy eyebrows.

Local police and the FBI checked out Rees' background, and the puzzle seemed to fit together. In 1953 Melvin David Rees had attended the University of Maryland—which would explain how he had gotten his hands on coed Wanda Tipson's picture and plastered it onto the wall of his shack near Annapolis.

Further checking revealed that Rees had been picked up on March 12, 1955, after being charged with assaulting a thirty-six-year-old woman by pulling her into his car when she refused to ride with him. Unfortunately, she had dropped the charges against him.

The FBI spread out its dragnet. Still, they came up with nothing. Finally, the musician's salesman friend got a letter from him post-

marked West Memphis, Arkansas. FBI men rushed to the area and located Rees in a music store where he was employed as a piano salesman.

"Mr. Rees?" an agent asked.

The tall, thin-faced man with the long hair nodded quietly.

"You are under arrest for flight to avoid prosecution for the murder of Margaret Harold."

Though Rees screamed he was innocent, the Army sergeant who had seen him kill his girl picked him out of a police line-up the same day.

More FBI agents went to the home of Rees' parents near Washington with a search warrant. Going through two floors of the home, they found nothing. Finally, in the attic, their search was rewarded. They found a nickel-plated .38 pistol in a saxophone case. With it were numerous notes written by Rees which described in detail his demented, brutal crimes against women.

Clipped to a newspaper photo of Mildred Jackson was a note containing the following words, which damned him: "Caught on a lonely road . . . after pulling them over, leveled pistol and ordered them out and into car trunk which was opened by husband and both bound.

"Drove to select area and killed husband and baby. Now the mother and daughter were all mine." Rees then described in his twisted memoirs the abnormal sex act he had compelled Mrs. Jackson to perform with him. He described this disgusting brutality with glee. "I was her master," he concluded.

A postscript to this letter told how Rees, acting as a religious cultist, caused Mildred Jackson's slow, agonizing death—a nightmare of sadism.

Other overwhelming evidence linked the berserk Rees to the slaughterhouse murders of four other females—Marie Shomette, sixteen, and Ann Ryan, fourteen, both killed after being sexually assaulted in College Park near the University of Maryland; and the naked, torn bodies of Mary Elizabeth Fellers, eighteen, and Shelby Jean Venable, sixteen, who were found floating in Maryland rivers.

It was all over for the "Sex Beast." Rees faced trial in Baltimore in 1961 and was condemned to life imprisonment. But the "swinging" musician was not to get off with languishing in a prison cell.

Virginia tried him for the murders of the Jackson family, and he was convicted and sentenced to the fate he had so mercilessly meted out to nine others—death.

John Reno was captured by Pinkerton detectives in front of his own gang. (Pinkerton, Inc.)

RENO BROTHERS

BACKGROUND: BORN AND RAISED IN INDIANA. MINOR PUBLIC EDUCATION. FOUGHT IN THE UNION ARMY DURING THE CIVIL WAR. THE BROTHERS WERE CLINTON, FRANK, JOHN, SIMON, AND WILLIAM. ORIGINAL OCCUPATIONS, FARMERS. DESCRIPTION: ALL TALL AND SWARTHY. ALIASES: TRICK RENO (FRANK RENO), WILK RENO (WILLIAM RENO). RECORD: ORGANIZED CRIMINAL BANDS IN SOUTHERN INDIANA INTO ONE UNIT FOLLOWING THE CIVIL WAR, PREYING UPON FARMERS AND SMALL TOWNS, MURDERING SEVERAL PEOPLE; ROBBED WITH SEVERAL BANDITS THE OHIO AND MISSISSIPPI RAILROAD AT SEYMOUR, IND., 10/6/1866, THE FIRST TRAIN ROBBERY IN THE HISTORY OF THE U.S. ($10,000); ROBBED THE FOLLOWING YEAR THE DAVIESS COUNTY TREASURY IN MISSOURI ($22,000); JOHN RENO CAPTURED SHORTLY THEREAFTER BY PINKERTON DETECTIVES AND SENTENCED TO TWO YEARS IN JAIL; ROBBED THE HARRISON COUNTY BANK IN MAGNOLIA, IOWA, IN 1868 ($14,000); ROBBED THE JEFFERSON, MISSOURI, AND INDIANAPOLIS RAILROAD 5/22/68, WOUNDING AN ENGINEER WHO DIED OF INJURIES RECEIVED IN THIS HOLDUP ON 12/7/68 ($96,000 IN CASH, GOLD, AND GOVERNMENT BONDS); WILLIAM, FRANK, AND SIMON RENO AND CHARLES ANDERSON, A MEMBER OF THE GANG, LYNCHED BY VIGILANTES AT THE NEW ALBANY COUNTY JAIL IN SEYMOUR, IND., 12/11/68.

The Renos, as far as Western outlaws go, didn't last long. They robbed and murdered throughout southern Indiana with sorties into Iowa and Missouri for little better than two years, yet their single strike against the Ohio and Mississippi Railroad on October 6, 1866, marked them for distinction in criminal history. It was the first train robbery in America, an act popularly and mistakenly attributed to Jesse James.

On that night, the brothers and several others in their recently organized band waited for the fast express outside Seymour, Indiana. When the train slowed for a curve, Frank and John Reno flagged it down. A startled messenger was made to open the Adams Express car, and the robbers hauled away $10,000 in gold

and cash. William Reno labored for close to an hour to open the safe, but it was too sturdy for him and he gave up only after cursing, kicking, and emptying his pistol at it.

In the spring of 1867 the brothers rode into Daviess, Missouri, and robbed the county bank of $22,000. Jesse and Frank James would relieve the same bank of considerably less money years later. The Renos then rode home to Indiana with the Pinkertons hot on their trail. The detective agency had been hired to protect Adams Express car shipments.

The brothers weren't hard to find. They operated openly around Seymour and brazenly made the train station their meeting place. There, while the outlaws were gathering one day to plan another strike, Allan Pinkerton and six men swooped down on them and captured John Reno. It was more of a kidnapping; Pinkerton did not wish to take on the entire clan at the time and tricked Reno into getting aboard a departing train before the gang became alerted. The outlaws blinked in surprise and stood empty-handed as the train pulled out of the station with one of their chieftains under arrest.

Incensed, Frank Reno loaded his men onto another train and ordered the engineer to run down the flyer. A frantic chase ensued, but the outlaw train was diverted onto another track at Quincy, Illinois, and Pinkerton successfully delivered Reno to authorities. He was sent to jail for two years.

The loss of one brother did not deter the gang, who struck again in early 1868, robbing the Harrison Bank in Magnolia, Iowa, of $14,000. Pinkerton again pursued them and, with a large posse, surrounded them in their Council Bluffs, Iowa, camp. The bandits were packed into a small jail but escaped en masse on April 1, 1868. One rather capricious member of the gang had painted on the side of the jail before departing the galling words: "APRIL FOOL."

At least two dozen men reportedly participated in the Reno-led raid against the Jefferson, Missouri, and Indianapolis Railroad flyer that was stopped on the night of May 22, 1868, outside Marshfield, Indiana, where a guard was wounded fatally when the outlaws forced the express car door. The amount stolen from the express car was a staggering $96,000 in gold, cash, and government bonds, one of the largest amounts ever taken in a train holdup, far surpassing anything ever stolen by the James gang.

Frank Reno, the acknowledged leader of the gang, was an elementary robber. He reasoned that the previous successes enjoyed by the band in robbing trains around Seymour would continue indefinitely. Pinkerton detectives, who had studied the gang's predictable moves for some time, were of the same mind. They spread the report that $100,000 in gold would be shipped through Seymour. When the outlaws stopped the train and threw open the express car doors, a well-armed posse opened up on them, wounding several men. The bandits fled with the detectives in close pursuit.

Simon and William Reno were taken quickly. Pinkerton operatives tracked Frank Reno and four of his men—Michael Rogers, Miles Ogle, Charles Spencer, and Albert Perkins—to Canada, where they were arrested and returned to Indiana for trial.

Housed in the New Albany County Jail, the Reno brothers and one of their lieutenants,

Frank Reno and his brothers committed the first train robbery in American history. He was later hanged by vigilantes. (Pinkerton, Inc.)

Charlie Anderson, never saw the inside of a courtroom. Vigilantes, angered over the two years of terror and killing the brothers had conducted throughout the area, broke into the jail on the night of December 11, 1868. Sheriff Fullenlove was wounded as he attempted to protect his prisoners.

At gunpoint, two deputies turned over the keys to the cells, and one by one, the Renos were dragged out and hanged from a second-story tier. Frank Reno prayed and begged. He was hanged from the tier and died immediately of a broken neck as his body was hurled over the railing. William Reno reminded the vigilantes that his father's ghost would haunt them. He, too, was hanged and died in seconds.

When Simon Reno's turn came, he put up a bone-crushing fight, swinging as a bludgeon an iron sink he had torn from the wall of his cell in desperation. He knocked several vigilantes senseless, and then, his arms weary, he dropped his makeshift club. He was hanged while cursing his executioners. Charlie Anderson, without a whimper of protest, joined the three swaying corpses moments later.

Seconds after the vigilantes departed, Simon Reno, hanging by his neck, suddenly revived. While prisoners screamed for the wardens to help, he fought frantically with the rope that was slowly choking him to death. For a half hour Simon attempted to grab the rope and pull himself upward overhand, but the feat required superhuman strength and, giant though he was, he had expended his energy in his fight with the vigilantes. The absence of the wounded Fullenlove and his deputies was never explained. They arrived in the cell block about an hour later, and by then Simon Reno, in full view of the prisoners, had slowly strangled to death.

The mass execution ended the gang's power around Seymour. The vigilante committee issued a warning to other outlaws who might be inspired to follow in the footsteps of the Reno brothers. The committee's proclamation read: "Having first lopped off the branches, and finally uprooted the tree of evil which was in our midst, in defiance of us and our laws, we beg to be allowed to rest here, and be not forced again to take the law into our own hands. We are very loth [sic] to shed blood again, and will not do so unless compelled in defense of our lives."

RICCA, PAUL ("THE WAITER")
Syndicate Gangster ● (1897-1972)

BACKGROUND: BORN 11/14/97 IN NAPLES, ITALY, AS FELICE DELUCIA. MINOR PUBLIC EDUCATION. IMMIGRATED TO THE U.S. IN 1920. DESCRIPTION: 5'8", BROWN EYES, WHITE HAIR, HEAVYSET, GLASSES. ALIASES: THE WAITER, ANTHONY DELUCIA, PAUL VIELA, THE PORTER, MOPS, PAUL MAGLIO, PAUL VILLA, PAUL SALVI, PAUL BARSTOW. RECORD: ARRESTED AND CONVICTED OF MURDERING EMILIA PARILLO IN 1917 IN NAPLES; RELEASED AFTER SERVING TWO YEARS IN PRISON; MURDERED WITNESS AGAINST HIM IN THE PARILLO TRIAL, VINCENZO CAPASSO, IN 1919, FLED TO U.S. TO AVOID PROSECUTION; TRIED IN ABSENTIA AND CONVICTED AND SENTENCED TO TWENTY-TWO-YEAR TERM; TRAVELED TO CHICAGO AND BECAME A BODYGUARD FOR AL CAPONE; FIRST ARRESTED IN CHICAGO IN 1927 WITH MORE THAN A DOZEN ARRESTS SINCE THAT TIME, INCLUDING CHARGES OF CONSPIRACY, INCOME-TAX EVASION, EXTORTION AND POSTAL FRAUD, FALSIFYING APPLICATION PAPERS FOR CITIZENSHIP; CONVICTED ALONG WITH PHIL D'ANDREA, LOUIS "LITTLE NEW YORK" CAMPAGNA (ALSO ONE-TIME BODYGUARDS OF CAPONE), CHARLES "CHERRY NOSE" GIOE, RALPH PIERCE, JOHN ROSELLI, AND LOUIS "POTATOES" KAUFMAN OF CONSPIRING TO EXTORT $1 MILLION FROM FILM STUDIOS 20TH-CENTURY FOX, LOEW'S AND WARNER BROS. FROM 1941-42 ON THE TESTIMONY OF INFORMERS WILLIE BIOFF (LATER KILLED) AND GEORGE BROWNE; SENTENCED TO TEN YEARS, SENT TO THE FEDERAL PENITENTIARY AT ATLANTA IN 1943, TRANSFERRED TO LEAVENWORTH, RELEASED IN 1946; ARRESTED ON INCOME-TAX EVASION AND CONSPIRACY TO MAKE FALSE STATEMENTS (ACQUITTED ON THE LATTER CHARGE, CONVICTED OF THE FORMER) IN 1959, SENTENCED TO NINE YEARS IN THE FEDERAL PRISON AT TERRE HAUTE, IND., AND FINED $5,000; RELEASED IN TWENTY-SEVEN MONTHS (ON 10/1/61); DENATURALIZED AND FINED $500 FOR CONTEMPT OF COURT, DEPORTATION ORDERED IN 1959, FREED ON $20,000 BOND PENDING APPEAL, NEVER DEPORTED; DIED 10/11/72 IN CHICAGO OF NATURAL CAUSES.

Mafia chief in Chicago, Paul "The Waiter" Ricca (in hat, eyes closed) stands for a line-up at detective headquarters; next to him is one-time Capone bodyguard, Louis "Little New York" Campagna. (UPI)

After the imprisonment of Al Capone in the early 1930s, Ricca, an escaped murderer from Italy, became a top syndicate leader under the nominal command of Frank "The Enforcer" Nitti. He, Louis "Little New York" Campagna, Tony Accardo, and Phil D'Andrea became the ruling members of the syndicate with the suicide of Nitti in 1943.

Ricca traveled to the West Coast in 1940 and, with a number of other gangsters, attempted to extort an estimated $1 million from several movie studios, using as a lever the syndicate's control of the motion-picture projectionists' union. Ricca and others were arrested and convicted on a charge of extortion and, because of the testimony of informers Willie Bioff and George Browne, were sentenced to ten years in the federal penitentiary at Atlanta. Ricca was later transferred to Leavenworth and then released after serving only three years. A national scandal erupted because of Ricca's ridiculously shortened term, and a Congressional investigation resulted. The probe concluded that Ricca's release had been effected by the syndicate, whose power and influence had reached into the Justice Department and the White House.

The Waiter's name was prominent in early attempts to organize a national syndicate in the late 1920s. Founders Lucky Luciano and Meyer Lansky considered him "the brains" behind the Chicago mob as early as 1929, when the first significant gangster conclave was held in Atlantic City.

The importance of Ricca's position with the Chicago mob by 1930 was illustrated by Nicola "Culicchia" Gentile, who eventually turned informer. Gentile had been elected to a Mafia commission (which also included other Mustache Petes of the Mafia in New York—Peppino Siracusa, Salvatore Mangiaracina, Vincenzo Troia, Toto Lo Verde, and Giuseppe "The Peasant" Traina) created to order Salvatore Maranzano to cease his bloody intra-gang war with Joe the Boss Masseria.

Representatives from every major American city came to the commission and stated which side they supported. Capone was still in power in Chicago, and he chose to back Masseria. He sent Ricca to see Gentile in New York. At that time, Ricca approached Gentile and said: "I have been sent by Al Capone himself to talk exclusively with you. We of Chicago follow attentively the development of the situation and we are sure that all the components of the Commission are working in favor of Maranzano. The only one who is faithful to the mandate among all the representatives is you, for which we invite you to make your voice heard and to set aside the nonsense which does not bring anybody to agreement . . . Either Maranzano decides to receive you or otherwise we authorize you to dissolve the Commission. Maranzano should know of the war we of Chicago will wage, and if it is necessary we will even employ airplanes, because those means are ready and concentrated in a specified place."

Neither the delivering of Capone's threat by Ricca, nor the Mafia commission's order, prevented Maranzano from pursuing his war with Masseria. The fact that Ricca had spoke of bombing Maranzano's forces from the air in December, 1930, gave the Eastern gangsters a nightmarish image of the Chicago mob, one that caused the organizers of the syndicate four years later to deal with the more level-headed Ricca in cementing relationships rather than with Capone's savage killer, Nitti.

At the time the national syndicate was being organized, Meyer Lansky flew to Chicago and held private conferences with Ricca. He was their choice to head up the Chicago faction of the syndicate, Lansky told him. "We'll make you rich," little Meyer stated. "Play the waiting game . . . keep your name out of the newspapers and build your own organization."

Ricca, unknown to his boss, Nitti, flew East several times in 1934 and 1935 and represented Chicago in meetings of the national syndicate; he was the acknowledged leader of the Chicago faction and was elected to the board of directors.

Affiliating himself with strong man Tony Accardo, Ricca took control of the Chicago mob in the late 1940s and held on to it until his death in 1972, except for a brief retirement period in the mid-1960s when federal heat was on him for income-tax evasion and deportation proceedings against him were being inaugurated. His short-lived step-down saw Sam "Momo" Giancana assume leadership duties of the syndicate for a period of about two years, until he was forced to leave the city under government pressure and go into permanent hiding in South America.

Ricca faced deportation from 1959 on, but successfully stalled it. In 1966 his lawyer, Jack Wasserman, flew to Italy and filed a petition in Rome asking the government to declare that Ricca was not a citizen of that country. Months later the Italian government dropped a warrant for Ricca on an old murder charge.

Emilia Parillo, who had dared to ask for the hand of Amelia DeLucia, Ricca's sister, was killed by the Waiter in 1917. Ricca was convicted of the murder and sent to prison for a scant two years. Upon his release he murdered Vincenzo Capasso, a witness against him in the Parillo trial. He then fled Italy. Tried in absentia, Ricca was convicted of killing Capasso and sentenced to twenty-two years in prison, not a day of which did he serve.

The gangster later discouraged Italy from taking him back, should deportation proceedings be successful, by mailing to Italian authorities a great number of newspaper clippings about his nefarious activities and past criminal history in America.

Through clever legal maneuvering, Ricca managed to avoid several convictions for tax evasion through the years. In 1965 he claimed that his stated income of $80,159 for 1963 had been earned from wagers he had made at various racetracks. In court he offered an elaborate chart showing how he had made eighty-six bets on thirty-seven races in which the horse had always come in first.

John J. McDonnell, Assistant U.S. Attorney, shook his head at the display. "It's utterly ridiculous," McDonnell said. "His horses never came in second or third. They always came in first. Isn't that the silliest thing you have ever heard of!"

The jury members, believers in long shots all, acquitted Ricca.

Ricca's death on October 11, 1972, left Tony Accardo, an aging don, as the supreme ruler of Chicago's syndicate. In a rare interview, Accardo lamented: "It ain't like the old days . . . most of the boys are gone. Not much to do anymore . . . I go to dinner at Paul's [Ricca] sometimes." Now, it's dinner for one.

[ALSO SEE Salvatore Maranzano.]

RICHARDSON, LEVI
Gunfighter ● (1851-1879)

The gunfight between Levi Richardson and Cockeyed Frank Loving in Dodge City's Long Branch Saloon was one of passion-struck motives and reached comic proportions before its conclusion. The Wisconsin-born Richardson, who worked in Dodge as a freight handler, had a solid reputation as a feisty gunfighter, having dispatched several men who had mistaken his awkward gestures and clodlike manner for sluggishness and ineptitude with a six-gun. He was fast on the trigger.

Loving was a cool-headed, handsome young gambler of twenty-five who had no gunfights to his credit. The two men had known each other for years, and Richardson had played poker in games where Loving served as the dealer. Then they fell in love with the same girl.

In early March, 1879, Richardson passed Loving on the street. The two men argued about their dance-hall Delilah and Levi hit Loving across the face. Unarmed, Loving stalked off without a word. Richardson told a crony, P. L. Beatty, that the next time he "would shoot the guts out of the cock-eyed son-of-a-bitch anyway."

Blood boiled over between the gunmen on the night of April 5, 1879. Richardson sauntered into the Long Branch at 9 p.m. with his .44 Remington pistol strapped to his side. Although Wyatt Earp, Bat Masterson, and other redoubtable lawmen who kept the peace in Dodge City had banned the wearing of all side arms north of the dividing line, the rule was ignored. Loving, after his first encounter with Richardson, had also gone armed at all times.

Ten feet separated the two as they stood at the bar sipping whiskey and watching each other in the mirror. Richardson mumbled some inaudible words from the corner of his mouth. Loving pushed away from the bar and faced his antagonist. "You damned son-of-a-bitch," Cockeyed Frank said. "If you have anything to say to me, say it to my face."

"I don't believe you will fight," Richardson replied and dropped his hand to his pistol.

"Try me and see," Loving gritted.

They moved away from the bar together, closing in until they were on opposite sides of a stove. Each man jerked out his pistol. For several seconds they dodged back and forth around the stove, neither firing and each man waiting for the other to be off-guard. Richardson then fired a shot which whizzed past Loving's head. The men were so close, according to one report, that "their pistols almost touched each other."

The experienced gunfighter, Richardson, then resorted to fanning his pistol—the sign of an amateur gunman—either in desperation or fear of Loving. After Richardson's fifth shot, Loving jumped on Richardson and emptied his pistol into him, hitting him in the chest. Richardson died almost immediately, and Loving was arrested.

After a brief hearing, the gambler was acquitted on the grounds of self-defense.

ROBINSON, PETER
Murderer ● (1809-1841)

An impoverished farmer, Robinson could discover no way to redeem the mortgage on his home from businesslike Abraham Suydam, president of the Farmers' and Mechanics' Bank of New Brunswick, New Jersey. Being a simple-minded fellow, Robinson concluded that sheer brute force would solve his problem.

The farmer asked Suydam to his house and told him to bring the mortgage, implying that he intended to pay it off. As soon as the bank president arrived, Robinson clubbed him with a mallet and took the mortgage. He then dragged Suydam to his basement where he kept him tied up for three days. On the night of the third day, December 3, 1840, Robinson walked calmly to his cellar, dug a grave while Suydam watched, terrified, and threw the bank president into it. He stepped forward and bashed in his victim's skull with a shovel and then buried the body.

Friends discovered Robinson in possession of the mortgage days later and reported this curious fact to authorities, who knew full well that the farmer had no funds with which to retrieve this document. Robinson was arrested and quickly confessed to the murder (he was compelled to dig up the corpse himself).

Following a speedy trial, Robinson was hanged in New Brunswick on April 16, 1841. Bands played, families picnicked, and colorful bunting adorned the gallows.

ROBINSON, SARAH JANE
Murderer ● (? -1905)

Born in Ireland, Sarah Jane Tennent and her sister Annie immigrated to Boston, Massachusetts, with their parents in the 1860s. Both daughters married, but Sarah, who had wedded a man named Robinson, was widowed in 1882 when her husband was killed by a mysterious illness. Mrs. Robinson, who had borne eight children (five died at childbirth) was awarded a handsome settlement from the family's insurance company, the United Order of Pilgrim Fathers.

Mrs. Robinson's gossiping neighbors found it curious that Mr. Robinson succumbed in the same fashion as the landlord who had leased the building to the family had done several months previously. Poor Mrs. Robinson was to be plagued by untimely deaths in her family during the next few years.

Her sister Annie, married to Prince Arthur Freeman, was the next to go. Suffering from pneumonia, Annie was attentively nursed by her sister Sarah. At first Mrs. Freeman rallied and her health improved, then her condition worsened and she suddenly died. Again, the insurance people paid. Sarah insisted that her widowed brother-in-law, Prince, move into her

Cambridge home with his two children. He did.

A month later, Mr. Freeman died of a strange illness. Then, within two months, Sarah's own children William and Lizzie died; and seven-year-old Thomas Freeman followed them.

The insurance company, which had paid heavily on all these deaths, began a routine and turgid investigation. Months dragged on before an investigator ordered an examination of all of the bodies. They were loaded with arsenic.

Two trials later, Mrs. Robinson was found guilty of murdering her brother-in-law and sentenced to death. She received a commuted sentence, but was never paroled, dying in prison in 1905, a lonely hag of a woman scorned by her fellow prisoners, who deemed themselves above the exploits of a common poisoner who killed her relatives for money.

ROGERS, DAYTON LEROY
Serial Killer ● (1953-   )

Operator of an engine repair shop in Oregon City, Oregon, Dayton Rogers was also a devout Seventh-Day Adventist, or so he appeared. Inside this nineteen-year-old seethed a deep hatred for women that finally exploded in 1972 when he took Melody Dahlman Myers for a ride in the woods around Oregon City.

Rogers had picked up Myers and then abruptly stabbed her in the abdomen. He suddenly rebelled against his own violence and told Myers that he would marry her (even though he had married another girl just six weeks earlier) and take her to a hospital if she would tell everyone that she had fallen on the knife by accident. Myers wisely promised to do as Rogers asked.

When she arrived at the hospital, however, Myers told the truth and Rogers was arrested. He pleaded guilty to second-degree assault and received probation. Next Rogers picked up a woman and took her for a drive. He stripped her and hog-tied her, then played with her feet. Though he threatened to kill her, Rogers released the woman. She went straight to the police. Rogers went to prison for violating his parole.

Upon his release, Rogers pursued his "hobby" with a vengeance. He picked up countless prostitutes, drove them into the woods, and hog-tied them. Then he played with their feet. If they protested or fought against their ropes, Rogers cut them on the feet and breasts. As soon as they became submissive, he was no longer interested in the game.

Seven women fought too hard against Rogers and he killed them, leaving their bodies in the woods. On August 6, 1987, Rogers picked up a Portland prostitute, hog-tying her. He drove her back to town on her promise that she would say nothing. When they approached a Wendy's restaurant, the girl leaped form the pickup truck. Rogers, incensed, pursued her, and stabbed her to death. This time he was identified and was arrested a short time later.

Eleven of the more than fifty prostitutes Rogers had tortured testified in court against him at his trial. Rogers was found guilty of murdering six women by an all-woman jury on May 4, 1989. The jury recommended that Rogers be put to death by lethal injection. He is, at this writing, awaiting execution on Oregon's Death Row.

ROMAINE, HENRY G.
Graverobber ● (? - ?)

When wealthy New York department store owner Alexander T. Stewart died in 1876, leaving an estate of $30 million, great pains were made to protect his remains buried in the venerable churchyard of St. Mark's-in-the-Bouwerie. The Stewart family had been warned that the famous bank robber George Leonidas Leslie might attempt with his gang to dig up the remains of the merchant prince and hold them for ransom.

First, a guard was posted in the churchyard. For months the armed sentry marched back and forth on eerie night duty, but nothing happened. The guard was finally dismissed in early November, 1876. On the morning of November 17, 1876, the church's assistant sexton,

An artist's conception of graverobber "Henry G. Romaine," ransoming the bones of millionaire Alexander T. Stewart in 1877.

Frank Parker, discovered that the marble slab covering the Stewart tomb had been turned over and that the remains of Alexander T. Stewart had been stolen.

In a day where the violation of graves was considered a mortal offense against God and man, the incident caused widespread publicity and public indignation. Stewart's heirs offered $25,000 as a reward for anyone who could recover the remains and capture the ghouls.

The following January, lawyers for the Stewarts received a letter signed by Harry G. Romaine, an obvious alias, stating that he and others in his grave-robbing gang possessed the Stewart bones and demanding a ransom of $200,000 for their return. After much haggling by mail and through intermediaries whispering at secret rendezvous along dark roads, Romaine and his gang accepted $20,000 as payment for the human artifacts.

Romaine and two others met a Stewart relative and turned over to him a sack of bones. As way of proof that the contents were truly the remains of Stewart, the masked Romaine displayed strips of velvet taken from Stewart's coffin plus the silver handles from his specially built casket. The Stewart family took no chances with ghouls in the future, reburying the remains in the basement of the Garden City Cathedral on Long Island. An intricate alarm system of springs and bells was constructed and set up around the Stewart casket, lest anyone dare approach the expensive bones of Alexander T. Stewart in the future.

Romaine, whoever he was, went on to enjoy the fruits of his grim plunder, never being apprehended. Some historians identify him as Traveling Mike Grady, others as the bank robber Leslie.

ROSELLI, JOHN
Syndicate Gangster • (1905-1976)

Born in Esteria, Italy, Roselli immigrated to this country on September 16, 1911, after changing his name from Fillippo Sacco. He was first arrested in 1921 for violation of federal narcotics laws. After posting bail, Roselli fled to the West Coast where he worked for the underworld boss, Jack I. Dragna, who liked to be called "the Al Capone of Los Angeles."

Roselli extorted money from motion-picture studios for years and was finally convicted of this racket in 1944. Though sentenced to ten years in prison, Roselli served only three and was released on parole on August 13, 1947.

With the death of Jack Dragna in 1957, Roselli became the syndicate boss of the West Coast.

[ALSO SEE The Syndicate.]

ROTHSTEIN, ARNOLD
Gambler • (1882-1928)

BACKGROUND: BORN AND RAISED IN NEW YORK, N.Y., THE SON OF A SHOPKEEPER. MINOR PUBLIC EDUCATION. MARRIED, NO CHILDREN. DESCRIPTION: 5'10", BROWN EYES, BROWN HAIR, HEAVYSET. ALIASES: MR. BIG, THE BRAIN, MR. A., A. R., THE MAN TO SEE, THE MAN UPTOWN, THE BIG BANKROLL. RECORD: ARRESTED UNDER SUSPICION OF FENCING THE NOTORIOUS MAIL-BOND-ROBBERY BONDS STOLEN FROM WALL STREET BANKS IN 1918, DISMISSED; ARRESTED IN NEW YORK, JANUARY, 1919, FOR HOLDING AN ILLEGAL CRAP GAME AND WOUNDING TWO CITY DETECTIVES MAKING THE ARREST, DISMISSED; APPEARED BEFORE A CHICAGO GRAND JURY IN 1920 ON SUSPICION OF FIXING BASE-BALL'S 1919 WORLD SERIES, DISMISSED WITHOUT INDICTMENT; FINANCED ILLEGAL SPEAKEASIES THROUGHOUT MANHATTAN AND GANGS LED BY JACK "LEGS" DIAMOND, JACOB "LITTLE AUGIE" ORGEN, AND LARRY FAY WHICH INVADED THE UNIONS THROUGHOUT THE 1920S; SHOT IN A POKER GAME AT THE PARK CENTRAL HOTEL IN NEW YORK 11/4/28, DYING AT POLYCLINIC HOSPITAL WITHOUT NAMING HIS KILLERS.

Arnold Rothstein was Mr. Big for so long that gamblers, murderers, and common prostitutes alike had only to whisper his initials, "A. R.," up and down the Broadway strip for anyone to get the meaning.

And the meaning was always clear. Rothstein, who had been a millionaire gambler in Manhattan for twenty years, could fix anything. A. R. could fix a bet, a night in bed with a Broadway star—or someone's violent death.

Rothstein's criminal gift, and the reason why he remained Mr. Big on Broadway for so long, was that no one could ever prove anything incriminating against him. His hands were always clean, his henchmen took the falls for him. And nobody ever disagreed or talked back to Mr. Big.

But Rothstein began small, as the son of a respected Jewish immigrant merchant. The father was called Rothstein the Just for his high-principled life and business transactions, but Arnie was completely different.

Rothstein began to gamble impulsively as a child. He had a quick mind that could handle numbers like a modern-day computer. All day long he figured odds.

His friend Nicky Arnstein (Jules W. Arndt Stein, who later became Fanny Brice's lover) tossed random numbers to him. Rothstein added, multiplied, or subtracted the lengthy numbers instantly and belched out the correct answer.

"It isn't good for you, A. R.," Nicky said. "It isn't normal and you'll hurt your brain."

"Just exercise," Rothstein replied.

As a teenager, Rothstein gambled his way into a fortune. His nerves and ruthless composure betrayed no emotion whether he was shooting craps in a Manhattan alleyway or drawing three cards at poker. He always won.

He was a close friend of gambler Herman Rosenthal, who was killed by Charles Becker in 1912.

By the time he was twenty, Rothstein was half-owner of a high-toned New York gambling den which sported thick carpets, glass chandeliers, and champagne at every table. Upstairs, Rothstein had a string of sultry, expensive whores for customers wanting more diversion.

His take at such a tender age was more than $10,000 a week. For most, this kind of super-livelihood would have been more than enough. But A. R. was greedy. Money was power in

New York, and power was what Rothstein most lusted after.

He began to steal from his partner by skimming off huge gobs of money from the nightly take. His partner discovered the thefts and told Rothstein to beat it or take a bullet in the head. Rothstein went elsewhere.

Probably the greatest scandal in American sports—the fixing of the 1919 World Series by bribing eight Chicago White Sox players (afterward called "The Black Sox")—was attributed to Rothstein.

The fixing of the 1919 World Series was a bumbling, awkward affair handled by ex-featherweight boxing champion Abe Attell and almost certainly masterminded by his good friend and employer, Arnold Rothstein. Eight players of the winning Chicago White Sox—Eddie Cicotte, "Shoeless" Joe Jackson, Charles "Swede" Risberg, George "Buck" Weaver, Claude Williams, Oscar "Happy" Felsch, Chick Gandil, and Freddie McMullin—were bribed by Attell (for approximately $70,000) to throw the first and second games of the series.

The cry that went up for Rothstein's head after the fix was discovered was mighty, but the nerveless gambler, acting under the advice of his shrewd lawyer, William Fallon, traveled to Chicago in 1920, where he faced a grand jury investigating the baseball scandal.

Rothstein leaped to the attack, challenging the city's pride. "Gentlemen," he roared at the jurors, "what kind of courtesy is this? What kind of a city is this? I came here voluntarily, and what happens? A gang of thugs bar my path with cameras [newsmen], as though I was a notorious person—a criminal even! I'm entitled to an apology. I demand one! Such a thing couldn't happen in New York. I'm surprised at you."

This audacity proved to be the right ploy, and Rothstein was not indicted.

Though no one ever proved that A. R. did the bribing, Mr. Big never denied it; he liked having that kind of fame. Fixing a World Series was big-time crime, and that's where Rothstein wanted his name and image.

Friends meant nothing to Rothstein. For instance, his closest associate for years was Nicky Arnstein. But when police captured a gang of killers and heistmen who were robbing Wall Street messengers carrying securities between brokerage houses, Rothstein threw Nicky to the wolves.

The thieves only knew their boss, they said, as "Mr. A." They told police that Mr. A. directed all the robberies and killings from a comfortable office uptown. They had never met him.

But they had glimpsed him—or so they thought.

Before the thefts, when the thieves demanded Arnstein's stooges to tell them who Mr. A. was, Rothstein sent another stooge to take them to an all-night restaurant. The flunky told the thieves that Mr. A. sat in the big window table there every evening.

The man in the window was hapless Nicky Arnstein.

Arnstein was identified as Mr. A. after the thieves were caught. He was sent to a federal penitentiary in 1922. That was the way Mr. Big dealt with his "friends."

As the twenties roared, so did Rothstein. He bet heavily on just about anything, fixing the odds and, when possible, the outcome. He never seemed to lose.

Rothstein's interests grew. He bought racehorses, nightclubs, gambling casinos, and red-plush whorehouses.

To protect this ever-increasing empire, he hired one of the most fanatical killers in America—Jack "Legs" Diamond, who saved his life on numerous occasions.

For instance, when Dutch Schultz tried to take over some of Rothstein's gambling interests, Legs—at A. R.'s orders—killed six of the Dutchman's boys within three days.

Dutch Schultz got the message and backed off. Rothstein became such a power in the New York underworld that his orders were obeyed even by rival gangs. For example, when the Owney Madden and Waxey Gordon gangs began blasting each other in an all-out war, it was Rothstein who arranged a truce.

He settled the argument—with Legs Diamond standing behind him—in twenty minutes. It was his singular pride that he could wield such power. His plan was simple; he described how the boys could carve up the rackets and all make money.

Reportedly, A. R. got $500,000 to mediate this first gangland summit conference in America.

No one got in Rothstein's way now. He lived high, with an estimated fortune of $50 million salted away in banks.

Every night his chauffeur-driven limousine

pulled to the curb at Broadway and 49th Street. Rothstein got out and walked down to 42nd and back. On his walk, Rothstein laid down his bets with sharpers waiting on the street. He carried $200,000 on him all the time in crisp $1,000 bills. He collected and paid off as he walked. Mostly, he collected.

Sometimes, to keep his name in kingly status, Rothstein would pass on a tip. Within minutes, thousands of tongues were wagging: "Get in on this. A. R.'s got the fix in."

Rothstein, after making the rounds of several nightclubs, wound up at Lindy's and continued to take bets there until dawn.

Then he drove either home to his beautiful wife or to one of the two-dozen plush apartments he kept and the showgirl mistresses waiting there for him.

The money rolled in so fast that Rothstein couldn't find enough ways to gamble or invest it. So he loaned it for more power. He loaned vast sums to judges, police captains, commissioners, stage stars, and politicians. His interest rates were high, and Legs Diamond did the collecting.

But some of A. R.'s loan-shark clients—judges especially—were not pushed to repay. Instead, he took his interest in other ways, such as having indictments quashed against his hired killers, gambling-den managers, and call girls.

He literally owned Broadway and almost all of Manhattan. And he dressed like it. All of his suits cost $400 or more. His shoes were $50 a pair.

At forty-six, Arnold Rothstein had not only arrived, he was uncrowned king of the underworld and almost everything on top of it.

Then, for reasons no one has ever explained, Rothstein went to pieces in 1928. His face took on a sickly pallor, his dress became unkempt, his hands shook. His confidence seemed to fade.

Worse, Rothstein started to lose and lose big.

His bets still went down, but now he was coming up a loser. He dropped tens, then hundreds of thousands of dollars on the horses and at poker tables.

The financial crash came in September, 1928. Between the 8th and 10th of that month, Rothstein tried to recoup his losses in what was, perhaps, the biggest poker game of the decade.

Sitting in the expensive apartment of George

Gambler Arnold Rothstein was known as Mr. Big in New York until his luck ran out in 1928. (UPI)

"Hump" McManus at the Park Central, Rothstein lost hand after hand to two newcomers from California—sharp, fast gamblers "Nigger Nate" Raymond and "Titanic" Thompson.

For two days, these men battled back and forth, with A. R. losing consistently. He lost his nerve and his sophistication. He screamed that they were cheating. They laughed. Laughed! At Mr. Big!

After forty-eight hours, the play came down to Rothstein and Nigger Nate. A. R. foolishly bet $50,000 on a high-card draw. Nigger Nate agreed.

Rothstein drew a queen and smiled.

Nigger Nate drew an ace.

Rothstein jumped from his chair, exploding in a hail of curses. McManus tallied A. R.'s losses. They came to $320,000.

Snarling, Rothstein headed for the door. "I'll pay off in a day or two," he yelled over his shoulder. "I don't carry that sort of dough under my fingernails!"

He was lying, of course. Rothstein had that and more in his inside coat pocket. Nigger Nate nodded coolly.

In twenty-four hours, A. R. told waiters from his reserved table at Lindy's that the game was fixed. "I don't pay off on fixed poker," Rothstein said.

His words were like a shock wave down Broadway. Arnold Rothstein was welshing on a bet!

Weeks went by, and Rothstein was contacted by unknown parties who wanted the account closed.

"I won't pay off!" several heard him yell over the phone. "The game was rigged!"

On November 4, 1928, Rothstein laid down more than a half million dollars that Herbert Hoover would beat Al Smith in the Presidential election. He took bets that night in Lindy's.

A. R. was called to the phone.

Soon he was putting on his coat. "I'm going up to the Park Central," he told intimates, "to see Hump McManus."

Less than a half hour later, a bellboy in the Park Central found Mr. Big holding his stomach in the service entrance. Blood was gushing from a bullet wound.

Detectives later followed the trail of blood to the suite rented by Hump McManus. Rothstein was rushed by police ambulance to the Polyclinic Hospital, where police asked him to name his killer. But A. R. kept the underworld code to the last. Smiling, he raised his finger to his lips. Then his head slumped forward and he was dead.

Nigger Nate Raymond was arrested but released. He had a beautiful alibi—a blonde who told the judge brassily that Nigger Nate was her bed partner at the time A. R. was being killed.

Hump McManus had no blonde, and he went to trial. But there was no substantial evidence against him either and he, too, was released.

The story that A. R. had drawn a royal flush in his last poker hand was untrue. There were five sets of cards on the table in McManus' room. One hand was a disaster—not even an ace high. It had A. R.'s blood on it.

RUDENSKY, MORRIS ("RED")
Safecracker, Robber ● (1908-1986)

He was a man of many names. The one name he didn't use was the one he was born with—Max Motel Friedman. He was best known as Morris "Red" Rudensky, ex-master thief, ex-king of the cons, ex-escape artist extraordinaire.

He called himself the Gonif, a Jewish word meaning thief. And thief he was. Nobody robbed like Rudensky—often in the millions of dollars.

Born in the teeming, squalid poverty that was the Lower East Side of New York in 1908, Rudensky began to steal early. "I remember, when I was just an ordinary undisciplined young punk," he recalled. "Nobody ever really paid particular attention to me except when I swiped something from a pushcart. Then the chase began. I kept running for nearly forty years, rotting in prisons for at least thirty-five of those years."

Rudensky's years on the outside were jammed with some of the most astounding thefts in American crime. Rudensky started small, stealing clothes, appliances, trinkets. Judged an incorrigible, he was sent to a reformatory. His conduct grew worse, and he was transferred to the state reformatory at Elmira, New York. "Elmira was a sophisticated crime school," he stated.

Once there, Rudensky began to learn from the older, more experienced convicts. A locksmith taught him the intricacies of breaking into and blowing up safes and of picking locks, every kind imaginable, until he was one of the best petermen (safecrackers) in the business.

Superintendent Doc Kristian at Elmira was the typical sadistic warden often portrayed in gangster movies. Long before prison reform was even whispered in America, men like Kristian did what they pleased with prisoners. Their brutal tactics transformed wayward boys into professional criminals.

One day at mess, Rudensky tripped a fellow inmate. Kristian pounced on him. "You're the only one giving me trouble today," Doc roared as he grabbed the boy by the neck. "So we'll make it special, you Heeb son-of-a-bitch. You've got long thumbs so we'll put them to use!"

Kristian ordered the "Thumb Hook" treatment for Rudensky to last for three days. "They stretched out my arms, fastened my thumbs to small steel eyelets and left me hanging in solitary, my back to a damp wall and bugs crawling the length of me. The stench would nauseate a garbage man."

For seventy-two hours Red hung there without food and water. Finally released, he collapsed and was taken to the infirmary. There was only one though on his mind—escape.

"Oh, God. I can't stay alive like this. I have to get out."

Once in the infirmary, Rudensky noticed that everybody, including the drunken quack doctor, avoided the TB patients. After his release, he hoarded scraps of soap containing lye.

Munching small doses of the soap, he achieved the required effect. His skin took on the appearance of jaundice, and "the Croaker took only a glancing observation before condemning me to the tubercular ward."

Once there, Red dangerously mixed his sputum with sick patients. Everyone was convinced that he was dying of TB and stayed away from him. After one day in the infirmary he learned that the wall behind the TB compound was not patrolled during the night.

He fashioned a makeshift ladder, and days later, in a black night splattered with drizzle, Rudensky let himself over the wall. He had taken pains to discover the time schedule of a passing freight train (the tracks were only a few hundred feet from the wall), and he was right on time.

Rudensky was headed back to New York in minutes.

With his new knowledge of safecracking and lock-picking, Rudensky quickly earned a reputation in the underworld. He moved to the Midwest and cracked several safes for the Bugs Moran gang before starting to free-lance.

His first big theft was in Kansas City in the early 1920s. There, with the help of some confederates, he robbed a jewelry store—including its giant safe—of over $300,000 in rare gems. His cut was $25,000.

Rudensky then flitted to Detroit and performed several burglaries for the Purple Mob. He returned to Chicago and free-lanced for Al Capone.

But Red, heading back to Kansas City, intended to go it alone. His biggest theft earned him the grudging respect of every criminal in America. For months, Rudensky cased a federal warehouse in Kansas City that held millions of dollars of pre-Prohibition liquor. He went to such lengths as getting himself hired as a workman in the warehouse.

He picked up specialists—an electrician, a top gunman, professional barrel handlers and truckers. He called himself "Red" Manion then. After elaborate planning with timetables and fences, plus bribing two guards at the warehouse, he was ready.

In the space of several hours, Rudensky and his crew loaded 2,420 barrels of bonded whiskey aboard trucks—a take of $2,105,400! There were no problems. Paid off by a man Rudensky still refers to today as "The Commissioner," Red's share was more than $100,000. He had over twenty other men to pay off. One gangster didn't like the split. He wanted more.

"Before the creep got the last word out of his mouth," Rudensky remembered, "I had leaped on him, pistol drawn. I iron-whipped him with all the pent-up hate and fury of a warped childhood again coming out of me! I clubbed, raked and hammered his face until it was a bloody pulp.

"I heard a bone crack and red pumped out of his mouth like gas from a hose. I hit him again and again until he was senseless. Then I kicked him viciously three times in the groin and stomach, his convulsed form finally quieting into a mass of raw, bleeding still flesh.

"I didn't have to pour it on—but I wanted a reputation. I wanted to be known as the smartest, youngest, and toughest hood." Few thought otherwise.

After that, Rudensky and such experienced strong-arm hoods as Smitty Kreuger went on a crime spree unequaled by modern-day safecrackers and stickup men. They robbed a bakery in Indianapolis of $7,000. They stuck up a shoe firm for $20,000. They stole $5,000 from a burial firm in Michigan. They robbed $30,000 from a company payroll truck in rural Indiana. They knocked over a distillery in Peoria, Illinois, for $30,000.

Then, dressed as policemen, Rudensky and others stopped a mail train just outside Springfield, Illinois, and made off with eleven mailbags of uncertain contents. Back in Decatur, Illinois, in the upstairs bedroom of an old house they had rented, Rudensky and Kreuger threw the sacks on a bed.

"The first bag we opened had nothing but bonds and securities. The second, too, and panic began to clutch my belly.

"But the third bag that we ripped open was full of cash, mostly small bills. The next bag had bigger bills, and the last bag had nothing but centuries—sparkling $100 greens.

"It took us, Dago, Chink, Smitty and myself, forty-five minutes to count the loot. The final total was commendable—just over $300,-000! It meant nearly $43,000 apiece. It was almost as good as the booze bash!"

Spectacular was the rise of Red Rudensky, and all of those crimes were accomplished before he was twenty-one years old. He had been lucky until then. His luck ran out in St. Louis.

There while trying to rob a jewelry store, Red and his gang were caught by police and a wild shoot-out took place. All the gang members were captured, and Rudensky was sent to Leavenworth.

He was far from a model prisoner. Nobody sassed Rudensky. He would fight anyone. He used his fists, a knife, a hammer—anything with which to destroy an opponent. Soon he earned the reputation of being Leavenworth's "King of the Cons."

He also earned solitary confinement and additional years on his sentence, for Rudensky was a confirmed escape artist by the time he hit Leavenworth.

Once, he walked out of Leavenworth through the front door, pretending to be a visitor. He was recaptured. Another time, he tried to smuggle himself out of prison by squeezing into a gunny sack with a corpse—a dead convict being sent out for burial. Again he was caught.

Red's most spectacular escape consisted of squeezing into a magazine box in the prison's print shop. Leavenworth's guards merely ran razor-sharp bamboo rods through the box to check the contents. One of the rods barely missed him before he was shipped through the front gate to a waiting freight car.

Even though he had made sure the box was stamped "This Side Up" so that he would not be placed on his head in the railcar, packing agents ignored the sign. The crate was placed upside-down and Rudensky rode for seven-and-a-half hours on a jangling, jumping, pulsating freightcar until he hemorrhaged. An alert train guard saw the blood flowing from the box, and Rudensky was broken loose.

He returned to Leavenworth with even more years added to his sentence. But his reputation was almost international by then. The FBI placed the bloody magazine box on display at the Philadelphia Sesquecentennial International Exposition in 1926. It was a left-handed compliment to Rudensky's ingenuity if nothing else.

This time, Red stayed in Leavenworth, meeting such notables as Machine Gun Kelly

Safecracker Morris "Red" Rudensky stole close to a million before he was twenty, then totally reformed; shown here setting type for his magazine, *The Atlantian*, in the Atlanta Federal Prison.

and Jack Johnson, the ex-heavyweight champ, who was serving a term for violation of the Mann Act. Johnson was a jovial type and taught Red how to box.

He also met the strange Robert Stroud, later known as "The Birdman of Alcatraz." "He was a homo," Rudensky remembered. "I was younger and somewhat repulsively attractive, he wanted me as young meat. I just ignored his hints."

Rudensky also met Al Capone and was his cellmate when he was moved to Atlanta. He watched Capone go stir crazy before they shipped him to Alcatraz.

But long before he was sent to Atlanta, two things happened in Leavenworth that were to change his life. First he met Charles Ward, an inmate who had totally reformed himself and when released worked for the national advertising agency Brown and Bigelow in St. Paul.

Ward finally became president of Brown and Bigelow and continued to encourage Rudensky to improve his life while in prison. Red began to read and then write.

On August 1, 1929, Rudensky stopped a suicidal riot in Leavenworth's mess hall and saved warden Tom White's life from a vengeance-seeking mob of convicts. He decided to reform. It came slowly. In Atlanta, Rudensky's persistent literary efforts were rewarded. He was made editor of the prison magazine, *The Atlantian*. This new prison job won him notice from such people as Margaret Mitchell, author of *Gone With the Wind*, and crusading newsman Ralph McGill.

During the Second World War Rudensky penned an editorial calling for convicts in prisons all over America to support the war effort. It earned him praise from the White House. He went on to organize prisoner labor all over America and totally reform himself into a useful citizen behind prison walls.

When Rudensky was finally released, Charles Ward appointed him copy chief at Brown and Bigelow. Later, he became the Chief Consultant of Security Systems for the 3M Company.

No one was more grateful for this amazing transformation from arch-criminal to responsible citizen than Red Rudensky.

He summed it up best himself in a letter to a young boy seeking help in avoiding a life of crime: "During my long prison stretch, I personally have known many of the crime big shots of the last fifty years. I haven't found a single one who wouldn't have traded everything he possessed for thirty days of freedom and peace of mind, if not for themselves, certainly for their families.

"Don't lock yourself up like I did."

RULOFF, EDWARD H.
Murderer, Burglar ● (? -1871)

Ruloff was a man who prided himself on his cunning and glib ability to persuade others to his way of thinking. His background was extremely shadowy, but it is known that he lived for a while in Ithaca, New York, and that, sometime in 1846, he killed his wife and child, dropping their bodies into Lake Cayuga (they were never found).

Arrested for these murders, Ruloff smugly languished in jail knowing that the state had to produce a body to convict him of murder in the first degree. He was convicted of kidnapping his wife, but that was all. After serving ten years in prison, Ruloff was again tried for killing his child and convicted of murder. The court sentenced him to hang. He escaped before the execution could be carried out.

In his absence, a court of appeals reversed the death sentence, but by then, Ruloff, who had mastered several languages while in prison, began impersonating a professor, giving lectures at various colleges for large fees. The academic life bored Ruloff, so he enlisted the aid of two burglars and, for a decade, robbed stores and offices throughout New York. One August night in 1870 Ruloff was discovered in a Binghamton store by two clerks who slept there.

The surprised Ruloff turned his pistol on one of the clerks, Fred Mirick, and shot him dead; the trio of burglars ran from the premises and dove into the nearby Chenango River in an attempt to escape. Ruloff, an excellent swimmer, got away, but his accomplices drowned.

Days later, a man in rags begging for food was found wandering near the river. He was identified as Ruloff by the absence of the big toe on his left foot, the result of a previous accident. By the time of his apprehension, eight murders were attributed to Ruloff, who was promptly convicted of murdering the clerk Mirick and hanged. Physicians from Cornell University's medical college received permission to dissect the killer's brain, which was then compared with that of Daniel Webster's, an effort the great barrister would, no doubt, have found less than creative.

The murderer's skull remained on display at Cornell for many years; Ruloff had strangely returned to the place of his highest aspirations—college.

SALTIS-MC ERLANE GANG

The sprawling Southwest Side of Chicago served as the bailiwick of the Saltis-McErlane gang during Prohibition. The leader was a behemoth of a man called Polock Joe Saltis who had been a saloon keeper before the First World War in Joliet, Ill. Aligned with Saltis was the politically ambitious John "Dingbat" O'Berta (Oberta before he anglicized the name) who at one time had been a Republican committeeman in the district and had run for state senator and alderman in several elections.

Saltis served his bootleg hooch to more than 200,000 heavy-fisted drinkers, mostly Slavic in origin, who worked in the stockyards and factories. Saltis grew so rich that by 1925 he purchased a huge estate in Wisconsin near Eagle River from his bootlegging activities. A nearby Wisconsin community was later called Saltisville to fatten the gangster's ego.

Though he openly paid allegiance to Capone, Saltis secretly joined North Side gangster Earl "Hymie" Weiss to put Scarface out of business. To protect his barony, Saltis employed the murderous talents of such men as Frank "Lefty" Koncil and Charlie "Big Hayes" Hubacek. His right-hand man and chief killer was Frankie McErlane who eventually became a full partner in Saltis's enterprises.

Anyone invading Polock Joe's territory usually went out feet first—as did John "Mitters"

Foley, killed by Saltis and Koncil in 1925. O'Berta was indicted for this killing as well as Saltis and Koncil—but all three were acquitted. The Dingbat's political clout was awe-inspiring.

It was O'Berta who arranged for a truce among the gangs during the mid-1920s. On October 20, 1926, the suave O'Berta presided at a gangland summit meeting at the Hotel Sherman. In attendance were Al Capone, Maxie Eisen, George "Bugs" Moran, Vincent "The Schemer" Drucci, Jake "Greasy Thumb" Guzik, Ralph Sheldon, William Skidmore, Christian P. Barney Bertsche, and Jack Zuta.

Capone opened the meeting under O'Berta's smiling approval with the line: "We're a bunch of saps killing each other." More than 150 gangsters from all the factions had been killed up to 1926 (the number would increase to a thousand by 1931). It was at this meeting that Capone established the deadline—Madison Street—which would permanently divide his domain from that of the powerful North Side gang under Moran.

The gangsters also agreed to (1) general amnesty, (2) no more murders or beatings, (3) all past killings between the mobs to be considered closed incidents, (4) all malicious gossip spread by the press or police concerning the factions to be ignored, and (5) leaders of each gang to report to the governing body any infractions caused by their minions.

The peace held up for two months. Then Hillory Clements, a gunman in Ralph Sheldon's gang, was killed by a Saltis gunner on December 30, 1926, and the wars were rejoined. Sheldon and Saltis had been battling over the Southwest territory for about a year. Sheldon was really acting under Capone's orders to invade Polock Joe's domain, since Scarface did not want to openly wage war with a man already paying him tribute. Al merely wanted more, and he could get it from his obsequious vassal Sheldon.

Saltis and McErlane had already killed two of Sheldon's best beer runners, John Tucillo, who was Diamond Joe Esposito's brother-in-law, and Frank DeLaurentis in April of 1926. With Clements' murder at the end of the year, Sheldon declared all-out war on the Saltis gang. The intrepid but foolish Frank "Lefty" Koncil was led into a trap on March 11, 1927 and machine-gunned to death. Killed with him was Charlie "Big Hayes" Hubacek. Saltis and Mc-

The deadliest gangster in Chicago during the 1920s—
Frankie McErlane, who used the machinegun for the first
time in the gang wars. (UPI)

Polack Joe Saltis, South Side Chicago bootlegger and gangster, lived to have a town named after him. (UPI)

Erlane went scurrying to Capone, frightened.
He could handle Sheldon, he promised, for a
price. Saltis upped his ante and lived in comparative peace.

McErlane, one of the city's most vicious killers who had murdered at least ten gang rivals
and introduced the use of the Thompson submachinegun to the underworld, quit Saltis
in late 1929 when he felt he was being
cheated out of his share of Polock Joe's bootleg
profits. McErlane was shot and wounded in
the leg on January 28, 1930.

Police figured Saltis had ordered the shooting and tried to get Frankie to talk. He
laughed at them from a hospital bed where his
leg was suspended in mid-air by weights and
pulleys. "Shoo, shoo!" he told them. "Just say
the war's on again. It's been brewing since last
November. You'll all know about it in two
weeks."

On March 25, 1930, John "Dingbat" O'Berta
was shot to death, killed with his chauffeur,
Sam Malaga. The two men had been abducted
in O'Berta's own Lincoln and taken for a ride.
O'Berta had fought for his life, getting off three
bullets from his belly gun—a .38 pistol with
the barrel sawed down to one inch—before his
head was blown away by a shotgun blast.

Saltis quit the racket that year, telling police chief John Stege: "I got a fine country
home and farm at Saltisville on Barker Lake,
Wisconsin. I'm out of the racket. I got mine all
in a pile and I got $100,000 sunk in my farm—
a nine-hole golf course, a clubhouse that sleeps

twenty-six people, ponies, deer, plenty of fishing."

Stege glowered at the jowl-cheeked gangster. "How come the place is named Saltisville?"

Saltis grinned. "I named it. It's honorary
now, but we're going to make it stick. You see,
there are only sixty-two voters in the township, and I got twenty-six of them working for
me. I'm going to hire five more, which will
give me majority control. At the election this
spring when we ballot on it, I'll have enough
to put it across. What I want is for my kids
to be able to look in the United States Postal
Guide and see their town, Saltisville. Okay,
Chief?"

By 1930 Capone had absorbed the Saltis-
McErlane territory and the gang ceased to
operate as an independant mob thereafter.
Saltis did retire to Wisconsin, pleased with the
thought that he was the only gangster in America to have a town named after him.

SAUL, NICHOLAS
Gangleader, Robber ● (1833-1853)

Of the fifty gangs running wild through
New York's troubled Fourth Ward in
the 1850s, the Daybreak Boys were the

most fearsome. It was compulsory for each member of the gang to commit at least one murder before being accepted as part of the mob. Leader Nicholas Saul, twenty, and his sidekick, William Howlett, only nineteen, had qualified many times over.

The Daybreak Boys gang got its name from the period of time when its members were most active, at dawn. They usually preyed upon the barges and sloops that were docked along the Hudson and East Rivers. Stealing cargo and cash from a captain's chest was but a prelude to killing the crew and scuttling the ship. Saul was ever conscious of future witnesses against him.

Skull cracking became a sport for this gang and soon the most desperate gangsters in New York joined its ranks—Slobbery Jim, Cowlegged Sam McCarthy, Sow Madden, Patsy the Barber. In the two years that Saul led the gang, its members committed at least forty murders and stole $200,000 in cash and goods.

Saul's fortunes ebbed on the night of August 25, 1852 when he, Howlett, and Bill Johnson invaded the brig *William Watson* anchored in the East River between Olive Street and James slip. While Johnson waited in a dinghy alongside the brig, Saul and Howlett climbed aboard, found the captain's chest, and were dragging it to the railing when a watchman, Charles Baxter, rushed them. Both Saul and Howlett drew their pistols and fired, killing Baxter with a bullet in the heart and one in the head.

A detective spotted the trio pulling to shore with their loot and called for aid. A squad of heavily armed policemen, twenty in all, rushed into Pete Williams' Slaughter House Inn where Saul, Howlett, and Williams had taken their spoils. It took almost three hours to arrest the gangleaders. When the cops entered the inn, two dozen Daybreak Boys engaged the police in a slugmatch, attempting to save their captain from capture.

Convicted of Baxter's murder, Saul and Howlett were hanged in the Tombs Courtyard on January 28, 1853. Before they were executed, two hundred of their fellow gangsters, as well as political big-wigs including Butcher Bill Poole and Tom Hyer, formed a line and passed the two men, already with ropes about their necks, enthusiastically shaking their hands and telling them what swell fellows they had been.

SCHILD, JOHN
Murderer ● (? -1813)

A farmer in Reading, Berks County, Pa., Schild seemed obviously insane when, on August 12, 1812, he accused his wife of putting poison in his tea and, moments later, dashed to the barnyard where he wildly pursued chickens with an axe. Failing to catch any of the hurrying hens, the madman ran to his house and, wielding the axe, bashed in his father's skull and cut off his mother's head.

Schild then took to the house furniture with a vengeance, whopping it to pieces. He concluded his murderous tantrum by setting fire to his home. Naturally, his defense at his trial was that of insanity but this was thrown out and he was ordered to hang. Schild was executed January 20, 1813.

SCHMID, CHARLES HOWARD, JR.
Murderer ● (1942-   )

BACKGROUND: BORN AND RAISED IN TUCSON, ARIZ. HIGH SCHOOL GRADUATE. MARRIED 15-YEAR-OLD DIANE LYNCH 9/9/65. DESCRIPTION: 5'3", BLUE EYES, RED HAIR (DYED BLACK), STOCKY. ALIASES: ANGEL RODRIGUEZ. RECORD: MURDERED WITH JOHN SAUNDERS 15-YEAR-OLD ALLEEN ROWE ON 5/31/64 NEAR TUCSON, ARIZ.; ADMITTED THE KILLING OF 17-YEAR-OLD GRETCHEN FRITZ AND HER 13-YEAR-OLD SISTER WENDY ON 8/16/65 NEAR TUCSON; ARRESTED FOR IMPERSONATING AN FBI AGENT IN SUMMER, 1965 IN SAN DIEGO, CALIF., RELEASED; ARRESTED 11/11/65 AND TRIED FOR MURDER; CONVICTED AND SENTENCED TO DEATH FOR THE MURDERS OF GRETCHEN AND WENDY FRITZ; TRIED THE FOLLOWING YEAR FOR THE MURDER OF ALLEEN ROWE, PLEADED GUILTY TO SECOND DEGREE MURDER; SENTENCED ON THIS MURDER TO 50 YEARS TO LIFE IMPRISONMENT; EXECUTION NULLIFIED BY THE SUPREME COURT DECISION TO ELIMINATE CAPITAL PUNISHMENT (GIVEN TWO LIFE TERMS); BROKE OUT OF THE ARIZONA STATE PRISON 11/11/72 WITH RAYMOND HUDGENS, KILLER OF THREE IN KINGMAN, ARIZ.; BOTH HELD FOUR HOSTAGES ON RANCH NEAR TEMPE, ARIZ.; SCHMID, WEARING A BLOND WIG, THEN HOPPED A FREIGHT, BUT WAS SHORTLY RECAPTURED (AS WAS HUDGENS) AND RETURNED TO PRISON; HE NOW FACES KIDNAPPING CHARGES IN ADDITION TO THE TWO LIFE SENTENCES HE IS PRESENTLY SERVING.

Schmid was a habitue of the Speedway Boulevard area in Tucson, a strip where speed-crazy, thrill-seeking motorcyclists gathered and mixed with teenage rock-and-roll guitarists. It was a melting pot of oddballs and Charles Howard Schmid was one of the oddest.

Schmid's small stature was a constant worry to him and he strove to excel in sports and social popularity while in high school. He became an expert gymnast specializing in the flying and still rings. In his senior year Schmid won the overall Arizona State gymnastic championship. Upon graduation, however, he gave up athletics and took to bumming about Tucson, dating young girls by the score and expanding his already-eccentric behavior.

To increase his height, Schmid bought oversized cowboy boots and stuffed them with rags and crushed tin cans. As a result, he added several inches to his height but found it difficult to walk. He explained his odd, lumbering gait as the after effects of a battle with Mafia hoods who had crippled him for life. Such wild fabrications were normal for Schmid, or Smitty, as his friends called him. Five years after graduating high school and murdering three young girls, Schmid could no longer distinguish between reality and his sordid imagination.

A mama's boy, Schmid created all kinds of stories in which he triumphed over impossible odds, thinking such tales would fascinate the young girls he dated. To gain sympathy, he told several girls that he was an adopted child and that his real name was Angel Rodriguez (an alias he used in the future to cover his wanderings). He also stated that he was stricken with terminal leukemia. He smeared his face with cosmetic cream, dyed his red hair inky black and even designed an "ugly" mark on his left cheek—a self-made mole. constructed of putty and darkened with axle grease—to give him a tougher appearance.

All manner of gobbledygook drooled from Smitty's non-stop mouth. One of Smitty's favorite expressions was: "I can manifest my neurotical emotions, emancipate an epicureal instinct, and elaborate on my heterosexual tendencies." Richard Bruns, one of his best friends, thought him a "phony perfector" but was fascinated by Schmid and, like so many others in his weird clique, did his bidding.

Mary Rae French, an 18-year-old brunette, fell madly in love with Schmid. He told her he needed money and if she wanted to see him she would have to work for the privilege. He got her a job in his parents' nursing home and she dutifully, slavishly deposited most of her weekly earnings to his bank account.

Schmid rented a small cottage on the edge of Tucson, obtained a beat-up car, and then proceeded to become the center of attention along Speedway Boulevard through his wild antics, his impossible tales, and his bizarre appearance. He bragged that he had more than one hundred teenage prostitutes working for him.

Such stories, Richard Bruns later stated, ". . . were out of proportion, all the stories about how great he was, how many girls he knew, how many girls he went out with, and most of all, how many girls he laid."

In spring of 1964, friends noticed a change in Schmid. He seemed bored with talking about his sexual exploits. He lusted for "higher excitement." On the evening of May 31, 1964, Schmid was guzzling beer with his friends John Saunders and Mary French in the latter's home. Suddenly, the strange-eyed Schmid jumped to his feet and said: "I want to kill a girl! I want to do it tonight. I think I can get away with it!"

At Mary's suggestion, Alleen Rowe, age fifteen, slipped unnoticed from her home in Tucson that night about 11 p.m. and joined Schmid, Saunders and Miss French in Smitty's car. They drove to the desert. Once there, Saunders and Schmid led the younger girl to a lonely spot while Mary French sat in the car. After raping her, Schmid told Saunders to "hit her over the head with a rock." Saunders obeyed but the terrified girl broke away and ran. Schmid raced after her, knocked her down, and then crushed her skull with the rock.

Both men then walked back to the car. Before driving off, Smitty kissed Mary French and laconically stated: "We killed her. Whatever happens, remember I love you." Minutes later, the three returned to the murder scene and dug a shallow grave, placing Alleen Rowe's body in it. Mary French remembered looking at the corpse and noting: "She was lying on the ground on her back with blood all over her head and face."

When questioned by police, Schmid shook his head puzzled. No, he didn't know where Alleen Rowe was. He had planned to pick her up on the night of May 31, 1964, but when he had arrived at her home she was gone.

Saunders and Mary French supported his story. Police listed Alleen as another runaway and told her mother, Mrs. Norma Rowe, that she would likely turn up some day. The matter was forgotten.

The brutal slaying only served to increase Schmid's appetite for killing. He began to date a girl named Gretchen Fritz who came from a socially prominent family. Gretchen, 17, was almost as odd as Schmid. She had a habit of "borrowing" cars, and stealing liquor and gasoline. Gretchen attended a private school, and during classes she took to smoking and spitting on the floor to show contempt for the institution.

Gretchen and Schmid fought incessantly. "They were a mess," Bruns stated. "They were always arguing, always accusing each other of everything."

Bruns also stated that in August, 1965, he was present when Schmid received a phone call from Gretchen, telling him that "she'd gone all the way with this guy in California. He burst into tears." Later, Smitty danced crazily about the small cottage where he was staying and kicked and punched the walls, screaming at the top of his lungs: "I really loved that girl! I'll kill her! I'll kill her! I'll kill that bitch!"

Driving a red Pontiac with her 13-year-old sister Wendy at her side, Gretchen Fritz went to a drive-in movie on the night of August 16, 1965. She was never seen alive again. Once more, Schmid was questioned by police and he told them that Gretchen probably went to California where she was dating someone. The Fritz sisters were listed as runaways.

Days later Schmid calmly walked up to Richard Bruns and said: "You know I killed Gretchen?" Bruns blinked astonishment. Smitty then told him that he had taken the Fritz sisters into the desert and strangled both of them. He said he threw their bodies into a ditch alongside a deserted road.

Bruns chalked up the statement to braggadocio. Then two men—Bruns later termed them "Mafia types"—showed up and questioned both young men. They said they had been hired by friends of the Fritz family and if Schmid knew where the girls were he had better tell them. Schmid and Bruns feigned ignorance.

Later, frightened, Bruns felt implicated in the murders since it was well known that he disliked Gretchen Fritz. He challenged Schmid to produce the bodies. "Let's go bury them," he said. "Either you got some bodies out there or you don't. If you do, I'm in trouble."

Smitty agreed and the two drove to the desert where the bodies were easily spotted. Both hammered out shallow graves from the baked desert floor and placed the half-decomposed bodies into them. "It stunk like hell," Bruns later remembered.

With this grisly work completed, Schmid turned to his friend and said, "Now you're in this as deep as I am."

The "Mafia types" returned and, according to Bruns, they took Schmid to San Diego to look for the Fritz sisters. Weeks later, Schmid was arrested on a beach after posing as an FBI agent and questioning three bikini-clad girls. "He looked too crummy to be an FBI agent," one of the girls stated.

Released by San Diego police, Schmid made his way back to Tucson. His behavior became more erratic. When one of his friends asked why he, a man of twenty-three, was dating such young teenage girls, Schmid erupted, screaming, "Shut up! Shut up!" and sent his fist through the flimsy plaster walls of his much abused cottage. He then ran outside and yelled, "God is going to punish me! God is going to punish me!"

Richard Bruns' nerves were also strained. He had fitful nightmares. He believed Schmid was about to kill his own girl, Kathy Morath. He even took to patroling the Morath home late at night to guard against Schmid's appearance. Smitty had once given Kathy a cheap ring, claiming it was a diamond. She had thrown it back in his face. Schmid, Bruns figured, would brood over such an insult and ultimately seek revenge.

"I started having this dream," Bruns later told police. "It was the same dream every night. Smitty would have Kathy out in the desert and he had her all stripped down and he'd be doing all these things to her and strangling her. And it was like I was two hundred miles away and I'd be running across the desert with a gun in my hand, but I could never get there."

His dread of Schmid finally led Bruns to call the police and tell them everything he knew. Schmid was arrested November 11, 1965 and placed on trial for murdering the Fritz sisters.

Charls Howard Schmid of Tucson, Ariz., murderer of three young girls in 1965.

Mary French and John Saunders were also arrested for aiding Schmid to murder Alleen Rowe. They turned state's evidence against their berserk mentor.

Schmid appeared in court without his usual oddball garb and make-up. He was dressed in a conservative sportcoat, white shirt and tie. The testimony against him was damning. All the gruesome aspects of the murders were exposed and detailed to a shocked jury. In summation, prosecutor William Schafer III told the jury: "There is no sympathy, no mercy in this case. This man must be shown no mercy!"

None was forthcoming. Schmid was convicted by the jury in a two-hour session. He was condemned to death. Mary French, for turning state's evidence, was sentenced to four-to-five years in prison. Saunders got life.

A year later Schmid, already tried for the Fritz slayings, pleaded guilty to second-degree murder in the Rowe case and was given an additional 50 years to life imprisonment. Appeals held up Schmid's execution and he finally beat the death penalty when the U.S. Supreme Court abolished such "cruel and unusual punishment."

After being re-sentenced to two life terms, Schmid and another inmate escaped from the Arizona State Prison on November 11, 1972 but were recaptured days later.

SCHMIDT, HELMUTH
Serial Killer ● (? -1918)

Schmidt, like Belle Gunness and Harry Powers, found his victims in the lovelorn columns of newspapers. Unlike Powers, who answerd the ads of lonely, wealthy widows, Schmidt followed the technique of Belle Gunness. He placed the ads, always using an alias, advertising for "a suitable lady to marry soon." He was not out to bilk rich widows. Powers planned to entice young immigrant girls to his bedside and kill them for whatever little money they carried.

Dozens of young girls recently arrived from Europe answered Schmidt's ads before WWI. He had placed these ads in newspapers published in New York, New Jersey, Missouri, and Michigan, traveling to those areas to meet any prospect. He finally used the money he robbed from his murder victims to settle down in Royal Oak, Michigan, where he went to work on the assembly line of the Ford Motor Manufacturing Co.

Schmidt could not resist returning to his old ploy, however, and ran another ad in the New York Herald in 1918. Augusta Steinbach answered and Schmidt invited her to Royal Oak. He killed her after taking her money and jewels. This time, Schmidt was caught. The victim's friend, Agnes Dominicki, upon the disappearance of her friend, learned Schmidt's identity and informed police.

Schmidt was arrested on April 23, 1918. Police found the blood-soaked clothing of Mrs. Steinbach beneath Schmidt's front porch. He was jailed but Schmidt cheated the hangman. He pulled a heavy iron railing down on himself in his cell. It crushed his skull. The press had dubbed Schmidt "The American Bluebeard," and law enforcement officials estimated that he may have killed as many as three dozen gullible women.

SCHULTZ, DUTCH
(ARTHUR FLEGENHEIMER)
Bootlegger ● (1902-1935)

BACKGROUND: BORN IN BRONX, N.Y., 8/6/02 TO EMMA (NEU) AND HERMAN FLEGENHEIMER, OWNER OF A SALOON AND STABLE. ATTENDED P.S. 12 IN THE BRONX THROUGE 4TH GRADE. WIFE, FRANCES, NO CHILDREN. ORIGINAL OCCUPATION, PRINTER. DESCRIPTION: 5'9", BLUE EYES, LIGHT BROWN HAIR, STOCKY BUILD. ALIASES: THE DUTCHMAN, DUTCH SCHULTZ. RECORD: BECAME A MEMBER OF THE BERGEN AVENUE GANG AT AGE 14 (FOLLOWING HIS FATHER'S DESERTION OF THE FAMILY); COMMITTED SEVERAL PETTY HOLDUPS AND BURGLARIES; ARRESTED IN 1919 FOR BURGLARY AND CONVICTED, SENTENCED TO FIFTEEN MONTHS IN JAIL WHICH HE SERVED; UPON RELEASE PURCHASED A BRONX SALOON AND ADOPTED THE NAME DUTCH SCHULTZ FROM AN INFAMOUS MEMBER OF THE DEFUNCT FROG HOLLOW GANG WHICH HAD OPERATED IN THE BRONX BEFORE THE TURN OF THE CENTURY; ENLISTED SUCH TOUGHS AS JOEY RAO AND FORMED A GANG THAT CONTROLLED BOOTLEGGING IN THE BRONX AND PARTS OF MANHATTAN FROM THE MIDDLE 1920S TO HIS DEATH; ALSO TOOK OVER CONTROL OF THE POLICY GAME IN HARLEM; WENT INTO SLOT MACHINES THROUGHOUT NEW YORK WITH DANDY PHIL KASTEL, JOEY RAO AND FRANK COSTELLO; PROMINENT IN RESTAURANT RACKETS IN MANHATTAN FROM LATE 1920S TO EARLY 1930S; ORDERED GANGSTER RIVAL JACK "LEGS" DIAMOND SHOT TO DEATH IN 1931; ORDERED GANSTER VINCENT "MAD DOG" COLL KILLED THE FOLLOWING YEAR; TRIED FOR INCOME-TAX EVASION (REPUTEDLY MADE $481,000 FROM 1929 TO 1931 FROM THE SALE OF HIS BOOTLEGGED NEEDLE BEER ALONE) IN 1933; ACQUITTED; ORDERED HIS FIRST LIEUTENANT, BO WEINBERG, KILLED (MURDERED BY BENJAMIN "BUGSY" SIEGEL) IN 1933; DEMANDED THAT SPECIAL PROSECUTOR THOMAS E. DEWEY OF N.Y.C. BE KILLED BUT THE BOARD MEMBERS OF THE NEWLY-CREATED NATIONAL CRIME SYNDICATE, NOTABLY LOUIS LEPKE BUCHALTER AND CHARLES LUCKY LUCIANO VETOED THE ACTION; WHEN SCHULTZ INSISTED UPON KILLING DEWEY, THE BOARD CONDEMNED HIM TO DEATH; SHOT AND KILLED WITH THREE BODYGUARDS IN THE PALACE CHOPHOUSE IN NEWARK, N.J., 10/23/35 BY CHARLES "THE BUG" WORKMAN AND MENDY WEISS.

New York's mobsters in the 1920s were slick. In Capone's wild and woolly Chicago 1,000 rival gangsters died in the streets over a ten-year period. But in Little Old New York, "the boys" knew better. You only killed for business, not pleasure or loyalty or anger. Kid stuff. Kill for money!

At first such suave mobsters as Owney Madden, Waxey Gorden (Irving Wexler), Vannie Higgins, and Little Augie Orgen ran things. No pistol-smoking shootouts on busy corners. Keep it smooth, work with Tammany Hall and the politicians. Is everybody happy?

There was one who wasn't. He was a wild Third Avenue punk named Arthur Flegenheimer. The Roaring Twenties and all its bootleg riches were passing him by.

A product of Bronx's Bergen Avenue Street Gang, Flegenheimer stole his nickname from a once-feared thug named Dutch Schultz. Schultz's early years were misspent in gang battles but he did manage to go through four years of grade school at P.S. 12 in the Bronx. Oddly enough, his principal then was Dr. J. F. Condon who was to become famous years later as the mysterious "Jafsie," the go-between who handed the Lindbergh ransom money over to kidnapper-murderer Bruno Richard Hauptmann.

The Dutchman turned bad shortly after his father deserted the family in 1916. His mother, a pious, warm-hearted woman who worked hard to keep Schultz in clothes and food, took in washing. Dutch took up a bag of burglar tools.

He began by opening a few speakeasies, supplying them with hooch run down from Canada in his own trucks. He also manufactured his own needle beer, the worst in town.

He lined up his own gunsels, over one hundred of them, and he muscled in on the bigger boys. Jack "Legs" Diamond worked for him briefly, then branched out on his own.

At first Dutch didn't care. It was when Legs and his troop started hijacking Schultz beer that the Dutchman blew his top. New York's first full-scale gang war broke out.

Legs, who got his nickname by turning on the speed after swiping packages from horse-drawn delivery wagons, was also known as the Clay Pigeon. Diamond carried so many bullets in him that he jingled when he walked.

For years, the Dutchman and Legs battled it out while Luciano, Genovese, and Costello bided their time.

Then, on December 19, 1931, luck ran out for Legs. Celebrating with his girl, Kiki Roberts, after being released on a kidnapping charge, Diamond saw his number come up. An ace Schultz gunner, Bo Weinberg, slipped the latch on the door of his dingy room, quietly crept up on the sleeping Legs and pumped seventeen steel-jacketed shells into him.

Dutch Schultz's epitaph for Legs was succinct: "Just another punk caught with his hands in my pockets. That's why Bo took him." The Dutchman's philosophy in a nutshell.

As his debonair mouthpiece, Dixie Davis (also rubbed out later), once said about Dutch, "You can insult Arthur's girl, spit in his face, push him around—and he'll laugh. But don't steal a dollar from his accounts. If you do, you're dead."

Another young man with ideas, Vincent Coll, didn't believe Dixie. He and his brother Pete went to work as part of Dutch's army of hired guns. But in three months Coll went single.

"The Mick," as Dutch called Coll, wasn't content with his own operation; he wanted Dutch's $20 million-a-year booze and policy racket empires, too.

The Dutchman's war with Vincent Coll was brief but bloody. In one attempt to kill Schultz lieutenant Joey Rao, Coll sprayed a crowded Manhattan street with machinegun bullets, killing a small child and wounding a half dozen more.

This kind of insanity earned for Coll his nickname "Mad Dog" and the Dutchman's fear. Once, in June, 1931, while being accompanied by his bodyguard Dannie Iamascia, Schultz spotted two figures lurking in the shadows near his headquarters on upper Fifth Avenue.

"The Mick!" he hissed to Iamascia and both drew their guns, popping away at two city detectives, Steve DiRosa and Julius Salke, who had been keeping the Dutchman under surveillance. The policemen returned the fire and Iamascia fell to the pavement, critcally wounded.

Schultz, after glancing at his fallen henchman, threw his pistol down an alleyway and ran. DiRosa charged after him (although one well-aimed bullet could have rid the city of Schultz) and tackled him. Dutch quickly yanked $18,600 from his pockets and offered it to DiRosa as a bribe to let him go.

"Here, take it all," he said.

DiRosa became incensed. "You miserable bum!" he yelled. "I'll shove that dough down your throat!" When Sergeant Salke ran up, he found DiRosa trying to do exactly that.

It was darkly clever, the way they got Coll. The movies have used it a thousand times since. While Dutch's friend, Owney Madden, stalled the Mad Dog on the phone (Coll was blackmailing Owney at the time) Schultz had the call traced. Several minutes later three men pulled up to a drugstore on West Twenty-Third Street. Coll stood in the phone booth threatening Madden. Bo Weinberg hauled out a machinegun from beneath his long overcoat and opened up.

The glass booth exploded, and Coll tumbled out dead.

The Dutchman's troubles were just beginning. He was charged with income-tax fraud and went to trial. After getting a change of venue to a small town court in upstate New York, Dutch became a nice guy. He hired a public relations firm to spread his money around to needy charities. He became a model family man.

One admirer seeing him in his drab, cheap clothes said he should improve his attire. "Such display is vulgar," Schultz said. "Personally, I think only queers wear silk shirts . . . I never bought one in my life. A guy's a sucker to spend fifteen or twenty dollars on a shirt. Hell, a guy can get a good one for two bucks!"

His thrifty chatter hoodwinked the hayseeds. They said he wasn't guilty.

While Schultz was on trial, Luciano, Genovese, and the others of the newly-established crime syndicate seized his rackets. Bo Weinberg complained to Lucky Luciano, "But what if Schultz comes back?"

"That loudmouth is never coming back," Luciano promised. But the Dutchman did come back. With murder in his eyes. He knew that he was outnumbered but he wasn't out. So Dutch went across the river to Newark, N. J. to lick his wounds and rebuild his forces. Bo Weinberg was his first order of business— he had his disloyal minion stabbed to death.

In 1935, Special Prosecutor Thomas E. Dewey was appointed to bust up the N. Y. rackets. Mayor Fiorello LaGuardia wanted the Dutchman's blood.

Dewey went to work attacking and raiding Schultz's policy rackets with a vengeance. The Dutchman went crazy. He called a meeting of the syndicate's board members. "Dewey's my nemesis," he told the crime lords. "He's gotta go."

Johnny Torrio, who'd left the palmy-though-bloody Chicago days behind, tried reasoning with Schultz. "You just can't go around bumping off big shots like him, Dutch."

"It'll bring down the heat on all of us," Luciano said.

"It's bad for business," Joe Adonis said.

Schultz went berserk. He shouted, he waved his arms. "You guys stole my rackets and now you're feeding me to the law. Dewey's gotta go. I'm hitting him myself . . . and in forty-eight hours!" He stomped out.

Every eye in the room turned to the deadly-looking Albert Anastasia, the new head of Murder, Incorporated, the syndicate's enforcer arm. "Okay," he said coldly. "Schultz goes tonight."

Dutch was in the Palace Chophouse in Newark with some of his men that night, plotting how he'd kill Dewey. Outside a car pulled up. Charlie "The Bug" Workman, Mendy Weiss, and a man named Piggy got out and, like little boys, pressed their faces to the window of the restaurant. "He's in there!" Piggy said.

"You guys wait here," the Bug said, "I'll hit the Dutchman alone." Piggy sat behind the wheel of the car. Mendy stood watch on the sidewalk.

Workman sauntered through the half-empty bar area, heading toward the rear where the Dutchman held court. "I'd better check the john," he told himself. He kicked the door open, gun drawn, and saw a heavy-set man washing his hands. He looked familiar but the Bug didn't ask his name. He fired rapidly and the man crashed to the floor.

Then, like a Western marshal, Workman waded into the back area of the Chophouse, two .38's blazing. Schultz's startled gunsels returned fire but missed. In ten seconds Abe "Misfit" Landau, Lulu Rosencranz, and Otto "Abbadabba" Berman were all dead.

"But where's Schultz?" the Bug wondered. "The guy in the john!" He went back to the washroom and rifled the Dutchman's pockets, taking several thousand dollars. Workman still resides in the New Jersey State Prison for this mass slaying.

The Dutchman was hit all right, but he wasn't dead. Rushed to the Newark City Hospital, Schultz lay dying and raving. His last words, as he slipped in and out of a coma, his body leaking blood like a sieve (five hundred cubic centimeters of blood were administered to him in fruitless, massive transfusions), was a grim ode to the short, brutal life of a gangster.

The Dutchman's last words (taken down by

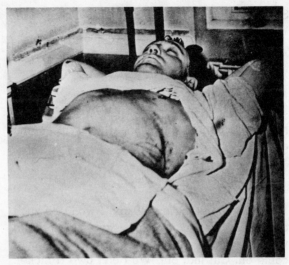

New York gangster Dutch Schultz mortally wounded, 10/23/35, babbled and raved before dying. (UPI)

police stenographer, F. J. Long): "George, don't make no full moves. What have you done with him? Oh, mama, mama, mama. Oh, stop it, stop it; oh, oh, oh. Sure, sure, mama.

"Now listen, Phil, [possibly referring to his ex-partner policy king Dandy Phil Kastel], fun is fun. Ah, please, papa. What happened to the sixteen? Oh, oh, he done it. Please.

"John, [a reference to Johnny Torrio?] please, oh, did you buy the hotel? You promised a million, sure. Get out. I wished I knew.

"Please make it quick, fast and furious. Please. Fast and furious. Please help me get out. I am getting my wind back, thank God. Please, please, oh, please. You will have to please tell him, you got no case.

"You get ahead with the dot-dash system. Didn't I speak that time last night? Whose number is that in your pocket book, Phil—13780.

"Who was it? Oh—please, please. Reserve decision. Police, police. Henry and Frankie.

"Oh, oh, dog biscuits and when he is happy, he doesn't get snappy . . . please, please to do this. Then Henry, Henry, Frankie you didn't meet him, you didn't even meet me. The glove will fit what I say. Oh, Kayiyi, Kayiyi. Sure, who cares when you are through? How do you know this?

"How do you know this? Well, then—oh, Cocao know—thinks he is a grandpa again. He is jumping around. No Hobo and Poboe. I think it means the same thing."

Police Sergeant L. Conlon attempted to quiz

Schultz about the shooting at the Chophouse. "Who shot you?" he asked Dutch.

"The boss himself."

"He did?"

"Yes, I don't know."

"What did he shoot you for?"

"I showed him boss. Do you hear me meet him? An appointment. Appeal stuck. All right, mother."

"Was it the boss who shot you?"

"Who shot me? No one."

"We will help you."

"Will you get me up? Okay, I won't be such a big creep. Oh, mama, I can't go through with it. Please. Oh—and then he clips me; come on. Cut that out. We don't owe a nickel. Hold it. Instead, hold it against him. I am a pretty good pretzler. Winnifred. Department of Justice. I even got it from the department. Sir, please stop it. Say listen the—last night."

"Don't holler," Conlon told the delirious gangster.

"I don't want to holler."

"What did they shoot you for?"

"I don't know, sir, honestly I don't. I don't even know who was with me, honestly. I went to the toilet. I was in the toilet and when I reach the—the boy came at me."

"The big fellow gave it to you?"

"Yes, he gave it to me."

"Do you know who this big fellow was?"

"No." Schultz rolled back into raving: "If we wanted to break the ring . . . No, please—I get a month. They did it. Come on, ——[name garbled], cut me off and says you are not to be the beneficiary of this will. Is that right? I will be checked and double checked and please pull for me. Will you pull? How many good ones and how many bad ones? Please, I had nothing with him; he was a cowboy in one of the seven days a week fight. No business. No hangouts. No friends. Nothing. Just what you pick up and what you need.

"I don't know who shot me. Don't put anyone near this check. You might have. Please do it for me. Let me get up, heh? In the olden days, they waited and they waited. Please give me shot. It is from the factory. Sure, that is a bad—well. Oh, good, ahead. That happens for trying. I don't want harmony. I want harmony. Oh, mama, mama! Who give it to him? Who give it to him? Let me in the district—fire—factory that he was nowhere near. It smoldered.

"No, no. There are only ten of us. There are ten million fighting somewhere of you, so get your onions up and we will throw up the truce flag. Oh, please let me up. Please shift me. Police are here. Communistic—strike—baloney—honestly this is a habit I get. Sometimes I give it and sometimes I don't. Oh, I am still in. That settles it. Are you sure? Please let me get in and eat. Let him harness himself to you and then bother you.

"Please don't ask me to go there. I don't want to. I still don't want him in the path. It is no use to stage a riot. The sidewalk was in trouble and the bears were in trouble and I broke it up. Please put me in that room. Please keep him in control. My gilt-edged stuff and those dirty rats have tuned in. Please, mother, don't tear, don't rip; that is something that shouldn't be spoken about. Please get me up, my friends. Please look out, the shooting is a bit wild and that kind of shooting saved a man's life.

"No payrolls. No walls. No coupons. That would be entirely out. Pardon me, I forgot. I am plaintiff and not defendant. Look out. Look out for him. Please. He owes me money; he owes everyone money. Why can't he just pull out and give me control?

"Please, mother, you pick me up now. Please, you know me.

"No, don't scare me. My friends and I think I do a better job. Police are looking for you all over. Be instrumental in letting us know. They are Englishmen [a possible reference to British-born Owney Madden] and they are a type and I don't know who is best, they or us. Oh, sir, get the doll a roofing. You can play jacks and girls do that with a soft ball and do tricks with it. It takes all events into consideration. No. No. And it is no. A boy has never wept nor dashed a thousand kim. Did you hear me?"

"Who shot you," Conlon again asked the Dutchman.

"I don't know."

"The doctor wants you to lie quiet."

"That is what I want to do."

"How many shots were fired?"

"I don't know."

"How many?"

"Two thousand. Come on, get some money in that treasury. We need it. Come on, please get it. I can't tell you to. That is not what you have in the book. Oh, please, warden. What am I going to do for money? Please put me up on my feet at once. You are a hard-boiled man. Did you hear me? I would hear it, the Circuit Court would hear it, and the Supreme Court might hear it. If that ain't the payoff. Please crack down on the Chinaman's [Chink Sherman, a Schultz rival] friends and Hitler's commander. I am sore and I am going up and I am going to give you honey if I can. Mother is the best bet and don't let Satan draw you too fast."

Conlon persisted in his questioning. "What did the big fellow shoot you for?"

"Him? John? Over a million, five million dollars."

"You want to get well, don't you?"

"Yes."

"Then lie quiet."

"Yes. I will lie quiet."

"John shot you," Conlon said, "and we will take care of John."

"That is what caused the trouble. Look out. Please get me up. If you do this, you can go on and jump right here in the lake. I know who they are. They are French people [perhaps a reference to Owney Madden's chief enforcer, Big Frenchy DeMange]. All right. Look out, look out. Phhhh . . . my memory is gone. A work relief. Police. Who gets it? I don't know and I don't want to know, but look out. It can be traced. He changed for the worse. Please look out; my fortunes have changed and come back and went back since that. It was desperate. I am wobbly. You ain't got nothing on him but we got it on his helper."

Conlon leaned forward. "Control yourself."

"But I am dying."

"No, you are not."

"Come on, mama. All right, dear, you have to get it."

At this point, Schultz's wife entered the room and sat next to the babbling gangster. "This is Frances," she said.

"Then pull me out. I am half crazy. They won't let me get up. They dyed my shoes. Give me something. I am so sick. Give me some water, the only thing that I want. Open this up and break it so I can touch you. Dannie [obviously Dannie Iamascia], please get me in the car."

Mrs. Schultz left the room and Conlon resumed his questioning.

"Who shot you?"

"I don't know. I didn't even get a look. I don't know who could have done it. Anybody.

Kindly take my shoes off."

"They are off."

"No, there's a handcuff on them. The Baron says these things. I know what I am doing here with my collection of papers. It isn't worth a nickel to two guys like you or me, but to a collector it is worth a fortune. It is priceless. I am going to turn it over to . . . Turn your back to me, please. Henry, I am so sick now. The police are getting many complaints. Look out. I want that G-note. Look out for Jimmy Valentine for he is an old pal of mine. Come on, come on, Jim. Okay, okay, I am all through. Can't do another thing.

"Look out, mama, look out for her. You can't beat him. Police, mama, Helen, mother, please take me out. I will settle the indictment. Shut up, you got a big mouth! Please help me up, Henry. Max, come over here. French-Canadian bean soup. I want to pay. Let them leave me alone."

Then, for two hours, the Dutchman said nothing. He died at 8:40 p.m.

[ALSO SEE Louis "Lepke" Buchalter, Vincent "Mad Dog" Coll, John T. "Legs" Diamond, Meyer Lansky, Charles "Lucky" Luciano, Owney Madden, Benjamin "Bugsy" Siegel, The Syndicate.]

SCHWARTZ, CHARLES HENRY
Murderer, Swindler ● (1895-1925)

An enterprising young man, Schwartz hurriedly built a chemical plant in the sleepy California town of Walnut Creek, close to San Francisco, in 1925 and claimed that his Pacific Cellulose Plant would begin the manufacturing of synthetic silk. Schwartz boasted that he possessed a secret formula by which such magic could be performed.

But the only activity in Schwartz's cavernous plant of any consequence was a bizarre murder scheme to collect a $185,000 life insurance policy the owner had taken out on himself. A trained chemist, Schwartz decided to blow up his building and himself along with it—or a reasonable facsimile of himself. He planned meticulously.

On July 25, 1925, Schwartz had a molar on the upper right side of his jaw removed. Then he waited for a *doppleganger* to appear. Days later, on July 30, 1925, a traveling missionary, Gilbert Warren Barbe, who looked enough like Schwartz to be his twin, was in the chemist's office. How he came to be there was never discovered, but Schwartz made good use of the man. After clubbing him to death, the chemist dragged the body to a nearby closet and then returned to his desk.

Schwartz then called in his shop foreman, Walter Gonzales, and, while talking to him about routine matters, withdrew his coin purse and deliberately counted out his change which came to $1.73. Gonzales was then excused and went back to work. So did Schwartz. He went to the closet with a chisel in his hand, opened the closet door and promptly knocked out Barbe's upper right molar.

After his employees had left the plant for the night, Schwartz placed Barbe's corpse on the floor of his office and soaked the place with inflammable chemicals. These he ignited and then fled.

The plant exploded minutes later. By the time firemen arrived and fought their way into Schwartz's office, only the charred hulk of a man whose face had been totally obliterated by the fire was found. Inside his pocket was a coin purse containing $1.73. Walter Gonzales, who rushed in to identify his employer, did not hesitate.

"It's Mr. Schwartz," Gonzales gasped, noting the coin purse and its contents. "I left him here only a while ago."

The incident might have ended there, written off as an accidental death (also covered in Schwartz's insurance policy) had it not been for the disturbing fact discovered by insurance investigators, that the deceased was three inches taller than Schwartz.

In addition, the indomitable private criminologist Edward O. Heinrich was called in on the case and, through painstaking examination, learned the dead man's true identity after determining that the missing molar had been chiseled out of the mouth. Burned, but recognizable pages of Scripture found on the body, along with other scraps of paper having the dead man's handwriting brought about the identification of evangelist Gilbert Warren Barbe.

A manhunt for Schwartz ensued. Authorities

Subtle murderer Charles Henry Schwartz tried to pass off another's body as his own for insurance money in 1925. (UPI)

were denied the use of photos; the chemist had quietly slipped into his home while his wife was out and removed every picture of himself. An early photo was finally unearthed and printed repeatedly in several West Coast newspapers. A reader caught sight of the wanted Schwartz's picture and identified him to police as a man living under the name of Harold Warren (employing Barbe's middle name as an alias, no less), a resident of Oakland.

Police closed in on the address given to them by the informant. Locating his apartment in a cheap rooming house, officers banged loudly on the door. "Open the door! We're police!" they shouted.

They were greeted by silence. Then the officers threatened to smash down the door. With this a single shot rang out and they broke down the door. Charles Henry Schwartz was found lying on the floor with a bullet through his temple, quite dead.

On the table in the center of the room was a note the killer chemist had penned to his wife in which he attempted to exonerate himself:

"My dear wife:

I am writing you without making any excuses; but one thing I will tell you, I am not guilty of the crime they accuse me of.

Last Monday a man called at the factory for work. I was in the lab. He came straight in. We talked a little while, when suddenly the man told me if I didn't give him work, I would have to give him money.

He attacked me. I gave him a blow on his head. He fell. I gave him another. Suddenly, I knew he was dead. . . .

I decided to run away, but made a dirty job of it. I put the man in the closet, got ready. Can you imagine how I felt all this time? Oh, God, how I suffered. . . .

I wish to tell you, my dear little girl, I do not know the man [Barbe], never looked how he was dressed, never touched him after that. The only thing I did was I tried to burn him, to wipe out and go—go I do not know where. . . . .

I kiss this in bidding and kissing you goodbye. My last kiss is for you, Alice."

SCOTT, JAMES
Causing A Catastrophe ● (1970-   )

On July 17, 1993, the wall of sandbags holding back the swollen Mississippi River at West Quincy, Mo., gave way and flooded more than 14,000 acres of rich farmland. This disaster, it was later learned, was caused by 24-year-old James Scott, an Illinois resident who removed the crucial sandbags.

Scott's reported reason for bringing about the disaster was so that his estranged wife would be stranded on the other side of the river and he could hold a party without her. Scott was tried and convicted of causing a catastrophe and, on December 5, 1993, was sentenced to life imprisonment.

SEADLUND, JOHN HENRY
Murderer, Kidnapper ● (1910-1938)

BACKGROUND: BORN AND RAISED IN RURAL MINNESOTA. MINOR PUBLIC EDUCATION. ORIGINAL OCCUPATION, LABORER. DESCRIPTION: 5'9", BROWN EYES, BROWN CURLY HAIR, SLENDER. ALIASES: PETER ANDERS. RECORD: ARRESTED FOR BURGLARIZING A RESTAURANT IN MINN., IN 1927; GIVEN MINOR JAIL TERM, ESCAPED; BECAME PETTY THIEF, HOLDING UP STORES, FILLING STATIONS AND BURGLARIZING HOMES; KIDNAPPED WITH JAMES ATWOOD GRAY NEAR FRANKLIN PARK, ILL., CHARLES S. ROSS, 72-YEAR-OLD GREETING CARD MANUFACTURER, ON 9/25/37, HOLDING HIM FOR $50,000 RANSOM WHICH WAS PAID ON 10/8/37; MURDERED ROSS AND GRAY SOMETIME IN EARLY OCTOBER, 1937 NEAR SPOONER, WIS.; ARRESTED AT SANTA ANITA RACETRACK, 1/14/38; CONVICTED AND SENTENCED TO DEATH IN THE ELECTRIC CHAIR; EXECUTED AT THE COOK COUNTY JAIL IN SPRING OF 1938.

For ten years, John Henry Seadlund, born and bred in Minnesota, tramped throughout the country. He had never been much good to anyone, even himself. Embarking on a criminal career at age seventeen, he quickly discovered his incompetence as a thief when in 1927 he attempted to burglarize a restaurant and was caught in the act. He was jailed for a short term, but he escaped, making his way across the country on freight trains.

When Seadlund worked, which was rarely, he took odd day laborer chores, earning just enough money to travel on and, perhaps, place a few bets at racetracks since he was an inveterate gambler. During the Depression years even odd jobs were impossible to find; Seadlund turned to petty crime, holding up a gas station in Illinois, robbing a store in Minnesota.

He drifted without purpose or plan. Then, in 1937, Seadlund met a 22-year-old sneak thief named James Atwood Gray, who was from Kentucky. Gray ached to become an armed bandit and he showed Seadlund two pistols he had obtained to achieve that end. The two robbed a few homes and blackjacked a couple of drunks. Their pattern of crime drastically changed when they drove into Illinois in a stolen car in September of 1937.

On the night of September 25, 1937, Seadlund and Gray spotted an expensive, late-model car cruising down a lonely road in Franklin Park, Ill. Inside and at the wheel was 72-year-old Charles S. Ross, a wealthy manufacturer of greeting cards from Chicago. At his side was his secretary, Florence Freihage. The couple had just dined in the exclusive Fargo Hotel Restaurant in Sycamore, Ill. and were returning to Chicago at a leisurely speed.

Seadlund and Gray thought the occupants of the expensive-looking car ideal prospects for robbery and zoomed ahead of them, forcing the car to a halt by cutting in front of it. Seadlund jumped out and ran back to the car with a pistol in his hand.

Ross studied the man approaching, saw the

gun in his hand, and said, in an almost philosophical way: "I've often thought of being kidnapped." Apparently the thought had never occurred to a small-time crook like Seadlund but once the words were spoken, he hugged the idea like a long-lost safety deposit box.

Seadlund ordered Ross out of the car and into his own, telling Miss Freihage to stay where she was. After the kidnappers had departed, Florence Freihage frantically drove to a filling station, clambered out of Ross' car and raced to a phone. She babbled hysterically to police that her escort had been kidnapped.

When Mrs. Ross was notified at her fashionable Commonwealth Avenue home in Chicago, she, too, became hysterical. She explained that her husband had a slight heart ailment but "if he's kidnapped, my husband can't live long. His doctors say he must have constant attention."

The FBI, along with local police, at first did not believe Ross was kidnapped. Upon investigation, Miss Freihage's story held up. The search for Ross and his kidnappers commenced.

Seadlund drove to Wisconsin, where, Ross informed him, he had a friend who could act as an intermediary in handling any ransom money. The friend, Harvey Brackett of Williams Bay, was contacted by letter on September 30, 1937. It was written in Ross' hand and succinctly stated: "I am held for ransom. I have stated I am worth $100,000. Try and raise $50,000."

Brackett sent the note to Mrs. Ross in Chicago and she turned it over to Special Agent Earl Connelley, who had been sent from Washington, D.C. by J. Edgar Hoover to personally supervise the case. Connelley verified the note as having been written by Ross and instructed the businessman's wife to turn over the money. A second note followed, also in Ross' handwriting, outlining the details of how the money was to be turned over to the kidnappers.

Mrs. Ross followed directions and placed an ad in a Chicago paper reading: "For Sale: 1934 Dodge Sedan. $250. William Gegenwarth, 5043 South Western Avenue." The amount stated in the ad indicated that Mrs. Ross was offering $25,000, not the amount demanded, $50,000.

Seadlund wrote back in a carefully typed note, demanding the $50,000 and instructing

Mrs. Ross' lawyers to contact a motorcycle shop, one he had picked at random, and obtain a driver "for a dangerous mission." A rider from the shop was employed and waited for the next move.

The FBI, meanwhile, had developed a print from one of the ransom notes. The typeface on the notes indicated that the kidnapper was using a new typewriter. Agents then checked all typewriter shops in Chicago which had recently sold a new typewriter. More than 150 agents scoured the city and finally got a description of a curly-haired man who had purchased a new portable typewriter. Using this description they tracked down an address in a cheap rooming house where a "Peter Anders" had stayed. He had moved days before, leaving no forwarding address. Prints in the room matched the one the agents had taken from the ransom note.

In one of the most massive FBI investigations ever, the Bureau had determined the description and fingerprints of the kidnapper in a matter of weeks. They also learned that the kidnapper was addicted to gambling, a student of racing forms.

Another note demanding the payment of $50,000 arrived at Mrs. Ross' residence. With it was a picture taken of her husband, standing in a wooded area and holding a Chicago newspaper dated October 2, 1937. The motorcyclist, George Kukovac, was given $50,000 in marked bills and sent to deliver the ransom.

He headed Northwest in a strange stop-and-start pattern, following Seadlund's orders to the letter. On the road to Rockford, Ill., a car came slowly up behind him. Kukovac was dressed all in white. His cycle had also been painted white, as per Seadlund's orders, to distinguish him as the one delivering the ransom money.

By pre-arranged plan, the car's lights blinked three times, and, without looking behind him, Kukovac unzipped a package containing the ransom money and dropped it as he scooted forward. Seadlund stopped his car as Kukovac drove out of sight and picked up the money.

With that, Seadlund, Gray and Ross disappeared for close to three months. Seadlund had sent Mrs. Ross a last note stating that he would return Mr. Ross to Chicago, "if I collect, and if I have an opportunity to get rid of the bills by that time."

Agent Connelley knew the letter was a sham. He stated that he knew the kidnapper was aware of the fact that the bills were marked and that it would take months to dump them. Mrs. Ross gave up hope of ever seeing her husband alive again.

FBI agents throughout the country were alerted to look for the marked bills. They turned up almost everywhere—Philadelphia, New York, Washington, Cincinnati, Cleveland, Toledo, Detroit, Atlanta, Miami, Palm Beach. The Bureau concluded that "Anders" was spending money almost exclusively in race tracks across the country. Then the pins on their map indicating where the bills had turned up began to trail West, first in Arkansas, then in Denver. Agents reasoned that "Anders" was heading for the Santa Anita Race Track in Los Angeles which was about to hold some well-touted races.

Hoover flew to Los Angeles and took charge. The FBI had performed poorly in the Lindbergh kidnapping case and the Director did not want any cause for error this time. He ordered agents to man every betting window at Santa Anita. Each agent had a list of the serial numbers of the hot Ross bills. The hunch that the kidnapper would show up at the track was accurate.

Seadlund stepped up to the $10 window on January 14, 1938 to make a bet. An agent identified his bill as one of those listed as Ross ransom money. He signaled to other agents standing by and Seadlund was arrested without a fight.

Once in custody, the kidnapper calmly admitted his guilt. When asked where Ross was, he said without inflection: "Dead, of course. I shot him. I also killed the fellow with me, a punk named James Atwood Gray. They're dead in a hole up in Wisconsin."

After confessing, Seadlund looked up at agents around him and asked: "Will I get hanged or fried?"

The ransom money, $47,345 of it, was recovered, found by agents following Seadlund's directions. (Seadlund explained that he had been lucky and won at the track.) Agents also found the slain bodies of Ross and Atwood in a pit in Spooner, Wisconsin. Seadlund had taken them to the spot personally and told them to "dig there."

As to Seadlund's fate, his question was answered two months later when he was strapped

Murderer and kidnapper John Henry Seadlund received his death sentence with a smile and phony brow-mopping; he was the most vicious killer J. Edgar Hoover ever knew. (UPI)

into the electric chair in the Cook County, Ill. jail. "The most vicious cold-blooded killer" J. Edgar Hoover "ever knew" died without uttering a word of regret.

SELZ, RALPH JEROME VON BRAUN
Murderer ● (1909-   )

"I am sulky, whiny, cry too much and am inclined to outbreaks of brutality." This was one of the strange comments Ralph Jerome Von Braun Selz, better known as "The Laughing Killer," made to reporters during his sensational 1936 murder trial. Selz, at the time, was being tried for the murder of Ada Franch Rice, the estranged wife of the mayor of Gnome, Alaska. He mugged for photographers then, smiling ridiculously, sticking out his tongue through a leering grin, plugging his ears with his thumbs and finger-waving to news cameras.

Moments later he grew somber and stated: "I am a happy-go-lucky fellow by nature. I've roamed a lot and laughed my way through life; but fellow, I'm not laughing now, no matter what you may think." The reporter was aghast. All the while Selz was talking a maniacal smile stretched wide his pudgy cheeks.

In late 1935, Selz, a vagabond lothario who prided himself on his handsome features and his ability to attract females, arrived in San Francisco. "All the girls are plenty crazy about me," he was fond of saying. He was 27 at the time and looking to live on "the sunny side of the street."

Only a few days in town, Selz literally bumped into Ada Franch Rice, 58, who had left her connubial bed forever. Mrs. Rice was surfeited with cash and an unrelenting sex drive. The two moved into a small cottage in Palo Alto.

Many months later, on February 27, 1936, Selz was picked up on a charge of stealing an auto. Police discovered that he was unemployed yet had plenty of money. They then learned that he had been forging the signature of Mrs. Rice and cashing her checks on her Palo Alto bank account.

Mrs. Rice had been reported missing months before. Police grilled Selz for two weeks, keeping him incommunicado. Deputy Sheriff Thomas Maloney of San Mateo County told newsmen that Selz was "a hot one" (murder suspect) and added: "We are positive that we can force a confession from Selz in a few more days. He is starting to crack."

The fact that Selz was denied any legal counsel during this time later helped to get him released from prison. Selz finally did "crack" and confessed to killing Mrs. Rice and burying her body on a lonely ridge in the Santa Cruz Mountains. He claimed her death had been an accident. One night, he explained to authorities, he had entered Mrs. Rice's cabin and was attacked by "a Bulgarian." In desperation, he grabbed a poker and wildly flayed at his assailant.

When he managed to turn on the lights, Selz stated, he was greeted with the surprise of his life. There, dressed only in "scanties" was the body of Mrs. Rice sprawling before him.

Selz's admission provoked Sheriff James J. McGrath to tell newsmen: "[He] is almost a proven wholesale killer . . . [He has] already killed at least ten or eleven people in the Bay Area and six or seven in other parts of California." These charges, however, were never upheld.

Selz went on trial for his life. Before entering the courtroom, Selz led his guards to the remote spot where he had secreted Mrs. Rice's body in the Santa Cruz Mountains. A host of newsmen and cameramen accompanied the expedition. Selz acted queerly throughout the

trip. He joked and laughed with newsmen. He clowned before the cameras.

When deputies began to unearth the body from a shallow grave, Selz spouted cornball one-liners. He laughed uproariously while the corpse was being lifted from the pit and spectators held handkerchiefs to their noses to fight the stench.

"If you guys want a sensation," he squealed, "try hauling a corpse around in a car with the hoot owls hooting at night." He did "clog dances" about the makeshift grave. "I'm going to Hollywood when I get through here," he said through his chilling smile. He danced another jig before stunned newsmen. He stuck out his tongue and smiled. He pulled his nose and rolled his eyes. He beat his chest, ruffled his hair. Grim photographers recorded it all. "Say," he said, as deputies led him away, "I haven't had any breakfast yet. You guys got any gum?"

Selz's trial was brief. Only one material witness testified for him, a 25-year-old woman with whom he had been living, named Dorothy Hemmer. She, too, had been a vagabond, riding the rails and sleeping in hobo camps. Her appearance in court moved one writer to state: "Perhaps no better description of her general character could be given than plain recitation of the fact that she wears bell bottom trousers instead of a skirt (shockingly unconventional for 1936), and a sweater bearing on its bosom the approximation of a baseball player's picture with the insignia, 'Babe Ruth, Sultan of Swat.' "

After pleading guilty, Selz was convicted of murder on March 13, 1936 in a three-and-a-half-hour courtroom appearance and sentenced to life imprisonment. He was still smiling when the door of his prison cell closed upon him. The Laughing Killer was again heard from in 1945 when he escaped from the Chino State Prison. He was recaptured almost a year later in Calgary, Alberta. Oddly enough, lawmen found him in a barracks there; Selz had enlisted in the Canadian Army.

Again in 1962, Selz escaped, this time from the minimum-security San Luis Obispo jail. He was captured three days later only a few miles away while munching happily on a candy bar.

The Laughing Killer never stopped filing petitions for release. In one attempt at parole he stated that his strange actions following

The laughing killer—Ralph Jerome von Braun Selz; he did dances around his victim's grave. (UPI)

his arrest in 1936 were the result of being starved by the police. This caused him to become hallucinatory, he claimed. "The only release from the hallucinatory fears," Selz wrote, "was a pretense of infectious humor whose parallel is akin to a small boy, shouting or whistling as he passes a graveyard at night time."

Selz was paroled in 1966 after spending thirty years in jail but was picked up and returned to prison a little more than a year later for welfare fraud. He claimed that his duplicating of welfare applications was the result of, again, "hallucinations." He is presently in prison, ailing from hardening of the arteries, dropsy, and high blood pressure.

Mention of the Rice killing no longer brings a smile to Selz's lips. He merely stares and states: "No comment on that one."

SHAEFFER, DANIEL
Murderer ● (? -1832)

The only thing on handyman Shaeffer's mind was the voluptuous body of Mrs. Elizabeth Bowers, a well-to-do resident of Lancaster, Pa., whom he accosted in No-

vember, 1831. Entering the pretty young widow's home, Shaeffer extracted her promise not to resist him or scream out, but twice she asked him "not to kill" her.

Mrs. Bowers' statement obviously took hold in Shaeffer's mind and he suffocated her with a pillow after he had taken his pleasure. Neighbors finding the woman days later assumed she had merely died in her sleep and quietly buried her; Schaeffer escaped without suspicion. He could not, however, elude his conscience, and after listening to a moving sermon delivered from the gallows in Frederick, Md., where another murderer was to meet his fate, Shaeffer went to the local sheriff and confessed the killing of Mrs. Bowers.

The sheriff thought him drunk and threw him out of his office. Shaeffer persisted and his statement was finally and seriously written down. He was promptly tried, convicted, and hanged April 13, 1832.

SHELDON GANG

Chicago's Sheldon gang was strictly a bootlegging mob that operated on the city's Southwest Side and served as a satellite to Al Capone. Ralph Sheldon led a small band of killers and still operators from about 1920 to 1932, warring at times with the neighboring Saltis-McErlane gang and the South Side O'Donnells gang led by Edward "Spike" O'Donnell.

Sheldon and his boys were not above making deals, however, with such anti-Capone stalwarts as George "Bugs" Moran, particularly when it came to purchasing truckloads of hijacked liquor from Moran to supply their thirsty speakeasy drops.

The Sheldon gang disappeared with the coming of the national syndicate in the early 1930s.

[ALSO SEE Saltis-McErlane Gang.]

SHERMAN, LYDIA
Murderer ● (? -1879)

Mass poisoners Lucrezia Borgia and the Marchioness of Brinvilliers would have found it difficult indeed to match the sheer ruthlessness of America's Lydia Sherman, who admitted to killing at least eight persons. The true count was probably closer to an even dozen.

Lydia's first husband, Edward Struck, was dismissed from the New York City Police Department with a charge of cowardice. Struck took to drink and became violent when soused. Lydia's eighteen-year marriage with this man ended when she administered to him a fatal dose of arsenic in his soup. The poison seemed to solve her marital problems with such ease that Lydia decided to eliminate her responsibility to the four children she had borne. They were given lethal amounts of poison in their meals and died.

Authorities did not grow suspicious of the deaths since Lydia never made any insurance claims; her murdering was merely an expeditious way of canceling troublesome people—her family. The next to die was a man named Hurlburt, whom Lydia married after he promised her his estate following his death. His demise came fourteen months later.

A widower, Horatio Nelson Sherman from Derby, Conn., was her next victim. After marrying Sherman, a drunkard, Lydia grew to despise his two small children. She poisoned them to death. Then she poisoned Sherman.

With the death of Lydia's husband Sherman, doctors became suspicious and examined the body. The corpse contained heavy amounts of arsenic. Mrs. Sherman was arrested and broke down almost immediately, admitting the murders of two husbands (she stated that Hurlburt may have died because some arsenic "accidentally" got into his salad) and six children. In explaining why she murdered her first husband Struck, Lydia stated: "I gave him the arsenic because I was discouraged. I know now that that is not much of an excuse, but I felt so much trouble that I did not think about that." As far as Sherman, his two children and her own four offspring, Lydia simply reported that she felt that by giving them poison they "would be better off."

Convicted of second degree murder, Lydia Sherman, mass murderer, was given a life sentence and died in prison.

SHIRT TAILS GANG

An early New York gang, circa 1825, the Shirt Tails got their names from several sloppy members who habitually wore their shirts outside their pants. Basically sneak thieves and muggers, the Shirt Tails centered their activities around the Five Points section. In their battles with other gangs, the Shirt Tails generally sided with the more heavily-staffed Plug Uglies, Chichesters, and Dead Rabbits gangs. The Shirt Tails disappeared in the 1890s, making way for the last of New York's street-terror gangs, The Five Pointers.

SICA, JOSEPH
Syndicate Gangster ● (1911-1983)

Sica was, according to the McClellan committee, a long-time Mafia power in Newark, N. J., the place of his birth. His arrest record dates back to 1928 and includes charges of robbery, murder, extortion, and narcotics trafficking. He had maintained coast-to-coast contacts with underworld notables for years.

Sica, along with a dozen other syndicate gangsters, was indicted for conspiracy to sell narcotics in California in 1950. Abraham Davidian, the chief witness against him, was shot in bed shortly thereafter and the case was dropped.

SIEGEL, BENJAMIN ("BUGSY")
Syndicate Gangster ● (1906-1947)

BACKGROUND: BORN 2/28/06 IN WILLIAMSBURG SECTION OF BROOKLYN, N. Y. ONE BROTHER, MAURICE; THREE SISTERS, ESTHER, ETHEL, ESSIE. MARRIED ESTHER KRAKOWER, TWO DAUGHTERS MILLICENT, BARBARA. MINOR PUBLIC EDUCATION. DESCRIPTION: 5'10", BLUE EYES, BLACK HAIR, SLENDER. ALIASES: HARRY ROSEN. RECORD: ROBBED, CIRCA 1921, A LOAN COMPANY IN THE LOWER EAST SIDE OF MANHATTAN; JOINED A JUVENILE GANG ABOUT THIS TIME LED BY MEYER LANSKY; EARLY CRIMINAL ASSOCIATES INCLUDED ALBERT ANASTASIA, CHARLES "LUCKY" LUCIANO, MOE SEDWAY (MORRIS SEDWITZ); ARRESTED FOR RAPE, 1926 IN BROOKLYN, RELEASED; ARRESTED FOR CARRYING CONCEALED WEAPONS IN APRIL, 1928 IN PHILADELPHIA, DISMISSED; MURDERED WITH ALBERT ANASTASIA, JOE ADONIS, AND VITO GENOVESE, JOE THE BOSS MASSERIA ON 4/15/31 IN SCARPATO'S RESTAURANT, CONEY ISLAND, BROOKLYN, ON ORDERS FROM MEYER LANSKY AND CHARLES "LUCKY" LUCIANO; ARRESTED 11/11/31 AT A GANGSTER CONCLAVE IN NEW YORK'S HOTEL FRANCONIA (THOSE ATTENDING INCLUDED LOUIS "LEPKE" BUCHALTER, JACOB "GURRAH" SHAPIRO, PHILIP "LITTLE FARVEL" KOVALICK (ALIAS COHN), HARRY TEITELBAUM, LOUIS "SHADOWS" KRAVITZ, HYMAN "CURLY" HOLTZ, JOSEPH "DOC" STACHER, AND HARRY "BIG GREENIE" GREENBERG), NO CHARGE MADE, RELEASED; ARRESTED IN 1932 IN MIAMI BEACH FOR GAMBLING, $100 FINE; AS CO-LEADER OF THE BUGS-MEYER MOB (WITH MEYER LANSKY) CONVOYED ILLEGAL LIQUOR SHIPMENTS FROM PHILADELPHIA TO MANHATTAN DURING THE ERALY 1930S. HELPED TO ORGANIZE MURDER, INC. WITH LANSKY, LEPKE, AND SHAPIRO IN EARLY 1930S WITH BODYGUARD ABE "KID TWIST" RELES BECOMING ONE OF THE ORGANIZATION'S TOP "HIT" MEN; INVOLVED WITH A NUMBER OF MURDERS WHILE PARTICIPATING IN GANG WARFARE WITH WAXEY GORDON AND HIS CHIEF LIEUTENANT CHARLES "CHINK" SHERMAN, 1931-33; INJURED IN THIS GANG WAR IN 1934 WHEN A BOMB WAS LOWERED DOWN THE CHIMNEY OF THE BUGS-MEYER HEADQUARTERS ON GRAND STREET IN MANHATTAN BY RIVAL GANGSTER, FRANCIS ANTHONY "TONY" FABRIZZO, A GORDON GUNMAN; MURDERED FABRIZZO DAYS LATER IN SOUTHWEST BROOKLYN; MURDERED LOAN SHARKS JOSEPH "JOEY" AND LOUIS "PRETTY" AMBERG, 9/30/35; MURDERED BO WEINBERG, A LIEUTENANT OF DUTCH SCHULTZ IN 1935 AS A "FAVOR" TO SCHULTZ (WEINBERG HAD DOUBLE-CROSSED THE DUTCHMAN); SENT BY SYNDICATE LEADERS TO THE WEST COAST IN 1937 TO DEVELOP RACKETS THERE WITH UNDERWORLD BOSS JACK I. DRAGNA; BEGAN SYNDICATE-CONTROLLED GAMBLING IN LOS ANGELES, SMUGGLING OF HEROIN FROM MEXICO INTO CALIFORNIA, 1937-46; MURDERED HARRY "BIG

Benjamin "Bugsy" Siegel, friend of Hollywood stars, was first to establish rackets on the West Coast for the crime syndicate and then pioneered big time gambling in Nevada. (UPI)

GREENIE" GREENBERG WITH AL "ALLIE" TANNENBAUM, FRANKIE CARBO, AND WHITEY KRAKOWER ON 11/22/39 IN LOS ANGELES; MURDERED WHITEY KRAKOWER ON 7/31/40 IN BROOKLYN; MOVED INTO LAS VEGAS IN 1945, BUILT THE FLAMINGO HOTEL AND CASINO WHICH OPENED THE FOLLOWING YEAR; MURDERED IN THE BEVERLY HILLS HOME OF HIS MISTRESS, VIRGINIA HILL, ON 6/20/47, REPORTEDLY EXECUTED BY A SYNDICATE MURDER SQUAD.

The mob said Dutch Schultz would never come back. They said that the IRS had a solid case for his conviction in 1935. Bo Weinberg, Dutch's right-hand man, believed Vito Genovese and Lucky Luciano. Quickly, he snatched the Dutchman's empire of union rackets, brothels, and gambling. After swagging what he could, Weinberg turned over the Dutchman's numbers game in Harlem to Lucky Luciano and Vito Genovese.

But unlucky Bo had made a mistake. The Dutchman slipped out of the conviction and came back, and when he came back he ordered his bosom pal and hatchet man, Weinberg, killed.

The man who took the "contract" was one of the most ruthless killers in the underworld —Benjamin "Bugsy" Siegel, later to become the dapper consort of movie queens, countesses, and a high hob-nobber of West Coast society.

Under the pretense of having dinner with his old pal, Bugsy lured Weinberg to Brooklyn. There, on a dusky, garbage-strewn, and almost deserted street, Siegel got out of his car and suddenly ran around to where Weinberg was seated. He reached in and clubbed him on the head with a pistol.

The stunned gangster couldn't believe it— Bugsy had been one of the gangsters who told him to take over Schultz's rackets. As Weinberg looked up at Benny Siegel whom he had known as a child in Hell's Kitchen, seeing the knife in Bugsy's hand he must have realized that his friend was going to kill him.

"This is for being a rat and a double-crosser, you bastard!" Bugsy pumped the knife quickly into Weinberg's throat. Bo tried to scream out his pain but only a bubble of blood came from his mouth. Siegel then thrust the long blade into Weinberg's stomach. He concentrated on the stomach, puncturing the huge gangster several times. He had a specific reason for this last bit of savagery.

Professional syndicate killers had learned in the early gang wars during the 1920s that once a body was thrown into a lake, regardless of how it was weighted down, the air in a victim's stomach would cause the body to bob to the surface, creating messy inquiries.

Siegel knew this well since he developed the stomach puncture routine to let the air out and thus prevent the body from surfacing. He was very professional with Weinberg.

Driving casually to a hill overlooking the silvery Hudson River, Siegel got out wires and weights. He tied them securely about Weinberg's body and rolled the dead man into the river. After watching him go down, Siegel headed for his Broadway haunts. That night he promptly attacked and raped a chorus girl who was friendly with syndicate chieftain Joey Adonis. A favor for Dutch Schultz and a fight with "Joey A" in the same day—Bugsy didn't care. He was on his way up in the rackets with his pals Meyer Lansky (the two captained the Bug and Meyer outfit) and little Moe Sedway. Nobody was going to get in his way.

Benjamin Siegel, born of poor Jewish parents in Brooklyn, 1906, had to claw for life from the moment of his birth. All about him was corruption, poverty, disease, and early death. As a boy, he vowed to rise above the slums.

He grew fast and developed a fine athletic body. He was roughly handsome and little Moey Sedway followed him like a lapdog everywhere he went. Pushcart and stand peddlers along Lafayette Street in New York's Lower East Side hated to see this pair ambling toward them. It was always the same routine.

Benny would pause before a peddler and thumb through his merchandise. Then he would look up with a half grin and make the usual demand: "Give me a dollar."

"No," the meek answer would come.

"No?" Bugsy would say almost sweetly. "Okay, give me five dollars!"

"No, get outa here, youse bums. Leave me make my livin'!"

Benny would look at little Sedway who habitually lugged a quart jar of kerosene. "Okay," the Bug ordered Moey, "pour the stuff on his junk." Sedway would then gleefully dump the kerosene over the seller's merchandise.

Bugsy would drop a match to it and the whole stand would flare into consuming flames while the peddler cringed in horror and anguish. Next time he would pay the $5 and stay in business. And just to show the proprietors that he was a good fellow after all, Bugsy would patrol the street, making sure nobody bothered his "clients."

This boyhood protection racket was only the beginning for Bugsy. He was destined, he told Moe Sedway and later Meyer Lansky, for bigger things. "Class, that's the only thing that counts in life. Class. Without class and style a man's a bum, he might as well be dead."

As the Bug & Meyer gang took over hot cars, bootlegging, gambling rackets in sections of New York, New Jersey, and Philadelphia, the syndicate was formed. Everything was going well for the Bug until the early 1930s. Then, he, like Capone twenty years before him, got involved in a killing. At first Siegel hid out as a patient in a Catholic hospital, guarded by thugs. But, after several attempts on his life, Siegel decided to quit New York and convinced the syndicate to finance his move to the West Coast where he would develop new rackets for the "combine."

California was virgin territory for the syndicate in 1937. Alone, Jack Dragna held the reins on the underworld. The ruling six of the Cosa Nostra told Bugsy to consolidate things with Dragna and send them back a piece of the action. He was reportedly given a half million dollars to establish himself.

Another story had it that Siegel moved West to be near pretty French ingenue Ketti Gallion; though Bugsy never divorced his wife, who followed him with his two daughters to Hollywood, he remained a field-playing ladies' man to his dying days.

Bugsy rented a mansion owned by singer Lawrence Tibbet after arriving in Hollywood. He looked up an old friend—George Raft, who was a gossamer star in the movies by 1937 making $5,000 a week; they had grown up together in New York's Lower East Side. Siegel's plan was simple. George was associated with Hollywood's bigwigs and he was going to provide Bugsy with the proper introductions.

Raft, who had a genuine fondness for the gangster—Bugsy did have his charming, boyishly smiling side—did exactly that. Siegel passed himself off as a "sportsman." He began attending Santa Anita Race Track daily, betting heavily and almost always winning on "sure things."

The New York thugs who had grown up from the gutter would have been flabbergasted to see the Bug. He had met the Countess Dorothy Dendice Taylor DiFrasso, a wealthy joy-lusting woman who was madly in love with the handsome gangster.

Bugsy—who hated the nickname—cultivated this wild woman beyond the bedroom door whenever the whim moved her. The Countess and the gangster provided the Los Angeles press with many hot items. They were seen everywhere and with everyone—Jack Warner had them to his house; they socialized with Clark Gable, Cary Grant, Gary Cooper, and Jean Harlow. (Jean Harlow had originally been sent to Hollywood to seek her filmic fortune by none other than New Jersey gangster and Siegel chum, Abner "Longy" Zwillman who provided her and her family with money for years before she reached stardom. Harlow was one of Siegel's first "sponsors" in Hollywood.)

Bugsy had made the big time.

With strong-arm help such as Dragna, luna-tic Mickey Cohen, who brandished pistols at the drop of his 10-gallon hat, and faithful Moe Sedway, Bugsy also made it big in the rackets. Siegel backed and operated gambling dives along Los Angeles' waterfront and purchased a 15 per cent interest in a dog track in Culver City. He also financed old fashioned bootlegger, Anthony Cornero Stralla, in the establishment of a posh gambling ship, *The Rex*, which operated beyond the twelve-mile limit. Siegel and Dragna also set up a bookmaking wire service which stretched across the U.S., relaying West Coast racetrack results to bookies. In addition, Siegel inaugurated an elaborate and successful relay system whereby narcotics, such as heroin and opium, were smuggled into the U.S. from Mexico.

Reports also had it that the real reason Bugsy pursued the friendships of big name movie people was to blackmail them for indiscretions known to him. Nevertheless, Bugsy lived lavishly, throwing $5,000-a-night parties, spending as much as $10,000 a day at the track, and building up his wardrobe.

Siegel and the Countess had some high times together. Once, after listening to a repulsive Bowery bum tell them that there was $90,000,000 buried somewhere on Cocos Island 300 miles off the coast of Costa Rica (from the famous wreck of the *Mary Deere*), they formed an expedition.

With a crew that would have rivaled anything Damon Runyon could have mustered, Siegel and the Countess DiFrasso sailed southward on the sloop, the *Metha Nelson*. Bugsy kept his treasure hunters in the dark until the ship was well out to sea. Then he called them together and explained that millions in Spanish treasure was awaiting them. "We're gonna grab the stuff and then beat it," he said, his blue eyes blazing. "And then we're all gonna go home rich!"

They spent weeks cruising to the forlorn island (picked clean years before) only to blast half the isle away in search of the lost treasure. They found nothing. One report had it that Siegel, disgusted after wandering around Cocos for days without turning up anything, produced several hand grenades and, dressed in a stylish pinstripe suit and pointed two-tone shoes, stood lobbing the "potato-mashers" into the jungle.

Blasting was also another scheme Bugsy and the Countess developed. They unearthed two wacky scientists who claimed to have developed a super explosive called Atomite. They tested it for Bugsy and the Countess and blew away half a mountain.

"Terrific!" exclaimed Siegel, "but where do we sell this stuff?"

The Countess, an enterprising businesswoman and millionairess herself, knew. She winked wisely. "Mussolini."

So, before the Second World War broke out, the Countess DiFrasso and Bugsy sailed for Europe to demonstrate their miracle explosive for the power-mad Italian warlord. Mussolini had even put up $40,000 down payment to develop the munition.

After a great deal of fanfaronade, the demonstration came off—and fizzled. When the detonation button was pushed, only a small puff of smoke drifted upward. Il Duce blew his stack and demanded the return of his $40,-000. The Countess paid it back.

While staying in Italy at the DiFrasso estate, Siegel met the Germans Herman Goering and Dr. Joseph Goebbels. He hated both Nazis and, the story goes, threatened to kill them—but the Countess stopped him. (History might have thought differently of Benjamin "Bugsy" Siegel if he had.)

Bugsy met his pal George Raft on the Riviera that year but he didn't have much time to chat. He received a cable from the states, packed his bag, and flew home. His associates in America, namely Lansky, had informed Siegel that Harry "Big Greenie" Greenberg, an old-time Murder, Inc. associate, was about to turn police informer. Greenberg never got the chance.

Frankie Carbo, Siegel, and another boyhood chum, Whitey Krakower, killed Big Greenie as he was coming home one night in Los Angeles.

Shortly after that Whitey Krakower was gunned down in Manhattan. Ironically, George Raft, who was riding around with two plain-clothes cops in New York that night, went to the scene of the shooting. Whitey had been a boyhood pal of his, too. As he stood on the dark street looking down at the riddled body he knew that his pal Bugsy hadn't changed a bit.

Siegel's exploits after that became more subdued. Acquitted of the Greenberg murder he moved into the trans-America bookie wire service from which he earned millions both for himself and the syndicate.

He also acquired new women. One of them was the film star Wendy Barrie. Next it was the all-time syndicate call girl, Virginia Hill, who had slept with just about every big time gangster in America, including Joe Adonis. Bugsy had a habit of stealing Adonis's girls.

In 1945 Bugsy got the brainstorm of his life. He was going to transform the desert just east of Los Angeles to a gambling paradise . . . and he did. He sunk $6,000,000 into the building of the Flamingo Hotel in undeveloped Las Vegas—the living end of all plush gambling casinos.

He commuted between Los Angeles and Las Vegas, keeping his crime empire going in both places. For leisure, he would visit Raft on the studio set when he was filming and tell him he could act just as well.

To prove it, Bugsy would re-do one of Raft's scenes in front of the actor with little Moey Sedway taking a 16mm film of the vain gangster doing his bit. Moey Sedway would do anything for the Bug.

Meanwhile, with construction of the Flamingo (which was Virginia Hill's nickname) completed, Siegel began to reap huge profits as the suckers came to gamble at his legalized casino. Bugsy hadn't overlooked anything in the graciously styled hotel and gambling spa. Everything was tastefully appointed. Siegel even ordered his employees to wear tuxedos throughout the day. The Bug hadn't forgotten anything, except the syndicate.

Lucky Luciano, then deported but secretly in Havana to confer with syndicate board members, called the Bug to a meeting there. He wanted the $3,000,000 the syndicate put up for the Flamingo and the Bug told him to go to hell. Luciano said nothing and Siegel flew back to his crime empire in the sun.

But the sun went out suddenly on June 20, 1947 as Bugsy Siegel sat in Virginia Hill's $500,000 palatial home on Linden Drive in Beverly Hills. As he talked with one of his associates, Allen Smiley, somebody pumped three 30.30 rifle bullets into the Bug's head, killing him instantly. One of his eyes was blown clear out of his handsome head and across the expensively decorated living room.

Almost at the same moment, little Moey Sedway walked into the Flamingo Hotel in Las Vegas and shouted at Bugsy's manager: "We're taking over!"

Only five people—all members of the Siegel

family—went to Benjamin Siegel's funeral (Bugsy was buried in a closed $5,000 casket). The Countess DiFrasso was in Europe with no comment. Virginia Hill was in Europe . . . no comment. George Raft was at home with asthma. All of Hollywood stayed away and the boy who made it big being bad went into a marbled vault at age 41.

"We only kill each other," Siegel once told construction tycoon Del Webb when Webb was building the Flamingo. Meyer Lansky was the man who proved Bugsy's point.

[ALSO SEE Meyer Lansky, Charles "Lucky" Luciano, Murder, Inc., The Syndicate, Abner "Longy" Zwillman.]

SIRHAN, SIRHAN BISHARA
Assassin ● (1946-   )

"I think we can end the divisions within the United States," Robert Kennedy was saying to his supporters from the podium of the Embassy Ballroom of the Los Angeles Ambassador Hotel. The date was June 5, 1968 and Kennedy had just won the California primary.

He was happy, tired, jubilant, and grateful. "What I think is quite clear . . . is that we can work together. We are a great country, a selfless and compassionate country . . . so my thanks to all of you and on to Chicago and let's win there."

As Kennedy made his way off stage and toward a rear exit via a serving pantry, a young, dark-faced man waited in a group of well wishers with a rolled-up Kennedy campaign poster in his hand. Inside the poster was a .22-caliber revolver. His name was Sirhan Bishara Sirhan, a Palestinian, and he intended to assassinate Robert Kennedy.

Sirhan worked his way through the crowd and, dropping the poster, raised the pistol only ten inches from the candidate's face. He fired several times, hitting the Senator in the head.

Andrew West, a reporter for Mutual Radio, was next to Kennedy when he was shot. The reporter had been interviewing the candidate and his tape recorder was still whirring when Sirhan's shots were fired. As Kennedy's bodyguards, Roosevelt Grier and Rafer Johnson, rushed forward to grapple with the assassin, West excitedly blurted: "Senator Kennedy has been . . . Senator Kennedy has been shot! Is that possible, ladies and gentlemen? It *is* possible! . . . He has . . . Not only Senator Kennedy! Oh my God! . . . I am right here, and Rafer Johnson has hold of the man who apparently fired the shot. He still has the gun! The gun is pointed at *me* right this moment! Get the gun! Get the gun! Stay away from that guy! Get his thumb! Break it if you have to! Get the gun, Rafer! Hold him! We don't want another Oswald! Hold him, Rafer! Hold him! . . . The Senator is on the ground! . . . He is bleeding profusely . . . The ambulance has been called for, and this is a terrible thing! . . . The shock is so great that my mouth is dry . . . We are shaking as is everyone else . . . I do not know if the Senator is dead or alive. . . ."

The athletes Johnson and Grier finally subdued Sirhan. At their feet, Robert Kennedy was dying, from a bullet wound in the brain. Police arrived and began to lead the assassin from the hotel, forming a flying wedge with

Sirhan's victim, Senator Robert Kennedy, lies dying with a rosary on his chest, 6/5/68. (UPI)

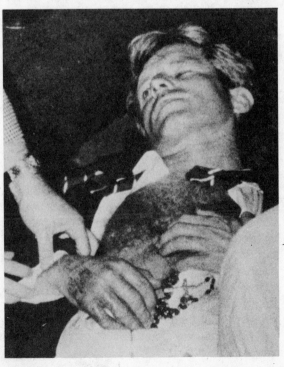

Sirhan Bishara Sirhan, Robert Kennedy's assassin, photographed only minutes after the shooting. (UPI)

their bodies as they raced through the ballroom crowd, now livid with rage. "Kill that bastard!" one woman shouted. "Kill him! Hang him!" others screamed.

Roosevelt Grier wept. "It's my fault . . . I should have been in front of him."

Kennedy was rushed to the Central Receiving Hospital but it was a futile race. His wound was fatal and he died twenty-five hours later.

Sirhan Sirhan was sitting in police headquarters joking with his guards while Kennedy slipped deeper into death. "You are a lazy man," he told John Howard, deputy district attorney. "You should exercise." Before a sergeant handed him a cup of coffee, the murderer jokingly asked him to sample it. The officer did.

"If anything happens," the sergeant said, "we both go together."

Sirhan laughed. "I'll hold you to that."

The sergeant, W. C. Johnson, somehow got drawn into a discussion with Sirhan concerning the Boston strangler. The police sergeant explained how the killer made a fancy bow out of a stocking he used in strangling his victims.

"That's really cruel," Sirhan Bishara Sirhan said solemnly. "I wonder often what would cause a man to do such a thing."

Tried in 1969 over a period of fifteen weeks, Sirhan was found guilty of murdering Robert Kennedy. He confessed the killing before his jury. On April 24, 1969 he was sentenced to death and then began the customary lengthy appeals. He cheated the gas chamber when the U.S. Supreme Court abolished capital punishment.

SKAGGS, ELIJAH
Gambler, Con Man ● (1810-1870)

Kentucky born, Skaggs mastered the art of card sharping before his twenty-first birthday. He could conceal cards on his person, make a pass, deal from the bottom of the deck and arrange card positions in the deck with such proficiency that even the most experienced gamblers of his time fell prey to his black art.

Nashville was Skaggs's first area of gambling activity. Here, he won enough money to attire himself in what became the almost traditional garb of professional gamblers. He was described by criminal historian John Morris thusly: "He appeared in Nashville, dressed in frock coat and pants of black broadcloth, a black silk vest, and patent leather boots, a white shirt with standing collar and around his neck was wound a white choker, while, resting on his cranium, was a black stovepipe hat, which completed his attire."

Elijah's game was faro and he schooled himself in every conceivable trick known to dealers. He studied dealers suspected of being dishonest and, if he could not detect them, would then take them aside and offer large amounts of money for their secrets; if they refused, he threatened to expose them. Skaggs began operating along the Mississippi, appearing in New Orleans and St. Louis. As his fortunes grew, enterprising Elijah added employed teams to work the riverboats, fleecing the gullible. He made an estimated $100,000 a month from his crooked faro games.

In 1847, Skaggs was a thriving millionaire but word about his crooked faro operations had spread—"the true character of his games leaked out, and a cry was raised against them throughout the country, till the name of Skaggs patent dealers, as they were termed, was a synonym for all sorts of frauds and dishonesty at the gaming table."

At thirty-seven, Elijah retired to a lavish plantation in Louisiana, but he lost his millions by banking too heavily in Confederate Bonds. When the South collapsed following the Civil War, Skaggs' fortunes went with it.

He wandered through Texas for five years, dying a hopeless drunk in 1870.

SLADE, JOSEPH A. ("JACK")
Murderer, Gunfighter ● (1824-1864)

BACKGROUND: BORN IN CARLYLE, ILL., IN 1824. NO PUBLIC EDUCATION. MARRIED, NO CHILDREN. SERVED IN THE U.S. ARMY DURING THE MEXICAN WAR, SEEING ACTION ON NUMEROUS OCCASIONS. ORIGINAL OCCUPATION, STAGECOACH LINE SUPERINTENDENT. DESCRIPTION: SHORT, HEAVYSET. ALIASES: NONE. RECORD: MURDERED JULES BENE (OR RENI) AT COLD SPRINGS, COLO., IN 1859; ARRESTED FOR SHOOTING UP THE U.S. ARMY POST AT FORT HALLECK, COLO., 1861, RELEASED; INDICTED BY A GRAND JURY ON A CHARGE OF ASSAULT WITH INTENT TO MURDER A FORT HALLECK RESIDENT, 1861; FLED TO VIRGINIA CITY, MONT., WHERE HE WAS HANGED BY VIGILANTES 3/10/64 FOLLOWING A WEEK-LONG SPREE OF "HURRAHING" THE TOWN WITH HIS PISTOL WHILE DRUNK. BURIED IN THE MORMON CEMETERY AT SALT LAKE CITY, UTAH, 7/20/64.

There was much of the Jekyll and Hyde in Joseph Slade, better known as Jack. When sober, he was the kindliest, most thoughtful of men. In his cups, Jack Slade was one of the most savage gunmen and killers the West had ever seen.

Born in the sleepy town of Carlyle, Ill., Slade moved away from home while still a youth and wandered the cowboy trails of the Southwest until joining the army during the Mexican War. He was hired by the Central Overland California and Pike's Peak Express Company in 1858 as a line superintendent.

Slade's position made him responsible for a long stretch of roadway the stage traveled, through Colorado. Company officials suspected that another superintendent, a French Canadian named Jules Bene, was stealing horses from the line and using the company offices at Julesburg, Colo. to shelter wanted criminals. The firm's general superintendent, Ben Ficklin, ordered Slade to investigate Bene's operation.

Julesburg was a hellish eyesore, a bloody blot on the map where a killing a day was usual even though the town never numbered more than 2,000 souls. Slade arrived full of business. He looked up an ex-overland employee, one Bene had fired, and found him to be extremely conscientious. Slade rehired the man and Bene, upon learning this, traced Slade down with shotgun in hand. Bene fired twice at close range into Jack Slade who thumped face first into the street. Three more blasts from Bene's shotgun tore into the fallen man.

"Bury him," was Bene's terse remark as he stood over Slade's body. The barbarous shooting, however, so incensed a crowd at the scene that several men turned on Bene, tied a rope about his neck, and prepared to hang him for murder. Ben Ficklin arrived and stopped the lynching. Amazingly, Jack Slade, shot five times, staggered to his feet still alive. Ficklin offered Bene his life if he promised to leave the state. Bene accepted and departed.

Gunfighter Jack Slade was one of the most feared men of the early West; he was hanged in Virginia City, Mont. by vigilantes, 3/10/1864. (Western History Collection, U. of Okla. Library)

Inside of a year, Slade had fully recovered from his wounds and was back at work for the Overland Company. Then he received word that Bene had returned to the territory. Slade sent several cronies to locate him and Bene was shortly found at Slade's ranch near Cold Springs. It appeared that Bene was lying in ambush and waiting for Slade to appear so that he could kill him. The would-be bushwhacker was lashed to a post in front of Slade's home.

When Slade arrived, he stood before Bene and proceeded to take long pulls from a whiskey bottle. Between drinks, Slade used Bene for a target, shooting him in the legs and arms. "To hell with it," he finally said, and walked up to his victim, placed the barrel of his pistol in Bene's mouth and blew out the back of his head. Legend then has it that Jack Slade pulled out a knife and sliced off Bene's ears. Most reports state that Slade used one of these ears as a watch fob. The other he sold as a souvenir to have drinking money.

The bestial mutilation of Bene earned Jack Slade a neck-turning reputation, one that sent chills up the spines and, fortunately for Slade, down the hands of gunslingers who might otherwise have tried their luck with him. Whenever, he entered a saloon, which was often, Slade would find a wide space at the bar. He reveled in the attention heaped upon him by greenhorns eager to look at his grisly watch fob.

Even the noted author Mark Twain found this tough, unfeeling killer fascinating. Twain, however, was fascinated by most gunmen and robbers; he once wrote that "some time ago I was making a purchase in a small town store in Missouri. A man walked in and, seeing me, came over with outstretched hand and said, 'You're Mark Twain, ain't you?'

"I nodded.

"'Guess you and I are 'bout the greatest in our line,' he remarked. To this I couldn't nod, but I began to wonder as to what throne of greatness he held.

"'What is your name?' I inquired.

"'Jesse James,' he replied, gathering up his packages."

Of Jack Slade, Twain waxed fondly, following their meeting in 1861. Twain wrote that he discovered Slade to be "so friendly and so gentle-spoken that I warmed to him in spite of his awful history."

Slade's history degenerated further by the time his wife Virginia had convinced him to move from Colorado to the rip-snorting town of Virginia City, Montana. There was little argument in moving on; Slade was on the run from an arrest warrant charging him with assault with intent to kill a Julesburg citizen.

At first, Slade tried his hand at running a small ranch outside of Virginia City, but his alcoholism increased and he soon became the cause of small riots, mass fights, and general bedlam.

A vigilante group, hardened by their harsh dealings with swarms of bandits who had raided their town, wanted no more trouble from Jack Slade. The tough gunman was ordered to leave Virginia City for good. He promised he would do exactly that, but made the mistake of stopping by a local saloon for a drink, which was followed by a bitter tongue-lashing hurled against the bartender. Hands on his guns, Slade defied anyone to draw against him.

Several vigilantes rushed him, tied him up, and dragged him down the street. A rope was placed about his neck and then thrown over a sturdy beam holding a saloon sign. The tough killer realized his predicament and burst into great sobs. As the tears rolled down his bearded cheeks, Slade gasped, "My, God! My God! Must I die like this? Oh, my poor wife!" A boy raced off to bring Virginia Slade to plead for the outlaw's life.

It was too late. The vigilantes were determined to make an example of this most feared of men. "Do your duty, boys!" someone in the crowd shouted and Slade was hanged. His body was taken to a local hotel and laid out. Slade's wife appeared and threw herself across the corpse. Weeping hysterically, Virginia Slade spat out insults to Slade's friends standing nearby. Why had they not, she demanded to know, shot her husband like a man rather than allow him to be hanged like an animal?

Days later, Mrs. Slade packed her husband's body in a tin coffin filled with raw alcohol to preserve the remains and set off for Slade's birthplace in Illinois where she intended the burial to be. The alcohol did not do its work; the body began to decompose and gave off a knockout odor by the time it reached Salt Lake City, Utah. Mrs. Slade buried the remains of her man in the Mormon Cemetery there on July 20, 1864, a peaceful spot for those who had fled religious oppression but a most unlikely resting place for the imbruted Jack Slade.

SMITH, JEFFERSON RANDOLPH ("SOAPY") Gambler ● (1860-1898)

Times were hard for Jefferson Randolph Smith as a boy in Georgia. The South had lost the Civil War and was in the desperate Reconstruction period when young

Smith decided to run away from home; he moved to San Antonio where he became a cowpuncher. In his wide-sweeping travels from Texas to the northern cities of Kansas and Missouri, Smith met the famous gunmen, gamblers, and cattle barons of the West.

In San Antonio, Smith was relieved of six month's pay by an old shell game expert, Clubfoot Hall. The man's prestidigitation so impressed Smith that he began to hang about with card sharps and con men, learning piecemeal their nefarious trades. He mastered the pea-in-the-shell routine and three card monte. He then teamed up with a bunco artist named Taylor. Their con game was simple but it worked on the naive settlers and cowboys in Colorado.

Taylor would set up a soap stand in a small town and shout out to the residents that several of the bars of soap he was selling contained a twenty dollar bill inside the wrapper. Smith would rush up to Taylor, buy a bar of soap and excitedly unwrap it, shouting to the startled citizens that he had struck it, waving a twenty dollar certificate aloft.

Smith, by the time he arrived in booming Leadville, had naturally acquired the nickname "Soapy" from his routine. He ran his own soap stand game so profitably that he was able to hire several shills to help him con the curious crowds.

Leadville was a wild and different world from even the roaring cattle towns of Kansas and Texas. Smith once held a race between two prostitutes who ran naked down the town's main street; the winner received a quart of bonded whiskey. The town's leading residents protested not. When Soapy had a man arrested as insane because he spent all day in prayer, the citizens roared appreciation.

In 1892, Soapy opened a saloon, the Orleans Club, in nearby Creede, Colorado, following the rush of miners to that pesthole where silver veins two feet wide had been discovered. The Orleans Club stayed open 24 hours a day and Soapy freed the suckers from every cent in their pockets. Every game in his establishment was rigged and crooked. This brought about a few gunfights from vituperative customers, but Soapy displayed his own truculence by shooting several.

When the silver veins ran out in Creede, Soapy moved on to the gold rush scene in Alaska, establishing another saloon, Jeff's Place, in teaming Skagway. This grubby, mud-filled town was the crossroads of the great Alaska Gold Rush. Gold-fevered miners passed through the little hell-hole on their way northward to the gold fields and straggled back through it with saddle bags laden with nuggets and gold ore. Soapy got them going both ways.

One of Smith's money-producing devices was a ramshackled cabin with a huge sign atop its roof which read: "Telegraph Office." He charged each person $5 to send a telegram to the U.S. The money rolled in from prospectors desperate to inform their families that they had arrived safe in the golden kingdom, had struck it rich, or had been broken by their own hardscrabble dream and needed grubstaking.

No one noticed that there wasn't a single wire stretching from Soapy's telegraph office and that the messages tapped out incoherently by one of his sharpers disappeared into air at the final tap of the key.

Those who became suspicious of Soapy's rigged card games, pea-in-the-shell trick, and tilted roulette wheel, hid their gold in their mattresses. It did them no good. Soapy's roaming toughs merely held them up. Those who protested too much were shot and killed. Soapy virtually owned Skagway. Though not officially or clerically endowed with the authority, Soapy took upon himself to marry and divorce the lonely miners from his shill-bound dance hall girls. He administered justice as a self-appointed marshal and handled court cases, also as a self-appointed judge, from behind the bar of his saloon.

As Skagway grew, its permanent residents yearned for relief from Soapy's baronial dictatorship. Religious leaders arose and condemned him. One Methodist minister went so far as to solicit money from Soapy to help rid Skagway of its corrupting influences. The wily gambler smiled and then stood up on his bar, handing down to the preacher $1,000 in cash and announcing loudly that he personally backed such a noble effort.

The minister, guarded by Soapy's men, made the rounds that day in Skagway, telling saloon owners and prospectors that Soapy Smith was behind his drive to clean up the town. By evening, the preacher sweated heavily as he toted three large grain sacks brimming with more than $36,000, the fruits of his collection. At this point, Smith's guards merely relieved the preacher of the money for "safe keeping."

Soapy roared long and loud that night. "Thirty-six for one is pretty good odds," he told his junior partner, Wilson Mizner.

The reign of Soapy Smith roared to an end in July, 1898. Three days after he led the town's Independence Day parade astride a resplendent white horse, a vigilante committee called the Committe of 101, tired of trying to persuade the gambler to reform, stormed his saloon, and shot him to pieces.

Soapy Smith was laid to rest with honors. Three shells and a pea were ceremoniously tossed into his open grave.

SMITH, RICHARD
Murderer ● (? -1816)

Smith, a lieutenant in the regular U.S. Army who was stationed near Philadelphia, met the beautiful and vivacious Mrs. Ann Carson in 1812. Her husband, Captain John Carson, had been away for two years on missions against the Indians and was presumed dead. Following a brief courtship, Smith married Mrs. Carson. Four years later, on January 20, 1816, Carson staggered out of the wilderness and made for his home.

Banging loudly on the door of his house, he announced himself to a befuddled Smith, who refused him entry. A scuffle took place and Smith drew a revolver, sending a ball into Captain Carson's brain.

While Smith stood trial for the murder, Ann Carson Smith attempted to boldly kidnap the governor of Pennsylvania, Simon Snyder, and hold him until her husband was released. The plot failed and Smith was promptly convicted, his prosecution all but directed by Judge Rush. The hapless lieutenant was sentenced to death and was hanged on a Philadelphia scaffold, February 4, 1816.

His wife, Ann, became embittered against all forms of justice and turned to crime, establishing a counterfeiting ring. As a daughter of a naval officer and the wife of two army officers, Ann knew well how to command her brigands. Her cohorts—William Butler, Sarah Maland, Sarah Willis, and a Dr. Loring—operated successfully for close to six years, passing phony notes throughout Pennsylvania.

The gang was finally captured in June, 1823, for passing counterfeit notes on Girard's Bank in Philadelphia and on July 12, 1823, all received stiff prison sentences. Ann died writing her memoirs in the Philadelphia prison in 1838.

SMITH, SUSAN
Murderer ● (1971-   )

Almost everyone in Union, South Carolina, thought 23-year-old Susan Smith was a bright, cheerful, and responsible person. "She was the best friend and the best mother," said one friend. But this same Susan Smith, on October 25, 1994, strapped her two young sons, Michael, 3, and Alexander, 14 months, into their car seats and drove to a lake. She let the burgundy Mazda Protege roll down a boat ramp and watched as it sank into the dark waters. Her children drowned, still helplessly strapped in their seats.

Smith then went to a nearby house and reported that her car had been carjacked by a black man wearing a stocking cap. First, the entire town of Union was up in arms. As the story of this horrible abduction spread, the nation was shocked. Susan Smith appeared for nine days on national television, pleading with the kidnapper to return her children to her, telling her young sons, as if they were still alive, that she loved them and missed them.

Oddly, in all of her appearances, the mother in Susan Smith was not very much in evidence. She did not shed tears, although she sounded as if she were weeping. In her first appearance on TV shortly after the kidnapping, she was not hysterical nor visibly upset as one might expect a normal mother to be. A few at that time asked the question, "Why is this woman alive?" They added that any nomral mother would have fought to the death with a kidnapper before giving them up, or, at least, have gone with her children.

More perversely, Smith released a video of her children playing at home, and doubled her pleas to the mythical kidnapper to return her boys to her. Over and over again, the slightly distraught mother went on national television to beg for the lives of her two children with the cold and calculating knowledge that she had already murdered them.

The case did not sit well with local police officers and FBI agents working on the case. Smith's statements from the start did not work with her story. She said, for instance, that on the night of the murder that she was driving to see a friend when her boys were kidnapped by the carjacker. The friend was interviewed and said he was not expecting to see Susan that night.

Smith said she went to a Wal-Mart store from the time she left home at 6 p.m. to about 9 p.m. when she appeared before a stranger's door to report the carjacking. No one at the store remembered seeing her or the two small boys. She said her car was stopped at a deserted intersection where she had waited for a light to turn green. The intersection has a constant green light, which trips red only when a car approaches on the interconnecting street, a street very seldom used.

The FBI conducted a polygraph test on Smith, which was reported inconclusive but the machine did become erratic when Susan Smith was asked "Do you know where your children are?" The fact that she was asked this question by law enforcement officials indicated that they already suspected her.

Sheriff Howard Wells was diplomatic while the investigation was under way, careful not to reveal his innermost suspicions, but three days into the case, he called the investigation "impossible." Meanwhile, the nation hung on every word slipping quietly from the mouth of Susan Smith. Thousands of concerned people wrote their condolences. Thousands more joined in the search for the boys.

Susan Smith fooled her relatives, her estranged husband, David (she had filed for a divorce a few weeks earlier, on October 7, 1994), and her neighbors. She went on fooling everyone in Union and the state of South Carolina, as well as the rest of the nation. Finally, on November 3, 1994, only hours after she and David had appeared on the *Today Show* to once more plead for the lives of their children, Susan Smith confessed her terrible crime to Sheriff Wells.

She told him where her car and her children could be located. The car with the dead little boys still strapped in the back seat was hauled up from eighteen feet of water. Smith was placed under arrest. The same people who had given her en-couragement and hung on her every word, assembled at a police building as Smith was being transferred (for her own safety) to another undisclosed destination. They railed and shouted their hatred. "Baby-killing bitch!" screamed one mother who held her own infant in her arms.

Many reasons for the murders have since been given. Smith believed that, after dating the son of the richest man in town, she would marry 27-year-old Thomas Findley. She had been rejected, however, by Findley, who broke off their relationship because, as he reportedly stated in a note to Smith, he did "not want the responsibility of children."

Smith had played the wrong hand. She had filed for divorce believing she was about to enter a life of money, luxury, and ease. Instead, she had been thrown back into her own blue collar class with no hope of escaping. She would have to face raising her children alone.

It was later pointed out that Smith herself came from a broken home and that she had a history of psychological problems. She had once thought of suicide. None of this, however, excused, mitigated, or exonerated her heinous act. The first sentence of her confession displays the real focus of Susan Smith, herself, not her innocent, helpless sons. "Because of my romantic and financial situation, I've never been so low . . . " Smith awaits trial at this writing.

SOCCO THE BRACER
Gangster ● (1844-1873)

Born Joseph Gayles, Socco the Bracer was the chief lieutenant of the New York Patsy Conroy Gang. Under the command of Socco the Bracer were such ruthless thugs as Scotchy Lavelle, Kid Shanahan, Pugsy Hurley, Benny Kane, Wreck Donovan, Piggy Noles, and Johnny Dobbs (Mike Kerrigan).

River pirates mostly, the gang operated in the early 1870s from the Corlears' Hook district and preyed on cargo ships docked in the East River. Socco the Bracer was reported to have killed at least twenty men and always went heavily armed into the streets.

On the night of May 29, 1873, Socco the Bracer and two of his cohorts, Billy Woods and

Bum Mahoney, robbed the brig *Margaret*. They made such commotion in stealing the captain's sea chest that the ship's crew was alerted and shot at them as they rowed for shore. Two policemen patroling the river in a rowboat gave chase through the fog-bound waters.

As the thieves neared shore, Socco the Bracer lit a lantern to find his way and one of the policemen, Officer Musgrave, traded shots with him. Socco the Bracer was hit below the heart. His two companions rowed furiously for the middle of the river where they unceremoniously tossed their leader overboard, thinking him dead. The water revived the wounded Socco and he held on to the boat.

The pursuing policemen could hear the gangleader somewhere in the mists begging his men to pull him into the boat. Woods said, "Aw, give 'em one in the knuckles." Mahoney, however, pulled Socco into the rowboat where he promptly died. "Ah, hell, *now* he's dead," Mahoney said and they threw Socco the Bracer once again into the churling waters. His body floated ashore four days later.

SONTAG BROTHERS

George and John Sontag, owners of a quartz mine in California, traveled throughout Wisconsin and Minnesota in 1892, holding up trains. Returning to California, the brothers, along with Chris Evans, held up another train near Collis Station in Fresno, California in August, 1892.

Local police and Pinkertons tracked down the three men days later and a deputy was killed and several wounded when the outlaws attempted to shoot their way out of the trap. George Sontag was captured and sent to Folsom Prison for life.

After robbing several stages and terrorizing the residents of the San Joaquin Valley, John Sontag and Evans were surrounded at their hideout and a terrific gun battle ensued. Evans was captured but John Sontag was killed, pierced by two dozen possemen's bullets.

California trainrobber John Sontag (front, center) lies dead at the feet of the posse which tracked him down and shot him full of holes. (Western History Collection, U. of Okla. Library)

George Sontag, when hearing of his brother John's killing, went berserk in Folsom Prison, staged a riot, and was shot to death while scaling a wall. (Western History Collection, U. of Okla. Library)

When George Sontag heard of his brother's death he staged a one-man riot in Folsom prison and was shot while trying to escape over a wall. Evans was sent to jail for life.

SPECK, RICHARD FRANKLIN
Murderer ● (1941-1991)

BACKGROUND: BORN 12/6/41 IN KIRKWOOD, ILL. TO MARY MARGARET AND BENJAMIN SPECK, A POTTER. TWO BROTHERS (ONE DIED IN 1954) AND FIVE SISTERS. FAMILY MOVED TO MONMOUTH, ILL. IN 1942, LIVING THERE UNTIL 1947. MOVED TO DALLAS, TEX. GRADUATED J. L. LONG JUNIOR HIGH SCHOOL (EIGHTH GRADE). MARRIED 15-YEAR-OLD SHIRLEY MALONE IN 1961, ONE DAUGHTER. ORIGINAL OCCUPATION, GARBAGEMAN. DESCRIPTION: 6'1", BLUE EYES, BLOND HAIR, THIN, TATTOO ON LEFT FOREARM READING "BORN TO RAISE HELL." ALIASES: B. BRIAN, RICHARD FRANKLIN LINDBERGH, RICHARD BENJAMIN SPECK. RECORD: ARRESTED TEN TIMES IN DALLAS, TEX. BEFORE HE WAS TWENTY ON CHARGES OF TRESPASSING, DISORDERLY CONDUCT, BURGLARY; A TOTAL OF THIRTY-SEVEN ARRESTS BEFORE COMING TO CHICAGO IN 1966 WHEN HE WAS STILL WANTED FOR BURGLARY IN DALLAS; ARRESTED FOR DISORDERLY CONDUCT IN MONMOUTH, ILL., MARCH, 1966; MURDERED, ON THE NIGHT OF 7/13-

14/66, EIGHT STUDENT NURSES FROM SOUTH CHICAGO COMMUNITY HOSPITAL—SUZANNE FARRIS, VALENTINA PASION, PAMELA WILKENING, MERLITA GARGULLO, PATRICIA MATUSEK, NINA SCHMALE, MARY ANN JORDAN, AND GLORIA DAVY (WHOM HE RAPED); ARRESTED BY CHICAGO POLICE 7/17/66 AFTER HE ATTEMPTED TO COMMIT SUICIDE IN A SKIDROW FLOPHOUSE; INDICTED FOR MURDER BY A CHICAGO GRAND JURY 7/26/66; TRIED AND CONVICTED OF MURDER IN THE FIRST DEGREE IN APRIL, 1967; SENTENCED TO DEATH IN THE ELECTRIC CHAIR BY JUDGE HERBERT C. PASCHEN 6/6/67; FOLLOWING THE U.S. SUPREME COURT'S DECISION TO ABOLISH CAPITAL PUNISHMENT, RICHARD SPECK WAS RE-SENTENCED TO SEVERAL LIFE SENTENCES AMOUNTING TO MORE THAN 400 YEARS, MAKING FUTURE PAROLE IMPOSSIBLE. DIED IN PRISON, 1991.

Dallas-bred Richard Speck knew nothing but violence and vagrancy by the time he drifted back to Illinois, the place of his birth, in the spring of 1966. He was a drunk and a pill head who worked sporadically as a crew member on board freighters sailing the Great Lakes.

Speck—who later attributed his plight to several blows to his head received in fights, his alcoholism, his drug addiction, a poor home life, and an unfaithful wife—spent his sober moments avidly staring at comic books and photo magazines. He was almost totally illiterate but possessed a cunning sense of self-survival. He had the ominous words "Born to Raise Hell" tattooed on his left forearm in Dallas when he was nineteen.

In early 1966, Speck worked on board an ore boat in Lake Superior. An appendicitis attack caused him to be hospitalized in Hancock, Michigan. While recovering, he spent a great deal of time with 28-year-old Judy Laakaniemi, a nurse, who thought him "gentle and quiet." Speck would spend approximately six hours with nine other nurses in Chicago months later, leaving eight of them dead, bestially slaughtered.

At the end of June, 1966, Speck was fired from the cargo vessel *Randall*, owned by the Inland Steel Company, after fighting with a ship officer. Out of work, he sought help from one of his sisters in Chicago, Mrs. Martha Thornton. She and her husband gave him money and drove him to the National Maritime Union hiring hall on July 10, 1966. Speck wanted to go to New Orleans and attempted to find work on board a ship destined for that

Corazon Amurao, 24-year-old Filipino nurse, hid from Speck's carnage and lived to identify him in court as the mass murderer of her eight friends. (UPI)

port. There were no available berths. Speck hung about several bars patronized by merchant mariners. He drank heavily and sometime on the night of July 13, 1966 injected an unknown drug into his veins.

Stinking of alcohol, Speck strolled along East 100th Street on Chicago's South Side about 11 p.m. that night, stopping in front of a two-story townhouse, number 2319, one of three houses rented by the South Chicago Community Hospital as residences for their student nurses. He walked to the front door and knocked. He then slid his hands into the pockets of a black jacket and withdrew a knife and a gun.

Pretty 23-year-old Corazon Amurao, an exchange nurse from the Philippines, answered the door with two of her roommates. "I opened the door and a man was standing there," Miss Amurao later told police. "The first thing I noticed about him was the strong smell of alcohol."

She saw the gun and knife.

"I'm not going to hurt you," Speck told her. "I'm only going to tie you up. I need your money to go to New Orleans." He waved his gun and ordered Miss Amurao and her two friends to an upstairs back bedroom where he found three more student nurses. Speck told the six women to lie on the floor. They meekly obeyed. While reminding them several times he would not hurt them, Speck methodically tore a sheet from one of the beds into strips and bound each nurse by the hands and feet.

Gloria Davy, another nurse, returned from a date at 11:30 p.m. and Speck met her at the door. He marched her to the back bedroom and she too was tied up. At midnight, two more nurses, Suzanne Farris and Mary Ann Jordan, arrived. They were also tied up

Of the nine girls menaced by Speck that night, one, Mary Ann Jordan, did not live at the address. She had planned to spend the night with her friend, Miss Farris.

Speck asked the girls where they kept their money. They told him. He pocketed what cash they had on hand and then studied his captives for a moment as they stared wide-eyed up at him from their positions on the floor where they were bound hand and foot.

He looked at Miss Davy the longest; she was reportedly the prettiest of the group. The daughter of a steel company foreman in Dyer, Ind., she was twenty-two, one of six children. Miss Davy had worked as a nurses' aide at Our Lady of Mercy Hospital in Dyer and she was president of the Illinois Student Nurses Association. She had planned on joining the Peace Corps after her training program was completed.

It was Miss Davy who asked Speck when he was tying her feet: "Why are you doing this? . . . We are student nurses."

"Oh," Speck said through a wide smile, "you are a student nurse?" He continued tying her up. "Don't be afraid . . . I'm not going to kill you."

When all nine nurses were tied up, Speck plunked down to the floor and played with the gun in his hand, talking to the girls. "Do you know karate?" he asked Merlita Gargullo. He kept looking from the bedroom window and, according to the later testimony of Miss Amurao, became tense and nervous. He then untied Pamela Wilkening and led her from the room. (Pamela Wilkening, age twenty, from Lansing, Ill. Her father was a steam fitter. Pamela's career as a nurse had been the dream of a lifetime. Her twenty-first birthday was but nine days away.)

Moments after Speck and Miss Wilkening left the room, Miss Amurao heard a deep "ahh"—then silence. Speck had taken Miss Wilkening into another bedroom and there stabbed her with his knife in the left breast. He then twisted a strip of sheet about her throat and, without uttering a word, strangled her to death.

From later findings, the murder apparently caused Speck to be sexually stimulated. One killing, however, failed to satiate him.

Minutes later, Speck returned to the back bedroom and, waving his gun, took Mary Ann Jordan and Suzanne Farris to the door of another bedroom. (Mary Ann Jordan, age twenty, from Chicago. One of six children, her father worked for the city of Chicago as a civil engineer.)

Speck suddenly flashed his knife in front of the two girls. Viciously he lunged at Mary Ann Jordan, stabbing her three times in the neck, breast, and eye, killing her. He then turned to Suzanne Farris. (Suzanne Farris, age twenty-one, from Chicago. Her father worked for the Transit Authority. She was one of three children.) Miss Farris resisted. Speck tore at her with his knife, plunging the blade into her again and again and again, eighteen times in all, in the back, neck, chin. When she fell on her back, Speck leaped on her and strangled her. He then grabbed her underclothes and ripped them in several places.

Getting up, Speck went to the bathroom and washed his hands. He then walked back

One-time garbageman and apprentice seaman Richard Franklin Speck slaughtered eight Chicago nurses in 1966; he was sentenced to 1,200 years in jail. (UPI)

to the south back bedroom of the townhouse for his next victim, Nina Schmale. (Nina Schmale, age twenty-four, from Wheaton, Ill. Her father was a cement mason. Before entering nurses' training at South Chicago Community Hospital, she had taught Sunday School for

Speck's docile victims: Valentina Passion, Pamela Wilkening, Patricia Matuse, Suzanne Farris, Mary Ann Jordan, Marlita Gargullo, Gloria Davy, and Nina Schmale. (UPI)

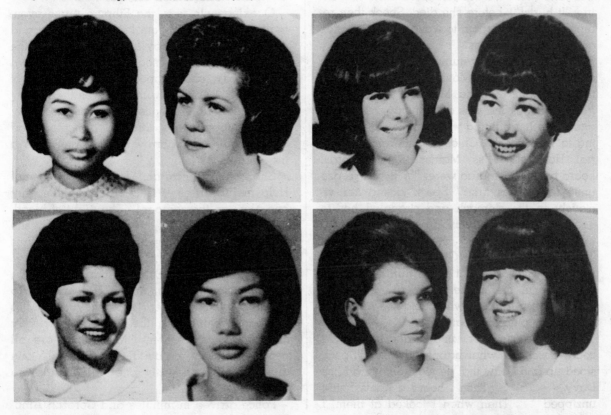

four years and worked as a volunteer nurse's aide in the DuPage Convalescent Home.)

Speck ordered Miss Schmale to lie on the bed in another bedroom. He then stabbed her in the neck and strangled her. He was doing his sinister work at a leisurely pace, spending about twenty to twenty-five minutes with each girl. The girls remaining in the back bedroom, after Nina Schmale was taken out, attempted to hide under beds. Speck found them all, except Corazon Amurao, who squirmed far beneath one of the beds and stayed there, quiet and terror-struck.

Valentina Pasion and Merlita Gargullo were next. (Valentina Pasion, age twenty-three, from Jones City, Philippines. Merlita Gargullo, age twenty-two, from Santa Cruz, Philippines. Both nurses were on an exchange program and had come to the U.S. for the first time a month before.)

Speck took the two women into the front upstairs bedroom. He instantly stabbed Miss Pasion in the neck, killing her. He then stabbed Miss Gargullo, who toppled across the body of Miss Pasion. Speck fell upon Miss Gargullo and strangled her to death.

Corazon Amurao heard both girls give loud "ahhs" as they were struck. She heard Merlita Gargullo yell out in Tagalog, "Maskit!" (meaning "It hurts!"), before she died. Speck then returned to the bathroom to wash the blood once again from his hands.

The mass killer returned to the bedroom and carried Patricia Matusek, still bound, into the bathroom. (Patricia Matusek, age twenty, from Chicago. She was a swimming champion and, once her training was completed, was going to work for the Chicago Children's Memorial Hospital.) Miss Matusek's last words, heard by Miss Amurao were: "Will you please untie my ankles first?" Speck kicked her viciously in the stomach and strangled her to death, leaving her body on the floor.

Speck walked into the South bedroom. There, on the bed, was Gloria Davy. Apparently Speck had lost count of the number of girls originally in the house. He didn't bother to look for Miss Amurao who could see him from her hiding place beneath a bed.

The lone survivor, under questioning in court, described what happened next: "Speck stood up and I saw that he was removing Miss Davy's jeans . . . Then I heard a pants being unzipped . . . Then when I looked at them, I saw that Speck was already on top of Miss Davy . . . [the witness wept bitterly] . . . I saw Speck was on top of Davy. Then, when I saw he was right on top of Davy, I put my face down. And then I heard the bedsprings moving . . . After a few minutes, Speck asked: 'Will you please put your legs around my back?' . . . I heard it [the movement of the springs] for about twenty, twenty-five minutes . . . About five minutes after the bedsprings stopped, I looked up and saw that Davy and Speck was not there anymore."

Speck then led Gloria Davy naked downstairs to the front room and ordered her to lie face down on a divan. He then assaulted her again or used some sort of implement on her, according to an official police report which stated that Miss Davy's anus was mutilated. He then strangled his last victim with a strip of sheet.

Upstairs, Corazon Amurao was petrified with fear. She waited until there were no more noises in the house. Then she waited some more. She waited, she waited. At 5 p.m. an alarm clock went off in another bedroom and kept buzzing—it was the usual time the nurses got up and got ready to go to the hospital. Miss Amurao thought Speck might still be in the house. She waited another hour.

Quaking with fear, the Filipino nurse eventually eased herself from beneath the bed and crept along the hallway to her bedroom in the front of the house. As she made her way down the hallway, she stepped over the bodies of her friends, avoiding with her eyes the bloody carnage before her. Once in the front bedroom, Miss Amurao broke through a screen and crawled out onto a narrow ledge ten feet above the ground.

She began to scream: "Help me! Help me! Help me! Everybody is dead! I am the only one alive on the sampan!" The night of blood, no doubt, had jarred her mind to think she was back in her Filipino home in San Luis Batanga.

A neighbor, Mrs. Betty Windmiller, and a man walking his dog, Robert Hall, rushed to the front of the house. There they saw Miss Amurao cowering on the ledge, hysterically shouting down to them: "My friends are all dead, all dead, all dead! I'm the only one alive, oh God, the only one! My friends are all dead!"

Police arrived in minutes and Corazon Amurao was taken to a hospital and put under sedation. Detectives found more than thirty telltale fingerprints in the house belonging to the intruder. They also found a man's T-shirt wrapped in Miss Davy's white panties. When Miss Amurao could speak, she described the mass murderer in detail and police artist Otis Rathel put together a sketch which bore a remarkable likeness to Richard Franklin Speck. This portrait was reprinted by all the Chicago newspapers in their next editions which carried the grisly story of the mass slayings.

The killer, meanwhile, walked to the heart of skid row on Madison Street and began to hit a number of bars. In one bar, Speck heard two men talking about the killings. He turned to the man next to him and said: "I hope they catch the son-of-a-bitch!" Later, Speck would claim that he wasn't even aware that the police were looking for him, that he remembered nothing of the murders.

He spent the next few days drinking incessantly, shooting pool, buying the favors of a $3 whore, and ending up on July 16, 1966, in the 90-cents-a-night Starr Hotel, a bug-ridden flophouse on West Madison Street, registering under the alias B. Brian. He carried into stall 584 a newspaper folded to a banner headline which read: "POLICE SAY NURSE SURVIVOR CAN IDENTIFY SLAYER OF 8."

By then the police, indeed, knew Richard Speck was the murderer. A gas station attendant told police a man answering Rathel's excellent police sketch had left two bags with him for safekeeping. The attendant told officers that the man stated he was looking for work at the National Maritime Union. Union authorities then told police that a man had been trying to get assigned to a New Orleans bound ship recently. His application was found in a waste can where it had been discarded. The name on the card read Richard Franklin Speck. The killer's fingerprints were then matched to Speck's Dallas police record by the FBI. The police then knew their man but had no idea where he might be found.

Late on the night of July 16, 1966, Speck, lying on his flea-bitten bunk in the Starr Hotel, reached out and slashed his right wrist and then his left arm. His blood began to run onto the floor in a steady stream. He called out to a man in the next stall: "Come and see me . . . You got to come and see me . . . I done something bad . . ."

George Gregorich, the man in the next stall, heard the weak voice and replied: "Leave me alone. You're a hill-billy. You just want to get at me. I don't trust no hill-billy."

"I'm going to die if you don't come and see me," Speck said.

"No!"

Speck got up on buckling legs and staggered into the hallway. Someone in the hall noticed him and shouted: "Hey! This guy's bleeding himself to death!"

A police ambulance rushed the killer to Cook County Hospital where he arrived in the trauma ward at 12:30 a.m. and was cared for by Dr. LeRoy Smith.

"What's your name?" Smith asked him.

"Richard. Richard Speck."

The police had their man.

Speck's sensational trial for murder took place the following spring. Miss Amurao dramatically appeared in court and recounted in detail the events of the previous summer in the murder house. Without hesitation, she identified the pock-marked Richard Speck as the mass slayer of her friends. Fingerprints taken from the death scene matched those of Speck. The case was conclusive.

The jury was out only forty-nine minutes. Its deliberation, read by the foreman, was concise: "We, the jury, find the defendant, Richard Franklin Speck, guilty of murder in the manner and form as charged in the indictment, and we fix his punishment at death."

The following June, Speck was sentenced to die in the electric chair. He had once asked the staff psychiatrist of the Cook County jail, Dr. Marvin Ziporyn: "If they don't burn me, what will they do with me? Put me in some kind of nuthouse?"

Speck stalled off his execution through various appeals. His life was spared by the U.S. Supreme Court's decision to abolish capital punishment. He was re-sentenced in 1972 to several life terms totalling more than 400 years.

A grim comment about Speck's fate came more than six years after his wholesale slaughter of eight nurses. Accused mass murderer Michael Clark, a member of the alleged Chicago killer cult, De Mau Mau, stated: ". . . you know what happened to Speck? Nothin'. And that's what's gonna happen to us, too."

Speck suffered a fatal heart attack in 1991 and died in his cell at age forty-nine.

SPENCER, AL
Bankrobber ● (? -1923)

Spencer was a onetime member of Henry Starr's gang. He was an attentive pupil. When Starr inaugurated the use of the auto in robbing banks, Spencer was the first to carry on the tradition. A resident of the wild Cookson Hills in Oklahoma, Spencer gathered about him the first formidable bank robbing gang of the early 1920s which included Frank "Jelly" Nash (later killed in the Kansas City Massacre), Earl Thayer, and Ray Terrill.

All the raids executed by this gang were meticulously planned, sometimes in the Tulsa home owned by Ma Barker. The gang operated so professionally that its members never bothered to use aliases. Speed was what Spencer and his gang relied upon. Unlike Henry Starr, they took great pains to "soup up" their cars, using them in relays when escaping from lawmen.

After robbing several banks in 1920-23, raiding two or three of them a week, the Spencer gang stopped the Katy Limited of the Missouri, Kansas & Texas Railroad on August 21, 1923 near the whistle stop of Okesa, Okla. They took $20,000 in Liberty Bonds and cash from the baggage car and then, each driving a different auto, split up and went into hiding.

Spencer, however, was tracked down in Coffeyville, Kan. and, after an informer's call to police, surrounded in a hideout only blocks away from the spot where the Dalton brothers had been gunned to death by vigilantes thirty years before. Spencer made a fight of it. He was killed in a hail of bullets as he attempted to escape.

Frank Nash, Thayer, and three others were captured and sent to Leavenworth for twenty-five years. Terrill, the lone member of the band who escaped, joined Matt and George Kimes, Cookson Hills outlaws, and embarked on another bank robbing spree which culminated with the 1927 robbery of the Pampa bank in Texas. Terrill and the Kimes boys hauled the safe out of the bank with a winch and later broke it open to discover their biggest strike—$35,000.

Terrill later joined Herman Barker in robbing Missouri banks and was subsequently killed by lawmen in 1931.

[ALSO SEE The Barkers, Kansas City Massacre, Henry Starr.]

SPENCER, HENRY
Murderer, Robber ● (1880-1914)

In June of 1914, a blonde-haired young man got off the train at Wheaton, Ill. His name was Henry Spencer and his origins and background were mysterious. He was an affable sort and soon ingratiated himself with the town's leading citizens. Spencer was well-groomed, had money in his pocket, and told everyone he was a salesman.

He met and wooed a spinster, Allison Rexroat, who was ten years his senior. Miss Rexroat confided to him that she possessed an ample bank account. After having seduced her and with the promise of marriage on his lips, Henry suggested a quiet little picnic outside of Wheaton. The two journeyed to a remote hillside with picnic basket in hand. Spencer had brought along the tools necessary for the completion of his mission—a hammer and shovel.

As Miss Rexroat lay on her back, awaiting the amorous advances of her sweetheart, her eyes fluttering closed, Henry Spencer quickly moved to her side and, lifting the hammer high in the air, bashed out her brains. He then dug a small grave and, after removing two rings on Miss Rexroat's fingers, threw her body in the hole and covered her up.

Spencer then returned to Wheaton and went to the bank. He had previously convinced the trusting Miss Rexroat to put her savings in his name. He promptly withdrew these funds and then calmly walked to the train station where he waited for the 1 p.m. flyer to spirit him from town.

As the train pulled in, the Wheaton sheriff and the local banker collared Spencer. The banker, an old friend of the Rexroat family, had grown suspicious when he saw Spencer withdrawing Miss Rexroat's life savings. Spencer was arrested and thrown into jail. He was interrogated for a week as to the whereabouts of his intended bride. The prisoner claimed to know nothing. He was a victim of circumstances. How should he know where Miss Rexroat was?

A farmer who had seen the couple picnicking on his property soon answered that question by locating the spinster's grave and digging up the body. The murder weapon, however, was missing. Again sheriff's deputies grilled Spencer. He protested mightily, he screamed, he ranted. Finally a deputy hit him in the mouth, breaking several of his teeth. At the sight of his own blood, Spencer shakily told the lawmen where they could find the murder weapon. He then confessed his crime and was scheduled for trial.

Though his lawyers claimed that Spencer had confessed under severe beatings, the fact that he was able to lead lawmen to the flesh-caked hammer condemned him. He was convicted and sentenced to death on the gallows. A day before his execution, several members of the Chicago press trained to Wheaton to interview the killer.

Wallace Smith and Ben Hecht of the *Daily News* arrived and found Spencer in his cell with two evangelists, the MacAuslins, brother and sister, smiling cherubically at the murderer's side. Spencer explained that he had embraced religion, that he had reformed his entire evil character, and had joined "God's holy crusade."

"Cut out the act," Smith said to Spencer, who looked hurt.

"It's no act. I've joined the ranks of God's children," he replied.

"Have you admitted the killing?" Hecht said.

"That's not important anymore," Spencer stated. "I was a sinner, a black sinner. I did evil. Evil was in me. Now it's gone."

"Did you kill Miss Rexroat?" Hecht persisted.

Spencer and the MacAuslins, one of whom was squeezing a melodeon while the other hummed a hymn, then knelt in prayer. The reporters poured themselves glasses of lemonade from a pitcher on a stand in the cell and marveled at the redeemed man. The MacAuslins, who had saved Spencer's soul, so he claimed, flanked him and the three lifted their voices in prayer.

Wheaton, Ill. killer Henry Spencer (in shirtsleeves, wearing spectacles) dines with detectives who arrested him in 1914. (UPI)

Getting up slowly and dusting his gray flannel trousers, Spencer looked peacefully at the newsmen and said: "Yes, I killed her. I have no secrets from God." The MacAuslins beamed. "He knows me. I am a brand snatched from the burning. I have repented. My soul is washed of all wickedness. God can look into it and see that there is nothing evil left. That's why He will let me into Heaven. Because there is not a single lie in me—only truth!"

The MacAuslins filled the air with hallelujahs. They had spent ten days and nights in the cell with Spencer preparing his soul for eternity. And, from Spencer's sanctimonious mouthings, they appeared to have triumphed.

Hecht and Smith left and walked to their hotel. They would have to stay overnight and cover the execution at six in the morning in the Wheaton stockade. The two men argued over Spencer's character.

"He's a fraud," Smith said. "It's holier-than-thou gibberish. He hasn't changed. He's as sly and rotten as ever."

Hecht disagreed. He felt Spencer sincerely believed in his repentance.

"That son-of-a-bitch is providing himself with his own hop," Smith said. "He's scared pissless and he's found something that he thinks will keep his knees from buckling when he starts up the gallows' steps. There is no faith or repentance involved . . . Henry's a rat and he'll die like a rat. I'll give you three to one on it."

They made their bet. In addition, other reporters joined Smith and Hecht in betting on what step Spencer would stumble in his fear of being hanged while climbing the stairs to the waiting rope.

The next morning, thousands of county employees brought their families to the massive stockade at Wheaton. Men, women, and children carried picnic baskets and balloons. The hanging was a great event in Wheaton that August of 1914.

Spencer appeared at 6 a.m. wearing white tennis shoes, gray flannel pants, a white shirt opened at the collar, and a red carnation pinned to his breast pocket. The flower was a parting gift from his evangelist friends. He surprised the reporters by ascending the gallows stairs without stumbling once. A long white robe was put over him. He smiled. His hands were strapped to his side. He smiled. The rope was placed about his neck and brought up behind the ears. He smiled.

The sheriff approached him almost apologetically and said, "Have you got anything to say, Henry Spencer?"

The smile had not faded from his face. "Yes, I have. This is the happiest moment of my life," he bubbled joyously. He glanced at the MacAuslins who stood on either side of him, their hands clasped in prayer. "I have never had a mother or father. Now I have a Father. He is up there waiting to receive me—waiting to welcome me home to a place beside His eternal spirit and His great kindness. My heart is full of happiness because I have made my peace with God. I have given Him the truth of my soul and the truth unlocks the gates of Heaven.

"I can see my new home. Its streets are golden. Its houses are white and pure. I never knew any home before. Now I have one finer than any in the world—with its door open and waiting for me and God holding out His hand to me. And my soul is clean and happy. And I give thanks to this wonderful thing. I give thanks to God. The Lord is my shepherd, I shall not want. He maketh me to lie down in green pastures . . ."

After reciting several psalms, Spencer was silent, still strangely smiling and lifting his face to the sky.

"You finished talkin'?" the sheriff said. He raised his hand to signal the trap door to be sprung.

Desperately, Spencer looked at the upraised hand and shouted: "No, wait! I ain't through . . . I got something else to say! Something else!"

The sheriff's hand dropped limply to his side. "Say it."

"What I got to say is that I'm innocent of the murder of Allison Rexroat! I never killed her! It's a lie! You're all dirty bastards! You got no right! I never touched her! So help me, God, I never harmed a hair on her head! So help me God!"

The sheriff waved to the executioner and the trap sprung open sending Henry Spencer to his eternity. Smith turned to Hecht and said: "I told you, like a rat! In order to live an extra forty-five seconds he spit in the eye of God and the truth and squealed out a lie for the finish."

As Hecht was writing out the details of the hanging he received a wire from his editor telling him to "keep story of hanging brief . . . omit all gruesome details . . . the world has just gone to war." Hecht fired back his own telegram reading: "Will try to make hanging as cheerful and optimistic as possible."

SPENCER, TIMOTHY W.
Rapist-Murderer ● (1962-   )

Spencer raped and killed four women in Richmond, Virginia in Autumn 1987. Following his arrest in January 1988, Spencer was tried for killing Susan Tucker. He was convicted on the strength of DNA testing of sperm traces left at the scene of the crime. This was the first case where DNA brought about a conviction in America.

DNA tests were applied to other murders Spencer might have committed and pinpointed three more homicides he committed, including that of Carol Hamm who had been raped and murdered in her Arlington, Virginia home in January 1984, a crime for which David Vasquez had already served five years of a 35-year sentence.

Timothy Spencer, the first person to be convicted of murder (in 1988) through the DNA identification system.

SPOONER, BATHSHEBA
Murderer ● (1746-1778)

Bathsheba was the daughter of General Timothy Ruggles, who had served in several campaigns under Lord Amherst. His vast estates in Massachusetts were taken over by the colonials at the advent of the Revolution after Ruggles declared himself for the king. Ruggles went into exile in Nova Scotia but Bathsheba, who had married a squire named Joshua Spooner in 1766, remained behind.

Ezra Ross, a young revolutionary soldier returning from a battle, stopped by Bathsheba's Brookfield, Mass. home, asking to be fed. The attractive Mrs. Spooner not only fed him but bedded him and a romance between the two blossomed. The thought of murdering her wealthy husband then occurred to Bathsheba and she tried to convince Ross to perform the deed. The young man was squeamish and Bathsheba enlisted the aid of two passing British soldiers, James Buchanan and William Brooks, to help perform the killing.

The trio waited for Joshua Spooner outside of his home on the night of March 1, 1778 and cracked his skull as he stepped into his porchway. The three men then dragged Spooner's body to a nearby well and threw it in. They were not clever men. All three were found days later wearing Spooner's clothing and carrying his watch and silver buckles.

In the first capital case of American jurisdiction in Massachusetts, the three men and Bathsheba were convicted and sentenced to death. Mrs. Spooner begged for her life on the grounds that she was pregnant with child. A group of midwives called in by the court examined her and stated she was not about to have a baby.

Bathsheba, her lover Ross, Brooks, and Buchanan were hanged at Worcester, Mass., July 2, 1778. Mrs. Spooner's body was then inspected and doctors discovered the midwives had erred. The fetus Bathsheba carried was already close to five months old.

SPORTSMEN'S HALL

From about 1845, Kit Burns owned and operated this notorious dive in the Fourth Ward of New York City. A three-story frame building at 273 Water Street, Sportsmen's Hall featured a stinking pit on its

A daily scene in Kit Burns' Sportsman's Hall where thieves and killers hovered about the popular Death Pit to witness two terriers destroy each other.

first floor, where fights to the death were held between terriers and enormous gray rats.

The infamous killer, George Leese, a leader of the Slaughter House Gang, frequented Sportsmen's every night. Leese was known as "Snatchem" because of his adroitness in lifting wallets from customers in the dive. He was described as a "beastly, obscene ruffian, with bulging, bulbous, watery-blue eyes, bloated face and coarse swaggering gait." Leese would pick up pin money by attending boxers who had been cut and slashed in matches. He would suck the blood from their wounds, once considered medicinal, for the right stipend.

Another denizen of Sportsmen's was Jack the Rat. The peculiar entertainment this obnoxious character offered customers consisted of gnawing the head from a mouse for a dime. For twenty-five cents he would chew off the head of a live rat.

The place had an odd bouncer, a giant woman known as Gallus Mag. She was English and well over six feet. Gallus Mag carried several daggers and pistols in a belt strapped around her skirt and stalked through the saloon eager to cripple or kill any troublesome customer. This odd creature specialized in biting off the ears of those who caused disturbances. The ears were kept pickled in a jar behind the bar as a warning to boastful drunks.

There wasn't a police officer in the district who would speak to Gallus Mag, let alone stop her from beating someone half to death on the street. They shuddered at the sight of her as she walked down the alleyways, heavy-booted and snapping exposed galluses (suspenders). Sportsmen's Hall served as a gathering place for the most devastating gangs in New York during the Nineteenth Century—the Daybreak Boys, Border Gang, Patsy Conroys, Shirt Tails, Hookers, Buckoos, Swamp Angels, and Slaughter Housers all met there.

Seven murders were committed inside the hall within two months during 1845. Such hulking murderers as Slobbery Jim, Patsy the Barber, and One-Armed Charlie clod-marched their way through the dimly lit passageways and gambling rooms of the hall seeking likely victims to rob and kill.

Sportsmen's Hall was torn down in 1870 as part of a redevelopment program in the district and the gangsters moved off to the Five Points section to continue their criminal careers.

ST. VALENTINE'S DAY MASSACRE

The battle for control of Chicago's North Side between Al Capone and George "Bugs" Moran reached its peak in 1929. Several of Capone's top lieutenants had been killed by Moran's gunners while Scarface retreated to his home in Palm Island, Florida. Capone decided that drastic measures were called for and ordered Moran's entire gang annihilated. His scheme was diabolically clever.

Through a contact in Detroit, reportedly Abe Bernstein, leader of the Purple Gang, Capone arranged for someone to call Bugs Moran on the phone, telling him that a special shipment of hijacked bonded whiskey was going to be delivered to Moran's North Side headquarters, a garage at 2122 North Clark Street. Adam Heyer, a Moran flunkie, owned the garage, a front with the sign "S.M.C. Cartage Company" plastered on its street window.

Moran received a call at the garage on the morning of February 13, 1929, probably from Abe Bernstein. The caller told Moran that he had a wonderful load of booze available, recently hijacked "right off the river."

"How much?" Moran asked.

"Fifty-seven dollars a case."

"Okay, deliver it to the garage."

"When?"

"By ten-thirty tomorrow morning. All the boys will be here. We're short and they'll want a cut."

Bernstein, who had previously been Capone's chief supplier of Canadian liquor, probably had begun to send Moran shipments of quality booze months before, working his way into the leery gangleader's confidence. The caller was both known and trusted by Moran.

The following morning, February 14, 1929 —St. Valentine's Day—Moran's gang, such as it was after years of being ravaged by the bootleg wars, assembled at the garage. Thief and bootlegger Adam Heyer attended. Also waiting were Moran's top gunners, the deadly brothers Frank and Pete Gusenberg. John May, a safe-blower, speakeasy owner Al Weinshank, bankrobber James Clark, and Dr. Reinhardt H. Schwimmer, an optometrist fascinated by gangsters, lounged about on the premises. A German shepherd named Highball, belonging to May, scampered about the trucks and cars parked in the garage. The men impatiently waited for Moran to arrive with Willie Marks and Ted Newbury.

Moran was late. He, Newbury, and Marks had stopped to attend to some business and just as he rounded a corner he saw a black Cadillac, similar to that used by police detectives, roll up to the curb and stop before the garage. Five men, three dressed as policemen, two in plainclothes, went inside. Bugs waved Newbury and Marks into a nearby coffee shop. They waited until the expected pinch was over. Moran talked of sending Newbury down to precinct headquarters with bond money. The Gusenbergs always went armed and were sure to be arrested for carrying concealed weapons, he said.

Neighbors in adjoining buildings then heard what they later described to police as "pneumatic drills." The police emerged minutes later with two men apparently under arrest. The "squad car" drove off leisurely. Then May's dog began to howl.

The landlady in the next building, Mrs. Jeanette Landesman, was disturbed at the dog's whining and sent one of her roomers, C. L. McAllister, to the garage to investigate. He came outside two minutes later, his mouth gaping, his face ashen. McAllister ran up the stairs to tell Mrs. Landesman: "The place is full of dead men!"

The police were called and, upon entering the garage, stepped back in shock at the sight of the carnage. It was obvious to police that seven men had been lined up against the north brick wall of the building and machine-gunned while their backs had been turned. One reporter later described the victims as models of "upkeep and dress—shave, hair trim, manicure; the silk shirt, the flashy tie; here and there a diamond stickpin and ring; in Dr. Schwimmer's case a carnation boutonniere; fedoras with brims slanted down over the right eyes; spats; tailored suits and overcoats; each with the customary roll—Heyer, $1,135; Weinshank, $1,250; May, $1,200. . . ."

Capone's killers had not bothered to rummage through their victims' pockets. Their assignment was mass murder plain and simple. They performed their duty so adroitly, using the police raid ruse, that they were never com-

The front of the garage Bugs Moran used to store his bootleg liquor or North Clark Street.

pletely identified. The only person named without reservation as one of the machinegunners was Fred "Killer" Burke, an out-of-town gunsel who was never brought to trial for the St. Valentine's Day slaughter. Others thought to be part of the extermination party were John Scalise, Albert Anselmi, and "Machine Gun" Jack McGrun, all top Capone hit men.

Seven men (five shown) were lined up against the wall in the North Clark Street garage by Capon's machinegunners on 2/14/29 and slaughtered. It was the end of the Moran gang. (UPI)

Fred R. "Killer" Burke (with cigar and manacles) was the only man positively linked with the St. Valentine's Day shooting; he was never tried for this crime. (UPI)

One man survived the slaughter for a few hours. Frank Gusenberg had worked his way from the blood-splattered wall where his brother Pete had died kneeling, slumped against a chair, where James Clark had fallen on his face with half his head blown off, where Heyer, Schwimmer, Weinshank, and May sprawled lifeless on their backs, their brains spilling onto the greasy garage floor.

Sergeant Tom Loftus found Gusenberg crawling toward the garage door and called an ambulance. An hour later police sergeant Clarence Sweeney, at a bedside in Alexian Brothers Hospital, his head bent close to the mortally wounded gangster, asked Gusenberg: "Who shot you, Frank?"

Gusenberg could only whimper a reply: "No one—nobody shot me."

The gangster was tough but he was dying and he knew it. He had been with O'Bannion since the beginning and upon that gangleader's assassination, had gone on working for Earl "Hymie" Weiss and then Bugs Moran. He had been part of the car cavalcade that drove past Capone's Cicero headquarters and sprayed the place with machinegun bullets in broad daylight. He had, with his brother Pete, cornered "Machine-Gun" Jack McGurn in a McCormick Hotel phone booth and shot him to pieces only to see McGurn recover and swear revenge; he had helped to shoot down Capone's *Unione Siciliane* appointee as president, Pasqualino Lolordo.

"You don't have long to live, Frank," Sweeney told him. "They got Pete and all the others. Tell us who did it. We'll get them for you."

Gusenberg's eyes flashed open for a moment. "Nobody shot me."

Sweeney could see Gusenberg slipping into death. "Want a preacher, Frank?" he asked.

The gangster moved his lips and the word "No" was barely heard in a last sigh.

Gusenberg died at 1:30 p.m., bringing the Clark Street toll to seven.

Moran exploded when he heard of the almost total destruction of his gang. When police asked him who the caller was who set up the gang, "he raved like a madman." Where Frank Gusenberg staunchly upheld the underworld's code of silence, even on his deathbed, Moran did not. Pressured by newsmen for a comment, he finally blurted: "Only Capone kills like that!"

The St. Valentine's Day Massacre marked the end of any significant gangland opposition to Capone in Chicago. It also heralded a wave of reform in reaction to the slaughter that would sweep Scarface from power forever.

(ALSO SEE Al Capone, Capone Gang, "Machine-Gun" Jack McGurn, George "Bugs" Moran.)

STACHER, JOSEPH ("DOC")
Syndicate Gangster ● (1902-1977)

BACKGROUND: BORN IN POLAND IN 1902. IMMIGRATED TO THE U.S. IN 1912. MINOR PUBLIC EDUCATION. DESCRIPTION: 5'11", BROWN EYES, BROWN HAIR, SLENDER. ALIASES: JOSEPH ROSEN, DOC ROSEN, MORRIS ROSE, JOE J. STEIN, DOC HARRIS, DOC WEINER, GEORGE KENT, J. P. HARRIS, HARRY GOLDMAN. RECORD: ARRESTED UNDER THE ALIAS OF JOSEPH ROSEN IN NEWARK, N.J. FROM 1924 TO 1930—BREAKING AND ENTERING, LARCENY, 11/26/24, DISPOSITION; LARCENY, 4/21/26; DISMISSED; ASSAULT AND BATTERY, 8/18/26, DISMISSED; TWO CHARGES OF ASSAULT AND BATTERY, 6/7/27, DISMISSED; ROBBERY, 8/15/27, NOLLE PROSSED; VIOLATING PROHIBITION LAWS, 12/4/27, ADJOURNED WITHOUT FUTURE DATE; ASSAULT AND BATTERY, 12/9/27, FINED $50; ASSAULT AND BATTERY, 11/5/30, DISMISSED; TRAVELED TO THE WEST COAST IN THE MID-1930S AND BECAME MEYER LANSKY'S REPRESENTATIVE IN GAMBLING INTERESTS THERE; INVOLVED IN LAS VEGAS GAMBLING IN 1950S; CONVICTED OF INCOME TAX EVASION AFTER PLEADING GUILTY ON 7/31/64; SENTENCED TO FIVE

YEARS IN PRISON AND A $10,000 FINE, SENTENCE SUSPENDED AFTER HE AGREED TO BE DEPORTED TO ISRAEL.

Stacher began as a petty thief in Newark N. J., stealing from pushcarts. He met and formed close ties with future New Jersey syndicate thugs Abner "Longy" Zwillman, Gerardo "Jerry" Catena, and Willie Moretti. During the 1920s, Stacher worked as an underboss to Zwillman, concentrating in gambling.

In 1931, Stacher, at the instigation of Meyer Lansky, another strong ally, held the first summit meeting of what was then termed the "Jewish Mafia," gathering the top Jewish mobsters in New York. Attending the meeting at the Franconia Hotel on November 11, 1931 were Bugsy Siegel, Louis "Lepke" Buchalter, Jacob "Gurrah" Shapiro, Hyman "Curly" Holtz, Louis "Shadows" Kravitz, Philip "Little Farvel" Kovalick, Harry Tietlebaum, and Harry "Big Greenie" Greenberg, who would be murdered eight years later in Los Angeles by Bugsy Siegel.

Stacher went on to the West Coast in the mid-1930s to develop gambling for Meyer Lansky, with brief stints performed for Little Meyer in the casinos nestling in the Caribbean islands.

During the Las Vegas boom of the early 1950s, Stacher, representing Lansky, moved into gambling and was linked with various casinos such as the Fremont and the Sands.

In 1964, federal authorities brought charges of income tax evasion against Doc Stacher and he pleaded guilty. He was sentenced to five years in jail and fined $10,000. Rather than imprison Stacher, the courts chose to offer him a deal. The prison term would be suspended if he would accept deportation to a country of his choice. A ban existed at the time which prevented anyone being deported to Iron Curtain countries. Since Stacher proved he had been born in Poland, he was allowed to opt for Israel.

Stacher left for Israel in 1965 and died there in 1977.

STARKWEATHER, CHARLES
Murderer, Robber ● (1940-1959)

BACKGROUND: BORN AND RAISED IN LINCOLN, NEB., ONE OF SEVEN CHILDREN. MINOR PUBLIC EDUCATION. ORIGINAL OCCUPATION, GARBAGEMAN. DESCRIPTION: 52", BROWN EYES, RED HAIR, STOCKY BUILD. ALIASES: NONE. RECORD: ROBBED A SERVICE STATION IN LINCOLN, NEB., KILLING ATTENDANT ROBERT COLVERT 12/1/57; MURDERED VELDA, MARION, AND BETTY JEAN BARTLETT 1/28/58; SHOT AND KILLED ROBERT JENSEN AND CAROL KING 1/30/58; SHOT, STABBED, AND KILLED THE SAME DAY MR. AND MRS. C. LAUER WARD AND THEIR HOUSEKEEPER MISS LILLIAN FENCI; SHOT AND KILLED SHOE SALESMAN MERLE COLLISON NEAR DOUGLAS WYOMING TWO DAYS LATER; APPREHENDED AND SENTENCED TO DEATH; EXECUTED IN THE ELECTRIC CHAIR AT NEBRASKA STATE PENITENTIARY, 6/24/59.

There was always something a little odd about Charlie Starkweather. Not his all-American love of comic books, hot rods, and hunting; he did strange things.

Once when he was driving a garbage truck in Lincoln, Neb., Charlie sat behind the wheel and shouted obscenities at passersby.

(From his confession: "The more I looked at people the more I hated them because I knowed they wasn't any place for me with the kind of people I knowed. I used to wonder why they was here, anyhow? A bunch of goddamned sons of bitches looking for somebody to make fun of . . . some poor fellow who ain't done nothin' but feed chickens.")

Still no one suspected little Charlie would become one of the bloodiest mass murderers of all time.

Starkweather, nineteen, was infatuated with the James Dean image and wore his red hair long (by 1950s standards). Small, stocky, and pigeon-toed, he wore a cheap pair of cowboy boots several sizes too large, the toes of which he stuffed with crumpled newspapers.

His small stature kept him from dating girls his own age. So he selected diminutive Caril Ann Fugate for his sweetheart.

Caril Ann was only fourteen but well developed. She had a sexy, hip-swinging way about her. And she was a rebel, like Charlie. She delighted in telling her stepfather, Marion Bartlett, to go to hell.

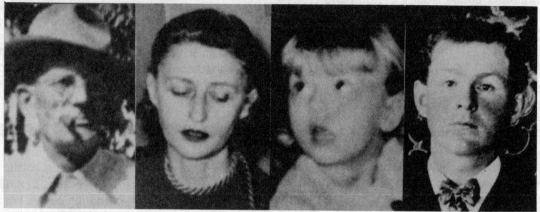

Victims of Starkweather's weeklong murder spree: (left to right, top) Carol King, Robert Jensen, C. Lauer Ward, Mrs. Ward, Lillian Fencl, (left to right, bottom) Marion Bartlett, Mrs. Bartlett, Betty Jean Bartlett, and August Meyer.

Little Red, as Starkweather was called by his friends, and Caril Ann made a mumbling, awkward pair of lovebirds. Charlie was on the shy side.

Yet it was this withdrawn boy who would blithely slaughter eleven people and terrify the Plains States area in the late, wintry days of January, 1958.

A lone victim of Starkweather's wrath was gas station attendant Robert Colvert. Little Red drove into Colvert's station on December 1, 1957 and robbed him at gunpoint. He then drove the 21-year-old Colvert to the open plains beyond Lincoln and killed him, shooting him several times in the head.

The mass slaughter began in Caril Ann's living room two months later. Charlie was waiting for her to come home from school. He had brought along his slide-action .22-caliber hunting rifle, the one possession he was seldom without.

Mrs. Bartlett was annoyed. She didn't like Charlie, and his fondling of the rifle made her uneasy. Suddenly she started shouting angrily at him.

As Little Red remembered later: "They said they were tired of me hanging around. I told Mrs. Bartlett off and she got so mad that she slapped me. When I hit her back, her husband started to come at me, so I had to let both of them have it with my rifle."

Caril Ann arrived just as the argument began. She watched the berserk bantam saunter into her little sister's room and choke two-year-old Betty Jean to death by pushing his rifle down her throat.

Then she switched on one of her favorite TV programs while Charlie made sandwiches in the kitchen.

Charlie hid Bartlett's body under rags and newspapers in the chicken coop behind the house. He dragged Mrs. Bartlett's corpse to an abandoned outhouse a few yards away and covered it with newspapers.

Next he dumped the baby's body into a cardboard box and joined Caril Ann to watch television.

(From his confession: "Don't know why it was but being alone with her [Caril] was like owning a little world all our own . . . lying there with our arms around each other and not talking much, just kind of tightening up and listening to the wind blow or looking at the same star and moving our hands over each other's face . . . I forgot about my bow-legs when we was havin' excitement. When I'd hold her in my arms and do the things we done together, I didn't think about bein' a red-headed peckerwood then . . . We knowed that the world had give us to each other. We was goin' to make it leave us alone . . . if we'd a been let a lone we wouldn't hurt nobody . . .")

Caril Ann worried that relatives might show up. So Charlie wrote on a piece of paper: "Stay a Way. Every Body is Sick With the Flu." They tacked the note to the front door.

It wasn't long before Mrs. Bartlett's older daughter stopped to visit. She thought the note fishy and pounded on the door. Caril Ann refused to let her in.

Puzzled and angry, the sister told her husband the fourteen-year-old was acting strangely. He called the police.

When officers arrived, Caril Ann again refused to open up.

"Everybody in this house is sick with the flu," she said. "The doctor told me not to let anybody inside."

"He didn't mean your relatives, did he?"

"I certainly wouldn't let my sister come in here with her baby."

Caril Ann played her role faultlessly. Perhaps, as her lawyer argued later, she was protecting visitors from the killer who lurked behind the door.

The officers were persistent. "Why would your brother-in-law call us over something like this?" one asked.

"Ask him. I don't know what goes on in his head. He doesn't like me, for one thing. And he always has to be worrying about something."

Two days later, Caril Ann turned her grandmother away. The woman angrily went to Lincoln's assistant police chief, Eugene Masters.

"There's something fishy going on," she asserted. "Caril's voice just didn't sound right, like she was covering something up."

Two officers accompanied the woman back to the Bartlett house. Ignoring the "Flu" sign, they entered. The house was empty.

At first they thought the entire family may have gone to the doctor. Then the Bartlett son-in-law, followed by Starkweather's brother, found the bodies.

Police quickly learned that Caril Ann and Charlie had packed bags into Little Red's hot rod and roared off. They ordered their arrest on "suspicion."

"Suspicion" hardened to belief when a gas station attendant in Bennet, sixteen miles away, reported Charlie and Caril had stopped for gas and to repair a flat.

Little Red bought a box each of .22 rifle cartridges and .410 shotgun shells.

On January 29 Charlie's car was reported to be parked next to August Meyer's farmhouse. Sheriff Merle Karnopp, with a large body of officers, crept up on the house at dawn.

"Charles Starkweather!" Karnopp roared through a bullhorn. "Come out with your hands in the air!"

No response. At Karnopp's signal nine tear gas bombs were shot through the farmhouse windows. The deputies moved in, guns drawn.

An officer kicked open a door and almost vomited. "Starkweather and the girl are gone," he told Karnopp. "They left the farmer with his head nearly torn off by a shotgun."

A short time later a nearby farmer, Evert Broening, found the bodies of Robert Jensen, 17, and Carol King, 16, shot through their heads in an abandoned storm cellar near the Meyer place.

Police figured that Jensen was killed for his automobile. Carol, the coroner reported, had been stripped naked and viciously raped before being killed.

(From his confession: "I began to wonder what kind of life I did live in this world, and even to this day, I'm wondering about it, but it don't matter how much I used to think about it. I don't believe I ever would have found a personal world or live in a worth-while world maybe, because I don't know life, or for what it was. They say this is a wonderful world to live in, but I don't believe I ever did really live in a wonderful world.")

Two hundred lawmen combed the plains around Lincoln, but they were too late for wealthy industrialist C. Lauer Ward. A relative got suspicious when the businessman failed to appear at work; he found a 1950 Ford in Ward's garage in place of Ward's '56 Packard.

Officers broke into the Ward home to find Ward sprawled in the foyer with a bullet in his head.

In a bedroom were the mutilated bodies of Clara Ward and her maid, Lillian Fenci. Both women had been tied and gagged, then stabbed repeatedly.

(From his confession: "Nobody knowed better than to say nothin' to me when I was a-heavin' their goddamn garbage.")

By now 1,200 men, including 200 National Guardsmen, were looking for Little Red and his girlfriend. Charlie had made the Big Time.

Luck let Charlie slip through massive dragnets into Wyoming. Outside the small town of Douglas, he came on a car parked along the highway.

Shoe salesman Merle Collison, Starkweather's last victim, had pulled over for a nap. Starkweather sent a bullet through the window.

Collison, frightened, got up.

"Come on outta that car, mister!" Starkweather shouted, gesturing wildly with his rifle.

Mass murderer Charles Starkweather; he was executed. (UPI)

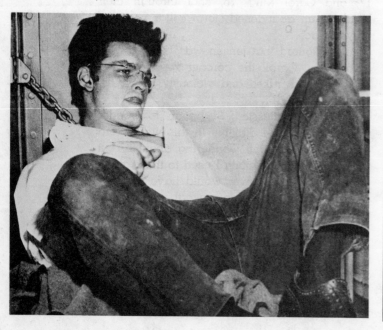

As Collison stepped out of the car, Starkweather pumped nine bullets into him, killing him instantly and blowing him back into the car.

"We got us another car, honey!" Charlie shouted.

(From his confession: "People will remember that last shot. I hope they'll read my story. They'll know why then. They'll know that the salesman just happened to be there. I didn't put him there and he didn't know I was coming. I had hated and been hated. I had my little world to keep alive as long as possible, and my gun. That was my answer.")

The killer leaned over Collison's body and tried to release the emergency brake, but it was stuck. Passing oil agent Joseph Sprinkle, pulled over to help what he thought were motorists in trouble. Starkweather brandished his rifle.

"Help me release this brake or I'll kill you!" Starkweather yelled.

Sprinkle spotted Collison's body and knew what he could expect. When Charlie reached forward to help the oil man release the brake, he grabbed the rifle.

"You bastard!" Starkweather screamed. "Gimme my rifle! Jump him Caril! Get my shotgun!"

The fourteen-year-old girl stared, petrified as she saw another car, a police squad, approaching fast, red warning light spinning. As Deputy Sheriff William Rohmer drove up, Caril Ann ran toward him.

"Help! It's Starkweather!" she yelped. "He's going to kill me! He's crazy! Arrest him!"

Sprinkle tore the rifle out of Starkweather's hands and the killer darted for his car. Rohmer couldn't fire because Caril Ann was in the way.

The deputy threw the girl into his car and took after Charlie, radioing to police ahead. Another sheriff's car took up the chase at 115 miles an hour. A shot blew out the rear window of Little Red's car.

Outside Douglas, Wyo., Starkweather suddenly braked and staggered out, holding his right ear. "I'm hit!" he squealed. "You lousy bastards shot me!"

While Sheriff Earl Heflin held a shotgun on the killer, Police Chief Robert Ainsley looked him over.

"You're a real tough guy, aren't you?" he

Starkweather's girlfriend, fourteen-year-old Caril Fugate, is still in jail fighting to get out. A recent parole board denied her pardon. (UPI)

asked in disgust. Charlie had a superficial cut from flying glass.

At first, Starkweather tried to protect Caril Ann: "Don't take it out on the girl. She had no part in any of it." He shouted that Caril had been his hostage.

Later when she cried innocence and branded him a killer in court he turned on her.

"She could have escaped any time she wanted," he said. "I left her alone lots of times. Sometimes when I would go in and get hamburgers, she would be sitting in the car with all the guns. There would have been nothing to stop her from running away.

"One time she said that some hamburgers were lousy and we ought to go back and shoot all them people in the restaurant.

"After I shot her folks and killed her baby sister, Caril sat and watched television while I wrapped the bodies up in rags and newspapers.

"We just cooked up that hostage story between us."

As Starkweather had no mercy for his playmate in death, the jury ignored her plea of innocence. Caril Ann Fugate was sentenced to life in prison, though she continued to sob her not guilty plea as they led her from the courtroom.

Starkweather went to his death in the Nebraska State Penitentiary only a few miles from the shack he called his home. He entered the death room on June 24, 1959. Only hours before, the Lions Club in Beatrice, Nebraska had asked that he donate his eyes to their eye bank following his death.

"Hell no!" Little Red roared from his cell. "No one ever did anything for me. Why in the hell should I do anything for anyone else?"

Starkweather sat down in the electric chair at exactly midnight, saying nothing. He wore a badly-fitted death mask that made the ritual all the more grotesque. Five jolts of electricity —2,200 volts in each charge—were sent into his body and at 12:03 a.m. prison doctor Paul Getscher dramatically announced to witnesses present: "Charles Starkweather is dead!"

Outside the prison gates, thirty teenagers in blue jeans and bobby socks milled around. A young girl stepped forward and told a reporter: "Some of us knew him. Some of us wanted to be with him at the end."

STARR, BELLE
Horse Thief, Fence ● (1848-1889)

BACKGROUND: BORN 2/5/48 AS MYRA BELLE SHIRLEY IN A LOG CABIN NEAR CARTHAGE, MO. TO ELIZABETH AND JOHN SHIRLEY. ONE BROTHER KILLED IN THE BORDER WARS (1860) WHILE RIDING WITH REDLEGS UNDER THE COMMAND OF JIM LANE AT SARCOXIE, MO. MOVED WITH THE FAMILY AT AGE 16 TO SCYENE, TEX., NEAR DALLAS. GRADUATED CARTHAGE FEMALE ACADEMY (EIGHTH GRADE). MARRIED OUTLAW SAM STARR IN 1876. TWO CHILDREN, PEARL (BY OUTLAW COLE YOUNGER) AND EDWARD (BY BANKROBBER JIM REED). DESCRIPTION: 5'1", BLACK EYES, BLACK HAIR, SLENDER. ALIASES: UNKNOWN. RECORD: HARBORED FUGITIVE COLE YOUNGER IN 1866; WITH JIM REED TORTURED AND ROBBED A SETTLER IN CALIFORNIA NEAR THE NORTH CANADIAN RIVER, STEALING APPROXIMATELY $30,000 IN GOLD; HEADED A BAND OF HORSE AND CATTLE THIEVES IN OKLAHOMA FROM 1875 TO 1880; TRIED WITH HER HUSBAND SAM STARR BEFORE JUDGE ISAAC PARKER IN FORT SMITH, ARK. AS HORSE THIEVES IN 1883, CONVICTED AND SENTENCED TO SIX MONTHS IN JAIL; ARRESTED IN 1886 FOR HORSE STEALING, DISMISSED FOR LACK OF EVIDENCE; SHOT

Belle Starr, the so-called "Bandit Queen," sporting a small arsenal. (Western History Collection, U. of Okla. Library)

Horse thief Belle Starr playing the role. (Oklahoma Historical Society)

Of all the legends of the Old West, that of Belle Starr, bandit queen, was the most totally fabricated. Belle was ridiculously romanticized by the dime novelists of the day. To them she was a daring and noble woman endowed with beauteous charms who fulfilled the role of a female Robin Hood. It was all far from the truth. Belle Starr was a cheap, free-living horse thief with the morals of an alley cat.

Born Myra Belle Shirley, the future "bandit queen" lived a docile life in Carthage, Mo. until she was twelve, attending the Carthage Female Academy and finishing eighth grade. Her father was reportedly a judge at one time or other and stemmed from Southern aristocracy.

To avoid the violence of the border wars between Redlegs and Slaveholders, John Shirley moved his small family to Scyene, Tex., about ten miles from Dallas. Six years later, Belle met and fell in love with bankrobber Cole Younger, right-hand man to Jesse James.

Cole was on the run, having just robbed the Liberty bank in Missouri. Belle took him to a small cabin squatting on the Oklahoma Strip, a place she renamed Younger's Bend, where they hid. Months after Cole rode away to rejoin the James gang, Belle gave birth to a daughter, Pearl. It was generally acknowledged that the child was Younger's offspring.

Next Belle took up with bankrobber Jim Reed. In 1869, Belle, Reed, and two others rode to California and, hearing that a wealthy prospector living near the North Canadian River had a huge cache of gold hidden in his shack, attacked him one night and tortured him into telling them where his riches were secreted. The band rode off with about $30,000 in gold.

Supplied with new wealth, Belle returned to Texas and sported about Scyene in long velvet gowns, plumed hats and a leather girdle crammed with six guns. She bought an expensive race horse, Venus, and whipped it up and down the streets, her angular features grimly set; Belle was a truly ugly woman with razor thin lips, beady eyes, and a sliver of slicked down hair slapped to her forehead.

When Reed was killed in a gun fight in August of 1874, Belle began living with an Indian outlaw named Blue Duck, who appeared about 1876. At this time she organized a band of horse thieves and they regularly raided the ranches and small towns through the Oklahoma Strip.

Then Sam Starr, a Cherokee Indian gone bad, arrived at Younger's Bend and Belle married him. Belle and Sam Starr embarked upon a rampage of horse and cattle stealing unequalled in the history of Oklahoma. She and her husband were arrested in 1883 and given six months in jail. Upon their release, the Starrs resumed their brigandry. They were again arrested in 1886, but the "hanging judge" for Fort Smith, Judge Isaac Parker, released them for lack of evidence.

One of the deputies who had arrested the pair felt that their trial had been a farce and, in December, 1886, started an argument with Sam Starr in a local saloon which ended when both men drew their guns and shot each other to death.

Belle Starr's paramour days were not at an end, however. She found a new lover, a Creek Indian named Jim July. He was wanted for robbery but Belle convinced him to turn himself in since the law had little evidence with which to convict him. He agreed and, on February 3, 1889, the pair headed for Fort Smith. Belle rode half-way to the town and then turned around to ride back to her home at Younger's Bend.

Alone on the trail, Belle was shot from her horse by an unknown gunman lying in ambush. Some said he was one of the many lovers Belle had discarded. Hours later, a traveler found Belle and took her home. She died in her daughter's arms. Pearl Starr had an elegant monument erected over her mother's grave with the following poem inscribed at its base:

"Shed not for her the bitter tear,
Nor give the heart to vain regret,
'Tis but the casket that lies here,
The gem that fills it sparkles yet."

STARR, HENRY
Bankrobber ● (1881-1921)

Allegedly a nephew of Belle Starr, Henry began a life of crime while a teenager living in the Oklahoma Strip; he rustled cows and horses. The part Cherokee Indian organized a small band of hard-riding desperadoes in the late 1890s and began to rob one-horse banks in Oklahoma, Texas, and Arkansas, forty-eight of them by the end of his career according to one literary accountant.

In 1903, Starr shot and killed one of Judge Isaac Parker's deputies, Floyd Wilson. He was convicted and sentenced to death by the rope but was saved through appeals. Judge Parker tried him again for the same crime and sentenced him to death again. President Theodore Roosevelt stepped in and pardoned Starr.

A month later, Starr, Kid Wilson, and three others held up the Bentonville, Arkansas bank, getting more than $11,000 from the vault. Posse members trapped Starr and Wilson in Colorado Springs, Col. in July, 1903 as they were eating steaks in the Cafe Royal. The lawmen asked the outlaws where they had hidden their loot. Starr stared at them in silence.

When asked his real name Kid Wilson replied: "My kinfolks have never done a thing to place me where I am, so I prefer to say nothing of them." He, too, refused to turn over the stolen money.

Bankrobber Henry Starr was the first bandit to use the auto in a robbery. (Oklahoma Historical Society)

Starr's young wife, however, was found sleeping in a nearby hotel. Possemen plucked close to $2,000 in gold from beneath her pillow. She had been safeguarding it for him. Starr was sentenced to five years in the State Penitentiary. He was far from reformed when he was released in 1908. Starr continued to rob banks regularly. In 1914, Henry was thunderstruck with an idea. The automobile, he had seen, could certainly outdistance any posse on horseback. He purchased one and used it in his next bank raid, becoming the first American criminal to employ a car in a robbery. The new gimmick worked successfully for six years until lawmen also equipped themselves with autos. After he robbed the bank in Harrison, Arkansas in 1921, Henry Starr's car broke down on a dusty road. A sheriff's posse, riding a string of cars, caught up to him and he was killed in a wild gun battle.

[ALSO SEE Al Spencer.]

STEINBERG, JOEL B.
Murderer ● (1941-   )

A disbarred New York lawyer, Steinberg lived with Hedda Nussbaum, beginning in 1976. A year later she served as Steinberg's human punching bag. He broke her teeth, ribs, and nose. She still continued to live with him. The sadistic Steinberg ordered Nussbaum not to eat unless he gave her permission and when she broke this rule he forced her to take ice baths.

The couple took hard drugs and somehow managed to obtain two children, a boy and a girl, through illegal adoption. Steinberg was brutal toward the girl, Lisa, slapping her and hitting her without provocation. He claimed that she was "staring" at him. On November 1, 1987, Steinberg punched the little girl three times so that she collapsed to the floor.

He went to dinner, telling Nussbaum to hold Lisa and "stay in harmony with her." The next day the girl was unconscious and rushed to a hospital where she was declared "brain dead." She died three days later of a brain hemorrhage resulting from a severe blow to the head. She was one of 1,200 children who died from neglect or abuse in the U.S. in 1987.

Investigators examining the Steinberg–Nussbaum apartment were shocked to see food and excrement littering the floor. They found burglary tools, handcuffs, drugs of all kinds. Both Nussbaum and Steinberg were charged with murdering Lisa in November 1987 but all charges against Nussbaum were dismissed when she agreed to testify against her berserk lover.

Steinberg was convicted of first-degree manslaughter on January 30, 1989 and sentenced the following March to 8 to 25 years in prison.

STEVENS, WALTER
Gangster ● (1877-1939)

Stevens was a lone gunman and slugger who occasionally hired out to Johnny Torrio and Al Capone, to administer either a beating or a bullet to their enemies. The last remaining member of the old Maurice "Mossy" Enright labor-slugging gang, Stevens was a sanctimonious murderer who would kill a man for $50 or beat him half to death for $25, but would rage against short skirts, rouge, and "Flaming Youth."

He was an avid reader of Robert Louis Stevenson and Jack London; he particularly enjoyed the poetry of Robert Burns which he often quoted to brow-furrowing hoodlums. Stevens was considered "the dean of Chicago gunmen" and he is credited with shooting down at least five of Spike O'Donnell's stalwarts in the bootleg war between Capone and the South Side Irish gang.

The clout Stevens carried with Illinois Governor Len Small was considerable and was made available to the Capone-Torrio faction whenever Scarface needed an important political favor. Years before, Stevens had bribed and threatened several jury members sitting on a case involving Len Small. A Kankakee farmer and stooge for Mayor Big Bill Thompson, Small had been accused of embezzling

$600,000 while serving as State Treasurer. With the help of Walter Stevens he was freed.

It was quite well known that Stevens had ruthlessly killed several people for Enright before Mossy was murdered by Sunny Jim Cosmano in February of 1920. Enright and Stevens had openly shot down gunman Pete Gentleman a year before Mossy's own death. Small, obviously out of gratitude, pardoned Stevens after he was convicted of murdering a policeman in Aurora, Ill.

Walter Stevens tried to show a good side to the world. He cared for his incurably invalided wife for twenty years and adopted three children. He didn't drink, never ran about with women, and didn't learn to smoke until he was fifty. He refused to allow his children to attend plays and films, condemning them as immoral. He also ripped out passages of novels he thought questionable before his children were permitted to read them.

He was credited with killing sixty men before he died in 1939.

STOKES, EDWARD S. ("NED")
Murderer ● (? -1901)

Stokes was a minor robber baron who hitched his wagon to Big Jim Fisk, stock manipulator and Jay Gould's erstwhile partner in bilking Cornelius Vanderbilt of the $19 million Erie Railroad. Handsome, cultured Ned Stokes first came into business contact with Fisk through stock manipulations concerned with oil. He profited enormously but was not content with merely sharing in the spoils of Fisk's schemes; he stole Big Jim's ravishing mistress, Helen Josephine "Josie" Mansfield.

Josie had long been "Jubilee Jim's" mistress and he had squandered untold tens of thousands of dollars on her; her jewelry collection was the toast of New York's high society. (Fisk's wife Lucy didn't seem to mind since she publically proclaimed that she "owned the man.")

Fisk, pompous and jealous, reacted angrily at losing his mistress to Stokes (whom he had brought to dinner one night at Josie's plush home). He accused Stokes of embezzling oil stock funds which they jointly owned. Stokes countered with a suit charging slander. Josie, who felt she was losing a fortune by throwing over Fisk for Stokes, then entered the battle and charged Big Jim with alienation of affections. Fisk sued Stokes for blackmail.

Stokes, on trial, bristled at the insulting questions put to him by Fisk's lawyer while on the stand. He was still seething as he downed a gourmet meal at Delmonico's on January 6, 1872 where he received word that he had been found guilty of blackmailing Jim Fisk.

Possessed of a violent temper, Stokes rushed to the street and caught a hansom cab to his hotel. There he pocketed a Colt revolver and went to see Josie Mansfield. Where was Fisk, Stokes wanted to know. The enterprising mistress had kept careful watch on the multimillionaire's movements and told her paramour that Fisk would be at the Broadway Central Hotel, meeting a friend from Boston who was arriving that afternoon.

Ned went to the hotel and secreted himself at the top of its magnificent, richly-carpeted stairway. Fisk arrived there promptly at 4 p.m. dressed in his usual flamboyant cape and top hat, carrying a gold-knobbed cane. As the robber baron began to ascend the stairway, he saw Stokes on the top landing, pointing a revolver down at him.

"Now I have you!" Stokes yelled out.

Fisk gasped: "For God's sake, will no one help me?"

Stokes fired twice. The first shot only wounded Fisk superficially in the arm. The second bullet was lodged deeply in Fisk's ample stomach. Doctors refused to operate for fear of killing the patient. "Prince Erie," as Fisk was sometimes called, died hours later.

Stokes, quickly apprehended, was given three trials. At the end of the second trial a jury found him guilty of murder and he was given the death sentence. His deft lawyers used a legal loophole to win him a third trial where the verdict was reduced to manslaughter; he was sentenced to six years in jail.

Josie Mansfield, who had begged for her lover's life on the witness stand, did not wait for him. When Stokes was released from Sing Sing, she had already disappeared.

Miss Mansfield journeyed to Paris where, for a brief time, she was the rage of the City of Light, lecturing the French on matters of the heart. She died in 1931 in a small Left Bank flat with pictures of both Fisk and Stokes above her bed.

STORMS, CHARLES
Gunfighter ● (? -1881)

Charlie Storms was a professional gunfighter who hungered after a reputation that would put him in contention with such top gunslingers as Bat Masterson and Wild Bill Hickok. Storms was sitting at the card table in Carl Mann's Saloon on August 2, 1876 in Deadwood when the cross-eyed lush, Jack McCall, walked up behind Hickok and blew out his brains, a wild act prompted by nothing more than drunkenness. (Hickok was uncustomarily sitting with his back to the door and was killed holding aces and eights, forever after known as "The Dead Man's Hand".)

Storms immediately took one of Wild Bill's famous pearl-handled pistols, a handsome .45-caliber single-action Colt, and kept it at his side till the day of his death. According to most reports, the weapon served more as a jinx to Storms than an asset. After several gunfights in Deadwood, Storms moved to Tombstone, Ariz. There, on the night of February 21, 1881, Charlie went up against diminutive but deadly Luke Short.

Short was a professional gambler and was employed at the time as a faro dealer in the Oriental Saloon. Storms, who had never met Short, thought of him as an undersized gunman with an inflated reputation. Emboldened by whiskey, Storms argued with Short at the gambler's table and then foolishly slapped the little man. A moment before Short went for his gun, his friend Bat Masterson leaped between the two adversaries.

Masterson convinced Storms to go home and sleep. Storms mumbled an apology to Short and walked away.

An hour later Masterson and Short were standing in front of the Oriental when Storms appeared. He grabbed Short by the arm as if to swing him around and into the street, while pulling Hickok's famed pistol from his scabbard. Masterson later stated that Storms "was too slow, although he succeeded in getting his pistol out. Luke stuck the muzzle of his own pistol against Storms' heart and pulled the trigger. The bullet tore the heart asunder, and as he was falling, Luke shot him again. Storms was dead before he hit the ground."

Luke Short was acquitted of the killing by a local judge on grounds of self-defense.

STOUDENMIRE, DALLAS
Gunfighter ● (1843-1882)

BACKGROUND: BORN AND RAISED IN TEXAS. MINOR PUBLIC EDUCATION. SERVED IN THE CONFEDERATE ARMY DURING THE CIVIL WAR. MARRIED ISABELLA SHERRINGTON, 2/20/82, NO CHILDREN. ORIGINAL OCCUPATION, MARSHAL. DESCRIPTION: 6'2", BROWN EYES, AUBURN HAIR, HEAVYSET. ALIASES: NONE. RECORD: AFTER A SHORT BUT DISTINGUISHED CAREER AS THE MARSHAL OF EL PASO, TEX., STOUDENMIRE WAS REPLACED BY JAMES B. GILLETT AND ATTEMPTED TO KILL DR. GEORGE FELIX "DOC" MANNING, HEAD OF THE MANNING BROTHERS CLAN; SHOT TO DEATH, 9/18/82.

When El Paso, Tex. was at the zenith of its gun madness, Dallas Stoudenmire, one of the most feared gunmen in the Southwest, was made its new marshal, April 11, 1881. In the year of his reign, Stoudenmire was involved in several shootings from which he emerged victorious. The marshal was a silent type who, like Wild Bill Hickok and Wyatt Earp, shot first and talked later.

While serving as marshal, Stoudenmire developed a feud with the Manning brothers—Dr. George, Frank, and James—who owned interests in almost all of El Paso's riotous saloons and one of the largest cattle ranches in Texas.

Stoudenmire and his close friend and one-time deputy, Doc Cummings, repeatedly claimed that the Mannings had hired gunslingers to kill them. Six days after he was made marshal, Stoudenmire, who was patroling the town's streets with Cummings, was shot at by assassins hidden in the darkness. Though he charged his assailants with two blazing six-guns (the marshal wore his pistols tucked into his belt, refusing to use holsters as being too cumbersome), Stoudenmire failed to capture anyone and received a slight wound in the heel.

On and off for a year, alleged Manning gunmen took pot-shots at Stoudenmire until he left El Paso to get married to pretty Isabella Sherrington in Columbus. Upon his return, the marshal learned that his good friend Cummings had been shot and killed in the Coliseum Saloon owned and operated by the Mannings. The brothers had been freed following this killing, their action termed self-defense. Cummings had come gunning for them, they insisted, and they had fired out of necessity.

Stoudenmire brooded over the loss of Cummings and took to heavy drinking. He became loud and threatened the Mannings with death on several occasions. The Vigilance Committee which had hired Stoudenmire suddenly lost faith in El Paso's fearless marshal and asked him to resign. He did, but he continued to hang about the saloons, cursing and insulting the Mannings.

Thoroughly drunk on the night of September 18, 1882, Stoudenmire staggered into Doc Manning's saloon and began to argue heatedly with the proprietor. (The feud had intensified to the extent where Stoudenmire and the Mannings had actually signed a truce months before).

In the middle of their shouting match, Stoudenmire and Manning reached for their pistols. A Manning henchman, Walter Jones, attempted to stop the ex-marshal but was shoved aside. Manning fired a shot that was stopped by a packet of letters in the gunfighter's left breast pocket.

Stoudenmire fired and wounded Manning in the arm. Doc dropped his pistol and dashed forward, locking himself around the big ex-lawman, attempting to prevent him from firing another shot. The two men grappled and fought their way out of the saloon. James Manning then arrived, gun in hand, and fired two shots, the second entering Stoudenmire's head, killing him.

Doc Manning, enraged, leaped upon the dead man, and, grabbing one of Stoudenmire's

Lawman turned gunfighter Dallas Stoudenmire of El Paso, Tex. (Western History Collection, U. of Okla. Library)

own pistols, beat at the corpse's head with the gun butt.

The Mannings were exonerated once again. A judge called it self-defense.

STOUT, MARION IRA
Murderer ● (? -1858)

Sarah Stout was anything but a fickle woman. Her strange allegiance to her criminal father and brother, both serving time in prison for robbery, was unswerving. The beautiful woman caught the eye of a Rochester, N. Y. man, Charles W. Littles. He courted the moody Sarah.

Before accepting Littles's hand in marriage, Sarah told him, in a rare burst of honesty, the truth about her relatives. Littles was in love. Nothing she could say or do, he vowed, would prevent him from wedding her.

A few years later, when Sarah's brother, Marion Ira Stout, was released from jail, a conspiracy immediately took place. Sarah was bored with her easy-going husband, she told Marion. There was a simple solution to that, Marion told Sarah. On the night of December 19, 1857 the brother and sister entered Littles' bedroom and, as he struggled to get out of bed, beat his head in with a hammer.

Both were arrested, tried, and convicted of the murder. Sarah was sent to serve a long term in Sing Sing Prison. Marion avoided returning to jail; he was hanged at Rochester, N. Y., October 22, 1858.

STOUT, PETER
Murderer ● (? -1803)

A youth living in Dover, New Jersey, Stout was mad as a hatter. Murderous thoughts entered his mind at the slightest insult. One local lad, fourteen-year-old Thomas Williams, had passed a mild criticism about his appearance. Stout did not immediately react but, days later, he saw Williams on the street and engaged him in conversation. As the two walked along, Stout suddenly produced an axe and sank it into the boy's skull, killing him instantly.

Throwing down the murder weapon, Stout leaned forward, reddened his hands with blood from his victim's wound and smeared the gore all over his body. He then waited for a constable to arrest him.

After a speedy trial, Stout was hanged at Monmouth Court House, N. J., May 13, 1803.

STRANG, JESSE
Murderer ● (? -1827)

Strang deserted his wife and child sometime in 1825 and went to live in Albany, N. Y., residing on the Van Rensselear estate under the name Joseph Orton. He went to work as a hired hand for a neighbor, John Whipple. Elsie Whipple, the squire's wife, had a long history of promiscuity.

Only days after he went to work on the Whipple estate, Elsie enticed the young man to bed. Then she began to encourage Jesse to murder her husband. First the conspirators decided to kill their victim by giving him doses of arsenic (Strang purchased large amounts of poison on three separate occasions), but abandoned this idea and ultimately thought up a quicker death for Whipple.

The lovers decided to shoot Whipple through the glass of a window as he was preparing to retire for the night. For months, Strang practiced such a shot with an expensive rifle Mrs. Whipple purchased for him. On the night of May 7, 1827, Strange fired accurately and killed the unsuspecting husband.

A stray bullet fired by a passing drunk was the excuse Mrs. Whipple and Strang gave to authorities in explaining the squire's death. Oddly enough, Strang was a member of the coroner's jury and voted with other members a verdict of murder by "persons unknown."

Mrs. Whipple and Strang, however, could not stay apart, and suspicion against them grew. They were arrested and the weak-willed Strang soon confessed the killing to the Rev. Mr. Lacey, Rector of St. Peter's Church of Albany.

The lovers fell out at their trials. After his own conviction, Strang attempted to testify at Mrs. Whipple's trial. He figured that if the woman was convicted, his chances for commutation would be aligned with her own. The judge trying Mrs. Whipple, however, refused to allow the young man to testify and Elsie was acquitted of the murder.

Strang was executed on the gallows in Albany August 24, 1827. Mrs. Whipple lived out her life in seclusion on her murdered husband's estate.

STRAWHIM, SAMUEL
Gunfighter ● (? -1869)

Sam Strawhim earned his reputation as a gunfighter and killer in Hays City, Kan. just after the Civil War. He was a vicious, rowdy drunk who shot first and then asked the name of his victim. Hays was a wide-open cowtown for a number of years but a Vigilance Committee soon hired Wild Bill Hickok to keep the peace and the shootings abated. Strawhim was ordered to leave town and, angered by the directive, proceeded, with Joseph Weiss, to beat up a vigilante named Alonzo Webster.

Webster grabbed his pistol and shot Weiss; Strawhim fled, going to Ellsworth. The outlaw returned to Hays on September 27, 1869, still brooding about his exile. He entered Bittle's Saloon with about eighteen cowboys, old friends, and the mob began to shoot up the place. Bittles sent for Hickok, who arrived in a jovial mood.

At first, Wild Bill tried to joke Strawhim out of any gunplay. The gunfighter and his friends were then in the street, having taken all the saloon's beer glasses with them. Hickok ignored Strawhim's threat: "I shall kill someone tonight just for luck." The marshal smilingly collected several beer glasses from the drunken cowboys and took them back to the saloon. Strawhim followed him.

As Hickok stood at the bar, staring into a mirror, Strawhim threatened to break every glass in the place. Wild Bill's lips curled into an ugly snarl, "Do, and they will carry you out." Hickok, watching in the mirror, saw

Strawhim step behind him and reach for his pistol. The marshal whirled about, gun already in hand, and shot Strawhim dead.

STROLLO, ANTHONY C. ("TONY BENDER")
Syndicate Gangster ● (1899-1962)

Born in New York City on June 18, 1899, Strollo, better known as Tony Bender to his Mafia intimates, rose through the underworld ranks in the 1920s as a bootlegger, strong-arm man, and killer. He was made a lieutenant in the Lucky Luciano Cosa Nostra family in 1931, upon the assassination of Salvatore Maranzano. Bender controlled crime in Greenwich Village.

Bender concentrated in gambling, especially in slot machines and organized crap games. In 1932, Bender ordered Joseph Valachi, Petey Muggins (Peter Mione), and another man, all members of his "troop," to murder Michael Reggione, alias "Little Apples." Reggione was shot to death with three bullets in the head on November 25, 1932.

When Luciano was deported and Vito Genovese fled to Italy, Frank Costello took over the Luciano family. Bender went on working for Costello in this family as an underboss, opening up several nightclubs in the Village in the late 1930s and early 1940s such as The Hollywood, the Black Cat, the Village Inn, and the 19th Hole.

Upon the expulsion of Frank Costello from the Mafia-syndicate, Bender became Vito Genovese's chief underboss in Manhattan. Genovese returned to the U.S. after a seven-year exile in Italy. Bender ordered Joseph Valachi, Joseph and Pasquale Pagano, and Fiore Siano (Valachi's nephew) to kill one Eugenio Giannini, who was then shot to death in Manhattan on September 20, 1952. The following year, on June 19, 1953, Bender ordered the killing of Steven Franse, who had been telling narcotic agents all he knew about Bender's drug trafficking. Franse was strangled to death in Joseph Valachi's nightclub, The Lido, in Greenwich Village.

Bender disappeared on the night of April 8, 1962. According to later testimony by Valachi and others, he was murdered and his body destroyed by a syndicate murder squad.

STROUD, ROBERT FRANKLIN
Murderer ● (1887-1963)

The international status Robert Stroud earned as "The Birdman of Alcatraz" reflected little upon his shabby beginnings. At nineteen, Stroud employed himself in Alaska as a pimp. His chief protege, according to one report, was an attractive dance hall girl named Kitty O'Brien. Stroud was extremely jealous of Kitty, and particularly of her nightly receipts. When a bartender refused to pay Kitty's $10 price for an evening of fun and frolic, Stroud got into a fight with him and killed him.

Convicted of manslaughter and sentenced to twelve years in prison, Stroud was sent to McNeil Island, a federal penitentiary in Pu-

get Sound off the coast of the State of Washington. He was later transferred to Leavenworth, where he kept to himself. His fellow prisoners thought little of him and resented his closed-lip attitude.

One convict, Morris "Red" Rudensky, described him thusly: "Physically, he was a disgrace—tall, thin and as attractive as a barracuda or a herring bone without herring. He seldom spoke to anyone, including the cons, and vice versa. He was a ferocious misanthrope." Rudensky also reported Stroud to be a flagrant homosexual.

Inexplicably, just before his sentence was completed, Stroud entered Leavenworth's mess hall on March 26, 1916, and, before twelve hundred convicts and prison officials, stabbed and killed prison guard Andrew F. Turner. The motivation for this murder was never adequately explained but Stroud did tell Rudensky: "The guard took sick and died all of a sudden. He died of heart trouble. I guess you would call it a puncture of the heart. Anyhow, there was a knife hole in the guard's heart. I never have given any reason for doing it, so they won't have much to work on; only that I killed him, and that won't do much good. I admit that much."

Stroud was convicted and sentenced to die

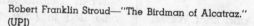

Robert Franklin Stroud—"The Birdman of Alcatraz."
(UPI)

on the gallows which were constructed in the exercise yard not more than two hundred feet from his cell.

The reputation Stroud had built up as a lover of canaries and an expert on their diseases (probably the most knowledgeable "canary doctor" in the U.S.) stood him in good stead. In 1920, his mother went to President Woodrow Wilson to seek a special commutation. Wilson was ailing and his wife, Elizabeth Bolling Wilson, had all but assumed his responsibilities of office.

Through the President's wife, who was impressed with Stroud's work in ornithology, Mrs. Elizabeth Stroud managed to obtain a presidential commutation which became effective just eight days before Stroud was scheduled to die. Wilson's commutation to life imprisonment carried with it the stipulation that Stroud be placed in solitary confinement for the remainder of his days.

Prison officials were more than kind to "The Birdman." He was allowed to use two adjoining cells (the wall separating them being torn down) to carry on his experiments in canary diseases and ornithology. He also penned a massive and hypercritical manuscript dealing with prison reform entitled *Looking Outward* (never published).

Stroud was eventually transferred to Alcatraz. His sobriquet came from the years he spent on The Rock. He died in prison in 1963, of old age.

STUART, CHARLES
Murderer ● (1960-1990)

Charles Stuart sold furs in an exclusive Boston store. He made good money but he wanted a better life. When his wife Carol, 30, informed him that she was pregnant in 1989, Stuart became upset. He did not want the extra burden of raising a child and he suggested that his wife have an abortion, as one story had it.

Carol Stuart wanted to give birth and planned to do so. On October 23, 1989, while driving through Mission Hill, a predominately black neighborhood in Boston, the Stuarts were shot by a black assailant, according to Charles who survived the attack. Carol was killed but she was still rushed to the hospital where her baby was delivered alive. The child died a short time later.

In a bizarre but truthful twist of events, Stuart's brother Matthew later revealed to police that Matthew gave him the gun which he, Charles Stuart, had used to shoot his own wife to death. The gun, along with some of Carol Stuart's jewelry, Matthew Stuart threw away.

The gun was found and its serial number matched that of a gun kept at the store where Charles Stuart worked. Learning that he was about to be arrested and that all the evidence would point to his conviction, Charles Stuart committed suicide by jumping off a bridge.

SUTTON, WILLIE ("THE ACTOR")
Bankrobber ● (1901-1982)

Sutton was a lone wolf bankrobber who gleaned, according to some reports, close to a million dollars in cash and securities from the twenty-odd banks he held up. He was a master at disguises, making up his face with false beards, plastic noses, and face putty, and affecting odd limps, gaits, and peculiar mannerisms which won for him his underworld nickname, "The Actor."

Never a member of organized crime, Sutton became the beau ideal among crooks, particularly during his heyday in the 1940s and 1950s. His ability to escape prisons and jails (with the agility of a circus-trained contortionist) earned him a place on the FBI's "Ten Most Wanted" list in 1951. While starting his car, he was captured the following year in Brooklyn, by two alert patrolmen. Sutton wasn't wearing any disguise. One story recounted the following dialogue:

"You're Willie Sutton aren't you?" one of the officers inquired.

"Who's Willie Sutton?"

"You are. The bankrobber."

Willie "The Actor" Sutton (right), notorious bankrobber out of disguise; shown here in 1952 being grilled by police following an uneventful capture. (UPI)

The bankrobber clucked his tongue in disgust. "Honestly, officer, you just can't go around stopping people and accusing them of being thieves. Do I look like a bankrobber to you?"

"You're not supposed to. That's the point. C'mon."

Sutton, released from prison in 1969, began to write his memoirs, no doubt finding it difficult to remember just who he was and what roles he had been playing throughout his incredible criminal career.

[ALSO SEE Albert Anastasia.]

SWEARINGEN, GEORGE
Murderer ● (? -1829)

Rachel Cunningham was the most beautiful harlot in Washington County, Md. and her amorous adventures were not unknown to the local sheriff, George Swearingen. The sheriff cautioned her on several occasions to quit the area, but his arguments soon softened into love.

Swearingen was wealthy and married but, after openly taking up with Miss Cunningham, he neglected his estate and his wife. Nothing his friends could say could convince the sheriff to give up his mad romance. In the summer of 1829, Swearingen decided to do away with his wife. He took her riding and on the Hagerstown Road, he later claimed, she fell from her mount and was killed.

Authorities grew suspicious and Swearingen fled with his mistress to New Orleans. They were arrested there and returned to Maryland. Though the evidence was flimsy, after a brief trial the sheriff was convicted and sentenced to death for the murder. He was hanged at Cumberland, Md., October 2, 1829.

SYNDICATE, THE

Known as the syndicate, the combine, the outfit, this criminal cartel presently controls all organized crime in the U.S. It is basically Mafia-oriented and its board members represent every American city throughout the country. The national crime syndicate was officially established in 1934 by the then-ruling monarchs of crime—Charles "Lucky" Luciano, Johnny Torrio, Meyer Lansky, Louis "Lepke" Buchalter, Jacob "Gurrah" Shapiro, Abner "Longy" Zwillman, Dutch Schultz, Vito Genovese, Frank Costello, and Thomas "Three-Finger Brown" Lucchese, in a non-stop gangster conclave in New York City.

The Mafia or Cosa Nostra, as it is called in the East by members of New York's Mafia families, did not at first exercise control of this organization. It remained a fraternal criminal brotherhood separate and apart from the syndicate, albeit several syndicate members were also members of the Mafia.

Several attempts had been made in the late 1920s by Luciano, Lansky, Torrio, and others to organize the various gangs across the country under one standard. Prohibition gangleaders such as Al Capone met with Luciano, Lansky, and Torrio in Atlantic City in 1929. There were subsequent meetings held in New York, Chicago, and Philadelphia.

Though Johnny Torrio has been credited with formally outlining the organization of the syndicate, most of the dubious credit should go to Luciano and Lansky. Most crime historians now agree that these two men formally launched the syndicate and detailed its protocol.

The original purpose of the syndicate was to do away with intragang wars and to consolidate power and lines of communication: establishing franchises, as it were, in the narcotics, vice, gambling, and union rackets throughout the U.S., with each city having its boss of bosses, bosses, underbosses, lieutenants and "soldiers."

In the early 1930s the Jewish and Irish gangleaders still possessed considerable power throughout the U.S., thus preventing the establishment of a syndicate as being an all Italian or Mafia-controlled organization. Since that time, however, the Mafia has come to entirely dominate the syndicate.

As of this writing those syndicate bosses of major American cities sitting on the board of directors of the syndicate (according to the most reliable sources) are: New York: Gerardo Vito Catena, Joseph Magliocco; New England, Raymond Patriarca, Philip Bruccola, Genaro Angulo; Florida, Santo Trafficante, Jr.; Detroit, Peter Licavoli, Angelo Meli, John Priziola, William Tocco; Chicago, Anthony Accardo, Fiore Buccieri; New Orleans, Carlos Marcello; with many sub-bosses based in smaller cities.

The power of the syndicate today is absolute in the underworld. Its decrees are carried out to the letter, even to the extermination of members of the board of directors, a policy established when members voted to kill Dutch Schultz in 1935 when he disregarded a board edict. Chief rackets concerning the syndicate today are narcotics and gambling, rigidly controlled throughout the U.S. by board members of the combine.

[ALSO SEE Anthony Accardo, Joe Adonis, Albert Anastasia, Louis "Lepke" Buchalter, Gerardo Catena, Frank Costello, Carlo Gambino, Vito Genovese, Meyer Lansky, Thomas "Three-Finger Brown" Lucchese, Charles "Lucky" Luciano, Stefano Magaddino, Carlos Marcello, Michele Miranda, Raymond Patriarca, John Roselli, Dutch Schultz, John Torrio, Santo Trafficante, Jr., Joseph Zerilli, Abner "Longy" Zwillman.]

TALBOTT, CHARLES E.
Murderer ● (? -1881)

Charles Talbott and his brother Albert had plotted the death of their father for several months. The old man was a tyrant who beat his wife, sons, and hired man unmercifully and at whim. One evening, after the Talbott brothers had waited until their father was about to retire for the night, Charles shot him to death with a hunting rifle.

They were quickly tried, convicted, and hanged.

TENNES, MONT
Gambler ● (1865-1941)

Tennes was a high roller in the plush gambling era dominated by Mike McDonald in Chicago and Richard Canfield in New York. He was one of McDonald's protéges and was part of a Chicago gambling clique which included Hot Stove Jimmy Quinn, Big Jim O'Leary, and John Condon, whose underworld nickname was "Johnny Fix-'Em."

By the turn of the century, Tennes estab-lished a gambling syndicate in Chicago and, in 1901, sent out an army of sluggers and bombers to subdue independent gamblers. Dozens of saloons and gambling dens were destroyed and many men were killed. By 1904, Tennes was king of the handbook and pool-room gambling concessions in Chicago.

With his partner, Johnny Rogers, Tennes monopolized the racing news by exclusively buying the Payne Telegraph Service of Cincinnati for $300 a day. Tennes relayed a nationwide racing results service to saloon owners and gambling dives at a cost of $100 a day to each proprietor. He became a millionaire within a year.

Gamblers were at Tennes's mercy and, with the exception of a South Side bloc led by John O'Malley, to a man turned over half their daily receipts to him. (Tennes, in turn, paid for half of their daily losses.)

O'Malley fought the combine in 1907, first by slugging Tennes in front of his home as he was taking the air one warm June evening. Next he bombed several Tennes-backed gambling dens; several persons were killed and injured. The Chicago gambling war lasted for a year. During this period, Police Chief George M. Shippy made his paradoxical comment: "It looks as if there was a big gambler's war on in Chicago. I still maintain, however, that there is no gambling worthy of the name in existence here at the present time."

First Ward politico Michael "Hinky Dink" Kenna, finally arbitrated a truce between Tennes and O'Malley factions in 1908, outlining strict borders in which the Chicago gamblers could operate. Tennes still wound up with the winning hand and virtual control of all handbook operations in the city.

Reformed gambler Henry Brolaski publicly indicted Kenna by snickering: "Some guys said Little Mike got forty thousand out of it."

"Brolaski," Kenna intoned, upon hearing this accusation, "is a big liar!" Unscathed, Hinky Dink and his erstwhile sidekick Bathhouse John Coughlin went on to greater booty.

Tennes, in 1910, established the General News Bureau to compete with the Payne Service in an attempt to avoid paying exorbitant rates and to eliminate competition. The General News Bureau virtually destroyed the Cincinnati operation and Tennes became the most influential gambler in the U.S., becoming, as one writer of the day put it, ". . . the boss of racetrack gambling all over the United States and Canada. He had corrupted the police of a score of cities, was enforcing his decrees with guns and dynamite, and was making profits of several million dollars a year."

For fourteen years, Tennes was the king of the gamblers in the country, arrested not once throughout his long and immensely successful career (one indictment was handed down but was quashed for "lack of evidence"). Reform Mayor William Dever changed all that in 1924 shortly after taking office in Chicago. At his direction Police Chief Morgan Collins raided hundreds of gambling dens in the Loop and drove gamblers by the scores from the city.

His poolhall and handbook operations wrecked, Tennes retired in June, 1924. In 1927, Tennes sold half of his interest in the decaying General News Service to Moe Annenberg, a publisher of newspapers and magazines in Chicago and New York. Two years later he sold Chicago gambler Jack Lynch, owner of the Sportsmen's Club, forty per cent of his remaining interest and parceled the rest out to a set of nephews. He died peacefully in 1941, rich, unscarred, and memorable.

TENTH AVENUE GANG

A band of robbers, the Tenth Avenue Gang operated throughout Manhattan during the 1860s and were led by Ike Marsh. This gang reached great notoriety in 1868 when Marsh and others stopped an express train of the Hudson Railroad and, after tying and gagging the express car guard, escaped with $5,000 in cash and government bonds.

The gang was finally absorbed by the Hell's Kitchen Gang led by Dutch Heinrich in the 1870s.

TERRANOVA, CIRO
Syndicate Gangster ● (1891-1938)

A Mafia boss of Harlem, Terranova took control of the district following the imprisonment of Ignazio Saietta ("Lupo the Wolf"), a sadistic blackhander who was sent to Sing Sing in 1918. Terranova was known as "The Artichoke King." His arch enemy, Joseph Valachi, later stated: "He got his name because he tied up all the artichokes in the city. The way I understand it he would buy all the artichokes that came into New York. I didn't know where they all came from, but I know he was buying them all out. Being artichokes, they hold; they can keep. Then Ciro would make his own price, and as you know, Italians got to have artichokes to eat."

Terranova was a powerful Cosa Nostra gangster throughout the 1920s but his influence began to fade during the Maranzano-Masseria war of 1930-31. On April 15, 1931, it was Terranova's car that was used to transport Joe the Boss Masseria to Coney Island where he would be killed on Lucky Luciano's orders. Terranova, Luciano, and Vito Genovese accompanied Masseria there. When Genovese and Luciano noticed that Terranova's hands shook with fear as he tried to start the car, he was ordered to sit in the back seat with the unsuspecting Masseria.

"Ever since then," Valachi stated, "Ciro Terranova was getting what was called buckwheats, you know, like he was being stripped

Mobster Ciro Terranova, "The Artichoke King."

. . . a little at a time, he was being taken . . . his power was being taken from him."

When Terranova attempted to take over Dutch Schultz's policy rackets following the Dutchman's execution in 1935, he was ordered to "beat it" by Luciano and Genovese. He died an ineffectual Mafia flunky three years later.

THAW, HARRY KENDALL
Murderer ● (1872-1947)

Probably the most famous of murder cases involving America's super rich was Harry K. Thaw's murder of the architectural genius, Stanford White.

Thaw was a product of an ambitious Pittsburgh family who engineered a vast fortune —close to $40 million—in a short time by cornering the coke market and forcing their way into New York high society.

Though well-educated, Thaw was weird. Harry's wild behavior caused his tycoon father to cut his considerable allowance to $2,-000 a year. His doting mother, however, supplemented this paltry income with an additional $80,000 annually. Thaw whined that such pin money was hardly enough for a man of his stature and manner of living. His manner of living was anything but normal.

He was at times insane with rage and strange sexual compulsions. He kept an apartment in a New York brothel to which he enticed young girls under the promise of a show business career.

Once there, as the house madam Susan Merrill later testified, he ravished the girls and beat them senseless.

"I could hear the screams coming from his apartment," she later testified, "and once I could stand it no longer. I rushed into his rooms. He had tied the girl to the bed, naked, and was whipping her. She was covered with welts. Thaw's eyes protruded and he looked mad."

At times, a jury later concluded, Harry K. Thaw indeed was mad.

Still, Thaw probably would never have been

Thaw's victim, world famous architect Stanford White.

known to the American public if it had not been for a sultry lovely, Evelyn Nesbit, who came from Pittsburgh to New York at age sixteen. Evelyn became one of the Floradora Chorus, and the mistress of millionaire Stanford White.

The corpulent White, a red-haired, 250-pound girl-chaser, was the most distinguished architect of his day. More than fifty of New York's most elegant buildings were monuments to his talents, including the resplendent Washington Square Arch. White was a spectacular rake who kept several mistresses at once. In one of his many love nests—in the tower of Madison Square Garden—was a red velvet swing hanging from the ceiling. In this, he would swing his women wildly to peer lasciviously up their billowing skirts as a prelude to more primitive passions, according to Miss Nesbit.

White fell madly in love with chorus girl Nesbit almost at first sight and gave her large amounts of money and expensive jewels. He gave Evelyn's mother considerable money, too.

From poverty to fame and wealth was not enough for Miss Nesbit. At nineteen, she left White to marry multi-millionaire Harry Thaw.

For almost three years, Thaw persecuted Evelyn about her relationship with White. He forced the girl to never use White's name but to refer to his as "The Beast," or "The Bastard."

At these times, Thaw became insane. Once, while crossing the ocean on a European vacation, Thaw chained his young wife to the bed in their stateroom and took his belt to her for hours until she confessed every horrible atrocity of the flesh she could imagine Stanford White had ever done to her.

She told her insanely jealous husband that White had lied to her with promises of marriage to get her to come to his New York love nest and, once there, stripped her and raped her and made her pose and swing naked on the red velvet swing.

Evelyn Nesbit, one-time Floradora Girl, became "The Girl in the Red Velvet Swing" and the reason Thaw gave for killing White.

Later, at Harry's murder trial, Evelyn Nesbit Thaw stated that White had invited her and a girl friend to his love nest one evening. She and another girl had gone to his Madison Square Garden penthouse and, after mounting two flights of stairs, they had entered a strange room: ". . . and in this room was a red velvet swing and Mr. White would put us in this swing and we would swing up to the ceiling. He would put the other girl in the swing, and then it would be my turn . . . He would push us until we would swing to the ceiling. There was a big Japanese umbrella on the ceiling, so when he pushed us our feet would crash through."

A few nights later, Evelyn recounted, White invited her to a big party. The architect had given her mother a large amount of cash to return to Pittsburgh for a visit with relatives. When Evelyn arrived at White's place, she discovered no one present except the architect. He proceeded to get her drunk with champagne, she claimed, until she blacked out.

"When I woke up all my clothes were pulled off me. I was in bed. I sat up in bed and I started to scream. Mr. White got up and put on one of his kimonos which was on a chair. I moved up and pulled some covers over me, and there were mirrors all around the bed; mirrors on the sides of the wall and on the ceiling. Then I looked down and saw blotches of blood on the sheets. Then I screamed and screamed and screamed, and he came over and asked me to please keep quiet, and that I must not make so much noise. He said, 'It's all over, it's all over.'

"Then I screamed, 'Oh, no!' and then he brought a kimono over to me and he went out of the room. Then as I got out of the bed, I began to scream more than ever. Then he came back into room and tried to quiet me. I don't remember how I got my clothes on or how I went home. But he took me home and left me and I sat up all night."

This is essentially the story Harry Thaw whipped out of his wife while the couple sailed the Atlantic to Europe and the same story she would repeat at her husband's trial.

Such was the intensity of his madness that Thaw, who had whipped the accusations against White out of his wife, believed every word and vowed revenge.

Revenge came on the warm summer evening of June 25, 1906. That night Harry and

Evelyn, accompanied by two effeminate males, attended the opening of a light Victorian musical farce, *Mam'zelle Champagne* at the dining theater on the roof of Madison Square Garden.

It was the gathering place for high society, most of whom were attending this play.

In the audience was architect Stanford White. He sat alone at one of the tables. Evelyn placed a gloved hand on her husband's sleeve. Harry, dressed in a heavy overcoat even though it was a balmy summer night, turned his boyish face to her. "The Bastard is here," she told him. As he glared at White, Thaw's whole being seemed to change.

During one of the production numbers, Thaw calmly got up from his table, walked over to White and fired three shots. The architect took two bullets in the brain and died immediately, his heavy frame crashing to the floor.

Thaw changed his grip on the pistol, holding it by the muzzle to signify that he meant no harm to anyone else. He was arrested, hurried off to the Center Street Station, charged with murder, and locked in the Tombs.

While awaiting trial, Thaw had all his meals

Millionaire murderer Harry K. Thaw in his N.Y. Tombs cell, dining on catered meals from Delmonico's after slaying Stanford White in 1912.

catered from the finest New York restaurant, Delmonico's. He had whiskey smuggled to him and he continued to play the stock market, visiting with his broker in the jail at all hours.

After his arraignment for murder, Harry's mother publicly announced that she would spend all of her $40,000,000 fortune to save her boy from dying in the electric chair. Mrs. Thaw imported the famous trial lawyer Delphin Delmas from California to defend her son. Delmas was called "The Little Napoleon of the West Coast Bar."

The equally famous William Travers Jerome, New York's district attorney, opposed him. When Jerome learned that the Thaw millions would be spent down to the last penny to save Harry, he thundered: "With all his millions, Thaw is a fiend! No matter how rich a man is, he cannot get away with murder—not in New York County!"

It seemed like an open-and-shut case but from the first moment of his lengthy seven-month trial, Thaw claimed that he was innocent, that a form of insanity took him over and made him kill White.

"I never wanted to shoot that man," Thaw pleadingly told a jury. "I never wanted to kill him . . . Providence took charge of the situation."

This claim of being controlled from the great beyond was supported, strangely enough, by a doctor of medicine and member of the American Association for the Advancement of Science, Dr. Carl Wickland of Chicago.

Dr. Wickland's wife, it seems, was endowed with powerful visions of mediumship. Three weeks after Thaw's arrest and months before his trial, on July 5, 1906, Mrs. Wickland insisted, a spiritual voice admitted through her that he had killed White!

At this seance, the spirit stated, "I killed Stanford White. He deserved death. He had trifled too long with our daughters."

According to Mrs. Wickland, the voice that spoke through the medium identified himself as a man named Johnson. The manners and articulation of his speech indicated he was from a low social scale, the same as Evelyn Nesbit.

Johnson denounced the rich such as White as society rakes and ne'er-do-wells. "They steal our children from us and put fine clothes on them, and the parents do not know what becomes of them."

Another spirit broke into Mrs. Wickland's busy trance, speaking rapidly. He identified himself as the long-dead father of Harry K. Thaw!

Thaw's spiritual father fought for his son's innocence. "He is sensitive to spirit influence and has been all his life. He was always erratic and so excitable that we were afraid to correct him for fear he would become insane. But I see our mistake now."

The voice claiming to be Thaw's father went on to add that though he never understood his son's actions when he was alive, he now knew that Harry "had been a tool in the hands of earth-bound spirits, evil spirits that ordered death.

"He was obsessed by revengeful spirits when he killed Stanford White," the voice went on.

Incredibly, the Wicklands reported that the spirit-father implored Wickland to write to Thaw's attorney informing him of these spiritual truths.

Counsel Delmas and other attorneys representing Shaw apparently ignored the Chicago mediums but did advance the theory to the court that Harry, at the moment of killing White, suffered a severe attack of what they termed "dementia Americana," a singularly American neurosis among males in the U.S. who believed that every man's wife was sacred.

Apparently, the jury listening to evidence in the White killing came to the conclusion that something had taken temporary control over Thaw's reasoning at the time of the murder. They returned the verdict, "Not guilty, on the ground of his insanity at the time of the commission of the act."

But Thaw was not free. He was imprisoned for life in the New York State Asylum for the Criminally Insane at Matteawan, N. Y. He spent years in this institution while his mother spent tens of thousands of dollars attempting to get him judged sane. Harry grew tired of waiting for psychiatrists to make up their minds and escaped from the Matteawan asylum in 1913. He was captured in Canada and returned.

Evelyn Nesbit went on to become a vaudeville attraction. A son was born to her which she stubbornly insisted was Harry K. Thaw's offspring (she filed for huge support money). When newsmen politely pointed out that Mr. Thaw had been inside a mental institution for the past seven years, Evelyn blithely told them that Harry had bribed a guard at Matteawan to allow her to spend a heavenly and quite fruitful night with her.

When Thaw was finally pronounced sane by a New York court in 1915, he barreled out of Matteawan, cursing Evelyn Nesbit and denying he had anything to do with fathering her child. He divorced her and went on a buying spree.

In 1916 Thaw was again arrested, this time for horsewhipping a teenager named Frederick B. Gump. He attempted to buy the Gump family off and made a huge settlement reported to be a half million dollars. He was nevertheless returned to Matteawan and kept under close security until his second release in 1922. Fifty, Harry Thaw then embarked on another career of fast living, which would not end until his death in 1947.

He roamed the world, a pathetic playboy, sporting attractive young girls on his arm, billing himself to reporters as a producer of plays and motion pictures.

Of course, it was all imagination—or something else, especially when Harry would get that wild stare in his eyes, his mouth would sag, and strange words would tumble incoherently from him.

THOMAS, HENRY
Murderer, Burglar ● (? -1846)

Burglary was Thomas's business and he worked his trade effectively for a number of years in the Ohio River country. While robbing the store of Frederick Edwards in Bourneville, O., on November 20, 1844, Thomas and his accomplices were interrupted when the proprietor burst in on them. Thomas stabbed Edwards to death with a hunting knife. He was captured and held on suspicion of murder days later.

While in jail, Thomas talked too much to a fellow prisoner, who informed authorities that the burglar had admitted the killing to him. This evidence was used to convict Thomas of Edwards's murder and he was quickly executed.

THOMPSON, BEN
Gunfighter ● (1842-1884)

BACKGROUND: BORN 11/11/42 IN NOTTINGLEY, YORK-SHIRE, ENGLAND. IMMIGRATED WITH FAMILY TO TEXAS IN 1849. MINOR PUBLIC EDUCATION. SERVED IN THE SECOND TEXAS CAVALRY DURING THE CIVIL WAR. WOUNDED IN 1863. MARRIED CATHERINE MOORE, 1863. ONE SON. ORIGINAL OCCUPATION, SALOONKEEPER. DESCRIPTION: 5'7", BROWN EYES, BROWN HAIR, STOCKY. ALIASES: UNKNOWN. RECORD: INVOLVED IN A NUMBER OF GUNFIGHTS, ALLEGEDLY KILLING TEN MEN BEFORE LEAVING TEXAS IN 1870; SHOT AND WOUNDED HIS BROTHER-IN-LAW, JAMES MOORE, IN 1864; CONVICTED OF ASSAULT AND ATTEMPTED MUR-DER, SENTENCED TO PRISON FOR FOUR YEARS; RE-LEASED IN 1866; INVOLVED IN SEVERAL GUNFIGHTS IN ABILENE AND DODGE CITY, KAN., SEVERAL KILL-INGS CREDITED TO HIM; MURDERED, ALONG WITH HIS FRIEND JOHN "KING" FISHER, BY JOE FOSTER, BILLY SIMMS AND A MAN NAMED COY IN THE VAUDEVILLE THEATER IN SAN ANTONIO, 3/11/84.

Guns were Ben Thompson's way of life. Not long after his family immigrated to Texas from England, Ben began to practice shooting with an old six-shooter. By the time he was into his teens, he was considered an expert shot in Austin, his home town. He was involved in several gunfights before he was twenty, when he joined the Confederate Army, riding with the Second Texas Cavalry. Thompson was wounded in 1863, returned to Austin, and married pretty Catherine Moore.

His bride's brother, James Moore, was a man with a mean disposition, used to knocking his sister about. One day Thompson arrived home to find his wife unconscious. Moore had knocked her down and upon seeing Ben approaching, ran across an open field to escape. Thompson grabbed his gun and took off after his brother-in-law, wounding him in the leg.

Arrested by military authorities then in control of Northern Texas, Thompson was tried and sent to prison for four years. He was released in two years. Ben Thompson then became a roving professional gambler and gunfighter. His ability with a gun was demonstrated in a minor shootout in the small town of Ogallalie, Kansas in 1869. Thompson, wearing a black frock coat and sporting two pistols, was playing cards in the Crystal Palace. A young man entered the saloon, stood at the bar and began twirling his guns.

"The fellow was making a spectacle of himself," wrote noted Oklahoma lawman Jim Herron years later, "twisting his gun around and spinning it and pointing it at various men along the bar. Now this was something that a man never did in Texas or Oklahoma unless he was asking for trouble. . . . Suddenly I heard a shot, and this gun-flashing fellow let out a squeal like a javelina. His gun flew out of his hand and went clattering off across the floor, and as he grasped his hand in pain I could see he was minus a perfectly good finger for a bullet had hit him in his gun hand."

Ben Thompson had gotten up from his card game and fired a single shot from the end of the bar. Then he walked closer, blowing smoke from the muzzle of his pistol. "I never want to see you do a thing like that again, hear?" Thompson told the terrified cowboy.

Later, Thompson told Herron that he had no intention of killing the showoff. "I just wanted to slow him down a bit before he got himself into real trouble."

By 1871, Thompson had moved on to Abilene, Kansas and built up a lucrative saloon business there. He had a number of gunfights with gunslingers in Abilene from which he emerged victorious. Otherwise, his luck was poor. When his wife and son arrived in Kansas City to join him, he took them for a ride. The buckboard hit a hole in the road and spilled over. His son's foot was broken and his wife's arm was smashed, which later caused it to be amputated. Thompson himself suffered a broken leg.

Ellsworth, Kansas, another cowboy hell-town, beckoned Thompson next. He plied his gambling trade there and often backed other gamblers in high stake monte games. One of these was John Sterling, who on August 15, 1873 won more than $1,000 playing monte while using Thompson's bankroll.

Sterling proceeded to get drunk on the money, not bothering to pay Thompson. Hours later, Thompson cornered Sterling in Nick Lentz's saloon and demanded his spoils. Sterling slapped Thompson in the face and Ben went for his gun. Before he could fire, policeman John "Happy Jack" Morco stepped between the two men.

Morco, who was later described by a historian as "an illiterate, surly fellow," had come to Ellsworth from California where, it was said, he had killed twelve men in separate gun duels. Morco persuaded Thompson to leave the saloon and "cool off." Ben went to Brennan's Saloon and waited. Minutes later he looked up from the bar to see Morco at the door of the tavern. With him, grinning, was Sterling.

"C'mon outside, Ben," Sterling said.

Thompson noticed both men were holding shotguns. He turned, dashed out of Brennan's, and ran to another saloon owned by Jack New, where he had left his pistol and rifle. His homicidal brother, Billy, an habitual drunk, joined him there carrying Ben's English-made $150 shotgun. The brothers stepped into the street. Bill Thompson stumbled and discharged one barrel of the shotgun, almost shooting a cowboy in the foot.

Ben Thompson shouted to Sheriff Chauncey B. Whitney, Sterling, and Morco: "We're going down by the railroad. More room there. Bring out your men if you want to fight."

Whitney walked up to the brothers and convinced them to settle the whole matter over a friendly drink in Brennan's saloon. The Thompsons had no sooner entered the bar when Ben saw Morco advancing toward him with a drawn pistol. Ben got off a quick shot as Morco dashed outside. Bill Thompson and Sheriff Whitney also ran outside.

Thinking the sheriff had trapped them, Billy Thompson turned his shotgun in Whitney's direction.

"Don't shoot!" Whitney yelled.

Billy Thompson fired both barrels at him from close range. With a scream, Whitney crumpled in the street and Billy Thompson ran back into the saloon to face his enraged brother. "For God's sake," Ben told his brother, "leave town, you have shot Whitney, our best friend."

Lifting a shot of rye to his lips, Billy Thompson said he would have fired "if it had been Jesus Christ." He then fled town.

Ben Thompson stayed in the saloon. Several friendly fellow Texans joined him. Ellsworth's Mayor Jim Miller begged him to surrender his guns and give up to the law. He refused. Miller then went outside where he saw several members of the town police force loading shotguns, preparing to shoot it out with Thompson. Miller fired them on the spot and Thompson then surrendered. He was soon released, after explaining that his brother had shot Whitney. "He was drunk and didn't know what he was doing."

Whitney gallantly supported this claim on his deathbed hours later, stating to friends: "He did not intend to do it. It was an accident . . . send for my family." (Billy Thompson was tried for the killing in September, 1877, but was acquitted; the shooting was ruled an accident.)

The biographer of Wyatt Earp insists that this gunfight was highlighted by Earp's appearance after Mayor Miller had fired his police force. According to this version, Miller ordered his deputies Ed Crawford, Charlie Brown, and Marshal J. S. "Brocky Jack" Norton to close in on Ben Thompson, who was menacing people with his shotgun from the platform of the Kansas Pacific depot. "Arrest that man," Miller reportedly called to his men. They did not move. "You're fired," Miller shouted angrily.

At this moment, a tall, mustachioed young man stepped from a nearby barber shop and said to Miller, "Can't a fellow even get a shave in this town without gunplay?" He was Wyatt Earp, soon to become legend. Miller shrugged helplessly.

"It's none of my business," Earp allegedly told Miller, "but if it was me I'd get me a gun and arrest Ben Thompson or kill him."

"I'll make this your business," Miller replied and tore the badge from Sheriff Norton's shirt and pinned it on Earp. "Go into Beebe's and get some guns. I order you to arrest Ben Thompson." Earp then obtained two second-hand .45s and walked across the plaza toward Thompson.

Biographer Stuart N. Lake wrote later that the two men glared at each other and that the following conversation took place while Earp stalked his prey:

"I'd rather talk than fight," Thompson said.

"I'll get you either way, Ben," replied Earp, still walking forward.

"Wait a minute," Thompson shouted. "What do you want me to do?"

"Throw your shotgun in the road, put up your hands, and tell your friends to stay out of this play."

"Will you stop and let me talk to you?"

Earp stopped walking.

"What are you going to do with me?" Ben Thompson asked.

"Kill you or take you to jail."

"Brown's over there by the depot with a rifle. The minute I give up my guns he'll cut loose at me."

"If he does, I'll give you back your guns and we'll shoot it out with him. As long as you're my prisoner, the man that gets you will have to get me."

Thompson threw out his gun. "You win."

If Earp truly got involved in the Thompson-Sterling feud in Ellsworth, his appearance and backing down of Thompson was one of the great dramatic scenes of the Old West. However, no records, newspaper accounts, or official testimony exists to support this story, other than the heady narrative penned by Lake.

In addition to leading the fearsome Ben Thompson meekly to jail, Earp, in Lake's version, backs down an entire mob of Texans, including such notorious gunslingers as Cad Pierce, Neil Kane, John Good, and George Peshaur, who were bent on releasing Thompson.

After many years in Abilene, Ellsworth, and Dodge City, Thompson tried his hand at law enforcement, becoming City Marshal in Austin, Texas. He kept the job briefly, quitting when he became bored.

Gunfighter Ben Thompson, who served briefly as a city marshal in Austin, Tex., was shot to death in a theater. (Kansas State Historical Society, Topeka)

Though he survived many a gunfight, Ben Thompson was to be killed in a most inglorious fashion—shot to death while sitting in a theater seat, watching a song-and-dance act. He was attending a show with his friend John King Fisher in San Antonio when three gunfighters—Joe Foster, Billy Simms, and an ex-policeman named Coy—walked in and shot both men to death on March 11, 1884.

THOMPSON, GERALD
Murderer, Rapist ● (1910-1935)

BACKGROUND: BORN AND RAISED IN PEORIA, ILL. HIGH SCHOOL EDUCATION. OCCUPATION, FACTORY WORKER. DESCRIPTION: 5'8", BROWN EYES, BROWN HAIR, SLENDER. ALIASES: NONE. RECORD: RAPED SIXTEEN WOMEN IN THE PEORIA, ILL., AREA BETWEEN NOVEMBER AND JUNE, 1935, HIS LAST VICTIM BEING MILDRED HALLMARK, WHOM HE ALSO MURDERED 6/16/35; APPREHENDED 6/22/35 BY POLICE AND CONFESSED TO THE MURDER AND RAPES; CONVICTED OF MURDER AND SENTENCED TO DEATH. EXECUTED AT THE ILLINOIS STATE PENITENTIARY IN JOLIET, ILL., IN THE ELECTRIC CHAIR, 10/15/35.

He was an ineffectual-looking young man with a weak chin. Fingerwaves of hair poked from the top of his high forehead. Quiet, soft-spoken, he lived with his grandmother and labored diligently as a toolmaker for the Caterpillar Tractor company in Peoria, Ill. His name was Gerald Thompson.

Another toolmaker at the same factory, John Hallmark, had just lost his daughter, an attractive young woman who had been a hostess in a popular Peoria restaurant. Mildred Hallmark had not died of natural causes. She had been brutally raped, beaten, and murdered a few days before. Her naked body had been found in a shallow ravine in Peoria's Springdale Cemetery on June 17, 1935.

Someone came to Gerald Thompson while he was at work in the plant and asked for a donation for flowers and mass cards for the murdered girl. He gave willingly.

Meanwhile an army of police and reporters were trying to sift the grisly facts surrounding the discovery of the corpse. The pretty auburn-haired girl had had her neck broken.

Police, inspecting the body, noticed that human skin was curled in shreds under the dead girl's fingernails.

Another curious item: Mildred Hallmark's fountain pen had a badly bent point. It wasn't much to go on, but the town of Peoria—where rape and murder was not the norm of, say, Chicago—demanded instant apprehension of Mildred's killer. The police stepped up the manhunt, frantically scooping up suspects.

Gerald Thompson watched as startled young men all over Peoria were arrested as murder suspects. He watched and waited and said nothing.

As a result of the widespread publicity and waves of gossip buzzing through the community, dozens of young women and girls came forward with bizarre tales of being raped by a lone, charming young man who used his auto as a bedroom.

The stories the young women told about this lone wolf dated back several years and were mostly the same. The young man carried a pair of razor-sharp scissors in his glove compartment. After charming his female victims into his car, he prevented their escape through a cleverly devised wiring system hooked from his battery to the car's door handle. If a young woman attempted to flee, she was jolted back into the arms of the unwanted lover, trapped.

Then the young man would go to work with his scissors, carefully cutting away with precision the bra straps and panties of each woman. After satisfying himself against their unwilling flesh, he would switch on the lights of the car and the beams would poke eerily into the dark reaches of lonely roadways he always chose.

He would then force each woman to the front of the car and in the glare of car lights, while a self-timing camera clicked lewdly away, compelled each victim to pose naked with him in wildly-invented sexual positions.

The rape victims told Peoria's enraged police officials that these pictures would subsequently be used by the young pervert to blackmail them into silence.

Gerald Thompson, meanwhile, reported to work at the Caterpillar factory promptly, performed his duties conscientiously, and went home each evening to dine with his elderly grandmother.

The police frantically pulled in more suspects.

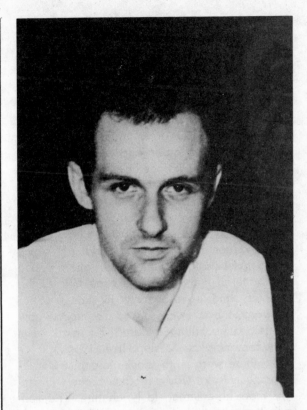

Mass rapist and murderer Gerald Thompson in 1935. (UPI)

The man hunt went on and Gerald Thompson waited and waited. Six days after the murder, on June 22, 1935, the police, on a tip, came for him. They grilled Thompson for hours and he finally broke down.

Thompson explained that he had picked Mildred up as she was waiting for a streetcar after having left her date, John McGinnis. Thompson explained that he had joked and charmed her into his car with the promise of a lift home. Once in the car, he drove immediately to his favorite deserted spot, the cemetery, and took out his trusty scissors.

Mildred had not been submissive and frightened like the other young women. As Thompson cut her clothes away, Mildred did the unexpected—she fought back, clawing desperately at his face with her fingernails, gashing and slashing him. Thompson told police he laughed at her. As they struggled, the not-so-helpless girl slashed Thompson's neck with her long fingernails and he felt his hot blood run out.

Seething with anger, Thompson smashed

the girl blindly and her head whipped back with a snap and she collapsed unconscious. He then went at the limp body again with his scissors.

Mildred awoke screaming and struggling as Thompson groped at her body. Again she clawed at his face and more of the rapist's blood ran down his face. In desperation she reached into her purse and using her fountain pen, jammed the needle-sharp point again and again into Thompson.

He went wild, he admitted, and began to hammer the young girl's face with flailing fists until she sagged silent against the now blood-spattered car seat. She was dead.

Thompson said he threw the girl's naked and battered body into the ravine next to the cemetery and drove away to his home where he went to bed. Police asked Thompson how he felt after killing Mildred Hallmark. His only remark was: "I slept like a baby."

But there were more shocks to come. Gerald Thompson's trial was a regular circus with angry mobs threatening to lynch him. The self-admitted rapist and murderer had to be spirited away to another town until Peoria citizens quieted.

The prosecution had more evidence to convict Thompson than was really necessary. On top of his signed confession, police investigators produced Thompson's bloodstained trousers, a bloodstained car cushion from his auto and a diary that would have made Bluebeard blanch.

Thompson had recorded in his diary the names and addresses of sixteen pickup and rape victims. Along with the list of names were many obscene photos showing Thompson and his victims naked under the glare of his car's headlights.

It was enough to convict him ten times over. One more startling detail was added by a former friend of Thompson's. The ex-friend stated from the witness stand: "Thompson boasted that he would use this sinister pattern of action to rape fifty-two girls within the year. By the middle of November last year he told me he had already exceeded his quota— one for every week of that year."

Gerald Thompson's twisted calendar ended abruptly on October 15, 1935, when he was strapped into the electric chair at Joliet State Penitentiary and three massive electrical charges were sent through his body.

THORN, MARTIN GEORGE
Murderer ● (1868-1897)

Police were baffled in June of 1897 when chunks of a body began turning up in the rivers about Manhattan. First a torso with a tattoo of a naked woman on its chest appeared wrapped in oilcloth. Next a pair of legs was turned in to police. The identity of the dissected corpse was impossible to determine.

Quite by accident, a reporter for the New York World heard two rubbers in a Turkish bath complaining that Willie Guldensuppe, a fellow worker, had failed to show up for a week. Knowing of the chopped up body the police possessed, the reporter asked: "Was your pal Willie tattooed?"

"Sure," one of them replied. "There was a pretty girl on his chest." The reporter obtained Guldensuppe's address—439 Ninth Ave.—and hurried there. He discovered that Mrs. Augusta Nack, who had immigrated from Germany several years before, an unlicensed midwife, ran the boarding house where Guldensuppe had lived.

Immediately following the location of Willie's address, a reporter for the New York Journal—both the Journal and the World were locked in desperate competition for such grisly stories—found a hardware merchant in Queens who stated he had sold an oilcloth to a woman who looked like Mrs. Nack. Police whisked the landlady to the station.

A buxom, pleasant-faced woman, Mrs. Nack was unperturbed. Police thought to shock her into a confession by seating her in a chair and then abruptly thrusting Guldensuppe's badly decomposed legs under her nose. "Are those Willie's?" she was asked.

Mrs. Nack never batted an eyelash. "I would not know as I never saw the gentleman naked."

This, of course, was far from the truth. Mrs. Nack, neighbors testified, had taken Willie Guldensuppe as a lover years ago. About ten months before his slaying, however, they reported a new tenant, one Martin George Thorn, had moved into Mrs. Nack's rooming house and into Mrs. Nack's bed, substituting for Mr. Guldensuppe.

There were reports of how the two men argued and fought. Mrs. Nack suggested to both men that further consternation could easily be avoided. All three of them would share the same bed, she stated. Guldensuppe declined and began to date another girl. Mrs. Nack felt Willie was slighting her and demanded Thorn kill him. (Another story had it that Thorn wanted to kill Guldensuppe because Willie had beaten him up in a bloody fistfight.)

Thorn and Mrs. Nack rented a farm in Woodside, a suburb of Queens. Mrs. Nack told Willie she intended to practice her mid-wifery there and lured him to the "baby farm" under the pretext of getting his ideas about setting up such a clinic, though Guldensuppe's experience as a rubber in a Turkish bath hardly qualified him as expert in such matters. Flattered, Willie journeyed to the Woodside retreat.

"Look around, Willie. Check everything for me like a nice fellow, will you?" Mrs. Nack asked. Guldensuppe wandered about the place, casually opening closets and idiotically staring at cobwebs while rendering such critical comments as "that's nice," and "that'll do."

One of the closets contained a surprise—Martin George Thorn. When Guldensuppe opened the closet where he was hiding, Thorn leapt out with a pistol in one hand and a dagger in the other. He first shot the beefy Guldensuppe and then stabbed him repeatedly until he was sure Willie was dead. Mrs. Nack appeared and she and her lover dragged the corpse into the kitchen.

There, Thorn carefully removed the head and went about slicing up the body in manageable chunks while Mrs. Nack obtained an oilcloth in which to wrap them. There was no sewer system leading from the Woodside cottage pipes, a fact Thorn overlooked when he turned on the taps to repeatedly wash his hands of blood while he butchered Guldensuppe's body.

Though Thorn and Mrs. Nack were suspected, they were not arrested immediately, even with the hot gossip of their neighbors sizzling police ears. A Woodside farmer noticed days later that his pure white ducks had turned pink. Upon investigating, he was shocked to find that a drainage pool near Mrs. Nack's cottage had turned red with human blood. The police had their murder scene and they also found in the cottage a saw and butcher knife caked with flesh and blood.

Both Thorn and Mrs. Nack were arrested and brought to trial. A barber testified that Thorn had bragged to him how he had murdered poor Willie and then cut him to pieces. The next day, Mrs. Nack abruptly stood up and described in detail how Thorn butchered her ex-boyfriend after shooting and stabbing him. She was so explicit in her description of the crime that several female members of the jury fainted and a mistrial was declared.

In the second trial, Thorn took the stand and told how Mrs. Nack burst into his room one day in June, 1897 and shouted: "Willie's upstairs! I just killed him!"

The jury was sympathetic to Mrs. Nack even though the press universally branded her the catalyst of the murder. She was sentenced to twenty years in jail. Thorn got the electric chair, dying a few months later. When they strapped Martin George Thorn into the electric chair, he commented: "I have no fear. I'm

Killer Martin Thorn and his dominating lover, Mrs. Augusta Nack, made the front page of the *New York World* in 1897 after murdering Willie Guldensuppe; Thorn went to the chair, Mrs. Nack got ten years in prison. (N.Y. Historical Society)

MURDERER OF GULDENSUPPE, MARTIN THORN, WILL PAY THE PENALTY AND BE KILLED TO-DAY.

Condemned Murderer Is Calm, Says He Has No Fear, and Is Sure of Forgiveness.

not afraid." Then, "I am positive God will forgive me."

Mrs. Nack served only ten years of her prison term. When she was released she returned to her old neighborhood and opened a delicatessen which few persons patronized. She vanished before the First World War.

___

THURMOND, THOMAS HAROLD
Kidnapper, Murderer ● (1909-1933)

BACKGROUND: BORN AND RAISED IN SAN JOSE, CALIF. ONE BROTHER, A MINISTER. GRADUATE OF SAN JOSE HIGH SCHOOL, BRIEFLY ATTENDED SAN JOSE STATE COLLEGE. ORIGINAL OCCUPATION, FILLING STATION ATTENDANT. DESCRIPTION: 5'10", BROWN EYES, BROWN HAIR, SLENDER. ALIASES: NONE. RECORD: KIDNAPPED WITH JOHN MAURICE HOLMES, A HIGH SCHOOL CLASSMATE, 22-YEAR-OLD BROOKE HART, SON OF A WEALTHY HOTEL AND DEPARTMENT STORE OWNER ON 11/9/33, KILLING HIM BY THROWING HIM BOUND INTO SAN FRANCISCO BAY THAT SAME NIGHT; ARRESTED BY POLICE 11/15/33 IN SAN JOSE, INFORMED AUTHORITIES OF HOLMES' COMPLICITY IN THE MURDER. BOTH MEN IMPRISONED IN THE SANTA CLARA COUNTY JAIL IN SAN JOSE. ON 11/26/33 HART'S BODY WAS FOUND; THAT NIGHT A MOB, ESTIMATED TO BE 15,000 OR MORE, LYNCHED BOTH PRISONERS.

___

Thurmond came from a middle-class family in San Jose where he had lived all his life. He had never committed a crime and the only explanation he ever gave for kidnapping and killing 22-year-old Brooke Hart, scion of a department store fortune, was that he was "driven half crazy" by the thought of not being able to marry his high school sweetheart for lack of funds. He later changed this story, insisting that he was in love with another woman several years his senior who rejected him because he was poor. "I don't even know that man," the woman said when confronted.

Whatever the reason, Thurmond and a boy who had gone to school with him, John Maurice Holmes, abducted blonde-haired Brooke Hart as he drove away from his father's store (where he had recently been made a vice president following his graduation from Santa Clara College). The two forced Hart's Studebaker to the side of the road.

Then, using Hart's car, the three men drove to the San Mateo-Hayward Bridge arching across the southern part of San Francisco Bay. They stopped on the bridge late on the night of November 9, 1933 and Hart was forced to get out. He was then hit by a brick and knocked unconscious. Thurmond and Holmes then bound him tightly with wire and tied chunks of cement to his body to weight it down. They threw him into the Bay. Regaining consciousness, Hart began to scream that he couldn't swim. Thurmond fired several shots at him and his body quickly disappeared.

An hour later Thurmond was on the phone to Alex Hart demanding $40,000 for the release of his son. "Keep the police out of this," Thurmond said, "if you want to see him alive."

Hart, however, instantly called the police after talking to the kidnapper. Authorities at first did not believe the tale. Hart was probably kidding around with some college chums, they said.

The kidding theory exploded when Hart failed to return to his home in several days and two more ransom notes followed, one reading: "We have Brooke and are treating him right." The second note instructed Alex Hart to put an "L" in the window of his department store if he was willing to pay the $40,000 ransom. Hart did as directed. Next, Hart was told to drive a car south on the Los Angeles highway bringing the money in small bills. This Alex Hart did not do.

He received a call the next day. "What gives, Mr. Hart?" Thurmond said. "You didn't show up last night. You got one more chance."

"I don't drive," Hart said.

There was a pause. "We'll call you back," Thurmond said and hung up. This time the police were ready. When Thurmond rang up the Hart residence again on November 15, 1933, his call was traced while Alex Hart stalled him on the phone. Officers located Thurmond in a San Jose garage, still arguing on the phone with Hart about a pickup spot for the ransom money. They entered and arrested him.

Thurmond quickly confessed, signing a statement which put most of the guilt for the kidnapping and murder on his partner Holmes. When Holmes was arrested, he, too, confessed but blamed Thurmond for planning and executing the crime. The two were locked up in separate cells in the Santa Clara County Jail

Kidnapper and murderer Thomas Harold Thurmond in custody (center); to his right is FBI agent R. E. Vetterli, who had guarded gangster Frank Nash in 1933 and survived the Kansas City Massacre. (Wide World Photos)

in downtown San Jose.

Nine days later Brooke Hart's body washed ashore and was found by duck hunters. Upon hearing the news, the citizens of San Jose, especially the college community where Hart was well-liked, went berserk with rage. By early evening a giant crowd of at least 15,000 collected in a park across from the jail.

Women with babies, small boys, elderly men with canes joined the students in shouting thunderous calls like "We want a touchdown!" and "Get that ball!" Staring down from his second floor office, Sheriff William Emig got jittery. Days before he had stated: "We are not at all alarmed at the threat of possible violence." Now it was at hand and he turned out his men to guard all windows and doors on the first floor of the jail. He then got on the phone and asked California Governor James "Sunny Jim" Rolfe for troops.

Rolfe said no, it wasn't necessary. Emig glanced out the window to see dozens of youths pick up planks and pipes from a nearby construction area. The mob was now howling for the blood of Thurmond and Holmes. "You hear that?" Emig said, holding the phone's mouthpiece toward the window. Rolfe heard nothing. No troops, he repeated. Then he hung up.

At about 9:30 p.m., the crowd surged forward with its pipes and planks, battling the state and local police officers on duty for close to two hours. The police did everything but fire on the jostling vigilantes. They sprayed them with high-powered hoses and drove them back. The mob came on again. They bombarded the mob with tear gas shells. Again, the crowd pushed forward, demanding Holmes and Thurmond be turned over to them. Alex Hart appeared and begged the self-appointed avengers to go home, but he was brushed aside and within two hours, a young boy of about sixteen appeared and shouted as he waved an iron bar: "I want fifty men with guts enough to follow me!" At least that number raced after him in a charge against the front door of the jail; it was promptly battered down.

They poured into the jail, sweeping past the handful of guards. When members of the lynch mob flung wide Holmes's cell door, the young man snarled like a trapped cougar. Several went in after him and he put up a terrific fight. His clothes were stripped from him in the raging battle and he was beaten so badly that his face was turned to raw pulp. He was led half unconscious out of his cell with an eyeball dangling from its socket.

Someone called down from a second-floor window to the hooting mob below: "We've got Holmes and he's coming down to you! Now we'll get Thurmond!"

Thurmond was no where to be found. His cell was empty and the vigilantes foraged through the cell block looking for him. One of them entered his open cell and stood silently listening. Then he heard the heavy breathing and looked up. There, hanging high from the water pipes above the cell's toilet, was Thurmond. He was dragged down. The lynch mob punched him senseless as they descended the jail stairs and then into the park.

The two largest trees in the park facing each other were used to string up the two prisoners. First Thurmond was lynched as he pleaded with his captives. As his lifeless corpse swayed in the breeze, Holmes was led over to him and made to look at the dead body. "How do you like your pal now?" someone asked him.

"For God's sake, give me a chance?" Holmes said.

A roar of laughter greeted his plea.

He was led to the other tree and promptly hanged. Spotlights were trained on both bod-

His clothes torn from his body by enraged citizens of San Jose, Calif., kidnapper Thurmond was lynched, 11/26/33. (Wide World Photos)

ies. The two dead kidnappers, half naked and almost unidentifiable from beatings swung solemnly in the midnight air as the stark and eerie lights played upon them.

A small army of state police arrived on motorcycles and bullied its way through the hostile crowd. Boos and jeers greeted them when they cut the bodies down and placed them on stretchers.

"Throw them into the Bay, too!" someone shouted.

"Why waste time? They're headed for hell anyway," another said.

As the bodies passed through the throng, men, women and small boys spat on them and punched them with vicious swipes. No one was ever indicted for the killings.

Though newspapers throughout California condemned the mob violence, Governor Rolfe stated that the lynch mob provided "the best lesson ever given the country. I would pardon those fellows if they were charged. I would like to parole all kidnappers in San Quentin and Folsom to the fine patriotic citizens of San Jose."

For years after the lynchings, members of the mob held onto grisly souvenirs taken that November night in 1933, pieces of clothing from the prisoners, bits of bark of the trees from which they were hanged. It was a night to remember.

TINKER, EDWARD
Murderer, Swindler ● (? -1811)

A captain of a small cargo schooner, Tinker plotted to defraud the company insuring his vessel. Two of his crewmen, Durand and Potts, were in on the plan but a third member, known only as Edward, was not. After scuttling his ship off Roanoke Island, Tinker moved to Newbern, N. C., so he could be near Edward in an attempt to convince him to support his story about losing his ship.

The young seaman seemed reluctant to testify for Tinker so the captain, under the ruse of a duck-hunting trip, shot Edward in the back, weighed down his body with rocks, and threw him into the sea. The body, however, floated back into Newbern harbor and the captain was arrested.

Tinker immediately sent off a letter to his co-conspirator Durand, pleading with him to blame Potts for the loss of his ship and the murder of Edward. The worst that could happen, Tinker pointed out, if Durand was convicted of perjury, was that he could lose a piece of his ear, an early practice by the courts.

Durand was having none of Tinker's involved schemes and informed authorities. The captain was taken to Carteret, N. C., and was there convicted of Edward's murder. He was hanged in September, 1811.

TINNING, MARYBETH ROE
Serial Killer ● (1943-   )

Marybeth Tinning and her husband Joseph lived their entire married life in Schenctady, N.Y. They appeared to be a friendly, outgoing couple but they moved many times, and always seemed to be seeking a new apartment. One other fact of their lives seemed strange. Marybeth kept having children and they kept dying, some in infancy, some within a few years. All nine of her children died before they reached the age of five.

Not until a curious physician, Dr. Thomas F.D. Oram, looked into the case, was it resolved that Marybeth Tinning had been systematically murdering her children. Oram studied the strange deaths, beginning with Joseph Tinning, Jr., in 1973 and ending with the death of Tammi Lynne in 1985. "There's only one explanation for all this," he concluded, "and it has to be smothering."

Marybeth was questioned but she did not confess murdering eight of her nine children until February 1987. Only her first child, Jennifer, born in 1972, had died of natural causes. "I smothered each of them with a pillow because I am not a good mother," Tinning said in her confession. "I'm not a good mother because of what happened to the other children."

After a lengthy trial, Tinning was convicted of second-degree murder "with a depraved indifference to human life." She was sent to prison for 25 years on October 1, 1987.

TORRIO, JOHN ("JOHNNY")
Prohibition Gangster, Syndicate Chief (1882-1957)

BACKGROUND: BORN IN FEBRUARY, 1882 IN ORSARA, ITALY TO MARIA (CARLUCCI) AND THOMAS TORRIO. IMMIGRATED WITH HIS MOTHER IN 1884 TO NEW YORK. MINOR PUBLIC EDUCATION (13 MONTHS). MARRIED ANNA JACOBS, 1912. OBTAINED CITIZENSHIP IN 1923. ORIGINAL OCCUPATION, SALOON AND BROTHEL KEEPER. DESCRIPTION: 5'6", BROWN EYES, BROWN HAIR, STOCKY. ALIASES: FRANK LANGLEY, J. T. MCCARTHY, "J. T." RECORD: OPENED A SALOON AT JAMES AND WALKER STREETS IN NEW YORK IN 1904, CONCENTRATING ON PROSTITUTION, WHORES KEPT UPSTAIRS OF SALOON AND IN AN ADJOINING BUILDING; BECAME LEADER OF THE SO-CALLED JAMES STREET GANG, INSTRUCTED YOUNG BOYS HOW TO STEAL POCKETBOOKS AND BURGLARIZE STORES; FENCED STOLEN GOODS; LED GANG OF POLITICAL SLUGGERS, ORGANIZED VOTE FRAUD FOR TAMMANY POLITICIANS RUNNING AGAINST THE TICKET OF WILLIAM RANDOLPH HEARST IN 1905; BROUGHT JAMES STREET GANG INTO THE POWERFUL FIVE POINTS GANG THAT YEAR, CEMENTING CLOSE RELATIONSHIPS WITH ARCH KILLER AND GANGSTER PAUL KELLY (PAOLO VACCARELLI); LEFT JAMES STREET AND FIVE POINTS GANGS IN 1908 AND OPENED A SALOON, THE HARVARD INN, WITH FRANK UALE (FRANKIE YALE) IN BROOKLYN WHERE HE OPERATED A BLACKHAND RING, TRAFFICKED IN PROSTITUTION; MOVED TO CHICAGO, 1909, TO OPERATE BROTHELS FOR GANGSTER BIG JIM COLOSIMO; MURDERED THREE BLACKHAND GANGSTERS, 1909, WHO WERE ATTEMPTING TO EXTORT $50,000 FROM COLOSIMO; ACTED AS MALE MADAM IN COLOSIMO'S WHOREHOUSE, THE SARATOGA, 1910-11; ESTABLISHED BROTHELS IN CHICAGO'S SUBURBS—STICKNEY, SOUTH CHICAGO, POSEN, FOREST VIEW, BLUE ISLAND, CHICAGO HEIGHTS, (AND IN INDIANA) EAST CHICAGO, WHITING, AND GARY, 1914; HIRED AL CAPONE, A FELLOW FIVE POINTS GANGSTER IMPORTED FROM NEW YORK AS A $35-A-WEEK BOUNCER FOR THE FOUR DEUCES BROTHEL; ORDERED AL CAPONE TO MURDER JIM COLOSIMO 5/11/20; TOOK OVER COLOSIMO'S BROTHEL EMPIRE, ESTABLISHING BROAD-BASED BOOTLEGGING OPERATIONS WITH CAPONE AS LIEUTENANT; ORGANIZED WHITE SLAVERY IN BROTHELS, 1920 UNDER DIRECTION OF HARRY GUZIK; ORDERED THE MURDER OF SEVERAL HENCHMEN IN THE SOUTH SIDE O'DONNELL GANG, SENDING WALTER STEVENS TO MAKE "HITS" IN LIAISON WITH THE SALTIS-MCERLANE GANG 1922-24; ARRESTED JUNE, 1923 FOR ILLEGALLY BREWING BEER, PLEADED GUILTY, POSTED $2,500 BOND, RELEASED 12/17/23 AFTER PAYING $2,000 FINE; OPENED WIDESPREAD GAMBLING CASINOS THROUGHOUT CHICAGO, 1922-24, THE LARGEST OF WHICH WAS THE SHIP, JOINTLY OWNED BY TORRIO, CAPONE, AND DION O'BANNION; ARRESTED 5/19/24 WITH DION O'BANNION AND EARL "HYMIE" WEISS AT SIEBEN'S BREWERY, 1470 N. LARRABEE STREET FOR VIOLATION OF THE PROHIBITION ACT, POSTED $7,500 BOND; ORDERED AL CAPONE TO HAVE HIS MEN KILL O'BANNION, 11/10/24 FOR TRAPPING HIM IN BREWERY RAID; SHOT AND SEVERELY WOUNDED ON 1/20/25 BY EARL "HYMIE" WEISS, GEORGE "BUGS" MORAN, AND VINCENT "THE SCHEMER" DRUCCI; SENTENCED TO NINE MONTHS IMPRISONMENT IN THE WAUKEGAN, ILL. JAIL AND FINED $5,000 FOR ILLEGALLY OPERATING SIEBEN'S BREWERY; DEPARTED CHICAGO UPON RELEASE, TURNING RACKETS ESTIMATED AT $105,000,000 A YEAR OVER TO AL CAPONE; RETIRED TO NAPLES, ITALY, 1925-28, RETURNED TO U.S., 1928, BECAME HEAD OF BOOTLEGGING CARTEL FOR EASTERN SEABOARD; HELPED CHARLES "LUCKY" LUCIANO AND MEYER LANSKY FORM THE NATIONAL CRIME SYNDICATE IN 1934; ARRESTED 4/22/36 IN WHITE PLAINS, N.Y. ON CHARGES OF INCOME-TAX EVASION, POSTED $100,000 BOND; SENTENCED IN 1939 TO TWO YEARS AND SIX MONTHS IN PRISON AND $86,000 PAYMENT FOR BACK TAXES DUE, SENT TO LEAVENWORTH TO SERVE SENTENCE, PAROLED 4/14/41; WENT INTO SEMI-RETIREMENT 1945-57; DIED OF A HEART ATTACK, 4/16/57.

The most careful of gangsters, Johnny Torrio was an enigma. Throughout his criminal career he operated from shadowy offices letting others, such as Al Capone, hog the limelight. Torrio was the only gangster to emerge from the vicious streetgangs of New York as a top mobster without establishing a police record. He was a pimp, bootlegger, and arch murderer who bridged the old fashioned brass knuckles gangs to the Prohibition era and then went on to a ranking position in organized crime.

Survival meant secrecy to Torrio. Even the slightest mention of his name in connection with crime produced in him fits of nervousness and icy fear. Through his fifty years of crime, Torrio's abiding credo and standing order to his stooges and killers, including Capone, was: "No one is ever to mention my name. No one!"

In 1884, Torrio arrived in this country with his mother from Orsara, Italy. His father, Thomas Torrio, had worked in a vineyard for twenty years, saving to immigrate to the U.S. He died in an accident before sailing. His two-and-a-half-year-old son toddled off the boat wearing a girl's dress and a note pinned to his chest which read "John Torrio."

After working two years as a seamstress, Torrio's mother remarried. Little Johnny's stepfather was Salvatore Caputo, who ran an illegal bar behind a small grocery front at 86 James Street on the Lower East Side of Manhattan. Though Torrio was later to claim that he had completed grade school and his first year of high school, his real education consisted only of thirteen months on and off in a public school. The rest of his childhood was spent as a swamper, cleaning the tables in his stepfather's unlicensed saloon. He was too busy working to get into trouble then. As a teenager, he did join a local gang but performed thefts and muggings alone. No police blotter in New York possessed John Torrio's name. He was much too crafty and cautious ever to put himself in a position to be caught.

When he was twenty-two, Torrio, using the alias J. T. McCarthy, bought a bar at James and Walker Streets. He rented the upper floors and the building adjoining his saloon. There he housed about twenty-five whores and went into the brothel business. For protection, Torrio enlisted a number of brutal thugs, forming a mob which would later be known as the James Street Gang. He cemented a strong friendship with Paul Kelly of the Five Points Gang and eventually became Kelly's sub-chief.

As Torrio looked up to Kelly, imitating the gangleader's conservative, tasteful attire and glib mannerisms, apprentice hoodlums such as Al Capone and Frankie Yale aped Torrio. Johnny taught his followers how to pick pockets, burglarize stores, and murder. Stealth was everything; toe-to-toe shootouts were too risky, he emphasized. He also taught them how to terrorize whores into kicking back their nightly earnings. Capone learned so well that he killed one of Torrio's prostitutes in 1918 in an insane rage over $10, and was forced to flee to Chicago to avoid prosecution.

Torrio paid his thugs with shares of the spoils from the robberies he planned, as well as allowing them to drink free of charge in his bar and enjoy the blatant charms of his whores without the usual fees. He himself seldom drank and never touched the women who peddled their flesh for him. "He was terrified of the disease," one ex-gang member commented.

When the mob war between Five Points and Monk Eastman gangs reached fever pitch in 1908, with more than one hundred bodies strewn about the Lower East Side in a three-month period, word came down from Tammany sachem, Big Tim Murphey, to "cut out the wild stuff or you're through, all of you."

To Torrio that meant the James Street Gang, too. In fear of political reprisal, Torrio sold his holdings along James Street, disbanded his gang, and moved to Brooklyn with Frankie Yale where, for about a year, he became a blackhander, extorting money from wealthy Italian businessmen. He and Yale opened a notorious dive called The Harvard Inn on Navy Street, the scene of several murders.

Blackhanding, however, was dangerous business. There was always a possibility of having deaththreat letters traced. Torrio was always looking about for safer criminal pursuits and, in 1909, his problem was solved. Big Jim Colosimo's first wife, Victoria (Moresco), who was Torrio's cousin in Chicago, wrote stating that her husband could use a hand running some of his "businesses" in the Windy City.

Torrio was on a west bound train days later. Chicago, at the time of Torrio's arrival, was a wide-open city, particularly the First Ward, the Red Light district controlled by the clownishly corrupt politicians "Bathhouse" John Coughlin and Michael "Hinky Dink" Kenna. This was also the province of Big Jim Colosimo. Of the 35,000 inhabitants of the ward, one fourth were involved in criminal activities; one third of the women in this group were prostitutes, and almost all worked for Colosimo.

Handling Colosimo's army of whores was a big job, one that consumed Torrio's days and nights. Especially rankling to the assembly-line pimp was the fact that he was compelled briefly to serve as a male madam of Colosimo's classy brothel, the Saratoga.

Torrio's stint at the Saratoga, he felt, was undeserved; it was not the kind of reward one received for saving a man's life. When Torrio first arrived in Chicago, Colosimo had sent for him and asked him to handle a little matter of murder. Big Jim had been receiving blackhand notes for years and he had paid off. The extortion amounts, however, rose with Colosimo's fortunes, which, by 1909, were considerable.

Little Johnny, who claimed to abhor violence, first attempted to talk the Blackhanders into leaving Colosimo alone. They were adamant, demanding $50,000. Either pay up they said or several brothels owned by Big Jim would be burned and the boss himself would be shot. Torrio shrugged and arranged a meeting for the next night when he promised to pay. The three blackhanders were paid off the next night with bullets. Infamous Chicago Blackhander "Sunny Jim" Cosmano headed the Blackhand terrorists, but once he learned that his men had been killed, he sent no more death notes to Colosimo.

When Colosimo asked Torrio what had happened to the blackhanders, Little Johnny laconically stated: "I looked back and they didn't wave goodbye."

Such ruthless tactics were appreciated by Colosimo and he showed his gratitude by appointing Torrio his right hand man in running his rackets. Colosimo's cafe on South Wabash Avenue, the pride of the underworld, was the most lavish in town. Here, society mixed with the cream of gangsterdom. Its many rooms were elegantly designed and its sumptuous meals were made by a dozen chefs.

Such finery was not for Torrio. Colosimo relegated his lieutenant to headquarters in the dilapidated bar and whorehouse, the Four Dueces at 2222 S. State St. Torrio kept to himself in a small office off the bar which was heavily guarded. When he learned that one of his guards had been paid to kill him, Torrio sent for Five Points gangster, Al Capone, a strong-arm boy of blind allegiance.

Torrio had many reasons to send for Capone. He had expanded Colosimo's brothel empire into a half dozen suburbs and had gotten married. The job was simply too big and Torrio needed a night assistant (so he could go home at night to his young bride Anna) and a bully boy to keep his men in line.

Capone was eager to leave New York. He had murdered one of Torrio's prostitutes in a dispute over kickbacks from her take, and another gang murder was about to be charged to him by police. Al Capone came to Chicago in 1918 ostensibly as the Four Dueces' $35-a-week bouncer. He was extremely grateful to Torrio whom he called "Johnny Papa."

Scarface (jagged scars ran across Capone's left cheek, a gift from a Brooklyn knifefighter) was ambitious and fairly imaginative for a man of his brutish reputation. When Prohibition came into effect the following year, he urged Torrio to enter the bootlegging field. "There's millions in it," he said. Torrio didn't require too much urging. He was alert to his opportunities. But first, out of respect, he sought Colosimo's approval. It was old fashioned, such permission seeking, but Torrio's parents had always stressed manners.

Big Jim said no. He had made his millions already. "We got the whorehouses, we got the gambling, we don't need that other stuff."

"But, Jim. Prohibition is here to stay."

"So what? We're fixed. No. Let the other guys kill themselves over cheap beer."

Big Jim, wearing $50,000 worth of diamonds and carrying $10,000 in cash, was shot to death in the vestibule of his posh club on the afternoon of May 11, 1920. Al Capone, from all reports, fired the fatal bullet while hiding in a nearby phone booth. Colosimo's bankroll and diamonds were taken.

Torrio and Capone went far and fast after Big Jim's death. The gangs of the South Side, where Torrio's influence and Capone's muscle dominated, fell into line. From the Stenson brewery and other breweries across the state line in Indiana, Torrio's beer began to flow to Ragen's Colts and Ralph Sheldon's Gang on the South Side at $45 a barrel (each barrel cost $5 to produce). On the West Side, Capone and Torrio sold their beer to the Circus Gang headed by Claude Maddox; Marty Guifoyle's mob; and the Druggan-Lake combine.

Up to 1922, comparative peace reigned throughout Chicago gangland. Then, led by Spike O'Donnell, the South Side O'Donnells rose against Torrio. They were shotgunned back into line over a period of two years, 1923 to 1925, by Torrio gunmen "Sonny" Dunn and Walter Stevens, along with a bloody assist from Frankie McErlane, loaned from the Polock Joe Saltis gang.

The Genna brothers, who supplied Torrio with their poorly made liquor which was manufactured in hundreds of crude stills in Little Italy, began to get greedy, demanding a larger slice of the reported $100,000,000 filling Torrio's coffers (Capone was a 25% partner at the time). The West Side O'Donnells were becoming edgy under Torrio-Capone edicts. Little Johnny didn't like it. He could see the wars about to erupt.

The worst trouble emanated from the North Side Gang, a wacky legion of gunmen under the direction of the gangster gadfly, Dion O'Bannion. The high quality Canadian liquor being shipped to Torrio by the Purple Mob in Detroit was constantly being hijacked by the North Siders. O'Bannion also moved his bootlegging operations into virgin Cicero, which Capone and Torrio had already staked out as their exclusive domain.

At every turn, Torrio attempted to arbitrate, rather than use the gun as Capone wildly urged. Dozens of meetings were held between Torrio, Capone, and the North Siders. The result was always the same. O'Bannion promised to acknowledge the South Siders' territory and then systematically began a series of encroachments.

The Irish gangleader insulted the Genna brothers. They came to Torrio and said they wanted to kill O'Bannion. He convinced them to wait. O'Bannion insulted Capone (and killed several of his gunmen). Scarface went to Torrio and said he wanted to kill Dion. Wait, wait, Torrio cautioned.

All of O'Bannion's threatening banter amazingly evaporated in early May, 1924 when he came to see Torrio and Capone. He stated his offer flatly. He, Torrio, and Capone jointly owned the largest gambling spa in Chicago, The Ship. O'Bannion also owned controlling interest in the finest brewery in Chicago, Sieben's (also known as Mid-City).

O'Bannion sat back in a chair in Torrio's Four Deuces office. "I'm getting tired, Johnny," he said, masking his impish face with a woebegone expression. "The rackets are wearing me down and the Gennas are making me weary. I've been thinking of retiring. I'm gonna buy some nice ranchland in Colorado near Louis Alterie's spread and settle down. I want to unload The Ship and Sieben's."

"Just like that?" Capone said, snapping his fingers.

"Yeah, Al, me boy," O'Bannion winked. He, too, snapped his fingers. "Like that."

Torrio beamed. This was the way he liked to do business—buy out the opposition, not blast them out. He agreed to buy up O'Bannion's concerns and reportedly paid him a half million dollars in cash two days later. The two gangleaders arranged to meet at Sieben's on May 19, 1924. Torrio wanted to inspect his new property.

Torrio was not inside the brewery for more than ten minutes when Police Chief Collins, leading twenty men, raided the place, arresting O'Bannion, Earl "Hymie" Weiss, and Little Johnny. Dion and Hymie smiled happily; this was their first arrest for violating Prohibition laws. Torrio fumed. He had been arrested in June, 1923 and had been freed after paying a fine. A second arrest would mean a jail term, which O'Bannion knew.

Bond for Torrio was set at $7,500. He peeled the amount from his heavy roll and strolled out of the federal building free and seething with anger. He realized then that O'Bannion had had no intention of retiring from the rackets and had hoodwinked him into buying the brewery for a fortune while knowing it was about to be closed up by police.

It was time, Torrio decided, to get rid of Dion O'Bannion. He waited for five months. Then, under the pretext of buying flowers from O'Bannion, who ran a floral shop on North State Street, three of Torrio's gunmen (reportedly Albert Anselmi, John Scalise, and Little Johnny's old Brooklyn pal Frankie Yale) approached the unsuspecting Dion and shot him to death at close range while one man held his hand (the handshake murder) and the other two pumped six bullets into his body.

O'Bannion's death ignited what one crime historian termed "The Bootleg Battle of the Marne." Johnny Torrio was the first to feel the wrath of the revenge-seeking North Siders. On the evening of November 10, 1924, Torrio and his wife alighted from their chauffeur-driven limousine in front of their home at 7011 Clyde Avenue (where Torrio lived under the alias of Frank Langley). Anna Torrio began

Johnny Torrio, who organized crime on a grand scale in Chicago during Prohibition, is shown here in 1925 with a silk scarf, hiding wounds received in a recent gun attack. (UPI)

to walk inside. Johnny stopped to scoop up some packages from their recent shopping trip. As he did, a black Cadillac rolled up to the curb opposite his home. Inside, four men armed with pistols and shotguns watched for a moment. Then two of them, Hymie Weiss and Bugs Moran jumped from the car and dashed across the street, automatics barking. Torrio fell down instantly, a bullet in his chest and one in the neck.

The other two men in the Cadillac, Schemer Drucci and Frank Gusenberg, opened up on Torrio's limousine with shotguns. The chauffeur, Robert Barton, was hit in the leg with a load of buckshot and slipped down on the seat. Weiss and Moran ran to the fallen Torrio and, standing over him, fired a bullet into his right arm and another into his groin. Moran leaned over to fire the fatal bullet, the *coup de grace*, into Torrio's head. His trigger clicked. His gun was empty. As he reached for a new clip, the driver of the Cadillac, Drucci, slammed the horn frantically, the signal to leave immediately. Swearing, Moran and Weiss raced to their car and sped away.

Little Johnny began to scrawl toward his home. Anna Torrio ran to him screaming incoherently and dragged him into the house. A neighbor, Mrs. James Putnam, who had witnessed the shooting from her home, called a police ambulance. As he was being raced to Jackson Park Hospital, aware that his opponents might have tipped their bullets with garlic to cause gangrene, Torrio cried out: "Cauterize it! Cauterize it!"

It wasn't necessary. Torrio lived, the bullet wound in his neck creating a permanent scar. A bevy of reporters surrounded his hospital bed. "Sure, I know all four men," he told them. "I'll never tell their names."

With his jaw bandaged, Torrio stood before Federal Judge Adam Cliffe on February 9, 1925 (convicted of operating Sieben's brewery). He was fined $5,000 and received a nine-month sentence in jail—the maximum was five years—to be served in the DuPage County jail in Wheaton. The defendant's counsel, Robert W. Childs, asked Judge Cliffe to send Torrio to the Waukegan County Jail since it was better equipped to provide his client with the medical attention he required because of his wounds. Judge Cliffe granted the request. By most authorities, it was considered a lenient sentence, and brought to mind the report of a $50,000 bribe offered to First Assistant U.S. District Attorney William F. Waugh. The bribe, made in a round-about way by a Torrio representative, would be paid if Waugh recommended that the court merely fine Little Johnny. Waugh told the emissary to "get the hell out of here."

Earl "Hymie" Weiss, who had taken over the leadership of the North Side Gang after his mentor, Dion O'Bannion, had been slain, received only a $2,000 fine as a first offender of the Prohibition Act in the Sieben case.

When the clerk called the name, "Dion O'Bannion," the third party arrested in the Sieben raid the previous summer, Prosecutor Waugh said: "Defendant is deceased, Your Honor."

With that Earl "Hymie" Weiss gave Torrio a ferocious look and then walked to the clerk to pay his fine. Little Johnny took the hint. Weiss, Moran, and Drucci may have botched their first attempt to kill him but such ineptitude or luck would not reoccur. Torrio was packed off to the Waukegan jail, jangling with fear.

The treatment Torrio received in the Waukegan jail was no less than lavish. Sheriff Edwin Ahlstrom, Johnny's warden, was more than happy to fit the windows of his cell with bullet-proof plating. His cell was guarded night and day by extra deputies. Easy chairs, throw rugs and other comforts were provided for the rackets czar.

Torrio even took his evening meals in the Sheriff's home and was permitted for several hours in the evening to relax on the Sheriff's front porch, at which time he visited with his wife and numerous associates such as Al Capone.

There was plenty of time for meditation and Torrio could think of himself as a lucky man. He had survived the New York gang wars as leader of the James Street mob and the precarious position of Paul Kelly's top lieutenant in the Five Pointers. He had established a city-wide brothel system that stretched into the wealthiest suburbs of Illinois for Big Jim Colosimo. He had survived Big Jim. He and Capone had organized the largest booze and beer cartel in Chicago and Little Johnny had grown startlingly rich with a personal fortune estimated to be $75,000,000.

He also realized that he would never live out the year to spend a dime of his wealth as long as he continued to stay in Chicago. Calling in Capone and his lawyers, Torrio transferred all his holdings to Scarface—the brothels, the gambling casinos, the bootlegging empire, even the legitimate businesses he had insisted the gang purchase.

"I'm through," he told Capone. "It's all yours, Al. I'm going back to Italy . . . if I can get out of this city alive."

"I'll see to that," the jubilant 26-year-old Capone promised. When he took Torrio's hand he was shaking hello to a gross annual income of $105,000,000 (which would later win Scarface a place in the *Guinness Book of World Records* as the all-time record-holder of yearly earnings). Capone would also have to enter an arena of death to hold onto Torrio's original investments, a blood bath that would cause the deaths of at least one thousand gangsters and churn even his cast-iron stomach.

Torrio and his wife Anna were escorted out of town in Capone's $26,000 armor-plated limousine. In front and behind this car were two other roadsters jammed with heavily armed gunmen bristling with machineguns.

Thus, Johnny Torrio exited from Chicago.

The gangster caravan took Torrio, his wife, and their trunks to the Indiana state line and then into Gary, where the party waited for the East bound train. It was a solemn affair and a strange one. A dozen armed men patrolling the small Gary station made it appear that the governor of the state was leaving on the afternoon flyer, or, at least, the local mayor.

Capone said goodbye to Torrio in his state room. "So long, Johnny Papa, you come back when you feel better."

"Me? I'll never be back here again." He kept his word. The Torrios traveled to Florida, where they were trailed by Hymie Weiss' gunmen. They then left for Italy and stayed three years in Naples.

The warm Italian climate bored Torrio. He fidgeted. There was nothing to do, nothing that held his interest. He longed for his old profession, the work of it was in his system. But he could not return to Chicago. He finally settled on New York. He had no police record there.

The Torrios had another reason for moving. Mussolini had bombastically stated that he had had enough of Italian gangsters returning to Italy to victimize their own people. He told his fanatics that he would round them up and parade them through the streets of Rome in animal cages. Days after this pronouncement, Torrio and Anna were sailing back to the U.S.

In New York, Torrio bought several office and apartment buildings and went into the real estate business. In cooperation with Abner "Longy" Zwillman, Meyer Lansky, and Charles "Lucky" Luciano he also began a liquor cartel that would stretch from Florida to New England along the Atlantic seaboard. His job was to keep track of the mob's warehouses and liquor shipments, see that bills were paid, keep records, and maintain open lines of transportation.

Torrio performed amazingly well, building up a multi-million dollar business within a year. More and more he began to drift into the comfortable role of "crime's elder statesman." He enjoyed the respect the Eastern gangsters awarded him. This status allowed him to sit on the board of directors of the national crime syndicate once it was formed in 1934.

On many occasions, Torrio settled the most

heated of disputes between the members and, reportedly, his was the deciding vote to kill Dutch Schultz in 1935 when the Dutchman defied the board's ruling that District Attorney Thomas E. Dewey was not to be assassinated.

Year after year, Torrio went about his liquor business, thriving just as well after Repeal as it had during Prohibition. He puttered in real estate and enjoyed a sedate life. Then, on April 22, 1936, Torrio was arrested by federal officers in a post office in White Plains, N. Y., charged with income-tax evasion. His bond was set at $100,000. Hours later, authorities gaped as Mrs. Anna Torrio posted bond, appearing with $100,000 in crisp $1,000 bills rolled up in a newspaper.

There followed a long trial and several appeals. Torrio was finally convicted and was sent to Leavenworth for two and a half years. He was ordered to pay $86,000 in back income taxes. He promptly paid the money and, in 1939, stepped behind the walls of Leavenworth.

When Johnny Torrio was paroled on April 14, 1941 he went into semi-retirement. As underworld battles raged between Frank Costello and Vito Genovese, as Joe Bananas rose and fell, as the Gallo brothers were exterminated, Torrio sat quietly in his penthouse apartment reading newspapers.

On April 16, 1957, when most of the world thought Torrio had long passed to his fate, the dapper little gangster, chubby in later years, entered a barbershop and sat down for a shave. As the hot towel was placed about his bullet-scarred neck, Johnny Torrio groaned in pain, twitched, and then slipped from the chair. He died six hours later in the Cumberland Hospital with his faithful wife Anna at his side.

Torrio's passing was completely overlooked by the press and it was three weeks before obituary writers got around to linking him with the bootleg wars of Chicago. By then a mere half dozen people had already buried him in Greenwood Cemetery. Johnny Torrio, the gangster the Chicago press once chided as a man "who could dish it out but couldn't take it," went as unspectacularly to his grave as he had to Chicago in 1909, when everything seemed so terribly easy.

[ALSO SEE Al Capone, James Colosimo, Five Points Gang, Genna Brothers, James Street Gang, George "Bugs" Moran, Dion O'Bannion, Saltis-McErlane Gang, Walter Stevens, The Syndicate, Earl "Hymie" Weiss, Frank Yale.]

TOUHY, ROGER ("THE TERRIBLE") Bootlegger ● (1898-1959)

BACKGROUND: BORN IN CHICAGO, 1898. TWO SISTERS, FIVE BROTHERS (FATHER A POLICEMAN). MOVED TO DOWNER'S GROVE, ILL. IN 1908. GRADUATED ST. JOSEPH'S CATHOLIC SCHOOL IN 1911 (EIGHTH GRADE). MARRIED WIFE, CLARA, 4/22/22. ONE SON. ORIGINAL OCCUPATION, TELEGRAPHER. DESCRIPTION: 5'6", BLUE EYES, GREYING HAIR, SLENDER. ALIASES: NONE. RECORD: OPENED BOOKMAKING OPERATION IN CHICAGO WITH BROTHER TOMMY (ALSO KNOWN AS "TERRIBLE TOMMY" TOUHY) IN 1926; BEGAN BOOTLEGGING ACTIVITIES IN NORTHWESTERN SUBURBS OF CHICAGO ABOUT 1927 IN PARTNERSHIP WITH MATT KOLB AND BROTHER EDDIE; ENTERED SLOT MACHINE ACTIVITIES IN NORTHERN COOK COUNTY, ILL. IN LATE 1920S; ARRESTED WITH EDWARD MCFADDEN, PETER STEVENS (ALIAS GUS SCHAFER), AND WILLIE SHARKEY BY FBI AGENTS IN ELKHORN, WIS. IN AUGUST, 1933 FOR THE KIDNAPPING OF WEALTHY ST. PAUL BREWER, WILLIAM A. HAMM, JR. WHICH HAD OCCURRED ON 6/15/33; TAKEN TO ST. PAUL AND INDICTED THERE FOR KIDNAPPING BY A GRAND JURY ON 8/13/33; ALL FOUR DEFENDANTS FOUND NOT GUILTY BY JURY (ALVIN KARPIS AND OTHER MEMBERS OF THE BARKER/KARPIS GANG LATER CONVICTED OF THE HAMM KIDNAPPING); ARRESTED WITH STEVENS, MCFADDEN (SHARKEY HAD COMMITTED SUICIDE IN THE RAMSEY COUNTY JAIL IN ST. PAUL DURING THE HAMM TRIAL), AND ALBERT KATOR FOR THE ALLEGED KIDNAPPING OF JOHN "JAKE THE BARBER" FACTOR, WHICH SUPPOSEDLY OCCURRED ON 6/31-7/1/33; TRIED IN TWO TRIALS, 1/11-2/2/34 (FIRST JURY DISCHARGED FOR FAILING TO COME TO A DECISION) AND A SECOND TRIAL BEGINNING 2/13/34, BOTH BEFORE JUDGE MICHAEL J. FEINBERG IN THE COOK COUNTY CRIMINAL COURT; CONVICTED AND SENTENCED TO 199 YEARS IN STATEVILLE PRISON AT JOLIET, ILL.; ESCAPED STATEVILLE PRISON WITH BASIL "THE OWL" BANGHART, EUGENE O'CONNOR, EDWARD DARLAK, MARTLICK NELSON, EDWARD STEWART, AND ST. CLAIR MCINERNEY ON 10/9/42; RECAPTURED BY FBI AGENTS (WHO SHOT AND KILLED O'CONNOR AND MCINERNEY WHEN THEY RESISTED ARREST) ON 12/29/42 IN AN APARTMENT AT KENMORE AND LAWRENCE IN CHICAGO; GIVEN AN ADDITIONAL 199 YEARS FOR "AIDING AND ABETTING" THE ESCAPE OF EDWARD DARLAK; AFTER SEVERAL YEARS OF LEGAL MANEUVERING, RELEASED IN 1959 ON THE DECISION OF FEDERAL JUDGE JOHN P. BARNES, WHO PROCLAIMED THE FACTOR KIDNAPPING A HOAX AND THE "AIDING AND ABETTING" CHARGE A FRAUD; SHOT DOWN IN FRONT OF HIS SISTER'S HOME IN CHICAGO BY UNKNOWN PARTIES

The early childhood of Roger Touhy was about as normal as that of any other American boy in a large middle-class family. When he was ten, however, a stove blew up in his Chicago home, killing his mother. His father, a policeman, moved his eight children to Downer's Grove and there Roger attended St. Joseph's Grade School, graduating in 1911. He was an altar boy in the church and did odd jobs on weekends. There was nothing in his background to suggest a future life of crime.

Upon graduation from grade school, Touhy went to work for Western Union as a telegrapher and manager of a small office. He kept at this trade until 1915, when he was fired by the firm for union activities. For a brief time, Roger became involved in union work; then he moved on to be employed by the Denver & Rio Grand Railroad as a telegraph operator in Colorado.

At the outbreak of the First World War, Touhy enlisted in the Navy and between 1917 and 1918 taught code to naval officers at Harvard. Following his discharge, he traveled to Oklahoma where he worked as an oil rigger and engineer. Soon he began to buy and sell oil leases, until he had accumulated $25,000; with this small fortune he returned to Chicago and, in 1922, married.

Settling in Des Plaines, Touhy established a trucking company. By 1926 his business had run down and he thought of using his trucks to haul beer. "It happened that I knew most of the bootleggers and saloon owners in my area," he wrote later. "Why not? They were the guys who had money to buy fancy cars. If Chicago's best stores catered to them and their wives, why shouldn't Roger Touhy?"

At first Touhy began trucking beer for others; then he decided to make his own brew. He hired a chemist who brewed the finest beer in the Midwest for him, using the best ingredients available. "We're not going to need any salesmen," he told his partner Matt Kolb. "We're going to put out the best beer in America. The saloonkeepers will come to us begging to buy it."

He then bought his own cooperage to make leak-proof beer barrels and placed his brother Eddie in charge of the brewery and packaging operation. He then disguised his beer shipments by buying several oil tank trucks, painting them so they resembled Texaco Oil Company trucks. His business went smoothly, and most agreed that the quality of Touhy beer was superior to that of anything available. His delivery route was small but he managed to unload 1,000 barrels of beer at $55 a barrel (it cost him $4.50 a barrel to produce).

Police and city officials were paid off in barrels of beer and specially brewed bottled beer. Touhy invested heavily in making his bottled beer, paying more than $10,000 for a bottle washer and pasteurizer. The bottled beer was not sold; it was distributed solely to policemen and politicians as "gifts."

Soon Al Capone heard of Touhy's highly successful bootlegging racket. About the time when Touhy and Kolb were distributing slot machines to 225 outlets in the suburbs, Capone called Roger and said that he had heard Touhy had the best beer available. Touhy agreed. Capone ordered five hundred barrels, saying his own sources had dried up temporarily. "I gave him a discount price of $37.50 a barrel because of the big order. The brew must have sold well. He called me a few days later and asked for three hundred more." Touhy shipped the beer, telling Scarface he wanted to collect for both orders on the following Tuesday.

On Monday Capone called Touhy. "Rog," he said, "fifty of those barrels were leakers. I'll pay you for 750, okay?"

Touhy laughed and told him that that was impossible. His professionally run cooperage hadn't had a leaker in years and every barrel was sealed with powerful air pressure. "Don't chisel me, Al. You owe me for eight hundred and I expect to get paid for eight hundred."

"Well, the boys told me there were fifty leakers," Capone squirmed.

"I'll check on it."

Touhy received $30,000 in cash from Capone the next day. Though he had backed Capone down, Touhy was playing a dangerous game. Unknown to Capone, Touhy was not a mobster, but merely a middle class bootlegger with no gang of armed killers protecting his suburban racket from the invasion of the Chicago mobs. Capone knew little about suburbs such as Des Plaines but planned to move brothels and gambling casinos into the untapped area. Touhy's presence worried him. He knew less about Roger Touhy than he did about this new territory.

"Capone envied me my anonymity and he begrudged me my income," Touhy stated in 1959. Two of Capone's torpedoes, Frank Rio and Willie Heeney, appeared at the Touhy-owned roadhouse, The Arch in Schiller Park. Touhy was prepared for them. He had hung a dozen shotguns on the walls and placed two machineguns in a nearby closet, the door of which was purposely left open. The nervy bootlegger arranged for a filling station attendant to call him every time he made some motions with his hands. The attendant was directly across the road and could see Touhy through the large window of his office.

"Don't pay any attention to what I tell you when you call," Touhy told the attendant. "I'm only playing a joke on some friends."

Rio and Heeney showed up and approached Touhy with swaggers and boasts. Then the two mobsters saw the machineguns—borrowed from a local police station for the sham —and grew docile. Heeney then said: "Al wants to move cathouses, some taxi-dance joints and punchboards out here. Al wants you should go along with this deal."

Touhy went into his act, blowing his nose, scratching his head and brushing lint from his suit. The phone rang. Touhy scowled at the mouthpiece. "Yeah?" he roared. "Well, send some of the boys over there and take care of those bums. Nobody can hijack our slots."

Heeney and Rio exchanged nervous glances. Heeney then meekly went on to say that Capone thought Schiller Park was "virgin territory for whorehouses." Touhy laughed and replied that the local people were devout churchgoers and that the male population were serious family men.

When Rio pulled out a map marked with pins indicating where Capone wanted to establish his brothels, Touhy coughed loudly, another signal for his second act. A giant off-duty policeman, who drove a truck for Touhy on occasions, rumbled into the office, walked over to the closet and grabbed the two machineguns, cursing. "Me and Louie are going to give those bastards a good scare—or maybe worse, boss," the burly cop said to Touhy.

"Do what you think best, Joe, but don't let 'em bluff you," Touhy shot back. The cop

Frank "The Enforcer" Nitti, Capone's top gun, tried to invade Touhy's bootlegging territory but was frightened of Touhy's imaginary gang. (UPI)

walked out of the office to return the machineguns to the local police arsenal. Rio and Heeney kept talking but didn't get far.

"The telephone rang constantly," Touhy reported, "and I made gangster-type ·remarks into the mouthpiece. I acted like a one-man Murder Incorporated, and Heeney and Rio got a little pale around their noses and mouths. They said they would go back and report to Capone. I waved them cheerily on their way."

Scarface kept after Touhy. He next sent Louis "Little New York" Campagna and "Machine Gun" Jack McGurn to reason with Touhy. They got nowhere. Then Sam "Golf Bag" Hunt, Frank Diamond, and Frank Rio showed up with the same pitch. Ex-policemen and farmers who worked in Touhy's brewery and drove his trucks, none of them gunmen, stomped back and forth through his office brandishing firearms.

Rio blurted: "You got a big organization, huh, Rog?"

Touhy shrugged. "There are two hundred guys out here from every penitentiary in the United States and some from Canada," he lied. "Say, we're having a big party tonight. Most of my guys will be here. Why don't you come out and bring Al and some of the other boys?"

Capone's gunners accepted the invitation with alacrity. Touhy closed the Arch down the minute they left. That night six Chicago police squads raided the place to find it locked and empty. "Remarkable coincidence, wasn't it?" Touhy chuckled.

Roger's next two visitors from Capone were James "Red" Fawcett and Murray "The Camel" Humphreys. Humphreys asked Touhy to drive back to Chicago with them and talk over their proposition with Frank "The Enforcer" Nitti.

"To hell with that," Touhy said in his toughest voice. He walked to a rack of weapons in his office and fingered a shotgun.

"You know, Rog," Humphreys said, "We can take care of you anytime we want."

"Yeah?" Touhy grinned.

Then Humphreys' hands began to shake and he amazed Touhy by stating: "Look, Touhy. I've got a swell car parked outside." He pointed at the window to a 16-cylinder limousine. "If you drive me back inside the Chicago City Limits, I'll give you the car. I want to get home alive!"

Fawcett gave Humphreys a contemptuous smirk.

"Go on back to Chicago, both of you," Touhy said. "You won't get hurt."

The pair almost ran to their car. Fawcett reappeared moments later and leaned across Touhy's desk, saying, "Listen, Touhy, for five thousand I'll kill that son-of-a-bitch Hum-

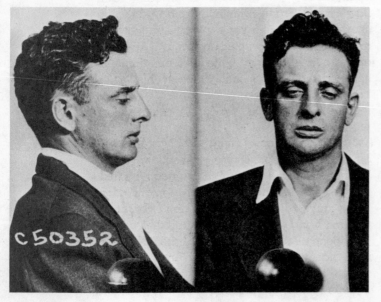

Bootlegger Roger "The Terrible" Touhy, who wasn't so terrible after all, shown here in 1934 while on trial for kidnapping.

phreys on the way to the city and for another five grand I'll go to Cicero and knock off Nitti, too."

Roger Touhy only laughed and sent Fawcett on his way. Capone grew tired of talking to Touhy through his gunmen and kidnapped Touhy's partner, Matt Kolb, holding him for $50,000 ransom, a way of getting back his investment in Touhy's beer shipments.

Capone called Touhy and said: "Rog—some people have got Matt. They want $50,000 to set him loose and asked me to act as a go-between." Touhy got the message and Capone got the $50,000. Touhy delivered the money personally and alone, marching through an army of gunmen at The Metropole Hotel, a Capone fortress.

Plunking the ransom money down in front of Scarface he said: "Where's Matt?"

Capone eagerly tore off the newspapers wrapped around the money. "Now, Rog," he said sweetly, "I want you to know I had nothing to do with this. I like Matt. I'm trying to help him."

Kolb was released several blocks away by Capone gunmen minutes after Touhy delivered the money. The non-shooting feud between Capone and Touhy went on for several years, culminating with the Capone-directed murder of Matt Kolb in 1931. Touhy struck back by aligning himself with labor leaders resisting Capone's attempt to take over unions.

In 1933, Touhy was set up in two phony kidnapping charges. One was unwittingly perpetrated by the reckless Melvin Purvis of the FBI, in which Touhy and three others were charged with kidnapping William A. Hamm, Jr., wealthy St. Paul brewer. The four were found not guilty. Then Touhy was charged with kidnapping Jake "The Barber" Factor, a shadowy Chicago figure. This time, through perjured testimony, as was later revealed, he was convicted and sent to the Illinois State Prison in Joliet for 199 years.

For almost a decade, Touhy attempted to prove his innocence in the Factor kidnapping, claiming that he had been framed so that the Capone mob could take over his interests in the suburbs and also in revenge for Touhy's siding with labor leaders against the mob. After exhausting all legal avenues, Touhy, who had been a model prisoner at Stateville, agreed to go along on a prison break led by Basil "The Owl" Banghart and Eugene O'Con-

Burglar Basil "The Owl" Banghart escaped with Roger Touhy and others from the Illinois State Penitentiary in a sensational 1942 prison break.

nor. Others in the break included Edward Darlak, St. Clair McInerney, Martlick Nelson, and Edward Stewart.

The seven men broke out of Stateville on October 9, 1942, scaling a wall to a guard's tower, then climbing down through the tower to an outside door where a car was waiting. They were all recaptured the following December. O'Connor and McInerney resisted FBI agents and were shot to death in a gun battle in a North Side Chicago apartment building where they were hiding.

Though Touhy received no added sentence for the prison break, he was sentenced to an additional 199 years for "aiding and abetting" Edward Darlak's escape. (Oddly enough, a prison break was not punishable in Illinois unless someone was hurt during the break, or unless crimes were committed during the escapee's time at large; the Illinois legislature finally passed a bill in 1949 stating that it was a crime to break out of jail.)

Touhy's lawyers persisted in filing appeals and in the early 1950s, Federal Judge John P. Barnes reviewed the Factor kidnapping case and declared it a "hoax." He pointed out that Factor, who was wanted at the time in England for perpetrating a $7,000,000 swindle under the alias Norman D. Spencer (two other aliases Factor had used in scams were Har-

ry Wise and J. Gest) had desperately engineered the fake kidnapping to prevent his extradition to England to stand trial. Jake the Barber's long career was pock-marked by such schemes; he was jailed from August of 1943 to February, 1948 in the federal penitentiary at Sandstone, Minn. after pleading guilty to a plot to swindle Catholic priests and others out of $1 million while using whiskey warehouse receipts.

Barnes also went on to indict Chicago district attorney Thomas J. Courtney for his role in the case. Courtney had gone to Washington and conferred with President Franklin D. Roosevelt in 1933 and persuaded the President to allow Factor to stay in the U.S. so that he could testify in an important kidnapping case. Roosevelt unwittingly sanctioned this move and the lengthy case provided Factor with enough time in the U.S. to escape extradition through a time lapse.

The end of Roger Touhy; the old bootlegger lies mortally wounded, shot down by unknown gangsters in Chicago, just twenty-three days after being released from prison in 1959.

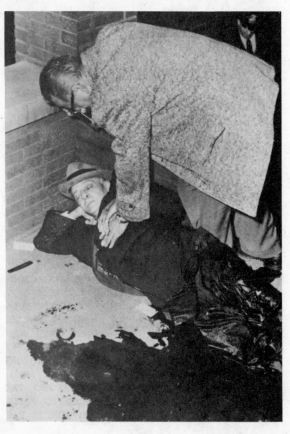

Another suspicious character in the trumped-up kidnapping case was police captain Daniel A. "Tubbo" Gilbert, who was later called "The World's Richest Cop" by the Chicago press. Gilbert was Factor's constant companion during the kidnapping trial and Barnes later stated that Gilbert convinced a witness, convicted thief Isaac Costner, to lie in his testimony in the Touhy trial on the promise that he would receive a reduced prison sentence.

It took several years of legal juggling before Touhy was released from Stateville on November 25, 1959. The old bootlegger went to live with his sister in Chicago, no longer called Roger "The Terrible" Touhy by the press, once his story had been finally made clear. But there were those who would not forgive and forget and on December 17, 1959, as he was entering his sister's home, Roger Touhy was hit by several shotgun blasts from unknown gunners on the street. He fell onto a porch with his legs half blown away and wordlessly waited for the ambulance to arrive.

"I've been expecting it," he mumbled to an attendant on the way to the hospital. "The bastards never forget." He died four hours later in the hospital.

TOURBILLON, ROBERT ARTHUR
Swindler, Robber ● (1885- ?)

BACKGROUND: BORN IN ATLANTA, GA., 1885. MINOR PUBLIC EDUCATION. ORIGINAL OCCUPATION, CIRCUS PERFORMER. DESCRIPTION: 5'9", BROWN EYES, BROWN HAIR, SLENDER. ALIASES: DAPPER CON COLLINS, HARRY HUSSEY, CROMWALL, RATSY. RECORD: ARRESTED FOR THEFT IN NYC, 1908, RELEASED; ROBBED THE HOTEL ROY. 6/15/11 ($160), RECEIVED A MINOR SENTENCE; BECAME A MEMBER OF A TELEPHONE COIN BOX RING; ARRESTED 1916 AND SENTENCED TO TWO YEARS IN THE FEDERAL PRISON OF ATLANTA AFTER BEING CONVICTED OF INTERSTATE WHITE SLAVE BLACKMAILING; ROBBED A WEALTHY MERCHANT IN UPSTATE NEW YORK, 1918; ARRESTED AND FREED; ARRESTED, TRIED AND CONVICTED OF ROBBING AN AMERICAN EXPRESS GUARD, FREDERICK C. ROBB, OF $5,000 CASH AND SOME JEWELRY; RELEASED ON $5,000 BOND PENDING APPEAL; JUMPED BOND; SUSPECTED OF SHOOTING JOHN H. REID IN NYC OVER A WOMAN ON 5/15/21; BECAME AN IMPORTANT RUMRUNNER ALONG THE EAST COAST IN THE EARLY 1920S; FLED TO PARIS, FRANCE TO AVOID ARREST AFTER BEING INDICTED FOR ROBBING FREDERICK C. ROBB; ARRESTED IN PARIS IN 1924 AND RETURNED UNDER GUARD TO THE U.S.; ARRESTED FOR SWINDLING AN APPLE FARMER, THOMAS WEBER, IN EGG HARBOR, N.J.; AND SENTENCED TO THREE YEARS IN THE NEW JERSEY STATE PRISON AT TRENTON ON 4/26/29; RELEASED ON PAROLE, AUGUST, 1930; DISAPPEARED.

Tourbillon's first known job was that of riding a bicycle down a chute, through a hoop, and past a cage loaded with well-fed lions; his act was known as "The Circle of Death." Life with a Southern circus, however, bored Bobby Tourbillon. Seeking higher adventure, he made his way to New York, arriving at Curly Bennett's celebrated pool hall in 1908 where, at the age of 23, he promptly and happily fell in with thieves.

Within a month Tourbillon was arrested for burglary, but the charge was dismissed. Tourbillon's reputation as a clothes horse and highly-polished con man grew among the shifty denizens who inhabited off-Broadway haunts. They dubbed him "Rat," an unsavory moniker derived from the initials of his three names, an appellative he understandably refused to cherish.

Late on the night of June 15, 1911, accompanied by two gunmen, Tourbillon entered the Hotel Roy in mid-town Manhattan and robbed the clerk of $160. The three were caught hours later and convicted. Receiving a light sentence, Tourbillon heard his reputation dramatized by Judge Edward Swann, who told reporters that "He is as smooth a rascal as ever came before me . . . He is a real Raffles. I consider this man a very dangerous character, for he is a smooth talker and such a fine dresser."

Four years later, Tourbillon was back on the crime circuit, this time allied with a ring who robbed telephone coin boxes. Detectives apprehended the gang but Tourbillon was turned over to federal authorities holding a warrant for his arrest on a charge of interstate white-slave blackmail. He was convicted of this charge and given two years in the Atlanta federal penitentiary.

Once back on the streets, Tourbillon decided to bilk an upstate New York landowner named Julius Scholtz. Bobby had learned that Scholtz kept a trunk full of savings which was purported to be in the neighborhood of $20,-000. He obtained a fake badge and journeyed to the Scholtz farm with an accomplice. The penny-pinching farmer met them without alarm when the two con men informed him that they were "from the Department of Internal Revenue." Tourbillon quickly flashed his badge.

"Mr. Scholtz, we are compelled to search your farm," Bobby told him.

"I gat nuddings," Scholtz insisted.

Bobby told the farmer that they were looking for illegal caches of liquor. Scholtz replied that all he had on hand was apple cider and offered the two men some. After having downed several tart-tasting cups, Tourbillon searched the premises, discovered the farmer's much-vaunted trunk, and was horrified to learn that it contained nothing more than old German newspapers. He apologized to the farmer for the inconvenience, took his hand and said: "Goodbye, Julius."

After the pair left, the farmer grew suspicious. He concluded that the men were imposters by the fact that they knew his first name. Scholtz went to the local police, repeating to officers: "How he know I gat name Julius?"

Tourbillon was arrested for impersonating a federal officer, but this time he took the precaution of enlisting the services of the greatest criminal lawyer in the land, William Fallon. The agile Fallon speedily won an acquittal, but Tourbillon, being sought by police for robbing an American Express guard of $5,000 in 1920, was convicted of this charge. Fallon arranged bail pending an appeal; Tourbillon jumped bail and went into hiding. Police intensified their search for Tourbillon after one John H. Reid was shot on May 15, 1921, since it appeared that Bobby had performed the marksmanship. He and Reid had been vying for the same woman, a curvacious cutie, Mrs. Hazel D. Warner.

In the summer of 1921, Tourbillon went into rum-running on a large scale. He purchased a luxury yacht, the *Nomad*, noted for its speed (some say its price was paid by gambler and Tourbillon friend, Arnold Rothstein), and began smuggling Canadian liquor into New York harbor.

No one could match Tourbillon for sheer brazenness. He once sailed up to a New York dock and informed the suspicious night watchman that the *Nomad* was putting in for repairs, that the ship would be lifted onto the Marine railway in the morning.

"You can't dock here," the watchman ordered.

"Do you want to be responsible for us sinking here?" Tourbillon said.

"No, you can dock," the watchman said.

A truck then appeared and the watchman returned. "Now what's going on?" he said anxiously.

"We're taking off the furniture, stupid," Tourbillon griped, injecting annoyance into his words.

"Oh, sure," the watchman mumbled and sauntered away.

Two hours later, Bobby Tourbillon and his rum-runners loaded more than 1,800 bottles of whiskey into the truck and then quietly sailed out to sea.

Accumulating a small fortune, Bobby decided to visit Europe, his move undoubtedly prompted by the fact that he was about to face a charge of grand larceny. By 1924, Tourbillon was residing in Paris, living under the alias of Harry Hussey and bilking gullible, wealthy, expatriate women.

Mrs. Helen Petterson, the estranged wife of an American industrialist, fell madly in love with the sneak thief. She plied him with money and even gave him some of her own jewelry. Nothing Tourbillon did daunted her affection for him. One festive New Year's Eve party culminated when Bobby pushed Mrs. Petterson, according to authorities, off her third-floor balcony at the Hotel Majestic. She broke her leg in the fall, yet when Tourbillon was thrown into debtor's prison for failing to pay his hotel bill, the indomitable Mrs. Petterson hobbled each day to the jail to visit her Bobby, telling reporters: "We are going to be married."

Coincidence and luck worked against the adventurous thief in early 1924, while he was serving out the last days of his sentence in Sante Prison. Two American police officers, Lieutenants McCoy and Kane of the NYPD, arrived to extradite an American burglar named Mourey to the U.S. The warden's courtesy extended to showing the officers his well-disciplined inmates.

McCoy was startled to see Tourbillon in the line-up. "I'll be damned if that isn't Ratsy Tourbillon," he told Kane.

"Hello, Rats," McCoy called and wiggled his index finger in Tourbillon's direction, indicating he wanted him to walk forward.

Bobby arched his eyebrows. "Are you addressing me?" he said airily.

"Yes, Rats, you." McCoy smiled. "You remember us, don't you?"

"Never had the pleasure," the suave Bobby replied.

Minutes later, the two officers were arranging Tourbillon's extradition to the U.S.

Tourbillon returned home in a first-class cabin aboard the luxury liner, *Paris*, accompanied by a detective named Daley whom Bobby referred to as his "secretary." The good-natured cop played out the role rather than embarrass his prisoner.

The wacky and ironic Roaring Twenties were never more in evidence than at the moment the *Paris* docked. A cluster of reporters, hearing that Tourbillon was on board, rushed to the smoking lounge where they found the criminal coolly puffing a cigar.

One newsman showed him a clipping and photo of Mrs. Petterson. "You going to marry this dame?"

"Ask my secretary." Bobby turned to his "secretary" and quipped: "I suppose every milk bottle and door mat stolen since I went away will be attributed to me."

The wily crook was taken to Tombs Prison. While Tourbillon was being booked, an officer asked the accompanying detective what charge was being leveled against the prisoner.

"Moprey!" the insouciant Bobby responded. (Moprey, a joke among criminals, consists of exhibiting the naked body before a blind woman.)

Tourbillon's odd fame faded in the late 1920s when he was sentenced on April 26, 1929 to three years in the New Jersey State Prison for swindling a New Jersey farmer, Thomas Weber, out of $30,000. He served sixteen months.

Upon his release, reporters once again interviewed the dapper con man.

"This was an excellent prison," he told them. "I recommend it as a wonderful vacation spot." When asked what his plans were, Tourbillon became pensive and then replied: "I'm going back to Paris." No one knows whether he ever did. Bobby Tourbillon, or Dapper Don Collins, completely disappeared at this time, leaving behind many news-hungry reporters and a lovesick Mrs. Petterson.

TRACY, ANN GIBSON
Murderer ● (1935-   )

BACKGROUND: BORN AND RAISED IN LAGUNA BEACH, CALIF. ONE OF THREE CHILDREN. PARENTS DIVORCED AT AN EARLY AGE. HIGH SCHOOL GRADUATE. ORIGINAL OCCUPATION, COCKTAIL WAITRESS. DESCRIPTION: 5'2", BROWN EYES, BROWN HAIR, SLENDER. ALIASES: NONE. RECORD: SHOT AND KILLED WEALTHY LAGUNA BEACH BUILDING CONTRACTOR AMOS STRICKER ON 11/14/60; ARRESTED 11/16/60; ARRAIGNED 12/2/60, CHARGED WITH FIRST DEGREE MURDER, PLEADED NOT GUILTY; TRIED 1/23-2/1/61, ADMITTED GUILT; CONVICTED OF SECOND DEGREE MURDER, SENTENCED TO LIFE IMPRISONMENT IN THE CALIFORNIA STATE WOMEN'S PRISON AT CORONA.

Ann Tracy murdered out of love, or out of the lack of it. She had been born into an unhappy marriage and shuttled about between her father and mother all her life, until she moved out on her own, becoming a cocktail waitress in her home town of Laguna Beach, California.

In 1958, a cultured, well-dressed customer asked her to dinner. She accepted and so began a two-year romance with 44-year-old Amos Stricker, a well-to-do building contractor, divorced and the father of three children, who lived comfortably in his plush hilltop residence overlooking Laguna Beach.

Shortly after meeting Ann, Stricker took ill and Ann nursed him back to health, spending several months at his bedside. Their love affair was a bit strange. Stricker recovered and then began to run around with other women, while he continued to see Ann. She knew about his other flames but was content to see him when he saw fit, asking only that "If you do run around, please don't tell me about it."

Stricker did tell her, however, in graphic detail about the women he dated. He tortured her incessantly with such talk, she later claimed at her trial. On one occasion, returning with a woman to his apartment and finding Ann there, Stricker asked her to leave without being seen; she did, exiting through a trap door to the wine cellar and from there into the street.

Stricker took advantage of her love for him at every turn. He increasingly delighted in telling Ann that he would be having women visit-

Amos Stricker taunted his girlfriend Ann Tracy with tales of other women. Her response came out of the end of a gun. (Wide World Photos)

A woman scorned, Ann Tracy shot her beloved, wealthy building contractor Amos Stricker of Laguna Beach, and then bundled him in a blanket. (Wide World Photos)

ing him on certain days. On the night of November 13, 1960, Stricker called Miss Tracy at her home and told her he had a female house guest and "forget about coming up here."

The following day, Stricker called Ann and asked her to dinner. She arrived at 4 p.m. Within minutes the couple went to bed. Then they prepared dinner. As they were sipping Manhattans, Stricker looked up at Ann Tracy and said: "Why do you waste your love on me?"

"Because I love you, that's all."

They drank champagne with dinner. Stricker, reserved, detached, began to talk about jealousy. He mentioned that his female companion of the previous night would return.

"You do as you please but don't tell me about it," Ann said. She went into the bedroom and lay down.

Stricker came to the bedroom door. "It won't do you any good to pout," Stricker said, "because there are going to be a lot of other women up here on weekends, too."

Ann Tracy had been a patient woman. She had also been ridiculed and humiliated. This final insult provoked in her the universal wrath of the woman scorned. Knowing Stricker kept a gun in a bedstand drawer, she reached for it and then followed him into the living room. Stricker was sitting in a chair. She walked behind it. He turned to face her. He mentioned a woman's name and then said: "She hasn't

been up here for a long time. I think I'll call her."

Lifting the gun to his face, Ann Tracy closed her eyes and fired.

The first bullet struck Amos Stricker in the neck. He stood up shakily and advanced upon Miss Tracy, haltingly saying: "If I have to go, I'm taking you with me."

"Sit down," she told him, noticing that he was bleeding freely from the neck wound.

Stricker came on. He lunged for the weapon and Miss Tracy emptied the gun into him. He fell backward into a chair. Ann went to him, propped him up. When she realized that he was dead she covered him with a blanket and put a pillow under his head. "And his mouth and his eyes were open," she stated later, "and I closed them." The murder was a model of orderliness.

Miss Tracy admitted the killing to a friend hours later. She was arrested, tried, and quickly convicted of second degree murder, after first denying her guilt and then admitting it. Before going into the Corona Women's Prison for life, she was asked why she had killed Amos Stricker. Her answer was in the classical tradition of the crime of passion.

"Because I loved him," she said without hesitation. ". . . I didn't mean to hurt him . . . I wouldn't have hurt him for anything in the world."

TRAVELING MIKE GRADY GANG

A group of mobile sneak thieves who plied their nefarious trade throughout New York City about the time of the Civil War, this gang included montebanks like Greedy Jake Rand, Boston Pete Anderson, Hod Ennis, Eddie Pettengill, and, naturally, Traveling Mike, an infamous fence whose traffic in stolen goods approached, at times, that of Marm Mandelbaum, queen of the fences.

The mob hit it lucky when they entered the offices of the eccentric and penurious financier Rufus L. Lord. Though he possessed a fortune of more than $4 million, Lord's hole-in-the-wall office afforded him light from only one window. He was a thorny investor in stocks and bonds and his financial acumen was the talk of Wall Street. Personally, his mien could best be described as dingy. Lord clothed himself in rotting rags and torn slippers. To conserve expenses, he refused to have more than one candle burning in his offices at the rear of 38 Exchange Place.

On March 7, 1866, Traveling Mike and his minions confronted Lord, who was alone at his desk. Grady spoke of taking out a loan in the grand manner of a moneyed man. He airily prattled that a loan at twenty per cent would not be unreasonable. At this, Lord leapt to his feet and with quaking hands clutched Grady's lapels, demanding that he close the deal at once.

While thus distracted, Lord failed to see Pettengill and Anderson slip behind him and go to his burglar-proof safe. It was open, which was not unusual for Lord. Growing feeble-minded, he often left the safe open when leaving at night. He kept millions of dollars in cash and negotiable bonds inside.

Pettengill and Anderson removed a large tin box from Lord's safe while its owner urgently attempted to foist a loan upon Grady. The thieves then left. The effervescent Grady stated that he would return within an hour and sign the papers for the loan.

Upon opening the tin box, the robbers discovered $1,900,000 in cash and securities, the largest theft ever engineered by sneak thieves in the U.S. Almost all the bonds were negotiable. Every member of the gang retired on the spot except Traveling Mike, who continued selling stolen goods for years, proving he was just as parsimonious as Lord. The financier never quite recovered from the shock of the theft and installed a steel door in his office, where he died years later among his dusty money bags.

TULLY, SAMUEL
Murderer, Pirate ● (? -1812)

Sam Tully was a thorough blackguard who worked on board the schooner *George Washington* under the alias R. Heathcoate, being sought in England for the murder of his father.

On January 21, 1812, Tully and his messmate, John Dalton, seized control of the ship while the captain was ashore at Cape Verde. They sailed the small craft to the West Indies and sank it near St. Lucie, but not before killing a protesting crewman, one George Cummings.

Both Tully and Dalton were captured and sent to Boston for trial. Tully shouted in court that he was compelled to take over the schooner because the captain was usually drunk and his seamanship would surely cause the deaths of the crew in any kind of storm. His arguments against the charges of murder and piracy fell on deaf ears and both he and Dalton were sentenced to death on the gallows.

The gallows scene in South Boston on December 10, 1812 was bizarre. Venders hawked hot pastries beneath the scaffold as thousands gathered to watch the two men die. An enterprising publisher named Coverly sold broadsheets on the case to the mob; he had to correct his pamphlets which reported the execution of the two men, however, because Dalton, at the last moment, was reprieved. Still the blood-thirsty crowd was not totally disappointed. Tully was hanged on schedule.

TURLEY, PRESTON S.
Murderer ● (? -1858)

Drink was Preston Turley's downfall. His acute alcoholism caused him to be driven from the Baptist Church in Charleston, Va. (now West Virginia). The ex-minister hit the bottle harder than ever, enticing his wife Mary Susan to join in his revels.

One late summer night in 1858, the couple began to quarrel while both were well into their staggers. Turley abruptly turned on his wife and, while raging scripture, strangled her in front of his three children.

Despite the witnesses, Turley attempted to conceal his wife's body by dumping her weighted corpse into the nearby Coal River. He was quickly taken into custody and sentenced to death.

On September 17, 1858, Turley addressed a large throng for more than three hours, lecturing them on the wages of demon rum. He was noticeably disappointed as the hangman approached him with the noose. His death mattered little to him, it seemed, but the fact that his children had not come to see him die saddened him. He had repeatedly encouraged them, in letters from jail, to attend the ceremonies. One note stated: "Don't you want to go and see Pa hung?"

TURNER, NAT
Murderer ● (1800-1831)

In late August of 1831, a field slave foreman and Baptist preacher, Nat Turner, decided to revolt against his white masters, claiming to have had a vision from God who commanded him to free his people. Armed with knifes and hatchets, he and eight other blacks invaded his owner's house and hacked to death four adults and an infant.

Turner sent word to slaves on neighboring plantations throughout Southampton County, Virginia, to join him in his revolt. About sixty more slaves joined him and his small band and then began one of the most bloody uprisings ever witnessed in the antebellum South. The slaves took weapons and horses as they swept through each plantation, slaughtering every white person in sight.

Several blacks who refused to join Turner were beaten senseless and killed while shielding their masters with their own bodies. The burly foreman of one plantation, upon seeing his master knifed to death, strode up to Turner and said: "Now that you have killed him, you may kill me. I have nothing to live for."

Small children were tracked down in corn and cotton fields where they sought refuge; they were hacked to bits. The slaughter went on for forty-eight hours and caused the deaths of close to fifty whites.

While en route to the county seat, ironically named Jerusalem, Turner and his rebels stopped at the Parker plantation. Several of his men went into the plantation to recruit more slaves to the rebellion. Instead, they broke into the large wine cellar and proceeded to get drunk. Within an hour, Turner went into the cellar after them, exhorting them to continue along the bloodpath of their sacred revolution.

While Turner was thus occupied, a band of eighteen whites arrived at the plantation gates on horseback and shot up the runaway slaves who were waiting there for their leader. Turner and his men rushed out of the wine cellar and drove them off, but it was clear that the whites had begun a ruthless counterattack. Word came to Turner that troops were marching on his position; he and his men retreated. First they attacked a farm, but five whites, barricaded inside, drove them off with fowling pieces. His numbers reduced, the slave general fled with the remnants of his army into the brush.

For three months white militiamen hunted Turner throughout Virginia. Reprisals against anyone who even sympathized with Turner and his men were vicious and quick. More than one hundred slaves were hanged, shot, or beaten to death. A few were drawn and quartered, their dissected bodies nailed to the entrance of certain slave quarters as a warning.

Turner was finally apprehended along with eighteen others in early November, 1831. He was condemned to death. Before his public hanging, Turner confessed to his crimes. In describing the 48-hour bloodbath, he stated:

"I took my station in the rear and it was my object to carry terror and devastation wherever we went. I placed fifteen or twenty of the best-armed and most to be relied on in front, who generally approached the houses as fast as their horses could run.

"This was for two purposes—to prevent their [whites] escape, and strike terror to the inhabitants . . . I sometimes got in sight to see the work of death completed . . . viewed the mangled bodies as they lay in silent satisfaction, and immediately started in quest of other victims. . . ."

TUTT, DAVID (OR DAVIS)
Gunfighter ● (? -1865)

Tutt had the reputation of a mean gunfighter a dozen years before he ran headlong into James Butler "Wild Bill" Hickok in Springfield, Mo. The cause of the argument between the two men is still uncertain.

Hickok had been recently mustered out of the Union Army and was apparently wooing a wild girl from the Ozarks, one Susannah Moore. Tutt, who was passing through town on his way West, was also attracted to Susannah's ravishing beauty. One report has it that the two men quarreled over her while playing cards and that Hickok challenged Tutt to face him in the town square at high noon. Tutt accepted.

At about noon on July 21, 1865, Tutt, whose background indicated that he had shot several men in similar duels, began walking toward Hickok who stood passively waiting for him in the middle of the square. It was *the* storybook gunfight which Hollywood would ceaselessly employ a century later.

Tutt went for his guns first (he wore two) and began banging away at Hickok. His hurried shots went wide. Hickok, who was to dispose of a plethora of gunmen in future cow towns, then displayed the coolness under fire that would make him legend. While Tutt was slinging slugs at him, Hickok carefully and slowly drew his own pistol and, holding it with both hands, took deliberate aim and squeezed off one round. The bullet hit Tutt square in the heart from an estimated distance of seventy-five yards, killing him instantly.

UDDERZOOK, WILLIAM E.
Murderer, Swindler ● (? -1873)

With his brother-in-law W. S. Goss, Udderzook entered into a plot to defraud an insurance company of $25,000. The Goss home—a small cottage in Baltimore, Md.—was burned to cinders in early 1873 and Mrs. Goss immediately pressed the Baltimore insurance company for payment, claiming her husband had been consumed by the flames.

The insurance company investigated and found the remains of a man who was totally unrecognizable. Company officials immediately smelled fraud, thinking the cadaver to be a corpse stolen from a nearby medical college (a technique perfected years later by mass murderer Herman W. Mudgett), but could prove nothing. The company refused to pay off and Mrs. Goss sued.

Though the jury awarded the sum to the bereaved Mrs. Goss, the insurance firm appealed. Authorities wanted time to find the living Goss, whom they suspected was in hiding. They were right. Udderzook had been secreting his brother-in-law in dozens of places for weeks, compelling Goss to don ridiculous disguises complete with flowing red beards, frocks, wigs, and false faces.

When the insurance detectives appeared to be catching up with the pair near Chester, Pa., Udderzook decided to make Goss's demise a reality. He beat Goss to death, and hurriedly buried the body in a wooded area. The grave was soon found and Udderzook was apprehended.

He was sentenced to death on the gallows. Before he was hanged Udderzook wrote an emotional appeal, requesting that his body be buried as close to that of his brother-in-law's as possible—"that our bodies may return to the mother dust, and our spirits may mingle together on the bright, sunny banks of deliverance, where pleasures never end."

UNDERHILL, WILBUR
Bankrobber ● (1897-1934)

Underhill was an impulsive bankrobber who belonged to the genre that produced Charles Arthur "Pretty Boy" Floyd of the Oklahoma Cookson Hills. He was known as the "Tri-State Terror" and robbed dozens of banks in Oklahoma, Kansas, and Arkansas with such other notorious bad men of 1930s as Ford Bradshaw, Bob Brady, Ed Newt Clanton, Aussie Elliott, Troy Love, Jim Benge, Jim Clark, and Tom Carlisle.

After robbing a number of small town banks in the late 1920s, Underhill was sent to the Kansas State Penitentiary at Lansing. In September, 1933, Underhill, Bob Brady, and Jim Clark escaped and went into hiding in the Cookson Hills. Underhill joined the Ford Bradshaw gang, and Brady and Clark decided to strike out on their own. On October 7, 1933 Clark was apprehended in Tucumari, N. M. Brady lasted until the following year, being surrounded by a posse on January 9, 1934 in Paoloa, Kan. He chose to make a fight of it and was torn to ribbons by a dozen shotgun blasts.

During the fall of 1933, Underhill, Bradshaw, and others went on a bankrobbing spree which included the banks in Stuttgart, Arkansas; Coalgate, Okla.; Helena, Kan.; and Okmulgee, Okla. On November 2, 1933, they took more than $13,000 from the Okmulgee bank vault.

Bankrobber Wilbur Underhill was known as the "Tri-State Terror." (UPI)

Underhill decided to marry his childhood sweetheart and with his loot moved to Shawnee, Okla. His honeymoon was interrupted by federal agents under the command of R. H. Colvin, who surrounded his cottage on New Year's Day 1934 and ordered him to surrender. Underhill answered them with two pistols spitting bullets. He darted from window to window for nearly a half hour, battling the agents who poured more than one thousand shells into the cottage. Leaking from a dozen wounds and wearing only his long underwear, Wilbur dashed from the house firing a shotgun and broke through the police cordon.

He staggered down a street, dove through the plate glass window of a furniture store, and there passed out. Taken to the hospital, he lingered for five days, dying in McAlester, Okla. on January 6, 1934. Told he was about to die, Underhill cryptically said with a sigh: "Tell the boys I'm coming home."

UNIONE SICILIANE

In the late 1880s, the Sicilian immigrants in New York organized a fraternal organization, the *Unione Siciliane*, to look after their special interests. Members paid small dues and received life insurance and attended social affairs sponsored by the *Unione*. Through the years the *Unione* became a political power and could exercise enough voting strength to win over several wards during elections.

Before the First World War, Ignazio Saietta ("Lupo the Wolf"), a vicious blackhanding terrorist, took over the *Unione* through murder and beatings. He turned the once peaceloving fraternity into a national crime cartel secretly operating among Sicilians in dozens of cities and active in white slavery, extortion, kidnapping, robbery, labor and union rackets, and murder, with umbilical ties to the Mafia.

Under Saietta's direction *Unione* thugs murdered close to seventy people in a six year period, according to the U.S. Secret Service, using the organization's offices in Harlem as a murder den where Saietta installed meathooks from which he would dangle his victims. The basement afforded another avenue of disposing bodies; Lupo the Wolf burned alive at least six Black Hand victims in the furnace there.

When Saietta was sent to prison in 1918, Brooklyn gangster Frankie Yale, a one-time partner of Johnny Torrio's in extortion, took over the *Unione* and broadened its criminal activities. Yale was to hold this all-powerful position for ten years until he was murdered by Al Capone's gunmen in New York.

Capone, a Neapolitan, was much disliked by many Sicilians. He therefore attempted to dominate the *Unione* in order to shore up his own criminal interests.

In the early 1920s, Mike Merlo was president of the *Unione* branch in Chicago. He was an on-and-off Capone ally and when he died in 1924, Angelo "Bloody Angelo" Genna of the six terrible Genna brothers, appointed himself president of the *Unione*. Genna was quickly killed in early 1925 by the North Side mob run by Earl "Hymie" Weiss, Bugs Moran, and Vin-

The 1925 gangster funeral of *Unione Siciliane* president Angelo "Bloody Angelo" Genna in Chicago. (UPI)

cent Drucci. He was replaced by another self-appointed president, Samuzzo "Samoots" Amatuna. Vincent Drucci killed Samoots in a barber shop months later. Upon Amatuna's death, Capone moved in and appointed Anthony Lombardo to the exalted post. Tony was a modest fellow who immediately penned his own brief autobiography and sent it out as a press release to all Chicago newspapers. It read:

"Chicago owes much of its progress and its hope of future greatness to the intelligence and industry of its 200,000 Italians, whose rise in prestige and importance is one of the modern miracles of a great city.

"No people have achieved so much from such small beginnings, or given so much for what they received in the land of promise to which many of them came penniless. Each life story is a romance, an epic of human accomplishment.

"Antonio Lombardo is one of the most outstanding of these modern conquerors . . . Mr. Lombardo came to America twenty-one years ago. He was one of hundreds who cheered joyously, when, from the deck of the steamer, they saw the Statue of Liberty, and the skyline of New York, their first sight of the fabled land, America. With his fellow countrymen he suffered the hardships and indignities to which the United States subjects its prospective citizens at Ellis Island without complaint, for in his heart was a great hope and a great ambition.

"After he landed, he paid his railroad fare to Chicago, and came here with just $12 as his initial capital . . . Mr. Lombardo, however, accepted the hardships as part of the game, and with confidence in his own ability and assurance of unlimited opportunities, began his career . . . He became an importer and exporter . . . His political influence is due largely to his interest in civic affairs and his championship of measures for maintaining and improving standards of living, as well as his activity in the support of charities and benevolent institutions. Like most successful men, he has received much, but has given more to the community in which he lives. It is to such men that Chicago owes her greatness."

One of Lombardo's "interests in civic affairs" was apparently acting as a go-between for Blackhanders and their victims. A sewer contractor, A. Frank Ranieri, was informed by Blackhanders that they had kidnapped his ten-year-old son, William, and were holding him for $50,000 ransom. Desperate, Ranieri attempted to raise the money, gleaning only $10,000 from every available source. He spread the word that he was unable to raise more and begged advice.

An unidentified caller phoned Ranieri on September 6, 1928 and said only two words before hanging up: "See Lombardo."

Ranieri raced to the Unione headquarters and, after he had explained his mission, was told by a secretary to return the following day. "The Chief will have some word for you by then," the girl told him.

The distraught father waited the next day in Lombardo's office but Tony Lombardo was absent. Ranieri never did see Lombardo until the day after, when he spotted a newspaper picture of his lifeless body lying on the sidewalk at State and Madison. He did, however, pay off the Blackhanders and retrieve his son.

Lombardo had taken an evening stroll September 7, 1928 on Dearborn Street with two bodyguards, Joseph Lolordo and Joseph Ferraro. As they turned onto the "World's Busiest Corner," State and Madison, with thousands of people streaming by, two men came up behind the trio and opened fire. Two dum-dum bullets crashed into Lombardo's brain, killing him instantly. Ferraro, wounded in the spine, was helpless next to him. He drew his .45 automatic but was so weak from the loss of blood that he feebly dropped the weapon. He, too, died that day. Lolordo, unharmed, drew his gun and chased the killers, but Patrolman John Marcusson, thinking him to be one of the murderers, arrested him.

Pasqualino Lolordo assumed the presidency of the Unione next; he, too, met Lombardo's fate. Joseph Aiello and his brothers much coveted the Unione leadership and the three Aiellos went calling on Lolordo on January 8, 1929.

Thinking the Aiellos his close friends, Lolordo invited them into his home at 1921 W. North Avenue. Lolordo's wife, Aleina, brought the four men sandwiches, relishes, pastries, wine, and a box of cigars.

Lolordo closed the door to his den and his wife could hear the foursome enjoying themselves for close to an hour. There was much laughter and toasting. Joseph Aiello lifted his glass and shouted, "Here's to Pasqualino!"

Beaming, the Unione president lifted his glass of wine to his lips and at that precise moment three guns barked in unison. The Aiellos emptied their revolvers into the shocked Lolordo, eleven bullets hitting him in the face, neck, and shoulders. He fell dead.

Mrs. Lolordo ran down the hall and threw open the door to the den. The Aiellos rudely shoved her aside. Joe Aiello tossed a .38 revolver into the room and the brothers departed, casually stepping into the street and talking unexcitedly among themselves. Later, Mrs. Lolordo told police she had never met them before.

Joseph Aiello took over the Unione the following day. He lasted until October 23, 1930 when Capone machinegunners found him leaving a friend's home on Kolmar Avenue and stitched his body with a hundred shells.

The position of President of the Unione became so lethal that occupants became increasingly hard to find. The Unione, which had changed its name to the Italo-American National Union in 1924, began to ebb as a power in the early 1930s and became totally impotent when the great, dark Depression settled over the land.

UNRUH, HOWARD
Murderer ● (1921-   )

BACKGROUND: BORN AND RAISED IN CAMDEN, NEW JERSEY. GRADUATED PUBLIC HIGH SCHOOL. SERVED AS A TANK GUNNER IN ARMORED DIVISION, DISTINGUISHING HIMSELF IN BATTLES DURING THE ITALIAN CAMPAIGN AND THE BATTLE OF THE BULGE. PREPARED TO ENTER TEMPLE UNIVERSITY AFTER WORLD WAR II TO STUDY PHARMACY WHILE LIVING WITH HIS PARENTS. DESCRIPTION: 6'2", BLUE EYES, BROWN HAIR, SLENDER BUILD. ALIASES: NONE. RECORD: USING A 9MM GERMAN LUGER, UNRUH KILLED 13 PEOPLE IN TWELVE MINUTES ON THE STREETS OF CAMDEN, N.J., 9/6/49 AND THEN SURRENDERED TO POLICE; NEVER BROUGHT TO TRIAL BUT SENT TO NEW JERSEY STATE MENTAL HOSPITAL AT TRENTON FOR LIFE.

He was a Bible reader. Throughout his youth he had been a quiet boy, withdrawn, reserved, expressionless. An only child, he had religion ingrained into his daily life by his parents. He lived in Camden, New Jersey and before he was uprooted from his home like so many other millions by World War II, Howard Unruh planned on going to college.

Just out of high school, Unruh was called up and went willingly into the army. He was introduced to weapons for the first time and they infatuated him.

Howard Unruh became a sharpshooter early in his training. Fellow GIs would notice him sitting quietly in his barracks bunk fondling his rifle, taking it apart, cleaning it lovingly, and putting it back together.

The young soldier never went out with the rest of the soldiers to look for girls. He stayed in the barracks, read his Bible, and cleaned his rifle. Finally, he was shipped overseas and fought up the boot of Italy as a machinegunner in a tank. German resistance was tough but Howard didn't mind. He enjoyed his work.

After Italy it was France, and Howard Unruh's tank contingent helped to liberate Bastogne in the violent and bloody Battle of the Bulge. A fellow soldier, who later became a policeman in New York, remembered sneaking a look into Unruh's diary—a private day-to-day account of his life.

The friend was shocked. Unruh had listed all of the Germans he had personally killed with his machinegun, the day he killed them, the hour, the place, and how they looked in death.

When the war ended, Unruh was honorably discharged and given several commendations for his cool service under fire. Little was said or noted of him upon his return to Camden. He was just another serviceman being mustered out.

Howard's only immediate plan was to become a pharmacist. He kept to himself, brushed up on some high school refresher courses, and entered Temple University in Philadelphia.

He continued his Bible Class studies, where he met and dated the only girl in his life—a mild flirtation that led nowhere. Unruh grew embittered and by 1949 he had become a recluse in his own home, never talking to his parents. His one recreation was acquiring weapons and setting up his targets in the basement where he practiced his excellent marksmanship daily.

The smallest slights from the neighbors, people he had known all his life, became raging insults to Howard. His mind imagined great wrongs and he slowly sank into what doctors later termed acute paranoia and schizophrenia.

Just as he had kept a death list during the war, Unruh began another diary, this time entering all the petty grievances he had with his neighbors.

Once, while cutting through the backyard of his next-door neighbor, Unruh was startled to hear Mrs. Cohen yell at him, "Hey, you! Do you have to go through the yard?"

Howard gritted his teeth and said nothing. It was another item to add to his hate list. He wrote it down next to all the "violations" the Cohens had committed against him, such as their Christmas gift to their twelve-year-old son: a new bugle.

Howard hated the sound of the bugle. It was a serious offense in his book. After each offense, Howard jotted down the abbreviation, "retal"—retaliate.

But Howard didn't retaliate, not immediately. He tried desperately to seal himself away from the imagined insults of his neighbors by constructing a high wooden fence around the pathetically small Unruh backyard.

He labored long and hard, with his father's assistance, to build a massive gate that would lock away the rest of the world.

Its completion was his one triumph—next to the ample arsenal he kept in his room: a $40 9mm German Luger with several clips, several pistols, a large hunting knife, and a massive machete, honed razor-sharp.

Disaster struck when Howard came home at 3 a.m. on September 5, 1949. Someone had stolen his elaborate gate—now there was only a gaping hole leering at him. Of course, it was the work of local pranksters but Howard, as usual, kept silent and blamed the neighbors with hatred fanned to white heat. He went to his room and as he sprawled on his bed, eyes wide open at the ceiling, the reality of the world he had tried to close out blinked off forever in Howard Unruh's mind.

He did not know who had stolen his gate but he did conclude exactly who had been hurting him emotionally for the past four years . . . so he decided to kill them all.

Unruh decided to kill his mother, too. It would spare her the grief of what he was about to do.

At 8 a.m. Howard went down to breakfast. His mother had prepared eggs and cereal for him. He sat down and stared at her. The desperation and wild hate inside of him blazed like a torch and she sensed it.

Suddenly, he wheeled from his chair, ran to the basement, and, eyes still blazing, walked upstairs and toward his mother. She became hysterical and ran from the Unruh home to a neighbor's where she confided her fears.

Unruh was disturbed. His mother's reaction had fouled up his schedule. He would have to begin earlier than planned.

Methodically, Unruh went to his room and loaded his Luger and another pistol. He placed them into his pocket along with a knife. He jammed spare clips into the other pocket. He was ready.

Howard walked outside, through his backyard, and vaulted the fence he had built instead of merely walking through the open area where the gate had been.

By 9:20 a.m. Unruh arrived at a small shoeshop only a few doors away from his home. Cobbler John Pilarchik was busy repairing children's shoes for the school season.

The shoemaker had just finished paying for the shop. He looked up to see the tall, 28-year-old Unruh standing in his doorway, the bright sunny day filtering past him. It was his last mortal vision.

Howard lifted his arm mechanically, the Luger pointing toward the little cobbler. He squeezed the trigger twice and Pilarchik fell to the floor, dead.

Unruh turned about quickly and walked out. At the door next to Pilarchik's shop, he paused and turned in. Barber Clark Hoover, a man who had known Howard most of his life (as had Pilarchik), blinked as he spotted the deadly Luger in Unruh's hand.

Hoover tried to shield the little boy perched on a plastic horse in the barber chair. Mrs. Edward Smith and her eleven-year-old daughter stood by in shock.

Unruh raised the Luger and shot six-year-old Orris Smith in the head. Then, expressionless, he shot the barber in the head and body.

He ignored the screams of Mrs. Smith as she held her dead little boy in her arms and walked calmly back out onto the pleasant Camden street. Hurriedly now, Unruh moved toward the corner drugstore owned and operated by the man he hated most, his next-door neighbor, Cohen.

But before he could enter, James Hutton came out and blocked his path. Hutton had known Howard for years—he was the Unruh's insurance agent.

"Hello, Howard," Hutton said.

"Excuse me," Unruh said.

Hutton's eyes bulged when he saw the Luger in Unruh's hand. The insurance man was petrified. Unruh was annoyed. He had nothing personal against Hutton, but he was in the way. Unruh fired twice. The insurance man fell to the sidewalk with fatal wounds in his head and body. Unruh's marksmanship was true.

Cohen had seen the cold-blooded murder in front of his shop and ran upstairs to warn his family. Not finding the druggist in his shop, Howard plodded up the steps to his apartment, carefully inserting another clip into his Luger.

Mrs. Cohen hid in one closet and her son hid in another. Unruh listened quietly and heard her move. He fired once through the door, opened it to see the woman sag to the floor, and then shot her again through the head.

The Cohen boy ran to his father.

Unruh moved into the next room and found the elderly Mrs. Cohen on the phone trying to call police. His Luger thundered twice again. The phone in Mrs. Cohen's hand slapped the table as she released it and she sank to the floor dead.

Howard was again annoyed. He had not found Mr. Cohen. Then he heard desperate scraping and looked out a window. He saw Cohen and his boy trying to escape across a sloping roof.

Unruh aimed carefully and fired a bullet into Mr. Cohen's back. Cohen fell to the sidewalk. Howard wanted to make sure with this victim; he took deadly aim again and sent another bullet into Cohen's head.

He ignored the Cohen boy, who clung to the roof screaming.

Unruh retraced his steps until he emerged in front of the drugstore. There, Alvin Day had stopped his car to help the man lying on the sidewalk—James Hutton, a man beyond help.

Day's Good Samaritanism was fatal. Howard Unruh shot him to death. He again reloaded and proceeded across the street, at a leisurely stroll. He saw a car waiting for the light to change.

Unruh walked over to it and leaned in the window. The horror-struck woman driver stared into the barrel of his Luger. He fired once, killing her. Then he poked the weapon inside and emptied it into the woman's elderly mother and her ten-year-old son who were in the back seat. Both were killed instantly.

Then, acting as if he were on a Sunday walk, Unruh recrossed the street. He noticed a truckdriver climbing out of his cab a block away. He fired one round—a long shot—in his direction and dropped him with a wound in the leg.

He seemed to be walking in circles now. He was back to the cobbler's store. He moved on to the next shop, after unsuccessfully trying to get through the locked doors of a supermarket and bar-restaurant (proprietors and patrons huddled in fear behind the closed doors). He had blasted the bar door twice but the lock held.

The next shop was the tailor's, operated by Tom Fegrino who was away. But his wife was hiding in the back room. He found her there on her knees, begging.

"Oh, my God, don't," she said to him.

He didn't blink an eye as he banged two shots into her, ending her life.

By now most of the residents of the neigh-

Howard Unruh at Camden Police Headquarters 9/6/49.

borhood had taken refuge behind locked doors against the madman. However, when Unruh walked outside again he spotted three-year-old Tommy Hamilton standing at a nearby window. Unruh's stare met that of the boy. He fired once, the bullet smashing the glass and killing the child immediately.

It was then that Howard realized that he was running low on ammunition. He walked to a nearby house and found Mrs. Madeline Harris with her two sons in the kitchen. Mrs. Harris' older son, a brave lad, dove for the tall killer.

Unruh shot twice, wounding the boy and his mother. He sauntered from the house and then broke into a light trot toward his home. Far in the distance, perhaps not at all in Unruh's twisted mind, could be heard the wail of police sirens.

Howard again vaulted the fence at the rear of his home and climbed the stairs to his room where he barricaded the door and reloaded.

The police arrived outside.

At this moment, the dogged editor of the

Camden *Courier Post*, who had already been informed of the berserk killer's identity, called Howard Unruh. It was one of the strangest phone conversations in the annals of crime.

"Hello," Unruh said picking up the phone.

"Is this Howard?" editor Phillip Buxton said.

"Yes, this is Howard. What is the last name of the party you want?" Unruh's voice was calm and courteous.

"Unruh."

"Who are you and what do you want?"

"I'm a friend," Buxton said smoothly, "and I want to know what they're doing to you."

"Well, they haven't done anything to me yet, but I'm doing plenty to them."

"How many have you killed?"

"I don't know yet—I haven't counted 'em, but it looks like a pretty good score." The score was thirteen killed in a space of 12 minutes.

Buxton went on, writing everything down wildly. "Why are you killing people, Howard?"

There was a short silence and then Unruh said, "I don't know. I can't answer that yet—I am too busy. I'll have to talk to you later." He hung up the receiver.

By now police were heaving tear gas cannisters through the windows of his tiny room. Their small-arms fire cracked into the cheap plaster all about him. Unruh stared down at the weapons in his hands, shrugged, and then took down the barricade and walked out.

Over fifty guns were trained on him as he walked forward, hands high in the air.

Police frisked him and held him. Detective Vince Connelly stared at the good-looking young man. "What's the matter with you?" Connelly said with a quaking voice as he looked around at the dead bodies littering the street. "Are you a psycho?"

Howard Unruh was offended. "I'm no psycho. I have a good mind."

But Howard Unruh, Bible student, courageous war veteran, killer, did not have a good mind at all. According to twenty medical specialists he was incurably insane.

Unruh never faced trial. He was placed in the New Jersey State Mental Hospital for life, where he now resides.

Is he sorry for the mass murder he committed? He answered that one on the day he told a psychiatrist: "I'd have killed a thousand if I'd had bullets enough."

VALACHI, JOSEPH MICHAEL
Syndicate Gangster ● (1904-1971)

BACKGROUND: BORN 9/22/04 IN NEW YORK CITY. MINOR PUBLIC EDUCATION. DESCRIPTION: 5'6", BROWN EYES, BROWN-GREY HAIR, STOCKY. ALIASES: JOE CARGO, JOE CAGO, ANTHONY SORGE, MICHAEL VALACHI, JOE KATO, JOE SIANO. RECORD: ARRESTED 11/10/21 IN JERSEY CITY, N.J. FOR CARRYING CONCEALED WEAPONS, FINED $100 AND PLACED ON PROBATION; ARRESTED FOR BURGLARY IN BRONX, N.Y. 8/17/23; CONVICTED AND SENTENCED TO ONE TO TWO YEARS IN SING SING ON 10/23/23, PAROLED 8/20/24; ARRESTED FOR BURGLARY, IN NEW YORK, 4/9/25; SENTENCED TO THREE YEARS IN SING SING, PAROLED 6/15/28; ARRESTED FOR ARMED ROBBERY 3/14/29 IN NYC, DISCHARGED; ARRESTED IN NYC FOR ASSAULT AND BATTERY 9/29/29, DISCHARGED; TOOK AN ACTIVE PART IN SEVERAL SLAYINGS DURING THE CASTELLEMMARESE WAR BETWEEN SALVATORE MARANZANO AND GIUSEPPE "JOE THE BOSS" MASSERIA, 1930-31; MURDERED WITH THREE OTHERS MICHAEL "LITTLE APPLES" REGGIONE ON 11/25/32; WORKED AS A "SOLDIER" UNDER TONY BENDER (ANTHONY STROLLO) IN THE LUCKY LUCIANO FAMILY OF THE NYC MAFIA-COSA NOSTRA, 1931-59; INVOLVED IN POLICY, GAMBLING, NARCOTICS, AND OTHER ILLEGAL ACTIVITIES IN THE GREENWICH VILLAGE AREA IN THE 1940S AND 1950S; ARRESTED IN NYC FOR ROBBERY, 1/13/36, DISMISSED; ARRESTED FOR PEDDLING NARCOTICS IN BROOKLYN, N.Y., 11/1/44, DISMISSED; ARRESTED IN DALTO, MD., 3/23/48 ON NARCOTICS CHARGES, DISMISSED; MURDERED WITH THREE OTHERS, EUGENIO GIANNINI ON 9/20/52; MURDERED WITH OTHERS STEVEN FRANSE IN GREENWICH VILLAGE ON 6/19/53; ARRESTED 5/20/55 FOR NARCOTICS PEDDLING, SENTENCED TO FIVE YEARS IN PRISON AND A $10,000 FINE; ARRESTED SEVERAL TIMES IN THE 1950S FOR VIOLATION OF NARCOTICS LAWS AND RELEASED; ARRESTED 11/19/69 BY FEDERAL OFFICERS FOR VIOLATING NARCOTICS LAWS; CONVICTED AND SENT TO THE FEDERAL PRISON IN ATLANTA, GA. FOR FIFTEEN YEARS AND FINED $10,000;

MURDERED ATLANTA PRISON INMATE JOHN JOSEPH SAUPP ON 6/22/62; DIED OF A HEART ATTACK IN LA TUNA FEDERAL PRISON IN TEXAS IN 1971.

"Someone put a gun and a knife on the table in front of me. I remember the gun was a .38, and the knife was what you call a dagger. After that, Maranzano motions us up again, and we all hold hands and he says some words in Italian. Then we sit down and, he turns to me, still in Italian, and talks about the gun and knife. 'This represents that you live by the gun and the knife,' he says, 'and you die by the gun and the knife.'

"Next he asked me, 'Which finger do you shoot with?'

"I said, 'This one,' and I hold up my right forefinger.

"I was still wondering what he meant by this when he told me to make a cup out of my hands. Then he put a piece of paper in them and lit it with a match and told me to say after him, as I was moving the paper back and forth, 'This is the way I will burn if I betray the secret of this Cosa Nostra.' "

In his own words, this is the way Joseph Valachi became part of the dreaded Mafia society, known in the Eastern states as the Cosa Nostra. [SEE Camorra, Tony Notaro's description of initiation rites.]

Salvatore Maranzano, the man who administered the blood oath in his baronial estate in upstate New York, was at that time conducting a full-scale war against top Mafia chieftain Joe the Boss Masseria. It was 1930 and Prohibition was going full blast. Maranzano was organizing all of the anti-Masseria New York gangs against Joe the Boss and also laying the foundation of the modern Mafia or Cosa Nostra.

The inside workings of this Cosa Nostra—meaning "our thing" or "this thing of ours" was first revealed to a shocked nation by Joseph Valachi who sang a loud and unheard-of song to a Senate Investigations subcommittee in 1962. Joe Cago, (Valachi's syndicate name) also sang on every important gangster in the crime cartel.

His was a story of brutal murder, corruption, and organized crime on a scale so vast and held together so strongly by blood oaths and "kiss of death" techniques, that America reeled in horror. (Valachi's "facts," however, offered little fresh information to the overall picture of the syndicate.)

Valachi was a man who had lived in constant fear ever since the syndicate tried to exterminate him in Sing Sing. After receiving a "carving" from a fellow inmate in the Twenties on the specific orders of the Artichoke King and gangster, Ciro Terranova, Valachi made a deal.

He took no action against his attacker, Peter LaTempa, a Mafia hit man. (LaTempa later decided to testify against Mafia don Vito Genovese and was poisoned to death in his jail cell.) Valachi played ball with everyone and was finally taken into the Salvatore Maranzano gang when the younger mobsters—Willie Moretti, Tommy Lucchese, and finally Joe the Boss' own lieutenants, Vito Genovese and Charles "Lucky" Luciano—made up their minds to get rid of Masseria.

Valachi's criminal career began when he was fifteen; he had no formal schooling and was constantly in jail or at the sides of gangsters. He survived an incredibly long period of time.

This may be due to the fact that he always remained a strong-armed type, a muscleman, a hit artist, and never rose to a rank of authority. The ones who did, with only a few exceptions like Luciano and Genovese, did not survive. And it was Genovese who finally drove Valachi to squeal.

Valachi was essentially a policy or numbers racket man who helped to take over Dutch Schultz's Harlem empire of numbers after the Dutchman was killed in 1935. But during the Thirties, Valachi graduated to narcotics peddling. During the war he bought and sold ration stamps and coupons that netted him $100,000 a year. Then it was back to narcotics.

After several arrests on narcotics charges, Valachi was safely tucked away in Atlanta Federal Prison to rot. It was in Atlanta where Valachi's problems really began.

Even though Joe Bonanno (also known as family chief Joe Bananas) had sponsored him and was his "gombah," his godfather, that long ago night in Maranzano's home, he could not help or protect Valachi from the insane wrath of Vito Genovese. There was only one gang overlord in Atlanta—Vito Genovese, the most feared man in the Cosa Nostra. It was Vito who with Lucky Luciano had killed his own leader, Joe the Boss. It was Vito who was the only man powerful enough in the syndicate to order the deaths of other gang chiefs—Willie Moretti, Albert Anastasia (who headed up Murder, Inc.), and even crime czar, Frank Costello.

Though Genovese was serving time at Atlanta, he was still in power. Cons had to report to Vito every day and they made appointments. When speaking with him in the yard, they backed courteously away from him after the conversation was ended.

His laundry and his chores were done for him; his food was specially prepared. Luciano was in exile in Italy and Genovese was in jail, but they were both still running things.

Cosa Nostra hit man and informer Joseph Valachi testifying before the Senate Investigations Subcommittee in 1963. (UPI)

Valachi was singled out for persecution by Genovese. The minor muscleman thought it was because of his former association with other Cosa Nostra members. He was right.

He pleaded and argued with the Mafia chieftain, that he meant him no ill will, that he hadn't informed on Genovese's narcotics operations as "Don Vito" suspected. Geneovese said nothing.

Genovese, still believing Valachi was part of a Mafia faction against him, invited him into his cell one night. Valachi later recalled the chilling conversation: "Vito starts saying to me, 'You know, we take a barrel of apples, and in this barrel of apples there might be a bad apple. Well, this apple has to be removed, and if it ain't removed, it would hurt the rest of the apples.' "

Valachi was terrified. He knew what Genovese meant and tried to stop him from going on. He blurted, "If I done anything wrong show it to me and bring me the pills—meaning poison—and I will take them in front of you."

"He said, 'Who said you done anything wrong?' " Valachi later recounted.

"Then he said to me that we had known each other for a long time and he wanted to give me a kiss for old time's sake. Okay, I said to myself, two can play the game. So I grabbed Vito and kissed him back.

"After I did this, he asked me, 'How many grand-kids you got?'

"I said, 'Three, how many you got?' I think he said six. So I said, 'It's good to know.' In other words, if he's going to be concentrating on my grand-kids, I'm letting him know I'll concentrate on his."

But Valachi wasn't fooling anyone. Genovese had the power to have him murdered anytime right there in prison. Valachi asked for the hole, solitary confinement, and got it. He brooded. Even in the hole he wasn't safe. Finally, he was released, and, thinking one of Genovese's men, Joseph DiPalermo, was waiting for him, he picked up a pipe in the exercise yard and killed him on June 22, 1962. He had killed the wrong man, John Joseph Saupp, a forger who resembled DiPalermo.

The killing brought Valachi to the attention of federal investigators, who questioned him. His fear of Genovese was so great that he cracked, singing a song the Mafia is not likely ever to forget.

Month after month he squealed in Washington for the Justice Department. Genovese put a $100,000 price tag on his head for anyone who could get to him. But the authorities were careful and placed Valachi in a maximum security cell in Atlanta, later moving him to La Tuna Federal Prison in Texas.

It was here that Joseph Valachi died of a heart attack. The ex Cosa Nostra "soldier" had no regrets and lived long enough to see Vito Genovese die of old age in Atlanta.

Just before his death, a reporter asked Valachi what would happen if the prison authorities had not taken special precautions with his custody. The old gangster grinned ruefully.

"I'd have to kill or be killed. If they got me, I wouldn't last five minutes."

But nobody ever got Joe Valachi, ironically, even in death. Not one person in the world wanted to claim his body.

[ALSO SEE The Camorra, Frank Costello, Vito Genovese, The Mafia, Salvatore Maranzano, Raymond Patriarca, Anthony Strollo (Tony Bender), Ciro Terranova.]

VAN VALKENBURGH, ELIZABETH
Murderer ● (? -1846)

Mrs. Van Valkenburgh became annoyed with her husband and spiked his tea with arsenic—which killed him. She was indifferent at her trial, claiming that she had poisoned her husband to cure him of his drinking.

In addition to the murder of John Van Valkenburgh, Elizabeth admitted to killing a former husband in the same fashion and for the same reasons. It was never learned whether or not zealous temperance leaders were ever reached for comment on Mrs. Van Valkenburgh's drastic measures to reform drunks.

Elizabeth was hanged January 24, 1846 in Fulton, N. Y.

VASQUEZ, TIBURCIO
Murderer, Bandit ● (? -1875)

California bandit Tiburcio Vasquez. (Denver Public Library)

A robber since his teens, Tiburcio Vasquez was released from San Quentin in 1870 and immediately launched a five-year spree of holdups in Southern California. Amazingly, Vasquez's dozens of robberies never ended in violence. This changed on August 26, 1873 when, with a band of men, the outlaw invaded the hamlet of Tres Pinos (also called Paicines), looting the town and killing three unarmed residents: George Redford and two others named Davidson and Martin.

Giant rewards were offered for the capture of Vasquez and dozens of posses combed the Cahuenga Pass, his reputed hiding place. Before his capture, Vasquez hit yet another town, Kingston, robbing the local hotel and all the stores. As he and his men made for their mountain hideout, they robbed several stages and travelers.

A posse led by George Beers, a sharpshooter, cornered the band in Cahuenga Pass (now the site of Hollywood) and shot it out with the outlaws. Beers brought down Vasquez himself with a shotgun blast but the outlaw leader lived to face trial for the murders of the three Tres Pinos men. He was found guilty and sentenced to hang.

His execution took place at San Jose, Calif., March 19, 1875.

WADDELL, REED
Swindler ● (1859-1895)

Waddell was the son of a wealthy Springfield, Illinois family. He was college trained and was expected to enter the family business. Gambling and confidence games, however, were the primary interests of Waddell, and he was ostracized by his family for the many scams he perpetrated in Springfield. Journeying to New York, Waddell was the first to employ the gold brick con game.

He had a lead brick triple gold-plated and made up with a rough finish. A hole was cut out of the brick and a gold plug inserted. The brick was stamped "U.S." in the same fashion the United States Assayer's Office marked authentic gold bricks. With this device, Waddell approached the gullible and offered to sell his brick, a family keepsake, he said, to shore up debts. If the sucker was suspicious, Waddell dug out the gold plug and suggested the dupe check it with a jeweler. Invariably, he did and was amazed to find out that the metal was, indeed, solid gold.

Waddell sold his first gold brick for $4,000. Inside of ten years, the sharper made $250,000 through the sale of his spurious bricks. He moved to Paris to fleece more suckers but was killed there in March, 1895 by gambler Tom O'Brien in an argument over a rigged banco game.

WANDERER, CARL OTTO
Murderer ● (1887-1921)

BACKGROUND: BORN AND RAISED IN CHICAGO. GRADE SCHOOL EDUCATION. ORIGINAL OCCUPATION, BUTCHER. SERVED IN THE FIRST ILLINOIS CAVALRY DURING PERSHING'S CAMPAIGN AGAINST PANCHO VILLA IN 1916; SERVED AS A LIEUTENANT OF INFANTRY IN WORLD WAR I ON THE WESTERN FRONT, EARNING SEVERAL IMPORTANT CITATIONS FOR HEROIC DUTY. DESCRIPTION: 5'10", BROWN EYES, BROWN HAIR (BALDING), SLIGHT BUILD. ALIASES: NONE. RECORD: SHOT AND KILLED HIS WIFE AND AN UNKNOWN DRIFTER 6/21/20 IN A BIZARRE PLOT DESIGNED TO THROW GUILT ON ANOTHER MAN; APPREHENDED THROUGH THE EFFORTS OF NEWSMEN AND CONVICTED OF MURDER; EXECUTED BY HANGING ON THE GALLOWS IN CHICAGO, 3/19/21.

Probably no other murder case in the country was solved in a more colorful manner than the one that dealt with the Ragged Stranger. Thanks to the ingenuity, suspicious natures, and natural cunning of two of America's finest reporters, Ben Hecht and Charles MacArthur, one of Chicago's most ruthless murderers was brought to justice.

Carl Otto Wanderer looked like anything but a murderer. He came from a penny-conscious German family and by the time he was twenty-seven years old had saved enough money to begin a successful butcher shop with his father. In 1916, adventure called to Wanderer when he read about how Pancho Villa had raided the United States, and how American volunteers were sought to pursue his wild bands.

Wanderer enlisted and went to the Southwest to serve under Black Jack Pershing as a cavalry soldier. His experience with the First Illinois Cavalry gave him enough military stature to become a lieutenant with the first American units sent to France when the U.S. entered World War I.

He saw action on the western front and by the time he returned home in the spring of 1919 his chest was coated with medals.

In the fall of that year, Wanderer, then thirty-two, married pretty Ruth Johnson, twenty, and the couple moved into an apartment shared by Ruth's parents. Before Christmas, Ruth told her husband that he would be a father the following summer.

Wanderer did not rejoice. Instead he fell into somber, sullen moods, rarely speaking. This went on for several months until the night of June 21, 1920.

That night Wanderer and Ruth were returning from a movie. They didn't notice the man who followed them into the dark vestibule of their apartment building.

"My wife was feeling for the hall switch," Wanderer later reported to police, "when I heard a voice say, 'Don't turn on the light.' I reached for my gun."

The war hero said that he heard the man shout out a string of obscenities and then the stranger fired once at them. This was followed by several more shots from the stranger's gun. Carl whipped out his Colt .45 service automatic which he habitually carried with him, emptying the clip in the direction of the intruder.

Fourteen bullets roared in heavy explosions in the space of a few seconds. Ruth's mother rushed down to the small vestibule to find Ruth on the floor with two bullets in her. Wanderer was berserk with rage, smashing his gun and fists against a man dressed in rags who was also on the floor, shot full of holes.

Ruth Wanderer lived just long enough to utter the pathetic words: "My baby. . . . my baby is dead."

The stranger in the hallway was rushed to Raveswood Hospital where he died without speaking. In his pockets, police found only $3.80.

It was an unspeakable crime, especially in 1920. Here was a great war hero who had fought to protect America from its enemies left destitute by the murder of his lovely wife and unborn child, even though he valiantly fought and slew the killer.

It was a heartless, devastating crime and the public reacted in shock and outrage. Wanderer was praised for his bravery. Poor, poor Carl Wanderer.

The story was big for the Chicago press. Every newspaper in town gave it great gulps of space. Even the two weapons used in the shooting, both big .45-caliber automatics, were photographed side by side.

Ben Hecht was sitting at his desk in the vast city room of the *Daily News*, looking over the story. He kept turning back to the picture of the two automatics. Something was not right with the photo.

Then he remembered that the Ragged Stranger had but $3.80 in his pockets when killed by Wanderer. It occurred to Hecht that a man down on his luck would hock a hefty automatic for $15 or more rather than risk being shot up by a war hero known to carry a gun.

It didn't make sense. Hecht reasoned that Wanderer's automatic was merely his army-issued sidearm which he kept with him out of habit. But it was more than curious that the Ragged Stranger had an identical weapon in his hand at the time of the murder.

Charles MacArthur, who worked for the rival *Examiner*, also thought the story of the two automatics suspicious. He called the Colt Arms Manufacturing Company and gave the firm the serial number of the stranger's gun. He was told that the weapon was first sold in 1913 to a sporting goods store in Chicago.

MacArthur checked with the store and found that the gun had been bought by one Peter Hoffman, a telephone repairman who lived on Crawford Avenue.

The next day, MacArthur went to see Hoffman and discovered that Hoffman had sold the gun to a mailman several years before. The mailman was Fred Wanderer, Carl's cousin.

MacArthur confronted Fred Wanderer who told him that the weapon was his and that he had loaned it to his cousin the day Ruth Johnson Wanderer was murdered. When he realized the implication of such information the cousin collapsed in a dead faint.

There was still a chance that Wanderer was not involved. The guns might have gotten mixed up. Hecht, who had interviewed the war hero several times after the shooting, went to see Carl Wanderer. He walked up the back porchway. The Johnsons' back porch door was open and Hecht stood there as he listened to Carl Wanderer hum and happily whistle through the screen door.

When Hecht showed himself he could see Wanderer, shirtless, ironing a pair of pants.

"Hi," Hecht said amiably. "Mind if I come in?"

"Oh, Mr. Hecht," Wanderer said in a pleasant voice. "Sure come in. What is it?"

"Just a few more routine questions for a follow-up story. I hope you don't mind."

Wanderer smiled. "No, not at all."

It was unreal. Only a few days ago, Hecht thought, this man's young wife and unborn child had been shot to death by a cold-blooded killer and here he was happy as a lark.

"Mind if I use your bathroom, Carl?"

Wanderer pointed to a small door off the hall. "Help yourself, Mr. Hecht."

Hecht went into the washroom and as he pondered the curiosities of the weapons and Wanderer's attitude he noticed something strange sticking from a bathrobe that belonged to the war hero. He reached forward and withdrew a woman's silk stocking from the pocket. Then another. Then he discovered lipstick, rouge, mascara, all the essential make-up items that women habitually carry around.

Then he found some incriminating letters Wanderer had written . . . to a man. Love letters of deep devotion. Standing there in that cramped little bathroom, holding these strange items all taken from Wanderer's bathrobe pocket, Hecht realized that the war hero was a wild-eyed homosexual.

That would account for a lot of things, Hecht reasoned. He walked out to Wanderer and talked to him briefly and then he raced to police headquarters. MacArthur arrived at about the same time. MacArthur told Lieutenant Mike Loftus of the discrepancies in the gun traced to the Ragged Stranger. Hecht felt Wanderer was a confirmed homosexual and that he had arranged for his wife's death.

The police brought Wanderer in for questioning.

Wanderer told the police that, sure, Fred's weapon was the one he used. The other one used by the Ragged Stranger, who was yet to be identified, was mistakenly identified as his.

That was a possibility. The other .45 automatic had been part of a massive shipment sent to several training camps during the war.

"It's all a mistake, don't you see?" Wanderer said innocently.

While police interrogated Wanderer, Hecht had learned that Ruth Wanderer had withdrawn $1,500 from her own account—money she had saved before marrying Carl—at the Second Security Bank the morning before she was killed.

Hecht ran back to the Johnson apartment and ransacked Wanderer's bedroom. He found the money taped to the back of Wanderer's bureau behind a shirt drawer.

He took his find to the police.

Confronted with this, Wanderer still protested his innocence. Then Hecht threw down the female items he had found in Wanderer's room and the letters to his homosexual lover whose name was James.

"James is coming to see you," Hecht bluffed. "I just talked with him." Hecht had no idea who and where James was.

Wanderer's hands shook, the blood drained from his face. "No, not here. Don't let him come here . . . Oh, My God!"

Then Carl Otto Wanderer confessed. He told the police that he had always been homosexual and that he had married Ruth for her money, that he hated her, he hated all women. The idea of having a child by a woman, he said, was repugnant to him. It disgusted him and sickened him. He was in love with James.

He arranged for her death very simply. He said he hung around several skid row bars until he met a drifter named Al Watson, a Canadian ex-soldier down on his luck. Wanderer had a way for him to make money.

His wife had begun to doubt his war record and his image as a hero, Wanderer said he told Watson. It was his feminine manner that upset her. He couldn't help it; he had always been that way. But he needed to pull a stunt to revive the romantic image of himself as a hero in her eyes.

Wanderer told Watson that he would pay him well to stage a holdup. He would hand Watson a gun when the couple went into the dark hallway and when Ruth turned on the light, he would floor him with a punch. Watson would then run away and he, Carl Wanderer, would once again be the hero of his wife's dreams.

Watson thought it was a harmless way to make a few bucks; he agreed. It was to mean his death. That night when Wanderer came into the hallway with Ruth, he did not hand any gun to Watson. Instead he cocked both weapons and fired at both his wife and Watson. After they had fallen he fired several more bullets into them to make sure they were dead.

Then he went into his avenging husband act for the benefit of Mrs. Johnson, who he knew would race to the scene.

After two sensational trials, one for the murder of Ruth Johnson Wanderer and the other for Al Watson, Carl Wanderer was sentenced

War hero and wife killer Carl Otto Wanderer was trapped into confessing by two nimble-witted reporters—he sang loudly for the press when standing on the gallows. (UPI)

down helplessly to the typewritten speeches strapped to his side. He did the next best thing. Throwing back his head he burst into an old ditty entitled, "Dear Old Pal O' Mine."

The hangman came forward after the first chorus. Wanderer warded him off with a shake of his head and went into the second. By this time, pranksters Hecht and MacArthur were unnerved to see tears streaming down the murderer's cheeks, his eyes rolling crazily in his to death on the gallows.

Hecht and his friend, fellow newsman Charles MacArthur, stood on the gallows on March 19, 1921 when Wanderer approached the dangling rope.

Hecht and MacArthur became quite chummy with Wanderer during his last days on death row, playing poker with him into the early dawn (they won). They convinced the killer to read attacks on their editors which they had meticulously written just before he was to be hanged on the gallows.

The newsmen, however, forgot that those executed on the gallows were tied hand and foot and the pathetic Wanderer could only glance

head like a man whose mind has snapped once and for all.

Carl was still singing when the hangman placed the black shroud on his head and lowered the rope to his neck. The pathetic voice sang on behind the mask. "Glub . . . glub . . . glub" were his last words.

The trap sprung open and Wanderer shot down till the rope snapped him up into space and instant death.

The world-hardened MacArthur turned to his friend and co-author Ben Hecht and said, "You know, Ben, that son-of-a-bitch should have been a song plugger."

WARD, RETURN J. M.
Murderer ● (? -1857)

Ward was a brutish, illiterate, and psychotic giant of a man who made life unbearable for his petite wife, Olive. The woman had been beaten numerous times by her cretinous husband and, to spare herself further agony, moved away from his Sylvania, Ohio home.

At his pleading, the woman returned for a brief visit in early 1857, whereupon Ward killed her. He hid her body under the bed for safekeeping and neighbors, aroused at Mrs. Ward's disappearance (she had informed them of her worst fears before rejoining her husband), charged Ward with the killing but failed to find Olive's body after searching the house. Apparently it occurred to no one in the search party to look under the bed.

As soon as the suspicious crowd departed, Ward rushed to the bedroom, dragged his wife's corpse forth and dissected it in the kitchen with an axe and carving knife. He threw the bloody pieces into the open hearth and burned them.

Ward then cleaned out the fireplace the next day and placed the ashes by the steps of his front door (as stated, he was none too bright). Neighbors inspected the ashes and found parts of Olive's jaw bone. Ward was arrested and tried.

At his trial, the killer insisted that he struck his wife only after she had inflicted a terrific blow on him (the jury roared with laughter), and that he had accidentally killed her. In his panic, Ward claimed, he cut up the body and attempted to dispose of it by burning it in the fireplace. The murderer's vivid description of how he minced Olive's torso was so sickeningly detailed that the jury condemned him halfway through his testimony.

Before he was hanged, Ward admitted killing at least two other persons near Richland, Ohio.

WARDLAW SISTERS

BACKGROUND: BORN BEFORE THE CIVIL WAR IN SOUTH CAROLINA. THE WARDLAWS WERE DAUGHTERS OF A STATE SUPREME COURT JUSTICE. VIRGINIA WARDLAW GRADUATED WELLESLEY COLLEGE WITH A DEGREE IN EDUCATION. CAROLINE AND MARY WARDLAW BOTH MARRIED. DESCRIPTION: ALL THREE SISTERS WERE SHORT AND STOUTISH. ADDICTED TO BLACK GARB. ALIASES: NONE. RECORD: MURDERED JOHN SNEAD (MARY WARDLAW'S SON) TO COLLECT AN INSURANCE POLICY ($12,000) THE SISTERS HAD TAKEN OUT FOR HIM IN 1900; CAROLINE WARDLAW MURDERED HER HUSBAND, A COLONEL MARTIN, SHORTLY THEREAFTER BY ADMINISTERING POISON TO HIM AND COLLECTING HIS INSURANCE POLICY ($10,000); MURDERED OSCEY MARTIN SNEAD (CAROLINE'S DAUGHTER) IN 1909 AND ATTEMPTED TO COLLECT HER INSURANCE POLICY ($32,000); VIRGINIA WARDLAW COMMITTED SUICIDE BY STARVING HERSELF TO DEATH IN PRISON WHILE AWAITING TRIAL; CAROLINE WARDLAW WAS COMMITTED TO AN INSANE ASYLUM, DYING THERE IN 1913; MARY WARDLAW WAS ACQUITTED OF THE MURDER OF OSCEY MARTIN SNEAD.

The doctor approached the Wardlaw house—a huge, gabled building. It was a routine house call. Oscey Martin was sick again.

Once inside the dark and musty-smelling place, the doctor was led into a small bedroom. Lying on a mattress, drained of blood and wearing rags, Oscey Martin, a beautiful young girl, blinked up at him in obvious pain. Her mother, Caroline Wardlaw Martin, stood with a grim look on her face saying nothing.

The doctor was shocked to discover that the young girl was in acute stages of starvation. "My God, this girl is hungry," he told Oscey's mother. "All she needs is food."

Caroline Wardlaw Martin clucked her tongue in disgust. "Eat, eat, that's all she ever does."

"Well, apparently she hasn't been eating enough. Feed her."

The doctor left the house in a rage. How the wealthy Wardlaw sisters could treat their daughter and niece in such a fashion was beyond him. It was inhuman.

"The women were her blood relatives," he remembered later. "I simply could not believe what my eyes told me."

There was much about the Wardlaw sisters that was hard to believe. They were recluses who dressed in funeral black at all hours of the day, every day. No one knew where their money came from, but they could afford to travel extensively and owned large, expensive houses.

Their travels were mysterious; it was known that they had moved from house to house through Virginia, Tennessee, New Jersey, and New York. They had a very good reason to keep their strange activities secret—they were murderesses.

For years, the sisters, now ugly little spinsters shriveled of body and pinched of face, had been starving Oscey Martin to death. Killing seemed to come naturally to them. They had been doing it for years.

Caroline Wardlaw Martin and her two sisters, Mary Wardlaw Snead and Virginia Wardlaw, were all daughters of a supreme court justice of South Carolina and were raised in the tradition of the Old Gentry of the South. They were anything but gentle.

The Wardlaws of South Carolina had fought in almost all the major battles of the Civil War, naturally for the Confederacy. When young, the sisters were inseparable. They had the bad habit of plotting and executing evil little tricks such as tripping the upstairs maid at the head of the stairs.

Mary Wardlaw married first to a man named Snead and they produced two sons, John and Fletcher. Then Caroline Wardlaw married a Southern war hero, a Colonel Martin, who had led a battalion of Kentucky cavalry. Their only child was Oscey.

Oscey wasn't her real name. It was Bessie, but she garbled the name in her baby talk and it came out Oscey. All through her brief life, the sisters taunted and tortured the child with this name she hated.

Virginia Wardlaw, who was the leader of the deadly trio, never married. After attending Wellesley College, Virginia became a prominent female educator. She was appointed head of the Montgomery Female College in 1900.

Without any apparent reason, as soon as Virginia took over the college, her two sisters deserted their husbands and joined her, taking their children with them.

Residents of the small college town eyed the three sisters apprehensively when they appeared in their long black dresses, shawls, scarves, and heavy veils. Apprehension soon turned to horror.

When John Snead ran away with a Montgomery student, the sisters chased him and brought him back. A few days later, breathless residents broke into the Wardlaw's campus home to find John screaming in pain. His clothing was on fire and he died before them, a writhing human ember.

The sisters said that he had committed suicide—but it was a strange way to do oneself in. There were some who whispered that they thought they smelled kerosene in the room where John burned to death.

The sisters were awarded $12,000 on an insurance policy they had recently taken out on John. Yet no one questioned their actions. They were members of an old-line family, above reproach and criticism. Murder? Unthinkable!

The whispers increased, however, and people in the street were openly talking murder. The Wardlaws suddenly packed valises and scattered.

Mrs. Martin rejoined her husband, dragging twelve-year-old Oscey along with her. The Martins lived in a drab, run-down rooming house on 57th Street in New York.

Shortly after Mrs. Martin moved back with her husband, the landlady heard terrible moans coming from the Martin apartment. She forced the door. The scene was a nightmare.

Little Oscey, frightened, cowered in a dark corner, dressed in rags, a thin, undernourished child. On the floor, Colonel Martin groaned in deep pain, his legs doubled into his chest. Caroline Wardlaw Martin was sprawled on the bed, looking down at her dying husband with indifference. The landlady's mouth gaped open at the incredible scene as she watched Colonel Martin die before her eyes.

His widow suddenly became grief-stricken and begged Confederate veterans in New York for money to bury the hero of the South. No sooner was Colonel Martin beneath the sod than Mrs. Martin suddenly remembered a $10,000 insurance policy she had recently taken out on her husband.

While Caroline Wardlaw Martin was busy poisoning her husband, her sister Virginia schemed her way into becoming the head of Soule College in Murfreesboro, Tennessee. Her sisters then joined her there, moving into a mammoth house. The eerie mansion's only furnishings, it seemed, consisted of a few iron cots.

Murfreesboro residents were amazed by the black-clad sisters who prowled their streets day and night. Their eccentric behavior, however, only amused the college fathers and Virginia held onto her job.

Oscey, however, was rarely seen. She was always ill, bedridden. One doctor who called to check on her was appalled at the conditions in the old, dark house.

"Why do you live this way?" he asked Mrs. Martin.

She snapped back at him: "Because it suits us."

The sisters became alarmed when another doctor threatened to have them hauled into court unless Oscey was properly fed.

When he showed up to check on the young girl, the weird sisters announced that she wasn't there, that she had married her first cousin Fletcher! This time, they were telling the truth. The Wardlaws even showed him the marriage certificate.

The doctor became even more suspicious and told the women he was going for the police. Before he returned, the sisters fled. Oscey and Fletcher were deposited in a small Louisville cottage. The sisters went on to New York.

Oscey became pregnant and when the sisters heard of it, they returned to Louisville, chased Fletcher to Canada, and scooped up Oscey, who was taken to another gloomy rooming house in Brooklyn.

A kindly doctor who attended the girl in her pregnancy smuggled her food and watched, amazed, as she wolfed it down like

Mrs. Caroline Wardlaw Martin and Mary Wardlaw Snead, two of the three murderous sisters in black. (N.Y. Historical Society)

an animal. As soon as the child was born, the doctor found himself locked out.

His fears led him to climb through a window of the Wardlaw rooms, but he was met by a sinister-looking Virginia who screamed hysterically and shoved him from the premises. A lawyer told the doctor there was nothing he could do and to mind his own business. Unfortunately for Oscey, he did.

There was no limit to the viciousness practiced by the three women. They told Oscey her child was dead, and then they placed the boy in an orphanage. They then moved to another ghastly-looking house in East Orange, New Jersey.

A doctor found Oscey there, weeping for her dead child. He thought she was drugged as well as starving.

The girl who never had a chance came to her untimely end on November 29, 1909; the sisters called police, stating Oscey had committed suicide. Investigators found her in a bathtub with only enough water in it to cover her attractive face.

A pathologist found a small quantity of water in her stomach. There were also traces of morphine. He listed the cause of her death as starvation.

Police grew more suspicious when they discovered that the Wardlaw sisters had long ago insured the girl for $32,000 which they now demanded. A premium, they peevishly pointed out, had been promptly paid only a few days before Oscey's suicide.

This was one policy the sisters would not collect. They were arrested and charged with murder. Awaiting trial, Virginia Wardlaw refused all food and slowly starved herself to death in prison. The other two sisters were brought to trial and the state proved that Oscey's mother was murderously mad.

Mrs. Snead was acquitted but Mrs. Martin went to prison. She was removed to an insane asylum where she died in 1913.

The Sisters in Black where by then only a shuddering memory in yellowing newspapers.

WATKINS, JESSE
Murderer ● (1903- ?)

As a young itinerant, Watkins went to work for Henry Chambers in 1927 as a stablehand; his job was to care for the horses housed at the Presidio, an Army post outside San Francisco. Stablemaster Chambers accused Watkins of being lazy and neglecting the horses. Watkins was fired and vowed to "get" Chambers, according to one soldier, William Nelson, who overheard a row between the two men.

On the night of August 21, 1927, Watkins let himself into Chambers' rooms above the stable. The stablemaster awoke, grabbed his pistol, and fired three rapid shots at Watkins who was advancing upon him in a wild rage. One bullet hit Watkins in the cheek but the wound was only superficial and did not prevent him from pouncing upon the old man, wresting the pistol from him, and clubbing him to death with it. Following the murder, Watkins ransacked the apartment and then took Chambers' large pension check (for services rendered in the Spanish-American War) and left.

The killer raced back to his rooms on Lombard Street in San Francisco. No one saw him approach the building or anxiously run up the stairs to his flat, such was the dense fog that swept through the streets. His hands, Watkins noted, were coated with blood; he set to scrubbing them furiously. Watkins then saw that the white shirt he was wearing was also speckled with Chambers' blood. He scrubbed that, too. As an added precaution, he sent the shirt to the laundry the following day.

The murder baffled San Francisco police for several weeks. After Army private William Nelson told officers about Watkins' dislike for Chambers, they immediately visited his apartment. Watkins' roommate, a man named Cahill, told them that Jesse had returned home one night recently with an incredible story: He had been held up and shot by a bandit. Cahill reported that Watkins had returned with the bullet still sticking from his cheek. "I took it out for him with a pair of tweezers," Cahill stated.

The police, having found Chambers' pistol with three shots fired, instantly surmised that Watkins was the man they were looking for and when he arrived home he was arrested and held for questioning. Witnesses, fingerprints, anything that could be considered as important evidence, however, was missing.

Two months later Watkins went on trial for murder, still maintaining his innocence. The prosecution, at first, presented little evidence. Then came their surprise witness, independent criminologist Edward O. Heinrich of Berkeley, Calif. Police had called him into the case and, as his testimony bore out, he had accumulated enough circumstantial evidence to smother Watkins' case.

The bullet, he proved through extensive ballistics displays, plucked from Watkins' cheek had been turned over to police by Cahill and was one of the three shots fired by Chambers at his killer on the night of his murder. Next, Heinrich displayed the shirt Watkins had worn on the night of the slaying.

Freshly laundered, it was immaculate to the naked eye. Using ultraviolet rays, however, Heinrich had discovered the fabric was still flecked with blood, Chambers' blood.

Another odd piece of evidence was then related by the meticulous Heinrich. Police investigating Chambers' apartment noted an odd name—"vere"—imprinted on the floor with the old man's blood. Heinrich told the jury how he had examined an old pair of shoes owned by the defendant. Watkins, Heinrich reported, had a curious way of walking so that the heels of his shoes wore down on the inner sides; each heel was marked with the word "vere." Upon microscopic examination, Heinrich found that two other letters, "Re," were discernible, letters worn off on the inner sides of the heels, and pieced with the letters obvious to the naked eye, spelled out the trade name for the heels, "Revere."

Not long after the criminologist had testified, the jury returned a verdict of guilty against Watkins and he was sentenced to life imprisonment at McNeil Island. "Believe me," Watkins stated later about the laundered shirt that had trapped him, "if I had known about those violet lights or whatever you call them, you can be sure I'd have burned the damned thing up." Watkins was later paroled and has since vanished.

WATSON, ELLA ("CATTLE KATE")
Cattle Thief ● (1866-1888)

Ella Watson thrived in the broad expanses of Wyoming's cattle ranches near Rawlins. Born to a prosperous farmer in Smith County, Kan., she had run away from home and worked as a dancehall girl in Denver, where she married at eighteen. Her husband, however, was a woman chaser and she soon left him. Ella then drifted to Cheyenne and then Rawlins, Wyo. where she worked in a bar as a shill.

Clever Jim Averill, who had moved West after allegedly receiving a diploma from Cornell University, spotted Ella in the Rawlins saloon and soon asked her to move to Sweetwater where he ran a post office and bar operation. He would back her in a brothel, he said, and they would split the profits.

Ella agreed and arrived in Rawlins in early 1888. A local paper described the 26-year-old woman as having "a robust physique," and being "a dark devil in the saddle, handy with a six-shooter and a Winchester, and an expert with a branding iron."

She would soon get plenty of practice with the branding iron. Averill, who wrote vituperative letters to local papers in protest of the cattle barons and their evil ways, began to steal cattle on a wholesale basis, keeping them penned up in a corral next to Ella's bordello. Ella, practically surrounded with cows, came to be known as "Cattle Kate."

On several occasions, local cattlemen spied their brands on cows in Kate's pens but were driven off when Kate appeared brandishing a rifle. In July of 1888, a large vigilante group showed up at Kate's bordello and caught her off guard. She fought wildly and then asked, "Where are you taking me?"

"To Rawlins," one of the men shouted.

"You can't do that!" she screamed.

"Why not?"

"I haven't got my print dress on, that's why not!"

They loaded her in a wagon and drove off to Jim Averill's ranch which was a half mile distant. There they took Averill prisoner and he was thrown into the wagon alongside Kate. As the cowboys rode along toward a remote canyon, it became apparent that they weren't headed for Rawlins. One of them mumbled something about lynching Cattle Kate and Averill but they were unconcerned. They laughed and joked as they rode along, poking fun at the riders galloping next to them.

Reaching the Sweetwater River, the cattlemen stopped. They fixed ropes around the necks of Cattle Kate and Averill. "Jump," one rancher told Averill as he was standing on a boulder, the rope around his neck attached to a limb of a cottonwood tree.

Averill smiled. "Stop your fooling fellows," he said.

They weren't fooling. One man came up and pushed Averill into space and another shoved Cattle Kate from her rocky perch. Both fought for their lives with unbound hands. "The kicking and writhing of those people was awful to witness," one newspaper re-

Cattle Kate Watson looking over the stolen herds of cows penned next to her brothel in 1888. (Wyoming State Archives and Historical Department)

ported.

Days later the bodies were taken down and seven of the lynching party were arrested. They posted bonds for each other but never faced trial. One of the vigilantes felt a tinge of remorse and later told a reporter: "We didn't mean to hang 'em, only scare 'em a little."

WATTS, CORAL EUGENE
Serial Killer ● (1953-   )

To Coral Watts all women were unfaithful and deceitful. He hated them and showed that hate by killing as many as forty females before he was apprehended and put behind bars. Watts attended Western Michigan University at Kalamazoo. He tried to choke a woman to death in 1974 but he was arrested and jailed for a few days.

Released on bail, Watts, a few days later, killed university student Gloria Steele, stabbing her thirty-six times before mutilating her body. He then appeared in court on the assault charge a few days later and was given a one-year prison term. By then police knew of the Steele killing and believed Watts had committed the murder but they lacked evidence to prove it.

Upon his release from prison in 1975, Watts moved to Ann Arbor, Michigan where he worked as a bus mechanic which allowed him to travel freely. He committed a series of stabbing murders, killing several young women and creating what the press then called "The Sunday Morning Slasher."

Watts, at the same time, was traveling to Detroit and Windsor, Ontario, Canada where he also stabbed and killed several more women. In 1981, after losing his job, Watts moved to Houston, Texas. Here, Watts hanged a jogger, Phyllis Tam, with her own clothes in January 1982. He then killed a female university student and stuffed her body into a car. He beat Margaret Fossi to death and left her body alongside a road.

On May 23, 1982, Watts broke into the Houston apartment of twenty-year-old Lori Ann Lister, catching her in her bath. He bent a hanger around her throat and tried to drown her but her screams brought a neighbor to the rescue. Watts fled, but was quickly identified and arrested. He was charged with burglary, aggravated kidnapping and attempted murder.

Watts plea bargained his way out of an execution. He said that he would provide information on several murders if the charge against him was for simple burglary. Prosecutors agreed and Watts rattled off a list of 22 murders he had committed in three states. Ironically, he was not tried for any of these horrendous murders, but received a 60 year term for burglary, the maximum sentence Judge Doug Shaver could give him under the prosecutor's agreement. As Watts was leaving the courtroom, Shaver said to him. "I hope you serve each and every minute of the sixty years."

WEBSTER, JOHN WHITE
Murderer ● (? -1850)

America's first "classic" murder, which focused national attention on distinguished educator Dr. John White Webster, was for all practical purposes brought about through an act of unpremeditated wrath.

Dr. Webster (M.A., M.D., Harvard) was a corpulent, ineffectual-looking man who peered mildly over loose-fitting spectacles, but he was also a much-respected professor of chemistry and mineralogy at the Massachusetts Medical College during the 1840s. Webster's office was directly below that of Oliver Wendell Holmes (who would testify at his trial, as would Drs. W. T. G. Morton and C. T. Jackson, discoverers of ether, and Jared Sparks, President of Harvard and one of George Washington's biographers).

The professor was not the reclusive type, but gave handsome parties and delighted in long, sumptuous meals brightened with the best wines and illustrious company of Boston intellectuals such as poet Henry Wadsworth Longfellow. His expensive tastes were costly to the point where Webster spent far beyond what his annual salary of $1,200 would allow. Such extravagances compelled Webster to seek financial aid in the form of loans. First he borrowed $2,432 from a local group of lenders. He next went to an opulent member of this group, Dr. George Parkman, and borrowed an additional $400.

Parkman was an odd creature, tall, gangling, razor-thin, with a jutting, squared-off jaw (he was called "Chin" by students), pointed nose, and small, squinty eyes. A graduate of the University of Aberdeen, Parkman had given up medicine to become one of the school's wealthiest landlords. Though miserly, Parkman ostentatiously donated the ground on which the Massachusetts Medical School stood and for whom the Parkman Chair of Anatomy was established (occupied at one time by Oliver Wendell Holmes). Parkman was not so generous with those to whom he lent money, particularly with the pudgy-faced Dr. Webster. Parkman originally loaned Webster money in a sham spirit of friendliness. This attitude soon dissolved when, in the fall of 1849, the rod-like Parkman entered Webster's classes wearing a stovepipe hat and a long, black frock coat to goad him with sarcastic remarks while the professor attempted to deliver lectures.

Webster ignored Parkman; he also ignored the loan he promised to repay. On one occasion, Parkman told Webster: "The world does not owe you a living." Webster only smiled good naturedly and walked away. Parkman continued to hound Webster. The money shark learned that Webster had accumulated more than $1,000 after selling his valuable minerals collection. Still no payment came to him from the professor.

Parkman's dark mood became even blacker on November 23, 1849 until he worked himself into an indignant rage, raced to the college grounds, and entered Webster's office.

"Have you got the money?" Parkman demanded of Webster.

"No, I have not," the professor replied.

Parkman was beside himself with anger. "I got you your professorship and I'll get you out of it!" This was patently untrue but at this impassioned juncture, Parkman actually believed he was responsible for Webster's appointment.

The threat was too much for Webster. "I felt nothing but the sting of his words," the professor wrote later, "I was excited by them to the highest degree of passion." Webster grabbed a heavy piece of kindling wood from a pile near the fireplace and crashed it down on Parkman's head with great force. The blow crushed Parkman's stovepipe hat and his head. He collapsed to the floor, bleeding from the mouth.

Parkman was sprawled on the floor for ten minutes while Webster frantically used spirits of ammonia and other drugs to revive him. It was hopeless. Parkman was dead. And it was murder, Webster realized with a shudder.

The professor was a practical man. There appeared to him no reason why he should face such a charge. The solution was simple—merely dissect and destroy Parkman's body. Calmly, Webster dragged the corpse into his washroom after locking all the doors. There he labored long to lift the body into a sink and then, using a butcher knife (careful not to employ any of the dissecting knives) meticulous-

This early drawing illustrates Webster's killing of Dr. Parkman. (N.Y. Historical Society)

ly cut up his creditor's body.

The college janitor, Empraim Littlefield, was a born meddler. He had witnessed an argument between Parkman and Webster weeks before, at which time Parkman dunned Webster for the money due him. He had watched the determined Parkman enter the college grounds on the day of the murder and go into Webster's office. He checked the doors when Parkman did not reappear, only to find himself locked out.

Entering another office, next to Webster's assay furnace, Littlefield felt the wall. It was scalding hot. Webster had built a fire so intense that the brick wall backing the furance burned to the touch. On the other side of that wall, Webster was burning Parkman's head and other sections of his body.

Three days later, November 26, 1849, a reward of $3,000 was offered for the return of Dr. Parkman. Authorities believed him kidnapped and held for ransom, such was his vast wealth. Janitor Littlefield suspected something else. He tried to inspect Dr. Webster's dissecting vault where bones were stored. It was locked.

The enterprising janitor then spent two days removing parts of a wall, brick by brick, surrounding this chamber. In an eerie midnight scene, Littlefield finally broke through and, holding his oil lantern through a small aperture, spied the bloody pelvis and parts of a leg belonging to Dr. Parkman. He scurried off to babble his story to officials.

Webster was arrested and an investigation of his premises revealed a thigh and thorax secreted in a tea chest, bits of bone lodged in the grate of the furnace and, most damning of all, Parkman's identifiable teeth intact at the back of the furnace.

While Webster was being taken to jail, he gulped down a vial of strychnine which he had prepared for just such an occasion. He had developed a nervous stomach, however, and could not hold the poison.

His trial was a national spectacle. The press heightened the drama by devoting pages and pages to the case. Thousands journeyed to Boston from as far as New Orleans to view the murderer. So many visitors arrived that the judge ordered that spectators could only sit in the gallery during the proceedings for a period of ten minutes (and they were timed) in order to enable all to enjoy the macabre scene. In this way, more than 60,000 bugeyed spectators visited the trial.

Webster's only defense was that he had acted out of anger and that he had not intended to kill Parkman. The dissecting and hiding of the body convinced the jury otherwise and he was convicted and sentenced to death. Dr. Webster was hanged in August, 1850.

Professor John Webster's "classic" murder of Dr. George Parkman was fully described in this 1850 chapbook issued by the Boston Globe. (N.Y. Historical Society).

WEIL, JOSEPH ("YELLOW KID") Swindler ● (1875-1976)

I never cheated an honest man, only rascals," said the greatest confidence man of them all after his retirement. "They may have been respectable but they were never any good. They wanted someting for nothing. I gave them nothing for something."

With that philosophy ever in mind, Joseph "Yellow Kid" Weil embarked at an early age to take the wealthy suckers of this country through the most ingenious schemes ever concocted. Born and raised in Chicago, the Kid became famous early when members of the press adopted him, delighting in Weil's high-minded confidence games.

The Kid often operated with confederates such as Fred Buckminster, but generally preferred to pull his swindles alone. His greatest asset was his presence. Weil's sartorial splendor was unequalled in his trade. He was always immaculately dressed and was partial to silk cravats spliced with pearl stickpins, winged collars, expensive vested suits, and spats. His sobriquet stemmed from his youthful habit of reading the Ocault cartoon strip character, "Yellow Kid" in the 1890s.

From about 1900 to 1934, when the Kid claimed to have gone straight, Weil was involved with so many bunco plots that he often had to perform some frenzied juggling to keep up with them. His quick wit, razor sharp tongue, and stolid appearance pulled him through colossal bluffs.

One of his more ambitious schemes involved the buying of a bank, or rather the renting of one. Upon hearing that the Merchants National Bank in Muncie, Ind., was moving to a new location, he went to Muncie and set in motion an elaborate swindle. Before the teller cages and other banking accouterments were removed, the Kid rented the vacated bank building. He then had children go to other banks and snatch piles of deposit and withdrawal slips which were placed in the slots of his bank. Streetcar conductors were hired to act as bank guards. His tellers were, of course, some of the most notorious confidence men in the Midwest.

Into this bear trap, the Kid led his lamb. Days before renting the old Muncie Bank Building, Weil had primed an out-of-town millionaire with the prospect of investing $50,000 in a fake land deal. After his bank was established, the Yellow Kid approached his sucker and stated "Why, the president of the Muncie Bank vouches for it."

The sucker was led into the bank by the austere-looking Weil. The building was jammed with customers who hauled sacks of money across the floor and thrust wads of greenbacks upon the tellers as deposits. To Weil's victim the phony bank appeared to be booming with business. Of course, the customers were prostitutes, racetrack touts, and gamblers Weil had employed purposely for his swindle.

After waiting an hour, Weil and his pigeon were shown into the bank president's office. The president, a Weil associate who acted with great dignity and sophisticated bearing, sanctioned the $50,000 investment while spouting financial gibberish. By the evening of that day, Yellow Kid was far from Muncie with $50,000 in his pocket.

Another scheme enacted in Youngstown, Ohio, also involved a bank, a real one. Here Weil approached the president of the bank pretending to be a millionaire passing through town. He talked of depositing a great deal of money in the bank but intimated that there was a pressing matter to be cleared up first. "Please be kind enough to use my office for any business transactions," the bank president obligingly said.

Weil used the offices for an hour—just enough time for him to pass himself off as the bank president and take another sucker in a quick swindle.

The Kid was publicity-minded, convinced that most people were gullible and believed almost anything that appeared in print. He stumbled across a financial magazine of great repute which carried the story of an investor who had purchased an abandoned gold mine and subsequently made millions from it. Weil took the magazine to a friend who was a printer. His friend ingeniously reprinted the page in the magazine that dealt with the mining millionaire and substituted Weil's picture for the investor, and then carefully rebound the magazine.

Armed with this tool, Weil traveled throughout the Midwest. His first stop in each town was the library. There he would take out an authentic copy of the magazine, substituting it with his doctored copy. He would then buttonhole his victims with a stock pitch, pretending to be the mining millionaire. "You can find it in the library," he would point out to the sucker. When the prospective victim checked, he found the article with Yellow Kid's picture and invariably foisted his money upon Weil within hours. Before leaving town, the Kid was careful to replace the doctored copy of the magazine with the original.

The Kid plotted and schemed his way into some of the most fantastic swindles imaginable. One story had it that he took a Detroit car manufacturer for several thousand dollars by selling him pills that could turn water into gasoline.

Not all of the Kid's swindles were successful. He served a number of prison terms in local and federal jails. The Yellow Kid looked upon these periodical jolts of incarceration as temporary setbacks. Fame became his ultimate undoing. Addicted to a pince nez and a full, luxurious, and carefully combed and trimmed beard, he soon realized that his appearance had become a trademark and caused him to be identified by his victims. After serving a long term in the Illinois State Prison at Joliet, Weil attempted to bilk youthful Detroit millionaire George Malcolmson, of $30,000 in a fake copper mine proposition. Malcolmson recognized Weil and brought charges on February 11, 1924.

Outwardly, such police rousts did not ruffle Weil, but he became increasingly aware that the great glut of stories concerning his activities stripped away his most important tool, anonymity.

In Peoria, Ill. on February 3, 1934, the Kid's hotel room was invaded by an army of local

The greatest con man of them all—Joseph "Yellow Kid" Weil, shown here in 1924 in the palmy days of his fabulous swindles. (UPI)

police just as he was preparing another swindle. Weil had been in town only a few days with two partners, both named Smith. The trio had been negotiating the rental of a whole floor of the largest business building in Peoria. Weil had asked real estate brokers to locate "a palatial residence" for him in town. The Kid and his partners then received dozens of telegrams at their hotel which reported the meteoric rise of something called "Soviet Gold Mine Stock."

That's as far as Weil's intended swindle got. Police recognized the dapper crook and stormed into his room, finding in one suitcase bundles of paper cut to bank bill size and carefully wrapped and marked: "$20,000." Whatever the Kid's scheme was, it never materialized.

He was hauled into jail but police authorities were nonplussed. There was no real evidence upon which to convict the Kid of a crime. Police Chief Walter Williams realized his raid had been premature.

"Give me proof that I've broken the law," the Kid insisted.

"I don't have any," Williams said, "but you're up to something." Williams was compelled to free Weil and his associates.

It was a close shave and for Weil spelled the end of his career. He had been defeated by his own notoriety. The Yellow Kid decided to go straight.

The Kid disappeared after that and did not emerge until the late 1940s. A policeman passed him on a Gold Coast street in Chicago while he was walking his dog. Weil recognized the officer and waved at him. The policeman recognized the Kid and arrested him. Taken to court on "suspicion," Weil grew indignant and then, with an impassioned speech made before the judge, the Kid insisted that he had gone straight years ago and the pinch was a miscarriage of justice.

"Just what are you doing now, Mr. Weil?" the judge asked the chipper 72-year-old confidence man.

"I'm writing my memoirs," Weil announced proudly.

He was telling the truth. The Yellow Kid's autobiography, written with W. T. Brannon, appeared in 1948. Apparently the old master had not lost his touch. One report stated that "a legal battle is expected between Brannon and a moving picture company over film rights to the book as the Kid has been up to his old tricks and sold the rights to both Brannon and the film company."

WEISS, EARL ("HYMIE")
Bootlegger ● (1898-1926)

BACKGROUND: BORN EARL WAJCIECKOWSKI IN CHICAGO, ILL. MINOR PUBLIC EDUCATION. DESCRIPTION: 59", BROWN HAIR, BROWN EYES. STOCKY. ALIASES: HYMIE, LITTLE HYMIE, HYMIE THE POLACK. RECORD: BEGAN ROBBING AND BURGLARIZING STORES AND WAREHOUSES IN THE CHICAGO AREA IN 1908 AT AGE TEN; TEAMED UP WITH DION O'BANNION AND GEORGE "BUGS" MORAN IN SEVERAL ROBBERIES AND BURGLARIES, 1916; ARRESTED FOR BURGLARY, MARCH, 1921, CHARGE STRICKEN OFF WITH LEAVE TO REINSTATE; ARRESTED, MAY, 1921 FOR BURGLARY, STRICKEN OFF WITH LEAVE TO REINSTATE; MURDERED STEVEN WISNIEWSKI, JULY, 1921, USING THE AUTOMOBILE FOR THE FIRST TIME IN AMERICAN CRIMINAL HISTORY TO TAKE A VICTIM "FOR A ONE-WAY RIDE"; ARRESTED IN

JULY, 1922 FOR ROBBERY, POSTED BOND OF $10,000, CASE NOLLE PROSSED; ACTIVE AS DION O'BANNION'S LIEUTENANT IN OPERATING WIDE-SCALE BOOTLEGGING ON CHICAGO'S NORTH SIDE, 1920-24; ARRESTED WITH O'BANNION AND JOHNNY TORRIO FOR VIOLATION OF THE PROHIBITION ACT BY CHICAGO POLICE, 5/19/24, DISCHARGED ON 2/9/25 AFTER PAYING $2,000 FINE; TOOK OVER LEADERSHIP OF THE NORTH SIDE GANG (CONTROLLING THE 42ND AND 43RD WARDS) UPON THE CAPONE—DIRECTED MURDER OF O'BANNION, 11/10/24; ATTEMPTED TO MURDER WITH MORAN AND DRUCCI, CAPONE ON 1/12/25 AT STATE AND FIFTY-FIFTH STREETS IN A DAYLIGHT AMBUSH, WOUNDED CAPONE'S CHAUFFEUR SYLVESTER BARTON IN THE LEG; ATTEMPTED TO MURDER JOHNNY TORRIO 1/20/25 WITH MORAN, VINCENT "THE SCHEMER" DRUCCI, AND FRANK GUSENBERG; ATTEMPT MADE ON HIS LIFE 8/10/26 BY CAPONE GUNMEN LED BY LOUIS BARKO; ANOTHER ATTEMPT MADE ON HIS LIFE BY CAPONE GUNMEN ON 8/15/26; LED CARAVAN OF EIGHT CARS PAST CAPONE'S CICERO HEADQUARTERS, THE HAW-THORNE HOTEL, 9/20/26, FIRING MORE THAN 1,000 MACHINEGUN BULLETS INTO THE HOTEL AND NEIGH-BORING BUILDINGS, WOUNDING CAPONE HENCHMAN LOUIS BARKO AND A PASSERBY; SHOT AND KILLED ON 10/11/26 WHILE ENTERING HIS HEADQUARTERS AT 740 N. STATE STREET BY CAPONE'S GUNMEN.

Weiss, an habitual criminal since child-hood, first misled authorities into be-lieving he was merely a common and considerably inept burglar. In one of his first adult burglaries, Hymie upset a shelf in a perfume store and emerged minutes later smelling strongly like a prostitute. Two suspicious policemen stopped him and sniffed.

"Are you some sort of a pansy, fella?" one of them asked.

"Go to hell!" the ferocious Weiss replied. The press got hold of the story and branded Hymie Weiss "The Perfume Burglar." Weiss lived down the name through the years and became known as one of the craftiest criminals in Chicago; in cold blood he would murder anyone who stood in his path.

Weiss attended Holy Name Cathedral on Chicago's North Side as a youth and there met his bosom pal and future crime boss, Dion O'Bannion, an altar boy gone wrong. The two continued to attend church until their deaths; Weiss constantly carried a rosary in his pocket which he threaded nervously at times of great stress, particularly during a gang killing or while completing an important hijacking assign-ment for O'Bannion.

The devotion to religion for these two ended at the door of the Cathedral. They embarked upon a string of burglaries and robberies from 1920 to 1922 and were arrested several times, but O'Bannion's political friends managed to have the cases dismisssed. With the North Side police in their pockets during their bootleg-ging heyday, O'Bannion, Weiss, Vincent "The Schemer" Drucci, and Bugs Moran operated brazenly in the open.

Once police found their prints on the dial of a safe in the Parkway Tea Room, which they had robbed. A bribed jury quickly acquitted the burglars. Walking from court, O'Bannion jerked a thumb at Weiss and said to reporters: "It was an oversight. Hymie was supposed to wipe off the prints and he forgot."

The remark was inappropriate. Weiss sel-dom neglected such important details. He was a brainy crook who provided a prudent bal-ance to O'Bannion's impetuous nature. After they had built up the most lucrative boot-legging activities in Chicago during the early 1920s, Weiss had all he could do to moderate O'Bannion's rash decisions and wild temper. Hymie did, however, murder anyone he felt stood in his way of earning a living. One such person was hijacker Steve Wisniewski, who, in early July, 1921, stopped a shipment of O'Bannion's beer and drove off with the truck after pistol-whipping its driver and guard.

"That jerk needs a lesson," Weiss snarled. He found Wisniewski days later and lured him into his car. "Let's go for a ride, Steve," he said sweetly, "I got a proposition for you." Wisniewski got into Weiss' car and Hymie drove out to a remote spot where he put two bullets into the hijacker's head. Thus, Earl "Hymie" Weiss became the originator of the "one-way ride."

By 1923, the Northsiders were wealthy from their bootleg profits. "We're big business without high hats," O'Bannion said to Weiss. Little Hymie appeared every inch the busi-nessman, too, dressed in elegantly tailored suits and imported shoes, sedately riding about in a chauffeur-driven limousine. He always carried $10,000 in cash wherever he went.

"Ain't you afraid of a heist?" Schemer Drucci once asked him.

"Naw, you never can tell when you'll need dough quick. Besides, I got the roscoe with

Chicago gangster Earl "Hymie" Weiss invented the "one-way ride" and vowed to kill Al Capone. (UPI)

me." The "roscoe" was, of course, the large automatic Weiss packed in a shoulder holster beneath his suit.

One of the things Weiss needed ready cash for was women. A wild chaser, he often appeared at the opera with no less than three curvacious chorines on his arm. Hymie abruptly ceased being a womanizer in 1922 when he met blonde and busty Josephine Libby in the lobby of the Congress Hotel. Miss Libby and Weiss were a twosome after that and Little Hymie rented a swanky North Side apartment which they shared.

Josephine had once had a minor lead in the *Ziegfield Follies* and as such had come to appreciate men with money. Weiss had lots of it, hundreds of thousands of dollars. Oddly enough, once he moved in with Josephine, Weiss became a homebody.

"Earl was one of the finest men in the world," Miss Libby proudly stated following Hymie's gangland killing, "and I spent the happiest time of my life with him. You'd expect a rich bootlegger to be a man about town, always going to nightclubs and having his home full of rowdy friends. But Earl liked to be alone with me, just lounging about, listening to the radio or reading. He seemed to me pretty well read. He didn't waste time

on trash, but read histories and law books. If you hadn't known what he was, you might have mistaken him for a lawyer or college professor. He was crazy about children. 'I want a boy of my own some day,' he said. 'I don't amount to much, but maybe the youngster would turn out all right.'"

Hymie's law book reading convinced him that he could practice amateur legalistics. When a U.S. Marshal broke into his apartment with a warrant charging him with violating the Mann Act, Weiss ran him off at the point of a shotgun. The marshal returned with several heavily armed men and confiscated cases of whiskey, brandy, and champagne, boxes of ammunition, several revolvers, shotguns, rifles, knockout drops, blackjacks, handcuffs, a tripod for a heavy machinegun and two First World War issue grenades.

Hymie, spouting legal jargon, promptly sued the federal government, charging that two dozen of his best silk shirts had been stolen by the marshal. The suit, as well as government charges against Weiss, came to nothing.

As the bootleg era soared into 1924, minor gang wars erupted in Chicago. The first to be wiped out by the monolithic Capone gang were the South Side O'Donnells, close friends of Dion O'Bannion. O'Bannion had agreed with Johnny Torrio and Al Capone to keep his bootlegging activities north of Madison Street, but the brutal Capone-inspired slayings of Walter O'Donnell and Jerry O'Connor by Frank McErlane incensed O'Bannion. Shortly after these murders, an underworld figure entered O'Bannion's flower shop at 740 N. State Street across from Holy Name Cathedral.

O'Bannion and Weiss were fuming. "Goddamn that Capone!" O'Bannion said. "Those killings weren't Torrio's orders," he told the visitor. "They were all done by that dirty atheistic dago! Did you see poor Jerry O'Connor's face at the funeral home? It was blown off! Nothing left to it. And Walter O'Donnell, too . . . and all those other lads. That Capone kills like a beast in the jungle!"

As the visitor, a fringe friend of Capone's, began to leave, Hymie Weiss, who had been leaning against a glass case saying nothing, suddenly gritted: "You can tell Capone this for me. If he ever pulls anything like that on us, I'm going to get him if I have to kill everybody in front of him to do it. You can tell him that, and if I see him I'll tell it to him."

When Dion O'Bannion was gunned down in his flower shop on November 10, 1924 by Capone gunmen, Hymie went crazy. First he "cried as a woman might," at Deanie's funeral, according to one reporter. Next he vowed the slaughter of the entire Torrio-Capone gang. It was war and Hymie Weiss carried it to Capone, just barely missing Scarface on January 12, 1925 as Capone alighted from his car.

Weiss, Moran, and Drucci swept past Capone and his bodyguards in a fast-moving auto as the gangsters were about to enter a South Side restaurant. The Northsiders blasted Capone's car to shreds with shotguns, wounding Scarface's chauffeur, Sylvester Barton. A traffic cop, who witnessed the daylight bombardment, stated: "They let it have everything but the kitchen stove."

The stove was next. Weiss, Moran, Drucci, and Frank Gusenberg trapped Johnny Torrio outside of his South Side home on January 20, 1925 and shot him to pieces. They fled as police approached before they could send a bullet into Torrio's brain: The attack so frightened Torrio that he quit the Chicago rackets and briefly retired to Italy.

Angelo Genna, a Capone ally and member of the terrible Genna brothers clan, was next ambushed at Weiss' orders and killed on June 13, 1925. The bodies of Capone's gunmen began to litter the streets of Chicago. Scarface ordered a specially-built armored car for $26,000 and rode down side streets in terror, a wall of gunsels surrounding him every time he stepped into the street.

Capone struck back. Twice his gunmen, led by Louis Barko, attempted to kill Weiss and Drucci in broad daylight as the two walked along Michigan Avenue. Both times Weiss and Drucci beat back the attackers with intense pistol fire. Hymie decided to give Scarface a moment to remember for the rest of his life.

He loaded eight touring cars full of gangsters armed to the teeth with rifles, pistols, shotguns, and machineguns. The caravan passed Capone's stronghold, the Hawthorn Hotel, and then, in broad daylight, opened up, raking the building top to bottom. Weiss, Moran, Drucci, and the Gusenberg brothers, Henry, Frank, and Pete, got out of their cars and stood on the sidewalk, firing for a full minute into the hotel lobby. A thousand shells struck the building and neighboring stores but Capone, who dove to the floor of the Hawthorn coffee shop when the attack began, miraculously escaped.

The noonday assault badly frightened Scarface and he called for a truce. His emissary, Tony Lombardo, met with Weiss at the Morrison Hotel on October 4, 1926. Capone wanted no more killing and agreed "to live and let live," Lombardo told Weiss.

Hymie told Lombardo that he would make peace only if Albert Anselmi and John Scalise, the murderers of his friend Dion O'Bannion, were turned over to him. Lombardo called Capone on the spot and told Scarface Little Hymie's terms.

"What?" Capone screamed. "I wouldn't do that to a yellow dog!"

The momentary truce was over.

Capone waited for his chance. He sent Frank Diamond, Frank Nitti, Scalise, and Anselmi (and later reports state Anthony Accardo) to the North Side where they rented rooms facing Weiss' headquarters at 740 N. State, O'Bannion's old flower shop. For days, the crew manned two machinegun nests and waited, watching the corner in shifts.

Their vigil was rewarded on October 11, 1926 when Weiss, three of his bodyguards, Sam Peller, Benny Jacobs, and Paddy Murray, and his lawyer, William W. O'Brien, alighted from a car in front of the Holy Name Cathedral and began to walk across the street to the shop. The machineguns opened up on them as they were half-way across the street. Weiss, the main target, was shattered with ten bullets, killed instantly. Murray was dead before he hit the cement with sixteen bullets in him. Peller was wounded in the groin, O'Brien in the arm, Jacobs in the leg.

The vicious barrage raked half the street, hitting the cornerstone of Holy Name Cathedral. The cornerstone originally had an inscription (from St. Paul's *Epistle to the Philippians*, 2:10) on it which read: "At the name of Jesus every knee should bow in heaven and on earth." The stone was hit by so many bullets that only six words remained: ". . . every knee should . . . heaven and . . . earth."

Newspaper reporters rushed to Capone to get a statement from him about the death of his arch enemy (the only Chicago gangster Scarface ever really feared). Big Al met them in his posh office in the Hawthorn Hotel. He was wearing an imported silk bathrobe, was smoking a large Havana cigar, and felt quite talkative.

"That was butchery," he said shaking his head sadly. "Hymie was a good kid. He could have got out long ago and taken his and been alive today. When we were in business together in the old days, I got to know him well and used to go often to his room for a friendly visit. A lot of us guys did, Nitti, Diamond . . ."

"Torrio and me made Weiss and O'Bannion. Then they went on their own. When they broke away and went into business for themselves that was jake with us. We had no objections. Then they started to get real nasty, raiding our territory. We sent 'em word to stay in their own back yard, up North. We pleaded with 'em not to start no trouble, we begged them. They busted into our places, wrecking 'em and hijacking our trucks. They had a swell head . . . they thought they were bigger than we were.

"Then someone got O'Bannion. Then Torrio was shot—and he knew who shot him—and I had a little talk with Weiss. 'What do you want to do, Hymie' I asked him, 'get yourself killed before you're thirty?' He gave a wise answer, a smartcracker, he was. He said something like 'How old are you, Al?' Imagine that? He was a real bullhead, thought he was smarter than anybody in the world. That's why he's dead.

" 'You'd better get some sense while some of us are still alive,' I told him. He could have got along with me. But he wouldn't listen to me. Forty times I've tried to arrange things so we would have peace and life would be worth living. Who wants to be followed around night and day by guards? Not me! And that stupid shootout at noon in front of the hotel here . . . they might as well as come after me with a brass band with a day's warning . . . There was plenty to share for everyone. But Weiss couldn't be told anything. I suppose you couldn't have told him a week ago that he'd be dead today. There are some reasonable fellows in his outfit, and if they want peace I'm for it now, as I always have been.

"I'm sorry Hymie was killed but I didn't have anything to do with it. I phoned the detective bureau that I'd come in if they wanted me, but they told me they didn't want me. I knew I'd be blamed for it . . . Why should I kill Weiss?"

William Schoemaker, chief of detectives, was quoted as saying later: "Capone knows why and so does everybody else. He had Hymie killed . . . and all those others."

The least sympathetic over the loss of Earl Hymie Weiss was his brother, Frank Weiss. A reporter stopped Frank at Hymie's funeral and asked him for some family background. Frank Weiss stared solemnly at the reporter and then flatly stated: "I don't know nothing about Hymie's early life at home because I can't remember too much about it. And I don't know anything about his affairs. You see, I've seen him only once in twenty years. That was six years ago when he shot me."

[ALSO SEE Louis "Two Gun" Alterie, Al Capone, Vincent "The Schemer" Drucci, George "Bugs" Moran, Dion O'Bannion, John Torrio.]

WESTERVELT, WILLIAM
Kidnapper, Murderer ● (1831- ?)

Early in 1874, a discharged New York cop, William Westervelt, arrived in the quiet community of Germantown, Pa. After making several inquiries as to the financial status of grocer Christian Ross, he departed. Though Ross owned an impressive-looking mansion, he was not as well-to-do as Westervelt was made to believe by gossipy neighbors.

Mistaking Ross for a rich man, Westervelt sent two of his confederates, infamous burglars Joseph Douglass and William Mosher, to Germantown to kidnap Ross' youngest son, four-year-old Charles Brewster "Charley" Ross, and bring him to New York where he would be held for ransom.

On July 1, 1874, Douglass and Mosher abducted little Charley from in front of his home on the pretext of taking him to Philadelphia to buy fireworks for an upcoming Fourth of July celebration. He was never seen again but reports have it the boy was delivered to Wes-

Burglars and kidnappers Joseph Douglass and William Mosher abducted four-year-old Charley Ross for ex cop William Westervelt, who held him for ransom and then reportedly killed him when authorities closed in. (N.Y. Historical Society)

tervelt and held in New York while negotiations went on for the delivery of the ransom money, $20,000.

Christian Ross was told to pack the money in a suitcase and then board a specific New York-bound train. He was told to stand at the end of the platform car and toss the suitcase from the train when he saw a series of lights flash along the way. He followed these instructions, but all the way to New York, Ross saw no lights as he stood on the back platform of the car. The car was jammed with detectives, a fact Westervelt may have learned.

New York police authorities, by checking handwriting samples in their files, identified the ransom notes as having been written by William Mosher, a habitual burglar. Ironically, Westervelt, who was Mosher's brother-in-law, was called in by police to help. After several meetings it was obvious that Westervelt could not produce his brother-in-law. Then, on December 14, 1874, Mosher and Douglass were caught in the act of burglarizing a Brooklyn home and both were shot while resisting arrest.

With his dying breath, Mosher admitted to kidnapping Charley Ross. "We done it," he said. "We did it for money."

Westervelt was subsequently identified as having been in Germantown asking strange questions about the Ross family. He was brought to Philadelphia and there stood trial for the kidnapping. A woman identified him as being on a trolley car with little Charley

but the ex-cop would admit to nothing, repeatedly stating his innocence. He was tried, found guilty of perpetrating America'a first major kidnapping, and sentenced to seven years of solitary confinement which he served. Upon his release, Westervelt completely disappeared.

Underworld reports had it that Westervelt took the Ross child to New York and held him there while attempting to collect the ransom money. When the intensive manhunt for the child began and publicity on the case became widespread, he panicked and drowned the boy in the East River.

WHITE, ALEXANDER
Murderer ● (1762-1784)

White immigrated from Tyrone, Ireland to Boston where he fell in love with a local girl. He proposed marriage but soon realized that in his impoverished state he could ill afford a bride. To solve his dilemma, White, who worked as a seaman aboard a cutter, tried to rob his captain, killing him in the process while their ship was anchored in Cow Harbor, Long Island, N. Y.

A passenger witnessed the murder and escaped White's blade by diving overboard and swimming to shore where he made a report to harbor authorities. The seaman was arrested and quickly convicted of the killing and of piracy. He was hanged at Cambridge, Mass., on November 18, 1784.

WHITE HAND GANG

The White Handers were river terrorists who extorted money from dockworkers and boat captains alike on the East River, centering activities along the Brooklyn shore from 1900-1925. They were

Two leaders of the Brooklyn White Hand Gang of the early 1920s—W. L. "Wild Bill" Lovett and Richard "Peg Leg" Lonergan.

led by Wild Bill Lovett and Dinny Meehan. In 1920, White Hand lieutenant Meehan was stabbed to death by an underling who aspired to his rank. Wild Bill was shot to death in 1923, ambushed one evening as he made his way to his Brooklyn home.

Richard "Peg Leg" Lonergan, a scabrous murderer with twenty killings to his credit, then took over the White Hand mob. On the night of December 26, 1925, Lonergan entered the Adonis Social Club, a South Brooklyn saloon patronized by Italian gangsters. With him was Cornelius "Needles" Ferry, Jimmy Hart, Patrick "Happy" Maloney, and Aaron Harms.

By coincidence, Al Capone, who had become ganglord of Chicago, had returned to his old stomping grounds in Brooklyn for a brief nostalgic visit (and also to cement relationships with *Unione Siciliane* president Frankie Yale) and happened to also be in the club. With him were Italian mobsters Fiore "Fury" Agoglia, Jack "Stick-'em-Up" Stabile, George Carozza, Ralph Demato, Frank Piazza, and Tony Desso.

Lonergan was apparently spoiling for a fight, even though he and his band were considerably outnumbered. He slammed the bar for service and made loud, insulting remarks about "dagoes" and "ginzos." When he spotted two Irish girls entering the club on the arms of Italian youths, he chased them out, shouting after them: "Come back with white men!"

At 2 a.m., as if on cue, the lights of the Adonis Club suddenly went out. The place then lit up with blazing, snapping gunfire. When the lights went back on again, Lonergan, Harms, and Ferry were lying in the middle of the floor, all of them shot in the head.

The rest of the Irish gangsters had fled in the dark.

A gruesome jester had, while the lights were out, pinned some sheet music to Peg Leg's suitcoat. The title of the song was "She's My Baby."

The White Handers faded after that and disappeared altogether in 1928.

WHITE, JOHN DUNCAN
Murderer, Pirate ● (? -1826)

White, alias Charles Marchant, was wanted for several robberies in New England. He and his partner, Winslow Curtis, alias Sylvester Colson, signed on board the *Fairy*, a merchant vessel, in 1826 to avoid the pursuit of authorities.

While bound for Gottenburg, White and Curtis revolted and killed Captain Edward Selfridge, only 23, and first mate Tom Jenkins, throwing their bodies overboard. The two mutineers then sailed the *Fairy* to Louisburg, Nova Scotia and sank it.

The two pirates were soon captured and brought to Boston for trial. They were found guilty and sentenced to death. On the night before the execution, White hanged himself in his cell; Curtis mounted the scaffold the next day and died on time.

WHITMAN, CHARLES
Murderer ● (1941-1966)

BACKGROUND: BORN AND RAISED IN FLORIDA NEAR LAKE WORTH. AS A YOUTH BECAME AN EAGLE SCOUT. ATTENDED THE UNIVERSITY OF TEXAS IN AUSTIN. SERVED IN THE U.S. MARINE CORPS. MARRIED, NO CHILDREN. DESCRIPTION: 6', BLUE EYES, BLOND HAIR, HEAVYSET. ALIASES: NONE. RECORD: KILLED HIS MOTHER AND HIS WIFE 7/31/66; FROM THE TOWER OF THE UNIV. OF TEXAS CAMPUS IN AUSTIN, ON 8/1/66, SHOT 46 PEOPLE, KILLING SIXTEEN; DIED ON THE SAME DAY AT THE HANDS OF POLICE ATTEMPTING TO CAPTURE HIM.

When Don Walden and his girl, Cheryl Botts, stepped off the observation deck of the University of Texas' 300-foot tower, they saw him: a handsome young man with a rifle in each fist.

They also saw a pool of some red-black substance at the receptionist's desk.

"Oh, don't step in that mess, Don," Cheryl said.

The couple had been looking over the University of Texas campus and the city of Austin for about a half hour.

As they headed for the stairs, Miss Botts said, "Hello" to the young blond-haired man.

"Hi," the young man smiled affably, "how are you?"

As the couple walked to the 27th floor elevator, Miss Botts paused. "Why do you suppose he had those rifles with him?" she asked.

"I don't know," Walden replied. "I was about to ask him the same thing. He's probably a maintenance man who's supposed to shoot pigeons."

Up on the observatory platform, 25-year-old Charles Whitman was preparing to shoot a lot more than birds. In 96 minutes, this one-man army, seeking vengeance for imagined personal hurts, would kill sixteen innocent people and wound thirty more, a slaughter unequalled in modern American murder.

Whitman's mind had been jarred several months earlier, in March 1966. He stood weeping outside the home of his parents in Lake Worth, Fla., a pleasant resort by the sea.

On this day Whitman's mother, after years of browbeating and physical punishment, decided to leave his father.

Charles Whitman seemed as normal as the next man, but when his mother left his father he began to act strangely. By the time Whitman returned to Austin with his mother, he was a mass of jangled nerves. He strained to become a top student and the studies were telling on him. Elaine Fuess, a neighbor, remembered, "even when he looked perfectly normal, he gave you this feeling of trying to control himself."

Whitman's temper flared constantly at the smallest of agitations.

Charles was intelligent enough to realize he had problems so he went to a psychiatrist on March 29, 1966.

In a waiting room, he was handed a form to fill out. "What is your chief problem?" the form began.

Whitman puzzled over it.

Finally, he wrote, "That's why I'm here. I don't know."

During his visit with Dr. Maurice Heatly, Whitman told of his uncontrollable temper, a seething anger that had caused him to attack his wife twice—just as his father had brutally beaten his mother.

He admitted that there was a killer's wrath inside him that could erupt in the future. He couldn't explain exactly how.

Dr. Heatly wrote down his observations, after Whitman left. "The precipitating factor for this visit seemed to be the separation of his parents 30 days ago . . . He says his father has called him every 48 hours for several weeks petitioning him to persuade his mother to return.

"His real concern is for himself. He admits having overwhelming periods of hostility with a minimum of provocation.

"*At one point he said he was thinking about going up on the tower with a deer rifle and start shooting people* [italics added.]

On July 22, Charles Whitman, accompanied by his brother, went up to the tower and looked around. He noted the bastion-like wall around the observation deck and the commanding view of the campus.

Nine days later, at exactly 6:45 p.m., Whitman sat before his portable typewriter and

Sleeping peacefully is 25-year-old Charles Whitman, who, days after this picture was taken, shot 46 people (killing sixteen) from the tower of the Texas University campus in Austin, Tex., 7/31/66. (UPI)

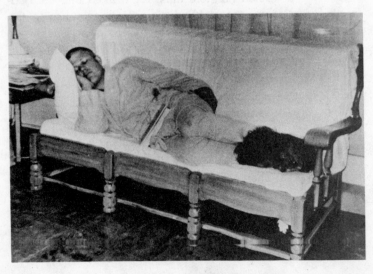

carefully typed out a terrifying note. It was addressed to no one:

"I don't quite understand what is compelling me to type this note," he tapped out gently. "I have been to a psychiatrist. I have been having fears and violent impulses. I've had some tremendous headaches in the past.

"I am prepared to die. After my death, I wish an autopsy on me be performed to see if there's any mental disorder."

At this point in Whitman's macabre letter, he began to attack his father viciously. Then he wrote:

"I've decided to kill Kathy tonight. I love her very much." Whitman then went back to writing attacks on his father and his invective was intense. Then back to his wife, Kathy:

"I intend to kill my wife after I pick her up from work. I don't want her to have to face the embarrassment my actions will surely cause her . . ."

His note-writing was interrupted by the Fuess neighbors. Shortly after they left, he picked up his wife but apparently changed his mind about killing her immediately. He dropped her off at their apartment and drove to his mother's residence.

Charles Whitman visited with his mother and then, about midnight, he drove a knife into her chest and followed this gruesome act by shooting her in the back of the head.

Quickly, he scribbled a note "To Whom It May Concern: I have just killed my mother. If there's a heaven, she's going there. If there's not a heaven, she's out of her pain and misery.

"I love my mother with all my heart."

Whitman got home around 1 a.m. and wasted no more time. He walked into the bedroom and stabbed his wife three times in the chest before bundling her in a bedsheet.

The tarnished Eagle Scout then went calmly back to his typewriter and tapped out the words: "12:00 a.m.—Mother already dead. 3 o'clock—both dead."

Whitman was not through communicating with his unseen and unknown readers. He poured out his feelings for his father, stating that he hated him "with a mortal passion."

Then, as a lame postscript, he ended his morbid epistle with: "Life is not worth living."

Like a man who knows his duty, Whitman set out on August 1, 1966, with several pistols and a 35-mm Remington rifle, heading for the tower where he would arbitrarily decide that the lives of forty-six other people were also not worth living and that he was the man to end them.

After renting a dolly with which to truck his arsenal to the top of the tower, he stopped off at a gunshop and purchased a powerful .30-caliber carbine and boxes of ammunition. Whitman wanted to do the job right.

He packed meats, peanuts, fruit cocktail, raisins, sandwiches, and water. He also stashed gasoline, toilet paper, a transistor radio, and even a bottle of spray deodorant. An ex-Marine, Whitman was prepared for anything.

Wheeling the dolly containing his weapons and a service foot locker, Whitman casually rolled his stores to the tower and took the elevator to the 27th floor. Receptionist Edna Townsley, just outside the observation deck, asked the young man what he wanted.

Whitman's answer was to tear half her skull away with a tremendous blow from the butt of his rifle. He threw her body behind a sofa just before Don Walden and Cheryl Botts walked to the elevator, noticing but not knowing it was Miss Townsley's blood which stained the floor.

After he had strangely spared their lives, Whitman barricaded the stairway with a desk.

He heard approaching footsteps and leveled his sawed-off shotgun at the visitors.

With two quick squeezes he blasted the heads off Mike Gabour and his aunt, who were coming up for the view. Relatives dragged the bodies back to the 27th floor.

Whitman headed for the tower deck, taking his Remington Rifle with its telescopic lens. As he went, he fired a blast into Miss Townsley's body.

Once on the deck, Whitman surveyed the strolling, unconcerned people beneath his gaze. They were sitting ducks.

He began shooting at 11:48 a.m. The killing of Miss Townsley had delayed him and he missed the 11:30 class-changing time when more than 1,000 students would have been in his sights.

Nonetheless, within minutes, Whitman shot down six students. He then hit Mrs. Claire Wilson in the abdomen. She survived, but the bullet crushed the skull of the baby she was carrying.

Next went student Thomas Eckman, killed

immediately with a bullet in the head. Newspaper boy Alec Hernandez was blasted from his bike as he made deliveries.

Patrolman Billy Speed, answering the alarm, was killed next as he tried for a shot at Whitman from behind a stone railing.

Whitman picked off Roy Dell Schmidt with a 500-yard shot that entered his stomach. Next came Peace Corps trainee Thomas Ashton. Robert Boyer got it in the back and died, leaving two children and a pregnant wife waiting for him in England.

An expert marksman in the service, Whitman never seemed to miss. He went on dropping students and townspeople alike.

More than 100 policemen tried to get a shot at Whitman, but his position was all but invulnerable. Authorities even sent a low-flying plane over the tower but Whitman drove it off with rapid fire from his carbine.

In desperation, an over-the-top charge was led up the stairs and onto the observation deck by intrepid Austin patrolman Ramiro Martinez.

They went in blasting. Martinez was wounded but Whitman was shot to pieces, finally finding the death he wanted so much.

He took eighteen people with him.

WHYOS GANG

Following the Civil War, the Whyos came into existence in New York and they soon proved to be the most vicious and terrifying street gang ever seen in the city. The origin of the name of the gang remains a mystery but one writer advanced the idea that it resulted from a "peculiar call sometimes employed by gangsters."

Evolving from the Chichesters and the old Five Points Gang, the Whyos dominated the Fourth Ward of the Lower East Side and headquartered at Mulberry Bend. Unlike any other gang in New York, the Whyos considered the whole of Manhattan their province and some of their five hundred members were, at one time or other, constantly raiding the territories of Greenwich Village or West Side

gangs. Their central drinking spa was aptly named The Morgue and was the scene of at least one hundred violent murders.

Gang fights between the members were not unusual. Often, Whyos factions drew guns on each other and blasted away for hours in The Morgue. Among the broad ranks of the Whyos were to be found the arch criminals of the day: Big Josh Hines, Hoggy Walsh, Bull Hurley, Fig McGerald, Baboon Connolly, Googy Corcoran, Red Rocks Farrell, Slops Connolly, Piker Ryan, Dorsey Doyle, and Mike Loyd: Irish to a man and not only professional killers, but also master burglars, pickpockets, and bandits.

Big Josh Hines delighted in holding up stuss games (a variation of faro), marching from one gambling den to another like a man following a milk route each night. He openly wore a brace of pistols and was utterly amazed by a police detective who stopped him one night and said "The boys are getting mad with your stickups."

"What?" Hines bellowed. "Them guys must be nuts! Don't I always leave 'em somethin'? All I want is me fair share!"

At the peak of the Whyos' reputation and power in the 1880s and 1890s, it became mandatory for an apprentice Whyo to kill a man before gaining full membership. This decree was handed down by gang captain Mike McGloin in 1883 when he was quoted as saying: "A guy ain't tough until he has knocked his man out!"

Living up to his own code, McGloin attempted to rob a West Twenty-fifth Street saloonkeeper named Louis Hanier, killing Hanier in the process before he was captured by police. McGloin died on the gallows in the Tombs prison on March 8, 1883.

Whyos killers hired out at all hours of the day to administer beatings and murder. One of the gangleaders, Piker Ryan, was arrested in 1884. In his pocket was found a printed list of services the Whyos offered and the cost of each. It read:

"Punching .... $	2
Both eyes blackened	4
Nose and jaw broke	10
Jacked out (knocked out with a blackjack)	15
Ear chawed off	15
Leg or arm broke	19

Some deadly members of the dreaded New York Whyos Gang (left to right) Big Josh Hines, Piker Ryan, Red Rocks Farrell, Slops Connolly.

Shot in leg	25
Stab	25
Doing the big job [murder]	100 and up."

Danny Lyons and Danny Driscoll headed the Whyos by 1887. The latter hanged on January 23, 1888. Driscoll had gotten into an argument with gangster John McCarthy over a prostitute named Beezy Garrity. They both drew guns in the girl's presence and banged away at each other. Though they missed each other, one of Driscoll's bullets struck Beezy and killed her. Lyons followed Driscoll to the gallows six months later on August 21, 1888 after shooting a fellow gangster, Joseph Quinn, in a noonday gun battle in the middle of Paradise Square at the Five Points on July 5, 1887. The duel was fought over a prostitute named Pretty Kitty McGown.

Two of Lyons' prostitutes, Lizzie the Dove and Gentle Maggie, were so upset by the gangleader's subsequent execution in the Tombs that they donned mourning black and refused customers for a whole week. Months later the two women fell to arguing in a bar over whose sadness at the loss of Lyons was greater.

"I'll settle it," Gentle Maggie said; she drew a knife and plunged it into Lizzie the Dove's throat.

As she was dying, Lizzie gurgled: "I'll meet you in hell soon and scratch your eyes out there!"

One of the Whyos gangsters turned inventor. Dandy John Dolan created a host of deadly implements for the gang members with which they could gouge out eyes and stomp the faces of gang rivals. Dolan used his eye gouger, made of copper and worn on the thumb, on many occasions. He once robbed, in the summer of 1875, a store owned by wealthy manufacturer James H. Noe. When Noe caught him in the act, Dolan crushed his skull with an iron bar and gouged out Noe's eyes for good measure. Dolan carried the eyeballs around in his vest pocket for a week, showing them to his pals.

Police Detective Joseph M. Dorcy tracked Dolan down and found Noe's jewelry in Dolan's pockets. Dolan was convicted of the murder and was hanged April 21, 1876.

For forty years the Whyos ruled the criminal underworld in New York but faded at the turn of the century with the coming of newer gangs led by Monk Eastman and Paul Kelly.

WILBER, LEWIS
Murderer ● (1816-1839)

Riverboat life on the Erie Canal was exciting and adventuresome to many early American pioneers, but it was routine and boring to Lewis Wilber. He had worked the boats for several years and was on board the *Oliver Newbury* heading West when he struck up an acquaintance with 53-year-old Robert Barber, a passenger who climbed aboard at Utica, N. Y., August 29, 1837.

Barber told Wilber that he was on his way to Buffalo where he intended to get married. Wilber smiled and nodded approvingly. The two, according to the other thirty-odd passengers, became great friends. When the boat stopped at New Boston for supplies the next morning, the two men got off and strolled leisurely into the woods, talking in animated fashion.

Four miles upstream, Wilber, alone, climbed back on board the *Oliver Newbury*, such was the snail's pace of the tow boat. When questioned as to Barber's whereabouts, Wilber explained that the older man had decided to walk to Syracuse. Barber's corpse, horribly cut to pieces, was found almost eight months later.

Wilber was remembered by the passengers and he was traced by lawmen to the Ohio River Valley where he was arrested and returned to New York for trial. Though he confessed to the murder, Wilber never volunteered his reasons for killing Barber.

The murderer was executed on the gallows October 3, 1839 at Morrisville, N. Y.

WILD BUNCH, THE

When the West as the outlaws knew it began to collapse like a Chinese magic box in the 1890s, the remnants of the robber bands straggled and romped toward their last bastion: Hole-in-the-Wall, an almost impenetrable and natural fortress of deep gorges, high cliffs, and rocky retreats that straddled the Wyoming, Colorado, and Utah state lines. Outlaws came there from all points of the land.

Some drifted in, crime weary and looking for a place to rest, even to permanently settle. Others roared into Hole-in-the-Wall to recruit gang members for sallies and raids into more civilized areas. Under the pressure of tens of thousands of settlers, farmers, and town-build-ers, the bandits were being penned in, like the Indians, sectored off into invisible reservations.

Before their demise, the outlaw gangs lashed out viciously in a decade-long battle with the forces of the law, a battle that reached across the plains of ten states. The victims were trainmen, bankers, and cattle ranchers, who were robbed by ravaging bands that left hundreds killed, wounded, and crippled. It was the last fling of the bad man on horseback, the last stand of a violent and uncompromising breed known as The Wild Bunch.

Here are the men who rode in and out of Hole-in-the-Wall for thirty some odd years, all of whom could be termed loosely or specifically members of the Wild Bunch:

—Dave Atkins, train robber and murderer from San Angelo, Texas. Orginally a farm hand, Atkins turned to crime early in his twenties. Pinkerton archives described him as having a "round face, thick lips . . . drops his head when talking . . . peculiar slouchy walk."

—Jack Bennett, who often brought supplies to his outlaw friends living in Hole-in-the-Wall. Bennett was caught after a shootout with a posse and was hanged from the crosspieces at the entrance of the Bassett ranch in March, 1898.

—Sam Carey, called "Laughing Sam," was anything but congenial. A meanstreaked bandit with an ugly knife scar under his right eye, Carey was one of the first outlaws to use Hole-in-the-Wall as a hideout in the 1880s. He had murdered several men by the time he embarked on a bank robbing career that led him through Wyoming, Montana, and South Dakota. With him rode the Taylor brothers and professional train robbers Bud Deslow and H. Wilcox.

Laughing Sam's robbery of the Spearfish bank in South Dakota was almost a repeat of the disastrous raids led by Jesse James at Northfield and the Daltons at Coffeyville. He alone escaped a citizen's ambush as the gang emerged from the bank, riding back to the Hole more dead than alive. A cowboy surgeon removed three bullets from his badly scarred body and Laughing Sam rode out again the next week to rob a train.

—William Todd Carver, one of Butch Cassidy's original riders, who rode with Butch

The Wild Bunch arrived in Fort Worth, Texas, and thought it would be fun to sit for a formal photograph; they are (standing, left to right) William Carver, Harvey Logan ("Kid Curry"), and (sitting, left to right) Harry Longbaugh ("The Sundance Kid"), Ben Kilpatrick, and the impish Butch Cassidy. (Pinkerton, Inc.)

and the Sundance Kid on a half dozen train robberies.

—Joseph Chancellor, a Texas-born bandit who first earned his reputation as a gunfighter and bankrobber in Oklahoma before moving to Hole-in-the-Wall. Chancellor had also served time in the Santa Fe, N. M. Penitentiary (released January 28, 1897) for rustling. He arrived in the Hole about 1904. This 37-year-old bandit was described by Pinkerton archivists as being nervous. "Constantly gets up two or three times during the night to smoke. Uses brown cigarette paper. Fingers stained from the use of this paper. Never drinks or chews tobacco."

—William Cruzan, 33 years old by the turn of the century, an ugly-tempered pistol-whipper who had served four years in jail for rustling and robbery. A lone wolf bandit, Cruzan raided several banks in the Dakotas, Wyoming, and Colorado before he was gunned down.

—George L. "Flat Nose" Curry (George

Parrott), once described as "the largest rustler in Wyoming." Also known as "Big Nose" Curry, this bandit served as a Western Fagin to the Logan brothers, Harvey, Lonny, and Johnny (another Logan brother, Henry, did not take up the outlaw trail). He also rode with Butch Cassidy as did Harvey Logan, in many raids. Logan's dog-like idolatry for George Curry caused him to adopt the name Kid Curry.

After participating in several bank and train robberies in the Southwest following the turn of the century, George Curry rode back to the Hole-in-the-Wall and began rustling cattle. He was caught red-handed while changing a brand by the sheriff of Vernal, Utah.

Instead of surrendering, Curry leaped on his horse and galloped off. The sheriff gave chase and for ten miles, the two men exchanged shots that boomed and echoed across the plain. A lucky shot hit Curry in the skull and he dropped from his saddle—dead.

The residents of Castle Gate, U. rushed to

the outskirts of their little town where Curry had been slain. Outlaws, like the buffalo, were becoming increasingly rare and some of the citizens enthusiastically sought souvenirs of this memorable pursuit and capture. They took out hunting knives and stripped away Big Nose George Curry's flesh from his chest. One ambitious townsman made a pair of shoes from the flesh. Another swatch wound up as a good luck charm and was carried from vest to vest through generations of outlaw *aficionados*. The final possessor of the skin swatch, before these gruesome artifacts were turned over to a Western museum, was a Professor Reed of the Wyoming University at Laramie.

—Frank "Peg Leg" Elliot, a 21-year-old bank robber was first arrested with Robert Eldredge in October, 1891. Elliot and Eldredge were caught robbing a train and shot to death by a posse.

—O. C. "Camilla" Hanks, also known as "Deaf Charley," was one of Butch Cassidy's original Wild Bunch. Hanks rode alongside Cassidy, Kid Curry, the Sundance Kid, Bill Carver, and Ben Kilpatrick in almost every raid the Wild Bunch committed.

Hanks was a short, squat outlaw from Las Vegas, N. M., where he murdered a man in a bar fight. In his twenties he robbed and killed in Utah and Montana under the alias Charley Jones. He was captured by a posse in Teton, Mont. in 1892 just after robbing a Northern

William Cruzan. (Pinkerton, Inc.)

Pacific train at Big Timber, Mont. Sentenced to ten years in jail at Deer Lodge, Hanks was released on April 30, 1901 and promptly rode to Hole-in-the-Wall where he joined Butch Cassidy and went on to rob trains at Tipton, Wyo. and Wagner, Mont. He was later shot and killed.

—Swede Johnson, an insane killer who pulled his six gun at the slightest insult. Johnson first appeared in Hole-in-the-Wall in 1898 and became friendly with arch killers and robbers Dave Lant and Harry Tracy, who was known as the "Mad Dog" of the Wild Bunch. Three months after his arrival, Johnson exploded when Willy Strang, a seventeen-year-old cowboy, kiddingly dumped a pitcher of water on him. Johnson jumped up and emptied his six gun into the boy. He, Tracy, and Lant were tracked down for this murder and Johnson was sent to Wyoming State Prison for life.

—Ben Kilpatrick, "The Tall Texan," was, next to the Sundance Kid, Butch Cassidy's top man. He was a mediocre gunfighter but nerveless when it came to robbing banks and trains. When Butch and Sundance fled to South America, Kilpatrick, using the alias Benjamin Arnold, struck out on his own. Laura Bullion, alias Della Rose, went with him. She was the last in a line of cowgirls who followed Kilpatrick's outlaw trail.

Both Kilpatrick and Laura Bullion were captured by police detectives in St. Louis on November 8, 1901. Found in their luggage was $7,000, part of the money Kilpatrick had helped Butch Cassidy to liberate from a Great Northern train at Wagner, Mont., on July 3 of that year.

The Tall Texan admitted taking part in the Wagner robbery, and on December 12, 1901 he was sentenced to fifteen years in the federal penitentiary at Atlanta, Ga. Laura Bullion was convicted as the gang's accomplice and drew a five year sentence in a Tennessee women's prison.

Released on June 11, 1911, Kilpatrick resumed his old ways, a trainrobber out of his own time. He didn't last long. On March 14, 1912, when Kilpatrick and Howard Benson, another ex-convict from Atlanta, walked into the baggage car of the Pacific's Sunset Flyer, they learned that the old times were gone forever.

Resistance to armed bandits before the

O. C. Camiella Hanks.

Harry Tracy.

Dave Lant. (Pinkerton, Inc.)

turn of the century had been unthinkable. But feisty David A. Trousdale, the baggage car guard, was not impressed by Kilpatrick and Benson who demanded he turn over the money in the safe. The two first attempted to dupe Trousdale.

"I'm a Union Pacific detective," Benson told him when they entered the car. "We just got wind of a robbery attempt on you."

Trousdale began to reach for his rifle when Kilpatrick poked his own rifle in the guard's stomach, saying, "Don't try it, young fellow."

The nervy guard, through a ruse, got Kilpatrick to turn his head and when he did so, Trousdale brought an ice mallet down on his skull, killing him with one blow. He then grabbed the Tall Texan's rifle and shot and killed Benson.

"They thought they were such smooth workers at the game," Trousdale told reporters later. "But it made me sore the way they acted, so I decided to take some of the conceit out of them . . . I am more worried about what to do with the vacation and the reward the company has given me than I am about killing those two."

A more humiliating end never befell a Western bad man.

—Elza Lay was another one of the hardcore members of the Wild Bunch who rode with Butch Cassidy on almost all of his rob-

bery sorties. Following the disappearance of Cassidy and Sundance, Lay was trapped by a posse in Clayton, N. M. and tried to shoot his way to freedom. He killed a sheriff in the attempt but was knocked senseless by gun butts and thrown into jail. He was sentenced to prison for life in the Santa Fe Penitentiary.

—Jesse Linsley, a horsethief and ex-convict, appeared briefly at Hole-in-the-Wall in the 1890s after committing some minor robberies. Linsley disappeared at the turn of the century.

—Harvey Logan, better known as "Kid Curry," was the real killer of the Wild Bunch, a ruthless gunslinger whose leadership abilities were marred by his quick temper and total reliance upon a six gun. One of four brothers, Logan came from Dodge, Mo. and gained Western fame in his early twenties as one of the most feared gunmen alive. He could not outdraw Sundance but was a deadly marksman. He killed eight men in street duels before joining the Wild Bunch.

Logan wore a pearl-handled Peacemaker with a fourteen inch barrel, and he used it often. Taught to rustle cattle by George Curry, Logan soon graduated to robbing banks and trains. He appeared at Hole-in-the-Wall with gunmen Bob Lee and Jim Thornhill about 1896, the same time his leader, Butch Cassidy, arrived there fresh from serving a two-year prison sentence. Logan participated in every major robbery committed by the Wild Bunch and it was often that Cassidy had to stop Kid Curry from needlessly killing train guards.

When Cassidy and Sundance left for South America Logan promised to join them, but he went on to rob banks and trains and by 1901 was the most hunted outlaw in America. He was trapped in a Knoxville, Tenn. poolroom in the fall of 1902, and was wounded as he attempted to escape squads of policemen. He was identified as the infamous Kid Curry by Pinkerton detective Lowell Spence.

As he was being taken to jail, five thousand people mobbed the police van to get a look at him. But Curry's mind was on Spence.

"Some day I'll kill that man," Logan told one of his captors. "He's very troublesome."

Logan was imprisoned in 1902 but escaped from the Knoxville Jail on June 27, 1903. Pinkertons led by Lowell Spence and other law enforcement officers trailed Logan all the way

Tom O'Day. (Pinkerton, Inc.)

to the Rockies in Colorado. There Logan formed a new band of robbers and stopped a train in Parachute, Colo., taking a small amount of money from the express car. Two days later Logan and his men were trapped in a dead end canyon by a large posse.

While jumping up and running for the cover of a large boulder, Kid Curry was wounded in the shoulder. The lawmen heard one of the outlaws call to him: "Are you hit?"

After a long silence, Kid Curry answered: "Yes, and I'm going to end it here." With that Harvey Logan, the most feared member of the Wild Bunch, sent a bullet into his left temple and died.

—James Lowe was a 32-year-old train robber who was in and out of Hole-in-the-Wall during the waning years of the Wild Bunch. He was killed in 1910.

—Tom O'Day, a cowboy from Wyoming, turned to crime in the late 1890s, centering his exploits on bank robbery. He sometimes rode with Butch Cassidy but preferred to be on his own. He was finally captured in Casper, Wyo. on November 23, 1903 while herding stolen horses through the center of town. He was given a long prison term.

—Will Roberts, also known as "Dixon," specialized in train robbery and was one of the last important outlaws to hide out in Hole-in-the-Wall.

—Harry Tracy, the most brutal member of the Wild Bunch, preceded Butch and his boys to Hole-in-the-Wall by two years and was addicted to murder. Tracy was sent to the Colorado State Prison at Aspen for life with Dave Lant, convicted with Swede Johnson for killing Willy Strang in 1898.

Tracy escaped from the Aspen jail on June 9, 1902 with Dave Merrill. Somehow, Tracy got his hands on a rifle and began picking guards off the prison wall. He killed one and wounded three. Then he and Merrill, using a wounded guard as a human shield, broke through a gate and dashed to freedom.

They traveled to Oregon, stealing guns and ammunition in Salem, and robbing a carriage in Portland. Hundreds of soldiers were put on their trail. Tracy and Merrill went into the woods and headed for Washington.

Tracy appeared alone in a small fishing town on Puget Sound on July 8, 1902. He had killed Merrill. While the two men were being hunted, they had taken refuge in a barn. There Tracy found a newspaper and began to read. He came across a story that reported Merrill had informed on Tracy years ago, a fact unknown to Tracy, in order to receive a lighter sentence for a robbery they had both committed. Laying aside the paper, Tracy reached over and strangled his fellow escapee to death.

Commandeering a motor launch in a fishing village, Tracy ordered the captain to pass close to the McNeil Island Penitentiary which jutted from the middle of Puget Sound.

"For God's sake, why?" the Captain asked.

"I want to pick a few guards off the wall," Tracy replied. The outlaw thought better of the idea when it occurred to him that the guards might fire back and possibly kill him. He ordered the captain to take him to Seattle. There he tied up the boat's crew and began walking inland. He bummed his way through Washington, begging meals from farmers.

The soldiers and possemen were still tracking him in August, 1902. Tired, hunted like an animal in alien territory, Tracy decided to turn about and make a fight of it. He hid in a tall stand of timber and traded shots with lawmen for several hours. As the sun began to set, Tracy realized his position was hopeless. Like Harvey Logan, he preferred to end his own life rather than return to prison.

At dusk, Harry Tracy put his six gun to his temple and fired.

The possemen listened for a while and then one said, "I guess he's through." They closed in, a hundred men gripping rifles, and stepping carefully around tall trees and through thick underbrush. Tracy was lying in a clearing with a pistol still gripped in his stiffened hand. He had pulled his trousers up to his knees to display his worn out cowboy boots, the dead Western outlaw lying in the woods of Washington, far from his native plain.

It was all over with the Wild Bunch.

[ALSO SEE Butch Cassidy.]

WITTROCK, FREDERICK
Trainrobber ● (1858-1921)

He was a victim of the potboilers and lurid dime novels churned out during the early 1880s to puff the imaginary exploits of Jesse James. Meek and mousy Fred Wittrock voraciously consumed any and all such blood-curdling accounts of Western bandits, spending more time on this literature than at his uneventful job as a clerk in a St. Louis store.

In November, 1886, his mind exploding with heady tales of robbery, Wittrock stopped the St. Louis and San Francisco flyer as it was slowing down to enter the St. Louis yards. He was masked with a black bandanna and he held two menacing six-guns. Within minutes he successfully escaped with $10,000 taken from the Adams Express Company's safe.

Wittrock returned to his job and whiled away the hours reading newspapers to see if detectives had picked up any clues from his great train robbery. They hadn't. Wittrock decided to help authorities and sent a letter to the St. Louis Globe, telling the paper that "the outlaw's tools" could be found in a St. Louis baggage room.

Detectives found the pistols, bandanna, and a copy of a dime novel with Wittrock's home address written on its cover. They tracked him down and arrested him. As they were leading him away, Wittrock asked deputies to please refer to him as "Terrible Fred," his much-feared underworld name.

Wittrock served a long prison term and was released to live out his life as a retired bad man, much like Al Jennings, spinning impossible yarns about himself for young school children who stared open-mouthed and believed.

WOOD, ISAAC L.
Murderer ● (? -1858)

Isaac Wood was a ruthless but careless murderer. His brother David owned a huge estate at Dansville, N. Y., but never lived to enjoy it. David Wood died unexpectedly in May, 1855, struck down by a strange illness. His wife Rhoda and her three children died of the same illness short months later.

The illness had been administered to the family in the form of arsenic by Isaac Wood, who promptly looted the estate once the members died. He moved to New Jersey, where he cold-bloodedly killed his wife and child and then moved on to Illinois.

Before leaving Dansville, Isaac, as administrator of the Wood estate, leased his brother's home to a man named Welch. The new tenant discovered three packs of arsenic in the barn wrapped in official papers, papers that had been exclusively in the possession of the estate's administrator, Isaac.

Wood was tracked down and brought back to New York for trial. He was speedily convicted and executed July 9, 1858 at Geneseo, N. Y.

St. Louis gangster Frank Buster Wortman glumly listens to his lawyer's advice while testifying at a Senate Rackets Committee hearing in 1958. (Wide World Photos)

WORTMAN, FRANK ("BUSTER")
Gangster ● (1903-1970)

Buster Wortman began his criminal career as a teenager and accumulated a string of robbery arrests that ran to 1926. At that time he joined the East St. Louis bootlegging gang operated by the three Shelton brothers. The Sheltons allied themselves with the vicious South St. Louis mob known as "The Cuckoos," commanded by killer Jimmy Michaels, to wipe out the Charlie Birger Gang. Wortman was linked to a number of killings involving Birger's gangsters.

In June, 1933, Wortman and another Shelton gunsel, Monroe "Blackie" Armes, shot and killed a Prohibition agent who had arrested them while they were operating a still in Collinsville, Mo. Both men were sent to prison for ten years, Armes to Leavenworth and Wortman to Alcatraz.

Released in 1941, Wortman attempted to take over the rackets in Southern Illinois operated by Earl, Bernie, and Carl Shelton. His troop of thugs included Armes (released from Leavenworth), Armes' brother Tony, Black Charlie Harris, and Elmer Sylvester "Dutch" Dowling.

Wortman's gang killed Carl Shelton in 1947; they killed his brother Bernie the following year. From then on Wortman dominated gambling, vice, and narcotics rackets in St. Louis and Southern Illinois. His influence reached into the highest offices of the states of Missouri and Illinois, according to most reports. Orville E. Hodge, one-time Illinois State Auditor who stole more than $1 million in public funds in 1953, was reported to be Wortman's "front man."

Wortman was convicted of tax evasion on February 26, 1962 but his case was set aside for further federal investigation. He was never sent to prison on this federal charge and died of cancer in 1970.

YALE, FRANKIE
Gangster ● (1885-1927)

Brooklyn-born Frankie Yale (christened Frank Uale) began his criminal career as a member of the Five Points gang in the late 1890s and several gangland killings were attributed to him before he was twenty. He joined Johnny Torrio in a Brooklyn black-hand ring in 1908, extorting money from fellow Italian residents under threats of kidnapping, bombings, and murder.

Murderer, extortionist, blackhander, and national president of the *Unione Siciliane*, Frankie Yale.

Yale took over the *Unione Siciliane*, the powerful Sicilian fraternal organization turned crime cartel, in 1918, following the imprisonment of its former president, Ignazio Saietta, a bloodthirsty killer. Yale assumed the presidency and began taking murder contracts to supplement his income. When asked by police what he did for a living, Yale wryly stated: "I'm an undertaker."

He owned the Harvard Inn with Torrio before Johnny went West to work for Big Jim Colosimo. Yale continued to run this dive throughout his criminal career. At least two dozen men were murdered on the premises of this Brooklyn bar from 1918 to 1928.

In addition to bootlegging and rumrunning during the 1920s, Yale forced tobacconists to buy cheap brands of cigars he manufactured, his company serving as a front for illegal activities. Yale's countenance—that of a smirking, pudgy-faced man with slicked-down hair, wearing a high starched collar and a narrow black tie—was stamped on each cigar box. His product was universally condemned; in the Brooklyn argot of the 1920s, "A Frankie Yale," meant anything cheap and rotten.

Yale functioned as Al Capone's chief supplier of bonded whiskey during Prohibition. He also did little favors for Capone, who had palled about with him as a fellow Five Pointer before the First World War. The favors consisted of murdering Capone's Chicago-based enemies. It was generally accepted that Yale was the man who held Dion O'Bannion's hand in a vise-like grip while Capone's gunmen, Albert Anselmi and John Scalise, shot the Irish mobster to death in his flower shop on November 10, 1924.

Chicago police picked up Yale and his bodyguard Sam Pollaccia at the LaSalle Street train station just after O'Bannion was killed, three minutes before Yale's New York-bound train was scheduled to depart.

To police questions, Yale replied: "I came here for Mike Merlo's funeral. Sure I know Capone. No, I don't know Torrio. I stayed over for a swell dinner that my friend Diamond Joe Esposito gave for me."

Police took two revolvers from Yale and Pollaccia. When Chief Morgan A. Collins confronted Yale with the weapons, he nonchalantly replied: "I have a permit from a Supreme Court justice of New York to carry it. I collect lots of money in New York."

He was let go, but Chief Collins felt with "moral certainty" that Yale had helped to kill O'Bannion.

When Yale refused to endorse Capone-sponsored candidates for the branch office presidency of the *Unione Siciliane* in Chicago, their relationship deteriorated. Capone began to suspect Yale was selling him liquor shipments and then having the trucks hijacked before they ever left New York State.

Yale told Johnny Torrio, who had returned from his brief exile in Italy in 1927, that Capone was complaining about his liquor shipments. "The bastard is beefing that I'm giving him a short count," Yale said.

Capone did suspect Yale of the short shrift and sent one of his hoodlums, James F. De-Amato, to Brooklyn to spy on Yale. DeAmato relayed information to Capone that his suspicions were correct, but he did not live long enough to report personally to Scarface. Yale had DeAmato killed.

Capone then sent Yale an unsigned wire stating: "Some day you'll get an answer to DeAmato."

On July 1, 1927, the answer came. In the early afternoon of that day Yale was called to the phone in a Brooklyn speakeasy and then rushed out to his car. The jaunty Yale—attired in a soft gray fedora, pinstripe suit, and spats—wheeled his roadster down Forty-fourth Street and was suddenly overtaken by a large touring car bristling with gunmen. They opened up on Yale who was half blown through the seat of his car by the blizzard of shotgun, rifle, pistol, and machinegun bullets.

Yale's car crashed wildly off the street and ploughed into a house, tearing half the facade away. The killers threw their weapons out on the street blocks away. A machinegun, the first to be used in New York in a gangland killing, was traced to Chicago gun shop owner, Peter von Frantzius, who was well-known as Capone's gun supplier. Obviously, Scarface wanted the New Yorkers to know who had taken care of Yale.

The funeral of Frankie Yale was the most impressive ever seen for Manhattan mobsters. Following Dion O'Bannion's lavish funeral of 1924, Yale had commented: "Boys, if they ever get me, give me a sendoff that good." The boys saw to it. Yale's silver and copper-lined casket cost $12,000 and twenty-eight trucks of flowers followed him to the cemetery.

On the last truck, a giant wreath bore the ominous inscription: "We'll See Them, Kid."

[ALSO SEE Al Capone, Dion O'Bannion, John Torrio, *Unione Siciliane*.]

ZANGARA, JOSEPH
Assassin ● (1902-1933)

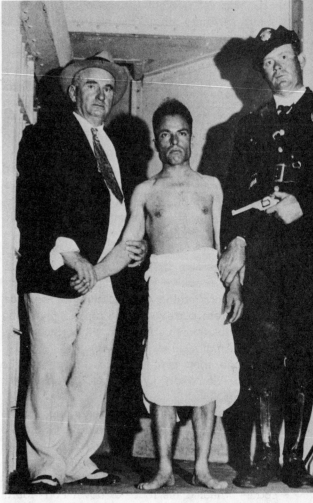

Would-be presidential assassin Joseph Zangara shown only hours after he attempted to kill FDR; he missed, but fatally wounded Chicago Mayor Anton Cermak. (UPI)

An unemployed New Jersey mill hand, Zangara hoboed his way to Miami, Florida in early 1933 where he attempted to find work. Unable to locate employment, as was the plight of most people in America at that time, Zangara began to rave wildly about "capitalists" and babbled Marxist double-talk to strangers on the street.

In the second week of February, 1933, newspapers in Miami announced that President-elect Franklin D. Roosevelt would arrive there accompanied by Chicago Mayor Anton J. Cermak. Zangara decided to kill Roosevelt.

The diminutive Zangara was plagued with stomach cramps on the morning of February 15, 1933, the day of Roosevelt's arrival in Miami. He swallowed several bottles of "medicine" and then loaded his revolver.

As President Roosevelt, with Cermak at his side, rode in the back seat of an open car through the Miami streets, enormous crowds gathered to cheer him. The reception became so enthusiastic that the mobs spilled into the street and pushed forward against the President's car until it was reduced to a crawl. At that moment, little Joe Zangara came barreling through the mass, knocking people down and shoving others aside. His mouth drooped and his black eyes smoldered.

One observer shoved aside by Zangara later stated: "It was like he was going to explode. I was going to hit him but something made me stop. He was like a nut."

When he was about eight feet from the President's car, Zangara raised his pistol and shouted: "There are too many people starving to death!" He fired wildly in the direction of the car. As he was squeezing off his rounds, a woman swung her handbag at him, knocking the pistol upward. Bullets hit 23-year-old Margaret Kruis, who was vacationing in Florida, and 22-year-old Russell Caldwell. Both received head wounds. Two bullets hit Mayor Cermak, wounding him fatally.

Roosevelt's only reaction to the shooting was a withering glance flashed in Zangara's direction. An FDR aide, Raymond Moley, later wrote: "There was not so much as the twitching of a muscle, the mopping of a brow, or even the hint of false gaiety."

Cermak died hours later and Zangara was convicted of murder in a whirlwind trial and sentenced to death. Hours before his execution, Zangara was interviewed by newsmen in his Raiford, Fla. cell.

"Was anyone in on this with you?" a reporter asked.

"No, I have no friends. It was my own idea."

"Do you realize you killed Mayor Cermak? How do you feel about that?"

"I feel nothing about that. Nothing."

"One of your bullets hit a woman, you know."

"She shouldn't have got in the way of the bullet."

"What made you do this? Why do you hate Mr. Roosevelt?"

Zangara stared and then said, "If I got out I would kill him at once."

He was strapped into the electric chair on March 21, 1933. His last words were: "Goodbye. Adios to the world."

New York gangster Big Jack Zelig; he was gunned down on a Manhattan trolley car in 1912. (UPI)

ZELIG, JACK ("BIG JACK")
Murderer, Gangleader ● (1882-1912)

Born William Alberts, Zelig took over a faction of the Monk Eastman Gang in New York when Monk was sent to prison. Big Jack's two lieutenants were Jack Sirocco (who had introduced Johnny Torrio into the Five Points gang) and Chick Tricker.

A minimum of seventy-five tough gangsters worked for this trio from 1910 until 1912, when Zelig was killed. Most of them had backgrounds similar to Zelig's, who began as a pickpocket at age fourteen and then went on to mugging, rolling drunks, and murdering for profit. Early in his career, Zelig, who always retained a youthful appearance, developed a gimmick used exclusively in courtrooms. He hired a consumptive-looking girl to act as his wife.

Arraigned before a judge, Zelig would hang his head in a remorseful manner, a signal to the girl who would then rush forward and tearfully cry out: "Oh, Judge, for God's sake, don't send my boy-husband, the father of my baby, to jail!" Big Jack was almost always released by a kind-hearted judge who instructed him to return home and take care of his family.

In Zelig's employ were the most unsavory murderers of the era—Gyp the Blood (Harry Horowitz), Lefty Louis (Louis Rosenberg), Dago Frank (Frank Cirofici), and Whitey Lewis (Jacob Siedenschner), all of whom helped to kill gambler, Herman "Beansy" Rosenthal, on orders from Zelig and the crooked cop, Charles Becker.

When Zelig robbed a brothel of $80 in 1911, he discovered the loyalty of his lieutenants Sirocco and Tricker was sadly wanting. He called them from a police station after the madam had had him arrested and told his men to pay her off. They ignored Zelig's plea, hoping to see him sent to prison so they could take over the gang.

Big Jack, however, called upon his political contacts, who were quite influential; he was freed. He vowed to kill Sirocco and Tricker. They, in turn, sent a gunman named Julie Morrell to kill Zelig. Big Jack was informed of Morrell's intent by Ike the Plug and went hunting his would-be executioner.

On the night of December 2, 1911, several Zelig-paid stooges got Morrell drunk in the Stuyvesant Casino on Second Avenue. Morrell staggered across the dance hall with a gun held limply in his hand and shouted: "Where's Zelig? . . . I'll fill that big Yid so full of holes he'll sink! . . . Where's that big Yid, Zelig? . . . I gotta cook that big Yid! . . ."

The casino's lights suddenly went out, and as dancers scattered for the exits they heard two words boom across the dance hall toward Morrell—"Right here!" A single shot followed and Morrell was dead with a bullet in his heart.

Gang warfare then broke out between Zelig's band and that of Tricker and Sirocco. It lasted until the following year when Zelig was shot and killed on a Thirteenth Street trolley car, October 5, 1912, by Red Phil Davidson.

ZERILLI, JOSEPH
Syndicate Gangster ● (1897-1977)

Considered by the McClellan Committee to have been one of the ruling "dons" of the Mafia-syndicate in Detroit for the past decade, Zerilli shared power with Peter Licavoli and others. Sicilian-born, Zerilli dates his criminal activities back to the days of the Purple Mob in Detroit; he had reportedly been involved in all forms of illegal pursuits, including extortion, burglary, robbery, larcency, bootlegging, illegal possession of weapons, and murder.

Zerilli planned to attend the Apalachin summit meeting of syndicate heads from across the country in 1957, but he turned back when he discovered police had raided the Barbera estate.

[ALSO SEE The Syndicate.]

ZWERBACH, MAX ("KID TWIST")
Gangster ● (1882-1908)

Zwerbach, best known to the criminal underworld in New York in the early 1900s as Kid Twist, was one of Monk Eastman's top killers. He was responsible for the murder of at least ten men, one of whom was gang rival Richie Fitzpatrick, who was lured to his death by Zwerbach on the promise of settling a gang war.

In tandem with his friend Cyclone Louie (Vach Lewis), Kid Twist then killed five more of Fitzpatrick's men within a week. A sadist by nature, Zwerbach enjoyed punishing others. One of his favorite victims was nineteen-year-old Louie the Lump (Louis Pioggi). Kid Twist and Cyclone Louie ran into Louie the Lump in a second-story bar in Coney Island on May 14, 1908. Zwerbach taunted Louie the Lump with caustic remarks about his girl, a tart named Carroll Terry, stating that he, Kid Twist, had made love to her and that she disliked Louie the Lump's awkward advances.

"She says youse was an active little cuss, Louis," Kid Twist said with a grin. "Always jumpin' around. Let's see how active youse is, kid. Take a jump out the window!" Zwerbach and Cyclone Louie pulled out guns and motioned Louie to jump from the broken second-story window. He did and survived with only a broken ankle.

Louie the Lump called Paul Kelly of the Five Points Gang and screamed: "I got to cook him!"

"Sure you got to cook him," Kelly smoothly assured. "I'll send some boys." Kelly dispatched twenty goons from the Five Points Gang to Coney Island and two hours later, as Zwerbach and Cyclone Louie swaggered from the bar, fifty bullets cut them down. Carroll Terry, the girl in question, suddenly arrived at the scene of the shooting, and Louie the Lump sent a bullet in her direction for good measure, wounding her in the shoulder.

Louie the Lump was apprehended and tried for the double murder. He pleaded guilty to manslaughter and received eleven months in jail.

ZWILLMAN, ABNER ("LONGY")
Syndicate Gangster ● (1899-1959)

Syndicate boss Abner "Longy" Zwillman, attempted to jog his memory for the Senate Rackets Investigation Committee in 1951. (UPI)

Zwillman worked his way up in the New York rackets during the 1920s, aligning himself at times with the Bug & Meyer Mob (Bugsy Siegel and Meyer Lansky) in various bootlegging and gambling enterprises. His association with Meyer Lansky would last a lifetime and eventually, according to some sources, cause his execution.

In the early 1930s, Zwillman moved into New Jersey and established gambling and vice rackets for the newly-born syndicate, of which he was a board member. Dutch Schultz had re-established his restaurant and gambling rackets in New Jersey after being ousted from Manhattan by Lucky Luciano.

In 1935, the Dutchman, also a member of the original board of directors for the national crime syndicate, insisted the cartel kill New York district attorney Thomas E. Dewey. Instead, the syndicate ordered Schultz killed on October 23, 1935 in the Palace Chophouse in Newark, N. J. Killers Mendy Weiss and Charlie the Bug Workman were directed to the restaurant by Zwillman and two of his men.

Upon Schultz's death, Zwillman became the crime czar of all the rackets in New Jersey; he held that position until his death in 1959. Late in life, Longy, who had had several murders attributed to him, and who, incidentally, had courted the actress Jean Harlow for a number of years before financing her initial trip to Hollywood, decided to quit the rackets.

He invested his illegal millions in legitimate enterprises in the 1950s and married a socialite, moving her into a $200,000 twenty-room mansion in West Orange, N. J. He attempted to change his image by donating huge sums of money to charity.

Zwillman went so far as to donate $250,000 to a Newark, N. J. slum clearance project. He was then ordered to appear before the McClellan sub-committee investigating rackets. Longy's new image exploded with the resultant publicity of his past gangland activities.

Facing a possible IRS probe and despondent over the McClellan expose, Zwillman committed suicide, according to one report, by strangling himself with a plastic cord in the basement of his luxurious West Orange home on February 27, 1959.

Another report flatly denied a suicide. Federal authorities believed, according to one account, that syndicate members felt Zwillman was showing signs of old age and feared he would turn informant if the federal authorities brought too much pressure to bear. Meyer Lansky favored the move to kill Zwillman and Gerald Catena performed the execution. The reason given for Lansky's decision was that he resented Zwillman's voting opposition on the syndicate board. Longy had opposed Lansky and others who wanted to remove Frank Costello from power in the middle 1950s.

Supporting this second theory is the fact that strangling oneself to death with a piece of cord hardly befits the end of a super ganglord like Zwillman, who possessed several guns that would have made the job quicker. Also, it must be noted that such an act is almost physically impossible.

Either way, Abner Longy Zwillman left no notes by which the world could judge his fate.

[ALSO SEE Meyer Lansky, Charles "Lucky" Luciano, The Syndicate.]

BIBLIOGRAPHY

Thousands of books, pamphlets, periodicals, and newspaper clippings, as well as personal interviews and extensive correspondence with law enforcement officials and criminals in and out of prison, were used in researching this work. What follows are only the basic reference sources employed in the writing, compiling, and preparation of this narrative encyclopedia.

BOOKS

Abbott, Wilbur C., *New York in the Revolution.* New York: Charles Scribner's Sons, 1929.

Adams, Ramon F., *Six Guns and Saddle Leather.* Norman: University of Oklahoma Press, 1954.

———, *A Fitting Death for Billy the Kid.* Norman: University of Oklahoma Press, 1960.

———, *Burs Under the Saddle.* Norman: University of Oklahoma Press, 1964.

———, *From the Pecos to the Powder.* Norman: University of Oklahoma Press, 1965.

Adler, Polly, *A House is Not a Home.* New York: Popular, 1954.

Agee, George W., *Rube Burrows, King of Outlaws, and His Band of Train Robbers.* Chicago: Hennebery Co., 1890.

Aikman, Duncan, *Calamity Jane and the Wildcats.* New York: Henry Holt and Co., 1927.

Akeny, Nesmith, *The West as I Knew It.* Lewiston, Id.: R. G. Bailey Printing Co., 1938.

Allan, A. A. ("Scotty"), *Gold, Men and Dogs.* New York: G. P. Putnam's Sons, 1931.

Allen, Edward J., *Merchants of Menace—The Mafia.* Springfield, Ill.; Charles C. Thomas, 1962.

Allen, Frederick Lewis, *Only Yesterday, An Informal History of the Nineteen Twenties.* New York: Harper & Bros., 1931.

———, *Since Yesterday.* New York: Harper & Bros., 1940.

Allsop, Kenneth, *The Bootleggers.* London: Hutchinson Pub. Co., 1961.

Altman, Jack, and Ziporyn, Marvin, *Born to Raise Hell.* New York: Grove Press, 1967.

Alvarez, N., *The James Boys in Missouri.* Clyde, Ohio: Ames Publishing Co., 1907.

American Guide Series (compiled by WPA writers)

Arizona, A State Guide. New York: Hastings House, 1940.

California, A Guide to the Golden State. New York: Hastings House, 1939.

Colorado, A Guide to the Highest State. New York: Hastings House, 1941.

Idaho, A Guide in Word and Picture. New York: Oxford University Press, 1937.

Kansas, A Guide to the Sunflower State. New York: The Viking Press, 1939.

Montana, A State Guide. New York: The Viking Press, 1939.

Oklahoma, A Guide to the Sooner State. Norman: University of Oklahoma Press, 1941.

The Oregon Trail. New York: Hastings House, 1939.

A South Dakota Guide. Pierre, S.D.: Pierre Publishing Co., 1938.

Tennessee, A Guide to the State. New York: Hastings House, 1939.

Texas, A Guide to the Lone Star State. New York: Hastings House, 1940.

Utah, A Guide to the State. New York: Hastings House, 1941.

Wyoming, A Guide to Its History, Highways, and People. New York: Oxford University Press, 1941.

Amory, Cleveland, *The Last Resorts.* New York: Harper & Bros., 1948.

Andreas, A. T., *History of the State of Nebraska.* Chicago: The Western Historical Co., 1882.

Andrews, C. L., *The Story of Alaska.* Caldwell, Id.: Caxton Printers, Ltd., 1938.

Angel, Myron (ed.), *History of Nevada.* Berkeley: University of California Press, 1958.

Angley, Edward, *Oh Yeah?* New York: The Viking Press, 1931.

Anonymous, *Alcatraz.* San Francisco: Crowell Mensch, 1937.

Anonymous, *Asmodeus in New York* New York: (n.p.), 1868.

Anonymous, *Hot Corn.* New York: (n.p., 1854.

Anthony, Irving, *Paddle Wheels and Pistols.* Philadelphia: Macrae Smith Co. 1929.

Applegate, Frank G., *Native Tales of New Mexico.* Philadelphia: J. B. Lippincott, 1932.

Appler, Augustus C., *The Guerrillas of the West; or The Life, Character and Daring Exploits of the Younger Brothers.* St. Louis: Eureka Pub. Co., 1876.

Aptheker, Herbert, *Nat Turner's Slave Rebellion.* New York: Grove Press, Inc., 1966.

Arthur, George Clinton, *Bushwhacker.* Rolla, Mo.: Rolla Printing Co., 1938.

Asbury, Herbert, *The Gangs of New York.* New York: Alfred A. Knopf, Inc., 1927.

———, *Sucker's Progress.* New York: Dodd, Mead and Company, Inc., 1938.

———, *Gem of the Prairie.* New York: Alfred A. Knopf, Inc., 1940.

———, *The French Quarter, An Informal History of the New Orleans Underworld.* New York: Alfred A. Knopf, Inc., 1940.

———, *The Great Illusion: An Informal History of Prohibition.* New York: Doubleday & Co., 1950.

Atherton, Lewis, *The Cattle Kings.* Bloomington: Indiana University Press, 1961.

Atkin, Ronald, *Revolution! Mexico 1910-20.* New York: The John Day Company, 1970.

Audett, James Henry ("Blackie"), *Rap Sheet.* New York: William Sloane Associates, 1954.

Axford, Joseph, *Around Western Campfires.* New York: Pageant Press, 1964.

Ayers, Col. James J., *Gold and Sunshine.* Boston: Richard G. Badger, 1922.

Baker, Pearl, *The Wild Bunch at Robbers Roost.* New York: Abelard-Schuman, 1971.

Bales, William A., *A Tiger in the Streets.* New York: Dodd, Mead and Co., 1962.

Bard, Floyd, *Horse Wrangler.* Norman: University of Oklahoma Press, 1960.

Barnard, William F., *Forty Years at the Five Points.* New York: (n.p.), 1893.

Barnes, David, *The Metropolitan Police.* New York: Baker & Godwin, 1863.

Bayer, Oliver Weld (ed.), *Cleveland Murders.* New York: Duell, Sloan and Pearce, 1947.

Beals, Carleton, *American Earth.* Philadelphia: J. B. Lippincott Co., 1939.

Bearss, Edwin C., and Gibson, A. M., *Fort Smith, Little Gibraltar on the Arkansas.* Norman: University of Oklahoma Press, 1969.

Beebe, Lucius, and Clegg, Charles, *U.S. West: The Saga of Wells Fargo.* New York: E. P. Dutton & Co., 1949.

———, *Hear the Train Blow.* New York: E. P. Dutton & Co., 1952.

Beers, George A., *Vasquez; or the Hunted Bandits of San Joaquin.* New York: Robert M. DeWitt, 1875.

Beidler, X., *X. Beidler, Vigilante.* Norman: University of Oklahoma Press, 1965.

Bell, John C., *The Pilgrim and the Pioneer.* Lincoln, Neb.: International Publishing Assn., 1906.

Bennett, James V., *I Chose Prison.* New York: Alfred A. Knopf, 1970.

Berger, Meyer, *The Eighty Million.* New York: Simon & Schuster, 1942.

Biddle, Francis, *In Brief Authority.* New York: Doubleday & Co., 1962.

Block, Eugene B., *The Wizard of Berkeley.* New York: Coward-McCann, 1958.

———, *Great Train Robberies of the West.* New York: Coward-McCann, 1959.

———, *Great Stagecoach Robbers in the West.* New York: Doubleday & Co., 1962.

———, *Fifteen Clues.* Garden City, N.Y.: Doubleday & Co., Inc., 1965.

———, *The Fabric of Guilt.* Garden City, N.Y.: Doubleday & Co., Inc., 1968.

Boettiger, John, *Jake Lingle.* New York: E. P. Dutton & Co., 1931.

Boggs, Mae Hélene Bacon, *My Playhouse was a Concord Coach.* Oakland, Calif.: Howell-North Press, 1942.

Boland, Charles, *They All Discovered America.* Garden City, N.Y.: Doubleday & Co., Inc., 1963.

Bolitho, William, *Murder for Profit.* New York: Harper & Bros., 1926.

Bonney, Edward, *Banditti of the Prairies.* Chicago: Homewood Publishing Co., 1890.

Bontham, Alan, *Sex Crimes and Sex Criminals.* New York: Wisdom House, 1961.

Borthwick, J. D., *The Gold Hunters.* New York: Outing Publishing Co., 1927.

Boswell, Charles, and Thompson, Lewis, *The Girls in Nightmare House.* New York: Gold Medal, 1955.

———, *Practitioners of Murder.* New York: Collier, 1962.

Botkin, Benjamin A., *The Treasury of American Folklore.* New York: Crown Publishers, 1944.

———, *A Treasury of Western Folklore.* New York: Crown Publishers, 1951.

Boynton, Percy Holmes, *The Rediscovery of the Frontier.* Chicago: University of Chicago Press, 1931.

Brace, Charles Loring, *The Dangerous Classes of New York.* New York: Wynkoop & Hallenbeck, 1880.

Bradley, Glenn Danford, *The Story of the Santa Fe.* Boston: R. G. Badger, 1920.

Bradley, Hugh, *Such Was Saratoga.* New York: Doubleday, Doran & Company, Inc., 1940.

Bragin, Charles, *Dime Novels, Bibliography, 1860-1928.* Brooklyn: Charles Bragin, publisher, 1938.

Breckenridge, William M., *Helldorado.* Boston: Houghton-Mifflin Co., 1928.

Breihan, Carl W., *The Complete and Authentic Life of Jesse James.* New York: Frederick Fell, Inc., 1953.

———, *Quantrill and His Civil War Guerrillas.* Denver: Sage Books, 1959.

———, *The Day Jesse James was Killed.* New York: Frederick Fell, Inc., 1961.

———, *The Outlaw Brothers: The True Story of Missouri's Younger Brothers.* San Antonio, Tex.: The Naylor Company, 1961.

Bright, John, *Hizzoner Big Bill Thompson.* New York: J. Cape & H. Smith, 1930.

Bronson, Edgar Beecher, *The Red-blooded Heroes of the Frontier.* New York: A. C. McClurg & Co., 1910.

Brown, Dee, and Schmitt, Martin F., *Trail Driving Days.* New York: Charles Scribner's Sons, 1952.

Brown, F. Yeats (ed.), *Escape.* New York: The Macmillan Company, 1933.

Brown, Mark H., *The Plainsmen of the Yellowstone.* New York: G. P. Putnam's Sons, 1961.

Brown, Robert L., *An Empire of Silver.* Caldwell, Id.: The Caxton Printers, Ltd., 1965.

Brownlee, Richard S., *Gray Ghosts of the Confederacy.* Baton Rouge: Louisiana State University Press, 1958.

Bryant, Will, *Great American Guns and Frontier Fighters.* New York: Grossett & Dunlap, 1961.

Brynes, Thomas, *Professional Criminals in America.* New York: Chelsea House, 1969.

Buel, James William, *The Border Outlaws.* St. Louis: Historical Publishing Co., 1882.

Bullough, Vern L., *The History of Prostitution.* New Hyde Park, N.Y.: University Books, 1964.

Burns, Walter Noble, *The Saga of Billy the Kid.* Garden City, N.Y.: Doubleday, Page & Company, 1926.

———, *Tombstone, An Iliad of the Southwest.* Garden City, N.Y.: Doubleday, Page & Company, 1927.

———, *The One-Way Ride.* Garden City, N.Y.: Doubleday, Doran & Co., Inc., 1931.

Burroughs, John Rolfe, *Where the Old West Stayed Young.* New York: William Morrow and Co., 1962.

Burt, Olive Woolley, *American Murder Ballads.* New York: Oxford University Press, 1958.

Busch, Francis X., *Enemies of the State.* New York: Bobbs-Merrill, 1954.

Butterfield, Roger, *The American Past.* New York: Simon and Schuster, 1947.

Caesar, Gene, *Incredible Detective: The Biography of William J. Burns.* Englewood Cliffs, N.J.: Prentice-Hall, 1968.

Canton, Frank M., *Frontier Trails.* Boston: Houghton Mifflin Co., 1930.

Carlson, John Roy, *Under Cover.* New York: E. P. Dutton & Co., Inc., 1943.

Carmer, Carl, *Stars Fell on Alabama.* New York: Farrar & Rinehart, Inc., 1934.

Carter, W. N., *Harry Tracy, The Desperate Outlaw.* Chicago: Laird & Lee Publishers, 1902.

Casey, Lee (ed.), *Denver Murders.* New York: Duell, Sloan and Pearce, 1947.

Casey, Robert J., *The Black Hills and Their Incredible Characters.* Indianapolis: Bobbs-Merrill Co., 1949.

Castel, Albert, *William Clarke Quantrill: His Life and Times.* New York: Frederick Fell, Inc., 1962.

Castleman, Harvey N., *Sam Bass, The Train Robber.* Girard, Kan.: Haldeman-Julius, 1944.

———, *The Texas Rangers.* Girard, Kan.: Haldeman-Julius, 1944.

Caughey, John Walton, *Their Majesties the Mob.* Chicago: University of Chicago Press, 1960.

Chaefetz, Henry, *Play the Devil.* New York: Clarkson N. Potter, Inc., 1960.

Chaplin, J. P., *Rumor, Fear and the Madness of Crowds.* New York: Ballantine Books, Inc., 1959.

Chapman, Arthur, *The Pony Express.* New York: G. P. Putnam's Sons, 1932.

Chidsey, Donald Barr, *On and Off the Wagon.* New York: Cowles, 1969.

Chrisman, Harry E., *The Ladder of Rivers: The Story of I. P. (Print) Olive.* Denver: Sage Books, 1962.

Churchill, Allen, *A Pictorial History of American Crime.* New York: Holt, Rinehart & Winston, 1964.

———, *The Year the World Went Mad.* New York: Thomas Y. Crowell Comany, 1960.

Cipes, Robert M., *The Crime War.* New York: New American Library, 1967.

Clarke, Donald Henderson, *In the Reign of Rothstein.* New York: Vanguard Press, 1929.

Clemens, Samuel Langhorne (Mark Twain, pseud.), *Roughing It.* Chicago: F. G. Gilmer and Co., 1872.

———, *Life on the Mississippi.* Boston: James R. Osgood and Co., 1883.

Cleveland, Agnes Morley, *No Life for A Lady.* Boston: Houghton Mifflin Co., 1941.

Clum, John P., *It All Happened in Tombstone.* Flagstaff, Ariz.: Northland Press, 1965.

Coates, Robert M., *The Outlaw Years: The History of the Land Pirates of the Natchez Trace.* New York: The Literary Guild of America, 1930.

Coblentz, Edmund D. (ed.), *William Randolph Hearst.* New York: Simon and Schuster, Inc. 1952.

Coe, George Washington, *Frontier Fighter.* Boston: Houghton Mifflin Co., 1934.

Cohen, Louis H., *Murder, Madness and the Law.* New York: World Publishing Co., 1952.

Cohn, Art, *The Joker Is Wild; The Story of Joe E. Lewis.* New York: Random House, 1955.

Collier, William Ross, and Westrate, Edwin Victor, *The Reign of Soapy Smith, Monarch of Misrule.* Garden City, N.Y.: Doubleday, Doran & Company, Inc., 1935.

Collins, Frederick Lewis, *Glamorous Sinners.* New York:

Ray Long and Richard R. Smith, Publishers, 1932.
———, *The F.B.I. in Peace and War.* New York: G. P. Putnam's Sons, 1943.
Collins, Ted (ed.), *New York Murders.* New York: Duell, Sloan and Pearce, 1944.
Comstock, Anthony, *Frauds Exposed.* New York: J. H. Brown, 1880.
Connable, Alfred, and Silberfarb, Edward, *Tigers of Tammany Hall.* New York: Holt, Rinehart & Winston, 1967.
Connelley, William Elsey, *Quantrill and the Border Wars.* Cedar Rapids, Iowa: The Torch Press, 1909.
———, *Wild Bill and His Era.* New York: The Press of the Pioneers, 1933.
Conot, Robert, *Rivers of Blood, Years of Darkness.* New York: Bantam Books, Inc., 1967.
Cook, David J., *Hands Up; or Twenty Years of Detective Life in the Mountains and on the Plains.* Denver: W. F. Robinson Printing Co., 1897.
Cook, Fred J., *A Two Dollar Bet Means Murder.* New York, Dial Press, 1961.
———, *The FBI Nobody Knows.* New York: The Macmillan Company, 1964.
———, *The Secret Rulers.* New York: Duell, Sloan and Pearce, 1966.
Cook, John R., *The Border and the Buffalo.* Topeka, Kan.: Crane & Co., 1907.
Coolidge, Dane, *Fighting Men of the West.* New York: E. P. Dutton & Co., Inc., 1932.
Cooper, Courtney Riley, *Ten Thousand Public Enemies.* Boston: Little, Brown and Company, 1935.
Corey, Herbert, *Farewell, Mr. Gangster!* New York: Appleton-Century-Crofts, Inc., 1936.
Costello, A. E., *Our Police Protectors: A History of the New York Police.* New York: C. F. Roper & Co., 1885.
Crabb, Richard E., *Empire on the Platte.* New York: World Publishing Co., 1967.
Crane, Milton (ed.), *Sins of New York.* New York: Bantam Books, 1950.
Crapsey, Edward, *The Nether Side of New York; or The Vice, Crime and Poverty of the Great Metropolis.* New York: Sheldon & Company, 1872.
Crawford, Samuel J., *Kansas in the Sixties.* Chicago: A. C. McClurg & Co., 1911.
Cressey, Donald, *Theft of the Nation.* New York: Harper & Row Publishers, 1969.
Crittenden, Henry Huston, *The Crittenden Memoirs.* New York: G. P. Putnam's Sons, 1936.
Cromie, Robert, and Pinkston, Joseph, *Dillinger, A Short and Violent Life.* New York: McGraw-Hill Co., 1962.
Croy, Homer, *Jesse James was My Neighbor.* New York: Duell, Sloan and Pearce, 1949.
———, *He Hanged Them High.* New York: Duell, Sloan and Pearce, 1952.
———, *Last of the Great Outlaws, The Story of Cole Younger.* New York: Duell, Sloan and Pearce, 1956.
———, *Trigger Marshall, The Story of Chris Madden.* New York: Duell, Sloan and Pearce, 1958.
Crump, Irving, and Newton, John W., *Our G-Men.* New York: Dodd, Mead & Company, Inc., 1937.
Cummings, Homer, *Selected Papers.* New York: Charles Scribner's Sons, 1939.
Cummins, Jim, *Jim Cummins' Book.* Denver: The Reed Publishing Co., 1903.
Cunningham, Eugene, *Triggernometry, A Gallery of Gunfighters.* New York: The Press of the Pioneers, 1934.
Curzon, Sam, *Legs Diamond.* New York: Tower Publications, Inc., 1962.
Cushman, Dan, *The Great North Trail.* New York: McGraw-Hill Book Co., 1966.
Dacus, Joseph A., *Illustrated Lives and Adventures of Frank and Jesse James and the Younger Brothers, The Noted Western Outlaws.* St. Louis: N. D. Thompson and Co., 1882.
Dale, Henry, *Adventures and Exploits of the Younger Brothers, Missouri's Most Daring Outlaws, and Companions of the James Boys.* New York: Street & Smith, 1890.
Dalton, Emmett, *When the Daltons Rode.* Garden City, N.Y.: Doubleday, Doran & Co., Inc., 1931.
Dane, G. Ezra, *Ghost Town.* New York: Tudor Publishing Co., 1941.
Danforth, Harold R., and Horan, James D., *The D.A.'s Man.* New York: Permabooks, 1959.
Daniels, Jonathan, *The Devil's Backbone.* New York: McGraw-Hill, 1962.
Darrow, Clarence, *The Story of My Life:* New York: Charles Scribner's Sons, 1932.
Davis, Clyde, *The Arkansas.* New York: Farrar & Rinehart, Inc., 1940.
Davis, Jean, *Shallow Diggin's.* Caldwell, Id.: Caxton Printers, 1963.
Davis, Mary Lee, *Sourdough Gold.* Boston: W. A. Wilder Co., 1933.
Dean, John, *The Indiana Torture Slaying.* Chicago: Bee-Line Books, 1967.
Debo, Angie, *The Cowman's Southwest.* Glendale, Calif.: The Arthur H. Clark Co., 1953.
Dedman, Emmett, *Fabulous Chicago.* New York: Random House, 1963.
deFord, Miriam Allen, *Murders Sane & Mad.* New York: Abelard-Schuman, Ltd., 1965.
De la Torre, Lillian, *The Truth About Belle Gunness.* New York: Gold Medal Books, 1955.
Demaris, Ovid, *Lucky Luciano.* Derby, Conn.: Monarch Books, 1960.
———, *Captive City.* New York: Lyle Stuart, Inc., 1969.
———, *America the Violent.* New York: Cowles Book Co., 1970.
Dennis, Charles H., *Victor Lawson, His Time and His Work.* Chicago: University of Chicago Press, 1935.
deRham, Edith, *How Could She Do That?* New York: Clarkson N. Potter, 1969.
Derleth, August, *Wisconsin Murders.* Sauk City, Wis.: Mycroft and Moran Pub., 1968.
DeVol, George, *Forty Years a Gambler on the Mississippi.* New York: H. Holt & Company, 1926.
DeVoto, Bernard, *The Course of Empire.* Boston: Houghton Mifflin Co., 1952.
Dibble, Roy Floyd, *Strenuous Americans.* New York: Boni and Liveright, 1923.
Dickson, Arthur Jerome, *Covered Wagon Days.* Cleveland: Arthur H. Clark Co., 1929.
Dillon, Richard, *Wells Fargo Detective, A Biography of James B. Hume.* New York: Coward-McCann, 1969.
Dimsdale, Thomas J., *Vigilantes of Montana.* Helena, Mont.: State Publishing Co., 1915.
Dobie, James Frank, *Coronado's Children.* Garden City, N.Y:. Garden City Publishing Co., 1930.
———, *The Longhorns.* Boston: Little, Brown & Co., 1941.
Dobyns, Fletcher, *The Underworld of American Politics.* New York: Fletcher Dobyns, Publisher, 1932.
Dolan, J. R., *The Yankee Peddlers of Early America.* New York: Clarkson N. Potter, 1964.
Donald, Jay, *Outlaws of the Border.* Philadelphia: Douglas Brothers, 1882.
Donovan, Frank, *River Boats of America.* New York: Thomas Y. Crowell Company, 1966.
Dorsett, Lyle W., *The Pendergast Machine.* New York: Oxford University Press, 1968.
Drago, Harry Sinclair, *Outlaws on Horseback,* New York: Dodd, Mead & Company, 1964.
Duke, Thomas S., *Celebrated Criminal Cases of America.* San Francisco: James H. Barry Co., 1910.
Duncan, Lee, *Over the Wall.* New York: E. P. Dutton & Co., Inc., 1936.
Dunlop, Richard, *Doctors of the American Frontier.* Garden City, N.Y.: Doubleday & Co., Inc., 1965.
Dykstra, Robert R., *The Cattle Towns.* New York: Alfred A Knopf, 1968.
Ellen, Mary; Murphy, Mark; and Weld, Ralph Foster, *A Treasury of Brooklyn.* New York: William Sloane Associates, 1949.
Ellis, Steve, *Alcatraz Number 1172.* Los Angeles: Holloway House Publishing Co., 1969.
Elliott, David Stewart, *Last Raid of the Daltons.* Coffeyville, Kan.: Coffeyville Journal, 1892.
Elman, Robert, *Fired in Anger.* Garden City, N.Y.: Doubleday & Co., Inc., 1968.
Emery, J. Gladston, *Court of the Damned.* New York: Comet Press, 1959.
Evans, Clyde (ed.), *Adventures of Great Crime Busters.* New York: New Power Publications, 1943.
Erbstein, Charles E., *The Show-Up: Stories Before the Bar.* Chicago: Pascal Covici, 1926.
Every, Edward Van, *Sins of America as 'Exposed' by the Police Gazette.* New York: Frederick A. Stokes Co., 1931.
Farley, Philip, *Criminals of America; or Tales of the Lives of Thieves.* New York: Published by author, 1876.
Feder, Sid, and Joesten, Joachim, *The Luciano Story.* New York: David McKay Co., 1954.
Fenwick, Robert W., *Alfred Packer.* Denver: Denver Post, 1963.
Fergusson, Erna, *Murder & Mystery in New Mexico.* Albuquerque, N.M.: Armitage Editions, 1948.
Fergusson, Harvey, *Rio Grande.* New York: Alfred A. Knopf, 1933.
Fisher, Vardis, and Holmes, Opal Laurel, *Gold Rushes and Mining Camps of the Early American West.* Caldwell, Id.: Caxton Printers, Ltd., 1968.
Flinn, John T., *History of the Chicago Police from the Settlement of the Community to the Present Time.* Chicago: Police Book Fund, 1887.
Fowler, Gene, *The Great Mouthpiece.* New York: Covici-Friede, 1931.
———, *Timberline.* New York: Covici-Friede Publishers, 1933.
Foy, Eddie, and Harlow, Alvin F., *Clowning Through Life.* New York: E. P. Dutton & Co., Inc., 1928.
Fulton, Maurice Garland, *Maurice Garland Fulton's History of the Lincoln County War.* Tucson, Ariz.: University of Arizona Press, 1968.
Furlong, Thomas, *Fifty Years A Detective.* St. Louis: C. E. Barnett, 1912.
Gaddis, Thomas E., *The Birdman of Alcatraz,* New York: New American Library, 1958.
———, and Long, James O., *Killer, A Journal of Murder.* New York: The Macmillan Co., 1970.
Gage, Nicholas, *The Mafia Is Not an Equal Opportunity Employer.* New York: McGraw-Hill Book Company, 1971.
Gantt, Paul H., *The Case of Alfred Packer, The Man Eater.* Denver: University of Denver, 1952.
Gardner, Raymond Hatfield, *The Old West.* San Antonio, Tex.: The Naylor Co., 1944.
Garrett, Patrick Floyd, with Upson, Ash, Maurice Garland Fulton (ed.), *The Authentic Life of Billy the Kid.* New York: Macmillan Company, 1927.
Garwood, Darrel, *Crossroads of America: The Story of Kansas City.* New York: W. W. Norton & Company, Inc., 1948.
Gaylord, Otis H., *The Rise and Fall of Legs Diamond.* New York: Bantam Books, 1960.
Geyer, Frank, *The Holmes-Pitezel Case.* Philadelphia: Frank Geyer, Publisher, 1896.
Gilbert, Paul Thomas, and Bryson, Charles Lee, *Chicago and Its Makers.* Chicago: University of Chicago Press, 1929.
Ginty, Elizabeth Beall, *Missouri Legend.* New York: Random House, 1938.
Gish, Anthony, *American Bandits.* Girard, Kan.: Haldeman-Julius, 1938.
Glasscock, Carl Burgess, *Bandits of the Southwest Pacific.* New York: Frederick A. Stokes Co., 1929.
Godwin, John, *Alcatraz 1868-1963.* New York: Doubleday & Co., 1963.
Gordon, Welche, *Jesse James and His Band of Notorious Outlaws.* Chicago: Laird and Lee, 1891.
Gosnell, Harold F., *Boss Platt and His New York Machine.* Chicago: F. Mendelsohn, 1933.
———, *Machine Politics, Chicago Model.* Chicago: F. Mendelsohn, 1937.
Graham, Stephen, *New York Nights.* New York: G. H. Doran and Co., 1927.
Graves, Richard S., *Oklahoma Outlaws.* Oklahoma City: State Publishing Co., 1915.
Green, J. H., *Report of Gambling in New York.* New York: Privately published, 1851.
———, *The Secret Band of Brothers; or The American Outlaws.* Philadelphia: Privately published, 1847.
———, *Gambling Unmasked! or The Personal Experience of J. H. Green, the Reformed Gambler,* Philadelphia: Privately published, 1847.
Green, Laurence, *The Era of Wonderful Nonsense.* Indianapolis: The Bobbs-Merrill Company, Inc., 1939.
Griffin, Bulkley S. (ed.), *Offbeat History.* New York: World Publishing Co., 1967.
Guttmacher, Manfred, *The Mind of the Murderer.* New York: Grove Press, 1962.
Hall, Frank O., and Whitten, Lindsey H., *Jesse James Rides Again.* Lawton, Okla.: LaHoma Publishing Co., 1948.
Hamer, Alvin C. (ed.), *Detroit Murders.* New York: Duell, Sloan and Pearce, 1948.
Hardin, John Wesley, *The Life of John Wesley Hardin.* Norman: University of Oklahoma Press, 1961.
Harkey, Dee, *Mean as Hell.* Albuquerque, N.M.: University of New Mexico Press, 1948.
Harlow, Alvin F., *The Old Waybills.* New York: Appleton-Century Company, 1934.
Harman, Samuel W., *Hell on the Border.* Fort Smith, Ark.: The Phoenix Pub. Co., 1898.
Harrington, Fred Harvey, *Hanging Judge.* Caldwell, Id.: Caxton Printers, Ltd., 1951.
Harrison, Carter H., *Stormy Years.* Indianapolis: Bobbs-Merrill, 1935.
———, *Growing Up With Chicago.* Chicago: Seymour Press, 1939.
Havighurst, Walter, *Voices on the River, The Story of the Mississippi Waterways.* New York: Macmillan Company, 1964.
Healy, Paul F., *Cissy, A Biography of Eleanor M. 'Cissy' Paterson.* Garden City, N.Y.: Doubleday & Company, Inc., 1966.
Hecht, Ben, *A Child of the Century.* New York: Simon & Schuster, 1954.
———, *Charlie, The Improbable Life and Times of Charles MacArthur.* New York: Harper & Bros., 1957.
Heimer, Mel, *The Cannibal, The Case of Albert Fish.* New York: Lyle Stuart, 1971.
Helmer, William J., *The Gun That Made the Twenties Roar.* New York: Macmillan Company, 1969.
Hendricks, George D., *The Bad Men of the West.* San Antonio, Tex.: The Naylor Company, 1941.
Henry, Will, *Death of A Legend.* New York: Random House, 1954.
———, *The Raiders.* New York: Bantam Books, 1956.
Hicks, Edward P., *Belle Starr and Her Pearl.* Little Rock, Ark.: Pioneer Press, 1963.
Hirsch, Phil (ed.), *Men Behind Bars.* New York: Pyramid Publications, 1962.
———, *The Law Enforcers.* New York: Pyramid, 1969.
———, *The Racketeers.* New York. Pyramid, 1970.
———, *The Killers.* New York: Pyramid, 1971.
Holbrook, Stewart H., *The Story of American Railroads.* New York: Crown Publishers, 1947.
Hoover, J. Edgar, *Persons in Hiding.* Boston: Little, Brown & Co., 1938.
Horan, James D., *Desperate Men.* New York: G. P. Putnam's Sons, 1949.
———, *Pictorial History of the Wild West.* New York: Crown Publishers, Inc., 1954.
———, *Across the Cimmaron.* New York: Crown Publishers, Inc., 1956.
———, *The Great American West.* New York: Crown Publishers, Inc., 1959.
———, *The Desperate Years.* New York: Crown Publishers, Inc., 1962.

————, The Pinkertons, The Detective Dynasty That Made History. New York: Crown Publishers, Inc., 1967.

Hough, Emerson, The Story of the Outlaw. New York: Outing Publishing Co., 1907.

House, Brant (ed.), Crimes That Shocked America. New York: Ace Books, 1961.

Houts, Marshall, They Asked for Death. New York: Cowles, 1970.

Howe, William F., and Hummel, Abraham, In Danger; or Life in New York, A True History of a Great City's Wiles and Temptations. New York: J. S. Ogilvie & Company, 1888.

Hunt, Frazier, Cap Mossman, Last of the Great Cowmen. New York: Hastings House, 1951.

Hynd, Alan, The Giant Killers. New York: Robert M. McBride & Co., 1945.

————, Murder, Mayhem and Mystery. New York: A. S. Barnes & Co., 1958.

————, Con Man. New York: Paperback Library, 1961.

Irey, Elmer, The Tax Dodgers. Garden City, N.Y.: Garden City Publishing Co., 1948.

Irving, Henry Brodribb, A Book of Remarkable Criminals. New York: George H. Doran Company, 1918.

Jackson, Joseph Henry (ed.), The Portable Murder Book. New York: The Viking Press, 1945.

————, Bad Company. New York: Harcourt, Brace and Co., 1949.

————, San Francisco Murders. New York: Duell, Sloan and Pearce, 1947.

James, Jesse Edward, Jesse James, My Father. Independence, Mo.: Sentinel Publishing Co., 1899.

Jennings, Alphonso J., Beating Back. New York: D. Appleton and Co., 1914.

Jennings, Dean, We Only Kill Each Other, The Life and Bad Times of Bugsy Siegel. Englewood Cliffs, N.J.: Prentice-Hall, Inc., 1968.

Johnson, Malcolm, Crime on the Labor Front. New York: McGraw-Hill, 1950.

Johnston, James A., Alcatraz Island Prison. New York: Charles Scribner's Sons, 1949.

Jones, Lloyd, Life and Adventures of Harry Tracy. Chicago: Jewett & Lindrooth Publishers, 1902.

Josephson, Matthew, The Robber Barons. New York: Harcourt, Brace and Company, 1934.

Juergens, George, Joseph Pulitzer and the New York World. Princeton, N.J.: Princeton University Press, 1966.

Karpis, Alvin, with Trent, Bill, The Alvin Karpis Story. New York: Coward McCann & Geoghegan, Inc., 1971.

Katcher, Leo, The Big Bankroll, The Life and Times of Arnold Rothstein. New York: Harper & Bros., 1959.

Kefauver, Estes, Crime in America. New York: Doubleday & Co., 1951.

Keleher, William A., The Fabulous Frontier. Santa Fe, N.M.: The Rydal Press, 1945.

Kelly, Charles, The Outlaw Trail. New York: Devin-Adair Pub., 1959.

Kelly, Joseph ("Bunco"), Thirteen Years in the Oregon Penitentiary. Portland, Ore.: Published by author, 1908.

Kelly, Thomas P., Jesse James, His Life and Death. New York: Export Publishing Enterprises, Ltd., 1950.

Kennedy, Michael S. (ed.), Cowboys and Cattleman. New York: Hastings House, 1964.

Kennedy, Robert F., The Enemy Within. New York: Popular Lib., 1960.

Kilgallen, Dorothy, Murder One. New York: Random House, 1967.

King, Ernest L., Main Line. Garden City, N.Y.: Doubleday & Co., Inc., 1948.

Kingston, Charles, Remarkable Rogues. New York: John Lane Co., 1921.

Kirkpatrick, Ernest E., Crime's Paradise. San Antonio, Tex.: The Naylor Company, 1934.

————, Voices from Alcatraz. San Antonio, Tex.: The Naylor Company, 1947.

Klein, Alexander (ed.), Grand Deception. New York: J. B. Lippincott & Company, 1955.

————, Double Dealers. Philadelphia and New York: J. B. Lippincott & Company, 1958.

Knox, Thomas W., Underground, or Life Below the Surface. Hartford, Conn.: J. B. Burr, Hyde & Co., 1873.

Kobler, John, Capone. New York: G. P. Putnam's Sons, 1971.

Krakel, Dean, The Saga of Tom Horn. Laramie, Wyo.: Powder River Publishers, 1954.

Kunstler, William M., First Degree. New York: Ocean Press, 1960.

Lait, Jack, and Mortimer, Lee, New York Confidential. Chicago: Ziff-Davis Pub. Co., 1948.

————, Chicago Confidential. New York: Crown Publishers, Inc., 1950.

————, Washington Confidential. New York: Crown Publishers, Inc., 1951.

————, U.S.A. Confidential. New York: Crown Publishers, Inc., 1952.

Lake, Stuart N., Wyatt Earp, Frontier Marshal. Boston: Houghton Mifflin Co., 1931.

Langford, Gerald, The Murder of Stanford White. Indianapolis: Bobbs-Merrill, 1962.

Langford, Nathaniel Pitt, Vigilante Days and Ways. Boston: J. G. Cupples Co., 1890.

Lardner, W. B., and Brock, M. J., History of Placer and Nevada Counties, California. Los Angeles: Historic Record Co., 1924.

Larkin, Margaret, Singing Cowboys. New York: Alfred A. Knopf, Inc., 1931.

Lavigne, Frank C., Crimes, Criminals and Detectives. Helena, Mont.: State Publishing Co., 1921.

Lavine, Sigmund, Allan Pinkerton, America's First Private Eye. New York: Dodd, Mead & Company, Inc., 1963.

Lawes, Warden Lewis Edward, Twenty Thousand Years In Sing Sing. New York: R. Long & R. R. Smith, Inc., 1932.

Leakey, John, The West that was from Texas to Montana. Dallas: Southern Methodist University Press, 1958.

LeBlanc, Jerry, and Davis, Ivor, 5 to Die. Los Angeles: Holloway House Publishing Co., 1970.

Leckie, William H., The Buffalo Soldiers. Norman: Oklahoma University Press, 1967.

LeFors, Joe, Wyoming Peace Officer. Laramie, Wyo.: Laramie Printing Co., 1953.

Lewis, Alfred Henry, The Apaches of New York. New York: G. W. Dillingham Company, 1912.

————, Nation-Famous New York Murders. New York: G. W. Dillingham Company, 1914.

Lewis, Lloyd, and Smith, Henry Justin, Chicago, the History of Its Reputation. New York: Harcourt, Brace, 1929.

Lockwood, Francis Cummins, Pioneer Days in Arizona. New York: Macmillan Co., 1932.

Logan, Guy B. H., Rope, Knife and Chair. London: S. Paul & Co., Ltd., 1930.

————, Wilful Murder. London: Eldon Press Ltd., 1935.

Lord, John, Frontier Dust. Hartford, Conn.: E. V. Mitchell, 1926.

Lord, Walter, The Good Years. New York: Harper & Bros., 1960.

Louderback, Lew, The Bad Ones. New York: Fawcett Publications, 1968.

Love, Robertus, The Rise and Fall of Jesse James. New York: G. P. Putnam's Sons, 1926.

Lowther, Charles C., Dodge City, Kansas. Philadelphia: Dorrance & Co., Inc., 1940.

Ludlow, Fitzhugh, The Heart of the Continent. New York: Hurd and Houghton, 1870.

Lundberg, Ferdinand, Imperial Hearst. New York: Modern Library, 1937.

Lustgarten, Edgar, The Murder and the Trial. New York: Charles Scribner's Sons, 1958.

Lyle, Judge John H., The Dry and Lawless Years. Englewood Cliffs, N.J.: Prentice-Hall, Inc., 1960.

Lynch, Dennis Tilden, Boss Tweed, the Story of a Grim Generation. New York: Boni and Liveright, 1927.

————, Criminals and Politicians. New York: Macmillan Co., 1932.

McClellan, John L., Crime Without Punishment. New York: Duell, Sloan & Pearce, 1962.

McComas, J. Francis, The Graveside Companion. New York: Obelensky, 1962.

McConaughy, John, From Cain to Capone, or Racketeering Down the Ages. New York: Brentano's, 1931.

McDade, Thomas, Annals of Murder. Norman: University of Oklahoma Press, 1961.

McIntire, Josephine, Boot Hill. Boston: Chapman & Grimes, Inc., 1945.

McNeil, Cora, Mizzoura. Minneapolis: Mizzoura Pub. Co., 1898.

McPhaul, Jack, Johnny Torrio. New Rochelle, N.Y.: Arlington House, 1970.

McPherren, Ida, Empire Builders. Sheridan, Wyo.: Star Publishing Co., 1942.

Maas, Peter, The Valachi Papers. New York: G. P. Putnam's Sons, 1968.

Mackaye, Milton, The Tin Box Parade. New York: Robert M. McBride & Company, 1934.

Makins, John R. (ed.), Boston Murders. New York: Duell, Sloan and Pearce, 1947.

Mangan, Frank J., Bordertown. El Paso, Tex.: Carl Hertzog, 1964.

Mariano, John Horace, The Second Generation of Italians in New York. Boston: Christopher Publishing House, 1921.

Marshal, James, Santa Fe, The Railroad that Built an Empire. New York: Random House, 1945.

Marshall, Theodora Britton, and Evans, Gladys Crail, They Found It in Natchez. New Orleans: Pelican Publishing Co., 1939.

Martin, Douglas D., Tombstone's Epitaph. Albuquerque, N.M.: University of New Mexico Press, 1951.

Martin, Edward Winslow (pseud. for James Dabney McCabe), Secrets of the Great City; the Virtues and the Vices, the Mysteries, Miseries and Crimes at New York City. New York: Published by author, 1868.

Martin, George Washington, The First Two Years in Kansas. Topeka, Kan.: State Printing Office, 1907.

Mason, Thomas Alpheus, Harlan Fiske Stone: Pillar of the Law. New York: The Viking Press, 1966.

Masterson, William Barclay ("Bat"), Famous Gunfighters of the Frontier. Houston, Tex.: The Frontier Press of Texas, 1957.

Merz, Charles, The Great American Bandwagon. New York: John Day Company, 1928.

————, The Dry Decade. New York: Doubleday, Doran and Co., 1931.

Mertz, Leon Claire, John Selman, Texas Gunfighter. New York: Hastings House, 1966.

Messick, Hank, The Silent Syndicate. New York: Macmillan Company, 1967.

————, Secret File. New York: G. P. Putnam's Sons, 196

————, Lansky. New York: G. P. Putnam's Sons, 1971.

Millar, Mara, Hail to Yesterday. New York: Farrar Rinehart, Inc., 1941.

Miller, Gene, with Mackle, Barbara Jane, 83 Hours Ti Dawn. Garden City, N.Y.: Doubleday & Company Inc., 1971.

Miller, George, Missouri's Memorable Decade. Columbic Mo.: E. W. Stephens Publishing Co., 1898.

Miller, Nyle H., and Snell, Joseph W., Why the West wa Wild, Topeka, Kan.: Kansas State Historical Societ 1963.

Mills, James, The Prosecutor. New York: Pocket Books 1970.

Mitgang, Herbert, The Man Who Rode the Tiger, Th Life and Times of Judge Samuel Seabury. Philadelphi and New York: J. B. Lippincott Company, 1963.

Mizner, Addison, The Many Mizners. New York: Sear Publishing Co., 1932.

Monagham, Jay, The Legend of Tom Horn, Last of the Ba Men. New York: Bobbs-Merrill, 1946.

Moody, Ralph, Wells Fargo. Boston: Houghton Mifflin, 1961

Moore, Dan Tyler, Wolves, Widows and Orphans, A Expose of the Ways and Wiles of Con Men, Card Sharps, Swindlers and Rogues. New York: World Publishing Company, 1967.

Morgan, Murray, Skid Road. New York: The Viking Press 1951.

Morrel, Ed, The Twenty-fifth Man. Montclair, N.J.: New Era Publishing Co., 1924.

Morrison, Samuel Elliot, The Story of the Old Colony of New Plymouth. New York: Alfred A. Knopf, 1956.

Morse, Frank P., Cavalcade of Rails. New York: E. P. Dutton & Co., Inc., 1940.

Musick, John R., Mysterious Mr. Howard. New York: G. W. Dillingham Co., 1896.

Myers, Gustavus, History of Tammany Hall. New York: Boni & Liveright, Inc., 1917.

————, History of Bigotry in the United States. Edited and revised by Henry M. Christman. New York: Capricorn Books, 1960.

Nash, Jay Robert, Citizen Hoover. Chicago: Nelson-Hall Co., 1972.

————, and Offen, Ron, Dillinger: Dead or Alive? Chicago: Henry Regnery Co., 1970.

Navasky, Victor S., Kennedy Justice. New York: Atheneum, 1971.

Neider, Charles (ed.), The Great West. New York: Coward-McCann, Inc., 1958.

Ness, Eliot, with Fraley, Oscar, The Untouchables. New York: Julian Messner, 1957.

Newmark, Harris, Sixty Years in Southern California. New York: Knickerbocker Press, 1916.

Nix, Evett Dumas, Oklahombres. St. Louis: n.p., 1929.

Nolan, Frederick W., The Life & Death of John Henry Tunstall. Albuquerque, N.M.: University of New Mexico Press, 1965.

Nordyke, Lewis, John Wesley Hardin, Texas Gunman. New York: William Morrow & Co., 1957.

Noyes, Alva Josiah, In the Land of the Chinook. Helena, Mont.: State Publishing Co., 1917.

O'Connor, Richard, Courtroom Warrior, The Combative Career of William Travers Jerome. Boston: Little, Brown and Company, 1963.

O'Neal, James Bradas, They Die But Once. New York: Knight Publications, 1935.

Orth, Samuel P., The Boss and the Machine. New Haven, Conn.: Yale University Press, 1920.

O'Sullivan, F. Dalton, Crime Detection. Chicago: The O'Sullivan Publishing House, 1928.

Otero, Miguel Antonio, My Life on the Frontier, 1864-1882. New York: The Press of the Pioneers, Inc., 1935.

Owen, Collinson, King Crime, an English Study of America's Greatest Problem. New York: H. Holt and Company, 1932.

Paine, Lauren, Texas Ben Thompson. Los Angeles: Westernlore Press, 1966.

Parish, Joe, Coffins, Cactus and Cowboys. El Paso, Tex.: Superior Publishing Co., 1954.

Parkhurst, Rev. Charles H., My Forty Years in New York. New York: The Macmillan Company, 1923.

Pasley, Fred D., Al Capone, The Biography of A Self-Made Man. New York: Ives Washburn, 1930.

————, Muscling In. New York: Ives Washburn, 1931.

Patterson, Robert T., The Great Boom and Panic. Chicago: Henry Regnery Co., 1965.

Pearson, Edmund L., Murder At Smutty Nose. New York: Doubleday & Company, Inc., 1926.

————, Studies in Murder. New York: Macmillan Company, 1926.

————, More Studies in Murder. New York: Harrison Smith & Robert Haas, Pub., 1936.

Penfield, Thomas, Dig Here! San Antonio, Tex.: The Naylor Co., 1962.

Peterson, Virgil, Barbarians in Our Midst. Boston: Little, Brown & Co., 1952.

Phares, Ross, Bible in Pocket, Gun in Hand. Garden City, N.Y.: Doubleday & Co., Inc., 1964.

————, Reverend Devil, A Biography of John A. Murrell. New Orleans: Pelican Publishing Co., 1941.

Pierce, Bessie Louise, As Others See Chicago. Chicago: University of Chicago Press, 1933.

Pinkerton, Allan, *Criminal Reminiscences and Detective Sketches*. New York: G. W. Dillingham, Co., 1878.

———, *Bankrobbers and the Detectives*. New York: G. W. Carleton & Co., 1883.

Pinkerton, Matthew Worth, *Murder in All Ages*. New York: A. E. Pinkerton & Co., 1898.

Poe, John William, *The Death of Billy the Kid*. Boston: Houghton Mifflin Co., 1933.

Porges, Irwin, *The Violent Americans*. Derby, Conn.: Monarch Books, 1963.

Powell, Addison M., *Trailing and Camping in Alaska*. New York: A. Wessels, 1909.

Prall, Robert H., and Mockridge, Norton, *This is Costello*. New York: Gold Medal Books, 1951.

Preece, Harold, *The Dalton Gang, End of An Outlaw Era*. New York: Hastings House, 1963.

———, *Lone Star Man*. New York: Hastings House, 1963.

Preston, John Hyde, *A Short History of the American Revolution*. New York: Pocket Books, 1952.

Purvis, Melvin, *American Agent*. New York: Doubleday, Doran & Co., Inc., 1936.

Quiett, Glen Chesney, *Pay Dirt, A Panorama of American Gold Rushes*. New York: D. Appleton-Century Co., Inc., 1936.

Quinn, John Philip, *Fools of Fortune*. Chicago: W. B. Conkey, 1890.

Radin, Edward D., *Crimes of Passion*. New York: G. P. Putnam's Sons, 1953.

Raine, William McLeod, *Famous Sheriffs and Western Outlaws*. Garden City, N.Y.: Doubleday, Doran & Co., 1929.

Rankin, Hugh F., *The Golden Age of Piracy*. New York: Holt, Rinehart and Winston, Inc., 1969.

Ransom, Rev. A., *A Terrible History of Fraud and Crime; The Twin Brothers of Texas*. Philadelphia: M. A. Milliette, 1858.

Rascoe, Burton, *Belle Starr, The Bandit Queen*. New York: Random House, 1941.

Ray, G. B., *Murder at the Corners*. San Antonio, Tex.: The Naylor Co., 1957.

Reckless, Walter, *Vice in Chicago*. Chicago: University of Chicago Press, 1933.

Redmond, Frank, *The Younger Brothers*. St. Louis: Dramatic Company, 1901.

Redston, George, and Crossen, Kendall F., *The Conspiracy of Death*. New York: Bobbs-Merrill Co., 1965.

Reid, Ed, *Mafia*. New York: Random House, 1952.

———, and Demaris, Ovid, *The Green Felt Jungle*. New York: Trident Press, 1963.

———, *The Grim Reapers, The Anatomy of Organized Crime in America*. Chicago: Henry Regnery Co., 1969.

Reid, Col. J. M., *Sketches and Anecdotes of the Old Settlers and New Comers*. Keokuk, Iowa: R. R. Ogden Publishers, 1876.

Reinhardt, James Melvin, *The Murderous Trail of Charles Starkweather*. Springfield, Ill.: Thomas Pub., 1962.

Reno, John, *Life and Career of John Reno*. Indianapolis: Indianapolis Journal Co., 1879.

Rickard, Mrs. "Tex", with Oboler, Arch, *Everything Happened to Him*. New York: Frederick A. Stokes Company, 1936.

Rickards, Collin, *Mysterious Dave Mathers*. Santa Fe, N.M.: Press of the Territorian, 1968.

Ridge, John Rollin (Yellow Bird), *Life and Adventure of Joaquin Murieta*. San Francisco: Frederick MacCrellish & Co., 1871.

Riegel, Robert E., *America Moves West*. New York: Henry Holt & Co., 1930.

Ripley, Thomas, *They Died with Their Boots On*. Garden City, N.Y.: Doubleday, Doran & Co., Inc., 1935.

Robertson, Frank C., and Harris, Beth Kay, *Soapy Smith, King of the Frontier Con Men*. New York: Hastings House, 1961.

Robertson, Mrs. Harriet M. (ed.), *Dishonest Elections and Why We Have Them*. Chicago: Published by author, 1934.

Rodell, Marie F., *New York Murders*. New York: Duell, Sloan and Pearce, 1944.

Roe, Clifford, *Panderers and Their White Slaves*. Chicago: Revell Pub. Co., 1910.

Roe, Edward Thomas, *The James Boys*. Chicago: A. E. Weeks & Co., 1893.

Rogers, Agnes, and Allen, Frederick Lewis, *I Remember Distinctly*. New York: Harper & Brothers, 1947.

Rogers, John William, *The Lusty Texans of Dallas*. New York: E. P. Dutton & Co., Inc., 1951.

Root, Frank A., and Connelley, William Elsey, *The Overland Stage to California*. Topeka, Kan.: Published by authors, 1901.

Root, Jonathin, *One Night in July*. New York: Coward-McCann, Inc., 1961.

Rosa, Joseph G., *They Called Him Wild Bill*. Norman: University of Oklahoma Press, 1964.

———, *The Gunfighter*. Norman: University of Oklahoma Press, 1969.

Roscoe, Theodore, *True Tales of Bold Escapes*. Englewood Cliffs, N.J.: Prentice-Hall, Inc., 1965.

Rosen, Rev. Peter, *Pa-ha-sa-pah; or the Black Hills of South Dakota*. St. Louis: Nixon-Jones, 1895.

Ross, Robert, *The Trial of Al Capone*. Chicago: Robert Ross, Pub., 1933.

Rothert, Otto A., *The Outlaws of Cave-in-Rock*. Cleveland: Arthur H. Clark Co., 1924.

Rowan, Richard Wilmer, *The Pinkertons, A Detective Dynasty*. Boston: Little, Brown and Co., 1931.

Rudensky, Morris ("Red"), and Riley, Don, *The Gonif*. Blue Earth, Minn.: The Piper Company, 1970.

Runyon, Damon, *Trials and Other Tribulations*. Philadelphia and New York: J. B. Lippincott & Company, 1926.

Russell, Jesse Lewis, *Behind These Ozark Hills*. New York: The Hobson Book Press, 1947.

Sabin, Edwin LeGrand, *Wild Men of the Wild West*. New York: Thomas Y. Crowell Co., 1929.

Salerno, Ralph, and Tompkins, John, *The Crime Confederation*. New York: Doubleday & Co., Inc. 1969.

Samuels, Charles, *The Girl in the Red Velvet Swing*. New York: Fawcett Publications, 1953.

———, *Death was the Bridegroom*. New York: Fawcett Publications, 1955.

Sandoe, James (ed.), *Murder: Plain & Fanciful*. New York: Sheridan Pub., 1948.

Sandoz, Mari, *Love Song of the Plains*. New York: Harper & Bros., 1961.

Sands, Frank, *A Pastoral Prince*. Santa Barbara, Calif.: n.p., 1893.

Sann, Paul, *The Lawless Decade*. New York: Crown Publishers, Inc., 1957.

Santee, Ross, *Apache Land*. New York: Charles Scribner's Sons, 1947.

Sawyer, Eugene Taylor, *The Life and Career of Tiburcio Vasquez*. San Francisco: Bacon and Co., 1875.

Schlesinger, Arthur Meier, *The Rise of the City, 1878-1898*. New York: The Macmillan Co., 1933.

Schmedding, Joseph, *Cowboy and Indian Trader*. Caldwell, Id.: The Caxton Printers Ltd., 1951.

Schultz, Gladys Denny, *How Many More Victims, Society and the Sex Criminal*. Philadelphia: J. B. Lippincott & Company, 1966.

Settle, William A., Jr., *Jesse James Was His Name*. Columbia, Mo.: University of Missouri Press, 1966.

Shackleford, William Yancey, *Belle Starr, The Bandit Queen*. Girard, Kan.: Haldemann-Julius Publications, 1943.

Sherman, James E., and Barbara H., *Ghost Towns of Arizona*. Norman: University of Oklahoma Press, 1969.

Shields, Robert William, *Seymour, Indiana and the Famous Story of the Reno Gang*. Indianapolis: H. Lieber and Co., 1939.

Shirley, Glenn, *Henry Starr, Last of the Real Bad Men*. New York: David McKay Co., Inc., 1965.

Shoemaker, Floyd C. (ed.), *Missouri, Day by Day*. Jefferson City, Mo.: Mid-State Printing Co., 1942.

Sims, Judge Orland L., *Gun-Toters I Have Known*. Austin, Tex.: The Encino Press, 1967.

Sinclair, Andrew, *Era of Excess*. New York: Harper & Row, 1964.

Singer, Kurt (ed.), *My Strangest Cases*. Garden City, N.Y.: Doubleday & Co., Inc., 1958.

Siringo, Charles A., *A Texas Cowboy, or Fifteen Years on the Hurricane Deck of A Spanish Pony*. Chicago: M. Umbdenstock & Co., 1885.

———, *A Cowboy Detective*. Chicago: W. B. Conkey Co., 1912.

Skinner, Emory Fiske, *Reminiscences*. Chicago: Vestal Printing Co., 1908.

Small, Kathleen Edwards, and Smith, J. Larry, *History of Tulare County, California*. Chicago: S. J. Clarke Publishing Co., 1926.

Smith, Alson J., *Syndicate City*. Chicago: Henry Regnery Co., 1954.

Smith, D. B., *Two Years in the Slave-Pen of Iowa*. Kansas City, Mo.: H. N. Farey & Co., 1885.

Smith, Duane A., *Rocky Mountain Mining Camps*. Bloomington, Ind.: Indiana University Press, 1967.

Smith, Edward H., *You Can Escape*. New York: The Macmillan Co., 1929.

Smith, Helena Huntington, *The War on Powder River*. New York: McGraw-Hill, 1966.

Smith, T. Marshall, *Legends of the War of Independence and of the Earlier Settlements in the West*. Louisville, Ky.: J. F. Brenan, 1855.

Smith, Wallace, *Prodigal Sons*. Boston: The Christopher Publishing House, 1951.

Sondern, Frederic, Jr., *Brotherhood of Evil: The Mafia*, New York: Farrar, Straus & Cudahy, 1959.

Sonnichsen, Charles Leland, *Cowboys and Cattle Kings*. Norman: University of Oklahoma Press, 1950.

———, *I'll Die Before I'll Run*. New York: Harper & Bros., 1951.

———, *Outlaw: Bill Mitchell Alias Baldy Russell*. Denver: Sage Books, 1965.

Sorenson, Alfred R., *Hands Up! or The History of a Crime*. Omaha, Neb.: Barkalow Brothers, 1877.

Sparrow, Gerald, *Women Who Murder*. New York: Abelard-Schuman, 1970.

Springs, Agnes Wright, *The Cheyenne and Black Hills Stage and Express Routes*. Glendale, Calif.: Arthur H. Clark Co., 1949.

Stanley, F. (pseud. for Father Stanley Crocchiola), *Clay Allison*. Denver: World Press, Inc., 1956.

———, *Desperadoes of New Mexico*. Denver: World Press, Inc., 1953.

Stanton, G. Smith, *When the Wildwood was in Flower*. New York: J. S. Ogilvie Publishing Co., 1910.

Starr, John, *The Purveyor*. New York: Holt, Rinehart & Winston, 1961.

Steffens, Lincoln, *Shame of the Cities*. New York: McClure, Phillips & Co., 1904.

Steiger, Brad, *The Mass Murderer*. New York: Award Books, 1967.

Stern, Philip Van Doren, *The Man Who Killed Lincoln*. New York: Random House, 1935.

Stone, Irving, *Clarence Darrow for the Defense*. New York: Doubleday & Co., 1941.

Stout, Ernest, *The Younger Brothers*. Chicago: Dramatic Company, 1902.

Streeter, Floyd Benjamin, *Prairie Trails and Cow Towns*. Boston: Chapman & Grimes, Inc., 1936.

———, *Ben Thompson, Man With A Gun*. New York: Frederick Fell, Inc., 1957.

Stuart, William H., *The 20 Incredible Years*. Chicago, New York: M. A. Donohue & Co., 1935.

Sullivan, Edward Dean, *Rattling the Cup on Chicago Crime*. New York: The Vanguard Press, 1929.

———, *Chicago Surrenders*. New York: The Vanguard Press, 1930.

———, *The Snatch Racket*. New York: The Vanguard Press, 1932.

———, *The Fabulous Wilson Mizner*. New York: The Henkle Co., 1935.

Sullivan, Mark, Our Times. (Vols I, II) New York: Charles Scribner's Sons, 1926, 1927.

Sullivan, W. John L., *Twelve Years in the Saddle for Law and Order on the Frontiers of Texas*. Austin, Tex.: Von Boeckman-Jones Co., 1909.

Sutherland, Edwin H., *White Collar Crime*. New York: Holt, Rinehart & Winston, 1949.

Sutley, Zachary Taylor, *The Last Frontier*. New York: The Macmillan Co., 1933.

Sutton, Charles Warden, *The New York Tombs; Its Secrets and Mysteries*. New York: n.p., 1874.

Sutton, Fred Ellsworth, *Hands Up! Stories of the Six Gun Fighters of the Old West*. Indianapolis: Bobbs-Merrill Company, 1927.

Swallow, Alan (ed.), *The Wild Bunch*. Denver: Sage Books, 1966.

Swan, Oliver G. (ed.), *Frontier Days*. Philadelphia: Macrae-Smith, 1928.

Swanberg, W. A., *Jim Fisk, The Career of An Improbable Rascal*. New York: Charles Scribner's Sons, 1959.

———, *Citizen Hearst*. New York: Charles Scribner's Sons, 1961.

———, *Pulitzer*. New York: Charles Scribner's Sons, 1967.

Tallant, Robert, *Ready to Hang*. New York: Harper & Bros., 1952.

Tannenbaum, Frank, *Crime and the Community*. New York: Columbia University Press, 1938.

Tanner, Louise, *All the Things We Were*. Garden City, N.Y.: Doubleday and Company, Inc., 1968.

Taylor, Drew Kirksey, *Taylor's Thrilling Tales of Texas*. San Antonio, Tex.: Guaranty Bond Printing Co., 1926.

Terret, Charles, *Traffic in Innocents*. New York: Bantam Books, 1961.

Thaw, Harry K., *The Traitor*. New York: Dorrance, 1926.

Thomas, Bob, *Winchell*. Garden City, N.Y.: Doubleday & Company, Inc., 1971.

Thompson, Craig, and Raymond, Allen, *Gang Rule in New York*. New York: Dial Press, 1940.

Thompson, George G., *Bat Masterson, The Dodge City Years*. Topeka, Kan.: Kansas State Printing Plant, 1943.

Thorndike, Thaddeus, *Lives and Exploits of the Daring Frank and Jesse James*. Baltimore: I. & M. Ottenheimer, 1909.

Thorp, Nathan Howard, *Story of the Southwestern Cowboy, Pardner of the Wind*. Caldwell, Id.: Caxton Printers, Ltd., 1945.

Thrasher, Frederick, *The Gang, A Study of 1,313 Gangs in Chicago*. Chicago: The University of Chicago Press, 1927.

Tilghman, Zoe A., *Marshal of the Last Frontier*. Glendale, Calif.: Arthur H. Clark Co., 1949.

Toland, John, *The Dillinger Days*. New York: Random House, 1963.

Touhy, Roger, with Brennan, Ray, *The Stolen Years*. Cleveland: Pennington Press, Inc. 1959.

Triplett, Col. Frank, *The Life, Times, and Treacherous Death of Jesse James*. St. Louis: J. H. Chambers and Company, 1882.

———, *Conquering the Wilderness*. New York and St. Louis: N. D. Thompson Publishing Co., 1883.

Truman, Benjamin Cummings, *Life, Adventures and Capture of Tiburcio Vasquez*. Los Angeles: Los Angeles Star, 1874.

Tully, Andrew, *Era of Elegance*. New York: Funk & Wagnalls Co., 1947.

Turkus, Burton B., and Feder, Sid, *Murder, Inc.: The Story of the Syndicate*. New York: Farrar, Straus and Young Co., 1951.

Turner, Wallace, *Gambler's Money*. Boston: Houghton Mifflin Co., 1965.

Turrou, Leon G., *Where My Shadow Falls*. Garden City, N.Y.: Doubleday & Co., Inc. 1949.

Tyler, George C., *Whatever Goes Up*. Indianapolis: Bobbs-Merrill Co., 1934.

Upshur, George Lyttleton, *As I Recall Them, Memories of Crowded Years*. New York: Wilson-Erickson, Inc. 1936.

Van Cise, Philip S., *Fighting the Underworld*. Boston: Houghton Mifflin Co., 1936.

Van Emery, Edward, *Sins of New York*. New York: Frederick A. Stokes, 1930.
Vestal, Stanley (pseud, of Walter S. Campbell), *Dodge City, Queen of Cow Towns*. New York: Harper & Bros., 1952.
Vitray, Laura, *The Great Lindbergh Hullabaloo: An Unorthodox Account*. New York: William Fargo, 1932.
Waldrop, Frank, *McCormick of Chicago*. Englewood Cliffs, N.J.: Prentice-Hall, 1966.
Walker, Stanley, *The Night Club Era*. New York: Frederick A Stokes Company, 1933.
Wallace, Betty, *Gunnison County*. Denver: Sage Books, 1960.
Walling, George, *Recollections of a New York Chief of Police*. New York: Caxton Book Concern, 1887.
Walton, William M., *Life and Adventures of Ben Thompson, the Famous Texan*. Houston, Tex.: Reprinted by Frontier Press, 1954.
———, *The James Boys of Old Missouri*. Cleveland: Arthur Westbrook Co., 1907.
Warden, Ernest A., *Infamous Kansas Killers*. Wichita, Kan.: McGuin Publishing Co., 1944.
Wardman, Cy, *The Story of the Railroad*. New York: D. Appleton & Co., 1911.
Warner, Matt, *The Last of the Bandit Riders*. Caldwell, Id.: Caxton Printers, Ltd. 1940.
Warren, John H., Jr., *Thirty Years' Battle with Crime, or The Crying Shame of New York As Seen Under the Broad Glare of An Old Detective's Lantern*. Poughkeepsie, N.Y.: A. J. White, 1874.
Washburn, Charles, *Come Into My Parlor*. New York: National Library Press, 1936.
Waters, Frank, *The Story of Mrs. Virgil Earp. The Earp Brothers of Tombstone*. New York: Clarkson N. Potter, Inc., 1960.
Webb, Jack, *The Badge*. Englewood Cliffs, N.J., Prentice-Hall, Inc., 1958.
Webb, Walter Prescott, *The Texas Rangers, A Century of Frontier Defense*. Boston: Houghton Mifflin Co., 1935.
Weinberg, Arthur (ed.), *Attorney for the Damned*. New York: Simon & Schuster, 1957.
Wellman, Manly Wade, *Dead and Gone*. Chapel Hill, N.C.: University of North Carolina Press, 1954.
Wellman, Paul I., *A Dynasty of Western Outlaws*. Garden City, N.Y.: Doubleday & Co., Inc., 1961.
———, *Spawn of Evil*. Garden City, N.Y.: Doubleday & Co., Inc., 1964.
Wendt, Lloyd, and Kogen, Herman, *Lords of the Levee*. New York: Bobbs-Merrill, 1943.
———, *Bet a Million!* Indianapolis: Bobbs-Merrill, 1948.
———, *Big Bill of Chicago*. New York: Bobbs-Merrill, 1953.
Werner, M. R., *Tammany Hall*. Garden City, N.Y.: Doubleday, Doran & Co., Inc., 1928.
Wertham, Dr. Fredric, *The Show of Violence*. New York: Doubleday & Co., Inc., 1949.
———, *A Sign for Cain*. New York: Paperback Library, 1969.
Willison, George Finlay, *Here They Dug the Gold*. New York: Brentano's, 1931.
Wilson, Frank J., and Day, Beth, *Special Agent*. New York: Holt, Rinehart & Winston, 1965.
Wilson, Neil C., *Treasure Express, Epic Days of the Wells Fargo*. New York: The Macmillan Co., 1936.
Wilson, Samuel Payntor, *Chicago and Its Cess Pools of Vice and Infamy*. Chicago: n.p., 1910.
Wilstach, Frank J., *Wild Bill Hickok, the Prince of Pistoleers*. New York: Doubleday, Page & Company, 1926.
Whitehead, Don, *The F.B.I. Story*. New York: Random House, 1956.
———, *Journey Into Crime*. New York: Random House, 1960.
Whyte, William Foote, *Street Corner Society*. Chicago: University of Chicago Press, 1943.
Wooldridge, Clifton R., *Hand Up! In the World of Crime or Twelve Years a Detective*. Chicago: Police Publishing Co., 1901.
Wormser, Richard, *The Yellowlegs, The Story of the United States Cavalry*. Garden City, N.Y.: Doubleday & Company, Inc., 1966.
Wright, Robert M., *Dodge City, The Cowboy and the Great Southwest*. Wichita, Kan.: Wichita Eagle Press, 1913.
Young, Art, *On My Way*. New York: Horace Liveright, 1928.
Young, Harry (Sam), *Hard Knocks, A Life Story of the Vanishing West*. Portland, Ore.: Wells & Company, 1915.
Younger, Coleman, *The Story of Cole Younger by Himself*. Chicago: The Henneberry Co., 1913.
Zorbaugh, Harvey W., *The Gold Coast and Slum*. Chicago: University of Chicago Press, 1929.
Zornow, William Frank, *Kansas, A History of the Jayhawk State*. Norman: University of Oklahoma Press, 1957.

PERIODICALS

Aiken, Duncan, "Deadwood the Dreadful." *American Mercury*, November, 1927.
Anderson, Robert T., "From Mafia to Cosa Nostra." *American Journal of Sociology*, November, 1965.
Anonymous, "Chicago as Seen by Herself." *McClure's Magazine*, May, 1907.
———, "Mild-Mannered Mr. Volstead, the 'Goat' of the Wets." *Literary Digest*, December 27, 1919.
Asbury, Herbert, "The St. Valentine's Day Massacre." *47 The Magazine of The Year*, September, 1947.
Barnes, Lela (ed.), "An Editor Looks at Early Day Kansas." *Kansas State Historical Society Quarterly*, Summer, 1960.
Bechdolt, Frederick, "The Rock." *The Saturday Evening Post*, November 2, 1935.
Bell, Daniel, "Crime as an American Way of Life." *Antioch Review*, June, 1953.
Bennett, James O'Donnell, "Chicago Gangland, The True Story of Chicago Crime." *Chicago Tribune* (series), 1929.
Bloch, Herbert A., "The Gambling Business: An American Paradox." *Crime and Delinquency*, October, 1962.
Bolitho, William, "The Natural History of Graft." *The Survey*, April, 1931.
Boder, Bartlett, "Jesse James was a Vaquero." *Museum Graphic*, Fall, 1954.
Bourke, Charles Francis, "Pinkerton's National Detective Agency." *Strand Magazine* (London), 1905.
———, "Great American Train Robberies." *Railroad Man's Magazine*, April, 1906.
Brannon, W. T., "The Modest Mr. Guzik." *True Detective*, April, 1946.
Breitel, Charles, "Controls in Criminal Law Enforcement." *University of Chicago Law Review*, 27: 1960 (p. 427).
Brennan, Ray, "The Capone I Knew." *True Detective*, June, 1947.
———, "Blood Money." *Coronet*, November, 1948.
———, "Dion O'Bannion." *True Detective*, June, 1961.
———, "Al Capone." *True Detective*, August, 1961.
———, "Inside the Outfit." *ChicagoLand Magazine*, April, 1969.
Brown, Carleton, "Confidence Games." *Life*, August 1, 1946.
Carson, Charles, "One Underworld." *Author and Journalist*, November, 1945.
Chapman, Arthur, "Getting the Drop and Living." *New York Herald Tribune Magazine*, January 3, 1932.
Childs, M. W., "The Inside Story of the Federal Government's Secret Operations in Convicting Al Capone." *St. Louis Post Dispatch Sunday Magazine*, September 25, 1932.
Conway, Bryan, "20 Months in Alcatraz." *Saturday Evening Post*, February 19, 1938.
Cooper, Courtney Ryley, "Draw, Stranger." *Saturday Evening Post*, January 2, 1926.
Cooper, Jeff, "How Good Was Hickok?" *Guns and Ammo*, March, 1960.
Coxe, John E., "The New Orleans Mafia Incident." *Louisiana Historical Quarterly*, 1937 (pp. 1067-1110).
Currie, Barton W., "American Bandits: Lone and Otherwise." *Harper's Weekly*, September 12, 1908.
Cushman, George L., "Abilene, First of the Kansas Cow Towns." *Kansas State Historical Society Quarterly*, August, 1940.
Darrow, Clarence, "Crime and the Alarmists." *Harper's*, Vol. 153, 1926.
Davidson, Bill, "How the Mobs Control Chicago." *Saturday Evening Post*, November 3, 1963.
———, "The Mafia: How It Bleeds New England." *Saturday Evening Post*, November 18, 1967.
Davis, J. Richard, "Things I Couldn't Tell Till Now." (series) *Collier's*, July 22, 29; August 12, 19, 26, 1939.
deFord, Miriam Allen, "The Case of Leopold and Loeb." *True Crime Detective Magazine*, October, 1952.
DeLacy, Charles, "The Inside on Chicago's Notorious St. Valentine's Day Massacre." *True Detective Mysteries*, March-April, 1931.
Dibble, R. F., "'SBlood!" *The Nation*, July 14, 1926.
Dillard, Jack (pseud. for R. A. Faherty), "How the U.S. Government Caught Al Capone." *The Master Detective*, February, 1932.
Dunlap, Al, "Why Dillinger's Gang is Doomed." *Liberty Magazine*, 0ctober 27, 1934.
Dykstra, Robert R., "Ellsworth, 1869-1875: The Rise and Fall of A Kansas Cowtown." *Kansas State Historical Society Quarterly*, Summer, 1961.
"The FBI's War on Organized Crime." *U.S. News and World Report*, April 18, 1966.
Flynt, Josiah, "In the World of Graft—Chi, an Honest City." *McClure's Magazine*, February, 1901.
Fuchs, Daniel, "Where Al Capone Grew Up." *The New Republic*, September 9, 1931.
Geis, Gilbert, "Crime and Politics." *The Nation*, August 14, 1967.
Gentile, Nicolo, interviews, *Paese Sera* (Rome), September, 1963.
Gillette, James B., "The Killing of Dallas Stoudenmire." *Frontier Times*, July, 1924.
Grinnell, Charles E., "Crime as a Political Power in the East and the West." *American Law Review*, May, 1882.
Gunther, John, "The High Cost of Hoodlums." *Harper's Monthly*, October, 1929.
Hallgren, Mauritz A., "Chicago Goes Tammany." *The Nation*, April 22, 1931.
Hauptmann, Bruno Richard, "Why Did You Kill Me?" *Liberty Magazine*, May 2, 1936.
Henshall, John A., "Tales of the Early California Bandits." (Part III, Black Bart) *Overland Monthly*, June, 1909.
Hess, Albert C., "Juvenile Delinquency, Then and Now." *Mankind Magazine*, February, 1970.
Irwin, John, and Cressey, Donald R., "Thieves, Convicts, and the Inmate Culture." *Social Problems*, Fall, 1962.
Irwin, Will, "Our New Civil War." *Liberty Magazine*, January 5, 1935.
Jarman, Rufus, "The Pinkerton Story." *The Saturday Evening Post*, (series) May 15, 22, 29; June 5, 1948.
Johnson, Earl, Jr., "Organized Crime: Challenge to the American Legal System." *Journal of Criminal Law, Criminology and Police Science*, December, 1962.
Jordan, Philip D., "The Adair Train Robbery." *The Palimpsest*, February, 1936.
Kamisar, Yale, "When Cops Were Not Handcuffed." *New York Times Magazine*, November 7, 1965.
Kirkpatrick, Arthur Roy, "Missouri on the Eve of the Civil War." *Missouri Historical Review*, January, 1961.
Koop, W. E., "Billy the Kid: The Trail of a Kansas Legend." *The Trail Guide*, September, 1964.
Lake, Stuart N., "Tales of the Kansas Cowtowns." (series) *Saturday Evening Post*, September, 1930.
Landesco, John, "The Criminal Underworld of Chicago in the 80s and 90s." *Journal of the American Institute of Criminal Law and Criminology*, May-June, 1934; March-April, 1935.
———, "The Woman and the Underworld." *Journal of the American Institute of Criminal Law and Criminology*, March, 1936.
Lee, Henry, "The Ten Most Wanted Criminals in the Past 50 Years." *Liberty Magazine*, Fall, 1972.
Lippmann, Walter, "The Underworld: A Stultified Conscience." *Forum*, February, 1931.
Long, James A., "Julesburg—Wickedest City of the Plains." *Frontier Times*, February-March, 1964.
Lord, John, "Picturesque Road Agents of Early Days." *Overland Monthly*, November, 1917.
"Mafia—Client Politics." *Saturday Review*, July 6, 1968.
"Mafia in New Orleans." *American Law Review*, May 6, 1891.
Mangil, William, "Torrio 'the Immune'." *True Detective*, September, 1940.
Martin, John Bartlow, "Al Capone's Successors." *American Mercury*, June, 1949.
Mason, Frank, "What Really Happened at the O.K. Corral?" *True West*, September-October, 1960.
Masterson, W. B. (William Barclay, "Bat"), "Famous Gunfighters of the Western Frontier, Wyatt Earp (Part II)." *Human Life*, February, 1907.
———, "The Tenderfoot's Turn." *Guns Quarterly*, Summer, 1960.
Mayer, Milton, "The Case of Roger Touhy." *The Reporter*, November, 1955.
Mencken, H. L., "What to do With Criminals." *Liberty Magazine*, July 28, 1934.
Michelson, Charles, "Stage Robbers of the West." *Munsey's Magazine*, July, 1901.
Milligan, Capt. Leo, "Pistol Aces of A Past Era." *Guns Review*, March, 1963.
Mills, James, "The Detective." *Life*, December 12, 1965.
Missouri World, March 1874 (on Jesse James).
Moynihan, Daniel P., "The Private Government of Crime." *Reporter*, July 6, 1961.
Nash, Jay Robert, "The Shakespeare Bandit." *Action Time Magazine*, March-April, 1967.
———, "Terrible Tommy and the Waiting Gallows." *ChicagoLand Magazine*, March, 1968.
———, "Heyday! Chicago's Golden Era of Journalism." *Mankind Magazine*, October, 1972.
Nathan, George Jean, "The Old Time Train Gambler." *Harper's Weekly*, May 21, 1910.
The Nation, January 6, 1891 (on Mafia in New Orleans).
Nichols, Col. George Ward, "Wild Bill." *Harper's New Monthly Magazine*, February, 1867.
Nolan, Warren, and White, Owen P., "The Bad Man From Missouri." *Collier's*, January 21, 1928.
Northlander, J. Philip, "Ma Barker's Last Stand." *Midwest Magazine*, June 21, 1970.
Ornduff, Donald R., "Aristocrats in the Cattle Country." *The Trail Guide*, June, 1964.
Osgood, Stacy, "Harry Tracy—Meanest Man, Alive or Dead." *Westerner's Brand Book*, August, 1959.
Palmer, John Williamson, "The Pinkertons." *Century Magazine*, February, 1892.
Peterson, Virgil, "Rackets in America." *Journal of Criminal Law, Criminology and Police Science*, March-April, 1959.
Pigg, Elmer L., "Bloody Bill, Noted Guerilla of the Civil War." *The Trail Guide*, December, 1956.
Pileggi, Nicholas, "The Lying, Thieving, Murdering, Upper-Middle-Class Respectable Crook." *Esquire*, January, 1966.
———, "How We Italians Discovered America and Kept it Pure, With Lots of Swell People." *Esquire*, June, 1968.
Pinkerton, William A., "Highwaymen of the Railroads." *North American Review*, November, 1893.
Portley, Ed, "The Barrow Gang." *Master Detective*, February, 1945.
Randolph, John A., "Alfred Packer, Cannibal." *Harper's Weekly*, October 17, 1874.

Randolph, Col. Robert Isham, "How to Wreck Capone's Gang." Collier's, March 7, 1931.

Reilly, Edward J., "Will Lindbergh Save Hauptmann?" Liberty Magazine, October 5, 1935.

Remington, Frank, "The Challenge of Crime." The New Republic, May 20, 1967.

Roberts, Gary L., "O.K. Corral: The Fight That Never Dies!" Frontier Times, October-November, 1965.

Rodann, Curtis, "Big Daddy of the Underworld." True Detective, August, 1960.

Rojas, Arnold R., "The Vaquero." The American West, Spring 1964.

Ruth, Henry S., Jr., "Why Organized Crime Thrives." Annals of the American Academy of Political and Social Science, November, 1967.

Ryder, David Warren, "Stage Coach Days." Sunset, September, 1927.

Salts, Dan, "Missouri's Forgotten Don Quixote." Focus/Midwest, October, 1962.

Scaduto, Anthony, "Vito Genovese." Master Detective, August, 1967.

Schrag, Clarence, "Leadership Among Prison Inmates." American Sociological Review, February, 1954.

Settle, William A., Jr., "The James Boys and Missouri Politics." Missouri Historical Review, July, 1942.

Shepherd, William G., "Can Capone Beat Washington, Too?" Collier's, October 16, 1931.

Sherman, Thomas G., "The Owners of America." Forum, November, 1889.

Sidran, Louis, "The Unmasking of Paul 'The Waiter' Ricca." Reader's Digest, November, 1959.

Smith, Duane A., "The Golden West." Montana, July, 1964.

———, "Painted Ladies of the Cowtown Frontier." The Trail Guide, December, 1965.

Smith, Sandy, "The Charmed Life of Tony Accardo." The Saturday Evening Post, November 24, 1962.

———, "The Fix." Life, September 1, 1967.

———, "Mobsters in the Market Place—Money, Muscle, Murder." Life, September 8, 1967.

———, and Lambert, William, "The Mob." Life, January 5, 1968.

———, "The Congressman and the Hoodlum." Life, August 9, 1968.

Stack, Andy, "The Killers' Week-Long Blood Orgy." Official Detective Magazine, May, 1971.

Strong, Dwight S., "New England: The Refined Yankees in Organized Crime." Annals of the American Academy of Political and Social Science, May, 1963.

Sullivan, Edward Dean, "I Know You, Al." North American Review, September, 1929.

Sutherland, Sidney, "The Machine-Gunning of McSwiggin and What Led Up to It." Liberty, July-August, 1926.

Talese, Gay, "The Ethics of Frank Costello." Esquire, September, 1961.

Thomas, Robert L., "Gunfight at Iron Springs." True West, January-February, 1965.

Toland, John, "Sad Ballad of the Real Bonnie & Clyde." New York Times Magazine, February 18, 1968.

Train, Arthur, "Imported Crime: The Story of the Camorra in America." McClure's Magazine, May, 1912.

Turner, George Kibbe, "The City of Chicago, A Study of the Great Immoralities." McClure's Magazine, April, 1907.

Tyler, Gus, "The Roots of Organized Crime." Crime and Delinquency, October, 1962.

"Unvarnishing Jesse James." Literary Digest, March 20, 1915.

Vanderbilt, Cornelius, Jr., "How Al Capone Would Run This Country." Liberty, October 17, 1931.

Wallace, Robert, "Crime in the U.S." Life, September 9, 1957.

Walwrath, Ellen F., "Stagecoach Holdups in the San Luis Valley." The Colorado Magazine, January, 1937.

Westford, Adam, "Jesse James and the Great Northfield Raid." Twin Citian Magazine, September, 1966.

White, Owen P., "Belle Starr, Bandit." Collier's, February 2, 1932.

———, "El Paso." American Mercury, August, 1924.

———, "Five El Paso Worthies." American Mercury, December, 1929.

———, and Nolan, Warren, "The Bad Man from Missouri." (Series) Collier's, January 14, 21, 28, 1928.

Wilson, Paul E., "Law on the Frontier." The Trail Guide, September, 1960.

Wolfe, Edgar Forest (pseud. for R. H. Faherty), "The Real Truth About Al Capone." The Master Detective, September, 1930.

Woolem, Dee, "Fast Draw—From Six to Sixty." Guns Quarterly, Spring, 1960.

REPORTS, PAMPHLETS, DOCUMENTS

Better Government Association of Chicago Report, 1969.

The Challenge of Crime in a Free Society. Report By President Johnson's Commission on Law Enforcement and Administration of Justice, 1968.

Chicago Crime Commission Annual Report (1919-1971).

Chicago Police Problems, The Citizen's Police Committee, 1931.

Chicago Vice Commission Report, Chicago, 1912.

Citizen's Association of Chicago Annual Report (1902-24).

Complete Trial of H. H. Holmes. Philadelphia: Bissel, 1897.

Early Day Gunmen Gave Picturesque Setting of Dodge City. Topeka Daily Capital, December 9, 1934.

Hearings Before the Permanent Subcommittee on Investigations: Organized Crime and Illicit Traffic in Narcotics. U.S. Senate, 1963.

Hearings Before the Special Committee to Investigate Organized Crime in Interstate Commerce. U.S. Senate, 1950.

Illinois Crime Survey, 1902, 1929.

National Commission on Law Observance and Enforcement: Report of the Prohibition Laws of the U.S., 1931.

Report of the Committee of 15 on Prostitution and Gambling in Chicago, Chicago, 1914.

Seabury, Samuel. Final Report of Investigation of the Magistrate's Courts in the First Judicial Departments (N.Y.), March, 1932.

Social Evils in Chicago, A Study of Existing Conditions with Recommendations by the Vice Commission of Chicago. Chicago, 1911.

Wickersham Report. Findings of President Hoover's National Commission on Law Enforcement and Observance. Washington, D.C., 1930.

Warren Commission. Report of the President's Commission on the Assassination of President Kennedy. (1964)

NEWSPAPERS

(The following newspapers were used extensively in research; years of reference are given in lieu of miscellaneous dates too numerous to cite here.)

Arizona Republic (1949-1971)
Arkansas Gazette (1874-75, 1971)
Boston Herald Traveler (1971)
Boston Sunday Globe (1930-1971)
Chicago Commercial Advertiser (1879-82)
Chicago Daily News (1913-1972)
Chicago Herald-Examiner, also Examiner (1914-1935)
Chicago Inter-Ocean (1874-1901)
Chicago Sun-Times (1960-1972)
Chicago Times (1890-1904)
Chicago Today, also Chicago Evening American and Chicago's American (1910-1971)
Chicago Tribune (1875-1972)
Cincinnati Enquirer (1875-1910)
Columbia Missouri Statesman (1863-1884)
Denver Daily News (1891)
Denver Post (1930-1970)
Denver Rocky Mountain News (1882-1897)
Denver Times (1891)
Grand Rapids Press (1971)
Hartford Courant (1971)
Indianapolis News (1922-1937)
Kansas City Daily (1866-1887)
Kansas City Star (1880-1971)
Kansas City Times (1870-1886)
Los Angeles Herald-Examiner (1924-1971)
Los Angeles Times (1929-1972)
Milwaukee Journal (1970-1972)
Missouri State Journal (1901)
Montreal Star (1971)
Newark Evening News (1971)
New Orleans Picayune (1890-1970)
New Orleans Times-Democrat (1890-1891)
New York Daily Graphic (1882-1930)
New York Press (1904)
New York Sun (1904)
New York Times (1891-1972)
New York Tribune (1904)
New York World (1874-1929)
Philadelphia Daily News (1939-1971)
St. Louis Evening Chronicle (1880-1885)
St. Louis Globe Democrat (1876-1950)
St. Louis Post Dispatch (1878-1972)
St. Louis Times (1875)
San Francisco Chronicle (1910-1971)
Toronto Star (1920-1971)
Washington Evening Star (1930-1971)

INDEX